THE OLD ENGLISH
OROSIUS

EARLY ENGLISH TEXT SOCIETY

S.S. 6

1980

Ure ieldran ealne þisne ymbhwyrft þises
middangeardes, cwæð Orosius, swa swa Oceanus
utan ymbligeð, þone garsecg hateð, on þreo todældon. 7 hie þa þrie dælas on þriw tonimdon, Asiam, 7
Europam, 7 Affricam; þeah þe sume men sædon þæt þær
nære buton twegen dælas, Asia, 7 þæt oðer Europe. Asia
is befangen mid Oceano þam garsecge suþan 7 norþan
7 eastan, 7 þære ealne middangeard fram þæm eastadæle
healfne behæfð. Þon on dæm norþdæle þæt is Asia on þa siþ-
ran healfe Indea þære is Dehasia, 7 Europe hira land
gemincu togædne licgað. Ond þon of þære ilcan is Danai
þæt andlang Nidel, 7 þon þis þ Asiam alle andþara þære
beþrig Asia 7 Affrica togædne licgead. Es Europe hio onginð
þar le cþæt of Danai þære is þ hir hunside of norþ dæle
of þære ðing þæm briþgiu þa þindon neh þam garsecge
þimon hateð þir mondþc, 7 þeo ea Danai þind forþ
þid þrþce on þþt healfe alle andþær heþiza. On In pocho
marco þære þeode hio þrped þæt þæt þimon hateð Moteða þe
7 þon þoþ þid micle flode neah þære þeode þimon hateð
Teodoþia, þið eastan ut on þær floþeð þimon hett
euximuy, 7 þon mid longre neaþoncþre þuþ þonan be
eastan con stantino polim Gitta þriz ligeð. 7 þonne norþ
þonan ut on Nidel þæ. Se þyrt þuþ inde Europe land ge
miþce iþ Inþþania þyrte þeundu ut þam garsecge 7
maþt ut þam iglunde þat te zadeþ hatte þæn reix þe
Nidel þæ up of þæm Garsecge þæn ete þncol þr þlu
fenoaþ on þam ilean Nidel þæ 7 Inþe on þyrt þide
iþ reot land. Affrica 7 Asia hiþalland ge miþcu on
ginnaþ of Alexandria Egypta burge 7 ligeð þat lond ge
miþe þuþ þonan of þinilus þa ea 7 þa oþ þt þinopica
þyrthne of þone þuþ garsecg 7 þæþe of þica norþ þyrt g meþe

THE
OLD ENGLISH
OROSIUS

EDITED BY

JANET BATELY

Published for

THE EARLY ENGLISH TEXT SOCIETY

by the

OXFORD UNIVERSITY PRESS

LONDON   NEW YORK   TORONTO

1980

Oxford University Press, Walton Street, Oxford OX2 6DP

OXFORD LONDON GLASGOW
NEW YORK TORONTO MELBOURNE WELLINGTON
IBADAN NAIROBI DAR ES SALAAM LUSAKA CAPE TOWN
KUALA LUMPUR SINGAPORE HONG KONG TOKYO
DELHI BOMBAY CALCUTTA MADRAS KARACHI

British Library Cataloguing in Publication Data
Orosius, Paulus
    The Old English Orosius. - (Early English Text
    Society. Supplementary series; 6)
    1. History, Ancient
    I. Title   II. Bately, Janet   III. Alfred,
    King of England   IV. Series
    930   PR1555.A1   77-30208
    ISBN 0-19-722406-7

Printed in Great Britain
at the University Press, Oxford
by Eric Buckley
Printer to the University

PREFACE

THIS edition had its beginning in a comparison of the Old English Orosius with the Old French poem *Les Empereors de Rome*, which I undertook at the instigation of my former colleague Professor D. J. A. Ross, to whom I owe considerable thanks not only for drawing my attention to the problem of the relationship between the two works but also for his subsequent encouragement. As a result of my investigations I was led to query Henry Sweet's choice of Haverkamp's text of Orosius as the 'Latin original' of the Old English translation and to examine the numerous MSS of the *Historiarum adversum Paganos Libri Septem*, a task which was only made possible by the generosity of the University of London Central Research Fund and of Birkbeck College, and by the helpfulness of the librarians of the many libraries that I visited. Since then I have received help and encouragement from a great variety of sources. Some of this help is acknowledged in the Introduction and Commentary. In addition I would like to express my special thanks to Professors Donald Booth, Andrew Colin, and Michael Levison, formerly of the Department of Numerical Automation at Birkbeck College, for programming a word-list and partial concordance of the OE Orosius for me at a time when computer concordances were in their infancy. Also to Mrs. Hilde Poltorak and Dr. Přemysl Janotá for their help in checking my translations from Polish and Czech, to Dr. Bruce Mitchell and Mr. Malcolm Parkes for their advice on syntactical and palaeographical matters respectively, to Professor Norman Davis for his comments on the finished edition, and to Dr. Pamela Gradon for her meticulously careful scrutiny of specimens of text and glossary and for the patience and promptness with which she has answered my many queries about presentation. I am particularly grateful to Professor Peter Clemoes for his detailed and most valuable criticism both of my earlier work on the sources of additional material in the OE Orosius and of the edition itself. However, it is to Professor Dorothy Whitelock that I owe the greatest debt. Not only have her published works—in particular the studies of the OE Bede and of Alfredian prose—suggested to me lines of inquiry and methods of approach which I have followed up with advantage, but over the years she has read and commented on drafts of my articles and generously shared with me her discoveries connected with the Orosius, spurring me to renewed efforts by her judicious questions.

Finally, I must express my gratitude to my husband and son, Leslie and Michael Summers, without whose tolerance and long-suffering this edition might still be unfinished.

CONTENTS

CONTENTS

PLATES

Reproduced by kind permission of the British Library.

SELECT BIBLIOGRAPHY, SHORT TITLES, AND ABBREVIATIONS

1. Editions and Facsimile

Barrington (1773). *The Anglo-Saxon Version from the historian Orosius by Aelfred the Great*, ed. D. Barrington (London, 1773).

Bosworth (1859). *King Alfred's Anglo-Saxon Version of the Compendious History of the World by Orosius*, ed. J. Bosworth (London, 1859).

Sweet (1883). *King Alfred's Orosius, Part I: Old English Text and Latin Original*, ed. H. Sweet, EETS o.s. 79 (London, 1883).

Thorpe (1853). B. Thorpe, *The Life of Alfred the Great . . . To which is appended Alfred's Anglo-Saxon version of Orosius* (London, 1853).

Campbell (1953). *The Tollemache Orosius (British Museum Additional MS 47967)*, ed. A. Campbell, *EEMF*, iii (Copenhagen, 1953).

2. Selections

Only a handful, valuable for their annotations, are listed here: a = voyages of Ohthere and Wulfstan; b = geography of Germania; c = geography of the world; d = other selections.

Bright (1971). *Bright's Old English Grammar and Reader*, 3rd ed., rev. F. G. Cassidy and R. N. Ringler (New York, 1971), a.

Labuda (1961). G. Labuda, *Źródła Skandynawskie i Anglosaskie do Dziejów Słowiańszczyzny* (Warsaw, 1961), abc, with a facsimile of ff. 7ᵛ–15 of the Cotton MS.

Mossé (1945). F. Mossé, *Manuel de l'anglais du Moyen Âge. I: Vieil-Anglais* (Paris, 1945), a.

Raith (1958). J. Raith, *Altenglisches Lesebuch: Prosa*, 2nd ed. (Munich, 1958), ab.

Sweet–Whitelock (1967). H. Sweet, *Anglo-Saxon Reader*, rev. D. Whitelock (Oxford, 1967), ad.

Wyatt (1919). A. J. Wyatt, *An Anglo-Saxon Reader* (Cambridge, 1919), ad.

3. Other Texts

(i) Old English.

Ælfric, *Homilies*, ed. Pope. *Homilies of Ælfric: A Supplementary Collection*, ed. J. C. Pope, EETS 259–60 (1967–8).

Ælfric, *Lives of Saints. Ælfric's Lives of Saints*, ed. W. W. Skeat, EETS o.s. 76, 82, 94, 114 (1881–1900, repr. in 2 vols. 1966).

Alfred's Boethius. King Alfred's Old English Version of Boethius' De Consolatione Philosophiae, ed. W. J. Sedgefield (Oxford, 1899).

Alfred's Soliloquies. King Alfred's Version of St. Augustine's Soliloquies, ed. T. A. Carnicelli (Harvard, 1969).

Anglo-Saxon Chronicle. Two of the Saxon Chronicles Parallel, ed. C. Plummer (Oxford, 1892–99, repr. with two notes by D. Whitelock, 1952).

Corpus (Glossary). *The Corpus Glossary*, ed. W. M. Lindsay (Cambridge, 1921).

Cura Pastoralis. King Alfred's West-Saxon version of Gregory's Pastoral Care, ed. H. Sweet, EETS o.s. 45, 50 (1871, repr. 1958).

Gregory's Dialogues. Bischof Wærferths von Worcester Übersetzung der Dialoge Gregors des Grossen, ed. H. Hecht, Bibliothek der angelsächsischen Prosa, v (Leipzig, 1900, 1907, repr. Darmstadt, 1965).

Laws. *Die Gesetze der Angelsachsen*, ed. F. L. Liebermann (Halle, 1903–16, repr. Aalen, 1960).

Leiden (Glossary). *A Late Eighth-century Latin–Anglo-Saxon Glossary preserved in the Library of the Leiden University*, ed. J. H. Hessels (Cambridge, 1906).

OE Bede. The Old English Version of Bede's Ecclesiastical History of the English People, ed. T. Miller, EETS o.s. 95, 96 (1890–1, repr. 1959).

OE Heptateuch. The Old English Version of the Heptateuch, ed. S. J. Crawford, EETS o.s. 160 (1922).

OE Martyrology. An Old English Martyrology, ed. G. Herzfeld, EETS o.s. 116 (1900).

Parker Chronicle. MS A of the Anglo-Saxon Chronicle, as above.

Rushworth Gospels. See W. W. Skeat, The Four Gospels in Anglo-Saxon, Northumbrian, and Old Mercian Versions (Cambridge, 1871–87).

St. Chad. The Life of St. Chad. An Old English Homily, ed. R. Vleeskruyer (Amsterdam, 1953).

Three Old English Prose Texts. Three Old English Prose Texts, ed. S. Rypins, EETS 161 (1921).

Vercelli Homilies. Die Vercelli-Homilien, ed. M. Förster (Hamburg, 1932, repr. Darmstadt, 1964).

Wright–Wülcker. *Anglo-Saxon and Old English Vocabularies*, ed. T. Wright and R. P. Wülcker (London, 1884, repr. Darmstadt, 1968).

(ii) Other languages.

For ease of reference I have normally cited those editions that are most likely to be readily accessible, e.g. from *PL*, and the Loeb and Teubner series.

Abavus (Glossary). See *Glossaria Latina*.

Abolita (Glossary). See *Glossaria Latina*.

Abstrusa (Glossary). See *Glossaria Latina*.

Acron. *Acronis et Porphyrionis Commentarii in Q. Horatium Flaccum*, ed. F. Hauthal (Berlin, 1864-6, repr. 1966).

Adam of Bremen. Adam of Bremen, *Gesta Pontificum Hammaburgensis Ecclesiae*, PL cxlvi, cols. 451-662.

Agrippa fragment. Printed in *Geographi Latini*.

Ammianus Marcellinus. *Ammianus Marcellinus*, ed. J. C. Rolfe (London, 1935-9).

Annales Fuldenses. *Annales Fuldenses*, ed. F. Kurze (Hanover, 1891).

Appendix Probi. See W. A. Baehrens, *Sprachlicher Kommentar zur Vulgärlateinischen Appendix Probi* (Halle, 1922).

Arma (Glossary). See *Glossaria Latina*.

Augustine, *Civ. Dei*. Augustine, *De Civitate Dei*, ed. E. Hoffmann, *CSEL*, xl.

Aurelius Victor. *Sexti Aurelii Victoris Liber de Caesaribus*, ed. F. Pichl-mayr (Leipzig, 1911, repr. 1970).

Bavarian Geographer. *Descriptio Civitatum ad Septentrionalem Plagam Danubii*, ed. B. Horák and D. Trávniček, *Rozpravy Československé Akademie Věd*, lxvi (1956).

Bede, *De Natura Rerum*. Bede, *De Natura Rerum Liber*, PL xc, cols. 187-278.

Bede, *De Temporum Ratione*. Bede, *De Temporum Ratione*, PL xc, cols. 293-578.

Bede, *HE*. Bede, *Historia Ecclesiastica Gentis Anglorum*, ed. C. Plummer (Oxford, 1896).

Calendre. Calendre, *Les Empereors de Rome*, ed. G. Millard (Ann Arbor, 1957).

Capella. *Martianus Capella*, ed. A. Dick (Leipzig, 1925).

Christian of Stavelot. *Christiani Druthmari Corbeiensis Monachi Expositio in Matthaeum Evangelistam*, PL cvi, cols. 1261-1504.

Chronicle of Æthelweard. *The Chronicle of Æthelweard*, ed. A. Campbell (London, 1962).

Cicero. *M. Tullii Ciceronis scripta quae manserunt omnia, pars IV*, II, ed. C. F. W. Mueller (Leipzig, 1878), and III, ed. R. Klotz (Leipzig, 1876).

Claudian. *Claudian*, ed. M. Platnauer (London, 1922).

Cornelius Nepos. *Cornelius Nepos*, ed. J. C. Rolfe (London, 1929).

Cosmographia. Printed in *Geographi Latini*.

De Situ Orbis. *Anonymi de Situ Orbis Libri Duo*, ed. M. Manitius (Stutt-gart, 1884).

De Viris Illustribus. Printed with Aurelius Victor, as above.

Dicuil. *Dicuili Liber de Mensura Orbis Terrae*, ed. J. J. Tierney (Dublin, 1967).

Dimensuratio. *Dimensuratio Provinciarum*. Printed in *Geographi Latini*.

Divisio. Divisio Orbis Terrarum. Printed in *Geographi Latini.*

Dunchad. *Glossae in Martianum Capellam,* ed. C. E. Lutz (Lancaster, Pa., 1944).

Einhard, *Life of Charlemagne. Einhard's Life of Charlemagne,* ed. H. W. Garrod and R. B. Mowat (Oxford, 1915).

Einhardi Annales. Annales regni Francorum. . . qui dicuntur Annales. . . Einhardi, ed. F. Kurze (Hanover, 1895).

Epitoma, ed. Thomas. *Epitoma Rerum Gestarum Alexandri Magni,* ed. P. H. Thomas (Leipzig, 1966).

Eutropius. *Eutropi Breviarium ab Urbe Condita,* ed. F. Ruehl (Leipzig 1887).

Expositio. Expositio Totius Mundi et Gentium. Printed in *Geographi Latini.*

Festus. *Festus, De Verborum Significatu.* Printed in *Glossaria Latina.*

Florus. *L. Annaei Flori Epitomae Libri II,* ed. O. Rossbach (Leipzig, 1896).

Freculph, *Freculphi Lexoviensis Episcopi Chronicon, PL* cvi, cols. 917–1258.

Frontinus. *Iuli Frontini Strategematon Libri IV,* ed. G. Gundermann (Leipzig, 1888).

Geographi Latini. Geographi Latini minores, ed. A. Riese (Heilbronn, 1878, repr. Leipzig, 1957).

Glossaria Latina. Glossaria Latina, ed. W. M. Lindsay et al. (Paris, 1926–31, repr. Hildesheim, 1965).

Gl(ossarium) Ansileubi. Printed in *Glossaria Latina.*

Gregory of Tours. *S. Georgii Florentii Gregorii Episcopi Turonensis Historiae Ecclesiasticae Francorum Libri Decem, PL* lxxi, cols. 161–572.

Herodotus. *Herodotus,* ed. J. E. Powell (Oxford, 1949).

Horace. *Q. Horati Flacci opera,* ed. F. Klingner (Leipzig, 1959).

Horace scholia. See Acron.

Hyginus. *Hyginus, Fabulae,* ed. H. I. Rose (Leiden, 1934).

Isidore, *Chronicon. Sancti Isidori Hispalensis Episcopi Chronicon, PL* lxxxiii, cols. 1017–58.

Isidore, *Etymologies. Isidori Hispalensis Episcopi Etymologiarum sive Originum Libri XX,* ed. W. M. Lindsay (Oxford, 1911).

Jerome, *Comm. in Daniel. S. Eusebii Hieronymi Stridonensis Presbyteri Commentaria in Danielem, PL* xxv, cols. 491–584.

Jerome, *De Viris. S. Eusebii Hieronymi Liber de Viribus Illustribus, PL* xxiii, cols. 631–764.

Jerome–Eusebius. *S. Eusebii Hieronymi Interpretatio Chronicae Eusebii Pamphili, PL* xxvii, cols. 33–677.

Jordanes. *Jordanes, De Gothorum Origine, PL* lxix, cols. 1251–96.

Julius Honorius. *Julius Honorius, Cosmographia.* Printed in *Geographi Latini.*

Julius Valerius. *Iuli Valeri Alexandri Polemi Res Gestae Alexandri Macedonis*, ed. B. Kuebler (Leipzig, 1888).

Justinus. M. *Iuniani Iustini epitoma Historiarum Philippicarum Pompei Trogi*, ed. O. Seel after F. Ruehl (Leipzig, 1956).

Juvenal scholia. *Scholia in Iuvenalem Vetustiora*, ed. P. Wessner (Leipzig, 1931, repr. Stuttgart, 1967).

Lactantius Placidus *in Achilleida*. *The Medieval Achilleid of Statius*, ed. P. M. Clogan (Leiden, 1968).

Lactantius Placidus *in Stat. Theb*. *Lactantii Placidi Commentarii in Statii Thebaida*, in P. *Papinius Statius, Opera*, III, ed. R. Jahnke (Leipzig, 1898).

Liber Nominum Locorum. Liber Nominum Locorum ex Actis, PL xxiii, cols. 1297–1306.

Livy. *Titi Livi Ab Urbe Condita Libri*, ed. G. Weissenborn and M. Müller (Leipzig, 1902 etc.)

Lucan scholia, ed. Endt. *Adnotationes super Lucanum*, ed. J. Endt (Leipzig, 1909).

Lucan scholia, ed. Weber. *Marci Annaei Lucani Pharsalia*, ed. H. Grotius and C. F. Weber III, Scholiastae (Leipzig, 1831).

Macrobius, *Saturnalia*. See *Macrobius*, ed. F. Eyssenhardt (Leipzig, 1893).

Mela, *Pomponii Melae de Chorographia Libri Tres*, ed. C. Frick (Leipzig, 1880).

Mythographus I and II. See *Classicorum Auctorum e Vaticanis Codicibus Editorum* III, ed. A. Mai (Rome, 1831).

OHG Tatian. *Tatian*, ed. E. Sievers, 2nd ed. (Paderborn, 1892, repr. 1960).

Orosius Commentary. Rome, Vatican Library, Reginenses Latini, 1650, ff. 1–10.

Orosius' History. *Pauli Orosii Historiarum adversus Paganos Libri VII*, ed. C. Zangemeister, *CSEL*, v (Vienna, 1882).

Otfrid. *Otfrids von Weissenburg Evangelienbuch*, ed. J. Kelle (Regensburg, 1856–81, repr. 1963).

Ovid. *P. Ovidius Naso, Opera*, ed. R. Merkel (Leipzig, 1896).

Paulus Diaconus. *Pauli Historia Langobardorum, MGHSS. rer. Germ.*

Paulus Diaconus. *Historia Romana*, ed. H. Droysen (Berlin, 1879).

Placidus Glosses. See *Glossaria Latina*.

Pliny. *C. Plini Secundi Naturalis Historiae Libri XXXVII*, ed. C. Mayhoff (Leipzig, 1906 etc.).

Plutarch. *Plutarch, Lives*, ed. B. Perrin (London, 1919).

Porphyrio. See Acron.

Priscian, *Periegesis. La Périégèse de Priscien*, ed. P. van de Woestijne (Bruges, 1953).

Quintus Curtius. *Q. Curti Rufi Historiarum Alexandri Magni Macedonis Libri*, ed. E. Hedicke (Leipzig, 1908).

Ravenna Geographer. *Ravennatis Anonymi Cosmographia*, ed. M. Pinder and G. Parthey (Berlin, 1860).

Regino of Prüm. *Reginonis Abbatis Prumiensis Chronicon*, ed. F. Kurze (Hanover, 1890).

Remigius *in Capellam. Remigii Autissiodorensis Commentum in Martianum Capellam*, ed. C. E. Lutz (Leiden, 1962).

Sallust. *Sallust, Bellum Iugurthinum*, ed. A. Kurfess (Leipzig, 1957).

Scriptores Historiae Augustae, ed. E. Hohl (Leipzig, 1971).

Servius. *Servii Grammatici qui Feruntur in Vergilii Carmina Commentarii*, ed. G. Thilo and H. Hagen (Leipzig, 1881, repr. Hildesheim, 1961).

Silius Italicus. *Sili Italici Punica*, ed. L. Bauer (Leipzig, 1890–2).

Solinus. *C. Iulii Solini Collectanea Rerum Memorabilium*, ed. T. Mommsen (Berlin, 1895, repr. 1958).

Steinmeyer and Sievers. *Die althochdeutschen Glossen*, ed. E. Steinmeyer and E. Sievers (Berlin, 1879–98, repr. Dublin, 1968–9).

Tacitus. *P. Cornelii Taciti Libri qui supersunt*, ed. E. Koestermann (Leipzig, 1969).

Tertullian, *Apol.* Tertullian, *Apologeticus adversus gentes pro Christianis*, *PL* i, cols. 257–536.

Valerius Maximus. *Valerii Maximi Factorum et Dictorum Memorabilium*, ed. C. Kempf (Leipzig, 1888).

Velleius Paterculus. *C. Vellei Paterculi ex Historiae Romanae Libris Duobus quae supersunt*, ed. C. Stegmann de Pritzwald (1933, repr. Stuttgart, 1965).

4. *Other Works*

Admiralty, *Norway Pilot*. See *Norway Pilot*.

Admiralty, *White Sea Pilot*. See *White Sea Pilot*.

Bately (1960). J. M. Bately, 'Alfred's *Orosius* and *Les Empereors de Rome*', *SP*, lvii (1960), 567–86.

Bately (1961). J. M. Bately, 'King Alfred and the Latin MSS of Orosius' History', *Class. et Med.*, xxii (1961), 69–105.

Bately (1964). J. M. Bately, 'The Vatican Fragment of the Old English Orosius', *ES*, xlv (1964), 224–30.

Bately (1966). J. M. Bately, 'The Old English Orosius: The Question of Dictation', *Anglia*, lxxxiv (1966), 255–304.

Bately (1967). J. M. Bately, 'The Relationship between the MSS of the Old English Orosius', *ES*, xlviii (1967), 410–16.

Bately (1970). J. M. Bately, 'King Alfred and the Old English Translation of Orosius', *Anglia*, lxxxviii (1970), 433–60.

Bately (1971). J. M. Bately, 'The Classical Additions in the Old English

Orosius', in *England before the Conquest*, ed. P. Clemoes and K. Hughes (Cambridge, 1971) pp. 237–51.

Bately (1972). J. M. Bately, 'The relationship between geographical information in the Old English Orosius and Latin texts other than Orosius', *ASE*, i (1972), 45–62.

Bately (1978). J. M. Bately, 'The Compilation of the Anglo-Saxon Chronicle 60 B.C. to A.D. 890: Vocabulary as Evidence', *PBA*, lxiv (1979, for 1978).

Bately and Ross. J. M. Bately and D. J. A. Ross, 'A Check List of Manuscripts of Orosius' "Historiarum adversum paganos libri septem"', *Scriptorium*, xv (1961), 329–34.

Binns (1961). A. L. Binns, 'Ohthere's Northern Voyage', *EGS*, vii (1961), 43–52.

Bosworth (1855). J. Bosworth, *A Literal English Translation of King Alfred's Anglo-Saxon Version of Orosius* (London, 1855, repr. in Bosworth, 1859).

Campbell, *OEG(rammar)*. A. Campbell, *Old English Grammar* (Oxford, 1959, corr. repr. 1962).

Cleasby–Vigfusson (1957). R. Cleasby and G. Vigfusson, *An Icelandic Dictionary*, 2nd ed., with Supplement by W. A. Craigie (Oxford, 1957).

Cosijn (1883–6). P. J. Cosijn, *Altwestsächsische Grammatik* (The Hague, 1883–6).

Cross (1931). S. H. Cross, 'Notes on King Alfred's North: Osti, Este', *Speculum*, vi (1931), 296–9.

Dahl (1938). I. Dahl. *Substantival Inflexion in Early Old English: Vocalic Stems* (Lund, 1938).

Dahlmann (1822). C. F. Dahlmann, *Forschungen auf dem Gebiete der Geschichte* (Altona, 1822), I.

Derolez (1971). R. Derolez, 'The orientation system in the Old English Orosius', in *England before the Conquest*, ed. P. Clemoes and K. Hughes (Cambridge, 1971), pp. 253–68.

Dvornik (1949). F. Dvornik, *The Making of Central and Eastern Europe* (London, 1949).

Dvornik (1956). F. Dvornik, *The Slavs, Their Early History and Civilization* (Boston, 1956).

Dvornik (1970). F. Dvornik, *Byzantine Missions among the Slavs* (Rutgers Univ., 1970).

East (1950, repr. 1962). W. G. East, *An Historical Geography of Europe*, 4th ed. (London, 1950, repr. 1962).

Ebert (1924). M. Ebert, *Reallexicon der Vorgeschichte* I (Berlin, 1924).

Ekblom (1940). R. Ekblom, 'Ohthere's Voyage from Skiringssal to Hedeby', *SN*, xii (1939–40), 177–90.

Ekblom (1941). R. Ekblom, 'Der Volksname Osti in Alfreds des Grossen Orosius-Übersetzung', *SN*, xiii (1940–1), 167–73.

b

Ekblom (1941–2). R. Ekblom, 'Alfred the Great as Geographer', *SN*, xiv (1941–2), 115–44.

Ekblom (1960). 'King Alfred, Ohthere and Wulfstan', *SN*, xxxii (1960), 3–13.

Ellegård (1960). A. Ellegård, 'The Old Scandinavian System of Orientation', *SN*, xxxii (1960), 241–8.

Foote and Wilson (1970). P. Foote and D. Wilson, *The Viking Achievement* (London, 1970).

Förster (1941). M. Förster, *Der Flussname Themse und seine Sippe* (Munich, 1941).

Geidel (1904). H. Geidel, *Alfred der Grosse als Geograph*, Münchener Geographische Studien, xv (Munich, 1904).

Grierson (1972). P. Grierson, *English Linear Measures*. The Stenton Lecture 1971 (Univ. of Reading, 1972).

Guldesku (1964). S. Guldesku, *The History of Mediaeval Croatia* (The Hague, 1964).

Hampson (1859). *Mr. Hampson's Essay on King Alfred's Geography*, printed in Bosworth (1859).

Havlík (1964). L. Havlík, 'Slované v anglosaské chorografii Alfréda velikého', *Vznik a počátky Slovanů*, v (1964), 53–85.

Helvig and Johannessen (1966). M. Helvig and V. Johannessen, *Norway* (Oslo, 1966).

Horgan (1963). D. M. Horgan, *West Saxon Dialect Criteria in the extant MSS of King Alfred's Translation of Gregory's Regula Pastoralis and Orosius's Historiae adversus paganos*, unpubl. diss. (Manchester Univ., 1963).

Hübener (1925–6). G. Hübener, 'König Alfred und Osteuropa', *ESn*, lx (1925–6), 37–57.

Hübener (1930). G. Hübener, *England und die Gesittungsgrundlage der europäischen Frühgeschichte* (Frankfurt, 1930).

Ingram (1807). J. Ingram, *An Inaugural Lecture on the Utility of Anglo-Saxon Literature; to which is added the Geography of Europe by King Alfred* (London, 1807).

Jackson (1953). K. Jackson, *Language and History in Early Britain* (Edinburgh, 1953).

Jones (1968). Gwyn Jones, *A History of the Vikings* (Oxford, 1968).

Ker (1957). N. R. Ker, *Catalogue of Manuscripts containing Anglo-Saxon* (Oxford, 1957). Cited by catalogue number.

Labuda (1960). G. Labuda, *Źródła, sagi i legendy do najdawniejszych dziejów Polski* (Warsaw, 1960).

Laistner (1957). M. L. W. Laistner, *Thought and Letters in Western Europe A.D. 500 to 900*, 2nd ed. (London 1957).

Leland, *Collectanea*. *J. Lelandi antiquarii de rebus Britannicis Collectanea*, ed. T. Hearn (Oxford, 1715).

Liggins (1970). E. Liggins, 'The Authorship of the Old English Orosius', *Anglia*, lxxxviii (1970), 289–322.

Linderski (1964). J. Linderski, 'Alfred the Great and the Tradition of Ancient Geography', *Speculum*, xxxix (1964), 434–9.

Malone (1930a). K. Malone, 'The date of Ohthere's voyage to Hæthum', *MLR*, xxv (1930), 78–81.

Malone (1930b). K. Malone, 'King Alfred's North: A Study in Mediaeval Geography', *Speculum*, v (1930), 139–67.

Malone (1931). K. Malone, 'On Wulfstan's Scandinavia', *SP*, xxviii (1931), pp. 574–9.

Malone (1933). K. Malone, 'On King Alfred's geographical treatise', *Speculum*, viii (1933), 67–78.

Mezger (1921). F. Mezger, *Angelsächsische Völker- und Ländernamen* (Berlin, 1921).

Miller, *Mappaemundi*. K. Miller, *Mappaemundi, die ältesten Weltkarten* (Stuttgart, 1895–8).

Mossé (1955). F. Mossé, 'Another lost manuscript of the OE Orosius?', *ES*, xxxvi (1955), 198–203.

Mustanoja (1960). T. F. Mustanoja, *A Middle English Syntax*, I (Helsinki, 1960).

Nickel (1966). G. Nickel, *Die Expanded Form im Altenglischen* (Neumünster, 1966).

Norway Pilot (1953). Admiralty, *Norway Pilot*, vol. iii, 4th ed. (London, 1953).

Pinkerton's Voyages. J. Pinkerton, *A General Collection of the best and most interesting voyages and travels in all parts of the world*, I (London, 1808–14).

Plummer (1920). C. Plummer, *The Life and Times of Alfred the Great* (Oxford, 1920).

Pope (1934). M. K. Pope, *From Latin to Modern French* (Manchester, 1934).

Porthan (1800). H. G. Porthan, *Försök at uplysa Konung Aelfreds geographiska beskrifning öfver den europeiska norden* (Stockholm, 1800, repr. *Opera Selecta*, v, Helsinki, 1873).

Potter (1931). S. Potter, *On the Relation of the Old English Bede to Werferth's Gregory and to Alfred's Translations* (Prague, 1931).

Potter (1952–3). S. Potter, 'Commentary on King Alfred's Orosius', *Anglia*, lxxi (1952–3), 385–437.

Purchas his Pilgrimes. S. Purchas, *Hakluytus Posthumus or Purchas his Pilgrimes* (London, 1625).

Rae (1881). E. Rae, *The White Sea Peninsula* (London, 1881).

Reuter (1934). O. S. Reuter, *Germanische Himmelskunde* (Munich, 1934).

Ross (1940). A. S. C. Ross, 'The Terfinnas and Beormas of Ohthere', *Leeds Texts and Monographs*, vii (Leeds, 1940).

Ross (1954). A. S. C. Ross, 'Ohthere's Cwenas and Lakes', *Geographical Journal*, cxx (1954), 337–46.

Ross (1978). A. S. C. Ross, 'The Este', *N & Q*, n.s. xxv (1978), 100–4.

Sawyer (1962). P. Sawyer, *The Age of the Vikings* (London, 1962).

Schilling (1886). H. Schilling, *König Alfreds angelsächsische Bearbeitung der Weltgeschichte des Orosius* (Halle, 1886).

Sievers–Brunner (1965). K. Brunner, *Altenglische Grammatik nach der angelsächsischen Grammatik von Eduard Sievers neubearbeitet*, 3rd ed. (Tübingen, 1965).

Simpson (1967). J. Simpson, *Everyday Life in the Viking Age* (London, 1967).

Sisam (1953). K. Sisam, *Studies in the History of Old English Literature* (Oxford, 1953).

Sprockel (1965). C. Sprockel, *The Language of the Parker Chronicle*, I (The Hague, 1965).

Stokoe (1957). W. C. Stokoe, 'On Ohthere's *Steorbord*', *Speculum*, xxxii (1957), 299–306.

Toynbee (1973). A. Toynbee, *Constantine Porphyrogenitus and his World* (London, 1973).

Vorren (1961). *Norway North of 65*, ed. Ø. Vorren (London, 1961).

Vorren and Manker (1962). Ø. Vorren and E. Manker, *Lapp Life and Customs* (London, 1962).

Whitelock (1962). D. Whitelock, 'The Old English Bede', *PBA*, xlviii (1963, for 1962), 57–90.

Whitelock (1966). D. Whitelock, 'The Prose of Alfred's Reign', *Continuations and Beginnings, Studies in Old English Literature*, ed. E. G. Stanley (London, 1966).

White Sea Pilot (1946). Admiralty, *White Sea Pilot*, 1st ed. (London, 1946).

White Sea Pilot (1958). Admiralty, *White Sea Pilot*, 2nd ed. (London, 1958).

Wright (1965). J. K. Wright, *The Geographical Lore of the Time of the Crusades*, 2nd ed. (New York, 1965).

Wülfing (1901). J. E. Wülfing, *Die Syntax in den Werken Alfreds des Großen* (Bonn, 1894–1901).

5. Abbreviations

Standard abbreviations such as adj., sg., etc. are not included.

ASE	*Anglo-Saxon England.*
Be.	*OE Bede.* See section 3(i).
BL	British Library, formerly British Museum.
BNL	Paris, Bibliothèque Nationale, fonds latin.
Bo.	*Alfred's Boethius.* See section 3(i).
BT, BTS	*An Anglo-Saxon Dictionary*, by J. Bosworth and T. N. Toller (Oxford, 1898); *Supplement*, by T. N. Toller (Oxford, 1921); *Enlarged Addenda and Corrigenda*, by A. Campbell and repr. of the dictionary and supplement (Oxford, 1972).

CFMA	*Classiques français du moyen âge.*
Class. et Med.	*Classica et Mediaevalia.*
CP	*Cura Pastoralis.* See section 3(i).
CSEL	*Corpus Scriptorum Ecclesiasticorum Latinorum.*
EEMF	*Early English Manuscripts in Facsimile.*
EETS	Early English Text Society.
EGS	*English and Germanic Studies.*
ES	*English Studies.*
ESn	*Englische Studien.*
Gc.	Germanic.
GD	*Gregory's Dialogues.* See section 3(i).
JEGPh	*Journal of English and Germanic Philology.*
Lat.	Latin.
LER	Calendre, *Les Empereors de Rome.* See section 3(ii).
MGHS	*Monumenta Germaniae Historica, Scriptores.*
MLR	*Modern Language Review.*
MS	*Medieval Studies.*
ODan.	Old Danish.
ODu.	Old Dutch.
OE	Old English.
OED	*The Oxford English Dictionary*, corrected reissue of *A New English Dictionary* (Oxford, 1933).
OEG	A. Campbell, *Old English Grammar.* See section 4.
OH	*Orosius' History.* See section 3(ii).
OHG	Old High German.
ON	Old Norse.
Or.	The Old English Orosius.
OS	Old Saxon.
OScand.	Old Scandinavian.
PBA	*Proceedings of the British Academy.*
PL	*Patrologia Latina*, ed. J. P. Migne (Paris, 1st ed.).
PMLA	*Publications of the Modern Language Association of America.*
Ru. 1	Rushworth Gospels. See section 3(i).
SN	*Studia Neophilologica.*
So.	*Alfred's Soliloquies.* See section 3(i).
SP	*Studies in Philology.*
WS	West Saxon.
ZfdA	*Zeitschrift für deutsches Altertum.*

INTRODUCTION

I. DESCRIPTION OF THE MANUSCRIPTS[1]

1. *British Library*, *Additional 47967*. The Lauderdale or Tolle-mache MS, here referred to as MS L and forming the basis of the text pp. 1/2–15/1, 28/12–156/23. Ker 133, saec. x[1]. Ff. i+8+ viii+71. *c.* 282×190 mm. Written space *c.* 212 ×130 mm. 31 long lines. Ff. 9–16 are supply and blank leaves, saec. xvii,[2] replacing a section of manuscript containing the last two-thirds of the report by Ohthere and presumably the whole of the report by Wulfstan, as well as chapters ii–viii of the early history of the world (15/1–28/11), which had earlier been lost or stolen.[3] Apart from a few corrections and notes in medieval and modern hands, the manuscript is the work of a single scribe, apparently identical with the second scribe of the Parker MS of the *Anglo-Saxon Chronicle* and possibly also the scribe of the Latin text of the Junius Psalter.[4] The script used is a prototypal form of 'square minuscule'[5] with occasional use of half-uncial *a* and *s* and uncial

[1] For the summary description of manuscripts in this section, I have relied heavily on Ker (1957), to which work the reader is referred for further details.

[2] The material in the new gathering (copied from Junius's transcript of MS C, MS Bodley Junius 15) is apparently the work of Thomas Marshall (d. 1685): see Campbell (1953), p. 14, n. 1 and the summary of J. Lawrence Mitchell's paper, 'Some notes on the Textual History of the Manuscripts of the OE Orosius', in 'The Second St. Louis Conference on Manuscript Studies', *Manuscripta*, xx (1976), 17.

[3] This material was already missing when Thomas Marshall annotated the Junius transcript of the Cotton MS (see below, p. xxv n. 2). Campbell (1953), p. 14, claims that 'there can be little doubt that the original second gathering was withdrawn . . . by some vandal who wished to possess the MS. of the *periplus* for himself' and this may be so. It should be noted, however, that the part of the *periplus* that attracted most interest in the sixteenth and seventeenth centuries, the account of Ohthere's northern voyage, has remained in its entirety. For early interest in the *periplus*, see D. S. Brewer, 'Sixteenth, Seventeenth and Eighteenth Century References to the Voyage of Ohthere', *Anglia*, lxxi (1952–3), 202–11.

[4] See Malcolm Parkes, 'The Palaeography of the Parker Manuscript of the *Chronicle*, Laws and Sedulius, and Historiography at Winchester in the late ninth and tenth centuries', *ASE*, v (1976), 156–7 and notes.

[5] See T. A. M. Bishop, 'An Early Example of the Square Minuscule', *Transactions of the Cambridge Bibliographical Society*, iv (1964–8), 246–52 and Parkes, pp. 158–9.

t^1 and with a mixture of square capitals and insular majuscule as the basis of a secondary display script.[2] In addition there are a number of elaborate initials in outline which are by the same artist as the initials in the Junius Psalter, and which are closely related to the initials in the Tanner MS of the OE Bede.[3] All the indications are that the scriptorium responsible for script and illustrations was at Winchester.[4] Corrections are few and are mainly the work of the original scribe. This scribe normally indicates omissions by placing either a single dot or two vertical dots on or below the line, inserting the omitted letters above.[5] Corrections indicated by a comma on or below the line are the work of a second scribe;[6] corrections with no omission mark are frequently indistinguishable from corrections by the main scribe, but sometimes written in what is clearly a later script.[7]

Although palaeographical evidence points to Winchester as its place of origin, nothing is known of the history of this manuscript before its appearance in the library of the Duke of Lauderdale at the end of the seventeenth century.[8] Before that, according to Thomas Marshall (d. 1685), who added a few variant readings from it to Junius's transcript of the Cotton MS, and George Hickes, who was the Duke of Lauderdale's chaplain from 1676 to 1678,[9] it was the property of Dr. John Dee (d. 1608), the Elizabethan astrologer and collector of manuscripts. There is, however, no mention of the Orosius in the list of Dee's books.[10] A detailed account of the subsequent history of MS L, as well as its physical appearance, is given in Alistair Campbell's introduction to the

---

[1] e.g. *beswac*, f. 2ᵛ, l. 2, *se*, f. 4, l. 27, *æfter* f. 19ᵛ, l. 6.

[2] See Parkes, pp. 159–60.

[3] See F. Wormald, 'Decorated Initials in English MSS from A.D. 900–1100', *Archaeologia*, xci (1945), 107–35, esp. p. 118; id., 'The Winchester School before St. Æthelwold' in *England before the Conquest*, ed. P. Clemoes and K. Hughes (Cambridge, 1971), pp. 305–13, and Parkes, p. 157.

[4] See Parkes, pp. 162 ff. Parkes suggests as the order of copying first Or., then the Junius Psalter, then the Parker Chronicle.

[5] e.g. f. 3, l. 16 *gewearð*, f. 17, l. 11 *hie*.

[6] e.g. f. 2, l. 16 *fo'lc'*.   [7] e.g. f. 45, l. 22 *lau'da'menda*.

[8] The signature Joan Davysun in a sixteenth-century hand appears on f. 1.

[9] See George Hickes, *Catalogus*, printed with *Institutiones Grammaticæ Anglo-Saxonicæ* (Oxford, 1689), p. 167 and Campbell (1953), pp. 21–2. Campbell suggests that Hickes either derived his information from Marshall's note or himself communicated it to Marshall. A third possibility is that they share a common source.

[10] See M. R. James, 'Lists of MSS formerly owned by Dr. John Dee' *Transactions of the Bibliographical Society*; Supplement No. 1 (1921).

EEMF facsimile. It forms the basis of the EETS edition by Henry Sweet.

2. *British Library, Cotton Tiberius B. i.* The Cotton MS, here referred to as MS C and used as the basis of the text pp. 15/1–28/11. Ker 191. Ff. vii+163+iv. *c.* 280×195 mm. Written space 224–215×136–130 mm. 27 long lines (25 on ff. 3–34). In addition to the OE Orosius this manuscript contains the verse Menologium (ff. 112–14^v) and Gnomic Verses (f. 115^{rv}) in a hand of s. xi med., and the C text of the *Anglo-Saxon Chronicle* (ff. 115^v–64), ending with the annal for 1066 and written in a number of hands of s. xi med. with an addition in a hand of s. xii², the first hand being that of the Menologium and Gnomic Verses.[1] The OE Orosius takes up ff. 3–111^v and seems to be written in four hands of s. xi¹: (1) ff. 3–32/25 (Or. 1/1–40/16); (2) ff. 32^v/1 *-ma cyning–*34^v/13 (Or. 40/16–43/19); (3) ff. 34^v/13 *þæt to secgenne–*45/3 (Or. 43/19–57/12); (4) ff. 45/4 *moston tawian–*111^v (Or. 57/12–156/23). A hand of s. xi/xii has made a number of alterations, notably *him* (dpl.) to *hiom, hi* to *hy,* and *hiora* to *heora,* and there are numerous annotations in the hand of Robert Talbot, by whom the manuscript was lent to Leland (d. 1552). Nothing is known of the place of origin of this manuscript; however, by the time the Chronicle annals for 491 to 1048 were added, it seems to have been at Abingdon. By 1621 it had entered the possession of Robert Cotton, having been acquired by him from Bowyer (see MS Harley 6018, f. 154^v). MS C forms the basis of the transcripts by Franciscus Junius, Elstob and Ballard, and of the editions by Daines Barrington, Thorpe, and Bosworth.[2]

---

[1] See further Ker (1957), 191. I give Ker's foliation here.

[2] The Junius transcript is now Bodleian MS Junius 15 (5127). For the subsequent annotation of the Junius MS by Thomas Marshall and Ballard and Elstob's transcripts of it, see Campbell (1953), p. 24. For Barrington and Thorpe's dependence on Elstob's transcript in their editions, see Campbell (1953) p. 25. Campbell (p. 24) also cites 'for completeness' the transcript of a few passages from the Cotton MS in MS Rawlinson A 310. However, apart from the printed extracts cited by Brewer (see p. xxiii n. 3 above) and a handful of readings from Cotton in Leland, *Collectanea,* iii, 121, I know of at least two other manuscripts containing transcripts which could be derived from the Cotton MS. These are BL MS Cotton Vitellius D. vii, with a passage from Book I, ch. i (the section now missing from MS L) transcribed by Joscelyn, the secretary of Archbishop Parker, and BL MS Addit. 43704, with a transcript of the opening of Book V, ch. xiii, apparently by Lawrence Nowell. The British Library catalogue says that the manuscript from which this last transcript was

3. *Bodleian, Eng. Hist. e. 49 (30481)*. The Bodley fragment, here referred to as MS B. Ker 323. saec. xi[1]. Ff. iii+2+xi. Ff. i–iii, 3–13 are modern paper, 4 leaves are missing between ff. 1 and 2, which were probably once a bifolium, the second sheet of a quire of 8 leaves, although they are now separate. Ruling on 1[v] and 2[r]. 234×168 mm. Written space 178×127 mm. 29 long lines. This fragment consists of two complete leaves, subsequently used as the wrapper of an octavo book, and contains parts of Bk. III of the OE Orosius, chs. iii–v and vii–ix (57/14–59/11 and 66/5–67/27). Its history is unknown. It was printed by Napier in *MLR*, viii (1913), 59–63.

4. *Vatican City, Reg. Lat. 497, f. 71*. The Vatican fragment, here referred to as MS V. Ker 391, saec. xi[1]. 1 leaf. 207×144 mm. Written space 178×112 mm. Probably 26 long lines. A complete leaf of the OE Orosius, Bk. IV, ch. xi, of which all but the last 13 lines on the verso have been erased. Legible parts correspond to 109/13–26. The leaf was at Trier in the late 11th century and used there, after erasure, for the conclusion of a life of St. Gertrude. The text has been printed by Steinmeyer in *ZfdA*, xxiv (1880), 192, and, after a re-examination under ultra-violet light, by Bately (1964), pp. 224–30.

II. LOST MANUSCRIPTS

These four manuscripts are the only ones still extant. However, there are indications that others once existed. Thus Leland records an *Orosius Saxonice* at Glastonbury in the early sixteenth century,[1]

made was neither Cotton nor Lauderdale; however, it could in fact be a careless copy of the former. For the accuracy of other transcripts by Joscelyn and Nowell see J. Sanders Gale, 'John Joscelyn's Notebook: a Study of the Contents and Sources of B.L. Cotton MS. Vitellius D. vii', unpublished dissertation, Nottingham, 1978, and A. Lutz, 'Zur Rekonstruktion der Version G der Angelsächsischen Chronik', *Anglia*, xcv (1977), 1–19.

[1] *Collectanea*, iii. 154. This may be the same as the Orosius *in Anglica* listed in a Glastonbury catalogue of the 13th century: see MS Trinity College Cambridge R. 5. 33 and T. W. Williams, *Somerset Mediæval Libraries* (Bristol, 1897), pp. 68 and 85. Since the manuscript seems to have contained only the Orosius it cannot be identified with the Cotton MS, nor, unless the palimpsest leaf had become separated from the rest of the manuscript before it reached Trier, can be it MS V. However, in spite of the comment in Campbell (1953), p. 24, that it is a MS 'not now known to exist', identification of the Glastonbury MS with the now fragmentary Bodley MS, or even the Winchester Lauderdale MS cannot be ruled out. For the evidence against a Hatton MS of the Orosius see

and a sentence on the flyleaf of Rouen MS 524 may point to the presence of yet another manuscript on the Continent in the early Middle Ages.[1] Evidence of a different kind is provided by an Old French poem, Calendre's *Les Empereors de Rome* (here referred to as LER), preserved in Paris, Bibliothèque Nationale, fonds français 794, saec. xiii. According to the poet, his source was a *queronique reongnie*, written in Latin and once in the possession of the Byzantine emperor, Manuel Comnenus;[2] however, close examination reveals that whatever form was taken by Calendre's immediate source, his poem must ultimately be based on the Old English version.[3] Not only does it share errors and additions found in Or.—for instance, like Or. it describes Cato as committing suicide by leaping from a wall and Titus as saying that he considered that day lost on which he did nothing good[4]—but some of its own errors seem to have arisen from the misreading or miscopying of Old English. Thus the similarity between OE *sweor*, 'father-in-law', and *sweord*, 'sword', seems to be responsible for the discrepancy between Calendre's claim that Numerianus was killed by a sword and that of OH and Or. that he was killed by his father-in-law.[5] The existence of an intransitive use of OE *geeode*, 'went', beside the transitive 'conquered' accounts for the difference between Or.'s statement that Constantius conquered Britain (*geeode Brettaniam*) and Calendre's that he merely went there

---

Campbell (1953), p. 21. For the claim that Nowell's transcript of a passage from Book V, ch. xiii is taken from a now lost manuscript, see above, p. xxv n. 2.

[1] See Mossé (1955), pp. 198–203. Mossé would date the four-line quotation as 'from the 10th or, more probably, the 11th century'; Ker 375, however, dates it as twelfth-century. Both agree that the manuscript on the flyleaf of which it is written, and which belonged to the abbey of Fécamp, was copied on the Continent in the ninth century and that there is no evidence that it was ever in England. For a discussion of the text see below, pp. xxxiii–xxxiv. Verbal similarities between Or. 152/15–16 and the *Anglo-Saxon Chronicle*, s.a. 975 (E) may imply that a manuscript of Or. was available to the author of the northern recension. However, I agree with Professor Whitelock, to whom I am indebted for this suggestion, that the similarity is probably accidental.

[2] LER 4864–8 'Li empereres Manuiax / Qui cest livre ot an conpaignie, / La queronique reongnie, / Clamoit cest livre et disoit tant / Nel doit avoir qui ne l'antant.' Could these words attributed to Manuel be based on an inscription on a flyleaf?

[3] See H. Nearing, 'The Legend of Julius Caesar's British Conquest', *PMLA*, lxiv (1949), 889–929, Galia Millard's edition of LER, pp. 6–18 and Bately (1960), pp. 567–86.

[4] LER 1797–801 and 3092–5, Or. 128/18–19 and 138/23–139/2.

[5] LER 3949, Or. 146/18.

(*passe an Bretaigne*).¹ Similarly the fact that OE *wif* and *bearn* are uninflected in nom. acc. sg. and pl. explains why Calendre describes Narseus as having one wife and one son, while Orosius refers to *uxores liberosque* (Or. *his wif 7 his bearn*).² As for Calendre's description of Cleopatra's suicide as taking place in a *fosse*, this is more easily accounted for as a rendering of Or. *byrgenne* than of OH *monumentum*.³

Moreover, where the extant manuscripts of Or. differ, Calendre's version often shares with one of them an error that can be shown to have arisen in the course of transmission of the OE text. Thus, for instance, because of an omission, MS L of the OE version confuses Theodosius the Elder with his son, the Roman emperor, and the same confusion appears in Calendre's poem:

> Si anvea Theodosie
> .i. haut baron qui soz lui ere
> Qui puis fu de Rome emperere,

corresponding not to MS C 'þa sende Ualens þyder þeodosius his ealdormon mid fyrde, þæs godan Theodosiuses fæder þe eft wæs casere', OH VII. xxxiii. 6 'comes Theodosius, Theodosii qui post imperio praefuit pater, a Valentiniano missus', but to the version found in MS L, 'þa sende Ualens þider Theodosius his ealdormon þe eft wæs casere'.⁴ Occasionally, however, Calendre's version differs significantly from that of the surviving manuscripts of Or., indicating that his source contained readings found in none of these.⁵

If Calendre is speaking the truth, then, we must assume the existence of a Latin translation of the OE Orosius, based on a no longer extant manuscript of that work. That such a translation of a translation should have been undertaken is perhaps less surprising than at first sight appears if we call to mind the popularity of Freculph's *Chronicon*, a history which like Or., though not in the vernacular, is an abridgement of OH, with added material from other sources. The Old English version could either have been considered to have independent worth, or have been used as a substitute for the Latin at a centre where this was not available.

---

¹ LER 3993, Or. 147/8.   ² LER 4069, OH VII. xxv. 11, Or. 147/18.
³ LER 2088, Or. 130/9–10, OH VI. xix. 17.
⁴ Or. 152/19–21, LER 4554–6. Like Or. Calendre incorrectly attaches the account of Theodosius the Elder's execution to Firmus.
⁵ See below, pp. xxxvi–xxxvii.

When and why it was undertaken and how it came to be first in Byzantium and then in Lorraine as Calendre claims must remain a matter for speculation. The Byzantine emperor named by Calendre—Manuel Comnenus, c. 1143–1180—was renowned for his interest in Latin culture and for his Frankish connections.[1] Thus, it might be not unreasonable to suppose that he could have acquired the hypothetical Latin manuscript from a Western European source (or even had an Old English version translated). However, Latin or Old English versions could have reached Byzantium earlier.[2] An even more eminent patron of the arts was Manuel Comnenus' predecessor Constantine VII Porphyrogenitus, emperor from 944 to 959. Like Manuel he had Frankish connections[3] and a splendid library, and more significantly he was the promoter of a huge programme of codification and extract. Since historical writing had now grown to an intractable bulk, he wrote, and since industry and scholarship, like everything else, were in decline, it was vain to expect people nowadays to read original works in full; so he would skim off the cream, and hope that practical men would be prevailed on to digest it for their profit.[4] Moreover, his appreciation of (the Latin) Orosius is also on record: in 949 he sent the Caliph of Cordova splendid manuscripts of Dioscorides and Orosius, saying, 'As for Orosius, he is no problem, as you will doubtless easily find someone who knows

---

[1] Not only were both of Manuel's consorts Latin princesses, respectively Bertha of Sulzbach and Mary of Antioch, but his daughter married Rainier of Montferrat and his son Alexios II was married while still a child to Agnes-Anna, daughter of Louis VII of France. His niece Maria married Stephen IV of Hungary, his niece Theodora married Duke Henry of Austria, and another niece of the same name married King Baldwin III of Jerusalem. Contemporaries actually commented on Manuel's policy of dynastic marriages with western royal houses: see Eustathius, *Opuscula*, ed. T. L. F. Tafel (repr. Amsterdam, 1964), 199. 57 ff. I am grateful to Professor Robert Browning for this information and for advice on this section.

[2] If the translation of Orosius had any part in King Alfred's plan, it is just conceivable that he could have sent a copy (or a Latin version of it) to the Emperor Leo VI, especially if he was aware of the fact that the Byzantines too were encouraging the making of translations in the vernacular. See *Cura Pastoralis* 6/4–6 and Dvornik (1970), *passim*. However, I have not been able to find a shred of evidence in support of what otherwise would seem an attractive theory.

[3] His sister was married to Louis of Italy and his son to the daughter of Hugh of Provence. For his Francophilism see Toynbee (1973), p. 18, n. 4.

[4] See Romilly Jenkins, *Byzantium: The Imperial Centuries: AD 610–1071* (London, 1966), p. 258.

Latin.'[1] It is therefore not impossible that the (hypothetical) presence of a Latin—or Old English—version of Calendre's source in Byzantium was the result of a gift by some Western dignitary,[2] aware of Constantine's interest.[3] Alternatively, a manuscript of the OE Orosius could have been taken to Byzantium by one of the Anglo-Saxon exiles that sought refuge there after the Norman Conquest.[4] As for the subsequent removal of Manuel's copy to Lorraine, it is tempting to see this as the result of the sack of Constantinople by the Crusaders in 1204,[5] though a peaceful transaction cannot of course be ruled out.

If Calendre is not speaking the truth, on the other hand, but merely using Manuel's name to give his work greater 'respectability',[6] then we must query also the veracity of his claim to be using a Latin chronicle. The evidence provided by the text is confused and confusing: there are some features that might lead us to suppose an intermediary Latin version, while there are other features that are more easily explained if we suppose a direct rendering from Old English into Old French.[7] There remains the problem of comprehension: could Old English have been intelligible to Calendre? There is certainly ample evidence of the understanding of Old English in England in the Middle English

---

[1] See Romilly Jenkins, *Byzantium*, pp. 265–6. Toynbee (1973), p. 552, however, casts doubts on Constantine's own Latinity: 'In the tenth century a knowledge of Latin was as rare in the Byzantine World as a knowledge of Greek was in the contemporary West. If any tenth-century Byzantine intellectual might have been expected to have acquired a mastery of Latin, it would have been Constantine Porphyrogenitus; for Constantine was both a scholar and a statesman, and in both capacities, he would have found a knowledge of Latin useful to him. However, Constantine's Latin was poorer than Liutprand's smattering of Greek . . . and, every time that Constantine undertakes to interpret a Latin word himself, he betrays his ignorance.'

[2] Liutprand, Bishop of Cremona, who visited Constantine in 949 and who was himself a scholar, is a name that comes to mind; another dignitary who came on a mission to Byzantium at this time was Siegfried of Parma.

[3] Constantine was interested not only in history but also in the geography of the lands beyond his empire (see Toynbee (1973), pp. 581–2), so the geographical additions in the OE Orosius might well have been of interest to him.

[4] See Christine Fell, 'The Icelandic version of the Anglo-Saxon emigration to Byzantium', *ASE*, iii (1974), 179–96 and Jonathan Shepard, 'The English and Byzantium', *Traditio*, xxix (1973), 53–92.

[5] See S. Runciman, *A History of the Crusades* (Cambridge, 1954), iii. 123–4.

[6] It is strange that Calendre at no point names Orosius as his ultimate authority, and the possibility must be considered that the person who excerpted the Roman material—and selected only a small part of that—was someone other than Calendre himself, and that this person did not include in these excerpts Or.'s reference to Orosius.   [7] See Bately (1960), pp. 583–6.

period, and the fact that Anglo-Saxon texts were still being copied
in the second half of the twelfth century demonstrates that these
could still be read with ease at that time. Whether a Frenchman
could be expected to understand Old English in the first quarter of
the thirteenth century would depend on the extent of his knowledge of contemporary English; in the last third of the twelfth
century Marie de France claimed that her Fables were translated
from English—and not just English but King Alfred's English:

> Li reis Alvrez, que mut l'ama,
> Le translata puis en engleis,
> E jeo l'ai rimee en frenceis;

but she was writing in England, not in Lorraine.[1]

III. THE RELATIONSHIP BETWEEN THE MANUSCRIPTS

1. *MSS L and C.* Joseph Bosworth, the editor of C, believed that
this manuscript was no more than a careless copy of L, citing in
support of his theory the fact that 'the omissions of L are omitted
by C', while 'some of the omissions of C are just such as would be
made by a copier of L, and some of the errors of L seem to be
copied by C'.[2] However, of the instances quoted by Bosworth only
two could possibly be taken to point to dependence of one manuscript on the other: C *Mæse* for L *Mæs`ian'e* and the shared error
Læcede for *Læcedemonia*.[3] Of the first, Bosworth says, 'In L . . . the
scribe first wrote the defective word mæse; but perceiving his error,
he put ian above in small letters . . .; C, observing only the larger
and more perceptible letters, and passing over the small super-
scribed ian copied the erroneous word mæse.' However, neither
the method of indicating the omission nor the manner of insertion
of the letters *ian* is that normally employed by the scribe of MS L
and there are good palaeographical reasons to suppose that the

---

[1] See A. Cameron, 'Middle English in Old English MSS' in *Chaucer and
Middle English Studies in Honour of Rossell Hope Robbins*, ed. B. Rowland (London,
1974), pp. 218–29, and for late twelfth-century OE manuscripts, Ker (1957),
pp. xviii–xix. That Marie de France's Alfred was the king of that name is disputed, though on slender evidence which deserves careful re-examination: see
Karl Warnke, *Die Fabeln der Marie de France* (Halle, 1898), pp. xliv–xlv and
A. Ewert and R. C. Johnston, *Marie de France: Fables* (Oxford, 1942) p. xi.

[2] Bosworth (1859), p. xix. Sweet, *Cura Pastoralis*, p. xxi, comments that
Bosworth has 'proved decisively that the later MS is a direct copy of the
earlier one'.   [3] See 35/3 and 55/23–4.

hand is that of corrector no. 2.[1] Although this corrector could have had access to another manuscript of Or., it is more likely that he made the addition independently, in order to bring *mæse* in line with the two examples of *Mesiane* for Latin *Messenii* that occur immediately before it in the text. L's *mæs'ian'e*, therefore, is of no value in determining manuscript relationship.

Of the second error, Bosworth says: 'At the end of sheet IIII . . . of the Lauderdale MS., the scribe had only room to write Læcede-; and in taking another sheet, and in beginning the next page, he omitted -monia . . . The scribe of C copied the incomplete word Læcede just as L left it, without the same reason for leaving it incomplete, as it does not conclude a sheet, nor come at the end of a line in C. It seems hardly possible, then, that such a glaring mistake could have been made in C, if it had not been copied from L.'[2] However, there are other 'glaring mistakes' in C—and in L too—not at the end of a line in either manuscript,[3] and it is quite possible that the position of the word *Læcede* in L—at the end not merely of a page but of a gathering—was, by chance or by design, identical with that in its exemplar,[4] the error being already present in L and C's common ancestor.

At the same time, there is plenty of evidence to suggest that C, far from being a copy of L, was independent of it. Among the proper names, for example, forms such as C *Aruhes, Assapias,*

[1] See above, p. xxiv. Presence of a 'correction' alongside the original reading in the common manuscript may well explain 45/11 *Cambisis* or *Cambises* (chapter headings *Cambisis*) where MS L has final *is* or *es* erased and MS C reads *Cambis*. In such a case, the scribe of L would seem not to have noticed the 'correction' until he had copied the name in its original form.

[2] Bosworth (1859), p. xx.

[3] e.g. the omission of *hlafordas* in 102/5 and the reading *Octauianuses* for *Antoniuses*, 129/29.

[4] See the description in P. Schmitz, *Histoire de l'ordre de Saint-Benoît* (Maredsous, 1948), ii. 71, of one of the methods of manuscript duplication current in *scriptoria* in this period: 'on détachait les cahiers d'un manuscrit et on les distribuait à plusieurs calligraphes. Chacun de ceux-ci reproduisait exactement le cahier reçu, de façon à terminer le verso du dernier feuillet de la même façon. Pour cela il suffisait souvent de resserrer ou d'élargir les mots des dernières lignes, de multiplier ou de négliger les abréviations. Ce système qui apparaît déjà au VIIIe siècle fut très usité.' In this connection, it may be noted that a number of leaves in MS L end with a run-over of a word or part of a word (once as many as five words: see f. 80[v]) to the space below the last line, yet elsewhere the scribe appears to have no objection to splitting a word so that the first part of it occurs at the bottom of one page and the remainder at the top of the next, whether facing or not (cf., for example, ff. 22[v]–23 and f. 24–24[v]).

Othono, and *Sostianus* are closer to the readings *Arucha, Assapios, Othonam*, and *Sostianos* or *Sosdianos* of the family of manuscripts of OH to which Or.'s exemplar belonged[1] than L *Arues, Aspanias, Thona*, and *Satianos*. *Folucius*, for the *Falucium* of the 'related' Latin manuscripts, a name omitted from L, cannot be the invention of the Cotton scribe, while an error such as C *Semuses* for *Remuses* can hardly be derived from L *Romuses*. Again, there are a number of passages where material has been omitted by L but not by C, and again the nature of this material precludes intelligent correction by the scribe of C. Thus, for instance, the detail that the *ceorlas* seize their masters' wives for themselves—OH IV. v. 5 'coniugiaque dominorum sibi per scelus usurpant'—is found only in C, as is the statement that as a result of Calatinus' stratagem the enemy left the pass undefended, so that the Roman army was able to go through it: cf. OH IV. viii. 2 (of Calpurnius Flamma) 'in se Poenos omnes pugnando conuertit, donec Romanus exercitus obsessas angustias hoste non urguente transiret.'[2] Of course, with medieval manuscripts one has always to bear in mind the possibility of correction through collation; however, the evidence as it stands indicates that MS C is not a copy of L, though apparently sharing with it a common ancestor in which a number of errors occurring in both L and C were already to be found. That this common ancestor was at least one remove from the original translation is demonstrated not only by the shared error *Læcede* but also by readings such as 149/3 *byrig* for *brycge* (OH VII. xxviii. 16 *pontem*) and 75/18 *Fumus* for *Fauius* (without exact correspondence in OH) and by omissions such as those in 52/34 and 102/5.

2. *MSS B and V and the Rouen Sentence.* The three surviving fragments of Or. are too short to provide much information about manuscript relationships. Of the sentence in the Rouen MS[3] the most that can be said is that it cannot have been copied from C and that it never agrees with C against L; where it agrees with L against C the reading corresponds to that of the Latin, while where it differs from both L and C, it is the latter which have the reading closest to the Latin. Its most interesting feature is its use of the formula 'from frimðe weron agane' to express the passing of time,

---

[1] See below, p. lvi, and, for details of forms in this section, see Glossary of Proper Names.   [2] See 87/22–3 and 93/3–4.   [3] See 35/22–6.

in place of MSS L and C 'þæt wæs from frymðe middangeardes'. The verb *agan* in this—or indeed in any—context is not found anywhere in Or. as we know it from the Lauderdale and Cotton MSS. However, it occurs several times in the early parts of the *Anglo-Saxon Chronicle*, for instance, s.a. 6 'From frymþe middangeardes oþ þis gear wæron agan .v. þusendu wintra 7 cc. wintra.' There is no way of telling whether the scribe of Rouen himself was responsible for this substitution, or whether, as Mossé believes, he 'had before his eyes a copy of the OE *Orosius* of which no other trace is left'.[1] In support of the theory of a written exemplar Mossé cites the peculiar use of the symbol *y* for *v* in *y.tiene* (for the numeral *v.tiene*) in both L and R, a reading the unfamiliarity of which is presumably responsible for C's variant *tyne*.

MS B's relationship to the two major manuscripts is again unclear through lack of evidence. If we discount the agreement of B with C in reading *murcniað* for L *murciað*, 67/7, as quite possibly the result of the later date of these two manuscripts,[2] then what evidence there is suggests agreement between B and L against C. Where L and C agree against B, e.g. in reading *forhergede*, 58/17, MS B *oferhergode*, there is no good reason to suppose that their version is not the original one. On the other hand, when L and B agree against C, the latter sometimes has the 'better' reading. Thus, for instance, MS C *swiðe fela*, 58/18, is a more accurate rendering of OH *plurimos* than L *fela*, B *feala*, while although L *gewicadon*, B *gewicodan*, 57/25-6, is contextually appropriate,[3] C *gewacodan* has the support of OH III. vi. 1 'nisi otio et lentitudine torpuisset'. Moreover, where both B and C differ significantly from L, they differ also from one another: thus, for instance, for MS L *lxxxviii* (57/24, OH III. vi. 1 *lxxxviii*), C reads *lxxviii* and B *lxxxvii*, while for L *besierede* (66/18), C reads *bismere*, B *bescyrede*.

---

[1] See Mossé (1955), p. 202. For a different formula using the verb *agan* see *An OE Martyrology* 2/8 'þa wæs agangen from middangeardes fruman fif þusend geara 7 ane geare læs þonne twa hund þa Crist acenned wæs'.

[2] In addition to the instances in Or., variants occur also in the manuscripts of Alfred's *Boethius* and *Cura Pastoralis*, in the case of the latter the form without *n* apparently representing the original reading: see Horgan (1963), p. 44. Later texts such as the Lambeth Psalter, the West Saxon Gospels and Ælfric's Homilies use the form with -*n*-, at least in the manuscript versions with which I am familiar.

[3] The Latin of the passage corresponding to 57/24-6 states that 'Gallorum inundatio ad quartum ab Vrbe lapidem consedit.'

However, MS B does not fall into L's error of reading *nan land* for *on an land* (58/7), and its use of *æt* for 57/24 *oð* (L and C) may indicate an underlying manuscript with the spelling *ot*. It is not possible, therefore, to determine whether MS B is a copy, or a copy of a copy, of MS L,[1] or whether it is derived from some lost manuscript, ancestor of MS L but not of MS C.[2]

As for MS V, this differs in several respects from both C and L and may well represent a separate manuscript tradition. Since the variations involved are of vocabulary, with apparently little or no corresponding alteration of meaning, e.g. V *burgleode*, L *burgware*, C *burhware*, 109/23, it is unfortunately not possible to decide which forms are those of the 'original' Or. However, one variant used by V—*ofworpod* for L and C *oftorfod*, 109/19—may be of some significance. The word *ofworpian* is cited by BT only from the Laws of Alfred, *Einleit*. ch. 21, where it occurs three times, the twelfth-century copy in the Textus Roffensis significantly substituting *oftorfod* for the first occurrence and *ofworpen* for the two others. The simple form *worpian* is equally rarely recorded, occurring in the *Cura Pastoralis*, *Elene*, and the *Poetic Dialogues of Solomon and Saturn*, all of which works, like the Laws of Alfred and Or. itself, were apparently composed before or during the ninth century. Instances of *(of)weorpan*, in the sense of 'throw and hit', and the compounds *oftorfian*, *-tyrfan*, on the other hand, are not only far more numerous but also occur in texts written right up to the end of the Old English period. It is possible, therefore, that *ofworpod* may be a typically early word which subsequently fell into disfavour and disuse and that the reading of MS V either represents the original version of Or. or replaced the original at an early date. If the former is the case, then we would appear to have in the Vatican fragment independent testimony of the Old English translation.

3. *The Old French Version, LER.* As I have argued in detail elsewhere,[3] the manuscript of Or. underlying Calendre's poem had many features in common with MS L and shared with it errors of transcription not found in C. Thus, for instance, when

---

[1] In which case B *on an land* would be an intelligent correction.

[2] In which case the correction in L of *Furculus* to *Furcules* (66/11, OH III. xv. 2 *furculas*, C *Furculus*, B *Furcules*) must be supposed to have been already present in some form in L's exemplar.

[3] Bately (1960), pp. 571–6. See also above, p. xxviii.

LER states that Domitian's pride was the cause of St. John's exile—

> Et Dex! comant fu il si os
> Qant il an l'isle de Pathmos
> Saint Jehan an essil anvoie—

it must be following a faulty text such as that of L 'wæs on swa micle ofermetto astigen þæt he bebead þæt mon Iohannes þone apostol gebrohte on Bothmose þæm iglande on wræcsiþe', from which the words 'bead þæt man on gelice to him onbugan sceolde swa to gode 7 he', found in MS C between *he* and *bebead*, had accidentally been dropped.[1] Like L, too, it refers to Rome as being saved because the Gauls camped outside—*se logierent*—, suggesting an underlying *gewicadon* rather than *gewacadon*, and has the reading *Maximianus* for C and OH *Maximinus*.[2]

However, on occasion LER provides a better reading than L, indicating that it is derived not from L but from a now lost manuscript, ancestor of L but not of C. Thus, for instance, it agrees with C and the Latin manuscripts closest to Or. in reading *Claudius* where L has *Gaius*,[3] and it seems to be inspired by a reading such as C 'Romane him geþancodon ealles his geswinces mid wyrsan leane þonne he to him geearnod hæfde', the second part of which is omitted by L, when it quotes what at first sight appears to be a proverb:

> Li vilains dit, nel puis noier,
> De bel servir malvés loier.[4]

That yet another lost manuscript intervened between the common ancestor of L and LER and LER itself is suggested by a number of readings which can be shown on metrical grounds to have been used by Calendre and not to have been introduced subsequently through scribal error. Thus, for instance, LER reads *Thitus* for OH V. xvi. 1 *Quintus*, Or. *Cuintinus*, and *Theodric* for Or. and OH *Tetricum*.[5] Very occasionally LER's reading is 'better' than that of both L and C, usually in contexts where intelligent correction is

---

[1] 139/6–9 and LER 3109–11.
[2] LER 153 and 4129, Or. 57/25 and 148/6.   [3] 137/12 and LER 2777.
[4] 119/4–5, LER 567–8. In spite of its prefatory 'Li vilains dit', this saying is not to be found in Adolf Tobler's *Li Proverbe au Vilain* (Leipzig, 1895). Dr. Millard identifies it with proverb no. 462 in J. Morawski's *Proverbes français antérieurs au XVᵉ siècle*, *CFMA* (Paris, 1925): 'De bien faire vient bien maus', but it seems to be formed rather on the type 'En biau servir covient eur avoir' (no. 631), with a twist of meaning which is very effective in this context.
[5] LER 884, 3881, Or. 122/7 and 145/25 and OH VII. xxiii. 5.

a possible explanation. Thus, LER *Pathmos* for L *Bothmose*, C *Thomore*, referring to the place of St. John's exile, is the correct form of a name likely to be familiar to anyone with a reasonable knowledge of the New Testament, while *Probus*, L and C *Brobus*, is not only the name of a Roman emperor but occurs in its correct form in the lists of chapter headings in both L and C.[1] The identification of *Geoweorþa* with Jugurtha could have been made by an intelligent reader, copyist, or translator conversant with Roman history; the name *Apuleius*, L and C *Apulcius*, could similarly be the result of correction by someone who had heard of Apuleius' namesake, the Platonic philosopher and author of the *Golden Ass*.[2] Even the reading *Sapor*, for OH *Sapore*, L and C *Sapan*,[3] could be the result of correction by someone (whether Calendre or an intermediary) familiar with one of the short world chronicles popular in the Middle Ages.[4] The great weight of evidence, therefore, suggests that the manuscript of Or. lying behind Calendre's poem was descended from a hypothetical MS 'X', ancestor also of Cotton, by way of a second hypothetical MS 'Y', ancestor also of Lauderdale, and, more immediately, a third hypothetical MS 'Z', based on 'Y' but not ancestor of Lauderdale.

4. *Text and Chapter Headings.* The text of Or. is divided into six books, each further subdivided into sections which may for convenience be called chapters. In MS L a list of chapter headings for all six books is placed before Book I. MS C has the same list (C1) in the same position and also repeats the entries relating to Books V and VI (C2) at the appropriate points in the text, with one set following the end of Book IV and another following the end of Book V. All these lists are derived ultimately from the same source, but each has individual errors or special readings which seem to rule out the possibility of any one being copied from another. On one occasion C2 avoids an error found in both L and C1, possibly indicating that the duplication of entries in MS C occurred at a very early stage in transmission (though intelligent correction cannot be ruled out).[5] Usually, however, significant

---

[1] 139/9, LER 3110; 146/9 and 7/24, LER 3893.
[2] 120/11, LER 580 and 122/27, LER 994.
[3] 145/2, LER 3807.   [4] See, e.g., Jerome–Eusebius, col. 693.
[5] 5/27 'hu þa þeowas wunnan wiþ þa hlafordas', with *wunnan* omitted from L and C1. In both L and C1 the word *þeowas* occurs at the end of a line, a position which may explain why neither text has corrected the error. In a second place, 5/20, L and C1 agree with the text, 114/5, against C2.

variation is between L and C2 on the one hand and C1 on the other, and this may well be the result of recollation of C1, or an ancestor of C1, with the text.[1] Although chapter headings are found in a number of manuscripts of OH, the list in Or. was without question drawn up from the OE text, sharing with it fundamental errors of comprehension, such as the reference to fifty men slain in one night by their sons, and the interpretation of OH V. xviii. 1 *Sex. Iulio Caesare* as 'in the sixth consulship of Julius Caesar'.[2] It also agrees verbally with the corresponding parts of the text, though there are several interesting variations of vocabulary.[3] However, in a significant number of details it seems to have differed from the version of that text preserved in L and C. Some of these differences are the result of error in the list itself and whether they arose in the course of compilation of the chapter headings or in subsequent copying cannot be determined.[4] Some, however, are the result of error in the text and must be taken as evidence that the chapter headings were drawn up at a time when the text had not yet acquired some of the corruptions shared by L and C. Thus, for instance, for 76/4 *Escolafius*, the chapter headings in both L and C have *Escolapius*, the form found also in the Latin manuscripts closest to Or.[5] For 93/12-13 'feower hunde scipa 7 þritigum', they have the reading 'þrim hunda (*MS C* hund) scipa 7 . . . xxx', corresponding to OH IV. viii. 6 'trecentis triginta nauibus',[6] while for 146/9 *Brobus* the lists in L and C2 have the correct form *Probus*.[7] It seems, therefore, that when the list of chapter headings was compiled, the text too contained these correct readings and had not yet acquired the corruptions of L and C. This gives support

[1] See, e.g., 6/19, where L reads *Ispanie*, C2 *Ispania*, C1 *Ispanie leode*, corresponding to 131/23 *Ispania leode* (C *Ispaniæ leode*), also 6/7, where L and C2 read *wæron*, C1 and text, 120/11, *wunnon*, and 1/2, where L reads *ealne þisne middangeard* and C1 *ealne ðysne ymbhwyrft*, text, 8/11, *ealne þisne ymbhwyrft þises middangeardes*. For a possible interaction between text of C and C2, see 114/12 *Ueriatus*, C text *Uariatus* and heading *be Uariato*, beside chapter heading 5/21 *Ueriatus*, C2 *Uariatus*.

[2] 1/17, 27/2, 6/10-11 and 123/9-10.   [3] See below, p. lxxii.

[4] See, e.g., 88/5 *Caperronie*, chapter headings 4/1 *Caperrone* (L), *Caperone* (C1), 110/24 *Emilius*, chapter headings 5/12 *Enilius*, and 57/24 *iiii mila*, chapter headings 3/4 *iii mila*. None of the three lists has an entry for V. viii.

[5] 3/19. See Glossary of Proper Names. For the possibility that dictation is responsible for some of the differences of spelling between chapter headings and text see below, pp. cxv-cxvii.   [6] 4/11.

[7] 7/24. The form *Probus* is also found in LER 3893 f. C1 agrees with the text in reading *Brobus*, perhaps as a result of recollation.

to the conclusions drawn from a comparison of the texts of L and C, that these manuscripts are at least two removes from the archetype and had a common ancestor in which certain corruptions had already occurred.

IV. THE LANGUAGE OF THE MANUSCRIPTS

1. *MS L*. Since the Lauderdale MS of the OE Orosius is one of the four manuscripts on which our idea of eWS is based, it is not surprising that its language is usually described as 'typically eWS'. However, as Wrenn has pointed out,[1] MS L, 'while evidently approximately of the same period as the Hatton *Cura Pastoralis*, shows, on the one hand, an absence of its more archaic features, and on the other, many forms which, if taken out of any context, might suggest W.S. of a rather later period'. And Wrenn concludes, 'The *Orosius* . . . may be regarded as presenting a decidedly regular type of W.S., somewhat later than that of the *Cura Pastoralis* and probably post-Alfredian.' At the same time, there are a number of spellings, and a handful of lexical, morphological, and syntactical items of a kind generally described as Mercian or even Northumbrian, whose presence in eWS texts is usually explained as due to Mercian influence.[2] How far the scribe of L is responsible for this state of affairs and how far his usage reflects that of his exemplar it is impossible to determine with any certainty. However, it may be significant that although in a large number of respects L's usage agrees with that of Parker II (the Parker Chronicle annals 892–912, which are apparently the work of the scribe of L), there are a number of differences. Some of these could be the result of changes in spelling habits by the scribe; some, however, could be due to the existence of variant usages in his two exemplars. Since a detailed survey of the phonology, morphology, and syntax of the Lauderdale MS is provided by Cosijn in his *Altwestsächsische Grammatik* and by Wülfing in *Die Syntax in den Werken Alfred des Großen* it is to the most important similarities and differences between MS L and Parker II, with occasional reference to the usage of Parker I and

---

[1] ' "Standard" Old English', *Trans. Phil. Soc.* (1933), 75–6.
[2] Since we know so little about the sub-dialects of eWS I do not propose to draw any conclusions from the mixture of forms in this manuscript.

the oldest MSS of CP, that I propose to confine myself here. Lexical features will be touched on in Sections V (iv) and VI.[1]

I. Stressed *vowels*

(i) *a* for WS *a*/*o*+nasal. Like CP, MS L has a marked preference for *o*-spellings, in this being unlike lWS texts, in which *a* preponderates. However, as Cosijn, following Sweet, observes, there is a tendency for *o* to be used in words of frequent occurrence and *a* in less common words. Cosijn also finds *a*+*n* to appear more frequently in MS L than in CP.[2] The situation in Parker II resembles that in Or.: it has *o*- and *a*-spellings in stressed syllables in the proportions 5:3, but roughly the same number of different words are involved in the two categories. However, there are some differences of distribution: thus, although in both L and Parker II the spellings *mon* and *lond* are preferred to *man* and *land*, L prefers *long* (39×) to *lang* (7×), the latter being the only form (8×) in Parker II, while Parker II has almost as many instances of *manig* (3×) as of *monig* (4×), the latter being the only form in L (112×). *Fram* occurs 1× in both L and Parker II with *from* 2× in Parker II and 90× in L.[3]

(ii) *a* for WS *ea*+*l*+cons. *a*-spellings are occasionally found for *ea* in this position, though less frequently than in CP and Parker I and mainly in forms of the word *onwald, anwald*. *a*-spellings in this word occur 139 times, beside 26 instances of *ea* and 1 of *o*. *a* occurs once in *alneg* and *aldormon*, 5 times in *nales*, and 3 times in *alle*. CP has *a* in a far wider range of words, though *ea* spellings predominate here too, while in Parker I *a*-spellings predominate. Parker II, like MS L, normally has *ea*—including 3 instances of

---

[1] For a study of the phonology and morphology of the whole of the Parker Chronicle see Sprockel (1965). The annals up to 891 (here referred to as Parker I) form Sprockel's Section A. His Section B covers annals 891–924 and thus includes material apparently not written by the scribe of the OE Orosius, MS L. For a comparative study of the language of the MSS of CP and OH see Horgan (1963).

[2] Cosijn, i § 5. See also Campbell, *OEG* § 130. No attempt is made here to check Cosijn's statistics for CP nor normally to cite inflexional or compound variants.

[3] Parker II also has single instances of *a*-spellings where MS L prefers *o*: e.g. *gesamnod, gang*, MS L *gesomn-* (4×), *gong* (9×), *gang* (3×), and a single instance of *o* in *hond*, where L prefers *a* (*hand* 19×, *hond* 5×). For further statistics for L see Cosijn i § 5.

weald, 'wood'—the exceptions (excluding personal names) being one instance each of *gewaldenum*, *onwalde*, and *gewald*.[1]

(iii) *e* for WS *ĕa* in (a) *forgef* (1×), *onget* (1×), *ger* (20×), *ongen* (2×), *flex* (2×), *neh* (11×), *toecan* (1×), *þeh* (114×), words for which there is normally a preponderance of *ea*-spellings, exceptions being *flex* (never *fleax*) and *þeh* (beside *þeah* 24×). This smoothing of *ĕa*>*e* after *g* and before *c* and *χ* occurs only very rarely in CP.[2] Parker II like L uses *e*-spellings in *agef* (1×), *-get* (2×), *ger* (11×), *ongen* (2×), and *þeh* (5×), alongside *gear* (10×) and single instances of *ageaf*, *ongean* and *þeah*. In addition it has *e* in the place and personal name elements *-cester* and *sex-*. It differs from L in its use of *neah*, never *neh*, L having both forms, with *neah* and compounds 29× and *neh* 11× along with 2 instances of *-næh*.[3] However, since Parker II has only 2 examples of *neah* and that is the form preferred by L this difference is probably non-significant.

(b) *mehte*. *Mehte*[4] is the normal form in both L and Parker II, occurring 164× in L, 17× in Parker II. *Meahte*, the most common form in CP, occurs only once in Parker II and twice in L, in the account of Ohthere's voyages. L also has four examples of *mæhte(n)*.[5]

(c) *herg* (2×, beside *hearg* 2×). Smoothing of *ea* to *e*+*rc*, *rg* is a feature of the Mercian Vespasian Psalter gloss and Ru. 1.[6] This combination does not occur in Parker II.

(iv) *æ* for WS *ea* in *scæl* (3×) and *e* for WS *ie* in *-geld* (1×), *gelp* (2×), *gered-* (2×), *sceld* (2×), *gescend* (1×). Absence of palatal diphthongization is a feature of Kentish and Mercian and Campbell sees the examples of *e* in L as 'no doubt to be attributed to the influence of Merc. spelling'.[7] Parker II has the form *gescæpene*, beside *-ceaster*, *-cester*, etc. (See above, I (iii).)

[1] See *OEG* § 143, Cosijn i § 8. 3 and, for a valuable discussion of the problem of such *a*-spellings, E. G. Stanley, 'Spellings of the *Waldend* Group', *Studies in Language, Literature and Culture of the Middle Ages and Later*, ed. E. Bagby Atwood and Archibald A. Hill (Austin, Texas, 1969), 38–69.

[2] See Cosijn i §§ 3. 1 and 7 and 61. 2. Single letter spellings in these positions are not confined to WS: see *OEG* §§ 164, 187, 222–6 and 312–14. The relatively large number of instances of *ger* has to be seen in the context of 106 examples of *gear*.

[3] MS L also has *þæh* (1×).   [4] *Mehton*, etc.

[5] See *OEG* § 767, Cosijn i § 3. 7 and below, p. li. Vleeskruyer, *St. Chad*, p. 88, n. 3, describes the form as 'conceivably' a Mercianism.

[6] *OEG* § 223. Apparent non-WS smoothing of *eo* is found in Parker II *gewerc*, *sex*.   [7] *OEG* § 185, Cosijn i § 14.

(v) *e* for WS *ie* in *alesan, fiftene, geflemde, geflemed, hehsta, hehste, opewed* (all 1×), *opewde* (2×). The *i*-mutation of *ēa* is *īe* in WS but *ē* elsewhere. This apparently non-WS feature is found also, with much greater frequency, in CP. Parker II has the forms *uneðelice* and *e* (2×).[1]

(vi) *i* for WS *ĭe*. *i*-spellings frequently occur in MS L as in CP alongside occasional examples of the converse—in MS L *fieftiene* (1×), *hierede* (2×), *tiema* (1×), *twie-* (1×), *wietena* (2×), *iernan* (4×), *biernan* (2×), *ondliefene* (1×), and normal *hiene* (231×) beside *hine* (16×)—and it seems that WS *ĭe* had undergone monophthongization before the period of our eWS manuscripts. L differs from CP in having only *i*-spellings for the *i*-mutation of Gc. *a+h+*cons. (e.g. *ælmihtig, niht, sliht, nihst*). Parker II, like L, has a number of *i*-spellings, including *niht*, but unlike L it has *ie* in *niehst* and invariable *i* in *hine* (7×).[2]

(vii) *y* for WS *ĭe*. Like *i*, instances of the spelling *y* for *ĭe* occur in all the eWS manuscripts. However, in MS L *y* is found in a wider range of contexts than in CP. Thus, for instance, L not only has *y* between labial consonants and *r*, as in *fyrra*, adv. *fyr, wyrþe*, etc., a development found also in CP, it has *y* before *l* in *abylgþ, scyll, ylde*, etc., before *t* in *-scyt* and *aprytton*, and before *r* after consonants other than labials in *cyrre, besyrede, eorþtyrewan*, with the inverted spelling *ie* for *y* in *afielde, awierged*.[3] Parker II has only three instances of *y*-spellings: *wyrþoste, -wyrþe*, and *syx* (beside *sex*). The first two of these are paralleled in L, the third is not, L having only the spellings *siex* and *six-*.

(viii) *y* for WS *i* in (*a*) *bysmerlic, bysmredan, symble* etc.; (*b*) *aspryngþ, drync, ryht*. *y* for *i* in the neighbourhood of labials is a feature of lWS but is found already in CP. *y* for *i* after *r* is normal eWS in the word *ryht*, lWS usually *riht*, and occurs sporadically in eWS in other words.[4] Parker II has *y* in only three words: *mycel, gerypon*, and (in the neighbourhood of neither labial nor *r*)

---

[1] *OEG* § 200, Cosijn i § 97. Parker II *efenehðe* may belong here. See also *e* for *ĭe* in Parker II *Mercna* etc.

[2] *OEG* § 300, Cosijn i §§ 14, 27 ff., 66, 70, 94.

[3] *OEG* § 300, Cosijn i §§ 51, 96, 106. For an important discussion of *y* and *i* spellings in Old English see P. Gradon, 'Studies in Late West-Saxon Labialization and Delabialization', *English Medieval Studies Presented to J. R. R. Tolkien*, ed. N. Davis and C. L. Wrenn (London, 1962), pp. 63–76.

[4] *OEG* §§ 305, n. 2, 315–18, Cosijn i § 35.

ylcan (2×), beside normal *micel* and *ilcan*, words in which L invariably has *i*.

(ix) *i* for WS *y*. *y* is unrounded to *i* in *cining* (1×), *genihtsumnisse* (1×). This unrounding is rare in eWS, and in lWS is found only before *h*, *c*, and *g* and groups containing them.[1] Parker II agrees with L in its use of *i* in *cinges* (1×) alongside the more usual *cyning*, *cyng*.

(x) *eo* for WS *e* in *seolf* (3×, beside 134 *self*). Breaking of *e+lf* is a non-WS feature, the normal WS development in this word being to *sylf*.[2] Parker II has a single example of *self*.

(xi) *oe* for WS *ē* in *oepel* (3×) and *soelest* (2×, beside *selest* 1×). The spelling *oe* for the *i*-mutation of *ō* is most unusual in WS except in the earliest texts.[3] Parker II has a single example of *selest*- and no *oe* spellings.

(xii) *io* and *eo* for WS *i* in *piosan* (5×), *peosan* (5×) beside *pissum* (1×). Back-mutation of *i* before *s* is not normally found in WS. Parker II has invariably *pysum* (3×).[4]

(xiii) *io* for WS *ěo*. In WS, the graphs *eo* and *io* had become equivalent in force by the time of the oldest manuscripts. *io*-spellings occur only in a limited number of contexts in L and far less frequently than in CP. Thus, with the possible exception of *swiostor* (1×), the inverted spelling *io* for 'original' *eo* is never found, while *io* for 'original' *ēo* occurs only in *diofol* (12×), *dior* (1×), *elpiod-* (2×) and *iower* (5×). None of these words is used in Parker II, which has *eo*, never *io*, for 'original' *ěo*. 'Original' *io*, standard WS *ěo*, is normally represented by the spelling *eo* in both MS L and Parker II. Exceptions in L are *bion* (3×), *hio* (40×), *hiora* (120×), *sio* (25×), *siofope* (1×), *siolfre(s)* (2×), and *prio* (3×). Exceptions in Parker II are confined to the forms *hiora* and *sio* and to the annals 893–5. *Hiora* occurs 8 times in the annals for 893 and 894, alongside 2 instances of *heora* and 4 of *hira* in 894; subsequently *hira* is the only form used (11×). Parker II's order of preference, *hira*, *hiora*, *heora*, is the reverse

---

[1] *OEG* §§ 315–17, Cosijn i § 51 and Gradon, op. cit. For the form *gingra* see *OEG* §§ 178 and 316 f. 2.
[2] *OEG* § 146. See also *St. Chad*, p. 111, n. 3.
[3] *OEG* § 198. Cosijn, i § 65, comments that *soelest* is 'schwerlich ächt ws.'.
[4] *OEG* §§ 212 f. and 711. L also has back-mutation of *i* > *eo*, once *io*, + *t* in *wiotodlice*, *weotum*, *sweotole*, etc. See Cosijn i § 29.

of L's, with *heora* (284×) the most frequently used form, then *hiora* (120×), *hiera* (77×) and finally *hira* (7×). Similarly, Parker II has equal numbers of *seo*, *sio* (each 6×), but L has more than three times as many instances of *seo* (80×) as of *sio* (25×).[1]

(xiv) *y* for WS *ǣ* in *dyde* (1×) and *ea* for WS *eo* in *gefeaht* (1×). These spellings, like the *eo* for *ēa* of *heofod-*, the *a* for *o* of *gewarhte*, the *æ* for *ĕ* of *stænc*, *gedæmde*, *garsæcg*, *wæst*, the *æ* for *ea* of *hwærfigiende*, and the *e* for *ĕ* of *se*, *ætsemne*, *et*, *festen*, *sede* etc., all isolated examples, may reflect non-WS usage.[2] However, they could equally well be 'non-significant' scribal errors. Parker II has the isolated spelling *wæst* for *west*.

II. *Consonants*

(i) *u* for WS *w* in *cuene* (1×). The spelling *u* for *w* after consonants is frequent in both CP and Parker I. In MS L, however, it is confined to this single occurrence and it is completely absent from Parker II.[3]

(ii) *m* for *n* in *benomam*, *gereniam*, *feorðam*, *om*, etc. See below, section III (ii), n. 2 and cf. Parker II, *miclam*. These forms have all been emended in the text.

III. *Inflections and inflectional endings*

The evidence of the spellings of MS L is that by the time the manuscript was written the unstressed back vowels *u*, *o*, and *a* had largely coalesced in a single unaccented back vowel, and that this was becoming—or had become—confused with unaccented *e*. This development is sometimes associated with eleventh-century West Saxon, though it appears to have taken place in Mercian and Northumbrian before Ru. 1 and the lNorth. glosses were written.[4]

---

[1] See further Cosijn i §§ 19, 25, 26, 29, 38, 74, 101, 102. For the possibility that *swiostor* has 'original' *eo* see *OEG* § 210. 2, n. 3.

[2] See *OEG* §§ 156, 164, 193(*d*), and f. 4, 198, 278–81, 288, 329 and f. 2, Cosijn i §§ 4, 18, 19, 44, 80, and 90. See also 144/11 *ætsæmne*. *Hett* (59/31, 60/5, 70/12) is more probably an error or scribal variant for pa. t. *het* than a form of 3rd pers. sg. pres. ind. *hætt*. In view of the occurrence of these forms here, we must treat with caution the suggestion that similar and equally rare forms in poetic texts may indicate a Northumbrian origin for the latter. See, e.g., *Daniel and Azarias*, ed. R. T. Farrell (London, 1974), pp. 14 f.

[3] See *OEG* § 60 and Cosijn § 147. The forms *cuom*, *cuomon*, common in CP and Parker I, are absent from Or. and Parker II, which have only *com* etc.

[4] *OEG* §§ 377–9 and § 379 n. 3. See also K. Malone, 'When did Middle

For the supporting evidence of the spellings of proper names see below, p. cviii. Parker II has mainly 'normal' spellings.

(i) neuter pl. *-u* appears as *-o* and *-a* in *geata, scipa, gemæru, wæpeno,* etc. Cosijn gives the statistics for *o-* and *a-* spellings in the early WS texts as Or. MS L 14 *o,* 23 *a,* CP MS H 4 *o,* 3 *a,* MS C 7 *o,* no *a,* Parker I 1 *o,* no *a.*[1] Parker II has only *u-* spellings.

(ii) dat. *-um* appears as *-un, -on,* and *-an.* Cf., e.g., *cierrun, mattucun, elpendon, gewealdon, beorgan, gifan* and adj. dsm. and dpl. *ælcon, godan, hwelcun, miclan.* CP has only a few instances: *weorcun, hwilon, yðon,* and dpl. *scearpan ramman.*[2]

(iii) *-an* appears as *-on* in *eacon, namon, nomon, þreoteopon* (all 1×), in inf. *geondwyrdon* (1×) and dat. inf. *healdonne* (2×). CP has a handful of similar spellings; Parker II has only standard spellings apart from a single example of *Eastron,* the normal form throughout the Parker Chronicle.[3]

(iv) pa. t. ind. pl. *-on* appears as *-an* on more than 200 occasions, compared with 3 in Parker I and (Cosijn's statistics) 14 in MS H of CP and 1 in MS C of CP. Parker II has four instances of *-an.*[4]

(v) pa. t. ind. pl. *-on* appears as *-un* in *fortendun* (1×). CP and Parker I have a number of *-un* spellings, which Cosijn takes to be archaisms but which in L at least could result from the falling

---

English begin?', Curme volume of linguistic studies (Baltimore, 1930), pp. 110–17, and D. Amborst, 'Evidence for Phonetic Weakening in Inflectional Syllables in *Beowulf*', *Leeds Studies in English,* NS. 9 (1977) 1–18. Not considered here is the frequent reduction of medial unaccented vowels to a sound written *e,* for which see *OEG* §§ 385–7.

[1] Cosijn ii § 3 ff. 30/29 *niwu* for expected *niwa* (or *niwe*) may be the result of a similar falling together of *u* and *a,* though simple scribal confusion of the two letter forms cannot be ruled out. Not considered here is the extension of mf. *e* to npl. of strong adjs., for which see *OEG* § 641. For noun inflexions (vocalic stems), see further Dahl (1938).

[2] Cosijn ii §§ 1, 3, 10, 13, 18, 20, 30, and 44–57. It is possible that the spellings *-am* for *-an* cited above, section II (ii), also reflect a reduction in unstressed syllables. However, in some cases of substitution of *m* for *n* assimilation is a possible explanation (thus, for instance, *om mergen,* 96/19, emended to *on mergen*), while in others we may have to do with incorrect expansion of the abbreviation ~, standing for either *m* or *n* as in the Parker Chronicle. As for *feorðam* for *feorðan,* 97/19, the line-end separates *feor* from *ðam* and the second element may have been incorrectly identified with the demonstrative by a scribe.

[3] Cosijn ii §§ 30–33, 51, 70. The most usual form of the dat. inf. in CP and MS L is *-anne,* with *-enne* a poor second.   [4] Cosijn ii § 76.

together of vowels in unstressed syllables.¹ Parker II has a single example, *worhtun*. We may compare L *tungul* (2×) for 'normal' WS *tungol*.

(vi) pa. t. ind. pl. *-on* appears as *-en* in *awriten, bæden, gesawen* (all 1×).

(vii) subj. pl. *-en* appears as *-an* in *ascian, gehulpan, pigedan* (all 1×), *sworan* (2×) and possibly also in other instances in contexts where either indicative or subjunctive forms are possible. Cosijn cites three instances of *-an* from CP, MS H.²

(viii) pa. t. subj. pl. *-en* appears as *-on* in *hiersumedon, gewacadon*, etc. Cosijn cites 48 instances in Or., beside 36 in MS H of CP, 30 in MS C of CP, and 3 in Parker I. However, on a number of occasions Or. uses unambiguous indicative forms where 'standard' OE has subjunctive and some at least of Cosijn's instances may be intended as indicatives.³ Apparently subjunctive is Parker II *foron* in annal 905 (second example).

(ix) pp. *-en* appears as *-an* in *hatan* (1×).

(x) npl. *-as* appears as *-es* in *beames, swicdomes, wealles* (all 1×).

(xi) gpl. *-a* appears as *-e* in *ærende, geare, scipe* (all 1×).

(xii) ds. *-a* appears as *-e* in *dure* (1×).⁴

(xiii) weak adj. nsm. *-a* appears as *-e* in *mæste* (1×).

(xiv) adj. gpl. *-ra* appears as *-re* in *gongendre, ofslagenre* (each 1×).

(xv) gs. *-es* appears as *-as* in *anwaldas, caseras* (each 1×).

(xvi) dsf. *-e* appears as *-a* in *dæda* and as *-æ* in *dædæ* (1×). Cf. Parker II *eæ*.⁵

(xvii) weak adj., nsf. *-e* appears as *-a* in *mæsta* (1×).⁶

(xviii) apl. *-e* appears as *-a* in *ealla* (1×).

¹ OEG § 373 and Cosijn i § 115 and ii § 76. See also below, p. xlvii, section III (xxii) and (xxiii).　　　　² Cosijn ii § 77.
³ See Cosijn ii § 77 and Liggins (1970), p. 300, also below, p. xlviii n. 3.
⁴ OEG § 613 cites eWS *dure* as an instance of the extension of *e* from the fem. ō-stems, such forms becoming increasingly frequent later. However, since the only example of eWS *dure* noted by Cosijn and Campbell is this one in MS L, confusion of unstressed vowels must be considered as an alternative explanation.
⁵ Cf. CP gs. *gæsðæs* and adj. aplf. *sumæ, eallæ*. Whether these are archaisms, scribal variants, or merely scribal errors is a matter for debate. See Cosijn ii §§ 1, 38, 39, OEG § 369 and f. 3. Not included here is the frequent use of *-a* in the a. and ds. of fem. nouns in *-ung*, for which see OEG § 589 and Cosijn ii § 16.
⁶ The scribe originally wrote *se mæsta wynn*, 52/21, but subsequently corrected *se* to *seo*.

(xix) *þe* appears for the unstressed conjunction *þa*, and *þa* for *þe*.

(xx) ds. *-e* is dropped in *cyning*, *fleam*, *land*, *wif* (all 1×). Cf. Parker II *efes*, sometimes taken as an endingless locative.[1] This could be interpreted as early syncretism of acc. and dat., a development that is found mainly in Northumbrian texts but which also occurs occasionally in the Mercian Ru. 1; however, in view of the loss of final *-e* of other origins in forms such as *hæfd*, *hier*, *ric*, a 'mechanical' explanation such as the use in an earlier manuscript of abbreviations such as Parker I *hæfd'*, *fierd'* should perhaps be sought.[2] I have accordingly emended all these forms in the text.

(xxi) *-e* is extended to the nom. sg. of *heardsælnesse* (1×). This extension of *-e* to the nom. sg. of abstract nouns in *-ness* is found also in CP and the Vespasian Psalter gloss and is frequent in Ru. 1 and in Northumbrian texts.[3]

(xxii) pa. t. *-ade* is preferred to *-ode*. Second class weak verbs form their pa. t. in *-ade* and *-ode*, pp. *-ad*, *-od*, with a marked preference for *-ad-*, unlike CP, which prefers *-od-*. Parker II in this differs from MS L, having only 8 *a*-forms to 23 *o* and 1 *u*. Elsewhere *-ade* is found predominantly in Anglian and Kentish texts, *-ode* in West Saxon.[4]

(xxiii) superlative *-ast* is preferred to *-ost*, *-ust*. The distribution of *u*, *o* and *a* in strong forms of the superlative adjective is also possibly a matter of dialect, though subsequent development to *-est* in the majority of extant texts makes this no more than a matter of conjecture. What is certain, however, is that the situation in MS L is very different from that in the other eWS texts. Thus, MS L has 20 *-ast*, 5 *-ost*, and 1 *-ust*, beside CP MS H 15 *o*, 7 *u*, never *a*, MS C 10 *o*, 6 *u*, never *a*, and Parker I 1 *o*, 1 *u*, never *a*. Parker II has 2 *o* and 1 *u*.[5]

---

[1] Sprockel (1965), 7. 4. 3, Note, however, finds the absence of an ending here 'difficult to account for'.

[2] See, e.g., 45/1 *hier*, 48/34 *sprecend*, 63/8 *ric*, 78/5 *hæfd* and 109/23 *fleam*, all emended in the text. Asf. *-e* is also dropped in 50/29 *tacnung*; however, this could be either a scribal error or due to the workings of analogy. For possible syncretism in Northumbrian and Mercian texts see Sievers–Brunner § 237 and L. Blakeley, 'Accusative–Dative Syncretism in the Lindisfarne Gospels', *EGS*, i (1947–8), 6–31.

[3] *OEG* § 592(f), Cosijn ii § 18. 4.

[4] *OEG* § 757, Cosijn ii § 129. For the complicated situation in CP see Horgan (1963), pp. 318 ff.

[5] *OEG* § 657, Cosijn ii § 46. In the weak form *-est* is normal in all texts.

(xxiv) *eam* for WS *eom. eam*, as 1st pers. sg. of the verb 'to be', which occurs twice in MS L, with no examples of *eom*, is found also in the Kentish Glosses, the Mercian Vespasian Psalter gloss, and Ru. 1. CP has only *iom, eom*.[1]

(xxv) uncontracted forms of the 3rd pers. sg. pres. ind. of strong verbs. Absence of syncope is a feature of Anglian and also of early Kentish. The eWS texts normally have the typically WS contracted forms, but both CP and MS L have a number of uncontracted forms. The distribution of these forms in MS L appears significant: not only does it have far fewer uncontracted forms than CP, involving only three different verbs—*floweþ* (1×), *hateþ* (5×), *ligeþ* (6×)—but all the instances of these forms occur in the first 65 lines of the main text.[2]

(xxvi) pa. t. pl. subj. *-en* appears as *-e*. The inflexion *-e* for WS *-en* is a feature of eWS and is found more than 20 times in MS L. It occurs also in CP and the OE Bede. There are no instances in Parker II, in which subjunctive forms are in any case rare.[3]

(xxvii) loss of final inflexional *-n* in infin. *besinca*, pa. t. pl. *gefuhto*, ds. *tweo* (all 1×). Cf. CP *(ge)læra* and, with *n* subsequently added, *(for)bera*, etc. Loss of final *n* is found in both Northumbrian and in the Mercian Ru. 1, though less widely in the latter. It should be noted, however, that the scribe of MS L frequently omits *n* in non-final position and that all the *n*-less forms he uses may be the result of scribal error.[4] I have accordingly emended all but the first of these forms in the text.

---

[1] *OEG* § 768(d), Cosijn ii § 136. 3b.

[2] *OEG* § 733, Cosijn ii § 112. See also the wk. vb. *nemneþ* (3×) and below, p. lii. The occasional uncontracted form is also found in Bo.

[3] See *OEG* § 473, Potter (1952–3), p. 396 and L. Bloomfield, 'Old English Plural Subjunctives in *-e*', *JEGPh*, xxix (1930), 100–13. However, as Dr. Bruce Mitchell (see *Daniel*, ed. R. T. Farrell, l. 77 n.) warns, 'pending a fully-documented study . . . it would seem dangerous to rely on *-e* in the preterite as an unambiguous sign of the singular, or subjunctive plural; sometimes it might well stand for an indicative plural.'

[4] *OEG* § 472, Cosijn i § 141. 7 and ii § 69. 'Non-inflexional' *n* is lost in *piunge* for *pinunge*, *buto* for *buton* (but cf. Parker II *bute*) and *forbærdon* for *forbærndon* etc., 34/1, 83/13, and 117/12. Elsewhere an omitted *n* is added above the line, unmarked by a dot and thus possibly by a later corrector. See, e.g., 41/3 *forbær`n´don*, 61/12 *stro`n´gan* and 63/14 *beluce`n´* (with second *e* altered to *o* and where an *n*-less form of the pa. t. subj. is a permissible variant), also above, p. xxiv. For loss of *n* in MS C see 16/11, Commentary.

(xxviii) *þe* for nsm. *se* (1×). A similar extension of *þ* from the rest of the paradigm is found in the Mercian Ru. 1.[1]

(xxix) *on* for *ond* (1×). *On* (or *an*) for *ond* occurs frequently in the OE Bede, Tanner MS, and is also found in Parker I and II, GD, the Leiden, Corpus, and Erfurt glossaries and Ru. 1. How far this form can be considered a dialect feature, however, is debatable: as Vleeskruyer comments, 'The spelling *on* might perhaps be considered an archaism in so far that it points to an older phase of Anglo-Saxon orthography, in which greater latitude as to the spelling of individual words still existed.'[2]

2. *MS C.* The language of the Cotton MS is standard lWS, as might be expected from the eleventh-century date assigned to that manuscript and its associations with Abingdon. However, it contains a number of features that are normally thought of as 'early' and thus presumably taken over from C's examplar, and others that are non-WS in type, while even the lWS usage varies from one part of the manuscript to another, usually coinciding with the observable changes in hand but sometimes concentrated within a more limited area, suggesting differences of scribal practice at an earlier stage of transmission. Hand 4 in particular stands apart from the other hands in its frequent use of late or non-standard forms such as *-on* in the infinitive and *siþþon* for *siþþan* (beginning not in III. iii with the change of hand but in V. vii), of *e* for *ēa* in *est* and for *ēo* in *betwenan, fregean, untwegendlice* etc., of *u* for *ȳ* in *feowertune, nurewitt, sullan, wurcean* etc., and of *feala* for *fela* and *spec-* for *sprec-*. Even forms occurring throughout the work often have different distribution patterns depending on the hand involved, as the following highly selective survey (designed to complement the study of L) shows.[3]

I. *Stressed Vowels*

(i) *a* for WS *a/o*+nasal. Since lWS spelling tradition prefers *a*-spellings in this position, it is not surprising to find *a* in the great

[1] *OEG* § 708.

[2] *St. Chad*, pp. 121–2. For a possible instance of *an* in Erfurt see J. D. Pheifer, *Old English Glosses in the Épinal–Erfurt Glossary* (Oxford, 1974), p. 1044 n. Parker II *on*, annal 894 (opening word), is interpreted as adv. by Plummer. Subsequent editors, however, emend it to *ond*.

[3] For a detailed survey of certain aspects of the language of MS C see Horgan (1963).

majority of words where L has *o*, the most common exceptions being *mon* and *monig* and compounds formed from them. However, the practice of the different scribes varies: Hands 1 and 3 both have *o* much less frequently than *a*; Hand 4 virtually ceases to use *o*-spellings from V. i onwards, while Hand 2 has only *a*-spellings except in prefix and preposition *on* and in *þonne*. Where *o*-spellings occur they normally correspond in position to similar spellings in MS L, suggesting ultimate derivation from a common exemplar.

(ii) *a* for WS *ea+l+*cons. *a*-spellings in this position are confined to a handful of words: *anwald*, *nales*, and *waldend*. *Waldend* occurs once, in the section missing from L and thus with no equivalent in MS L. *Anwald* (var. *onwald*) and *nales* are two of the five words with *a*-spellings in MS L and C's *a*-spellings usually occur in places where MS L also has *a*, though in the case of *anwald* occasionally where MS L has *ea*. However, C has far fewer *a*-spellings than L in this word (52× beside L 139×) and most of these are found in Hand 1. This distribution of *a*-spellings in MSS L and C again suggests ultimate derivation from a common exemplar containing these forms.

(iii) *e* for eWS *ĕa* through non-WS or lWS smoothing. MS L's *e*-spellings are usually interpreted as lWS.[1] However, only a handful of such forms are found in MS C, those in Hands 1, 2, and 3 usually corresponding in position to similar forms in MS L and so presumably derived from L and C's common exemplar. Thus Hand 1 agrees with L in its use of *neh* and *herga* (both 1×). Hand 3 has *mehte* (1×), as L; Hand 4 agrees with L using *flex* (2×), *þeh* (46×), *mehte*, *onget* and *hergas* (all 1×), as well as *toecon* (L *toeacan*, elsewhere once *toecan*), and in addition has a number of instances of lWS smoothing in forms where MS L has *ea*: e.g. *ehta*, *egan*, *wexande*, *ofscet*. MS L's spelling *ger* for *gear* does not occur anywhere in MS C.

(iv) *e* for eWS *ie*. *e*-spellings occur sporadically throughout the manuscript in all hands except Hand 2. Examples are *nehst-*, *hehst-*, *oþewde*, *uneþe*. Usually these *e*-spellings are ones found also in L, either in the same place or elsewhere; however, a few are

---

[1] However, see above, p. xli n. 2.

found only in C, e.g. *herra* L *hierra*, and *nehst-*, L invariably *nihst-*, Parker II *niehst*.

(v) *ea* in *meahte*, etc. MS C normally has the lWS forms *miht-*, *myht-*, though occasionally agreeing with MS L in using the apparently intermediate form *meht-*. However, Hand 1 has 5 instances of eWS *meaht-* (4 corresponding to MS L *meht-* and 1 in the section missing from L) and Hand 3 has one instance (MS L *meht-*). The occurrence of these 6 instances in MS C only, beside 2 in L only (MS C, Hand 1 *mihte*) and another in MS V (L *mehton*, C *mihton*) suggests that *ea* spellings in this word may have been a feature of the MS of Or. from which all these manuscripts are ultimately descended.[1]

(vi) eWS *ie*. The spelling *ie* is rare in MS C and is found only in Hands 1 (12×), 3 (4×), and 4 (16×), with no examples after IV. xiii except in foreign proper names such as *Hierusalem*, which are not under consideration here. Almost every instance of *ie* in MS C corresponds to an *ie* spelling in MS L, suggesting that this may also have been the usage in the MS from which they are ultimately descended.

(vii) *oe* for WS *ē* in *oepel*. *oe* spellings are found 2× in this word, in Hand 4, with *o* erased.

(viii) *eo* for WS *i*. In addition to forms such as *weotena*, *sweotol*, where *eo* spellings are common in WS, *eo* occurs for *i* in *peosan* (Hand III 1×).

(ix) eWS (and dialectal) *io*. *io* spellings are frequent in Hand 1, especially in the words *hio*, *hiora*, *sio*, but also elsewhere: e.g. *bion*, *bliotan*, *diofolgild*, *sioles*. Not only is *io* found where MS L has *io*, it also occurs on some fifty occasions where L has *eo*, *ie*, or *i*. Hand 2, in contrast, has no *io* spellings; Hands 3 and 4 have no more than a dozen between them, in the words *hio*, *hiora* (each 3×), *giong(a)* (2×), *iowra* (1×), and *diofolgyld* (3×), all but one having corresponding *io* spellings in MS L. This evidence, combined with that provided by a comparison of the usage in MS L and Parker II, suggests that *io*-spellings were a feature of the

---

[1] The existence of these instances of *meaht-* in MSS C and V suggests that we must treat as accidental the fact that in MS L the form is confined to the report of Ohthere's voyages.

manuscript from which L and C are ultimately descended,[1] and that they were much more common in that manuscript than in MS L.

II. *Consonants*

k for WS *c*. Hand 1 has a number of instances of *k* for WS *c* in *kyning, kynekynnes, akennes*, etc. The symbol *k* is not used in MS L, though it occurs occasionally in CP and Parker I. In view of the relative conservatism of Hand 1 it could be an early spelling taken over from MS C's exemplar. However, *k* occurs also in texts of later date.[2]

III. *Inflexions and inflexional endings*

(i) pa. t. *-ade* for lWS *-ode*. The pa. t. and pp. of Class II weak verbs, MS L *-ad(e), -od(e)* normally appears as *-od(e)* in all four hands. However, *-ade* etc. is found over 100 times, and though in the majority of instances it occurs in identical positions in both manuscripts, occasionally MS C has *-ad(e)* for MS L *-od(e)*, and even for pl. *-ed-*, suggesting that *-ad-* was also the usage of their common ancestor.

(ii) 3rd pers. sg. pres. ind. in *-eþ*. MS C, Hand 1, has 21 instances of forms without syncope, some corresponding to uncontracted forms in MS L in the opening section 8/11–10/15 and therefore to be traced back to L and C's common ancestor, some occurring in the account of Wulfstan's voyages, 16/21–18/2, which is missing from L, and one in the Old English *incipit*, which is found only in C. Although MS L sometimes has uncontracted forms where C has syncope, the converse never occurs.

(iii) eWS pa. t. subj. pl. in *-e*. Although *-an* is the most usual subj. pl. ending in MS C, *-on* and *-en* spellings are also found, with a substantial number of instances of eWS *-e*, apparently ultimately derived from L and C's common ancestor. In view of the distribution of *-e* forms in MS L, where they do not appear before 35/8 or in the section 104/8–127/25, it is significant that many of the instances of *-e* in MS C correspond to forms with *-en, -on* in MS L and a number of them are found in the sections from which they are absent in L.

---

[1] See above, pp. xxxi f., also D. G. Scragg, 'The Compilation of the Vercelli Book', *ASE*, ii (1973), 196–9.

[2] See Cosijn i § 131. For *k*-spellings in later OE texts see, e.g., the revision of *Gregory's Dialogues*, MS H, and MSS B and C of *The Anglo-Saxon Chronicle*.

From these features and a number of others,[1] it would appear that C's exemplar contained a large number of eWS spellings. Although the majority of these correspond to similar spellings in L, the fact that in a number of instances C has early forms not found in L would seem to provide confirmation for the theory advanced in section III above that the two manuscripts are descended not one from the other but both from a common archetype. Non-WS spellings found in C but not in L may also be derived from this manuscript; however, they could have been introduced subsequently by a scribe, or scribes, familiar with both WS and non-WS spelling traditions. It is possible that some of the peculiarities of the language of Hand 4 point to a scribe with southern connections,[2] but in the present state of our knowledge of late OE dialect features any degree of certainty on this matter is out of the question.

3. *MS B.* The language of the fragmentary MS B is mainly standard lWS. Thus, there are no instances of *io* spellings, while eWS *ie* occurs only in the word *hie*, though here it is found thirty-five times, to the exclusion of other variants and in agreement with the usage in MS L, which likewise has exclusively *hie* in this section. *a+l+*cons. occurs only in the word *onwald*, *anwald*, again in agreement with the usage in the corresponding passage in L. *a+*nasal is preferred to *o* in stressed syllables, the latter being confined to the words *onwald* (2×) and *mon* (2×) beside *anwald* (2×) and *man* (7×). The corresponding passages in L have only *a*-spellings in *anwald*, though the form *onwald* is more common in the work as a whole, and only *o*-spellings in *mon*.[3] lWS *miht-* is invariable, while *-an* is the normal pa.t.pl. ending for both ind. and subj. Unlike MS L, B has *-ode*, never

---

[1] e.g. the use of unstressed *u* in *heafud*, *brocude* etc. (though this could be an early Anglian characteristic), *worce* for *weorce*, *ryht* beside *riht*, and possibly the spellings *iu* and *oe* in *iu* and *oeþel* (with *o* subsequently erased).

[2] Notably the spelling *u* for WS *y*, cited above. Similar spellings occur in the Ælfric MS, Cambridge, University Library Ii. i. 33, saec. xii², and these Crawford, *OE Heptateuch*, Appendix II, takes to reflect a pronunciation current (in the ME period at least) in the Surrey area. See also *St. Chad*, § 27 and Ælfric, *Homilies* ed. Pope, i, pp. 38–9. Possibly but not conclusively southeastern, and not confined to Hand 4, is the interchange of *æ* and *e* in *wæredon*, L *weredon*, *gemoterne*, L *gemotærne*, *aleton* for L inf. *alætan*, *gedræfednesse* for L *gedrefednesse* etc., and the retention of *io* in *diofol-* referred to under (ix) above.

[3] For MS L's preference for *o* in *mon* and the use of this spelling also in MS C see above, pp. xl and xlix–l.

-ade, and *þeah* not *þeh*. In addition it has *gear* not *ger*; however, *gear* is the only form in this section in L. A few apparently non-WS forms without parallel in L also occur, most of which could be either Anglian or Kentish spellings: thus, *underfæng*, with *æ* for expected *e*, *meteleste* for L and C *metelieste*, with non-WS mutation of *ēa* to *ē*, and *seoþþan* for *siþþan*, with non-WS back-umlaut.[1]

4. *MS V.* Although the palimpsest leaf of MS V is dated saec. xi[1], it contains no features not found in eWS, and some features that are not normally found in lWS. Thus it retains *ie* in *hie*, it has *o* for *a/o*+nasal in *from* and *hond* (MS L *from, hand*),[2] and it normally distinguishes between pa. t. pl. ind. in *-on* and subj. in *-en*, the one exception being *loccodon*, L *aloccoden*, C *aloccodan*, in a context where the subjunctive might be expected.[3] Like MS L it has *firde* for eWS *fierde*, MS C *fyrde*, while gpl. *Romano*, altered to *Romana*, also has its counterpart in certain sections of MS L.[4] An early form not usually found in MS L is *meahton*, corresponding to L *mehton*, C *mihton*, while also possibly early though not found in L is *gefioht* (MS L *gefeoht*). This last form could, however, be a south-eastern spelling.[5] MS V differs from L in preferring *þam* to *þæm* and in its reading *hira*, L *hiera*.[6]

5. *The Rouen sentence.* In spite of its shortness, the extract from Or. in the Rouen MS, which Ker dates as twelfth-century, has a number of interesting features. Mossé, dating the sentence as tenth- or more probably eleventh-century and apparently assuming that its scribe copied his exemplar mechanically and faithfully, concludes that the copy of Or. used by the scribe was 'written in a form of Old English later than the language of the preserved MSS, which traditionally stand for typical Early West-Saxon', and suggests that 'some of the phonological features of R would point to the second half of the 11th century.'[7] However, these conclusions

---

[1] See *OEG* § 217 and above, p. xliii.
[2] For L's preference for *a* in *hand* see above, p. xl.
[3] See above, p. xlvi.   [4] See below, p. cviii.
[5] See *OEG* § 297, Sisam (1953), pp. 92–3, and above, p. li n. 1.
[6] MS L has only seven examples of *þam*, Parker II has exclusively *þæm*. For *hira, hiera* in these texts see above, pp. xliii–xliv.
[7] Mossé (1955), p. 202.

require much qualification. Certainly the use of *e* for WS *ǣ* in *er*, *were, weron, wes, þem*, can be very late OE, but it is also found much earlier in non-WS dialects,[1] while other features, considered to be 'late' by Mossé—the unrounding of *y* to *i* in *frimðe, drihtnes*, the simplification of double consonants in *acenes*, and the formation of the past of *timbran* according to Class II in *getimbroð*—can likewise all be cited from manuscripts of the ninth or early tenth centuries.[2] What is more, the Rouen sentence preserves a number of early WS spellings found in MS L but not in the corresponding section of C, which seem to have occurred also in the parent manuscript of L and C: thus, it has *ie* in *-tiene*, *o*+nasal in *from*, and final *g* in *burg*, L *-tiene, from, burg*, C *tyne, fram, burh*.[3] The copy of Or. supposedly used by the Rouen scribe, therefore, need not necessarily have been later in date than MS L and certainly not later than C. And like MSS L and C it has certain 'early' features which quite possibly ultimately reflect the translator's own usage.

V. THE SOURCES

1. Or.'s main source is the *Historiarum adversum Paganos Libri Septem* of Paulus Orosius, written in the second decade of the fifth century at the suggestion of St. Augustine. This work achieved very great popularity in the Middle Ages (its author appears among the blessed in Dante's heaven) and today over 250 manuscript copies of it are still in existence, as well as a number of early printed editions and translations. The Latin text used by Sweet in his edition of Or. is that of Haverkamp (1738, repr. as vol. xxxi of *PL*). However, neither this nor the text established by Zangemeister, *CSEL*, v, can be accurately described as the 'Latin original' of the OE version. As Zangemeister himself pointed out, the manuscript used by the OE translator was inferior to the

---

[1] Mossé calls attention to the presence of this feature in Kentish texts; however, all but two of the five instances in MS R could also be Anglian forms and even these two instances—*er* and *þem*—are spellings found in the Mercian Ru. 1. See further *St. Chad*, § 5. For *e* spellings in MS C, see above, p. liii n. 2.

[2] See Campbell, *OEG* §§ 315–16, 457, and 753(2). Only one form cited by Mossé—*feor* for expected *feower*—presents a special case and here it is possible that the scribe has been influenced by the form taken by the numeral in other Germanic languages: cf. OS *fior*, OHG *fiori*. For the expected development of OE *feower* see F. Mossé, *Handbook of Middle English* (Baltimore, 1952), p. 29.

[3] See above, pp. xlii, xl, and l and Campbell, *OEG* § 446.

manuscripts on which his standard text was based.[1] Accordingly, to appreciate the probable state of the Latin version used, it is necessary to look not at the 'best' manuscripts used by Zangemeister, but at others rejected by him because of the errors which they contained. It is extremely difficult to define relationship between the manuscripts of a text as frequently studied and copied in the Middle Ages as Orosius' History; however, it is possible to identify no fewer than 77 as 'related to' or connected with Or.'s exemplar.[2] Certain features are of common occurrence in these 'related' manuscripts—for instance, the forms *Libeum* for OH *Lilybaeum*, Or. *Libeum*, *Tenelaum* for OH *Sthenelan*, Or. *Tenelaus*, *Thelenus* for OH *Mytilenaeus*, Or. *Thelenus*, *Falucium* for OH *Plautium*, Or. *Folucius*, *Ithona* for OH *Python*, Or. *Ithona*, and the reading 'et vita et patrimonio damnauit' for OH II. vi. 12 'et uita et patrimonio donauit', referring to Cyrus' granting of life and patrimony to the captured Croesus, where Or. describes Cyrus as slaying him. Other features are found only in a handful of manuscripts, the two which may be described as 'closest' in type to Or. being Florence, Bibl. Riccardiana 627, Hand 1 (up to the middle of Book IV. xiii),[3] which is dated saec. xii, and Vienna, Österreichische Nationalbibliothek 366, which is dated saec. viii–ix. Somewhat less close are Oxford, Bodleian MS Auct. Selden B 16 (saec. xii) and Balliol MS 125 (saec. xv). The provenance of Ricc. 627 is unknown. The other three manuscripts, however, all have English or Irish connections. Vienna 366, according to Lowe, was 'written at Salzburg to judge from the script' and 'copied presumably from an Irish exemplar'.[4] Selden B 16 is the autograph copy of William of Malmesbury, and Balliol 125, a manuscript commissioned by William Gray for Balliol College and containing material connected with William of Malmesbury, is very closely related to it if not ultimately copied from it.[5] Distinc-

---

[1] OH, p. xxiii. Zangemeister's belief that this manuscript was written not earlier than the ninth century is incorrect, the chronological interpolation on whose presence he bases it being found in MS Vienna 366, saec. viii–ix.

[2] See Bately (1961), pp. 69–105. For the difficulties involved in such a study of manuscript relationship see G. Kane, *Piers Plowman: the A version* (London, 1960), pp. 53–64.

[3] Hand 2, which seems to be copying from a very different exemplar, is fourteenth century in date.

[4] See E. A. Lowe, *Codices Latini Antiquiores*, X (Oxford, 1963), 1476.

[5] See R. A. B. Mynors, *Catalogue of the MSS of Balliol College* (Oxford, 1963), pp. 103–4. According to Mynors, Selden B 16 is 'presumably the ultimate

tive features found in these manuscripts but not elsewhere include the following:[1]

OH	Or.	Ricc. 627, 1	Vienna 366	Selden B 16	Balliol 125
Gangis	Gandis	Gandis	Gandis	*Gangis*	*Gangis*
Caryatii	Ciarsathi	Ciarsathii	Ciarsathii	Ciarsati	*Caratassi*
Argiuos	Argi	Argios	Argios	*Argiuos*	*Arginos*
Amphyction	Ambictio	Ampictio	*Amphiction*	Ampictio	*Amphion*
Atheniensium	Othinentium	Athinentium	Athinensium	*Atheniensium*	*Atheniensium*
Lampeto	Lampida	Lampito	Lampito	Lampito	Lampito
Vulsci(que)	Fulcisci	Uulcisci(que)	Ulcisci(que)	*Uolsci(que)*	*Uolsci(que)*
Attalus	Catulusan	Catulus	Catulus	*Attalius*	*Attalus*
Leonnato	Leonantius	Leonantio	*Leonantho*	Leonantho	*Leonantho*
Python	Pison	Pyson	*Pithon*	——	*Fiton*
Pydnam	Fiðnam	Fydnam	Fidnam	*Pidnam*	Fiduam
Clipeam	Alpeam	Alpeam	*Clipeam*	Alpheam	*Clipeam*
Laomedon	Laumenda	*Laumedo*	Lamedon	Laumendo	Lamendo
Eurylochus	Eurilohus	*Eurilocus*	Eurilohus	*Eurilocus*	*Eurilocus*
Marco Liuio	Marcolia	——[2]	Marcolio	*Marco Liuio*	*Marco Liuio*
Cirtam	Cretan	——	Certam	*Cirtam*	*Cirtam*
Ponti	Ponto	——	Ponto	*Ponti*	*Ponti*
Psyllos	Uissilus	——	Phisillos[3]	*Psillos*	*Sillos*
Maximianum	Maximus	——	Maximum	*Maximianum*	*Maximianum*

The other 'related' manuscripts fall, with a handful of exceptions, into four large groups, each further subdivisible:

Group A: (i) Berne, Stadtb. 128.

(ii) Munich, Bayer. Staatsb. 492; Munich 22025.[4]

Group B: (i) Wolfenbüttel, Herzog August B., Gud. Lat. 80; Stuttgart, Württemberg B., HB v 19; Munich 6380; Leipzig, Stadtb. 155; Munich 13041.[5]

(ii) Venice, Marciana 350; Vienna Nat. B. 381; Vienna 3088.

(iii) Vienna 3149, Klagenfurt, Bundesst. Studienb., Pap. HS. 166; Gdańsk, Marienkirchen B., F. 311.

(iv) Geneva, B. Publ. et Univ. 18; Wolfenbüttel Guelf. 82. 10 Aug. in-12°; Vienna 480; Gdańsk, Mar. F. 285.

Group C: (i) Paris, Arsenal 983; Vatican, Lat. 1975; Bologna, B. Univ. 2298; Vatican, Archivio di San Pietro 23E; BL Addit. 26623.

parent of our MS'. However, occasionally Balliol 125 has readings which agree with Vienna 366 and Ricc. 627 (and Or.) against Selden B 16.

[1] See further Bately (1961), pp. 80–6.

[2] The last five names in this list occur in the last part of OH, where Hand 2 of Ricc. 627 takes over, using an 'unrelated' exemplar.

[3] See further Commentary on 130/19.

[4] These two MSS agree with Berne 128 up to about ch· xviii of Book V, when they suddenly diverge. See further Bately (1961), p. 103, n. 336.

[5] Munich 13041 has all the characteristics of a manuscript belonging to Group B up to ch. xi of Book V. See further Bately (1961), p. 103, n. 336.

(ii) Leiden, Univ. L., Voss. Lat. f. 13; Venice 349; Vatican, Reg. Lat. 296.

(iii) BNL 4877; BNL 4879; Berne 160; Clare College, Cambridge 18; New College, Oxford 151; Leiden, Bib. Pub. Lat. 80; Leiden, Univ. Lib., Voss. Lat. f. 18; Antwerp, Musaeum Plantin–Moretus, Lat. no. 38.[1]

(iv) BNL 4871; Vatican Lat. 7318; Boulogne-sur-mer, Munic. 126; St. Omer, Munic. 717; BNL 4880; Trinity College, Cambridge 1264; BNL 17567.

(v) BNL 17543; BL Burney 215; BNL 16012; BNL 16013.

(vi) Milan, Ambrosiana D 274 inf.; Rome, B. Angelica 1767; Belluno, B. Lolliniana 42; BNL 12496; Leipzig 156.

(vii) Lincoln, Cath. Lib. 102; BL Burney 216; BL Royal 6C viii; St. John's College, Oxford 95.

Group D: Jesus College, Oxford 34; Jesus College, Oxford 62; Bodley Laud Lat. 4; BL Royal 13A xx; BL Royal 7D xxv; St. John's College, Cambridge 98; Eton College BK 1.

Also belonging to Group C is Corpus Christi College, Cambridge 23, pt. 2. This manuscript falls into two parts, coinciding with changes in hand, one to be grouped with Trinity 1264 and Group C (iv), the other resembling Clare 18 and manuscripts of Group C (iii).[2]

The distribution of these manuscripts is perhaps significant: no English manuscript occurs in Groups A and B, but all members of Group C (vii) and of Group D have known English connections, as have three manuscripts of Group C (iii) and (iv).[3] Groups A and B have no significant forms that are not found also in at least one other group—usually at least two groups—as well as in one or more of the 'closest' manuscripts, while on a number of occasions where other groups have 'significant' readings, they have either the correct form or a minor variant of it. Group C, on the other hand, has examples of practically every significant form found

---

[1] The existence of this manuscript came to my knowledge after publication of my study of 1961.   [2] See further Bately (1961), pp. 87–96.

[3] See Bately and Ross (1961), pp. 329–34, and Bately (1961), pp. 101–2 and nn. 317 and 318.

in the other three groups, the only exceptions being *Rhobascorum,
Aracusia, Mathonam,* and *Picentes,* for OH *Rhobascorum, Arachosia,
Mothonam, Picentes,* where the significant forms *Rochobascorum,
Arocasia, Othonam,* and *Pincentes* are confined to the closest
manuscripts and Groups A and D in the first two instances and to
the closest manuscripts and Group D in the second two.[1] More-
over, it not only has a couple of significant readings otherwise
found only in the closest manuscripts—*Lautio* for Or. *Laucius,*
Ricc. 627 and Vienna 366 *Laucio,* OH *L(ucio),* and *Gradio* for Or.
Gratias, Ricc. 627 *Gracio,* OH *G(raccho),* it also has significant
readings not found in these closest manuscripts. Thus, for instance,
we find *Rogoditas* for Or. *Rogathitus,* OH *Trogodytas, Elio* for Or.
Eliuses, OH *Caecilio,* and *Mello* for Or. *Mella,* OH *Metello.*[2] Group
D, in contrast, has the smallest number of significant readings,[3]
but it has two not found elsewhere—*Ariathe* for Or. *Argeate,* OH
Ariarathe, and *Veteramonem* for Or. *Veteromonem,* OH *Vetranionem.*[4] Moreover, it has a handful of forms otherwise found only in
the closest manuscripts. Thus, for instance, where manuscripts of
Group C erroneously give the father-in-law of Perdiccas the name
Sinomen (Groups A and B no reading), Group D agrees with the
four closest manuscripts and with Or. in using the name *Stromen,*
a usage for which there is no justification, either in OH or in fact.[5]

Since only two or three of these 'related' manuscripts can be
dated as early as the eighth or ninth century,[6] and copies one
might have expected to belong to a number of important monastic
libraries including that of Rheims have apparently not survived,[7]

[1] See Bately (1961), pp. 87, 89, and 91.

[2] See Bately (1961), pp. 89, 91, and 95–8.

[3] Of the 'significant' forms listed in Bately (1961), pp. 86–96, 45 are found in
manuscripts of Group A, 63 in Group B, 80 in Group C, and 42 in Group D.
However, many such forms seem to have been removed by correction, particularly from the 'late' manuscripts. For an intermediate stage with correct and
incorrect forms side by side see, e.g., Belluno 42 *donavit vel dampnavit,* BN 17543
ythona vel phiton, and Corpus 23 *tenelaum vel stenelan.*

[4] Bately (1961), p. 96.

[5] See Bately (1961), pp. 81 and 90, and Or. 77/26, Commentary. It is possible
that Group C's *Sinomen* originated in a gloss *sine nomine* (cf. MS Geneva 18
'Nomen illius non dicitur') and that *Stromen* is the result of further corruption.

[6] Berne 128 (Group A) and Vat. Reg. 296 (Group C (ii)) are saec. ix, Vienna
366 is now dated saec. viii–ix.

[7] Eleventh-century manuscripts from St. Bertin and the Chapitre of St.
Omer belong with an English manuscript from Canterbury to 'related' Group
C (iv), and an eleventh-century manuscript from Fleury (?) to Group C (iii). See
further Bately and Ross (1961), pp. 329–34. The only early manuscript of

it is impossible to arrive at any safe conclusions as to the origins of Or.'s exemplar other than that it may have been of English or Irish provenance.[1] However, from a comparison of the distinctive features of the 'related' manuscripts and Or. it is obvious that Or.'s exemplar contained a large number of 'corrupt' or incorrect spellings and variant readings often reflecting Vulgar Latin changes in pronunciation and in spelling convention.[2] Since Or. is a translation, evidence of the existence of these spellings and variant readings is with very few exceptions[3] provided only by proper names. However, it must be considered a distinct possibility that, like other early Latin manuscripts, this exemplar had a certain amount of confusion of spelling in other words and that therefore a number of misunderstandings and incorrect renderings by the translator may be the result not of his ignorance of Latin but of corruption in the text he was using.[4]

It is also possible that this manuscript was either defective or abridged;[5] however, in the total absence of any evidence either to support or refute this theory, it is necessary here to proceed on the assumption that it was a complete but inaccurate copy, some stages removed from its original.

2. In addition to Orosius' *Historiarum adversum Paganos Libri Septem*, the translator has made use of material from a number of other sources. This is mainly explanatory, filling out allusions which Orosius expected his audience to understand, or adding details which Orosius himself had not seen fit to provide. However, in the opening chapter on the geography of the world, the translator produces information which Orosius was not in a position to furnish: details about the territorial divisions of Europe in the

Anglo-Saxon provenance, Düsseldorf, Staatsarchiv HS Z4, nr. 2, assigned by Lowe (Supplement, 1687) to Northumbria and the second half of the eighth century, is too fragmentary for its relationships to be determined.

[1] For Zangemeister's incorrect earliest possible date see above, p. lvi n. 1.

[2] e.g. *f* for *ph*, *i* for *y*, *e* for *i*, *e* for *ae*. See further below, pp. cix ff., and Glossary of Proper Names, *passim*.

[3] See, for instance, 43/7–8, 44/11, and 64/24, Commentary.

[4] If the translator were accustomed to reading manuscripts with confusion of inflexional endings, this might well explain some of his misconstructions, and his occasional apparent disregard of Latin inflexion. In Jordanes, for instance, *cum* and *sine* sometimes appear with the accusative, *inter* with the ablative, while nouns normally inflected change to indeclinables. See Fritz Werner, *Die Latinität der Getica des Jordanis* (Halle, 1908).

[5] A number of abridged versions of OH have survived: see Bately and Ross (1961), pp. 329–34.

ninth century and the reports of two seafarers, Ohthere and
Wulfstan.

(i) *Classical and patristic additions*[1]

As will be seen from the Commentary, the classical and patristic
additions in Or. are to be traced back to a variety of Latin sources,
including Livy, Sallust, Pliny the Elder, Quintus Curtius,
Frontinus, Valerius Maximus, Servius, Jerome, Bede, and (though
the evidence is not conclusive) probably also Augustine, Firmianus
Lactantius, and Suetonius.[2] In one instance, details added by Or.
appear to be derived from either Pomponius Mela or Lactantius
Placidus, in another from either Velleius Paterculus or Sidonius.[3]
A handful of additions use material from Ovid's *Fasti* and Julius
Valerius, but in the case of the former this may have reached Or.
via scholia on Juvenal or on Lucan, and in the case of the latter via
Fulgentius and either Jordanes or Servius.[4] Other possible sources
include Isidore, Eutropius (direct or via Paulus Diaconus),
Florus, Festus, and *De Viris Illustribus*, though of these only
Festus, *De Verborum Significatu*, contains material in common
with Or. that is not also to be found in two or more other Latin
works of which at least one is apparently elsewhere an actual
source of material in Or.[5]

This list of authorities is an impressive one, suggesting knowledge of a large number of classical and patristic texts. Access to
these texts in the ninth century is certainly possible: many are
extant in ninth-century copies,[6] while Lupus of Ferrières appears
to have been familiar with Florus, Aurelius Victor, the Latin
Josephus, Justinus, Valerius Maximus, Mela, Livy, and Sallust,[7]
and amongst the sources of Freculph's *Chronicon* other than
Orosius Grunauer has identified Alcuin, Augustine, Josephus,
Jerome–Eusebius, Florus, Rufinus, Aurelius Victor, Jerome,
Jordanes, and Bede.[8] However, the author of Or. need not have

[1] For a detailed study of these additions see Bately (1971), pp. 237–51.
[2] See, for instance, 106/9–11, 121/9–15, 28/20–1, 70/10, 73/11–17, 94/12–17,
101/4–13, 59/3–11, 60/8–10, 130/3–5, 128/13–21, and 124/19–20, Commentary.
[3] See 45/33–46/1 and 119/6, Commentary.
[4] See 39/13–16, 29/29–31 and 69/22–4.
[5] See Bately (1971), pp. 237–51 and Commentary, *passim*.
[6] See Laistner (1957), p. 254.
[7] See Laistner (1957), pp. 255–61 and M. Manitius, *Geschichte der lateinischen
Literatur des Mittelalters*, I (Munich, 1911).
[8] E. Grunauer, *De Fontibus Historiae Frechulphi* (Vitoduri, 1864).

been familiar with all these works (or indeed any of them) at first hand. Some of the additions may have been present in the manuscript of OH used by him—this certainly seems to be true of the Aeacida quotation from Ennius, less possibly the reference to the Dead Sea Fruit.[1] Others may have been derived from a Latin–Latin or Latin–Old English glossary,[2] from oral communications[3] or from a (Latin?) commentary.[4] There are a number of features which appear to support second-hand derivation of this kind. First of all, the translator sometimes shows ignorance of incidents or people described in the texts from which he is apparently quoting and occasionally incorporates a relevant comment in an irrelevant or even ludicrous manner. Thus, for instance, the Minotaur is half man, half lion, Cincinnatus is no more than 'a certain poor man', Smyrna, the title of a poem, becomes the deathplace of a consul with the same name as the poet, the story of Torquatus with its additions is attached to Decius Mus.[5] Tarquin is said to have been challenged by Brutus but to have sent *Arrunses sunu ðæs ofermodgan* in his stead, most probably because of a gloss or comment *pro Tarquinio*, intended to refer to the *Superbi* of OH *cum Arrunte, Superbi filio*.[6] Again, the description of Philip of Macedon as wounded in the thigh by a woman is surely most plausibly accounted for if we assume a gloss *femine* for OH *femore*, while Or.'s claim that Valerianus was *mid Emilitum þæm folce* appears to depend on a gloss or comment such as *a militibus* on OH *ab exercitu*.[7]

Yet another addition combines themes found in certain Latin texts in a way which suggests ignorance or at least independence

---

[1] See 84/8–11 and 23/7–11, Commentary, and Bately (1961), p. 97.

[2] See, for instance, 23/23–4 and 130/18–20, Commentary, also Bately (1961), pp. 98–9 and, for extensive quotation from Isidore, Augustine etc., the *Glossarium Ansileubi*.   [3] See 23/2, Commentary.

[4] For King Alfred's apparent use of a Latin commentary in translating Boethius see K. Otten, *König Alfreds Boethius* (Tübingen, 1964), pp. 119–57. For the commentaries of Remigius see Laistner (1957), pp. 260–1. The only known extant commentary on OH, Vat. Reg. Lat. 1650, ff. 1–10, a fragment covering OH I. i. 13–II. xiii. 5, has no more than a handful of details in common with Or.: see, e.g. 31/23–5 and 39/10–12, Commentary. For the Irish origin of this fragment, see P. Lehmann, *Erforschung des Mittelalters*, 2 (Stuttgart, 1959), 31.   [5] See 28/16, 50/3, 125/12 and 60/1, Commentary.

[6] 40/26–7, OH II. v. 2.

[7] See 64/29 and 144/21, Commentary. For material omitted by the translator in the course of his translation and added in the form of comment elsewhere see 133/16–19 and 142/3–5, Commentary.

of those texts. In its version of the Regulus story, Or., in making
Regulus oppose the exchange of prisoners because 'him to micel
æwisce wære þæt he swa emnlice wrixleden, 7 eac þæt hiora
gerisna nære þæt hie swa heane hie geþohten þæt hi heora gelican
wurden', seems to be elaborating on a source stating merely that
the opposition was on the grounds of shamefulness and inequality
and not to be using directly any of the Latin versions of the story
still extant. In these the themes of shamefulness and inequality
certainly appear, but in a different guise: the terms are shameful,
the Romans have become degraded and disgraced by their captivity, there is inequality between the prisoners on the two sides
as regards numbers, age, and vigour.[1] Again, although on the
one hand the use of certain passages from Livy, Frontinus, Sallust,
and Valerius Maximus suggests great interest in military stratagems, on the other hand the translator's rendering of them shows
an indifference to the manœuvres involved and a *naïveté* in handling them which cannot be explained away on the grounds of
faulty recollection or the translator's ignorance of Latin.[2]

(ii) *Geographical additions: general*

The best-known of the additions of a geographical nature are the
reports by Ohthere and Wulfstan and the description of northern
Europe which replaces OH I. ii. 53. However, there are a large
number of other pieces of additional geographical information,
not only in the first chapter but scattered throughout the work, and
before any attempt is made to assess the 'northern' material on its
own, it is necessary to examine the possible sources of the new
material as a whole.[3] Apart from oral communication—or, of
course, first-hand knowledge—this material could have been
derived from two very different types of source, that is, either
a Latin (or vernacular) text, or a map. The case for the use of a
map, more specifically a *mappa mundi*, or traditional map portray-
ing the *orbis terrarum* of classical geographers, into which additional information about Germanic, Slav, and Baltic countries was
inserted, has recently been put in detail by Dr. Havlík and Professor Derolez, following suggestions by Professor Labuda concerning the source of such features as the association of the Sabaei
with Arabia Eudaemon and the location of the legendary Land of

[1] See 95/28–31, Commentary.   [2] See below, p. xcix.
[3] For a detailed discussion of this material see Bately (1972), pp. 45–62.

Women and Rhipaean mountains north of the ninth-century Croats of Bohemia.[1] Havlík and Derolez suggest that the apparent clockwise deviation of a number of directions in Or.[2] may similarly be due to the use of an enlarged *mappa mundi*. According to them, the author of Or. describes the relative positions of peoples and countries from the standpoint not of true north, south, east, and west, but of cartographic *oriens*[3] (near the mouth of the Ganges), *meridies* (south of the Nile), *occidens* (near the Pillars of Hercules), and *septentrio* (in the region of the river Tanais). Thus, for instance, the Abodriti, whose 'centre', Mecklenburg, was true north-east of the Old Saxons, are cartographic north of them, by virtue of their location on an imaginary line between Saxonia and *septentrio*.[4]

This theory is a most attractive one. Certainly, the author of Or. could have been aided by a *mappa mundi*: there might even have been one in the manuscript of OH that he apparently used.[5] From such a source he could have obtained information about the relative positions of countries and of topographical features, about the direction of rivers, seas, and mountain ranges, and about such details as whether there were one or more Fortunate islands.[6] From such a source he could have learned of the 'labels' to be applied to certain proper names, such as 'town', or 'country' or 'river', and the identity of the country to which a place belonged.[7]

---

[1] See Labuda (1960), pp. 13–90, esp. pp. 38 ff, and Labuda (1961) esp. pp. 12–14 and commentary, nn. 12, 27, 38, 75, 76, 172, 173, 199, and 216; Havlík (1964) pp. 53–85, and Derolez (1971), pp. 253–68. For a useful study of medieval *mappae mundi* see Marcel Destombes, *Mappemondes A.D. 1200–1500*, Monumenta Cartographica Vetustioris Aevi 1 (Amsterdam, 1964).

[2] These and other apparently clockwise deviations have been much discussed from the time of Porthan and Rask onwards, two of the most detailed surveys being K. Malone (1930b), pp. 139–67, and Ekblom (1941–2), pp. 115–44. For a valuable discussion of the weaknesses of these surveys see Derolez (1971), pp. 256–60 and 264; for individual instances, see 10/25–18/31, Commentary, *passim*.

[3] In *mappae mundi* the east is normally put at the top.

[4] See Havlík (1964), p. 67.

[5] *Mappae mundi* are surprisingly rare in extant MSS of OH; however, there are two surviving from the eighth and ninth centuries: Albi, B. Rochegude, 28, 487ʳ, and St. Gallen Stiftsbibliothek, 621, p. 35, neither, unfortunately, of any special significance to this study. The map in BL Cotton Tiberius B. v. 1, 56ᵛ, usually dated to the tenth century and apparently the work of an Anglo-Saxon scribe, is associated not with OH but with Priscian's *Periegesis*, though a number of the names on it are (not surprisingly) similar to names occurring in OH.

[6] See, e.g., 10/25–6, 18/13–15, 9/1, 9/29–31, 11/27–12/1, and 9/16–17, Commentary.

[7] Some *mappae mundi* indicate towns and mountains pictorially.

If the *mappa mundi* was of the type incorporating legends, then from it he could even have derived a few pieces of general information, such as the cause of the Nile floods or the 'fact' that Olympus is the highest mountain.[1] However, this hypothetical map would need to have been far more detailed— and, incidentally, more accurate—than any *mappa mundi* still extant for the author of Or. to have derived from it more than a fraction of his new information. Moreover, although in theory a *mappa mundi* may seem a likely source for certain details, there is no feature that actually requires us to suppose that one was used by the author.[2] Invariably there are reasonable alternative sources. Thus, for instance, the inclusion of *Mægþa land, Sermende*, and the Rhipaean mountains in an account of ninth-century Europe could be due, as Labuda suggests, to the author's possession of a *mappa mundi* containing these traditional details and his insertion on it of 'contemporary' information with which he had been provided.[3] On the other hand, it could have formed part of that 'contemporary' information. As late as the twelfth century a writer as familiar with northern Europe as Adam of Bremen could not only accept the existence of a northern Land of Women but also believe in the reality of the Rhipaean mountains, which he locates on the borders of Sweden and Norway.[4] As for the Sarmatae, their name continues to appear in geographical treatises of the medieval period, and is sometimes applied to the Slavs.[5] Similarly, the substitution of *Arabia 7 Sabei 7 Eudomane* for OH *Arabia Eudaemon* could be due to the translator chancing to notice the word *Sab(a)ei* in close proximity to the words *Arabia Eudaemon* on his hypothetical *mappa mundi*;

[1] See 11/17–20 and 10/30, Commentary. I have found no legend relevant to this study, apart from Paris, BNL 8878, f 7ʳ 'Arabia . . . eodomon. Ipsa est et Saba appellata.' However, some *mappae mundi* depict the Asian Olympus, without comment, as a large mountain.

[2] For only one feature have I found a parallel in a *mappa mundi* but not in a Latin text: the misplacing of *Cilia* (i.e. Cilicia) and *Issaurio* between Cappadocia and Asia Minor. However, here the translator or an intermediary may have misunderstood the corresponding Latin of OH. See 10/25–6, Commentary.

[3] See Labuda (1960) p. 48 and (1961), commentary, nn. 75–6. What is particularly interesting about the forms *Riffen, Riffin*, and *Sermende* is that they are found not only in the geographical addition but also in the body of the text. *Riffen* could be derived from *Riphaei* as a result of scribal error (cf. MS C *Saben* for *Sabei* and the thirteenth-century *mappa mundi*, Paris BNL 8352, f. 100ᵛ *Rhephens*), the forms *Riffeng, Riffing* being due to subsequent confusion with the *-ing* suffix. *Sermende* too could be the result of error: cf. the reading *Sarmentarum* of Solinus 96, 1, MS A.

[4] See 13/12 and 13/13, Commentary.   [5] See 13/13, Commentary.

on the other hand, it is no less convincingly explained as arising from a gloss or comment *Ubi Sab(a)ei* or *Et Sab(a)ei*, incorrectly incorporated in either the original Latin or the translation.[1] Indeed, almost all the geographical additions and alterations in the text, apart from those concerning the divisions of ninth-century continental Europe, have the support of extant Latin texts. Positive identification of sources is, from the very nature of the material, impossible and as in the case of the classical and patristic additions some of the author's new information could have been derived not at first hand but from a commentary;[2] however, this material can be shown to have been available in geographical treatises such as *De Situ Orbis*, *Dimensuratio*, *Divisio Orbis*, Bede's *De Natura Rerum*, Priscian's *Periegesis*, and the works of Dicuil, Solinus, the Ravenna Geographer, and Martianus Capella and his commentators,[3] as well as a number of other texts already named as possible sources of classical information, e.g. Pliny, Livy, Frontinus, Valerius Maximus, Servius, Mela, and Isidore.[4]

Even in the case of the apparent clockwise shift affecting certain directions given in the section on *Germania*, which Havlík and Derolez argue could be due to interpretation of 'contemporary' information on a *mappa mundi* in terms not of true but of cartographical north, south, east and west, the evidence is far from conclusive. As Professor Derolez himself points out in an important study of earlier discussions of the problem, a number of apparent or supposed deviations are the result of modern methods of calculation, involving a mechanical choice of pivotal centres which it probably never entered the head of a medieval geographer to use;[5] at least one seems to be the result of modern

[1] See 10/15, Commentary.

[2] See above, p. lxii. Geographical material that seems to have been derived at second hand includes the reference in 19/16–18 to Ireland's climate as superior to Britain's 'for ðon þe sio sunne þær gæð near on setl þonne on oðrum lande', possibly the result of the misapplication of a comment on Ireland that 'propinquus sol collocatur'. See further, Bately (1972), p. 62.

[3] See, for instance, 9/1, 9/4, 10/14–15, 10/21, 11/1–2, 11/17, 12/5–6, and 43/12–13, Commentary.

[4] See, for instance, 20/33–21/2, 99/29–30, 85/31, 10/15, 9/29–31, and 8/21, Commentary.

[5] Derolez (1971), p. 259. The mouth of the Elbe, for instance, may be true north-west, not west, of the geographical centre of the Old Saxons, but it is certainly part of their western boundary. The location of the *Hæfeldan* and *Sysyle* can similarly be justified: see 13/1–2 and Commentary.

error.[1] Others in their turn may have arisen from medieval methods of calculation and presentation, from mistaken beliefs, or even from errors made by the author of Or. or by his informants. Thus, in some cases, the apparent shift may be due to the use of directions worked out in terms of travellers' routes, perhaps with deductions of the type 'x is north of y and has z on its west; therefore z must be north-west of y'.[2] In other cases, the direction given may refer to the general position of a complex of peoples, of which only one particular group is specifically named.[3] Again, on occasion two pieces of information may have been incorrectly combined.[4] Nowhere is cartographical explanation the only one possible.

The author of Or., then, in his revising of OH, may have had at his disposal a *mappa mundi*, though there is no conclusive evidence that this was actually the case. He was quite possibly aided by an annotated or glossed Latin manuscript or by a commentary on OH, though this too is a matter of conjecture.[5] What cannot be disputed is that he had access to a considerable body of geographical information in addition to that provided by OH and that he incorporated it in a generally intelligent and unobtrusive manner.

(iii) *Geographical additions: the description of continental Europe*

In the section dealing with the geography of continental Europe, 12/14-19/10, changes are so radical that it is possible to consider the whole section as rewritten to conform to the ninth-century situation as known to the author of Or. or his immediate source.[6] 'Contemporary' information could have reached the author in three different ways: via a Latin or vernacular text or texts, via a map or plan, or orally. That the accounts of Northern Europe by Ohthere and Wulfstan are based on notes made from their verbal reports seems obvious enough. It is also possible that they and

[1] See Ekblom (1941–2), p. 131, where it is claimed that the *Afdrede* were not north of the Saxons as stated by Or., but north-east of them, and 12/31–13/1, Commentary.

[2] See 12/30 and 18/34–5, Commentary, and Bately (1972), p. 61, n. 3.

[3] See Derolez (1971), p. 259 and also 13/1 and 12/29–30, Commentary.

[4] See 13/21–2 and 12/31, Commentary. For possible incorrect beliefs see, e.g., 18/33, Commentary.

[5] See above, p. lxii. Some manuscripts e.g. Vat. Reg. 691, have glosses of the type *nomina locorum, nomen civitatis*, etc.

[6] The only parts not significantly changed are those dealing with Italy and Spain: see 18/19–23, and 19/1–10, Commentary, and pp. lxxxix–xc. For knowledge of Italy and Spain revealed elsewhere in Or., see 21/18–19, 58/7–8, 97/4–5, 100/9, 102/12–13, and 104/29–30, Commentary.

other travellers provided other pieces of information now incorporated in the general discussion of northern Europe.[1] At the
same time, the survival of an account of ninth-century central
Europe by the so-called Bavarian Geographer shows that written
descriptions were current in the period when Or. was written,[2]
while the existence of maps as distinct from *mappae mundi* in
royal courts if not in monasteries seems a reasonable assumption.[3]
And whatever the immediate source of the author's information,
it must be remembered that it too had to have a source, and that a
map could have been compiled from written or oral information,
while written information in its turn could have been derived
from a map. Moreover, a minor inaccuracy in copying the contours
of a map or inserting details in it, and a minor error in describing
the location of a country, could both have major repercussions.[4]

The evidence of the text of Or. as we have it is sadly inconclusive. The method of description adopted by the author or his
immediate source is a simple one, though varying slightly from
section to section. Thus the section on Europe east of the Rhine
and north of the Danube falls into two parts, in both parts description of the region being based on a handful of 'pivotal' areas, each
one linked to its predecessor by a reference to it in the description
of the boundaries of that predecessor. In the first part the pivotal
areas selected are those of the politically important East Franks,
Saxons, and Moravians, followed by the politically unimportant
Daleminzi; in the second part the areas are those of the South
Danes, North Danes, Bornholmers, and Swedes. Each pivotal area
is described in terms of its surrounding territories or natural
boundaries, these being enumerated in clockwise or anti-clockwise

[1] For the suggestion that Wulfstan provided Scandinavian material and that
Slav and Germanic material may have come from Regensburg see Labuda
(1960) pp. 23–4 and (1961), pp. 14 and 17.

[2] These may have included Itineraries. For the route of a tenth-century
Anglo-Saxon archbishop, Sigeric, see F. P. Magoun, *MS*, ii (1940), 231–52.

[3] See Leo Bagrow, *History of Cartography*, rev. and enlarged by R. A.
Skelton (London, 1964), p. 42. (Monastic) scribes appear not to have taken
mappae mundi very seriously, distorting their shapes to fit the page and often
using them primarily as decoration.

[4] A map tilting the Danish peninsula just a little towards the bottom of the
page (supposing E to be at the top) would change its direction from N. to NW.;
similarly, a very slight inaccuracy would make Norway and Sweden lie N.–S.
not NE.–SW. See the suggestion of Havlík (1964), p. 67 that the Danish peninsula was put NW. to fit the curve of a spherical map, and 13/17–18 and 13/26,
Commentary.

order, sometimes with further details of their own positions.[1] In all but one instance, involving the Swedes,[2] the first direction given or the unexpressed link is west.[3]

In the section on Europe east of the Rhine and south of the Danube, the region is again described in terms of a select handful of linked pivotal points (in this case Constantinople, Dalmatia, and Istria) not, as in OH, country by country, As before, each pivotal point is described in terms of its surrounding territories or natural boundaries, these being enumerated in clockwise or anti-clockwise order, sometimes with further details of their own position.[4] In contrast with the previous section, however, the first direction given or the unexpressed link is always east.[5] As for the third section, Europe west of the Rhine, here too the author of Or. departs from the practice of OH in his use of pivotal points (*Gallia Bellica*, *Æquitania*, *Narbonense*, and *Profentse*) but this time he makes use of a regular pattern only in the case of the first two, where the enumeration of the surrounding territories is clockwise, beginning explicitly or implicitly in the east. However, there is no link between *Gallia Bellica* and *Æquitania* and we are told nothing about the northern boundary of the latter.

This element of incompleteness is hard to explain if we assume that the translator had a map in front of him when he was reshaping

[1] Thus, in 13/4–8 the Moravians are said to have *Carendre* to their south, and this in its turn to have first the 'waste-land' then the Bulgarians, then the Eastern Empire to its east. A number of studies of the translator's (or his source's) technique have been made: see, e.g., E. D. Laborde, 'King Alfred's System of Geographical Description in his Version of Orosius', *Geographical Journal*, lxii (1923), 133–8 and Derolez (1971), pp. 255–6. It is customary to refer to the peoples and countries named as 'tribes'; however, the majority are political units of some significance in the ninth century. See Commentary, *passim*.

[2] 13/24–8. The description here begins with the southern boundary, *þone sæs earm Osti*. This also diverges from normal practice, since not only is south the 'link' direction, but in the preceding description it is the Bornholmers who are said to have the Swedes to their north.

[3] It should be noted that information is not always complete: Moravia, for instance, is given no northern neighbour, the Osti no eastern one. See the comment on Aquitania below.

[4] Constantinople, for instance, is described as having Athens and Corinth to its south, with Achaia south-west of Corinth and Dalmatia north-west of Achaia; see 18/10–15 and Commentary.

[5] The translator could here have been influenced by OH, since the latter often, though far from invariably, begins with the east. It should be noted that OH is also inconsistent in the order in which it gives its directions, a clockwise or anti-clockwise arrangement being no more common than an apparently haphazard mixture.

OH's account of the Gauls, easy to explain if we assume that he was using only that account along with the information or knowledge that OH's reference to Gallia Lugdunensis as Aquitania's northern neighbour was no longer correct. Also difficult to explain in terms of a single map source are the two different forms of the name of the Bohemians. As the people east of the East Franks these are described as *Bæme*; as the people west of the Moravians, they are described as *Behemas*. In the first instance, the form seems to be based on the *Boemi* of Latin texts, in the second, it corresponds to OHG *Beheima*, *Behemi*. Havlík would explain this in terms of information from two different sources;[1] however, another possible explanation is that a commentary based on a map using a form of the vernacular *Beheima* replaced this by its Latin equivalent the first time it referred to it, but kept the form of its original on the second occasion.[2] Also possibly favouring the theory of an underlying written rather than map source is the repeated reference to part of Bavaria not the whole. A commentary defining the boundaries of the East Franks might well say that on the south-east was that part of Bavaria in which the important city of Regensburg was located, or that Regensburg was located in that part of Bavaria nearest to the territory of the East Franks. The consulter of a map on the other hand—unless that map had the legend *Bavariae pars*—would surely see that the whole of Bavaria was on the East Franks' south-east and would be unlikely to make such a qualification as occurs in Or. However, none of these details is in itself conclusive evidence that a map was not used and the precise source or sources of Or.'s new material in the account of the geography of continental Europe must be said to be not known.[3]

[1] Havlík (1964), p. 74.
[2] Or vice versa in the case of a map with Latin names.
[3] It is interesting to note that the same indecisive conclusion is reached by editors of Jordanes: see Jordanes, *The Gothic History in English version*, ed. C. C. Mierow (Cambridge, 1966, repr. of 2nd edn., 1915), pp. 36–7, 'it is Mommsen's belief that [certain] geographical passages . . . in which places are portrayed as they would appear on a map, are based upon an actual map. Even the list of the islands of the Indian Ocean is given in exactly the same order as in the work of Julius Honorius who wrote from a map. Mommsen would ascribe to a like source five passages in which countries or tribes are located with reference to the points of the compass. Now the provinces there mentioned are of the time before Diocletian and the descriptions do not hold good for the time of Cassiodorus or Jordanes, but for about the second century, whereas the other names of localities and races found in the *Getica* accord properly with

(iv) *Ohthere and Wulfstan*

All that we know of Ohthere and Wulfstan is what is contained in their reports as recorded in the geographical first chapter of Or.[1] Ohthere's name and his home in the most northern part of Norway suggest that he was a Norwegian. However, there is no evidence to connect him with either the jarl Ohthere of the *Anglo-Saxon Chronicle*, s.a. 918, or the hero of *Qrvar-Odds saga*.[2] Holger Arbman sees him as a merchant yeoman, that is, not a full-time merchant skipper but a man with his own estate to which he normally returned each harvest time. Others consider him to have been an exile, forced to sell up his estate and leave Norway by the stern measures of King Harald Fairhair.[3] Whether he spoke English or used the services of an interpreter is uncertain, though in the ninth century comprehension between Anglo-Saxon and Norseman should have provided no great difficulty.[4] As for Wulfstan, he is normally taken to be an Englishman and a Mercian, on the grounds that Wulfstan is a known Anglo-Saxon name, found very rarely in a continental Germanic form, while a number of non-West Saxon linguistic features are present in his report. However, these non-West Saxon features could be the work of a reporter or interpreter, while on the one hand Danish and OHG equivalents are indeed recorded, and on the other we do not know enough about the name-giving of ninth-century Frisia to be able to rule out a Frisian or similar origin for him.[5] Although it is

fifth-century conditions. It would be difficult, however, to decide whether Cassiodorus actually made use of a map of the world as it was in the second century or merely of an epitome from such a map.'

[1] One slightly surprising thing about the reports is the amount of information that is excluded from them. We are not told, for instance, the name of the part of Halgoland in which Ohthere lived, nor the name of the great river where his journey ended. We are told nothing of the conditions on the journey there apart from the wind direction on two occasions; we are told nothing at all of the journey back—though as Rae, who followed the same route in the nineteenth century, ruefully remarks (*White Sea Peninsula*, p. 198), 'It may be taken for granted that to travel southward in these regions by boat is easier than to travel northward.'

[2] See *Qrvar-Odds saga*, ed. R. C. Boer (Halle, 1892), p. xiv. I am indebted to Mr. Anthony Faulkes for this reference.

[3] See Holger Arbman, *The Vikings*, trans. and ed. A. Binns (London, 1961), p. 44, and Bright (1971), p. 186.

[4] Cf., e.g., *Egils saga*, ch. 62.

[5] See W. A. Craigie, 'The Nationality of King Alfred's Wulfstan', *JEGPh*, xxiv (1925), 396–7 and Ross (1978), p. 102. Arguments for a Danish origin for Wulfstan based on the supposition that an Englishman would have described

generally supposed that Wulfstan, like Ohthere, made his report to King Alfred, there is nothing at all in the text to support this. On the other hand, the counter-suggestion that he made his report to Ohthere and that Ohthere repeated it to Alfred[1] seems to be ruled out by the differences of vocabulary and morphology between the two accounts. Thus, for instance, where Ohthere's report has the constructions *on þæt bæcbord, on þæt steorbord*, that of Wulfstan has *on bæcbord, on steorbord*; where Ohthere has contracted forms of the strong 3rd person singular present indicative, Wulfstan has the Anglian full forms.[2] At the same time, the language of both reports differs from that of the body of Or., suggesting that the author could not have been responsible for the drafting of either of them. Peculiar to Ohthere's report is the use of *hyrð in on* (Wulfstan *hyrað to*, 107/24 *hierden to*) and *up in on*, of *aþer oþþe . . . oþþe* with the first *oþþe* immediately following the pronoun, of *æghwilc* not *gehwilc*, *sped*, *spedig* not *wela*, *welig*, and of *mor* for 'mountain', not as elsewhere in Or. *beorg*, *munt*, or *dun*.[3] Peculiar to Wulfstan is the apparently Anglian *nænig*, and neuter *twegen*, weak masculine *þeowa* not strong *þeow*.[4] Otherwise paralleled only in the list of chapter headings is Wulfstan's use of *on* in the sense 'at a distance of', a use not infrequently found in the Old English Bede and occurring also in the Martyrology, while restricted to these reports but occurring in both of them is the use of *biþ* and *beoþ*.[5]

the journey from England to Hedeby (see Hübener (1925–6), p. 44) seem to me completely unconvincing, especially in view of the use of Hedeby to link Wulfstan's report to that of Ohthere.

[1] Förster (1941), p. 259, n. 3.

[2] The only other uncontracted forms of this type in Or. are concentrated at the very beginning of the geographical chapter. See above, p. xlviii.

[3] See Bately (1970), pp. 450, 448, and 439, n. 31. King Alfred uses *mor* in the sense of 'marsh', 'boggy ground', but in the Old English Bede it translates Lat. *mons*: cf. Bo. 42/7, Be. 358/3. For 15/9 *unbebohtra* as a possible Anglian word see R. Jordan, *Eigentümlichkeiten des anglischen Wortschatzes* (Heidelberg, 1906), p. 104.

[4] See Bately (1970), pp. 439, n. 31 and 458, n. 205 and for the suggestion that *twegen* is an Anglian neuter see Bright (1971), p. 195. However, since *fætels* is elsewhere normally masc., erroneous expansion of an underlying *ii* cannot be ruled out. Possibly also of significance is the use of *byrdest* in Ohthere's report, *heahþungen* in Wulfstan's.

[5] See Wülfing (1901), p. 491, and Karl Jost, 'Beon und Wesan', *Anglistische Forschungen*, xxvi (Heidelberg, 1909). For the use of *on* in the list of chapter headings, see below, p. lxxxii and n. 7.

VI. AUTHORSHIP

1. The Body of the Text

The earliest surviving reference to the authorship of the OE Orosius occurs in William of Malmesbury's *Gesta Regum Anglorum*, where it is attributed to King Alfred along with the Old English versions of Boethius' *De Consolatione*, Gregory's *Cura Pastoralis*, and Bede's *Historia Ecclesiastica*.[1] That William of Malmesbury was wrong in considering the Old English Bede to be the work of Alfred was suggested as long ago as 1876[2] and has since been generally accepted; however, his claim that Alfred translated the Orosius also has gone largely unchallenged.[3] As a result, comparative studies of the 'Alfredian' texts have been mainly concerned with chronology. Thus, the different handling of the *duo* and *tria nomina* of Roman citizenship has been quoted as evidence that Alfred translated first Or. and then Bo., although it could more appropriately be used as evidence of an order Bo., Or., or even of two different translators at work.[4] Again, certain classical references in Bo. have been said to 'have their source in Orosius and serve to prove, if further proof were necessary, that Or. preceded Bo.'.[5] However, here too there is no need to assume common authorship. For instance, the sole point of contact between the references to Regulus in Or. and Bo. is the fact of his

---

[1] *De Gestis Regum Anglorum*, ed. W. Stubbs, Rolls Series (London, 1887), i, p. 132. Gaimar's comment in *L'Estoire des Engleis*, ll. 3445–8, where he says of Alfred that

> Il fit escrivre un livre engleis
> Des aventures e des leis
> E des batailles de la terre
> E des reis ki firent guerre

surely refers not to Or. but to the *Anglo-Saxon Chronicle*, and in any case merely claims that Alfred caused the book to be written, not that he translated it himself. See Dorothy Whitelock, 'William of Malmesbury on the Works of King Alfred', in *Medieval Literature and Civilization: Studies in Memory of G. N. Garmonsway*, ed. D. A. Pearsall and R. A. Waldron (London, 1969), pp. 78–93.

[2] By Henry Sweet, in his *Anglo-Saxon Reader*. For a most valuable survey of the problems connected with the OE Bede see Dorothy Whitelock (1962), pp. 57–90.

[3] Alfred's authorship of Or. was first questioned by Josef Raith, *Untersuchungen zum englischen Aspekt, I. Grundsätzliches Altenglisch* (Munich, 1951), pp. 54–61.

[4] See Potter (1931), p. 59, n. 1 and Bately (1970), pp. 435–7.

[5] Potter (1931), p. 62.

being kept in bonds by the Carthaginians, and this piece of information is in each case derived from the primary source. What is
more, there is an important difference of usage between the two
versions, Bo. employing the term *Affricanas* for Lat. *Poenorum*,
while Or. invariably translates *Poeni* and *Carthaginienses* by
Pene, *Cartainienses* and variants of these forms, 62 instances in all,
never in any context using the noun *Affricanas*.[1]

It is indeed not to the content but to the expression that we
must look for what must surely be conclusive evidence as to
authorship. A detailed examination of the vocabulary and syntax
of the so-called Alfredian texts reveals so many differences
between Or. on the one hand and Bo. and So. on the other that
although there is no evidence at all to suggest different dialect
origins (as in the case of the OE Bede), it seems quite impossible
that these works as we have them could have been produced by
one and the same man.[2] Thus, for instance, where Bo. and So. use
the adjectives *scyldig*, *eapmod*, *wynsum*, Or. has *-gyltig*, *eapmodig*
and *lustsumlic*;[3] where Bo. and So. use the verbs *befæstan*, *fultumian*, *(ge)teohhian*, *lician*, and *pyncan* and prefer *(ge)andswarian*
to *(ge)andwyrdan*, Or. has *betæcan*, *fylstan*, *gestihtian*, *(ge)lician*,
gepyncan, and *(ge)ondwyrdan*, never *(ge)ondswarian*; where Bo. and
So. use *geo*, *gefyrn*, and the constructions *a(w)per oppe . . . oppe*
and *oper twegea*, *oppe . . . oppe*, and prefer *fulneah* to *forneah*,
and *ge-eowian*, *eowan*, etc. to *opiewan*, Or. has *on ærdagum*, *on
ealddagum* with a single instance of *iu* in the geographical addition,
invariable *opiewan* and the construction *oper (aper) . . . oppe . . .
oppe*, with either a verb or *para* following immediately after
oper, and prefers *forneah* to *folneah*.[4] Bo. moreover differs from
Or. in having the construction *no pæt an pæt . . . ac (eac)* not
nales pæt an pæt . . . ac eac, and in using *betweoh* and its variants

---

[1] See further Bately (1970), pp. 437–9.

[2] Drastic revisions of Old English texts were sometimes undertaken: see, for
instance, MS H of *Gregory's Dialogues* and D. Yerkes, *Studies in the Manuscripts of Gregory's Dialogues*, unpublished dissertation, Oxford, 1976.

[3] For a detailed discussion of these and a number of other words not only in
Or., Bo., and So., but also the Alfredian Laws, *Cura Pastoralis*, and the prose
section of the Paris Psalter see Bately (1970), pp. 440–59. For the adjectives see
pp. 444, 451–3, 455, and 457.

[4] See Bately (1970), pp. 444–8, 450–3, 455–8. For the exceptional use of *aper
oppe . . . oppe* in Ohthere's report see p. lxxii. For *geeowian*, *opiewan*, etc. see
Bately (1978). Other differences include variations of the formula 'was called',
for which see Bately (1978).

as both preposition and adverb, while Or. normally makes a clearcut distinction between *betweoh* preposition and *betweonum* postposition.[1] Other differences of vocabulary include Bo.'s use of *gigant* for Latin *gigas*, Or. *ent*, Bo. *upwita* for Latin *philosophus*, Or. *philosoph* etc., and Bo. *heretoga* for Latin *consul*, Or. *consul*.[2] Syntactical differences are no less frequent, though because of the complexity of the material they cannot easily be summarized here.[3] Noteworthy are Or.'s preference for *þa* to introduce temporal clauses where Bo. and So. favour *þonne*, its preference for *for þon* (*þe*) where Bo. and So. favour *forþæm* (*þe*), *forþam* (*þe*), its use of *mid þæm þe*, *mid þæm þæt*, and *mid þon þe*, none of which is used in Bo. and So., and its fondness for periphrastic tenses[4] where Bo. and So. have simple verb forms.[5] A few of these differences could of course be due to scribal alteration; however, the overwhelming weight of evidence is that if Alfred was the author of Bo. and So., he could not also have been responsible for Or.

At the same time, there are certain internal differences of usage in Or. that have led to suggestions of the involvement of not one person but at least two people in the translation of Or. In the penultimate paragraph of her article on the authorship of Or., having drawn attention to Raith's detection of several hands in the work,[6] Dr. Liggins writes:

My investigation has shown that within the historical books there are differences from one part to another. In the case of a considerable number of different grammatical concepts and ideas, one construction is preferred in the earlier part and another in the later. The order of

[1] See Bately (1970), pp. 449–450, 452, 455–7.

[2] See Bately (1970), pp. 440–1 and 451. Also suggesting different authorship, though with nothing comparable in either Bo. or So., is Or.'s name for the Jews, *Iudan*, *Iuþan*, CP and Paris Psalter *Iudeas*.

[3] For a detailed study, including a valuable survey of the syntactical material in the OE Bede, see Liggins (1970), 289–322.

[4] See Liggins (1970), pp. 292–3, 302–3, and 310–13.

[5] Although this is the feature that led Raith to query Alfred's authorship of the OE Orosius, another scholar working on the same material seems unwilling to accept Raith's interpretation of the facts as necessarily conclusive: see Nickel (1966), pp. 107–133, especially pp. 108–9 and 115; also Bruce Mitchell, 'Some problems involving OE periphrases with *Beon/Wesan* and the present participle', *Neuphilologische Mitteilungen* lxxvii (1976), 479 n. However, if the handling of the expanded form in the Orosius does not necessarily prove that Alfred did not have a hand in the composition of the work, it certainly does not prove that he did—and Nickel's study produces no evidence whatsoever *for* Alfred's involvement, presumably accepting William of Malmesbury's statement without question.   [6] See above, p. lxxiii n. 3.

words in clauses, the arrangement of clauses in sentences, the length of sentences and some of the rhythmic patterns also show significant variations. There is some suggestion of a change of style about the beginning of Book III, section viii; and Potter has remarked on the great number of silly mistakes of interpretation in Books IV and V by comparison with the earlier ones. Several explanations are possible. There is, however, quite strong evidence that the author of Book VI, with its barer, flatter style and several peculiarities of grammatical construction, could not have been responsible for the earlier historical books, although he probably worked in close collaboration with the other man or men, sharing in many turns of phrase and constructions not found in other contemporary writings. He may also have been responsible for part or all of the geographical introduction, but the subject matter there is too different for any real comparison to be made.[1]

The 'differences from one part to another' which Dr. Liggins cites in the body of her article form an impressive list. However, none of them actually requires us to suppose multiple authorship. For some there are reasonable alternative explanations; others, on close examination, appear to be irrelevant to this particular question or at most to provide negative evidence. Thus, in the case of certain constructions, limited distribution seems to be the result of limited opportunity. For instance, *þæs þe*, 'after', which is 'almost confined to the second half' of Or., is, as Dr. Liggins points out, invariably used with a prepositional phrase of time.[2] If we extend our study to include all the contexts in which it may reasonably be expected to occur, we find that, excluding the *æfter þæm þe* formula which opens most of the chapters, there are only two such contexts in the first half of the work. The first of these, 38/31, has *þæs þe*, the other, 61/6, has *æfter þæm þe*, most probably under the influence of the *æfter þæm þe* formula.[3] In the second half there is likewise a single exception.[4] Again, although the pattern of two infinitives, one inflected, one not, is confined to Book VI, nowhere else do we find a comparable context,[5] and the same applies to Book VI *swa longe swa . . . swa longe*.[6]

---

[1] Liggins (1970), p. 322. [2] Liggins (1970), p. 296.

[3] It not only occurs shortly after the *æfter þæm þe* formula opening III. vii, but corresponds to the opening of a chapter in OH with the formula *Anno ab Vrbe condita*. [4] Or. 133/27. See below, p. lxxviii.

[5] *þencan* can be used with either the inflected or the uninflected infinitive and instances of both types are found in Or. (cf., e.g., 81/15 and 148/16), so that the variation is perhaps less surprising than at first appears. Sweet's *þuhte* I emend to *þohte*, the reading of MS C. [6] Liggins (1970), p. 296.

In other cases, it is scribal interference that may be responsible for the final distribution patterns. Thus the two exceptional instances in Book VI of the order auxiliary+participle in the *æfter þæm þe* formula are confined to MS L, Cotton having the normal order, while of the seven instances of *mid þæm þæt* in Books IV and VI only four appear in both manuscripts, Cotton having the more usual *mid þæm þe* twice and Lauderdale once,[1] so that it is impossible to reach any conclusion as to the situation in the original version of Or. Similarly, there is disagreement between the two manuscripts over the distribution of *se þe* forms[2]—though the absence of relative *se þe* from III. viii–xi noted by Dr. Liggins[3] can, in view of the small number of forms involved, in any case only have negative value and may be the result of chance.

Chance too may account for two features involving the use of *raþe þæs þe*.[4] First of all, the fact that the sole instance of *raþe þæs þe* without any other connective occurs in Book VI must be seen in the light of another fact—namely that of the connectives otherwise used two (*ac* and *þehhwæþre*) are semantically inappropriate and the third (*7*) would be stylistically undesirable. Secondly, that the three exceptions to the rule that *raþe þæs þe* normally occurs with the verb *cuman* (nine instances) are all verbs or verbal phrases of perception and are found in the last quarter of the book (i.e. in Books V and VI) need be no more than coincidence. If we enlarge the discussion to include clauses of immediate sequence introduced by *sona swa*, we find that where the verb is one of perception *sona swa* is used with *wiste* and *raþe þæs þe* with other verbs and verbal phrases; where the verb is not one of perception, either formula can be used, though *cuman* occurs only with *raþe þæs þe*.[5]

Even where limited distribution, scribal interference, and chance may have played little or no part, change of authorship is not the only possible explanation. Seemingly significant differences may be accounted for in terms of stylistic development. Thus, it does

---

[1] See 84/23, 85/13, 94/32, 100/1, 101/25, 144/8, 150/26, and Liggins (1970), pp. 292–3.

[2] See, e.g., 131/10 and 136/28, where L *se se þe* appears as *se þe* in C.

[3] p. 316.   [4] See Liggins (1970), p. 294.

[5] The picture given by Dr. Liggins is distorted by the exclusion from consideration of the three instances of *raþe þæs . . . þe* and *raþe . . . þæs þe*, which are used with the verbs *gefaran*, *cuman*, and *ofslean* respectively. It should be noted that the *raþe þæs þe* formula does not appear before Book IV.

at first sight seem 'curious that of the seven *siþþan* constructions
which occur before the end of *Or* III, vii, five either may or must
mean "from the time when", while of the fourteen which are used
in the later part eleven *cannot* have this meaning and hence appear
to be interchangeable with *æfter þæm þe*'.[1] However, put another
way, what we have is a slight reduction in the number of 'from the
time when' constructions, where *æfter þæm þe* is never used (a
maximum of five before III. vii and three after it), and a marked
increase in the number of 'after'-clauses of the other type, where
either *siþþan* or *æfter þæm þe* is appropriate.[2] If we take into consideration also the increased use of *þæs þe* and *sona swa* in the
second half of the work and the introduction of *raþe þæs þe* from
IV. i, then what is significant is surely the greater flexibility that
develops as the work progresses, and this could be the result of
increased confidence and experience on the part of a single author.

The gradual development of stylistic mannerisms or idiosyn-
crasies may also account for the fact that some constructions 'are
heavily concentrated in one or other of the sections of Or.'—
though, surely significantly, the lines of demarcation are never the
same and normally occur well after III. vii. Thus, although *ær
þæm þe* and *ær þæm (þon, þan)* are found only in the earlier books,
where they occur alongside simple *ær*, the section which uses
only *ær* cannot be said to begin before IV. x.[3] As for *oþ* and
oþ þæt (oþ þætte, oþ þe), the latter is certainly discarded in the
later part of Or., but at precisely what point is not clear. MS L's
last instance occurs in IV. viii, C's in V. i.[4] Neither this gradual
elimination of alternatives to the simple forms *ær* and *oþ*, nor the
gradual reduction in the number of expanded verb forms,[5] requires
us necessarily to suppose a change of translator.

A slightly different problem is posed by the distribution patterns
of *þeah* and *þeah þe*. According to Dr. Liggins, 'the earlier books
prefer *þeah* to *þeah þe* (35:12) and in III. viii–V the simple form is
less common than the compound (17:29). Book VI has only

---

[1] Liggins (1970), p. 298.

[2] There are 10 instances of non-formulaic *æfter þæm þe* before III. viii and
12 after.

[3] The last instance of *ær þæm þe* occurs in III. ix (see 69/26); however, after
this chapter *ær* is not found again until IV. x (see 105/31).

[4] See 100/23 and 113/27.

[5] See Liggins (1970) pp. 299 and 312. I find that Nickel (1966, p. 128) is here
in agreement with me.

þeah (5:0).'[1] This seems to me potentially the most significant of Dr. Liggins's findings, especially in the context of an apparent ninth-century preference for simple *þeah*. Here indeed there seems to be a change at III. viii. However, there are as always several ways of interpreting the figures, even allowing for scribal distortion.[2] First of all, they could be taken as support for the theory implicit in Dr. Liggins's penultimate paragraph, that at least three men were involved in the translation of the historical part of Or. Secondly, since there are several occasions where five or more examples of simple *þeah* occur consecutively and therefore the 5:0 of Book VI is statistically non-significant, it could be that only the practice in the middle section suggests a new translator or translators. Finally, they may quite reasonably be explained as the work of a single translator, who uses *þeah* and *þeah þe* interchangeably.[3]

It would seem then that in order to account for the differences cited by Dr. Liggins, there is no necessity to postulate multiple authorship. How far the other points she raises concerning the order of words, the length of sentences, and certain rhythmic patterns are relevant it is impossible to determine without repeating the whole of her extremely detailed research on the five 'Alfredian' texts, since she does not identify those that she finds significant. There are certainly variations throughout the work, but the obvious ones are open to the same explanations that I have suggested above for syntactical variations, while in the case of Book VI the 'barer, flatter style' may be due to waning of interest on the part of the translator, lack of time for revision, or merely absence of the opportunity for grammatical complexity.[4]

As for the 'great number of silly mistakes of interpretation in Books IV and V by comparison with the earlier ones', this is based on a comment by Professor Potter on the translator's erroneous supposition that a youth of 17 could be appointed dictator, which as he himself observes would not have seemed too impossible to an Anglo-Saxon: 'It is nevertheless surprising that in these later books so many near-incredible or ridiculous statements have

---

[1] p. 309.

[2] Cf., e.g., 118/10, where MS L has *þeh*, C *þeah þe*, and 34/16, where L has *þeh þe* and C *þeah*.

[3] The two forms are, for instance, found side by side in the Homilies of Ælfric, choice often being determined by the requirements of rhythm.

[4] See below, p. xcvii n. 5.

been left uncorrected.'[1] However, of the three other references that Professor Potter gives in this note—112/11, 115/1–2, and 125/11—only the first, the description of a citadel as two miles high, is of a type necessarily likely to strike a medieval writer as either near-incredible or ridiculous, while there are enough misunderstandings in the early books to make the errors of the last three books no indication of different authorship.

The possibility of a single translator, gradually developing a style, taking up new expressions, and occasionally discarding old ones as the translation progresses, is not contradicted by the vocabulary of the work. Random checks that I have made at various points of Or., combined with a detailed examination of the distribution of words with related semantic fields, have yielded no statistically significant results that might be considered to indicate multiple authorship. Differences of usage do occur, but the lines of demarcation of the ones that I have noted do not normally correspond with those suggested by Dr. Liggins, nor indeed with one another.[2] In any case, a 'control' is lacking; there is, for instance, no study dealing in detail with non-distinctive variations of usage in the work of a known single author to help us to determine the extent to which variation in Or. is likely to be significant.[3] What is more, we do not know how the translator set about his task. We do not know his previous experience of writing English or indeed of translating. We do not know the order of translation, nor whether rewriting or revision of part or whole was undertaken. We do not know if he had the help of an amanuensis, or succession of amanuenses, who might have done some revising for him and introduced their own mannerisms.[4] We do not know if he worked

---

[1] Potter (1952–3), p. 422.

[2] Thus, for instance, *on siml* and *fylstan* are the normal usage in the earlier part of Or., *simle* and *gefylstan* in the final chapters, but the distribution is *on siml* I. ii–VI. xxiv, with *simbel* II. iv, *simle* (the 'Alfredian' usage) V. ii–VI. xxxvii, and *fylstan* I. xii–IV. v, *gefylstan* III. xi–VI. xxxiii, with *gefultumian* (the 'Alfredian' usage) twice in III. vii. *Adræfan* and *adrifan*, on the other hand, occur in three and four 'blocks' respectively spread over the whole work.

[3] Recent important studies of vocabulary, such as that of Ælfric by J. C. Pope and of the Winchester School by Helmut Gneuss are mainly concerned with the identification of distinctive features, not with the distribution of non-distinctive ones. See Ælfric, *Homilies*, ed. Pope, and H. Gneuss, 'The Origin of Standard English', *ASE*, 1 (1972). Since this note was written I have undertaken such an investigation in respect of a limited number of concepts: see Bately (1978).

[4] See *Chronicle of Æthelweard*, p. xxxvii.

continuously on the translation, without a break, or (far more likely if he was someone of importance, undertaking the translation in the midst of other more urgent preoccupations) whether he had to put it aside from time to time, perhaps for months on end. Only at one point do we know precisely what he was doing—that is, in the geographical chapter, when he inserted an account of the reports of Ohthere and Wulfstan—and that is the one point where there is clear indication of differences of authorship.[1] In the light of our present knowledge, the case for multiple authorship must be considered as unproved.

2. The Chapter Headings

The question of the authorship of the list of chapter headings poses a special set of problems, since, as we have seen,[2] it is based on the text of Or. and therefore, no matter who its author was, might be expected to follow fairly faithfully the wording of the text. However, there seem to be reasonably good grounds for supposing that the compiler of the list of chapter headings was not also the author of Or. First of all, as a guide to the contents of the book it is little more useful than a list of first lines: often it is just the first item in the chapter that is referred to, though sometimes two or three—rarely more—additional items are included. Only one entry seems to show knowledge of other parts of the text: II. iii 'Hu Romulus 7 Brutus mid hwelcum mane hie gehalgedon Roma', corresponding to the second sentence of the chapter, 'Romulus heora forma cyning 7 Brutus heora forma consul wurdon emnreðe', but apparently echoing an earlier comment on Romulus' behaviour, 'Swa weorðlice 7 swa mildelice wæs Romeburg on fruman gehalgod.'[3] Otherwise the list is at once unselective, mechanical, and unhelpful, and nowhere reflects what the text suggests to have been the translator's special interests. There is, for instance, nothing to direct the reader to the stories of the Rape of the Sabines or of Lucretia, to the account of the fall of Babylon or the death of Cato, or even the birth of Christ. Indeed, the chapter on the signs and portents attending Christ's birth, which is one of those almost completely rewritten by the author of Or., is 'identified' in the list merely by the words 'Hu Octauianus se casere betynde Ianes duru', drawn from the opening sentence of the text.[4] Other entries

[1] See above, p. lxxii.   [2] See above, p. xxxviii.
[3] See 2/16–17, 40/16–19, and 39/16–17.   [4] 6/18 and 130/25–7.

suggesting general unfamiliarity with the text are those beginning 'Hu under ii consulum', as though the compiler had not realized that in the stereotyped chapter openings it was the date and the names of the consuls that mattered, not the latter's existence or their numbers. Thus, for instance, for III. iii 'Æfter þæm þe Romeburg getimbred wæs iii hund wintra 7 lxxxiii, þa þa Laucius, þe oþre noman wæs haten Genutius, 7 Quintus, þe oþre noman wæs haten Serfilius, ða hie wæron consulas on Rome, gewearð se micla moncwealm on þæm londe' is reduced in the chapter headings to the uninformative 'Hu se micla monncwealm wearð on Rome on twegra consula dæge'. At the same time, where names given in the list correspond to *duo nomina* in the text, it is normally only the praenomen that is cited.[1] Ignorance of the text is suggested by the entry for V. ii, one of the multiple entries, which includes the words 'hu Ueriatus se hierde ongon ricsian on Ispanium' and 'hu an cild wearþ geboren on Rome', the latter referring to the birth of Siamese twins, the former referring to a brigand who terrorized large areas of Spain.[2]

Secondly, although the list of chapter headings derives the bulk of its vocabulary from the text, it contains certain variant usages which are either not typical of or alien to the text. Thus, I. x 'from him ondredon' appears as 'him fore andredan', with a postpositional construction found in the text of Or. only in conjunction with *gielpan*.[3] III. viii *swiþe mære* appears as *swiþe widmære*, with a compound never used elsewhere in Or., though it is found once in Bo., beside the 'Alfredian' *foremære*.[4] Alexander's *æfterfylgendas*, III. xi, become *heretogan*, again a term alien to the body of the text,[5] while the noun *wiþerwinna* occurs twice with the possessive dative, although in the text it is always used with the genitive.[6] Finally, the list of chapter headings includes Or.'s only instance of *on* with the meaning 'at a distance of' outside Wulfstan's report.[7]

---

[1] e.g. 5/3 *Lucius*, for 102/15 *Lucius Postumius*. The only instances of *duo nomina* are 3/3 *Marcus Curtius*, 6/24 *Tiberius Claudius*, and 7/8 *Marcus Antonius*.

[2] See 5/21 and 24, 114/12–115/28, and 116/23–5.

[3] See 1/26, 4/24, 97/23, and 113/14. The construction with *from* occurs again in the body of the text, 116/21.   [4] See Bately (1970), pp. 444 and 455.

[5] See Bately (1970), p. 441.

[6] Cf. 3/22, 6/19, and 55/15. In the text the construction invariably involves 3rd person possessive *his*, *hiora*, etc.

[7] 3/4. See above, p. lxxii. The reading *on* here may be a scribal error for *oþ* (so MS C), since elsewhere the idiom is '*on* . . . mila *from* þære byrg', beside

Cumulatively, these features seem to indicate that the compiler of the list was not also the author of the OE Orosius.[1]

3. *Or. and the* Anglo-Saxon Chronicle

That there are certain verbal parallels between Or. and the *Anglo-Saxon Chronicle* has long been recognized. Some scholars consider these parallels to be 'such as would be expected in works with similar themes', while 'at the most these similarities of expression could only prove that the Chronicler and the translator of the Orosius were familiar with each other's work'.[2] Others, however, would go further and claim that the 'compiler of the Chronicle of [890] and the adapter of the Orosius were the same person, whom the king commissioned to do both works'.[3]

The question of the manner of compilation of the '890 Chronicle' and the sources its compiler(s) used is an involved one. However, even if allowance is made for the probability that more than one man's usage is reflected here, all the evidence points away from the author of Or. as the compiler also of the Chronicle. On the one hand, the verbal similarities observed by Plummer[4] and others continue into the annals for the tenth century, while in the majority of instances the words and constructions involved also occur elsewhere in Old English literature. On the other hand, there are numerous verbal dissimilarities which cannot be dismissed as non-significant variations of usage. Only a small part of the evidence can be given here; however, in view of Plummer's suggestion of resemblances between the post-890 Chronicle and the OE Orosius, the following survey is extended beyond 890 to include the annals 892–923 of the Parker Chronicle. The division into sections

'*oþ* . . . mila *to* þære byrg'. See Wülfing (1901), II § 801. For the use of a gpl. in -*o* in the chapter headings see below, p. cviii.

[1] For an important study of the compilation of the list of chapter headings of another (presumably) ninth-century text, see D. Whitelock, 'The list of chapter-headings in the Old English Bede', *Old English Studies in Honour of J. C. Pope*, ed. R. B. Burlin and E. B. Irving, Jr. (Toronto, 1974), 263–84.

[2] See *The Parker Chronicle, 832–900*, ed. A. H. Smith (London, 1935, 3rd edn. 1951), p. 7.

[3] See K. Sisam, 'Anglo-Saxon Royal Genealogies', *PBA*, xxxix (1953), 335. According to Sprockel (1965), p. xix, 'The close resemblance in phraseology between the Chronicle and Alfred's Orosius . . . cannot, I think, be dismissed as mere correspondences in contemporary works on similar themes.' For 890 as the final annal of the 'first' compilation, see Bately (1978).

[4] See Plummer, *Two of the Saxon Chronicles Parallel*, pp. cvi–cvii.

in this survey is an arbitrary one and is not intended to reflect precisely the various possible stages in composition.[1]

(i) From the opening to annal 409. This section deals with a period of history covered also in Or. and contains the one phrase cited by Plummer which could have been taken over by the Chronicle from Or.: the saying of Titus that 'he þone dæg forlure þe he noht to gode on ne gedyde'. However, the Chronicle's ultimate source here seems to be Isidore's *Chronicon*, while Or.'s source owes something at least to Jerome,[2] and apart from this allusion, there is nothing to suggest an intimate connection between this part of the Chronicle and Or. Thus, for instance, the Chronicle's allusion to Severus, s.a. 189, 'Her Seuerus onfeng rice, 7 ricsode xvii winter. Se Breten lond mid dice begyrdde from sæ oþ sæ' has a greater verbal affinity with Be. 32/11–18, 'Ða wæs ymb hundteontig wintra 7 nigan 7 hundeahtatig wintra fram Drihtnes menniscnysse, þæt Seuerus . . . rice onfeng, 7 þæt hæfde seofontyne gear... He com on Breotene mid fyrde... 7 hit begyrde 7 gefæstnade mid dice 7 mid eorðwealle from sæ to sæ', than with Or. 142/6–14, 'Æfter þæm þe Romeburg wæs getimbred dcccc wintra 7 xliii, feng Seuerus to Romana onwalde 7 hiene hæfde xvii ger . . . Siþþan he for on Brettanie . . . 7 het ænne weall þwyres ofer eall þæt lond asettan from sæ oþ sæ',[3] and differs significantly from Or. in a number of ways. Thus, not only does Or. never use *Breten(e)* for Britain as this part of the Chronicle normally does, it never has the idiom *onfon rice*, only *fon to rice* or *fon to onwalde*, nor is *ricsode xvii winter* its usual way of expressing the length of a man's reign.[4] Other words and phrases in this section which are alien to

---

[1] For a study of the compilation of the '890 Chronicle' and of the relationship of this earliest surviving version to other texts of the ninth century see Bately (1978). [2] See further below, pp. xc–xci and n. 2.

[3] The source of the Chronicle reference is the chronological summary, Bede *HE* V. xxiv 'Anno ab incarnatione Domini clxxxviiii, Seuerus imperator factus xvii annis regnauit, qui Brittaniam uallo a mari usque ad mare praecinxit.' Be.'s version is based on a passage in Bede, *HE* I. v, which in its turn is taken virtually word for word from OH VII. xvii. 1 and 7 'Anno ab Vrbe condita dccccxliiii (*HE* Anno ab incarnatione Domini clxxxviiii) Seuerus . . . adeptus imperium xviii (*HE* imperium adeptus x et vii) annis tenuit' and 7 'in Britannias . . . trahitur . . . receptam partem insulae a ceteris indomitis gentibus uallo distinguendam putauit. itaque magnam fossam firmissimumque uallum . . . a mari ad mare duxit'.

[4] In the whole of Or. the only construction which links the verb *ricsian* with an expression of time is 37/26 'ricsade on ðon eastrice lii wintra'. See further Bately (1978).

Or.'s established usage include the chronological formula with *agan* and the verb *forþferan*.[1]

(ii) Annals 418–855. Plummer's 'resemblances' here are non-significant, the constructions *beniman rices* and *on . . . gebærum* occurring in a range of texts. Words and phrases actually alien to Or. include the continued use of *forþferde, onfon rice*, and the *agan* formula as well as the words *nænig, herereaf, eaþmod, ofermede,* and *fultumian,* Or. *nan,*[2] *herefeoh, herehyþ, eaþmodig, (ge)fylstan,*[3] and the collocations *þære stowe þe is gecueden, þam wæs noma, þam wæs oþer noma nemned, tun (ge)niman, sige niman,* and *rice healdan,* for Or. *þe mon hætt, þe oþre noman wæs haten* (or *hatte*), etc. [*burg*] *abrecan, sige habban,* and *rice habban.*[4]

(iii) Annals 860–90. Apart from a number of clearly non-significant correspondences, Plummer cites from this section the expression 'þær wæs ungemetlic wæl geslægen', found also in Or., as a variant of the usual formula 'þær wæs micel wæl geslægen'—a variant which does not require us to postulate dependence of one text on the other—and the entry for 865 'hie genamon friþ wiþ Cantwarum 7 . . . under þam friþe . . . se here hiene on niht up bestæl', with which he compares two passages in Or., 116/7–8 'he genom friþ wiþ þæt folc 7 hiene siþþan aweg bestæl' and 111/20–1 'Galua . . . frið genam wið hie, 7 hi under þæm friþe beswac', passages using constructions which occur in a range of texts and whose association here and in the Chronicle (as I have shown elsewhere)[5] again does not require us to suppose an intimate connection between the two works. However, alongside these similarities there are a number of fundamental differences. These annals not only have a number of words alien to Or., including *geweorc, wælsliht, dræfan,* and *befæstan,*[6] they use *sige niman* and

---

[1] Or. *þæt wæs from frymðe middangeardes* and *gefaran*. See further Bately (1978).

[2] The sole instance of *nænig* in Or. is found in the report of Wulfstan's voyage: see p. lxxii, and Bately (1970), pp. 439, n. 31 and 458, n. 205.

[3] See Bately (1970), pp. 444–5 and Bately (1978). Or.'s two exceptional instances of *gefultuman* occur side by side, 63/15 and 16, along with the noun *fultum*.

[4] For further details see Bately (1978). It should be noted that some of these features distinguish this section not only from Or. but from the annals for the second half of the ninth century: see Bately (1978).

[5] See Bately (1978).

[6] For *befæstan*, Or. *betæcan*, see Bately (1970), p. 445. This section also has *gefultum(i)an*, for which see above, n. 3. Not considered here are apparent

sige agan beside *sige habban* the normal usage of Or.,[1] and they use *on gehwæþere hond* where Or. invariably has *on ægþere healfe.*

(iv) Annals 891–923.[2] Plummer's resemblances here include 901 'sæde þæt he wolde oðer oððe þær libban oððe þær licgan', beside Or. 75/27–8 'hie oþer woldon, oððe ealle libban oþþe ealle licgean', and 894 'hæfde se cyning his fierd on tu tonumen, swa þæt hie wæron simle healfe æt ham, healfe ute', beside Or. 30/2–3 'Hie heora here on tu todældon, oþer æt ham beon heora lond to healdanne, oðer ut faran to winnanne'. However, in both instances, the wording of the Chronicle contains features alien to Or. Not only is the verb *toniman* never found in Or., but the only instance in that work of *aþer oþþe* without an intervening word occurs in Ohthere's report.[3] At the same time, there are a number of other features alien to Or.'s usage: apart from the words *forþferde, geweorc, befæstan*, and *agan* and the collocation *on gehwæþere hond*, these include the use of *þiderweardes* and *hamweardes* not *þiderweard* and *hamweard, hergaþ* not *hergung, cwild* not *cwealm, eaca* not *fultum*, and the collocations *þe we gefyrn ymbe spræcon* and *gedon æt* (or *on*).[4]

On the basis of this evidence, it must be concluded that unless the author of Or. suddenly, drastically, and inexplicably changed his established usage, the verbal similarities between Or. and the Chronicle cannot be the result of common authorship.

VII. THE DATE OF THE TRANSLATION

Hitherto, most attempts to date the composition of the Old English Orosius have started with the assumption that King Alfred was its author and that it must therefore have been begun after 890, the earliest possible date for the publication of the *Cura Pastoralis*, and completed before Alfred's death at the end of 899. However,

differences in choice of conjunctions, since, although on several occasions the Chronicle uses forms which Dr. Liggins has shown not to be Or.'s preferred usage, they are too few to be statistically relevant.

[1] *Sige habban* occurs 35 times in Or., beside 2 instances each of *sige gefaran* and *sige gefeohtan*, 3 of *sige geræcan* and 1 of *sige þurhteon*. For the usage in the Chronicle see Bately (1978).

[2] The last of the 'principal' resemblances cited by Plummer is from the annal for 918.

[3] See above, p. lxxii.

[4] For Or.'s avoidance of *gefyrn* and its use of *swa we ær beforan sægden* and similar collocations see Bately (1970), pp. 447 and 448.

as we have seen, the assumption of Alfredian authorship is unfounded. Moreover, as Professor Whitelock has observed, although the preface to *Cura Pastoralis* implies that this was the first work to be circulated in connection with Alfred's scheme for the improvement of the state of learning, the possibility that other works had been undertaken before the full scheme took shape cannot be ruled out.[1] It is hard to believe that Alfred would have waited until his translation of CP was completed and copied and circulated before putting pressure on those of his learned men with whom he was in contact to undertake translations of their own. In order to date the OE Orosius, therefore, we have to rely on internal evidence alone.

1. *Ohthere's report*

Or.'s summary of Ohthere's report to King Alfred contains references to three journeys, for two of which terminal dates have been proposed.[2] Thus, Ohthere's voyage to Hedeby is supposed by Kemp Malone to have taken place before 870-1, and his visit to King Alfred is not only given the obvious termini of that king's accession and death, 871 and 899, but is put early rather than late in Alfred's reign.[3] However, recent research leads us to question some of these conclusions. First of all, Malone's dating of the journey to Hedeby as before 870-1 depends on Ohthere's statement that all the way from his home to *Sciringesheal* he had Norway to port, but that from *Sciringesheal* to Hedeby Danish territory was in this position for the first three days.[4] If Ohthere is being correctly reported, the implication is that Oslo Fjord marked the boundary between Norwegian and Danish territory at that time.[5] Now Snorri's *Heimskringla*, written in the thirteenth century, relates how, shortly before the battle of Hafrsfjord, the Norwegian king Harald Fairhair extended his dominions east of Oslo Fjord and annexed to Norway both the present-day Norwegian territory of Østfold and also the whole coastland as far down as the Göta

---

[1] See Whitelock (1966), p. 75.

[2] The account of Ohthere's journey round the North Cape, like that of Wulfstan's voyage to the Vistula, contains no datable details.

[3] Malone (1930a), pp. 78-81.

[4] 16/8 and 16/15-16. For Ohthere's possible route see 16/16-20, Commentary.

[5] Much earlier in the century Danish territory seems to have extended west of Oslo Fjord and to have included Vestfold, the (presumed) location of *Sciringesheal*: see *Einhardi Annales*, s.a. 813.

Älv in present-day Sweden. Before that, Snorri claims, the region was ruled by a retainer of the Swedish king, though he was not long in possession of it.[1] Malone, accepting the traditional date of the battle of Hafrsfjord as 872, assumes that the Norwegian expansion took place *c.* 871. However, according to a consensus of modern opinion, 872 is not only more precise a date for the battle than present knowledge allows but also too early and the most that can be claimed is that it was 'earlier than 900 but not before 885'.[2] Since Malone's other terminal date for the voyage, the conquest of Hedeby by the Swedes, must also be placed vaguely 'toward the end of the ninth century',[3] it is thus not possible to use the account of the journey to Hedeby to improve on 899, the year of Alfred's death, as a *terminus ad quem* for Ohthere's report.

As for Ohthere's journey to England, the date of this is equally uncertain.[4] Malone argues that the absence of any reference to Iceland, first settled by Norsemen in 874, stems from ignorance and that Ohthere must therefore have made his visit to England in the early part of Alfred's reign.[5] However, there is no particular reason why Ohthere should have mentioned Iceland if he did know of it, especially if we accept Stokoe's theory that his account of what lies to starboard on a journey down the coast of Norway is influenced by his knowledge of the major sea routes from Norway to England.[6] All that can be said about the dates of Ohthere's voyages, therefore, is that they took place in the second half of the ninth century and that the visit to England was made before Alfred's death at the end of 899. And the most that can be deduced from all this about the date of Or. itself—at least in the form that

---

[1] *Haraldz saga ins hárfagra*, ed. F. Jónsson (Copenhagen, 1893), ch. 13 and 15–17.   [2] See Jones (1968), p. 89 and n. 1.

[3] Malone (1930a), p. 79.

[4] We are not told whether Ohthere travelled to England directly after his voyage to Hedeby, or whether he came from his home by one of the sea routes described by Stokoe (1957), p. 304.

[5] See Malone (1930a), p. 81 and, for an attempt to emend *Iraland* to *Isaland* see Or. 16/6–7, Commentary. For probable knowledge of the existence of Iceland before this date see Jones (1968), pp. 270–1. For the suggestion that 'since Ohthere and his neighbours seem to be collecting finnskattr or Lapp-tax (for which see Egils Saga ch. x sq.) for themselves and not on behalf of King Harald —who made it into a royal monopoly as soon as he had gained control of the area—the account seems to reflect the state of affairs prior to *c.* 885' see Bright (1971), p. 188, n. 41. See, however, Jones (1968), pp. 90–1.

[6] See Stokoe (1957), p. 304.

we have it—is that the reference to Alfred as king indicates that it cannot have been completed before his accession in 871.[1]

2. The geography of Europe

Most of the details about continental Europe not taken from OH could apply to any period in the ninth century or even earlier.[2] However, two features seem to point to a date late in the ninth century but before its close:[3] the location of a *westen* between *Carendran* and the Bulgarians, and the absence from this section of any mention of the Hungarians. If the two references to the *westen*[4] are not derived from classical sources, then they could be the result of knowledge either of Charlemagne's devastation of the Pannonian Mark at the end of the eighth century or, more plausibly, of Svatopluk's ravages of the same area in 883 and 884.[5] The absence of any reference to the Hungarians in this section has to be seen in the context of a subsequent allusion in the main body of the work to the crossing of the Danube by a people 'þe mon þa het Basterne 7 nu hie mon hæt Hungerre'.[6] Now Magyar troops first appeared at the mouth of the Danube as early as the thirties of the ninth century according to Byzantine sources,[7] although they seem to have been unheard of in western Europe until 862, when the Annals of Hincmar of Rheims, Continuation 861–82, report what seems to have been an isolated raid on Pannonia: 'hostes antea illis populis inexperti, qui Ungri vocantur, regnum eiusdem populantur.' A second isolated appearance is recorded in the Annals of Admont, s.a. 881.[8] However, it was not until 889 that the Hungarians seem to have arrived as permanent settlers at the mouth of the Danube and to have become a major

---

[1] See further Malone (1930a), p. 78.

[2] See Commentary on 12/17–13/28 and 18/3–19/10.

[3] A third feature of possible significance is the reference to the Burgundians as located north-east of Provence, if these are to be identified with the inhabitants of the kingdom of Upper Burgundy established by Roþulf in 888. For other explanations see 18/34–5, Commentary.

[4] 13/7 and 18/17.

[5] It was not until the ninth century that the Bulgarians so extended their domination over eastern Europe that they could be said to be immediate neighbours of the Pannonian Mark. See 13/7–8 and 18/15, Commentary.

[6] 110/7–8.

[7] For a convenient bibliography and survey of Byzantine and other sources see A. B. Urbansky, *Byzantium and the Danube Frontier* (New York, 1968).

[8] See E. Klebel, *Mitteilungen der Gesellschaft für Salzburger Landeskunde* (1921), s.a. 881, where a conflict with the Hungarians is described as taking place at *Wenia*.

force in eastern Europe. In the entry for this year in the Annals of
Regino of Prüm they are referred to as *gens ferocissima*, the very
same words that Orosius uses of the Basternae,[1] and it may have
been a reference such as this that is ultimately responsible for the
identification of Hungarians and Basternae in Or. It appears then,
that the additional material in the account of the geography of
Europe relates to the situation before 889 (perhaps between 884
and 889), but that Or. itself was composed or completed after that
date.

3. *Other evidence*

In her important study of the prose of Alfred's reign, Professor
Whitelock draws attention to two details in Or. which seem to
connect it on the one hand with the *Anglo-Saxon Chronicle* and
on the other with Alfred's translation of Boethius and which may
throw light on the problem of dating. The Chronicle's allusion to
Titus, s.a. 81, 'seþe sæde þat he þone dæg forlure þe he noht to gode
on ne gedyde', bears, as she observes, a striking resemblance to Or.
138/23–139/2 'he wæs swa godes willan þæt he sægde þæt he forlure
þone dæg þe he noht on to gode ne gedyde'. It is obvious that
either both texts had a common source or one was borrowing
from the other. At first sight, the fact that Or. has a fuller version
of the reference to Titus, with an allusion to his 'good will' which
is obviously derived ultimately from Jerome,[2] seems to indicate
borrowing by the Chronicle from the Orosius and therefore a date
'earlier than about 890' (the date when manuscripts of the
Chronicle began to circulate)[3] for the completion of Or. However, a
study of all the Chronicle entries dealing with world history shows
that the compiler of this section had as one of his sources for these
the *Chronicon* of Isidore of Seville, and it is Isidore who records
Titus' *celebre dictum* in the form closest to that of the Chronicle

---

[1] Cf. OH IV. xx. 34 'Basternarum gens ferocissima . . . praedarum spe sol-
licitata et transeundi Histri fluminis facultate sine ulla pugna . . . deleta est',
Regino of Prüm, s.a. 889 'gens Hungarorum ferocissima et omni belua crudelior,
retro ante seculis ideo inaudita quia nec nominata, a Scythicis regnis et a paludibus quas Thanais sua refusione in immensum porrigit, egressa est.' Since Or.
renders *gens ferocissima* by *seo strengeste þeod*, this explanation seems to rule out
the possibility that the identification was made by a scribe or reader of the
Old English version.

[2] For this and other versions of the Titus reference see 138/23–139/2,
Commentary.   [3] See Whitelock (1966), pp. 73–4.

and Or.: 'perdidisse diem quo nihil boni fecerat'.[1] So the presence of Titus' saying in ASC does not of itself indicate that the composition of Or. must have preceded the circulation of the Chronicle. If there was borrowing, indeed, it must have been by Or. from the Chronicle. However, there are several possible explanations for the form taken by the allusion in Or. Since Isidore's *Chronicon* itself refers to Titus' *bonitas*—though not linking it directly with Titus' saying—the author of Or. or a hypothetical commentary could have had this as his primary source, but knowing also Jerome modified the wording accordingly. Alternatively, a version of Jerome could have provided the primary source and this was modified because of knowledge of Isidore (or a derivative of Isidore).[2] Finally, a version of Jerome could have provided the primary source and this was modified because of knowledge of the Chronicle's rendering of Isidore. So borrowing by Or. from the Chronicle is no more than one of several possibilities. As for the implications for the dating of Or., here too there must be uncertainty. If the resemblances between the two texts are not due to coincidence, then Or. must have been completed after the compilation of the earliest version of the Chronicle to include the pre-449 annals, and the most that can be said about the date of that version is that its *terminus ante quem* must be 'about 890', when manuscripts of it began to circulate.[3]

Quite impossible to explain as coincidence, on the other hand, is the presence of a reference to Gothic kings called *Rædgota* and *Eallerica* in Bo., and *Alrica* and *Rædgota* in Or. As Professor Whitelock observes,

Alfred jumps from the mention of Rædgota and Eallerica, who occur at the end of the *Orosius*, direct to Theodoric, without any mention of the intervening history of the Goths. The form *Rædgota* is in both

---

[1] See J. M. Bately (1980), pp. 185 and 190-1, 'World History in the *Anglo-Saxon Chronicle*: its sources and its separateness from the Old English Orosius', *ASE*, viii.

[2] Identity of vocabulary between the OE versions in the Chronicle and Or. is no stumbling-block: *forleosan* is the only word for 'lose' in both texts and the collocation *to gode gedon* is apparently a not uncommon one—it is found also in CP and in the homilies of Ælfric and Wulfstan (though Ælfric uses it not with *noht* but with *nan þing*).

[3] There are no lexical features that require us to suppose that the author of the World History annals was not also the author of the bulk of annals up to the mid-ninth century. See Bately (1978).

works, yet it is not the true Germanic equivalent of *Radagaisus*, which would be *Rædgar*.[1]

Moreover, in both works the two kings are linked as though they ruled together over the same people and invaded Italy together, a linking which has no justification in fact but which in Or. can be explained as inspired by material provided by OH VII. xxxvii. 8–9.[2] This suggests that Or. preceded Bo. and if so must have been in circulation before the end of 899, the year of Alfred's death, at the very latest. If we accept the order of composition *Cura Pastoralis, Boethius, Soliloquies*, prose psalms of the Paris Psalter,[3] then we may safely assume a somewhat earlier date as the *terminus ad quem*.

A third passage which may throw light on the problem of dating is 83/1–3, 'þæt we gewinn nu hatað, þonne us fremde 7 ellþeodge an becumaþ 7 lytles hwæt on us bereafiað 7 us eft hrædlice forlætað'. This comment neither has a basis in OH nor is applicable to the state of affairs in Rome at the time of the Gothic invasions but seems to describe admirably the situation in southern England after the implementation of the Treaty of Wedmore and before the Great Army of 892 became a serious menace, and thus may indicate a date of composition between 880 and 892.[4]

The cumulative evidence, then, though none of it is absolutely conclusive, appears to point to a date of completion for Or., at least in the form in which we have it, not before 889, when the Hungarians first became generally known to western Europe. The *terminus ante quem* seems to be Alfred's death in 899, the latest possible date for the Boethius, but could be as early as the period

---

[1] Whitelock (1966), p. 82, n. 3. *Radagaisus* is the reading of the 'related' manuscripts and Zangemeister's first family (L, D, and B); Zangemeister's second family (P and R) has the form *Ragadaisus*. See OH, p. xvi. It is tempting to suppose that the second element of the OE form *Rædgota* is the result of scribal error, an explanatory gloss *Gotus* or its OE equivalent *Gota(n)* being falsely incorporated as a correction. See Bately (1970), pp. 438–9.

[2] Radagaisus and Alaric are, however, linked in several Latin chronicles: see, e.g., *Prosperi Chronica*, ed. T. Mommsen, *MGH, Auct. Antiquiss.* 9 (Berlin, 1892), 464.　　　　　　　　[3] See Potter (1931), especially pp. 71–3.

[4] A date after the dispersal of the Great Army in 897 seems unlikely. Professor Whitelock, though not very convinced by my suggestion, believes that the occasion which would fit best would be 885. The events of that year as recorded by the *Anglo-Saxon Chronicle* and Æþelweard, she points out (in a private communication) 'may have seemed so little in comparison with those of 878 that the translator had them in mind when putting into Orosius' mouth a belittling of what the Romans had suffered from the Goths'.

890-1, before the coming of the Great Army but after the circulation of the 890 Chronicle. Either date would link it in a most satisfactory manner with Alfred's educational schemes and suggest that Bishop Wærferth was not the only scholar in Alfred's kingdom apart from the king himself to undertake the translation of those works that it was most necessary for all men to know.

VIII. TREATMENT OF THE SOURCES

Although it is normally thought of as a translation, a more accurate description of Or. would be paraphrase, a rendering of sense for sense not word for word[1] by an author who, like King Alfred in his version of Boethius, had no hesitation in making radical but unacknowledged alterations to his primary source, expanding freely but also cutting, rewriting some sections, but generally retaining the order and arrangement of his original. The most common of these alterations relate to Orosius' interpretation of events: whole sections of comment in OH are completely omitted,[2] others are reduced to a couple of sentences,[3] or replaced by the Anglo-Saxon author's own observations. The result of these alterations is a transformation of OH from an exercise in polemic using historical material to a survey of world history from a Christian standpoint. Or.'s main interest is seen to lie in events and actions, whereas Orosius' avowed concern is their (usually miserable) effects,[4] his primary aim being to answer the charge of his opponents that the times in which they lived were unusually beset with calamities and that the sole reason for this was that men now believed in Christ and worshipped God, while idols were increasingly neglected.[5] Orosius was writing against the background of the Gothic invasions of Italy and the disintegration of the Roman Empire; he himself had experienced physical sufferings and was driven to flight to save his life.[6] So in his answer to his opponents, men still following the old gods of Rome, he tries to show not only that calamities have occurred in cycles throughout

---

[1] Sweet, *Cura Pastoralis*, p. xli, suggests that 'In those days, when grammars and dictionaries were hardly known or used, Latin was studied much more as a living language than it is now; sentences were grasped as wholes, without the minute analysis of modern scholarship, and were consequently translated as wholes.' [2] e.g. OH I. vi and viii.

[3] Cf., e.g., OH IV. xii. 8-13 and Or. 97/28-98/2.

[4] See OH III, Praef. 1. [5] See OH I, Prol. 9.

[6] See OH III. xx. 6-7.

all the ages but also that present calamities though great are less bad than past calamities. One God has directed the course of history, he says, and it is only because of His mercy that we now live at all. The wars of his time are less cruel than previous wars and in any case are just a temporary setback in a general context of peace—a peace which was prearranged for Christ's coming. It is because of the presence of Christians in Rome that Rome has been shown some mercy.[1]

Or.'s general theme, on the other hand, has as its focal point not the sack of Rome by the Goths in 410—the reasons for which were hardly a burning issue in late ninth-century England[2]—but the birth of Christ and the coming of Christianity. Stress is still laid, and laid heavily, on the trials and tribulations suffered by mankind in the pre-Christian era, and Orosius' grumbling Romans are still reminded how dreadful life really was in what they chose to regard as the good old days,[3] but through careful selection and rearrangement of the material provided by OH special emphasis is given to Christ's birth as the dividing point, separating a past of unrelieved misery from a present characterized by universal manifestations of mercy and peace and an undeniable improvement in man's lot. Sometimes the ingredients for Or.'s argument are present in the corresponding passage of OH; thus, for instance, 38/10–13

Þis ic sprece nu for ðæm þe ic wolde þæt þa ongeaten, þe þa tida ures cristendomes leahtriað, hwelc mildsung siþþan wæs, siþþan se cristendom wæs, 7 hu monigfeald wolbærnes ðære worulde ær þæm wæs,

which draws its inspiration from a lengthy comment by Orosius in which the respective fates of Rome and Babylon are compared and Rome's relative good fortune attributed to God's mercy.[4] Sometimes, however, they are completely independent of their primary source at that point, as for instance, at the end of Book V (Book VI of OH), following the announcement of Christ's birth. Orosius' comment here is far from full of good cheer: having, he

---

[1] See OH III. xx. 5, I. xxi. 18, II. iii. 5, V. xxiv. 20, VII. i. 11, and II. iii. 7.

[2] See Whitelock (1966), p. 90.

[3] e.g. 103/30–104/2. Even where Or. is independent of OH, the translator makes Orosius address his fellow Romans, though occasionally the remarks are given a more general application: cf., e.g., 31/2–21, 52/23–4, 77/4–7, and 34/15–20.

[4] OH II. iii. 5–10. For other material from this passage see 38/13–30.

says, from the start declared that men are sinners and that they are punished for their sins, he now proposes to recount the various persecutions of the Christians and the retributions that followed. The words that Or. attributes to him are very different, linking the events of history with the doctrines of both atonement and redemption:

Nu ic hæbbe gesæd, cwæð Orosius, from frymþe þisses middangeardes hu eall moncyn angeald þæs ærestan monnes synna mid miclum teonum 7 witum. Nu ic wille eac forþ gesecgan hwelc mildsung 7 hwelc geþwærnes siþþan wæs siþþan se cristendom wæs, gelicost þæm þe monna heortan awende wurden, for þon þe þa ærran þing agoldene wæron.[1]

And even where, in his account of the history of the Christian era, he is forced to relate stories of persecutions and violence, the translator endeavours to sustain his claim of general amelioration, giving prominence to OH's point that some at least of the calamities were now justly deserved, befalling those who had incurred God's wrath, not, as hitherto, the innocent,[2] and on one occasion adding a comment to the effect that God's retribution was none the less tempered by mercy.[3] These themes of God's retribution and God's mercy appear again most effectively combined in the opening sentence of Or.'s last chapter, which describes the final catastrophe, the sack of Rome by the Goths: 'Æfter þæm þe Romeburg getimbred wæs m wintra 7 c 7 iiii 7 siextegum, God gedyde his miltsunge on Romanum, þa þa he hiora misdæda wrecan let, þæt hit þeh dyde Alrica se cristena cyning 7 se mildesta.'[4] The corresponding chapter heading reads simply 'Hu God gedyde Romanum his mildsunge'.

A second important group of alterations suggests not modification but an acceptance of Orosius' attitude to history: as Professor Whitelock has observed,

What Orosius did also was to give a Christian view of world history; he christianised the Roman historians' conception of the *pax Romana*, and

---

[1] 132/17–22, OH VI. xxii. 11. See also 34/15–20 and Commentary.
[2] See, e.g., 135/12–21, 136/28–31, and 134/31–135/3.
[3] See 134/24–6, where Or. having exclaimed 'Hu God þa þa mæstan ofermetto gewræc on þæm folce, 7 hu swiðe hi his anguldon from heora agnum casere!', a comment based on OH VII. iv. 10 'tanta libidinis et crudelitatis rabie efferbuit, ut, qui spreuerant Christo rege saluari, rege Caesare punirentur', adds, without the authority of OH, 'þeh hit eallum þæm folcum of oþrum londum swa swiþe gewrecen ne wurde swa hit oft ær wæs'.   [4] 156/11–14.

showed how the whole of history, through the empires of Babylon, Macedon and Carthage, had been leading to the universal empire of Rome, so that Christ should be born in the universal peace of Augustus's reign and the faith could be spread through a universal empire. The translator emphasises this in places, and he rearranges and rewrites the section on the symbolic interpretation of the events of Augustus's reign. When he made his selection from Orosius, he seems to have had this theme in mind, for in the first four books he keeps almost everything concerning the four empires, but omits quarrels between Greek cities, presumably as irrelevant to the central theme; and when in Books 5 and 6 he cuts heavily, he still retains the thread of the expansion of Rome.

In Book VII, on the emperors of the Christian era, he concentrates on those parts about their dealings with the Christians:

wars in Spain, Gaul or the East, by which the Empire was maintained, he mentions only when the defeat of a persecuting emperor or the victory of one friendly to Christianity is recorded.[1]

Other omissions are less easy to categorize. Some may be the result of carelessness or accident, as, for instance, the telescoping of two separate incidents in the Roman wars with the Gauls and the Tuscans,[2] the attaching of the name Sempronius Gracchus to an incident involving another general, Cn. Fulvius,[3] and the elimination of two Roman emperors from Book VII.[4] Some are apparently deliberate but surprising, as, for instance, the omission of the names of authorities such as Tacitus, Suetonius, and Plato,[5] and the passing over of a number of details—sometimes whole stories —that might have been expected to appeal to an Anglo-Saxon audience, as, for instance, the heroic death of Epaminondas, the victory in defeat of the Spartans at Thermopylae, the Persian preference for death rather than defeat, the distress of a soldier

---

[1] Whitelock (1966), p. 90. [2] See 58/2–4, Commentary.
[3] 102/31–3.
[4] These are Helvius Pertinax, the sixteenth emperor, OH VII. xvi. 5, and Opilius Macrinus the nineteenth, OH VII. xviii. 3. Neither gets more than a passing mention from OH and neither occupies a position of prominence in the text. Also omitted are the names of a number of men who seized the *imperium* temporarily, without achieving a place in the line of succession. In all these and similar instances, the possibility of a defective manuscript of OH must also be borne in mind.
[5] See OH I. v. 1 and I. ix. 3, etc. The only authorities quoted by Or. other than Orosius himself are Pompeius Trogus and Justinus: see 23/23 and 88/18.

who discovered that his dead adversary was his brother, and the
birds of prey and scavenging animals that followed a dying army.[1]
Most surprising of all is what seems to be a total lack of interest in
the history and geography of Britain. Nothing is added to the
sketchy and inaccurate description of Britannia in the first chapter,
while although a brief and somewhat misleading account of
Julius Caesar's invasions is included,[2] Caligula's expedition to the
English Channel is not, nor are Claudius' conquest of the island
and the subsequent rebellion of the Britons, later references being
similarly either omitted or drastically curtailed.[3]

Sometimes, omissions seem to indicate a reluctance to dwell on
sensitive or distasteful subjects, as, for instance, the defeat of
Germanic tribes and their barbarous customs,[4] popular insurrec-
tions, slave wars, and some of the more unsavoury stories of
atrocities by the Greeks and others;[5] however, in the context of a
reduction of OH's 236 chapters to 84 and the creation of a work
which in spite of numerous additions is little more than one-
fifth of the length of its primary source, this is not capable of
proof. What is incontrovertible, on the other hand, is that the
translator omits a number of details that might have been supposed
to be of interest to a military man, and at the same time lets slip
a number of opportunities that should have appealed to a cleric.
Thus, for instance, OH's description of the *velites* and their
tactics[6] is omitted along with biblical quotations, miraculous

[1] See OH III. ii. 8, II. ix. 7–8 (and Or. 47/9–11, Commentary), III. xvii. 2,
V. xix. 12–13, II. x. 11.   [2] See 126/3–10.
[3] See OH VII. v. 5, vi. 9–10, vii. 11, and xxv. 3–7, etc. Schilling, p. 21,
suggests that the omission of any reference to Claudius' conquest could be
from patriotic motives. For omissions of British material from Be. see Whitelock (1962), pp. 71–2 and n. 128.   [4] See Whitelock (1966), p. 93.
[5] Passages omitted by Or. include accounts of an uprising by slaves, OH IV.
vii. 12, of the rebellion of the gladiators and Spartacus, V. xxiv. 1–8, and of the
unhappy end of the second of the Gracchi, V. xii, while the episode relating to
the first Gracchus is drastically curtailed: cf. OH V. viii–ix and Or. 117/26–7.
Tales of physical violence, rape, and murder that are omitted include the
stories of Procne and Philomela, OH I. xi. 3, and Verginia, OH II. xiii. 6–7. The
majority of these omissions occur in the last three books of OH, which are the
ones most suitable for précis. The earlier books provide less detail and therefore
less scope for abridgement. It should be noted that a number of references to
popular uprisings and slave wars are retained (see, e.g., 87/16–24 and 117/28–
31).
[6] OH IV. xviii. 10–12. Also omitted are details of siege tactics, OH V. vii, of
the battle between Jugurtha and Marius, V. xv, and of Caesar's Gallic campaigns, VI. vii–xii.

stories such as the vision of Ambrose, and Orosius' claim to be a citizen not of this world but of the next.[1]

However, the translator not only omits a great deal of material, he also adds freely. Apart from the ubiquitous purely geographical information, these additions are mainly factual and fall into two main groups: those explaining terms which otherwise might not be understood by an Anglo-Saxon audience, or giving identificatory details about people who might otherwise be unknown to them, and those filling out brief allusions by Orosius, who either expected his audience to know the story already or did not think further detail relevant. To the first group belong comments on terms relating to Roman institutions, such as *consul*, *senatus*, *cohors*, *virgo Vestalis*, *triumphus*, *Iani portae*,[2] or to classical mythology, such as *centaurus*.[3] Identificatory or explanatory detail about people includes such information as that Darius was the kinsman of Cyrus, Cincinnatus a poor man, Seleucus king of the east, Dido founder of Carthage, Marius uncle of Caesar, and Cleopatra the latter's mistress, Julian the Apostate a former deacon of the Christian Church, and the Amazons so-called because of their seared breasts.[4] The majority of these are brief, as are a number of the additions, accurate or inaccurate, belonging to the second group: thus, for instance, the naming of Alexander the Great's father as Nectanebus and of Cinna's deathplace as Smyrna, and the comments that Darius was pierced by spears, Alexander stoned, Jerusalem rebuilt in another place, and Augustus so-called because his victory over Antony took place in the month of August.[5] However, a large number of the additions in this group are relatively detailed and are expansions of allusions to specific events. In a number of cases these involve the description of stratagems

[1] See OH VII. iii. 1–4 and 11, xxxvi. 7 and xxxix. 3–14, and V. ii. 6. Since we do not know the precise nature of Or.'s secondary sources, it is futile to speculate as to what has not been taken over from them. However, it should be noted that the translator does not normally include etymological comment or add fabulous stories such as are found in Isidore, *Etymologies*, Solinus and early medieval commentaries and glossaries. Nor does he refer to the legendary childhood of Romulus and Remus, though stories of this may have been known in Anglo-Saxon England: see M. Hunter, 'Germanic and Roman antiquity and the sense of the past in Anglo-Saxon England; *ASE*, iii (1974), 40.

[2] See 40/12–14, 42/14–21, 127/13–14, 60/8–10, 42/1–13, 59/3–11 and Commentary. [3] See 28/19–21 and Commentary.

[4] See 45/17, 50/3, 77/30–2, 133/9, 124/19–20, 129/19, 150/8, and 29/34–5, Commentary.

[5] See 69/22–4, 125/12, 70/10, 73/12, 140/19–20, 130/4–5, and Commentary.

employed in the Punic and (occasionally) other wars: for instance, the 'tricks' that Philip of Macedon used against the Scythians, and Fulvius against the Gallo-Greeks, and details of Xanthippus' fight against Regulus, of the battle of Trasimene, and of Claudius Marcellus' attack on Hannibal.[1] The strange thing about these additions is that they indicate a special interest in military stratagems that is not borne out by either the manner of their narration[2] or the translator's treatment of accounts of military matters provided by OH,[3] and it is tempting to conclude that the translator included them simply because they were for some reason readily available to him[4] and fitted in with his main object of providing a history of the world in the vernacular.

A second group of expansions similarly provides additional details about specific events—for instance, the Rape of the Sabines and Lucretia, and the suicide of Cato[5]—but, unlike the other additions, their effect is not merely to increase the usefulness of Or. as a geographical and historical text book, but also to bring about a subtle change of emphasis in the earlier part of the work, and, as Professor Whitelock has pointed out, a difference of tone.[6] Orosius was reluctant to praise anything before the Christian era, but the translator writes in detail of the bravery of Mucius Scaevola and the honourable behaviour of Regulus and stresses the renown of Papirius.[7] Scipio is described as *se betsta Romana þegna*, while although the translator is not greatly concerned, as Orosius was, with Julius Caesar's generalship, he adds references to his clemency and generosity and to his bravery in the face of apparently overwhelming odds.[8] This shift of emphasis is reinforced by comments suggesting that in some ways the Romans of the Christian era were inferior to their predecessors.[9] Not every

[1] See 64/19–22, 109/20–5, 94/12–17, 101/4–13, 102/18–20 and Commentary. See further Bately (1971), pp. 244–7.

[2] See, e.g., the account of the outwitting of the Numidians at Capsa, 121/9–15 and Commentary, and see also above, p. lxiii.

[3] For omissions of material connected with military matters see above, p. xcvii and n. 6.

[4] For the possibility that he used a commentary, see above, p. lxii. Alternatively, excerpts from Frontinus or Livy could have been included in a classbook.   [5] See 39/5–16, 40/5–12, and 128/13–19.

[6] *Continuations and Beginnings*, p. 91.

[7] 41/1–11, 95/21–96/5 and 67/17–21.

[8] See 118/24–5, 128/3–4, 128/15–16, 128/27–9, and 128/30–1.

[9] e.g. 103/3–7 'þæt wæs swiðe sweotol þæt hie þa wæron beteran þegnas þonne hie nu sien, þæt hie þeh þæs gewinnes geswican noldon, ac hie oft

one of these additions has the support of other extant texts: sometimes the translator's expansions appear to be based on suppositions,[1] sometimes they represent his desire as a medieval historian to describe good men's deeds in such a way as to excite emulation and evil men's evil deeds so as to inspire revulsion,[2] sometimes they seem to be due to misunderstanding of his original. Thus, Scipio and Julius Caesar can become 'examples of the ingratitude of states and the vanity of earthly success'[3] because the translator not only attaches to them references in OH to several different Scipios and Julius Caesars,[4] but also misinterprets an allusion to the senate putting off their garments of mourning and resuming the toga after a victory by one of these Julius Caesars as an insult to Caesar. When Orosius subsequently describes the senate's resumption of the *laticlavia* after victory by a Pompey (not the one who became Gaius Julius Caesar's chief rival), Or. interprets this as the granting of a triumph to Pompey and a slight to Caesar, increasing the enmity between the two men: 'þa brohton Romane þone triumphan angean Pompeius mid micelre weorþfulnesse for þæm lytlan sige þe he þa hæfde 7 noldon Iuliuse nænne weorþscipe don, þeh he maran dæd gedon hæfde, buton ane tunecan, 7 hi heora gewin mid þæm swiþe geiecton.'[5]

IX. STYLE

Perhaps because of the tendency to concentrate attention on the reports of Ohthere and Wulfstan as the most obvious pieces of

gebidon on lytlum staþole 7 on unwenlicum, þæt hie þa æt nihstan hæfdon ealra þara anwald þe ær neh heora hæfdon', a comment based on OH IV. xvi. 21, 'et tamen fortis in alterutrum desperatio in meliora profecit, nam in his omnibus desperando pugnarunt, pugnando uicerunt. ex quo euidenter ostenditur non tempora tunc fuisse tranquilliora otiis, sed homines miseriis fortiores.' See also 111/10–19 and 113/1–10 and Commentary.

[1] e.g. 41/2–4 and 116/9–13. Possibly also the translator's own is the vivid description of the senators leaping up and stabbing Caesar with their meatknives, 129/2–3.

[2] See Bede, *HE*, *Praefatio*. The majority of these are mildly condemnatory. Thus, for instance, suicide is described as *þæt þær wyrrest wæs* (89/28), the monks who were compelled by Valens to become soldiers are said to have been ordered 'þæt hie wæpena namen 7 mid þæm fuhte 7 yfel dyde mid oþrum monnum' (152/14–15, a somewhat surprising blanket condemnation of warfare), while the Gallic sacrificial victims are *ungyltige* (98/17) and the Ethiopians and Indians attacked by Sameramis and Liber Pater respectively are *underiende* (22/13 and 25/9). [3] See Whitelock (1966), p. 92.

[4] See, e.g., 111/10, 118/24, 123/10, and Commentary.

[5] 124/9–13, OH V. xviii. 15–17.

'independent' prose in the Old English Orosius, the stylistic
achievement of the author has gone largely unrecognized.[1]
However, although he may not have the literary sophistication
of an Ælfric, he can fairly be claimed to have achieved a fluent,
effective, and generally lucid style, which, while being relatively
simple, yet serves his purpose well.[2] The syntactical structures he
uses are varied and frequently complex, with not only the sentence
but often the paragraph conceived as a unit, and with plain prose
alternating with passages of emotive rhetoric.

This is not the place for a detailed survey of the basic sentence
structures of Or. or their stylistic implications.[3] However, I would
draw attention to a handful of features that seem to me of particular interest. First of all, although all possible types of subordinate
clause occur,[4] the most common, not surprisingly, being temporal
clauses, the author shows a marked fondness for paratactic sentences, with subordination made implicit by the juxtaposing of
non-dependent clauses,[5] a stylistic mannerism which on occasion
is used with great dramatic effect, as, for instance, in 136/1–2 '7
Pilatus he hæfde on þreatunge oþ he hiene selfne ofstong: he
gedæmde urne Dryhten to deaðe', the last clause of which corresponds to a relative clause in OH.[6] Secondly, he has a preference
for active rather than passive constructions and a tendency to
avoid abstractions: thus, for instance, 112/22 'Scipia het ealle þa
burg toweorpan' for OH 'diruta est . . . Carthago', and 29/3–5
'Heton him þeh þæt ondwyrde secgan, þæt him leofre wære wið
hiene to feohtanne þonne gafol to gieldanne', for OH 'respondent
. . . timendum ipsi magis uersa uice fuerit propter incertos belli

---

[1] The only study of any length is that of L. Borinski, *Der Stil König Alfreds*
(Leipzig, 1934).

[2] For an important study of the differences between medieval histories and
annals, and between Or. and the Chronicle in particular see Cecily Clark,
'The Narrative Mode of *The Anglo-Saxon Chronicle*', *England before the
Conquest*, ed. P. Clemoes and K. Hughes (Cambridge, 1971), pp. 215–35.

[3] For a useful analysis of a large number of such structures see Paul Bacquet,
La structure de la phrase verbale à l'époque alfrédienne (Paris, 1962).

[4] For the range of these clauses and the variety of the words used to introduce
them, see Liggins (1970), pp. 292–321.

[5] See S. O. Andrew, *Syntax and Style in Old English* (Cambridge, 1940),
p. 87.

[6] Cf. OH VII. v. 8 'Pilatus autem praeses, qui sententiam damnationis in
Christum dixerat, postquam plurimas seditiones in Hierosolymis excepit ac
fecit, tantis inrogante Gaio angoribus coartatus est, ut sua se transuerberans
manu malorum conpendium mortis celeritate quaesierit'.

euentus nulla praemia et damna manifesta', with a heroic cast that would have appealed to his Anglo-Saxon audience. Thirdly, he employs a large number of expanded verb forms, and whatever his primary motive may have been for the use of these forms,[1] their effect on sentence rhythms and patterns is profound: thus, for instance, 45/8–9 'þu þe þyrstende wære monnes blodes xxx wintra, drync nu þine fylle', for OH II. vii. 6 'Satia te . . . sanguine quem sitisti, cuius per annos triginta insatiabilis perseuerasti'.

No less significant from the point of view of sentence rhythm is the idiom combining possessive and demonstrative which is a feature also of Wærferth's literary Mercian,[2] as in 151/15–16 'He him bebead þæt he forlete þone his cristendom oððe his folgað', and 48/32 'þæt tacnade Leoniða on his þæm nihstan gefeohte 7 Persa' or 79/26–7 'Æfter þæm þa sendon to Antigone ymb heora þæt mæste bismer', while the combination of proper name and pronoun or possessive adjective, and similar constructions, not only helps to make clear the sense, but gives additional emphasis, as in 22/4–5 'And he Ninus Soroastrem Bactriana cyning, se cuðe manna ærest drycræftas, he hine oferwann 7 ofsloh' and 33/20–3 'Hi þa hiera wif him ongean iernende wæron 7 hie swiþe tornwyrdon, 7 acsedon, gif hie feohtan ne dorsten, hwider hie fleon woldon; þæt hie oðer gener næfden, buton hie on heora wifa hrif gewiton', where the rhythms would be destroyed by the omission of tautological *hi* and the use of simple past in place of the expanded form.

This last passage illustrates a number of different stylistic features employed by the author of Or. to achieve rhythmic balance and contrasts, and to draw attention to key words. The use of alliteration to link two clauses (*feohtan* : *fleon*) or elements within a clause (*gener* : *næfden* and *wifa* : *gewiton*) is a frequent practice in Or., as is the use of *similiter cadens* or end-rhyme: thus, for instance, 32/26–7 'hu *m*onege *m*issenlice *m*oncwealmas on ðæm gewinnum gewurdon', 39/14–15 '7 heora *f*æderum wæron to *f*otum *f*eallende' (with effective use of the expanded verb form), 27/23 'þa spell þe ic *s*ecge ic hi *s*ceal gescyrtan' (with tautological *hi* contributing to the rhythm) and 31/28 'hie *n*æfre *n*oldon on cyþþe *cuman*' (with possible end-rhyme, if, as the spellings of MS L suggest, unstressed *an* and *on* had fallen together in the same sound[3]).

---

[1] See Nickel (1966), pp. 107–33. [2] See *St. Chad*, pp. 48 and 140.
[3] See above, p. xliv.

Indisputable instances of end-rhyme include 26/16–18 'Hwæðre God þa miclan Pharones menge gelytlode 7 hyra ofermætan ofermetto genyðerode' (with alliteration linking *miclan* and *menge*, and alliteration and wordplay linking *ofermætan* and *ofermetto*[1]) and 109/18–19 'mid flanum ofscotod 7 mid stanum oftorfod' (with not only alliteration linking the two constituent parts but also equivalence of syntax).

Rhythmic balance and contrast is achieved in a number of ways, one of the most common being the use of pairs of constructions that are syntactically identical but semantically different, as in the last quotation. Thus, for instance, at the simplest level, constructions such as 26/4 'ge dæges ge nihtes', 25/21 'ge inne ge ute' and 141/12 'swa micel hæte 7 swa micel þurst', with one changed element, beside 48/29 'swa micel folc on swa lytlan firste' and 37/20–1 'ða ðæt eastrice in Asiria gefeoll, þa eac þæt westrice in Roma aras', with two or more changed elements. The use of word pairs is common throughout the work, particularly with adjectives and verbs. In the case of adjectives there is a tendency for the second of a pair to be separated from the first by the noun that they qualify as, for instance, 25/27 'þære bismerlicestan wrace 7 þære unweorðlicostan', an order that applies both where the two adjectives are nearly synonymous and where they are different in meaning, as in 113/5 'stronges modes 7 fæstes' and 103/5–6 'on lytlum staþole 7 on unwenlicum'. In the case of verb pairs, separation of this type is less common, but near-identity of meaning and linking by alliteration, end-rhyme, and repetition of prefixes much more frequent. Thus, for instance, 103/17 'afyrhtede wæron 7 agælwede', and 37/10 'weaxan ongann 7 miclian', beside 31/2–3 'bemurciað 7 bespreca ð', 119/6 'asmorodon 7 aþrysemodan' and, with assonance, 133/31 'fleah 7 forbead'.

However, the author's stylistic achievement is best illustrated not from isolated forms but from whole paragraphs, and not from the historical narrative but from passages of comment where the author's role changes from that of recorder of history to that of orator and he accordingly uses language not merely to inform but to move his audience. All these passages deserve careful scrutiny, though it is not possible to consider more than three (two of them excerpted from longer passages) in detail here. Each of these three

---

[1] For other instances of word-play see, e.g., *dæles* and *dæl*, 23/7–8 and *bebyrgean* and *byrg*, 70/12.

is inspired by commentary in OH, but is to all intents and purposes completely independent of it.

(i) Hit is *s*condlic, cwæð Orosius, ymb *s*welc to *s*precanne hwelc hit þa wæs, þa swa *e*arme wif 7 swa *e*lðeodge hæfdon gegan þone cræftgestan dæl 7 þa hwatestan men *e*alles þises middangeardes, þæt wæs *A*siam 7 *E*urope, þa hie forneah mid *e*alle *a*weston, 7 *e*alda ceastra 7 *e*alde byrig *to*wurpon, 7 æfter ðæm hie dydon ægþer ge cyninga ricu settan ge niwu ceastra timbredon, 7 *e*alle þa *w*orold on hiora *a*gen *ge*will *on*wendende *w*æron folneah c *w*intra, 7 swa *ge*mune *m*en wæron ælces broces þætte hie hit *fol*neah to *n*anum *f*acne ne to *n*anum laðe *n*æfdon þætte þa earman wifmen hie swa tintredon. (30/24–33)

Apart from alliteration and end-rhyme (*aweston : towurpon, facne : laðe,* and possibly *dydon : settan : timbredon*) and the balance achieved by the use of *swelc* and *hwelc* and of the pairs *ealda ceastra 7 ealde byrig, to nanum facne ne to nanum laðe, swa earme wif 7 swa elðeodge,* and *þone cræftgestan dæl 7 þa hwatestan men,* we may note in particular the use of hyperbole, the repetition of *eall* and *eald,* the variations *forneah* and *folneah, middangeard* and *worold, ceastra* and *byrig, wif* and *wifmen* (the second pair presumably for alliterative purposes, the third for 'poetic', and the fourth for rhythmical reasons[1]), the exploitation of the expanded verb form, the contrast between 'old' and 'new' expressed through chiasmus, and the envelope pattern, the passage beginning and ending with the *earme wif(men)* and their behaviour towards the men.

(ii) Seo ilce burg Babylonia, seo ðe mæst wæs 7 ærest ealra burga, seo is nu læst 7 westast. Nu seo burg swelc is, þe ær wæs ealra weorca fæstast 7 wunderlecast 7 mærast, gelice 7 heo wære to bisene asteald eallum middangearde, 7 eac swelce heo self sprecende sie to eallum moncynne 7 cweþe: 'Nu ic þuss gehroren eam 7 aweg gewiten, hwæt, ge magan on me ongietan 7 oncnawan þæt ge nanuht mid eow nabbað fæstes ne stronges þætte þurhwunigean mæge.' (43/33–44/6)

This passage introduces the rhetorical figure of prosopopoeia[2]

---

[1] The simplex *ceaster* occurs only here in Or. As for *wif* and *wifmon,* the former is normally used in the sense of 'wife' or 'married woman' in this text, while *wifmon* has the sense 'woman' and in the majority of instances is contrasted with *wæpnedmon,* 'man'. The first Amazons were wives whose husbands had been killed (see 29/14–35); here they are also thought of simply as women, terrorizing men.

[2] See Commentary on 43/34–44/6. For other effective instances of direct speech (though not prosopopoeia) see 45/8–9, 47/5–9, 48/35–6, 127/20–4 and 128/15–18.

and once again hyperbole. Although it depends heavily on word-pairs for its effect, these are skilfully deployed. Thus, the pair *mæst* and *ærest* is not only split up by a verb, it is balanced by a second pair of superlatives not so separated and of contrasting meaning but of identical composition, monosyllable followed by dissyllable. *Gehroren* and *aweg gewiten* are similarly separated by the auxiliary on which they depend syntactically, while *ongietan* and *oncnawan* are linked by their prefixes, *fæstes ne stronges* given special emphasis by their unusual position, *sprecende sie* and *cweþe* both separated and syntactically varied, and the whole system of pairs varied by the interposition of a series of three superlatives *fæstast 7 wunderlecast 7 mærast.*[1]

(iii) Hu þyncð eow nu, cwæð Orosius, þe þæs cristendomes tida leahtriað, siþþan Gallia ut of þære byrig aforan, hu bliðe tida Romane æfter ðæm hæfdon. Þa þa iermingas þe þær to lafe wurdon ut of þæm holan crupon þe heo on lutedan, swa bewopene swelce hie of oþerre worolde come, þonne hie besawon on þa besengdan burg 7 on þa westan, þæt him þa wæs syndrig ege þær him ær wæs seo mæsta wyn, eac buton þæm yfele nahton hie naþer ne þærinne mete ne þærute freond. (52/15-22)

This passage opens with a rhetorical question, a figure of which, along with exclamation, the author seems particularly fond.[2] Apart from the emotive diction (*iermingas, holan, lutedan*, etc.), it contains a number of features of interest, as, for instance, the use of balance (e.g. the relative clauses 'þe þær to lafe wurdon' and 'þe heo on lutedan') and antithesis ('him þa wæs syndrig ege þær him ær wæs seo mæsta wyn', 'ne þærinne mete ne þærute freond'), the separation of the linked adjectives *besengdan* and *westan*, the repetition of the verbal prefix *be* (*bewopene, besawon, besengdan*) and the most effective use of comparison in 'swelce hie of oþerre worolde come'.[3] Finally, it contains a number of key words and themes which are taken up and elaborated in the paragraphs of comment that follow.

---

[1] The clause in which these adjectives occur, 'þe ær wæs ealra weorca fæstast . . .', is at the same time linked with the preceding 'seo ðe mæst wæs 7 ærest ealra burga' through chiasmus and variation of vocabulary (*ealra weorca fæstast : ærest ealra burga*) and word-play (*ær : ærest*).
[2] Cf., e.g., 27/26-7, 116/19-22, and 74/13-26.
[3] For other effective comparisons (though unlike this one, these have their basis in OH) see 77/21-3, 97/29-98/1, and 52/3-4. For an effective use of metaphor see 113/1-10.

X. THE PROPER NAMES[1]

1. *Inflexions*

The author of Or., it has frequently been pointed out, is not consistent in his treatment of the inflexions of the proper names in his text. However, although he follows no one single method, the majority of the forms that he uses can be grouped according to a number of clearly defined patterns. These patterns are ones which occur fairly generally in medieval translations from Latin and, as in Or., are not infrequently used side by side in the same text.

 i. The appropriate Latin inflexion is used:

(*a*) taken over by the translator from his source; thus, for instance, 102/29 *Centenus Penula se consul* and 30/4 *Effesum þa burg* for OH *Centenius Penula centurio* and *Ephesum*. We may compare the accusative singular forms *Iohannem* and *Samariam* of the OHG Tatian and Otfrid and the *de Claudio* of the Old French *Brut*.[2] It should be noted that in a number of instances the proper names used by Or. have been transferred from one Latin declension to another, though whether by the translator himself or a copyist of either OH or Or. is often not clear.[3] Thus, for instance, *Anthiopa* replaces *Antiope*, *Diþa* is found for *Dido*, *Mecipsus* for *Micipsa*, and *Antigones* for *Antigonus*.

(*b*) introduced, apparently by the translator, when the construction of the original is altered in the translation; thus, for instance, 77/30, as. *Capadotiam 7 Paflagoniam* for OH *Cappadocia cum*

---

[1] For a concordance of the foreign proper names (excluding the forms of the geographical addition and certain other names, such as *Donua* and *Pulgare*) see Richard Olbrich, *Laut- und Flexionslehre der fremden Eigennamen in den Werken König Alfreds* (Strasburg, 1908). This contains a detailed discussion of phonology and inflexions based on the readings of Zangemeister's edition, and on classical quantities. See also Mezger (1921).

[2] See OHG *Tatian*, Luke i. 13; Otfrid ii. 14. 5; Wace, *Le Roman de Brut*, ed. I. Arnold, *SATF* (Paris, 1938), 5079.

[3] The possibility of the intervention of a copyist is demonstrated by the existence of numerous variant readings in MSS L and C. Changes found also in the 'related' manuscripts of OH include transference from the first to the third declension: see e.g. Or. *Garamantes*, OH *Garamantas*, 'related' MSS *Garamantes*. Substitutions within a declension include *-is* for *-es*, a change which seems to have been widespread in Vulgar Latin and is noted and condemned by Latin grammarians: see e.g. *Appendix Probi* 'fames non famis', and Or. *Araxis*, *Artecsersis*, *Eumenis*, etc.

Paphlagonia. We may compare Ælfric's *Homilies*, (xxiii, 127), as. *Euentium and Theodolum* where the corresponding Latin has nom. *Eventius* and *Theodolus*.[1] These Latin forms, both original and non-original, are most commonly found in the nom. and acc. cases, all declensions. They are very rare indeed in other cases, though exceptions do occur, as for instance gs. *Tigris, Xersis,* ds. (for Lat. dat. and abl.) *Constantino, Minotauro, Pausania, Perseo,* gpl. *Molosorum, Epirotarum, Lemniaðum,* and dpl. (Lat. abl.) *Faliscis.* We may compare Ælfric (*Homilies,* xvii, 221) gpl. *Gerasenorum* and 65 ds. *Tyro.*

ii. The Latin inflexion is replaced by one belonging to the language of the translator; thus, for instance, 37/30 *from Arbate,* OH *ab Arbato,* and 40/8 ns. *Lucretie,* Lat. *Lucretia.* We may compare OHG Tatian, St. John iv. 6, *brunno Jacobes,* Otfrid i. 5. 28, *Dauides sez thes kuninges* for Luke i. 32 *sedem David patris eius,* and Ælfric (*Homilies,* xxiii, 161) *þam cwellere Aureliane.* Belonging to this group are a number of names in n. and as. with neither Latin nor OE inflexions, as 77/30 *Eumen* OH ds. *Eumeni,* and 96/29 *Tiber seo ea,* OH ns. *Tiberis.* These may be supposed to have n. and as. zero inflection of OE strong masculine and neuter nouns and certain strong feminines.

iii. The native inflexion is added to the Lat. nom. form; thus, for example, 108/29 *to Antiochuse* OH *ad Antiochum.* We may compare the OHG Tatian CLXIX. 200 *fater Alexandres inti Rufuses,* Otfrid iv. 11. 19 *zi Petruse,* and *Heliand* 3794 *Erodeses thegan.*[2] In this group, which is an uncommon one in OE,[3] I would include nouns in the accusative case with Latin nominative forms, on the grounds that they may be thought of as formed by analogy with OE nouns, which have identity of nom. and acc. forms in the plural and usually also in the (strong) singular. Thus, for instance, 146/11 *ofslog Proculus,* OH *Proculum . . . interfecit,* and 28/18 *gesawon Thesali þæt folc,* where OH has apl. *Thessalos* (in a slightly different construction).

---

[1] For the problem of appropriate Latin inflexions in *LER* see Bately, (1960), pp. 583–6.   [2] *Heliand,* ed. E. Sievers (Halle, 1878).
[3] See e.g. *The OE Heptateuch,* Genesis 46. 12 ds. *Farase* (MSS L and O *Pharese*), beside ns. *Phares,* Vulgate *Phares*; see also the use by Or., MS C, of *-us* where L has *-uses, -use,* e.g. 114/25–6 L *Ueriatuses,* C *Feriatus* and 39/2 L *Romuluse,* C *Romulus,* beside 94/16 L *Reguluses,* C *Regules.*

The most usual native inflexions are those of the strong declension. However, there is a tendency for weak inflexions to be used with Latin nouns in *-a* and *-o* as, for instance, 88/16 *Elisan*, 102/2 *Scipian*, beside 129/18 *Cleopatron* etc. Weak inflexions are also found alongside their strong equivalents added to a Latin nom. sg., as, for instance, 58/25 *Pirrusan*, beside as. *Pirrus*, gs. *Pirruses*, etc. A similar situation occurs in Otfrid; cf. iv. 9. 3 *Petrusan*, beside iv. 11. 19 *Petruse*. In the case of plural nouns, the native *-as*, *-an*, and *-e* are all found, but in the nom. *-as* and *-an* are used mainly with native or naturalized names, such as *Crecas*, *Finnas*, *Swæfas*, *Gotan*, *Iudan*, *Dalamentsan*, *-e* being the most common inflexion, corresponding to Latin *-i*, as in *Romane*, *-ae* as in *Lapithe*, *Perse*, and *-es* as in *Somnite*, *Atheniense*. In the accusative *-as* is more frequent and is often used for OH *-as* and *-os*, as in *Drancas*, *Areas*, as well as for OH *-es*, as in *Amazanas*, *Hasterbalas*. The genitive plural is normally *-a*; however, occasionally, as with common nouns in Or., the spelling *-e* occurs (e.g. *Gotene*, *Mæðe*, *Romane*, *Somnite*),[1] and occasionally *-o*; *-o* is found twenty-seven times in the list of chapter headings in the word *Romano*, and possibly twice in the text, in the words *Ponto* and *Rochouasco*.[2] A similar gpl. form is found in the OE Bede, where, however, it is not limited to Latin proper names: see, e.g., 120/3 *Breotono*, 146/6 *Norðanhymbro*, 408/3 *gewrito*. A dpl. in *-an* for *-um* is found once in Or. in the form *Persan*.

The chief exception to these patterns is the use of inappropriate Latin forms, either based on the corresponding forms in OH or apparently independent of them. Often these seem to have been adopted through ignorance of the correct Latin nominative;[3] thus, for instance, ns. *Boho*, as. *Bohan*, for Latin *Bocchus*, OH abl. *Boccho*, and ns. *Perdice* for Lat. *Perdicca*, OH gs. *Perdiccae*. Sometimes they may be due to the adoption of the Latin nominative as an 'indeclinable' form, as, for instance. gs. *Claudius*, *Epna*, ds. *Affrica*, *Roma*, *Theuhaleon*, dpl. *Athenienses*, *Spartani*, etc.[4] Sometimes, however, the only obvious explanation is care-

[1] See above, p. xlvi.
[2] *Rochouasco* could, however, be taken as ds. or dpl., *Ponto* as gs. For gpl. *-o* see also *Three OE Prose Texts*, p. xxxix, and Sisam (1953), p. 64.
[3] A number of incorrectly reconstituted nominatives also occur, e.g. *Attalis*, *Camillis* and *Annianes*, for Lat. *Attalus*, *Camillus*, *Anio*, OH gs. *Attali*, *Camilli*, and as. *Anienem*.
[4] Possibly to be included here are a number of genitives in *-a*, e.g. *Affrica* (*burg*), *Mauritania* (*cyning*); however, these could be not gs. of a place name but

lessness on the part of either translator or scribe;[1] thus, for instance, ns. *Galliam, Italiam*, npl. *Atheniensium*.

2. Phonology

'There are phonetic spellings in Orosius which suggest the idea that it was written down to dictation, and in fact there is strong support for that view in some mistaken word-forms in the said translation.'[2] This theory, first expressed in the nineteenth century by scholars such as Schilling and Pogatscher[3] and based almost entirely on the numerous differences in form between the proper names in OH and those in the surviving manuscripts of Or., remains unchallenged, even though many of the variants cited by its first proponents can be shown to have existed already in the Latin manuscript used by the translator.[4] The only point of dispute seems to be the native language of the man who did the dictating. Ann Kirkman, arguing that 'the Latin text was probably explained to King Alfred by his scholars, and afterwards dictated by him to some amanuensis', suggests that these scholars may well have been foreigners:

The influence of foreign scholars seems the best explanation of some of the changes which we have noticed. Without such influence it is hardly possible to explain the consonantal variations, which cannot be due to the defective hearing or incapacity of the person who wrote down the OE text.[5]

Bøgholm goes further: 'What kind of man was he who did the

gpl. of the name of the people living in that place, (for Or.'s substitution of npl. *Mauritanie* for OH *Mauri* see Glossary of Proper Names). Certainly whatever the translator intended, his audience would probably have interpreted constructions such as *-a cyning* and *-a lond* as plurals of the type *Norðanhymbra cyning* and *Englalond*.

[1] See, e.g., ns. *Aruhes*, for OH ns. *Aruba*, 'related' MSS *Arucha*, which would seem to derive its form from the preceding OE-type gs. *Aruhes*. For carelessness or ignorance on the part of the compiler of the chapter headings see 5/21 ns. *Corinthum*, corresponding to 114/6 as. *Corinthum*, OH gs. *Corinthi*. Some 'inappropriate' Latin forms may be the result of scribal error: see, e.g., dpl. *Læcedemoniam* (though an 'inappropriate' ds. cannot be ruled out here), and above, p. xlv.

[2] N. Bøgholm, *English Speech from an Historical Point of View* (Copenhagen, 1939), p. 19.

[3] See. Schilling (1886), p. 56, and A. Pogatscher, *Zur Lautlehre der griechischen, lateinischen und romanischen Lehnworte im Altenglischen* (Strasburg, 1888), §§ 247 n, 310, 317, 325, 329, and 340 n.

[4] See Glossary of Proper Names, *passim*.

[5] A. Kirkman, 'Proper Names in the OE Orosius', *MLR*, xxv (1930), 149 f.

dictating? Evidently a man of Romance culture. He reads Latin as it was pronounced in his time.[1]

Certainly there were people in England in the second half of the ninth century who were familiar with 'Romance culture'; foreign scholars like Grimbald would have been trained in the pronunciation of Latin current in the western Frankish kingdom[2] and could have taught it to others. However, in addition to 'Romance culture' there was also a flourishing Celtic culture and at least one of Alfred's scholars—Asser—was a Welshman. A close examination of the whole range of variant forms in Or. reveals no features that need to be explained in terms of Romance pronunciation apart from a handful of forms which appear to represent contemporary usage, but many that coincide with what we know of Welsh pronunciation at that time. By way of illustration I would take the treatment of intervocalic plosives and groups containing plosives in Or.,[3] since it is on this, and particularly the representation of intervocalic *d* by *ð*, that the chief arguments in favour of a dictator of Romance (or Gallo-Roman) culture are based.

i. Intervocalic *t* and *p* are replaced by *d*, *b*, and intervocalic *tr* by *dr*: e.g. *Lampida*, *Abulia*, *Parcoadras*, OH *Lampeto* ('related' manuscripts *Lampito*), *Apulia*, *Parcohatras*.[4]

ii. Intervocalic *d* and *b* are replaced by *ð*, *þ*, *th*[5] and *f*, *u*;[6] and intervocalic *rd* by *rð*, *br* by *fr*, *lb* by *lu*: e.g. *Archimeðes*, *Aripeusses*, *Epithaurus*, *Beuius*, *Marðonius*, *Clafrione*, *Galua*, OH *Archimedis*, *Arridaei*, *Epidaurium*, *Baebius*, *Mardonius*, *Glabrione*, *Galba*.

iii. Intervocalic *dr*, *dn* are replaced by *ðr*, *ðn*, and *nd* by *nth*: *Aprametum*, *Ciðnus*, *Fiðnam*, *Ponthionis*, OH *Hadrumetum*, *Cydnum*, *Pydnam*, *Pandionis*.

iv. Intervocalic *g* is lost in the combination -*agi*- and is replaced by *w* in the combination -*ugu*-: e.g. *Astiai*, *Cartaina*, *Geoweorþa.*, OH *Astyagi*, *Carthagin-*, *Iugurtha*.

[1] Bøgholm, p. 19.

[2] See Bately, 'Grimbald of St. Bertin's', *Medium Aevum*, xxxv (1966), 1–10.

[3] I exclude changes involving the combinations *mp*, *lp*, *rp*, *sp*, and *st*, for which see Bately (1966), pp. 262–3. For the representation of OH -*dio*- and -*ntia* see below, p. cxiv.

[4] For full details of these and other forms see Bately (1966), pp. 261–296.

[5] That Latin *th* was equated with OE *ð*, *þ* is shown by spellings such as *Sciþþie*, *Sciþþia*, for OH *Scythae*, *Scythia*, and MS C *þeodosius*, for L and OH *Theodosius*. For the *þþ* of *Sciþþia* see Campbell, *OEG* § 558.

[6] The identification of OE *f* intervocalic with Latin *v* (written *u*) in this position is illustrated by spellings such as *Trefia* for OH *Treuiam*.

Now, although in Gallo-Roman intervocalic t, p, and tr certainly developed to d, b, and dr, and intervocalic d, b, and br, dr, dn to $\eth$, $\flat$, and $\flat r$, $\eth r$, $\eth n$ respectively, the groups rd, nd, and lb remained unchanged.[1] Moreover, one important result of the Carolingian reforms was a more conscious separation between the written and the spoken language and the introduction of a new pronunciation for the former based on the symbols used.[2] That a plosive pronunciation of the symbols d and b as well as a voiceless pronunciation of t and p was indeed restored seems evident, not only from the form taken by Latin loan-words in French borrowed in and after the ninth century and the spellings of contemporary Latin documents, but also from the attempts in the Strasburg Oaths to find a satisfactory spelling for the sound $\eth$.[3] What is more, Old French itself seems to have acquired a new set of intervocalic plosives as a result of the simplification of double consonants, so that $\eth$ was not, as Pogatscher and others believed, the only representative of the dental plosives and spirants in this position.[4] As for intervocalic g, although this became lost in the vernacular in the combination -agi- after an intervening stage d (the pronunciation in the ninth century is not certain), a plosive pronunciation was restored in Latin words, while in the combination -ugu- the plosive pronunciation remained unchanged.[5] In Old Welsh, on the other hand, not only did intervocalic t, p, d, b and tr, rd, br, lb become d, b, $\eth$, $\flat$ and dr, $r\eth$, $\flat r$, $l\flat$ respectively as a result of lenition, but these sounds continued to be written t, p, d, b and tr, rd, br, lb,[6] while g was lost not only in the combination -agi- but also in the combination -ugu-, though g was still normally written in both positions in the ninth century.[7] A Welshman therefore would have read *Iugurtha* as *Iuurtha and this might easily have been 'heard'

[1] See Bately (1966), pp. 262 and 266 and Pope (1934), §§ 333, 335, and 372.

[2] See C. Beaulieux, *Histoire de l'Orthographe Française* (Paris, 1927), pp. 18–26.

[3] See Pope (1934), § 647, C. C. Rice, *The Phonology of Gallic Clerical Latin after the Sixth Century* (Idaho, 1909), p. 62, and the spellings *aiudha, cadhuna* of the Strasburg Oaths.

[4] See Pogatscher, p. 177 and T. Pyles, 'Old English Pronunciation of Foreign Words', *PMLA*, lviii (1943), 904.

[5] See Pope (1934), §§ 290, 297, and 404 and Pyles, *PMLA*, lviii, 907. The symbol d Miss Pope uses to denote a voiced plosive palatal. In Gallo-Roman the g of -ugu- had disappeared (see Pope (1934), § 341) but by the ninth century it had been replaced by a new velar plosive from other sources.

[6] See Jackson (1953), §§ 50, 52, 131, 72, 64, 138, and pp. 68–9.

[7] See Jackson (1953), §§ 83, 89. For *Cartaina* see Bately (1966) p. 271.

as *Iuwurða (or even so pronounced),[1] and in line with OE spelling convention iu written geo and wurth written weorþ.[2] As for dr, dn, and nd there is evidence that in the ninth century these symbols could be used in Old Welsh to represent the sounds ðr, ðn, and nð as well as secondary dr, dn, and nd.[3] However, in this case an alternative explanation is that Or.'s variants may be due to medieval Latin or OE scribal practice.[4]

The possibility that the hypothetical dictator was a man using not Romance but Welsh pronunciations is supported by other spellings in the surviving manuscripts, though these are open to other explanations.[5] Thus, for instance, the replacing of initial p, t by b, d and of initial b, d, g by p, t, c could be the result of two separate characteristics of Old Welsh: first lenition, which affected not only consonants internal of a word but also consonants initial of a word but preceded in a close speech-group by a proclitic ending in a vowel, or in general terms internal between vowels and sonants:[6] second, the partial aspiration of initial c, t, p except before l, r, s, and the partial unvoicing of initial g, d, b, which has remained a feature of Welsh and is responsible for such spellings as Fluellen's preach, plow (for breach, blow), peard, peseech, tevil, and so on in Shakespeare's Henry V.[7] However, Old Welsh was not the only language whose consonant systems differed slightly in manner of articulation from Old English—another instance is Upper German[8]—and therefore other explanations cannot be ruled out.

As for the vowels, the frequent variant spellings of these do not point specifically to 'foreign intervention'; however, they do strongly support the theory of dictation.[9] Old English is notorious

---

[1] I am indebted to Professor Jackson for this suggestion, also for the information that the Old Welsh development -ugu- > -uɣu- was much too early to be responsible for this particular form.
[2] See Bately (1966), pp. 272 and 282, and Campbell, OEG §§ 172 and 321.
[3] See Jackson (1953), § 143 and p. 562, n. 1.
[4] See Bately (1966), p. 267.
[5] See further Bately (1966), pp. 272–96.
[6] See Jackson (1953), § 131.
[7] See J. Baudiš, Grammar of Early Welsh, Part I; Philologica ii, Supplement (Oxford, 1924), pp. 78–9. According to Baudiš, p. 83, initial g, d, b in Glamorgan are voiceless or the voice vibration is minimal.
[8] See L. Armitage, Introduction to the Study of Old High German (Oxford, 1911), p. 64 and for a discussion of the possibility of OHG influence here Bately (1966), pp. 275–9.
[9] Since virtually every proper name with altered vowels would need to be considered separately, no attempt is made here to discuss these variant spellings

for the sensitivity of its vowels to their surroundings and although by the end of the ninth century most of the changes involving stressed vowels were represented in writing, this was not yet normally the case as regards vowels in unstressed position. Thus, although there is evidence already in early WS for a reduction of unaccented vowels in certain positions to a sound written *e*, the usual representation for this sound is determined by spelling tradition.[1] Where a scribe had no such tradition to help him, he might be expected to use either the roughly phonetic *e* or a symbol suggested by the surrounding stressed vowels. Such a situation appears to occur in the surviving manuscripts of Or. For instance, *e* is frequently substituted for another vowel in probable unstressed position[2] where OE would have reduction to *e*, e.g. *Andregatia* and *Eacedam* for OH *Andragathius, Aeacida*, while choice of other vowels found in this position often appears to be not arbitrary but determined by the nature of surrounding stressed vowels, e.g. *Damaris* beside *Dameris* for OH *Thamyris*, related MSS *T(h)ameris, Taprabane* beside *Deprobane* for OH *Taprobane*, and *Ar(c)halaus* beside *Archolaus*[3] for OH *Archelaus*. Some of the confusion of vowels found in Latin inflexional endings may also be the result of the interchangeability of vowel symbols in unstressed position: thus, for instance, *Procos* for OH ns. *Procas*, *Poros* for OH ns. *Porus*, *Farnabuses* for OH as. *Pharnabazum*, *Fefles* for OH ns. *Afellas* and *Siracuses* for apl. *Syracusas*.[4]

in detail. Of particular interest are the seemingly 'Anglo-Saxon' *æ* for *a* spellings of *Læcedemonia* and *Mæcedonia* which occur some eighty times in MS L. See also *Gælle, Ciarsæthi*, and *Mærsum*.

[1] See Campbell, *OEG* §§ 369 and 385–7 and above, p. xliv.

[2] The problem of the position of stress in foreign proper names is a difficult one, especially if we assume dictation by a foreigner. The Late Latin rules for the position of the accent were different from those of classical Latin (see, e.g., Pope (1934), pp. 99–100), moreover they did not correspond to those for the position of stress as applied to Latin loan-words in OE (see Campbell, *OEG* § 493). In late loans, including proper names of foreign origin, the evidence of OE verse is that while the main stress was transferred to the first syllable a strong half-stress normally remained on the syllable which had borne the main stress in Latin (see Campbell, *OEG* § 548)—but did the dictator have a similar usage? and in any case, how did he know where the Latin stress would have fallen in corrupt forms such as *Laumendo*? Similar problems arise in connection with the quantity of the vowels in unusual foreign proper names, even where they appear correctly spelt.

[3] The form *Archolaus* is probably influenced by the name *Archos* which immediately precedes it.

[4] For similar spelling variants in words other than proper names see above, p. xlvi.

h

Only one group of forms outside the 'geographical addition' seems to point away from Old Welsh to a continental pronunciation and these are all names of people and places that the author of Or. could have known in their contemporary form. Thus, *Profentse* is presumably the ninth-century Provençal and French pronunciation of the name Provence, Latin *provincia*;[1] *Magentsan*, for OH *Mogontiacum*, corresponds to OHG *Maginza*;[2] *Megelan* for OH *Mediolanium* may represent a pronunciation such as is suggested by the thirteenth-century form *Meielan* for *Mediolanum*, mod. Meilen, near Zürich.[3] Finally, *Donua* for OH *Danuuius* and *Rin* for OH *Rhenus* both represent Germanic forms of these river-names, though conceivably forming part of the vocabulary of the Anglo-Saxons from an early date.[4]

It seems likely, therefore, that a large number of the variant spellings of proper names in Or. are the result of dictation, and that quite possibly dictation by either a Welshman or an Englishman trained in Latin pronunciation by a Welshman.[5] However, two problems remain: what form did this dictation take and at what point in the transmission of the text did it occur? In medieval times dictation could take two forms, dictation by one man to another and self-dictation, while the 'Welsh' features could have arisen in the course of transmission of either Latin or OE text. According to T. C. Skeat, the two systems, visual copying and dictation, do not produce two readily separable types of error:

The scribe copying visually may commit visual errors through misreading the exemplar, or audible errors through self-dictation. The scribe copying from dictation may reproduce visual errors of the dictator, or himself commit phonetic errors through faulty hearing.

However,

While identical visual errors and identical phonetic errors may be made by different scribes, the mistakes due to lack of liaison between scribe

---

[1] See Pope (1934), §§ 290 and 180, Bately (1966), p. 269.

[2] See Bately (1966), pp. 269–70. [3] See Bately (1966), p. 268.

[4] However, *Donua* is a form not found outside Or., while *Rin*, though declinable here (as masc.) and in Be. (as fem.), is indeclinable in the *Anglo-Saxon Chronicle*, s.a. 887, a fact which could suggest that for the Chronicler at least it may have been an unfamiliar word. However, see Campbell, *OEG* § 628(6), n. 2.

[5] Since a Welsh-trained Englishman would not use initial lenition or articulate his plosives in a Welsh manner, the former is perhaps to be preferred.

and dictator are more likely to be different in each case. As a result, a dictated manuscript may be expected to contain a larger or smaller number of *singular* errors.[1]

Much, of course, depends on the knowledge and experience of the man who is writing from dictation. Although the scribe of the eighth-century Donaueschingen MS of OH 'seems to have had no visual impression of Latin',[2] other scribes may have been reasonably competent Latin scholars, particularly after the Carolingian reforms and in scriptoria where dictation was not an exceptional occurrence,[3] while dictation in the scribe's own language might be expected to present very few difficulties to someone who was practised in it. Indeed, in the case of Or., if dictation took place before translation, to a scribe with a good knowledge of Latin, or after translation to an Anglo-Saxon, then one might expect that scribe to experience difficulty mainly in transcribing unfamiliar names. And as I have endeavoured to demonstrate elsewhere[4] the retention of correct Latin spellings such as *ch*, *ph*, *qu*, *th*, *x*, *z*, and consonantal *i*, *u* in no way rules out the possibility of dictation by one man to another, while the sheer volume of error makes it appear—in the absence of evidence to the contrary—a more attractive theory than self-dictation. As for the occasion of this dictation, this cannot be determined with any great degree of certainty. Certain forms, such as *Margas* and *Sceltiuerin*, would seem to have arisen in a Latin context, since they depend on faulty division of OH *Sicyonam Argos* and *ingens Celtiberorum*. 78/3 *Calonie þa þeode* for OH *colonias* may likewise have a 'Latin' origin, for it is hard to believe that the translator was unfamiliar with the name *colonia*. However, these forms are insufficient evidence on which to build a theory of dictation of the Latin text. The first two could equally well be explained as the fault of the translator, misreading his Latin exemplar, while *Calonie* is an error that could have arisen in the course of the transmission of the Latin text quite independently of the bulk of errors under discussion.

In favour of dictation of the text of Or., on the other hand, we have faulty word-divisions such as 68/4–5 *an Nilirice* for *on Ilirice*, differences between the spellings of proper names in text

---

[1] T. C. Skeat, 'The Use of Dictation in Ancient Book-production', *PBA*, xlii (1956), 207–8.   [2] Skeat, *PBA*, xlii, 200.
[3] See Skeat, *PBA*, xlii, 203.   [4] Bately (1966), pp. 297–300.

and chapter headings,[1] and, most significant of all, the use of the OE symbols ð and þ for Latin *d*. In Anglo-Saxon manuscripts whose language is OE, substitution of the native symbols ð and þ for Latin *th* in classical proper names is, if not very usual, at least not particularly rare.[2] However, in Anglo-Saxon manuscripts whose language is Latin, the use of ð or þ is, to my knowledge, confined to proper names of OE origin and even here these symbols normally take second place to Latin *th* except in charters. The lost manuscript of Asser's Life of Alfred, for instance, seems consistently to have used *th*, even for names taken from the *Anglo-Saxon Chronicle*. What is more, Latin manuscripts of Anglo-Saxon provenance never—again to my knowledge—substitute ð or þ for Latin *d*, in this agreeing with the great majority of OE manuscripts, where the only exceptions[3] that I know of outside Or. itself are *Achapemicos* for *Academicos* in Alfred's *Soliloquies* and *Ðeoðerius* for *Theoderius* in MS C of the *Old English Martyrology*.[4]

In a Latin text, then, even an occasional attempt to show fricative pronunciation of Latin *d* in a learned proper name would be unusual, while if such an attempt were made, one might expect the symbol *th*, not ð or þ to be used. The surviving manuscripts of Or., however, make a fairly careful distinction between *th* for Latin *th* and ð, þ for Latin *d*,[5] a distinction which cannot be derived from an exemplar using only *th*. It is tempting to conclude, in the absence of evidence to the contrary, that the treatment of Latin *d* in Or. is unique and the result of dictation of the text of Or.

---

[1] e.g. 146/9 *Brobus*, chapter headings *Probus*. These errors, however, need not necessarily have been introduced at the same time as the main body of errors. For evidence other than that of the proper names that may suggest dictation of the OE text see Cosijn, i § 148, and the six times repeated form *tictator(es)*.

[2] See Bately (1966), p. 302.

[3] The form *Dauið*, beside *Dauit*, of the Hatton MS of CP, Cotton *Dauid*, is a special case and does not belong here. In common names borrowed by OE from Latin, either *d* or ð, þ is found, depending on the date of borrowing and the sphere to which the word belongs. An apparently learned borrowing with ð is CP *aðamans*.

[4] So. 60/22, *An OE Martyrology* 126/1. We may compare the usage in words of Romance origin, where Latin *d* has become ð, e.g. *Anglo-Saxon Chronicle*, s.a. 883 *Cundoþ* (Asser *Cundoth*) for *Condé*, from Gall. *Condate* by way of a Vulgar Latin form with intervocalic *d*.

[5] Only four instances of *th* for OH *d* occur and of these three (*Rogathitus, Rogathite, Ponthionis*) are in the section found in C only, while the fourth (*Epithaurus*) has *th* only in MS L, C having the more usual ð.

NOTE ON THE TEXT

Except for the section 15/1–28/11, for which only the Cotton version has survived, passages enclosed in square brackets and expanded abbreviations, the text is taken from the Lauderdale manuscript, as the earlier and in many ways the 'better' of the two major manuscripts.[1] Abbreviations are normally expanded without notice, the chief exception being the tironian sign (7). Where this stands for the conjunction, the tironian sign is retained; where it occurs as part of other words, it is expanded to *ond* or *and* and italicized. The punctuation, including capitals, has been modernized throughout. Manuscript spacing is generally used as a guide in distinguishing between compound verbs and quasi-compounds involving postpositions. Accent marks, which are frequent, appearing mostly on long monosyllables and the prefix *a-*, are not reproduced. Interlineal and marginal insertions are enclosed in slanting lines, \ /. They are normally relegated to the apparatus if they do not appear to be the work of the original scribe. Irrelevant scribbles, and marginalia in later medieval and modern hands are not included, nor are the majority of the additions and corrections in later hands where MS C provides the text. Damage to the writing surface is normally noted in the apparatus only where examination by the naked eye or by modern scientific aids suggests that it can reasonably be supposed to result from erasure of letter forms. Square brackets indicate departures from the reading of the base manuscript by addition, substitution, or transposition but not omission. All readings in square brackets are explained in the apparatus. Emendation is kept to the minimum and in the case of proper names is not normally employed where MS C has a better reading than L but this could be the result of correction: æ with attenuated first element (printed ę by Sweet) is not distinguished from other forms of the letter. Numerals are throughout printed in small roman, with *v* not *u* generalized for 5. The division of the text into separate numbered sections is that of the manuscript. Occasional omission of section numbers by one or other manuscript is not normally indicated. Foliation is that given to the

[1] See, however, above, p. xxxii–xxxiii.

manuscript after its purchase by the British Museum. It corresponds to the gatherings and to the pagination of the *EEMF* facsimile as follows:

1. Unnumbered fly-leaf and pp. 1–14: ff. 1–8ᵛ.
2. Missing, replaced by a seventeenth century gathering, pp. 15-26: ff. 9–16ᵛ. In the text this is replaced by the corresponding section of MS C, ff. 12ᵛ–23 (10ᵛ–21 in the old foliation used by Bosworth and Sweet).
3. pp. 31–46: ff. 17–24ᵛ.
4. pp. 47–62: ff. 27–32ᵛ.
5. pp. 63–78: ff. 33–40ᵛ.
6. pp. 79–94: ff. 41–8ᵛ.
7. pp. 95–110: ff. 49–56ᵛ.
8. pp. 111–126: ff. 57–64ᵛ.
9. pp. 127–142: ff. 65–92ᵛ.
10. pp. 143–158: ff. 73–80ᵛ.
11. pp. 159–174: ff. 81–8ᵛ, the last folio being stuck down to the inside of the binding.

Primary Latin Source

References are to the corresponding sections of OH as printed in Zangemeister's edition. For details, see Commentary, passim.

Apparatus

Only substantive variations from manuscripts other than MS L are normally recorded. Excluded variants include obvious errors (including omissions) and phonological and morphological variants, also differences in the manner of recording numerals, whether by using roman numerals or the corresponding Old English words. Certain common variants such as *þæt* for *þætte*, *aspeon* for *aspon*, and *timbrian* for *timbran* are cited only once. Variant spellings of proper names, however, are more fully recorded. Alterations and corrections in the Cotton manuscript by hands other than those of the main scribes are normally excluded. In the apparatus / is used to indicate the end of a line, where this position is significant.

Sigla.

B　　Bodleian, Eng. Hist. e 49 (30481)
C　　British Library, Cotton Tib. B. i
C1　　The first set of chapter headings in MS C, ff. 3–7ᵛ (1–5, old foliation)

C2   The second set of chapter headings in MS C, ff. 83 and 96–7^v
(94–5, old foliation)
L   British Library, Addit. 47967
OH   The Latin text of Orosius' History, ed. Zangemeister
R   Rouen 524
V   Vatican City, Reg. Lat. 497

Abbreviations in the Apparatus.

alt.	altered.
er., eras.	erased, erasure.
l.h.	later hand.
om.	omitted.
orig.	originally.

[Her onginneð seo boc þe man Orosius nemneð]

|[I].I. Hu ure ieldran ealne þisne middangeard on þreo todældon. f. 2

II. Hu Ninus, Asiria cyning, ongon monna ærest ricsian on þiosan middangearde; 7 hu Sameramis his cwen feng to þæm rice æfter him mid micelre reðnesse 7 wrænnesse. 5

III. Hu þæt heofenisce fyr forbærnde þæt lond on þæm wæron þa twa byrig on getimbred, Sodome 7 Gomorre.

IIII. Hu Thelesci 7 Ciarsæthi þa leode him betweonum wunnon.

V. Hu Ioseph se ryhtwisa mon ahredde Egypta folc æt þæm seofan geara miclan hungre mid his wisdome; 7 hu hie siþþan ealra hiora 10 wæstma þone fiftan dæl ælce geare heora cyninge to gafole gesellað æfter his gesetnesse.

VI. Hu on Achaie wearþ micel flod on Ambictiones dagum þæs cyninges.

VII. Hu Moyses lædde Israhela fo[lc] from Egyptum ofer þone 15 Re`a´dan Sæ.

VIII. Hu on Egyptum wurdon on anre niht l monna ofslagen from hiora agnum sunum; 7 hu Bosiridis se cyning het don to geblote ealle þa cuman þe hiene gesohtan; 7 ymbe monegra oþerra folca gewinn. 20

VIIII. Hu Cretense 7 Athaniense, Creca leode, him betweonum wunnon.

X. Hu Uesoges, Egypta cyning, wolde him to geteon ge þone suðdæl, þæt is Asia, ge þone norþdæl, þæt sint Sciþþie; 7 hu ii æþelingas wurdon afliemed of Sciþþium; 7 ymbe þa wif þe mon 25 Amozenas het; 7 ymbe þa Gotan, þe him fore andredan ge Pirrus se reþa [Creca] cyning, ge se mæra Alexander, ge Iulius se casere.

1 Her . . . nemneð] *from* C, *no reading* L. 2 I.I] I *both MSS.* mid-dangeard] ymbhwyrft C. 3 Asiria] assyria C. 5 reðnesse] fæstnesse C. 6 heofenisce] heofonlice C. 8 Thelesci] telesci C. Ciarsæthi] ciarsað C. 10 geara] gearon C. 10–11 ealra . . . geare] þone fiftan dæl ealra hira wæstma C. 12 gesetnesse] gesette C. 13 Achaie] achiae C. Ambictiones] ambicsionis C. 15 folc] 'lc' *in l.h.* L. Egyptum] ægy-ptum C. 18 Bosiridis] bosiridus C. 21 Athaniense] athinense C. 23 ge] *om.* C. 24 suðdæl] suðdæl to C. Asia] aia C. 25 afliemed] aflymde C. 26 Amozenas het] het amathenas C. 27 Creca] *from* C, *om.* L.

XI. Hu Elena, þæs cyninges wif, wearð genumen on Læcedomonia þære byrig; 7 hu Eneas se cyning gefor mid fierde on Italie.

f. 2ᵛ |XII. Hu Sardanopolus wæs se siþemesta cyning in Asiria, ond
hu hiene beswac Arbatus his ealdormon; 7 hu þa wifmen bysmre-
5 dan hiora weras, þe hie fleon woldon; ond hu se argeotere geworhte
anes fearres onlicnesse þæm æþelinge.

XIII. Hu Pelopensium 7 Atheniensium þa folc him betweonum
wunnon.

XIIII. Hu Læcedemonie 7 Mesiane him betweonum wunnon for
10 hiora mægdena offrunga.

[II].I. Hu Orosius sæde þæt ure Dryhten þone ærestan mon swiþe
ryhtne 7 swiþe godne gesceope; 7 ymbe þa feower onwealdas
þises middangeardes.

II. Hu Remus 7 Romulus þa gebroþor getimbredan Romeburg on
15 Italiam.

III. Hu Romulus 7 Brutus mid hwelcum mane hie gehalgedon
Roma.

IIII. Hu Romane 7 Sabine him betweonum w[u]nnon; 7 hu Cirus
wearð ofslagen on Sciþþium.

20 V. Hu Cambisis se cyning forseah þa Egyptiscan diofolgield; 7
ymbe Dariuses gewinn 7 Xer's'is 7 Leoniþan.

VI. Hu Romanum wearð an wundor oþiewed, swelce se heofon
burne.

VII. Hu Sicilia leode wæron him betweonum winnende.

25 VIII. Hu Romane besæton Ueiorum þa burg x winter; 7 hu
Galliæ of Senno abræcan Romeburg.

[III].I. Hu sio bysmerlice sibb 7 facenlice wearð betweonum
Læcedemonium 7 Persum.

1–2 Læcedomonia] læcedemonium C. 2 gefor] for C. 3 siþemesta]
siðmesta C. Asiria] asyria C. 5 þe] þa C. 7 Pelopensium] pelopen-
tium C. Atheniensium] athinentium C. 9 Mesiane] messiane C.
11 II.I] I L, *om.* C. 14 gebroþor] gebroþra C. getimbredan Romeburg]
romana burh getimbredon C. 15 Italiam] italium C. 16 Brutus]
brutos C. 18 wunnon] *from* C, wonnon L. 20 Egyptiscan] *from* C,
egypti/escan L. 21 Dariuses] darius C. Xersis] xercis *with* 's' *above* c L,
exersis C. 22 Hu] 7 hu C. 25 Ueiorum] ueiorem C. 26 Galliæ]
gallie C. 27 III.I] I L, *om.* C.

II. Hu on Achaie wearð eorþbeofung.

III. Hu se micla monncwealm wearð on Rome on twegra consula dæge; 7 hu Marcus Curtius besceat on þa g[i]nigendan eorþan.

IIII. Hu Galliæ oferhergodon Romana lond on iii mila to þære byrg.

|V. Hu Cartaina ærendwracan comon to Rome 7 him frið gebudon.

VI. Hu Romane 7 Latine wunnon him betweonum; 7 hu an nunne wearþ cuca bebyrged.

VII. Hu Alexander se cyning wonn wið Romane, þæs maran Alexandres eam; 7 hu Philippus, þæs maran Alexandres fæder, feng to Mæcedonia rice. Ond he him geceas Bizantium þa burg.

VIII. Hu Caudenes Furculus sio stow wearþ swiþe widmære for Romana bismere.

VIIII. Hu se mæra Alexander feng to Mæcedonia rice; 7 hu he het sumne biscep secgan on his gewill hwa his fæder wære; 7 hu he Darius þone cyning oferwon; 7 hu he self wearð mid atre acweald.

X. Hu under ii consulum woldon iiii þa strengstan þeoda Romane oferwinnan; 7 hu se micla cwealm 'ge'wearð on Rome; 7 hu hi him heton gefeccean to Escolapius þone scinlacan mid þære scinlacan nædran.

XI. Hu under ii consulum wurdon Somnite 7 Gallie of Senno þære byrig Romanum wiþerwinnan. Ond hu Alexandres heretogan heora lif on unsibbe geendedon æfter Alexandres deaþe.

[IV].I. Hu Tarentine gesawan Romano scipa on ðæm sæ [irnan], þa hie plegedon on hiora theatrum.

II. Hu þa monegan yflan wundor wurdon on Rome.

III. Hu mon geseah weallan blod of eorþan 7 rinan meolc of heofonum.

---

1 Achaie] achie C. 3 ginigendan] genigendan L, gyniendan C. 4 Galliæ] gallie C. on] oð C. 6 Cartaina] cartaine C. 9 Romane] romanum C. 11 Mæcedonia] macedonia C. Bizantium] biszantium C. 14 Mæcedonia] macedonia C. 15 biscep] alt. from biscop L, bisceo C. 16 Darius] darium C. atre] atra with 'e' above the second a L, attre C. 18 cwealm] mancwealm C. 19–20 scinlacan] scinlæcan C. 23 lif] orig. life, with e er. L. 24 IV.I] I L, om. C. Romano] romana here and subsequently C. irnan] om. L, yrnan C. 27–8 weallan . . . heofonum] rinan meolc of heofenum 7 weallan blod of eorðan C.

IIII. Hu on Romane becom micel moncwealm; 7 hu Caperrone sio nunne wearþ ahangen. Ond hu þa burgleode on Cartaina bleo[tan] men hiora godum.

V. Hu Himeolco, Cartaina cyning, for mid fierde on Siciliae; ond hu Hanna an mon wæs | onwaldes giernende; ond hu Cartaine hierdon þæt se mæra Alexander hæfde abrocen Tirum þa burg.

VI. Hu Sicilia folc 7 Pena wunnon him betweonum; 7 hu Romane besæton Hannibalan, Pena cyning; 7 hu Calatinus se consul for mid fierde to Camerinan, Sicilia byrg; 7 hu Punice gesetton eft þone ealdan Hannibalan þæt he mid scipum wiþ Romane wunne; 7 hu Romane foron on Affrice mid þrim hunda scipa 7 mid xxx; 7 hu Regulus se consul ofslog þa ungemetlican nædran; 7 hu Regulus gefeaht wiþ iii Pena cyningas on anum gefeohte; 7 hu Enilius se consul for on Affricam mid iii hunde scipe; 7 hu ii consulas foran mid iii hunde scipa on Affrice; 7 hu Cotta se consul oferhergede Sicilie. Ond h[u] on þriora consula dæge com Hasterbal se niwa cyning to Libeum þæm iglande; 7 hu Claudius se consul for eft on Punice; 7 hu Gaius se consul for on Affrice 7 on þæm sæ forwearð; 7 hu Lutatia se consul for on Affrice mid iii hunde scipa.

VII. Hu se ungemetlica fyrbryne wearþ on Rome; 7 hu Gallie wurdon Romanum wiðerwearde; 7 hu Sardinie wunnon on Romane, swa hie Pene gelærdon; 7 hu Orosius sæde þæt he wære cumen to ðæm godan tidan þe Romane eft fore gulpon; 7 hu Gallie wunnon on Romane, 7 Pene on oþre healfe; 7 hu ii consulas fuhton on Gallium; 7 hu monig wundor wæron gesewene; 7 hu Claudius se consul ofslog Gallia xxx m.

VIII. Hu Hannibal, Pena cyning, besæt Saguntum, Ispania burg; 7 hu Hannibal abræc ofer Perenei þa beorgas; 7 hu Scipia se consul gefeaht on Ispanium; 7 hu monige wundor gewurdon on þære tide.

---

1 Caperrone] caperone C.   3 bleotan] bleo/ L, bliotan C.   men] m *partly era*. L.   4 Himeolco] himelco C.   Siciliae] sicilie C.   8 Hanniballan] hanniballan C.   9 gesetton] *alt. from* gesæton? L.   11 foron] f *on eras*. L.   hunda] hund C.   12–13 Regulus] regolus C.   14 scipe] scypa C.   14–16 ii consulas . . . Sicilie] hu cotta se consul oferhergode sicilie. hu twegen consulas foron on affrice mid þrim hund scipa C.   15–16 oferhergede] oferheargede L.   16 hu] *from* C, hio L.   Hasterbal] h *over eras*. L. 21 fyrbryne] *alt. rom* farbryne? L.   23 Romane] romanum C.   29 Hannibal] hannibal pena cynig C.

VIIII. Hu 'H'annibal beswac ii consulas on heora gefeohte; 7 hu
Romane him gesetton tictator 7 Scipian to consule; | 7 hu Romane f. 4
sendon Lucius þone consul on Gallie mid iii legian.

X. Hu Marcellus se consul for mid sciphere on Sicilie; 7 hu Hannibal gefeaht wiþ Marcellus þone consul iii dagas; 7 hu Hannibal 5
bestæl on Marcellus þone consul 7 hine ofslog; 7 hu Asterbal,
Hannibales broðor, for of Ispanium on Italie; 7 hu Cartainum
wearþ frið aliefed from Scipian þæm consule.

XI. Hu Romano æfterre gewinn 7 [P]unica wearð geendod; 7 hu
Sempronius se consul wearð ofslagen on Ispania; 7 hu Philippus, 10
Mæcedonia cyng, ofslog Romano ærenddracan. Ond hu þæt Mæcedonisce gewin gewearð; 7 hu Enilius se consul oferwon Perseus
þone cyning.

XII. Hu Romanum wearþ se mæste ege from Sceltiferin, Ispania
'folce'.   15

XIII. Hu þæt þridde gewinn wearþ geendod Romano 7 Cartaina.

[V].I. Hu Orosius spræc ymbe Romano gielp, hu hie monega folc
oferwunnon; 7 hu hie monege cyningas beforan hiora triumphan
wið Rome weard drifon.

II. Hu on anum geare wurdon þa twa byrg toworpena, Cartaina 20
7 Corinthum; 7 hu Ueriatus se hierde ongon ricsian on Ispanium;
7 hu Claudius se consul gefliemde Gallie; 7 hu Mantius se consul
genam friþ wið Ispanie; 7 hu Brutus se consul ofslog Ispania lx m;
7 hu an cild wearþ geboren on Rome.

III. Hu Romane sendon Scipian on Ispanie mid fierde; 7 hu 25
Craccus se consul wonn wið þa oðre consulas, oþ hi hine ofslogon;
7 hu þa þeowas [wunnan] wiþ þa hlafordas.

IIII. Hu Lucinius se consul, se þe eac wæs Romano ieldesta
biscep, for mid fierde angean Aristonocuse þæm cyninge; 7 hu

2 Romane (2)] Romane him gesetton L.   6 Asterbal] hasterbal C.
9 Romano] *second* o *alt. to* e L, romana C.   7 Punica] 7 sunica L, *om.*
C.   11 Mæcedonia] macedonia C.   11–12 Mæcedonisce] macedonisce C.
12 Perseus] persus C.   14 mæste] mæsta C.   16 Cartaina] cartaina
kyninge C.   17 V.I] I L *and* C2, *om.* C1.   18 triumphan] triumphum C2.
20 Cartaina] cartago C2.   21 Corinthum] corinþum C2.   Ueriatus] feriaatus
C1, uariatus C2.   Ispanium] ispanian C2.   22 Mantius] mantris C1.
23 genam] *on eras.* L.   m] manna C1.   26 wonn] *om.* C2.   27 wunnan]
from C2, *om.* L *and* C1.   28 Lucinius] n *alt. from* u L.   29 Aristonocuse]
aristonucuse C1.

Antiochus, Asia cyning, wilnade Partha onwaldes; 7 hu Scipia, se betsta Romano þegn, mænde his earfeþa to Romano weotum; 7 hu Eþna fyr upp afleow.

f. 4ᵛ |V. Hu Romane heton eft getimbran Cartaina; 7 hu se consul
5 Metellus oferwon þa wicingas.

VI. Hu Fauius se consul ofercom Betuitusan, Gallia cyning.

VII. Hu Romane [wunnon] wiþ Geoweorþan, Numedia cyninge.

VIII[I]. Hu Romane ongunnon unsibbe him betweonum up ahebban on þæm fiftan geare þe Marius wæs consul.

10 X. Hu ofer ealle Italie wearð ungeferlic unsibb on þæm siextan geare þe Iulius se casere wæs consul.

XI. Hu Romane sendon Sillan þone consul ongean Metredatis, Partha cyning.

XII. Hu Romane sealdon Gaiuse þæm consule seofon legian;
15 7 hu Iulius besæt Tarquatus, Pompeiuses ladteow, on anum fæstenne; 7 hu Iulius gefeaht wið Ptholomeus iii'a'.

XIII. Hu Octauianus feng to Romano onwalde hiora unwillum.

XIIII. Hu Octauianus se ca[se]re betynde Ianes duru.

XV. Hu sume Ispanie wæron Agustuse wiþerwinnan.

20 [VI].I. Hu Orosius wæs sprecende ymbe þa iiii onwaldas þara feower heafedrica þisses middangeardes.

II. Hu Tiberius feng to Romano anwalde se casere æfter Agustuse.

III. Hu Gaius wearþ casere iiii gear.

IIII. Hu Tiberius Claudius feng to Romano anwalde.

25 V. Hu Nero feng to Romano anwalde.

1 Asia] assia C1.   Scipia] scipio C2.   2 Romano weotum] romana wytum
C1, romanum C2.   3 upp] om. C2.   4 Romane] romana C1, C2.
getimbran] getimbrian *here and subsequently* C1, C2.   5 Metellus] metallus
C1.   6 Fauius] uauius C1.   Betuitusan] betwitusan C1.   Gallia] gallina C2.
7 wunnon]*from* C1, wæron L, C2.   Geoweorþan] geowyrðan C1.   Numedia]
numeþia C2.   cyninge] cyning C1.   8 VIIII] VIII L, *om.* C1, C2.
ongunnon] agunnan C1.   10 Italie] italia C2.   12 Sillan] willan C1.
13 Partha] parhta C1.   14 Gaiuse] iuse C1.   legian] legan C1.
15 Tarquatus] tarcwatus C1.   Pompeiuses] pompeius C1, pompiuses C2.
16 Ptholomeus] potholomeus C1, tholomeus C2.   17 Octauianus] octauianus se casere C2.   unwillum] unwil/willum L.   18 casere]*from* C1, C2, care L.
19 Ispanie] ispanie leode C1, ispania C2.   Agustuse] agustos C1, agustes C2.
20 VI.I] I L, C2, *om.* C1.   22 æfter Agustuse] æfter agustus C1, *om.* C2.
25 Nero feng] ner onfeng C1.

VI. Hu Galua feng to Romano anwalde se casere.

VII. Hu Uespasianus feng to Romano anwalde.

VIII. Hu Titus feng to Romano anwalde.

VIIII. Hu Domitianus, Tituses broðor, feng to Romano anwalde.

X. Hu Nerfa feng to Romano anwalde. 5

XI. Hu Adrianus feng to Romano anwalde.

XII. Hu Pompeius feng to Romano anwalde.

XIII. Hu Marcus Antonius feng to Romano anwalde mid Aureliuse his breðer.

XIIII. Hu Lucius feng to Romano anwalde. 10

|XV. Hu Seuerus feng to Romano rice. f. 5

XVI. Hu his sunu feng to rice, Antonius.

XVII. Hu Marcus feng to Romano anwalde.

XVIII. Hu Aurelius feng to Romano anwalde.

XVIIII. Hu Maximus feng to Romano anwalde. 15

XX. Hu Gordianus feng to Romano rice.

XXI. Hu Philippus feng to Romano rice.

XXII. Hu Decius feng to Romano rice.

XXIII. Hu Gallus feng to Romano rice.

XXIII'I'. Hu Romane gesetton ii caseras. 20

XXV. Hu Claudius feng to Romano rice.

XXVI. Hu Aurelius feng to Romana rice.

XXVI'I'. Hu Tacitus feng to Romana rice.

XXVII'I'. Hu Probus feng to Romana rice.

XXIX. Hu Carus feng to Romana rice. 25

XXX. Hu Dioclitianus feng to Romana rice.

XXXI. Hu Constantinus feng to Romana onwalde mid his ii broþrum.

---

1 Galua] galfa C1.　2 Uespasianus] fespassianus C1, uespassianus C2. 5 Nerfa] nerua C1, C2.　8 Aureliuse] aurelius C1, C2.　11 rice] anwalde C1.　15 Maximus] maximianus C2. Romano] roma C2. 16 rice] anwalde C1, anwealde C2.　18 rice] anwealde C2.　19 Gallus] gallius C2.　21 rice] anwealde C2.　23 rice] anwealde C2. 24 Probus] brobus C1.　25 Carus] curus C2. rice] anwealde C2. 26 Dioclitianus] diocitius C2.　27 onwalde] rice C1.

XXXII. Hu Iuuinianus feng to Romana rice.

XXXII'I'. Hu Ualentinianus feng to Romana rice.

XXXII'II'. Hu Ualens feng to Romana rice.

XXXV. Hu Gratianus feng to Romana rice; 7 hu Brettanie namon
5 Maximianum him to casere ofer his willan.

XXXVI. Hu Theodosius 'feng' to Romana onwalde; 7 hu Ualentinianus feng eft to rice.

XXXVI'I'. Hu Archadius feng to Romana rice, 7 Honorius to þam
westrice.

10 XXXVI'II'. Hu God gedyde Romanum his mildsunge.

I. i

f. 5ᵛ |Ure ieldran ealne þisne ymbhwyrft þises middangeardes, cwæþ
Orosius, swa swa Oceanus utan ymbligeþ, þone [mon] garsæcg
hateð, on þreo todældon 7 hie þa þrie dælas on þreo tonemdon:
Asiam 7 Europem 7 Affricam, þeah þe sume men sæden þæt þær
15 nære buton twegen dælas: Asia 7 þæ't' oþer Europe.

Asia is befangen mid Oceano þæm garsecge suþan 7 norþan 7
eastan 7 swa ealne middangeard from þæm eastdæle healfne
behæfð. þonne on ðæm norþdæle, þæt is Asia on þa swiþran
healfe, in Danai þære ie, ðær Asia 7 Europe hiera landgemircu
20 togædre licgað. Ond þonne of þære ilcan ie Danai suþ andlang
Wendelsæs 7 þonne wiþ westan Alexandria þære byrig Asia 7
Affrica togædre licgeað.

Europe hio onginð, swa ic ær cwæþ, of Danai þære ie, seo is
irnende of norþdæle, of Riffeng þæm beorgum, þa sindon neh
25 þæm garsecge þe mon hateð Sarmondisc, 7 seo ea Danai irnð

11–15] OH I. ii. 1.   16–22] OH I. ii. 2–3.   23–p. 9, 10] OH I. ii. 4–7.

---

1 Iuuinianus] iuuianus C1.   rice] anwalde C1.   2 Ualentinianus] ualentinus
C1.   Romana] roma C2.   rice] anwealde C2.   4 Gratianus] gratinianus C2;
rice] anwealde C2.   Brettanie] brittannie C1, brettannie C2.   5 Maximi-
anum] maximum C1, maximianus C2.   6 Theodosius] ðeodosius C1.   on-
walde] rice C2.   6–7 Ualentinianus] ualentinus C1.   7 rice] anwealde C2.
8 Archadius] archiadus C1.   12 utan ymbligeþ] ymbligeð utan C.   mon]
om. L, man C.   14 Europem] europam C.   sæden] orig. sægden, with g er.
L.   15 nære] næran C.   þæt] orig. þær, with 't' above er. r L.   Europe]
europa C.   16 Oceano] oceanus C.   17 ealne] ealne þysne C.
19 hiera landgemircu] om. C.   24 Riffeng] riffing C.

þonan suðryhte on westhealfe Alexandres herga. On in Rochouasco þære þeode heo wyrcð þæt fen þe mon hateð Meotedisc
7 þonne forþ mid micle flode, neah þære byrig þe mon hateð
Theodosia, wið eastan ut on þa sæ floweð þe mon hætt Euxinus, 7
þonne mid longre nearonesse suþ þonan be eastan Constantino- 5
polim Creca byrg ligeð, 7 þonne forþ þonan ut on Wendelsæ. Se
westsuþende Europe landgemirce is in Ispania westeweardum et
ðæm garsecge 7 mæst æt þæm iglande þætte Gaðes hatte (þær sciet
se Wendelsæ up of þæm garsecge, þær eac Ercoles syla stondað
on þæm ilcan Wendelsæ) 7 hire on westende is Scotland. 10

Affrica 7 Asia hiera landgemircu onginnað of Alexandria,
Egypta burge, 7 ligeð þæt londgemære suþ þonan ofer Nilus þa
ea 7 swa ofer Ethiopica westenne oþ þone suþgarsecg, 7 þære
Af'f'rica norþwestgemære | is æt þæm ilcan Wendelsæ þe of ðæm f. 6
garsecge scyt, ðær Ercoles syla stondað, 7 hire ryhtwestende is 15
æt þæm beorge þe mon Athlans nemneð 7 æt þæm iglande þe mon
hæt Fortunatus.

Scortlice ic hæbbe nu gesæd ymb þa þrie dælas ealles þises
middangeardes, ac ic wille nu, swa ic ær gehet, þara þreora
landrica gemære gereccan, hu hie mid hiera wætrum tolicgeað. 20

Asia ongen ðæm middeldæle on þæm eastende, þær ligeð se
muþa ut on þone garsecg þære ie þe mon hateð Gandis; þone
garsecg mon hæt Indisc. Be suþan þæm muþan wið þone garsecg
is se port þe mon hæt Caligardamana, 7 be suþaneastan þæm porte
is þæt igland Deprobane, 7 þonne be norþan þæm Gandes muþan, 25
þær þær Caucasis se beorg endað neh þæm garsecge, þær is se port
Samera; be norþan þæm porte is se muþa þære ie þe mon nemneð
Ottorogorre; þone garsecg mon hæt Sericus.

þæt sint India gemæro þær þær Caucasus se beorg is be norþan,
7 Indus seo ea be westan, 7 seo Reade Sæ be suþan, 7 garsecg be 30
eastan. On Indea londe is xliiii þeoda buton þæm iglande Taprabane, þæt hæfð on him x byrg, buton oðerum monegum gesetenum
iglondum. Of þære ie Indus, þe be westan eallum þæm lande ligeð,

11–17] OH I. ii. 8–11.   18–20] OH I. ii. 12.   21–8] OH I. ii. 13–14.
29–33] OH I. ii. 15.   33–p. 10, 9] OH I. ii. 16–19.

1–2 Rochouasco] uasco *over eras.* L.   9 eac] *om.* C.   10 7 . . . west-
ende] on hyre westende C.   11 Asia] assia C.   13 Ethiopica] æthiopica
C.   20 gereccan] reccan C.   21 middeldæle] middele C.   24 þe
mon hæt] *om.* C.   7] *om.* C.   25 Gandes muþan] gandis se muða C.
28 Ottorogorre] oðcorogorre C.   29 India] indea C.

betux þære ie Indus 7 þære þe be westan hiere is, Tigris hatte, þa
flowað buta suþ on þone Readan Sæ, 7 betux þæm twæm ean
sindon þas land: Arocasia 7 Parthia 7 Asilia 7 Persiða 7 Meðia,
þeh þe gewrito oft nemnen eal þa lond Meðia oþþe Asiria; 7 þa
5 lond sindon swiþe beorhtte, 7 þær sint swiþe scearpe wegas 7
stanihte; þara landa norþgemæro sindon æt ðæm beorgum Caucasus, 7 on suþhealfe se Reada Sæ; 7 on ðæm londe sindon twa micla
ea, Iþaspes 7 Arbis; on ðæm londe is xxxii þeoda. Nu hæt hit mon
eall Parthia.

10 þonne west from Tigres þære ie oþ Eufrates þa ea, þonne betux
þæm ean sindon þas land: Babylonia 7 Caldea 7 Mesopotamia;
f. 6ᵛ binnan þæm landum sindon xxviii ðeoda; heora norðgemæro | sin-
don æt þæm beorgum Tauro 7 Caucaso, 7 hiera suþgemæro
licgeað to þæm Readan Sæ. Ondlong þæs Re[a]dan Sæs, þæs
15 dæles þe þær norþ scyt, ligeð þæt land Arabia 7 Sabei 7 Eudomane.
Of þære ie Eufrate west oþ þone Wendelsæ 7 norþ forneah oþ þa
beorgas þe mon Tauros hæt, oþ þæt land þe mon hæt Armenie, 7
eft suþ oþ Egypte, monege þeoda sindon þæs landes: þæt is, Comagena 7 Fenitia 7 Damascena 7 Coelle 7 Moab 7 Amon 7 Idumei 7
20 Iudea 7 Palestina 7 Sarracene, 7 þeh hit mon hæt eal Syria. þonne
be norþan Syria sindon þa beorgas þe mon Tauros hætt, 7 be
norðan þæm beorgum sindon þa land Capodocia 7 Armenie, 7 heo
Armenia is be eastan Capodotia, 7 be westan Capodocia is þæt
land þe mon hætt seo læsse Asia, 7 be norþan Capodocia is þæt
25 gefilde þe mon hæt Temeseras; þonne betux Capodocia 7 þære
læssan Asiam is þæt land Cilia 7 Issaurio. Seo Asia, on ælce healfe
heo is befangen mid sealtum wætre buton on easthealfe. On
norþhealfe is seo sæ Euxinus, 7 on westhealfe se sæ þe mon hætt
Proponditis 7 Ellaspontus, 7 Wendelsæ be suþan. On þære ilcan
30 Asiam is se hehsta beorg Olimpus.

10-15] OH I. ii. 20-2.   16-20] OH I. ii. 23-4.   20-6] OH I. ii. 25.
26-30] OH I. ii. 26.

2 betux] betweoh C.   3 Arocasia] oracassia C.   Persiða] passiða C.   Meðia]
media C.   4 Meðia] media C.   5 beorhtte] beorhte C.   sint] followed
by eras. (7 þær sint?) L.   6 stanihte] stanige C.   7 se Reada] seo reade C.
8 xxxii] twa 7 twentig C.   10 Tigres] tigris C.   Eufrates] eufrate C.
14 Readan (2)] from C, redan L.   15 Sabei] saben C.   16 Of] ofer
C.   17 Tauros] tauris C.   19 Fenitia] uenicia C.   22 Capodocia]
capadocia C.   23 Capodotia] capadocia C.   Capodocia] capadocia C.
24 Capodocia] capadocia C.   25 Capodocia] capadocia C.   28 se]
seo C.   29 Ellaspontus] ealla spontus C.   30 Olimpus] olimphus C.

Seo Ægyptus þe us near is, be norþan hire is þæt land Palastine,
7 be eastan hiere Sarracene þæt land, 7 be westan hire Libia þæt
land 7 be suþan hire se beorg þe mon hæt Climax. Nilus seo ea
hire æwielme is neh þæm clife þære Readan Sæs, þeah sume men
secgen þæt hire æwielme sie on westende Affrica neh þam beorge 5
Athlans 7 þonne fol raðe þæs sie east irnende on þæt sond 7 þonne
besince eft on þæt sand 7 þær neh sie eft flowende up of þæm
sande 7 þær wyrcð micelne sæ; 7 þær hio ærest up wielð hie hatað
þa landmen Nuchul 7 sume men Dara. Ond þonne of þæm sæ
þær he up of þæm sonde scyt he is east irnende from eastdæle þurh 10
Æthiopica westenne, | 7 þær mon hæt þa ea Ion oþ þone eastdæl,   f. 7
7 þær þonne wyrþ to miclum sæ 7 þær þonne besincð eft in on þa
eorþan 7 þonne eft norþ þonan up aspryngð neh þæm clife wið
þone Readan Sæ, þe hit ær beforan sæde. þonne of þæm æwielme
mon hæt þæt wæter Nilus þa ea, 7 þonne forþ þonan west irnende 15
heo toliþ on twa ymb an igland þe mon hæt Meroen 7 þonan norþ
bugende ut on þone Wendelsæ. þonne on þæm wintregum tidum
wyrþ se muþa fordrifen foran from þæm no[r]þernum windum
þæt seo ea bið flowende ofer eal Ægypta land 7 heo gedeð mid
þæm flode swiþe þicce eorþwæstmas on Ægypta lande. Seo fyrre 20
Ægyptus liþ east ondlong þæs Readan Sæs on suþhealfe 7 on
easthealfe, 7 on suþhealfe þæs landes liþ garsecg, 7 on hire westhealfe is seo us nearre Ægyptus, 7 on þæm twæm Ægyptum sindon
xxiiii þeoda.

Nu hæbbe we awriten þære Asian suþdæl, nu wille we fon to hire 25
norðdæle, þæt is þonne of þæm beorgum þe mon hæt Caucasus,
þe we ær beforan sædon, þa þe be norþan India sindon, 7 hie
onginnað ærest eastane of þæm garsecge 7 þonne licgað westryhte
oþ Armenia beorgas þe þa landleode hi hatað Parcoadras. þær of
þæm beorgum wilþ seo ea suþweard Eufrates, 7 of þæm beorgum 30
þe mon Parcoadras hætt licgeað þa beorgas westryhte þe mon

---

1 Ægyptus] egyptus C.   Palastine] palastine C.   3 þe . . . Climax] ðe
climax hatte C.   6–7 7 þonne (2) . . . sand] om C.   7 neh] om. C.
9 landmen] men C.   10 he (1)] hio C.   scyt] cymð C.   he (2)] heo C.
11 Æthiopica] ethiopica C.   14 hit] ic C.   15 þonan west] west þanon
C.   16 Meroen] mereon C.   18 norþernum] from C, noþernum L.
19 Ægypta] egypta C.   20 Ægypta] egypta C.   21 Ægyptus] egyptus C.
22 7 on suþhealfe] om. C.   23 Ægyptus] egyptus C.   sindon] is C.
25 Asian] asiam C.   26 þe mon hæt] om. C.   27 sædon] spræcon
C.   India] indea C.   29 þe] om. C.   30 Eufrates] eufrate C.

Tauros hætt oþ Cilium þæt lond; þonne be norþan þæm beorgum
ondlang þæs garsecges oþ þone norðeastende þisses middangeardes, þær Bore seo ea scyt ut on þone garsecg, 7 þonan west ondlong þæs garsecges oþ þone sæ þe mon hætt Caspia, þe þær up
5 scyt to þæm beorgum Caucasus, þæt lond mon hætt þa ealdan
Sciþþian 7 Ircaniam. þæs landes is xliii þeoda, wide tosetene for
unwæstmbærnesse þæs londes. þonne be westan þæm sæ Caspia
oð Danais þa ea 7 oþ þæt fenn þe mon hætt Meotedisc 7 þonne
f. 7ᵛ suþ oþ þone Wendelsæ 7 | oþ þone beorg Tauros 7 norþ oþ þone
10 garsecg is eall Sciþþia lond binnan, þeh hit mon tonemne on twa
7 on þritig þeoda. Ac þa lond on easthealfe Danais þe þær nihst
sindon, Albani hi sint genemde in Latina, 7 we hie hataþ nu
Liubene.

Nu hæbbe we scortlice gesæd ymbe Asia londgemæro, nu wille
15 we ymbe Europe londgemære areccean swa micel swa we hit
fyrmest witon.

From þære ie Danais west oþ Rin þa ea, seo wilð of þæm beorge
þe mon Alpis hætt 7 irnð þonne norþryhte on þæs garsecges earm
þe þæt lond uton ymblið þe mon Bryttania hætt, 7 eft suþ oð
20 Donua þa ea, þære æwielme is neah Rines ofre þære ie, 7 is siþþan
east irnende wið norþan Creca lond ut on þone Wendelsæ, 7 norþ
oþ þone garsecg þe mon Cwensæ hæt: binnan þæm sindon monega
þeoda, ac hit mon hæt eall Germania.

þonne wið norþan Donua æwielme 7 be eastan Rine sindon
25 Eastfranc[an], 7 be suþan him sindon Swæfas, on oþre healfe þære
ie Donua, 7 be suþan him 7 be eastan sindon Bægware, se dæl þe
mon Regnesburg hætt, 7 ryhte be eastan him sindon Bæme, 7
eastnorþ sindon þyringa[s], 7 be norþan him sindon Ealdseaxan,
7 be norþanwestan him sindon Frisan. Be westan Ealdseaxum is
30 Ælfe muþa þære ie 7 Frisland, 7 þonan westnorð is þæt lond þe
mon Ongle hæt 7 Sillende 7 sumne dæl Dene, 7 be norþan him is

---

7–13] OH I. ii. 49–50.   14–16] OH I. ii. 51.   17–23] OH I. ii. 52–3.

4 oþ] on C.   8 Danais] donais C.   9 Tauros] taurus C.   11 nihst]
neah C.   12 genemde] genemned C.   13 Liubene] liobene C.   15 lond-
gemære] so L, with second e alt. to o, landgemære C.   areccean] reccan C.
19 Bryttania] bryttannia C.   20 Rines ... ie] þære ea rines C.   21 nor-
þan] om. C.   25 Eastfrancan] from C, eastfrancna L.   26 Bægware]
bægðware C.   27 Bæme] beme C.   28 þyringas] from C, þyringa L.
29 Be] 7 be C.   30. Frisland] frysland C.   31 Ongle] angle C.   Dene]
dena C.

Afdrede 7 eastnorþ Wilte þe mon Hæfeldan hætt, 7 be eastan him
is Wineda lond þe mon hætt Sysyle, 7 eastsuþ, ofer sumdæl,
Maroara; 7 hie Maroara habbað be westan him þyringas 7 Behemas 7 Begware healfe, 7 be suþan him on oþre healfe Donua þære
ie is þæt land Carendre suþ oþ þa beorgas þe mon Alpis hæt; to 5
þæm ilcan beorgan licgað Begwara landgemæro 7 Swæfa. þonne
be eastan Carendran londe, begeonda[n] þæm westenne, is Pul-
gara land, 7 be eastan þæm is | Creca land, 7 be eastan Maroara f. 8
londe is Wisle lond, 7 be eastan þæm sint Datia, þa þe iu wæron
Gotan. Be norþaneastan Maroara sindon Dalamentsan, 7 be 10
eastan Dalamentsan sindon Horigti, 7 be norþan Dalamentsan
sindon Surpe, 7 be westan him Sysyle. Be norþan Horoti is Mægþa
land, 7 be norþan Mægþa londe Sermende oþ þa beorgas Riffen.
Be westan Suþdenum is þæs garsecges earm þe liþ ymbutan þæt
land Brettannia, 7 be norþan him is þæs sæs earm þe mon hæt 15
Ostsæ, 7 be eastan him 7 be norþan sindon Norðdene, ægþer ge
on þæm maran landum ge on þæm iglandum, 7 be eastan him sindon Afdrede, 7 be suþan him is Ælfe muþa þære ie 7 Ealdseaxna
sumdæl. Norðdene habbað be norþan him þone ilcan sæs earm
þe mon hæt Ostsæ, 7 be eastan him sindon Osti þa leode, 7 Afrede 20
be suþan. Osti habbað be norþan him þone ilcan sæs earm 7
Winedas 7 Burgendan, 7 be suþan him sindon Hæfeldan. Burgendan habbað þone sæs earm be westan him 7 Sweon be norþan,
7 be eastan him sint Sermende, 7 be suþan him Surfe. Sweon
habbað be suþan him þone sæs earm Osti 7 be eastan him 25
Sermende, 7 be norþan him ofer þa westenne is Cwenland,
7 be westannorþan him sindon Scridefinne 7 be westan Norþmenn.

Ohthere sæde his hlaforde, Ælfrede cyninge, þæt he ealra Norð-
monna norþmest bude. He cwæð þæt he bude on þæm lande 30

1 Afdrede] apdrede C.　Wilte] wylte C.　Hæfeldan] æfeldan C.　2 sum-
dæl] sumne dæl C.　3 Maroara (1)] maroaro C.　Maroara (2)] maroaro
C.　4 Begware] bægware C.　5 Alpis hæt] hæt alpis C.　6 Begwara]
bægðwara C.　þonne] 7 þonne C.　7 begeondan] *from* C, begeondam L.
8 Maroara] maroaro C.　10 norþaneastan] eastannorðan C.　Dalament-
san] dalamensan C.　11 Dalamentsan (1)] dalamensam C.　Horigti]
horithi C.　Dalamentsan (2)] dalomensam C.　12 Sysyle] sindon sysele C.
Horoti] horiti C.　13 Riffen] riffin 7 C.　15 Brettannia] brittannia
C.　16 be norþan] be norðan him C.　19 be norþan him] him be norðan
C.　20 hæt Ostsæ] ostsæ hæt C.　Afrede] afdræde C.　22–3 Burgen-
dan] burgendas C.　23 þone] þone ylcan C.　26 be norþan him] be
norðan C.　westenne] westennu C.　27 Scridefinne] scridefinnas C.

norþweardum wiþ þa Westsæ. He sæde þeah þæt [þæt] land sie
swiþe lang norþ þonan, ac hit is eal weste, buton on feawum
stowum styccemælum wiciað Finnas, on huntoðe on wintra 7 on
sumera on fiscaþe be þære sæ.

5 He sæde þæt he æt sumum cirre wolde fandian hu longe þæt
land norþryhte læge, oþþe hwæðer ænig mon be norðan þæm
westenne bude. þa for he norþryhte be þæm lande; let him ealne
f. 8ᵛ weg | þæt weste land on ðæt steorbord 7 þa widsæ on ðæt bæcbord
þrie dagas. þa wæs he swa feor norþ swa þa hwælhuntan firrest
10 faraþ. þa for he þa giet norþryhte swa feor swa he meahte on þæm
oþrum þrim dagum gesiglan. þa beag þæt land þær eastryhte,
oþþe seo sæ in on ðæt lond, he nysse hwæðer, buton he wisse ðæt
he ðær bad westanwindes 7 hwon norþan 7 siglde ða east be lande
swa swa he meahte on feower dagum gesiglan. þa sceolde he ðær
15 bidan ryhtnorþanwindes, for ðæm þæt land beag þær suþryhte,
oþþe seo sæ in on ðæt land, he nysse hwæþer. þa siglde he þonan
suðryhte be lande swa swa he mehte on fif dagum gesiglan. Ða
læg þær an micel ea up in on þæt land. þa cirdon hie up in on ða
ea, for þæm hie ne dorston forþ bi þære ea siglan for unfriþe, for
20 þæm ðæt land wæs eall gebun on oþre healfe þære eas. Ne mette
he ær nan gebun land siþþan he from his agnum ham for, ac him
wæs ealne weg weste land on þæt steorbord, butan fiscerum 7
fugelerum 7 huntum, 7 þæt wæron eall Finnas, 7 him wæs a widsæ
on ðæt bæcbord. þa Beormas hæfdon swiþe wel gebud hira land, ac
25 hie ne dorston þæron cuman. Ac þara Terfinna land wæs eal weste,
buton 'ðær' huntan gewicodon, oþþe fisceras, oþþe fugel'er'as.

Fela spella him sædon þa Beormas ægþer ge of hiera agnum
lande ge of þæm landum þe ymb hie utan wæron, ac he nyste hwæt
þæs soþes wæs, for þæm he hit self ne geseah. þa Finnas, him
30 þuhte, 7 þa Beormas spræcon neah an geþeode. Swiþost he for
ðider, toeacan þæs landes sceawunge, for þæm horshwælum, for
ðæm hie habbað swiþe æþele ban on hiora toþum—þa teð hie

---

1 norþweardum] norðeweardum C. þæt (2)] from C, om. L. 8 on ðæt
bæcbord] on bæcbord C. 10 swa feor swa] swa C. 11 gesiglan]
geseglian C. 13 7 (1)] oððe C. siglde] seglede C. ða] þanon C.
14 gesiglan] geseglian C. ðær] om. C. 15 ryhtnorþanwindes] ryhte norðan
windes C. for ðæm] for ðan C. beag þær] þær beah C. 16 siglde]
seglede C. 17 gesiglan] geseglian C. 18 in on (1)] in C. ða] eras. after
a L. 19 siglan] seglian C. 20 eas] ea C. 23 eall] ealle C.
24 Beormas] first stroke of m er. L. gebud] gebun C. 27 Beormas] last
stroke of m er. L. 30 Beormas] first stroke of m. er. L. 31 hors-
hwælum] from C, horschwælum L.

brohton sume þæm cyninge—7 hiora hyd | bið swiðe god to scip- f. 10ᵛ
rapum. Se hwæl bið micle læssa þonne oðre hwalas: ne bið he
lengra ðonne syfan elna lang; ac on his agnum lande is se betsta
hwælhuntað: þa beoð eahta and feowertiges elna lange, 7 þa
mæstan fiftiges elna lange; þara he sæde þæt he syxa sum ofsloge 5
syxtig on twam dagum.

He wæs swyðe spedig man on þæm æhtum þe heora speda on
beoð, þæt is on wildrum. He hæfde þagyt, ða he þone cyningc
sohte, tamra deora unbebohtra syx hund. þa deor hi hatað hranas;
þara wæron syx stælhranas, ða beoð swyðe dyre mid Finnum, for 10
ðæm hy foð þa wildan hranas mid. He wæs mid þæm fyrstum
mannum on þæm lande; næfde he þeah ma ðonne twentig hryðera
7 twentig sceapa 7 twentig swyna, 7 þæt lytle þæt he erede he
erede mid horsan. Ac hyra ar is mæst on þæm gafole þe ða Finnas
him gyldað. þæt gafol bið on deora fellum 7 on fugela feðerum 7 15
hwales bane 7 on þæm sciprapum þe beoð of hwæles hyde geworht
7 of seoles. Æghwilc gylt be hys gebyrdum: se byrdesta sceall
gyldan fiftyne mearðes fell 7 fif hranes 7 an beran fel 7 tyn ambra
feðra 7 berenne kyrtel oððe yterenne 7 twegen sciprapas; ægþer sy
syxtig elna lang: oþer sy of hwæles hyde geworht, oþer of sioles. 20

He sæde ðæt Norðmanna land wære swyþe lang 7 swyðe | smæl. f. 11
Eal þæt his man aþer oððe ettan oððe erian mæg, þæt lið wið ða
sæ; 7 þæt is þeah on sumum stowum swyðe cludig, 7 licgað wilde
moras wið eastan 7 wið uppon, emnlange þæm bynum lande. On
þæm morum eardiað Finnas. 7 þæt byne land is easteweard bradost 25
7 symle swa norðor swa smælre; eastewerd hit mæg bion syxtig
mila brad oþþe hwene brædre, 7 middeweard þritig oððe bradre;
7 norðeweard, he cwæð, þær hit smalost wære, þæt hit mihte beon
þreora mila brad to þæm more, 7 se mor syðþan on sumum stowum
swa brad swa man mæg on twam wucum oferferan, 7 on sumum 30
stowum swa brad swa man mæg on syx dagum oferferan. Ðonne
is toemnes þæm lande suðeweardum, on oðre healfe þæs mores,
Sweoland, oþ þæt land norðeweard; 7 toemnes þæm lande norðeweardum Cwena land. þa Cwenas hergiað hwilum on ða Norðmen
ofer ðone mor, hwilum þa Norðmen on hy, 7 þær sint swiðe micle 35
meras fersce geond þa moras, 7 berað þa Cwenas hyra scypu ofer
land on ða meras 7 þanon hergiað on ða Norðmen; hy habbað
swyðe lytle scypa 7 swyðe leohte.

---

1 bið] *Since the second gathering is now missing from L, the text of 1–p. 28, 11 is
taken from C, with the foliation of Bosworth and Sweet: see Note on the Text.*

Ohthere sæde þæt sio scir hatte Halgoland þe he on bude. He
cwæð þæt nan man ne bude be norðan him. Þonne is an port on
suðeweardum þæm lande þone man hæt Sciringesheal. Þyder he
f. 11ᵛ cwæð þæt man ne mihte geseg|lian on anum monðe, gyf man on
5 niht wicode 7 ælce dæge hæfde ambyrne wind; 7 ealle ða hwile he
sceal seglian be lande; 7 on þæt steorbord him bið ærest Iraland,
7 þonne ða igland þe synd betux Iralande 7 þissum lande; þonne
is þis land oð he cymð to Scirincgesheale, 7 ealne weg on þæt
bæcbord Norðweg. Wið suðan þone Sciringesheal fylð swyðe
10 mycel sæ up in on ðæt land, seo is bradre þonne ænig man ofer
seon mæge, 7 is Gotland on oðre healfe ongean 7 siðða[n] Sillende.
Seo sæ lið mænig hund mila up in on þæt land. 7 of Sciringesheale
he cwæð þæt he seglode on fif dagan to þæm porte þe mon hæt æt
Hæþum, se stent betuh Winedum 7 Seaxum 7 Angle 7 hyrð in on
15 Dene. Ða he þiderweard seglode fram Sciringesheale, þa wæs him
on þæt bæcbord Denamearc 7 on þæt steorbord widsæ þry dagas;
7 þa, twegen dagas ær he to Hæþum come, him wæs on þæt steorbord Gotland 7 Sillende 7 iglanda fela—on þæm landum eardodon
Engle, ær hi hider on land coman—7 hym wæs ða twegen dagas
20 on ðæt bæcbord þa igland þe in Denemearce hyrað.

Wulfstan sæde þæt he gefore of Hæðum, þæt he wære on Truso
on syfan dagum 7 nihtum, þæt þæt scip wæs ealne weg yrnende
under segle. Weonoðland him wæs on steorbord 7 on bæcbord
f. 12 him wæs Langaland 7 Læland 7 Falster | 7 Sconeg, 7 þas land
25 eall hyrað to Denemearcan. 7 þonne Burgenda land wæs us on
bæcbord, 7 þa habbað him sylf cyning. Þonne æfter Burgenda
lande wæron us þas land þa synd hatene ærest Blecingaeg 7 Meore
7 Eowland 7 Gotland on bæcbord, 7 þas land hyrað to Sweon. 7
Weonodland wæs us ealne weg on steorbord oð Wislemuðan. Seo
30 Wisle is swyðe mycel ea 7 hio tolið Witland 7 Weonodland, 7 þæt
Witland belimpeð to Estum, 7 seo Wisle lið ut of Weonodlande
7 lið in Estmere, 7 se Estmere is huru fiftene mila brad; þonne
cymeð Ilfing eastan in Estmere of ðæm mere ðe Truso standeð in
staðe, 7 cumað ut samod in Estmere, Ilfing eastan of Estlande 7
35 Wisle suðan of Winodlande; 7 þonne benimð Wisle Ilfing hire
naman 7 ligeð of þæm mere west 7 norð on sæ: for ðy hit man
hæt Wislemuða.

---

3 þone] þonne MS.   4 ne] m *first written, then alt. to* ne MS.   11 siðððan]
siðða MS.   20 in] 'to' *added in l.h.* MS. *Cf.* 14 in on.   34 Estlande]
eastlande MS.

lian on anum monðe. gyf man on niht picode. ꝛ æl
ce dæge hæfde ambyrne pind. ꝛ ealle ða hƿile he sceal
seglian be lande. ꝛ on þæt steop bopd. him bið ærest
ipa land. ꝛ þonne ða igland. þe synd betux ipa lande
ꝛ þirrum lande. þonne ir þir land oð he cymð to
rcipincg heale. ꝛ ealne peg on þæt bæc bopd. nopð
pegpið ruðan. þone scipingey heal fyld spyðe my
cel pæ. up in onðæt land. seo ir bnaðpe þonne æniz
man ofep seon mæge. ꝛ ir got land on oðpe healfe
ongean. ꝛ ridða pillende. seo pæ lið mæniz hund mi
la up in onþæt land. ꝛ of rcipincgey heale. he cpæð
þ he reglode on fif dagan. to þæm popte þe mon hæt
æt hæþum. se sænt betux pinedum. ꝛ reaxum. ꝛ an
gle. ꝛ hypð in on dene. ða he þidep peapd reglode
fram scipincgey heale. þa pær him on þæt bæc bopd.
dena meapc. ꝛ on þæt steop bopd. pið pæ. þny dagay. ꝛ þa
tpegen dagar ær he to hæþum come. him pær on þæt
steop bopd gotland. ꝛ rillende. ꝛ iglanda fela. on þæ
landum eapdodon engle. ær hi hiðep on land coman.
ꝛ hym þær ða tpegen dagar. on ðæt bæc bopd. þa igland
þe in dene meapce hypað. Pulfrtan ræde þ he ge
fope of hæðum. þæt he þæp pe on truso. on syfan da
gum ꝛ nihtum. þæt þæt scip pær ealne peg ynnende
undep regle. peonoð land him pær on steop bopd.
ꝛ on bæc bopd. him pær langa land. ꝛ læland ɼ falstep

British Library, MS. Cotton Tiberius B. i, f. 13ᵛ (f. 11ᵛ *old foliation*)

þæt Estland is swyðe mycel, 7 þær bið swyðe manig burh, 7 on
ælcere byrig bið cyningc, 7 þær bið swyðe mycel hunig 7 fiscað,
7 se cyning 7 þa ricostan men drincað myran meolc, 7 þa unspedi-
gan 7 þa þeowan drincað medo. þær bið swyðe mycel gewinn
betweonan him. 7 ne bið ðær nænig ealo gebrowen mid Estum, ac 5
þær bið medo genoh. 7 þær is mid Estum ðeaw, þonne þær bið
man dead, þæt he lið inne unforbærned mid his magum 7 freon-
dum | monað ge hwilum twegen, 7 þa kyningas 7 þa oðre heahðun-   f. 12ᵛ
gene men swa micle lencg swa hi maran speda habbað, hwilum
healf gear þæt hi beoð unforbærned 7 licgað bufan eorðan on hyra 10
husum. 7 ealle þa hwile þe þæt lic bið inne, þær sceal beon gedrync 7
plega, oð ðone dæg þe hi hine forbærnað. þonne þy ylcan dæg [þe]
hi hine to þæm ade beran wyllað, þonne todælað hi his feoh, þæt
þær to lafe bið æfter þæm gedrynce 7 þæm plegan, on fif oððe syx,
hwylum on ma, swa swa þæs feos andefn bið. Alecgað hit ðonne   15
forhwæga on anre mile þone mæstan dæl fram þæm tune, þonne
oðerne, ðonne þæne þriddan, oþ þe hyt eall aled bið on þære anre
mile; 7 sceall beon se læsta dæl nyhst þæm tune ðe se deada man
on lið. Ðonne sceolon beon gesamnode ealle ða menn ðe swyftoste
hors habbað on þæm lande, forhwæga on fif milum oððe on syx   20
milum fram þæm feo. þonne ærnað hy ealle toweard þæm feo;
ðonne cymeð se man se þæt swift[ost]e hors hafað to þæm ærestan
dæle 7 to þæm mæstan, 7 swa ælc æfter oðrum, oþ hit bið eall
genumen; 7 se nimð þone læstan dæl se nyhst þæm tune þæt feoh
geærneð. 7 þonne rideð ælc hys weges mid ðan feo 7 hyt motan 25
habban eall, 7 for ðy þær | beoð þa swiftan hors ungefoge dyre.   f. 13
7 þonne hys gestreon beoð þus eall aspended, þonne byrð man
hine ut 7 forbærneð mid his wæpnum 7 hrægle, 7 swiðost ealle
hys speda hy forspendað mid þan langan legere þæs deadan
mannes inne 7 þæs þe hy be þæm wegum alecgað, þe ða fremdan 30
to ærnað 7 nimað. 7 þæt is mid Estum þeaw þæt þær sceal ælces
geðeodes man beon forbærned, 7 gyf þar man an ban findeð
unforbærned, hi hit sceolan miclum gebetan. 7 þær is mid
Estum an mægð þæt hi magon cyle gewyrcan, 7 þy þær licgað
þa deadan men swa lange 7 ne fuliað, þæt hy wyrcað þone 35
cyle hine on, 7 þeah man asette twegen fætels full ealað oððe

1 Estland] eastland MS.   2 fiscað] fisc'n'að *with* 'n' *in l.h.* MS.
12 dæg (2)] e *added in l.h.* MS.   þe (2)] *no reading* MS.   16 forhwæga] æ
prob. original MS.   20 forhwæga] æ *prob. orig. though alt. from* a *cannot be
ruled out.*   22 swiftoste] swifte MS.   26 ungefoge] 'h' *above second* g
in l.h. MS.   34 Estum] eastum MS.

wæteres, hy gedoð þæt oþer bið oferfroren, sam hit sy sumor, sam
winter.

Nu wille we secgan be suðan Donua þære ea ymbe Creca land,
[hu hit] liþ. Wyð eastan Constantinopolim Creca byrig is se sæ
5 Proponditis, 7 be norðan Constantinopolim Creca byrig scyt se
sæearm up of þæm sæ westrihte þe man hæt Euxinus, 7 be westannorðan þære byrig Donua muða þære ea scyt suðeast ut on ðone
sæ Euxinus—7 on suðhealfe 7 on westhealfe þæs muðan sindon
Mæsi, Creca leode—7 be westan þære byrig sindon Traci, 7 be
10 eastan þære byrig Macedonie, 7 be suþan þære byrig, on suðhealfe
f. 13ᵛ þæs sæs earmes | þe man hæt Egeum, sindon Athena 7 Corintus þa
land; 7 be westansuðan Corinton is Achie þæt land æt þæm
Wendelsæ. þas land syndon Creca leode. 7 be westan Achie
*and*lang þæs Wendelsæs is Dalmatia þæt land on norðhealfe þæs
15 sæs, 7 be norðan Dalmatia sindon Pulgare 7 Istria, 7 be suðan
Istria is se Wendelsæ þe man hæt Atriaticum, 7 be westan þa
beorgas þe man hæt Alpis, 7 be norðan þæt westen þæt is betux
Carendan 7 [P]ulgarum.

þonne is Italia land westnorðlang 7 eastsuðlang, 7 hit belið
20 Wendelsæ ymb eall utan buton westannorðan. Æt þæm ende hit
belicgað ða beorgas þe man hæt Alpis: þa onginnað westane fram
þæm Wendelsæ in [N]arbonense þære ðeode 7 endiað eft east in
Dalmatia þæm lande æt þæm sæ.

þa land þe man hæt Gallia Bellica, be eastan þæm is sio ea þe
25 man hæt Rin, 7 be suðan þa beorgas þe man hæt Alpis, 7 be
westansuðan se garsecg þe man hæt Brittanisca, 7 be norðan on
oðre healfe þæs garsegges earme is Brittannia þæt land. Be westan
Ligore is Aequitania land, 7 be suþan Æquitania is þæs landes
sumdæl Narbonense, 7 be westansuðan Ispania land, 7 be westan
30 garsegc. Be suðan Narbonense is se Wendelsæ, þær þær Rodan
seo ea utscyt, 7 be eastan him Profentsæ, 7 be westan him ofer ða
f. 14 westenu seo us nearre Ispania, 7 be westan him 7 | norðan Equi-
tania, 7 Wascan be norðan. Profentse hæfð be norðan hyre þa
beorgas þe man Alpis hæt, 7 be suðan hyre is Wendelsæ, 7 be
35 norðan hyre 7 eastan synd Burgende, 7 Wascan be westan.

3–18] OH I. ii. 54–60.　　　19–23] OH I. ii. 61–2.　　　24–35] OH I. ii.
63–8.

---

4 hu hit] *om.* MS.　　　18 Pulgarum] fulgarum MS.　　　22 in Narbonense]
innrbonense, *with second* n *alt. to* a MS.　　　31 him (2)] him profentsæ MS.

Ispania land is þryscyte 7 eall mid fleote utan ymbhæfd, ge eac
binnan ymbhæfd ofer ða land ægþer ge of þæm garsecge ge of ðam
Wendelsæ. An ðæra garena lið suðwest ongean þæt igland þe
Gades hatte, 7 oþer east ongean þæt land Narbonense, 7 se ðridda
norðwest ongean Brigantia Gallia burh 7 ongean Scotland ofer 5
ðone sæs earm, on geryhte ongean þæne muðan þe mon hæt
Scene. Seo us fyrre Ispania, hyre is be westan garsecg 7 be norðan,
Wendelsæ be suðan, 7 be eastan seo us nearre Ispania; be norðan
þære synt Equitania, 7 be norðaneastan is se weald Pireni, 7 be
eastan Narbonense, 7 be suðan Wendelsæ.   10
Brittannia þæt igland, hit is norðeastlang, 7 hit is eahta hund
mila lang 7 twa hund mila brad. þonne is be suðan him on oðre
healfe þæs sæs earmes Gallia Bellica, 7 on westhealfe on oþre
healfe þæs sæs earmes is Ibærnia þæt igland, 7 on norðhealfe
Orcadus þæt igland. Igbernia, þæt we Scotland hata ð, hit is on 15
ælce healfe ymbfangen mid garsecge, 7 for ðon þe sio sunne þær
gæð near on setl þonne on oðrum lande, þær syndon lyðran wedera
þonne on Brettan|nia. þonne be westannorðan Ibernia is þæt f. 14ᵛ
ytemeste land þæt man hæt Thila, 7 him is feawum mannum cuð
for ðære oferfyrre.   20
Nu hæbbe we gesæd ymbe ealle Europe landgemæro, hu hi
tolicgað. Nu wille we ymbe Affrica [secgan], hu ða landgemæro
tolicgað. Ure yldran cwædon þæt hio wære se ðridda dæl þyses
middangeardes: næs na for ðam þe þæs landes swa fela wære, ac
for ðam þe se Wendelsæ hit hæfð swa todæled, for ðan þe he brycð 25
swiðor on ðone suðdæl þonne he do on þone norðdæl, 7 sio hæte
hæfð genumen þæs suðdæles mare þonne se cyle þæs norðdæles
hæbbe, for ðon þe ælc wiht mæg bet wyð cyle þonne wið hæte.
For ðam þingon is Affrica ægþer ge on landum ge on mannum
læsse ðonne Europe.   30
Affrica onginð, swa we ær cwædon, eastan westwerd fram
Egyptum æt þære ee þe man Nilus hæt. þonne is sio eastemeste
þeod haten Libia Cirimacia. Hire is be eastan sio us nearre Aegyptus, 7 be norðan Wendelsæ, þe man hæt Libia Æthiopicum, 7 be
westan Syrtes Maiores. Be westan Libia Æthiopicum is sio us 35

1–10] OH I. ii. 69–75.   11–15] OH I. ii. 76–8.   15–18] OH I. ii. 80–1.
18–20] OH I. ii. 79.   21–2] OH I. ii. 82.   23–30] OH I. ii. 83–6.
31–p. 20, 2] OH I. ii. 87–9.

22 secgan] *no reading* MS.

fyrre Ægyptus, 7 be suðan se garsecg þe man hæt Æthiopicus, 7
be westan Rogathitus.

Tribulitania sio þiod, þe man oðre naman hæt Arzuges, hio
4 hæfð be eastan hyre þone Sirtes Maiores 7 Rogathite þa land, 7 be
f. 15 norðan þone Wendelsæ þe man hæt | Adriaticum 7 þa þeode þe
man hæt Sirtes Minores, 7 be westan Bizantium, oþ þone sealtan
mere, 7 be suðan hyre Natabres 7 Geothulas 7 Garamantes, oð
ðone garsegc.

Bizantium sio þiod, þær se[o] b[u]rh is Adrumetis, 7 Seuges sio
10 þiod, þær sio mycle burh is Cartaina, 7 Numedia sio þeod, hi
habbað be eastan him þæt land Syrtes Minores 7 þone sealtan
mere, 7 be norðan him is Wendelsæ, 7 be westan him Mauritania,
7 be suðan him Uzera þa beorgas, 7 be suðan þam beorgum þa
simbelfarendan Æthiopes oð ðone garsecg. Mauritania, hyre is
15 be eastan Numedia 7 be norðan Wendelsæ 7 be westan Malua sio
ea 7 be suðan Astrix[i]m ða beorgas, þa todælað þæt wæsmbære
land 7 þæt deadwylle sand þe syþþan lið suð on þone garsecg.
Mauritania þe man oþre naman hæt Tingetana, be eastan hyre is
Malua sio ea 7 be norðan Abbenas þa beorgas 7 Calpis, oþer beorh.
20 þær scyt se ende up of þam garsecge betuh þan twam beorgum
eastweard, þær Ercoles syla standað, 7 be westan him is se beorh
Athlans, oð ðone garsecg, 7 [be westan]suþan ða beorgas þe
man hæt Æsperos, 7 be suðan him Aulolum sio þiod, oð ðone
garsecg.

25 Nu hæbbe we ymb Affrica landgemæro gesæd, nu wille we
f. 15ᵛ secgan ymb þa ygland þe on þa[m] Wendelsæ | sindon. Cipros
þæt igland, hit lið ongean Cilicia 7 Issaurio on þam sæs earme þe
man hæt Mesicos 7 hit is an hund mila lang 7 fif 7 hundsyfantig,
7 an hund mila brad 7 twa 7 twentig. Creto þæt igland, him is be
30 eastan se sæ þe man Arfatium hæt, 7 westan 7 be norðan Creticum
se sæ, 7 be westan Sicilium, þe man oðre naman hæt Addriaticum;
hit is an hund mila lon[g] 7 hundsyfantig, 7 fiftig mila brad. Ðara
iglanda þe man hæt Ciclades, þara sindon þreo 7 fiftig, 7 be eastan

---

3–8] OH I. ii. 90.　　9–14] OH I. ii. 91–2.　　14–26] OH I. ii. 93–5.
26–p. 21, 2] OH I. ii. 96–8.

---

3 þiod] i *alt. to* e *in l.h. here and in a number of other instances* MS.　　9 seo
burh] se beorh MS.　　Seuges] seuges 7 MS.　　sio (2)] i *alt. to* e *in l.h. here and
in several other instances* MS.　　16 Astrixim] astrix ymb MS.　　22 be
westansuþan] suþan MS.　　25 landgemæro] landgemærco MS.　　26 þam]
þa MS.　　32 long] lond MS.

him is se [Ica]risca sæ, 7 be suðan se Cretisca, 7 be norðan se
Egisca, 7 be westan Addriaticum. Sicilia þæt igland is ðryscyte.
On ælces sceatan ende sindon beorgas. þone norðsceatan man
hæt Polores, þær is seo burh neah Mesana, 7 se suðsceata hatte
Bachinum, þær neah is sio burh Siracussana, 7 þone westsceatan 5
man hæt Libeum, þær is seo burh neah þe man hæt Libeum, 7 hit
is an hund 7 syfan 7 fiftig mila lang, suð 7 norð, 7 se þridda sceata
is an hund 7 syfan 7 hundsyfantig westlang. 7 be eastan þæm
lande is se Wendelsæ þe man hæt Adriati[c]um, 7 be suþan þ[e]
man hæt Affricum, 7 be westan þe man hæt Tirenum, 7 be norðan 10
is se sæ þe ægþer is ge nearo ge hreoh, wið Italia þam lande.
Sardina 7 Corsica þa igland todæleð an lytel sæs earm, se is twa
7 twentig mila brad. Sardina is þreo 7 þritti mila lang 7 twa | 7 f. 16
twentig mila brad. Him is be eastan se Wendelsæ þe man hæt
Tirrenum, þe Tiber sio ea ut scyt on, 7 be suðan se sæ þe lið 15
ongean Numedia lande, 7 be westan þa twa igland þe man hæt
Balearis, 7 be norðan Corsica þæt igland. Corsica him is Romeburh
be eastan 7 Sardine be suðan, 7 be westan þa igland Balearis, 7 be
norðan Tuscania þæt land; hit is syxtene mila lang 7 nygan mila
brad. Balearis þa tu igland, him is be [suðan] Affrica, 7 Gades be 20
westan, 7 Ispania be norðan. Scortlice hæbbe we nu gesæd be þæm
gesetenum iglandum þe on ðæm Wendelsæ sindon.

I. ii

Ær ðæm ðe Romeburh getimbred wære þrim hund wintra 7
þusend wintra, Ninus, Asyria kyning, ongan manna ærest ricsian
on ðysum middangearde. 7 mid ungemætlicre gewilnunge anwaldes 25
he wæs heriende 7 feohtende fiftig wintra, oð he hæfde ealle Asiam
on his geweald genyd suð fram þæm Readan Sæ 7 swa norð oþ
þone sæ þe man hæt Euxinus, butan þæm þe he eac oftrædlice for
mid miclum gefeohtum on Sciððie þa norðland, þa ðe gecwedene
syndon ða heardestan men, þeah hy syn on þyson woroldgesælþon 30
þa unspedgestan. 7 hy ða, under ðæm þe he him on winnende
wæs, wurdon gerade wigcræfta, þeah hi ær hyra lif bylwetlice

2–11] OH I. ii. 99–100.   12–22] OH I. ii. 101–5.   23–p. 22, 7] OH I.
iv. 1–3.

1 Icarisca] risca MS.   9 Adriaticum] adriatium MS.   þe (2)] þam MS.
20 suðan] norðan MS.   22 gesetenum] gesetenessum MS.   32 gerade]
gerade 'an' with 'an' in l.h. MS.

f. 16ᵛ alyfden; 7 hy him æfter þæm grimme for|guldon þone wigcræft
þe hy æt him geleornodon; 7 him ða wearð emleof on hyra mode
þæt hi gesawon mannes blod agoten swa him wæs þara nytena
meolc þe hy mæst bi libbað. And he Ninus Soroastrem Bactriana
5 cyning, se cuðe manna ærest drycræftas, he hine oferwann 7 ofsloh
7 þa æt nyhstan he wæs feohtende wið Sciððie on ane burh 7 þær
wearð ofscoten mid anre flane.

   7 æfter his deaðe Sameramis his cwen fengc ægþer ge to þæm
gewinne ge to þæm rice, 7 hio þæt ylce gewin þe hio hine on
10 bespon mid manigfealdon firenlustum twa 7 feowertig wintra wæs
dreogende. 7 hyre þagyt to lytel þuhte þæs anwaldes ðe se cyningc
ær gewunnen hæfde. Ac hio mid wiflice niðe wæs feohtende on
þæt underiende folc Æthiopiam 7 eac on Indeas, þa nan man ne
ær ne syððan mid gefeohte ne gefor buton Alexander. Hio wæs
15 wilniende mid gewinnum þæt hio hy oferswiðe, ða hio hit
ðu[r]hteon ne mihte. Sio gitsung þa 7 þa gewin wæron grimlicran
þonne hy nu syn, for ðon hy hyre nane bysene ær ne cuðan swa
men nu witon, ac on bilwitnesse hyra lif alyfdon.

   Seo ylce cwen Sameramis, syððan þæt rice wæs on hyre ge-
20 wealde, nales þæt an þæt hio ðyrste[n]de wæs on symbel mannes
blodes, ac eac swelce mid ungemetlicre wrænnesse manigfeald
f. 17 geligre fremmende wæs, swa þæt ælcne þara þe hio | geacsian
myhte þæt kynekynnes wæs, hio to hyre gespon for hyre geligernesse, 7 syððan hio hy ealle mid facne beswac to deaðe. 7 þa æt
25 nehstan hyre agene sunu hio genam hyre to geligere, 7 for ðon þe
hio hyre firenluste fulgan ne moste butan manna bysmrunge, hio
gesette ofer eall hyre rice þæt nan forbyrd nære æt geligere betwuh
nanre sibbe.

I. iii

   Ær ðam ðe Romeburh getimbred wære þusend wintra 7 an
30 hund 7 syxtig, þæt wæstmbære land on þæm Sodome 7 Gomorre
ða byrig on wæron, hit wearð fram heofonlicum fyre forbærned,
þæt wæs betuh Arabia 7 Palestina. Ða manigfealdan wæstmas

8–18] OH I. iv. 4–6.   19–28] OH I. iv. 7–8.   29–p. 23, 11] OH I. v. 1
and 6–10.

---

16 ðurhteon] ðuhteon *with* 'r' *added in l.h.* MS.   wæron] 'þe' *added in l.h.*
MS.   20 ðyrstende] ðyrstede MS.

wæron for þam swiþost ðe Iordanis seo ea ælce geare þæt land
middeweard oferfleow mid fotes þicce flode, 7 hit þonne mid ðam
gedynged wearð. þa wæs þæt folc þæs micclan welan ungemetlice
brucende, oð ðæt him on se miccla firenlust oninnan aweox.
7 him com of þæm firenluste Godes wraco, þæt he eal þæt land mid 5
sweflenum fyre forbærnde, 7 seððan ðær wæs standende wæter
ofer þam lande, swa hit þære ea flod ær gefleow; 7 þæs dæles se
dæl se þæt flod ne grette ys gyt todæg wæstmberende on ælces
cynnes blædum; 7 ða syndon swyþe fægere 7 lustsumlice on to
seonne, ac þonne hig man on hand nymð, þonne weorðað hig to 10
acxan.

I. iv

Ær ðæm ðe Romeburh ge|timbred wære þusend wintra 7 f. 17ᵛ
hundsyfantig, Thelescises 7 Ciarsathi þa leode betuh him gewin
up hofon, 7 þæt drugon oþ hi mid ealle ofslegene wæron butan
swiðe feawum. 7 swa þeah þæt þær to lafe wearð þara Thelescisa 15
hi hiora land ofgeafan 7 geforan Roðum þæt igland, wilniende þæt
hi ælcum gewinne oðflogen hæfdon. Ac hi Creacas þær onfundon
7 hi mid ealle fordydon.

I. v

Ær ðam ðe Romeburh getimbred wære eahta [hund] wintra, mid
Egyptum wearð syfan gear se ungemetlica eorðwela, 7 hi æfter 20
ðæm wæron on þan mæstan hungre oðre syfan gear. 7 him ða
Ioseph, rihtwis man, mid godcunde fultume gehealp. From ðæm
Iosepe Sompeius se hæþena scop 7 his cniht Iustinus wæran ðus
singende—Ioseph, se þe gin[g]st wæs hys gebroðra 7 eac gleawra
ofer hi ealle—þæt, him ða ondrædendum þæm gebroðrum, hy 25
genamon Ioseph 7 hine gesealdan cipemonnum, 7 hi hine gesealdon
in Egypta land. þa sæde he Pompeius þæt he þær drycræftas
geleornode, 7 of þæm drycræftum þæt he gewunode monigc
wundor to wyrcenne, 7 þæt he mihte swa wel swefn reccan, 7 eac
þæt he of ðæm cræfte Pharaone þæm cyninge swa leof wurde. 30
7 he sæde þæt he of þæm drycræfte geleornode godcundne wisdom,

12–18] OH I. vii. 1–2.   19–p. 24, 15] OH I. viii. 1–5, 7, and 9.

19 hund] *in l.h. on eras.* MS.   24 gingst] ginst MS.   27 Pompeius]
first p *er. and replaced by* s *in l.h.* MS.

f. 18 þæt he þæs landes wæstmbærnesse þara syfan | geara ær beforan
sæde 7 þara oþera syfan geara wædle þe þæræfter com, 7 hu
[he] gegaderode on þan ærran syfan gearan mid hys wisdome,
þæt he þa æfteran syfan gear eall þæt folc gescylde wið þone
5 miclan hungor. 7 sæde þæt Moyses wære þæs Iosepes sunu, þæt
him wæran fram hym drycræftas gecynde, for ðon þe he monige
wundor worhte in Egyptum. 7 for þæm wole þe on þæt land becom,
se scop wæs secgende þæt Egypti adrifen Moyses ut mid hys
leodum. For ðon sæde Pompeius 7 þa Egyptiscan bisceopas þæt
10 þa Godes wundor þe on hiora landum geworden wæron [wæron]
to þon gedon þæt hi hiora agnum godum getealde wæron, þæt sint
diofolgild, nales þam soþan Gode, for ðon þe hiora godu syndon
drycræfta lareowas. 7 þæt folc nugyt þæt tacn Iosepes gesetnesse
æfterfylgeað: þæt is, þæt hi geara gehwilce þone fiftan dæl ealra
15 hiora eorðwæstma þæm cyninge to gafole gesyllað.

Wæs se hunger on þæs cyninges dagum on Egyptum þe mon
hæt Amoses, þeah ðe hiora þeaw wære þæt hi ealle hiora cyningas
hetan Pharaon. On ðære ylcan tide ricsade Baleus se cyning in
Assirin, þær ær wæs Ninus. On þæm leodum þe mon Argi hæt
20 ricsade Apis se cyningc. On þære tide næs na ma cyninga anwalda
butan þysan þrim ricum. Ac syþþan wæs sio bysen of him ofer ealle
world. Ac þæt is to wundrianne þæt þa Egipti swa lytle þoncunge
f. 18ᵛ wiston Iosepe þæs þe he hi | æt hungre ahredde, þæt hi hys cyn
swa raðe geunaredon 7 hy ealle to nydlingum him gedydon. Swa
25 eac is gyt on ealre þysse worulde: þeah God langre tide wille
hwam hys willan to forlætan, 7 he þonne þæs eft lytelre tide
þolige, þæt he sona forgyt þæt god þæt he ær hæfde 7 geðencð
þæt yfel þæt he þonne hæfð.

I. vi

Ær ðæm ðe Romeburh getimbred wære eahta hund wintra 7
30 tyn gearan, ricsode Ambictio se cyning in Athena, Creca byrig. He
wæs se þridda cyning þe æfter Cicrope þæm cyninge ricsade, þe
ærest wæs þære burge cyning. On þæs Ambictiones tide wurdon
swa mycele wæterflod geond ealle world 7 þeah mæst in Thasalia,

16–28] OH I. viii. 10–14.   29–p. 25, 6] OH I. ix. 1–2.

3 he] 'he' in l.h. MS.   7 wole] wolde MS.   9 Pompeius] first letter
(p?) er. and replaced by s in l.h. MS.   10 wæron (2)] no reading MS.
28 þonne] þonnne MS.

Creca byrig, ymb þa beorgas þe man hæt Parnasus, þær se cyning
Theuhaleon ricsode, þæt forneah eall þæt folc forwearð, 7 se
cyningc Theuhale[on] ealle þa þe to him mid scypum oðflugon to
þæm beorgum he hi þær onfengc 7 hi þær afedde. Be þæm
Theuhaleon wæs gecweden, swilce mon bispel sæde, þæt he wære 5
moncynnes tydriend, swa swa Noe wæs.

On þæm dagum wæs se mæsta mancwealm in Æthiopian,
Affrica leode, swa þæt heora feawa to lafe wurdon. Eac on þæm
dagum wæs þæt Liber Pater oferwan þa underigendan Indea
ðeode 7 hi forneah mid ealle fordyde, ægþer ge mid druncennysse 10
ge mid firenlustum ge mid manslyhtum, | þeah hi hine eft æfter f. 19
hys dæge heom for god hæfdon 7 hy sædon þæt he wære ealles
gewinnes waldend.

I. vii

Ær ðam ðe Romeburh getimbred wære eahta hund wintra 7 fif
wintrum, gewearð þæt Moyses lædde Israhela folc of Egyptum 15
æfter þæm manegum wundrum þe he þær gedon hæfde. þæt wæs
þæt forme þæt hyra wæter wurdon to blode. þa wæs þæt æfterre
þæt froxas comon geond eall Egypta land, swa fela þæt man ne
mihte nan weorc wyrcan, ne nanne mete gegyrwan, þæt þara wyrma
nære emfela þæm mete, ær he gegearwod wære. þridde yfel wæs 20
æfter þam þæt gnættas comon ofer eall þæt land, ge inne ge ute,
mid fyrsmeortendum bitum 7 ægþær ge þa men ge ða nytenu
unaablinnendlice piniende wæron. þa wæs þæt feorðe, þæt ealra
scamlicost wæs, þæt hundes fleogan comon geond eall þæt mancyn
7 hy crupon þæm mannum betuh þa þeoh ge geond eall þa limu, 25
swa hyt eac well gedafenode þæt God ða mæstan ofermetto
geniðrode mid þære bismerlicestan wrace 7 þære unweorðlicostan.
þæt fif[te] wæs hyra nytena cwealm. þæt syxte wæs þæt eall
[þæt] folc wæs on blædran, 7 þa wæron swiðe hreowlice berstende
7 þa worms utsionde. þæt syfeðe wæs þæt þær com hagol se wæs 30
wið fyre gemenged, þæt he ægþer sloh ge ða menn ge ða nytenu,
ge eall þæt on þæm lande wæs | weaxendes 7 growendes. þæt f. 19ᵛ

7–13] OH I. ix. 3–4.   14–p. 26, 11] OH I. x. 1 and 10–13.

3 Theuhaleon] on *in l.h. on eras.* MS.   12 heom] *alt. from* hiom MS.
20 gegearwod] d *on alt.* MS.   28 fifte] fif *alt. to* fifte *in l.h.* MS.
29 þæt] *no reading* MS.   30 worms] 'v' *above* o *in l.h.* MS.

eahtoðe wæs þæt gærstapan comon 7 fræton ealle þa gærsciðas
þe bufan þære eorðan wæron, ge furðon þa wyrttruman sceorfende wæron. þæt nygoðe wæs þæt þær com hagol 7 swa mycel
þysþernes, ge dæges ge nihtes, 7 swa gedrefedlic, þæt hit man ge-
5 felan mihte. þæt teoðe wæs þæt ealle ða cnihtas 7 ealle ða mædena
þe on þæm lande [frumcennede] wæron wurdon on anre niht
acwealde, 7 þeah þæt folc nolde ær Gode abugan, hy hwæðre þa
hyra unðances him gehyrsume wæron: swa swyðe swa hi ær
Moyse 7 hys folce þæs utfæreldes wyrndon, swa micle hy wæron
10 geornran þæt hi him fram fulgen. Ac seo hreowsung þe him þa
gewearð [wearð] swyðe raðe on wyrsan geþanc gehwyrfed.

Hrædlice se cyningc þa mid his folce him wæs æfterfylgende, 7
hy gecyrran wolde eft to Egyptum. Se kyningc Pharon hæfde syx
hund wigwægna, 7 swa fela þæs oðres heres wæs þæt man mæg
15 þanon oncnawan, þa him swa fela manna ondredon swa mid
Moyse wæron: þæt wæs syx hund þusenda manna. Hwæðre God
þa miclan Pharones menge gelytlode 7 hyra ofermætan ofermetto
genyðerode; 7 beforan Moyse 7 hys folce he ðone Readan Sæ on
twelf wegas adrigde, þæt hi drigan fotan þæne sæ oferferdon. þa
20 þæt gesawon þa Egypte, hy ða getrymedon hyra dryas Geames
f. 20 7 Mambres 7 getruwedon mid hyra drycræftum þæt hi | on ðone
ilcan weg feran meahtan. Ða hi ða oninnan þæm sæfærelde wæron,
þa gedu[r]fon hi ealle 7 adruncon. þæt tacn nugyt is orgyte on
þæs sæs staðe, hwær þara wigwægna hweol on gongende wæron.
25 þæt deð God to tacne eallum monkynne þæt þeah hit wind oððe
sæs flod mid sonde oferdrifen, þæt hit ðeah bið eft swa gesyne
swa hit ær wæs.

On þære tide wæs sio ofermycelo hæto on ealre worulde: nales
þæt an þæt men wæron miclum geswencte, ac eac ealle nytenu
30 swyðe neah forwurdon. 7 ða suðmestan Æthiopian hæfdon bryne
for ðære hæte, 7 Sciþþie þa norðmestan hæfdon ungewunelice
hæton. þa hæfdon monige unwise menn him to worde 7 to
leasungspelle þæt sio hæte nære for hiora synnum, ac sædon þæt
hio wære for Fetontis forscapunge, anes mannes.

12–27] OH I. x. 14–17.   28–34] OH I. x. 19.

---

2 wyrttruman] gærsciðas 7 þa wyrttruman MS.   6 frumcennede] 'frum-
cennede' in l.h. MS.   9 utfæreldes] s alt. from l MS.   11 wearð] no
reading MS.   18 folce] folce 7 MS.   23 gedurfon] gedu fon with letter
er. before f MS.

I. viii

Ær ðæm ðe Romeburh getimbred wære syx hund wintran 7 fif, in Egyptum wearð on anre niht fiftig manna ofslegen, ealle fram hiora agnum sunum; 7 ealle ða men comon fram twam gebroðran. þa þis gedon wæs, þa gyt lyfedan ða gebroðra. Se yldra wæs haten Danaus, þe þæs yfeles ordfruma wæs. Se wearð of his rice adræfed, 5 7 on Arge þæt land he fleonde becom. 7 his se cyning þær Tenelaus mildelice onfeng; þeah [he] hit him eft mid yfele forgulde, þa he hine of his rice adræfde.

On þæm | dagum on Egyptan wæs þæs kyninges þeaw Bosiriðis f. 20ᵛ þæt ealle þa cuman þe hine gesohton he to blote gedyde 7 hys 10 godum bebead. Ic wolde nu, cwæð Orosius, þæt me ða geandwyr- dan þa þe secgað þæt þeos world sy nu wyrse on ðysan cristendome þonne hio ær on þæm hæþenscype wære, þonne hi swylc geblot 7 swylc morð donde wæron swylc her ær beforan sæde. Hwær is nu on ænigan cristendome betuh him sylfum þæt mon him þurfe 15 swilc ondrædan, þæt hine mon ænigum godum blote? oððe hwær syndon ure godas þe swylcra mana gyrnen swilce hiora wæron?

On þæm dagum Perseus se cyningc of Creca lande in Asiam mid fyrde for 7 on ða ðeode winnende wæs oþ hi him gehyrsume wæron, 7 þære þeode oþerne naman ascop be him syluum, swa hi mon 20 syððan het Persi.

Ic wat geare, cwæð Orosius, þæt ic his sceal her fela oferhebban, 7 þa spell þe ic secge ic hi sceal gescyrtan, for ðon þe Asyrie hæfdon lx wintra 7 an hund 7 an þusend under fiftiga cyninga rice, þæt hit na buton gewinne næs oþ þæt Sarðanopolim ofslegen 25 wearð, 7 se anwald siððan on Mæðe gehwearf. Hwa is þæt þe eall ða yfel þe hi donde wæron asecgean mæge oððe areccean? Eac ic wille geswigian Tontolis 7 Philopes þara scondlicestena spella; hu manega bismerlica gewin Tontolus gefremede syððan he cyningc wæs; ymb þone cniht þe he neadinga genam | Ganemeþis; 7 hu 29 he his agenne sunu his godum to blote acwealde 7 hine him sylf f. 21 siððan to mete gegyrede. Eac me sceal aðreotan ymbe Philopes 7 ymbe Tardanus 7 ymb ealra þara Troiana gewin to asecgenne,

---

1–8] OH I. xi. 1.   9–11] OH I. xi. 2.   18–21] OH I. xi. 4.
22–p. 28, 11] OH I. xii. 1–10.

---

7 he (1)] 'he' *in l.h.* MS.   14 swylc (2)] 'ic' *added in l.h.* MS.   24 fiftiga] fiftigan MS.

for ðon on spellum 7 on leoðum hiora gewin cuðe sindon. Ic
sceall eac ealle forlætan þa þe of Perseo 7 of Cathma gesæde
syndon, 7 eac þa ðe of Thebani 7 of Spartani gesæde syndon. Eac
ic wille geswigian þara mandæda þara Lemniaðum, 7 Ponthionis
5 þæs cyninges, hu hreowlice [he] wearð adræfed of Othinentium
his agenre þeode; 7 Atregsas 7 Thigesþres, hu hi heora fæderas
ofslogan, 7 ymb hiora hetelican forlignessa, ic hit eall forlæte. Eac
ic hit forlæte, Adipsus hu he ægþer ofsloh ge his agenne fæder,
ge his steopfæder, ge his steopsunu. On þæm dagum wæron swa
10 u[n]gemetlica yfel þæt þa men sylf sædon þæt hefones tungul
hiora yfel flugon.

I. ix

f. 17 | Ær ðæm þe Romeburg getimbred wære siex hunde wintrum 7
lxgum, wearð þæt ungemetlice mic[le] gefeoht betuh Cretense
7 Atheniense þæm folcum, 7 þa Cretense hæfdon þone grimlecan
15 sige, 7 ealle þa æðel'e'stan bearn þara Atheniensa hi genoman, 7
sealdon þæm Minotauro to etanne, þæt wæs healf mon, healf leo.
On ðæm dagum wæs þætte Lapithe 7 Thesali wæron winnende
him betweonum. þonne þa Lapithe gesawon Thesali þæt folc of
hiora horsum beon feohtende wið hie, þonne heton hi hie Centauri
20 —þæt sindon healf hors, healf men—for þon hie on horse feohtan
ne gesawen ær þa.

I. x

Ær þæm þe Romeburg getimbred wære iiii hu'n'de wintrum 7
hundeahtatigum, Uesoges, Egypta cyning, wæs winnende of
suðdæle Asiam, oð him se mæsta dæl wearð underþieded. 7 he
25 Uesoges, Egypta cyning, wæs siþþan mid firde farende on Sciþþie
on ða norðdælas, 7 his ærendracan beforan asende to þære ðeode,
7 him untweogendlice secgan het þæt hie [oðer] sceolden, oþþe
ðæt lond æt him alesan, oþþe he hie wolde mid gefeohte fordon 7

12–16] OH I. xiii. 1–2.   17–21] OH I. xiii. 3–4.   22–p. 28, 13] OH I. xiv. 1–4.

---

5 he] 'he' in l.h. MS.   10 ungemetlica] utgemetlica MS.   12 Ær]
MS L resumes here.   siex hunde] gloss sexaginta in l.h. L.   13 micle]
micel L, mycle C.   15 æðelestan] 'e' in l.h. L.   17 þætte] þæt here and
subsequently C.   Lapithe] laphite C.   Thesali] i on eras.? L.   18 Lapithe]
laphite C.   þæt] þæt 'þæt' L.   20 for þon] for ðon þe C.   horse] horse
'hie' L.   21 gesawen] gesawan C.   24 oð] oððe C.   27 oðer]
from C, eras. (ð. r?) L.

forherigan. Hie him þa gesceadwislice *ond*wyrdon, 7 cwædon þæt
hit gemalic wære 7 unryhtlic þæt swa oferwlenced cyning sceolde
winnan on swa earm folc swa hie wæron. Heton him þeh þæt
*ond*wyrde secgan, þæt him leofre wære wið hiene to feohtanne
þonne gafol to gieldanne. Hie þæt gelæstan swa, 7 sona þone cyning 5
gefliemdon mid his folce, 7 him æfterfolgiende wæron, 7 ealle
Ægypte awestan buton þæm fenlondum anum, 7 þa hie hamweard
wendon be westan þære ie Eufrate, ealle Asiam hie genieddon
þæt hie him gafol guldon, 7 þær wæron fiftene gear þæt lond
herigende 7 westende, oð heora wif him sendon ærendracan æfter 10
| 7 him sædon þæt hie oðer dyden, oðþe ham comen oððe hie f. 17ᵛ
him woldon oðerra wera ceosan. Hi þa þæt lond forleton 7 him
hamweard ferdon.

On þære ilcan tide wurdon twegen æþelingas afliemde of Sciþþian, Plenius 7 Scolopetius wæron hatene, 7 geforan þæt lond 15
7 gebudon betuh Capadotiam 7 Pontum neah þære læssan Asian,
7 þær winnende wæron oð hie him þær eard genamon, 7 hie ðær
æfter hrædlice tide from þæm londleodum þurh seara ofslægene
wurdon. þa wurdon hiora wif swa sarige on hiora mode 7 swa
swiðlice gedrefed, ægþær ge þara æþelinga wif ge þara oþerra 20
monna þe mid him ofslægene wæron, þætte 'hie' wæpna naman,
to þon ðæt hie heora weras wrecan þohton, 7 hi þa hrædlice æfter
þæm ofslogan ealle þa wæpnedmen þe him on neaweste wæron.
For þon hie dydon swa þe hie woldon þætte þa oþere wif wæren
emsarige him, þæt hie siþþan on him fultum hæfden, ðæt hie ma 25
mehten heora weras wrecan. Hi þa þa wif ealle togædere gecirdon
7 on ðæt folc winnende wæron 7 þa wæpnedmen sleande, oð hie
þæs londes hæfdon micel on hiora onwalde. þa under þæm gewinne
hie genamon friþ wið þa wæpnedmen, siþþan wæs hiera þeaw þæt
hie ælce geare ymbe twelf monað tosomne ferdon 7 þær þonne 30
bearna striendon. Eft þonne þa wif heora bearn cendon, þonne
feddon hie þa mædencild 7 slogon þa hysecild. 7 þæm mæden-
cildum hie fortendun þæt swiðre breost foran þæt hit weaxan ne
sceolde, þæt hie hæfden þy strengran scyte. For þon hi mon hæt
on Crecisc Amazanas, þæt is on Englisc fortende. 35

14–35] OH I. xv. 1–3.

2 gemalic] gemahlic C.   7 Ægypte] Egypte C.   14–15 Sciþþian] scyððian
C.   15 geforan] a *alt. from* o L.   16 Asian] asiam C.   17 oð] oþ þe C.
22 wrecan] *alt. from* wræcan L.   34 hæt] het C.   35 Crecisc] creacisc C.
Amazanas] *from* C, amazasanas L.

Heora twa wæron heora cwena, Marsepia 7 Lampida wæron
hatene: hie heora here on tu todældon, oþer æt ham beon heora
f. 18 lond | to healdanne, oðer ut faran to winnanne. Hie siþþan geeodon
Europe 7 Asiam þone mæstan dæl 7 getimbredon Effesum þa burg
5 7 monege oðere on ðære læssan Asiam, 7 siþþan hiera heres þone
mæstan dæl ham sendon mid hiora herehyþe, 7 þone oþerne dæl
þær leton þæt lond to healdonne. þær wearð Marsepia sio cwen
ofslagen, 7 micel þæs heres þe mid hiere beæftan wæs. Ðær wearð
hire dohtor cwen Sinope. Seo ilce cwen Sinope toeacan hiere
10 hwætscipe 7 hiere monigfealdum duguþum hiere lif geendade on
mægðhade.

On þæm dagum wæs swa micel ege from ðæm wifmonnum
þætte Europe ne Asiam ne ealle þa neahþeoda ne mehton aþencean
ne acræftan hu hi him wiðstondan mæhten, ær þon hie gecuron
15 Ercol þone ent þæt he hie sceolde mid eallum Creca cræftum
beswican; 7 þeah ne dorste he geneðan þæt he hie mid firde
gefore, ær he ongan mid Creca scipun þe mon dulmunus hætt, þe
mon sægð þæt on an scip mæge an þusend manna; 7 þa nihtes on
ungearwe hi on bestæl 7 hie swiþe forslog 7 fordyde, 7 hwæðere
20 ne mehte hie þæs londes benæman. On ðæm dagum þær wæron
twa cwena, þæt wæron gesweostor, Anthiopa 7 Orithia, 7 þær
wearð Orithia gefangen. Æfter hiere feng to ðæm rice Pentesilia,
sio on þæm Troianiscan gefeohte swiþe mære gewearð.

Hit is scondlic, cwæð Orosius, ymb swelc to sprecanne hwelc
25 hit þa wæs, þa swa earme wif 7 swa elðeodge hæfdon gegan þone
cræftgestan dæl 7 þa hwatestan men ealles þises middangeardes,
þæt wæs Asiam 7 Europe, þa hie forneah mid ealle aweston 7 ealda
ceastra 7 ealde byrig towurpon, 7 æfter ðæm hie dydon ægþer ge
29 cyninga ricu settan ge niwu ceastra timbredon, 7 ealle þa worold
f. 18ᵛ on hiora agen gewill on|wendende wæron folneah c wintra, 7 swa
gemune men wæron ælces broces þætte hie hit folneah to nanum
facne ne to nanum laðe næfdon þætte þa earman wifmen hie swa
tintredon, 7 nu, þa ða Gotan coman of þæm hwatestan monnum
Germania, þe ægðer ge Pirrus se reða Creca cyning, ge Alexander,

1–11] OH I. xv. 4–6.   12–23] OH I. xv. 7, 8, and 10.   24–p. 31, 21] OH
I. xvi. 1–4.

4 Europe] europam C.   13 Asiam] asia C.   15 Creca] creaca C.
17 Creca] creaca C.   21 þæt] þa C.   25–32 wif . . . earman] om. C.
34 Creca] creaca C.

ge Iulius se cræftega casere, hie alle from him ondredon þæt hi
hie mid gefeohte [sohte]. Hu ungemetlice ge Romware bemurciað
7 besprecað þæt eow nu wyrs [s]ie on þiosan cristendome þonne
þæm þeodum þa wære, for þon þa Gotan eow hwon oferhergedon
7 iowre burg abræcon 7 iower feawe ofslogon, 7 for hiora cræftum 5
7 for hiora hwætscipe iowra selfra anwaldes eoweres unþonces
habban mehton, þe nu lustlice sibbsumes friðes 7 sumne dæl
[landes] æt eow biddende sindon, to þon þæt hie eow on fultume
beon moten, 7 hit ær þiosan genog æmettig læg 7 genog weste,
7 ge his nane note ne hæfdon. Hu blindlice monege þeoda sprecað 10
ymb þone cristendom þæt hit nu wyrse sie þonne hit ær wære,
þæt hie nellað geþencean oþþe ne cunnon, hwær hit gewurde ær
þæm cristendome, þæt ænegu þeod oþre hiere willum friþes bæde,
buton hiere þearf wære, oþþe hwær ænegu þeod æt oþerre mehte
frið begietan, oððe mid golde, oððe mid seolfre, oþþe mid ænige 15
feo, buton he him underþiedd wære. Ac siþþan Crist geboren wæs,
þe ealles middangeardes is sibb 7 frið, nales þæt an þæt men hie
mehten aliesan mid feo of þeowdome, ac eac þeoda him betweonum
buton þeowdome gesibbsume wæron. Hu wene ge hwelce sibbe
þa weras hæfden ær þæm cristendome, þonne heora wif swa 20
monigfeald yfel donde wæron on þiosan middangearde?

I. xi

Ær þæm þe Romeburg getimbred wære feower hunde [wintrum]
7 xxxgum wintra, gewearð þætte Alexander, Priamises sunu | þæs f. 19
cyninges, of Troiana þære byrig, genom þæs cyninges wif Monelaus, of Læcedemonia, Creca byrig, Elena. Ymb hie wearð þæt 25
mære gewinn 7 þa miclan gefeoht Creca 7 Troiana, swa þætte
Crecas hæfdon m scipa þara miclana dulm[u]na, 7 him betweonum
gesworan þæt hie næfre noldon on cyþþe cuman ær hie hiora
teonan gewræcen. 7 hi ða x gear ymbe þa burg sittende wæron 7
feohtende. Hwa is þætte ariman mæge hwæt þær moncynnes for- 30
wearð on ægðere hand? þæt Omarus se scop sweotelicost sægde.

22–p. 32, 8] OH I. xvii. 1–3.

2 gefeohte sohte] *from C,* gefeohten L.   bemurciað] bemurcniað C.   3 wyrs
sie] *from* C, wyrsie L.   8 landes] *from* C, *om.* L.   10 ne hæfdon]
næfdon C.   15 ænige] ænigan C.   16 underþiedd] underðeoded C.
22 wintrum] wintran C, *no reading* L.   25 Creca] creaca C.   26 Creca]
creaca C.   27 Crecas] creacas C.   dulmuna] *from* C, dulmana L.
29 gear] *followed by eras.* L.   31 Omarus] omerus C.

For þon nis me þæs þearf, cwæð Orosius, to secgenne, for þon hit
longsum is 7 eac monegum cuð. þeah swa hwelcne mon swa lyste
þæt witan, ræde on his bocum hwelce ungetina 7 hwelce tibernessa
[hie dreogende wæron] ægðer ge on monslihtum ge on hungre ge
5 on scipgebroce ge on mislicre forscapunge, swa mon on spellum
sægð. þa folc him betweonum ful x winter þa gewin wraciende
wæron. Geþence þonne þara tida 7 nu þissa, hwæ'ð'r[e him bet
licien]!

þa sona of þæm gefeohte wæs oþer æfterfylgende. Eneas mid
10 his firde for of þæm Troianiscan gefeohte in Italiam. þæt mæg
mon eac on bocum sceawigean, hu monega gewin 7 hu monega
gefeoht he ðær dreogende wæs.

I. xii

Ær þæm þe Romeburg getimbred wære lxiiiigum wintra, ricsade
Sarda'no'polus se cyning in Asiria, þær Ninus se cyning ærest
15 ricsade. 7 Sardanopolus wæs se siðmesta cyning þe on ðæm londe
ricsade. He wæs swiþe furþumlic mon, 7 hnesclic 7 swiþe wræne,
swa þæt he swiðor lufade wifa gebæro þonne wæpnedmonna.
þæt þa onfunde Arbatus his ealdormon, þe he gesett hæfde ofer
Meðas ðæt lond. He angan sierwan mid þæm folce þe he ofer wæs,
20 hu he hiene beswican mehte, 7 aspon him from ealle þa þe he
ondred ðæt him on fyl's'te beon woldon. þa se cyning ðæt an-
f. 19ᵛ funde, | þæt him mon geswicen hæfde, he ða hiene selfne for-
bærnde, 7 siþþan hæfdon Mæðe onwald ofer Asirie. Hit is unieðe
to gesecgenne hu monege gewin siþþan wæron betuh Mæðum 7
25 Caldeum 7 Sciððian. Ac þæt mon mæg witan, þonne swa ofer-
mætlicu ricu onstyrede wæron, hu monege missenlice moncweal-
mas on ðæm gewinnum gewurdon.

Æfter þæm ricsade Fraortes se cyning in Meðen. Æfter þæm
Fraorte ricsade Diocles, se Mæðe rice swiðe gemiclade. Æfter
30 Diocle feng Astiai to rice, se næfde nan'ne' sunu. Ac he nam his

9–12] OH I. xviii. 1.   13–27] OH I. xix. 1–3.   28–p. 33, 12] OH I. xix. 4–8.

3 hwelce ungetina] hwilc ungetima C.   4 hie . . . wæron] *no reading* MSS.
6 ful] fulle C.   wraciende] wrecende C.   7–8 hwæðre . . . licien]
hwæ'ð'ran L, hwæþer him bet lycian C.   10 Troianiscan] troaniscan C.
14 Sardanopolus] sarda'nopo'polus *with* 'nopo' *in l.h.* L, sarþanapolus
C.   15 Sardanopolus] sarðanapolus C.   24 gesecgenne] secgenne C.
27 gewinnum] gewinne C.   29 Mæðe] mæþa C.   30 Diocle] ðam
diocle C.

nefan him to suna of Persan þære þeode, Cirus wæs haten. Se þa,
mid ðon þe he geweox, him þa ofþyncendum 7 ðæm Perseum
þæt hie on his eames anwalde wæron 7 on þara Meða, ac hie gewin
uphofan. He þa Ast[i]ai se cyning beþohte swiðost to Arpelles his
ealdormenn, þæt he mid his cræfte his nefan mid gefeohte wið- 5
stode; for þon ðe se cyning ne gemunde þara monigra teonena þe
hiora ægðer oþrum on ærdagum gedyde; 7 hu se cyning het his
sunu ofslean, 7 hiene siþþan þæm fæder to mete gegierwan, þeh
heora gewinn þa gesemed wære. He þa se ealdormon mid firde for
ongean þæm Perseum, 7 sona þæs folces þone mæstan dæl fleonde 10
mid ealle forlædde, 7 mid sea'r'we þæm Perseo cyninge on onwald
gedyde, 7 on þæm gefeohte Meða cræft 7 heora duguð gefeoll.

þa se cyning þæt facn anfunde þe se ealdormon wiþ hiene gedon
hæfde, he þeah gegaderade þone fultum þe he þa mæhte 7 wið
þæm nefan fird gelædde. 7 he Cirus Persea cyning hæfde þriddan 15
dæl his firde beæftan him, on þæt gerad, gif ænig wære þe fyr
fluge þe on ðæm gefeohte wæs þonne to þæm folce þe þær
beæftan wæs, þæt hine mon sloge swa raðe swa mon hiora fiend
wolde. þa þ'e'ahhwæ'ð're gebyrede him þæt hie hwæthwara
gebugan to fleonne. Hi þa hiera wif him ongean iernende [wæron] 20
7 hie swiþe torn|wyrdon, 7 acsedon, gif hie feohtan ne dorsten, f. 20
hwider hie fleon woldon; þæt hie oðer gener næfden, buton hie
on heora wifa hrif gewiton. Hi þa hrædlice, æfter þæm þe þa wif
hie swa scondlice geræht hæfdon, gewendan eft ongean þone
cyning 7 ealne his here gefliemdon 7 hiene selfne gefengon. He þa 25
Cirus ageaf þæm cyninge his eame ealle þa are þe he ær hæfde,
buton ðæt he cyning nære; 7 he þæt wæs eall forsacende, for þon
þe him Arpellas se ealdormon ær to beswice wearð mid his agenre
þeode. Ac him Cirus his nefa gesealde Ircaniam þa þeode on
anwald to habbanne. Ðær wearð Mæðe onwald geendod. Ac Cirus 30
mid Perseum to ðæm anwalde feng. Ac þa byrig þe on monegum
þeodum Mæðum ær gafol guldon wurdon Ciruse to monegum
gefeohtum.

On ðæm dagum wilnade sum æðeling to ricsianne in Argentine
þære ðeode, Falores wæs haten. He wæs of Si'ci'lia þæm londe, 35

13–33] OH I. xix. 8–11.   34–p. 34, 14] OH I. xx. 1–4.

1 Persan] *alt. to* persam *in l.h.* L.   4 Astiai] *from* C, astai L.   12 Meða]
mæþa C.   15 Persea] persa C.   20–1 wæron 7] 'waeron' *in l.h.* L, *om.* C.
30 Mæðe] *both MSS.* Cirus] i *alt. from* u *by eras.* L.   35 Sicilia] cilicia C.

7 mid ungemetlicre pi[n]unge he wæs þæt folc cwielmende, to
ðon þæt hie him anbugen. Ða wæs þær sum argeotere, se mehte
don missenlica anlicnessa. He þa se geotere gebead þæm æðelinge,
for ðon he him cweman þohte, þæt he him æ`t´ ðære pinunge
5 fylstan wolde þe he ðæm folce donde wæs. He þa swa dyde, 7
geworhte anes fearres anlicnesse of are, to ðon, þonne hit hat wære
7 mon þa earman men oninnan don wolde, hu se hlynn mæst wære,
þonne hie þæt susl þæron þrowiende wæron; 7 eac þæt se æþeling
ægðer hæfde, ge his plegan ge his gewill, þonne he þara manna
10 tintrego oferhierde. þa þæt þa onhæt wæs 7 eall gedon swa se
geotere þæm æðelinge ær behet, se æðeling þæt þa sceawode 7
cwæð þæt þæm weorce nanum men ær ne gerise bet to fandianne
þonne þæm wyrhtan þe hit worhte; het hiene þa niman 7 ðæron
bescufan.
15   For hwi besprecað nu men þas cristnan tida, 7 secgað þæt nu
wyrsan tida sien þonne þa wæren, þa, þeh þe hwa wære mid þæm
f. 20ᵛ cyningum on hiora gewill | yfel donde, þæt hie swa þeah æt him
ne mehton mid þy nane are findan? 7 nu cyningas 7 caseras, þeah
þe hwa wið hiora willan gegylte, hie ðeah for Godes lufan be ðæs
20 gyltes mæþe forgifnesse doð.

I. xiii

Ær þæm þe Romeburg getimbred wære xxx wintra, wæs þætte
Pelopensium 7 Atheniensium, Creca þeoda, mid eallum hiera
cræftum him betweonum winnende wæron, 7 hie to ðon swiðe
forslagene wurdon on ægþere hand, þæt hiera feawa to lafe wurdon.
25 On þære ilcan tide wæron eft oðre siþe þa wifmen winnende on
Asiam þe ær on Sciþþian wæron, 7 hie swiðe awestan 7 forhergedan.

I. xiiii

Ær þæm þe Romeburg getimbred wære xxgum wintrum, Læcedemoniæ 7 Mesiane, Creca leode, him betweonum winnende
30 wæron xx wintra, for þon Mesiane noldon ðæt Læcedemonia

15–20] OH I. xx. 6.   21–7] OH I. xxi. 1–2.   28–p. 35, 18] OH I. xxi. 3–8.

---

1 pinunge] *from* C, pi/unge L.   4 for ðon] forðon þe C.   15 be-
sprecað] beswicað C.   16 þeh þe] þeah C.   18–19 þeah þe] þeah C.
22 Atheniensium] athenientium C.   Creca] creaca C.   28–9 Læcedemoniæ]
læcedemonie C.   29 Creca] creaca C.

ffeldon de · ⁊ hie sƿa þeah æt him ne mehton mid þy nane
aɼie findan · ⁊ nu ᵹɼininᵹaɼ ⁊ caɼthaɼ þeah þe hƿa ƿið hiopu
pillan ᵹeᵹɼице · hie deah foɼᵹodþ laɼun be dæᵹ eɼ ицeɼ meþe
foɼ iᵹɼniþɼe doð :⁊

XIII· Æft þam þe hie me buɼᵹ ᵹ шmb þɼed ƿæɼe · xxx · ƿin tɼa
Ƿɼiɼ þæt te þelo þh ɼ ɼiшm · ⁊ æц hiɼ niɼi ɼ uiɼ ɼ ɼieca þɼoda
mid eallū hiɼ nu ɼpaɼ ш him be ipið nū ƿin иɼ nde paɼ
þon · ⁊ hie иdon ɼpið e · ɼoɼ ɼlaᵹ ɼne ƿuɼidon · on uцþ ne hand
⁊ hiɼ na ɼeaɼɼa tola ɼe ƿuɼidon · On þaɼie ilcan цide þaɼ hon
ɼæc odɼie ɼiþe þaɼiɼ meɼi ƿinn иide · on aɼiam þe иɼon ɼeiþ
þɼan ƿaɼ hon · ⁊ hie ɼpið e apɼɼ иn ⁊ þon hth ᵹ edan :⁊

XIIII· Æft þan þe hie me buɼiᵹ ᵹ иmb ƿɼed ƿæɼie · xx · ᵹшm ƿin иpɼū
Laцed ɼinoniᵹ · ⁊ miɼ iane ɼ hiecu læþde him be иpið nū ƿin
nɼ иde þaɼ hon · xx · ƿin иɼiu foɼ þon miɼ iane noldon dū.
Laцed ɼimonia mæᵹ þɼi in þnū mid hшpu oɼfɼied þɼi ⁊ hɼo
ƿaᵹodū on ɼiaᵹ þɼu · þaц · ни h frū hie hæᵹ þɼi ᵹ ин ᵹ ɼ eal
ɼhieca ɼole иdaɼ ᵹ ƿinnū þali ɼɼedɼ ino ria be ɼiцan þa
buɼiᵹ mɼɼ· x · ƿinc · ⁊ adaɼ ᵹ ɼ ɼo ɼan · ⁊ hie niɼiɼ ɼie nol
don æц ham ɼimun uþ hie ɼæц ᵹ ɼ ɼ ɼ iɼ n h ɼ þɼi · þaɼie
don hihim be иpið nū · ⁊ ɼpæd on þæц hi e иoɼiade poldɼi
ɼ ucū lea ɼe bion æц h шpu bea ɼan цumū þali иdaɼ ɼ ɼ a lonᵹ
doли иon bɼon ne · ⁊ þ mid lin ɼ iu þ ɼ n odū ᵹ ɼ æɼц nod hæᵹ þon
⁊ þæц hi h шpu ɼ ɼ n odū bɼæ ɼide þon þɼiɼ mid þæ ᵹ ɼ ɼ æþon
þaɼ þaþe uɼi uц hɼ иn nbu in nuɼ uɼ þ þaham ᵹ læи don ⁊ hi
eallū h шpa ɼiɼ цū beaɼna ɼɼ иɼ don · ⁊ þn oɼ ɼ ie ƿiц ude
þ иan ɼimb þabuɼiᵹ · oð hihie ᵹ ƿinn ɼ ie hæᵹ þon · þeah hie
hi lɼ иe hƿile ᵹ hiɼ ɼ ɼ ume ƿuɼ ion · и иoᵹe ɼu ƿon him
an ne ɼ ɼop иo ɼ iminᵹe oɼ æц hiɼ niɼ i ɼ ɼ m · ⁊ þæц mid ɼiɼ ide
ɼo ɼ an ƿiþ иam ɼ ɼ ие · þa hihi neal ɼ lиuп þaᵹ иp иude hie
hɼ иðɼ hie ɼið hi melиæ ɼ ɼe hшpa ɼiminᵹ on ᵹ anda

mægdenmenn mid heora ofreden 7 heora godum onsægden. þa
æt nihstan hie hæfden getogen eal Creca folc to ðæm gewinnum,
þa Læcedemonia besætan þa burg Mæse x winter 7 aðas gesworan
þæt hie næfre noldon æt ham cuman ær hie þæt gewrecen hæfden.
þa redon hi him betweonum, 7 cwædon þæt hie to raðe wolden 5
fultumlease beon æt heora bearnteamum, þa hi ðær swa longe
ðohton 'to' beonne, 7 þæt mid hiera we[d]dum gefæstnod hæfdon,
7 þæt hi heora feondum bet dyde þonne wyrs mid þæm. Gecwædon
þa þæt þa þe ær æt þæm aþum næren, þæt þa ham gelendon 7 bi
eallum heora wifum bearna striendon 7 þa oðere sittende wæran 10
ymb þa burg, oð hi hie gewunnene hæfdon, þeah hie him lytle
hwile gehiersume wæron. Ac gecuron him anne scop to cyninge
of Atheniensem 7 eft mid firde foran wiþ þa Messene. þa hi him
nealæhtan, þa getweode hie hwæðer hie wið him mæhten. Se heora 14
cyning ongan ða | singan 7 giddian 7 mid þæm scopleoðe heora   f. 21
mod swiðe getrymede, to þon þæt hie cwædon þæt hie Mesiana
folce wiðstondan mehten. [Heora] þeh wurdon feawa to lafe on
aðre hand, 7 þæt Creca folc fela geara him betweonum dreogende
wæron, ægþer ge of Læcedemonia, ge of Mesiane, ge of Boetium,
ge of Atheniensium; 7 monege oþera þeoda to ðæm ilcan gewinne 20
getugon.

Nu is hit scortlice ymbe þæt gesægd þætte ær gewearð ær
Romeburg getimbred wære, þæt wæs from frymðe middangeardes
feower þusend wintra 7 feower hund 7 twa 7 hundeahtatig, 7 æfter
þæm þe hio getimbred wæs, wæs ures Dryhtnes acennes ymb 25
seofon hund wintra 7 vtiene. Her en[d]aþ sio forme boc 7 onginð
sio æfterre.

II. i

Ic wene, cwæð Orosius, þæt nan wis mon ne sie, buton he genoh
geare wite þætte God þone ærestan monn ryhtne 7 godne gesceop,
7 eal monncynn mid him. Ond for þon þe he þæt god forlet þe him 30

18–21] OH I. xxi. 9–16.   22–7] OH I. xxi. 20–1.   28–p. 36, 11] OH
II. i. 1–4.

2 Creca] creaca C.   3 Læcedemonia] læcedemonian C.   Mæse] 'ian'
added in l.h. L.   5 redon] ræddan C.   7 weddum] from C, wendum
L.   11 oð] oððe C.   14 getweode] getweonode C.   17 Heora]
from C, no reading L.   18 Creca] creaca C.   20 Atheniensium]
athenientium C.   22 ær (2)] Rouen quotation begins.   23 þæt wæs]
om. R.   middangeardes] weron agane R.   24 feower (2)] feor R.   25 þæm]
þe R.   26 vtiene] alt. from ytiene L, ytiene R, tyne C. R ends.   endaþ]
from C, enðað L.

geseald wæs 7 wyrse geceas, hit God siþþan longsumlice wrecende
wæs, ærest on him selfum 7 siþþan on his bearnum gind ealne
þisne middangeard mid monigfealdum brocum 7 gewinnum, ge
eac þas eorþan, þe ealle cwice wyhta bi libbað, ealle hiere wæstm-
5 bæro [he] gelytlade. Nu 'we' witan þæt ure Dryhten us gesceop,
we witon eac þæt he ure reccend is 7 us mid ryhtlicran lufan lufað
þonne ænig mon. Nu we witon þæt ealle onwealdas from him
sindon, we witon eac þæt ealle ricu sint from him, for þon ealle
onwealdas of rice sindon. Nu he þara læssena rica reccend is, hu
10 micle swiþor wene we þæt he ofer þa maran sie, þe on swa unmetlican onwealdun ricsedon!

An wæs Babylonicum, þær Ninus ricsade. þæt oðer wæs Creca,
f. 21ᵛ þær Alexander ricsade. þridda wæs Affricanum, | þæ[r] Ptolome
ricsedon. Se feorða is Romane, þe giet ricsiende sindon. þas
15 feower heafodricu sindon on feower endum þyses middangeardes
mid unasecgendlicre Godes tacnunge. þæt Babylonicum wæs þæt
forme 7 on easteweardum. þæt æfterre wæs þæt Crecisce 7 on
norðeweardum. þæt þridde wæs þæt Affricanum 7 on suðwear-
dum. þæt feorþe is Romane 7 on westeweardum. Babylonisce þæt
20 æreste 7 Romane þæt siðmeste hie wæron swa fæder 7 sunu.
þonne hie heora willan moton wel wealdan, þæt Crecisce 7 þæt
Affri[c]anisce wæron swa swa hie him hiersumedon 7 him underþieded wære. þæt ic wille eac gescadwislecor gesecgean þæt hit
mon geornor ongietan [mæge].

25 Se æresta cyning wæs Ninus haten, swa we ær beforan sægden.
þa hiene mon ofslog, þa feng Sameramis his cwen to þæm rice 7
getimbrede þa burg Babylonie, to þon þæt heo wære heafod ealra
Asiria; 7 hit fela wintra siþþan on þæm stod, oð ðæt Arbatus,
Meþa ealdormon, Sardanopolum Babylonia cyning ofslog. þa
30 wearð Babylonia 7 Asiria anwald geendad 7 gehwearf on Meðas.
On þæm ilcan geare þe þiss wæs, Procos, Numetores fæder, ongon
ricsian in Italia þæm londe, þær eft Romeburg getimbred wearð.
Se Procos wæs Numetores fæder 7 Mulieses 7 wæs Siluian eam.

12–24] OH II. i. 4–6.　　25–p. 37, 4] OH II. ii. 1–4.

5 he] 'he' *in l.h.* C, *om.* L.　　6 ryhtlicran lufan] rihtlican þingan C.
10–11 unmetlican] ungemetlicum C.　　12 Creca] creaca C.　　13 þær (2)]
from C, þæp L.　　Ptolome] phtolome C.　　14 þe] þa *alt. to* þæ C.
15 heafodricu] heafodlicu ricu C.　　on] *om.* C.　　endum] endas C.　　18–19 suð-
weardum] suðeweardum C.　　22 Affricanisce] *from* C, affrianisce L.
24 ongietan] agytan C.　　mæge] *from* C, *om.* L.　　26 ofslog] sloh C.　　29 Sar-
danopolum] sarðanapolum C.

Seo Siluie wæs R[e]muses modor 7 Romules, þe Romeburg
getimbredon. Ðæt wille ic gecyþan, þæt þa ricu of nanes monnes
mihtum swa gecræftgade 'ne' wurdon, ne for nanre wyrde buton
from Godes gestihtunge.

Ealle stærwriteras secgað þæt Asiria rice æt Ninuse begunne 7   5
Romana rice æt Procose begunne. From ðæm ærestan geare
Ninuses rices oðþæt Babylonia burg getimbred wæs, wæron lxiiii
wintra; | eac of ðæm ilcan geare þe Procos ricsade in Italia wæron   f. 22
eac swilce lxiiii wintra, ær mon Romeburg getimbrede. þy ilcan
geare þe Romana rice weaxan ongann ond miclian, on Procos dæge   10
þæs cyninges, þy ilcan geare gefeoll Babylonia 7 eall Asiria rice 7
hiora anwald, æfter þæm ðe mon heora cyning ofslog Sardanopolum. Siþþan hæfdon Caldei þa lond gebun on freodome þe
nihst þære byrig wæron, þeh þe Mæðe hæfden þone anwald ofer
hie, oðþæt Cirus, Persea cyning, rics'i'an ongann 7 ealle Babylonia   15
aweste 7 ealle Asirie 7 ealle Mæþe on Persa anwald gedyde. þæt
þa swa gelomp ðætte on þære ilcan tide þe Babylonia ðiowdome
onfeng from Ciruse ðæm cyninge, þætte Roma aliesed wearð of
þeowdome þara unryhtwisestana cyninga 7 þara ofermodgestana,
þe mon hæt Tarcuinie; 7 ða ðæt eastrice in Asiria gefeoll, þa eac   20
þæt westrice in Roma aras.

Giet scæl ic, cwæð Orosius, monigfealdlecor sprecan wiþ þa þe
secgað þæt þa anwaldas sien of wyrda mægenum gewordene, nales
of Godes gestihtunge. Hu emnlice hit gelomp ymb ðas tu heofodricu, Asiria 7 Romana, swa swa we ær sægdon, þætte Ninus   25
ricsade on ðon eastrice lii wintra, 7 æfter him his cwen Sameramis
xlii wintra, 7 on middeweardum hire rice hio getimbrede Babylonia þa burg. From þæm geare þe heo getimbred wearð, wæs hire
anwald m wintra 7 c 7 lx 7 folnæh feower, ær hio hiere anwaldes
benumen wurde 7 beswicen from Arbate hiere agnum ealdormenn   30
7 Meþa cyninge; þeh þe siðþan ymbe þa burg lytle hwile freodom
wære buton onwalde, swa we ær sægdon, from Caldei þæm leodum.
Swa eac swilce wearð Romeburg ymb m wintra 7 c 7 lx 7 folneah
feower, þætte Alrica hiere ealdormon 7 Gotona cyning hiere

5–21] OH II. ii. 4–10.   22–p. 38, 9] OH II. iii. 1–4.

1 Remuses] romuses L, semuses C.   5 begunne] letter er. after first n L.
12–13 Sardanopolum] sarðanopolum C.   14 þeh þe] þeah C.   15 Persea]
persa C.   18 Roma] romana C.   20 hæt] het C.   21 Roma]
romana C.   30 hiere] hyra C.   31 þeh þe] þeah C.   33 Swa]
7 swa C.   34 Alrica] eallrica C.

f. 22ᵛ onwaldes hie beniman woldon, 7 heo | hwæþere onwealg on hiere
onwalde æfter þurhwunade. þeh þe ægþer þissa burga þurh Godes
diegelnessa þus getacnod wurde—ærest Babylonia þurh hiere
agenne ealdormon, þa he hiere cyning beswac, swa eac Roma, þa
5 hi hiere agen ealdormonn 7 Gotona cyning hiere anwaldes ben'i'man
woldon—hit þeh God for heora cristendome ne geþafode, naþer
ne for heora caseras ne for heora selfra, ac hie nugiet ricsiende
sindon ægþer ge mid hiera cristendome ge mid hiora anwalde ge
mid hiera caserum.

10 þis ic sprece nu for ðæm þe ic wolde þæt þa ongeaten þe þa
tida ures cristendomes leahtriað, hwelc mildsung siþþan wæs,
siþþan se cristendom wæs, 7 hu monigfeald wolbærnes ðære
worulde ær þæm wæs; 7 eac þæt hie oncnewen hu gelimplice ure
God on þæm ærran tidum þa anwaldas 7 þa ricu sette, se ilca 'se'
15 þe giet settende is 7 wendende ælce onwaldas 7 ælc rice to his
willan. Hu gelice onginn þa twa byrg hæfdon, 7 hu gelice heora
dagas wæron, ægðer ge on [ðæm] gode ge on ðæm yfele! Ac hiora
anwalda endas wæron swiþe ungelice; for þon þe Babylonie mid
monigfealdum unryhtum 7 firenlustum mid heora cyninge buton
20 ælcre hreowe libbende wæran, þæt hie hit na gebetan noldan ær
þon hie God mid þæm mæstan bismere geeaðmedde, þa he hie
ægðres benam ge heora cyninges ge heora anwaldes. Ac Romane
mid hiora cristnan cyninge Gode þ[e]owiende wæron, þætte he
him for þæm ægþres geuþe, ge hiora cyninges ge heora anwaldes.
25 For þæm magan hiora spræce gemetgian þa þe þæs cristendomes
wiþerflitan sint, gif hie gemunan willað hiora ieldrena unclænnessa
7 heora wolgewinna 7 hiora monigfealdan unsibbe 7 hiora unmilt-
f. 23 |sunge þe hie to gode hæfdon ge eac him selfum betweonum, ðæt
hie nane mildheortnesse þurhteon ne mehtan, ær þæm him seo
30 bot of ðæm cristendome com þe hie nu swiþost tælað.

II. ii

Ymb feower hunde wintra 7 ymb feowertig þæs þe Troia, Creca

31–p. 39, 24] OH II. iv. 1–6.

1 hwæþere] *orig.* hwægþere, *with* g *er.* L.   onwealg] on *followed by eras.* L.
2 æfter] æfter ðæm C.   þeh þe] ðeah C.   5 beniman] benaman *with*
'i' *above first* a L.   7 caseras] *both MSS.*   7–8 ricsiende sindon] synd
ricsiende C.   10 þe þa] þa ðe C.   13 oncnewen] *second* n *on eras.* L,
oncnawen C.   17 ðæm (1)] *from* C, *no reading* L.   23 þeowiende] *from* C,
þowiende L.   29 þæm] ðon C.   31 Troia] troiana C.   Creca] creaca C.

burg, awested wæs, wearð Romeburg getimbred from twam gebroðrum, Remuse 7 Romuluse, 7 raðe æfter Romulus hiora anginn
geunclænsade mid his broðor slege 7 eac siþþan mid his hiwunge
7 his geferena: hwelce bisena he ðær stellende wæs, mid þæm þe
hie bædon Sabini þa burgware þætte hi him geuðen hiora dohtra 5
him to wifum to habbanne, 7 hie him þara bena forwierndon. Hi
swaþeah heora unðances mid swicdome hie begeaton, mid þæm
þe hie bædon þæt hie him fylstan mosten ðæt hie hiera godum þe
ieð blotan mehten: þa hie him þæs getygðedon, þa hæfdon hi him
to wifum 7 heora fæderum eft agiefan noldon. Ymb þæt wearð 10
þæt mæste gewinn monig gear, oð hie fornæh mid ealle forslægene
7 forwordene wæron on ægþere healfe, þæt hie mid nanum þinge
ne mehton gesemede weorþan ær þara Romana wif mid heora
cildum iernende wæron gemong ðæm gefeohtum, 7 heora fæderum
wæron to fotum feallende 7 biddende þæt hie for þara cilda lufan 15
þæs gewinnes sumne ende gedyden. Swa weorðlice 7 swa mildelice
wæs Romeburg on fruman gehalgod, mid broðor blode 7 mid
sweora 7 mid Romuluses eame[s] Numetores, þone he eac ofslog,
ða he cyning wæs 7 him self siþþan to ðæm rice feng! þuss gebletsade Romulus Romana rice on fruman: mid his broðor blode þone 20
weall 7 mid þara sweora blode þa ciricean 7 mid his eames blode
þæt rice. Ond siþþan his agenne sweor to deaðe beswac, þa he
hiene to him aspon 7 him gehet | ðæt he his rice wið hiene dælan f. 23ᵛ
wolde 7 hiene under ðæm ofslog.

He þa Romulus æfter þiosan underfeng Cirinensa gewinn þara 25
burgwarana, for þon þe he þagiet lytel landrice hæfde buton þære
byrig anre, for þon þe Romulus 7 ealle Romware oþerum folcum
unweorðe wæran, for þon ðe hie on cnihthade wæron oþerra manna
niedlingas. þa hie ða hæfdon Cirinen þa burg ymbseten 7 ðær
micelne hungor þoliende wæron, þa gecwædan hie þæt him leofre 30
wære þæt hie on ðæm iermþum heora lif geendodon þonne hie
ðæt gewinn forleten oððe frið genamen. Hie ðær þa winnende
wæron oð hie þa burg abræcon 7 æfter þæm wið þa londleode on
ælce healfe unablinnendlice winnende wæron oð hie ðærymbutan
hæfdon monega byrig begietena.

35

25–35] OH II. iv. 7–8.

2 Remuse] remus C.   Romuluse] romulus C.   æfter] æfter ðan C.
5 Sabini] sabine C.   11 oð] oþ þe C.   14 gefeohtum] gefeohte C.
18 eames] eame *both MSS.*   29 Cirinen] cirinensa C.

Ac þa cyningas þe æfter Romuluse ricsedon wæron forcuðran 7
eargran þonne he wære, 7 þæm folcum laðran 7 ungetæsran, oð
þætte Tarcuinius, ðe we ær ymbe sædon þe hira [eallra] fracoþast
wæs—ægþer ge eargast, ge wrænast, ge ofermodgast—ealra þara
5 Romana wif, 'ða' þe he mehte, he to [ge]ligre geniedde 7 his suna
geþafode þæt he læg mid Latinus wife, Lucrettie hatte, Brutu[s]es
sweostor, [þa] heo on firde wæron, ðeh þe hie Romana bremuste
wæron to ðæm cyninge. Heo ða Lucretie hi selfe for þæm
acwealde. Ða þæt Latinus hiere wer geascade 7 Brutus hiere
10 broðor, þa forleton hie ða firde þe hie bewitan sceoldan, 7 þa hie
ham comon, þa adræfdon hie ægðer ge þone cyning ge his sunu ge
ealle þa þe þær cynecynnes wæron of þy rice mid ealle. Him ða
Romane æfter þæm ladteowas gesetton þe hie consulas heton, þæt
14 heora rice heolde an gear an monn.

II. iii

f. 24 Æfter þæm þe Romeburg getimbred wæs ii hunde | wintrum 7
iiii, þætte Brutus wæs se forma consul. Romulus heora forma
cyning 7 Brutus heora forma consul wurdon emnreðe. Romulus
slog his broðor 7 his eam 7 his sweor. Brutus slog his [ii] suna 7 his
wifes twegen broðor, for þon þe hie spræcon ðæt hit betere wære
20 þætte Romane eft heora cynecynne onfengen, swa hie ær hæfdon.
For þæm he hie het gebindan 7 beforan eallum þæm folce mid
besman swingan 7 siþþan mid æxsum heora heafda of aceorfan.
Tarcuinius [þa], ðe ær Romana cyning wæs, aspon Tuscea
cyning him on fultum, Porsenna wæs haten, þæt he ðe ieð mehte
25 winnan wið Brutuse 7 wið eallum Romanum. He ða Brutus gecwæð
anwig wið þone cyning ymb heora feondscipe. Ac him Tarcuinius
oðerne ðegn ongean sende, Arrunses sunu ðæs ofermodgan, 7
heora þær ægðer oðerne ofslog.
Æfter þæm Porsenna 7 Tarcuinius þa cyningas ymbsæton

3–12] OH II. iv. 12.   12–14] OH II. iv. 15.   15–22] OH II. v. 1.
23–8] OH II. v. 2.   29–p. 41, 11] OH II. v. 3.

---

3 eallra] *from* C, *no reading* L.   4 ealra] ealla C.   5 geligre] *from* C,
ligre L.   6 Lucrettie] lucretie C.   Brutuses] *from* C, brutues L.   7 þa]
from C, þe L.   ðeh þe] þeah C.   8 hi] his *with* s *er.* L.   13 ladteowas]
underlatteowas C.   15 wintrum] wintra C.   18 ii] v L, fif C.
22 heafda] heafod C.   23 Tarcuinius] tarcuinus C.   þa] *from* C, *no reading*
L.   24 ieð] eað C.   26 Tarcuinius] tarcuinus C.   29 Tarcuinius]
tarcuinus C.

Romeburg 7 hie eac begeaton, þær Mutius nære, an monn of
ðære byrig: he hi mid his wordum geegsade. Ða hie hiene gefengon,
ða pinedon hie hiene, mid þæm þæt hie his hand forbær'n'don,
anne finger 7 anne, 7 hiene secgan heton hu fela þæra manna wære
þe wið þæm cyninge Tarcuinie swiðost wiðsacen hæfde. þa he   5
ðæt secgean nolde, þa acsedon hie hine hu fela þær swelcerra
manna wære swelce he wæs. þa sægde he him ðæt ðær fela þara
monna [wære], 7 eac gesworen hæfdon ðæt hie oþer forleosan
woldon, oþþe hira 'agen' lif, oþþe Porsennes þæs cyninges. þa þæt
þa Porsenna gehierde, he ðæt setl 7 þæt gewin mid ealle for'let' þe   10
he ær þreo winter dreogende wæs.

II. iiii

Æfter þæm wæs þæt Sabinisce gewinn, 7 him Romane þæt
swiðe ondrædende wæron 7 him gesetton hir|an ladteow þonne   f. 24ᵛ
hiera consul wære, þone ðe hie tictatores heton, 7 hie mid þæm
tictatore micelne sige hæfdon. Æfter þæm Romane betux him   15
selfum, þa rican menn 7 þa earmran, micel gewinn upahofon, 7
him ðæt to longsumere wrace come, þær hie ðe raðor gesemed ne
wurden. On þæm dagum wæron þa mæstan ungetina on Romanum,
ægðer ge on hungre ge on moncwealme, under þæm twæm consulum, Tita 7 Publia hatton. 7 hie heora gefeohta þa hwile hie   20
gerestan, þeh hie þæs hungres 7 þæs moncwealmes ne mehte. Ac
þa monigfealdan iermþo þa werigan burg swiþe brociende wæran.

Ær ðæm þe seo wol geendod wære, Ueigentes 7 Etrusci þa
leode wið Romanum gewinn upahofon 7 wið þæm twæm consulum,
Marcuse 7 Grease, 7 þa Romane him ongean foran 7 him betweo-   25
num aþas gesworan þæt hiera nan nolde eft eard gesecan buton
hie sige hæfden. þær wæron Romane swa swiþe forslægene, þeh
hie sige hæfden, þæt heora an consul þe him to la[f]e wearð forsoc
þone trium[p]han þe him mon ongean brohte þa he hamweard
wæs, 7 sæde þæt hie hæfden bet gewyrh[t] þæt him mon mid heafe   30
ongean come þonne mid triumphan.

12–22] OH II. v. 4–6.   23–31] OH II. v. 7.

---

3 forbærndon] bærndon C.   5 Tarcuinie] tarcuine C.   8 wære]
from C, *om.* L.   12 Romane] romana C.   13–14 hiran . . . wære] þæt
hyra an latteow wære þon'n'e hyra consul C.   18 ungetina] ungetima C.
28 lafe] *from* C, laðe L.   29 triumphan] *from* C, triumhpan L.
30 gewyrht] gewyrh L, gewyrhte C.   heafe] heofe C.

þæt hie triumphan heton, þæt wæs þonne hie hwelc folc mid
gefeohte ofercumen hæfdon, þonne wæs heora þeaw þæt sceoldon
ealle hiera senatus cuman ongean heora consulas æfter þæm gefeohte, siex mila from ðære byrig, mid crætwæne mid golde 7 mid
5 gimstanum gefrætwedum, 7 hie sceoldon bringan feowerfetes twa
hwit. þonne hie hamweard foran, þonne sceoldon hiera senatus
ridan on crætwænum wiðæftan þæm consulum 7 þa menn beforan
him drifan gebundene þe þær gefongene wæron, ðæt heora mærþa
f. 25 sceoldon þy þrymlicran beon. | Ac þonne hie hwelc folc buton
10 gefeohte on heora geweald genieddon, þonne hie hamweard wæron,
þonne sceolde him man bringan ongean of þære byrig crætwæn,
se wæs mid siolfre gegiered, 7 ælces cynnes feowerfetes feos an,
hiora consulum to mærþe. þæt wæs þonne triumpheum.

Romulus gesette ærest monna senatum, ðæt wæs an hund
15 monna, þeh heora æfter fyrʼsʼte wære þreo hund. þa wæron simbel
binnan Romebyrg wuniende, to þon þæt hie heora rædþeahteras
wæron 7 consulas setton, 7 þæt ealle Romane him hirsumeden, 7
þæt hie bewisten eal þæt licgende feoh under anum hrofe þæt hie
begeaton oþþe on gafole oþþe on hergiunga, þæt hie hit siþþan
20 mehten him eallum gemænelice to nytte gedon, þæm þe þær buton
þeowdome wæron.

þa consulas þe on ðæm dagum þæt Sabinisce gewinn underfengon, þe mon het eall hiera cynn Fabiane, for þon hit ealra Romana
ænlicost wæs 7 cræftegast, nu giet todæge hit is on leoðum sungen
25 hwelcne demm hie Romanum gefeollan. Eac þæm monega ea sindon be noman nemnede for þæm gefeohte 7 eac þa geata, þa hie
ut of Romebyrig to þæm gefeohte ferdon, him mon ascop þa noman
þe hie giet habbað. Æfter þæm Romane curon iii hund cempena
7 siex, þæt sceolde to anwige gangan wið swa fela Sabina, 7 ge-
30 truwedon þæt hie mid hiera cræftum sceolden sige gefeohtan. Ac
Sabini mid heora searwum hie ealle þær ofslogon buton anum, se
þæt laðspel æt ham gebodade. Næs na on Romanum anum, ac
swa hit an scopleoðum sungen is þæt gind ealne middangeard
wære caru 7 gewin 7 ege.

22–34] OH II. v. 8–10.

3 senatus] senatas C.   cuman] coman, *with* ʻuʼ *above* o L.   6 hwit]
hwite C.   senatus] senatas C.   7–8 beforan him] *after eras.* (beforan him?)
L.   26 þa (2)] þe C.   27 ascop] a gesceop C.   29 siex] syx
cempan C.   32 Romanum] romane C.

Cirus, Persa cyning, þe we ær beforan sægdon, þa hwile ðe
Sabini 7 Romane wunnon on þæm westdæle, þa hwile wonn he
ægþer ge on Sciþþie ge on Indie, oþ he hæfde mæst ealne þone
eastdæl awest, | 7 æfter ðæm fird gelædde to Babylonia, þe þa f. 25ᵛ
welegre wæs þonne ænigu oþeru burg. Ac hiene Gandes seo 5
[ea] þæs oferfæreldes longe gelette, for þæm þe þær scipa næron.
þæt is ealra ferscra wætera mæst buton Eufrate. þa gebeotode an
his ðegna þæt he mid sunde þa ea oferfaran wolde mid twam
tyncenum, ac hiene se stream fordraf. Ða gebeotode Cirus ðæt he
his þegn on hire swa gewrecan wolde, þa he swa grom wearð on 10
his mode 7 wiþ þa ea gebolgen, þæt hie mehte wifmon be hiere
cneowe oferwadan, þær heo ær wæs nigon mila brad þonne heo
fledu wæs. He þæt mid dædum gelæste 7 hie upp forlet an feower
hund ea 7 on lx 7 siþþan mid his firde þær oferfor. 7 æfter þæm
Eufrate þa ea, seo is mæst eallra ferscra wætera 7 is irnende þurh 15
middewearde Babylonia burg, he hie eac mid gedelfe on monige
ea upp forlet 7 siþþan mid eallum his folce on ðære ea gong on þa
burg færende wæs 7 hie gerahte.

Swa ungeliefedlic is ænigum menn þæt to gesecgenne, hu ænig
mon mehte swelce burg gewyrcan swelce sio wæs, oððe eft abrecan. 20
Membrað se ent angan ærest timbran Babylonia 7 Ninus se cyning
æfter him. 7 Sameramis his cwen hie geendade æfter him on
middeweardum hiere rice. Seo burg wæs getimbred an fildum
lande 7 on swiþe emnum. 7 heo wæs swiþe fæger an to locianne.
7 heo is swiþe ryhte feowerscyte, 7 þæs wealles micelness 7 fæst- 25
ness is ungeliefedlic to secgenne: þæt is, þæt he is l elna brad 7 ii
hund elna heah, 7 his ymbgong is hundseofontig mila 7 seofeða
dæl anre mile, 7 he is geworht of tigelan 7 of eorðtyrewan. 7
ymbutan þone weall is se mæsta dic, on þæm is iernende se unge-
foglecesta stream; 7 wiðutan þæm dice is geworht twegea elna 30
heah weall, 7 bufan ðæm maran wealle ofer ealne þone ymbgong
he is mid stænenum wighusum beworht.

| Seo ilce burg Babylonia, seo ðe mæst wæs 7 ærest ealra burga, f. 26
seo is nu læst 7 westast. Nu seo burg swelc is, þe ær wæs ealra

1–18] OH II. vi. 1–6.   19–32] OH II. vi. 6–10.   32–p. 44, 6] OH
II. vi. 11 and 13.

3 Sciþþie] sciððige C.   4 Babylonia] babilonia C.   6 ea] *from* C,
om. L.   þæs ... gelette] lange gelette þæs oferfæreldes C.   11 hie]
i *partly* er. L.   mehte] mihton C.   wifmon] wifmenn C.   hiere] heora C.
14 lx] syxtig ea C.   16 Babylonia] babilonian C.   19 gesecgenne]
secgenne C.   21 Babylonia] babilonia C.   33 Babylonia] babilonia C.

weorca fæstast 7 wunderlecast 7 mærast, gelice 7 heo wære to
bisene asteald eallum middangearde, 7 eac swelce heo self sprecende
sie to eallum moncynne 7 cweþe: 'Nu ic þuss gehroren eam 7
aweg gewiten, hwæt, ge magan on me ongietan 7 oncnawan þæt
5 ge nanuht mid eow nabbað fæstes ne stronges þætte þurhwunigean
mæge.'

On ðæm dagum þe Cirus Persa cyning Babylonia abræc, ða wæs
Croesus se Liþa cyning mid firde gefaren Babylonium to fultume.
Ac þa he wiste þæt hie him on nanum fultome beon ne mæhte, 7
10 þæt seo burg abrocen wæs, he him hamweard ferde to his agnum
rice. 7 him Cirus wæs æfterfylgende oþ he hiene gefeng 7 ofslog.
Ond nu ure cristne Roma bespricð þæt hiere wealles for ealdunge
brosnien, nales na for þæm þe hio mid forheriunge swa gebis'm'rad
wære swa Babylonia wæs. Ac heo for hiere cristendome nugiet is
15 gescild, ðæt ægþer ge hio self ge hiere anweald is ma hreosende
for ealddome þonne 'of' æniges cyninges niede.

Æfter þæm Cirus gelædde fird on Sciþþie, 7 him ðær an giong
cyning mid firde ongean for, 7 his modor mid him Damaris. þa
Cirus for ofer þæt londgemære, ofer þa ea þe hatte Araxis, him
20 þær se gionga cyning þæs oferfæreldes forwiernan mehte. Ac he
for þæm nolde þy he mid his folce getruwade ðæt he hiene
beswican mehte, siþþan he binnan ðæm gemære wære 7 wicstowa
name. Ac þa Cirus geahsade þæt hiene se gionga cyning þær secean
wolde, 7 eac þæt þæm folce seldsiene 7 uncuðe wæron wines
25 dryncas, he for þæm of ðære wicstowe afor on ane digle stowe 7
þær beæftan forlet eall þæt þær liðes wæs 7 swetes, þæt þa se
gionga cyning swiðor micle wenende wæs þæt hie þonon fleonde
wæren þonne hie ænigne swicdom cyþan dorsten, þa hie hit þær
f. 26ᵛ swa æmenne | metton. Hie ðær þa mid micelre bliðnesse buton
30 gemetgunge þæt win drincende wæron, oð hi heora selfra lytel
geweald hæfdon. He þa Cirus hie þær besyrede 7 mid ealle ofslog;
7 siþþan wæs farende þær ðæs cyninges modor mid þæm twæm
dælum þæs folces wuniende wæs, þa he þone ðriddan dæl mid
ðæm cyninge beswicen hæfde. Hio þa seo cwen Dameris mid
35 micelre gnornunge ymb þæs cyninges slege hiere suna þencende
wæs, hu heo hit gewrecan mehte, 7 þæt eac mid dædum gelæste

7–11] OH II. vi. 12.   12–16] OH II. vi. 14.   17–p. 45, 9] OH II.
vii. 1–6.

---

8 Babylonium] babilonium C.   12 Roma] romana C.   wealles] weallas C.
25 dryncas] drencas C.   29 metton] gemetton C.

7 hier[e] folc on tu todælde, ægþer ge wifmen ge wæpnedmen, for
þon þe þær wifmenn feohtað swa same swa wæpnedmen. Hio mid
þæm healfan dæle beforan þæm cyninge farende wæs swelce heo
fleonde wære, oð hio hiene gelædde on an micel slæd, 7 se healfa
dæl wæs Ciruse æfterfylgende. þær wearþ Cirus ofslægen, 7 twa 5
þusend monna mid him. Seo cwen het þa ðæm cyninge þæt heafod
of aceorfan 7 beweorpan on anne cylle, se wæs afylled monnes
blodes, 7 þus cwæð: 'þu þe þyrstende wære monnes blodes xxx
wintra, drync nu þine fylle.'

II. v

Æfter þæm þe Romeburg getimbred wæs twa hunde wintra 7 10
iiiix, þætte Cambis[i]s feng to Persa rice, Ciruses sunu, se, mid
þon þe he Egypte oferwon, gedyde þæt nan hæþen cyning 'ær'
gedon ne dorste, þæt wæs þæt he heora godgieldum eallum wiðsoc
7 hie æfter þæm mid ealle towearp.

Æfter him ricsade Darius, se awende ealle Asiriæ 7 Caldei eft 15
to Perseum, þe ær from him gebogene wæron. Æfter þæm he wonn
on Sciþþie, ægþer ge for Ciruses slege þæs cyninges, his mæges,
ge eac for þæm þe him [mon] | ðær wifes forwiernde. His heres f. 27
wæs seofon hund þusenda, þa he on Sciðþie for. Hwæþere ða
Sciþþie noldon hiene gesecan to folcgefeohte. Ac þonne hie gind 20
þæt lond tofarene wæron, hie þonne hie floccmælum slogan. þa
wæron ða Perse mid þæm swiþe geegsade 7 eac ondredon þæt mon
þa brycge forwyrcan wolde þe æt þæm gemære wæs, þæt hie siþþan
nysten hu hie þonan comen. He þa se cyning, æfter ðæm þe his folc
swiþe forslægen wæs, þær forlet hundeahtatig þusenda beæftan 25
him, þæt hie ðær þagiet leng winnan sceoldon, 7 he self þonan
gewat on þa læssan Asiam 7 hie forhergeade, 7 siþþan on Mæcedoniam 7 on Ionas, Creca leode, [7] þa hie butu oferhergeade, 7
for siððan firr an Crecas 7 gewin upp ahof wið Athenienses, for
þæm hie Mæcedoniam on fultume wæron. Sona swa Atheniense 30
[wiston] þæt Darius hie mid gefeohte secan wolde, hie acuron
endlefan þusend monna 7 him ongean foran 7 þone cyning æt
ðære du'ne' metton þe mon hætt Morotthome. Heora ladteow

10–14] OH II. viii. 1–2.   15–p. 46, 5] OH II. viii. 4–13.

1 hiere] hyre C, hier L.   11 Cambisis] *final two letters* (es *or* is?) *er.* L,
cambis C.   15 Asiriæ] asirige C.   18 mon] *om.* L, man C.   28 7 (2)]
7' *in l.h.* (?) C, *no reading* L.   31 wiston] *om.* L, 'wysten' *in l.h.* C.

wæs haten Htesseus, se wæs mid his dædum snelra þonne he
mæ'ge'nes hæfde, se geworhte micelne dom on ðæm gefeohte.
þa wearð tu hund þusenda Persea ofslægen, 7 þa oþre gefliemed.
Ða he eft hæfde fird gegaderod on Perseum 7 þæt wrecan þohte,
5 þa gefor he.

Æfter him feng his sunu to Persea rice Xersis. þæt gewinn þæt
his fæder astealde he diegellice for þæm v gear scipa worhte ond
fultum gegaderode. þa wæs mid him an wræccea of Læcedamania,
Creca byrg, se wæs haten Damerað, se þæt facn to his cyþþe
10 gebodade 7 hit on anum brede awrat 7 siþþan mid weaxe beworhte.
Xersis, þa he an Crecas for, hæfde his agenes folces viii c þusenda,
7 he hæfde of oþerum þeodum abeden iiii c m; 7 he hæfde scipa,
þara miclena dulmuna, an m 7 ii hund, 7 þara scipa wæron iii m þe
f. 27ᵛ hiora mete bæran; 7 ealles his heres | wæs swelc ungemet þæt mon
15 eaðe cweþan mehte ðæt hit wundor wære, hwær hie landes hæfden
þæt hie mehten an gewician, oþþe wæteres þæt hie mehten him
þurst of adrincan. Swa þeah seo ungemetlice mengeo þæs folces
[wæs] þa ieðre to oferwinnanne þonne heo us sie nu to gerimanne
oþþe to geliefanne.

20 Leoniða, Læcedemonia cyning, Creca byrg, hæfde iiii þusend
monna þa he angean Xersis for on anum nearwan londfæstenne 7
him þær mid gefeohte wiðstod. Xersis þæt oþer folc swa swiðe
forseah, þæt he ascade hwæt sceolde æt swa lytlum weorode mara
fultum buton þa ane þe him þær ær abolgen wæs on ðæm ærran
25 gefeohte, þætte wæs on Merothonia þære dune. Ac gesette þa men
on ænne truman þe mon hiora mægas ær on ðæm londe slog, 7
wiste þæt hie woldon geornfulran beon þære wrace þonne oþere
men, 7 hie swa wæron oð hie þær mæst ealle ofslægene wurdon.
Xersis, swiþe him þa ofþyncendum þæt his folc swa forslagen
30 wæs, he self þa þærto for mid eallum þæm mægene þe he ðærto
gelædan mehte, 7 þær feohtende wæron iii dagas, oþ þara Persea
wæs ungemetlic wæl geslægen. He het þa þæt fæste lond utan
ymbfaran, þæt him mon sceolde an ma healfa on feohtan þonne on
ane. Leoniþa þæt þa geascade þæt hiene mon swa beþridian wolde.
35 He þonan afor 7 his fierd gelædde on an oþer fæstre land, 7 þær

6-19] OH II. ix. 1-3.   20-p. 47, 11] OH II. ix. 3-9.

8 Læcedamania] læcedamonia C.   17 ungemetlice] ungemætlice C.
18 wæs] 'wæs' in l.h. C, om. L.   22 Xersis] from C, cxersis (for exersis?)
L.   28 þær mæst ealle] ealle mæst þær C.

gewunedon oþ niht, 7 him from afaran het ealla þa burgware þe he
of oðerum londe him to fultome abeden hæfde, þæt hie him ge-
sunde burgen, for þæm he ne uþe þæt ænig ma folca for his
þingum forwurde þonne he self mid his agenre þeode. Ac he þus
wæs sprecende 7 geomriende: 'Nu we untweogendlice witan þæt 5
we ure agen lif forlætan sceolan for þæm ungemetlican feondscipe
þe ure ehtende [on] sindon. Uton þehhwæþere acræftan hu we
heora an þisse niht mægen mæst beswican 7 us selfum betst word
7 longsumast æt urum ende gewyrcan.' | Hu micel þæt is to sec- f. 28
ganne þætte Leoniða mid vi c monna vi c m swa gebismrade, sume 10
ofslog, sume gefliemde!

Xersis wæs þa æt twam cirrum on ðæm londe swa gescend mid
his ormætan menige. He þagiet þriddan siþe wæs wilniende mid
scipfierde þæt he þæs gewinnes mehte mare gefremman 7 him
Ionas, Creca leode, on fultum gespon, þeh hie ær ofer hiera willan 15
him to gecierdon; 7 hie him geheton þæt hie ðæt gefeoht ærest mid
him selfum þurhteon wolden, þeh hie him eft facen gelæsten, þa
hie on ðæm sæ feohtende wæron. Themestocles hatte Atheniensa
ladteow: hie wæron cumen Leoniðan to fultume, þeh hie æt þæm
ærran gefeohte him ne mehten to cuman. Se Themestocles 20
gemyndgade Ionas þære ealdan fæhþe þe Xersis him to geworht
hæfde, hu he hie mid forhergiunge 7 mid heora mæga slihtum on
his geweald geniedde. He bæd hie eac þæt hie gemunden þara
ealdena treowa 7 þæs unarimedlican freondscipes þe hie ægþer
hæfdon ge to Atheniensum ge to Læcedemoniam ær on ealddagum, 25
7 hie bidde[nde] wæs þæt hie mid sume searawrence from Xerse
þæm cyninge sume hwile awende, þæt hie 7 Læcedemonie mosten
wið Persum þæs gewinnes sumne ende gewyrcan; [7] hi him þære
bene getygþedon. þa þa Perse þæt gesawon þæt him þa from bugan
þe hie betst getriewdon þæt him sceolde sige gefeohtan, hie selfe 30
eac fleonde wæron, 7 hiora þær wearð fela ofslægen 7 adruncen 7
gefangen.

Xersis þegn wæs haten Marðonius, se hiene wæs georne lærende
þæt he ma hamweard fore þonne he þær leng bide, þylæs ænegu
ungeþwærnes on his agnum rice ahafen wurde, 7 cwæþ þæt hit 35

12–32] OH II. x. 1, 2, 4, 5.   33–p. 48, 18] OH II. x. 6–10.

---

1 gewunedon] gewunode C.   7 on] 'on' in l.h. C, no reading L.   26 bid-
dende] from C, bidde L.   Xerse] exerse with first e er. L.   28 7] from C,
no reading L.

gerisenlic're' wære þæt he þæt gewinn him betæhte mid þæm
fultume þe þær to lafe þagiet wæs leng to winnanne, 7 sæde þæt
hit þæm cyninge læsse edwit wære gif þæm folce buton him
þagiet misspeowe, swa him ær dyde. Se cyning þa Xersis swiþe
5 geliefedlice his þegne gehierde 7 mid sumum dæle his fultume
þonan afor. þa he þa hamweard | to þære ie com þe he ær west-
weard het þa ofermætan brycge mid stane ofer gewyrcan, his sige
'to' tacne þe he on þæm siþe þurhteon þohte, þa wæs seo ea to
þon flede þæt he ne mehte to þære brycge cuman. þa wæs ðæm
10 cyninge swiþe ange on his mode þæt naþær ne he mid his fultume
næs, ne ðæt he ofer þa ea cuman ne mehte; toeacan ðæm he him
wæs swiþe ondrædende þæt him his fiend wæren æfterfylgende.
Him þa to com an fiscere 7 uneaþe hiene ænne ofer brohte. Hu
God þa 'mæstan' ofermetto 7 þæt mæste angin on swa heanlice
15 ofermetto geniðerade, þæt se, se þe him ær geþuhte þæt him nan
sæ wiþhabban ne mehte þæt he hiene mid scipun 7 mid his fultume
afyllan ne mehte, þæt he eft wæs biddende anes lytles troges æt
anum earman men, þæt he mehte his feorh generian!

Morþonius, Xersis þegn, forlet þa scipa þe hie on farende wæron,
20 7 for to anre byrig on Boetium, Creca londe, 7 hie abræc. Him mon
þæt æfter ðæm hrædlice forgeald, þa hie mon gefliemde 7 swiþe
forslog, þeh þe Atheniensum se sige 7 seo reafung þæs Persiscan
feos to maran sconde wurde, for þon, siþþan hie welegran wæron, hie eac bleaðran gewurdon. Æfter þæm Xersis wearþ his
25 agenre þeode swiþe unweorþ, 7 hiene his agen ealdormon Artabatus
besirede 7 ofslog. Eala, cwæð Orosius, hu lustbærlice tida on ðæm
dagum wæron, swa swa þa secgað þe þæs cristendomes wiðerflitan
sint, þæt us nu æfter swelcum longian mæge swelce þa wæron, þa
swa micel folc on swa lytlan firste æt þrim folcgefeohtum for-
30 wurdon, þæt wæs nigon x hund þusenda of Persa anra anwealde
buton hiera wiþerwinnum, ægþer ge of Sciþþium ge of Crecum!
þæt tacnade Leoniða on his þæm nihstan gefeohte 7 Persa, hwelc
moncwealm on Creca londe wæs mid monigfealdum deaðum, mid
þæm þe he sprecend[e] wæs to his geferum | æt his underngereorde,
35 ær he to ðæm gefeohte fore: 'Uton nu brucan þisses undernmetes
swa þa sculon þe hiora æfengifl on helle gefeccean sculon.' þeh

---

19–24] OH II. xi. 1–3.   24–6] OH II. xi. 7.   26–p. 49, 9] OH II. xi. 8–10.

---

15 se (2)] *no reading* C.   24 bleaðran] bliðran C.   34 sprecende] *from* C,
sprecend L.

he swa þa cwæde, he cwæð eft oþer word: 'þeh ic ær sæde þæt
we to helle sceolden, þeh ne geortriewe ic na Gode þæt he us ne
mæge gescildan to beteran tidun þonne we nu on sint.' Leoniþa
sæde þæt þa tida þa yfele wæron 7 wilnade þæt him toweard
beteran wæron; 7 nu sume men secgað þæt þa beteran wæren 5
þonne nu sien. Nu hie swa twywyrdige sindon, þonne wæron
ægþer gode, ge þa ærran, swa sum[e m]en nu secgað, ge eac þas
æfterran, swa hie ær sædon, 7 næron naðere an þance; gif hie
þonne soð ne sædon, þonne næron naþer gode [ne þa], ne nu.

Nu we sculon eft, cwæð Orosius, hwierfan near Roma, þær we 10
hit ær forleton; for 'þon' ic ne mæg eal þa monigfealdan yfel
emdenes areccean, swa ic eac ealles þises middangeardes na maran
dæles ne angite buton ðætte on twam onwealdum gewearð, on
þæm ærestan 7 on ðæm siþemestan: þæt sint Asirie 7 Romane.

II. vi

Æfter þæm þe Romeburg getimbred wæs ii hunde wintra 7 15
hundeahtatigum—þy ilcan geare þe Sabini Romane swa beswicon,
þa hiora iii hund 7 siex men of ægðerre healfe to anwigge eodon—
wearð micel wundor on heofonum gesewen, swelce eal se hefon
birnende wære. þæt tacen wearð on Romanum swiþe gesweotolad
mid þæm miclan wolbryne monncwealmes þe him raðe ðæs æfter 20
com, swa ðæt hie healfe belifene wurdon, 7 heora twegen consulas
ðe hie ða hæfdon, ge þa æt nihstan ða þe þær to lafe beon moston
wæron to ðæm meðie þæt hie ne mehton þa gefarenan to eorþan
bringan.

Sona æfter þæm ealle heora þeowas wið þa hlafordas winnende 25
wæron 7 hie benoma[n] heora heafodstedes þæt hie Capitoliam
heton. 7 hie micla gefeoht ymb þæt hæfdon, oþ hie ofslogan | þone   f. 29ᵛ
ænne consul þe hie þa niwan geset hæfdon, þeh þa hlafordas on
þæm ende hæfden heanlicne sige. 7 sona þæs, þy æfterran geare,
Romane wunnan wið Fulcisci þæt folc 7 þær wurdon swiþe for- 30
slægene, 7 se dæl se þær to lafe 'wæs' wearð on an fæsten bedrifen,

10–14] OH II. xii. 1.   15–24] OH II. xii. 2–3.   25–p. 50, 5] OH II. xii. 5–8.

1 swa þa] þa swa C.   2 geortriewe] geortruwige C.   6 sien] synd C.
7 sume men] *from* C (menn), sumen L.   9 ne þa] *from* C, *om.* L.
12 emdenes] *alt. to* endemes L, endemes C.   14 ðæm] ðæm 'ðæm' L.
Asirie] asirige C.   26 benoman] benomam L, benamon C.   30 Fulcisci]
fucisci C.

7 þær wurdon mid hungre acwealde, þær heora þa ne gehulpe þa
þær æt ham wæron, mid ðæm þe hie gegaderedon eal moncynnes
þæt þær læfed wæs 7 genamon anne earmne mon him to consule,
þær he on his æcere eode 7 his sulh on handa hæfde, 7 siþþan to
5 Fulcisci þæm londe ferdon 7 hie ut forleton.

Æfter þæm wæs an ger full þæt ofer eall Romana rice seo eorþe
wæs cwaciende 7 berstende, 7 ælce dæg mon com unarimedlice
oft to senatum, 7 him sædon from burgum 7 from tunum on
eorþan besuncen[um], 7 hie selfe wæron ælce dæg on þære
10 ondrædinge hwonne hie on þa eorþan besuncene wurden. Æfter
ðæm com swa micel hæte giend Romane þæt ealle heora eorðwæst-
mas ge eac hie selfe neah forwurdon. Æfter þæm þær wearð se
mæsta hunger.

Æfter þæm Romane gesettan him x consulas þær hie ær twegen
15 hæfdon, to þon þæt hie hiera æ bewisten. Hiera an wæs Claudius
haten, se him wæs on teonde ealdordom ofer þa oþere, þeh hie him
þæs geþafiende næren, ac wið hiene winnende wæron oþ þo'ne'
first þe hie sume to him gecirdon, sume noldan. Ac swa on twa
todælde him betweonum wunnan þæt hie forgeatan þara utera
20 gefeohta þe him anhende wæron, oþ ealle þa consulas togædere
gecirdon 7 Claudium þone ænne mid saglum ofbeotan, 7 siþþan
heora agen lond wergende wæron.

Ieþelice, cwæð Orosius, 7 scortlice ic hæbbe nu gesæd hiora
ingewinn, þeh hi him wæron forneah þa mæstan 7 þa pleolecestan.
25 þæt eac Eðna þæt sweflene fyr tacnade, þa hit up of helle geate
asprong on Sicilia þæm londe, hwelc gewinn þa wæron be ðæm þe
f. 30 nu sindon, 7 Sicilia | fela ofslog mid bryne 7 mid stænce. Ac
siþþan hit cristen wearð, þæt helle fyr wæs siþþan geswiðrad, swa
ealle ungetina wæron, þæt hit nu is buton swelce tacnung þæs
30 yfeles þe hit ær dyde, þeh hit ælce geare sie bradre 7 bradre.

II. vii

Æfter þæm þe Romeburg getimbred wæs iii hunde wintra 7 an,
þætte Sicilie ungerade wæron him betweonum, 7 hie healfe asponan

6–13] OH II. xiii. 8–9.   14–22] OH II. xiii. 3–4.   25–30] OH II. xiv. 3.
31–p. 51, 4] OH II. xiv. 4–22.

---

6 full] ice *added in l.h.* L, fullice C.   9 besuncenum] besuncen/ L, besuncan C.   29 ungetina] ungetima C.   swelce] swylcum C.   tacnung]
tacnungum C.   30 bradre (1)] *alt. from* bladre L.

Læcedemonie him on fultum 7 healfe Athenienses, Creca þeoda, þe ær ætgædere wið Perse winnende wæron. Ac siþþan hie on Sicilium wunnon, hie eac siþþan betweonum him selfum winnende wæron, oþ þæt Darius, Persa cyning, Læcedemonium on fultume wearð wið þæm Athenienses, for þæm gewinnum his ieldrena. 5 Wæs ðæt micel wunder þæt eall Persa anweald 7 Læcedemonia, þæt hie ieð mehton Ahtene þa burg awestan þonne hie ðæt folc mehten to heora willum geniedan!

7 sona æfter þæm, þy ilcan geare, Darius gefor, Persa cyning, 7 his ii suna ymb þæt rice wunnon, Artecserses 7 Cirus, oþ hiora 10 ægþer þæt mæste folc ongean oþerne geteah, 7 þa unsibbe mid gefeohtum dreogende wæron oþ Cirus ofsˈlˈagen wearð, se þær gingra wæs. On þæm dagum wæs an burg in Affrica sio wæs neh þæm sæ, oð an sæflod com 7 hie aweste 7 þa men adrencte.

II. viii

Æfter þæm þe Romeburg getimbred wæs iii hunde wintra 7 lv, 15 þætte Romane besæton Ueiorum þa burg x winter, 7 him þæt setl swiþor derede þonne þam þe þærinne wæron, ægþer ge an ciele ge an hungre, buton ðæm þe mon oft hergeade ægðer ge on hie selfe ge on heora land æt ham. 7 hie þa hrædlice beforan heora feondum forweorþan sceoldon, þær hie ða burg ne abræcen mid þæm 20 cræfte þe þa scondlicost wæs, þeh he him eft se weorðesta wurde. þæt wæs þæt hie from heora wicstowum | under þære eorþan dul- f. 30ᵛ fon, oþ hie binnan þære byrig up eodon, 7 hie nihtes on frumslæpe on bestælan 7 þa burg mid ealle awestan. þysne nyttan cræft, þeh he arlic nære, funde heora tictator, Camillis hatte. 25

Sona æfter þæm wearð Romana gewinn 7 þara Gallia þe wæron of Senno þære byrig. þæt wæs ærest for þæm þa Gallia hæfdon beseten Tusci þa burg. þa sendon Romane ærendracan to Gallium 7 hie bædon þæt hie frið wið hie hæfden. þa on ðæm ilcan dæge æfter þæm þe hie þiss gesprecen hæfdon, fuhton Gallie on þa 30 burg. þa gesawan hie Romana ærendracan on hie feohtende mid þæm buˈrˈgwarum. Hie for þæm hie gebulgon 7 þa burg forleton 7 mid eallum heora fultume Romane sohton; 7 him Uauius se

---

4–8] OH II. xv. 4–5.   9–13] OH II. xviii. 1–2.   13–14] OH II.
xviii. 7.   15–25] OH II. xix. 1–3.   26–p. 52, 22] OH II. xix. 3–11.

6 Læcedemonia] lecedemonia C.   12 ofslagen] 'l' on eras. L.

consul mid gefeohte ongean com 7 eac raðe gefliemed wearð eft
into Romebyrig, 7 him Gallie wæron æfterfylgende oþ hie ealle
þærbinnan wæron: gelice 7 mon mæd mawe, hie wæron þa burg
hergende 7 sleande buton ælcre ware. þæt tacen nugiet cuþ is on
5 þære ea noman þæs consules sleges Fauiuses.

Ne wene ic, cwæð Orosius, þæt ænig mon atellan mæge ealne
þone demm þe Romanum æt þæm cirre gedon wearð, þeh hie þa
burg ne forbærnden swa hie þa gedydon, 7 þa feawan þe þær to
lafe wurdon gesealdon m punda goldes wið heora feore—7 hie
10 þæt dydon for þæm swiþost þe hie þohtan þæt hie siþþan hiora
underþeowas wæren—7 sume binnan þæt fæsten oðflugon þæt
hie Capitoliam heton. Hie þa eac besæton, oð hie sume hungre
acwælan, sume on hand eodan, 7 hie siþþan oþrum folcum him
wið feo gesealdon.

15 Hu þyncð eow nu, cwæð Orosius, þe þæs cristendomes tida
leahtriað, siþþan Gallia ut of þære byrig aforan, hu bliðe tida |Ro-
f. 31, mane æfter ðæm hæfdon. þa þa iermingas þe þær to lafe wurdon
ut of þæm holan crupon þe heo on lutedan, swa bewopene swelce
hie of oþerre worolde come, þonne hie besawon on þa besengdan
20 burg 7 on þa westan, þæt him þa wæs syndrig ege þær him ær wæs
se'o' mæsta wyn, eac buton þæm yfele nahton hie naþer ne
þærinne mete ne þærute freond.

þæt wæron þa tida þe Romane nu æfter sicað 7 cweþað þæt him
Gotan wyrsan tida gedon hæbben þonne hie ær hæfdon, 7 næron
25 on hie hergende buton þrie dagas; 7 Gallie wæron ær siex monað
binnan þære byrig hergende 7 þa burg bærnende, 7 him þæt þagiet to lytel yfel þuhte buton hie eac hie þæs naman bename þæt
hie nan folc næren. Eft þa Gotan þær læssan hwile hergedan þæt
hie for þæs cristendomes are 7 þurh Godes ege þæt hie naþer ne
30 þa burg ne bærndon ne þæs þone willan næfdon þæt hie heora
noman hie benamon, ne þara nanne yflian noldan þe to ðæm
Godes huse oðflugon, þeh hie hæþene wære. Ac swiþor micle
wæron wilniende þæt hie gemong him mid sibbe sittan mosten;
7 uneaðe mehte ær ænig þæm Gallium [oðfleon] oþþe oðhydan, 7
35 þa þa Gotan þær lytle hwile hergedan, ne mehte mon buton feawa
ofslagenre geahsian. Ðær wæs gesiene Godes irre, þa hiora ærenan

23–p. 53, 3] OH II. xix. 12–15.

---

21 mæsta] mæste C.   27 eac hie] *om.* C.   34 oðfleon] *om. both MSS.*
36 ofslagenre] ofslagenra C.

beames 7 hiora anlicnessa, þa hie ne mehton from Galliscum fyre
forbærnede weorþan, ac hi hefenisc fyr æt ðæm ilcan cyrre forbærnde.

Ne wene ic, cwæð Orosius, nu ic longe spell hæbbe to secgenne,
þæt ic hie on þisse bec geendian mæge. Ac ic oþere anginnan 5
sceal.

III. i

| Æfter ðæm þe Romeburg getimbred wæs iii hunde wintra 7   f. 31ᵛ
lvii, on þæm dagum þe Gallie Roma awest hæfdon, þa gewearð seo
mæste sibb 7 seo bismerleceste betwih Læcedemonium, Creca
londe, 7 Persum. Æfter þæm þe Læcedemonie hæfdon Perse oft 10
oferwunnen, þa gebudon him Perse þæt hie hæfden iii winter
sibbe wiþ hie, se þe þæt wolde, 7 se þe þæt nolde, þæt hie wolden
þa mid gefeohte gesecan. Hie þa Læcedemoniæ lustlice þære sibbe
hirsumedan, for þæm lytlan ege þe him mon gebead, on þæm mon
mæg sweotole oncnawan hu micelne willan hie to ðæm gewinne 15
hæfdon, swa heora scopas on heora leoðum giddiende sindon 7 on
heora leaspellengum. Ne geþyncð þe swelc gewin noht lustbære,
cwæð Orosius, ne þa tida þon ma, þætte him his feond mæge swa
eaþe his mid wordum gestieran?

Æfter þæm þe Læcedemonie hæfdon oferwunnen Ahtene þa 20
burg, hiora agene leode, hi hie þa up ahofon 7 winnan angunnan
on ælce healfe hiora, ge wið heora agen folc, ge wið Perse, ge wið
þa læssan Asiam, ge wið Ahtene þa burg, þe hie ær awestan, for
ðon þa feawan þe þær ut oþflugon hæfdon eft þa burg gebune 7
hæfdon Thebane, Creca leode, him on fultum asponon. Læcede- 25
monie wæron swa uppahæfene, þæt ægðer ge hie self wendon ge
ealle ða neahþeoda þæt hie ofer hie ealle mehte anwald habban.
Ac him Ahteniense mid Thebana fultume wiðstodon 7 hie mid
gefeohte cnysedan.

Æfter þæm Læcedemonie gecuron him to ladteowe Ircclidis 30
wæs haten, 7 hiene sendon on Perse mid fultume wið hie to
gefeohtanne. Him þa Perse mid heora twæm ealdormonnum

4–6] OH II. xix. 16.   7–19] OH III. i. 1–3.   20–9] OH III. i. 5.
30–p. 54, 8] OH III. i. 6.

---

1 beames] beamas C.   2 hefenisc] hefenlic C.   7 ðæm] *followed by*
eras. L.   8 Roma] rome C.   9 Læcedemonium] monium *on eras.* L.
10 þe Læcedemonie] *on eras.* L.   13 Læcedemoniæ] *orig.* læcedomoniæ
with first o *alt. to* e L.   24 gebune] gebogene C.

ongean coman. Oþer hatte Farnabuses, oþer Dissifarnon. Sona swa þara Læcedemonia ladteow wiste þæt he wið þa twegen heras sceolde, him þa rædlecre geþuhte þæt he wið oþerne frið gename,

f. 32 |þæt he þone oðerne þe ieð ofercuman mehte; 7 he swa gedyde 7 his
5 ærenddracan to oþrum onsende 7 him secgan het þæt he geornor wolde sibbe wið hiene þonne gewinn. He þa se ealdormon geliefedlice mid sibbe þara ærende anfeng, 7 Læcedemonie þa hwile gefliemdon þone oðerne ealdormon.

Æfter þæm Persa cyning benom þone ealdormon his scire, þe
10 ær þæm friþe anfeng æt Læcedemonium, 7 hie gesealde anum wræccean of Ahtena, Creca byrg, se wæs haten Conon, 7 hiene sende mid scipehere of Persum to Læcedemonium, 7 hie sendon to Egyptum Læcedemonie 7 him fultumes bædon, 7 hie him gesealdon an c þara miclena þriereðrena. Læcedemonie hæfdon
15 him to ladteowe ænne wisne mon, þeh he healt wære, se wæs hatan Ageselaus, 7 him to gielpworde hæfdon þæt him leofre wære þæt hie hæfdon healtne cyning þonne healt rice. Hie siþþan on ðæm sæ togædere foran 7 þær swa ungemetlice gefuhton þæt hie neah ealle forwurdon, þæt naðer ne mehte on oþrum sige geræcan. þær
20 wearð Læcedemonia anweald 7 heora dom alegen. Ne wene ic, cwæð Orosius, ðæt ænige twegen latteowas emnar gefuhten.

Æfter þæm Conon gelædde fierd eft on Læcedemonie 7 ðæt land buton þære byrig on ælcon þingun mid ealle aweste, þætte þa þe ær ute oþra ðeoda anwalda girndon, him þa god þuhte þær
25 hie mehten hie selfe æt ham wið ðeowdom bewerian. Pissandor hatte sum Læcedemonia latteow. He gesohte Conon mid scipun, þ[a] he of Læcedemonium for, 7 þara folca ægðer on oðerum micel wæl geslogan. þær wurdon Læcedemonie swa swiðe forslagen þæt hie naþer næfdon siþþan ne heora namon ne heora anweald. Ac
30 heora hryre wearð Ahtenum to arærnesse þæt hie ðone ealdan teonan gewrecan mehten þe him on ærdagum gemæne wæs, 7 hie 7 Thebane hie gegaderedon 7 Læcedemonie mid gefeohte sohton,

f. 32ᵛ |7 hie gefliemdon 7 hie on hiora burg bedrifon 7 siððan besætan. þa burgware sendon þa æfter Iesulause, þe mid heora here wæs

9–21] OH III. i. 7–9.   22–5] OH III. i. 10–11.   25–33] OH III. i.
12–19.   34–p. 55, 18] OH III. i. 20–5.

---

5 oþrum] 'þam' oðrum *with* 'þam' *in l.h.* C.   7 ærende] ærenda C.
Læcedemonie] læcedemonia C.   11 Ahtena] ahtene C.   14 þriere-
ðrena] þriereðrenena *both MSS.*   15 hatan] haten C.   27 þa] *from*
C, þe L.

in Asiam, 7 bædon þæt hie tidlice hamweard wære 7 heora gehulpe,
7 swa gedydon 7 on Ahtene ungearwe becoman 7 hie gefliemdon.
Ahteniense wæron þa him swiðe ondrædende þæt Læcedemonie
ofer hie ricsian mehten swa hie ær dydon, for þæm lytlan sige þe
hie þa ofer hie hæfdon. Hie sendon þa on Perse æfter Conone 7 5
hiene bædon þæt he him on fultume wære. 7 he him þæs getygþade
7 hie mid micle sciphere gesohte, 7 hie Læcedemonie mæst ealle
awestan, 7 hie to þon gedydon þæt hi hie selfe leton ægþer ge for
heane ge for unwræste. Æfter þæm Conon gelende to Ahtena þære
byrig, his ealdcyþþe, 7 þær mid micle gefean þa`ra´ burgleoda 10
onfangen wæs, 7 he ðær his selfes longe gemyndgunge gedyde mid
[þan] þe he geniedde ægþer ge Perse ge Læcedemonie þæt hie
gebetton þa burg þe hie ær tobræcon, 7 eac þæt Læcedemonie
þære byrig siþþan gehiersume wæron, þeh hie ær longe heora
wiþerwinnan wæren. Æfter þeosan gewinne gewearð þætte Perse 15
gebudan frið eallum Creca folce, næs na for þæm þe hie him
ænigra goda uþen, ac for þæm þe hie wunnon on Egypti, þæt hie
mosten for him þy bet þæm gewinne fullgongan. Ac Læcedemonie
hæfdon þa hwile maran unstillnessa þonne hie mægenes hæfden
7 wæron swiþor winnende on Thebane þonne hie fultumes hæfde 20
7 hloðum on hie staledon oð hie abræcan Arcadum heora burg.
Æfter þæm Thebane hie mid firde gesohton, 7 him Læcedemonie
oþre ongean brohton. þa hie longe fuhton, þa cleopade Læcede-
[monia] | ealdormon to Arcadium 7 bæden þæt hie ðæs gefeohtes f. 33
geswicen, þæt hie mosten þa deadan bebyrgean þe heora folces 25
ofslagen wæron. þæt is mid Crecum þeaw þæt mid ðæm worde
bið gecyþed hwæðer healf hæfð þonne sige.
For þon ic wolde gesecgan, cwæð Orosius, hu Creca gewinn
[angan], þe of Læ`ce´demonia ðærc byrg ærest onsteled wæs, 7
mid spellcwidum gemearcian, ærest on Athena þa burg 7 siþþan 30
on Thebane 7 siþþan on Boeti 7 siþþan on Macedaniæ—þiss
wæron ealle Creca leode—7 siþþan on þa læssan Asiam 7 ða on

18–27] OH III. ii. 1–3.   28–p. 56, 1] OH III. ii. 9–11.

1 hie] he *alt. from* hi C.   2 swa] he swa C.   gedydon] gedyde C.
6 hiene] *first* e *er.* L.   7 hie (1)] e *er.* L.   micle] micclum C.   hie (2)] e *er.* L.
8 hie (1)] e *er.* L.   hie (2)] e *er.* L.   9 Ahtena] ahtene C.   10 micle]
micclum C.   11 gemyndgunge] gemynegunge C.   12 þan] *from* C, *no*
reading L.   13 hie] e *er.* L.   23–4 Læcedemonia] læcede *both MSS.*
24 bæden] bædon C.   29 angan] *no reading* MSS.   31 Macedaniæ]
macedonie C.

þa maran, 7 siþþan on Perse 7 siþþan on Egypti, ic scæl eac þy
lator Romana istoria asecgan þe ic angunnen hæfde.

III. ii

Æfter þæm þe Romeburg getimbred wæs iii hunde wintra 7
lxxvi, wæs in Achie eorþbeofung, 7 twa byrig, Ebora 7 Elice, on
5 eorþan besuncon. Ic mæg eac on urum agnum tidum gelic anginn
þæm gesecgan, þeh hit swelcne ende næfde, þætte Constantinopolim, Creca burg, on swelcre cwacunge wæs, 7 hiere gewitgad
wæs of soðfæstum monnum þæt heo sceolde on eorþan besinca.
Ac heo wearð gescild þurh þone cristnan casere Arcadiusan 7 þurh
10 þæt cristene folc. On þæm burgum wæs getacnad þæt Crist is
eaðmodegra help 7 ofermodigra fiell. Mare ic þyses gemyndgade
þonne ic his mid ealle asæde; gif his hwa sie lustfull mare to
witanne, sece him þonne self þæt.

On þæm dagum gewearð þætte Wulchi 7 Falisci, þe ær wæron
15 lxx wintra wið Romane winnende, þæt hi hie þa oferwunnon 7
heora land oferhergedon. 7 raþe æfter þæm Suttrian þæt folc
wæron hergende on Romane oþ þære burge geata. Hit Romane
æfter þæm hrædlice mid gefeohte 7 mid hergiunge him forguldon
19 7 hie gefliemdon.

III. iii

f. 33ᵛ | Æfter þæm þe Romeburg getimbred wæs iii hund wintra 7
lxxxiii, þa þa Laucius, þe oþre noman wæs haten Genutius, 7
Quintus, þe oþre noman wæs haten Serfilius, ða hie wæron consulas on Rome, gewearð se micla moncwealm on þæm londe, nales,
swa hit gewuna is, of untidlican gewideran, þæt is, of wætum
25 sumerum 7 of drygum wintrum 7 of reðre 'lencten'hæte, 7 mid
ungemætre hærfestwætan 7 æfterhæþan, ac an wind com of Calabria wealde, 7 se wol mid þæm winde. þes moncwealm wæs on
Romanum full ii gear ofer ealle menn gelice, þeh þe sume deade

---

3–13] OH III. iii. 1–3.   14–19] OH III. iii. 4–5.   20–p. 57, 1] OH III.
iv. 1–3.

---

8 besinca] besincan C.   9 Arcadiusan] arcadiusas C.   10 folc] folc þe C.
getacnad] 'þæt' getacnode, with 'þæt' in l.h. C.   11 gemyndgade] first d
er. L, gemyngode C.   14 Wulchi] fulchi C.   15 Romane] rome C.
23 nales] last three letters er. L, nalæs C.   25 lenctenhæte] lenctenhætan
C.   26 ungemætre] ungemetlican C.   28 full] fulle C.

wæron, sume uneaþe gedrycnede aweg coman; oþ þæt heora
biscepas sædon þæt heora godas bædon þæt him man worhte
anfiteatra, þæt mon mehte þone hæðeniscan plegan þærinne don,
7 hiora diofolgield, þæt wæron openlice ealle unclænnessa.
Her [m]e magon nu, cwæð Orosius, þa geondwyrdon þe þæs cristen- 5
domes wiðerflitan sint, hu heora godas þurh heora blotunge 7
þurh hiera diofolgield þæs monncwealmes gehulpon, buton þæt
hie ne angeatan mid hwelcum scinncræfte 7 mid hwelcum lotwrence
hit deofla dydon—næs na se soða God—ðæt hie mid þy yfele þa
menn swenctan, to ðon þæt hie geliefdon heora ofrunga 7 heora 10
deofolgieldum, 7 þæt hie þonan mosten to þæm sawlum becuman,
7 þæt hie [hie] mosten tawian mid þære mæstan bismrunge æt
heora anfiteatra. þa wæron unarimede 7 me nu monigfeald to
secganne, for þon þu, fæder Agustinus, hie hæfst on þinum bocum
sweotole gesæd; 7 ic gehwam wille þærto tæcan þe hiene his lyst 15
ma to witanne.

Æfter þeosan on þæm ilcan geare tohlad seo eorþe binnan
Romebyrig. þa sædon heora biscepas eft þæt heora godas bædan
þæt him mon sealde ænne cucne mon, þa him þuhte þæt heo heora 19
deadra to lyt hæfden. | 7 seo eorþe swa giniende bad, oþ þæt Mar- f. 34
cus, þe oþre noman hatte Curtius, mid horse 7 mid wæpnum
þæroninnan besceat; 7 hio siþþan togædre behlad.

III. iiii

Æfter þæm þe Romeburg getimbred wæs iii hund wintra 7
lxxxviii, þætte Gallie oferhergedan Romana lond oð iiii mila to
ðære byrig 7 þa burg mehton eaðe begitan gif hie þær ne gew[a]ca- 25
don, for þon Romane wæron swa forhte 7 swa æmode þæt hie ne
wendon þæt hie þa burg bewerian mehton. Ac þæs on morgenne
Titus heora ladteow, þe oðre noman wæs haten Qui'n'tius, hie mid
firde gesohte. þær gefeaht Mallius anwig, þe oðre noman wæs

1–4] OH III. iv. 5.   4–13] OH III. iv. 4.   13–16] OH III. iv. 6.
17–22] OH III. v. 1–3.   23–p. 58, 4] OH III. vi. 1–3.

---

1 gedrycnede] gedrehte C.   5 me] so C, me (?) with m er. L.   9 yfele]
second e alt. from a L.   12 hie hie] hie L, hi C.   bismrunge] bism
on eras. L.   14 hæfst] fragment 1 of MS B begins. here   23 wintra]
wintrum B.   24 lxxxviii] lxxxvii B, lxxviii C.   Gallie] gallige B.   Romana]
roman C.   oð] æt B.   25–6 gewacadon] gewacodan C, gewicadon L,
gewicodan B.   26 for þon] for þon þe B, for þam C.   28 Titus]
tidus C.   oðre] oðran C.

haten Tarcwatus, wið anne Galliscne monn 7 hiene ofslog; 7 Titus
Cuintius þa oðre sume gefliemde, sume ofslog. Be þæm mon mehte
ongietan hwæt ðær ofslagen wæs, þa heora fela ðusenda gefongen
wæs.

III. v

5 Æfter þæm þe Romeburg getimbred wæs iiii hunde wintra 7 ii,
ðætte Cartaina þære burge ærendracan comon to Rome 7 him
gebudon þæt hie frið him betweonum hæfden, for þon hie [o]n an
land þa winnende wæron, þæt wæs on Benefente. Mid þæm þe þa
ærendracan to Rome comon, þa com eac mid him seo ofermæte
10 heardsælnesse 7 monegra ðeoda iermþa, seo longe æfter þæm
weaxende wæs, swa hit heofones tungul on þæm tidun cyþende
wæron, þæt hit wæs niht oð midne dæg, 7 on sumre tide hit
hagalade stanum ofer ealle Romane.

On þæm dagum wæs Alexander geboren on Crecum swa swa an
15 micel yst come ofer ealne middangeard. 7 Ocus, Persa cyning,
þone mon oþere noman het Artecsersis, æfter þæm þe he Egyptum
forhergede, he gefor siþþan on Iudana lond 7 hiera fela forhergeade.
Siþþan on Ircaniam þæm londe he heora [swiðe] fela gesette wið
19 þone sæ þe mon Caspia hætt, 7 hie þær gesetene sint giet oð þisne
f. 34ᵛ dæg | mid bradum folcum, on ðæm tohopan þæt hie sume siðe
God þonan ado to heora agnum lande. Siþþan Artecsersis abræc
Sidonem, Fenitia burg, seo wæs þa welegast on ðæm dagum.

Æfter þæm Romane angunnan þæt Somniticum gewinn ymbe
Campena land. Hie þa longe 7 oftrædlice ymb þæt fuhton on
25 hweorfendum sigum. þa getugon Somnite him on fultum Pirrusan,
Epira cyning, þone mæstan feond Romanum. þæt gewinn wearð
hwæðre sume hwile gestilled, for þon Punici wið Romane winnan
angunnan.

Siþþan þæt gewin angunnen wæs, gif ænig mon 'sie', cwæð
30 Orosius, þe on gewritun findan mæge þæt Ianas dura siþþan

5–13] OH III. vii. 2–4.   14–22] OH III. vii. 5–8.   23–8] OH III.
viii. 1.   29–p. 59, 3] OH III. viii. 3–4.

---

1 Tarcwatus] tarquatus B, tarcuatus C.   2 Cuintius] quintius B, C.
5 wintra] wintrum B.   7 on an] so B, C, nan L.   8 þa (1)] om. B.
14 Crecum] grecum C.   16 oþere] oðrum C.   Egyptum] ægypti B.
17 forhergede] oferhergode B.   siþþan] om. B.   Iudana] iudeana B, iuþana
C.   18 swiðe] from C, no reading L, B.   19 þone] þa B.   20 sume
siðe] om. B.   22 Sidonem] siþonem C.   29 Siþþan] on eras. and preceded by er. þ L.

belocen wurde buton anum geare—7 þæt wæs for þæm þe Romane
eallne þone gear an monncwealme lægan—ær eft Octauianus dæge
þæs caseres. þæt hus hæfdon Romane to ðæm anum tacne geworht
þæt on swelce healfe swelce hie þonne winnende beon woldan,
swa suþ, swa norþ, swa east, swa west, þonne andydan hie þa duru 5
þe on þa healfe open wæs, þæt hie be þæm wiston hwider hie
sceoldon. 7 mið þæm þe hie þara dura hwelce opene gesawon,
þonne tugon hie heora hrægl bufan cneow 7 giredon hie to wige,
7 be þæm wiston þæt hie wið sum folc frið ne hæfdon. 7 þonne hie
frið hæfdon, þonne wæron ealle þa dura betyneda, 7 hie leton hiera 10
hrægl ofdune to fotum. Ac þa þa Octauianus se casere to rice feng,
þa wurdon Ianas dura betyneda, 7 wearð sibb 7 friþ ofer ealne
middangeard.

Æfter þæm þe Perse frið genaman wið Romanum, siþþan
gelicade eallum folcum þæt hie Romanum underþieded wære 7 15
hiora æ to behealdanne, 7 swa swiþe þone frið lufedon þæt him
leofre wæs þæt hie Romanisce cyningas hæfden þonne of heora
agnum cynne. On þæm wæs sweotole getacnod | þæt nan eorþlic f. 35
man ne mehte swelce lufe 7 swelce sibbe ofer eallne middangeard
gedon swelce þa wæs. Ac heo for þæm wæs þe Crist on þæm dagum 20
geboren wæs, þe sibb is heofonwara 7 eorðwara. þæt eac Octauianus sweotole getacnade, þa þa Romane him woldon ofrian swa
heora gewuna wæs 7 sædon þæt sio sibb of his mihte wære; ac he
ægðer fleah ge þa dæd ge þa sægene 7 eac self sæde þæt seo dæd
his nære, ne eac beon ne mehte nanes eorðlices monnes, þætte ealre 25
worolde swelce sibbe bringan mehte, þætte twa þeoda ær habban
ne mehton, ne, ðætte læsse wæs, twa gemægþa.

III. vi

Æfter þæm þe Romeburg getimbred wæs iiii hunde wintrum 7
viii, gewearð þætte Romane 7 Latine wunnon. On þæm forman
gefeohte wearð Romane consul ofslagen Mallius, þe oðre noman 30
wæs haten Tarcuatus, 7 heora oþer consul, þe mon Detius hett 7

11–13] OH III. viii. 5.   14–27] OH III. viii. 5–8.   28–p. 60, 5] OH
III. ix. 1–2.

---

2 ær eft] ærest on C.   6 open] *om.* B.   7 mið] mid B, C.   9 ne
hæfdon] næfdan B.   11 ofdune] ondune B.   to (1)] *fragment 1 in B ends.*
22 Romane] romana C.   swa] swa swa C.   23 of] on C.   27 ne (2)]
na C.   30 Romane] romana C.   oðre] oðrum C.   31 Detius] decius C.

oðre noman Mure, his agenne sunu ofslog, for þon he oferbræc
heora gecwedrædenne, þæt wæs þæt [hie] hæfdon gecweden þæt
hie ealle emlice on Latine tengden. Ac þær an ut asceat of Latina
weorode 7 anwiges bæd, 7 him ðæs consules sunu ongean com 7
5 hiene þær ofslog. For þæm gylte hiene eft hett his fæder ofslean.
For þæm slege noldan Romane brengan þæm consule þone triumphan þe heora gewuna wæs, þeh he sige hæfde.

On ðæm æfterran geare þæs, Minutia hatte an wifmon þe on
heora wisan sceolde nunne beon, seo hæfde gehaten heora gydenne
10 Dianan þæt heo wolde hiere lif on fæmnhade alibban. þa forlæg
heo hie [sona]. Hie þa Romane, for þæm gylte þe heo hiere beot
aleag, swa cuce on eorþan bedulfan, 7 nugiet to dæge þæm gylte
to tacne mon hætt ðæt lond Manfeld þær hie mon byrgde.

Raþe æfter þæm on þara twegea consula dæge, Claudius, þe oðre
15 noman hatte Marcellus, 7 Ualerius, þe oðre noman hatte Flaccus, þa
f. 35ᵛ gewearð hit, þeh hit me scondlic sie, | cwæð Orosius, þætte sume
Romana wif on swelcum scinlace wurdon 7 on swelcum wodan
dreame, þæt hie woldon ælcne mon, ge wif ge wæpned, þara þe hie
mehton, mid atre acwellan 7 hit on mete oþþe on drynce to geþic-
20 genne gesellan 7 þæt longe donde wæron ær þæt folc wiste hwonan
þæt yfel come (buton þæt hie sædon þæt hit ufane of ðære lyfte come)
ær þon hit þurh ænne þeowne mon geypped wearð. þa wæron ealle
þa wif beforan Romana witan gelaðede, þara wæs iii hund 7 hundeahtatig, [7] þær wæron geniedde þæt hie þæt ilce þigedan þæt hie
25 ær oþrum sealdon, þæt hie þærryhte deade wæron beforan eallum
þæm monnum.

III. vii

Æfter þæm þe Romeburg getimbred wæs iiii hund wintra 7 xxii,
Alexander, Epirotarum cyning, þæs maran Alexandres eam, he mid
eallum his mægene wið Romane winnan angan 7 æt Somnite
30 gemære 7 Romana gesæt 7 þa nihstan landleode on ægþere healfe
him on fultum geteah, oþ Somnite him gefuhton wið 7 þone cyning

5–7] OH III. ix. 4.   8–13] OH III. ix. 5.   14–26] OH III. x. 1–3.
27–p. 61, 5] OH III. xi. 1–2.

1 oðre] oþrum C.   sunu] 'he' *in margin in l.h.* (?) L.   2 hie] hy C, *no
reading* L.   5–6 hiene (2) . . . slege] *om.* C.   6 brengan] bringan C.
10 fæmnhade] fæmnanhade C.   11 sona] *from* C, *no reading* L.   beot]
gehat C.   12 cuce] cuce hy C.   14 oðre] oðrum C.   15 Marcel-
lus] marcellius C.   Ualerius] ualerianus C.   oðre] oðrum C.   22 ær
þon] ær C.   24 7] *from* C, *om.* L.   25 þærryhte] þær C.

ofslogon. Nu ic þyses Alexandres her gemyndgade, cwæð Orosius,
nu ic wille eac þæs maran Alexandres gemunende beon, þæs oþres
nefan. Þeh ic ymbe Romana gewin on þæm gearrime forð ofer þæt
geteled hæbbe, ic sceal hwæðre eft gewendan þæt ic hwelcnehugu
dæl gesecge Alexa[n]dres dæda; 7 hu Philippus his fæder iiii hund 5
wintrum æfter þæm þe Romeburg getimbred wæs, he feng to
Mæcedonia rice on Crecum 7 þæt hæfde xxv wintra, 7 binnan
þæm gearum he geeode ealle þa cynericu þe on Crecum wæron.
An wæs Ahteniense, oþer wæs Thebane, iii wæs Thesali, iiii
Læcedemonie, v Focenses, vi Mesii, vii Macedonie, þæt he ærest 10
hæfde. Philippus, þa he | cniht wæs, wæs Thebanum to gisle f. 36
geseald, Paminunde, þæm stroʼnʼgan cyninge 7 þæm gelæredestan
philosophe, from his agnum breþer Alexandre, þe Læcedemonia
rice þa hæfde, 7 mid him gelæred wearð on þam þrim gearum þa
he ðær wæs. Þa wearð Alexander ofslagen his broðor from his 15
agenre meder, þeh heo hiere oþerne sunu eac ær ofsloge for hiere
geligernesse, 7 heo wæs Philippuses steo[p]modor. Þa feng
Philippus to Mæcedonia rice 7 hit ealle hwile on miclan pleo 7 on
miclan earfeþan hæfde, þæt ægþer ge him mon utane of oðrum
londum anwann, ge eac þæt his agen folc ymbe his feorh sierede, 20
þæt him þa æt nihstan leofre wæs þæt he ute wunne þonne he æt
ham wære. His forme gefeoht wæs wið Atheniense 7 hie oferwonn,
7 æfter þæm wið Hiliricos, þe we Pulgare hatað, 7 heora monig
ðusend ofslog, 7 heora mæstan burg geeode, Larisan. 7 siþþan on
Thesali he þæt gewinn swiþost dyde for þære gewilnunge þe he 25
wolde hi him on fultum geteon for heora wigcræfte, for þon hie
cuþon on horsum ealra folca ʼfeohtanʼ betst 7 ærest. Hie þa ægðer
ge ʼforʼ his ege ge for his olecunge him to gecierdon. He þa gegaderade mid heora fultume 7 mid his agene ægþer ge ridendra ge
gongendre unoferwunnendlic[n]e here. 30
Æfter þæm þe Philippus hæfde Atheniense 7 Thesali him

5–7] OH III. xii. 1.   11–30] OH III. xii. 2–7.   31–p. 62, 16] OH
III. xii. 8–11.

---

3 gearrime] geargerime C.   ofer] oð C.   4 hwelcnehugu] ælcnehugu C.
5 Alexandres] *from* C, alexaldres L.   7 on] 7 C.   8 Crecum] grecum C.
9 Ahteniense] atheniense C.   10 Focenses] folcenses C.   11 Philippus]
phipilpus C.   wæs (2)] he wæs C.   13 philosophe] philosofe C.   17 steop-
modor] *from* C, steowmodor L.   18 Philippus] philipus C.   20 his (2)]
his agen C.   25 gewilnunge] wilnunge C.   26 for þon] 7 for þon þe C.
27 feohtan] *om.* C.   29 agene] agenum C.   ridendra] ridende C.   30 gon-
gendre] gangendra C.   unoferwunnendlicne] unoferwunnendlice *both MSS.*

underðieded, he begeat Aru[h]es dohtor him to wife, Malosorum
cyninges, Olimphiade wæs hatenu. Aru[h]es wende þæt he his rice
gemiclian sceolde þa he his dohtor Philippuse sealde. Ac he hiene
on ðære wenunge geband 7 him ðæt an genam þæt he self hæfde
5 7 hiene siþþan forsende oþ he his lif forlet. Æfter þæm Philippus
feaht on [O]thona þa burg, on Thebana rice, 7 him ðær wearþ oþer
eage mid anre flan ut ascoten. He hwæðre þa burg gewann 7 eall
þæt moncynn acwealde þæt he ðærinne mette. 7 æfter þæm mid
f. 36ᵛ searewan he geeode eall Creca folc, | for þon heora gewuna wæs
10 þæt hie woldon of ælcerre byrig him self anwald habban 7 nan
oðerre underþied beon, ac wæron him swa betweonum winnende.
þa bædan hie Philippus æst of anre byrig, þonne of oþerre, þæt hie
him on fultume wære wiþ þa þe him on wunnon. þonne he þa
oferswiðed hæfde þe he þonne on winnende wæs mid þæm folce
15 þe hiene ær fultumes bæd, þonne dyde he him ægþer to gewealdon;
swa he belytegade ealle Crece on his geweald. þa Crece þæt þa
undergeaton, 7 eac him swiþe ofþyncendum þæt hie an cyning swa
ieðelice forneah buton ælcon gewinne on his geweald beþridian
sceolde, gelice 7 hie him þeowiende wæron—he hie eac oþrum
20 folcum oftrædlice on þeowot sealde þe ær nan folc ne mehte mid
gefeohte gewinnan—hie þa ealle wið hiene gewin up ahofan; 7 he
hiene geeaðmedde to þæm folce þe he him þær heardost ondred,
þæt wæron Thesalii, 7 on hie gelec þæt hie mid him on Athene
wunnon. þa hie to ðæm gemære comon mid heora firde, þa hæfdon
25 hie hiera clusan belocene. þa Philippus þærbinnan ne mehte þæt
he his teonan gewræce, he þa wende on þa ane þe him þa getriewe
wæron 7 heora burg gefor 7 þæt folc mid ealle fordyde 7 heora
hergas towearp, swa he ealle dyde þe he awer mette, ge eac his
agene, oþ him þa biscepas sædon þæt ealle godas him irre wæren
30 7 wiðwinnende; 7 þeh hie him ealle irre wæren, on þæm xxv wintrum þe he winnende wæs 7 feohtende he na oferwunnen ne wearð.
Æfter he gefor on Capadotiam þæt lond 7 þær ealle þa cyningas

21–4] OH III. xii. 14.   24–31] OH III. xii. 15–17.   32–p. 63, 6] OH
III. xii. 18–20.

---

1 Aruhes] *from* C, arues L.   Malosorum] malosolum C.   2 Olimphi-
ade] olimphiaðe heo C.   Aruhes] *from* C, arues L.   3 he (1)] he he L.
4 wenunge] wununge C.   6 Othona] othono C, thona L.   oþer] þæt
oðer C.   9 searewan] his searwum C.   12 hie (2)] he C.   15 geweal-
don] wealdan C.   18 forneah] *om.* C.   23 Athene] nathene L, thene C.
26 gewræce] *on eras.* L.   28 awer] ahwer C.   29 oþ] oð þæt C.
32 Æfter] æfter þam C.   Capadotiam] capodotiam C.

mid biswice ofslog. Siþþan ealle Capadotiam him gehiersumedon.
7 hiene siþþan wende on his þrie gebroðor, 7 ænne ofslog, 7 þa
twegen oðflugon on Olinthum þa burg, seo wæs fæstast 7 welegast
Mæcedonia | rices, 7 him Philippus æfter for 7 þa burg abræc 7 þa   f. 37
broðor ofslog 7 eall þæt þærinne wæs. þa þrie gebroðor næron na   5
Philippuse gemedren, ac wæron gefæderen.
      On þæm dagum on Tracia þæm londe wæron twegen cyningas
ymb þæt ric[e] winnende, þa wæron gebroþor. þa sendan hie to
Philippuse 7 bædon þæt he hie ymb þæt rice gesemde 7 on þære
gewitnesse wære þæt hit emne gedæled wære. He þa Philippus to   10
heora gemote com mid micelre firde 7 þa cyningas begen ofslog 7
ealle þa witan, 7 feng him to þæm ricum bæm. Æfter þæm Atheniense bædan Philippus þæt he heora ladteow wære wið Focenses
þæm folce, þeh hie ær hiera clusan him ongean beluce, 7 þæt he
oðer ðara dyde, oþþe hie gesemde, oþþe him gefultumade þæt hi   15
hie oferwinnan mehten. He him þa gehet þæt he him gefultuman
wolde þæt hie hie oferwunnen. Eac æt þæm ilcan cirre bædan
Focense his fultumes wið Athene. He him þa gehet þæt he hie
geseman wolde. Siþþan he buta þa clusan on his gewealde hæfde,
þa dyde he him eac þa ricu to gewealdon, 7 his here geond þa   20
byrig todælde 7 him bebead þæt hie ðæt lond hergiende wæron
oþ hie hit awesten, þæt þæm folce wæs ægþres waa, ge þæt hie
þæt mæste yfel forberan sceoldon, ge eac þæt hie his sciran ne
dorstan. Ac he ealle þa ricestan forslean het 7 þa oðre sume on
wræcsið forsende, sume on oðra mearca gesette. Swa he Philippus   25
þa miclan ricu geniþerade, þeh þe ær anra gehwelc wende þæt hit
ofer monig oþru anwald habban mehte, þæt hie þa æt nihstan hie
selfe to nohte bemætan.
      Philippuse geþuhte æfter þæm þæt he an land[e] ne mehte þæm
folce mid gifan gecweman þe him an simbel wæron mid winnende;   30
ac he scipa gegaderode, 7 wicingas wurdon 7 sona æt anum cirre
an c 7 eahtatig ceapscipa gefengon. | þa geceas he him ane burg   f. 37ᵛ
wið þone sæ, Bizantium wæs hatenu, to ðon þæt him gelicade þæt

7–12] OH III. xii. 22.   12–28] OH III. xii. 23–32.   29–p. 64, 27] OH
III. xiii. 1–7.

———

1 biswice] his swice C.   Capadotiam] capodotiam C.   6 gemedren]
gemedred C.   gefæderen] gefædred C.   7 Tracia] thracia C.   8 rice]
from C, ric L.   14 clusan] clusa C.   beluce] *so also* C, *alt. to* beluco'n' L.
19 buta] *om.* C.   22 oþ] oð þæt C.   ægþres] ægþer C.   29 lande]
from C, land L.   32 geceas] ceas C.

hie þær mehten betst friŏ binnan habban, 7 eac þæt hie þæ[r]
gehendaste wæren on gehwelc lond þonan to winnanne; ac him þa
burgleode þæs wiŏcwædon. Philippus mid his fultume hi besæt 7
him anwann. Seo ilce Bizantium wæs ærest getimbred from Pausa-
5 nia, Læcedemonia ladteowe, 7 æfter þæm from Constantino þæm
cristenan casere geieced, 7 be his noman heo wæs gehatenu Constantinopolim 7 is nu þæt hehste cynesetl 7 heafod ealles eastrices.
Æfter þæm þe Philippus longe þa burg beseten hæfde, þa ofþuhte
him þæt he þæt feoh to sellanne næfde his here swa hie bewuna
10 wæron. He þa his here on tu todælde. Sum ymb þa burg sætt 7 he
mid sumum hloþum for 7 monega byrg bereafode on Cheranisse,
Creca folce, 7 siþþan for an Sciþþie mid Alexandre his suna, þær
Atheas se cyning rice hæfde, þe ær his geþo[f]ta wæs wiŏ Hisdriana
gewinne, 7 þa on ŏæt lond faran wolde. Ac hie þa landleode wiŏ
15 þæt gewarnedon 7 him mid firde angean foran. þa þæt þa Philippus
geacsade, þa sende he æfter maran fultume to ŏæm þe þa burg
ymbseten hæfdon 7 mid ealle mægene an hie for. þeh þe Sciþþie
hæfdon maran monmenie 7 self hwætran wæron, hie þeh Philippus
besirede mid his lotwrencum, mid [þæm] þæt he his heres þriddan
20 dæl gehydde 7 him self mid wæs, 7 þæm twam dælum bebead, swa
hie feohtan angunnen, þæt hie wiŏ his flugen, þæt he siþþan mid
þæm ŏriddan dæle hie beswican mehte, þonne hie tofarene wæron.
þær wearŏ Sciþþia xx m ofslagen 7 gefangen wifmonna 7 wæpnedmonna, 7 þær wæs xx m horsa gefangen, þeh hie ŏær nan licgende
25 feoh ne metten, swa hie ær bewuna wæron þonne hie wælstowe
f. 38 geweald ahton. On þæm gefeohte wæs ærest | anfunden Sciþþia
wanspeda. Eft þa Philippus wæs þonan cirrende, þa offor hiene
oŏere Sciþþie mid lytelre firde, Tribaballe wæron hatene. Philippus
him dyde heora wig unweorŏ, oþ hiene an cwene sceat þurh þæt
30 þeoh, þæt þæt hors wæs dead þe he onufan sæt. þa his here geseah
þæt he mid þy horse afeoll, hie þa ealle flugon 7 eal þæt herefeoh
forleton þe hie ær gefangen hæfdon. Wæs þæt micel wundor þæt
swa micel here for þæs cynges [fielle] fleah, þe na ær ŏæm fleon nolde,
þeh his mon fela þusenda ofsloge. Philippus mid his lotwrence, þa

---

1 friŏ binnan] binnan friŏ C.   þær (2)] *from* C, þæt L.   2 on] *om.* C.
11 Cheranisse] cheranisce C.   13 geþofta] *from* C, geþohta L.   Hisdriana]
isŏriana C.   17 ealle] eallum C.   18 monmenie] manna mænige C.
self] hy selfe *with* e *in l.h. on eras.?* C.   19 mid þæm þæt] mid þam þe
C, mid þæt L.   25 bewuna] gewuna C.   33 fielle] fylle C, *om.* L.

hwile þe he wund wæs, aliefde eallum Crecum þæt heora anwaldas
moston standan him betweonum, swa hie ær on ealddagum dydon.
Ac sona swa he gelacnad wæs, swa hergeade he on Athene. þa
sendon hie to Læcedemonium '7 bædon' þæt hie gefriend wurden,
þeh hie ær longe gefiend wæren, 7 bædon þæt hie ealle gemænelice 5
cunnoden, mehten hi heora gemænan fiend him from adon. Hie
þa sume him getygðedon 7 gegaderodon maran monfultum þonne
Philippus hæfde, sume for his ege ne dorstan. Philippuse geþuhte
þa þæt he leng mid folc'g'efeohtum wið hie ne mehte. Ac oftrædlice he wæs mid hloþum on hi hergende 7 onbutan sierwende oþ 10
hie eft totwæmde wæron, 7 ða on ungearwe on Ahtene mid firde
gefor. Æt þæm cirre wurdon Ahteniense swa wælhreowlice forslagen 7 forhiened þæt hie na siþþan nanes anwaldes hi ne bemætan
ne nanes freodomes.

Æfter þæm Philippus gelædde fird on Læcedemonie 7 on The- 15
bane 7 hi miclum tintrade 7 bismrade, oþ hie mid ealle wæron
fordon 7 forhiened. Æfter þæm þe Philippus hæfde ealle Crecas
on his geweald gedon, he sealde his dohtor Alexandre þæm cyninge
his agnum mæge, þe he ær Æpira rice geseald hæfde. þa on ðæm
dæge plegedon hie of horsum, ægþer ge Philippus ge Alexander, 20
| þe he his dohtor him sellan wolde, ge Alexander his agen sunu, f. 38ᵛ
swa heora þeaw æt swelcum wæs, 7 eac monige oþere mid him.
þa Philippuse gebyrede þæt he for ðæm plegan ut of ðæm mon-
weorode arad, þa mette hiene his ealdgefana sum 7 hiene ofstang.

Ic nat, cwæð Orosius, for hwi eow Romanum sindon þa ærran 25
gewin swa wel gelicad 7 swa lustsumlice on leoðcwidum to gehieranne, 7 for hwy ge þa tida swelcra broca swa wel hergeað, 7
nu, þeh eow lytles hwæt swelcra gebroca on becume, þonne
gemænað gc hit to þæm wyrrestan tidum 7 magon hie swa hreowlice wepan swa ge magon þa'ra' oþra bliþelice hlihhan. Gif ge 30
swelce þegnas sint swelce ge wenað þæ[t] ge sien, þonne sceoldon
ge swa lustlice eowre agnu brocu aræfnan, þeh hie læssan sien,

15–17] OH III. xiv. 1.   18–24] OH III. xiv. 4 and 7.   25–p. 66, 6] OH
III. xiv. 8–10.

6 fiend] feond C.   8 his] *om*. C.   12 Ahteniense] atheniense C.
13 na] *om*. C.   15 Philippus gelædde] gelædde philippus C.   Læcede-
monie] læcedomonie C.   16 tintrade] tintregade C.   mid] *om*. C.
19 Æpira] epira C.   21 his . . . him] him his dohtor C.   24 his]
om. C.   29 gemænað] mænað C.   31 þæt ge] *from* C, þæte *with* t *alt.*
to g L.

swa ge heora sint to gehieranne. þonne þuhte eow þas tida beteran
þonne þa, for þon eowre brocu nu læssan sindon þonne heora þa
wære. For þon Philippus wæs xxv wintra Creca folc hienende,
ægþer ge heora byrig bærnende ge hiera folc sleande 7 sume on
5 elþiodige forsende, 7 eower Romana brocu, þe ge ðær ealneg
drifað, næs buton þrie dagas. Philippuses yfel mehte þeh þagiet
be sumum dæle gemetlic þyncan, ær se swelgend to rice feng,
Alexander his sunu, þeh ic nu his dæda sume hwile gesugian scyle,
oþ ic Romana gesecge þe on ðæm ilcan tidun gedon wæran.

III. viii

10 Æfter þæm þe Romeburg getimbred wæs iiii hunde wintra 7 vi 7
xxgum, Caudenes Furculus seo stow gewearþ swiþe mære, 7 giet
todæge is, for Romana bismere. þæt gewearð æfter þæm gefeohte
f. 39 þe Romane 7 Somnite hæfdon, swa we ær beforan sædon, | þa
þara Somnita xx m ofslagen wurdon under Fauia þæm consule. Ac
15 Somnite æt oþran gefeohte mid maran fultume 7 mid maran
wærscipe to Romana gemetinge coman þonne hie ær dyde, æt
þære stowe þe mon hætt Caudenes Furculus. 7 þær Romane
swiþost for þæm besierede wæron þe him þæt land uncuþre wæs
þonne hit Somnitum wære, 7 on ungewis on an nirewett beforan,
20 oþ hie Somnite utan beforan, þæt hie siþþan oþer sceoldon, oþþe
for metelieste heora lif alætan, oþþe Somnitum on hand gan. On
þæm anwalde wæron Somnite swa bealde þæt se æþeling þe heora
ladteow wæs, Pontius wæs haten, het ascian þone cyning his
fæder, þe þær æt ham wæs, hwæþer him leofre wære, þe he hie
25 ealle acwealde, þe hie libbende to bismre gerenia[n] hete. Hie þa
se æþeling to ðæm bismre getawade þe þa on ðæm dagum mæst
wæs, þæt he hie bereafade heora claþa 7 heora wæpna, 7 siex hund
gisla on his geweald underfeng, on þæt gerad þæt hie him siþþan
ece þeowas wæren. 7 se æþeling bebead sumum his folce þæt hie
30 gebrohten Romana consulas 7 heora witan æt heora agnum londe

6–9] OH III. xv. 1.   10–p. 67, 2] OH III. xv. 2–6.

---

5 elþiodige] ellþeode C.   eower] *fragment 2 of MS B begins here.*   6 drifað]
drifan B.   8 gesugian] gesuwian C.   9 oþ] þæt B.   gedon] gedone
C.   11 Furculus] *so* C, *third* u *alt. to* e L, furcules B.   14 Somnita]
somnite C.   17 hætt] hæt B, het C.   Furculus] furculas C.   18 be-
sierede] bescyrede B, bismere C.   20 oþ] þæt B.   25 gerenian] *so*
B, C, gereniam L.   30 gebrohten] bebrohtan B. 7 heora witan] *om.* C.
æt] on C.   londe] landum C.

7 him beforan drifen swa swa niedlingas, þæt heora bismer þy
mare wære.

Geornor we woldon, cwæð Orosius, iowra Romana bismra beon
forsugiende þonne secgende, þær we for eowerre agenre gnornunge
moste, þe ge wið þæm cristendome habbað. Hwæt, ge witon þæt 5
ge giet todæge wæron Somnitum þeowe, gif ge him ne alugen iowra
wedd 7 eowre aþas þe ge him sealdon; 7 ge murciað nu, for þæm
þe monega folc þe ge anwald ofer hæfdon noldon eow gelæstan þæt
hie eow beheton; 7 nellað geþencan hu lað eow selfum wæs to
gelæstanne eowre aþas þæm þe ofer eow anwald hæfdon.   10

Sona þæs on þæm æfterran geare forbræcon Romane heora aþas
þe hie Somnitum geseald hæfdon, 7 mid Papiria heora consule hie
mid firde gesohton 7 þær deadlicne | sige geforan, for þæm þe f. 39ᵛ
ægþer þara folca wæs þæs gefeohtes georn, Somnite for þæm
anwalde þe hie on ægþere healfe hæfdon, 7 Romane for þæm   15
bismere þe hie ær æt him geforan, oþ Romane gefengon Somnita
cyning 7 heora fæsten abræcon 7 hie to gafolgieldum gedydon. Se
ilca Papirius wæs æfter þæm gefeohte mid Romanum swelces
domes beled þæt hie hiene to ðon gecoren hæfdon þæt he mid
gefeohte mehte þæm maran Alexandre wiþstondan, gif he eastane 20
of Asiam Italiam gesohte, swa he gecweden hæfde.

III. viiii

Aefter þæm þe Romeburg getimbred wæs iiii hunde wintrum 7
xxvi, feng Alexander to Mæcedonia rice æfter Philippuse his fæder,
7 his ærestan ðegnscipe on ðon gecyþde þa he ealle Crecas mid his
snyttro on his geweald geniedde, ealle þa þe wið hiene gewin 25
up ahofon. Þæt wearð ærest from Persum, þa hie sealdon Demostanase þæm philosophe licgende feoh wið þæm þe he gelærde ealle
Crecas þæt hie Alexandre wiðsocen. Athene budon gefeoht
Alexandre, ac he hie sona forslog 7 gefliemde, þæt hie siþþan
ungemetlicne ege from him hæfdon, 7 Thebana fæsten abræc 7 30

3–10] OH III. xv. 7.   11–21] OH III. xv. 8–10.   22–p. 68, 12] OH
III. xvi. 1–3.

4 þær] þonn[e] *with last letter illegible* B.   6 alugen] lugon C.   7 mur-
ciað] murcniað B, C.   7–8 for þæm þe] for ðon þe B.   10 gelæstanne]
'ge'læstanne *with* 'ge' *in l.h.* C.   18 Papirius] papirus C.   19 ðon] ðæm B.
23 Mæcedonia] macedonia B.   Philippuse] philippus B.   27 philosophe]
fragment 2 of B ends.

mid ealle towearp, þætte ær wæs ealra Creca heafodstol, 7 siþþan
þæt folc eall on ellþeodge him wið feo gesealde; 7 ealle þa oðre
þeoda þe an Crecum wæron he to gafolgieldum gedyde, buton
Mæcedonium þe him æst to gecirdon, 7 þonan wæs farende an
5 Nilirice 7 on Thraci 7 hie ealle to him gebigde. 7 siþþan he gegaderode fird wið Perse, 7 þa hwile þe he hie gaderade, he ofslog
ealle his mægas þe he geræcan mehte. On his feðehere wæron
xxxii m, 7 þæs gehorsedan fifte healf m, 7 scipa an hund 7 eahtatig.
9 Nat ic, cwæð Orosius, hwæðer mare wundor wæs, þe þæt he swa
f. 40 mid lytle fultume þone mæstan dæl | þisses middangeardes gegan
mehte, þe þæt he mid swa lytle weorode swa micel anginnan
dorste.

On þæm ærestan gefeohte þe Alex[an]der gefeaht wið Darius an
Persum, Darius hæfde siex hund m folces. He wearþ þeh swiþor
15 beswicen for Alexandres searewe þonne for his gefeohte. þær wæs
ungemetlic wæl geslagen Persa, 7 Alexandres næs na ma þonne
hund twelftig on þæm rædehere 7 nigan on þæm feðan. þa afor
Alexander þonan on Frigam, Asiam lond 7 heora burg abræc 7
towearp þe mon hætt Sardis. þa sægde him mon þæt Darius [hæfde]
20 eft fird gegaderod on Persum. Alexander him þæt þa ondred for
þære nearwan stowe þe he þa on wæs, 7 hrædlice for þæm ege
þonan afor ofer Taurasan þone beorg 7 ungeliefedlicne micel[ne]
weg on þæm dæge gefor, oð he com to Tharsum þære byrg on
Cilicium þæm londe. On ðæm dæge he gemette ane ea, sio hæfde
25 ungemettlice ceald wæter, seo wæs Ciðnus haten. þa ongan he hine
baðian þæron swa swatigne; þa for þæm ciele him gescruncan ealle
þa ædra, þæt him mon þæs lifes ne wende.

Raðe æfter þæm com Darius mid firde to Alexandre. He hæfde
iii c [þusenda] feðena 7 an hund þusenda gehorsedra. Alexander
30 wæs þa him swiðe ondrædende for þære miclan menige 7 for þære
lytlan þe he self hæfde, þeh þe he ær mid þære ilcan Darius maran
ofercome. þæt gefeoht wæs gedon mid micelre geornfullnesse of

---

13–27] OH III. xvi. 4–5.   28–p. 69, 9] OH III. xvi. 6–11.

2 þæt folc eall] eall þæt folc C.   ellþeodge] ellþeode C.   4 Mæcedonium]
mæcedoniam C.   5 Thraci] thracii C.   5–6 gegaderode] gaderade C.
9 Orosius] orososius C.   9–10 swa mid] mid swa C.   11 lytle] lytlan C.
13 ærestan] forman C.   Alexander] *from* C, alex/der L.   19 hæfde] *from*
C, *om.* L.   22 micelne] *from* C, micel L.   25 ungemettlice] ungemetlicne C.   26 swatigne] ign (?) *erased* L.   27 þa] *om.* C.   29 þusenda]
from C, *om.* L.

þæm folcum bæm, 7 þær wæron þa cyningas begen gewundod.
þær wæs Persa x m ofslægen gehorsedra 7 eahtatig m feþena 7
eahtatig m gefangenra, 7 þær wæs ungemetlic micel licgende feoh
funden on ðæm wicstowum. þær wæs Darius modor gefangen, 7
his wif, sio wæs his swiostor, 7 his ii dohtor. Ða bead Darius healf 5
his rice Alexandre wiþ þæm wifmonnum, ah him nolde Alexander
þæs getygþ'i'an. Darius þa giet þriddan siþe gegaderade fird of
Persum 7 eac [of] oþrum londum | þone fultum þe he him to   f. 40ᵛ
aspanan mehte 7 wið Alexandres for. þa hwile þe Darius fird
gegaderode, þa hwile sende Alexander Parmenionem his ladteow 10
þæt he Darius sciphere gefliemde 7 'he' self for in Sirium, 7 hie
him ongean comon 7 his mid eaþmodnessun anfengon, 7 he ðeah
naþelæs heora land oferhergeade 7 þæt folc sum þær sittan let, sum
þonan adræfde, sume on elðiode him wið feo gesealde; 7 Tirus þa
ealdan burg 7 þa welegan he besætt 7 siþþan tobræc 7 mid ealle 15
towearp, for þon hi him lustlice anfon noldan. 7 siþþan for on
Cilicium 7 þæt folc to him geniedde; 7 siþþan on Roðum þæt iglond
7 þæt folc to him geniedde; 7 æfter þæm he for on Egypti 7 hi to
him geniedde; 7 þæ[r] het þa burg atimbran þe mon siþþan be
him het Alexandria; 7 siþþan he for to þæm hearge þe Egypti 20
sædon þæt he wære Amones heora godes, se wæs Iobeses sunu
heora oþres godes, to þon þæt he wolde beladian his modor
Nectanebuses þæs drys, þe mon sæde þæt heo hie wið forlæge 7
þæt he Alexandres fæder wære. þa bebead Alexander þæm hæðnan
biscepe þæt he becrupe on þæs Amones anlicnesse þe inne on þæm 25
hearge wæs, ær þæm þe he 7 þæt folc hie ðær gegaderede, 7 sæde
hu he him an his gewill beforan [þam] folce *ond*wyrdan sceolde
þæs he hiene ascade. Genoh sweotollice us gedyde nu to witanne
Alexander hwelce þa hæðnan godas sindon to weorþianne, þæt hit
swiþor is of þara biscepa gehlote 7 of heora agenre gewyrde þæt 30
þæt hie secgað þonne of þara goda mihte.

Of þære stowe for Alexander þriddan siþe ongean Darius, 7 hie
æt Tharse þære byrig hie gemetton. On þæm gefeohte wæron
Pɛrse swa swiþe forslagen þæt hie heora 'miclan' anwaldas 7

9–31] OH III. xvi. 11–13.   32–p. 70, 15] OH III. xvii. 1–17.

3 ungemetlic] ungemetlice C.   micel] *om.* C.   7 Darius] *alt. from* daruus
L.   8 of] *from* C, *om.* L.   9 fird] ge *er. after* fird L.   10 gegaderode]
gaderade C.   11 gefliemde] aflymde C.   13 sum (2)] sume C.
15 siþþan] *om.* C.   19 þær] *from* C, þæt L.   het] he het C.   26 gega-
derede] gaderade C.   27 þam] *from* C, *om.* L.   33 Tharse] þarse C.
34 anwaldas] anwealdes C.

longsuman hie selfe siþþan wið Alexander to nohte ne bemætan.

f. 41 þa Darius geseah þæt he oferwunnen | beon wolde, þa wolde he
hiene selfne on ðæm gefeohte forspillan, ac hine his þegnas ofer his
willan from atugon, þæt he siþþan wæs fleonde mid þære firde, 7
5 Alexander wæs xxxiii daga on þære stowe, ær he þa wicstowa 7 þæt
wæl bereafian mehte. 7 siþþan for on Perse 7 geeode Persi[p]ulis
þa burg heora cynestol, seo is giet welegast ealra burga. þa sede
man Alexandre þæt Darius hæfde gebunden his [agene] mægas
mid gyldenre racentan. þa for he wið his mid siex hund monna 7
10 funde hiene ænne be wege licgan, mid sperum tosticad, healfcucne.
He þa Alexander him anum deadum lytle mildheortnesse gedyde,
þæt he hiene hett bebyrgean an his ieldrena byrg, þe he siþþan
nanum ende his cynne gedon nolde, ne his wif[e], ne his meder,
ne his bearnum, ne þætte ealra læst wæs, his gingran dohtor he
15 nolde buton hæftniede habban, seo wæs lytel cild.

Uneaðe mæg mon to gel[e]afsuman gesecgan swa monigfeald
yfel swa on ðæm þrim gearum gewurdon, on þrim folcgefeohtum,
betux twæm cyningum. þæt wæron fieftiene hund þusend monna
þæt binnan þæm forwurdon, 7 of þæm ilcan folcum forwurdon
20 lytle ær, swa hit her beforan sægð, nigantiene hund m monna,
buton miclan hergiungum þe binnan þæm þrim gearum gewurdon
an monigre þeode. þæt is þæt Asirie eall seo þeod awest wearð
from Alexandre, 7 monega byrig on Asiam, 7 Tirus seo mære burg
eall toworpenu, 7 Cilicia þæt lond eall awest, 7 Capadotia ðæt lond
25 7 ealle Egypti on þeowote gebroht, 7 Roþum þæt iglond mid ealle
awest, 7 monog oþra land ymbe Tauros þa muntas.

Nales þæt an þæt heora twegea gewinn þa wære on ðæm eastende
þisses middangeardes, ac onemn þæm Agidis, Spartana cyning, 7
29 Antipater, oþer Creca cyning, wunnon him betweonum. 7 Alexan-
f. 41ᵛ der, Epira cyning, | þæs miclan Alexanderes [eam], se wilnade þæs
westdæles swa se oðer dyde þæs eastdæles 7 fird gelædde in Italiam
7 þær hrædlice ofslagen wearð. 7 on þære ilcan tide Zoffirion,

---

16–26] OH III. xvii. 8–9.   27–p. 71, 2] OH III. xviii. 1–4.

---

1 ne] *om.* C.   6 Persipulis] *from* C, persibulis L.   8 agene] *from* C,
om. L.   9 hund] m C.   10 ænne] *alt. from* anne (?) L.   13 wife] *from*
C, wif L.   16 geleafsuman] *from* C, gelafsuman L.   monigfeald] *Sweet, probably wrongly, sees an erased* e *after* d *in* L.   20 beforan] beforan an *with* an *on
eras.* L.   24 Cilicia] cecilia C.   28 Agidis] agiðis C.   29–30 Alexander]
alex/sander C.   30 Epira] *over eras.* L, epiria C.   Alexanderes] alexandres
C.   eam] *from* C, *om.* L.

Ponto cyning, in Sciþþie mid firde gefor, 7 he [7] his folc mid ealle [þær] forwearð.

Alexander æfter Darius deaþe gewonn ealle Mandos 7 ealle Ircaniam. 7 on ðære hwile þe he þær winnende wæs, frefelice hiene gesohte Minoth[e]o, seo Sciþþisce cwen, mid þrim [h]unde 5 wifmonna, to þon þæt heo woldon wið Alexander 7 wið his mærestan cempan bearna strienan. Æfter þæm wonn Alexander wið Parthim þæm folce, 7 he hie neah ealle forslog 7 fordyde, ær he hie gewinnan mehte. 7 æfter þæm he gewonn Drancas þæt folc 7 Euergetas 7 Paramomenas 7 As[sap]ias, 7 monega oþra þeoda þe 10 gesetene sint ymbe þa muntas Caucasus, 7 þær het ane burg atimbran, þe mon siþþan het Alexandria.

Næs his scinlac ne his hergiung on þa fremdan ane, ac he gelice slog 7 hiende þa þe him on siml wæron mid farende 7 winnende. Æst he ofslog Amintas his modrian sunu, 7 siþþan his broðor, 7 þa 15 P[a]rmenion his þegn, 7 þa Filiotes, 7 þa C[a]tulusan, þa Eurilohus, þa Pausanias, 7 monege oþre þe of Mæcedonian ricoste wæron. 7 Clitus, se wæs ægþer ge his þegn ge ær Philippuses his fæder, þa hie sume siþe druncne æt heora symble sætan, þa angunnon hi trea[h]tigean hwæðer ma mærlecra dæda gefremed hæfde, þe 20 Philippus þe Alexander. þa sægde se Clitus for ealdre hyldo þæt Philippus mare hæfde gedon þonne he. He þa Alexander ahleop 7 hiene for þære sægene ofslog. He Alexander toecan þæm þe he hienende wæs ægþer ge his [agen] folc ge oðerra cyninga, he wæs sin[þyrst]ende monnes blodes.   25

Raþe æfter þæm he for mid firde on Chorasmas 7 on Dacos | 7 f. 42 him to gafolgieldum hie geniedde. [Ch]alisten þone philosofum he ofslog, his emnscolere, ðe hi ætgædere gelærede wæron æt Aristotolese heora magistre, 7 monege men mid him, for þon hie noldon to him gebiddan swa to heora Gode.   30

3–12] OH III. xviii. 5–7.   13–30] OH III. xviii. 8–11.

---

1 cyning] *from* C, cyninges L.   in Sciþþie] *om.* C.   7 (2)] *from* C, *om.* L.
2 þær] *from* C, *no reading* L.   4 ðære] oþre C.   5 Minotheo] *from* C, minotho L.   hunde] unde L, hund C.   6 wifmonna] fif manna C.
8 forslog] ofsloh C.   10 Assapias] *from* C, aspanias L.   16 Parmenian] *from* C, permenion L.   Catulusan] *from* C, cutulusan L.   17 Mæcedonian] mæcedoniam C.   20 treahtigean] *from* C, treatigean L.   22 mare] ma C.   23 7 hiene] *om.* C.   24 agen] *from* C, *no reading* L.
25 sinþyrstende] *from* C, sinstyrsende L.   27 Chalisten] *from* C, hcalisten L.   philosofum] filosofum C.   28–9 Aristotolese] aristolose C.

Æfter þæm he for on Indie, to þon þæt he his rice gebrædde oþ
þone eastgarsecg. On þæm siþe he geeode Nisan, India heafodburg, 7 ealle þa beorgas þe mon Dædolas hætt, 7 eall þæt rice
Cleoffiles þære cwene, 7 hie to geligre geniedde, 7 for þæm he
5 hiere rice eft ageaf. Æfter þæm þe Alexander hæfde ealle Indie
him to gewildon gedon, buton anre byrg, seo wæs ungemettan
fæste mid cludum ymbweaxen, þa geascade he þæt Ercol se ent
þær wæs to gefaren on ærdagum, to ðon þæt he hie abrecan þohte;
ac he hit for þæm ne angan þe þær wæs eorþbeofung on þære tide.
10 He þa Alexander hit swiþost for þæm angann þe he wolde þæt his
mærþa wæren maran þonne Ercoles, þeh ðe he hie mid micle for-
lore þæs folces begeate.

Æfter þæm Alexander hæfde gefeoht wið Porose þæm strengstan
Indea cyninge; on ðæm gefeohte wæron þa mæstan blodgytas on
15 ægþere healfe þara folca. On ðæm gefeohte Poros 7 Alexander
gefuhton anwig of horsum. þa ofslog Poros Alexandres hors, þe
Bucefal wæs haten, 7 hiene selfne mehte, þær him his þegnas to
fultume ne comen, 7 he hæfde Poros monegum wundum gewun-
dodne 7 hiene eac gewildne gedyde, siþþan his þegnas him to
20 comon, 7 him eft his rice to forlet for his þegnscipe, þy he swa
swiðe wæs feohtende ongean hiene; 7 he Alexander him het siþþan
twa byrg atimbran: oþer wæs hatenu be his horse Bucefal, oþer
Nicea.

Siþþan he for on Ræstas þa leode 7 on Cathenas 7 on Presidas 7
25 an Gangeridas, 7 wið hie ealle gefeaht 7 oferwon. þa he com on
f. 42ᵛ India eastgemæra, þa com him þær ongean | twa hund þusenda
monna gehorsades folces, 7 hie Alexander uneaðe oferwonn ægþer
ge for þære sumorhæte ge eac for þæm oftrædlican gefeohtum.
Siþþan æfter þæm he wolde habban maran wicstowa þonne his
30 gewuna ær wære, for þon he him siþþan æfter þæm gefeohte
swiðor on sæt þonne he ær dyde.

Æfter þæm he for ut on garsecg of þæm muþan þe seo ea wæs
hatenu Eginense, on an iglond þær Siuos þæt folc 7 Iersomas on

1–12] OH III. xix. 1–2.   13–23] OH III. xix. 3–4.   24–31] OH III.
xix. 4–5.   32–p. 73, 6] OH III. xix. 6–7.

1 he (2)] *om.* C.   3 Dædolas] dedolas C.   4 he] *om.* C.   6 un-
gemettan] ungemetan C.   11 mid] *om.* C.   16 of] on C.   17 Buce-
fal] bucefall C.   19 gedyde] dyde C.   24 Ræstas] ræstan C.   25 an
Gangeridas] ongean geridas C.   oferwon] *alt. from* oforwon L.   27 monna]
om. C.

eardedon, 7 hi Ercol þær ær gebrohte 7 gesette; he him þa to
gewildum gedyde. Æfter þæm he for to þæm iglande þe monn þæt
folc Mandras hætt 7 Subagros, 7 hi him brohton ongean eahta c m
feþena 7 lx m gehorsades folces, 7 hie lange wæron þæt dreogende
ær heora aðer mehte on oþrum sige geræcan, ær Alexander late 5
unweorðlicne sige geræhte.

Æfter þæm he gefor to anum fæstenne. þa he þær to com, þa ne
mehton hie nanne monn on ðæm fæstenne utan geseon. þa wundrade Alexander hwy hit swa æmenne wære, 7 hrædlice þone weall
self oferclom, 7 he ðær wearð from þæm burgwarum in abroden, 10
7 hie his siþþan wæran swa swiðe ehtende swa hit is ungeliefedlic
to secganne, ge mid scotum, ge mid stana torfungum, ge mid eallum
heora wigcræftum, þæt swaþeah ealle þa burgware ne mehton
hiene ænne genieddan [þæt] he him an hand gan wolde. Ac þa him
þæt folc swiðost an þrang, þa gestop he to anes wealles byge 7 15
hiene ðær awerede. 7 swa eall þæt folc wearð mid him anum agæled
þæt hie þæs wealles nane gieman ne dydon, oð Alexandres þegnas
toemnes him þone weall abræcon 7 þær in coman. Ðær wearð
Alexander þurhscoten mid anre flan underneoðan oþer breost. 19
Nyte we nu hwæðer sie swiþor to wundrianne, þe þæt, 'hu' he | ana f. 43
wið ealle þa burgware hiene awerede, þe eft þa him fultum com,
hu he þurh þæt folc geþrang þæt he ðone ilcan ofslog þe hiene ær
þurhsceat, þe eft þara þegna angin þa hie untweogend[lice] wendon þæt heora hlaford wære on heora feonda gewealde, oððe cuca
oððe dead, þæt hie swaþeah noldon þæs weallgebreces geswican, 25
þæt hie heora hlaford ne gewræcen, þeh þe hie hiene meðigne on
cneowum sittende metten.

Siþþan he þa burg hæfde him to gewildum gedon, þa for he to
oðre byrg, þær Ambira se cyning on wunode. þær forwearþ micel
Alexandres heres for geætredum gescotum. Ac Alexandre wearð 30
on ðære ilcan niht an swefne an wyrt oðewed. þa nam he þa on
mergen 7 sealde hie ðæm gewundedum drincan, 7 hie wurdon mid
þæm gehæled, 7 siþþan þa burg gewann.

Ond he siþþan hwearf hamweard to Babylonia. þær wæron

7–27] OH III. xix. 7–10.   28–33] OH III. xix. 11.   34–p. 74, 12] OH
III. xx. 1–4.

---

1 he] '7' he C.   12 scotum] gesceotum C.   14 þæt] *from* C, þonne L.
19 oþer] þæt oðer C.   20 Nyte we nu] *written twice, scored through the first
time* L.   23 untweogendlice] *from* C, untweogend L.   30 geætredum]
'ge'ætredum *with* 'ge' *in l.h.* C.

ærendracan on anbide of eallre worolde: þæt wæs from Spaneum
7 of Affrica 7 of Gallium 7 of ealre Italia. Swa egefull wæs Alexander þa þa he wæs on Indeum, on easteweardum þissum middangeard[e], þætte þa from him ondredan þe wæron on westeweardum.
5 Eac him coman ærendracan ge of monegum þeo[d]um þe nan mon
Alexandres geferscipes ne wende þæt man his naman wiste, 7 him
friþes to him wilnedon. þagiet þa Alexander ham com to Babylonia, þagiet wæs on him se mæsta þurst monnes blodes. Ac þa þa
his geferan ongeatan þæt he ðæs gewinnes þagiet geswican nolde,
10 ac he sæde þæt he on African faran wolde, þa geleornedon his
byrelas him betweonum hu hie him mehten þæt lif oþþringan, 7
him gesealdon ator drincan. þa forlet he his lif.

Eala, cwæð Orosius, on hu micelre dysignesse men nu sindon on
f. 43ᵛ   þeosan cristendome. Swa þeh þe him lytles hwæt unieðe sie, | hu
15 earfeðlice hi hit gemænað. Oðer þara is, oððe hie hit nyton, oððe
hi hit witan nyllað, an hwelcun brocum þa lifdon þe ær him wæron.
Hu wenað hie hu ðam wære þe on Alexandres onwalde wæron, þa
him ða [swa] swiðe hiene ondredan þe on westeweardum þisses
middangeardes wæron þæt hie on swa micle neþinge 7 on swa
20 micel ungewiss, ægðer ge on sæs fyrhto, ge on westennum wildeora
7 wyrmcynna missenlicra, ge on þeoda gereordum, þæt hie hiene
æfter friþe sohton on easteweardum þeosan middangearde. Ac we
witon georne þæt hie nu ma for iergðe naþer ne durran, ne swa
feor frið gesecan, ne furþon hie selfe æt ham æt heora cotum hie
25 werian, þonne hie monn æt ham secð. Ac þæt hie magon þæt hie
þas tida leahtrien.

III. x

Aefter þæm þe Romeburg getimbred wæs iiii hunde win*tra* 7 l,
under þæm twæm consulum þe oðer wæs haten Fauius 7 oðre
naman Maximus, 7 un[d]er þæm þe Cwintus haten wæs 7 oðre
30 noman Decius, on heora feorþan consulatu, on Italium 'feo'wer

---

13–26] OH III. xx. 5–13.　　27–p. 75, 14] OH III. xxi. 1–6.

3–4 middangearde] middang*eard* L, middanearde C.　　4 ondredan] adredan
C.　þe] þa C.　　5 þeodum] *from* C, þeoðum L.　　10 African] affrica C.
17 onwalde] 'ge'walde *with* 'ge' *in l.h.* C.　　18 swa] *from* C, *no reading* L.
24 ham æt] *om.* C.　　hie (2)] *om.* C.　　25 magon þæt hie] *om.* C.
27 wintra] *so* C, wiñ L.　　28 oðre] oðran C.　　29 under] *from* C,
unðer L.　　haten wæs] wæs haten C.　　oðre] oðran C.　　30 feorþan]
om. C.

þa strengstan ðeoda hi him betweonum gespræcon—þæt wæron
Umbri 7 Ðrysci 7 Somnite 7 Galli—þæt hie wolden on Romane
winnan, 7 hi him þæt swiþe ondrædan hu hi wið him eallum
emdemes mehten 7 georne siredon hu hi hie totwæman mehten,
7 gewealdenne here on Ðrysci 7 on Umbre sendon an hergiunge 5
7 þæt folc to amierrenne. þa hie þæt geascedon, þa wendon hie
him hamweard to ðon þæt hie heora land bewereden. 7 Romane
ða hwile mid heora maran fultume þe hie æt ham hæfdon foron
ongean Somnite 7 ongean Gallie. Ðær on ðæm gefeohte wæs
Cuintus se consul ofslagen, 7 Fauius se oðer consul æfter þæs oðres 10
fielle sige hæfde. þær wearð Somnita 7 Gallia feowertig m ofslagen,
7 seofon m Romana on þæm dæle þe Decius on ofslagen wæs.
þonne sæde Libius | ðæt Somnita 7 Gallia wære oðer healf hund m f. 44
ofslægen þara feðena 7 seofon m gehorsedra.

Eac ic hierde to soþum secgan, cwæð Orosius, þæt hit na nære 15
on ðæm dagum mid Romanum buton gewinne, oþþe wið oþra folc,
oþþe on him selfum mid monigfealdum wolum 7 moncwealmum,
swa swa hit ða wæs þa [Fauius] se consul of þæm gefeohte hamweard for. þa dyde man ðone trium[ph]an him beforan þe heora
gewuna wæs þonne hie sige hæfdon. Ac se gefea wearð swiþe raðe 20
on heora mode to gedrefednesse gecierred, þa hie gesawan þa
deadan men swa þiclice to eorþan beran þe þær ær æt ham wæron,
for þy þær wæs se micla moncwealm on þære tide. 7 þæs ymb an
gear Somnite gefuhton wið Romanum 7 hie gefliemdon 7 hie
bedrifon into Romebyrg, 7 hrædlice æfter þæm Somnite awendan 25
on oþre wisan ægþer ge heora sceorp, ge eall heora wæpn ofersylefredan, to tacne þæt hie oþer woldon, oððe ealle libban oþþe
[ealle] licgean. On þæm dagum gecuron Romane him to consule
Papirius 7 raðe þæs fird gelæddon ongean Somnitum, þeh þe heora
biscopas from hiora godum sæden þæt hie ðæt gefeoht forbuden. 30
Ac he Pa[pi]rius þa biscepas for þære sægene swiþe bismrade 7
þæt færelt swa þeh gefor 7 swa weorþlicne sige hæfde swa he ær
unweorðlice þara goda biscepun oferhirde. þær wearð Somnita

15–23] OH III. xxi. 7–8.　　　23–p. 76, 7] OH III. xxii. 1–5.

2 Galli] gallie C.　　10 Cuintus] cwintus C.　　15 hierde] gehyrde C.
18 Fauius] fumus *both MSS.*　　19 triumphan] *from* C, triumhpan L.
23 for þy] for þon þe C.　　24 Romanum] romanam C.　　25 awendan]
awendan æfter þæm L.　　28 ealle] *from* C, *om.* L.　　28–9 him . . .
Papirius] papirius him to consule C.　　31 Papirius] *from* C, parius L.
33 biscepun] n *alt. to* m *in l.h.* (?) L, bisceopan C.

twelf m ofslagen 7 iiii m gefangen, 7 raðe æfter þæm mærlican sige
hie wurdon eft geunret mid moncwealme, 7 se wæs swa ungemetlic
7 swa longsum ðæt hie ða æt nihstan witende mid deofolcræftum
sohton hu hi hit gestillan mehte 7 gefetton Escolafius þone scin-
5 lacan mid þære ungemetlican nædran þe mon Epithaurus het, 7
onlicost dydon swelce him næfre ær þæm gelic yfel an ne become,
ne æfter þæm eft ne become.

f. 44ᵛ   þy æfterran geare þæs Fauius hiora | consul, þe oðre noman wæs
haten Gurius, gefeaht wið Somnitum 7 heanlice hamweard oðfleah.
10 þa woldan senatus hiene aweorpan, for þon he ðæt folc on fleame
gebrohte. þa bæd his fæder, wæs eac Fauius haten, þæt þa senatum
forgeafen þæm suna þone gylt 7 þæt hie gebiden þæt he moste mid
þæm suna æt oðrum cirre wið Somnitum mid heora ealra fultume;
7 hie him þæs getygþedon. þa bebead se fæder þæm consule þæt
15 he mid his fierde angean fore, 7 he beæftan gebad mid sumum þæm
fultume. þa he geseah þæt Pontius, Somnita cyning, hæfde þone
consul his sunu besired 7 mid his folce utan befangen, he him þa
to fultume com 7 hiene swiðe geanmette; 7 Pontius, Somnita
cyning, gefengon. þær wearð Somnita xx m ofslagen 7 iiii m ge-
20 fangen mið þæm cyninge. þær wearð Romana gewinn 7 Somnita
geendad—for þon þe hie heora cyning gefengon—þætte hie ær
dreogende wæron lviiii wintra.

þæs on oþrum geare Curius se consul mid Romanum gefeaht
wið Sabinan 7 heora ungemet ofslog 7 sige hæfde, be þæm mon
25 mehte witan, þa he 7 þa consulas hie atellan ne mehton.

III. xi

Æfter 'þæm' þe Romeburg getimbred wæs iiii hunde wintrum
7 lxiii, þa ða Dolabella 7 Dom[i]tius wæron consulas on Rome, þa
Lucani 7 Bruti 7 Somnite 7 Gallie of Senno angunnan wið
Romanum winnan. þa sendon Romane ærendracan to Gallium
30 ymbe frið. þa ofslogon hie ða ærendracan. þa sendon hie eft

---

8–22] OH III. xxii. 6–10.   23–5] OH III. xxii. 11.   26–p. 77, 7] OH
III. xxii. 12–15.

---

1 twelf] *letter* (x?) *er. before* t L.   3 deofolcræftum] deofol/cræftum *with* 'es'
in margin in l.h. L.   5 Epithaurus] epiðaurus C.   8 hiora] hieora L,
heora C.   oðre] oþrum C.   10 woldan] *from* C, wolde an L.   24 þæm]
þon C.   25 7] *om.* C.   26 þæm] *in l.h.* L.   27 Domitius] *from* C,
domotius L.   30 eft] eft 'to' *with* 'to' *in hand* 2 L.

Cecilium heora pretorium mid firde þær Gallie 7 Bryti ætgædere
wæron, 7 [he] þær wearð ofslægen 7 þæt folc mid him, þæt wæs
eahtatyne m. Swa oft swa Galli wið Romanum wunnan, swa
wurdon Romane gecnysede. For þon ge Romane, cwæð Orosius, 4
| þonne ge ymb þæt an gefeoht alneg ceoriað þe eow Gotan gedy- f. 45
don, hwy nyllað ge geþencan þa monegan ærran þe eow Gallie of ˈtˈ
rædlice bismerlice þurhtugon?

Ic sceal eac gemyndgian be sumum dæle þæs þe Alexandres
æfterfylgendas dydon on þæm tidun þe þis gewearð on Romebyrg, hu hie hie selfe mid missellican gefeohtum fordydon. Hit is, 10
cwæð he, þæm gelicost, þonne ic his geþencean sceal, þe ic sitte on
anre heare dune 7 geseo þonne o[n] smeðum felda fela fyra byrnan:
swa ofer eall Mæcedonia rice, þæt is ofer ealle þa maran Asiam 7
ofer Europe þone mæstan dæl 7 ealle Libium, þæt hit na næs buton
hete 7 gewinnum. þa þe under Alexandre fyrmest wæron, þær þær 15
hie æfter him ricsedon, hie ðæt mid gewinnum awestan; 7 þær
þær hie næron, hie gedydon þone mæstan ege, swelce se bitresta
smic upp astige 7 þonne wide tofare.

Alexander xii gear þisne middangeard under him þrysmde 7
egsade, 7 his æfterfolgeras feowertiene gear hit siþþan totugon 7 20
totæron þæm gelicost þonne seo leo bringð his hungregum hwel-
pum hwæt to etanne: hie ðonne gecyðað on ðæm æte hwelc heora
mæst mæg gehrifnian. Swa þonne dyde Pˈtˈholomeus, Alexandres
þegna an, þa he togædere gesweo[p] ealle Egyptum 7 Arabia, 7
Laumenda his oþer þegn, se befeng ealle Asirie, 7 Thelenus Cili- 25
cium, 7 Filotos Hiliricam, 7 Iecrapatas þa maran Meðian, 7 Stromen þa læssan Meðian, 7 Perdice þa læssan Asiam, 7 Susana þa
maran Frigan, 7 Antigonus Liciam 7 Pamphiliam, 7 Nearchus
Cariam, 7 Leo[n]ontus þa læssan Frigan, 7 Lisimachus Thraciam,
7 Eumen Capadotiam 7 Paflagoniam; 7 Seleucus hæfde ealle þa 30
æðelestan men Alexandres heres 7 on lengðe mid him he begeat
ealle þa eastlond, 7 Cassander þa cempan mid Chaldeum; 7 on

8–18] OH III. xxiii. 1–5.   19–p. 78, 9] OH III. xxiii. 6–13.

---

2 he] *from* C, *om.* L.   12 on] *from* C, om L.   21 þæm gelicost]
gelicost þam C.   23 gehrifnian] gehwyrftnian C.   Ptholomeus] p
scored through L, pholomeus C.   24 gesweop] gesweow L, gesceop C.
25 Laumenda] lauˈdaˈmenda, *with* ˈdaˈ *in l.h.* L.   25–6 Cilicium] cicilium C.
26 Iecrapatas] i *er.* L.   27 Perdice] perðice C.   28 Pamphiliam]
pamphilian C.   Nearchus] narchus C.   29 Leonontus] *from* C, leomontus L.
Frigan] frigam C.   30 Paflagoniam] paflago/goniam C.   32 Chaldeum]
caldeum C.

f. 45ᵛ Pactrium 7 on Indeum | wæron ða ealdormen þe Alexander gesette,
7 ðæt lond betux þæm twam ean Induse 7 Iðasfene hæfde Itaxiles,
7 Ithona hæfde Calonie þa þeode on Indeum, 7 Parap[a]menas
hæfde Uxiarches æt þæs beorges ende Caucasus, 7 Arachasihedros
5 hæfde Siburtus, 7 Stontos hæfd[e] [D]ranceas 7 Areas þa þeoda,
7 Omintos hæfde Atrianus, 7 S'i'cheus hæfde S[os]tianos þæt folc,
7 Itacanor hæfde Parthos, 7 Philippus Ircanus, 7 Fratauernis hæfde
Armenie, 7 Theleomommos hæfde Meþas, 7 Feucestas hæfde
Babylonias, 7 Polausus hæfde Archos, 7 Archolaus Mesopotamiam.
10   Eall heora gewinn awæcnedon ærest from Alexandres epistole,
for þon þe he þæron bebead þæt mon ealle þa wræccan an cyþþe
forlete þe on ðæm londum wæron þe he ær self gehergad hæfde.
þa noldan Crecas þæm bebode hieran for þon 'hie' ondredon,
þonne hie hie gegaderedon, þæt hie on him gewræcen þa teonan
15 ðe hie ær mid him geþoledon, ge eac wiðsocon þæt hie leng Læcedemonium hieran nolde, þær heora heafodstol wæs; 7 raðe ðæs
Atheniense gelæddon xxx m folces 7 twa hund scipa angean Antigone ðæm cyninge, þe eall Creca rice habban sceolde, for þon þe
he ðæs ærendes ærendra[ca] wæs from Alexandre, 7 ge'set'ton him
20 to ladteowe Demoste[n]on þone filosofum, 7 asponon him to fultume Corinthum þa burgleode 7 Sihonas 7 Margas, 7 besæton
Antipatrum þone cyning on anum fæstenne, for þon þe he wæs
Antigone on fultume. þær wearð Leostenas, oðer heora ladteowa,
mid anre flan ofscoten. þa hie from ðære byrg hamweard wæron,
25 þa metton hie Leonantius, þe sceolde Antipatrume to fultume
cuman, 7 þær ofslagen wearð.
   Æfter þæm Perðica, þe þa læssan Asiam hæfde, angan winnan
wið Ariarata, Capadoca cyninge, 7 hiene bedraf into anum fæs-
f. 46 tenne, 7 þa burgware self hit onbærndon an feower healfa, þæt | eall
30 forwearð þæt þærbinnan wæs. Æfter þæm Antigones 7 Perðica
gebeotedan þæt hie woldon him betweonum gefeohtan, 7 longe
ymb þæt siredon hwær hie hie gemetan wolden, 7 monig igland
awestan on ðæm geflite hwæðer hiera mehte maran fultum him to

10–26] OH III. xxiii. 14–16.   27–p. 79, 15] OH III. xxiii. 17–23.

---

3 Parapamenas] *from* C, parapemenas 7 L.   4 Arachasihedros] ara 7 aratha/
sihedros C.   5 hæfde (2)] *from* C, hæfd L.   Dranceas] *from* C, þranceas L.
6 Sostianos] satianos L, sostianus C.   7 Fratauernis] fratafernis C.
8 Meþas] mæðas C.   12 forlete] lete C.   19 ærendraca] *from* C,
ærendra L.   20 Demostenon] *from* C, demosteon L.   28 Ariarata]
ariata C.   29 self] selfe C.   32 hie (1)] e *er.* L.   hie (2)] e *er.* L.

geteon. On þæm anbide Perdica for mid firde an Egyptum, þær
Tholomeus wæs se cyning, for þon ðe him wæs gesæd þæt he
wolde Antigone fylstan þæm cyninge. þa gegaderade Pholomeus
micle fird ongean him. þa hwile þe hie togædereweard fundedon,
gefuhton twegen cyningas Neoptolomus 7 Umenis, 7 he Umenis 5
gefliemde Neoptolomus, þæt he com to Antigone þæm cyninge 7
hiene spon þæt he on Umenis unmyndlenga mid here become. þa
sende Antigones hiene selfne 7 'his' oþerne [þegn] Polipercon mid
micle fultume þæt hie hiene beswiceden. þa geascade þæt Umenis
7 forsætade hie ðær ðær hie geþoht hæfdon þæt hie hiene besæte- 10
don, 7 hie begen ofslog 7 þa oþre gefliemde. Æfter ðæm gefeaht
Perdica 7 Ptholomeus, 7 þær wearþ Perdica ofslagen. Æfter ðæm
wearð Mæcedonium cuð þæt Eumen 7 Pison 7 Ilirgus 7 Alceta,
Perdican broðor, wolden winnan on hie, 7 fundon þæt Antigones
him sceolde mid firde ongean cuman. On ðæm gefeohte gefliemde 15
Antigones Umenis 7 hiene bedraf into anum fæstenne 7 hiene ðær
hwile besæt. þa sende Umenis to Antipatre þæm cyninge 7 hiene
fultumes bæd. þa Antigones þæt angeat, þa forlet he þæt setl. Ac
he Umenis him wende from Antigones hamfærelte micelra un-
treowða 7 him to fultume aspon þa þe ær wæron Alexandres 20
cempan, þa wæron hatene Argiraspides, for þon ðe eall heora wæpn
wæron ofersylefreda. þa on ðæm tweon þe hie swa ungeorne his
willan fulleodon, þa becom him Antigones mid firde on 7 hie
benæmde ægþer ge heora wifa, ge heora bearna, ge heora eardes,
ge ealles þæs licgend[an] feos þe hie under Alexand'r'e begeatan, 25
| 7 hie selfe uneaðe oðflugon to Umene. Æfter þæm þa sendon to f. 46ᵛ
An'ti'gone ymb heora þæt mæste bismer 7 hiene bædon þæt he him
ageafe þæt he [ær] on him gereafade. þa onbead he him ðæt he him
ðæs getygðian wolde, gif hie him Umenes þone cyning, þe heora
hlaford þa wæs, gebundenne to him brohten, 7 hie þæt gefremedon 30
swa. Ac he heora eft ægþer ge mid bismere onfeng, ge hie eac on þone
bismerlecestan eard gesette, þæt wæs on ðæm ytemestan ende his

15–p. 80, 2] OH III. xxiii. 24–8.

1 Perdica] perðica C. 2 Tholomeus] ptholomeus C. 3 Pholomeus]
ptholomeus C. 5 Neoptolomus] neptolomus C. 6 Neoptolomus]
neptolomus C. 7 hiene] first e er. L. 8 þegn] from C, om. L.
9 micle] miclan C. 12 Perdica (1)] perðica C. Perdica (2)] perðica C.
13 Eumen] umen C. 14 Perdican] perþican C. 17 hwile] om. C.
21 Argiraspides] argiraspiðes C. 25 licgendan] from C, licgendes L.
26 sendon] sendon hy C. 28 ær] from C, him L. gereafade] bereafode C.

monna, 7 him swaðeah nanuht agiefan nolde þæs þe hie bena
wæron.

Æfter þæm Euredica, Ariþeusses cwen, Mæcedonia cyninges,
heo wæs þæm folce monig yfel donde þurh Cassander hiere hla-
5 fordes þegn, mid þæm heo hæfde dierne geligre. 7 under 'ðæm'
heo gelærde þone cyning þæt he hiene swa upp ahof þætte he wæs
bufan eallum ðæm þe on þæm rice wæron to ðæm cyninge, 7 heo
gedyde mid hiere lare þæt ealle Mæcedonie wæron þæm cyninge
wiðerwearde, oþ hie fundon þæt hie sendon æfter Olimpeadum,
10 Alexandres meder, þætte hio him gefylste þæt hie mehton ægðer
ge þone cyning ge þa cuene him to gewildum gedon. Hio þa
Olimpiade him to com mid Epira fultume hiere agnes rices 7 hiere
to fultume abæd Eacedam Molosorum cyning 7 hie butu ofslog,
ge þone cyning ge þa cwene; 7 Cassander oðfleah. 7 Olimpiade
15 feng to þæm rice 7 þæm folce fela laðes gedyde þa hwile þe hio þone
anweald hæfde. þa Cassander þæt geascade þæt hio ðæm folce
laðade, þa gegaderade he fird. þa hio þæt geascade þæt þæs folces
wæs swa fela to him gecirred, þa ne getriewde hio þæt hiere wolde
19 se oðer dæl gelastfull beon. Ac hio genom hiere snore Roxan,
f. 47 Alexandres lafe, 7 Alexandres sunu Ercoles, 7 fleah to | ðæm
fæstenne þe Fiðnam wæs haten, 7 Cassander hiere æfter for 7 þæt
fæsten abræc 7 Olimpiadum ofslog, 7 þa burgleode oþbrudon þa
snore mid hiere suna, þa hie ongeatan þæt þæt festen sceolde
abrocen bion, 7 hi sendon on oðer fæstre fæsten, 7 Cassander hie
25 het þær besittan 7 him ealles þæs anwaldes weold Mæcedonia
rices.

þa wende man þæt þæt gewin geendad wære betux Alexandres
folgerum, þa þa wæron gefeallen þe þær mæst gewunnan: þæt wæs
Perþica 7 Eumen 7 Alciþen 7 Polipercon 7 Olimpiadas 7 Antipater
30 7 monige oðre. Ac Antigones, se mid ungemete girnde anwalda
ofer oþre, 7 to þæm fæstenne for þær Alexandres laf wæs 7 his
sunu 7 hie þær begeat, to ðon þæt he wolde þæt þa folc him þy
swiþor to buge þe he hæfde hiera ealdhlafordes sunu on his

3–26] OH III. xxiii. 29–32.   27–p. 81, 7] OH III. xxiii. 33–5.

---

3 þæm] þæm 'ðe' L.   Euredica] eureðica C.   Ariþeusses] ariþeuses C.
9 hie (2)] e er. L.   Olimpeadum] olimpiaðum C.   10 hie] e er. L.
12 Olimpiade] olimphiaðe C.   14 Olimpiade] olimpiaðe C.   18 ge-
triewde] triewde C.   19 hio] om. C.   22 Olimpiadum] olimpiaðum C.
23 hie] e er. L.   28 wæron] 'we' wæron L.   29 Eumen] umen C.
Olimpiadas] olimpiaðas C.

gewealde. Siþþan Cassander þæt geascade, þa geþoftade he wið
Ptholomeus 7 wið Lisimachus 7 wið Seleucus þone eastcyning, 7
hie ealle winnende wæron wið Antigones 7 wið Demetrias his
sunu, sume on londe, sume on wætere. On þæm [gefeohte] gefeol
se mæsta dæl Mæcedonia duguðe on ægþere healfe, þeh hie sume 5
mid Antigone wære, sume mid Cassandre. þær wearð Antigones
gefliemed 7 his sunu. Æfter þæm Demetrias, Antigones sunu,
gefeaht on scipum wið Ptholomeus 7 hiene bedraf on his agen
lond. Æfter þæm Antigones bebead þæt mon ægðer hete cyning
ge hiene ge his sunu, for þon þe Alexandres æfterfolgeras næron 10
ær þæm swa gehatene, buton ladteowas. Gemong þæm gewinnum
Antigones him ondred Ercoles, Alexandres sunu, þæt þæt folc
hiene wolde to hlaforde geceosan, for þon þe he ryhtcynecynnes
[wæs]. Het þa ægþer ofslean ge hiene ge his modor. þa þæt þa
oþre geascedon þæt he hie ealle beswican þohte, hie þa eft hie 15
gegaderedon | 7 wið hiene wunnon. þa ne dorste Cassander self on f. 47ᵛ
ðæm færelte cuman, for his ðæm nihstan feondum þe him ymb
wæron. Ac sende his fultum to Lisimache his geþof[tan], 7 hæfde
his wisan swiþost beþoht to Seleucuse, for þon þe he monege
anwealdas mid gewinnum geeode on þæm eastlondum: þæt wæs 20
ærest Babylonie 7 Pactriane. Æfter he gefor on Indie, þær nan
mon ær ne siþþan mid firde gefaran ne dorste buton Alexandre.
7 he Seleucus geniedde ealle þa ladteowas to his hiersumnesse, 7
hie alle Antigones 7 Demetrias his sunu mid firde gesohton. On
þæm gefeohte wæs Antigones ofslagen 7 his sunu of þæm rice 25
adræfed. Ne wene ic, cwæð Orosius, þæt ænig wære þe þæt atellan
mehte þæt on ðæm gefeohte gefeoll.

On þære tide gefor Cassander, 7 his sunu feng to þæm rice
Philippus. þa wende man eft oþere siþe þæt þæt gewinn Alexandres
folgera geendad wære. Ac hie sona þæs him betweonum wunnon, 7 30
Seleucus 7 Demetrias, Antigones sunu, him togædere geþoftedan
7 wið þæm þrim wunnon, Philippuse, Cassandres suna, 7 wið
Ptholomeuse, 7 wið Lisimachuse. 7 hie þæt gewinn þa þæs licost

7–27] OH III. xxiii. 38–48.   28–p. 82, 5] OH III. xxiii. 49–51.

---

2 þone] þon'n'e L.   4 gefeohte] *from* C, *om.* L.   5 Mæcedonia] o *on eras.*
with space for 3 letters L.   10 æfterfolgeras] folgeras C.   14 wæs] *from*
C, *om.* L.   15 oþre] þry C.   16 hiene] *om.* C.   Cassander] cansander
C.   18 geþoftan] *from* C, geþof 'ton', *with* 'ton' *in l.h.* L.   21 Pactriane]
patriane C.   Æfter] æfter 'ðon', *with* 'ðon' *in l.h.* L, 7 æfter þon C.   27 ge-
feoll] gefor C.

angunnan þe hi hit ær ne angunnen. On þæm gewinne ofslog Antipater his modor, Cassandres lafe, þeh þe heo earmlice hiere feores to him wilnade. þa bæd Alexander, hiere sunu, Demetrias þæt he him gefylste þæt he his modor slege on his breðer gewrecan mehte, 5 7 hi hiene raðe þæs ofslogan. Æfter þæm gewunnon Demetrias 7 Lisimachus. Ac Lisimachus ne mehte Demetriase wiðstondan, for þon þe Dorus, Thracea cyning, him eac an wann. þa wæs Demetrias on þære hwile swiþe 9 geanmet 7 fird gelædde to Ptholomeuse. þa he þæt geascade, þa f. 48 begeat he Seleucus | him to fultume, 7 Pirrus, Epira cyning. 7 Pirrus him for þam swiþost fylste [þe] he him selfum facade Mæcedonia anweald, 7 hie þa Demetrias of þæm rice adrifon, 7 Pirrus to feng. Æfter þæm Lisimachus ofslog his agenne sunu Agothoclen 7 Antipater his aþum. On þæm dagum Lisimachus sio burg besanc 15 on eorþan mid folce mid ealle. Ond æfter þæm þe Lisimachus hæfde swa wið his sunu gedon 7 wið his aþum, þa anscunedon hiene his agene leode, 7 monige from him cirdon, 7 Seleucus sponan þæt he Lisimachus beswice. þagiet ne mehte se nið betux him twæm gelicgean, þeh heora na ma ne lifde þara þe Alexandres 20 folgeras wæron, ac swa ealde swa hie þa wæron hie gefuhton. Seleucus hæfde seofon 7 seofontig wintra, 7 Lisimachus hæfde þreo 7 seofontig wintra. þær wearð Lisimachus ofslagen. 7 þæs ymb þreo niht com Ptolomeus, þe Lisimahhus his sweostor hæfde, 7 diegellice æfter Seleucuse for, þa he hamweard wæs, oþ his fird 25 tofaren wæs, 7 hiene þær ofslog. Ða wæs seo sibb 7 seo mildheortnes geendad þe hie æt Alexandre geleornedon: þæt wæs þæt hie twegen þe þær lengest lifdon hæfdon þritig cyninga ofslagen heora agenra ealdgeferena 7 him hæfdon siþþan ealle þa anwealdas þe hie ealle ær hæfdon. Gemong þæm gewinnum Lisimachus forlet his xv 30 suna: sume he self ofslog, sume an gefeohtum beforan him selfum mon afslog.

Ðyllicne gebroðorscipe, cwæð Orosius, hie heoldon him betweonum þe an anum hierede wæron afedde 7 getyde, þætte hit is us

6–14] OH III. xxiii. 52–6.   14–31] OH III. xxiii. 57–64.   32–p. 83, 7] OH III. xxiii. 65–7.

6 Lisimachus (2)] silimachus C.   8 swiþe] 'þearle' added in l.h. L.   11 þe] from C, þa L.   12 rice] om. C.   19 heora] heora þa C.   21 seofontig] hund seofontig C.   23 Ptolomeus] ptholomeus C.   Lisimahhus] lisimachus C.   25 þær] om. C.   33 afedde] afedde 'wæron' L.

nu swiþor bismre gelic þæt we þæ[t] besprecað, 7 þæt þæt we
gewinn nu hatað, þonne us fremde 7 ellþeodge an becumaþ 7
lytles hwæt on us bereafiað 7 us eft hrædlice forlætað, | 7 nyllað f. 48ᵛ
geþencan hwelc hit þa wæs þa nan mon ne mehte æt oþrum his
feorh gebycggan, ne furþon þætte þa wolden gefriend beon þe 5
wæron gebroðor of fæder 7 of meder. 7 her endað sio þridde boc
7 onginð seo feorþe.

IV. i

Æfter þæm þe Romeburg getimbred wæs feower hunde wintrum
7 feower 7 siextegum, þætte Tarentine þæt folc plegedon binnan
Tarentan heora byrg æt heora [þeatra] þe þærbinnan geworht wæs. 10
þa gesawon hie Romane scipa on ðæm sæ irnan. þa hrædlice comon
Tarentine to heora agnum scipum 7 þa oþre hindan offoran 7 hie
ealle him to gewildum gedydan buto[n] v, 7 þa þe þær gefongne
wæron hie tawedan mid þære mæstan unieðnesse: sume ofslogon,
sume ofswungon, sume him wið feo gesealdon. 15

Ða Romane þæt geacsedan, þa sendon hie ærendracan to him 7
bædon þæt him man gebette þæt him ðær to abylgðe gedon wæs.
Ða tawedan hie eft þa ærendracan mid þæm mæstan bismere, swa
hie þa oþre ær dydon, 7 hie siþþan ham forleton.

Æfter þæm foran Romane on Tarentine. 7 swa clæne hie namon 20
heora fultum mid him, þætte heora proletarii ne moston him
beæftan beon—þæt wæron þa þe hie gesett hæfdon þæt sceoldon
be heora wifum bearna strienan þonne hie on gewin foron—7
cwædon þæt him wislecre þuhte þæt hie ða ne forluren þe þær ut
fore, hæfde bearn se þe mehte. Hie þa Romane comon on Taren- 25
tine 7 þær eall aweston þæt hie metton 7 monega byrg abræcon.

þa sendon Tarentine ægwern æfter fultume þær hie him æniges
wendon. 7 Pirrus, Epira cyning, him com to | mid þæm mæstan f. 49
fultume, ægþer ge an gangehere, ge on rædehere, ge an sciphere.
He wæs on ðæm dagum gemærsad ofer ealle oþere cyningas, ægþer 30
ge mid his miclan fultume, ge mid his rædþeahtunge, ge mid his

8–19] OH IV. i. 1–2.   20–6] OH IV. i. 3–4.   27–p. 84, 11] OH
IV. i. 5–7.

1 þæt (2)] þær *both MSS.*   3 bereafiað] gerefað C.   6–7 7 her . . . feorþe]
incipit liber quartus C.   10 þeatra] *from* C, þreata L.   11 Romane]
romana C.   ðæm] þære C.   13 buton] *from* C, buto L.   17 abylgðe]
æbylgðe C.   22 gesett] gesette C.   26 metton] gemettan C.
27 ægwern] ægwar C.   29 gangehere] ganghere C.   rædehere] radhere
C.   ge an sciphere] *om.* C.

wigcræfte. For þon fyl's'te Pirrus Tarentinum for þon þe Tarente
seo burg wæs getimbred of Læcedemonium, þe his rice þa wæs,
7 he hæfde Thesalium him to fultume 7 Mæcedonie. 7 he hæfde
xx elpenda to þæm gefeohte mid him, þe Romane ær nane ne
5 gesawon. He wæs se forma mon þe hie ærest on Italium brohte.
He wæs eac on þæm dagum gleawast to wige 7 to gewinne, buton
þæm anum þe hie[ne] his godas 7 his deofolgeld beswicon þe he
begon[gen]de wæs. þa he hie ascade his [godas] hwæþer heora
sceolde on oþrum sige habban, þe he on Romanum, þe Romane
10 on him, þa ondwyrdon hie him tweolice 7 cwædon, 'þu hæfst oþþe
næfst.'
þæt forme gefeoht þæt he wið Romanum hæfde, hit wæs in
Compania, neah þære ie þe mon Lisum hætt. þa æfter þæm þe
þær on ægþere healfe micel wæl geslagen wæs, þa het Pirrus don
15 þa elpendas on þæt gefeoht. Siþþan Romane þæt gesawan þæt him
mon swelcne wrenc to dyde swelcne hie ær ne gesawon ne secgan
ne hirdon, þa flugon hie ealle buton anum men, se wæs Minutius
haten. He genedde under ænne elpent þæt he hiene on þone
nafelan ofstang. þa, siþþan he irre wæs 7 gewundod, he ofslog
20 micel þæs folces, þæt ægþer ge þa forwurdon þe him onufan wæron,
ge eac þa oþre elpendas sticade 7 gremede, þæt þa eac mæst ealle
forwurdon þe þæronufan wæron, 7 þeh þe Romane gefliemed
wæren, hie wæron þeh gebielde mid þæm þæt hie wiston hu hie to
ðæm elpendon sceoldon. On ðæm gefeohte wæs Romana iiii x m
25 ofslagen feþena 7 eahtatig 7 'viii' hund gefangen, 7 þara gehorsedra
f. 49ᵛ wæron ofslagen | iii hund 7 an m, 7 þær wæron seofon hund
guðfonena genumen. Hit næs na gesæd hwæt Pirruses folces
gefeallen wære, for þon hit næs þeaw on þæm tidun þæt mon ænig
wæl on þa healfe rimde þe þonne wieldre wæs, buton þær þy læs
30 ofslagen wære, swa mid Alexandre wæs on 'ðæm' forman gefeohte
þe he wið Darius feaht. þær næs his folces na ma ofslagen þonne
nigon. Ac Pirrus gebicnede eft hu him se sige gelicade þe he ofer
Romane hæfde, þa he cwæð æt his godes dure 7 hit swa on awrat,

12–p. 85, 9] OH IV. i. 8–18.

---

1 þon (1)] þam C.   3 Thesalium] thesali C.   Mæcedonie] from C, mæce-
demonie L.   7 þe hiene] þe hie/ L, þæt hine C.   8 begongende]
from C, begonde L.   godas] from C, om. L.   10 þa] so C, 7 þa L.
17 Minutius] minuntius C.   18 genedde] geneðde C.   elpent] elpend C.
24 iiii x] xiiii C.   25 eahtatig] hund eahtatig C.   28 for þon] alt. to for
þæm L.   29 wæs] followed by eras. L.   33 dure] dura C.   on] þæron C.

'þonc hafa þu, Iofes, þæt ic þa moste oferwinnan þe ær wæron
unoferwunnen, 7 ic eac from him oferwunnen eam.' þa ascedan
hiene his þegnas hwy he swa heanlice word be him selfum gecwæde,
þæt he oferwunnen wære. þa *ond*wyrde he him 7 cwæð, 'Gif ic eft
gefare swelc'n'e sige æt Romanum, þonne mæg ic siþþan buton 5
ælcon þegne Creca lond secan.' þæt wearð eac Romanum an
yfelum tacne oþiewed ær þæm gefeohte, þa hie on firde wæron,
þæt þæs folces sceolde micel hryre beon, þa þunor ofslog xxiiii
heora fodrera, 7 þa oþre gebrocade aweg coman.

Æfter þæm gefuhton Pirrus 7 Romane in Abulia þære þeode. 10
þær wearð Pirrus wund on oþran earme; 7 Romane hæfdon sige,
7 hæfdon geleornad ma cræfta hu hie þa elpendas beswican mehton,
mid þæm þæt hie namon treowu 7 slogon on oþerne ende monige
scearpe isene næglas 7 hie mid flexe bewundon 7 onbærndon hit
7 beþyddan hit þonne on þone elpend hindan, þæt hie þonne foran 15
wedende ægþer ge for þæs flexes bryne ge for þara nægla sticunge,
þæt æt ælcon þa forwurdon ærest þe him onufan wæron, 7 siþþan
þæt oþer folc wæron [swa swiðe] sleande swa hi him scildan
sceoldon. On þæm gefeohte wæs Romana eahta þusend ofslagen 7 19
enlefan guðfonan | genumen, 7 Pirruses heres wæs xx m ofslagen f. 50
7 his guðfona genumen. þær wearð Pirruse cuð þæt Agathocles,
Siraccusa cyning þa[ra] burgleoda, wæs gefaren on Sicilia þæm
londe. þa for he þider 7 þæt rice to him geniedde.

Sona swa þæt gewinn mid Romanum geendad wæs, swa wæs þær
seo monigfealdeste wol, mid moncwealme, ge eac þætte nanuht 25
beren[des], ne wif ne nieten, ne mehton nanuht libbendes geberan;
þæt hie þa æt nihstan wæron ortriewe hwæþer him ænig moneaca
cuman sceolde.

þa wende Pirrus from Sicilium eft to Romanum, 7 him angean
com Curius se consul, 7 hiora þæt þridde gefeoht wæs on Luca- 30
niam, on Arosinis þære dune; þeh þe Romane sume hwile hæfdon
swiþor fleam geþoht þonne gefeoht, ær þan hie gesawon þæt mon
þa elpendas on þæt gefeoht dyde. Ac siþþan hi þa gesawan, hie hie
gegremedan, þæt hie þa wæron swiþe sleande þe hie fylstan

10–23] OH IV. i. 19–23.   24–8] OH IV. ii. 1–2.   29–p. 86, 6] OH
IV. ii. 3–7.

4–5 eft gefare] gefare eft C.   13 þæt] þe C.   15 foran] *alt. to* wæran L.
18 swa swiðe] *from* C, *no reading* L.   21 þær] þa C.   Agathocles]
agothocles C.   22 Siraccusa] siraccasa C.   þara] þæra C. þa L.
26 berendes] *from* C, beren L.   31 Arosinis] arosiuss C.

sceoldon; 7 Pirruses here wearð for þæm swiþost on fleame. On
ðæm gefeohte Pirrus hæfde eahtatig m feþena 7 v m gehorsedra.
7 þær wæs xxxvi m ofslagen 7 iiii hund gefangen. Æfter þæm
Pirrus for of Italium ymb fif gear þæs þe he ær þæron com. 7 raþe
5 þæs þe he ham com, he wolde abrecan Argus þa burg 7 þær wearð
mid ane stane ofworpen.

Æfter þæm þe Tarentine geacsedan þæ‘t′ Pirrus dead wæs, þa
sendon hie on Affrice to Cartaginenses æfter fultume, 7 eft wið
Romanum wunnon; 7 raðe þæs þe hie togædere coman Romane
10 hæfdon sige. þær anfundan Cartaginenses þæt hie mon oferswiþan
mehte, þeh hie nan folc ær mid gefeohte oferwinnan ne mehte.
Gemong þæm þe Pirrus wið Romane winnende wæs, hi hæfdon
f. 50ᵛ eahta legian. | þa hæfdon hie þa eahteðan Regiense to fultume
gesette. þa ne getruwade se eahteþa dæl þara legian þæt Romane
15 Pirruse wiðstondan mehte; angunnan þa hergean 7 hienan þa þe
hie friþian sceoldon. þa Romane þæt geacsedan, þa sendon hie
þider Genutius heora consul mid fultume, to þon þæt he an him
gewræce þæt hie þa slogon 7 hiendon þe ealle Romane friþian
woldon, 7 he þa swa gedyde. Sume he ofslog, sume geband 7 ham
20 sende; 7 þær wæron siþþan witnade 7 siþþan þa heafda mid
ceorfæxsum of acorfena.

IV. ii

Æfter þæm þe Romeburg getimbred wæs feower hunde wintrum
7 lxxvii, gewurdon on Rome þa yfelan wundor. þæt wæs ærest þæt
þunor toslog heora hiehstan godes hus Iofeses. 7 eac þære burge
25 weall micel to eorþan gehreas. 7 eac þætte þrie wulfas on anre niht
brohton anes deades monnes lichoman binnan þa burg 7 hiene þær
siþþan styccemælum tobrudon, oþ þa men onwocan 7 ut urnon, 7
hie siþþan aweg flugon. On þæm dagum gewearð þætte on anre
dune neah Romebyrig tohlad seo eorþe, 7 wæs byrnende fyr up of
30 þære eorþan, þæt on ælce healfe þæs fyres seo eorþe wæs fif æcra
bræde to axan geburnen. Sona þæs on þæm æfterran geare gefor
Sempronius se consul mid firde wið Pencentes, Italia folc. þa mið
þæm þe hi hie getrymed hæfdon 7 togædere woldon, þa wearð

7-21] OH IV. iii. 1-5.   22-p. 87, 7] OH IV. iv. 1-7.

---

2 eahtatig] hund eahtatig C.   7 þæt] þær *with* ‘t’ *above* r L.   8 Affrice]
africe C.   Cartaginenses] cartaniginienses C.   10 Cartaginenses] cartaginigenses C.   15 Pirruse] piruse C.   22 Romeburg] romane burh C.

eorþbeofung, þæt ægðer þara folca wende untweogendlice þæt hie
sceoldon on þa eorþan besincan, 7 hie þeah swa ondrædendlice
gebidon þæt se ege ofergongen wæs, | 7 þær siþþan wælgrimlice f. 51
gefuhton. þær wæs se mæsta blodgyte on ægðere healfe þara folca,
þeh þe Romane sige hæfden, þa feawa þe þær to lafe wurdon. þær 5
wæs gesiene þæt seo eorþbeofung tacnade þa miclan bloddryncas
þe hiere mon on þære tide to forlet.

IV. iii

Æfter þæm þe Romeburg getimbred wæs iiii hunde wintrum 7
lxxx, gemong þæm oþrum [monegum] wundrum þe on þæm
dagum gelumpan, þæt mon geseah weallan blod of eorþan 7 rinan 10
meolc of heofonum. On ðæm dagum Cartaginenses sendon fultum
Tarentinum, þæt hie þe ið mehton wiþ Romanum. þa sendon
Romane ærendracan to him 7 hie acsedon for hwy hie ðæt dyden.
þa oðsworan hie þæm ærendracan mid þæm bismerlicestan aðe
þæt hie him næfre on fultume nære, þeh þe þa aðas wæren near 15
mane þonne soðe. On ðæm dagum Ulcinienses 7 Thrusci ða folc
forneah ealle forwurdon for hiora agnum dysige, for þæm þe hie
sume heora þeowas gefreodon 7 eac him eallum wurdon to milde
7 to forgiefene. þa ofþuhte heora ceorlum þæt mon þa þeowas
freode 7 hi nolde. þa wiðsawon hie þæm hlafordum 7 þa þeowas 20
mid him, oþ hie wyldran wæron þonne hie 7 hie siþþan mid ealle
of þæm earde adrifon [7 him to wifum dydon þa þe ær wæran heora
hlæfdian]. þa siþþan gesohton þa hlafordas Romane, 7 hi him
gefylstan þæt hie eft to hiora agnum becoman.

IV. iiii

Æfter þæm þe Romeburg getimbred wæs iiii hunde wintrum 25
7 lxxxi, becom on Romane micel moncwealm, þæt hie ða æt nihstan
ne acsedon hwæt þara gefarenra wære, ac hwæt heora þonne to lafe
wære. Ond eac þa diofla þe hie an simbel weorþedon hi amirdon,
toeac[an] þæm oþrum monigfealdum bismrum þe hi him lærende

8–24] OH IV. v. 1–5.   25–p. 88, 4] OH IV. v. 6–8.

2 ondrædendlice] andrædende C.   3 ofergongen] ofergan C.   5 feawa
þe] feawan C.   9 monegum] *from* C, *no reading* L.   11 Cartaginenses]
cartaginigenses C.   22–3 7 ... hlæfdian] *from* C, *om.* L.   26 lxxxi]
lxxx C.   29 toeacan] *from* C, toeac/ L.   him] *om.* C.

f. 51ᵛ wæron, þæt hie ne cuþan angitan þæt hit Godes wracu wæs, | ac
heton þa biscepas þæt hie sædon ðæm folce þæt heora godas him
wæron irre, to þon þæt hie him þagit swiþor ofreden 7 bloten
þonne hie ær dyden.

5   On ðære ilcan tide Caperronie wæs hatenu heora goda nunne.
þa gebyrede hiere þæt heo hie forlæg. Hie þa Romane for þæm
gylte hi ahengon, 7 eac þone þe þone gylt mid hiere geworhte,
7 ealle þa þe þone gylt mid hi[m] ʽwiston' 7 mid him hælan. Hu
wene we, nu Romane him self þyllic writon 7 setton for heora
10   agnum gielpe 7 heringe 7 þeah gemong þære heringe þyllica bismra
on hie selfe asædon, hu wene we hu monegra maran bismra hie
forsugedon, ægþer ge for hiora agenre lufan 7 londleoda, ge eac
for hiora senatum ege?

Nu we sculon ʽfon', cwæð Orosius, ymb þæt Punica gewin, þæt
15   wæs of þæm folce of Cartaina þære byrig. Sio wæs getimbred from
Elisan þæm wifmen, lxxiitigum wintra ær Romeburg. Swa some
þara burgwarena yfel 7 heora bismeres wearð lytel asæd 7 awriten,
swa swa Trogus 7 Iustinianus sedon heora stærwriteras, for þon þe
heora wise on nænne sæl wel ne gefor, naþer ne innan from him
20   selfum, ne utane from oþrum folcum. Swa þeah toeacan þæm yflum,
hie gesetton, þonne him micel moncwealm on becom, þæt hie
sceolden men hiera godum blotan, swa eac ða diofla [þe] hie on
geliefdon gelærdon hie þæt þa ðe þær on unhæle wæran, þæt hie
hale for hie cwealdon, 7 wæron þa men to ðon dysige þæt hie
25   wendon þæt hie mehten þæt yfel mid þæm gestillan, 7 þa diofla to
þon lytige þæt hie hit mid þæm gemicledan. 7 for þon þe hie swa
swiðe dysige wæron, him com on Godes wracu an gefeohtum
f. 52 toeacan oþrum yflum. þæt wæs oftost on Sicilium | 7 on Sardinium
þæm iglondum, on þa hie gelomlicost wunnon.

30   Æfter þæm þe him swa oftrædlice mislamp, hie angunnan hit
witan heora latteowum 7 heora cempum heora earfeþa, 7 him
bebudan þæt hie on wræcsiþas foran 7 on ellþiede. Raþe æfter
þæm hie bædon þæt hie mon to hiora earde forlete, þæt hie mosten

5–13] OH IV. v. 9–13.   14–29] OH IV. vi. 1–7.   30–p. 89, 11] OH IV.
vi. 7–9.

3 þon] þam C.   bloten] blotten C.   4 hie] om. C.   8 him wiston]
so C, hiere geworhte with ere geworhte scored through and ʽwiston' written above
line L.   10 gielpe] p on eras. L.   14 Nu] the heading be cartaima gewinne
added C.   16 Elisan] elisann C.   lxxiitigum] lxxxiitigum C.   wintra]
wintrum C.   18 heora] om. C.   22 þe] from C, no reading L.
23 on unhæle] onhælede C.   30 hie] þæt hi C.

gefandian hweðer hie heora medselða oferswiþan mehte. þa him
mon þæs forwiernde, þa gesohton hie hie mid firde. On þære
heriunge gemette se ieldesta ladteow Macheus his agenne sunu
mid purpurum gegieredne on biscephade. He hiene þa for þæm
girelan gebealg 7 hiene oferfon het 7 ahon; 7 wende þæt he for his 5
forsewennesse swelc sceorp werede, for þon þe hit næs þeaw mid
him þæt ænig oþer purpuran werede buton cyningum. Raþe æfter
þæm hie begeaton Cartaina þa burg 7 ealle þa æltæwestan ofslogon
þe þærinne wæron 7 þa oþre to him genieddon. þa æt nihstan he
wearþ self besiered 7 ofslagen. þis wæs gew[o]rden on Ciruses 10
dæge Persa cyninges.

IV. v

Æfter þæm Himelco, Cartaina cyning, gefor mid firde an Siciliæ,
7 him þær becom swa færlic yfel þæt þa men wæron swa raðe deade
swa hit him an becom, þæt hie þa æt nihstan hie bebyrgean ne
mehton. 7 he for ðæm ege his unwillum þonan wende 7 ham for 15
mid þæm þe þær to lafe wæron. Sona swa ðæt forme scip land
gesohte ond þæt egeslice spell gebodade, swa wæron ealle þa burgware Cartaginenses mid swiðlice heafe 7 wope anstyred, 7 ælc
acsiende 7 frinende æfter his friend; 7 hie untweogendlice nanra
treowþa him ne wendon, buton þæt hie mid ealle forweorþan 20
sceolde. Mid þæm þe þa burgware swa geomor|lic angin hæfdon, f. 52ᵛ
þa co[m] se cyning self mid his scipe 7 land gesohte mid swiþe
lyþerlicum gegierelan, 7 ægþe[r] ge he [self] wepende hamweard
for, ge þæt folc þæt him ongean com, eall hit him wepende hamweard folgade. 7 he se cyning his handa wæs uppweardes brædende 25
wið þæs heofones, 7 mid oferheortnesse him wæs waniende ægþer
ge his agene heardsælða ge ealles þæs folces. 7 he þagiet him selfum
gedyde þæt þær wyrrest wæs, þa he to his inne com, þa he þæt folc
þærute bctynde 7 hiene ænne þærinne beleac 7 hiene selfne ofslog.

12–29] OH IV. vi. 10–15.

2 hie hie] hy C.   3 Macheus] maceus C.   4 purpurum] *alt. from*
puppurum L.   5 hiene] he, *with* 'hine' *in l.h.* C.   6 for þon þe] for
þon C.   10 geworden] *from* C, gewurden L.   12 Himelco, Car-] *on
eras.* L.   Siciliæ] sicilie C.   15 he] *om.* C.   þonan] *om.* C.   16 to
lafe] *om.* C.   18 Cartaginenses] cartaginigenses C.   swiðlice] swiðe-
lice C.   22 com] *from* C, con L.   23 ægþer] *from* C, ægþe L.
self] sylf C, *om.* L.   wepende] *om.* C.   27 agene] agenne MSS, *with
first* n *dotted to indicate error,* L.

Æfter þæm wæs sum welig mon binnan Cartaina, se wæs haten
Hanna 7 wæs mid ungemete girnende þæs cynedomes; ac him
geþuhte þæt he mid þara wietena willum him ne mehte to cuman
7 him to ræde genom þæt he hie ealle to gereordum to him gehete,
5 þæt he hie siþþan mehte mid attre acwellan. Ac hit wearð þurh þa
ameldad þe he geþoht hæfde þæt him to þære dæde fylstan sceolde.
þa he anfunde þæt þæt cuþ wæs, þa gegaderade he ealle þa þeowas
7 þa yfelan menn þe he mehte 7 þohte þæt he on þa burgware on
ungearwe become; ac hit him wearð æror cuþ. þa him æt þære
10 byrig ne gespeow, þa gelende he mid xxiiii m to anre oþerre byrig
7 þohte þæt he þa abræce. þa hæfdon þa burgleode Mauritanie him
to fultome 7 him ongean comon butan fæstenne 7 Hannan gefengon
7 þa oþre gefliemdon. 7 þær siþþan tintregad wearð: ærest hiene
mon swong, þa sticode him mon þa eagan ut, 7 siþþan him mon
15 slog þa handa of, þa þæt heafod, 7 eall his cynn mon ofslog, þy læs
f. 53 hit monn uferan dogore wræce, oþþe ænig oþer dorste eft | swelc
anginnan. þis gewearð on Philippuses dæge þæs cyninges.

Æfter þæm hierdon Cartainenses þæt se mæra Alexander hæfde
abrocen Tirum þa burg, seo wæs on ærdagum heora ieldrena
20 *oeþel*, 7 ondredon þæt he eac to him cuman wolde. þa sendon hie
þider Amilchor, heora þone gleawestan mon, þæt he Alexandres
wisan besceawade, swa he hit him eft ham bebead on anum brede
awriten; 7 siþþan hit awriten wæs, he hit oferworhte mid weaxe.
Eft þa Alexander gefaren wæs, 7 he ham com, þa tugon hie hiene
25 þære burge witan þæt he heora swicdomes wið Alexander fremmende wære, 7 hiene for þære tihtlan ofslogon.

Æfter þæm Cartainenses wunnon on Siciliæ, þær him seldon
teola gespeow, 7 besæton hiora heafedburg, Siracuses wæs hatenu.
þa ne anhagode Agathocle heora cyninge þæt he wið hie mehte

1–17] OH IV. vi. 16–20.   18–26] OH IV. vi. 21–2.   27–p. 91, 14] OH
IV. vi. 23–7.

---

1 Cartaina] cartania C.   2 girnende þæs cynedomes] þæs cynedomes
gyrnende C.   4 gehete] gehet C.   5 wearð] gewearð C.   10 ge-
speow] *alt. from* gesweow (?) L.   anre] anre byrig *with* byrig *scored through* L.
11 Mauritanie] mauritane C.   16 dogore] dagum C.   wræce] *orig.*
wræcce L.   17 Philippuses] philippus C.   18 Cartainenses] cartanienses C.   19 Tirum] trium C.   20 oeþel] *so* C, *expressed by the rune*
L.   he] hy C.   wolde] woldon C.   22 bebead] onbead C.   24 hie]
om. C.   27 Cartainenses] cartanienses C.   Siciliæ] sicilie C.   28 Sira-
cuses] siraccuses C.   29 Agathocle] agothocle C.

buton fæstenne gefeohtan, ne eac þæt hie ealle mehten for metelieste
þærbinnan gebidan. Ac leton heora fultum þærbinnan beon, be
þæm dæle þæt hie ægðer mehton, ge heora fæsten gehealdan, ge
eac þæt þa mete hæfdon þa hwile. Ond se cyning mið þæm oþrum
dæle on scipum for on Cartainense 7 hie raðe þæs forbærnnan het 5
þe he to lande gefor, for þon he nolde þæt his find heora eft ænigne
anwald hæfde. 7 him þær raðe fæsten geworhte 7 wæs þæt folc
þonan ut sleande 7 hienende, oþ þæt Hanna, þæs folces oþer
cyning, hiene æt þæm fæstenne gesohte mid xx m. Ac hiene
Agothocles gefliemde 7 his folces ofslog ii m, 7 him æfterfylgende 10
wæs oþ v mila to þære byrig Cartanense. Ond þær oþer fæsten
geworhte 7 þær ymbutan wæs hergende 7 bærnende, þætte Cartai-
nense mehton geseon of heora byrg | þæt fyr 7 þone teonan, þonne f. 53ᵛ
hie on fore wæron.

Ymbe ðone timan þe þiss wæs, Andra wæs haten, Agothocles 15
broðor, þone he æt ham on þære byrig him beæftan let, he besierede þæt folc þe hie ymbseten hæfden on anre niht ungearwe, 7 hit
mæst eall ofslog; 7 þa oþre to scipun oðflugon. 7 raðe þæs þe [hie]
ham coman 7 þæt spell cuð wearð Cartainiensium, swa wurdon
hie swa swiþe forþohte þætte nales þæt an þætte Agothocle monega 20
byrg to gafolgieldum wurdon, ac eac hie him heapmælum selfe on
hand eodon. Swa eac Fefles se cyng mid Cerene his folce hiene eac
gesohte. Ac Agothocles gedyde untreowlice wið hiene, þæt he
hiene on his w[æ]rum beswac 7 ofslog, swa him eac selfum siþþan
æfter lamp. Gif he þa þa ane untreowþa ne gedyde, from ðæm 25
dæge he mehte butan gebroce eallra Cartaina onwald begietan. On
þære hwile þe he þone unræd þurhteah, Amicor, Pena cyning, wæs
mid sibbe wið his farende mid eallum his folce, ac betux Agothocle
7 his folce wearð ungerædnes, þæt he self ofslagen wearð. Æfter
his deaðe foran eft Cartainienses an Sicilie mid scipum. þa hie 30
ðæt geacsedan, þa sendon hie æfter Piruse, Epira cyninge, 7 he
him sume hwile gefylste.

15–32] OH IV. vi. 28–33.

---

2 gebidan] n *on eras.?* L.   3 þæt] þe C.   5 Cartainense] cartanienses *with final* s *er.* C.   11 Cartanense] cartaniense C.   12–13 Car-
tainense] cartaniiense *alt. to* cartainiense C.   18 hie] hy C,*no reading* L.
19 Cartainiensium] cartainiensum C.   24 wærum] *from* C, warum L.
26 gebroce] broce C.   31 Piruse]pirruse C.

IV. vi

Æfter þæm þe Romeburg getimbred wæs feower hunde wintrum
7 lxx[x]iii, sendon Momertine, Sicilia folc, æfter Romana fultume,
þæt hie wið Pena folce mehte. þa sendon hie him Appius Claudius
þone consul mid fultume. Eft, þa hie togædereweard foron [mid
5 heora folcum], þa flugon Pene, swa hie eft selfe sædon, 7 his
wundredan þæt hie ær flugon ær hie togædere genealæcten. For
þæm fleame Hanna, Pena cyning, mid eallum his folce wearð
Romanum to gafolgieldum, 7 him ælce geare gesealde twa hund
9 talentana siolfres. On ælcre anre talentan wæs lxxx punda.

f. 54　Æfter Romane | besæton þone ieldran Hannibalan, Pena cyning,
on Argentine, Sicilia byrig, oð he forneah hungre swealt. þa com
him Pena oþer cyning to fultume mid sciphere, Hanna wæs haten,
7 þær gefliemed wearð. 7 Romane siþþan þæt fæsten abræcon. 7
Hannibal se cyning on niht ut oðfleah mid feawum monnum 7
15 hundeahtatig scipa gegaderade 7 on Romana londgemæro hergeade.
On ða wrace fundon Romane ærest þæt hie scipa worhton. þæt
gefremede Diulius hiora consul, þæt þæt angin wearð tidlice
þurhtogen, swa þætte æfter siextegum daga þæs þe ðæt timber
acorfen wæs, þær wæron xxx 7 c gearora ge mid mæste ge mid
20 segle. 7 oþer consul, wæs haten Cornelius Asina, se gefor on
Liparis þæt iglond to Hannibale to sundorspræce mid xvi scipun;
þa ofslog he hiene. Swa þæt þa se oðer consul gehierde Diulius,
swa gefor he to ðæm iglonde mid xxx scipun 7 Hannibales folces
iii hund ofslog 7 his xxx scipa genom 7 xiii on sæ besencte 7 hiene
25 selfne gefliemde.

Æfter þæm Punici, þæt sindon Cartainense, hie gesetton Hannonan ofer hiora scipa, swa Hannibales wæs ær, þæt he bewerede
Sardiniam 7 Corsicam þa iglond wið Romanum, 7 he raðe þæs wið
[hie] gefeaht mid sciphere 7 ofslagen wearð.

30　þæs on þæm æfterran geare Calatinus se consul for mid firde to
Camerinam, Sicilia byrg. Ac him hæfdon Pene þone weg forseten

---

1–9] OH IV. vii. 1–3.　　　10–25] OH IV. vii. 4–10.　　　26–9] OH IV.
vii. 11.　　　30–p. 93, 6] OH IV. viii. 1–3.

---

2 lxxxiii] *from* C, lxxiii L.　　4–5 mid heora folcum] *from* C, *no reading* L.
10 Æfter] æfter þam C.　　17 Diulius] duulius C.　　20 wæs] se wæs C.
22 Diulius] diiulius C.　　26 Cartainense] cartaniense C.　　28 Sardiniam]
sarðiniam C, sardianiam L.　　29 hie] hy C, *no reading* L.　　31 Sicilia]
secilia C.

þær he ofer þone munt faran sceolde. þa genom Calatinus iii
hund monna mid him 7 on anre diegelre stowe þone munt oferstag
7 þa men afærde, þæt hie ealle ongean hiene wæron feohtende [7
þone weg letan butan ware, þæt seo fierd siððan þær þurhfor]. 7
þær wearð þæt iii hund monna ofslagen, ealle buton ðæm consule 5
anum: he com wund aweg.

Æfter þæm Punice gesetton eft þone ealdan Hannibalan þæt he
mid scipum on Romane wunne. Ac eft þa he ðær hergean sceolde,
he wearð raðe gefliemed, 7 on ðæm fleame hiene oftyrfdon his
agene geferan.   10

Æfter þæm | Atilius se consul aweste Liparum 7 Melitam, f. 54ᵛ
Sicilia iglond. Æfter þæm foron Romane on Africe mid feower
hunde scipa 7 þritigum. þa sendon [hie] heora twegen cyningas
him ongean, Hannan 7 Amilcor, mid scipum. 7 þær wurdon
begen geflemed, 7 Romane genamon on him lxxxiiii scipa, 7 15
siþþan hie abræcon Alpeam heora burg 7 wæron hergende oð
Cartaina heora heafedburg.

Æfter þæm Regulus se consul underfeng Cartaina gewinn. þa
he æst þider mid firde farende wæs, þa gewicade he neah anre ie
seo wæs haten Bagrada. þa com of ðæm wætre an nædre, seo wæs 20
ungemetlice micel 7 þa men ealle ofslog þe neh ðæm wætre coman.
þa gegaderade Regulus ealle þa scyttan þe on ðæm 'fæ'relte
wæron, þæt hie mon mid flanum ofercome. Ac þonne hie mon slog
oþþe sceat, þonne glad hit on þæm scyllum swelc[e] hit wære
smeðe isen. þa het he mid þæm palistas, mid þæm hie weallas 25
bræcon þonne hie on fæstenne fuhton, þæt hiere mon mid þæm
þwyres on wurpe. þa wearð hiere mid anum wierpe an ribb forod,
þæt hio siþþan mægen ne hæfde hie to gescildanne, ac raðe þæs hio
wearð ofslagen, for þon hit is nædrena gecynd þæt heora mægen 7
hiera feþe bið on heora ribbum, swa oþerra creopendra wyrma bið 30
on heora fotum. þa hio gefylled wæs, he het hie behyldan 7 þa
hyde to Rome bringan 7 hie ðær to mærðe aðenian, for þon heo
wæs hund twelftiges fota lang.

Æfter þæm gefeaht Regulus wið iii Pena cyningas on anum

7–17] OH IV. viii. 4–8.   18–33] OH IV. viii. 10–15.   34–p. 94, 4] OH
IV. viii. 16.

3–4 7 (2) ... þurhfor] *based on* C, *no reading* L.   4 fierd] fyrd C, *no reading* L.
12 Africe] affrice C.   13 hie] hy C, *no reading* L.   15 Romane] *from*
C, romanane L.   22 þa] *preceded by the heading* Be þære nædran C.
24 swelce] swylce C, swelc L.

gefeohte, wið twegen Hasterbalas 7 se þridda wæs haten Amilcor,
se wæs on Sicilium him to fultume gefett. On ðæm gefeohte wæs
Cartainiensa vii m ofslagen 7 vx m gefangen 7 xi elpendas genumen
7 lxxxii tuna him eodon on hand.

5   Þa, æfter þæm þe Cartainiense gefliemde wæron, hie wilnedon
f. 55 friþes to Regule. Ac eft þa hie angeatan þæt he | ungemetlic gafol
       wið þæm friþe habban wolde, þa cwædon hie þæt him leofre
       wære þæt hie an swelcan niede deað fornome þonne hie mid
       swelcan niede frið begeate. Þa sendon hie æfter fultume ægþer ge
10   on Gallie ge on Ispanie, ge on Læcedemonie æfter Exantipuse
       þæm cyninge. Eft, þa hie ealle gesomnad wæron, þa [be]þohtan hie
       ealle heora wigcræftas to Exantipuse 7 he siþþan þa folc gelædde
       þær hie togædere gecweden hæfdon, 7 gesette twa folc diegellice
       on twa healfa his 7 þridde beæftan him, 7 bebead þæm twam
15   folcum, þonne he self mid þæm fyrmestan dæle wið þæs æftemes-
       tan fluge, þæt hie þonne on Reguluses fird on twa healfa þwyres on
       fore. Þær wearð Romana xxx m ofslagen 7 Regulus gefangen mid
       v hunde monna. Þiss gewearþ Punicum on þæm teoðan geare
       hiora gewinnes 7 Romana. Raðe þæs Exantipus for eft to his
20   agnum rice 7 him Romane andred, for þon hie for his lare æt
       hiora gemettinge beswicene wurdon.

       Æfter þæm Enilius Paulus se con῾sul῾ for on African mid þrim
       hunde scipa to Clepeam þæm iglonde. 7 him comon þær ongean
       Punice mid swa fela scipa 7 þær gefliemde wæron, 7 hiora folces
25   wæs v m ofslagen 7 hiora [scipa] [xxx] gefan[gen] 7 iiii 7 an hund
       adruncen 7 Romana wæs an c 7 an m ofslagen 7 heora scipa ix
       adruncen. 7 hie on þæm iglande fæsten worhton. 7 hie ðær eft
       Pene gesohton mid heora twam cyningum, þa wæron begen Hannan
       hatene. Þær heora wæron ix m ofslagen 7 þa oþre gefliemed. Mid
30   þære herehyþe Romane oferhlæstan heora scipa, þa hi hamweard
       wæron, þæt heora gedearf ii cc 7 xxx, 7 lxx wearð to lafe 7 uneaðe
       genered mid þæm þæt hie mæst eall ut awurpon þæt ðæron wæs.

5–21] OH IV. ix. 1–4.   22–32] OH IV. ix. 5–8.

3 vx] xv C.   xi] ix C.   8 niede] nide, with d alt. to ð in l.h. C.
11 beþohtan] from C, þohtan L.   16 Reguluses] regules C.   18 þiss]
þes sige C.   21 gemettinge] gemittinge C.   22 African] affricam C.
25 scipa] from C, om. L.   xxx] from C, twentig L.   gefangen] from C, gefan/
L.   31 gedearf] r er. L, gedraf C.   ii cc] twa cc C.   32 eall]
ealle C.

Æfter þæm Amilcor, Pena cyning, for on Numedian 7 on
Mauritaniam 7 hie oferhergeade 7 to gafolgieldum gesette, | for f. 55ᵛ
þon þe hie Regule ær on hand eodon.

þæs ymb iii gear Serfilius Cepio 7 Sempronius Blesus þa consulas foran mid iii hund scipa 7 lxgum on Africe 7 on Cartainien- 5
sium monega byrg abræcon, 7 siþþan mid miclum þingum
hamweard foran 7 eft hiora scipa oferhlæston, þæt hiora gedurfon
l 7 c.

Æfter þæm Cotta se consul for on Sicilie 7 'hie' ealle oferhergeade. þær wæron swa micle monslihtas on ægþere healfe þæt 10
hie mon æt nihstan bebyrgan ne mehte.

On Luciuses dæge [E]liuses þas consules 7 on Metelluses
Gaiuses 7 on Foriuses Blaciduses, com Hasterbal se niwa cyning
of Cartainum on Libeum þæt igland mid xxx m gehorsedra 7 mid
xxx elpenda 7 cgum, 7 raðe þæs gefeaht wið Metellus þone cyning. 15
Ac siþþan Metellus þa elpendas ofercom, siþþan he hæfde eac
raðe þæt oþer folc gefliemed. Æf'ter' þæm fleame Hasterbal wearð
ofslagen from his agnum folce.

þa wæron Cartainiense swa ofercumene 7 swa gedrefde betux
him selfum, þæt hie hie to nanum anwalde ne bemæton; ac hie 20
gewearð þæt hie wolden to Romanum friþes wilnian. þa sendon
hie Regulus þone consul, þone hie hæfdon mid him fif winter on
bendum, 7 he him geswor on his goda noman þæt he ægþer wolde,
ge þæt ærende abeodan swa swa hi hiene heton, ge eac him þæt
anwyrde eft gecyþan. 7 he hit swa gelæste, 7 abead þæt ægþer þara 25
folca oþrum ageafe ealle þa men þe hie gehergead hæfden 7 siþþan
him betweonum sibbe heolden. 7 æfter þæm þe he hit aboden
hæfde, he hie healsade þæt hie nanuht þara ærenda ne underfenge
7 cwæð þæt him to micel æwisce wære þæt he swa emnlice wrixleden, 7 eac þæt hiora gerisna nære þæt hie swa heane hie geþohten 30
þæt hi heora gelican wurden. þa æfter þæm wordum hie budon him
þæt he on cyþþe mid him wunade 7 to his rice fenge. þa *ond*wyrde

1–3] OH IV. ix. 9.   4–8] OH IV. ix. 10–11.   9–11] OH IV.
ix. 13.   12–18] OH IV. ix. 14–15.   19–p. 96, 5] OH IV. x. 1.

1 Amilcor] amicor C.   3 Regule ær] ær regule C.   eodon] *first* o *alt.
from* a L.   4 iii] vi C.   5–6 Cartainiensium] cartaniensum C.
9–10 oferhergeade] forhergade C.   12 Eliuses] iliuses L, heliuses C.
13 Foriuses] foruses C.   15 xxx] xxxgum C.   elpenda] helpenda
C.   16 elpendas] helpendas C.   19 Cartainiense] *first* e *smudged and
possibly alt. in l.h.* L.   25 anwyrde] *and*wyrde C.

f. 56 he him 7 cwæð | þæt hit na geweorþan sceolde þæt se wære leoda
cyning se þe ær wæs folce þeow. þa he eft [to] Cartainum com, þa
asædon his geferan hu he heora ærenda abead. þa forcurfon hie
him þa twa ædran on twa healfa þara eagena, þæt he æfter þæm
5 slapan ne mehte, oþ he swa searigende his lif forlet.

Æfter þæm Atilius Regulus 7 Mallius Ulsca þa consulas foron
on Cartaine, on Libeum þæt igland, mid twam hunde scipa, 7
þær besæton an fæsten. þa befor hiene þær Hannibal se geonga
cyning, Amilcores sunu, þær hie ungearwe butan fæstenne sæton,
10 7 þær ealle ofslagene wæron buton feawum. Æfter þæm Claudius
se consul for eft an Punice, 7 him Hannibal ut on sæ ongean com 7
ealle ofslog buton xxx sciphlæsta: þa oðflugon to Libeum þæm
iglande. þær wæs ofslagen ix m 7 xx m gefangen. Æfter þæm for
Gaius Iunius se consul on Affrice 7 mid eallum his færelte on se
15 forwearð.

þæs on þæm æfterran geare Hannibal sende sciphere on Rome
7 þær ungemetlice gehergeadon. Æfter þæm Lutatia se consul for
on Africe mid iii hunde scipa to Sicilium, 7 him Punice þær wið
gefuhto[n]. þær wearð Lutatia wund þurh oþer cneow. þæs o[n]
20 mergen com Hanna mid Hannibales firde 7 him þær gefeaht wið
Lutatia, þeh he wund wære, 7 Hannan gefliemde 7 him æfter for,
oþ he com to Cinam þære byrg. Raðe þæs coman eft Pene mid
firde to him 7 gefliemde wurdon, 7 ofslagen ii m. þa wilnedon
Cartaine oþre siþe friþes to Romanum, 7 hie hit him on þæt gerad
25 geafon þæt hie him Siciliam to ne tugen, ne Sardiniam, 7 eac him
gesealden þæronufan iii m talentana ælce geare.

IV. vii

Æfter þæm þe Romeburg getimbred wæs v hunde wintrum 7 vii,
f. 56ᵛ wearð ungemetlic fyrbryne mid Romanum, | þæt nan mon nyste
hwonan hit com. þa þæt fyr hie alet, þa wearð Tiber seo ea swa
30 fledu swa heo næfre ær næs ne siþþan, þæt heo mæst eall genom
þæt binnan þære byrg wæs þæra monna ondliefene, ge eac on heora
getimbrum.

6–15] OH IV. x. 2–3.   16–23] OH IV. x. 4–8.   23–6] OH IV. xi. 1–2.
27–32] OH IV. xi. 5–8.

2 þa ... com] om. C.   to] of L, om. C.   6 Mallius] nallius C.   17 Lu-
tatia] lutalia C.   19 gefuhton] from C, gefuhto L.   on] from C, om L.
21 Hannan] from C, hannannan L.   29 hie] om. C.   30 eall] from
C, ealle L.

On þæm dagum þe Titus Sempronius 7 Gratias Gaius wæron consulas on Rome, [hie] gefuhton wið Faliscis þæm folce 7 hiora ofslogan xii m.

On þæm geare wurdon þa Gallie Romanum wiðerwearde þe mon nu hæt Longbeardas, 7 raþe þæs heora folc togædere gelæddon. On 5 hiora þæm forman gefeohte wæs Romana iii m ofslagen, 7 on þæm æfterran geare wæs Gallia iiii m ofslagen 7 ii m gefangen. þa Romane hamweard foran, þa noldan hie don þone triumphan beforan hiora consulum þe hiora gewuna wæs þonne hie sige hæfdon, for þon þe he æt ðæm ærran gefeohte fleah, 7 hie þæt siþþan fela 10 geare an missenlicum sigum dreogende wæron.

þa þa Titus Mallius 7 Torcuatus Gaius 7 Atirius Bubulcus wæron consulas on Rome, þa ongun[non] Sardinie, swa hie Pene gelærdon, winnan wið Romanum 7 raþe oferswiðde wæron. Æfter þæm Romane wunnon on Cartaine, for þæm þe hie frið 15 abrocen hæfdon. þa sendon hie tua hiera ærendracan to Romanum æfter friþe 7 hit abiddan ne mehton. þa æt þæm þriddan cirre hie sendon x hie[ra] ie'l'dstena wietena, 7 hi hit abiddan ne mehton. Æt þæm feorða[n] cirre hie sendon Hannan heora þone unweorðestan þegn, 7 he hit abæd.   20

Wiotodlice, cwæð Orosius, nu we sindon cumen to þæm godan tidun þe us Romane oþwitað 7 to ðære genihtsumnisse þe hie us ealneg fore gielpað þæt ure ne sien ðæm gelican. Ac frine hie mon þonne æfter hu monegum wintrum sio sibb gewurde þæs þe hie æst unsibbe wið monegum folcum hæfdon: þonne is þæt æfter | 25 wintra 7 feower hundum. Ahsige þonne eft hu longe sio sibb gestode: þonne wæs þæt an gear. Sona þæs on ðæm æfterran geare Gallie wunnon wið Romane, 7 Pene | on oþre healfe. Hu þyncð   f. 57 eow Romanum hu seo sibb gefæstnad wære, hwæþer hio sie þæm gelicost þe mon nime ænne eles dropan 7 drype on an micel fyr 30 7 þence hit mid þæm adwæscan? þonne is wen, swa micle swiðor swa he þencð þæt he hit adwæsce, þæt he hit swa micle swiðor

---

1–3] OH IV. xi. 10.   4–11] OH IV. xii. 1.   12–20] OH IV. xii. 2–3.
21–p. 98, 2] OH IV. xii. 5–9.

2 hie] *no reading* L, hy *in margin in l.h.* C.   5 Longbeardas] langbeardas C.
8 foran] wæran C.   12 Torcuatus] torcwatus C.   13 ongunnon] *from*
C, ongun L.   15 for þæm þe] for þon þe C.   18 hiera] hie/ L, heora C.
19 feorðan] *from* C, feor/ðam L.   20 abæd] abead C.   21 sindon] i
alt. to e *in l.h.* L.   29 eow] eow nu C.

ontydre. Swa þonne wæs mid Romanum þæt an gear þæt hie sibbe
hæfdon, þæt hie under þære sibbe to þære mæstan sace become.

On hiora ðæm ærestan gewinne Amilcor, Cartaina cynig, þa he
to Romanum mid firde faran wolde, þa wearð he from Spenum
5 beþridad 7 ofslagen.

On ðæm geare Ilirice ofslogon Romana ærendracan. Æfter þæm
Fuluius Postumius se consul for þæm on hie fird gelædde, 7 fela
ofslagen wearð on ægðere healfe, 7 he þæh sige hæfde.

Sona þæs on þæm æfterran gere gelærdan Romana biscepas
10 swelce niwe rædas swelce hie fol oft ær ealde gedydan, þa him mon
on þreo healfe onwinnende wæs, ægþer ge Gallie be suþan muntum, ge Gallie be norþan muntum, ge Pene, þæt hie sceolden mid
monnum for hie heora godum blotan, 7 þæt sceolde beon an Gallisc wæpnedmon 7 an Gallisc wifmon, 7 hie þa Romane be þara
15 biscepa lare hie swa cuce bebyrgdan. Ac hit God wræc on him swa
he ær ealneg dyde, swa oft swa hie mid monnum ofredan, þæt hie
mid hiera cucum onguldon þæt hie ungyltige cwealdon. þæt wæs
ærest gesiene on þæm gefeohte þe hie wið Gallium hæfdon, þeh
þe heora agnes fultumes wære eahta hund m, buton oþrum
20 folcum þe hi him hæfdon to aspanen, þæt hie raðe flugon þæs þe
heora consul ofslagen wæs 7 hiora oþres folces iii m, þæt him þa
geþuhte swelc þæt mæste wæl swelc hie oft ær for noht hæfdon.
Æt hiora oþran gefeohte wæs Gallia ix m ofslagen.

f. 57ᵛ   þæs on þæm þriddan geare Mallius Tarcuatus | 7 Fuluius
25 Flaccus wæron consulas on Rome. Hie gefuhton wið Gallium 7
hiora iii m ofslogon 7 vi m gefengon.

On þæm æfterran geare wæron monege wundor gesewene. An
wæs þæt on Piceno þæm wuda an wielle weol blode, 7 on Tracio
þæm londe mon geseah swelce se heofen burne, 7 on Ariminio
30 þære byrg wæs niht oð midne dæg, 7 wearð swa micel eorþbeofung
þæt on Caria 7 on Roþum þæm iglondum wurdon micle hryras,
ond Colosus gehreas.

þy geare Fiaminius se consul forseah þa sægene þe þa hlyttan
him sædon 7 him logan þæt he æt þæm gefeohte ne come wið

3–5] OH IV. xiii. 1.   6–8] OH IV. xiii. 2.   9–23] OH IV. xiii. 3–10.
24–6] OH IV. xiii. 11.   27–32] OH IV. xiii. 12–13.   33–p. 99, 8] OH
IV. xiii. 14–16.

11 healfe] healfa C.   17 onguldon] guldon C.   20 þe (1)] þeh *with* h
dotted for correction L.   24 Mallius] *from* C, malllius L.   26 iii m] iii
hund m C.   28 Tracio] thracio C.   29 geseah] seah C.

Gallie. Ac he hit þurhteah 7 mid weorþscipe geendade. þær wæs
Gallia vii m ofslagen 7 xvii m gefangen. Æfter þæm Claudius se
consul gefeaht wið Gælle 7 hiora ofslog xxx m, 7 he self gefeaht
wið þone cyning anwig 7 hine ofslog 7 Megelan þa burg geeode.
Æfter þæm wunnon Isþrie on Romane. þa sendon hi heora 5
consulas angean, Cornelius 7 Minutius. þær wæs micel wæl
geslagen on ægþere healfe, 7 Isþrie wurdon þeh Romanum
underþiedde.

IV. viii

Æfter þæm þe Romeburg getimbred wæs v hunde wintrum 7
xxxiii, Hannibal, Pena cyning, besæt Saguntum, Ispania burg, for 10
þon hie on symbel wið Romanum sibbe heoldon, 7 þær wæs
sittende eahta monað, oþ he hie ealle hungre acwealde 7 þa burg
towearp, þeh þe Romane heora ærendracan him to sendon 7 hie
firmetton þæt hie þæt gewinn forleten; ac he hie swa unweorðlice
forseah, þæt he heora self onseon nolde. On þam gewinne, 7 eac 15
on monegum oðrum æfter þæm, Hannibal gecyþde þone niþ
7 þone hete þe he beforan his fæder geswor, þa he nigonwintre
cniht wæs, | þæt he næfre ne wurde Romana freo'n'd.   f. 58

þa þa Publius Cornelius 7 Scipa Publius 7 Sempronius Longus,
þa hie wæron [consulas], Hannibal abræc mid gefeohte ofer þa 20
beorgas þe mon hæt Perenei, þa sindon betux Galleum 7 Spaneum,
7 siþþan he gefor ofer þa monegan þeoda, oþ he com to Alpis þæm
muntum 7 þær eac ofer abræc, þeh him mon oftrædlice mid
gefeohtum wiðstode, 7 þone weg geworhte ofer munt Iof. Swa
þonne he to ðæm syndrigum stane com, þonne het he hiene mid 25
fyre onhætan 7 siþþan mid mattucun heawan, 7 mid þæm mæstan
geswince þa muntas oferfor. His heres [wæs] an m feðena 7 xx m
gehorsedra.

þa he hæfde on þæm emnete gefaren oþ he com to Ticenan
þære ie, þa com him ðær ongean Scipio se consul 7 ðær frecenlice 30
gewundod wearð 7 eac ofslagen wære, gif his sunu his ne gehulpe,

9–18] OH IV. xiv. 1–3.   19–28] OH IV. xiv. 3–5.   29–p. 100, 2] OH
IV. xiv. 6.

2 xvii] xv C.   3 Gælle] gallie C.   5 Romane] *from* C, romanane L.
7 Isþrie] istrie C.   9 v] vi C.   10–11 for þon] for þon þe C.
11 Romanum] romane C.   13 him to] to him C.   16 oðrum] *no reading*
C.   17 geswor] *form of* r *alt. in l.h.* L.   20 consulas] *from* C, *om.* L.
24 munt Iof] munti for C.   27 wæs] *from* C, *om.* L.

mid þæm þæt he hiene foran forstod oð he on fleame fealh. þær
wearð Romana micel wæl geslagen.

Hiora ðæt æfterre gefeoht wæs æt Trefia ðære ie, 7 eft wæron
Romane forslægen 7 gefliemed. þa þæt Sempronius hierde, heora
5 oþer consul, se wæs on Sicilium mid firde gefaren, he þonan afor,
7 begen þa consulas wæron mid firde angean Hannibal, 7 heora
gemetting wæs eft æt Trefia þære ie, 7 eac Romane gefliemed 7
swiþor forslagen, 7 Hannibal gewundod.

Æfter þæm for Hannibal ofer Bardan þone beorg, þeh þe ymb
10 þone tieman wæren swa micel snawgebland swa þætte ægþer ge
þara horsa fela forwurdon ge þa elpendas ealle buton anum, ge þa
men selfe uneaðe þone ciele genæson. Ac for þæm he geneðde
swiþost ofer þone munt þe he wiste þæt Flamineus se consul
wende þæt he buton sorge mehte on þæm wintersetle gewunian þe
15 he þa on wæs mid þæm folce þe he ða gegaderad hæfde, 7 untweogendlice wende þæt nan nære þætte þæt færelt ymbe þone timan
f. 58ᵛ anginnan dorste | oþþe mehte for þæm ungemetlican cile. Mid þæm
þe Hannibal to ðæm londe becom, swa gewicade he an anre diegelre
stowe, neah þæm oþrum folce, 7 sum his folc sende gind þæt lond
20 to bærnanne 7 to hergenne, þætte se consul wæs wenende þæt eall
þæt folc wære gind þæt lond tobræd, 7 þiderweard farende wæs 7
þencende þæt he hie on þære hergunge beswice, 7 þæt folc buton
truman lædde, swa he wiste þæt þæt oþer wæs, oþþæt Hannibal
him com þwyres on mid þæm fultume þe he ætgædere hæfde,
25 7 þone consul ofslog 7 þæs oþres folces xxv m, 7 vi gefengon, 7
Hannibales folces wæs twa m ofslagen.

Æfter þæm Scipia se consul, þæs oþres Scipian broþor, wæs
monega gefeoht donde on Ispanium 7 Magonem, Pena latteow,
gefeng; 7 monega wundor gewurdon on þære tide. Ærest wæs
30 þæt seo sunne wæs swelce heo wære eall geˈlytˈladu. Oþer wæs
ðæt mon geseah swelce seo sunne 7 se mona fuhte. þas wundor
gewurdon on Arpis þæm londe. 7 on Sardinium mon geseah
twegen sceldas blode swætan, 7 Falisci þæt folc hie gesawon swelce
se hefon wære tohliden, 7 Athium þæt folc him geþuhte, þa hie
35 heora corn ripon 7 heora cawelas afylled hæfdon þæt ealle þa ear
wæron blodege.

3–8] OH IV. xiv. 7.   9–12] OH IV. xiv. 8.   12–26] OH IV. xv. 2–5.
27–9] OH IV. xiv. 9.   29–36] OH IV. xv. 1.

3 ðæt] om. C.   7 gemetting] gemitting C.   9 ymb] hit ymbe C.
17 þæm (1)] þon C.   25 gefengon] on eras. L, gefangen C.

IV. ix

Æfter þæm þe Romeburg getimbred wæs v hunde win*trum* 7
feowertegum, þa þa Lucius Amilius 7 Paulus Publius 7 Terrentius
Uarra, þa hie wæron consulas, hie geforan mid firde angean Hannibal. Ac he hie mid þæm ilcan wrence beswac þe he æt heora ærran
ʾgeʾmetingge dyde 7 eac mid þæm niwan þe hie ær ne c[u]ðon,   5
þæt wæs, ðæt he on fæstre stowe let sum his folc 7 mid sumum for
angean þa consulas; 7 raðe þæs þe hie tosomne comon, he fleah
wið þara þe þær beæftan wæron, 7 him þa consulas wæron æfter-
fylgende | 7 þæt folc sleande 7 wendon þæt hie on ðæm dæge   f. 59
sceoldon habban þone mæstan sige. Ac raðe þæs þe Hannibal   10
to his fultume com, he gefliemde ealle þa consulas 7 on Romanum swa micel wæl geslog swa heora næfre næs ne ær ne siþþan
æt anum gefeohte, þæt wæs feower 7 feowertig m, 7 þara consula
twegen ofslog 7 þone þriddan gefeng. 7 þa on dæg he mehte
cuman to ealra Romana anwealde, þær he forþ gefore to ðære   15
byrg. Æfter þæm Hannibal sende ham to Cartaina þrio mydd
gyldenra hringa his sige to tacne. Be þæm hringum mon mehte
witan hwæt Romana duguðe gefeallen wæs, for þon þe hit wæs
þeaw mid him on ðæm dagum þæt nan oþer ne moste gyldenne
hring werian buton he æþeles cynnes wære.   20

Æfter þæm gefeohte wæron Romane swa swiðe forþohte þætte
Celius Metellus, þe þa heora consul wæs, ge ealle heora senatus,
hæfdon geþoht þæt hie sceoldon Romeburg forlætan, ge furþum
ealle Italiam, 7 hie þæt swa gelæsten, gif him Scipia ne gestirde, se
wæs þara cempena ieldest, mid þæm þæt he his sweorde gebræd   25
7 swor ðæt him leofre wære þæt he hiene selfne acwealde þonne
he forlete his fæder oeþel; 7 sæde eac þæt he þara ælces ehtend
wolde beon swa [swa] his feondes, þe þæs wordes wære þæt from
Romebyrg þohte. 7 he hie ealle mid þæm geniedde þæt hie aþas
sworan þæt hie ealle ætgædere wolden, oþþe on heora earde   30
licggean, oþþe on heora earde libban.

Æfter ðæm hie gesetton tictator, þæt he sceolde bion hierra ofer

1–20] OH IV. xvi. 1–5.   21–31] OH IV. xvi. 6.   32–p. 102, 13] OH
IV. xvi. 7–10.

1 wintrum] *so* C, wĩnt L.   5 cuðon] cuðan C, coðon L.   11 to] on
C.   16 Cartaina] carina C.   mydd] .m.ydd L, midd C.   21 Romane]
romana C.   25 mid þæm þæt] mid þam þe C.   28 swa (2)] *from* C,
no reading L.   32 hierra] herra C.

þa consulas, se wæs haten Decius Iunius. He næs buton seofontienewintre. 7 Scipian hie gesetton to consule, 7 ealle þa men þe
hie on ðeowdome hæfdon hie gefreodon, on þæt gerad þæt hie him
4 aðas sworan þæt hie him æt þæm gewinnum gelæsten. Ond sume,
f. 59ᵛ þa þe heora [hlafordas] freogean noldon, oþþe hie ne | anhagade
þæt hie mehten, þonne guldon hie þa consulas mid hiera gemænan
feo 7 siþþan freodon, 7 ealle þa þe fordemede wæron ær þæm, oþþe
hie selfe forworht hæfdon, hie hit eall forgeafon wið þæm þe hie
him æt þæm gewinnum fuleoden. þara mon'n'a wæs siex m, þa
10 hie gegaderad wæron. 7 ealle Italiam geswicon Romanum 7 to
Hannibale gecirdon, for þon þe hie wæron orwene hwæðer æfre
Romane to heora anwealde becomen. þa gefor Hannibal on Benefente, 7 hie him ongean coman 7 him to gecirdon.

Æfter þæm Romane hæfdon gegaderad feower legian heora
15 folces 7 sendon Lucius Postumius þone consul on þa Gallie þe mon
nu Longbeardan hæt, 7 þær ofslagen wearð 7 þæs folces fela mid
him. Æfter þæm Romane gesetton Claudius Marcellus to consule,
se wæs ær Scipian gefera. He for dearnenga mid gewealdene fultume on þone ende Hannibales folces þe he self on wæs 7 fela þæs
20 folces ofslog 7 hiene selfne gefliemde. þa hæfde Marcellus Romanum cuð gedon þæt mon Hannibal geflieman mehte, ðeh þe hie
ær tweode hwæðer hiene mon mid ænige monfultume geflieman
mehte.

Gemong ðæm gewinnum þa twegen Scipian þe þa wæron
25 consulas 7 eac gebroðor, hie wæron on Ispanium mid firde 7
gefuhton wið Hasterbale, Hannibales fædran, 7 hiene ofslogon 7
his folces xxx m sume ofslogan, sume gefengon. Se wæs eac Pena
oþer cyning.

Æfter þæm Centenus Penula se consul bæd þætte senatus him
30 fultum sealdon, þæt he mehte Han'n'ibal mid gefeohte gesecan, 7
þær ofslagen wearð 7 eahta þusend his folces. Æfter þæm Sempronius Craccus se consul for eft mid fierde angean Hannibal 7
gefliemed wearð, 7 his heres wæs micel wæl geslagen.

34 Hu magon nu Romane, cwæð Orosius, to soþe gesecge'a'n þæt
f. 60 hie þa hæfden beteran tida | þonne hie nu hæbben, þa hie swa

14-17] OH IV. xvi. 11.   17-23] OH IV. xvi. 12.   24-8] OH IV.
xvi. 13.   29-33] OH IV. xvi. 15-17.   34-p. 103, 7] OH IV. xvi. 18-21.

3 him] hy C.   5 hlafordas] *om. both MSS.*   16 Longbeardan]
langbeardas C.   18 gewealdene] gewealdenan C.   22 ænige] ænigon C.
31 þær] he þær C.   33 geslagen] ofslagen C.

monega gewin hæfdon emdenes underfongen? i wæs on Ispania,
ii on Mæcedonia, iii on Capadotia, iiii æt ham wið Hannibal, 7
hie eac oftost gefliemde wurdon 7 gebismrade. Ac þæt wæs swiðe
sweotol þæt hie þa wæron beteran þegnas þonne hie nu sien, þæt
hie þeh þæs gewinnes geswican noldon, ac hie oft gebidon on 5
lytlum staþole 7 on unwenlicum, þæt hie þa æt nihstan hæfdon
ealra þara anwald þe ær neh heora hæfdon.

IV. x

Aefter þæm þe Romeburg getimbred wæs v hunde wintrum 7
xliii, þætte Marcellus Claudius se consul for mid sciphere on
Sicilie 7 begeat Siracuses, heora þa welegestan burg, þeh he hie 10
æt þæm ærran færelte begietan ne mehte, þa he hie beseten hæfde,
for Archimeðes cræfte, sumes Sicilia ðegnes.

On þæm teoþan geare þæs þe Hannibal won on Italie, he for
of Campaina þæm londe oþ þrio mila to Romebyrg 7 æt þære ie
gewicade þe mon Annianes hætt, eallum Romanum to ðæm mæstan 15
ege, swa hit mon on þara wæpnedmonna gebærum ongitan mehte,
hu hie afyrhtede wæron 7 agælwede, þa þa wifmen urnon mid
stanum wið þara wealla 7 cwædon þæt hie þa burg werian wolden,
gif þa wæpnedmen ne dorsten. þæs on mergen Hannibal gefor to
þære byrig 7 beforan ðæm geate his folc getrymede þe mon hætt 20
Collina. Ac þa consulas noldon hie selfe swa earge geþencan swa
hie þa wifmen ær forcwædon, þæt hi hie binnan þære byrg werian
ne dorsten, ac hie hie butan þæm geate angean Hannibal trymedon.
Ac þa hie togædere woldon, þa com swa ungemetlic ren þæt
heora nan ne mehte nanes wæpnes gewealdan, 7 for þæm toforan. 25
þa se ren ablon, hie foran | eft togædere, 7 eft wearð oþer swelc f. 60ᵛ
ren þæt hie eft toforan. þa angeat Hannibal, 7 him self sæde, ðeh
ðe he wilniende wære 7 wenende Romana anwealdes, þæt hit
God ne geþafode.

Gesecgað me nu, Romane, cwæð Orosius, hwonne þæt gewurde 30
oþþe hwara, ær ðæm cristendome, [þæt] oþþe ge oþþe oðere æt

1 emdenes] endemes C.   2 ii] ii oþer L, oþer C.   iii] þridde C.   iiii]
feorðe C.   8 wintrum] wiñt both mss.   10 Siracuses] siraccuses C.
þeh] þeh þe C.   19 mergen] morgen C.   gefor] for C.   23 hie (2)]
er. L.   31 þæt] om. both MSS.

ænegum godum mehten ren abiddan, swa mon siþþan mehte
siþþan se cristendom wæs, 7 nugiet magon monege gode æt urum
Hælendum Criste, þonne him þearf bið. Hit wæs þeh swiþe
sweotol þæt se ilca Crist se þe hie eft to cristendome onwende,
5 þæt se him þone ren to gescildnisse onsende, þeh hie þæs wyrþe
næron, to þon þæt hie selfe, 7 eac monege oþere þurh [h]ie, to ðæm
cristendome 7 to 'ðæm' soþan geleafan become.

On þæm dagum þe þis gewearð, wæron twegen consulas
ofslagen on Ispania, þa wæron gebroðor 7 wæron begen Scipian
10 hatene; hie wæron beswicene from Hasterbale, Pena cyninge. On
þære tide Cuintus Fuluius se consul geegsade ealle þa ieldestan
men þe on Campaina wæron, þæt hie hie selfe mid atre acwealdon,
7 ealle þa ieldestan men þe wæron on Capu þære byrg he ofslog, for
þon þe he wende þæt hie wolden Hannibale on fultume beon, þeh
15 þa senatus him hæfden þa dæd fæste forboden.

þa Romane geacsedan þæt þa consulas on Ispanium ofslagen
wæron, þa ne mehton þa senatus nænne consul under him findan
þe dorste on Ispanie mid firde gefaran buton þara consula oþres
sunu, Scipia wæs haten, se wæs cniht, se wæs georne biddende
20 þæt him mon fultum sealde, þæt he moste on Ispanie fird gelædan,
7 he þæt færelt swiþost for þæm þur[h]teah þe he þohte þæt he
f. 61 his fæder 7 his fæderan gewræce, þeh þe he hit fæste | wið þa sena-
tus hæle. Ac Romane wæron þæs færeltes swa geornfulle, þeh þe
hie swiðe gebrocode wæren on hiora licgendan feo þe hie gemæne
25 hæfdon, for þæm gewinnum þe hie þa hæfdon on feower healfa,
þæt hie eall him gesealdon þæt hie þa hæfdon on þæm færelte to
fultume, buton þæt ælc wifmon hæfde ane yndsan goldes 7 an
pund seolfres, 7 ælc wæpnedmon ænne hring 7 ane hoppan.

þa Scipia hæfde gefaren to ðære niwan byrig Cartaina, þe mon
30 nu Cordofa hætt, he besætt Magonem, Hannibales broðor, 7 for
þon þe he on þa burgleode on ungearwe becom, he hie on lytlan
firste mid hungre on his geweald genie'd'de, þæt him se cyning

8–15] OH IV. xvii. 12.   16–28] OH IV. xvii. 13–14.   29–p. 105, 5] OH
IV. xviii. 1.

4 hie] e er. L.   6 þurh hie] þurhie L, þurh hy C.   10 wæron]
wurdon C.   11 Cuintus] quintus C.   12 Campaina] campina C.   hie
hie] alt. to hi by eras. L.   14 þeh] þeh þe C.   17 wæron] wurdon C.
21 þurhteah] from C, þurteah L.   22 þa] om. C.   24 hie (1)]
e er. L.   hie (2)] e er. L.   25 hie] e er. L.   26 hie (1)] e er. L.   on]
no reading C.   27 yndsan] ynd'san'san with 'san' in hand 2 L.   32 his]
no reading C.

self on hand eode, 7 he ealle þa oðre sume ofslog, sume geband, 7
þone cyning gebundenne to Rome sende 7 monege mid him þara
ieldestena witena. Binnan ðære byrig wæs micel li῾c῾ggende feoh
funden. Sum hit Scipia to Rome sende, sum he hit het ðæm folce
dælan.   5

On ðære tide for Leui[n]us se consul of Mæcedonia on Sicilie
mid sciphere 7 þær geeode Agrigentum þa burg 7 gefeng Hannonam heora latteow. Siþþan him eodon on hand feowertig burga, 7
xxvi he geeode mid gefeohte. On ðære tide Hannibal ofslog Gneus
Fuluius þone consul on Italium 7 eahta m mid him. Æfter þæm   10
Hannibal feaht wið Marcellus þone consul þrie dagas. þy forman
dæge þa folc feollon on ægðere healfe gelice. þy æfterran dæge
Hannibal hæfde sige. þy þriddan dæge hæfde se consul. Æfter
þæm Fauius Maximus se consul for mid sciphere to Tarentan
þære byrg, swa Hannibal nyste, 7 þa burg on niht abræc, swa þa   15
nyston þe þærinne wæron, 7 Hannibales latteow ofslog Cartalon
7 xxx m mid him.

þæs on þæm æfterran geare | Hannibal bestæl on Marcellus   f. 61ᵛ
Claudius þone consul, ðær he on firde sætt, 7 hiene ofslog 7 his
folc mid him. On þæm dagum Scipia geflemde Hasterbal on Ispa- 20
nium, Hannibales operne broðor, 7 þæs folces him eode on hand
eahtatig burga. Swa lað wæs Pena folc Scipian þa he hie gefliemed
hæfde, swa, þeh þe he hie sume wið feo gesealde, ðæt he þæt
weorð nolde agan þæt him mon wið sealde, ac he hit oþrum monnum sealde. On ðæm ilcan geare beswac eft Hannibal twegen   25
consulas, Marcellus 7 Cirspinus, 7 hie ofslog.

þa Claudius Nerone 7 Marcolia Salinatore wæron consulas,
Hasterbal, Hannibales broðor, for mid firde of Ispanium on
Italie, Hannibale to fultume. þa geacsedon þa consulas þæt ær,
ær Hannibal, 7 him ongean coman, swa he þa muntas oferfaren   30
hæfde, 7 þær hæfdon longsum gefeoht, ær þara folca aþer fluge.
þæt wæs swiþost on ðæm gelong þæt Hasterbal swa late fleah for
þon þe he elpendas mid him hæfde, 7 Romane hæfdon sige. þær
wæs Hasterbal ofslagen 7 liii m his heres, 7 v m gefangen. þa

6–17] OH IV. xviii. 2–5.   18–26] OH IV. xviii. 6–8.   27–p. 106,
12] OH IV. xviii. 9–10 and 14–18.

6 Leuinus] *from* C, leuius L.   11 Hannibal] hanniball C.   Marcellus]
macerllus C.   16 Cartalon] cartolon C.   22 eahtatig] hund eahtatig C.
24 he] *no reading* C.   29 Italie] italia C.   Hannibale] hannile C.
30 he] he swa L.   32 swiþost] swiþor C.   34 wæs] wearð C.

heton þa consulas Hasterbale þæt heafod of aceorfan 7 aweorpan
hit beforan Hannibales wicstowe. þa Hannibale cuð wæs þæt his
broðor ofslagen wæs 7 þæs folces swa fela mid him, þa wearð him
ærest ege from Romanum, 7 gefor on Bruti þæt lond. þa hæfde
5 Hannibal 7 Romane an gear stilnesse him betweonum, for ðon þe
þa folc butu on feferadle mid ungemete swulton. On ðære stilnesse
Scipia geeode ealle Ispanie 7 siþþan com to Rome 7 Romanum to
ræde gelærde þæt hie mid scipum foren on Hannibales land. þa
9 sendon Romane hiene þæt he þæs færeltes consul wære, 7 raðe þæs
f. 62 þe he on Pene com, him com ongen Hanno se cyni'n'g | unwærlice
7 þær ofslagen wearð. On þære tide Hannibal gefeaht wið Sempronius þone consul on Italiam 7 hiene bedraf into Romebyrig.

Æfter þæm Pene foran ongean Scipian mid eallum hiera fultume
7 wicstowa namon on twam stowum, neah þære byrg þe mon Utica
15 hæt. On oþerre wæron Pene, on oþerre Numeðe, þe him on fultume wæron 7 geþoht hæfdon þæt hie ðær sceoldon wintersetl
habban. Ac siþþan Scipia geascade þæt þa foreweardas wæron
feor ðæm fæstenne gesette, 7 eac þæt þær nane oðre near næran,
he þa diegellice gelædde his fird betuh þæm weardum 7 feawe
20 men to oþrum þara fæstenna onsende to þon þæt hie his ænne
ende onbærndon, þæt siþþan mæst ealle þe þærbinnan wæron
wæron wið þæs fyres weard, to þon þæt hie hit acwencean
þohton. He þa Scipia gemong þæm hie mæst ealle ofslog. þa þæt
þa oþre onfundon þe on ðæm oþrum fæstenne wæron, hie wæron
25 flocmælum þiderweard þæm oþrum to fultume, 7 hie Scipia wæs
ealle þa niht sleande, swa hie þonne comon, oð dæg, 7 siþþan he
hie slog ofer ealne þone dæg fleonde. 7 hiera twegen cyningas,
Hasterbal 7 Sifax, oþflugon to Cartaina þære byrg 7 gegaderodon
þone fultum þe hie þa hæfdon 7 ongean Scipian comon, 7 eft
30 wurdon gefliemde into Cartaina. Sume oþflugon to Cretan þæm
iglande, 7 him Scipia sende sciphere æfter, þæt mon sume
ofslog, sume gefeng, 7 Sifax wearð gefangen, hiera oþer cyning, 7
siþþan wæs to Rome on racentan sended.

On þæm gefeohtum wæron Pene swa forhiende þæt hie na
35 siþþan hie wiþ Romane to nohte ne bemætan, 7 sendon on Italie

13–33] OH IV. xviii. 18–21.   34–p. 107, 21] OH IV. xix. 1–4.

1 aweorpan] ã weorpan L.   8 scipum] *alt. to* scipium L.   11 ofslagen
wearð] wearð ofslagen C.   gefeaht] feaht C.   13 Pene foran] foran pene C.
15 hæt] het C.   27 hie] *om.* C.

æfter Hannibale 7 bædon þæt he him to fultume come, 7 he him
wepende [þære bene] getygðade, for þon þe [he] sceolde Italiam
forlætan on þæm þreoteoðon geare þæs þe he ær on com.
7 he ealle
ofslog þe of þæm landum his men wæron 7 mid him ofer sæ 4
noldon. þa he hamweard | seglde, þa het he ænne mon stigan on f. 62ᵛ
þone mæst 7 locian hwæþer he þæt land gecneowe þæt hie toweard
wæron. þa sæde he him þæt he gesawe ane tobrocene byrgenne,
swelce hiera þeaw wæs þæt mon ricum monnum bufan eorðan of
stanum worhte. þa wæs Hannibale æfter hiera hæðeniscum gewunan þæt *ond*wyrde swiþe lað, 7 him unþanc sæde þæs *ond*wyrdes, 10
7 ealne þone here he het mid þæm scipum þonan wendan þe he
ær to geþoht hæfde, 7 up comon æt Leptan þæm tune, 7 hrædlice
for to Cartaina 7 biddende wæs þæt he moste wið Scipian sprecan,
7 wilniende wæs þæt he frið betwux þæm folcum findan sceolde.
Ac he hiera sundorspræce þe hie betux þæm folcum togædere- 15
weard gespræcan to unsibbe brohton 7 hie to gefeohte geredon. 7
raþe þæs þe hie togædere comon, Hannibales folc wearð gefliemed
7 xx m ofslagen 7 d, 7 lxxx elpenda, 7 Hannibal oþfleah feowera
sum to Aþrametum þæm fæstenne. þa sendon þa burgleode of
Cartaina æfter Hannibale 7 cwædon þæt him soelest wære þæt hie 20
friþes to Romanum wilnaden. þa þa Gaius Cornelius 7 Lentulus
Publius wæron consulas, wearð Cartainum frið aliefed from
Scipian mid þara senata willan, on þæt gerad þæt þa igland Sicilia
7 Sarþinia hierden to Romanum, 7 þæt hie him ælce geare gesealden swa fela talentena seolfres swa hie him þonne aliefden. 7 25
Scipia het d hira scipa up ateon 7 forbærnan, 7 siþþan to Rome
hamweard for. þa him mon þone triumphan ongean brohte, þa
eode þær mid Terrentius, se mæra Cartaina scop, 7 bær hæt on
his heafde, for þon Romane hæfdon þa niwlice gesett þæt þa þe
hæt beran moston, þonne hie hwelc folc oferwunnen hæfdon, þæt 30
þa moston ægþer habban ge feorh ge freodom.

IV. xi

| Æfter þæm þe Romeburg getimbred wæs d wintrum 7 l, wæs f. 63
geendad Punica þæt æfterre gewin 7 Romana, þæt hie dreogende

21–31] OH IV. xix. 5–6.   32–p. 108, 11] OH IV. xx. 1–3.

2 þære bene] *from* C, *om.* L.   he] *from* C, *om.* L.   3 þæs] *om.* C.
9–10 gewunan] *from* C, gewunnan L.   12 ær to] *om.* C.   15 he] hy C.
23 þara senata] þæra senatuses C.   24 Sarþinia] sardinia C.   30 hwelc]
swylc C.   33 Punica . . . gewin] þæt æfт̃ punica gewinn C.

wæron xiiii winter. Ac Romane 'raðe' þæs oþer angunnon wið
Mæcedonie. þa hluton þa consulas hwelc hiera ærest þæt gewinn
underfenge. þa gehleat hit Quintius Flaminius 7 on þæm gewinne
monega gefeoht þurhteah 7 oftost sige hæfde, oð Philippus hira
5 cyning friðes bæd, 7 hit him Romane aliefdon. 7 siþþan he for on
Læcedemonie, 7 Quintius Flaminius geniedde begen þa cyningas
þæt hie sealdon hiera suna to gislum. Philippus, Mæcedonia
cyning, sealde Demetrias his sunu, 7 Nauiða sealde, Læcedemonia
cyning, Armenan his sunu. 7 ealle þa Romaniscan men þe Hanni-
10 bal on Crece geseald hæfde, him bebad se consul þæt hie eal
hiera heafod bescearen, to tacne þæt he hie of ðeowdome dyde.
      On þære tide Subres 7 Euoi 7 Ce'no'manni þa folc hie togædere
gesomnedon for Amilcores lare, Hannibales broðor, þone he ær
on Italiam him beæftan forlet, 7 siþþan for on Placentiæ 7 on
15 Cremone þa land 7 hie mid ealle aweston. þa sendon Romane
ðider Claudius Fuluius þone consul, 7 he hiene uneaðe oferwan.
Æfter þæm Flamineus se consul gefeaht wið Philippus, Mæcedonia cyning, 7 wið Thraci 7 wið Ilirice 7 wið monega oþera
þeoda on anum gefeohte 7 hie ealle gefliemde. þær wæs Mæc[e]-
20 doniæ eahta m ofslagen 7 vi m gefangen. Æfter þæm Sempronius
se consul wearð ofslagen on Ispania mid ealre his firde. On þære
tide Marcellus se consul [wearð gefliemed] on Etruria þæm lande.
þa com Furius, oþer consul, him to fultume 7 sige hæfde, 7 hie
siþþan þæt land eall aweston.
25   þa þa Lucius Ualerius 7 Flaccus Marcus wæron consulas, þa
f. 63ᵛ ongon Antiochus, Sira cyning, winnan wið Romanum 7 of Assia
on Europe mid firde gefor. On þære tide bebudan Romane | þæt
mon Hannibal, Cartaina cyning, [gefenge] 7 hiene siþþan to Rome
brohte. þa he þæt hierde, þa fleah he to Antiochuse, Sira cyninge,
30 þær he on tweogendlican onbide wæs hwæðer he wið Romanum
winnan dorste swa he ongunnen hæfde. Ac hiene Hannibal aspon

12–20] OH IV. xx. 4–6.   20–4] OH IV. xx. 10–11.   25–p. 109, 1] OH
IV. xx. 12–13.

2–3 ærest . . . underfenge] þæt gewinn ærest underfon sceolde C.   8–9 Nauiða
. . . cyning] læcedemonia cyning sealde C.   11 dyde] adyde C.   12 tide]
written twice, the first erased L.   7 Euoi] *om.* C.   togædere] togædere hy C.
14 Italiam] italium C.   Placentiæ] placentie C.   16 hiene] hy C.
19–20 Mæcedoniæ] mæcdoniæ L, mæcedonia C.   22 wearð gefliemed]
wearð geflymed C, *om.* L.   26 Sira] siria C.   Assia] asia C.   28 gefenge]
from C, *om.* L, *with space for some eight letters.*   29 hierde] gehyrde C.
Sira] siria C.

þæt he þæt gewin leng ne ongan. þa sendon Romane Scipian
Affricanus hiera ærendracan to Antiochuse. þa het he Hannibal
þæt he wið þa ærendracan spræce 7 him geandwyrde. þa hie nanre
sibbe ne gewearð, þa com æfter þæm Scipia se consul mid Clafrione,
oþrum consule, 7 Antiochuses folces ofslog xl m.   5
þæs on ðæm æfterran gere gefeaht Scipia wið Hannibal ute on
sæ 7 sige hæfde. þa Antiochus þæt gehierde, þa bæd he Scipian
friþes 7 him his sunu ham onsende, se wæs on his gewealde swa
he nyste hu he him to com, butan swa sume [me]n sædon, þæt he
sceolde beon gefangen on hergiunge oþþe æt wearde.   10
On þære firran Ispanie forwearð Emilius se consul mid eallum
his folce from Lusitaniam þære þeode. On þæm dagum forwearð
Lucius Beuius se consul mid eallum his folce from Etusci þæm
leodum, þæt ðær nan to lafe ne wearð þæt hit to Rome gebodode.
Æfter ðæm Fuluius se consul for mid firde on Crece to þæm   15
beorgum þe mon Olimphus hæt. þa wæs þæs folces fela on an
fæsten oþflogen. þa on ðæm gefeohte þe hie þæt fæsten brecan
woldon, wæs Romana fela mid flanum ofscotod 7 mid stanum
oftorfod. þa se consul ongeat þæt hie ðæt fæsten abrecan ne
mehton, þa bebead he sumum þæm folce þæt hie from þæm   20
fæstenne aforen, 7 þa oþre he het þæt hie wið þara oþerra flugen,
þonne þæt gefeoht mæst wære, þæt hie mið þæm aloccoden ut þa
[þe] þærbinnan wæron. On þæm fleam[e] þe þa burgware eft wið
þæs fæstennes flugon, hiera wearð ofslagen xl m, 7 þa þe þær to
lafe wurdon him on hand eodon. On þæm dagum for Marcus se   25
consul | on Ligor þæt land 7 gefliemed wearð, 7 his folces ofslagen   f. 64
fe'o'wer m.
þa þa Marcus Claudius 7 Marcellus Quintus wæron consulas,
Philippus, Mæcedonia cyning, ofslog Romana ærendracan 7 sende
Demetrias his sunu to þæm senatum þæt he þæt irre gesette wið   30
hie, 7 þeh þe he swa gedyde, þa he ham com, Philippus het his
oþerne sunu þæt he hiene mid atre acwealde, for þon þe he teah

---

1–5] OH IV. xx. 18, 20, 21.   6–10] OH IV. xx. 22.   11–14] OH IV.
xx. 23–4.   15–27] OH IV. xx. 25–6.   28–p. 110, 5] OH IV. xx. 27–31.

---

1 ne] *om.* C.   8 gewealde] wealde C.   9 sume men] sumen L, sume
menn C.   10 gefangen on hergiunge] on hergunge gefangen C.   æt] on C.
13 Etusci] *MS V begins.*   18 Romana fela] fela romana C.   ofscotod] ofscoten V.   19 oftorfod] ofworpod V.   20 he] se consul V.   22 aloccoden]
loccodon V.   23 þe (1)] *from* C, *om.* L, V.   fleame] *from* C, V, fleam L.
burgware] burgleude v.   26 gefliemed] *MS V ends* (ge).

hiene þæt he his ungerisno spræce wið þa senatos. On ðære ilcan
tide Hannibal his agnum willum hine selfne mid atre acwealde.
On þære tide oðewde Fulcania þæt iglond on Sicilium, þæt næs
gesewen ær þa. On þære tide Quintius Fuluius se consul gefeaht
5 wið þa firran Ispanie 7 sige hæfde.

þa þa Lapidus Mutius wæs consul, wolde seo strengeste þeod
winnan on Romane, þe mon þa het Basterne 7 nu hie mon hæt
Hungerre. Hie woldon Perseuse to fultume Mæcedonia cyninge.
þa wæs Donua seo ea [swa] swiþe oferfroren þæt hie getruwedon
10 þæt hie ofer þæm ise faran mehten; ac hie [mæst ealle] þær forwurdon.

þa þa Plicinius Crassus 7 Gaius Casius wæron consulas, þa
gewearð þæt Mæcedonisce gewin þæt mon eaðe mæg to þæm
mæstum gewinnum getellan, for þæm þe on þæm dagum wæron
15 ealle Italie Romanum on fultume 7 eac Ptholomeus, Egypta
cyning, 7 Argeatas, Capadocia cyning, 7 Eumenis, Asia cyning, 7
Masinissa, Numeðia cyning, 7 Perseuse, Mæcedonia cyning[e],
him wæron on fultume ealle Thraci 7 Ilirice, 7 raðe þæs þe hie
tosomne comon, Romane wurdon gefliemde, 7 raðe þæs æt oþrum
20 gefeohte hie wurdon eac gefliemede, 7 æfter þæm gefeohtum
Perseus wæs ealne þone gear Romane swiþe swencende, 7 siþþan
he for on Ilirice 7 abræc Sulcanum hira burg, seo wæs Romanum
f. 64ᵛ underþeow, 7 micel þæs moncynnes, | sum acwealde, sum on
Mæcedonie lædde. Æfter þæm gefeaht Lucius Emilius se consul
25 wið Perseus 7 hiene oferwon 7 his folces ofslog xx m. 7 he self æt
þæm cirre oþfleah 7 raþe æfter þæm gefangen wearð 7 to Rome
broht 7 þær ofslagen. 7 monega gefeoht gewurdon on þæm dagum
on monegum landum, þæt hit nu is to longsum eall to gesecgenne.

IV. xii

Æfter þæm þe Romeburg getimbred wæs dc wintrum, þa þa
30 Lucius Lucinius 7 Lucullus Aula wæron consulas, wearþ Romanum

6–11] OH IV. xx. 34–5.   12–28] OH IV. xx. 36–40.   29–p. 111, 8] OH
IV. xxi. 1–3.

---

1 senatos] senatus C.   4 Quintius] quintus C.   8 Hungerre] *second* r
alt. to i C.   woldon] woldan cumon C.   9 swa] *from C, no reading*
L.   10 mæst ealle] *from C, om.* L.   15 Ptholomeus] phtolomeus C.
16 Argeatas] argeatus C.   Capadocia] capadotia C.   Eumenis] emenis C.
17 Numeðia] nameþia C.   cyninge] *from C,* cyning L.   23 under-
þeow] underþeod C.   28 gesecgenne] secganne C.

se mæsta ege from Sceltiuerin, Ispania folce, 7 nænne mon næfdon
þe þider mid firde dorste gefaran butan Scipian þæm consule, se
wæs æfter þæm færelte Affricanus haten, for þon þe he þa oþre
siðe þider for þa nan oþer ne do'r'ste, þeh þe Romane hæfde
geworden hwene ær þæt he on Asiam faran sceolde. Ac he 5
monega gefeoht on Ispanium 7 on mislecum sigum þurhteah. On
þæm dagum Serius Galua, Scipian gefera, feaht wið Lusitaniam,
Ispania folce, 7 gefliemed wearð.
   On þæm dagum bebudon Romana godas þæm senatum þæt
mon theatrum worhte him to plegan. Ac hit Scipia oftrædlice ham 10
onbead þæt hie hit ne angunnen, 7 eac self sæde, þa he ham of
Ispanium com, þæt hit wære se mæsta unræd 7 se mæsta gedwola.
Hie þa Romane for his cidinge 7 þurh his lare oferhierdon þæm
godum, 7 eall þæt feoh þæt hie þærto gesomnad hæfdon, þe
hie wiþ þæm sylum 7 wið þæm weorce sellan woldon, hie hit 15
wið oþrum þingum sealdon. Nu mæg þa cristenan gescomian þe
swelc deofolgild lufiað 7 bigongað, þa se se þe cristen næs hit
[swa swiðe] forseah, se þe hit fyrþran sceolde æfter hiera agnum
gewunan.
   Æfter þæm Serius Galua for eft on Lusitanie 7 frið genam wið 20
hie, 7 hi under þæm friþe beswac. Seo dæd wearð forneah Roma-
num to ðæm mæstan hearme, | þæt him nan folc ne getruwade f. 65
þe him underþeow wæs.

IV. xiii

Æfter þæm þe Romeburg getimbred wæs dc wintrum 7 ii,
þa þa Censorinus Marcus 7 Mallius Lucius wæron consulas, þa 25
gewearð þæt þridde gewinn Romana 7 Cartaina, 7 gewearð þa
senatos him betweonum, gif hie mon þriddan siþe oferwunne,
þæt mon ealle [Cartaina] towurpe, 7 eft sendon Scipian þider, 7
he hie æt heora forman gefeohte gefliemde 7 bedraf into Cartaina.
Æfter þæm hie bædon friðes Romane. Ac hit Scipia nolde him 30
aliefan wið nanum oþrum þinge butan hie him ealle hiera wæpeno

9–16] OH IV. xxi. 4.   16–19] OH IV. xxi. 5–9.   20–3] OH IV. xxi. 10.
24–p. 112, 6] OH IV. xxii. 1–4.

1 Sceltiuerin] sceltiferin C.   6 7] om. C.   mislecum] missenlicum C.
7 feaht] gefeaht C.   11 onbead] abead alt. to forbead in l.h. C.   14 gesom-
nad] samnod C.   16 þa] þam C.   18 swa swiðe] from C, no reading L.
20 genam] genamon C.   23 underþeow] underþeod C.   25 7] om. C.
27 senatos] senatus C.   28 Cartaina] from C, om. L.

ageafen 7 þa burg forleten, 7 þæt nan ne sæte hiere x milum neah. Æfter þæm þe ðæt gedon wæs, hie cwædon þæt him leofre wære þæt hie mid þære byrig ætgædere forwurdon þonne hie mon butan him towurpe, 7 him [eft] wæpeno worhton, þa þe isen
5 hæfdon, 7 þa þe næfdon, hie worhton sume of seolfre, sume of treowum, 7 gesetton him to cyningum twegen Hasterbalas.

Nu ic wille, cwæð Orosius, secgean hulucu heo wæs. Hiere ymbegong wæs xxx mila, 7 eall heo wæs mid sæ utan befangen, butan þrim milum, 7 se weall wæs xx fota ðicce 7 xl elna heah, 7
10 þær wæs binnan oþer læsse fæsten on ðæm sæs clife, þæt wæs twegea mila heah. Hie þa Cartainenses æt þæm cirre þa burg aweredon, þeh þe Scipia ær fela þæs wealles tobrocen hæfde, 7 siþþan hamweard for.

Þa þa Gneo Cornelius 7 Lentulus Lucinius wæron consulas, ða
15 for Scipia þriddan siþe on Affrice, to þon þæt he þohte Cartainan toweorpan, 7 þa he þærto com, he wæs vi dagas on þa burg feohtende, oþ þa burgware bædon þæt hie mosten beon hiera underþeowas, þa hi hie bewerian ne mehton. Þa het Scipia ealle þa
19 wifmen ærest utgan, þara wæs xxvi m, 7 þa þa wæpnedmen, þara
f. 65ᵛ wæs xxx m. 7 se cyning | Hasterbal hiene selfne acwealde, 7 his wif mid hiere twæm sunum hie selfe forbærnde for þæs cyninges deaðe. 7 Scipia het ealle þa burg toweorpan 7 ælcne hiewestan tobeatan, þæt hie to nanum wealle siþþan ne mehton, 7 seo burg inneweard barn xvi dagas, ymb dcc wintra þæs þe heo ær getimbred
25 wæs.

Þa wæs þæt þridde gewin geendad Punica 7 Romana on þæm feorþan geare þæs þe hit ær ongunnen wæs, þeh þe Romane hæfden ær longsum gemot ymb þæt, hwæþer him rædlecre wære, þe hie þa burg mid ealle fordyden, þæt hie a siþþan on þa healfe frið hæf-
30 den, þe hi hie stondan forleten, to þon þæt him gewin eft þonan onwoce, for þon þe hie ondredon, gif hie hwilum ne wunnen, þæt hie to raþe aslawoden 7 aeargoden.

7–13] OH IV. xxii. 4–7.   14–25] OH IV. xxiii. 1–6.   26–32] OH IV. xxiii. 7–9.

---

2 him] 'heom' in l.h. C.   4 eft] from C, om. L.   8 ymbegong wæs] ymbeganges C.   mila] brad, with 'mila' in l.h. in margin C.   befangen] begangen C.   11 Cartainenses] cartainienses C.   12 hæfde] orig. hæfden with n er. L.   14 Lucinius] lucilius C.   18 hie] om. C.   het] t in l.h. on eras. L.   19 ærest utgan] om. C.   20 acwealde] followed by eras. of half a line L.   28 hie] e alt. from o? L.   31 onwoce] awoce C.   for þon þe] for þon C.

Swa þæt eow Romanum nu eft cuþ wearþ, siþþan se cristendom
wæs, cwæð Orosius, þæt ge eowerra ieldrena hwetstan forluran
eowerra gewinna 7 eowres hwætscipes, for þon ge sindon nu utan
fætte 7 innan hlæne, 7 eowre ieldran wæron utan hlæne 7 innan
fætte, stronges modes 7 fæstes. Ic nat [eac], cwæð he, hu nyt ic 5
þa hwile beo þe ic þas word sprece, butan þæt ic min geswinc
amirre. Hit biþ eac geornlic þæt mon heardlice gnide þone
hnescestan mealmstan æfter þæm þæt he þence þone soelestan
hwetstan on to geræceanne. Swa þonne is me nu swiþe earfeðe hiera
mod to ahwettanne, nu hit nawþer nyle beon, ne scearp ne heard. 10

V. i

Ic wat, cwæð Orosius, hwæt se Romana gelp swiþost is, for þon
þe hie monega folc oferwunnan 7 monege cyningas beforan hiera
triumphan oftrædlice drifon. þæt sindon þa godan tida þe hie
ealneg fore gielpað, gelicost þæm þe hie nu cweþen þæt þa tida
him anum gesealde wæron 7 næren eallum folcum. Ac þær hie hit 15
georne ongitan cuþen, þonne wisten hie | þæt hie wæron eallum   f. 66
folcum gemæne. Gif hie þonne cweðað þæt þa tida goda wæron,
for þon þe hie þa ane burg welge gedydan, þonne magon hie ryhtor
cweþan þæt þæt wæren þa ungesælgestan, for þon þe þurh þære
anre burge wlenco wurdon ealle oþra to wædlan gedone. Gif hie 20
þonne þæs ne geliefen, ascian þonne Italie hiera agne londleode hu
him þa tida gelicoden, þa hie mon slog 7 hiende 7 on oþru land
sealde xx wintra 7 c. Gif hie þonne him ne geliefen, ascien þon[ne]
Ispanie, þe þæt ilce wæron dreogende cc wintra, 7 monege oþre
þeoda; 7 eac þa monegan cyningas, hu him licade, þonne hie 25
'm'on on geocum 7 on racentum beforan hiera triumphan drifon
him to gelpe, wið Rome weard, 7 siþþan on carcernum lægon, oþ
hie deaðe swulton; 7 hie monege cyningas geswencton, to þon þæt
hie eall gesealdon þæt hie þonne hæfdon wiþ hiera earman life.
Ac for þon hit is us uncuð 7 ungeliefedlic for þon þe we sint on 30

1–10] OH IV. xxiii. 10–11.   11–p. 114, 3] OH V. i. 1–12.

5 eac] *from* C, *no reading* L.   11 Ic] *preceded by list of chapter headings* C, *see*
above, p. xxxvii.   13 godan] godcundan C.   14 cweþen] cwædon C.
15 folcum] folce C.   16 wisten hie þæt] *om.* C.   hie wæron] wæron hi C.
18 for þon þe] for þon C.   21 Italie] italia C.   23 geliefen] i *on eras.* (?)
L.   þonne (2)] *from* C, þon L.   26 mon] non *with* 'm' *above first* n L.
27 Rome] romane C.   oþ] oð ðe C.   29 eall] ealle *with final* e *er.* L.

6730 O 77   I

þæm friþe geborene þe hie þa uneaðe hiera feorh [mid] geceapedon. þæt wæs siþþan Crist geboren wæs þæt we wæron of ælcum þeowdome aliesde 7 of ælcum ege, gif we him fulgongan willaþ.

V. ii

Æfter þæm þe Romeburg getimbred wæs dc wintrum 7 vi, þæt
5　wæs þy ilcan geare þe Cartaina toworpen wæs, æfter hiere hryre Gneo Cornelius 7 Lentulus Lucio towurpon Corinthum, ealra Creca heafedburg. On hiere bryne gemulton ealle 'þa' onlicnessa togædere þe þærbinnan wæron, ge gyldene, ge sylfrene, ge ærene, ge cyprene, 7 on pyttas besuncan. Giet todæge mon hæt Corrinthisce
10　fatu ealle þe þærof gewarhte wæron, for þon þe hie sint fægran 7 dierran þonne ænegu oþru.

On þæm dagum wæs an hirde on Ispanium, se wæs Ueriatus haten 7 wæs micel þeofmon, 7 on þære stalunge he wearð reafere,
14　7 on ðæm reaflace he him geteah to micelne monfultum 7 monege
f. 66ᵛ　| tunas oferhergeade. Æfter þæm his weorod weox to þon swiþe þæt he monega land forhergeade, 7 Romanum wearð micel ege from him 7 Uecilius þone consul ongean hiene mid firde sendon, 7 he þær gefliemed wearð 7 his folces se mæsta dæl ofslagen. Æt oþrum cirre þider for Gaius [Folucius] se consul 7 eac gefliemed wearð.
20　Æt þriddan cirre þider for Claudius se con[sul] 7 þohte þæt he Romana bismer gewrecan sceolde; ac he hit on þæm færelte swiþor geiecte 7 uneaþe self com aweg.

Æfter þæm Ueriatus gemette mid þrim hunde monna Romana an m on anum wuda. þær wæs Ueriatuses folces ofslagen lxx, 7
25　Romana ccc, 7 þa oþre gefliemde. On þæm fleame wearð an Ueriatuses þegn þæm oþrum to longe æfterfylgende, oþ mon his hors under him ofsceat. þa woldon þa oþre ealle hiene ænne ofslean

---

4-11] OH V. iii. 1, 5, and 7.　　12-22] OH V. iv. 1-4.　　23-p. 115, 3] OH V. iv. 5-6.

---

1 mid] *from* C, *no reading* L.　　4 Romeburg] romanaburh *here and frequently in this formula in Book V* C.　　7 Creca] creaca C.　　9 pyttas] *first* t *on eras.* L.　　Corrinthisce] corinthisce C.　　12 On] *preceded by heading* be þam yrde uariato C.　　Ispanium] hispanium C.　　Ueriatus] uariatus C.　　19 Folucius] *from* C, *om.* L.　　20 consul] *from* C, con L.　　21 gewrecan] gebetan C.　　22 swiþor geiecte] geiecte swiþor *marked for transposition* L, swyðor geycte C.　　com aweg] aweg com C.　　24 ofslagen lxx] hundseofontig ofslagen C.　　25 gefliemde] geflymede wurdan C.　　25-6 Ueriatuses] feriatus C.

oþþe gebindan. þa slog he anes monnes hors mid his sweorde
þæt him wand þæt heafod of. Siþþan wæs eallum þæm oþrum
swa micel ege from him þæt hi hiene leng gretan ne dorstan.

Æfter þæm Apius Claudius se consul gefeaht wið Gælle 7 þær
gefliemed wearð, 7 raþe þæs eft fird gelædde wiþ hie 7 sige hæfde 5
7 hiera ofslog vi m. þa he hamweard wæs, þa bæd he þæt mon dyde
beforan him þone triumphan. Ac him Romane untreowlice his
forwierndon 7 hit under þæt ladedon for þon þe he ær æt þæm
oþrum cirre sige næfde.

Æfter þæm wearþ swa micel moncwealm on Rome þæt þær nan 10
utancymen mon cuman ne dorste, 7 monega land binnan þære
byrig wæron butan ælcum ierfwearde. Hie witon þeah þæt þæt
ilce yfel ofereode butan geblote, swa þa monegan ær dydan þe hie
wendon þæt hie mid hiera deofolgildum gestiered hæfden. Butan
tweo[n], gif hie þa blotan mehten, hie woldon secgean þæt him hiera 15
[godas] gehulpan. Ac hit wæs Godes gifu þæt ealle þa lægon þe
hit don sceoldon, | oþ hit self ofereode. f. 67

Æfter þæm Fauius se consul for mid firde ongean Ueriatus 7
gefliemed wearð. Se ilca consul gedyde eallum Romanum þa
bismerlecestan dæd, þa he aspon of Sciþþium dc monna to him 20
his geþoftena, 7 þa hie him to coman, he het him eallum þa honda
of aceorfan. Æfter þæm Pompeius se consul for on Numentinas,
Ispania þeode, 7 gefliemed wearþ. Ymb xiiii gear þæs þe Ueriatus
wið Romane winnan ongan, he wearð from his agnum monnum
ofslagen, 7 swa oft swa hiene Romane mid gefeohte gesohton, he 25
hie simle gefliemde. þær dydon [þeah] Romane lytla triewþa þæt
him þa wæron laðe 7 unweorþe þe hiera hlaford beswican, þeh þe
hie him leana to þære dæde wenden.

Ic sceal eac niede þara monegena gewinna geswigian þe on [þæm]
eastlondum gewurdon: his me sceal aþreotan for Romana gewin- 30
num. On þære tide Mitridatis, Partha cyning, geeode Babyloniam
7 ealle þa land þe betwux þæm twæm eaum wæron, Induse 7

4–9] OH V. iv. 7.   10–17] OH V. iv. 8–11.   18–28] OH V. iv. 12–14.
29–31] OH V. iv. 15.   31–p. 116, 5] OH V. iv. 16–17.

---

3 leng] *om.* C.   7 him Romane] romane him C.   10 Æfter] *preceded in*
C *by the heading* be þam manncwealme.   wearþ] wæs C.   11 utancymen]
utencumen C.   12 ierfwearde] yrfewearde C.   13 ilce] *om.* C.
15 tweon] *from* C, tweo L.   16 godas] *from* C, *om.* L.   18 Ueriatus]
feriatus C.   19 ilca] *om.* C.   24 winnan] *om.* C.   26 þeah]
from C, *om.* L.   28 dæde] tide C.   29 þæm] þam C, *no reading* L.
32 Induse] hiduse C.

Iþasfe, þ'a' wæron ær on Romana anwalde. 7 siþþan he gebrædde
his rice east oþ India gemæro, 7 Demetrias, Asia cyning, hiene
t'u'wa mid firde gesohte. Æt oþrum cirre he wearð gefliemed, æt
oþrum gefangen. He wæs on Romana onwalde, for þon þe hie
5 hiene þær gesetton.

Æfter þæm Mantius se consul for on Numentine, Ispania folc,
7 þær wæs winnende oþ he genom friþ wiþ þæt folc 7 hiene siþþan
aweg bestæl. þa he ham com, þa heton hiene Romane gebindan 7
gebringean beforan Numentia fæstennes geate. þa nawþer ne hine
10 þa eft ham lædan ne dorston þe hiene þider læddon, ne his þa onfon
noldon þe hiene mon to brohte, ac swiþe hreowlice swa gebend
he on a'n're stowe beforan þæm geate wæs wuniende, oþ he his lif
forlet.

On þæm dagum Brutus se consul ofslog Ispania folces lx m, þa
15 wæron Lusitaniam on fultume, 7 raþe þæs he for eft on Lusitanie
f. 67ᵛ 7 hiera ofslog | l m, 7 vi m gefeng. On þæm dagum for Lapidus
se consul on þa nearran Ispanie 7 gefliemed wearð, 7 his folces
wæs ofslagen vi m, 7 þa þe þær aweg comon, hie oþflugon mid
þæm mæstan bismre. Hwæþer Romane hit witen nu ænegum men
20 to secganne, hwæt hiera folces on Ispanium on feawum gearum
forwurde? þonne hie from gesælgum tidum gilpað, þonne wæron
þa him selfum þa ungesælgestan.

Ða þa Seruius Fuluius 7 Flaccus Quintus wæron consulas,
wearþ on Rome an cild geboren, þæt hæfde iiii fet 7 iiii handa 7
25 iiii eagan 7 iiii earan. On þæm geare asprong up Æþna fyr [on
Sicilium] 7 mare þæs landes forbærnde þonne hit æfre ær dyde.

V. iii

Æfter þæm þe Romeburg getimbred wæs dc wintrum 7 xx, þa
þa Mantius gedyde þone yfelan friþ on Numaantium swa hit
Romane selfe sædon þæt under hiera anwalde nan bismerlecre
30 dæd ne gewurde buton on þæm gefeohte æt Caudenes Furculus,
þa sendon Romane Scipian on Numantie mid firde. Hie sindon

6–13] OH V. iv. 20–1.   14–19] OH V. v. 12–13.   19–22] OH V. v.
14–15.   23–6] OH V. vi. 1–2.   27–p. 117, 15] OH V. vii. 1–18.

1 Iþasfe] idasfe C.   þa] alt. from þær L.   2 India] indea C.   Deme-
trias] demetria C.   7 genom] nam C.   hiene siþþan] syððan hine C.
19 nu] om. C.   20 Ispanium] ispaniam C.   23 Seruius] seruus C.
25 Æþna] etna C.   25–6 on Sicilium] from C, no reading L.   28 Nu-
maantium] numantium C.

on þæm norðwestende Ispania; 7 heo hie selfe ær þæm mid feower m aweredon xiiii winter wið Romana xl m, 7 oftost sige hæfdon. þa besæt Scipia hie healf gear on hiera fæstenne 7 hie to þon gebrocode þæt him leofre wæs þæt hie hie seolfe forneðdon þonne hie þa iermþo leng þrowoden. þa Scipia onget þæt hie swelces modes wæron, þa het he sum his folc feohtan on þæt fæsten þæt hie mid þæm þæt folc ut aloccoden. þa wæron þa burgware to þon fægene 7 to þon bliðe þæt hie feohtan moston, 7 gemong ðæm gefean hie hie selfe mid ealoð oferdrencton 7 ut irnende wæron æt twæm geatum. On þære byrig wæs ærest ealogeweorc ongunnen for þon þe hie win næfdon. On þæm swicdome wearþ Numantia dugu[ð] gefeallen, 7 | se dæl þe þær to lafe wearð forbær[n]don ealle þa burg, for ðon þe hie ne uþon þæt hiera fiend to hiera ealdgestreonum fengon; 7 æfter þæm hie hie selfe on þæm fyre forspildon.

þa Scipia hiene hamweard wende of þæm lande, þa com him to an eald mon se wæs Numentisc. þa frægn Scipia hiene an hwy hit gelang wære þæt Numentiæ swa raðe ahnescaden, swa hearde swa hie longe wæron. Ða sæde he him þæt hie wæren [hearde], þa hwile þe hie hira anrædnesse geheoldon him betweonum 7 anfealdnesse, 7 sona swa hie him betweonum ungerædnesse upahofon, swa forwurdon hie ealle. Ða wearð Scipian þæt *ond*wyrde swiþe andrysne, 7 ealle Romana weotan for ðæm *ond*wyrde [7 for þam wordum hi wurdon swiðe mid] geegsade, þa he ham com, for þon þe hie þa hæfdon ungerædnesse him betweonum.

On þære tide Craccus wæs h[a]ten, an þara consula, 7 [he] winnan ongon wið ealle þa oþre, oþ hie hiene ofslogon. 7 eac on þære tide on Sicilium þa þeowas wunnan wið þa hlafordas 7 uneaþe oferwunnene wurdon, 7 vi m ofslagen, ær hie mon gebiggiean mehte, 7 æt þære anre byrg Minturnan hiera mon aheng fifte healf hund.

16–25] OH V. viii. 1–2.   26–7] OH V. ix. 1–2.   27–31] OH V. ix. 4–7.

---

3 Scipia hie] hi scipia C.   5 Scipia] se scipio C.   11 Numantia] numentia C.   12 duguð] *from* C, dugud L.   7] *om*. C.   forbærndon] *from* C, forbærdon L.   14 ealdgestreonum] ealdan gestreonon C. 16 Scipia] se scipio C.   17 Scipia] se scipio C.   19 hearde] *from* C, *om*. L.   22 Scipian] þam scipian C.   23 ealle Romana weotan] eallum Romanum witum C.   24 7 . . . mid] *from* C, mid wordum swiþe L. 26 Craccus] creaccus C.   haten] *from* C, heten L.   he] *from* C, *om*. L.   29 vi] vii C.   hie mon] man hi C.   29–30 gebiggiean] gebigan C. 31 hund] hundred C.

V. iiii

Æfter þæm þe Romeburg getimbred wæs dc wint*rum* 7 xxi,
Luci[n]ius Crassus se consul—wæs eac Romana ieldesta bisce*p*—
he gefor mid firde ongean Aristonocuse þæm cyninge, se wolde
geagnian him þa læssan Asiam, þeh þe hie ær Attalis his agen
5 broðor hæfde Romanum to boclande geseald. Cra[ss]use wæron
monege cyningas of monegum landum to fultume cumene. An
wæs of Nicomedia, oþer of Biþþinia, þridda of Ponto, feorþa of
Armenia, fifta of Argeate, sixta of Cappadocia, seofoða of Filimine,
eahteþa of Paflogoniam, 7 þehhwæþre, raðe þæs ðe hie togædere
10 comon, se con'sul' wearð gefliemed, þeh he micelne fultum hæfde.
f. 68ᵛ þa þæt Perpena gehierde, se oþer consul, he þa hrædlice | fird
gegaderade 7 on þone cyning ungearone becom, þa his fird [eall]
tofaren wæs, 7 hiene bedraf into anum fæstenne 7 hiene besæt, oþ
hiene þa burgleode ageafan þæm consule, 7 hiene het siþþan to
15 Rome bringan 7 on carcern bescufan, 7 he þær læg oþ he his lif
forlet.

On þære tide Antiochuse, Asia cyninge, geþuhte ðæt he rice
genoh næfde 7 wilnade þæt he Parthe begeate 7 þider for mid
monegum þusendum, 7 hiene þær Parthe ieþelice oferwunnan 7
20 þone cyning ofslogan 7 him þæt rice geagnedan; for þon A[n]tio-
chus giemde hwæt he hæfde monna gerimes 7 ne nom nane
ware hulice hie wæron, for þon hiera wæs ma forcuþra þonne
æltæwra.

On þære tide Scipia, se betsta [7 se selesta Romana witena 7
25 þegna], mænde his earfoða to Romana witum, þær hie æt hiera
gemote wæron, hwy hie hiene swa unweorðne on his ylde dyden; 7
ascade hie for hwy hie nolden geþencan ealle þa brocu 7 þa geswinc
þe he for hira willan 7 eac for hiera niedþearfe fela wintra dreogende

1–16] OH V. x. 1–5.   17–23] OH V. x. 8.   24–p. 119, 8] OH V. x. 9.

1 wintrum] so C, wiñt L.   2 Lucinius] from C, luciuius L.   wæs] he
wæs C.   4 geagnian him] him geagnian C.   5 Crassuse] from C,
craccuse L.   7 of (1)] om. C.   oþer] twegen C.   Biþþinia] bithinia
C.   þridda] þry C.   Ponto] panto C.   feorþa] iiii C.   8 fifta] v
C.   Argeate] argeata C.   sixta] vi C.   seofoða] vii C.   9 eahteþa] viii C.
10 gefliemed] aflymed C.   þeh] þeah þe C.   12 ungearone] unwærne C.
eall] from C, om. L.   14 þa] ealle þa C.   7] 7 he C.   17 Asia]
asiria C.   20 ofslogan] ofsloh C.   20–1 Antiochus] from C, actiochus L.
21 giemde] ne gymde C.   22 hulice] hwilce C.   24–5 se (1) . . . þegna] from C
(þegena), se betsta romana þegn L.   26 hwy hie] for hwy C.   28 hiera]
om. C.

wæs unarimedlice oft; 7 hu he hie adyde of Hannibales þeowdome
7 of monegre oþerre þeode; 7 hu he him to þeowdome gewylde
ealle Ispanie 7 ealle Africe. On þære ilcan niht [þe he on dæg
þas word spræc], Romane him geþancodon ealles his geswinces
[mid wyrsan leane þonne he to him geearnod hæfde], þa hie hiene 5
on his bedde asmorodon [7 aþrysemodan, þæt he his lif alet. Eala,
Romane, hwa mæg eow nu truwian þa ge swylc lean dydon eowrum
þam getrywestan witan?]

Ða þa Emilius Orestes wæs consul, Eþna fyr afleow up swa brad
7 swa micel þætte feawe men þara monna mehten beon eardfæste 10
þe on Lipare wæron þæm iglande, þe þær nihst wæs, for þære
hæte 7 for þæm stence; ge ealle ða clifu þe neah þæm sæ wæron
forburnan to ascan, 7 ealle þa scipu formulton þe neah þæm sæ
færende wæron, ge ealle þa fiscas þe on þæm sæ wæron acwælan
for þære hæte. 15

Ða þa Marcus Flaccus wæs consul, | comon gærstapan on f. 69
Affrice 7 ælc wuht forscurfon þæs þe on þæm lande wæs weaxendes
7 growendes. Æfter þæm com an wind 7 forbleow hie ut on sæ.
Æfter þæm þe hie adruncne wæron, hie wearp se sæ up, 7 siþþan
mæst eall forwearð þæt on þæm lande wæs, ge mo'n'na, ge nietena, 20
ge wildeora, for þæm stence.

V. v

Æfter þæm þe Romeburg getimbred wæs dc wintrum 7 xxvii,
þa þa Lucius Mella 7 Quintus Flamineus wæron consulas, þa
gewearð þa senatos þæt mon eft sceolde getimbran Cartainam.
Ac þære ilcan niht þe mon on dæg hæfde þa burg mid stacum 25
gemearcod, swa swa hie hie þa wyrcean woldon, wulfas atugan þa
stacan up, 7 þa men forleton þæt weorc for þæm 7 longe gemot

9–15] OH V. x. 11.　　16–21] OH V. xi. 1–5.　　22–p. 120, 2] OH V. xii. 1–2.

1 oft] oftsiþum C.　　　3 Ispanie] ispaniæ C.　　Africe] affrice C.　　On]
7 þa on C.　　　3–4 þe . . . spræc] *from* C, *no reading* L.　　　5 mid . . .
hæfde] *from* C, *no reading* L.　　　6–8 7 . . . witan] *from* C, *no reading* L.
9 Orestes] orestestes L, ærestes *with final* es *dotted for eras.* C.　　Eþna] etna C.
10 feawe men] feawa C.　　11 Lipare] liware C.　　12 þæm (2)] þære C.
15 hæte] hætan C.　　　17 Affrice] africe C.　　　18 Æfter . . . sæ] *om.*
C.　　19 se] seo C.　　22 xxvii] xxiiii C.　　24 senatos] senatus C.　　ge-
timbran] timbrian C.　　Cartainam] cartaina C.　　26 wulfas atugan] þa tugon
wulfas C.　　　27 7 . . . forleton] þa for'leton' hi C.　　longe] lang C.

ymb þæt hæfdon hwæðer hit tacnade, þe sibbe þe unsibbe, 7 hie hie swa þeah eft getimbredon.

On þære tide Metellus se consul for on Belearis þæt land 7 oferwan þa wicingas þe on þæt land hergedon, þeh þara londleoda
5   eac fela forwurde.

V. vi

Æfter þæm þe Romeburg getimbred wæs dc wintrum 7 xxvii, Fauius se consul gemette Betui[tu]san, Gallia cyning, 7 hiene mid lytlum fultume ofercom.

V. vii

Æfter þæm þe Romeburg getimbred wæs dc wintra 7 xxxv, þa
10 þa Scipia Nasica 7 Lucius [Cal]furnius wæron consulas on Rome, Romane wunnon wið Geoweorþan, Numeðia cyninge. Se ilca Geoweorða wæs Mecipsuses mæg, Numeðia cyninges, 7 he hiene on his geogoðe underfeng 7 hiene fedan het 7 tyhtan mid his twam sunum. 7 þa se cyning gefor, he bebead his twæm sunum þæt hie
15 þæs rices þriddan dæl Geoweorþan sealden. Ac siþþan se þridda dæl on his gewealde wæs, he beswac begen þa suna: oþerne he
f. 69ᵛ ofslog, oþerne adræfde. 7 he siþþan gesohte Romane | him to friþe. 7 hie sendon Calfurnan þone consul mid him mid firde. Ac Geoweorða geceapade mid his feo æt þæm consule þæt he þæs
20 gewinnes lytel þurhteah. Æfter þæm Geoweorþa com to Rome 7 diegellice geceapade to þæm senatum, 'to' anum 7 to anum, þæt hie ealle [wæron] ymb hiene twywyrdige. þa he hiene hamweard of þære byrig wende, þa tælde he Romane 7 hie swiþe bismrade mid his wordum 7 sæde þæt mon nane burg ne mehte ieð mid feo
25 geceapian, gif hiere ænig mon ceapode.

þæs on þæm æfterran geare Romane sendon Anilius Mostumius þone consul mid lx m angean Geoweorþan. Heora gemeti[n]g

3–5] OH V. xiii. 1.   6–8] OH V. xiv. 1–4.   9–25] OH V. xv. 1 and 3–5.   26–p. 121, 15] OH V. xv. 6–8.

---

1 ymb þæt] *om.* C.   4 þeh] þeah þe C.   5 eac] *om.* C.   6 wintrum] *so* C, wiñt L.   7 Betuitusan] *from* C, betuisan L.   9 wintra] wintrum C.   10 Nasica] nusica C.   Calfurnius] calfurmus C, furnius L.   on Rome] *om.* C.   11 Geoweorþan] r *er.* L.   Numeðia] numeþa C.   12 Numeðia] numeþa C.   13 tyhtan] læran C.   15 Geoweorþan] geoweoþan C.   17 oþerne] oþerne he C.   22 wæron] *from* C, *om.* L.   27 gemeting] gemetig L, gemittincg C.

wæs æt Colima þære byrig, 7 þær wæron Romane oferwunnen. 7
siþþan lytle hwile hie genamon friþ him betweonum, 7 siþþan
mæst ealle Africe gecirdon to Geoweorþan. Æfter þæm Romane
sendon eft Metellus mid firde angean Geoweorþan, 7 he sige
hæfde æt twam cierrun 7 æt þriddan cierre he bedraf Geoweorþan   5
on Numeðiam his agen lond 7 hiene geniedde þæt he sealde
Romanum þreo hund gisla. 7 he þeh siþþan na þy læs ne hergeade
on Romane. þa sendon hie eft Marius þone consul angean Geoweorþan, a swa lytigne 7 a swa brægdenne swa he wæs, 7 for to
anre byrg gelicost þæm þe he hie abrecan þohte. Ac sona swa   10
Geoweorþa hæfde his fultum to þære byrg gelædd angean Marius,
þa forlet he Marius þæt fæsten 7 for to oþrum, þær he geascade
þæt Geoweorþan goldhord wæs. 7 ge[ni]edde þa burgleode þæt
hie him eodon on hond 7 him ageafon eall þæt licge[n]de feoh þæt
þærbinnan wæs. þa ne getruwade Geoweorþa his agnum folce   15
ofer þæt, ac geþoftade him wiþ Bohan, Ma'u'ritania cyning. 7 he
him com to mid micle monfultume 7 oftrædlice on Romane stalade,
oþ hie gecwædon folcgefeoht him betweonum. To þæm gefeohte
hæfde Boho Geoweorþan broht to fultume lx m gehor|sedra bu-   f. 70
tan feþan. Næs na mid Romanum ær ne siþþan swa heard gefeoht   20
swa þær wæs, for þon þe hie wurdon on ælce healfe utan befangen,
7 heora eac mæst for þon forwearþ þe hiora gemitting wæs on
sondihtre dune, þæt hie for duste ne mehton geseon hu hi hi
behealdan sceolden. Toeacan þæm hie derede ægþer ge þurst ge
hæte 7 ealne ðone dæg wæron þæt þafiende oþ niht. þa on mergen   25
hie wæron þæt ilce donde 7 eft wæron on ælce healfe utan befangen,
swa hie ær wæron. 7 þa hie swiðost tweode hwæðer hie aweg
comen, þa gecwædon hie þæt hie sume hie beæftan wereden 7
sume þu[r]h ealle þa truman ut afuhten, gif hie mehten. þa hie swa
gedon hæfdon, þa com a[n] ren, 7 swiþe Mauritaniæ wæron mid   30
þæm gewergade, for þon þe hiera sceldas wæron betogen mid
elpenda hydum, þæt hie heora feawa [for þam wætan] ahebban

15–p. 122, 5] OH V. xv. 9–19.

---

6 Numeðiam] numeþian C.   9 brægdenne] bredende C.   13 geniedde]
genydde C, gemedde L.   14 licgende] *from* C, licgede L.   16 him]
om. C.   cyning] cynicge C.   17 micle] miclum C.   19 broht]
gebroht C.   21 utan befangen] befangen utan, *marked for reversal* L.
22 gemitting] mitinc C.   29 þurh] þuh L, þuruh C.   ut] utan C.
30 an] *from* C, a L.   swiþe] swiðe þæt C.   Mauritaniæ] mauritanie C.
31 betogen] betogene C.   32 elpenda] ylpendan C.   for þam wætan]
from C, *no reading* L.

mehton, 7 for þæm gefliemde wurdon, for þon þe elpendes hyd
wile drincan wætan gelice 7 spynge deð. þær wearð Mauritania
ofslagen lx m 7 an hund. Æfter þæm Boho genom friþ wið Romanum 7 him Geoweorþan gebundenne ageaf, 7 hiene mon dyde
5 siþþan on carcern 7 his twegen suna, oþ hie þær ealle acwælon.

V. viii

Æfter þæm þe Romeburg getimbred wæs vi hunde wintra 7
xlii, þa þa Mallius 7 Cuintinus wæron consulas, Romane gefuhton
wið Cimbros 7 wið Teutonas 7 wið Ambronos—þas þeoda wæron
on Gallium—7 þær ealle ofslagene wurdon buton x mon[num], þæt
10 wæs xl m. 7 þær wæs Romane ofslagen eahtatig þusenda, 7 heora
consul 7 his twegen suna. Æfter þæm þa ilcan ðeoda besætan
Marius þone consul on anum fæstenne, 7 hit long first wæs ær
he ut wolde faran to gefeohte, ær him mon sæde þæt hie wolden
f. 70ᵛ faran on Italiam, Romana lond. | Ac siþþan he him for to ut of
15 þæm fæstenne, þa hi hi on anre dune gemetton, þa mænde þæs
consules folc to him heora þurst þe him getenge wæs. þa ondwyrde
he him 7 cwæð: 'Eaþe we magon geseon on oþre healfe urra
feonda hwær se drinca is gelang þe us nihst is; ac for þæm þe hie
us near sint, we him ne magon buton gefeohte to cuman.' þær
20 hæfdon Romane sige, 7 þær wæs Gallia ofslagen twa hund m 7
hiora latteow, 7 eahtatig m gefangen.

V. ix

Æfter þæm þe Romeburg getimbred wæs vi hunde wintrum 7
xlv, on þæm fiftan geare þe Marius wæs consul 7 eac þa mid Romanum wæs sibb of oþrum folcum, þa ongunnon Romane þa mæstan
25 sace him betweonum up aræran, þeh ic hit nu scortlice secgan
scyle, cwæð Orosius, hwa þæs ordfruman wæron. þæt wæs ærest
Marius se consul 7 Lucius 7 Apulcius 7 Saturninus, þæt hie

6–11] OH V. xvi. 1–4.   11–21] OH V. xvi. 9–12.   22–p. 123, 8] OH
V. xvii. 1–11.

---

3 lx] xl C.   hund] hund manna C.   6 wintra] wintrum C.   7 Mallius]
pallius C.   7] 7 7 with first 7 er. L.   Cuintinus] quintinus C.   9 mon-
num] mannum C, mon L.   10 Romane] romana C.   eahtatig] hund
eahtatig C.   13 wolde faran] faran wolde C.   20 Romane] romana C.
21 eahtatig] hund eahtatig C.   23–4 Romanum] romana C.   27 Saturni-
nus] saturius C.

adræfdon Metellus þone consul on elþeode, se wæs consul ær
Marius. Hit wæs þa swiþe oþþyncende þam oþrum consulum,
Pompeiuse 7 Caton; þeh þe hie mid þære wrace þæm adræfdan on
nanum stale beon ne mehton, hie þeh þurhtugon þæt hie ofslogon
Lucius 7 Saturninus 7 eft wæron biddende þæt Metellus to Rome 5
moste. Ac him þagiet Marius 7 Furius forwierndon, 7 him þa
siþþan se feondscipe wæs betweonum weaxende, þeh þe hie hit
openlice cyþan ne dorsten for þara senatum ege.

V. x

Æfter þæm þe Romeburg getimbred wæs vi c wintra 7 lxi, on
þæm siextan geare þe Iulius se ca[se]re wæs consul 7 Lucius 10
Martius, wearþ ofer ealle [Italia] ungeferlic unsibb 7 openlice cuð
betuh Iuliuse 7 Pompeiuse, þeh hie hit ær swiþe him betweonum
diernden. 7 eac on þæm geare gewurdon monega wu[n]dor on
monegum londum. | An wæs þæt mon geseah swelce an fyren f. 71
hring norðan cumen mid micle swege. Oþer wearþ on Tarentan 15
þære byrig æt anre feorme: þonne mon þa hlafas wrat to þicgeanne,
þonne orn þær blod ut. þæt þridde wæs þæt hit hagolade seofon
niht, dæges 7 nihtes, ofer ealle Romane. 7 on Somnia þæm londe
seo eorþe tobærst, 7 þonan up wæs biernende fyr wið þæs hefones.
7 mon geseah swelce hit wære an gylden hring on heofonum 20
brædre þonne sunne, 7 wæs from þæm heofone bradiende niþer
oþ þa eorþan 7 wæs eft farende wið þæs heofones.

On þære tide Pincente þæt folc 7 Uestine 7 Marse 7 Peligni 7
Marrucine 7 Somnite 7 Lucani hie ealle gewearð him betweonum
þæt hie wolden Romanum geswican, 7 ofslogon Gaius Seruius, 25
Romana ealdormon, se wæs mid ærendum to him onsended. On ðæm
dagum aweddon þa nietenu 7 þa hundas þe wæron on Somnitum.

Æfter þæm gefeaht Pompeius se consul wið eal þa folc 7 gefliemed wearþ, 7 Iulius se cesar gefeaht wið Marse þæm folce 7

9–22] OH V. xviii. 1–6.   23–7] OH V. xviii. 8–9.   28–p. 124, 6] OH
V. xviii. 10–15.

2 þa] swa C.   oþþyncende] ofþincende C.   3 Caton] catan C.   4 stale]
stæle C.   5 Saturninus] saturnius C.   7 hie hit] hit hi C.   9 wintra]
wintrum C.   10 casere] from C, care L.   11 Italia] from C, om. L.
12 Pompeiuse] pompeniuse C.   13 wundor] from C, wurdor L.   15 micle]
mycclum C.   Tarentan] tarentam C.   23 Pincente] pincende C.
Peligni] weligni C.   24 Lucani] a added in diff. ink L.   25 Gaius] canis
C.   26 onsended] asended C.   28 eal] om. C.   29 cesar] casere C.

gefliemed wearð. Raþe þæs Iulius gefeaht wið Somnitum 7 wið
Lucanum 7 hie gefliemde. Æfter þæm hiene mon het casere. þa
bæd he þæt mon þone triumphan him ongean brohte. þa sende
him mon ane blace hacelan angean, him on bismer, for triumphan,
5 7 eft hie him sendon ane tunecan ongean, þa þe hie toge heton,
þæt he ealles buton arunge to Rome ne com.
Æfter þæm Silla se consul, Pompeiuses gefera, gefeaht wið
Esernium þæm folce 7 hie gefliemde. Æfter þæm gefeaht Pompeius
wið Pincentes þæm folce 7 hie gefliemde. þa brohton Romane
10 þone triumphan angean Pompeius mid micelre weorþfulnesse for
þæm lytlan sige þe he þa hæfde, 7 noldon Iuliuse nænne weorþscipe
f. 71ᵛ don, þeh he maran | dæd gedon hæfde, buton ane tunecan, 7 hi
heora gewin mid þæm swiþe geiecton. Æfter þæm Iulius 7 Pompeius abræcan Asculum þa burg on [M]ærsum 7 þær ofslogon
15 eahtatiene m. Æfter þæm gefeaht Silla se consul wið Somnitum 7
heora ofslog eahtatiene m.

V. xi

Æfter þæm þe Romeburg getimbred wæs vi hunde wintra 7
lxii, þætte Romane sendon Sillan þone consul ongean Metreþatis
Partha cyning. þa ofþuhte þæt Mariuse þæm consule, Iuliuses
20 eame, þæt mon ðæt gewin nolde him betæcan, 7 bæd þæt him mon
sealde þone seofoþan consulatum 7 eac þæt gewin, for þon þe
hit wæs þeaw mid him þæt mon ymbe xii monað dyde ælces consules setl ane pyle hierre þonne hit ær wæs. þa Silla geacsade on
hwelc gerad Marius com to Rome, he þa hrædlice mid ealre his
25 firde wið Rome weard farende wæs 7 Marius bedraf into Romeburg mid eallum his folce, 7 hiene siþþan þa burgleode gefengon
7 gebundon 7 hiene siþþan þohton Sillan agifan. Ac he fealh

7–13] OH V. xviii. 16–17.   13–15] OH V. xviii. 18.   15–16] OH V.
xviii. 22–3.   17–p. 125, 13] OH V. xix. 1–xxiii. 16.

---

1 Raþe] 7 raðe C.   5 ongean] om. C.   6 arunge] aringe with n alt.
from m C.   9 Romane] romana C.   12 tunecan] tunican C.   hi]
om. C.   13 geiecton] gesettan C.   14 Asculum] ofculum C.
Mærsum] from C, nærsum L.   17 wintra] wintrum C.   18 Metre-
þatis] metridatis C.   19 cyning] cynincge C.   20 nolde him betæcan]
him betæcean nolde C.   him mon] man him C.   21 for þon þe] for
þon C.   23 ane] anum C.   25–6 Romeburg] romebyrig C.   27 fealh]
fleah C.

þære ilcan niht of þæm bendum þe hiene mon on dæg gebende 7
siþþan fleah suþ ofer sæ [on Africam, þær his fultum mæst wæs],
7 raþe eft wæs cirrende wið Rome weard. Him wæron twegen
consulas on fultume, Cinna 7 Sertorius, þa wæron simle ælces
yfles ordfruman. 7 raðe þæs þe þa senatus gehierdon þæt Marius 5
Rome nealæcte, hie ealle ut aflugon on Creca lond æfter Sillan 7
æfter Pompeiuse, þider hi þa mid firde gefaren wæron. þa wæs
Silla mid micelre geornfulnisse farende of Crecum wiþ Rome
weard 7 wið Marius heardlice gefeaht þurhteah 7 hiene gefliemde
7 ealle ofslog binnan Romebyrg þe Mariuse on fultume wæron. 10
Raðe þæs ealle þa consulas wæron deade buton twæm. Marius 7
Silla geforan him self, 7 Cinna wæs ofslagen | on Smyrna, Asia f. 72
byrg, 7 Sertorius wæs ofslagen on Ispania.

þa underfeng Pompeius Partha gewin, for þon Metreþatis
heora cyning teah him to þa læssan Asiam 7 eall Creca lond. Ac 15
hiene Pompeius of eallum þæm londe afliemde 7 hiene bedraf on
Armenie 7 him æfterfylgende wæs, oþ hiene oþþre men ofslogan
7 geniedde Ar[c]halaus þone latteow þæt he wæs his underþeow.
Hit is ungeliefedlic to secganne, cwæð Orosius, hwæt on þæm
gewinne forwearþ þæt hie wæron dreogende xl wintra, ær hit 20
geendad mehte beon, ægþer ge on þeoda forhergiunge ge on cyninga slihtum ge on hungre.

þa Pompeius hamweard wæs, þa noldan him þa londleode þæt
fæsten aliefan æt Hierusalem. Him wæron on fultume xxii cyninga.
þa het Pompeius þæt mon þæt fæsten bræce 7 on fuhte dæges 7 25
nihtes, simle an leg[ie] æfter oþerre unwerig, 7 þæt folc mid þæm
aþrytton þæt hie him on hond eodon, ymbe þreo mo'n'að þæs
þe hie mon ær ongon. þær wæs Iudea ofslagen xiii m, 7 mon
towearp þone weal niþer oþ þone grund. 7 mon lædde Aristobolus
to Rome gebundenne; se wæs ægþer ge heora cyning ge heora 30
biscop.

14–22] OH VI. ii. 1–4 and iv. 3–7, v.   23–31] OH VI. vi. 1–4.

---

2 on . . . wæs] *from* C, *om.* L.   6 Rome] to rome C.   aflugon] flugon
C.   Creca] greaca C.   7 gefaren] gefarene C.   8 Crecum] grecum C.   9 gefeaht] gefeoht C.   13 Ispania] *from* C, is/spania L.
14 Metreþatis] metredatis C.   15 Creca] creaca C.   18 Archalaus] *from*
C, arhalaus L.   19 Hit is] his nu *alt. to* hit is nu *in l.h.* C.   21 mehte beon]
beon mihte C.   26 an legie] anleg L, on læg C.   unwerig] unwerige C.
27 monað] moþað *with* 'n' *above er.* þ L.   28 ongon] began C.   29 Aristo-
bolus] aristopolus C.

V. xii

Æfter þæm þe Romeburg getimbred wæs vi hunde wintra 7
lxvii, Romane gesealdon Gaiuse Iuliuse seofon legan, to þon þæt
he sceolde fif winter winnan on Gallie. Æfter þæm þe he hie
oferwunnen hæfde, he for on Bretanie þæt iglond 7 wið þa Brettas
5 gefeaht 7 gefliemed wearð on þæm londe þe mon hæt Centlond.
Raþe þæs he gefeaht wiþ þa Brettas [eft] on Centlonde, 7 hie wurdon gefliemede. Heora þridde gefeoht wæs neah þære ie þe mon
f. 72ᵛ hæt Temes, neh þæm forda | þe mon hæt Welengaford. Æfter
þæm gefeohte him eode on hond se cyning 7 þa burgware þe
10 wæron on Cirenceastre, 7 siþþan ealle þe on þæm iglonde wæron.
Æfter þæm Iulius for to Rome 7 bæd þæt him mon brohte þone
triumphan ongean. þa onbudon hie him þæt he come mid feawum
monnum to Rome 7 ealne his fultum beæftan him lete. Ac þa he
hamweard for, him coman angean þa iii ealdormen þe him on
15 fultume wæron 7 him sædon þæt hie for his þingun adræfde wæron,
7 eac þæt ealle þa legean wæron Pompeiuse to fultume gesealde
þe on Romana anwalde wæron, þæt he þy fæstlecre gewinn mehte
habban wið hiene. þa wende eft Iulius to his agnum folce 7 wepende mænde þa unare þe him mon buton gewyrhton dyde 7
20 swiþost þara monna þe for his þingun forwurdon. 7 he him siþðan
aspon to þa seofan legian þe wæron on Silomone þæm londe.
    þa Pompeius 7 Cato 7 ealle þa senatus þæt hierdon, þa foran hi
on Crecas 7 micelne fultum gegaderedon on Thraci þære dune.
þa for Iulius to Rome 7 abræc hiera maðmhus 7 eall gedælde his
25 firde þæt þærinne wæs. þæt is ungeliefedlic to gesecganne, cwæð
Orosius, hwæt þæs ealles wæs. Æfter þæm he for on Marisiam
þæt lond 7 þær let þreo legian beæftan him, to þon þæt hie þæt

---

1–3] OH VI. vii. 1–viii. 23.   3–10] OH VI. ix. 2–9.   11–23] OH VI.
xv. 1–4.   24–p. 127, 3] OH VI. xv. 5–7.

---

1 wintra] wintrum C.   2 Gaiuse] caiuse C.   Iuliuse] iulius C.   legan]
legion C.   4 Bretanie] bryttoniæ C.   Brettas] bryttas C.   6 Brettas]
bryttas C.   eft] *from* C, *no reading* L.   7 gefliemede] aflymede C.
8 Temes] temese C.   Welengaford] welingaford C.   10 Cirenceastre]
cyrnceastre C.   12 onbudon] bebudon C.   16 legean] legian C.
to] on C.   gesealde] geseald C.   17 Romana] romane C.   20–1 siþðan
aspon to] aspeon to siþþan C.   22 hierdon] gehyrdon C.   23 Crecas]
greacas] C.   24 abræc] tobræc C.   24–5 his firde] *om.* C.   25 unge-
liefedlic] ungeliefedlice L, unalyfedlic C.   gesecganne] secganne C.   26 on
Marisiam] to samariam C.

folc to him genieddon. 7 he self mid þæm oþrum dæle for on
Ispanie, þær Pompeiuses legian wæron mid his [þrim] ladteowum,
7 he hie ealle to him geniedde. 7 æfter þæm he for on Creca lond,
þær his Pompeius on anre dune onbad mid xxxgum cyningum, 4
buton his agnum fultume. | þa for Pompeius þær Marcellus wæs, f. 73
Iuliuses ladteow, 7 hiene ofslog mid eallum his folce. Æfter þæm
Iulius besæt Tarquatus, Pompeius ladteow, on anum fæstenne,
7 him Pompeius æfter for. þær wearð [Iulius] gefliemed, 7 his
folces fela forslagen, for þon þe him mon feaht on on twa healfe,
on oþre Pompeus, on oþre se ladteow. Siþþan for Iulius on 10
Thesaliam 7 þær eft his fultum gegaderade.

þa Pompeius þæt hierde, þa for he him æfter mid ungemetlican
fultume. He hæfde eahta 7 eahtatig coortana, þæt we nu truman
hatað, þæt wæs on þæm dagum v hund monna 7 an m. þis eall he
hæfde buton his agnum fultume 7 buton Caton, his geferan, 7 15
buton þara senatuses; 7 Iulius hæfde eahtatig coortena. Heora
ægþer hæfde his folc on þrim heapum, 7 hie selfe wæron on þæm
midmestan, 7 þa oþre on twa healfa hiera. þa Iulius hæfde ænne
þara dæla gefliemed, þa cleopode Pompeius him to ymbe Romana
ealde gecwedrædenne, þeh þe he hie self læstan ne þohte: 'Gefera, 20
gefera, gemyne þæt ðu ure gecwedrædenne 7 geferrædenne to
longe ne oferbrec.' þa ondwyrde he him 7 cwæð: 'On sumre tide
þu wære min gefera; 7 for þæm þe þu nu [ne] eart, me is eal leofast
þæt þe laþost is.' þæt [wæs] sio gecwedræden þe Romane geset
hæfdon, þæt hiora nan oðerne on þone ondwlitan ne sloge, þær 25
þær hie æt gefeohtum gemette. Æfter þæm wordum Pompeius
wearð gefliemed mid eallum his folce, 7 he self siþþan oþfleah on
Asiam mid his wife 7 mid his bearnum, 7 siþþan he for on Ægyptum 7 him fultumes bæd æt Pholomeuse þæm cyninge. 7 raðe þæs

3–p. 128, 4] OH VI. xv. 22–9.

2 Ispanie] ispaniæ C.   Pompeiuses] pompeius C.   þrim] *from* C, twæm
L.   3 7 (2)] *om.* C.   Creca] creaca C.   5 fultume] *followed
by eras. of about two lines of MS* L.   7 Pompeius] pompeiuses C.
anum] *from* C, annum L.   8 Iulius] *from* C, *om.* L.   9 þon] þam C.
on (2)] *om.* C.   10 oþre (1)] oþre healfe C.   oþre (2)] oðre healfe C.   11 eft]
om. C.   12 hierde] gehyrde C.   13 eahta 7 eahtatig] hund eahtatig C.
15 Caton] catone C.   16 eahtatig] hund eahtatig C.   20 gecwedræ-
denne] *two letters* (en?) *er. after* ed L.   he] *om.* C.   læstan] gelæstan C.
21 gecwedrædenne 7 geferrædenne] geferædenne 7 cwydrædenne C.   23 ne]
from C, *om.* L.   24 laþost is] is laðost C.   wæs] *from* C, *om.* L.   26 hie]
hi hi C.   28–9 Ægyptum] egyptum C.   29 him] his C.

f. 73ᵛ þe he to him com, he him het þæt heafod of aceorfan | 7 hit siþþan
het Iuliuse onsendan 7 his hring mid. Ac þa hit mon to him brohte,
he wæs mænende þa dæd mid micle wope, for þon he wæs eallra
monna mildheortast on þæm dagum.

5   Æfter þæm Photolomeus gelædde fird wið Iuliuse, 7 eall his
folc wearð gefliemed 7 he self gefangen. 7 ealle þa men [Iulius] het
ofslean þe æt þære lare wæron þæt mon [Pom]peius ofslog; 7 he
swaþeah eft forlet Phtolomeus to his rice. Æfter þæm Iulius
gefeaht wið Phtolomeus þriwa 7 æt ælcum cirre sige hæfde. Æfter

10   þæm gefeohte ealle Egypti wurdon Iuliuse underþeowas, 7 he him
siþþan hwearf to Rome 7 eft sette senatus, 7 hiene seolfne mon
gesette þæt he wæs hierra þonne consul: þæt hi heton tictator.
Æfter þæm he for on Affrice æfter Caton þæm consule. þa he þæt
geascade, þa lærde he his sunu þæt he him ongean fore 7 hiene him

15   to friðe gesohte; 'For þon', cwæð he, 'þe ic wat þæt nan swa god
ne leofað swa he is on þeosan life, þeh þe he me sie se laþesta, 7
for þon eac ic ne mæg findan æt me seolfum þæt ic hine æfre
geseo.' Æfter þæm wordum he eode to þære burge wealle 7
fleah ut ofer, þæt he eall tobærst. Ac þa Iulius to þære byrig com,

20   he him wæs swiþe waniende þæt he to him cucan ne com 7 þæt
he swelce deaðe swealt. Æfter þæm Iulius gefeaht wið Pompeiuses
nefan 7 wið monige his mægas 7 hie ealle ofslog, 7 siþþan to Rome
for 7 þær wæs swa onddrysne þæt him mon dyde feower siþan þone
triumphan þa he ham com. Siþþan he for on Ispanie 7 gefeaht

25   wið Pompeiuses twæm sunum; 7 þær wæs his folc swa swiðe
forslagen þæt he sume hwile wende þæt hine mon gefon sceolde,
7 he for þære ondrædinge þæs þe swiþor on þæt weorod þrong, for
þon þe him wæs leofre þæt hiene mon ofsloge þonne hiene mon

29   gebunde.
f. 74 | Æfter þæm he com to Rome 7 ealle þa gesetnessa þe þær to
stronge wæron 7 to hearde he hie ealle g[e]dyde leohtran 7 liþran.

5–12] OH VI. xv. 30–xvi. 3.   13–21] OH VI. xvi. 4.   21–9] OH VI.
xvi. 5–7.   30–p. 129, 4] OH VI. xvii. 1–2.

2 hit mon] man hit C.   3 micle] miclum C.   5 Photolomeus] pholomeus C.   6 Iulius] *from* C, Alexander L.   7 Pompeius] *from* C,
peius L.   8 Phtolomeus] ptholomeus C.   9 Phtolomeus] ptholomeus
C.   13 Caton] catone C.   15 god] god man C.   18 wordum]
worde C.   wealle] weallum C.   19 eall] ealle, *with final* e *er.* L.
21 swelce] swylcon C.   22 nefan] genefon C.   hie] he hi C.
23 onddrysne] andrysne C.   26 hine mon] man hine C.   31 gedyde]
from C, gydyde L.

Hit þa eallum þæm senatum ofþyncendum 7 þæm consulum þæt
he heora ealdan gesetnessa tobrecan wolde, ahleopon þa ealle 7
hiene mid heora metseacsum ofsticedon inne on heora gemotærne.
þara wunda wæs xxvii.

V. xiii

Æfter þæm þe Romeburg getimbred wæs vii hunde wintra 7 x,   5
feng Octauianus to Romana onwealde, hiora unþonces, æfter
Iuliuses slege his mæges, for þon þe hiene hæfde Iulius him ær
mid gewritum gefæstnod þæt he æfter him to eallum his gestreo-
num fenge, for þon þe he hiene for mægrædenne gelærde 7 getyde.
7 he siþþan v gefeoht ungeferlice þurhteah swa Iulius dyde ær: 10
an wiþ Pompeius; an wæs wið Antonius þone consul; oþer wið
Cassus 7 wið Brutus; þridde wið Lepidus, þeh þe he raþe þæs his
freond wurde; 7 he eac gedyde þæt Antonius his freond wearð 7
þæt he his dohtor sealde [Octauiane] to wife 7 eac þæt Octauianus
sealde his swostor Antoniuse.   15
Siþþan him geteah Antonius to gewealdon ealle Asiam. Æfter
þæm he forlet Octauianuses swostor 7 him selfum onbead gewin
7 openne feondscipe, 7 he him het to wife gefeccan Cleopatron þa
cwene, þa hæfde Iulius ær 7 hiere for þæm hæfde geseald ealle
Egypti. Raðe þæs Octauianus gelædde fird wiþ Antonius 7 hiene   20
raðe gefliemde þæs þe hie togædere comon. þæs ymb iii niht hie
gefuhton [ut] on sæ. Octauianus hæfde xxx scipa 7 cc þara miclena
þriereðrena, on þæm wæron farende eahta legian, 7 Antonius
hæfde eahtatig scipa, on þæm wæron farende x legian, for þon
swa micle swa he læs hæfde, swa micle hie wæron beteran 7   25
maran, for þon hie wæron swa geworht þæt hie mon ne mehte
mid monnum oferhlæstan, þæt hie næren x | fota hea bufan wætere.   f. 74ᵛ
þæt gefeoht wearð swiþe mære, þeh þe Octauianus sige hæfde.
þær wæs [Antoniuses] folces ofslagen xii m, 7 Cleopatra his cwen

5–15] OH VI. xviii, esp. 1, 2, 8.   16–p. 130, 1] OH VI. xix. 4–12.

---

4 xxvii] v made into i by eras. L.   5 wintra] wintrum C.   x] lxx C.
10 v] iiii C.   ungeferlice] wel cynelice C.   þurhteah] gefeaht 7 þurhteah C.   swa] swa swa C.   Iulius] iulius his mæg C.   11 an wæs]
oþer C.   oþer] þridde C.   12 7 wið Brutus] om. C.   þridde] feorðe C.
Lepidus] lepiðus C.   13 7 (2)] om. C.   14 Octauiane] from C, iuliuse L.
18 Cleopatron] cleopatran C.   19–20 ealle Egypti] eall egypta C.   22 ut]
from C, om. L.   24 eahtatig] hund eahtatig C.   29 wæs . . . folces]
octauianuses folces wæs C.   Antoniuses] octauianuses both MSS.

6730 C 77   K

wearð gefliemed, swa hie togædere coman, mid hiere here. Æfter
þæm Octauianus gefeaht wið Antonius 7 wið Cleopatron 7 hie
gefliemde. þæt [wæs] on þære tide calendas Agustus, 7 on þæm
dæge þe we hatað hlafmæsse. Siþþan wæs Octauianus Agustus
5 haten, for þon þe he on þære tide sige hæfde.
   Æfter þæm Antonius 7 Cleopatro hæfdon gegaderod sciphere
on þæm Readan Sæ. Ac þa him mon sæde þæt Octauianus þiderweard wæs, þa gecierde eall þæt folc to Octauianuse, 7 hie selfe
opflugon to anum tune lytle werode. Hio þa Cleopatra het adelfan
10 hiere byrgenne 7 þæroninnan eode. þa heo þæron gelegen wæs,
þa het hio niman ipnalis þa nædran 7 don to hiere earme, þæt hio
hie abite; for þon þe hiere þuhte þæt hit on þæm lime unsarast
wære, for þon þe þære nædran gecynd is þæt ælc uht þæs þe hio
abitt scæl his lif on slæpe geendian. 7 hio þæt for þæm dyde þe
15 hio nolde þæt hie mon drife beforan þæm triumphan wiþ Rome
weard. þa Antonius geseah þæt hio hie to deaþe gerede, þa ofsticade
he hiene selfne 7 bebead þæt hiene mon on þa ilcan byrgenne to
hiere swa somcucre alegde. þa Octauianus þider com, þa het 'he'
niman oþres cynnes nædran, uissillus is haten, sio mæg ateon
20 ælces cynnes ator ut of men, gif hie mon tidlice to bringð. Ac hio
wæs gefaren ær he þider come. Siþþan Octauianus begeat Alexandriam, Egypta heafedburg, 7 mid hiere gestreone he gewelgade
Romeburg swa swiþe þæt mon ælcne ceap mehte be twiefealdan
bet geceapian þonne mon ær mehte.

V. xiiii

25 Æfter þæm þe Romeburg getimbred wæs vii hunde wintra 7
xxxv, gewearð þætte Octauianus Cesar on his fiftan consulato |
f. 75 betynde Ianes duru, 7 gewearð þæt he hæfde onweald ealles
middangeardes. þa wæs sweotole getacnad, þa he cniht wæs 7
hiene mon wið Rome weard lædde æfter Iuliuses slege, þy ilcan
30 dæge þe hiene mon to consule dyde, þæt mon geseah ymbe þa

1-4] OH VI. xix. 16.   6-24] OH VI. xix. 13-19.   25-p. 131, 21]
OH VI. xx.

2 Cleopatron] cleopatran C.   3 wæs] *from* C, *om.* L.   4 hlafmæsse]
hlafmæssan C.   6 Cleopatro] cleopatran C.   7-8 þiderweard] þyder
with 'ward' *in l.h.* C.   11 ipnalis] upnalis C.   12-13 for þon . . . wære]
om. C.   14 þæt] *om.* C.   þe] þæt C.   21 gefaren] forðfaren C.
24 geceapian] cepian C.   25 wintra] wintrum C.   26 Cesar] ceasar C.
consulato] consolato C.   30 dyde] sette C.

sunnan swelce an gylden hring, 7 binnan Rome weoll an wille ele
ealne dæg. On þæm hringe wæs getacnad þæt on his dagum sceolde
weorþan geboren se se þe leohtra is 7 scinendra þonne sio sunne þa
wære, 7 se ele getacnade miltsunge eallum moncynne. Swa he
eac monig tacen self gedyde þe eft gewurdon, þeh he hie unwitende 5
dyde on Godes bisene.

Sum wæs ærest þæt he bebead ofer ealne middangeard þæt ælc
mægþ ymbe geares ryne togædere come, þæt ælc [mon] þy gearor
wiste hwær he gesibbe hæfde. þæt tacnade þæt on his dagum
sceolde beon geboren se se þe us ealle to anum mæggemote gelaþaþ; 10
þæt bið on þæm toweardan life.

Oþer is þæt he bebead þæt eall moncynn ane sibbe hæfde 7 an
gafol guldon. þæt tacnade þæt we ealle sculon ænne geleafan
habban 7 ænne willan godra weorca.

þridde wæs þæt he bebead þæt ælc þara þe on elðeodignesse 15
wære, come to his agnum earde 7 to his fæder oeþle, ge þeowe ge
frige, 7 se þe þæt nolde, he bebead þæt mon þa ealle sloge; þara
wæron vi m, þa hie gegaderad wæron. þæt tacnade þæt us eallum
is beboden þæt we sculon cuman of þisse worolde to ures fæder
oeðle, þæt is to heofonrice; 7 se þe þæt nele, he wyrþ aworpen 7 20
ofslagen.

V. xv

Æfter þæm þe Romeburg getimbred [wæs] vii hunde wintrum
7 xxxvi, wurdon sume Ispania leode Agustuse wiþerwearde. þa
ondyde he eft Ianes duru 7 wið hie fird gelædde 7 hie gefliemde 7
hie siþþan on anum fæstenne besæt, þæt hie siþþan hie selfe sume 25
ofslogon, sume mid atre acwealdon, sume hungre acwælan.

After þæm monege þeoda wunnon wið Agustus, | ægþer ge f. 75ᵛ
Ilirice ge Pannonii ge Sermende ge monege oþra þeoda, 7 Agustuses
ladteowas monega micla gefeoht wiþ him þurhtugon, buton Agustuse selfum, ær hie hie ofercuman mehten. 30

22–6] OH VI. xxi. 1–8.   27–30] OH VI. xxi. 14–25.

1 Rome] romebyrig C.   3 se se] se C.   8 mon] man C, *no reading* L.
9 he . . . hæfde] hi sibbe hæfdon *with* o *alt. to* a C.   10 se se] se C.
12 is] wæs C.   16 earde] gearde C.   oeþle] o *er.* L.   17 sloge]
ofsloge C.   20 oeðle] o *er.* L.   22 wæs] *from* C, *om.* L.   wintrum]
so C, winṫ L.   23 Ispania] ispaniæ C.   wiþerwearde] wiþerwinnan C.
24 gelædde] lædde C.   26 sume (2) . . . acwælan] *om.* C.   28 Ilirice]
illirice C.   Sermende] sermenne C.   7] a *partly written and alt. to* 7 L, *om.*
C.   30 hie hie] hi C.

Æfter þæm Agustus sende Quintillus þone consul on Germanie mid þrim legian. Ac hiora wearþ ælc ofslagen buton þæm consule anum. For þære d[æ]de wearþ Agustus swa sarig þæt he oft unwitende slog mid his heafde on þone wag, þonne he on his setle sæt,
5 7 þone consul he het ofslean. Æfter þæm Germanie gesohton Agustus ungeniedde him to friþe, 7 he him forgeaf þone nið þe he to him wiste.

Æfter þæm eall þeos worold geceas Agustuses frið 7 his sibbe, 7 eallum monnum nanuht swa god ne þuhte swa hie to his hyldo
10 become 7 þæt hie his underþeowas wurden, ne ferþan þætte ænigum folce his æ[gen]u æ gelicade to healdenne, buton on þa wisan þe him Agustus bebead. þa wurdon Ianes dura fæste betyned 7 his loca rustega, swa hie næfre ær næron. On þæm ilcan *gere* þe þis eall gewearð—þæt wæs on þæm twæm 7 feowerteoþan wintra
15 Agustuses rices—þa wearð geboren se þe þa sibbe brohte eallre worolde, þæt is ure Dryhten Hælende Crist.

Nu ic hæbbe gesæd, cwæð Orosius, from frymþe þisses middangeard[es] hu eall moncyn angeald þæs ærestan monnes synna mid miclum teonum 7 witum. Nu ic wille eac forþ gesecgan hwelc
20 mildsung 7 hwelc geþwærnes siþþan wæs siþþan [se] cristendom wæs, gelicost þæm þe monna heortan awende wurden, for þon þe þa ærran þing agoldene wæron. Her en[d]aþ sio sixte boc, 7 onginð seo siofoðe.

VI. i

[Nu] ic wille, cwæð Orosius, on foreweardre þisse seofeþan bec
25 gereccean þæt hit þeh Godes bebod wæs, þeh hit strong wære, hu emnlice þa feower onwealdas þara feower heafedrica þisses middangeardes gestodon. þæt æreste wæs on Asirium, on þæm
f. 76 eastemestan onwalde, on Babylonia þære byrig. Sio gestod | tuwa

---

1–5] OH VI. xxi. 26–7.   5–7] OH VI. xxi. 29.   8–13] OH VI. xxii. 1–3.   13–16] OH VI. xxii. 5.   17–23] OH VI. xxii. 9–11. 24–7] OH VII. i (*see Commentary*).   27–p. 133, 10] OH VII. ii. 1–9.

---

3 dæde] *from* C, dyde L.   8 eall þeos worold] þeos woruld eall C. 9 hyldo] hyldon C.   11 ægenu] ænegu L, agenum C.   12 fæste] eft C.   15 wearð] wearð se C.   17–18 middangeardes] *from* C, middangeard L.   19 7 witum] *om*. C.   20 se] *from* C, *no reading* L. 22 endaþ] *from* C, enþaþ L.   sixte] v C.   23 siofoðe] vi. C.   *In C, Book VI is preceded by a list of chapter headings, for which see above,* p. xxxvii. 24 Nu] *from* C, *space left blank for ornamental letter* L.   seofeþan] vi C.

seofon hund wintra on hiere onwealde ær hio gefeolle, from Ninuse
hiora ærestan cyninge oþ Sardanopolim heora nihstan: þæt is
[i]iii c wintra 7 i m. þa Cirus benom Babylonia hiere onwealde,
þa ongon ærest Romana weaxan. Eac on þæm dagum wæs þæt
norþmeste micliende on Mæcedonium. þæt gestod lytle leng 5
þonne seofon hund wintra from heora ærestan cyninge Canone
oþ Perseus heora æftemæstan. Swa eac on Affricum, on þæm
suðmestan, Cartaina sio burg hio gefeoll eac ymb seofon hund
wintra 7 ymb lytelne first þæs þe hie ærest Diþa þe wifmon getimbrede, oþ hi eft Scipia towearp se consul.   10
  Swa eac Romana, se is mæst 7 westmest. Ymb vii c wintra 7
ymb lytelne eacon, com micel fyr[cyn 7 micel] bryne on Romeburg,
þæt þærbinnan forburnon xv tunas, swa nan mon nyste hwonan
þæt fyr com. 7 þær forwearð mæst eall þæt þærbinnan wæs, þæt
þær uneaþe ænig grot staþoles aðstod. Mid þæm bryne hio wæs 15
swa swiþe forhiened þæt hio næfre siþþan swelc næs, ær hie eft
Agustus swa micle bet getimbrede þonne hio æfre ær wære, þy
geare þe Crist geboren wæs, swa þætte sume men cwædon þæt
hio wære mid gimstanum gefrætwed. þone fultum 7 þæt weorc
Agustus gebohte mid fela m talentana.   20
  Hit wæs eac sweotole gesiene þæt hit wæs Godes stihtung ymb
þara rica anwaldas, þa þa Abrahame wæs gehaten Cristes cyme
on þæm twæm 7 on feowerteoþan wintra þæs þe Ninus ricsade on
Babylonia. Swa eac eft on þæm siþmestan onwalde 7 on þæm
westemestan, þæt is Roma, wearð se ilca geboren þe ær Abrahame 25
gehaten wæs, on þæm twæm 7 on feowerteogþan geare þæs þe
Agustus ricsade, þæt wæs siþþan Romeburg getimbred wæs vii
c wintra 7 lii.
  Siþþan gestod Romeburg xii winter mid miclum welum, þa
hwile þ[e] Agustus þa eaðmetto wiþ God geheold þe he angunnen 30
hæfde, þæt wæs þæt he fleah 7 forbead þæt hiene mon god hete,

11–20] OH VII. ii. 10–11.   21–8] OH VII. ii. 13–14.   29–p. 134, 10]
OH VII. iii. 4–7 and 9.

2 Sardanopolim] sarþanopolum C.   3 iiii] iii *both MSS.*   onwealde]
anwealdes C.   5 norþmeste] norþemeste C.   Mæcedonium] macedoniam
C.   8 suðmestan] suðemestan C.   hio] hie *with* 'o' *above* e L, heo C.
ymb] *om.* C.   9 þe (2)] se C.   11 westmest] westemest C.   12 fyrcyn
. . . bryne] fyrcyn 7 mycel bryne C, fyrbryne L.   13 forburnon] forbarn
C.   16–17 eft Agustus] agustus eft C.   20 talentana] *orig.* talentata
with 'n' *above dotted third* t L.   23 feowerteoþan] feowertigan C.
25 Roma] rome C.   26 on (2)] *om.* C.   30 þe (1)] *from* C, þa L.

f. 76ᵛ swa nan cyning nolde þe ær him wæs, | ac woldon þæt mon to him
gebæde 7 him ofrede. Ac þæs on þæm twelftan geare Gaius his
nefa for of Egyptum on Siriæ—hit hæfde Agustus him to onwalde
geseald—þa nolde he him gebiddan to þæm ælmihtigum Gode, þa
5 he to Hierusalem com. þa hit mon Agustuse sæde, þa herede he
þa ofermetto 7 nanuht ne leahtrade. Raþe þæs Romane anguldon
þæs wordes mid swa miclum hungre þæt Agustus adraf of Romebyrig healfe þe þærbinnan wæron. þa wearð eft Ianes duru andon,
for þon þe þa latteowas wæron Agustuse of monegum landum
10 ungerade, þeh þær nan gefeoht þurhtogen ne wurde.

VI. ii

Æfter 'þæm' þe Romeburg getimbred wæs vii hunde wintra 7
lxvii, feng Tiberius to rice se cesar æfter Agustuse. He wæs Romanum swa forgiefen 7 swa milde swa him nan onwald[a] næs ær
þæm, oþ him Pilatus onbead from Hierusalem ymbe Cristes
15 tacnunga 7 ymbe his 'mar'tyrunga, 7 eac þæt hiene monige for
god hæfde. Ac þa he hit sæde þæm senatum, þa wurdon hie alle
wið hiene [swiþe] wiðerwearde, for þon þe hit mon ne sæde him
æror swa hit mid him gewuna wæs, þæt hie hit siþþan mehten
eallum Romanum cyþan, 7 cwædon þæt hie hiene for god habban
20 noldon. þa wearð Tiberius Romanum swa wrað 7 swa heard swa
he him ær wæs milde 7 ieþe, þæt he forneah nanne þara senatusa
ne let cucne, ne þara twa 7 twentigra monna þe he him to fultume
hæfde acoren, þæt his rædþeahteras wæren, þa mon het patricius;
ealle þa he het ofslean buton twam, ge his agene twegen suna. Hu
25 God þa þa mæstan ofermetto gewræc on þæm folce, 7 hu swiðe hi
his anguldon from heora agnum casere; þeh hit eallum þæm
folcum of oþrum londum swa swiþe gewrecen ne wurde swa hit
oft ær wæs!

f. 77   On þæm twelftan geare Tiberiuses | rices wearþ eft Godes wracu
30 Romanum, þa hie æt hiora theatrum wæron mid heora plegan,
þa hit eall tofeoll 7 heora ofslog xx m. Wyrþigre wrace hie forwur-

---

11–28] OH VII. iv. 1–10.   29–p. 135, 3] OH VII. iv. 11–12.

---

2 gebæde] to bæde C.   3 nefa] genefa C.   5 Agustuse] aguste C.
8 andon] undon C.   11 wintra] wintrum C.   13 onwalda] anwealda
C, onwald L.   14 him Pilatus] pilatus him C.   17 swiþe] swyðe C,
no reading L.   him] om. C.   21 7 ieþe] om. C.   senatusa] senatussa
C.   27 of] on C.   28 wæs] hwæs with h er. L.

don ða, cwæð Orosius, þæt þa heora synna sceoldon hreowsian 7
dædbote don swiþor þonne heora plegan [began], swa hiora
gewuna wæs ær þæm cristendome.

On þæm eahtateoþan geare his rices, þa Crist wæs ahangen,
wearð micel þeosternes ofer eallne middangeard, 7 swa micel 5
eorðbeofung þæt cludas feollon of muntum 7, þætte þara wundra
mæst wæs, þa se mona ful wæs 7 þære sunnan firrest, þæt hio þa
aþeostrade. Æfter þæm Romane acwealdon Tiberius mid attre.
He hæfde rice xxiii wintra.

VI. iii

Æfter ðæm þe Romeburg getimbred wæs vii hunde wintra 7 10
lxxxx, wearþ Gaius Gallica casere iiii gear. He wæs swiþe gefylled
mid unþeawum 7 mid firenlustum, 7 ealle he wæs swelce Romane
þa wyrþe wæron, for þon þe hie Cristes bebod hyspton 7 hit
forsawon. Ac he hit on him swiþe wræc, 7 hi him swa laðe wæron
þæt he oft wyscte þæt ealle Romane hæfden ænne sweoran, þæt 15
he hiene raþost forceorfan mehte, 7 mid ungemete mænde þæt
þær þa næs swelc sacu swelc þær oft ær wæs. 7 he self for oft on
oþra lond 7 wolde gewin findan, ac he ne mehte buton sibbe.
Ungelice wæron þa tida, cwæð Orosius, siþþan Crist geboren
wæs: siþþan mon ne mehte unsibbe findan, 7 ær þæm hie mon ne 20
mehte mid nanum þingan forbugan.

On þæm dagum com eac Godes wracu ofer Iuþan, þæt hie
ægþer hæfdon ungeþwærnesse ge betweonum him selfum ge to
eallum folcum, swa þeh hio wæs swiþost on Alexandria þære 24
byrig, 7 hie Gaius het ut adrifan. þa sendon hie Filonem | hiora   f. 77ᵛ
þone gelæredestan mon to þon þæt he him sceolde Gaiuses mildse
geærendian. Ac he hie for þære gewilnunga swiþe bismrade 7
bebead þæt hie mon on ælce healfe hiende þær mon þænne mehte,
7 bebead þæt mon afielde diofolgielda þa cirican æt Hierusalem, 7
þæt mon his agen deofolgield þærtomiddes asette, þæt wæs his 30

4–8] OH VII. iv. 13–15.   8] OH VII. iv. 18.   9] OH VII. iv. 1.
10–21] OH VII. v. 1–5.   22–p. 136, 2] OH VII. v. 6–8.

---

2 began] *from* C, *om.* L.   4 ahangen] onhangen C.   8 Romane]
romana C.   10 wintra] wintrum C.   12 ealle] eall C.   Romane]
romana C.   14 swiþe] swa swiðe C.   16 mænde] mænende wæs C.
22 Iuþan] iudam C.   25 Filonem] filionem C.

[agen] onlicnes, 7 Pilatus he hæfde on þreatunge oþ he hiene selfne ofstong: he gedæmde urne Dryhten to deaðe.

Raþe þæs Romane ofslogon Gaius slæpendne. þa funde mon on his maðmhuse twa cista, þa wæron attres fulle, 7 on oþerre wæs an gewrit, þær wæron on awritene ealra þara ricestena monna noman þe he acwellan þohte [þæt he hi þe læs forgeate]. þa geat mon þæt attor ut on þone sæ. Raþe þæs þær com upp micel wæl deadra fisca. Ægþær wæs swiðe gesiene, ge Godes wracu þa he þæt folc costigan let, ge eft his mildsung þa he hie fordon ne let, swa hit Gaius geþoht hæfde.

VI. iiii

Æfter þæm þe Romeburg getimbred wæs vii hunde wintra 7 xc[v], þa feng Tiberius Claudius to Romana onwalde. On þæm ærestan geare his rices Petrus se apostol com to Rome, 7 þær wurdon ærest cristene men þurh his lare. þa woldon Romane ofslean Claudius for Gaiuses þingum his mæges, þæs ærran cesares, 7 ealle þa þe þære mægþe wæron. Ac mid þon þe hie þæs cristendomes onfengon, hie wæron swa geþwære 7 swa gesibsume þæt hie ealle forgeafon þæm casere þa fæhþe þe his mæg hæfde wið hie ær geworht, ond he forgeaf him eallum þæt unryht 7 þæt facn þæt [hie] him don þohte.

On þære tide gewearð eac oþer tacen on Romana onwalde, siþþan him se cristendom to com. þæt wæs þæt Dalmatie woldon gesellan Scribanianuse þæm latteowe hiora cynerice 7 siþþan wið Romane | winnan. Ac þa hie gesomnod wæron 7 hiene to cyninge don woldon, þa ne mehton hie þa guðfonan upahebban, swa hiora þeaw wæs þonne hie onwaldas setton, ac wurdon him selfum wiðerwearde þæt hie hit æfre ongunnon 7 Scribani[an]us ofslogon. Oðsace nu, cwæð Orosius, se se þe wille oþþe se þe dyrre, þæt þæt angin nære gestilled for þæs cristendomes Gode, 7 gesecge hwær ænig gewin ær þæm cristendome swa gehwurfe, gif hit ongunnen wære.

3-10] OH VII. v. 9-11.   11-20] OH VII. vi. 1-4.   21-31] OH VII. vi. 6-8.

1 agen] *from* C, *no reading* L.   2 gedæmde] gedemde C.   6 þæt (1) . . . forgeate] *from* C, *no reading* L.   8 þa] þæt C.   12 xcv] *from* C, xci *with* i *over eras.* L.   13 apostol] apostolus C.   15 cesares] caseres C. 19 ær] *om.* C.   20 hie] he L, hi C.   þohte] þohton C.   22 Dalmatie] dalmatiæ C.   27 Scribanianus] *from* C, scribanius L.   28 Oðsace] oð *on eras.* L, ætsace C.   se se] se C.

Oþer wundor gewearð eac þy feorþan geare Claudiuses rices,
þæt he self æfter gewinne for 7 nan findan ne mehte. On þæm
geare wæs micel hungor on Siria 7 on Palestina, buton þæt Elena,
Ætiubena cwen, sealde þæm munucum corn genog þe wæron æt
Hierusalem, for þon þe hio þa wæs niwlice cristen.   5
On þæm fiftan geare Claudiuses rices wearð oþiewed an igland
betuh Theram 7 Therasiam, v mila brad 7 v mila long. On þæm
seofeþan geare his rices wearð swa micel ungeþwærnes on Hierusalem betuh þæm þe þær cristene [n]æron, þæt þær wæron xxx m
ofslagen 7 æt þæm geate oftredd, swa nan mon nyste hwonon sio   10
wro'h't com. On þæm nigeþan geare his rices wearð micel hunger
on Rome, 7 [Claudius] het ut adrifan ealle þa Iudan þe þærbinnan
wæron. Æfter þæm Romane witan Claudiuse þone hunger þe him
getenge wæs, 7 he wearð him swa grom þæt he het ofslean þara
senatorum xxxv 7 þara oþerra iii hund þe þær ieldeste wæron.   15
Æfter þæm Romane hiene acwealdon mid atre.

VI. v

Æfter þæm þe Romeburg getimbred wæs viii hunde wintra 7
ix, feng Nero to Romana onwalde 7 hiene hæfde xiiii gear. He
hæfde giet þe ma unþeawa þonne his eam hæfde ær Gaius. Toeacan
þæm monigfealdum bismrum þe he donde wæs, he het æt sumum   20
cierre onbærnan | Romeburg 7 bebead his agnum monnum þæt hie   f. 78ᵛ
simle gegripen þæs licgendan feos swa hie mæst mehten 7 to him
brohten, þonne hit mon ut oþbrude, 7 gestod him self on þæm
hiehstan torre þe þærbinnan wæs 7 ongon wyrcan scopleoð be
þæm bryne. Se wæs vi dagas biernende 7 vii niht. Ac he wræc his 25
ungewealdes ærest on þære byrig hiora misdæda 7 siþþan on him
selfum, þa he hiene ofstong, þæt hie Petrus 7 Paulus gemartredon.
He wæs monna ærest ehtend cristenra monna. Æfter his fielle
wearð þara casera mægð offeallen.

1–2] OH VII. vi. 9.   2–5] OH VII. vi. 12.   6–16] OH VII. vi. 13–18.
17–19] OH VII. vii. 1.   19–25] OH VII. vii. 4–6.   25–9] OH VII. vii.
10–13.

2 æfter gewinne for] for æfter gewinne C.   4 æt] *from* C, þæt L.
7 v (1)] seofon C.   8 seofeþan] feorðan C.   9 næron] næran C,
wæron L.   10 oftredd] oftreden C.   11 wroht] 'h' *in l.h.* L.
12 Claudius] *from* C, gaius L.   Iudan] iudeas C.   13 Romane]
romana C.   16 Romane] romana C.   18 He] 7 he C.   19 þe]
om. C.   þonne] *from* C, þoñne L.   29 offeallen] oðfeallen C.

VI. vi

[Æf]ter þæm þe Romeburg getimbred wæs viii hunde wintra 7
xxiiii, feng Galua se casere to Romana onwalde. þæs on þæm
seofeþan monðe hiene ofslog Othon an mon 7 him to þon anwalde
feng.

5 Sona swa Romane ærest cristenra monna ehton, swa hit Nero
onstealde, swa wurdon ealle þa folc hiora wiðerwinnan þe be
eastan Siria wæron, ge eac hie selfe him betweonum hæfdon ungerædnesse. Uitellus, Germania cyning, gefeaht þriwa wið Othon 7
hiene ofslog on þæm þriddan monðe þæs þe hie winnan ongunnon.

VI. vii

10 [Æ]fter þæm þe Romeburg getimbred wæs dccc wintra 7 xxv,
feng Uespasianus to Romana onwalde. þa wearð eft sibb ofer
ealne Romana anwald, 7 'he' bebead Tituse his suna þæt he towearp
þæt templ on Hierusalem 7 ealle þa burg, for þon þe God nolde
þæt hie þone cristendom mierde leng, 7 forbead þæt mon na ðær
15 eft ne timbrede. 7 he fordyde þara Iudena xi hund m: sume he
ofslog, sume on oþer land gesealde, sume he mid hungre acwealde.
f. 79 Æfter þæm | mon dyde him twæm þone triumphan, Uespasiane
7 Tituse. Seo onsien wearð þa micel wundor Romanum, for þon
hi ær ne gesawon ii men ætsæmne ðæron sittan. Hi betyndan
20 Ianes dura. Æfter þæm Wespa[s]ianus gefor on utsihte, on ðæm
nigeþa[n] geare his rices, on anum tune 'b'uton Rome.

VI. viii

[Æ]fter þæm ðe Romeburh getimbred wæs viii hunde wintra
7 xxix, feng Titus to Romana onwalde 7 hine hæfde ii gear. He

1–9] OH VII. viii. 1–6.   10–12] OH VII. ix. 1.   12–16] OH VII. ix.
3–7.   17–20] OH VII. ix. 8–9.   20–1] OH VII. ix. 12.   22–3] OH
VII. ix. 13.

VI. vi] eras. L, vi C.   1 Æfter] from C, ter, with space left blank for
ornamental initial here and subsequently L.   wintra] wintrum C.   2 Galua]
galfa C.   se casere] om. C.   8 Germania] germana C.   10 Æfter]
fter L.   11 Uespasianus] uespassianus C.   12 bebead] bead C.
14 mierde leng] lencg myrdon C.   15 Iudena] iudea C.   xi] endlufon
siþon C.   17 Uespasiane] uespassiane C.   18 þa] om. C.   Romanum] a
alt. from o ? L.   for þon] for þon þe C.   20 Wespasianus] wespanianus
L, uespassianus C.   21 nigeþan] nigeþam L, ix C.   buton] tuton with 'b'
above first t L.   22 Æfter] from C, fter L.

wæs swa godes willan þæt he sægde þæt he forlure þone dæg þe
he noht on to gode ne gedyde. He gefor eac on þæm ilcan tune ðe
his fæder dyde 7 on þære ilcan adle.

VI. viiii

[Æ]fter þæm þe Romeburg getimbred wæs viii hunde wintra 7
xxx, feng Domitianus to Romana onwalde, Tituses broþor, 7 hit 5
hæfde xv gear. He wearþ eft [eh]tend cristenra monna 7 wæs on
swa micle ofermetto astigen þæt he] bead þæt man on gelice to
him onbugan sceolde swa to Gode, 7 he] bebead þæt mon Iohannes
þone apostol gebrohte on Bothmose þæm iglande, on wræcsiþe
from oþrum cristenum monnum, 7 he bebead þæt mon acwealde 10
eall Dauides cynn, to þon, gif Crist geboren nære þa giet, þæt he
na siþþan geboren ne wurde, for þon þe witgan sædon þæt he of
þæm cynne cuman sceolde. Æfter þæm bebode he wearð self
unweorðlice ofslagen.

VI. x

[Æf]ter þæm þe Romeburg getimbred wæs viii hund wintra 15
7 xlvi, þa feng Nerfa to Romana onwalde, 7 for þon þe [he] eald
wæs, he geceas him to fultume Traianus þone mon. þa gespræcon
hie him betweonum þæt hie wolden anwendan ealle þa gesetnessa
7 ealle þa gebodu þe Domitianus hæfde ær gesett, for þon þe he
him wæs ær bæm lað, 7 heton eft Iohannes æt his mynstre | 20
gebrengan on Effesum from þæm [woruld]ier[m]þum þe he [h]wile f. 79ᵛ
on wæs.

þa gefor Nerfa, 7 Traianus hæfde þone anwald x[ix] ger æfter
him. 7 he underþiedde Romanum eall þa folc þe him niwlice
geswicen hæfdon, 7 he bebead his aldormon[n]um þæt hie wæren 25

2–3] OH VII. ix. 15.　　4–8] OH VII. x. 1–2.　　8–14] OH VII. x. 5–7.
15–23] OH VII. xi. 1–2.　　23–p. 140, 3] OH VII. xii. 1–3.

4 Æfter] *from* C, fter L.　　5 Domitianus] domicianus C.　　6 ehtend]
from C, hetend L.　　7–8 he... 7] *from* C (onbugon), *om.* L.　　9 Bothmose]
thomore C.　　10 he] *om.* C.　　11 geboren... giet] þa git geboren nære C.
12 na siþþan] siþþon na C.　　for þon þe] for þon C.　　15 Æfter] *from* C. ter
L. Romeburg] romaburh C.　　16 þon] þam C.　　he] *from* C, *om.* L.
18 anwendan] an-*partly er.* L, towendon C.　　19 Domitianus] domicianus C.
20–1 æt... gebrengan] gebringan æt his mynstre C.　　21 woruldiermþum]
woruldyrmþum C, ierþum L.　　hwile] *from* C, wile L.　　23 xix] *from*
C, x L.　　25 he] *om.* C.　　aldormonnum] ealdormannum C, aldormonum L.

cristenra monna ehtend. þa sæde him hiora an, Plenius wæs
haten, þæt he woh bude 7 miclum on þæm syngade. He hit þa
hrædlice eft forbead.

On þære tide wæron Iudan on miclum geflite 7 on micelre
5 unsibbe wið þa londleode þær þær hie þonne wæron, oþ hiora fela
m forwurdon on ægþere hand. On þære tide Traianus gefor on
utsihte on Seleutia þære byrig.

VI. xi

[Æf]ter þæm þe Romeburg getimbred wæs dccc wintra 7 [lx]vii
feng Adrianus to Romana onwalde, Tr[a]ianuses nefa, 7 hiene
10 hæfde xxi wintra, 7 raðe þæs þe him cristne bec cuþe wæron þurh
ænne þara apostola geongrena, Quadratus wæs haten, he forbead
ofer ealne his onwald þæt mon nanum cristenum men ne abulge,
7 gif ænig cristen agylte, þæt se þonne wære beforan him gelædd,
7 he him þonne demde self, swa him ryht þuhte. He wearð þa
15 Romanum swa leof 7 swa weorð þæt hie hiene nanuht ne heton
buton fæder, 7 him to weorðscipe hie heton his wif casern, 7
het ofslean ealle þa Iudiscan men, for þon þe hie cristene men
pinedon—þa wæron on Palestina, þæt mon het Iudena lond—7
he bebead þæt mon timbrede on oþerre stowe Hierusalem þa
20 burg 7 þæt hie mon siþþan hete be noman Heli[a]m.

VI. xii

[Æf]ter þæm þe Romeburg getimbred wæs dccc wintra 7
lxxxviii, feng Ponpeius to Romana onwalde þe mon oþre nomon
het Pius, 7 him sealde Iustinus se philosophus ane cristene boc for
f. 80 hiora freondscipe. | Siþþan he þa geleornod hæfde, he wearð
25 cristnum monnum [swa leof 7] swiþe hold oþ his lifes ende.

4–7] OH VII. xii. 6–8.   8–20] OH VII. xiii. 1–5.   21–5] OH VII. xiv.
1–2.

---

4 Iudan] iudei C.   8 Æfter] from C, ter L.   lxvii] from C, xlvii L.
9 Traianuses] from C, trianuses L.   nefa] genefa C.   17 Iudiscan] iudeis-
cean C.   17–18 for . . . lond] þe wæron on palestina þæt man het iudea land
for þon þe hi cristene men pinedon C.   19 oþerre] þære C.   20 Heliam]
helium L, eliam C.   21 Æfter] from C, ter L.   25 swa leof 7] from
C, no reading L.

VI. xiii

[Æf]ter þæm þe Romeburg getimbred wæs dcccc wintra 7 iii, feng Marcus Antonius to Romana onwalde mid his breðer Aureliuse. Hie wæron þa ærestan men þe Romana onwald on tu todældon 7 hiene hæfden xiiii winter, 7 hie bebudon þæt mon ælcne cristenne mon ofsloge. Æfter þæm hie hæfdon micel gewin 5 wið Parthe, for þon þe hie hæfdon awest ealle Capodotiam 7 Armeniam 7 ealle Siriam. Æfter þæm hie genamon frið [w]ið Parthe, 7 him siþþan becom on [swa] micel hungor 7 micel moncwealm þæt heora feawa to lafe wurdon.

Æfter þæm him becom on þæt Deniscæ gewinn mid eallum 10 Germanium. þa on þæm dæge þe hie gefeohtan sceoldon, him com on swa micel hæte 7 swa micel þurst þæt hie him heora feores ne wendan. þa bædon hie þa cristnan men þæt hi heora an sume wisan gehulpen, 7 ongeaton þæt hit wæs Godes wracu. þa abædon hie æt þæm ælmihtegum Gode þæt hit swa swiðe rinde þæt hie 15 hæfdon wæter genog onufan þære dune 7 þæt þær wæs swa micel þunor þæt he ofslog fela þusend monna gemong þæm gefeohte.

þa æfter þæm ealle Romane wurdon cristnum monnum swa holde þæt hie on monegum templum awriten þæt ælc cristen mon hæfde frið 7 sibbe, 7 eac þæt ælc þara moste cristendome onfon se 20 þe wolde. 7 Antonius forgef eall þæt gafol þæt mon to Rome sellan sceolde 7 het forbærnan þæt gewrit þe hit on awriten wæs, hwæt mon on geare agiefan sceolde, 7 þæs on þæm æfterran geare he gefor.

VI. xiiii

[Æf]ter þæm þe Romeburg getimbred wæs dcccc [wintra] 7 25 xxx, feng Lucius Antonius to rice 7 hit hæfde xiii ger. | He wæs f. 80 swiþe yfel monn ealra þeawa, buton þæt he wæs cene 7 oft feaht anwig, 7 fela þara senatorum he het ofslean þe þær betste wæron.

1–9] OH VII. xv. 1–6. 10–17] OH VII. xv. 7–9. 18–24] OH VII. xv. 12. 25–p. 142, 5] OH VII. xvi. 1–3.

---

1 Æfter] from C, ter L. dcccc . . . iii] dcccc 7 iii wintra C. 4 7 (1)] 7 hi C. winter] gear C. 6 Parthe] parðe C. Capodotiam] capedociam C. 7 wið] from C, pið L. 8 swa] from C, no reading L. 10 Deniscæ] denisce C. 11 Germanium] germanum C. gefeohtan] feohton C. 18 ealle Romane] romana ealle C. 23 agiefan] gyldan C. 25 Æfter] from C, ter L. wintra] from C, om. L.

Æfter an þunor toslog hiora Capitoliam, þæt hus þe hiora godas
inne wæron 7 hiora diofolgield, 7 hiora bibliotheoco wearð onbær-
ned from ligette, 7 ealle heora ealdan bec forburnon þærinne. þær
wæs a swa micel dem geburnen swa on Alexandria wæs þære
5 byrig on hiora b[i]bliotheoco, þær forburnon iiii hund m boca.

VI. xv

Æfter þæm þe Romeburg wæs getimbred dcccc wintra 7 xliii,
feng Seuerus to Romana onwalde 7 hiene hæfde xvii ger. He
besæt Piscenius on anum fæstenne, oþ he him on hond eode, 7
he hiene siþþan het ofslean, for þon he wolde ricsian on Sirie 7
10 on Egypte. Æfter þæm [he] ofslog Albinus þone mon on Gallium,
for þon þe he eac wolde on hine winnan. Siþþan he for on Brettanie 7 þær oft gefeaht wið Peohtas 7 wið Scottas, ær he þa Brettas
mehte wið hie bewerian, 7 het ænne weall þwyres ofer eall þæt
lond asettan from sæ oþ sæ, 7 raþe þæs he gefor on Eforwicceastre.

VI. xvi

15 Æ[f]ter þæm þe Romeburg getimbred wæs dcccc wintra 7 lxii,
feng his sunu to rice Antonius, 7 hit hæfde vii ger. He hæfde twa
geswostor him to wifum. He hæfde folc gegaderad 7 wolde winnan
on Parthe, ac he wearð ofslagen on þæm færelte from his agnum
monnum.

VI. xvii

20 Æ[f]ter þæm þe Romeburg getimbred wæs dcccc wintra 7 lxx,
feng Marcus Aurelius to Romana onwalde 7 hiene hæfde iiii ger.
Hiene ofslogon eac his agene men 7 his modor mid.

6–10] OH VII. xvii. 1–2.   10–14] OH VII. xvii. 6–8.   15–19] OH VII.
xviii. 1–2.   20–22] OH VII. xviii. 4–5.

---

1 Æfter] æfter þam C.   Capitoliam] capitolium C.   þæt hus] om. C.
2 bibliotheoco] bibliþeca C.   2–3 onbærned] forbærnend C.   3 from]
fram þam C.   4 a] an C.   5 bibliotheoco] bbliotheoco L, bibliþecan C.
6 wæs getimbred] getimbred wæs C.   8 Piscenius] from C, pisceninus L.
10 he] from C, om. L.   11–12 Brettanie] brytannie C.   12 Scottas]
sceottas C.   he þa] he C.   Brettas] bryttas C.   15 Æfter] from C, æter L.
18 on (1)] wið C.   20 Æfter] from C, æter L.   wintra] so C, wint̃ L.

VI. xviii

| Æfter þæm þe Romeburg getimbred wæs dcccc wintra 7   f. 81
lxxiiii, feng Aurelianus Alexander to Romana onwalde 7 hiene
hæfde xvi gear. 7 Mammea his sio gode modor sende æfter Origenise þæm gelæredestan mæssepreoste 7 hio wearð siþþan cristen
from him 7 welgelæred 7 gedyde þæt hiere sunu wæs cristenum   5
monnum swiþe hold. He gefor mid fierde on Perse 7 ofslog Xersan
hiora cyning. Æfter þæm he forlet his lif on Magentsan þære
byrig.

VI. xix

Æfter þæm þe Romeburg getimbred wæs dcccc wintra 7 lxxxvii,
feng Maximus to Romana onwalde. He bebead eft þæt mon   10
cristene men brocode 7 þæt mon þa godan Mammeam gemartrade
7 ealle þa preostas þe hiere folgodan buton Origenis: [he] opfleah on
Aegypte. 7 Maximus ofslog his agen ealdormon on þæm þriddan
geare his rices on Aquilegia þære byrig.

VI. xx

Æfter þæm þe Romeburg getimbred wæs dcccc wintra 7 xc,   15
feng Gordianus to rice 7 hit hæfde vi ger, 7 he ofslog þa twegen
gebroðor þe ær Maximus ofslogan, 7 he self raþe þæs gefor.

VI. xxi

Æfter þæm þe Romeburg getimbred wæs dcccc wintra 7 xcvii,
feng Philippus to Romana onwalde 7 hiene hæfde vii ger. He
wearð diegellice cristen, for þon he eawenga ne dorste. On þæm   20
þriddan geare his rices hit gewearð swa hit God gestihtade, þæt
wæs ymb an m wintra þæs þe Romeburg getimbred wæs, þæt
ægþer ge hiora casere wearð cristen, ge eac þæt hie þa miclan
feorme þigedon Cristes þonces æt þæs caseres palendsan þe hie

---

1–8] OH VII. xviii. 6–8.   9–14] OH VII. xix. 1–2.   15–17] OH VII.
xix. 3 and 5.   18–p. 144, 5] OH VII. xx. 1–4.

---

2 Aurelianus] aureliusnus (aureliu'nu') C.   3–4 Origenise] oriense C.
6 Xersan] persan C.   7 Magentsan] magestan C.   9 lxxxvii] lxxxvi
C.   12 Origenis] orienis C.   he] *from* C, *om.* L.   13 Aegypte]
egypte C.   15 wintra] *so* C, wiñt L.   24 palendsan] palentsan C.

ær ælce geare þigedon æt hiora deofolgildum, deofla þonces: þæt
wæs þæt ealle Romane woldon ymb xii monað bringan togædere
þone selestan dæl hiora goda [gegearod to heora geblote] 7 hiora
4 siþþan fela wucena ætgædere brucan. Æfter þæm Decius, an rice
f. 81ᵛ mon, | beswac þone casere 7 feng him [siþþan] to þon anwalde.

VI. xxii

Æfter [þæm] þe Romeburg getimbred wæs m wintra 7 iiii, feng
Decius to Romana onwalde 7 hiene hæfde iii ger, 7 sona gedyde
sweotol tacn þæt he Philippus ær besierede, mid þæm þe he het
cristenra monna ehtan 7 monege gedyde to halgum martyrum 7
10 gesette his sunu to þæm onwalde to him, 7 ra[ð]e þæs hie wurdon
begen ætsemne ofslagen.

VI. xxiii

Æfter þæm þe Romeburg getimbred was m wintra 7 viii, feng
Gallus Ostilianus to rice 7 hit hæfde ii ger. þa wearð eft Godes
wracu on Rome: swa longe swa seo ehtnes wæs þara cristenra
15 monna, swa longe him wæs ungemetlic moncwealm getenge, þæt
nan hus næs binnan þære byrig þæt hit næfde þære wrace angolden.
Æfter þæm Emilianus ofslog Gallus 7 hæfde him þone anweald.
þæs eac on þæm þriddan monðe hiene mon ofslog.

VI. xxiiii

Æfter þæm þe Romeburg getimbred wæs m wintra 7 x, þa
20 gesetton Romane ii caseras. Oþer wæs binnan Romebyrig, Gallienus wæs haten, oþer wæs mid Emilitum þæm folce, Ualerianus
wæs haten. þa sceoldon on siml beon winnende þær hit þonne
þearf wæs. þa bebudon hie begen cristenra monna ehtnesse. Ac

6–11] OH VII. xxi. 1–3.   12–18] OH VII. xxi. 4–6.   19–22] OH VII.
xxii. 1.   23–p. 145, 5] OH VII. xxii. 3–4.

1 deofolgildum] followed by þæt wæs both MSS, with dots for eras. above
letters L.   1–2 þæt wæs] om. C.   2 Romane] romana C.   3 goda]
from C, godra L.   gegearod . . . geblote] from C, gearwa L.   5 siþþan]
siþþon C, no reading L.   6 þæm] þam C, om. L.   8 þe] þæt C.
10 raðe] from C, rade L.   11 ætsemne] ætsomne C.   16 byrig]
byrige L.   17 Emilianus] emelianus C.   20 Romane] romana C.
20–1 Oþer . . . haten] placed after following clause C.

hrædlíce on hie begen com Godes wracu. Ualerianus for mid
fierde ongean Sapan, Persa cyning, 7 þær gefongen wæs, 7 siþþan
he wæs Sapan þæm cyninge to ðon geset, oþ his lifes ende, þæt he
swa oft sceolde stupian swa he to his horse wolde, 7 he þonne se
cyning hæfde his hri[c]g him to hliepan, 7 þæm oþrum, Gallienuse, 5
wæron monog folc onwinnende, þæt he his rice mid micellre
unweorðnesse 7 mid micelre unieðnesse gehæfde. Ærest Germanie
þe be Donua wæron forhergedon Italiam oþ Rafennan þa burg, 7
Swæfas forhergedon ealle Galliam, 7 Gotan oferhergedon eall 9
Creca lond 7 þa læssan Asiam, 7 Sermende genieddon | ealle f. 82
Datie from Romana onwalde, 7 Hunas forhergedon Pannoniam, 7
Parthe forhergedon Mesopotamiam 7 ealle Sirie. Toeacan þæm
Romane hæfdon gewin betuh him selfum. Æfter þæm Gallienus
wearð ofslagen on Medialane þære byrig from his agnum monnum.

VI. xxv

Æfter þæm þe Romeburg getimbred wæs m wintra 7 xxv, feng 15
Claudius to Romana onwalde. þy ilcan geare he oferwon Gotan
7 hie adraf ut of Crecum, 7 him Romane gedydan ænne gyldenne
scield, þære dæda to weorðmynte, 7 an[e] gyldene anlicnesse, 7
ahengon [hie] up on hiora Capitoliam. þæs on þæm æfterran
geare he gefor, 7 his broþor Quintillus feng to þæm onwalde, 7 20
þæs on þæm seofonteoþan dæge he wearð ofslagen.

VI. xxvi

Æfter þæm þe Romeburg getimbred wæs m wintra 7 xxvii, feng
Aurelius to Romana onwalde 7 hiene hæfde v ger 7 vi monað, 7
adraf Gotan be norþan Donua 7 þonan for on Sirie 7 hie geniedde
eft to Romana onwalde. 7 siþþan he for on Gallie 7 ofslog Tetricum 25

5–14] OH VII. xxii. 6–13.   15–21] OH VII. xxiii. 1–2.   22–p. 146, 2]
OH VII. xxiii. 3–6.

1 com] becom C.   2 Sapan] saphan C.   3 ðon] þam C.   4 swa
oft sceolde] sceolde swa oft C.   5 hricg] hring with n er. L, hric C.
Gallienuse] gallianuse C.   6 monog] mænige C.   7 Germanie] gear-
maniæ C.   8 Rafennan] refennan C.   10 Creca] grecon C. Sermende]
sermenne C.   12 Sirie] siriæ C.   14 Medialane] mediolane C.
17 Crecum] creacum C.   Romane] romana C.   18 dæda] dæde C.   ane]
from C, an L.   19 ahengon] hengon C.   hie] hi C, single er. letter (h?) L.
Capitoliam] capitolium C.   23 Aurelius] aurilius C.   24 Sirie]
syrie C.

þone mon, for þy þe he hi him teah to anwalde. Æfter þæm he bebead cristenra monna ehtnesse 7 raðe þæs wearþ ofslagen.

VI. xxvii

Æfter þæm þe Romeburg getimbred wæs m wintra 7 xxxii,
feng Tacitus to Romana onwalde, 7 þæs on þæm sixtan monþe he
5 wearþ ofslagen on Ponto þæm londe. Æfter þæm Floriam feng to
þæm onwalde 7 wæs ofslagen [þæs] on þæm þriddan monþe on
Tharsa þæm londe.

VI. xxviii

Æfter þæm þe Romeburg wæs getimbred m wintra 7 xxxiii,
feng Brobus to Romana onwalde 7 hiene hæfde vi ger 7 iiii monað,
10 7 he adyde [Hu]nas of Gallium, 7 he ofslog Saturninus, þe æfter
þæm onwalde wonn. Æfter þæm he ofslog Proculus 7 Bo[n]orum,
þa gierndon eac æfter þæm onwalde. Æfter þæm he wearð self
ofslagen on Sirmie þære dune.

VI. xxix

f. 82ᵛ | [Æ]fter þæm þe Romeburg getimbred wæs m wintra 7 xxxix,
15 feng Carus to Romana onwalde 7 hiene hæfde ii ger, 7 gefeaht
tuwwa wið Parthe 7 geeode hiora burga twa, þa wæron on Tigris
staþe þære ie. Raþe þæs hiene ofslog an þunor, 7 his sunu Numerianus feng to þæm onwalde, 7 raþe þæs hiene ofslog his agen sweor.

VI. xxx

[Æ]fter þæm þe Romeburg getimbred wæs m wintra 7 xli, feng
20 Dioclitianus to Romano onwalde 7 hiene hæfde xx wintra. He
gesette under him gingran casere, Maximus wæs haten, 7 hiene

3–7] OH VII. xxiv. 1.   8–13] OH VII. xxiv. 2–3.   14–18] OH VII.
xxiv. 4.   19–p. 147, 19] OH VII. xxv. 1–11.

---

5 þæm (1)] *om.* C.   6 þæs] *from* C, *no reading* L.   8 wæs getimbred]
getimbred wæs C.   wintra] *from* C, wiñt L   10 Hunas] *from* C, minas L.
Saturninus] saturninum C.   11 þæm] *om.* C.   Bonorum] *from* C, bororum
L.   13 Sirmie] syrmie C.   14 Æfter] *from* C, fter L.   18 agen
sweor] sweortor C.   19 Æfter] *from* C, fter L.   20 Dioclitianus]
dioclicianus C.   Romano] romana C.

sende on Gallie, for þon ðe hie þa niwlice hæfdon gewinn up
ahæfen, ac he hie þa ieðelice ofercom. On þære tide wæron Dioclitie iii cyningas on winnende: Caucarius on Bretlande, 7 Achileus
of Egypta londe, 7 Marseus of Persum. þa gesette he iii caseras
under him: an wæs Maximianus, oþer Constantius, þridda Galerius. 5
Maximianus he sende on Affricam, 7 he oferwonn hiora wiþerwinnan, 7 Constantius he sende on Gallie, 7 he oferwonn Alamanni
þæt folc 7 siþþan he geeode Brettaniam þæt igland, 7 he self
Dioclitianus for on Ægypte 7 besæt Achileus þone cyning eahta
monað on Alexandria þære byrig, oð hiene þa burgleode him 10
ageafon, 7 he siþþan oferhergeade ealle Egypte. 7 Galerius he
sende on Perse 7 gefeaht ii wið Marseus þone cyning, þæt hiera
naþer næfde sige. Æt heora þriddan gefeohte Galerius wearþ
gefliemed 7 mid micelre fyrhtnesse com ʼtoʼ Dioclitiane. Ac he his
onfeng mid micelre unweorðnesse 7 hiene het iernan on his 15
a[ge]num purpurum fela mila beforan his rædwæne. After þæm þe
his mod wæs mid þæm bismre ahwet, he for eft on Perse 7 hie
gefliemʼdʼe 7 Marseus gefeng 7 his wif 7 his bearn. þa onfeng
Dioclitianus Galeriuse weorðlice. 19

Æfter þæm Dioclitianus 7 Maximianus bebudon ehtnes|se f. 83
cristenra monna, Dioclitianus eastane 7 Maximianus westane, 7
for þon gebode gewurdon fela martyra on x wintra firste.

þa gewearð hi him betweonum þæt hie woldon þa onwaldas
forlætan 7 þa purpuran alecgan þa hie weredon, 7 woldon hiera
dagas on seftnesse geendian, 7 þæt swa gelæston. Dioclitianus 25
gesæt on Nicomidio þære byrig [7 Maximianus gesæt on Mediolane
þære byrig] 7 leton þa onwealdas to Galeriuse 7 to Constantiuse, 7
hi hiene todældon siþþan on tu: Galerius nom Ilirice 7 begeondan
þæm þone eastende 7 þone mæstan dæl þisses middangeardes, 7

20–p. 148, 9] OH VII. xxv. 13–16.

---

1 þa] *om.* C.   2 þa] *om.* C.   2–3 Dioclitie] dioclitiæ C.   3 7] *om.*
C.   4 of (1)] on C.   5 Maximianus] maximus C.   Constantius] constantinus C.   6 Affricam] africe C.   7 Constantius] constantinus C.
Gallie] galliæ C.   Alamanni] alamaniæ C.   9 Dioclitianus] diacli-
tianus C.   11 he (1)] *om.* C.   Egypte] ægypte C.   12 Marseus]
marserius C.   13 Galerius] gallerius C.   15 onfeng] afeng C.
16 agenum] *from* C, anum L.   purpurum] pupuran C.   19 Dioclitianus]
dioclicius C.   Galeriuse] ualeriuse C.   weorðlice] weorðfullice C.
20 Æfter þæm] *om.* C.   Dioclitianus] dioclicianus C.   21 Dioclitianus]
dioclicianus C.   22 þon] þam C.   gewurdon] wurdon C.   25 Dio-
clitianus] dioclicianus C.   26 Nicomidio] nicomedia C.   26–7 7 . . .
byrig] *from* C, *om.* L.   27 Constantiuse] constantinuse C.

Constantius nom ealle Italie 7 Affricam 7 Ispanie 7 Gallie 7 Brettannie. Ac he wæs hwon giernende þissa woroldþinga 7 micelra
onwalda, 7 for þæm he forlet his agnum willan Italiam 7 Affricam to Galeriuse. þa gesette Galerius ii cyningas under him:
5 oþer wæs haten Seuerus, þæm he gesealde Italiam 7 Africam, 7
Maximinus he gesette on þa eastlond.

On þæm dagum Constantius, se mildesta monn, for on Brettannie 7 þær gefor, 7 gesealde his suna þæt rice Constanti[n]use, þone
he hæfde be Elenan his ciefese.

10 þa wolde Maxentius, Maximianuses sunu, habban þone anwald
on Italiam. þa sende Galerius him ongean Seuerus mid fierde, þe
him se onweald ær geseald wæs, 7 he þær beswicen wearð from
his agnum monnum 7 ofslagen neah [Rafenna] þære byrig. þa
Maximianus geacsade þæt his sunu feng to þæm onwalde, he þa
15 hrædlice forlet þa burg þe he on ge'se'ten wæs 7 þohte his sunu
'to' beswicanne 7 him siþþan fon to þæm onwalde. Ac þa hit se
sunu anfunde, þa adræfde he þone fæder, 7 he fleah on Gallie 7
wolde Constanti[n]us beswican his aþum 7 habban him þæt rice.
Ac hit anfunde his dohtor 7 hit Constanti[n]use asæde, 7 he hiene
20 afliemde siþþan on Masiliam, 7 he þær ofslagen wearð.

f. 83ᵛ   þa gesealde Galerius | Lucinuse Italiam 7 Affricam, 7 he het
ealle þa cristnan þe þær betst[e] wæron gebringan on elþeode.
Æfter þæm he wearð on micelre untrumnesse 7 him to gehet
monigne læce, 7 heora nan him ne mehte bion nane gode. Ac him
25 sæde heora an þæt hit wære Godes wracu. þa het he þæt mon þa
cristnan eft gebrohte on heora earde, ælcne þær he ær wæs; swa
þeah he gefor on þære mettrymnesse 7 Luci[ni]us feng to þæm onwalde.

10–20] OH VII. xxviii. 5–10.   21–8] OH VII. xxviii. 11–13.

---

1 Constantius] constantinus C.   Italie] italiæ C.   Ispanie] ispaniæ C.
Gallie] galliæ C.   1–2 Brettannie] bryttanie C.   4 Galeriuse] galleriuse C.
Galerius] galius C.   5 Africam] affricam C.   6 Maximinus] from C, maximianus L.   7 Constantius] constantinus C.   mildesta] mildeortesta C.
7–8 Brettannie] bryttannie C.   8 Constantinuse] from C, constantiuse with ti
er. L.   9 ciefese] wife in l.h. on eras. (room for 6 or 7 letters, final se still
visible) C.   10 Maximianuses] maximianus C.   13 Rafenna] from C,
refanne L.   16 him] he C.   17 Gallie] galliæ C.   18 Constantinus] from
C, constantius L.   19 Constantinuse] from C, constantiuse L.   asæde]
gesæde C.   20 afliemde] geflymde C.   22 betste] beste C, betst L.
24 monigne læce] manige læceas C.   nane] on nanum C.   26 cristnan]
cristenan men C.   27 Lucinius] from C, lucius L.

Æfter þæm wearþ gewinn betuh Constantinuse 7 Maxentiuse, 7 raðe þæs Constantinus ofslog Maxentius binnan Rome, æt þære [brycge] þe mon Moluia het. On þæm dagum Maximinus bebead cristenra monna ehtnesse 7 raðe þæs gefor on Tharsa þære byrig. On þæm dagum Lucin[i]us bebead þæt nan cristen mon ne come 5 on his hierede ne on his færelte, 7 raþe þæs wearð gewin betuh him 7 betuh Constantinuse 7 oftrædlica gefeoht, oþ Constantinus gefeng Lucinius 7 hiene siþþan het beheafdian 7 siþþan feng to eallum Romana onwalde. On ðæm dagum Arrius se mæssepresbyter wearþ on gedwolan 10 ymb þone ryhtan geleafan. Ymb þone timan wæs gegaderad iii hund biscepa 7 eahtatiene, hiene to oferflitanne 7 to amansumia[nne]. On þæm dagum Constantinus ofslog Crispum his sunu 7 Lucinius his swostor sunu, þæt nan monn nyste hwæt se gylt wæs buton him anum. Æfter þæm he underþiedde him selfum monege 15 þeoda þe ær wæron Romanum ungewilde, 7 het atimbran ane burg on Crecum 7 het hie be him hatan Constanti[no]polim. He bebead ærest monna þæt mon cirican timbrede 7 þæt mon beluce ælc diofolgield[hus]. He gefor ymb xxxi wintra þæs þe he rice 19 hæfde, on anum tune neah Nicomedio | þære byrig. f. 84

VI. xxxi

[Æ]fter þæm þe Romeburg getimbred wæs m wintra 7 xci, feng Constantius to þæm onwalde mid his ii broþrum, Constantine 7 Constante, 7 he Constantius hit hæfde xxiiii wintra. Hie wurdon ealle þa gebroþor on þæm Ar[i]aniscan gedwolan. Constantinus 7 Constans wunnon him betweonum oþ Constan[tinu]s wearð 25 ofslagen. Æfter þæm Magnentius ofslog Constans 7 feng him to þæm rice, þæt wæs Galliam 7 Italiam. On þæm dagum Ilirice

1–9] OH VII. xxviii. 16–20.   10–12] OH VII. xxviii. 23–5.   13–20] OH VII. xxviii. 26–31.   21–4] OH VII. xxix. 1 and 3.   24–p. 150, 13] OH VII. xxix. 5–17.

3 brycge] byrig *both MSS*.   het] hæt C.   4 Tharsa] tharra C. 5 Lucinius] *from* C, lucinus L.   10 mæssepresbyter] mæssepreost C. 11 timan] teonan C.   hund] hundred C.   12 amansumianne] *from* C, amansumiam L.   17 Crecum] grecum C.   Constantinopolim] *from* C, constantipolim L.   18 bebead] het C.   19 diofolgieldhus] deofulgyldhus C, diofolgield L.   20 Nicomedio] nicomedia C.   21 Æfter] *from* C, fter L.   getimbred] *from* C, gebtimbred L.   22 Constantius] constantinus C.   23 Constantius] constantinus C.   xxiiii] xxiii C. 24 Arianiscan] *from* C, araniscan L.   25 Constantinus] constans *both MSS*.

gesetton Ueteromonem þone mon to hiora anwealde, to þon þæt hie
siþþan mehten winnan wið Magnentiuse, 7 hi hiene nieddon to
leornunga, þeh he gewintred wære. Ac Constantius hiene benæmde
ægþer ge þæs onwaldes, ge þære purpuran þe he werede, ge þære
5 scole þe he on leornode. Æfter he gefeaht wið Magnentiuse 7
hiene gefliemde 7 bedraf into Luchina þære byrig, 7 he hiene selfne
siþþan ofsticode. Æfter þæm Constantius gesette Iulianus to casere
under him, se wæs ær þæm to diacone gehalgod, 7 sende hiene on
Gallie mid firde, 7 he hrædlice oferwon ealle þe þa on Gallie wun-
10 non 7 wæs æfter þære dædæ swa up ahæfen þæt he wolde ealne
Romana onwald him geagnian, 7 mid firde wæs farende þær
Constantius wæs mid oþerre fierde wiþ Parhte. þa he þæt geacsade
7 him ongeanweard wæs, þa he gefor on þæm færelte, 7 Iulianus
feng to þæm onwalde 7 hiene hæfde an gear 7 eahta monað. þa
15 wæs he sona geornfull þæt he wolde diegellice þone cristendom
onwendan, 7 forbead openlice þæt mon nane fæste boc ne leornode,
7 sæde eac þæt nan cristen mon ne moste habban nænne his
sunderfolgeþa, 7 hie mid þæm þohte beswican. Ac ealle hie wæron
19 þæs wordes, swa we hit [eft] secgan hierdon, cwæð Orosius, þæt
f. 84ᵛ him leofre wæs se cristendom | to beganne þonne his scira to
habbanne.

Æfter þæm he gegaderade fierd 7 wolde faran on Perse 7 bebead,
þonne he eft wære eastane hamweard, þæt mon hæfde anfiteatrum
geworht æt Hierusalem, þæt he mehte Godes þeowas on don, þæt
25 hie dior þærinne abite. Ac God gewræc on þæm færelte swiþe
gedafenlice on þæm arleasan men his arlease geþoht, mid þæm
þæt hiene gemette an mon, þa he for from Actesifonte þære
byrig, gelicost þæm þe he fliema wære, 7 him sæde þæt he hiene
mehte lædan þurh þæt westen, þæt he on Perse on ungearwe
30 become. Ac þa he hiene tomiddes þæs westennes hæfde gelædd,
þa geswac he him þæt nan mon nyste þæs færeltes hwær he com,
ac foran hwærfigiende geond þæt westen, þæt he nyste hwær he

13–21] OH VII. xxx. 1–3.   22–p. 151, 2] OH VII. xxx. 4–6.

---

3 Constantius] constantinus *both MSS.*   5 Æfter] æfter þam C.
6 Luchina] lucthina C.   7 Constantius] constantinus *both MSS.*
9 Gallie (1)] galliæ C.   þe þa] þa þe C.   12 Constantius] *from* C,
constantinus L.   Parhte] parthe C.   13 he gefor] gefor he C.   18 sunder-
folgeþa] underfolgoþa C.   19 eft] *from* C, *om.* L.   hierdon] gehyrdon C.
25 abite] abitan C.   32 hwærfigiende] hwearfiende C.

ut sceolde, oþ þæs folces wæs fela forworden, ægþer ge for þurste
ge for hæte. þa com him ongean an uncuð mon 7 ofstong Iulianus.

VI. xxxii

[Æ]fter þæm þe Romeburg getimbred wæs m wintra 7 i hund 7
xvii, feng Iuuinianus to Romana onwalde. Hiene mon geceas on
þæm westenne, þy ilcan dæge þe mon Iulianus ofstong. He ge- 5
sealde Persum Nissibi þa burg 7 healfe Mesopotamiam þæt lond,
wiþ þæm þe hie of þæm londe mosten buton laþe. On þæm eahto-
þan monþe þæs þe he to þæm onwalde feng, he wolde faran on
Ilirice. þa wæs he sume niht an anum nicealtan huse. þa het he
betan þærinne micel fyr, for þon hit wæs ceald weder. þa ongon 10
se cealc mid ungemete stincan; þa wearþ Iuuini[an]us mid þæm
bræþe ofsmorod.

VI. xxxiii

[Æ]fter þæm þe Romeburg getimbred wæs m wintra 7 xcviii,
feng Ualentinianus to Romana onwalde 7 hiene hæfde endlefan 14
gear. He wæs ær þæm Iulianuses cempena ealdormon. | He him f. 85
bebead þæt he forlete þone his cristendom oððe his folgað. þa wæs
him leofre þæt he forlete his folgað þonne þone cristendom, ac him
gefylste God eft to maran are, þa he þa læssan for his lufan forlet,
7 þæt he þæs ilcan rices ahte geweald þe his wiðerwinna ær ahte.
Raðe þæs he gesealde Ualente his breðer healf his rice, 7 he het 20
ofslean Percopiosus, þe þa ricsian wolde, 7 monege oðre mid him.
Ualens wæs gelæred from anum Arrianiscan biscepe, Eudoxius
wæs haten, ac he hit hæl swiþe fæste wið his broðor, for þon he
wiste þæt he hit on him wrecan wolde, gif he anfunde þæt he on
oþran geleafan wære, on oþran he self wæs, for þon he wiste hu 25
fæstmod he wæs ær on his geleafan, þa he læssan onwald hæfde.
On þæm ilcan geare Godenric, Gotena cyning, gedyde fela

3–12] OH VII. xxxi. 1–3.   13–26] OH VII. xxxii. 1–7.   27–p. 152, 7]
OH VII. xxxii. 9–14.

---

2 ge] ge eac C.   hæte] hungre C.   ofstong] ofsloh C.   3 Æfter]
from C, fter L.   7 þe] þæt C.   hie . . . mosten] hi mostan of þam
lande C.   9 nicealtan] niwcilctan C.   11 Iuuinianus] iuuinius
both MSS.   13 Æfter] *from* C, fter L.   18 gefylste] *from* C, gefylsted
L.   lufan] lufe C.   22 Arrianiscan] arrianisco C.   Eudoxius] eudoxus
C.

martyra on his þeode cristenra monna. On þæm dagum Ualentinianus geniedde eft þa Seaxan to hiera agnum lande, þa hie woldon
winnan on Romane; þa wæron eardfæste neh þæm garsecge. 7
Burgendum he gestierde eac þæt hie on Gallie ne wunnon; mid
5 þæm him wæs swiþost gestiered þæt him mon gehet fulwiht. On
þæm enleftan geare his rices Sermende hergedon on Pannoniam;
þa he þiderweard wæs mid fierde, þa gefor he on blodryne.

VI. xxxiiii

[Æ]fter þæm þe Romeburg getimbred wæs m wintra 7 an hund
7 xxviiii, feng Ualens, Ualenti[ni]anuses broþor, to Romana
10 onwalde, 7 Gratianus, Ualenti[ni]anuses sunu, feng to Italia
anwalde 7 to Gallia 7 to Ispania under Ualense. He þa Ualens
o[ð]ewde openlice þæt he ær diegellice gehyd hæfde, swa þæt he
bebead þæt munecas, þe woroldlica þing forgan sculon 7 wæpna
gefeoht, þæt hie wæpena namen 7 mid þæm fuhte 7 yfel dyde mid
15 oþrum monnum, 7 sende on Egypte 7 het toweorpan eal þa
munuclif þe his broðor ær gestaþelade, 7 sume þa munecas he het
ofslean, sume on elþiede fordrifan.

On þæm dagum Firmus wæs haten sum mon on Africum, se
wæs þær wilniende þæs onwaldes. þa sende Ualens þider Theodo-
20 sius his ealdormon [mid fierde, þæs godan Theodosiuses fæder]
f. 85ᵛ þe eft wæs casere. On þæm færelte | Firmus wearð gefangen 7 forþ
gelæded to sleanne. þa bæd he self þæt hiene mon ær gefulwade,
7 þa he gefulwad wæs, he wæs þurh þæs mæssepreostes lare þe
hiene fulwade on swa fullum geleafan heofonrices, þæt he cwæð
25 to ðæm folce, 'Doð nu swa ge willen', 7 him self leat forþ þæt him
mon aslog þæt heafod of 7 wearð Cristes martyre.

On ðæm dagum Gratianus gefeaht on Gallium wið Alomonne
þæm folce 7 heora fela m ofslog. On þæm ðriddan geare his rices,

---

8–17] OH VII. xxxii. 15, xxxiii. 1–4.   18–26] OH VII. xxxiii. 5–7.
27–p. 153, 17] OH VII. xxxiii. 8–15 and 19.

---

3 on] wið C.   Romane] romana C.   4 Burgendum] burhgendum C.
4–5 mid þæm] mid þam þe C.   6 Sermende] sermenne C.   8 Æfter]
from C, fter L.   9 Ualentinianuses] ualentianuses L, ualerianuses C.
10 Ualentinianuses] *from* C, ualentianuses L.   12 oðewde] oðywde C,
odewde L.   13 sculon] sceoldan C.   15 Egypte] ægypte C.
18 Africum] affricum C.   19–20 Theodosius] þeodosius C.   20 mid . . .
fæder] *from* C (fyrde), *om.* L.   21 wearð] wæs C.   26 martyre] martir C.
27 Alomonne] alamanne C.

þa he þæt mæste woh dyde wið þa Godes þeowas, þa adrifon hine
Gotan ut of hiora earde 7 hie foran siþþan ofer Donua þa ea on
Ualenses rice, 7 wilnedon to him þæt hie mosten on his rice mid
friðe gesittan. þa oferho[go]de he þæt he him aðer dyde, oþþe
wiernde, oþþe tigþade, ac hie let sittan þær þær hie woldon. Ac his 5
gerefan 7 his ealdormen nieddon hi æfter gafole 7 micel geflit
hæfdon ymb þæt, oþ þa Gotan hie mid gefeohte gefliemdon. þa
Ualens þæt 'ge'acsade on Antiochia þære byrig, þa wearð he swiþe
sarig 7 geþohte his misdæda, hu hi hiene bædon ryhtes geleafan 7
fulwihtes bæðes, 7 he him sende Arrianisce biscepas to lareowum 10
7 gedwolmen, swa he self wæs, 7 hwæt he hæfde Godes þeowum on
oftsiþas to laðe gedon; het þeh sendon æfter, þær he ænigne
libbendne wiste, þeh he þæt to late dyde, 7 him siþþan het gearian.

On þæm feorþan geare his rices he gefeaht wiþ Gotan 7 gefliemed wearð 7 bedrifen on anne tun, 7 þær wearð on anum huse 15
forbærned. þær wæs swiþe ryht dom geendad þæt hie þone woroldlice forbærndon þe hie þohte bærnan on ecnesse.

VI. xxxv

[Æ]fter þæm þe Romeburg getimbred wæs m wintra 7 c 7 xxxiii,
feng Gratianus to Romana onwalde 7 hiene hæfde vi ger, 7 gesette
Theodosius him 'to' fultume, for þon him geþuhte þæt þa þeoda 20
þe hiora wiðerwinnan wæron wæren to swiðe gestrongade þæt hie
mon leng ne mehte mid gefeohtum oferswiþan. Ac Theodosius
genam friþ wið hie 7 on þære sibbe he lædde Athanaricus hiora
cyning mid him to Constantinopolim | þære byrig, 7 þær raðe þæs his f. 86
lif geendade. Raðe þæs þe Gotan angeaton hu god Theodosius 25
wæs, ægþer ge hie, ge ealle þa þeoda þc on Sciþþium wæron,
gecuron his frið.

On þæm dagum gecuron Brettanie Maximianus him to casere
ofer his willan. Se wære wierðe ealra Romana onwaldes for his
monigfealdum duguðum, buton þæt he þa wiþ his hlaford won 30

18–22] OH VII. xxxiv. 1–2.   22–7] OH VII. xxxiv. 6–7.   28–p. 154, 3]
OH VII. xxxiv. 9–10.

1 hine] i alt. from u L.   4 oferhogode] from C, oferhode L.   10 Arria-
nisce] arrienisce C.   12 ænigne] ænne C.   13 libbendne wiste] wiste
libbendne, marked for transposition L, libbendene wiste C.   to late] late C.
14 gefeaht] feaht C.   15 þær] om. C.   18 Æfter] from C, fter L.
wintra] from C, wiñt L.   21 wiðerwinnan] winnan C.   26 þa] om. C.
28 Brettanie] bryttannie C.   29 onwaldes] anwealda C.

for oðra monna lare, 7 raðe þæs for on Gallie 7 Gratianus ofslog, 7
Ualentinianus his broðor he adraf ut of Italiam, þæt he oðfleah to
Theodosiuse.

VI. xxxvi

[Æ]fter þæm þe Romeburg getimbred wæs m wintra 7 c 7
5 xxxviii, feng Theodosius to Romana onwalde 7 hiene hæfde xi ger.
He hæfde vi gearum ær onwald ofer þa eastdælas. He þa Theodosius
wæs þencende hu he Gratianus his hlaford gewrecan mehte 7 eac
his broðor on þæm onwalde gebringan, 7 fird gelædde on Italie,
þær Maximus mid firde bad æt Aquilegia þære byrig 7 his ealdor-
10 men Andregatia hæfde beboden þa clusan to healdanne. Ac se
ealdormon hie betæhte lyþrum monnum to healdonne 7 þ[o]hte
him self on scipun to farenne east ymbutan 7 þonne bestelan on
Theodosius hindan. Ac mid þæm þe he from þære clusan afaren
wæs wiþ þara scipa, þa com Theodosius þærto 7 funde þæræt
15 f'e'awa men, þa wæron yfele 7 earge, 7 he hie ra[ð]e [aweg]
aþewde 7 þa clusan tobræc 7 siþþan for ofer þa muntas, oþ he
com to Aquilegia 7 Maximus ofslog. þa þæt se ealdormon hierde,
þa adrencte he hiene selfne. Hu ieðelice God geendade þæt micle
gewin mid hiora twegea fielle, þ[e] Maximus 7 his ealdormon
20 hæfdon up ahæfen mid monigum þeodum!

Æfter þæm feng eft Ualentinianus to his rice, 7 þæs ymb ii ger,
þa he on Gallie com, hiene ofsmorode Ambogestes his ealdormon
7 hiene siþþan mid rapum be þæm sweoran up aheng, gelicost
24 þæm þe he hiene self unwitende hæfde awierged, 7 gesette Euge-
f. 86ᵛ nius to þæm rices noman, þæt he casere wære, | 7 feng him self to
þæm onwalde, for þon þe he ne mehte self habban þæs onwaldes
noman, for þy he [n]æs Romanisc, ac lærde þone oþerne þæt he
diofolgield georne beeode. þa gelædde Theodosius eft fird wið him
twæm to þære ilcan clusan þe he ær hæfde wið Maximus. þa sende
30 Theodosius Gotene fultum beforan him, þæt hie þa clusan tobræcon, ac hie wurdon utan ymbfaren of þæm muntum 7 ealle ofslagen:

4–20] OH VII. xxxv. 1–8.   21–p. 155, 12] OH VII. xxxv. 10–23.

---

1 for (2)] he for C.   on] in C.   4 Æfter] from C, fter L.   8 Italie]
italia C.   9 bad] abad C.   11 þohte] from C, þuhte L.   13 þæm]
þæm þæt, with þæt er. L.   15 raðe] from C, rade L.   aweg] from C, om.
L.   17 hierde] gehyrde C.   19 þe] from C, þa L.   22 Gallie]
gallium C.   Ambogestes] ambogæstes C.   25 þæm] þæs C.   26 þon
þe] þam C.   27 næs] from C, wæs L.   28 Theodosius eft fird] eft
Theodosius fyrde C.   30 Gotene] gotena C.

þæt wæron x m. þa for Theodosius þiderweard 7 wiste þæt hiene
mon wolde mid þæm ilcan wrence beþridian. þa hie togædereweard foran, þa þohton Eugenius 7 Arbogestes þæt hie sceoldon
ærest of þam muntum hie 'ge'bigan mid hiora flana gescotum, ac
him onsende God swelcne wind ongean þæt hie ne mehton from 5
him nænne flan asceotan, ac ælc com oþer þara, oþþe on hie selfe,
oþþe on þa eorþan, 7 Theodosius hæfde þone wind mid him þæt
his fultum mehte mæstra ælcne heora flana on hiora feondum
afæstnian. þær wearð Eugenius ofslagen, 7 Arbogastes ofstang
hiene selfne. Æfter þæm Theodosius for on Italie. þa he com to 10
Mægelan þære byrig, þa geendade he his lif 7 betahte his twæm
sunum þone onwald.

VI. xxxvii

[Æ]fter þæm þe Romeburg getimbred wæs m wintra 7 c 7 xlix,
feng Archadius to anwalde to þæm eastdæle 7 hine hæfde xii ger, 7
Onorius to þæm wæstdæle 7 nugiet hæfð, cwæð Orosius, 7 for 15
þæm þe hie geonge wæron, he hie beta'h'te his twæm ealdormonnum to bewitanne: Archadius wæs betaht Rufinuse 7 Onorius
wæs betaht Stilecan. Ac hie gecyðdon raðe þæs hwelce hlafordhyldo hi þohton to gecyþanne on hiora ealdhlafordes bearnum,
gif hi hit þurhteon mehten: Rufinus wolde habban him self þone 20
a'n'wold þær east, 7 Stileca wolde sellan his suna þisne her west, 7
for þæm feondscipe he forlet Gotan on Italie mid hiora twam
ciningum, Alrican 7 Rædgotan, 7 þohte, siþþan þæt folc oferfunden
wære, | þæt hie siþþan wolde eall þæt he wold[e], 7 wende eac f. 87
þæt he þæm Gotan þæs gewinnes mehte raðe gestieran, for þon 25
he of hiora lande geboren wæs. Raðe þæs Alrica wearð cristen, 7
Rædgota hæþen þu[rhw]unade 7 dæghwamlice wæs blotende
diofolgildum mid monslihtum, 7 simle him wæs leofast þæt þa
wæron Romanisce.

13–15] OH VII. xxxvi. 1.   16–p. 156, 10] OH VII. xxxvii, *esp.* 1–2, 4–10,
13–15, and xxxviii. 1–2.

4–6 ac . . . asceotan] *om.* C.   9 Arbogastes] arbogæstes C.   10 Italie]
italiæ C.   11 Mægelan] mægelange C.   13 Æfter] *from* C, fter L.
15 Onorius] honorius C.   17 Onorius] honorius C.   19 gecyþanne]
cyðonne C.   22 Italie] italiæ C.   24 wolde (2)] *from* C, wold L.
25 þon]þam C.   27 þurhwunade] þu unade, *with hole in MS* L, þuruh-
wunode C.   28 monslihtum] *most of letter* o *missing* L.

Nugiet eow Romane mæg gescomian, cwæð Oros'i'us, þæt ge
swa heanlic geþoht sceoldon on eow geniman for anes monnes ege
7 for anes mo'n'nes geblote, þæt ge sædon þæt þa hæðnan tida
wæron beteran þonne þa cristnan, 7 eac þæt eow selfum wære
5 betere þæt ge eower[ne] cristendom forleten 7 to þæm hæðeniscan
þeawum fenge þe eowre ieldran ær beeodon. Ge magon eac
geþencan hu hean he eft wearþ his geblota 7 his diofolgilda þe he
on gelifde, þa þa ge hiene gebundenne hæfdon 7 hiene siþþan
atugon swa swa ge woldon 7 ealne his fultum. Þæt wæs, swa swa
10 ge selfe sædon, ii c m, swa eower nan ne wearð gewundod.

VI. xxxviii

Æfter þæm þe Romeburg getimbred wæs m wintra 7 c [7] iiii
7 siextegum, God gedyde his miltsunge on Romanum, þa þa he
hiora misdæda wrecan let, þæt hit þeh dyde Alrica se cristena
cyning 7 se mildesta, 7 he mid swa lytle niþe abræc Romeburg
15 þæt he bebead þæt mon nænne mon ne sloge, 7 eac þæt man nanuht
ne wanade ne ne yfelade þæs þe on þæm ciricum wære, 7 sona
þæs on þæm þriddan dæge hie aforan ut of þære byrig hiora
agnum willan, swa þær ne wearð nan hus hiora willum forbærned.

Þær genom Hettulf, Alrican mæg, Onorius swostor þæs cyninges
20 7 siþþan wið hine geþingade 7 hi him to wife nam. Siþþan sæton
þa Gotan þær on lande, sume be þæs caseres willan, sume his
unwillan; sume hi foron on Ispanie 7 þær gesæton, sume on
Affrice.

11–23] OH VII. xxxviii–xliii, *esp.* xliii. 1 and 11.

---

5 eowerne] *from* C, eower L.   8 gelifde] lyfde C.   11 wintra] *from*
C, wiñt L. 7 (2)] *from* C, *added in l.h.* L.   13 cristena] cristenesta C.
14 lytle] lytlum C.   17 aforan] geforan C.   19 Onorius] honoriuses C.
20 nam] genam C.   22 Ispanie] ispaniæ C.

COMMENTARY

1/2. For a discussion of the chapter headings and their relationship to the text, see Introduction, pp. xxxvii–xxxix and lxxxi–lxxxiii.

1/13. In the corresponding section of the text, 24/29–25/13, the flood is described as being greatest in *Thasalia, Creca byrig*.

2/5. For *þe*, 'because', see J. van Dam, *The Causal Clause and Causal Prepositions in Early Old English Prose* (Groningen, 1957), p. 73.

6/8. VIII[I]. The chapter heading for Bk. V. viii is omitted from all three lists.

8/11–13. *ealne . . . hateð*. OH I. ii. 1 'orbem totius terrae, oceani limbo circumsaeptum'. Cf. *The Poetical Dialogues of Solomon and Saturn*, ed. Robert J. Menner (New York, 1941), Appendix: The Prose Dialogue, p. 170, 'seo line ðe wile xxxiiitigum siða ealle eorðan ymbehwyrft utan ymblicggan'. For the persistence in the early Middle Ages of the classical view of the world as a disk or sphere, with the portion inhabited by men completely encircled by ocean, see Isidore, *Etymologies* XIV. ii. 1 and Wright (1965), pp. 53–4. For the term *garsecg* see *Exodus*, ed. Lucas l. 490, note.

8/13. *hie*. MS C reads *hu hie*, suggesting the proximity at some stage in transmission of a chapter heading.

8/14–15. *sume . . . Europe*. OH I. ii. 1 explains that Africa and Europe were grouped by these authorities as one continent.

8/16–17. *suþan 7 norþan 7 eastan*. OH I. ii. 2 *tribus partibus*.

8/17–18. *ealne . . . behæfð*. A clumsy rendering of OH I. ii. 2 'per totam transuersi plagam orientis extenditur'.

8/18–22. *þonne . . . licgeað*. In this rewriting of OH I. ii. 3 'haec occasum uersus a dextra sui sub axe septentrionis incipientem contingit Europam, a sinistra autem Africam dimittit, sub Aegypto uero et Syria mare nostrum quod Magnum generaliter dicimus habet', the translator may have been influenced by a map or commentary. Cf. Mela I. ii. 9, 'Dein cum iam in suum finem aliarumque terrarum confinia devenit media nostris aequoribus excipitur, reliqua altero cornu pergit ad Nilum altero ad Tanain'; also Remigius, *in Capellam*, VI. 304. 6, 'Per maria: id est in Meroe intrat Nilus ad terraneum mare, inde per Danaum ad septentrionem', and Introduction, pp. lxiii ff.

8/19. *Asia 7 Europe hiera landgemircu*. For later instances of the construction noun + dependent 3rd person possessive, see Mustanoja (1960), p. 160. Mustanoja's example from Ælfric, *Enac his*, is, however, better taken as a Latin genitive *Enachis*: see BT Suppl. *he*.

8/21. *Wendelsæs*. Or.'s *Wendelsæ* corresponds in extent to the *mare*

Nostrum (or *mare Magnum*) of writers such as Mela and Isidore, who define it as stretching from the Straits of Gibraltar not merely to the Aegean, as in OH, but on through the Black Sea to the Sea of Azov: see Mela I. i. 7 and Isidore, *Etymologies* XIII. xvi.

8/21. *wiþ westan Alexandria*. Or.'s addition. See 9/11 and Commentary, also Isidore, *Etymologies* XV. i. 34 and Mela I. ix. 60.

8/21–2. *Asia . . . licgeað*. For the inclusion of Egypt in Asia see 9/11–13, Commentary, 11/1–3, and Wright (1965), p. 298.

8/23–5. For a discussion of the terms *Riffeng* and *Sarmondisc* see Introduction, p. lxv, n. 3. The *Sarmondisc garsecg*, OH I. ii. 4 *Sarmatico oceano*, has been variously identified with the White Sea and the East Baltic (see Hübener (1925–6), p. 41 and Malone (1930b) pp. 151 and 154). It is also associated with the *Cwensæ*. See, however, 12/21–2, Commentary.

9/1. *suðryhte*. Or.'s addition. For the classical tradition that the Tanais flowed *a septentrione ad meridiem* see, e.g., Mela I. i. 8 and *De Situ Orbis* 41, 8–9. This course is shown on some *mappae mundi*, including the possibly tenth-century Cotton map.

9/1. *on westhealfe Alexandres herga*. OH I. ii. 5 merely describes the river as 'praeteriens aras ac terminos Alexandri Magni'. That the altars were in Asia is information found both in late medieval *mappae mundi* and in Latin texts: see e.g. Capella VI. 692 and 694, *De Situ Orbis* 78, 13–14 and 80, 3–4, and Solinus 180, 17 and 184, 15–16.

9/1–2. *On in Rochouasco*. I retain the reading *on* of the manuscripts as a variant of *ond* (see Introduction, p. xlix), though a rare form *onin* 'within' cannot be ruled out: see BM Stowe 2, Psalm 38. 4 *onin*, other psalters *binnan* or *on*. The interpretation *on* 'and', supported by the punctuation of MS L, requires us to suppose that the translator construed OH I. ii. 5 *sitos* with *Maeotidas paludes*, either disregarding its masc. inflexion or having in his Latin exemplar the incorrect reading *sitas*. See e.g. Zangemeister's MS R *situs*, altered to *sitas*, and Introduction, p. lx.

9/2. *þæt fen*. OH I. ii. 5 *paludes*. The Maeotis Palus was a *lacus* or inland sea; see e.g. Pliny IV. xii. 78, Mela I. ii. 14, Remigius, *in Capellam* VI. 304. 4. In Jordanes, col. 1268, however, *palus* is given its alternative meaning of 'swamp', as here, and hunters are said to cross on foot 'paludem Mæotidem, quam imperviam ut pelagus existimabant'.

9/4. *wið eastan*. OH I. ii. 5 *late*. The mouth of the Palus was considered by classical writers to be in the centre of the northern curve of the Pontus Euxinus: see e.g. Pliny IV. xii. 76. However, according to Priscian, *Periegesis*, 138–9, 'Panditur hinc Ponti pelagus Titanis ad ortus;/Quod petit obliquo boream solemque meatu', while on the Cotton map the Tanais is depicted as flowing into an (unnamed) *mare Magnum*, which at this point turns sharp east. The name *Meotides Paludes* is written on its northern shore. For another interpretation—that *wið eastan* relates to *Theodosia*—see Malone (1930b), p. 140. Knowledge that Theodosia was in Europe and thus had the sea to its east could have been derived from a number of Latin texts, e.g. Pliny IV. xii. 87 and Mela II. i. 3.

9/5. *be eastan.* OH I. ii. 6 *iuxta.* Cf. 18/4–5, where *se sæ Proponditis* is said to be *wyð eastan Constantinopolim.*

9/6. *þonne . . . Wendelsæ.* A mechanical rendering of OH I. ii. 6 'eas mare . . . Nostrum accipiat'. See 8/21, Commentary.

9/6–10. *Se westsupende . . . Scotland.* OH I. ii. 7 'Europae in Hispania occidentalis oceanus termino est, maxime ubi apud Gades insulas Herculis columnae uisuntur et Tyrrheni maris faucibus oceani aestus inmittitur.' The translator appears to have construed OH *occidentalis* with *Hispania* instead of with *oceanus*, perhaps influenced by the spacing of his exemplar: see the 'related' manuscript, Vienna 366, where *oceanus* begins a new paragraph. That the Strait of Gibraltar is the south-west point of Europe is easily deducible from OH; for Ireland as west of Europe see e.g. the Ravenna Geographer, 9, 13–17, 'Scotorum insula . . . quae et Ybernia conscribitur. nam iam ultra illam, ut ad occidentalem dicamus plagam, nullo modo ab hominibus terra invenitur.' However, a translator working in England could be drawing on his personal experience for this particular piece of information. See further below, 19/15–17. For parallel adjustments to OH's account of the western boundary of Africa, see below, 9/13–17 and Commentary. For *westsupende* and related terms see Derolez (1971), pp. 261–2.

9/8. *þæm iglande þætte Gaðes hatte.* OH I. ii. 7 *Gades insulas.* For a singular *Gades insula* see Mela II. vii. 97, Isidore, *Etymologies* XIV. vi. 7, *De Situ Orbis* 8, 12, and the version of OH in the *Cosmographia*, p. 91.

9/10. *hire.* i.e. of Europe. See Malone (1930b), p. 140. Bosworth's belief that the translator has 'fallen into the error of the time' of considering Ireland to be on the west of Spain (1855, p. 30, n. 7) is itself erroneous, requiring fem. *hire* to have as its antecedent masc. *se Wendelsæ.* Equally incorrect, at least without emendation, is the equation of *hire* with the plural *syla* by Labuda (1961), p. 91, n. 12.

9/10. *Scotland.* i.e. Ireland. Cf. *Iralande,* 16/7 and Commentary.

9/11–13. *Affrica . . . supgarsecg.* OH I. ii. 8–9, though stating that Africa begins with the land of Egypt and city of Alexandria (cf. 9/11–12), puts the actual boundary at Paraetonium and goes on to describe it as leading through Catabathmon and over Lake Chalearzum, then near the lands of the Upper Avasitae and across *Aethiopica deserta* to the Ocean. Or.'s account may be based on an identification of Lake Chalearzum with the 'vast lake' said to swallow up the Nile, OH I. ii. 30, Or. 11/8. Alternatively, the translator may have been influenced by a map showing the supposed course of the Nile, or by the knowledge that the Nile was believed to form the boundary between Egypt and Africa. See e.g. Mela I. i. 8, Solinus 40, 1 and Bede, *De Natura Rerum,* col. 276.

9/13–17. *þære Affrica . . . Fortunatus.* OH I. ii. 10–11 'termini Africae ad occidentem idem sunt qui et Europae, id est fauces Gaditani freti. ultimus autem finis eius est mons Athlans et insulae quas Fortunatas uocant.' Cf. Mela III. x. 101, where Atlas is described as situated in the middle of the west coast of Africa.

The Fortunate Islands, said by Isidore, *Etymologies* XIV. vi. 8, to be *occiduo proximae*, served as datum point for the western prime meridian (see Wright (1965), p. 334). For parallel adjustments in the description of Europe, see 9/6–10 and Commentary.

9/16–17. *þæm iglande* ... *Fortunatus*. OH I. ii. 11 'insulae quas Fortunatas uocant'. The use of singular for plural here may be an error; cf., however, the single *Furtunatus insula* of the early twelfth-century London Beatus map (reproduced by Miller, *Mappaemundi*, II, Tafel VII), the *Fortunatae insula* of MS A of Julius Honorius, p. 46, and the two islands, 'una Beata, et alia quae dicitur Fortunata', of Jordanes, col. 1251.

9/20. *mid hiera wætrum*. Or.'s addition.

9/21–8. A rearrangement of OH I. ii. 13–14, 'Asia ad mediam frontem orientis habet in oceano Eoo ostia fluminis Gangis, a sinistra promunturium Caligardamana, cui subiacet ad Eurum insula Taprobane, ex qua oceanus Indicus uocari incipit; a dextra habet Imaui montis—ubi Caucasus deficit—promunturium Samarae, cui ad aquilonem subiacent ostia fluminis Ottorogorrae, ex quo oceanus Sericus appellatur', with OH *a sinistra* and *a dextra* replaced by the geographically more precise *be suþan* and *be norþan*, and with OH's three oceans, *Eous*, *Indicus* and *Sericus*, reduced to two, *Indisc* and *Sericus*. Or. apparently takes OH *ex qua* to refer to the mouth of the Ganges. For the equation *Eous : Indicus* cf. Remigius, *in Capellam* VI. 303. 1, 'ab eoo mari: id est Indico'. Or.'s use of *port* for OH *promunturium* is hard to explain except in terms of manuscript corruption: cf. 20/19, where *promunturia* is rendered *beorgas*.

9/27. *be norþan*. OH I. ii. 14 *ad aquilonem*. Although OH uses *aquilo* in the sense of 'north-east', Latin texts frequently employ the word loosely as an alternative to *septentrio* (see e.g. Remigius, *in Capellam* VIII. 440. 11, 'Aquilonis igitur: id est septentrionis') and it is as 'north' that *aquilo* is regularly translated in Or. See further Derolez (1971), pp. 257–8 and 260–3, and Bately (1972), p. 52.

9/29–31. *þæt sint* ... *be eastan*. OH I. ii. 15 'In his finibus India est, quae habet ab occidente flumen Indum, quod Rubrum mari accipitur, a septentrione montem Caucasum; reliqua ... Eoo et Indico oceano terminatur.' Cf. Mela III. vii. 61, where *oceanus Eous* is said to be on the east of India, *oceanus Indicus* on the south. The translator, again equating *Eous* with *Indicus* (see above, 9/21–8, Commentary) is probably basing his assumption that *mare Rubrum* is the southern boundary of India on OH's statement that the Indus flows into this sea: see Malone (1930b) p. 163. However, some medieval maps depict the *mare Rubrum* as extending east as far as Taprobane.

10/1–2. *þa flowað* ... *Sæ*. Possibly deduced from OH I. ii. 15 and 18, Or. 10/7. However, a secondary source cannot be ruled out: see e.g. Mela III. viii. 76 and Julius Honorius, p. 30.

10/4. *þeh þe gewrito . . . Asiria.* OH I. ii. 19 'quamuis Scripturae Sanctae uniuersam saepe Mediam uocent'. For Assyrian supremacy over this area, see 21/26–8.

10/7. *se Reada Sæ.* OH I. ii. 18 'mare Rubrum et sinum Persicum'. For *sinus Persicus* and *sinus Arabicus* as part of *mare Rubrum*, see e.g. Isidore, *Etymologies* XIII. xvii. 4 and Bede, *De Natura Rerum*, col. 262.

10/8. *Nu.* OH I. ii. 19 'sed generaliter Parthia dicitur.' The name Parthia continued to be used in Latin texts and *mappae mundi* in the medieval period. However, by the ninth century, the area between Tigris and Indus was under the domination of Islam and the greater part of Persia was divided into the provinces of Media or Persian Iraq, Khurasan, Seistan, Khuzistan, and Fars.

10/10. *west.* Or.'s addition.

10/12. *binnan . . . ðeoda.* OH I. ii. 22 'in his sunt gentes xxviii.' OH's *his*, however, includes Arabia Eudaemon, which Or. treats separately.

10/13. *hiera suþgemæro.* Or.'s addition. Cf. Dicuil II. 6, 'Mesopotamia, Babillonia, Chaldea finiuntur . . . a meridie mari Persico.' For the equation *sinus Persicus : mare Rubrum* see 10/7, Commentary.

10/14–15. *þæs dæles . . . scyt.* OH I. ii. 21 'Arabia Eudaemon . . . inter sinum Persicum et Arabicum angusto terrae tractu orientem uersus extenditur.' The translator may here be following Bede, *De Natura Rerum*, PL xc, col. 262, where it is said that *sinus Persicus aquilonem petit*, while *sinus Arabicus* lies (as in OH) in the general direction of *mare Rubrum* up to that point. For the rendering of *aquilo* by 'north' in Or., see above, 9/27, Commentary; for the identification of *sinus Persicus* and *sinus Arabicus* with *mare Rubrum*, see 10/7, Commentary.

10/15. *þæt land . . . Eudomane.* OH I. ii. 21 *Arabia Eudaemon.* The Sabaei were the inhabitants of the greater part of Arabia Eudaemon: see Mela III. viii. 79, Isidore, *Etymologies* IX. ii. 14, Servius, *Aen.* I. 416, etc. Labuda (1961), p. 91, n. 27, suggests that the translator may have taken the interpolated name from a map. However, a gloss *Ubi Sabaei*, or *Sabei* is an equally possible source. See Introduction, pp. lxv f.

10/16–17. *norþ . . . Armenie.* OH I. ii. 23 'a septentrione id est a ciuitate Dagusa, quae in confinio Cappadociae et Armeniae sita est haud procul a loco ubi Euphrates nascitur'. Cf. OH I. ii. 38, where we are told that the Euphrates rises in the Parcohatras range of Armenia and 'Taurum excludit ad dextram' (cf. also I. ii. 37). For the siting of Taurus north of Syria see 10/21 and Commentary.

10/18–20. *monege þeoda . . . Sarracene.* OH I. ii. 24 'maximas prouincias Commagenam Phoeniciam et Palaestinam, absque Saracenis et Nabathaeis'. The translator appears to have overlooked or misunderstood the word *absque*, if that was indeed the reading of the Latin manuscript he used. The Nabathaei and Saraceni belonged not to Syria but to Arabia, as did the Moabitae, Ammonitae, and Idumaei (see e.g. Isidore, *Etymologies* XIV. iii. 26 and the *Liber Nominum Locorum*, col. 1297); however, the mid-twelfth-century Jerome map, reproduced in Miller, *Mappaemundi* II, Tafel 12, has an entry *Idumea regio Sirie*. For Coele, Damascene, and Judaea as provinces of Syria see Mela I. xi. 62 and Remigius, *in Capellam* VI. 337. 14 and 15. See further Bately (1972), p. 50.

10/21–2. *be norþan . . . Capodocia 7 Armenie*. OH I. ii. 25 'In capite Syriae Cappadocia est, quae habet ab oriente Armeniam . . . a meridie Taurum montem.' For the interpretation of *in capite* as *be norþan* see *Liber Nominum Locorum*, col. 1299, where *in capite Syriae* is explained as *ad septentrionem*. Armenia is said to have Taurus on its south by Dicuil I. 19, and by *Dimensuratio, Divisio*, and the Agrippa fragment, in *Geographi Latini*, §§ 6, 18, and 30.

10/24. *seo læsse Asia*. OH I. ii. 25 *Asiam*. Cf. OH I. ii. 26 'Asia regio, uel, ut proprie dicam, Asia minor'.

10/24. *be norþan*. OH I. ii. 25 *ab aquilone*. See 9/27, Commentary. OH puts *mare Cimmericum* as well as *Themiscyrios campos* in this position.

10/25–6. *betux Capodocia . . . Issaurio*. OH I. ii. 25 'Cappadocia . . . habet . . . a meridie Taurum montem, cui subiacet Cilicia et Isauria (*var*. Issauria) usque ad Cilicium sinum.' Cilicia and Isauria both formed part of Asia Minor (see Isidore, *Etymologies* XIV. iii. 38), Cilicia bordering on Syria to the east and on Cappadocia and Lycaonia to the north, while Isauria lay between Pisidia and Cilicia. The translator may have been puzzled by *cui subiacet* and supposed it to have *Cappadocia* as its antecedent. However, an inaccurate map source cannot be ruled out. See the eleventh-century St. Sever Beatus map (Miller, *Mappaemundi*, I), where Isauria and Cilicia (as represented by Tarsus) are sited between Asia Minor and *Capadocia*, one to the north and the other to the south. For the suggestion of a 'genuine, though indirectly expressed, displacement of the term of direction 45° clockwise' see Malone (1930b), p. 164 and Introduction, p. lxiv.

10/27–9. *On norþhealfe . . . be suþan*. OH I. ii. 26 'a septentrione Ponto Euxino, ab occasu Propontide atque Hellesponto, ad meridiem mari Nostro'. For the normal extent of the *Wendelsæ* in Or., including Euxine, Propontis, and Hellespont, see 8/21, Commentary.

10/30. *se hehsta beorg Olimpus*. OH I. ii. 26 *mons Olympus*. The translator appears to be confusing the Mysian with the European Olympus. References to the great height of the latter are numerous in Latin texts: see e.g. Isidore, *Etymologies* XIV. iv. 13 and viii. 9, Remigius, *in Capellam* VI. 285. 12. According to the Latin and Old English *Wonders of the East*, however, the world's highest mountain is indeed in Asia, between Media and Armenia. See *Three OE Prose Texts*, pp. 64 and 105.

11/1–2. *Seo Ægyptus . . . þæt land*. OH I. ii. 27 'Aegyptus inferior ab oriente habet Syriam Palaestinam . . . a septentrione mare Nostrum.' In his revision the translator seems to have been influenced by a combination of OH I. ii. 23–4 (Or. 10/16–20), where Syria, including Palestine, is said to have Egypt on its south, and a statement such as the 'Aegyptus inferior. Finitur ab oriente Scenitarum Arabia Trogodytice' of Dicuil

IV. 1 and *Divisio*, § 20. For the identification of Scenitae Arabes with the Saracens see Ammianus Marcellinus, XXII. xv. 2.

11/3. *Climax*. OH I. ii. 27 'Climax, et Aegyptum superiorem fluuiumque Nilum'. By omitting the reference to the Nile here, Or. loses the smooth transition between this and the following section of OH.

11/3–20. *Nilus seo ea . . . Ægypta lande.* A rearrangement of OH I. ii. 28–33, which first traces the course of the Nile from its supposed source near the Red Sea to Egypt (Or. 11/3–4 and 11/14–19) and then gives the alternative possible source and the river's subsequent course (Or. 11/4–8, 9–11, 8–9, 12–14). The directions which Or. adds (11/5 *westende*, 11/6 *east*, 11/10 *eastdæle*, 11/13 *norþ*) are all deducible from OH.

11/4. *clife*. OH I. ii. 28 *litore* 'shore'. Cf. *The OE Prudentius glosses at Boulogne-sur-Mer*, ed. H. D. Meritt (Stanford, 1959), p. 92, *litora* : *næssun*.

11/8. *micelne sæ*. OH I. ii. 30 *uastissimo lacu*. See also 11/12 and cf. 20/6–7 *þone sealtan mere*, OH *lacum Salinarum*.

11/8–9. *þær hio ærest . . . Dara.* A misunderstanding of OH I. ii. 31 'quem utique prope fontem barbari Dara nominant, ceteri uero accolae Nuhul uocant'.

11/10. *he*. The expected pronoun is *heo* or *hio*, as in the Cotton manuscript, referring to *seo ea*. If not a scribal error, the masculine form may be due to the influence of the Latin *fluvius* or the immediately preceding *þæm sæ*.

11/11. *þær mon . . . eastdæl*. Or.'s addition. The Gihon, one of the four rivers of Paradise, is frequently identified with the Nile in Latin writings: see e.g. Bede, *De Temporum Ratione*, col. 526. Or.'s restriction of the name to one small section of the Nile could be due to the use of a map by either the translator or his (hypothetical) commentary source; however, the Gihon is linked with Aethiopia in a number of texts: see e.g. Isidore, *Etymologies* XIII. xxi. 7, 'Geon . . . uniuersam Aethiopiam cingens' and Vulgate, Genesis 2: 13, 'Geon: ipse est qui circumit omnem terram Aethiopiae.'

11/17. *ut on þone Wendelsæ.* Cf. OH I. ii. 27 'Aegyptus inferior . . . habet . . . a septentrione mare Nostrum'; also OH i. ii. 8.

11/17–20. *þonne . . . Ægypta lande*. OH I. ii. 28 'tempestiuis auctus incrementis plana Aegypti rigat.' Latin texts normally give more than one possible cause of the Nile floods, which they describe as occurring in summer (see e.g. Mela I. ix. 53 and Bede, *De Natura Rerum*, col. 262). The translator, however, appears to be using a source such as Isidore, *Etymologies* XIII. xxi. 7, 'Aquilonis flatibus repercussus aquis retro-luctantibus intumescit et inundationem Aegypti facit', where only one cause is mentioned and the time of year not specified. It seems likely that Or.'s reference to winter in this connection is due to an association of the wind *aquilo* with that season: cf. Servius, *Aen.* IV. 310, 'Mediis Aquilonibus: media hieme, ut per Aquilones "hiemem" significet'; also

Gl. Ansileubi ME 102. *Aquilo* is generally used of the north wind in Latin texts.

11/20–3. *Seo fyrre Ægyptus . . . nearre Ægyptus*. OH I. ii. 34 'Aegyptus superior in orientem per longum extenditur. cui est a septentrione sinus Arabicus, a meridie oceanus. nam ab occasu ex inferiore Aegypto incipit, ad orientem Rubro mari terminatur.' Sweet's punctuation puts the ocean on both east and south of *Aegyptus superior*; however, 11/21–2 *on easthealfe* is best explained as due to a careless midstream switch of construction by the translator. To correspond with OH the passage should have read 'Seo fyrre Ægyptus liþ east ondlong þæs Readan Sæs on suþhealfe, 7 se Reada Sæ liþ eac on easthealfe.' For the identification of *sinus Arabicus* with *mare Rubrum* see 10/7, Commentary.

11/27. *þa þe be norþan India sindon*. See above, 9/29.

11/27–12/1. *hie onginnað . . . Cilium þæt lond*. A greatly modified and simplified version of OH I. ii. 36–46, omissions including all references to mountains not part of the east–west range Caucasus–Parcohatras–Taurus. Although this could be based solely upon OH, the translator may have been influenced in his selection by a map depicting such a chain, or by a text describing it. See e.g. Mela I. xv. 81, 'Taurus ipse ab Eois litoribus exsurgens vaste satis attollitur, dein dextro latere ad septentrionem, sinistro ad meridiem versus it in occidentem rectus et perpetuo iugo', and Wright (1965), p. 270, and p. 465, nn. 78 and 81.

12/1. *oþ Cilium þæt lond*. Or.'s addition; cf. *De Situ Orbis* 72, 3–4, 'Cilicia, qua incipit mons Taurus'; also Solinus 38, 13. For the variant *Cilium* see *Cosmographia*, p. 93, MS L *Cilium sinum*, and forms in manuscripts of OH such as *Cili\`ci'a, Cili\`ci'um*.

12/2. *oþ . . . middangeardes*. OH I. ii. 47 *ad promunturium Boreum*.

12/5–6. *þa ealdan Sciþþian*. OH I. ii. 47 *Scytharum gentes*. Or.'s modification seems to have originated in an attempt to distinguish between these Scythians, living east of the Caspians, and another group living west of the Caspians (see 12/7–10). It may well be based on descriptions of the eastern group as *gens antiquissima* (see Isidore, *Etymologies* IX. ii. 62), or on allusions to *antiqua Scythia* (see the Ravenna Geographer 30, 9). Less likely is the possibility that Or.'s usage was prompted by the knowledge that the Amazons' menfolk had been driven out of their original homeland (see OH I. xv). We may compare the use in OE of the term *Ealdseaxan* for the continental Saxons.

12/6. *xliii*. OH I. ii. 47 *xlii*, 'related' manuscripts including Vienna 366 *xliii*.

12/6–7. *wide . . . londes*. OH I. ii. 47 'propter terrarum infecundam diffusionem late oberrantes'.

12/9. *suþ . . . Tauros*. OH I. ii. 49 'per litus Cimmerici maris quod est ab Africo, usque ad caput et portas Caucasi quae sunt ad meridiem'. For the inclusion of the Cimmerian Bosphorus in *mare Magnum* see Mela I. i. 7, and Capella VI. 662. The substitution of Taurus for Caucasus, if not a running 'correction' due to failure to understand OH's geography here, could be based on OH I. ii. 37, where we are told that some people consider the Caucasus to be part of the Taurian range, or derived from a secondary source such as Isidore, *Etymologies* XIV. viii. 3, 'Mons Taurus a plerisque idem vocatur et Caucasus.' The section of Caucasus referred to by OH is one of those that do not conform to the east–west pattern and which are not mentioned in the translation of OH I. ii. 36–46.

12/10. *Sciþþia lond*. Or.'s addition, OH I. ii. 50 merely assigning this area to Albani and Amazons. That the Amazons were of Scythian stock the translator would know from OH I. xv; that the Albani too were Scythians, and that Scythia extended to Sarmatia and the Tanais he could have learned from a number of sources including Mela III. v. 36 and 39 and Isidore, *Etymologies* XIV. iii. 31.

12/10–11. *on twa 7 on þritig þeoda*. OH I. ii. 49 *xxxiiii*; 'related' manuscripts, including Ricc. 627, *xxxii*.

12/11. *on easthealfe Danais*. OH I. ii. 50 *regio proxima*, the area nearest to Europe and the Tanais. OH's *regio ulterior*, the land of the Amazons, is not referred to by Or., perhaps because it was felt to be synonymous with the *Sciþþia lond* of 12/10.

12/12–13. *we ... Liubene*. Or.'s addition. In spite of the use of the word 'we', the authenticity of the name *Liubene* is doubtful. It is hard to believe that the Anglo-Saxons of the late ninth century were familiar enough with the inhabitants of the Roman province of Albania—an Asiatic country bordering on the Caspian Sea, mod. *Dagestan* in the U.S.S.R.— to have a name for them other than the Latin one, though Scandinavians appear to have visited this remote area. It is more likely that the name arose as a result either of textual corruption (see the reading *Libani* for *Albani* of *Cosmographia*, p. 95, MS L) or of wrong identification (note the placing of the Albani (equated with the Wizzi) in the Baltic area by Adam of Bremen, col. 635), and the existence as suitable candidates in that area of the *Livi* or Livonians, for whom see *Saxonis Gesta Danorum*, ed. J. Olrik and H. Ræder (Copenhagen, 1931), VIII. iv. 1.

12/17–23. A rewriting of OH I. ii. 52–3. Or. retains the boundaries named by OH, but instead of assigning the area to fifty-four peoples and the three nations Alania, Dacia, and Germania, it merely says that it contains many peoples and is all called Germania. For the extension of Germania to the Rhipaean mountains see Capella VI. 665 and Isidore, *Etymologies* XIV. viii. 8.

12/17–19. *seo wilð ... Bryttania hætt*. Or.'s addition. That the Rhine had its source in the Alps could have been known to the translator either from accounts by traders and other travellers or from Latin texts: see e.g. Isidore, *Etymologies* XIII. xxi. 30, Mela III. ii. 24, Dicuil VI. 48 and—remarkably close in wording to Or.—the description in the twelfth-century *De Imagine Mundi*, PL clxxii, col. 129, 'Rhenus ab Alpibus nascitur et contra aquilonem vergens, sinu Oceani excipitur.' For Or.'s use of 'north' to translate *aquilo* see 9/27, Commentary.

12/20. *þære æwielme . . . ie.* Or.'s addition. Although this detail could have been well known by report, written sources cannot be ruled out. Cf. Priscian, *Periegesis* 288, 'Hunc (viz. the Rhine) prope consurgit fons Histri flumine longo', and the thirteenth-century Ebsdorf Map inscription (Miller, *Mappaemundi*, V), 'mons a quo Danubio oritur, parum distat ab illo a quo Renus oritur.'

12/21. *wið norþan Creca lond.* Cf. OH I. ii. 54 and 55. For *Creca lond,* the European part of the Byzantine Empire, see 18/3–13 and Commentary. For Germanic peoples living south of the Danube see 12/25–6.

12/21. *þone Wendelsæ.* OH I. ii. 52 *Ponto.* For the inclusion of Pontus Euxinus in *mare Magnum* see 8/21, Commentary, and Isidore, *Etymologies* XIII. xvi. 7.

12/21–2. *norþ . . . Cwensæ hæt.* OH I. ii. 52 'per litus septentrionalis oceani', i.e. the extreme northern limit of the *oikoumene,* the known land mass. The *Cwensæ* has been variously identified with the White Sea, as the furthest point of Ohthere's exploration (see Hampson (1859), pp. 16–17), with the Gulf of Bothnia, which was supposed to form part of the Sarmatian Ocean and on the shores of which *Cwenas* appear to have lived (see e.g. Malone (1930b), pp. 151 and 154, and Ekblom (1941–2), p. 130, n. 1), with the Arctic (see K. Grotenfelt, 'Über die alten kvänen und Kvänland', *Annales Academiae Scientiarum Fennicae* B. I (Helsinki, 1909), i, p. 3, and J. Svennung, 'Belt und Baltisch', *Uppsala Universitets Årsskrift,* 1953:4 (Uppsala–Wiesbaden, 1953), p. 23), and with some sea or other by which the *Cwenas* lived and which was imagined by the translator to connect the *Ostsæ,* or Baltic, with the Sarmatian Ocean, the actual configurations of Gulf of Bothnia and White Sea being completely unknown to him (see Labuda (1961), p. 92, n. 50). However, Ohthere refers not to *Cwenas* but to *Finnas, Terfinnas,* and *Beormas* in the neighbourhood of the White Sea, while his report suggests complete ignorance of the Arctic. Moreover, although identification of *Cwenas* with the Gulf of Bothnia depends on the assumption that the author of Or. supposed the Baltic to be connected with the Ocean at both ends, Ohthere at least seems to have known that it connected with the Ocean only at one end (see 16/12). I would therefore propose a fifth identification: that *Cwensæ* is a (known or unknown) stretch of water forming the northernmost boundary of *Germania* and taking its name from the people living, or believed to live, in that area, the *Cwenas.* For *Cwenas* living north of the Swedes, in the extreme north of Scandinavia, see 13/26 and Commentary. For the inclusion in *Germania* of races other than those known today as Germanic, see Einhard, *Life of Charlemagne,* ch. xv. Whether *Cwensæ* was a name current in the ninth century, or whether it was invented for the occasion, is a matter for conjecture.

12/23. At this point, OH's account of northern Europe comes to an end. Or., however, continues with a detailed survey, for which no written sources have been discovered and which seems to describe the area as it was known in the second half of the ninth century. This section, extending from 12/24 to 18/2, has been the subject of a great deal of discussion, of which only the most important features can be repeated here. Articles and books referred to are not necessarily the first to make the point quoted, but are the most easily accessible or the most comprehensive. For detailed surveys of Eastern European material see Labuda (1961) and Havlík (1964), the former including an invaluable bibliography.

12/24. *be eastan Rine*. See above, 12/17. The Rhine was the traditional boundary between Germania and Gaul and is still described as such in ninth-century texts, although at that time there were Franks settled west of the river who were considered to be of the East Franks; see Ekblom (1941–2), p. 127.

12/25. *Eastfrancan*. The inhabitants of Franconia, which, after the Treaty of Verdun in 843, formed the most important part of Austrasia, or *Orientalis Francia*; see further East (1950, repr. 1962) p. 158.

12/25. *Swæfas*. The inhabitants of the country known as *Swabia* or *Alamannia*, which in the ninth century formed part of the East Frankish kingdom, under the governance of the counts of Raetia. Swabia is generally assumed to have extended north as well as south of the Danube; however, Einhard, *Life of Charlemagne*, ch. xv, implies that the Danube formed its boundary: 'pars Germaniae quae, inter Saxoniam et Danubium Rhenumque ac Salam fluuium qui Thuringos et Sorabos diuidit posita, a Francis qui orientales dicuntur incolitur et praeter haec Alamanni atque Baioarii'. See further East (1950, repr. 1962), p. 158.

12/26. *be suþan him 7 be eastan*. Probably to be interpreted as 'to their (i.e. the East Franks') south-east'; see Derolez (1971), p. 263.

12/26–7. *Bægware . . . hætt*. Bavaria, which was assigned to Louis the German, king of the East Franks, in 817, was divided naturally into two parts by the Danube, which turns course at Regensburg. See further below, 13/4, and East (1950, repr. 1962), p. 158. Labuda (1961), p. 14, finds the allusion to Regensburg significant, suggesting that the translator's informant may have come from that area; we may compare J. A. Endres, *Honorius Augustodunensis* (Kempten–Munich, 1906), section 12, where the reference in the *De Imagine Mundi* I. xxiii to 'Noricus quae et Bauaria, in qua est ciuitas Ratispona' (Ratisbon being another name for Regensburg) is similarly taken to indicate that the author of this work was a native of Regensburg, or at least knew Germany! Regensburg, however, was a city of great importance, being not only a trading centre and a seat of a bishop, but also the capital of the East Frankish kings Louis the German and Arnulf.

12/27. *Bæme*. Cf. the variant *Behemas*, 13/3–4, and see Introduction, p. lxx. The Bohemians lived in the vicinity of Prague: see R. Turek, 'Kmenová území v Čechách', *Časopis Národního Musea*, cxxi (1952), 30. Conquered by Charlemagne, they seem to have remained nominally under Frankish authority for most of the ninth century. However, there is evidence that some time after 880 the Bohemian Duke Bořivoj recognized the political suzerainty of the Moravian Svatopluk and it was not until 895 that the Bohemian princes again became vassals of the Franks under Arnulf. See Dvornik (1949), p. 21.

12/28. *þyringas*. It is possible that MS L *þyringa*, like *Maroara* (13/3 and 10) retains an original OHG nom. pl. a-stem ending, corresponding to OE *-as* (Old Saxon *-os*, beside *-as* and *-a*): cf. the OHG gloss *Turingii*: *duringa*, Steinmeyer and Sievers III. 131. In the ninth century, Thuringia formed part of the East Frankish kingdom; for its location, see East (1950, repr. 1962), p. 147.

12/28. *Ealdseaxan*. The *Saxones* of continental Latin chroniclers, the *Antiqui Saxones* of Bede and Asser. Saxonia, first brought under Frankish rule by Charlemagne, fell to Louis the German, king of the East Franks, under the treaties of Verdun and Mersen. See further East (1950, repr. 1962), pp. 146–7.

12/29. *Frisan*. In the ninth century Frisia appears to have stretched from the mouth of the Scheldt to the Weser (see P. C. J. A. Boeles, *Friesland, tot de elfde eeuw* (The Hague, 2nd ed., 1951), p. 592). Between it and Franconia lay Lotharingian and Saxon territory. The Treaty of Mersen shared the country between Charles the Bald and Louis the German, the latter getting the coastal area. However, part of Frisia was under Danish control right up to 885.

12/29–30. *Be westan Ealdseaxum . . . Frisland*. Ekblom (1941–2), p. 127, explains the reference to Frisians and Elbe mouth lying in the same direction as due to the translator having in mind not the centre of the Frisians but 'the easternmost Frisian area round present-day Cuxhaven, near the Elbe estuary' (see, however, Boeles, *Friesland*, p. 592). The direction 'west' he takes to be Old Scandinavian, the actual direction being rather north-west. However, it is surely possible to interpret Or.'s *be westan* as referring to a range of west (cf. 13/3–4), in which case it is not incorrect to envisage *Saxonia* as having on its western borders first Frisia (west) then the mouth of the Elbe (north-west). See further Derolez (1971), p. 259, and Introduction, p. lxvi, n. 5.

12/30. *westnorð*. The Jutland peninsula is north rather than north-west of the geographical centre of Saxonia. However, Danish territory touched Saxonia only on the north-west part of the latter's northern borders; see 13/18–19, Commentary. What is more, to the traveller along the important trade route from Lüneburg via Lübeck to the West Jutland coast the peninsula would indeed be north-west. See further Introduction, p. lxvii.

12/31. *Ongle*. Cf. 16/14 *Angle*. Bede, *HE* I. xv, describes *Angulus*, the homeland of the Angles, as situated 'inter prouincias Iutarum et Saxonum' in the south of the Jutland peninsula.

12/31. *Sillende*. See also below, 16/11. Not Zealand, as suggested by Bosworth (1855), p. 35, n. 10, but the *Sinlendi* of *Einhardi Annales*, s.a. 815, where the Franks are said to advance 'trans Aegidoram fluuium in terram Nordmannorum uocabulo Sinlendi' and then camp 'in litore oceani'. Of the various etymologies put forward for this name, the most convincing is that which interprets it as 'the great land', i.e. the mainland,

ON *Sílende: see further Ekblom, (1940) pp. 177–90. Ekblom would limit its application to the eastern coastal district of south Jutland, from the narrowest part of the Little Belt to the Flensburg Fjord or to the Schlei, on the grounds that the western coast cannot have been so designated, since the dangerous waters of the western part were 'little known to voyagers from the Cattegat and Baltic'. However, if the name *Sinlendi* in fact originated in the mouths of seafarers, these need not have been travelling from Cattegat to Baltic: see 'Völker und Stämme Südostschleswigs im frühen Mittelalter', *Gottorfer Schriften zur Landeskunde Schleswig-Holsteins*, I, ed. S. Gutenbrunner, H. Jankuhn, W. Laur (Schleswig, 1952), p. 151, 'Sinlendi ist "Grossland, continens terra", im Gegensatz zu Inseln; der Begriff deutet darauf hin, dass dieser Landesname für das Gebiet von Schleswig von Seefahrern stammt, welche die Haithabu-Route befuhren: wo sie keine Durchfahrt fanden, sondern die Landenge überwinden mussten, war für sie die "kontinentale Strecke".' The Hedeby-route seems to have followed the line Eider–Treene–Schlei (see H. Jankuhn, 'Der fränkisch-friesische Handel zur Ostsee im frühen Mittelalter', *Vierteljahrschrift für Sozial- und Wirtschaftsgeschichte*, xl (1953), n. 115). Labuda (1961), p. 105, n. 121, on the other hand, restricts *Sillende* to the area north of the Schlei, on the grounds that Or. treats it as distinct from the land of the Angles. However, according to the author's practice elsewhere in this section (cf. 13/8–9, 13/12–13, and 13/21–2), *Ongle, Sillende*, and Danes should be not north one of the other in the order given, but all north of the centre, Saxonia. Since ninth-century Latin sources put the Danish border fixed by Charlemagne at the Eider River (a boundary apparently maintained until 934) and since Or. itself subsequently refers to the South Danes as having the Saxons to their south (13/18–19) and to Hedeby as situated *betuh Winedum 7 Seaxum 7 Angle* but belonging to the Danes (16/14–15, q.v.), it seems reasonable to suppose that the Eider was the boundary of both Danish territory and (as implied by *Einhardi Annales*, quoted above) *Sillende*. Perhaps the information on which Or.'s statement is based was that northwest of the Saxons was part of the Danish state, that that part was called *Sillende*, and that in it was situated *Angulus*, the homeland of the Angles.

12/31. *sumne dæl Dene*. Although the reading of MS C *Dena* suggests that MS L *Dene* is gpl. (see Introduction, p. xlvi), apl. cannot be ruled out: cf. 48/5 *sumum dæle his fultume* (both manuscripts). Raith's emendation of *sumne* to *sum* is not necessary, since the accusative form may be explained as obj. of *hæt*. For possible restriction of these Danes to Jutland see Raith (1958), p. 67; see, however, the comment on Sillende above.

12/31–13/1. *be norþan . . . Afdrede*. Ekblom (1941–2), p. 131, restricts the *Afdrede* (the *Abodriti* of continental writers) to Mecklenburg, with their geographical centre the district round Wismar and Schwerin, and sees here an example of OScand. orientation, the 'true' direction being northeast; for Havlík (1964), p. 74, the 'true' direction is east. However, the Bavarian Geographer, 2, 1 f., refers to one group of Abodriti as neighbours of the Danes ('isti sunt, qui propinquiores resident finibus Danaorum,

quos uocant Nortabtrezi') and in the ninth century the name seems to
have been used for a complex of tribes including Vagrians and Polabians,
stretching from the Danish border along the Baltic Sea and the Elbe to
the lower Oder (roughly modern Schleswig-Holstein and Mecklenburg).
See Dvornik (1949), p. 14, idem (1956), p. 295, and Wolfgang Fritze,
'Probleme der abodritischen Stammes- und Reichsverfassung', in H.
Ludat, *Siedlung und Verfassung der Slawen zwischen Elbe, Saale und Oder*
(Giessen, 1960), pp. 141–227. The traveller on the great road from
Lüneburg (see above, 12/30, Commentary) would have this area not on
his north-east but on his north.

13/1. *eastnorþ* . . . *Hæfeldan hætt*. The *Hæfeldan*—the *Hehfeldi* of the
Bavarian Geographer—held the Havel valley, their principal town being
Brandenburg and their geographical centre, according to Ekblom (1941–2),
p. 131, being round present-day Nauen. They were, therefore, not north-
east but east of the Saxons: Havlík (1964), p. 75, would even describe
them as south-east. However, the Wilti, of whom they are said to be part,
lived in an area extending between the mouths of the Oder and Warnow
rivers and the middle Elbe (see Dvornik (1956), p. 295) and this larger
group could certainly be described as north-east of the Saxons. It is
possible that the apparent deviation is due to a reference in Or.'s source
to the Wilte as living generally north-east of the Saxons and the subsequent naming of the *Hæfeldan* as the tribe of the *Wilte* nearest to the
Saxon borders. For the suggestion that the Havolans may have been the
most important of the southern Veleti, see J. Nalepa, 'Wyprawa Franków
na Wieletów', *Slavia Antiqua*, iv (1954), 210–31.

13/1–2. *be eastan* . . . *Sysyle*. The Slavs were known collectively as Wends
to their Germanic neighbours. The *Sysyle* (OHG *Siusili, Siusli* etc.) were
a Sorbian tribe, forming part of a complex of tribes living in the Leipzig
area between Elbe and Saale. Ekblom (1941–2), p. 131, calculating their
geographical centre to be in the district between Delitzsch and Wurzen,
north-east of Leipzig, interprets Or.'s *be eastan* as OScand. east, true
south-east, though he notes that there is a noteworthy deviation from
E 60° S, 'but not so large that the choice of direction is not the readiest'.
Him he takes rightly to refer to the *Ealdseaxe*; see Labuda (1961), p. 94,
n. 63, where it is assumed to refer to the East Franks and the direction
accordingly supposed to be accurate. Certainly, the *Sysyle* appear to have
lived south-east not east of the geographical centre of Saxonia. However,
it is also true to say that they were on the Saxons' eastern borders, while
to a native of, say, Quedlinburg or Halberstadt, the *Sysyle* would live
east, the *Hæfeldan* north-east and the *Afdrede* north. See further Introduction, p. lxvi.

13/2–3. *eastsuþ* . . . *Maroara*. It is not clear whether *ofer* here means 'on
the other side of' or 'throughout': see also 15/35 (with which cf. 13/7
begeondan þæm westenne) and Wülfing, § 777. Moravia proper was a
considerable distance from Saxonia, being centred on the district north
of Brno, with Mikulčice as its political capital. Thus, if *ofer sumdæl*
is interpreted as 'some distance away', then the intervening lands could

be Sorbian territory and Bohemia. However, in the time of Svatopluk, that is, after the peace treaty of 874, when the Moravians threw off Frankish rule, Moravian influence spread over all the lands between the Saale, Elbe, and Bober, with Bohemians as well as the Sorbs of modern Saxony joining the new Slavonic federation (see Dvornik (1956), p. 94, and (1970), map facing p. 234), and it may be Great Moravia, rather than the nucleus of Moravian tribes, that is located south-east of the Saxons. In that case, *ofer sumdæl* could mean 'extending over a considerable area'.

13/3–4. *Maroara . . . healfe.* The Moravians indeed had Bavaria and Bohemia on their western frontier; Thuringia was north-west, but over some considerable distance, with Bohemia and Sorbian territory intervening (see the preceding note). For a similar list in inverse order relating to the East Franks, see 12/26–8 and Introduction, p. lxx.

13/4–5. *be supan . . . Carendre.* Ekblom (1941–2, p. 131), calculating the geographical centre of Carentania to be in the district west of Graz, considers the deviation of 19° from true south to be an 'acceptable' one. Carentania adjoined Great Moravia on the south between the Wienerwald and the confluence of the Mura and Drava rivers. Further west there was no common boundary, the two countries being separated by the Ostmark. In the second half of the ninth century, the Slovene population of this area was ruled by the East Franks.

13/7. *þæm westenne.* See also below, 18/17–18 and Commentary. East of Carentania was the Pannonian Mark, extending between the Wienerwald, the Tisza, the Sava, and the Danube. At the end of the eighth century, this country, which had been overrun by the Avars, was laid waste by Charlemagne, and it is possible that Or.'s use of the term *westen* reflects knowledge of that event, perhaps by way of the memorable allusion in Einhard's *Life of Charlemagne*, ch. xiii: 'Quot proelia in eo gesta, quantum sanguinis effusum sit, testatur uacua omni habitatore Pannonia et locus in quo regia kagani erat ita desertus ut ne uestigium quidem in eo humanae habitationis appareat. Tota in hoc bello Hunorum nobilitas periit, tota gloria decidit.' However, Or.'s source could be contemporary. Svatopluk invaded Pannonia in 883 and devastated a great part of the country. He repeated the invasion in 884 and the *Annales Fuldenses* claim in the entry for that year that 'Pannonia de Hraba flumine ad orientem tota deleta est.' A few years later, in the Chronicle of Regino of Prüm, s.a. 889, we find an allusion to the Hungarians invading 'Pannoniorum et Auarum solitudines'. For the alternative suggestion, that Or.'s source may be classical, the *westen* being the *deserta Boiorum* of Pliny III. xxiv. 146 and *Dimensuratio*, § 12, see Linderski (1964), pp. 437–9. Linderski's argument in this instance seems less convincing than the arguments for a contemporary source.

13/7–8. *Pulgara land.* According to the Ravenna Geographer, p. 185, 'Inter uero Traciam uel Macedoniam et Mysiam inferiorem modo Bulgari habitant.' However, eastern Pannonia fell into the hands of the Bulgarians in the first half of the ninth century, and through the rest of the ninth century and for the whole of the tenth century the kingdom of Bulgaria extended in the north-west as far as Belgrade and Sirmium. See further Dvornik (1970), p. 334, n. 172, Guldesku (1964), pp. 96–8 and below, 18/15, and 61/23, Commentary.

13/8. *be eastan . . . Creca land*. According to Or.'s usual practice, the co-referent of *þæm* is *Pulgare*, not, as Ekblom (1941–2), pp. 131, suggests, *Carendre*. Byzantine territory as a whole was, strictly speaking, south-east and south of Bulgaria. However, Or. subsequently assigns the easternmost part of Bulgaria—ancient Moesia—to *Creca land*, locating the *Pulgare* inland (see 18/8–9 and 18/13–15, Commentary), and according to this distribution of territory the description of *Creca land* as east of Bulgaria is correct.

13/9. *Wisle lond*. The (Upper) Vistula was outside Moravia proper; however, there is evidence to suggest that the Wislans, or Vistulanians, were conquered by the Moravian ruler Svatopluk towards the end of the ninth century: see Dvornik (1970), p. 169. North-east would be a more accurate direction than east for this region, whose people are given the name *Uuislane* by the Bavarian Geographer, 3, 7. However, Havlík (1964), p. 76, observes that the main route from Moravia would have lain east.

13/9. *be eastan . . . Datia*. Ekblom (1941–2), p. 131, taking *þæm* to refer to Moravia (so also Havlík, (1964), p. 77) identifies Dacia with Transylvania and the neighbouring districts, i.e. south-east rather than east. However, according to Or.'s practice, *þæm* should refer to *Wisle lond* and the author may well be following the classical tradition according to which the Vistula formed the western boundary of Dacia. See e.g. Dicuil I. 16, 'Datia et Alania finiuntur ab oriente desertis Sarmatiae, ab occidente flumine Hiustia [*read* Uistla]', Pliny IV. xii. 81, and Linderski (1964), p. 436. For the location of Roman Dacia see East (1950, repr. 1962), pp. 46–7.

13/9–10. *þa þe iu wæron Gotan*. Cf. OH I. ii. 53 'Dacia ubi et Gothia' and the Ravenna Geographer, 202, 13–15, 'Datia . . . quae et Gipidia appellatur, ubi modo Uni qui et Avari inhabitant'. The Goths conquered Dacia in the third century A.D., but their empire was destroyed *c.* 370 by the Huns, who in their turn were conquered by the Avars in the second half of the sixth century. In the ninth century, the area was mainly under Bulgarian domination.

13/10. *Dalamentsan*. Cf. the Chronicle of Thietmar of Merseburg (973–1018), *PL* cxxxix, col. 1185, 'provinciam quam nos teutonice Deleminci vocamus, Sclavi autem Glomaci appellant'. The Daleminci appear to have lived on either side of the Elbe north-west of Dresden, in the Meissen area. Or.'s placing of them north-east of the Moravians raises considerable problems, for which the only solution may be emendation. See Malone (1930b), p. 153, where it is suggested that either 'north-west' should be read for 'north-east' (the generally accepted emendation) or *Maroara* should be altered to *þyringum*—an emendation which Malone admits is 'too drastic to be more than conjectural'.

13/11. *Horigti.* MS C *Horithi*; cf. 13/12 *Horoti,* MS C *Horiti,* the Chorvati or Croats. In the ninth century, in addition to the Croats of Pannonia, Illyricum and Dalmatia, there appear to have been Croats still living north of the Carpathians. One group was settled in Galicia or Little Poland; others seem to have lived in Bohemia, and it is to these that Or.'s *Horiti* are generally supposed to belong: see Malone (1930b), p. 153, Labuda (1961), p. 96, n. 73, and R. Turek, *Časopis Národního Musea,* cxxi, 3–46. On Turek's map, p. 30, east and west *Charvati* are put roughly east and north of Prague, i.e. north-west of Brno, Ekblom's geographical centre of the Moravians. Havlík (1964), p. 79, however, locates the second group of Chorvati in the region of the middle Oder, which, he says, along with the upper Oder region, was considered to be part of the Great Moravian kingdom in the time of Alfred. For recent discussions in English of the complicated problem of White Croatia, see Dvornik (1949), pp. 283–304, and Guldesku (1964), pp. 30–3.

13/12. *Surpe.* Cf. 13/24 *Surfe.* The Sorbs, called *Surbi* by the Bavarian Geographer, 2, 7, were a group of western Slavonic tribes living between Oder and Saale, north of Bohemia. This group included Daleminci and Siusli (treated separately by Or.) and Milčani. It may be the Milčani, the easternmost Sorbian tribe, whose stronghold was Bautzen in the Mark of Lausitz, that are referred to here. According to the *Annales Fuldenses,* the Sorbs submitted to Arnulf, king of the East Franks, on the death of the Moravian ruler Svatopluk.

13/12. *Horoti.* See 13/11, Commentary. Ekblom (1941–2), p. 133 identifies these Chorvati with the main group in Galicia.

13/12–13. *Mægþa land.* Three different interpretations have been proposed for *Mægþa*: (i) gpl. of OE *mægþ,* 'tribe', 'people': see E. Rask, 'Ottárs og Ulfstens korte Rejseberetninger', *Det skandinaviske Litteraturselskabs Skrifter,* xi (Copenhagen, 1815), pp. 85–6, where *Mægþa land* is identified with *Gardariki,* i.e. Russia (though there is no evidence that the latter name was in use in the ninth century, nor does *mægþa* appear the obvious translation of *garda* 'stronghold'); also Malone (1930b), p. 154, where *Mægþa land* 'land of tribes' is more plausibly explained as a title invented by the translator to cover the remainder of OH's fifty-four tribes, 'north' standing for actual 'north-east'. (ii) gpl. of OE *mægþ* 'woman': thus many commentators, from Sprengel, *Geschichte von Grossbritannien* (Halle, 1783), to Labuda (1961), p. 96, n. 75. These, with the exception of Dahlmann (1822), p. 456 (who sees here an alternative to *Cwenland*), equate *Mægþa land* with the Land of Amazons or Land of Women, referred to by Paulus Diaconus and Adam of Bremen: see *Pauli Historia Langobardorum,* i. 15: 'ego referri a quibusdam audiui, usque hodie in intimis Germaniae finibus gentem harum existere feminarum (*sc.* gentem Amazonum)', also Adam of Bremen, col. 634, where it is claimed that the Swedes' rule extends to the land of the Amazons, 'quod nunc terra feminarum dicitur', and id., col. 569, where an eleventh-century Swedish expeditionary force is said to have perished in this land. Tacitus, *Germania* ch. 45, similarly locates a tribe with women as the ruling sex (the *Sithones*) next to the *Suiones*. For a Town of Women, reported by the tenth-century Arab geographer, Ibrahim ibn Yakub, see T. Kowalski, *Relacja Ibrahima ibn Jakuba z podróży do krajów słowiańskich w przekazie al-Bekriego* (Kraków, 1946), p. 50; for the equation *Provincia Amazonum : provincia matronum* see the early twelfth-century Lambert Map, Miller, *Mappaemundi* III, 48 (though here it is sited in Asia). For the theory that Or. is at this point combining information from OH I. ii. 50 and an Orosian map see Labuda (1961), p. 97, n. 75 and Introduction, p. lxv. The only objection that can be raised against the interpretation 'land of women' is that although Or. elsewhere uses *mægþ* in the sense of 'tribe', it never has *mægþ*, 'woman', a sense which is generally restricted to OE poetry; the Amazons it refers to as *wif* or *wifmenn*. However, the translator could here be influenced by his source. (iii) a proper name, declension unknown; possibly a reference to the Magyars (the *Majghari* of Ibn Rusta), who 'seem to have tarried sometime in Wolhynia or thereabouts (where [the translator] locates them), before they decided to enter Pannonia in 896 under Arpad'; so Raith (1958), p. 68, also Mezger (1921), pp. 23–4, and Hübener (1925–6), pp. 39–42 (later retracted, *Speculum*, vi, 432). As Raith admits, the phonology presents some difficulties; however, in view of the frequent corruption of proper names in Or., these difficulties are not insuperable. For knowledge of the Magyars (under the name *Hungari*) in Western Europe in the ninth century, see 110/6–8, Commentary; for the etymology of the name Magyar see Imre Boba, *Nomads, Northmen and Slavs* (The Hague, 1967), p. 75.

Of these three interpretations, the second is the most attractive; however, the fact that it is attractive does not necessarily mean that it is also correct. As for the location of *Mægþa land*, since we know neither the identity of the people involved nor the source—and accuracy—of Or.'s information, speculation is valueless.

13/13. *Sermende*. Cf. 13/24 and 26, where the *Sermende* are put east of Bornholm and of the Swedes, a position which tallies with the placing of Bornholm north of the Sorbs (13/22–4), the Sorbs north of the Daleminci (13/11–12) and the *Horigti* east of the Daleminci (13/10–11). The Sarmatians disappeared from history long before the ninth century; however, their name continued to appear in medieval texts: see e.g. Dicuil VII. 22, where it is reported that according to some authorities the region as far as the Vistula is inhabited by Sarmatae, Venedi, and Sciri. Ekblom (1941–2), p. 133, claims that the Sarmatae were thought of in Alfred's time as living in present-day central Russia in the radius of the sources of the Niemen, Dnieper, and Don, their district being believed to extend to the Baltic and include roughly the then Lithuanian and Latvian tribes; however, it seems more likely that they were thought of merely as living in the extreme north-east of Europe and were made Germania's (north-)eastern neighbours on the strength of classical references such as Mela I. iii *Germani ad Sarmatas porriguntur*. See further Remigius, *in Capellam* VI. 325. 4, *Sarmatae: Sclavi*, and VI. 303. 15, *Sarmatorum id est Guinedorum* [i.e. *Winedorum*].

13/13. *þa beorgas Riffen*. See above, 8/24. In view of the statement of later classical writers that the river Tanais, or Don, rises in the Rhipaean mountains, the latter are often identified with a western branch of the Ural Mountains, though Havlík (1964), p. 81, on the strength of their position on the Cotton Map, would equate them with the Valdayskaya Vozvyshennost' and the Central Russian elevation. However, it seems unlikely that any Western writer in the early Middle Ages would possess geographical knowledge as precise as this. Adam of Bremen, col. 637, indeed describes the highland regions of Sweden as extending up to the Rhipaean mountains, quoting Orosius and Solinus as his authorities! For the possibility of a traditional source for Or.'s reference see Labuda (1960), p. 48 and (1961), p. 98, n. 76, and Introduction, p. lxv.

13/14. *Suþdenum*. Cf. 12/31, 'sumne dæl Dene' and 13/16–17 'Norðdene, ægþer ge on þæm maran landum ge on þæm iglandum'. Or. is generally supposed to be making a distinction between the Danes of the Jutland peninsula on the one hand and 'the Danes of the islands (except Fyn and its small neighbours) and of the Scandinavian mainland' on the other; see Malone (1930b), p. 155, also Ekblom (1941–2), pp. 127 and 134, and Raith (1958), p. 68. However, in such a case, as Raith points out, 'more accurate terms would be South-west and North-east, since *be eastan him* [*Suþdenum*] *and be norþan syndon Norðdene*; moreover, if the usual displacement of the cardinal points is considered, Ælfred's South and North Danes are in reality West and East Danes.' What is more, it is not clear whether the author intends all or merely some of the islands to be considered North Danish—arguments for the latter are based on Ohthere's comments, for which see below, 16/11–20 and Commentary—while, in view of the plural *þæm maran landum*, 13/17, it cannot be assumed that he excludes the possibility of some North Danes living on the Jutland peninsula; see F. P. Magoun, 'Danes, North, South, East and West in *Beowulf*', *Philologica: the Malone Anniversary Studies* (Baltimore, 1949), p. 22 and note. In the latter case, the terms North and South could have arisen as the result of the existence in the Jutland peninsula of two groups of Danes, the most northerly (north-easterly?) being associated with the Danes of the islands and of the Swedish peninsula. On the other hand, if, as is commonly supposed, the spread of the Danes into Jutland was comparatively late and their first expansion was from Zealand and the neighbouring islands north to the Swedish peninsula, or, as tradition would have it, south from the Swedish peninsula into Zealand (see Gwyn Jones (1968), pp. 44 ff., especially 49), then the terms North and South could reflect this earlier state of affairs, their geographical appropriateness having been lost as a result of subsequent expansions and new alignments.

Unfortunately, references to North and South Danes outside the Old English Orosius shed no light on the problem. The only known Scandinavian reference to South Danes—in the tenth-century runic inscription on the Sædinge-stone from Laaland, where Thyre's husband is described as 'the very strongest (?) of the separate Swedes and the South Danes', *sutrsuia auk supr[tana]*—does not make it clear who these South Danes are supposed to be (if they are the men of Laaland, then they ought to be North Danes according to Or.'s grouping), and in any case depends on a suspect reading; see L. Jacobsen, E. Moltke, *Danmarks Runeindskrifter* (Copenhagen, 1941–2), p. 264. References to North, South, East, and West Danes in *Beowulf*, *Widsith*, and the *Rune Poem*, though possibly chosen for their semantic appropriateness as well as their alliteration, do not require us to suppose that the land of the Danes was normally divided up according to the points of the compass; see G. Storms, *Compounded Names of Peoples in Beowulf* (Utrecht–Nijmegen, 1958). On the other hand, there is a considerable body of opinion that Denmark did not become a united kingdom in any acceptable sense of the term till the time of Harald Bluetooth in the second half of the tenth century.

13/15–16. *þæs sæs earm . . . Ostsæ*. This stretch of water is said to be not only north of the South Danes, but also north of the North Danes (13/19–20), north of the Osti (13/21), west of Bornholm (13/22–3), and south of the Swedes (13/24–5), and thus appears to consist of Skagerrak, Kattegat, and Baltic as far as Bornholm and most probably beyond (see 13/22–3, Commentary): i.e. the *mare orientale* or *Balticum* of Adam of Bremen, col. 511 (following Einhard, *Charlemagne*, ch. xii) and the *Eystrasalt* of ON sources. Although attempts have been made to identify the element *ost* with ON *aust* 'east' (see e.g. Geidel (1904), p. 40, Malone, *MLR*, xx (1925), pp. 3–4, Sievers–Brunner, *Altenglische Grammatik* (1965) § 26, n.) or even with the name *Aestii* (see 13/20, Commentary), it is most simply explained as a direct borrowing from OS or OHG *ost* 'east' (see Forster, in Bosworth (1855), p. 38, n. and Raith (1958), p. 69). The main argument levelled against this interpretation—that a designation 'east sea' can only be Norse—is completely unfounded: see *Einhardi Annales*, s.a. 808 *orientali maris sinu quem illi* [sc. the Scandinavians] *Ostarsalt* (var. *Estarsalt*) *dicunt*.

13/16. *be eastan . . . Norðdene*. It is not clear whether Or. is putting the North Danes both north and east of the South Danes or merely north-east. For the first interpretation see Ekblom (1941–2), p. 127, Labuda (1961), p. 99, n. 78; for the second, see Malone (1930b), p. 155 and Ekblom (1941–2), p. 134. Ekblom considers 'north-east' to represent actual 'east'; however, in view of the uncertainty as to the location of the North Danes (see 13/14, Commentary), this must remain conjecture. See further Introduction, pp. lxiii ff.

13/17. *þæm maran landum*. Normally taken to refer to Danish territories on the Swedish peninsula, i.e. in Skåne, central and southern Halland, and western Blekinge; see Ekblom (1941–2), p. 134, Malone (1930b), p. 155 and Raith (1958), p. 69. However, see above, 13/14, Commentary.

13/17. *þæm iglandum*. See 13/14, Commentary and Ekblom (1940), pp. 186 ff.

13/17–18. *be eastan . . . Afdrede*. Ekblom (1941–2), p. 134, interprets *be eastan* as OScand. east. i.e. true south-east; see also Malone (1930b), p. 155. Havlík (1964), p. 74, takes the Afdrede to be true south. However, the direction may be derived from a map showing South Danes as north-west of the Saxons, and the Abodriti as north, or depicting the Jutland peninsula as stretching north-west not north. See further above, 12/30–13/1 and Commentary, and Introduction, p. lxviii.

13/18–19. *be suþan . . . sumdæl.* For justification of *be suþan* as 'normal' south, see Ekblom (1941–2), p. 134 (on the grounds that the Old Saxons referred to are North Albingians, living in the north-west of Saxonia, for which see above, 12/30–1) and Labuda (1961), p. 99, n. 81 (on the grounds that the course of the Elbe from Hamburg to its mouth is south–north).

13/19–20. *Norðdene . . . Ostsæ.* Ekblom (1941–2), p. 134, finds this statement 'decidedly wrong', on the grounds that OScand. north of the North Danes lies the territory of *Finnveden*, the south-western part of the province of Småland. He suggests, (1960, p. 11), that *Norðdene* is an error for *Suðdene*. However, though the Danes of the Swedish peninsula may not have had the sea to the north, the Danes of the islands certainly did so. See Malone (1930b), p. 155, and Raith (1958), p. 69.

13/20. *be eastan . . . Osti þa leode.* A number of commentators have attempted to identify the *Osti* with the Ests of Wulfstan's account, 16/31; see e.g. Labuda (1961), p. 99, n. 83. The variant *o* is explained as due to the borrowing of the name **au(e)-ist-i* 'people who live on the water' by western contacts before contraction to *Aisti* took place. The resulting form **Austi* would give OS, OHG **Osti*. However, even if *Osti* and *Estas* are possible variants of the same name, resulting from two separate borrowings (and against this see below, 16/31, Commentary), and even taking allowing for the use of distorted directions, it seems unlikely that an informed commentator would describe a people living east of the Vistula as east of the North Danes, north of the Hæfeldan, and south of the Wends, Bornholm, and possibly also Sweden (see below, 13/21–2 and 25, Commentary). Much more likely is the theory put forward by S. H. Cross that the author's informant may have had in mind the Wostroze, a Slav tribe of Hither Pomerania, whose *pagus* is described by L. Niederle, *Manuel de l'Antiquité Slave*, I (Paris, 1923), p. 152 as 'entre le cours inférieur de l'Oder, le cours supérieur de la Havola et la Pěna', and by H. Böttger, *Diöcesan- and Gau-Grenzen Norddeutschlands* IV (Halle, 1876), p. 169 ff., as on the left bank of the Oder, in the region of Stettin: see Malone (1933), 67–77, where Cross's theory is coupled with Malone's earlier suggestion of a possible relationship between Osti and Ostrogoths. The identification with the Wostroze is supported by Ekblom (1941), p. 170, who explains the initial *w* as prosthetic, the common Slav form being **Ostrije*, and puts the Wostroze, or Wostze, 'in the area embraced by the Schwinge, the Peene and the Greifswalder Bodden'. However, according to W. Brüske, *Untersuchungen zur Geschichte des Lutizenbundes*, p. 179 and note (quoted by Labuda (1961), p. 99, n. 83), this territory was submerged right up to the end of the twelfth century. The exact location of the Wostroze in the ninth century, though presumably somewhere in the vicinity of the Oder, must therefore be a matter for conjecture. And since the author's location of the North Danes and the contours he attributes to the south coast of the Baltic are equally uncertain, it is futile to speculate on Or.'s use of the direction *be eastan*. There is nothing in the text to justify S. H. Cross's assumption, (1931), p. 298, that *him* may have as its antecedent not *Norðdene* but *Ostsæ*.

13/20–1. *Afrede be supan*. For the Abodriti see 12/31–13/1, Commentary. Ekblom (1941–2), p. 135, sees here an instance of normal orientation.

13/21–2. *Osti . . . Burgendan*. A. Gäters, 'Osti und Ostsee', *Beiträge zur Namenforschung*, v (1954), 245, followed by Labuda (1961), p. 100, n. 85, makes *Winedas 7 Burgendan* part of the subject and thus also of the 'centre' at this point. However, such a word order, if not impossible, seems most unlikely: cf. the 'normal' usage of 13/3–4. There is, moreover, no need to postulate such an order if the Osti are dissociated from the Ests. The *Winedas* of this passage are usually identified with the inhabitants of Rügen, living north-west of the Wostroze, Or.'s 'north' being interpreted as a blanket-term; see Porthan (1800), p. 60, Malone (1930b), pp. 155–6, Ekblom (1941–2), p. 135, and groups of directions such as 12/30–1 and 13/3–4. However, we may have here an original statement that the Osti had the Baltic and Bornholm to their north, modified in the light of the knowledge that the whole south shore of the Baltic as far as the Vistula was inhabited by Wends. See Wulfstan's statement, 16/23 and 29.

13/22. *be supan . . . Hæfeldan*. The possibility that this people is located south not of the Osti but of either *þone ilcan sæs earm* (see Labuda (1961), p. 100, n. 87) or the Wends and Bornholmers (see Cross (1931), p. 298) seems to be ruled out by the use of *him* not *þæm* in the text.

13/22–3. *Burgendan . . . be westan him*. It has been assumed from this that the *Ostsæ* was believed to end at Bornholm; see Ekblom (1941–2), p. 134 and (1960), p. 11. However, there is ample evidence of sea being mentioned only when there is no nearby land to help in localization: cf., e.g., the accounts of the positions of North and South Danes, 13/14–21, and of Corsica, 21/17–19.

13/23. *Sweon*. For the probable extent of Swedish territory at this time— east of the Keel and excluding Halland and Skåne—see Foote and Wilson (1970), p. 25.

13/24. *be eastan him sint Sermende*. See 13/13 and Commentary and 13/24–6. Bornholm has mod. Lithuania to its east, while Sweden has Latvia, Estonia, and Finland in this position, in each case with the Baltic intervening.

13/24. *Surfe*. Malone (1930b), pp. 153 and 156, distinguishes between the *Surfe* of this passage and the *Surpe* of 13/12, whom he identifies with the Sorbs of Germany proper and the Sorbs of Lusatia respectively. However, the latter can quite properly be described as south of Bornholm. See 13/12, Commentary. The variation in form is most simply explained as scribal, due to confusion of *f* and *þ* in Anglo-Saxon minuscule. The *b* of *Sorabi*, *Surbi* (see Glossary of Proper Names) would be fricative in OS and the more northern OHG dialects.

13/25. *þone sæs earm Osti*. Some commentators have argued from this that the old name of the Baltic may have meant not 'the eastern sea' but rather 'the sea of the Osti': see e.g. Porthan (1800), p. 61, Malone (1930b), pp. 156–7, and Labuda (1961), p. 101, n. 90. However, there are weighty arguments in favour of the interpretation of *Ostsæ* as 'eastern sea'; see above, 13/15–16, Commentary. *þone sæs earm Osti* in that case could be an error for (i) *þone sæs earm 7 Osti*; see Ekblom (1941), p. 164; (ii) *þone sæs earm Ostsæ*, with confusion between the forms *Ostsæ* and *Osti*; (iii) *þone sæs earm Ostsæ 7 Osti*; or (the explanation that I prefer) (iv) *þone sæs earm*, with *Osti* subsequently erroneously added. Cf. 13/21, *þone ilcan sæs earm* and 13/23, *þone sæs earm*.

13/26. *be norþan . . . Cwenland*. Cf. Ohthere's account of Norway, 15/31–4. The *Cwenas*, Old West Norse *Kvenir*, are generally identified with the Kainulaiset of present-day Finnish, i.e. a northern Suomi-Finnish tribe that appears to have been widespread over both north Norway and north Sweden in the ninth century. See e.g. A. S. C. Ross (1954), p. 338. Both Malone (1930b) p. 157, and Ekblom (1941–2), p. 135, restricting the *Cwenas* to the inmost part of the Gulf of Bothnia and the region north and north-east of it, see the true direction here as roughly north-east. For a discussion of the implications of this and other possible 'shifted' directions connected with the Scandinavian peninsula, see Introduction, p. xliv. For the ambiguity of *ofer* here, see above, 13/2–3, Commentary.

13/27. *be westannorþan . . . Scridefinne*. Cf. Ohthere's account of Norway, 14/1–3, where *Finnas* are said to live north of the Norwegians, also 15/24–5, where they are located in the *moras* that lie *wið eastan 7 wið uppon, emnlange þæm bynum lande*. The *Scridefinne* (MS C *-finnas*; cf. *Meþe, Meþas* etc.) are generally supposed to have lived in Finnmark, i.e. north not north-west of Sweden; see e.g. Malone (1930b), p. 157. Adam of Bremen, col. 641, however, puts them north-east of Sweden, while scholion 132 adds that Halsingaland, the land of the Scritefingi, is situated in the midst of the Rhipaean mountains!

13/27–8. *be westan Norþmenn*. Ekblom (1941–2), p. 136, and Raith (1958), p. 69, interpret *be westan* as OScand. west, i.e. north-west, on the ground that at this time *Norðmen* was the term used for the Teutonic settlers of the Arctic and Atlantic coast, those east and south-east of the mountains being called *Austrmen*. Cf., however, 16/8–9, where Ohthere seems to be applying the term to south-east Norway too. Ohthere is also quoted as putting *Norðmanna land* west of Sweden; see 15/31–3. See further Introduction, pp. lxxxvii f.

13/29. *his hlaforde*. The precise significance of the term *hlaford* in this context is uncertain. Some commentators assume that Ohthere must have entered Alfred's service, possibly as an exile, like the 'Franci . . . multi, Frisones, Galli, pagani, Britones, et Scotti, Armorici' who, according to Asser, ch. lxxvi, 'sponte se suo dominio subdiderant'; others suggest that he may have been a merchant and have merely gone through the formality of *primsigling*, or *prima signatio*: see e.g. Hübener (1930), pp. 172 ff. and Bright (1971), p. 186. On the other hand, it is reasonable to suppose that the visitor to the king's court addressed Alfred politely as 'my lord', and these words could have been recorded in the notes made of his report. For the possible date of Ohthere's visit and for a general discussion of this section, see Introduction, pp. lxxxvii ff.

13/29–30. *he . . . bude.* All we know of the whereabouts of Ohthere's home is that it was situated in *Halgoland*; see below, 16/1 and Commentary. Since Or.'s narrative is a second-hand account of Ohthere's report to King Alfred, presumably based on notes made at the time by a scribe, we cannot tell whether Ohthere actually said that he personally lived furthest north of all the Norwegians, or whether a statement by him that his home was in the most northerly district of Norway was subsequently so interpreted. Accordingly suggestions that he came from the island of Senja, or, even more precisely, from Lenvik Sound (see e.g. G. Storm, 'Om Opdagelsen af "Nordkap" og Veien til "det hvide Hav" ', *Norske Geografiske Selskabs Aarbog*, v (1893–4), 93, and Binns (1961), p. 44, n. 4), are pure conjecture. For Viking settlements in this northern area see G. Gjessing, *Viking*, iii (1939), 46–7.

14/2. *swiþe lang norþ þonan.* It is some 450 km, 280 miles, from northern Halgoland to Nordkyn, the actual trend of the coast being north-east. See below, 14/7, Commentary.

14/2–4. *on feawum . . . sæ.* Even in recent times, the coast Lapps seem to have been half-nomads, with hunting and fishing forming the basis of their economy: see Samuel Purchas, *Hakluytus Posthumus or Purchas his Pilgrimes* (London, 1625) iii, p. 223, 'the people of [Lappia] liue in the Summer time neere the Sea side and vse to take fish, of the which they make bread, and in the Winter they remoue vp into the Countrey into the Woods, where they vse hunting, and kill Deere, Beares, Wolues, Foxes, and other beasts.' See also Vorren and Manker (1962), p. 54. Pelts were of course at their best in the winter. For the name *Finnas* 'Lapps' see Glossary of Proper Names.

14/5–6. *He sæde . . . læge.* It does not automatically follow from this statement—as is often supposed—that Ohthere either thought himself to be or was the first to make this exploration. Archaeological evidence appears to suggest that Norsemen were very active in the Arctic regions beyond the North Cape in the second half of the ninth century, while according to Norse literary sources an expedition was made to *Bjarmaland* in King Harald Fairhair's reign, *c.* 870. See E. Oxenstierna, *The Norsemen*, trans. and ed. C. Hutter (London, 1966), p. 147, J. Simpson (1967), p. 97, and *Heimskringla*, ed. Bjarni Aðalbjarnarson (Reykjavík, 1941) I, p. 135. For Binns's suggestion (1961), p. 43, that Ohthere already had 'a vague general knowledge of the area' before he set out, see 14/13, Commentary. For the significance of *norþryhte* see 14/7, Commentary.

14/7. *þa for he norþryhte be þæm lande.* The general trend of the coastline beyond Halgoland is north-east, and it has been assumed by some commentators that we have here an instance of a 45° shift, or 'OScand. orientation'; see e.g. Ekblom (1941–2), p. 136, and, in refutation, Introduction, pp. lxiii ff. However, although *norþryhte* is normally interpreted as 'due north'—and indeed in the account of Germania, 12/27, the related expression *ryhte be eastan* is used in series with 'north-east' and 'south-east'—we cannot assume that this is the term that Ohthere himself used. If negative evidence is to be trusted, it would appear that ON had nothing to correspond to Mod. Icelandic *há-norður*, Danish *stiknord*, or Norwegian *rettnord*, 'due north', the only term for this direction in surviving texts being plain 'north': see Reuter (1934), p. 6, and S. Einarsson, 'Terms of Direction in Old Icelandic', *JEGPh*, xliii (1944), 282. Moreover, in the sentence immediately preceding, *norþryhte* is used quite inappropriately and must surely represent an original 'north', subsequently modified by the note-taking scribe, the author of Or., or even a hypothetical interpreter, unaware that he was distorting Ohthere's information.

If we assume that in this instance too *norþryhte* represents an alteration of Ohthere's own usage, then the apparent inaccuracy or shift can easily be explained. Either (i) Ohthere used the ON term *landnorð*, 'north-east', and this was interpreted as 'north along the land', or (ii) Ohthere used the term 'north' for a range of north, as part of a four-point system of directions, referring not merely to a point but to a quadrant of a circle. The latter theory appears to have the backing of surviving ON texts. The ON words for north-east, north-west, etc. seem to have been virtually restricted to a technical use as wind and weather terms. In other contexts, the norm was 'north' for a range of north, 'east' for a range of east, etc., with pregnant meanings for these terms in special contexts. See Einarsson, *JEGPh*, xliii, 283, and id., 'Terms of Direction in Modern Icelandic', *Scandinavian Studies presented to George T. Flom*, Illinois Studies in Language and Literature xxix nr. 1 (1942), 37–48, E. Haugen, 'The Semantics of Icelandic Orientation', *Word*, xiii (1957), 447–59, and Ellegård (1960), pp. 241–8. Such a use of north could have been clarified by the addition of the words *með landi*; cf. *Egils Saga*, ed. G. Jónsson (Reykjavík, 1945), xxi, 'taka þeir landnyrðing ut eftir firðinum, en þat er andviðri norðr með landi'.

Apparent confirmation of the theory that Ohthere used a four-point system of directions is provided by the report of his description of Norway's eastern neighbours, 15/31–4. Here, Sweden is located 'toemnes þæm lande suðeweardum, on oðre healfe þæs mores, oþ þæt land norðeweard' (i.e. south-east, possibly also due east) and the Cwenas 'toemnes þæm lande norðeweardum' (i.e. north-east), in both cases a four-bearing system apparently being used, where an eight-bearing one might have been preferable. See also below, 14/11–17 and Commentary.

14/7–8. *let . . . bæcbord.* Cf. ON *láta landit á bakborða* and *á stjórnborða*. The steering oar was attached to the starboard side and the aftermost frame of the viking ship. If Ohthere is correctly reported here, he would appear to have chosen to sail outside the islands off the coast of Norway in preference to following Indreleia, the inshore route. One possible reason for this is that he was hunting walrus (see below, 14/30–1). Another may be that, although Indreleia is much used today by steamships, conditions for sailing vessels are hazardous. I am informed by Mrs. Prudence Maxfield, who has sailed in these waters, that the inner passage has either virtually no wind or the most appalling unheralded squall off the mountains. In her opinion, Ohthere would most likely have stood from four to five miles off the coast. See also Admiralty, *Norway Pilot* (1953), pp. 28–9.

14/9. *þrie dagas*. Presumably a day of 24 hours is intended. Even as far south as Trondheim, Norway has practically full daylight from May 23 to July 20, while in the region of Nordkapp, continuous daylight occurs between May 12 and July 29. The opening of the White Sea is on the average May 15–December 15 (see Admiralty, *White Sea Pilot* (1946), p. 22).

14/10. *norþryhte*. See above, 14/7, Commentary. In this instance, it should be noted, there is no accompanying *be þæm lande*. Ekblom (1941–2), p. 136, n. 3, observing that Ohthere does not describe how the sea lay during these three days, suggests that he sailed inside Söröya and other islands. See, however, 14/23–4 below.

14/11. *þa beag . . . eastryhte*. Some commentators believe this point to be the North Cape or Knivkjerodden on the island of Magerøy: see e.g. Hampson, in Bosworth (1859), p. 56, Reuter (1934), p. 5, and the Admiralty *Norway Pilot*, (1953), p. 675: 'when approaching Nordkapp either from eastward or westward Magerøy will be easily identified as the land's end.' However, if Ohthere is correctly reported, the place referred to is where the *mainland* turns (see next note), and this continues to trend north-east for another 40 miles, 64 km, or so to Nordkyn. See Binns (1961), p. 48, also Ekblom (1960), p. 8, where it is suggested that Ohthere sailed south of Magerøy, a reversal of Ekblom's earlier theory (1941–2, p. 136) that he sailed outside Magerøy to Nordkyn, turning to starboard at Sletnes.

If Ohthere's turning point was Nordkapp, the direction named is correct enough. However, if the area round Nordkyn is meant, then the *eastryhte* of the text (for *east?*) refers to actual south-east. Assuming the use of a four-point system to describe general land directions (see 14/7, Commentary), Ohthere's choice here would have been between 'east' and 'south', and since he had previously been sailing 'north' and was subsequently to sail 'south' (see 14/17), 'east' would be the obvious term to select. See further Binns (1961), p. 51. Yet another factor might be Ohthere's recollection of the winds. Conditions in those parts render difficult any estimation of the main trend of the coast (see Binns, pp. 50–1). If a marked change in the trend of the coastline coincided, as apparently here, with the need to wait for a favourable wind, then an experienced sailor would spend the intervening period not so much attempting to assess the angle of the coast as observing such phenomena as direction and speed of current and tidal flow and determining what kind of wind he could safely use. Ohthere's recollection that the wind he waited for was 'west and slightly north' would be not unlikely to influence him in his attempt to answer (hypothetical) questions about the geography of the area, some considerable time after the event.

14/12. *he nysse hwæðer.* Hübener (1925–6), p. 45, sees here an echo of patristic views on geography and the question, first posed by Zeno, *PL* xi, col. 446, 'Quis terram aqua portari an aquam terrae gremio contineri se nosse praesumat?' However, Ohthere's caution surely needs no such justification. Since he does not explore further north, he cannot tell whether he has reached the extreme north of the continent of Europe, or whether the sea on which he is sailing penetrates the continent as the Baltic does. Cf. Remigius, *in Capellam* VI. 302. 5, 'sinus est mare intrans in terram.'

14/13. *he . . . norþan.* Suggested identifications for the place where Ohthere waited include Gjesvær (so Carl C. Rafn, *Antiquités russes* (Copenhagen, 1850–2) II, pp. 458 ff.) and Hornsviken (so Reuter (1934), p. 7); see the *Norway Pilot* (1953), p. 674: 'most of the harbours between Nordkapp and Vardø are small and exposed, therefore though the absence of outlying dangers renders them easy of access they should only be sought in case of emergency.' Ekblom (1960), p. 9, considers the wind to be in fact roughly real north, striking the coast of the Kola peninsula at an angle of 40° to 50°, 'in those parts the most favourable wind for a sailing boat of the period'. Binns (1961), p. 47, however, takes it to be north-west 'or perhaps WNW', the latter being in my opinion the most likely interpretation (cf. ON *útnyrðingr* 'north-west wind', with its emphasis on the northern element). Binns's further suggestion that Ohthere had a vague general knowledge of the area before he set out and may have been taking advantage of a depression to make his difficult journey is also plausible. However, it should be noted that (i) we are told nothing of the direction of the winds on Ohthere's journey up the Norwegian coast or during the four days after he obtained his west-north-west wind and before he waited for the due north wind of 14/15 and (ii) we are not told whether Ohthere waited for the west-north-west wind because it was the ideal one for the next stage of his journey or because it was the first one that was at all suitable. A west-north-west or north-west wind would certainly be particularly favourable, in view of the fact that both coastline and general current run south-east; however, since the Viking ship, though it could not sail before the wind, was perfectly well able to sail close to the wind, probably only south, south-east, and east winds would be completely unsuitable. From June to September winds in the southern part of the Barents Sea are most frequent between west and north. See Admiralty, *White Sea Pilot* (1958), pp. 36–7; Rae (1881), p. 7; Foote and Wilson (1970), p. 248 and Sawyer (1962), p. 74.

14/13. *east be lande.* Actual south-east, if the Murmanski coast is here referred to. See above, 14/11, Commentary. Reuter (1934), p. 9, suggests that the expression Ohthere used was ON *austr með landi*, i.e. *landaustr* 'south-east', a form not recorded in ON, which uses the term *landsuðr* for south-east on the rare occasions that it employs an eight-point system (though cf. the Lofoten dialect word *landaust* : *sudostlig vind* (*ost til sud*), cited by I. Aasen, *Norsk Ordbog* (Christiania, 1873)). However, *east* is correct if we assume a four-point system of directions (see 14/7, Commentary) and surprisingly corresponds to the usage of more modern accounts of the area: cf. Rae (1881), p. 70, where Svyatoy Nos is described as east of Sem Ostrova—it is in fact south-east—and Gerat de Veer's account of 'The Third Voyage Northward to the Kingdomes of Cathaia, and China, in Anno 1596', in *Purchas his Pilgrimes*, iii, p. 516, where Kola and Kildina are put west of Sem Ostrova, although they are true north-west: 'We got to the Seuen Ilands, where we found many Fishermen, of whom we enquired after *Cool* and *Kilduin*, and they made signes that they lay West from vs (which we likewise ghest to bee so).'

14/14–15. *þa sceolde . . . supryhte*. The second stopping-place has been variously identified with Varangerfjord (see e.g. Kuznetsov, quoted by E. Koutaissoff, 'Ohtheriana I', *EGS*, ii (1948–9), 21), Svyatoy Nos Bay (see e.g. Storm, *Det Norske Geografiske Selskabs Aarbog*, v, 94), Korabelnyy (see e.g. Bright (1970), p. 187), Mys Sazónov (see e.g. L. Weibull, 'De gamle nordbornas väderstrecksbegrepp', *Scandia*, i (1928), 294 f.), and Mys Orlov (see e.g. Ekblom (1941–2), p. 137). Assuming that Ohthere's journey ended south of the Kola peninsula (see below, 14/18 Commentary), the most likely places are in the vicinity of Mys Sazónov or the neighbouring Mys Gorodetskiy, where the coast changes general direction from south-east to south, and Mys Orlov, some thirty miles further on, where the trend changes to south-west. Although Binns claims that the only inviting stopping-places along the Murmanski coast, apart from Svyatoy Nos Bay, are Kildin, Teriberka, and the inlet behind the Sem Islands, or Sem Ostrova (1961, p. 49)—all three seemingly too far from the White Sea to be eligible—Rae (1881), p. 57, states that along this coast 'there are some of the best sheltered anchorages in the world', while the Admiralty *White Sea Pilot* (1958), pp. 204 f., gives quite a choice of anchorages for small vessels along the Terski coast.

A stopping-place in the vicinity of Mys Orlov may be indicated by the fact that Ohthere had at this point to wait for a due north wind. If the original west-north-west wind had shifted in the course of the previous four days or even blown itself out, then Ohthere could have waited for any of a range of favourable winds, the first he encountered happening to be north. Such a wind would be favourable for either the southerly stretch from Mys Mályy Gorodetskiy or the south-westerly stretch just past Mys Orlov but not the (hypothetical) rounding of the Kola peninsula into Kandalakshkaya Guba. On the other hand, had a west-north-west wind persisted up to that point, then a change of wind direction would not be necessary until the boat reached the Gorlo and the south-west stretch of the Kola peninsula. According to the *White Sea Pilot* (1946), p. 67, northerly winds in the northern zone of the White Sea raise a heavy sea, which increases with the south-west-going tidal stream, the general direction of the current being north off the coast between Mys Orlov and Svyatoy Nos. In the Gorlo, on the other hand, the current in the summer generally sets in a north-east direction, with wind and seas following the channel. Here it is seas from the north-east that are heavy, north and north-west winds causing smaller seas but in the same direction. If Ohthere waited deliberately for a due north wind, then it seems plausible that he should have done so at the entrance to the Gorlo, i.e. in the vicinity of Mys Orlov, rather than earlier, in the vicinity of Mys Mályy Gorodetskiy. Since winds are variable in the White Sea area from June to August, but northerly on-shore winds tend to prevail, especially in the afternoon (see *White Sea Pilot* (1946), p. 66), his wait need not have been a long one. That the trend of the coast after Mys Orlov is south-west not south presents no difficulty: Ohthere may have deduced land direction long after the voyage from his recollection of the wind he used, or alternatively *suþryhte* may represent an original *suþ* which in its turn formed part of a four-point system of directions (see 14/7, Commentary).

14/17. *suðryhte be lande.* See 14/14–15, Commentary. Those commentators who take Ohthere's destination to be the Varzuga explain the resultant discrepancy between Ohthere's *suðryhte* and an actual south, south-west, west and finally west by north-west in a variety of ways. See e.g. Binns (1961), p. 51 'this alteration is a gradual one . . . with no prominent cape to be doubled, and its omission suggests that his compass directions are to be taken much more with reference to an assumed trend of the coast-line than to any quarter of the heavens. The wind and general run of the sea which were probably his other criteria would not here help him to detect the curve in the coast as they tend to follow it', also Ekblom (1941–2), p. 137, 'The voyage went in a curve along the coast, but it is worth noting that the mouth of the Varzuga lies S 60° W of Cape Orlov', and Malone (1930b), p. 159, 'Ohthere, it would seem, did not bother to tell Alfred all this, but contented himself with a loose description of the course as southerly.' Of these explanations (assuming that Ohthere is correctly reported), Malone's seems the most convincing. Although it is possible that Ohthere might not have noticed a curve in the coast on his journey from Norway, it is hard to believe that on his way home again he could have been misled into interpreting an initial 80 miles, 128 km, or more of coast stretching south-east and then east as tending 'due north'. For the calculation of latitude by the Vikings see Simpson (1967), pp. 92–5.

14/18. *an micel ea.* This has been variously identified with the Dvina, the Varzuga, the Umba, the head of Kandalaks Bay and even the entrance to the White Sea: see e.g. Dahlmann (1822), p. 423, Reuter (1934), pp. 9 f., Storm, *Det Norske Geografiske Selskabs Aarbog,* v, 95, Ross (1940), p. 24, and Hampson, in Bosworth (1859), p. 56. On the evidence that we have, the first of these can be ruled out. Ohthere is reported—rightly or wrongly—as saying that throughout his voyage he kept the land on his port and the open sea on his starboard, and this would not be possible if he crossed the White Sea to the Dvina. The fourth too can be ruled out, on negative evidence: as Ross points out, p. 24, n. 3, the head of Kandalaks Bay is unlikely to have been meant, since to 'sail on past' the latter would involve a complete reversal of the course: 'Ohthere can hardly have meant this by "sailing on past" and, if he had been so far up the Bay that he thought it was a river, he would have been able to see across it and must therefore have been aware that a reversal of the course would have been necessary.' Of the remaining two identifications, commentators prefer the former: see e.g. Ross (1940), p. 24, n. 3, who cites in its favour the 'Karelian parishes' mentioned in this area in 1419 and 'the find at its mouth'. However, we have no evidence that Ohthere in fact passed through the Gorlo and round the bottom of the Kola peninsula. That he may have done so is admittedly suggested by the reference to *Terfinnas*, a people tentatively identified with the Lapps of the mod. *Terskij bereg*, the coast stretching from Mys Svyatoy Nos to Mys Ludoshnyy some 28 miles west of Varzuga (see *White Sea Pilot* (1958), p. 203; but cf. Ross (1940), pp. 24–8, where it is limited to the region from the entrance of the White Sea to the Varzuga). However, the allusion to *Beormas* cannot in the light of present knowledge be said to support this. What evidence there is for the location of the Biarmians in the early Middle Ages points almost without exception to an area round the River Dvina, east of the White Sea, and I am informed by Dr. Michael Branch that modern scholarly opinion would rule out Ross's suggestion (1940, p. 58) that in the ninth century the Biarmian (i.e. Karelian) population 'stretched right round the shores of the White Sea' and that the Varzuga was the then Biarmian–Lappish frontier. See also below, 14/24, Commentary. In any case, the Biarmian settlement referred to may have been in the middle of Lappish territory. Ohthere is reported as saying that he did not sail on past the river: therefore, we are not justified in making any deductions whatsoever as to the extent of the cultivated land that he noted on the other side of that river. Moreover, the Varzuga is not the only large river that Ohthere would have encountered in the latter part of his journey. We may compare with its present-day 1 cable width at its mouth the 3 cables of the Stryél'naya and the 2 cables of the Pyálka, the 1 cable of the Chapomá and the 1 cable of the Pyálitsa.

Finally, the number of days that Ohthere is reported as spending under sail is sometimes quoted in discussions of this problem (for calculations of speeds and distances see e.g. Binns (1961), pp. 48–9). However, we do not know how often he sailed faster or slower than average, nor can we be sure that the report does not include waiting times in its figures. As one of Ohthere's objects was walrus-hunting, it would be strange if he did not pause occasionally for this purpose, while variable weather is another complicating factor: on one occasion Rae ran nearly 20 miles in two hours 'which in an open boat is considerable', having just covered 120 versts in 12 hours (i.e. at a rate of 6½ m.p.h.), while he 'ran from Tschavanga after many hours' patience with a strong north-easterly wind' (see Rae (1881), pp. 114 and 119). An expedition described in

Purchas his Pilgrimes, iii, 223, took a week to sail from the North Cape to Cape Grace (60° 45′N), leaving on July 2 and arriving on July 9. All we can say, therefore, is that Ohthere could have reached the Varzuga in the time stated. We cannot claim that he did so.

14/24. *þa Beormas.* For a detailed examination of the material relating to the Beormas see Ross (1940), pp. 6–7, 24, 29, 44, and 57, where they are identified with the north Karelians—Baltic Fenns dwelling in the south of the Kola peninsula. However, Dr. Michael Branch kindly informs me that the leading authorities on Finno-Ugrian matters now believe that the northern Ladoga region was the furthest point reached by the Karelians in the ninth century: Karelian settlements on the Kola peninsula at this time seem to be out of the question.

14/24. *þa Beormas . . . land.* Cf. 14/20–1, 'ne mette he ær nan gebun land siþþan he from his agnum ham for'. Binns (1961), p. 49, claims support for the identification of the great river with the Varzuga from the Admiralty *White Sea Pilot's* description of the coast. 'Evidently at the present day the river marks a noticeable difference in vegetation; "many plants are absent, particularly E of the Varzuga river".' However, according to *White Sea Pilot* (1958), pp. 5 and 224, observable difference does not coincide with the banks of the river—beyond which Ohthere is reported not to have sailed.

14/25. *þara Terfinna.* For the *Terfinnas* see above, 14/18, Commentary, M. Vasmer, 'Zum Namen der Terfinnas in König Ælfreds Orosius-Übersetzung', *ESn*, lvi (1922), 169–71, and Ross (1940), pp. 24–8.

14/28–9. *hwæt þæs soþes wæs.* Cf. 'hwæt þæs ealles wæs', 126/26, and *Anglo-Saxon Chronicle*, s.a. 1046E.

14/29–30. *þa Finnas . . . geþeode.* From this statement it appears that like the Lapps the Beormas (whom Ohthere must be supposed to have met in Terfinnas' territory) spoke a form of Finno-Ugrian. Living in northern Norway, Ohthere might be expected to have some acquaintance with Lappish. However, he presumably used an interpreter to communicate with the Beormas since, as Dr. Michael Branch kindly informs me, Ross's belief in a very striking natural similarity between ninth-century Baltic-Fennic and Lappish (Ross (1940), pp. 50–1 and 57) is unfounded. To understand Karelian Ohthere would need a knowledge not of Lappish but of Finnish.

14/30–1. *Swiþost . . . horshwælum.* Today, constant persecution has driven the walrus, *Odobenus rosmarus*, northward, so that its normal habitat is the northern circumpolar region; however, migrations still take it to the Barents Sea, north-east of the Kola peninsula. An island at the entrance to the Gorlo bears the name Morzhovets, or 'Walrus Island', though according to the Admiralty, *White Sea Pilot* (1958), p. 6, neither walruses nor whales are found in the White Sea.

The reading of MS L, *horschwælum*, is most probably a scribal error for *horshwælum* (so Cotton MS): cf. ON *hross-hvalr.* However, V. Kiparsky, *L'Histoire du morse* (Helsinki, 1952), p. 37, sees a connection

between *horsc-* and the Lappish name for walrus, *moršša*, and quotes
A. S. C. Ross as having informed him that 'in *horschwælum* the division is
surely *horsc-hwælum* (*horsc* 'lebhaft', presumably); misunderstood later
because *chw* is a possible spelling for *hw*.' I do not find this explanation
convincing.

14/32. *swiþe æþele ban*. Walrus tusks were greatly prized for their ivory,
and a number of carved objects made of this material have survived from
the Middle Ages. An Anglo-Saxon example is the Gandersheim Casket,
probably late eighth century from Ely; see John Beckwith, *Ivory Carving
in Early Medieval England* (London, 1972).

15/1–2. *sciprapum*. In addition to ropes of bast and hemp, the Vikings
used walrus and sealskin ropes, probably made by cutting the hide in a
spiral round the body of the creature. See Foote and Wilson (1970), p. 245.

15/2–5. *ne bið . . . lange*. We do not know precisely what length was
represented by the term 'ell' in either Wessex or Norway in the second
half of the ninth century, although in Anglo-Saxon texts it is used to
translate Latin *cubitus*, a measure which seems to have varied in length
between 18″ and 22″. However, later evidence suggests that the Anglo-
Saxon ell may have been between 22″ and 24″ in length: see Grierson
(1972), p. 16. Such a length agrees very well with the figures attributed
to Ohthere. For instance, since the bull walrus ranges in length from 3 to
4·5 m (9′10″–14′9″), the largest are the equivalent of 7 ells at 24″, 8 ells
at 22″ per ell. The Blue Whale ranges from 22 to 30 (33) m, i.e. 72′–100′,
and a 30 m maximum is equivalent to 49 ells at 24″, 53 at 22″. An ell of
18″, on the other hand, while yielding lengths applicable to Rorqual and
Greenland Whales, the biggest of which are normally 25 m and 21 m
(82′ and 68′10″) respectively, would require us to suppose that the
largest walrus ever encountered by Ohthere was no more than 3·2 m or
10′ 6″ in length.

15/5. *syxa sum*. Rask's emendation to *syx ascum* ('six ships?' or 'six
harpoons?'), which is favoured by Labuda (1961), p. 103, n. 106, is both
forced and unnecessary. The idiom *syxa sum* can mean either 'one of six'
(cf. *Beowulf* 3123–4) or 'one of seven' (cf. *Beowulf* 2401, also—if the
numerals have been accurately transmitted—OE *Bede* 154/5 and *Or*.
107/18–19) and may refer not merely to six or seven men but to six or
seven men and their crews. Right up to the 1860s whales were hunted
from sailing ships by means of rowboats and harpoons. For an OE
reference to whalehunting with many boats, see *Ælfric's Colloquy*, ed.
G. N. Garmonsway (London, 1939), pp. 29–30: 'Gebeorhlicre ys me faran
to ea mid scype mynan, þænne faran mid manegum scypum on huntunge
hranes.'

15/6. *syxtig . . . dagum*. Serious doubts have been raised as to the possibility of a small band of men killing sixty of the biggest whales in two
days: see Bosworth (1855), p. 43, n. 46. Certainly this would be quite out
of the question at sea: Rae (1881), p. 60, referring to the whale fisheries
established by Tsar Peter the First in 1723, reports that in five years the

three whalers took only four whales, while half a century later a single vessel in Kola fjord wounded eleven whales but killed none, owing to the defective form of harpoon. Moreover, although slaughter on this scale might be technically feasible on land if the whales had been beached or trapped in very shallow water, it is most improbable that Blue Whales or Greenland Whales or even the Common Rorqual would have been stranded in such numbers. It is much more likely that we have here to do with condensed or inaccurate reporting and that Ohthere had at this point passed from an account of the size of some of the whales caught to an illustration of how good on occasion whale-hunting off Norway could be. In this case, the obvious candidate would be the Pilot or Ca'ing Whale, 4·30–8·70 m, irregular now off the Norwegian coast but very frequent off the Faroes, living in schools of up to several hundreds and even thousands and usually led by a very large adult which they follow almost blindly. See K. Leems, 'An account of the Laplanders of Finmark', *Pinkerton's Voyages*, (1808), I, p. 432, 'About the festival of the purification of the Virgin, and therefore about the middle of winter, a great quantity of whales is seen, not only near the shores extending far into the sea, but even in the recesses themselves of the inner bays, which, as if by the express command of Heaven, drive into those places the larger codfish, and other fish in great quantities.' See further, Vorren and Manker (1962), p. 59, Helvig and Johannessen (1966), p. 78 and Vorren (1961), p. 214.

15/8. *on wildrum*. See below, 15/14–20 and Commentary.

15/9. *tamra . . . hund*. For the suggestion that Ohthere may have attempted (and failed) to realize the value of his reindeer herd see Bright (1970), p. 188. For the size of the herd, see Vorren (1961), p. 183, 'It is usual to reckon that the *subsistence level* for an average family of about five members lies around 200 animals before calving.' It is possible that Ohthere's herd remained in one place all the year round, but much more probable that it stayed by the coast only in summer, migrating to the interior for winter grazing; see Vorren (1961), pp. 172 and 181 and, for a different point of view, Vorren and Manker (1962), pp. 13–16. According to the latter, 'not until the sixteenth century is it definitely established . . . that the keeping of domesticated reindeer by the Lapps had developed into reindeer breeding, with the consequent nomadism', while 'it is not impossible that in reality [Ohthere's reindeer herd] was owned by the Lapps who paid taxes to him, in which case it would be divided into several herds.' Reindeer were used as draught and milch animals as well as for their meat and skins.

15/10–11. *stælhranas . . . hranas mid*. Even in modern times the Lapps continued to use tame reindeer to catch wild ones. Johannes Tornaeus, writing in the seventeenth century in Johannes Schefferus's book *Lapponia*, describes how the Lapps keep a number of specially trained does (*vaja*). 'Once they have located the bucks they tie the does together with a thin white rope (the hunters, who are clad in reindeer skins, wear white linen hats); one of the does, however, is encouraged to move a short distance away from her companions. When she has gone far enough one of the hunters pulls gently on the rope. The doe stops and begins to graze as if everything were normal. When the wild bucks notice this and immediately attempt to mate, they are shot by the Lapps. This method is not employed by all Lapps, only by those who have acquired the skill and have the opportunity to hunt in this way' (unpublished translation by Michael Branch of Israel Ruong, *Samerna*). See also Knud Leems's account, in *Pinkerton's Voyages* (1808), pp. 406 and 414. According to Leems, p. 414, the Laplander goes with some of his reindeer, 'tamed for that intent', and fastens them to trees with halters. A second method employed by the Lapps was to use tame draught reindeer to round up the wild reindeer and then pursue them on skis (see Vorren and Manker (1962), p. 56), and it may be that it was wild reindeer rounded up in this way that were driven into the funnel of converging fences described by Leems, p. 414.

Whether *stæl-* is OE in origin or like *hranas* a Norse loan is a matter for conjecture. Its etymology is also uncertain. Association with *stelan* 'to steal' is possible (cf. OE *stælgiest* 'thievish stranger', *stælhere* 'predatory army') but not particularly appropriate in this context, while a connection with mod. Norwegian *stæla* 'to be in milk', is also unlikely, in spite of Tornaeus's reference to does, some more specific description than 'milch reindeer' being required here. More attractive is the suggestion, OED *stale* sb. 3, that *stæl* has the root of *steall* 'place', i.e. the Gc. root **stal* 'standing, stall, position' etc. However, whether it should be taken to refer to the way in which the animals were kept (in stalls, as opposed to in the open, where the Lapps of the period normally kept their reindeer: cf. German *Stallpferd* and *Weidepferd*) or the way in in which they were used (tethered, like those described by Tornaeus) is open to question. The interpretation adopted by the OED is 'decoy', though on its own admission there is no direct connection between this form and lME *stale* 'decoy duck', Old French *estalon* (see W. v. Wartburg, *Französisches Etymologisches Wörterbuch* (Bonn etc., 1928–70), XVII, p. 212). The development of such a meaning in OE is of course possible; however, to render the concept 'decoy' Ohthere himself might have been expected to use an ancestor of Mod. Norwegian *lokke-* (see *lokkedyr* and cf. German *Lockvogel*, Dutch *lokvogel*, and ON *lokka*, OE *(a)loccian* 'to entice, decoy').

For a possible underlying Norse form *tál* 'bait, allurement' see Cleasby–Vigfusson *tál*. However, I am assured by my Norse colleagues that this identification is highly improbable.

15/14. *mid horsan*. In Viking times both horses and oxen were used in Scandinavia as draught animals and to pull sledges. For the two types of plough used see Foote and Wilson (1970), p. 176. In Anglo-Saxon England the ox seems to have been the standard draught animal in preference to the slighter horse (see R. I. Page, *Life in Anglo-Saxon England* (London, 1970, p. 91)) and it is possible that Or.'s observation here is to be interpreted either as another instance of Ohthere's relative poverty in terms of domestic livestock, or as an indication of the small amount of arable land he cultivated.

15/14. *gafole.* i.e. *Finnskattr*. See Introduction, p. lxxxviii, n. 5.

15/15. *deora fellum*. The skins of martens, otters, seals, reindeer, and bears (see below, 15/17–20), perhaps also other skins, such as those of the beaver, Arctic fox, red squirrel, and sable, mentioned in medieval sources as passing through the hands of Scandinavian merchants. Furs were an important commodity then as now and one of the chief exports of Scandinavia.

15/15. *fugela feðerum*. Eiderdown-type bed-coverings were found at Oseberg, a down-filled pillow is recorded from a Danish grave at Mammen, Jytland, while bedding and feathers are mentioned as part of the booty taken after the sack of Dublin in 1000.

15/16. *hwales bane*. The reference here may be to *whalebone*, i.e. baleen, a light, flexible, tough and fibrous substance formed in the palate on the roof of the mouth of Baleen or Whalebone whales, *mystacoceti*, varying in colour from black to grey to yellowish white to white and used in modern times for fishing-rods, brushes, corsets, frames for portmanteaux etc. However, *whale's bone* (misleadingly also called whalebone by some modern writers) was likewise a useful commodity: see the carved board made from a whale's shoulder-blade in Tromsö museum and decorative objects such as the Franks Casket. Other possible referents are the tusk of the narwhal and the teeth of the sperm whale, which, like the tusks of the walrus, were much valued for their ivory.

15/16. *hwæles hyde*. Probably walrus hide (see 15/1–2), though the skin of the white whale can be used for leather.

15/18. *mearðes fell*. Pine marten (*martes martes*) or possibly sable (*martes zibellina*).

15/18. *ambra*. The capacity of the amber, which was used both as a liquid and a dry measure, is altogether unknown. It seems originally to have been an adaptation of the Roman *amphora*, which was equivalent to about six gallons: see F. Harmer, *Select English Historical Documents* (Cambridge, 1914), p. 73.

15/21–4. For a useful profile diagram of the Scandinavian peninsula and description of the terrain, see Foote and Wilson (1970), pp. 36–9. Even today only some 3% of Norway is cultivated, and, with the exception of the central parts of Østlandet, the areas in which agriculture is carried out have a marine climate. See Helvig and Johannessen (1966), p. 5.

15/22. *Eal . . . mæg*. Cf. 25/32 'eall þæt on þæm lande wæs weaxendes 7 growendes'.

15/25. *easteweard*. From the context it appears that the southern part of Norway is here referred to: cf. the Norse practice of describing a traveller going to the south coast of Norway (the area from Lindesnes to the inner end of the Christiania Fjord) as travelling 'east'. Later, however, Ohthere is reported as referring to *Sciringesheal*, a port in this area, as *on suðewear-dum þæm lande*. See below, 16/2–3, and Introduction, p. lxvii.

15/26–7. *syxtig mila brad*. The term *mila* was not normally used as a measure of distance in ON, its rare occurrences being mainly in texts where foreign influence is strong. On land the normal measure was the røst, derived from the *rasta*, the primitive Germanic itinerary measure, which apparently represented the distance or stage travelled between rests, i.e. about an hour's journey or 3–5 miles: see Grierson (1972), pp. 24–32. Such distances were not measured but roughly guessed, and varied according to the nature of the ground traversed. Some commentators have assumed that the figures attributed to Ohthere are based on the later Scandinavian measure of an 8–9 km 'mile'. Bosworth (1855), p. 45, n. 49, quotes Rask's calculations that the broadest part referred to should be not 60 but 300 miles wide, the narrowest not 3 miles but 15. However, if we discount the possibility of a simple substitution røst : mile, a stage of 3–4 English miles, 5–6 km, would seem to be more appropriate. Certainly today the greatest breadth of Norway is about 276 miles, the narrowest part, just south of Hinnøy being only 3·9 miles broad. However, Ohthere is reported as referring not to the width of Norway but to the width of the cultivated land between the sea and the mountains, a very much smaller distance.

15/30. *swa brad . . . oferferan*. Cf. Adam of Bremen's statement, col. 637, that Norway can hardly be traversed in the course of a month and that Sweden is not easily traversed in two months.

15/33. *Sweoland*. See above, 13/23, Commentary.

15/34. *Cwena land*. See above, 13/26, Commentary.

15/35–6. *þær sint . . . moras*. Ross (1954), p. 340, believes that Ohthere is here referring to Lakes Alta and Leina.

15/35–6. *micle meras fersce*. For the word-order here, see Fred C. Robin-son, 'Syntactical Glosses in Latin MSS of Anglo-Saxon Provenance', *Speculum*, xlviii (1973), 472–3.

15/36–7. *berað . . . Norðmen*. According to Ross (1954), pp. 339–40, the Cwenas would have gone up the waterways of their south-easterly draining system; then they would have portaged over the watershed to a north-westerly draining system and down its waterways until they reached the Norwegian settlements. Their actual route Ross calculates to have been from the extreme western end of Lake Torne, up to Lake Vuosko, to Lake Leina and Lake Alta, and thence down the Bardu and Målselva to the Malangenfjord.

15/38. *swyðe lytle . . . leohte*. Ross (1954), pp. 343–5, suggests that these may have been sewn wooden boats, not very dissimilar to the one de-scribed by Linnaeus, *Skrifter*, ed. T. M. Fries (Stockholm, 1905–7), v, 40–1. See also Vorren and Manker (1962), p. 60.

16/1. *Halgoland*. This covered a larger area than modern Helgeland, extending beyond N 69° 30′. For theories as to where in *Halgoland* Ohthere may have lived, see above, 13/29–30, Commentary.

16/2–3. *on suðeweardum.* Compare the use of *easteweard*, above, 15/25 and see Commentary.

16/3. *Sciringesheal.* A trading station, plausibly identified with Kaupang in Vestfold, Norway, where archaeologists have recently found traces of a settlement of some size with 'the character of a local market-town with international connections'; see Foote and Wilson (1970), pp. 213–14, and Sawyer (1962), pp. 168 and 180–2. The ON equivalent is generally supposed to be *Skiringssalr*, with the second element *salr*, 'hall', replaced in the OE by *heall*. However, *heall*, 'hall', is feminine in OE, while 16/9 refers to masculine *þone Sciringesheal*; and 16/8, 12, and 15 dative *Sciringesheale* seems to indicate a second element *healh*. What form the name took in the original record must remain a matter for conjecture.

16/3–5. *þyder . . . wicode.* The average *døgr-sigling* of Viking ships has been estimated as 12 hours at 2 knots. According to A. W. Brøgger and H. Shetelig, *Viking Ships*, trans. Katherine John (Oslo, 1953), pp. 230–2, the long-distance average from harbour to harbour was between 3·5 and 4 miles per hour, the 1893 replica of the Gokstad ship covering an average of about 11 miles per hour with a very favourable wind. The distance between Tromsö and Larvik is about 1,960 km, 1,218 miles. For a similar use of the negative, to indicate minimum travelling time, see Adam of Bremen, col. 637, quoted above, 15/30, Commentary.

16/4–5. *gyf man . . . wicode.* Crews normally went ashore each night on coastal voyages and pitched their tents on land; see Simpson (1967), p. 83.

16/5. *ambyrne wind.* *Ambyrne* has been linked with modern Icelandic *andbyrr*, 'contrary wind' (see the corrections appended to BT Suppl., p. 756); however, the interpretation 'favourable', 'suitable', 'appropriate' is on a number of counts a more satisfactory one. See BT, p. 36, *ambyr*, E. Ekwall, in *Mélanges de Philologie offerts à M. Johan Melander* (Uppsala, 1943), pp. 275–84 and Ælfric, *Homilies*, ed. Pope, I, 257–8. Of the possible etymologies, Ekwall prefers that identifying *am-* with *and-* in the sense 'having a useful purpose' and *byrne* (nom. *byre*) with the noun *byre*, 'opportunity', 'time', 'period', and sees the compound adjective as a *bahuvrîhi* formation, meaning 'with (affording) good opportunity', or more generally 'useful, helpful, serviceable'. J. C. Pope, however, considers that a more satisfactory range of meaning is 'suitable, appropriate, opportune', in view of the apparent connection between *ambyrne* and the adverb *amberlice* in Ælfric, *Feria VI in Secunda Ebdomada Quadragesimae* 141, which he would, on contextual grounds, translate as 'appropriately'. In medieval texts, estimates of travelling times by sea are not infrequently accompanied by the proviso 'if the wind is favourable'; see e.g. Dicuil VII. 14.

16/6. *on þæt steorbord . . . Iraland.* This statement has caused commentators a great deal of trouble. For a résumé of early views, including the untenable theory that *Iraland* here refers to Scotland, see Bosworth (1855), p. 46, n. 54. For the case for emendation to *Isaland* (first proposed by Ingram in 1807), see W. A. Craigie, ' "Iraland" in King Alfred's "Orosius" ', *MLR*, xii (1917), 200–1. For arguments for the retention of the manuscript reading, depending on medieval views of the position of Ireland, see O. F. Emerson, '*Iraland*', *MLR*, xi (1916), 458, and Malone, (1930b) p. 143 and (1933), p. 78. However, the basic problem— that even in the most northerly part of a voyage such as that described by Ohthere Ireland would not be the land on the seafarer's starboard, since Britain would intervene—is most neatly and easily resolved if we adopt W. C. Stokoe's convincing argument, (1957, p. 304) that Ohthere is thinking in terms of sea-routes: 'Ireland is first on the starboard . . . in one sense: at this early stage in his voyage, had [the seafarer] been bound for Ireland, he would have changed course to starboard, sheered away from the coast of Norway, beat to westward as far as possible without making too much southing, and then, having left the Shetlands and Orkneys well to south and east of him, made straight for Ireland by the long, open-sea route.'

That Ireland is here described as *Iraland* but elsewhere as *Scotland* (cf. 9/10 and 19/15) presents no real difficulty. There are several differences in terminology between the reports of Ohthere and Wulfstan and the rest of the work (see Introduction, p. lxxii), and while *Scottas* and *Scotland* seem to have been the names used by the West Saxons and Mercians at this time (see *The Anglo-Saxon Chronicle* 891 'þrie Scottas . . . of Hibernia', and Be. 28/30 'Hibernia, Scotta ealonde' etc.), the Norse names for the Irish and Ireland were *Írar* (from OIr. *Ériu*) and *Írland*. The earliest instance of *Irland* that I know of in English sources occurs in the Parker Chronicle entry for 918.

16/7. *ða igland . . . þissum lande.* The identification of these islands is bound up with the identification of *Iralande*. Suggestions include Faroe, Shetlands, and Orkneys (see Bosworth (1855), p. 47, n. 54), Hebrides and Man (see Malone (1930b) p. 143). Stokoe (1957), p. 305 argues convincingly for the Orkneys: 'The Shetlands and Orkneys do not lie between Ireland and England in a physical or geographical sense of "between"; but to Ohthere or any other shipmaster of his time, between Ireland and England is where they do lie. When one takes the shorter route to Ireland, he makes directly for them, the larger Orkneys particularly.' For the shorter route to Ireland, see Stokoe's map, p. 303.

16/7. *þissum lande.* Britain. For a different identification see the following note.

16/7–8. *þonne . . . Sciringesheale.* This is true only for the stretch south to Lindesnes. Ekblom (1960), p. 10, would therefore insert 7 'and', after the word *land* and treat the following clause as referring to Norway. However, neither this device nor the identification of *þis land* with Norway, Labuda (1961), p. 105, n. 118, is convincing. It must be remembered that what we have here is not Ohthere's verbatim report but Or.'s version of what we may presume to have been some official's notes made at the time. Ohthere may merely have observed that Britain lies on the starboard for the rest of the journey south.

16/9. *Norðweg.* Cf. 15/21 *Norðmanna land.*

16/9–10. *swyðe mycel sæ.* The Skagerrak, Kattegat, and Baltic. Ohthere has no doubts here as to whether or not the sea penetrates the land. See above, 14/11–12 and Commentary.

16/11. *Gotland.* Jutland. It is generally assumed that the reference is to the northern part of the Jutland peninsula only. For the form of this name see Malone, 'King Alfred's Geats', *MLR*, xx (1925), 1–11, and 'King Alfred's Gotland', *MLR*, xxiii (1928), 336–9. Malone argues for an underlying Norse form *Gautland* and against the ON *Jótland* postulated by earlier commentators. However, even assuming that the form used by Ohthere was correctly transcribed, the original spelling could well have been subsequently modified by a scribe—or even by the author of Or. himself—perhaps under the influence of the *Gotland* of Wulfstan's account, 16/28. Cf. the variant *Ion* for *Geon*, 11/11.

16/11. *siððan Sillende.* For the manuscript reading *siðða* see Campbell, *OEG* § 217, and Introduction, p. xlviii. For *Sillende* see above, 12/31, Commentary. In Bright (1970), p. 190, it is said to designate roughly the East Jutland coast from Fredericia south to the Schlei.

16/13–14. *æt Hæþum.* For the use of *æt* with place names in OE see e.g. *The Anglo-Saxon Chronicle*, s.a. 552 and 926D, and D. Whitelock, *The Genuine Asser. Stenton Lecture, 1967* (University of Reading, 1968), p. 18 and n. 7. In Norse, the preposition *í* was similarly used: see e.g. *í Rípum.* Hedeby was an important trading station on the edge of Haddebyer Noor, an inlet of the river Schlei, on the eastern side of the neck of the Jutland peninsula; see Foote and Wilson (1970), p. 210, Sawyer (1962), pp. 177 f., and H. Jankuhn, *Haithabu: ein Handelsplatz der Wikingerzeit*, 4th edn. (Neumünster, 1963). See also W. Laur, *Die Ortsnamen in Schleswig-Holstein, Gottorfer Schriften* VI (Hamburg, 1960), p. 21.

16/14–15. *se stent . . . Dene.* Cf. *The Chronicle of Æthelweard*, ed. A. Campbell (London, 1962), p. 9 'Anglia uetus sita est inter Saxones et Giotos, habens oppidum capitale, quod sermone Saxonico Slesuuic nuncupatur, secundum uero Danos, Haithaby.' Or.'s Wends are presumably the *Afdrede* or Abodriti: see above, 13/18, Commentary. Hedeby certainly appears to have been under Danish rule in the ninth century. The Danish king Godfrid, for instance, is said to have brought there the merchants from Reric, *c.* 808, in order to make it an important centre of trade. However, according to Adam of Bremen and other sources, the Swedes conquered the area at the end of the ninth century. See Introduction, pp. lxxxvii f.

16/16. *Denamearc.* The context suggests that the section of the western coast of the Swedish peninsula from the present-day Norwegian border to the Göta Älv is thus designated. Ohthere's placing of Danes here is surprising. Though Halland and Skåne were Danish in the second half of the ninth century, the region north of the Göta Älv seems to have been annexed to Norway by Harald Harfagr. However, there is evidence that Danes once ruled in this area. See *Einhardi Annales*, s.a. 813 and Introduction, pp. lxxxvii f. The name Denmark (*Denemarca*) occurs also in the Annals of Regino of Prüm, s.a. 884 and in *The Chronicle of Æthelweard*, p. 6 ('Doniam, quae Danmarc nuncupatur'), while the earliest known Danish use of the word is on the lesser Jelling stone (*c.* 935–40) in Central Jutland. None of these references supports Ekblom's suggestion that Ohthere distinguished between the land of the Danes and Denmark, for which see below, 16/17–20, Commentary. A similar duality of naming is found in Ohthere's(?) use of both *Norðmanna land* and *Norðweg* for Norway.

16/16. *on þæt steorbord . . . dagas.* Ohthere could have crossed directly from Skiringssalr to north Jutland: see Adam of Bremen, col. 650: 'The route is of a kind that . . . they may in a day's journey cross the sea from Aalborg or Wendila of the Danes to Viken, a city of the Norwegians' (i.e. the district of Larvik). However, it would appear from this statement that he followed the west coast of the Swedish peninsula, down the eastern channel of the Kattegat, probably as far as Anholt, subsequently entering the Samsø Belt. *Widsæ* would then refer to the Skagerrak and Kattegat.

16/17–20. *on þæt steorbord . . . hyrað.* Ekblom (1940), pp. 177–90, taking *Denemearc* to refer to Zealand and present-day southern and south-west Sweden, assumes that Ohthere went through the Little Belt and that therefore the islands to starboard were Hjelm, Vejrö, Samsö, Endelave, Brandsö, Baagö, Aarö, and Als, and the islands to port were Sejrö, Æbelö, Fyn, Fænö, Lyö, Avernakö and Ærö. Malone (1930b) p. 161, on the other hand, sees Ohthere as traversing the Samsö Belt, the Great Belt and Langeland's Belt, thus having Jutland, Fyn, Langeland, etc. on his starboard. He would finally cross Kiel Bay to Haddeby. Malone's theory seems the more convincing of the two, especially in view of the Anglian pots from the early migration period on Fyn and Langeland: see Albert Genrich, *Formenkreise und Stammesgruppen in Schleswig-Holstein* (Neumünster, Wachholtz, 1954), Karte 6.

16/18–19. *on þæm landum . . . coman.* Cf. Be. 52/7–10 'And of Engle coman Eastengle 7 Middelengle 7 Myrce 7 eall Norðhembra cynn; is þæt land ðe Angulus is nemned, betwyh Geatum 7 Seaxum; is sæd of þære tide þe hi ðanon gewiton oð to dæge, þæt hit weste wunige', *HE* I. xv. It is reasonable to suppose that Or. too is referring to Angles, not more generally to the English, as coming from Angeln. The usual term for the English in texts of this period is *Angelcynn* (Be. also *Angel-*, *Ongelþeod*): see e.g. *Anglo-Saxon Chronicle*, s.a. 897, Be. 64/1, *OE Martyrology* 18/2. However, the proper names used in Or. not infrequently take different forms from those in the surviving contemporary texts and since there is no other reference in Or. to either the Angles or the English, the translator's usage must remain a matter of conjecture. For a detailed discussion of the accuracy of the tradition reported by Bede see H. M. Chadwick, *The Origin of the English Nation* (Cambridge,

1924), esp. pp. 51–84 and 97–110, also J. N. L. Myres, 'The Angles, the Saxons, and the Jutes', *PBA*, lvi (1972 for 1970), 145–74.

16/21. *Wulfstan*. For theories about Wulfstan's nationality see Introduction, p. lxxi. For the length of his day's journey see Labuda (1960), p. 63. It should be noted that although the shift to the first person suggests that Wulfstan's report was, like Ohthere's, an oral one, there is nothing to indicate when or to whom this report was made.

16/21. *Truso*. See below, 16/33–4, Commentary.

16/28. *Gotland*. Foote and Wilson (1970), p. 225, argue from this allusion that Wulfstan must have known the sea-route to Birka: 'Öland and Gotland are not visible from the south Baltic [but] they, and the province of Blekinge . . . must have been familiar to anyone sailing along the east coast of Sweden to Gotland or Birka.' For the phonology of the names in this section see Malone (1931), pp. 574–9.

16/30. *Witland*. *Withlandia* is one of five provinces east of Pomerania referred to by the monk Alberic: see *Scriptores rerum Prussicarum*, ed. T. Hirsch (Leipzig, 1861), I. 241 and II. 404, 'terram Sambie, que tunc Weydelant uocabatur'. For a detailed discussion of the possible extent of Witland and the etymology of the name, see Labuda (1961), p. 107, n. 145.

16/31. *Estum*. Probably the same as the *Aestii* of Tacitus. For the etymology of the name see above, 13/20, Commentary, Labuda (1961), p. 109, n. 147, and Ross (1978), pp. 100–4. Ross makes no mention of the possibility of a connection with 13/20 *Osti*, taking the Indo-European root to be either **oist-* or **aist-*.

16/31–2. *seo Wisle . . . in Estmere*. According to Jordanes, col. 1255, the Vistula has three mouths: 'ad litus Oceani ubi tribus faucibus fluenta Vistulae fluminis ebibuntur Vidioarii (*al.* Vidivarii) resident. Post quos ripam Oceani item Aestii tenent.' The arm referred to by Wulfstan seems to be the river today known as the Nogat, which he would reach *after* passing the present-day Vistula.

16/32. *Estmere*. Świeży Zalew, a large fresh-water lake formerly known as Frisches Haff, separated from the Baltic by a chain of sandbanks. In the Middle Ages this covered a considerably larger area than it does today. See e.g. K. Soecknick, 'Die Wasserläufe Elbings', *Elbinger Jahrbuch*, xiv (1937), 213–30, and H. Bertram, W. La Baume, O. Kloeppel, 'Das Weichsel-Nogat Delta', *Quellen und Darstellungen zur Geschichte Westpreußens* (1924), 11. Following G. H. F. Nesselmann, *Wörterbuch der Littauischen Sprache* (Königsberg, 1850), pp. 13 and 383, most commentators have linked this name with Lit. *Aismares*. However, the authenticity of the form *Aismares* has recently been questioned. See e.g. R. Schmittlein, *Études sur la nationalité des Aestii* (Bade, 1948), I, p. 62, n. 5, and Ross, (1978), p. 101.

16/33. *Ilfing*. The Elbing flows from Lake Druzno, past the town of Elbing (Elblag) and into Świeży Zalew. The origin of the name is usually said to be Germanic; see e.g. T. E. Karsten, *Die Germanen* (Berlin, 1928),

p. 73 and Ekblom, 'Der Name Elbing', *Arkiv för nordisk filologi*, lviii (1944), 209–20. However, *-ing* is a common Prussian suffix in names of rivers and lakes and the word may be of Old Prussian origin; see e.g. G. Gerullis, *Die altpreußischen Ortsnamen* (Berlin–Leipzig, 1922).

16/33. *eastan.* Malone (1930b), p. 162, and Ekblom (1941–2), p. 142 see here yet another instance of clockwise deviation. However, as Ellegård points out, (1960), p. 247, 'The Elbing estuary was east of the Vistula estuary and . . . the Elbing opened up the country to the east, the Vistula that to the south.'

16/33–4. *ðæm mere . . . staðe.* The lake is probably Lake Druzno (Drausensee). As for Truso, see Foote and Wilson (1970), pp. 218–19, 'from Wulfstan's description, [this] could be anywhere between Danzig and Kaliningrad (formerly Königsberg) and although Elblag (formerly Elbing) is favoured as the site of this town, no real evidence for the identification exists, save for a small cemetery with Viking elements which has been found in Elblag itself. Recent research would identify the village of Druzno as Truso, but excavations have only just begun and are as yet inconclusive.' For possible explanations of the initial *t* here see Bately (1966), p. 274 f. For possible etymologies see Labuda (1961), pp. 110–11, nn. 150 and 151.

16/35–6. *þonne . . . naman.* This statement, coupled with the use of the word *samod*, 16/34, suggests that the Elbing was in the ninth century a tributary of the Nogat. However, today the rivers do not lose their separate identities until after they have flowed—virtually side by side—into Świeży Zalew. For a detailed discussion of the problem, see R. Ekblom, 'King Alfred and Bearings in the Borderland between the West Slavs and the Balts', *Scando-Slavica*, iv (1958), 117–26. That a lesser river loses its name in a great one is a statement to be found in classical texts; see e.g. Ovid, *Fasti* IV. 338. However, it may well be that *Ilfing* not *Wisle* is the subject of the sentence: see the study (with valuable bibliography) by E. G. Stanley, 'How the Elbing Deprives the Vistula of its Name and Converts it to the Elbing's own Use in "Vistula-Mouth"', *Notes and Queries*, 24 (1977), 1–11.

16/36. *ligeð . . . on sæ.* Today the only opening from Świeży Zalew to the Baltic lies in the north-east, near the old fortress of Pillau.

17/2. *mycel hunig.* In the days before the introduction of sugar into Europe, honey was a most valuable commodity and one of Scandinavia's chief items of trade; see Foote and Wilson (1970), p. 200, and *The Poetic Edda I, Heroic Poems*, ed. Ursula Dronke (Oxford, 1969), p. 70.

17/3. *myran meolc.* Possibly in a fermented form, like the kumiss of the Mongols. Adam of Bremen, col. 634, relates of the Prussians, the inhabitants of Samland, that they use the milk and blood of their draught animals so freely that they are said to become intoxicated. See also the report of a ninth-century Arab geographer (quoted *Cambridge Mediaeval History*, II, 432) 'the seat of their (i.e. Avars) prince lies in the middle of the Slav land . . . The food of their princes is [mare's] milk.'

17/5–6. *ne bið . . . genoh.* Cf. Peter of Dusburg, *Chronica terrae Prussiae,* *Script. rer. Pruss.,* I, p. 54: 'Pro potu habent simplicem aquam et mellicratum seu medonem, et lac equarum, quod lac quondam non biberunt, nisi prius sanctificaretur. Alium potum antiquis temporibus non noverunt.' However, ale is mentioned in connection with the Ests' freezing methods, 17/36, while as Ross (1978), p. 103, comments, 'The remarks about ale and mead seem to be in direct opposition to the linguistic evidence.'

17/6. *þær is . . . ðeaw.* For a survey of early funerary customs in the Baltic area, see Hübener (1930), pp. 192 f., and G. Gerullis's entry 'Baltische Völker', in *Reallexicon,* ed. Max Ebert, I.

17/16. *þone mæstan . . . tune.* The biggest portion is placed furthest from the town and nearest to the competitors; it is the first to be reached by the contestants and thus constitutes the first prize. Next comes the second biggest and second prize, and so on. For a somewhat different ceremony see the account given by Jan Meletius in the sixteenth century: 'A stake is driven in the ground with a shilling placed on it. All those who are on horseback race back to the stake and the first takes the shilling' (quoted by Gerullis in *Reallexicon,* ed. Ebert, I, p. 336). See also the version of this attributed to Lukas David and quoted by Hübener (1930), p. 195. Ingram (1807), p. 83, n. *g,* observes that the race was 'more than equivalent to two *three-mile-heats* in the present day!'

17/22. *þæt swiftoste hors.* Bright (1971), p. 194, n. 116 argues for the retention of the manuscript reading *swifte* here: 'there is at least a chance that it ought to be retained as being the kind of intensified positive which is indicated by stress in spoken Mn.E and by italics in print: "the man who has the *fast* horse", i.e. the really fast one.'

17/28. *forbærneð.* Cremation was still practised in Scandinavian and Baltic countries in the ninth century, though it had been discontinued in Kent and Wessex by this time.

17/34. *cyle gewyrcan.* Wulfstan's allusion to freezing in summer as well as winter seems to imply the use of ice-chambers: see A. Macdonald, 'Wulfstan's Voyage and Freezing', *MLR,* xliii (1948), 73–4. However, Macdonald's suggestion that the Ests may have tricked the 'credulous sailor' by concealing blocks of ice under poplar leaves, on top of which one of two vessels of ale or water was resting, is, at least without further qualification, scientifically unsatisfactory. Moreover, the account does not state that there was no sign of ice. Assuming that Wulfstan has been adequately reported, the trick could have been performed either by the introduction of an anti-freeze such as salt into one of the vessels before it was placed in freezing conditions, or by packing one vessel in crushed ice mixed with salt and the other into crushed ice alone. Ale has of course a lower freezing point than water. For the possibility of radiation freezing, producing a film of ice, see Bright (1971), p. 194, n. See further W. R. Woolrich, *The Men who Created Cold: A History of Refrigeration* (New York, 1967), pp. 30–7. The art of deep freezing persisted in this area: see e.g. Fynes Moryson, *Itinerary* (London, 1593),

IV. 4 (quoted by G. Waterhouse, 'Wulfstan's account of the Esthonians', *MLR*, xxv (1930), 327).

17/36. *hine on*. For retention of the manuscript reading *hine on* see Bright (1971), p. 194, n. 128.

17/36. *ealað*. The reference to ale is surprising: see above, 17/5, where it is claimed that the Ests did not brew ale.

18/3. At this point, the translator, like Orosius, turns his attention to eastern Europe south of the Danube. However, whereas OH I. ii. 54–60 deals with the Roman provinces of Moesia, Thracia, Macedonia, Achaia, and Dalmatia separately and in turn, followed by the group Pannonia, Noricus, and Raetia, the translator selects three centres, all of importance in his own day: Constantinople, Dalmatia, and Istria. If he took his facts from OH, it is hard to see how he could have done so without first making a sketch map or plan of the area. See Introduction, p. lxix.

18/3–4. *Nu . . . liþ*. For *Creca land* see below, 18/13 and Commentary. OH's reference is to a larger area: see I. ii. 54 'Nunc quidquid Danuuius a barbarico ad mare Nostrum secludit expediam.'

18/4–9. *Wyð eastan . . . Traci*. Cf. OH I. ii. 55 'Moesia ab oriente habet ostia fluminis Danuuii, ab euro Thraciam . . . a septentrione Danuuium', and I. ii. 56 'Thracia habet ab oriente Propontidis sinum et ciuitatem Constantinopolim . . . , a septentrione . . . sinum Euxini ponti.' That the gulf of the Euxine stretches *westrihte* could be a deduction from OH I. ii. 5 and 52, while the reference to the Danube as flowing into the Euxine could be taken from OH I. ii. 52. The south-easterly direction of the Danube may have been deduced from OH's allusion to Moesia as having the Danube on its north but the Danube mouth on its east; see, however, OH I. ii. 52 '[Danuuius] qui est a meridie et ad orientem directus', which could have been misunderstood by the translator or transmitted to him in corrupt form. Zangemeister's MS D, for instance, reads 'ad meridiae et ad oriente'. For *Mæsi, Creca leode* see below, 18/13, Commentary.

18/9–10. *7 be eastan . . . Macedonie*. A strange statement, which, in view of the otherwise clockwise sequence, appears to have originated in error subsequent to the rewriting of the material in OH. Emendation to *westan-suþan*, though drastic, would be in line with OH I. ii. 56, where Thrace is said to have Macedonia 'ab occasu et Africo', and with OH I. ii. 57, where Macedonia is said to have Thrace *a borea*. For similar errors see Or. 19/35 and 21/20.

18/10–12. *be suþan . . . þa land*. OH I. ii. 56 puts the *Aegaeum mare* south of Thrace, and the translator may have assumed from this that it is also south of Constantinople—though it is in fact the Propontis that has this position. Similarly, the placing of Athens and Corinth south of Constantinople could be derived from OH I. ii. 57–8, where it is implied that Athens is south-east of Thrace. However, a source other than OH cannot be ruled out, particularly in view of the description of Athens and Corinth as lands, whereas OH I. ii. 58 refers explicitly to *Athenas ciuitatem.* For the correct designation of these places as cities, see Or. 24/30 and 78/21 etc.

18/11. *sæs earmes.* OH refers only to *Aegaeum mare.* For *Aegaeus sinus* see e.g. Solinus 71, 9 and 12, and Mela I. iii. 17.

18/12. *be westansuðan.* In view of Or.'s consistent use of the term 'north' to translate *aquilo* (see above, 9/27, Commentary), it is tempting to see here not a reversal of OH I. ii. 58 *ab aquilone* but a comment based on an entirely different source. However, the translator may have been forced to recognize the alternative meaning 'north-east' by the context, with its sequence E., SE., S., SW., W., N., and NE.

18/12–13. *æt þæm Wendelsæ.* OH's section on Achaia, I. ii. 58, refers to three seas: *Myrtoum, Creticum,* and *Ionium.* That all these formed part of *mare Magnum* is a piece of information derivable from a text such as Isidore, *Etymologies* XIII. xvi.

18/13. *þas land . . . leode.* OH makes no mention of *Graecia* in its geographical chapter; however, it is included in Isidore, *Etymologies* XIV. iv. 7, where it has assigned to it seven provinces: Dalmatia, Epirus, Hellas, Thessalia, Macedonia, Achaia, and (presumably grouped together) Creta and the Cyclades. In the ninth century, Macedonia and Thrace were both Themes of the Eastern Roman Empire, the capital of which was Constantinople, while Athens, Corinth, and Achaia formed part of the Themes of Hellas and of the Peloponnesus. Moesia, though not included in Isidore's *Graecia,* was one of Alexander the Great's conquests and, after becoming part of the Roman Empire in the time of Augustus, fell to the lot of the Eastern emperors. In the seventh century it was over-run by the Bulgarians. However, Bulgarian control of the territory was hotly contested by the Byzantines, and the West may have thought of it as Greek: see *Einhardi Annales,* s.a. 812, 'Niciforus imperator post multas et insignes uictorias in Moesia prouincia commisso cum Bulgaris proelio moritur'; ibid., s.a. 813, 'Crumas, rex Bulgarorum, qui Niciforum imperatorem ante duos annos interfecit, et Michaelem de Moesia fugauit'.

18/13–15. *be westan . . . þæs sæs.* OH makes no mention of the relative positions of these countries, though it puts Achaia south of Macedonia (I. ii. 57) and Dalmatia west of Macedonia, with the Adriatic on its south (I. ii. 59), thus implying that Dalmatia is north-west of Achaia. Since Dalmatia is indeed north-west of Achaia, Malone (1930b), p. 150, sees Or.'s use of west here as an instance of a 45° clockwise shift. However, there are other possible explanations. (i) Or.'s 'west' may be modified by the subsequent description of Dalmatia as on the *northern* shore of *mare Magnum,* i.e. north-west; (ii) the coastline from Achaia to Istria may have been thought of as running roughly east–west: see Jordanes, col. 1272 and *Expositio* § 53, also the statement in Or. 13/8, that *Creca land* is east of the *Pulgare,* who in their turn are east of Carentania; (iii) a map may have depicted Dalmatia in this position; see Derolez (1971), p. 268.

18/15. *be norðan . . . Istria.* Cf. OH I. ii. 59 'Dalmatia habet . . . a septen-trione Moesiam, ab occasu Histriam et sinum Liburnicum et insulas

Liburnicas.' Although Isidore, writing in the seventh century, included it in *Graecia*, ninth-century Dalmatia was Croat territory, but with Franks and Byzantines struggling for overlordship. At first, Byzantium controlled some of its cities and islands as the Theme of Dalmatia, while its interior was controlled by the Franks: see Einhard, *Life of Charlemagne*, ch. xv. However, this jurisdiction seems often to have been purely nominal, Dalmatian (or White) Croatia apparently becoming fully independent of both great powers in the time of its leader Branimir, 879–92. By the end of the ninth century, its dukes had acquired authority also over Red Croatia and at least part of Pannonian Croatia. Istria was on the north-west of Dalmatian Croatia: it was the site of Venetian–Croat wars in the 880s, when Branimir seems to have extended his power along the coast to the Arsa river in Istria (see Guldesku (1964), pp. 91–106). As for Bulgaria, this too bordered upon the territory of the Dalmatian Croats: according to the testimony of Constantine Porphyrogenitus, Bulgar soil touched the lands of their duke Trpimir (d. about 864) in NE Bosnia, near Tuzla and Zvornik (see Guldesku (1964), p. 101). It is possible, therefore, that Or.'s 'north' is here a blanket term, comprising north-west and north-east (see Malone (1930b), p. 150 and Or. 12/29–30 and 13/3–4). However, an emendation of *7 Istria* to *7 be westan Istria* or *7 Istria be westan*, would not only put Istria in its 'classical' position but also complete the clockwise pattern of boundaries for that country (see Introduction, pp. lxviii f.). In that case, Or.'s *Pulgare* could include also the Bulgarians of eastern Pannonia, with western Pannonia—Or.'s *westen*—where Or. puts it, north of Istria. See above, 13/7–8, Commentary, also below, 61/23, Commentary.

18/15–18. *7 be suðan . . . Pulgarum*. Malone (1930b), p. 150, considers that all these items are the translator's own and show a shift of 45° clockwise. However, although Istria is not used as a centre in OH (which at this point deals with Pannonia, Noricus, and Raetia) the directions tally with ones in OH. Thus, OH I. ii. 59 'ab occasu Histriam et sinum Liburnicum et insulas Liburnicas' could be interpreted as siting the sea south of Istria (where it in fact lies); OH I. ii. 60, 'Pannonia, Noricus et Raetia . . . a meridie Histriam, ab Africo Alpes Poeninas', places the Alps west of Istria, and, if Or.'s *westen* is to be identified with Pannonia (see above, 13/7, Commentary), at the same time locates the *westen* north of it. Either a map incorporating material from OH, or alternatively a written or oral source combining traditional and contemporary information could be responsible for these correspondences.

In the ninth century, Istria—which had been settled by Slovenes in the Slav migrations of the fifth and sixth centuries—formed part of the Markgraf of Friuli and was controlled by the Frankish kingdom of Italy. To its true north it had Friuli and Carniola.

18/19–23. A simplified version of OH's account of Italy and the Alps, I. ii. 61.

18/20. *Wendelsæ*. OH's reference is to *Tyrrhenum mare* and *Hadriaticum sinum*, both considered to form part of *mare Magnum* by authorities such as Isidore, *Etymologies* XIII. xvi.

18/21–2. *westane . . . ðeode.* OH I. ii. 62 '[Alpes] a Gallico mari super Ligusticum sinum exsurgentes, primum Narbonensium fines, deinde Galliam Raetiamque secludunt.' For *mare Gallicum* as part of *mare Magnum* see Isidore, *Etymologies* XIII. xvi. 2. For the possibility that the translator connected *primum* with *exsurgentes* and took *fines* to be a second object of *super*, see Malone (1930b), p. 148.

18/22–3. *east . . . sæ.* OH I. ii. 62 'in sinu Liburnico defigantur.' According to OH I. ii. 59 the *sinus Liburnicus* is west of Dalmatia.

18/24–35. Or. here revises OH I. ii. 63–8 to give what is on the whole a reasonably accurate description of the ninth-century divisions of present-day France, only Brittany (not part of the western Frankish kingdom at that time) being excluded. Instead of OH's Gallia Belgica, Gallia Lugdunensis, Gallia Narbonensis, and Aquitania, we find accounts of Gallia Bellica, Æquitania, Narbonense and Profentse, in that order.

18/24–7. *þa land . . . þæt land.* OH I. ii. 63 similarly describes the geographical position of Gallia Belgica in terms of Rhine, Alps, British Ocean, and Britain, but in addition locates Gallia Narbonensis on the south and Lugdunensis on the west. By the ninth century, Gallia Narbonensis had shrunk in size and was no longer Gallia Belgica's neighbour; in its place Or. puts the Alps (see 18/25 and 18/34 and Commentary). Gallia Lugdunensis, which by this time had ceased to exist, is unmentioned but surprisingly not replaced by Or., which might have been expected to refer to *Britannia*, 'Brittany', in this position. One possible explanation for the consequent absence of a western boundary from Or.'s description is the identity in form between *Britannia* 'Brittany' and *Britannia* 'Britain', which Or., like OH, subsequently locates to the north of Gallia Belgica.

18/24. *þa land . . . Bellica.* For the form *Bellica* see Glossary of Proper Names. The Roman name Gallia Belgica is still used of northern France in ninth-century annals; see e.g. *Annales Fuldenses*, s.a. 888. The area which it denotes consisted of several units, hence perhaps Or.'s use of the plural *þa land*.

18/25. *be suðan.* OH *ab euro.* Malone (1930b), p. 145, suggests that the translator may have either taken OH *Alpes Poeninas* with the immediately following *a meridie* or deliberately departed from his source. 'His location of the Alps to the south of Gallia Belgica agrees strikingly with his later location of them to the north of Provence.' See further below, 18/32–4.

18/25–6. *be westansuðan.* OH *a circio.* Or.'s reading is best accounted for as an error in translation.

18/26–7. *on oðre healfe . . . earme.* No equivalent in OH. Cf. Or. 12/18–19; 13/14–15; 19/12–13, 19/13–14.

18/27–8. *Be westan . . . land.* The abrupt transition may be due to the influence of OH I. ii. 67, 'Aquitanica prouincia obliquo cursu Ligeris fluminis, qui ex plurima parte terminus eius est, in orbem agitur.' For the suggestion that only the Upper Loire is here referred to, see Malone (1930b), p. 145. OH itself puts Gallia Lugdunensis on the east (and also the north) of Aquitania; however, this province was no longer in existence in the ninth century. Or.'s form *Ligore* has no counterpart in extant 'related' Latin manuscripts, nor does it bear any resemblance to the various stages of development of the river name in Gallo-Roman. It may be that an original **Ligere* was written *Ligore* by a scribe, by analogy with the OE (British) *Ligora* (cf. *Ligora ceaster*), the *o* of which may well have been pronounced *e* by this date; see Bately (1966), p. 295. For *Æquitania*, first a kingdom then a duchy in the ninth century, see Glossary of Proper Names.

18/28–9. *be supan . . . Narbonense*. Possibly based on OH I. ii. 68 'ab euro et meridie Narbonensem prouinciam contingit'. However, see below, 18/32–3 and Commentary.

18/29–30. *be westansuðan . . . garsegc*. OH here incorrectly describes Spain as west and the 'oceanu[s] qui Aquitanicus sinus dicitur' as north-west. Since Or.'s version represents the true situation, the 45° clockwise shift must be treated as coincidental. See Introduction, p. lxiv, and Malone (1930b), p. 146.

18/30–3. *Be suðan Narbonense . . . Wascan be norðan*. Cf. OH I. ii. 66 'Narbonensis Provincia . . . habet ab oriente Alpes Cottias, ab occidente Hispaniam, a circio Aquitanicam, a septentrione Lugdunensem, ab aquilone Belgicam Galliam, a meridie mare Gallicum quod est inter Sardiniam et insulas Baleares, habens in fronte, qua Rhodanus fluuius in mare exit, insulas Stoechadas.' In his use of the name Narbonensis, the author of Or. may have been influenced by OH, although the designation *provincia Narbonensis* continues to be used, albeit rarely, in eighth- and ninth-century annals: see e.g. *Einhardi Annales*, s.a. 813. However, Or.'s Narbonensis represents only a portion of OH's—that part round Narbonne, often called *Septimania* or *Gothia* in contemporary sources. For the other part, Provence, see 18/33–5.

18/31. *Profentsæ*. Malone (1930b), p. 146, sees here a reference to a Sea of Provence, which he would locate not east but south-east of Narbonense, thus producing another instance of clockwise shift. However, although one reason for this interpretation is a wish to avoid emendation, it surely requires us to assume an underlying **Profentse sæ*, while on the other hand *Profentsæ* as a variant spelling for *Profentse* 'Provence' has the support of such forms as *Galliæ*, Or. 2/26 etc.

18/31–2. *ða westenu*. This is generally taken to refer to the Pyrenees; however, it may be that the allusion is to the *Hispanica marca* (established 801) that lay as a buffer between France and Spain. See OE *mearcland* 'a borderland, waste land lying outside the cultivated', etc., and E. Norden, *Altgermanien* (Leipzig and Berlin, 1934), pp. 14–17.

18/33. *Wascan*. The Vascones invaded Novempopulane, or Aquitania Tertia, between 561 and 602, the name Vasconia or Guasconia, OHG

UUasconoland, being adopted in the seventh century. In the ninth century, Gascony was a duchy, ruled by West Frankish dukes.

18/33. *Wascan be norðan.* Cf. 18/35, where the Vascones are put west of Provence. Since Gascony is in the south-west of France, Malone (1930b), p. 146, punctuates in such a way as to place *be norðan* in the following sentence (where it then appears twice, requiring us to suppose that the author changed his construction in midstream) and defines Or.'s Provence as 'the whole of ancient Narbonensis'. However, this and related problems are more simply solved if we assume that either the author of Or. or his source wrongly located Gascony in the south-east instead of the south-west of Aquitania. A south-eastern Gascony would be north of Septimania; the latter would then have Aquitania solely on its north-west and Aquitania would indeed have only part of Septimania on its south. For a similar error see Johann Honter, *Rudimenta Cosmographia* (Basle, 1542), where a woodcut map of France puts *Gasconia* next to *Gallia Narbonensis* and *Provincia.*

18/33–4. *Profentse . . . Alpis hæt.* Provence, which became a kingdom, with a Frankish ruler, in the mid-ninth century, was situated between the Alps, Cevennes and the Mediterranean, extending north at least as far as Isère. According to *Annales Vedastini, MGHS rer. Germ.*, s.a. 877, Charles had to cross the *Alpes Provintiae* to return to Francia. For a tradition of mountains south of Gallia Comata and north of Narbonensis (in its Orosian sense, including Provence), see *Divisio,* §§ 7 and 8.

18/34–5. *be norðan hyre 7 eastan.* Interpreting the direction as north-east, Malone (1930b), p. 147, observes that Burgundy is actual north of Provence proper (i.e. east of the Rhône) and concludes that the author's accuracy can be maintained only if we define his *Profentse* as the whole of ancient Narbonensis east and west of the Rhône. Labuda (1961), p. 116, n. 173, on the other hand, sees here a reflection of the situation in the fourth and fifth centuries and suggests that Or.'s information came from a *mappa mundi.* However, there are two other possibilities: (i) the Burgundians may have been thought of as living north-east, because to the traveller along the Grande Route d'Italie (passing from Bar s. Aube to Langres, Besançon, Pontarlier, Lausanne, and then via either the St. Bernard or Simplon passes to Milan), Provence would be for much of the way on the south-west (see Introduction, p. lxvii); (ii) the author may be referring not to the ancient province of Burgundy, nor to the French duchy of that name set up by Charles the Bald after the Treaty of Verdun, 843, but to the kingdom of Burgundy built up by Roþulf, which included the Helvetian *pagi* as well as the ancient diocese of Besançon and which was indisputably north-east of Provence.

18/35. *be westan.* For the misplacing of the Vascones, see 18/33, Commentary.

19/1–10. Or. here rearranges and abridges the account given by OH I. ii. 69–74, reversing the order in which the two Hispanias are described and showing no awareness of the ninth-century political divisions. See, however, 104/30 where Cartago Nova is equated with *Cordofa*, ninth-century capital of the Emirate of Cordova.

19/1–3. *Ispania . . . Wendelsæ.* OH I. ii. 69 'Hispania uniuersa terrarum situ trigona *est* et circumfusione oceani Tyrrhenique pelagi paene insula efficitur.' *Est* is omitted by the best manuscripts of OH.

19/3–4. *þæt igland . . . Gades.* OH I. ii. 72 *Gades insulae.* See above, 9/8, Commentary. For the direction south-west (not given by OH) see 9/6–8.

19/4–7. *se ðridda . . . Scene.* OH I. ii. 71 'secundus angulus circium intendit; ubi Brigantia Gallaeciae (*var.* Galliae) ciuitas sita altissimam pharum et inter pauca memorandi operis ad speculam Britanniae erigit.' See also the section on *Hibernia*, I. ii. 81, where it is said that Brigantia is most clearly visible from the promontory *ubi Scenae fluminis ostium est.* For the equation of Hibernia with *Scotland* see 16/6–7 and 19/15, Commentary.

19/5. *Gallia burh.* OH I. ii. 71 *Gallaeciae ciuitas,* 'related' MSS *Galliae civitas.*

19/8. *Wendelsæ be suðan.* OH I. ii. 74 'a meridie Gaditanum oceani fretum; unde mare Nostrum . . . inmittitur.'

19/8. *7 be eastan . . . Ispania.* OH I. ii. 74 'Hispania ulterior habet ab oriente Vaccaeos, Celtiberos et Oretanos.' Cf. I. ii. 73, where *Hispania citerior* is said to have the Vaccaei and Oretani on its west.

19/8–9. *be norðan . . . Equitania.* Possibly based on OH I. ii. 70, where the first corner of Spain is said to be walled in on the right (*a dextris*) by *Aquitanica prouincia.* Cf., however, 18/29, where Aquitania is said by Or. to have Spain on its south-west. Could the author of Or. here have used a Latin source giving the direction as north-east, i.e. *ab aquilone*, the term he normally translates as 'north'?

19/9. *be norðaneastan . . . Pireni.* Cf. OH I. ii. 73 'Hispaniam citeriorem ab oriente incipientem Pyrenaei saltus a parte septentrionis usque ad Cantabros Asturesque deducit.' For the translation of *saltus* by *weald* see 56/27 and *Abstrusa* SA 17 *saltus: silva vel mons.*

19/9–10. *be eastan Narbonense.* Not OH. See above, 18/28–9 and 18/30–3.

19/11–20. Or. surprisingly adds virtually nothing to the meagre account of Britain and the neighbouring islands given in OH I. ii. 76–82, actually omitting references to the Isle of Man and to Portus Rutupi (Richborough), which, OH claims, affords the nearest landing place for those who cross the Channel from Gaul. It also omits details about Ireland that it has already used elsewhere (see 19/4–7 and Commentary.) In mitigation, it may be pointed out that OH's inaccurate description of the position and size of Britain continued to be accepted well into the late Middle Ages.

19/12–13. *þonne . . . Bellica.* OH I. ii. 76 'a meridie Gallias habet'. Cf. *OE Bede*, 26/1–2, 'Hit hafað fram suðdæle . . . Gallia Bellica.'

19/13–15. *on westhealfe . . . þæt igland.* OH I. ii. 78 'a tergo . . . unde oceano infinito patet Orcadas insulas habet quarum xx desertae sunt, xiii coluntur.' Ireland OH elsewhere (I. ii. 80) locates between Spain and Britain. For a singular Orcades island, see the Ravenna Geographer, 439, 6–7.

19/15. *Igbernia . . . hataŏ.* Cf. *OE Bede,* 28/9, where *Scotland* translates Latin *Hiberniam;* also *Anglo-Saxon Chronicle,* s.a. 891. For the alternative name *Iraland* see 16/6 and Commentary.

19/16–18. *sio sunne . . . Brettannia.* OH I. ii. 81 'haec propior Britanniae, spatio terrarum angustior, sed caeli solique temperie magis utilis.' Could the source of this statement be a gloss or comment such as 'propinquus sol collocatur', which the translator took to be an explanation of OH's comment on the climate? Cf. the Ravenna Geographer, 12, 6–11: 'ad quos dicimus quomodo verbi gratia stat homo in Scotia, ubi iam terra ultra nullo modo invenitur apud humanos oculos, ei comparet quod certissime duodecim horas diei expleat et propinquus sol collocetur.'

19/18–19. *þonne . . . Thila.* OH I. ii. 79 merely locates *insula Thyle* 'in the middle of the ocean towards the north-west', while, according to Isidore, *Etymologies* XIV. vi. 4, it is 'inter septentrionalem et occidentalem plagam ultra Brittaniam'. References to *ultima Thule* in Latin texts are too numerous for Or.'s source here to be identified. Later writers appear to have equated Thule with Iceland, an island first settled by Norsemen in the second half of the ninth century; however, there is no evidence that the author of Or. did likewise.

19/21–20/24. In its description of Africa, Or. follows OH I. ii. 83–94 fairly closely, occasionally simplifying, occasionally misunderstanding, but apparently only once adding material from another source.

19/23–6. *Ure . . . norŏdæl.* According to OH I. ii. 83, Africa, between *mare Magnum* and the ocean, is narrower than Europe, because *mare Magnum* inclines more to the south.

19/26–8. *sio hæte . . . hæte.* OH's claim, I. ii. 86, is that more land remains uncultivated and unexplored in Africa because of the heat of the sun than in Europe because of the intensity of the cold.

19/31. *eastan westwerd.* Or.'s addition.

19/32. *æt . . . hæt.* OH I. ii. 88 puts the boundary at the city of Paraetonium. For the Nile as boundary, see e.g. Mela I. i. 8, Solinus 166, 1, and Bede, *De Natura Rerum,* col. 276.

19/32–3. *sio eastemeste þeod.* OH I. ii. 87 'Libya Cyrenaica et Pentapolis post Aegyptum in parte Africae prima est.'

19/33–20/2. *Hire . . . Rogathitus.* A rearrangement in two parts of OH I. ii. 87–9, which gives one set of boundaries for both Libya Cyrenaica and the territory of 'gentes Libyoaethiopum et Garamantum'. OH *Aegyptus* is split into Nearer and Further Egypt, and the former assigned, along with the Syrtes Maiores, to *Libia Cirimacia,* the latter, along with *Rogathitus* (the Troglodytes), to *Libia Æthiopicum.*

19/34. *Wendelsæ . . . Æthiopicum.* OH I. ii. 89 *mare Libycum.* The strange allusion in Or. is best explained as due to scribal error, with an original *Libicum* written *Libia Æthiopicum* in anticipation of the *Libia Æthiopicum* (for OH *gentes Libyoaethiopum*) that occurs only eight words later. *Mare Libycum* is identified with *mare Hadriaticum* in OH I. ii. 97. See further below, 20/5, Commentary.

19/35. *Be westan.* An error for *be eastan.*

20/4. *þone Sirtes . . . land.* OH I. ii. 90 'aras Philaenorum inter Syrtes maiores et Trogodytas'.

20/5. *þone Wendelsæ . . . Adriaticum.* OH I. ii. 90 'mare Siculum uel potius Hadriaticum'. For the identification with *mare Magnum,* see Isidore, *Etymologies* XIII. xvi.

20/5–6. *þa þeode . . . Minores.* OH I. ii. 90 *Syrtes minores.* Cf. 20/4, 'þone Sirtes Maiores', and 20/11, 'þæt land Syrtes Minores'. The Lesser and Greater Syrtes are in fact gulfs, as the translator could have learned from glosses such as *Abolita* SI 8 'Sirtes, duo sinus Africae'. For an error similar to Or.'s, see *Liber Generationis,* and *Ex Chronographo Anni P. Chr. 354 excerptum,* in *Geographi Latini* pp. 164 and 172, where names of provinces include *Syrtes.* According to Isidore, *Etymologies* XIII. xviii. 6 *De Æstibus et Fretis,* 'Syrtes sunt harenosa in mari loca.'

20/9. *Bizantium.* OH I. ii. 90 *Byzacium,* 'related' MSS *Bizantium.*

20/9. *seo burh.* MS *se beorh.* For confusion of *beorg* and *burg* see also *Exodus,* ed. Lucas, l. 70a, note, and 72/6–7, below.

20/10. *mycle . . . Cartaina.* OH I. ii. 92 *Carthago magna.*

20/12. *Mauritania.* OH I. ii. 93 'Sitifensis et Caesariensis Mauretaniae'.

20/16. *Astrixim ða beorgas.* OH I. ii. 93 *montem Astrixim. Mons* often has the meaning 'mountain range' in OH.

20/16–17. *þæt wæsmbære . . . sand.* OH I. ii. 93 'inter uiuam terram et harenas'. For *uiuam terram,* some manuscripts read *fecundas terras;* see e.g. Munich 6250.

20/17. *suð.* Or.'s addition.

20/19. *Abbenas þa beorgas.* Cf. OH I. ii. 94 'inter Auenae et Calpes duo contraria sibi promunturia'. OH's genitive singular *Auenae* appears to have been interpreted as a plural form, either by the translator or by a copyist of the Latin text incorrectly 'emending' *inter Auenae* to *inter Auenas.* See Introduction, p. lx.

20/21. *þær . . . standað.* Or.'s addition. See *Divisio,* § 2 and Isidore, *Etymologies* XIII. xv. 2, also above, 9/9 and 15.

20/26–8. *Cipros . . . Mesicos.* OH I. ii. 96 'Insula Cypros ab oriente mari Syrio, quem Issicum (*var.* Misicum) sinum uocant, ab occidente mari Pamphylico, a septentrione Aulone Cilicio, a meridie Syriae et Phoenices pelago cingitur.' Cf. OH I. ii. 25 'Taurum montem, cui subiacet Cilicia et Isauria usque ad Cilicium sinum, qui spectat contra insulam Cyprum.'

20/29. *an hund* . . . *twentig*. OH I. ii. 96 'in lato milia passuum cxxv'. The discrepancy between the two sets of figures is probably due to confusion of *v* (or *u*) and *ii* in an underlying manuscript. For a similar error, see below, 40/18.

20/30–1. *westan* . . . *Addriaticum*. OH I. ii. 97 'ab occasu et septentrione mari Cretico'. See Isidore, *Etymologies* XIII. xvi. 2 and Solinus 23, 15, where the Sicilian sea is said to lie between Sicily and Crete, i.e. west of Crete as here. For the identification of this sea with the Adriatic, see OH I. ii. 100. Or. strangely omits all reference to the Adriatic as *southern* boundary, though OH puts 'mari Libyco, quod et Hadriaticum uocant' in this position.

20/32. *an hund* . . . *hundsyfantig*. OH I. ii. 97 'habet in longo milia passuum clxxii.' See MS Vienna 366 *clxxi*.

20/33. *þreo 7 fiftig*. OH I. ii. 98 *liiii*, Vienna 366, Ricc. 627 and other 'related' MSS *liii*.

20/33–21/2. *be eastan* . . . *Addriaticum*. OH I. ii. 98 'ab oriente finiuntur litoribus Asiae, ab occidente mari Icario, a septentrione mari Aegaeo, a meridie mari Carpathio.' Or.'s source here appears to be Pliny IV. xii. 71, 'Cyclades et Sporades ab oriente litoribus Icariis Asiae, ab occidente Myrtois Atticae, a septentrione Aegaeo mari, a meridie Cretico et Carpathio inclusae.' Or. omits the measurements given by OH as well as individual island names.

21/2. *ðryscyte*. Possibly based on OH I. ii. 99, where Sicily is said to have three promontories; see, however, Isidore's entry on Sicily, *Etymologies* XIV. vi. 32, where the old name Trinacria is explained as the equivalent of Latin *triquetra*.

21/3. *norðsceatan*. See OH I. ii. 99 'Pelorum . . . aspicit ad aquilonem' and above, 9/27, Commentary.

21/4. *se suðsceata*. OH I. ii. 99 'Pachynum . . . respicit ad euronotum'. See Derolez (1971), p. 257, n. 3.

21/7. *an hund* . . . *norð*. OH I. ii. 100 'habet a Peloro in Pachynum milia passuum clviiii.' The 'related' manuscripts closest to Or. give the distance as 157 miles.

21/7–8. *se þridda* . . . *westlang*. OH I. ii. 100 'a Pachyno in Lilybaeum clxxxvii'. The numeral given by Zangemeister is an editorial emendation: both his base manuscripts and the manuscripts closest to Or. have the reading *clxxvii*.

21/9. *se Wendelsæ*. Or.'s addition.

21/10–11. *be westan* . . . *þam lande*. OH I. ii. 100 'ab occidente et septentrione habet mare Tyrrhenum, a borea usque subsolanum fretum Hadriaticum quod diuidit Tauromenitanos Siciliae et Bruttios Italiae.' Or. appears to be echoing a definition of *fretum* such as is found in Isidore, *Etymologies* XIII. xviii. 2: 'Fretum autem appellatum quod ibi semper mare ferveat; nam fretum est angustum et quasi fervens mare, ab undarum fervore nominatum, ut Gaditanum vel Siculum.' See also

Horace scholia, ed. Hauthal, *Carm.* II. xiii. 13. The position of the strait is altered by Or. from north-east to north, just as is the direction of the promontory of Pelorus lying on it; however, the term *borea* should have presented no problem to the translator: cf. 12/2 and 19/11 where it is taken to represent the direction 'north-east'.

21/12–13. *twa 7 twentig.* OH I. ii. 101 *xx.*

21/13. *þreo 7 þritti.* OH I. ii. 102 *ccxxx,* Vienna 366 and other 'related' MSS *cccxxx.* The word *hund* appears to have dropped out of the OE text.

21/13–14. *twa . . . brad.* Cf. the 'twa 7 twentig mila brad' of the sentence immediately preceding. OH reads *lxxx*; however, many manuscripts have the variant *ccxxx.*

21/14–15. *Him . . . scyt on.* OH I. ii. 102 'habet ab oriente et borea Tyrrhenicum mare quod spectat ad portum urbis Romae.' That the Tiber was the river on which Rome and its port both lay is a detail which could have been learned from a variety of sources; see e.g. Servius, *Aen.* VII. 31, Isidore, *Etymologies* XV. i. 56.

21/16. *be westan.* OH I. ii. 102 puts the Baleares *ab Africo*; however, in the section on the two Baleares, I. ii. 104, Sardinia is said to be on their east, as here in Or.

21/17. *Romeburh.* OH I. ii. 103 *portum Vrbis*; cf. I. ii. 102, 'portum urbis Romae'.

21/18–19. *be norðan . . . land.* OH I. ii. 103 'a circio et a septentrione Ligusticum sinum'. The reason for Or.'s alteration is unclear, unless it is based on misunderstanding of a comment such as Servius, *Aen.* X. 709, 'Liguria cohaeret Tusciae.' See also Mela II. vii. 122 and p. xi, n. 20, where a scribe (?) makes Corsica 'Etrusco litori propior'. For the equation of Etruria with Liguria elsewhere in Or., see 109/13, Commentary. For the name *Tuscania*, see *Glossarium Ansileubi*, TI 171, 'Tuscania: pars est Italiae, idem est Etruria.'

21/19–20. *syxtene . . . brad.* OH I. ii. 103 'in longo milia passuum clx, in lato milia xxvi'.

21/20. *him is . . . Affrica.* OH I. ii. 104 'a meridie et Africo Mauretanicum pelagus'. The translator may have been using a manuscript in which *Africo* had been corrupted to *Africa* or *Africae*: cf. the version of OH in *Cosmographia,* p. 102, 'a meridie africae Mauritanicum pelagus'. The error 'north' for 'south' may be his or a subsequent scribe's.

21/20–1. *Gades be westan.* OH I. ii. 104 'ab occasu Hibericum pelagus'. Labuda (1961), p. 118, n. 216, sees the introduction of Gades on the west as due to the use of a map. However, there are a number of written sources from which this information could have been derived: see e.g. Isidore, *Etymologies* XIII. xv. 2 and xvi. 2.

21/21. *Ispania be norðan.* OH I. ii. 104 'ab aquilone mare Gallicum'. Cf. OH I. ii. 70, where Spain's 'angulus prior' is said to have the Balearic sea on its left, i.e. to its south.

21/24. *manna ærest*. OH I. iv. 1 'rex Assyriorum, primus ut ipsi uolunt'. Cf. OH VII. ii. 14 'Nino primo rege' and Christian of Stavelot, col. 1280, 'Nini qui primus rex in mundo fuit'. According to Berosus, Ninus was the third king of Babylon; however, he came to be ranked first (e.g. by Diodorus), because of his preeminence.

21/29–31. *Sciððie . . . unspedgestan*. OH I. iv. 2 *Scythicam barbariem*. For the 'hardness' of the Scythians see Justinus II. i. 13, 'Et quanto Scythis sit caelum asperius quam Aegyptiis, tanto et corpora et ingenia esse duriora'; see also Acron, *Comm. in Horatium Flaccum, Carm.* iii. 24. 11, where *rigidi Getae* is glossed *fortes, asperi*. For the Scythians' poverty see OH I. xiv. 2, where the Scythians describe themselves as *inopes*; see also comments such as Justinus II. ii. 7, 'aurum et argentum . . . non adpetunt.'

21/31–22/2. *hy ða . . . geleornodon*. An effective rewriting of OH I. iv. 2, 'Scythicam . . . barbariem, adhuc tunc inbellem et innocentem, torpentem excitare saeuitiam, uires suas nosse . . . ad postremum uincere dum uincitur edocuit.'

22/2–4. *him ða . . . libbað*. Based on OH I. iv. 2, 'non lacte iam pecudum sed sanguinem hominum bibere', probably as a result of manuscript corruption. *Bibere* appears in a number of manuscripts of OH in the form *uiuere* and Professor Dorothy Whitelock has suggested to me that this may have been further corrupted to *uidere*. For milk as the Scythians' staple diet, see e.g. Justinus II. ii. 8, 'lacte et melle uescuntur', and Regino of Prüm, s.a. 889.

22/6. *wið Sciððie . . . burh*. Apparently a contextual guess, possibly influenced by OH's comment, I. iv. 2, that Ninus taught the Scythians 'ad postremum uincere'. OH I. iv. 3 refers merely to 'deficientem a se . . . urbem'.

22/9–10. *þe hio . . . bespon*. There is nothing in OH to suggest that Semiramis incited Ninus to make war.

22/12. *mid wiflice niðe*. Cf. OH I. iv. 5 'non contenta terminis mulier, quos a uiro suo tunc solo bellatore in quinquaginta annis adquisitos susceperat, Aethiopiam . . . imperio adiecit.'

22/13. *þæt underiende folc Æthiopiam*. OH I. iv. 5 'Aethiopiam bello pressam, sanguine interlitam'. See Introduction, p. c, n. 2.

22/13–14. *Indeas . . . Alexander*. OH I. iv. 5 'Indis . . . quo praeter illam et Alexandrum Magnum nullus intrauit'. OH is here following Justinus; however, see below, 81/22 and 43/2–4 and Commentary.

22/15–16. *ða hio . . . mihte*. *Ða* is here used concessively in the sense of 'although' and it is tempting to suppose that Or.'s source at this point had concessive *cum*. However, there is nothing comparable to this statement in OH and I have been unable to find a Latin source for the information that Semiramis failed to conquer India—though this is implicit in the statement by Freculph, *Chronicon*, col. 987, that she conquered '[totum] Orientem usque ad terminos Indiae'. (Augustine, *Civ. Dei* XVI. xvii, makes a similar claim on behalf of her husband,

Ninus.) For Greek references to Semiramis' failure, see *Diodorus Siculus*, ed. C. H. Oldfather (London, 1933–67), II, 19, and Arrian, *History of Alexander*, ed. E. I. Robson (London, 1929), VI. 24.

22/16–18. *Sio gitsung . . . alyfdon*. Cf. OH I. iv. 6 'quod eo tempore ideo crudelius grauiusque erat quam nunc est, persequi et trucidare populos in pace uiuentes, quia tunc apud illos nec foris erant ulla incendia bellorum, nec domi tanta exercitia cupiditatum'.

22/22–3. *ælcne . . . kynekynnes wæs*. Based on a misunderstanding of OH I. iv. 7 'omnes quos regie arcessitos'. For *þæt* as conjunction in this combination of adjective and noun clauses, see Bruce Mitchell, *A Guide to Old English* (Oxford, 2nd edn., 1968), p. 77.

23/1. *ælce geare*. Or.'s addition. For the annual flooding of the river Jordan, see Joshua 3: 15 and 1 Chron. 12: 15.

23/2. *mid . . . flode*. I have been unable to find a written source for this additional material. However, as Professor Cross points out, *Notes and Queries*, N.S. xxi, no. 5 (1974), 189, it could derive ultimately from observation: 'Adamnan, *De Locis Sanctis*, II, 16, reports Arculph as seeing a cross in Jordan marking the spot where Christ was baptized: "close to which the water comes up to the neck of the tallest man, or, at time of great drought . . . up to his breast, but when the river is in flood, the whole of the cross is covered". Breast to neck may approach one foot and there were other travellers to the Holy Places before the *Orosius* was written.'

23/7 *þæs dæles*. OH I. v. 10 *conuallem*.

23/7–8. *se dæl se*. I have retained the manuscript reading here. However, *se dæl þe* would make better sense.

23/7–11. *se dæl . . . acxan*. OH I. v. 10 refers merely to a *regio cineris*. However, at this point a number of manuscripts interpolate the comment (derived ultimately from Josephus by way of Hegesippus) 'Illic poma virentia et formatos uvarum racemos, ut edentibus (*var*. edendi) generent (*var*. gignant) cupiditatem, si carpas, fatiscunt in cinerem fumumque excitant quasi adhuc ardeant, ut nunc quoque appareat.' It is generally assumed that this interpolation was present in the manuscript of OH used by the translator. However, although it is found in certain manuscripts of the related groups, A, B, and C (see Introduction, pp. lvii f., and Bately (1961), p. 97), it is absent from the manuscripts apparently closest to Or. Accordingly, the possibility that the translator had some other source cannot be ruled out. Apart from Hegesippus IV. xviii itself (ed. V. Ussani, *CSEL*, lxvi (Leipzig, 1932–)) likely candidates include Isidore, *Etymologies* XIV. iii. 25, Augustine, *Civ. Dei* xxi. 5 and 8, Tertullian, *Apol*., *PL* i, cols. 483–4 and Tacitus, *Histories* 5. 7. However, the version of Hegesippus closest in wording to Or. is Bede, *De Locis Sanctis*, *PL* xciv, col. 1187: 'servat adhuc regio speciem poenae: nascuntur enim ibi poma pulcherrima, quae et edendi cupiditatem spectantibus generant: si carpas, fatiscunt ac resoluuntur in cinerem, fumumque excitant, quasi adhuc ardeant.' This passage is not used by Bede in his account of the holy places in *HE* V. xvi–xvii, nor is it found in Adamnan.

23/13 *betuh him.* According to OH I. vii. 1 the Telchises and Caryathii fight not each other but Foroneus, king of the Argives, and the Parrhasii.

23/14–15. *þæt drugon . . . feawum.* OH I. vii. 1–2 merely says that 'ancipiti spe sine fructu uictoriae gesserunt' and that the Telchises were shortly afterwards defeated in battle. Since similar comments without a basis in OH are found on a number of occasions in Or. (see e.g. 35/17–18), this may be the translator's own assumption.

23/17. *ælcum gewinne.* The translator appears to have interpreted the *congressu* 'friendly meeting' of OH I. vii. 2, 'a congressu totius humanae habitationis', in its alternative sense of 'combat'.

23/17–18. *Ac hi . . . fordydon.* OH I. vii. 2 merely hints that Rhodes may not have been the place of safety that the Telchises thought it. According to Greek sources, however, the Telchises abandoned Rhodes, foreseeing that the island would be inundated. Or.'s version of the story appears to combine two separate pieces of information: (i) that Rhodes subsequently became Greek territory (see e.g. Isidore, *Etymologies* XIV. vi. 19, Freculph, *Chronicon*, col. 947, and Juvenal, scholia VI. 295); (ii) that the Telchises were wiped out (see Ovid, *Metamorphoses* VII. 367, where Zeus is said to have caused their destruction by inundation, and Servius, *Aen.* IV. 377, where it is claimed that they were destroyed by Apollo in the shape of a wolf).

23/19. *eahta hund wintra.* *Hund* is in a later hand on an erasure and a marginal note, also in a later hand, has the reading 'þusend 7 eahta wintra': cf. OH I. viii. 1 *mviii.* Did MS C (our sole authority at this point) have the reading *eahta þusend* for *eahta 7 þusend*?

23/20. *syfan gear.* Or.'s addition. Cf. OH I. viii. 11 'fuerunt autem ante annos famis septem praecedentes alii septem ubertatis anni.'

23/23–4. *Sompeius . . . singende.* OH I. viii. 1 'Pompeius historicus eiusque breuiator Iustinus docet'. The expected translation of *historicus* is *stærwritere*; see below, 37/5 and 88/18 and Commentary. *Scop* Or. elsewhere uses to render OH *poeta* (see 31/31, 35/12, 53/16) and *comicus*, a term used of both comic actors and comic poets in classical Latin (see 107/28, referring to the poet Terence). Is it possible that underlying Or.'s rendering here is a confusion between *historicus* and *histrio*? See Corpus H 119, 'Historicus pantomimus qui historias scribit' (so also *Abstrusa*) and *Gl. Ansileubi*, HI 215, 'Hisdrio: historia (-icus)'. See also Solinus 20, 11, where MS H has the reading *historicus* for the *histrio* of the best texts. As for the 'translation' of *breuiator* by *cniht*, it is possible that the translator was puzzled by this rare word and assumed that the element *brev-* denoted shortness of stature.

24/1–2. *he þæs landes . . . sæde.* Or.'s addition. That Joseph foresaw the seven years of plenty is a detail given in Genesis 41 : 29.

24/9–13. *For ðon . . . lareowas.* OH I. viii. 7 goes no further than to claim that the Egyptian priests told a confused story, 'ne in contumeliam idolorum suorum eum colendum merito ostenderent, cuius consilio adnuntiata haec mala et auxilio euitata docuissent'. For the translator's attitude to idols and pagan gods see below 57/7–13 and Commentary, also 84/7.

24/16–18. *Wæs . . . Pharaon.* OH I. viii. 10 'sub rege Aegyptiorum Diopolita, cui nomen erat Amosis'. The 'related' manuscript, Balliol 125, has the gloss *Pharao* at this point, while the Orosius commentary, f. 5ᵛ, explains *diupolitana* as 'nomine genti' and then comments 'Amoisis . . . nomen regis quia verius ut farao'. Of the numerous Latin references to Pharaoh as a title, however, the one that is closest to this addition in Or. is the entry in Jerome–Eusebius, cols. 150–2, under the heading *Dynastia Diospolitanorum*, 'Aegyptiorum reges omnes tunc Pharaones dicebantur.'

24/20–2. *On . . . world.* No equivalent in OH. Isidore, *Etymologies* V. xxxix. 6 f., names four kingdoms as arising in the second and third ages of the world: *regnum Scytharum, regnum Aegyptiorum, regnum Assyriorum et Siciniorum,* and *regnum Argivorum*; however, at least one manuscript, Kⁱ, omits the reference to the Scythians. Or. could be following some such corrupt source, though an incorrect contextual guess is more likely.

24/24–8. *Swa eac . . . þonne hæfð.* OH's moral is quite different: we must not be surprised if there are some men today who would save themselves by pretending to be Christians but who maintain that they are sorely oppressed in Christian times. See, however, OH I. xxi. 17–18, and Introduction, pp. xciii ff.

24/29–30. *eahta hund . . . gearan.* According to Or.'s usage elsewhere, we would expect either 'eahta hund wintra 7 tyn wintrum' or 'eahta hund wintra 7 tyn'.

24/30. *Athena, Creca byrig.* OH I. ix. 1 *Athenis.* Cf. 18/11, where Athens is described as a 'land'.

24/31–2. *þe ærest . . . cyning.* Or.'s addition. Possible sources include Jerome–Eusebius, col. 168, Bede, *De Temporum Ratione*, col. 530, and Isidore, *Etymologies* XV. i. 44.

24/33. *geond ealle world.* Or.'s addition. Isidore, *Etymologies* XIII. xxii. 4, describes this as the third flood, confined to Thessalia, only the first (Noah's) being world-wide.

24/33–25/1. *Thasalia, Creca byrig.* OH I. ix. 1 *Thessaliae.* Thessaly was not a town but a province of Greece: see e.g. Isidore, *Etymologies* XIV. iv. 7. Did Or. here use a source which merely located Thessalia in *Graecia,* without further specification? For a comparable error see, however, *Glossaria Latina* AA T 374 *Thracia: civitas in Graecia.*

25/2. *Theuhaleon.* Sweet reads *Theuhale on.* However, there are no other instances in Or. of a construction *þær X on ricsade,* while *þær X ricsade* occurs 4 times; see 32/14–15, 36/12, 36/13, and 36/13–14.

25/3. *mid scypum.* OH I. ix. 2 *ratibus,* 'rafts'. See e.g. Isidore, *Etymologies*

XIX. i. 9, 'Nunc iam rates abusive naves', and *Abolita* RA 5 *ratibus*: *navibus*.

25/4–6. *Be þæm . . . Noe wæs*. OH I. ix. 2 'a quo propterea genus hominum reparatum ferunt'. Potter (1952–3), p. 390, believes that *reparatum* was misread or misheard as *repartum* or *reparitum*. However, the use of the word *bispell* 'fable' by Or. suggests knowledge of the myth of Deucalion and Pyrrha, according to which Deucalion became the progenitor of the human race: see e.g. *Mythographus I*, 189, Lactantius Placidus, *in Stat. Theb*. III. 560, Servius, *Buc*. VI. 41 and *App. Serviana, ibid.*, p. 113, on Virgil's *lapides iactos*: 'idest quos Pyrrha et Deucalion iactaverunt, id est in terra post diluvium Deucalionis homines nati sunt de illis viri et feminae'.

25/7–8. *Æthiopian, Affrica leode*. OH I. ix. 3 *Aethiopia*. See above, 20/13–14.

25/10. *mid druncennysse*. This addition may have been prompted by knowledge that Liber was reputedly the inventor of wine and identified with Bacchus, or Dionysus: see e.g. Isidore, *Etymologies* XVII. v. 1 and VIII. xi. 44.

25/11–13. *hi hine . . . waldend*. Or.'s addition. Potter (1952–3), p. 391, suggests that *gewinnes* is an error for *wines*. However, Liber was renowned not only for his introduction of wine but also for his military prowess; see e.g. Macrobius, ed. F. Eyssenhardt (Leipzig, 1868), *Saturnalia* I. 19, 'Hinc etiam Liber pater bellorum potens probatur, quod eum primum ediderunt auctorem triumphi', and Isidore, *Etymologies* IX. iii. 32. References to Liber's deification are also commonplace, see e.g. Isidore, *Etymologies* VIII. xi. 4 and XVII. v. 1, Augustine, *Civ. Dei* XVIII. 12, and Freculph, *Chronicon*, col. 956.

25/18–20. *froxas . . . gegearwod wære*. OH I. x. 10 'post horridos ranarum squalores per omnia munda inmundaque reptantes'. See also OH VII. xxvii. 5, where the frogs are said to have caused the inhabitants to starve. Or.'s rendering may owe something to the warning to Pharaoh, Exodus 8: 3, that the frogs shall come 'in furnos tuos, et in reliquias ciborum tuorum'.

25/19. *wyrma*. Isidore, *Etymologies* XII. vi. 5 and 58, classifies *ranae* not under *vermes* or *serpentes* but under *pisces*. However, in Old and Middle English, and indeed still in Early Modern English, the term 'worm' was used to denote any creature that creeps or crawls, including reptiles, amphibia, and insects; see e.g. *Genesis and Exodus*, ed. R. Morris, EETS, os 7 (1865), 2982 'Ðis wirmes [i.e. frogs and toads] storuen in ðe stede', and George Turbervile, *Tragical Tales* (London, 1587), ix. 128ᵛ, 'Vnderneath this bed of Sage, The fellow that did dig, Turnd vp a toade, a loathsome sight, A worme exceeding big.' See also below, 93/30–1.

25/21–3. *gnættas . . . piniende wæron*. OH I. x. 10 'ignitas sciniphes et nusquam, toto aere uibrante, uitabiles'. Cf. OH VII. xxvii. 6, where *sciniphes* are described as 'musculas . . . paruissimas ac saeuissimas, quae mediis saepe aestibus per loca squalida coadunatim uibrando densatae tinnulo uolatu adlabi solent capillisque hominum ac pecudum saetis cum urente morsu interseri'.

25/26–7. *ða mæstan ofermetto geniðrode.* OH makes no mention of the pride of Pharaoh and the Egyptians; however, this is a commonplace in both Bible texts and patristic writings; see e.g. Nehemiah 9: 10 and Augustine, *In Ioannis Evangelium Tractatus CXXIV, PL* xxxv, col. 1387; also Isidore, *Etymologies* XII. viii. 14 (of the third plague), 'superbus Aegyptiorum populus caesus est.'

25/32. *eall . . . growendes.* OH I. x. 12 *arbores.* Cf. Exodus 9: 25, 'cunctamque herbam agri percussit grando, et omne lignum regionis confregit.' The phrase is repeated in Or. 119/17–18, where it renders OH V. xi. 2 'herbasque omnes . . . folia arborum'.

26/3–4. *þær com . . . þysþernes.* OH I. x. 12 *tenebras.* Hail is a feature of the seventh plague.

26/6. *on anre niht.* Or.'s addition. Cf. Exodus 12: 29 *in noctis medio.*

26/7–10. *þeah . . . fulgen.* This appears to be based on a combination of OH I. x. 13 'qui iubenti Deo non cesserant cessere punienti' and I. x. 9 'tandem quos dimittere noluerant, etiam festinare coegerunt.'

26/13. *hy gecyrran . . . Egyptum.* See OH I. x. 2 and VII. xxvii.

26/13. *Se kyningc Pharon.* Pharaoh is not named by OH. See Exodus 14.

26/16–18. *God . . . genyðerode.* OH I. x. 15 *ultor contumacium Deus.* For Pharaoh's pride see 25/26–7, Commentary.

26/18–19. *on twelf wegas.* Or.'s addition. This detail is to be found in Jerome, *Tractatus LIX in Librum Psalmorum, PL, Suppl.* ii, col. 124, and Rabanus Maurus, *Commentarii in Exodum,* II, *PL,* cviii, col. 66, translating Origen on Exodus, ch. 5. Gregory of Tours, *Historia Francorum,* col. 168, also refers to the theory that the Red Sea opened to form twelve ways, but considers it to be based on a misuse of the testimony of the Psalms.

26/19. *drigan fotan.* OH I. x. 16 *per sicca.* Cf. the translation *drium fotum* for this same phrase in *The Old English Heptateuch,* Exodus XIV: 16, *Vercelli Homilies* III, p. 65, and *Salisbury Psalter,* Hymn IV, p. 290.

26/19–22. *þa þæt . . . meahtan.* I have found no source for this statement. For *Geames* and *Mambres* as the names of the magicians cf. 2 Timothy 3: 8 and Glossary of Proper Names.

26/25–7. *þeah . . . ær wæs.* According to OH I. x. 17, it is the winds and waves that restore the marks: 'si forte ad tempus uel casu uel curiositate turbantur, continuo diuinitus in pristinam faciem uentis fluctibusque reparantur.' See, however, Gregory of Tours, col. 168, 'Quos si modicum commotio maris obtexerit, illo quiescente, rursum divinitus renovantur ut fuerant.'

26/29–30. *ealle . . . forwurdon.* Or.'s addition.

26/30. *suðmestan.* Like the accompanying *norðmestan* this is Or.'s addition. Cf. Or. 9/13 and 12/9–10.

26/33. *for hiora synnum.* Or.'s addition. For this theme in OH, see e.g.
I. vi. 6.

26/34. *for Fetontis forscapunge.* OH I. x. 19 refers merely to 'ridiculam
Phaethontis fabulam'. That Phaethon suffered a 'mishap' is a piece of
information that could have been derived from a variety of sources: see
e.g. Isidore, *Etymologies* XVI. viii. 6, Hyginus, *Fabulae*, p. 109, and
Mythographus II, 57.

27/1. *syx . . . fif.* OH I. xi. 1 reads *dcclxxv* here.

27/2-3. *in Egyptum . . . gebroðran.* A strange perversion of OH I. xi. 1,
'inter Danai atque Aegypti fratrum filios quinquaginta parricidia una
nocte commissa sunt.' The personal name *Aegyptus* appears to have been
interpreted as a place name, while *parricidia* is taken to refer to the murder,
not of unspecified kinsmen, but of fathers: see Isidore, *Etymologies* V.
xxvi. 16, 'Parricidii actio non solum in eum dabatur qui parentem, id est
vel patrem vel matrem interemisset, sed et in eum qui fratrem occiderat.'
It is possible that the Latin manuscript used by the translator was one of
those with the variant *Aegysti* (see e.g. the 'related' MS Ricc. 627, and A.
la Penna, *Scholia in P. Ovidi Nasonis Ibin* (Florence, 1959), p. 19 (com-
menting on this story): 'Aegypti: Ubi est Aegypti non legas Aegisti') and
that a corrective gloss *Aegypti* was taken by him to be an additional
piece of information about the brothers. Alternatively, he may have
known the reference in Servius, *Aen.* IV. 377, to 'Danaus trahens ab
Aegypto originem'.

27/4. *Se yldra.* Or.'s addition, perhaps based on OH's reference to
Danaus as king. The brothers were in fact twins.

27/6. *Arge þæt land.* OH I. xi. 1 *Argos*.

27/11-17. *Ic . . . wæron.* OH I. xi. 2 merely inquires 'quod exsecrabile
sine dubio hominibus uiderim an ipsis etiam diis exsecrabile uideretur'.
For Or.'s theme that things are much better in Christian times, see
Introduction, pp. xciv f.

27/18. *Perseus se cyningc.* OH I. xi. 4 *Perseus.* See Isidore, *Etymologies*
IX. ii. 47, *Perseo rege*, also *Gl. Ansileubi*, P 1048, etc.

27/26. *se anwald . . . gehwearf.* See OH I. xix. 1 'regnum Assyriorum in
Medos concessit'.

27/26-7. *Hwa . . . areccean.* This effective rhetorical question replaces
OH I. xii. 2 'quis finis reperietur, si ea commemorare numerando, ut non
dicam describendo, conemur?'

27/28-30. *hu manega . . . cyningc wæs.* Is this based on OH I. xii. 4,
maximum bellum excitatum?

28/1. *on spellum 7 on leoðum.* OH I. xii. 6 *in fabulis.*

28/6-7. *hi . . . ofslogan.* For Or.'s interpretation of OH I. xii. 8 *parricidia*,
see 27/2-3, Commentary. Atreus and Thyestes were in fact supposed to
have killed their half-brother, while Atreus subsequently killed his own
son and the sons of Thyestes.

28/7. *hiora hetelican forlignessa.* OH I. xii. 8 *odia stupra.* The translator has apparently construed *odia* as an adjective.

28/8-9. *hu . . . steopsunu.* OH I. xii. 9 'interfectorem patris, matris maritum, filiorum fratrem, uitricum suum'. Potter (1952-3), p. 392, convicts the translator here of 'ignorance of mythology and reluctance to mention incestuous relationships'. The former charge is manifestly correct. However, in place of the second should be substituted careless reading (always supposing that the Latin exemplar was free from corruption at this point). *Maritum, fratrem,* and *uitricum* seem to have been interpreted not as in apposition to *interfectorem* but—with a shift of construction—as objects of the corresponding verb *interfecit. Filiorum fratrem,* 'the brother of his sons' then automatically becomes equated with 'his step-son'. See Introduction, p. lx.

28/12-13. *siex hunde . . . 7 lxgum.* OH I. xiii. 1 here reads *dlx,* but some manuscripts, including those closest to Or., read *dc et lx.*

28/15. *ealle . . . bearn.* OH I. xiii. 2 *nobilium Atheniensium filios.* The translator apparently does not know the story of the dispatching in tribute of seven youths and seven maidens, as related, for instance, by Servius, *Aen.* III. 74.

28/16. *healf mon, healf leo.* OH I. xiii. 2 'utrum fero homini an humanae bestiae aptius dicam nescio.' Or.'s error is a strange one, particularly in view of the frequency with which the name Minotaur is explained in Latin texts (see e.g. Isidore, *Etymologies* XI. iii. 38). Schilling, followed by Potter (1952-3), p. 392, attributes it to confusion between the Minotaur and the Sphinx. However, in early medieval sources the sphinx is described as 'animal quasi ad similitudinem pardorum, quam alii lamias dicunt' (see e.g. *Abolita* Y 8 *Ypinx*), while for Augustine, *Civ. Dei* XVIII. 13, it is a quadruped with a human face. Perhaps Or.'s error is based on an equation *ferus, bestia = leo* (see Isidore, *Etymologies* XII. ii. 1, 'bestiarum vocabulum proprie convenit leonibus, pardis . . .') or on a careless reading of Isidore, *Etymologies* XI. iii. 9, 'Alia . . . qui leonis habent vultum vel canis vel taurinum caput aut corpus, ut ex Pasiphae memorant genitum Minotaurum'.

28/20. *healf hors, healf men.* Or.'s addition, for which there are many possible sources: see e.g. Isidore, *Etymologies* XI. iii. 37, 'Centauris . . . id est hominem equo mixtum'; *Gl. Ansileubi,* CE 344, 'Centaurus: bestia medius equus, medius homo'; also Augustine, *Civ. Dei* XVIII. 13.

28/20-1. *for þon . . . ær þa.* OH I. xiii. 4 'quod discurrentes in bello equites ueluti unum corpus equorum et hominum uiderentur'. For Or.'s explanation cf. Pliny VII. 56. 202, where it is said that fighting on horseback was invented by the Thessalians called Centaurs. For the related claim that the Lapiths were given the name Centaur because 'primo equos frenis domuerunt', see Isidore, *Etymologies* XIV. iv. 12, also Servius, *Georg.* III. 115, and *Mythographus I,* 163.

28/23-4. *Uesoges . . . underþieded.* Based on OH I. xiv. 1, 'Vesozes rex Aegypti meridiem et septentrionem, diuisas paene toto caelo ac pelago plagas, aut miscere bello aut regno iungere studens'. Unless its exemplar was corrupt at this point, Or.'s version appears to be partly due to mis-understanding of the phrase 'diuisas *paene toto* caelo ac pelago plagas'.

28/27–29/1. *hie . . . forherigan*. For a similar construction see 29/11–12.

28/28. *ðæt lond . . . alesan*. OH I. xiv. 1 says that he ordered them to obey his laws.

29/4–5. *him leofre . . . gieldanne*. A most effective rendering of OH I. xiv. 2, 'timendum ipsi magis uersa uice fuerit propter incertos belli euentus nulla praemia et damna manifesta', with *praemium* interpreted in its sense of 'booty'.

29/6–7. *ealle . . . anum*. The translator appears to have misunderstood OH I. xiv. 3, 'uniuersam quoque Aegyptum populauissent, ni paludibus inpediti repellerentur.' Although OH's point is that the swamps acted as a barrier, Or. takes it to be that only the swamps were unconquered, thus preventing the Scythians' victory from being complete.

29/8. *be westan . . . Eufrate*. I have found no source for this addition. However, according to OH I. xiv. 4, Vesozes, returning, conquered *Asiam*, and it may be significant that Asia Minor was bounded on the east by the mountains on the west of the upper course of the Euphrates.

29/16. *betuh . . . Pontum*. OH I. xv. 1 'in Cappadociae Ponticae ora', 'related' MSS Ricc. 627 and Vienna 366 'ponti et cappadociæ ora'.

29/16. *neah . . . Asian*. OH I. xv. 1 'iuxta amnem Thermodontem'. Cf. OH I. ii. 26, where Asia Minor is said to have Cappadocia on its east and Pontus Euxinus on its north.

29/18. *æfter hrædlice tide*. OH I. xv. 1 *diu*. See also 35/11–12 and 107/17, beside 78/31–2, etc.

29/22 *to þon . . . þohton*. To þon ðæt is here used in the sense of 'because', rather than 'in order to': cf. Sweet–Whitelock (1967), p. 232 and see also Or. 72/8, 106/22–3 etc.

29/27–8. *oð hie . . . onwalde*. Or.'s addition.

29/29–31. *siþþan . . . striendon*. OH I. xv. 3 'externos concubitus ineunt'. Or.'s knowledge that this happened once a year seems to be ultimately derived from Julius Valerius III. 45, possibly via Jordanes, col. 1258, Servius, *Aen*. XI. 659, or a commentary. Cf. the Orosius Commen-tary, 7ʳ, 'concubitus ineunt: quia non habebant viros, semel in anno sicut animalia circa vernale equinoctium miscebantur viris.'

29/34. *strengran scyte*. Cf. OH I. xv. 3 'ne sagittarum iactus impedirentur'.

29/35. *þæt is . . . fortende*. Or.'s addition. Among the alternative etymo-logies for *Amazon* given by Isidore, *Etymologies* IX. ii. 64, is ἄνευ μαζῶν, 'quod adustis dexterioribus mammis essent'; so also Servius, *Aen*. I. 490, Remigius, *in Capellam* IX. 491. 20, and Lactantius Placidus, *in Achill*. 353 etc. However, in none of these works is the 'burnt breast' etymology mentioned first, and Or.'s immediate source may well have been a glos-sary, commentary, or manuscript gloss; see e.g. Leiden XXXVI. 15,

Amazones : *semiuste*, OH MS Stuttgart 410 'sine mammis, vel mammis inuste', and, in the company of other etymologies, Orosius Commentary, f. 7ʳ 'quasi semiuste' and 'adustis dexterioribus mammis'.

30/2–3. *hie . . . winnanne*. It is frequently claimed that King Alfred copied this particular strategy in his campaigns against the Danes: see e.g. Plummer's comment on annal 894 of the *Anglo-Saxon Chronicle*, also Potter (1952–3), p. 395. However, we have no evidence that Alfred knew either Latin or Old English versions of Orosius' History.

30/5. *ðære læssan Asiam*. OH I. xv. 5 *Asiae*. For the location of Ephesus in Asia Minor, see e.g. Solinus 166, 7.

30/8. *micel þæs heres*. OH I. xv. 5 *reliquae*.

30/13–16. *Europe . . . beswican*. An embroidery on OH I. xv. 7 'hac fama excitas gentes tanta admiratio et formido inuaserat, ut Hercules quoque cum iussus fuisset a domino suo exhibere arma reginae quasi ad ineuitabile periculum destinatus, uniuersam Graeciae lectam ac nobilem iuuentutem contraxerit.' The translator obviously did not know the story of the Labours of Hercules.

30/15. *þone ent*. Or.'s addition. Cf. Ælfric, *Lives of Saints*, xxxv. 112 f., 'þam hetelan ercule þam ormætan ente'. There are several possible explanations for the name 'giant' attached to Hercules. On the one hand, he may have been so called because of his great height: see e.g. Solinus 21, 16–18, 'licet ergo plerique definiant nullum posse excedere longitudinem pedum septem, quod intra mensuram istam Hercules fuerit'. On the other hand, if giants are the result of union between the sons of God and the daughters of men (see Genesis 6 : 4), then Hercules might qualify for membership of this select band, either because he was son of Jove and Alcmene (see e.g. Servius, *Aen.* VIII. 103), or because he had the title *heros* 'demi-god' (see e.g. Servius, *Aen.* I. 196, 'heros: vir fortis, semideus').

30/17. *dulmunus*. Cf. OH I. xv. 7 *longas naues*. For the identification of *dulmunus* with the Latin plural *dromones*, from Greek *drómōn* 'light sailing vessel' (a term applied to Greek ships from the fifth century A.D.), see Sweet–Whitelock (1967); p. 233. The translator's ultimate source appears to be Isidore, *Etymologies* XIX. i. 14, 'longae naves sunt quas dromones vocamus'; see below, 46/13, Commentary.

30/18. *on an scip . . . manna*. Or.'s addition. Has a gloss *naves militarias* (or *militares*) been misread or miscopied as *naves miliarias*?

30/18. *nihtes*. Or.'s addition. See below, 91/16–17.

30/19–20. *hwæðere . . . benæman*. Or.'s addition, without foundation in legend, since Hercules' aim was not conquest of the kingdom.

30/21–2. *þær . . . gefangen*. Or.'s addition, possibly deduced from either OH I. xv. 10 *post Orithyiam* or OH I. xv. 8 'inter caesas captasque conplurimas duae sorores Antiopae', though OH goes on to name the sisters as Melanippe and Hippolyte. According to classical tradition, Orithyia was elsewhere at the time of the attack.

30/27–9. *ealda . . . timbredon.* OH I. xvi. 1 'euertendo urbes plurimas atque alias constituendo'.

30/29. *niwu. Niwu* for expected *niwa* may be under the influence of the preceding form *ricu.* See further Introduction, p. xlv, n. 1.

30/30–3. *swa gemune . . . tintredon.* OH I. xvi. 1 'nec tamen miseriae hominum pressura temporum deputata est.'

30/33–4. *of þæm hwatestan . . . Germania.* Or.'s addition. For the trans-lator's attitude to the Germanic races see Sweet–Whitelock (1967), p. 233 and Introduction, p. xcvii.

30/34. *Pirrus . . . cyning.* OH I. xvi. 2, *Pyrrhus.* Pyrrhus is normally described in Or. as *Epira cyning,* corresponding to OH *rex Epiri.* See, however, the *Pyrrhus, rex Graeciae* of writers such as Augustine (*Civ. Dei* III. xvii) and Florus (I. xiii. 18).

31/1. *Iulius . . . casere.* OH I. xvi. 2 *Caesar. Iulius* is the normal designation for Julius Caesar in Or. See below, Book V. xii.

31/2–21. This section is virtually independent of OH I. xvi. 2–4, though it takes from it details such as the request for an alliance and for a small amount of land, the offering of their services by the Goths, the power of the Goths to take what they wanted by force, and the blindness of the opponents of Christianity.

31/2–5. *Hu . . . ofslogon.* There is no vocative in the corresponding passage of OH, which merely comments that the Goths invaded the Roman provinces. However, Orosius does address the Romans by name elsewhere; see e.g. OH V. v. 1. For the capture of Rome itself by the Goths and for the claim that damage and casualties were light, see OH VII. xxxix.

31/9–10. *hit ær þiosan . . . hæfdon.* Or.'s addition, possibly inspired by a misunderstanding of OH I. xvi. 3, 'quibus subiecta et patente uniuersa terra praesumere, quam esset libitum, liberum fuit'. See however, Jordanes, col. 1272, where Honorius is said to have allowed the Goths to take Gaul and Spain for their home, since at this time he had almost lost them and moreover they had been devastated by the invasion of Gaiseric, King of the Vandals.

31/10–11. *Hu . . . ær wære.* The *caeca gentilitas* of OH I. xvi. 4 is said to be unable to see that present improvements were won through Chris-tianity. For the complaint that things were now worse than before, see e.g. OH II. xix. 12, and Introduction. p. xciii.

31/12–21. *hie nellað . . . middangearde.* Only the last clause of this is derived directly from OH I. xvi; cf. OH III. viii, V. i, and VI. xxii. For Or.'s theme that life in the Christian era was far superior to life before Christ, see Introduction, pp. xciv f.

31/19–21. *Hu wene . . . middangearde.* For the construction *hu wene ge (we)* see also 88/11 and (*hu þyncð eow hu*) 52/15–17 and 97/28–9: 'What peace do you suppose the men had . . .?' OH's allusion is intended to stress the potential threat presented by the Gothic men: if their womenfolk were so terrible, how much more dangerous they themselves could have been.

31/23–5. *Alexander . . . Elena.* Cf. OH I. xvii. 1 *raptus Helenae.* Or.'s additional information could have been derived directly from a 'primary' source such as Dares' or Dictys' histories of the Trojan War. However, the form it takes suggests a commentary origin: cf. the Orosius Commentary, f. 7ʳ, 'Raptus Helene: quam Alexander qui et Paris pastor Priami filius Elena filia Tindaridis et que Lacena id Sporta (*sc.* Sparta) dicitur Helena uxor Minelici et pro cuius raptu Troia capta est.' That Lacedaemonia was in Greece could have been known to the translator from a variety of sources: see e.g. Lucan scholia, III. 270 'Lacedaemonia est in Graecia.'

31/27. *m scipa . . . dulmuna.* OH I. xvii. 1 *mille nauium.* For the term *dulmuna* see 30/17, Commentary.

31/27–9. *him betweonum . . . gewrǣcen.* OH I. xvii. 1 *coniuratio Graecorum.* Possible sources of Or.'s knowledge of the form taken by the vow include Dares, *De Excidio Troiae Historia,* ed. F. Meister (Leipzig, 1873), 20, 6.

31/30–1. *Hwa is . . . sǣgde.* OH I. xvii. 2 'quas nationes quantosque populos idem turbo inuoluerit atque adflixerit, Homerus poeta in primis clarus luculentissimo carmine palam fecit.' The translator seems to have taken OH's indirect question out of its context, with the addition of 'hwa is þætte ariman mæge', and then reverted to OH's construction. Some 'related' manuscripts, e.g. Vienna 366, have a point after *adflixerit.*

32/2. *monegum cuð.* OH I. xvii. 2 *omnibus notum.* It is hard to believe that even Or.'s modified claim was true of ninth-century England. However, Professor Whitelock points out (in a private communication) that although the laity would be ignorant of the Trojan legend, ecclesiastics with some pretence to education might be expected to be familiar with at least the outlines of it, from Latin poets, commentators, and the like.

32/2–6. *þeah . . . sǣgð.* The case of *swa hwelcne mon* is here determined by *lyste,* an impersonal verb taking the accusative of the person. Cf. OH I. xvii. 3, 'uerumtamen qui diuturnitatem illius obsidionis, euersionis atrocitatem caedem captiuitatemque didicerunt, uideant, si recte isto qualiscumque est praesentis temporis statu offenduntur quos hostes occulta misericordia Dei cum per omnes terras instructis copiis bello persequi possint, pacis gratia praetentis obsidibus per omnia maria sequuntur.'

32/11. *on bocum.* OH I. xviii. 1 refers to *ludi litterarii.*

32/14–15. *þær . . . ricsade.* Or.'s addition. See above, 21/24–5.

32/16–17. *He . . . wǣpnedmonna.* OH I. xix. 1 describes Sardanapallus as 'uir muliere corruptior . . . inter scortorum greges feminae habitu purpuram colo tractans a praefecto suo Arbato . . . uisus'. BT treats *furðumlic* (which seems to occur only here) as a derivative in -*lic* of *furðum,* itself derived from *forð*; to *furðum* BT attributes, for this purpose, a sense defined as 'to onwards, excessive?', and then translates *furðumlic* as 'luxurious, extravagant'. To this most unsatisfactory interpretation I can find no reasonable alternative without emendation, since I am informed by my Norse colleagues that ON *furðu-ligr*, *furðan-ligr* 'wonderful, remarkable' is too late to be used in this passage, while ME *forðlice*, *forthely* 'healthy, likely to live, full of energy' (see OED, *forthly*), though apparently the same sort of formation, does not appear to fit the sense. If the possibility of scribal error is allowed, then *furðumlic* may represent an original *fordomlic 'very glorious, very powerful' (see BT *domlic*) or *fordemedlic* 'deserving condemnation'. A third word *forþweorlic 'extremely depraved' (see BT *þweorlic*) is too dissimilar in form to be given serious consideration. I am indebted to Professor Norman Davis for his helpful suggestions concerning this word.

32/18. *his ealdormon.* OH I. xix. 1 *praefecto suo.* See H. Loyn, 'The Term "Ealdorman" in Translations prepared at the Time of King Alfred', *EHR*, lxviii (1953), 513–25.

32/19–21. *He angan . . . woldon.* An expansion of OH I. xix. 1 *excitis Medorum populis*, for which no source other than OH need be sought. Cf., however, Justinus I. iii. 3–4, where Arbactus is said to report back to his associates. 'Fit igitur coniuratio.'

32/21–2. *anfunde.* According to OH, this was when he was defeated.

32/23–7. *Hit . . . gewurdon.* Or. once again rewrites OH's indirect questions; cf. OH I. xix. 3 'in qua breuitate pensandum est: quantae ruinae cladesque gentium fuere, quanta bella fluxerunt ubi totiens tot et talia regna mutata sunt'.

33/1–4. *Se þa . . . uphofan.* OH I. xix. 6 'sed Cyrus mox ut adoleuit congregata Persarum manu auo certamen indixit.' Or.'s confused syntax is apparently the result of a shift of subject from Cyrus alone to Cyrus and the Persians. *Se* could be said to anticipate either the *him* of line 2 or part of the *hie* of line 3. Modern idiom would require *ac* to stand at the head of the sentence.

33/3. *eames.* OH I. xix. 6 *auo.* Cf. Freculph, *Chronicon*, col. 990, 'Astiage avunculo suo'.

33/6–7. *se cyning . . . gedyde.* OH I. xix. 7 'oblitus sceleris sui quod in Harpalum dudum admiserat'. Astyages' wicked deed was an act of reprisal: Harpalus had, on the king's orders, exposed the infant Cyrus, but the latter's life was saved by a herdsman, and Astyages held Harpalus responsible for this.

33/9–12. *He þa . . . gefeoll.* OH I. xix. 8 'qui acceptum exercitum statim Cyro per proditionem tradit'. According to Herodotus, some of the Medes deserted to Cyrus as promised by Harpalus, a few who were not in the plot did their duty, while the rest of the army took to its heels and fled.

33/15. *he . . . cyning.* OH I. xix. 8 *ipse*, referring not to Cyrus but to Astyages. The translator seems to have been misled by the reference to the subsequent flight of the Persians.

33/15–19. *Cirus . . . wolde.* OH I. xix. 8 refers to Astyages not Cyrus, saying merely that Astyages 'acrius . . . certamen instaurat, proposito suis, metu si quis a proelio cedere moliretur, ferro exciperetur'. According to Justinus, I. vi. 10–11, however, 'repetito alacrius certamine pugnantibus suis partem exercitus de tergo ponit et tergiversantes ferro agi in hostes iubet ac denuntiat suis, ni vincerent, non minus fortes post terga inventuros, quam a frontibus viros.' The attribution of this stratagem to Cyrus in Or. suggests that the translator did not have first-hand knowledge of Justinus' account. For the convention of dividing an army into three parts see also 44/32–4 and 64/19–20.

33/20. *hiera wif.* OH I. xix. 9 *matres et uxores.* Or. now agrees with OH in referring to the Persians.

33/21–3. *acsedon . . . gewiton.* OH I. xix. 9 'quaerentes, num in uteros matrum uel uxorum uellent refugere'.

33/25–31. *He . . . feng.* OH I. xix. 10 'cui Cyrus nil aliud quam regnum abstulit, eumque maximae Hyrcanorum genti praeposuit. in Medos uero reuerti ipse noluit.' For Arpelles' treachery see above, 33/9–12.

34/6–8. *geworhte . . . wæron.* According to OH I. xx. 3, the bull was constructed so that the hollow bronze would magnify the victim's cries. For the construction *to ðon . . . hu* see BTS p. 569, *Hu* IV. 3.

34/12–14. *cwæð . . . bescufan.* OH I. xx. 4 'Phalaris, factum amplexus factorem exsecratus, et ultioni materiam praebuit et crudelitati: nam ipsum opificem sua inuentione puniuit.'

34/15–20. *For hwi . . . doð.* A rewriting of OH I. xx. 6 'Eligant nunc, si uidetur, Latini et Siculi, utrum in diebus Aremuli et Phalaridis esse maluissent innocentum uitas poenis extorquentium, an his temporibus Christianis, cum imperatores Romani, ipsa in primis religione conpositi, post comminutas reipublicae bono tyrannides ne ipsorum quidem iniurias exigunt tyrannorum.' See Introduction, pp. xciv f.

34/22. *Creca þeoda.* Or.'s addition. That the Peloponnenses as well as the Athenians were Greeks could have been learned from a number of sources including Isidore, *Etymologies* XIV. iv. 11.

34/24. *hiera . . . wurdon.* Or.'s addition.

34/25–6. *þa wifmen . . . wæron.* OH I. xxi. 2 'Amazonum gentis et Cimmeriorum'. The Placidus glosses, P 30, describe the Amazons as 'ex genere Scytharum descendentes'; however, there is no need to look for an external source for this piece of information: see above, 29/14–35.

34/29. *Creca leode.* Or.'s addition. See OH I. xxi. 3 and Or. 35/2 and 35/18–19, also above 31/25.

34/30–35/1. *Mesiane . . . onsægden.* OH I. xxi. 3 'propter spretas uirgines suas in sollemni Messeniorum sacrificio'. Ignorant of the facts, the translator has assumed that the contempt shown to the Lacedaemonian girls consisted of their exclusion from the ceremonies. However, it was their inclusion that caused the war: see OH's source, Justinus III. iv. 1

'propter *stupratas* virgines suas in sollemni Messeniorum sacrificio'. That the Messenii were Greeks could be a contextual guess.

35/5–8. *cwædon . . . mid þæm*. OH I. xxi. 5 'consultatione habita ueriti, ne intercepta spe subolis sibi magis hac perseuerantia quam Messeniis perditio nutriretur'.

35/11–12. *lytle hwile*. OH I. xxi. 6 *diu*. For a similar reversal of sense see 29/18 and Commentary.

35/13. *eft*. OH I. xxi. 7 refers to four conflicts, of which the one described here is the last.

35/17–18. *Heora . . . hand*. OH I. xxi. 8 'raro umquam cruentius proelium exarserit'. See 23/14–15 and Commentary.

35/19–21. *ægþer . . . getugon*. A condensation of OH I. xxi. 9–16, which relates the outcome of the battle between Lacedaemonians and Messenians and the subsequent involvement of the Athenians.

35/19. *of Boetium*. OH I. xxi. 13 tells how the Lacedaemonians promised to restore to the Thebans rule over the Boeotians, on the condition that the Thebans would enter the war as their allies.

35/23–6. *þæt wæs . . . vtiene*. This passage is based on an addition found in many manuscripts of OH, 'Ab orbe condito usque ad Vrbem conditam anni iiii cccc lxxv iiii (*var*. vii), ab Vrbe condita usque ad natiuitatem Christi dccxv colliguntur, ergo ab origine mundi in aduentum domini nostri Iesu Christi anni v̄ c lxl viiii.' See Bately (1961), pp. 72, 73, 82, 92, and 101.

35/28–30. *nan . . . mid him*. OH II. i. 1 merely states that there is no man alive today who does not acknowledge that 'hominem in hoc mundo Deus fecerit'. However, in some of the manuscripts of OH closest to Or. the word *rectum* is interpolated after *hominem* (see e.g. MS Ricc. 627), while OH I. iii. 1 refers to 'homo, quem rectum atque inmaculatum fecerat Deus'.

35/30–36/5. *Ond . . . gelytlade*. Cf. OH II. i. 1 'unde etiam peccante homine mundus arguitur ac propter nostram intemperantiam conprimendam terra haec, in qua uiuimus, defectu ceterorum animalium et sterilitate suorum fructuum castigatur.' See Introduction, pp. xciii ff.

36/8–9. *ealle . . . sindon*. Cf. OH II. i. 3 'regna, a quibus reliquae potestates progrediuntur'.

36/9–11. *Nu he . . . ricsedon*. Cf. OH II. i. 4 'si autem regna diuersa, quanto aequius regnum aliquod maximum, cui reliquorum regnorum potestas uniuersa subicitur'.

36/12. *þær Ninus ricsade*. Or.'s addition. See above, 21/24–5.

36/12–13. *Creca . . . ricsade*. OH II. i. 4 *Macedonicum*. See below, 67/23–68/4.

36/13–14. *Affricanum . . . ricsedon*. OH II. i. 4 *Africanum*, referring to the Carthaginian empire; see below, 133/7, where *Africanum regnum* is correctly linked with Carthage. According to OH III. xxiii. 7, *Africae . . .*

pars is one of the territories assigned to Ptolomeus after the death of Alexander. However, Or.'s translation of this passage, 77/24, refers only to 'ealle Egyptum 7 Arabia'.

36/16. *mid . . . tacnunge.* OH II. i. 5 'eademque ineffabili ordinatione'.

36/19–23. *Babylonisce . . . wære.* Apparently based on a misunderstanding of OH II. i. 6, 'quorum inter primum ac nouissimum, id est inter Babylonium et Romanum, quasi inter patrem senem ac filium paruum, Africanum ac Macedonicum breuia et media, quasi tutor curatorque uenerunt potestate temporis non iure hereditatis admissi'. *Tutor curatorque* may have been taken to refer to Babylon and Rome, while for *admissi* Or.'s immediate source may have had the reading *amissi* as in OH, MS L.

36/23–4. *þæt . . . mæge.* Cf. OH II. i. 6 'quod utrum ita sit, apertissime expedire curabo.'

36/25. *Se æresta . . . sægden.* OH II. ii. 1 'Rex primus apud Assyrios, qui eminere ceteris potuit, Ninus fuit.' See above, 21/24–5.

36/27. *getimbrede.* The *instaurauit* 'repair', 'restore' of OH II. ii. 1 has been taken in its secondary sense of 'erect', 'make'; see below, 43/21–3.

36/28. *hit . . . stod.* The construction *hit stod* is probably impersonal: cf. *Alfred's Boethius,* Metre I. 28, 'stod þrage on ðam' and the Laws of Ethelred, in *Laws,* p. 470, 'Ðus hit stod on ðam dagum mid Englum.' However, the corresponding passage in OH, II. ii. 2, reads 'regnum Assyriorum diu inconcussa potentia stetit', and it is possible that *hit* refers back to *þa burg,* replacing the earlier *heo* under the influence of the neuter *regnum Assyriorum* of OH.

36/32. *in Italia . . . wearð.* OH II. ii. 3 *apud Latinos.* Surprisingly, Latin writers often find it necessary to comment on the name Latini: see e.g. Bede, *De Temporum Ratione,* col. 530, 'Latinis, qui postea Romani nuncupati sunt . . . in Italia'.

36/33. *Siluian eam.* Cf. OH II. ii. 3 'auus autem Rheae Siluiae'. It is normally assumed that the translator has confused Latin *auus* (OE *ealdfæder*) with *auunculus* (OE *eam*). However, here as elsewhere in Or. there are alternative explanations: (i) the Latin manuscript used by the translator could have had the reading *auunculus* (see 33/3, Commentary); (ii) a commentary or gloss stating that Amulius was Rhea Silvia's uncle could have been misapplied to Procas (see 39/18, Commentary); and (iii) what we have may be the result of error by a scribe of Or., the translator having written '7 *he* (*i.e.* Amulius) wæs Siluian eam'.

37/1–2. *Remuses . . . getimbredon.* OH II. ii. 3 *mater Romuli fuit.* See 39/1–2.

37/2–4. *þa ricu . . . gestihtunge.* OH II. ii. 4 'omnia haec ineffabilibus mysteriis et profundissimis Dei iudiciis disposita, non aut humanis uiribus aut incertis casibus accidisse'. *Omnia haec* refers not to kingdoms but to the various historical events just mentioned.

37/3 *wyrde.* See also 37/23 and cf. Bo., where the term is used of 'the course of events for which God is responsible', the realization of Divine Providence.

37/5–6. *Ealle . . . begunne.* OH II. ii. 4 merely claims that 'omnes historiae antiquae a Nino incipiunt, omnes historiae Romanae a Proca exoriuntur.' See 21/24, Commentary.

37/9–11. *þy ilcan . . . cyninges.* Cf. OH II. ii. 5 'regnante Proca futurae Romae sementis iacta est, etsi nondum germen apparet.'

37/11–13. *gefeoll . . . Sardanopolum.* An expansion of OH II. ii. 5 'Babylonis regnum defecit'. See 36/28–30.

37/13–15. *Sippan . . . ofer hie.* OH II. ii. 6–7 'discedente autem Arbato in Medos, partem regni penes se retinuere Chaldaei, qui Babylonam sibi aduersum Medos uindicauerunt. ita Babyloniae potestas apud Medos, proprietas apud Chaldaeos fuit.' Cf. Jerome–Eusebius, col. 339, 'In medio autem tempore Chaldæi prope prævalebant quorum separatæ quædam successiones regum feruntur.'

37/19–20. *þara unryhtwisestana . . . Tarcuinie.* OH II. ii. 9–10 refers to the *dominatio* of the Tarquin line and its *fastidium*. See below, 40/1–4.

37/22–4. *Giet . . . gestihtunge.* See above, 37/2–4. OH II. ii. 11 merely comments 'Et ne diutius uerbis morer, committo me dentibus insanientium, sed ueritatis praesidio liberandum.' *Diutius* here has been correctly interpreted; cf. above, 29/18, Commentary.

37/31–2. *þeh . . . leodum.* OH II. iii. 2 'ipsa tamen postea aliquamdiu mansit incolumis.' See above, 37/13–14.

37/34–38/1. *Alrica . . . woldon.* OH II. iii. 3–4 states that Rome was invaded 'a Gothis et Alaricho rege eorum, comite autem suo', the city was despoiled of her wealth but was not deprived of her sovereignty. The plural *woldon* (unless a scribal alteration of original *wolde*) seems to be the result of the erroneous identification of *comite suo* with Attalus, not with Alaric: see further below, 38/5, Commentary.

38/2–3. *þeh þe . . . getacnod wurde.* OH II. iii. 4 'quamuis in tantum arcanis statutis inter utramque urbem conuenientiae totius ordo seruatus sit'.

38/4. *þa . . . beswac.* Or.'s addition. See 32/19–23.

38/5. *hiere agen . . . cyning.* OH II. iii. 4 'hic praefectus huius Attalus regnare temptarit'. Once again the verb used in Or. is plural instead of the expected singular, though here the Latin refers not to Alaric but to Attalus. That Alaric made the praefectus Attalus Roman emperor for a short space of time is reported by OH VII. xlii, a section not represented in Or. However, the parallelism in wording with 37/34–38/1 suggests that Or. may here be influenced by its immediate context and not by a much later section of the Latin.

38/6–7. *naþer ne . . . selfra.* OH II. iii. 4 'merito Christiani imperatoris'.

38/10–30. *þis . . . tælað.* A free rendering of OH II. iii. 5–10, with much simplification and rearrangement, for the significance of which see Introduction, p. xciv.

38/31. *feower hunde . . . feowertig*. OH II. iv. 1 *ccccxiiii*. Confusion between the numerals *14* and *40* is perhaps more easily explained in the context of Anglo-Saxon than in that of Latin.

38/31–39/1. *Troia, Creca burg*. OH II. iv. 1 *Troiae*. Potter (1952–3), p. 397, describes the words *Creca burg* as 'a flagrantly erroneous addition'. However, Troy, or Ilium, was in an area that formed part of Alexander the Great's *Creca rice* and subsequently belonged to the Byzantine empire.

39/2. *hiora* In view of MS L's confusion of final unstressed *a* and *e* (see Introduction, pp. xliv f.) it is possible that the original reading here is gsf. referring to *Romeburg*: cf. OH II. iv. 2 *cuius regnum*.

39/3–16. *eac sipþan . . . gedyden*. An expansion of two brief allusions in OH: II. iv. 2 'sine more raptas Sabinas, inprobis nuptiis confoederatas maritorum et parentum cruore dotauit' and II. iv. 5 'Sabinorum, quos foedere ludisque pellexerat, feminas tam inhoneste praesumpsit quam nefarie defendit'. See the notes following.

39/5–6. *hie bædon . . . forwierndon*. This detail is to be found in a number of Latin texts narrating the story of the Rape of the Sabines. See e.g. Augustine, *Civ. Dei* II. xvii, Florus I. i, Ovid, *Fasti* III. 189, Livy I. ix, and Orosius Commentary, f. 7ᵛ.

39/8–9. *hie bædon . . . mehten*. For the information that the *ludi* referred to by OH were held in honour of pagan gods see e.g. Isidore, *Etymologies* XVIII. xvi, and Livy I. ix.

39/10–12. *Ymb . . . healfe*. Possibly inspired by OH's reference, II. iv. 6, to Titus Tatius, the leader of the Sabines, as 'diu armis propulsatum'. However, according to the Lucan scholia, ed. Weber, MS B, I. 118, the war lasted for fifteen years, while Ovid, *Fasti* III. 204, alludes to *longa bella*. That almost all the participants were killed is a claim made by Augustine, *Civ. Dei* III. xiii, and Orosius Commentary, f. 7ᵛ.

39/13–16. *þara Romana . . . gedyden*. Although the intervention of the women is a feature of a number of versions of this story, that they prostrated themselves at their fathers' feet is a detail that I have found only in Ovid, *Fasti* iii. 220, and Augustine, *Civ. Dei* III. xiii, while that they took their children with them is a detail that I have only found in Ovid, *Fasti* III. 217–24, in Lucan scholia, ed. Endt I. 118, and in Juvenal scholia VI. 163, 2.

39/18. *sweora*. i.e. the fathers of the Sabine women.

39/18. *eames*. OH II. iv. 3 *auo*. Did the translator misunderstand a gloss or comment on this passage of OH, which pointed out that Romulus in fact killed not his grandfather but his great uncle? Or was he influenced by the discrepancy between this reference in OH to Numitor as grandfather and a subsequent reference, OH VI. i. 14, to *Amulius auus*? See also above, 36/33 and Commentary.

39/22. *his agenne sweor*. OH II. iv. 6 'ducem eorum Titum Tatium'. I have found no allusion in Latin texts to Titus Tatius as the father-in-law of

Romulus. However, such a relationship may have been deduced from the allusion to *templum soceri*, OH II. iv. 3, coupled with a claim such as that of Servius, *Aen*. I. 291, that Tatius and Romulus together built the temple of Janus.

39/25–35. *He þa . . . begietena.* This replaces OH II. iv. 7–8, 'cum Veientibus proelium adhuc paruo nomine, iam magnis uiribus, agitatum. Caeninensium captum ac dirutum oppidum. adsumptis semel armis numquam quies, quippe quibus egestas turpis atque obscena fames domi timerentur, si umquam paci adquieuissent.'

39/26–9. *for þon þe . . . niedlingas.* Or.'s addition. That the Romans had once been other men's slaves is a detail that could have been derived from allusions to the *asylum* established by Romulus, to which fled slaves, criminals and deserters; see e.g. Livy I. viii, Florus I. i. 9 and Servius, *Aen*. VIII. 635. That the Romans were despised by their neighbours is a feature of the story of the Rape of the Sabines; see e.g. Silius Italicus XIII. 812 f. That they possessed no land beyond their city walls is stated by Florus I. iii. 7.

40/1–14. *Ac . . . an monn.* At this point OH gives a brief survey of events leading up to the establishment of the Republic, of which the only part preserved by Or. is an allusion to Tarquinius Superbus and the rape of Lucretia.

40/1–2. *Ac . . . ungetæsran.* Probably inspired by OH II. iv. 13, 'Romani quanta mala per ccxliii annos continua illa regum dominatione pertulerint, non solum unius regis expulsio uerum etiam eiuratio regii nominis et potestatis ostendit. nam si unius tantum superbia fuisset in culpa, ipsum solum oportuisset expelli seruata regia dignitate melioribus.'

40/3. *ðe . . . sædon.* See the reference to the Tarquin dynasty, 37/19–20.

40/3–5. *þe . . . geniedde.* All that OH II. iv. 12 has to say about Tarquinius Superbus is that he gained control of the state by murdering his father-in-law, that he held on to it by brutal attacks on citizens, and that he finally lost it, 'flagitio adulteratae Lucretiae'.

40/5–12. *his suna . . . mid ealle.* An expansion of OH II. iv. 12, 'Tarquinii Superbi regnum . . . flagitio adulteratae Lucretiae amissum'. There are many allusions in Latin texts to the Rape of Lucretia, and in stating that Lucretia was the wife of (Col)latinus, that she was raped by Tarquin's son, and that Brutus and Collatinus were responsible for driving out the Tarquins, Or. is using details common to a number of versions of the story: see e.g. Livy I. lvii–lx, Ovid, *Fasti* II. 721–852, Eutropius (and Paulus Diaconus) I. 8, Servius, *Aen*. VIII. 646, Mythographus *I*, 74, and Augustine, *Civ. Dei* I. 19. The absence of Brutus and Collatinus with the army is a feature of the accounts of Livy, Ovid, Paulus Diaconus, Servius and Mythographus I. Only the surprising claim that Lucretia was Brutus' sister has, to my knowledge, no more than three possible sources: Augustine's reference to Brutus as *propinquus* of Lucretia; the description in *De Viris Illustribus* 9. 1 and 10. 1 of first Collatinus and then Brutus as 'sorore *Tarquinii* Superbi genitus'; and a misreading of Eutropius I. 8

'Brutus, parens et ipse Tarquini, populum concitavit' as 'parens et ipsae (*sc.* Lucretiae) Tarquini populum concitavit'. *-e* for *-ae* is common in Latin manuscripts of the early Middle Ages.

40/12–14. *Him . . . monn.* OH II. iv. 15 *consules creauerunt.* For the annual appointment of consuls, see e.g. Livy II. i, Isidore, *Etymologies* IX. iii. 7 and Augustine, *Civ. Dei* V. xii.

40/15–16. *ii hunde . . . iiii.* OH. II. v. 1 *ccxliiii.*

40/16–18. *Romulus . . . sweor.* An expansion of OH's comment, II. v. 1, that Brutus desired not only to equal but to surpass the number of parricides committed by the founder and first king of Rome. See above II. **iv**.

40/18–19. *his ii . . . broðor.* OH II. v. 1 'duos filios suos adulescentes totidemque uxoris suae fratres'. In view of the wording of the Latin, it seems necessary to suppose that the *u* of the manuscripts of Or. is the result of scribal error after the translation was made. For confusion of *u* and *ii* see also 20/29.

40/21. *he . . . gebindan.* Or.'s addition: see Livy II. v.

40/23–5. *Tarcuinius . . . Romanum.* OH II. v. 3 'Porsenna rex Etruscorum, grauissimus regii nominis suffragator, Tarquinium manu ingerens'. Or. has reversed the order of the entries in OH concerning the death of Brutus and the involvement of Porsenna. The translator's assumption that Brutus was one of Porsenna's adversaries may be the result of his ignorance of Roman history. However, although, according to Livy II. viii–x, Porsenna did not take part in the wars with Rome during Brutus' lifetime, Florus I. iv. 8 and Freculph, *Chronicon*, col. 997, both place their account of the combat after the stories of Mucius and Cloelia and the withdrawal of Porsenna.

40/25–8. *He ða . . . ofslog.* OH II. v. 2 'ipse [sc. Brutus] . . . cum Arrunte, Superbi filio, congresso sibi commortuoque procubuit.' Or.'s strange perversion of the facts here could be the result of misapplication of a gloss or comment 'pro Tarquinio', intended to refer to the *Superbi* of OH. There was no formal single combat between the two men, though Latin texts such as Livy II. vi. 8 and *De Viris Illustribus* 10. 6 use the terminology of single combat to describe the encounter.

41/1–11. *Mutius . . . dreogende wæs.* OH II. v. 3, which links Mucius Scaevola with Cloelia as saviour of the Romans, relates no more of his actions than that he made a profound impression on the enemy, 'constanti urendae manus patientia'.

41/2–4. *Đa . . . 7 anne.* The translator is unaware that the burning of Mucius' hand was a voluntary act of courage and describes it graphically as a torture inflicted by Porsenna.

41/4–9. *hiene . . . cyninges.* This is ultimately based on Livy II. xii, where Porsenna, having been told by Mucius, 'Nec unus in te ego hos animos gessi: longus post me ordo est idem petentium decus', orders him to be burnt alive, 'nisi expromeret propere, quas insidiarum sibi minas per ambages iaceret'. Mucius, having then placed his hand in the fire of his own accord and been told that he may go free, tells Porsenna, as it were in gratitude, what he could not force from him by threats, 'trecenti coniuravimus principes iuventutis Romanae, ut in te hac via grassaremur.' See also Florus I. iv, Freculph, col. 997, *De Viris Illustribus* 12. 4, Augustine *Civ. Dei* V. xviii and Lactantius Placidus, *in Stat. Theb.* II. 703. It is impossible to identify Or.'s source here; however, only two of the versions do not specify the number of men involved as 300, and thus the vague reply given in Or. that there were *many* such as Mucius who had sworn to kill Porsenna may point to either the *multos tales* of Augustine or the *plures* of Lactantius as an intermediary between Livy and the Old English account.

41/9–10. *þa . . . forlet*. The immediate withdrawal of Porsenna is a feature of the accounts of Livy, Augustine, and *De Viris Illustribus*.

41/14–15. *7 hie . . . hæfdon*. OH II. v. 4 merely states that the appointment of a dictator 'plurimum emolumenti tulit'. According to Livy, one of the results of the appointment of the first dictator was that although war was formally declared against the Sabines, no action was taken. Subsequent dictators, however, were victorious in battle. See Livy II. xviii and xix.

41/16. *þa rican . . . earmran*. The *patres* and the *plebs*.

41/20. *Tita 7 Publia*. OH II. v. 6 'T. Gesonio et P. Minucio', with *T* expanded to *Tito* and *P* to *Publio* in a large number of manuscripts, including those closest to Or. With this use of *praenomen* alone compare 25/9 *Liber Pater* and 37/1 *Siluie* (for OH *Rheae Siluiae*) and see Bately (1970) pp. 436–7.

41/23. *Ær . . . wære*. Possibly inspired by OH II. v. 6 'Cessatum est paulisper a proeliis, cessatum tamen a mortibus non est.'

41/26. *eard gesecan*. OH II. v. 7 'ad castra redituros'.

41/28–31. *heora an . . . triumphan*. This rewriting of OH II. v. 7, 'M. Fabius consul oblatum sibi a senatu triumphum suscipere recusarit, quia tantis reipublicae detrimentis luctus potius debebatur', appears to be based on an interpretation of *oblatum* 'offered' in its alternative sense of 'brought'.

42/1–13. Or.'s addition.

42/2–4. *sceoldon . . . gefeohte*. See Servius, *Aen.* IV. 543.

42/4. *siex . . . byrig*. I have found no source for this detail. Roman triumphs normally started from the Campus Martius, though Claudian XXVIII. 544 f. describes the welcoming crowd as extending as far as the Mulvian Bridge.

42/4–5. *mid crætwæne . . . gefrætwedum*. Since in classical sources—e.g. Livy X. vii. 10 and Florus I. i. 5—the triumphal chariot is normally described as of gold, the gems may be a figment of the translator's imagination. See, however, the *Life of Aurelian*, in *Scriptores Historiae Augustae* II. xxxiii. 2, where the first chariot in a triumph is described as 'argento, auro, gemmis operosus atque distinctus' and Appian XII. xvii, where Pompey as triumpher rides in a chariot studded with gems.

42/5–6. *feowerfetes . . . hwit.* Latin accounts usually refer to four white horses drawing the triumphal chariot (see e.g. Livy V. xxiii. 5, Ovid, *Ars Amatoria* I. 214 and Servius, *Aen.* IV. 543), though Claudian, *Panegyricus* XXVIII, 369–70, gives the number as two. Or.'s use of *feowerfetes* is puzzling, even if we assume manuscript corruption and an original 'two white specimens of each kind of four-footed cattle', parallel-ing 42/12 'ælces cynnes feowerfetes feos an'. However, confusion between *quadrupes* and *quadriga* or *quadriiugi* is one possible explanation: see e.g. Statius, *Thebaid*, ed. A. Klotz (Leipzig, 1908), XII. 531 *niveis quadriiugis* and Apuleius, *Apologia*, ed. R. Helm, *Opera* (Leipzig, 1959), xxii *quadrigas albas*, both in descriptions of triumphs. Alternatively, the four-footed cattle may owe their presence in the ceremonies to a reference—perhaps Servius'—to bulls or oxen as well as horses preceding the triumpher: see Servius, *Georgics* II. 147, '*Perfusi* autem tauri, qui ante triumphantes usque ad templa ducebantur: aut certe *perfusi greges* intellegamus, quod ad equos triumphales potest referri'. See also Servius, *Aen.* IV. 543: 'qui autem triumphat albis equis utitur quattuor et senatu praeeunte in Capitolio de tauris sacrificat, et bene duo diversa posuit.'

42/6–7. *þonne . . . consulum.* According to Servius, *Aen.* IV. 543, the senators preceded the triumpher. However, in certain other Latin accounts, they are said to follow on foot: see Valerius Maximus VII. v. 4 and the *Life of Aurelian*, *Scriptores Historiae Augustae* II, xxxiv. 4. See also Aulus Gellius' reference to such an order in the *ovatio*, in *Noctium Atticarum Libri XX*, ed. C. Hosius (Leipzig, 1903), V. vi. 27, and Honorius' refusal to let the fathers march back before his chariot, Clau-dian XXVIII. 551. That the senators ride back to Rome in carriages may well be Or.'s own assumption.

42/7–8. *þa menn . . . wæron.* See below, 113/25–7, and OH V. i. That the captives were bound may be Or.'s own assumption; see, however, *The Life of Aurelian*, *Scriptores Historiae Augustae* II, xxxiii. 4, 'religatis manibus captivi', and OH V. i. 9.

42/9–10. *Ac . . . genieddon.* In such circumstances, the victor was awarded an *ovatio* or *minor triumphus*; see e.g. Festus, p. 306, *ovalis corona* and (for *triumphus* and *tropaeum*) Servius, *Aen.* X. 775 and Isidore, *Etymolo-gies* XVIII. ii. 3–4.

42/10–12. *þonne . . . an.* Or.'s account of the minor triumph seems entirely fanciful. In fact the ovator either walked, or rode on horseback. The translator, or a hypothetical gloss or commentary source, may have thought it appropriate that a silver chariot drawn by two animals should correspond and contrast with the gold chariot drawn by four animals assigned to the major triumph. Alternatively, the description may be based on a misunderstanding of Servius, *Aen.* IV. 543, 'proprie ovatio est minor triumphus. qui enim ovationem meretur . . . uno equo utitur' with *equo* identified with *aequo*. For a two-horse chariot, or *biga*, drawn by one white horse and one black, see e.g. Isidore, *Etymologies* XVIII. xxxvi. 2 and Lucan scholia ed. Weber, I. 78.

42/14–21. *Romulus . . . wæron.* A second passage of added comment, this time explaining OH II. v. 7 *senatu.* For the possible sources of individual details see below.

42/14–15. *Romulus . . . monna.* See e.g. Festus, p. 428, Jerome–Eusebius, cols. 374–6, Livy I. viii. 7 and Servius, *Aen.* VIII. 105.

42/15. *þeh . . . hund.* See Livy II. i. 10 and Festus, p. 362.

42/15–16. *þa . . . wuniende.* I have found no source for this detail, which may have its origin in knowledge that the senate normally met in Rome.

42/16–17. *hie . . . wæron.* See Eutropius I. ii. 1, 'quorum consilio omnia ageret', also Isidore, *Etymologies* IX. iv. 9.

42/17. *consulas setton.* It was in fact the centuries not the senate that appointed consuls; see, however, Livy II. lvi. 5 where it is said that the *patres* (a term habitually used of senators as well as *patricii*) 'Ap. Claudium . . . consulem faciunt'.

42/18–21. *hie bewisten . . . wæron.* In the time of the republic, the entire management of the revenues of the state belonged to the senate. For the custom of paying captured enemy assets into the treasury see e.g. Livy V. xx. 5.

42/22–4. *þa consulas . . . cræftegast.* Cf. OH II. v. 8 'Gloriosissima illa numero et uiribus Fabiorum familia Veientanum sortita certamen' and II. v. 7, where the consul offered the triumph is named as M. Fabius. Potter (1952–3), p. 399, suggests that the translator 'cannot resist the temptation to proffer an etymology, associating *gloriosissima illa . . . Fabiorum familia* with *faber* "smith" ' and compares *Alfred's Boethius* 46. 16, where the name *Fabricius* is replaced by that of the 'goldsmith', Weland. However, the author of Or. is not proffering an etymology, merely misrelating elements already present in his primary source: thus, *ænlicost* translates *gloriosissima*, while *cræftegast* ('most powerful', not 'most skilful') is prompted by OH *uiribus*. In view of the replacing of *Fabiorum* by an adjective of Latin origin, *Fabiane*, it is possible that the discrepancies between Or. and OH are due to the use by the translator of a (hypothetical) comment or gloss, **'Fabiorum: Fabii uel Fabiani, electi quia gloriosissimi et potentissimi erant', with *electi*, or its equivalent, taken to refer not to the family but to the name.

42/22. *þæt Sabinisce gewinn.* OH II. v. 8 *Veientanum certamen.* The Veientes are not infrequently mentioned in conjunction with the Sabines in the chapters of Livy dealing with this period: see e.g. II. xlviii and liii (where the two peoples are said to be in alliance with one another), III. xvi and xvii.

42/24–8. *nu giet . . . habbað.* OH II. v. 8 'quantam reipublicae orbitatem occasu suo intulerit, infamibus usque ad nunc uocabulis testes sunt fluuius qui perdidit et porta quae misit.' The river referred to by OH is the Cremera; Or.'s plural may include also the Allia, where another Fabius was ignominiously slain: see Or. 52/4–5 and OH II. xix. 6

'testatur hanc Fabii cladem fluuius Halia, sicut Cremera Fabiorum.' The poetry referred to by Or. may be that quoted by OH II. v. 10.

42/28–32. *Æfter . . . gebodade.* The translator has split OH's account of the exploits of the Fabii, II. v. 8–9, into two parts, linking the first part with the disastrous victory of M. Fabius, 41/27–31 (OH II. v. 7) treating the second part as a completely independent episode. This splitting corresponds with 'paragraph' divisions in some of the 'related' manuscripts, e.g. Vienna 366.

42/28. *cempena.* OH II. v. 9 *Fabii.*

42/29. *þæt . . . Sabina.* cf. OH II. v. 9 'Fabii . . . speciale sibi aduersum Veientes decerni bellum expetiuissent'. For the substitution of the Sabines for the Veientes see 42/22, Commentary. The idea of single combat was presumably suggested by the word *speciale,* though no such encounter as that between the three Horatii and three Curiatii was in fact involved.

42/29–30. *getruwedon . . . gefeohtan.* OH II. v. 9 'spem temere sumptae expeditionis primis successibus firmauerunt.'

42/31. *mid heora searwum.* According to OH the Veientes drew the Fabii into an ambush.

42/32–4. *Næs . . . ege.* OH II. v. 10 'ad haec non Romae tantum talia gerebantur, sed quaeque prouincia suis ignibus aestuabat et, quod poeta praecipuus in una urbe descripsit, ego de toto orbe dixerim:

> crudelis ubique
> Luctus, ubique pauor et plurima mortis imago.'

43/1–2. *þa hwile . . . westdæle.* OH II. vi. 1 *eodem tempore.*

43/2–4. *þa hwile . . . awest.* Cf. OH II. vi. 1 'Asiam Scythiam totumque Orientem armis peruagabatur.' Cyrus in fact never invaded India.

43/6. *for þæm . . . næron.* Or.'s addition.

43/7–8. *an his ðegna.* OH II. vi. 3 'unum regiorum equorum'. A number of manuscripts, including some of those closest to Or., e.g. Vienna 366, and that used by Freculph, *PL* cvi, col. 991, replace *equorum* by *equitum.*

43/8–9. *twam tyncenum.* The otherwise unrecorded word *tyncen* is generally taken to be a diminutive with double suffix, meaning 'small cask'; see e.g. Campbell, *OE Grammar* § 574. 6. Potter (1952–3), p. 400, suggests that the translator has misinterpreted the word *alueus* 'channel', taking it in its alternative sense of 'deep vessel', in support of which see e.g. *Corpus* A 437 *aluuium : meeli* ('cup'), beside A 490 *alueum : eduaelle* ('whirlpool'). For the interesting theory that the account in Or. has possibly been influenced by OH VI. ii, where a messenger in the Mithridatic wars performs a feat of swimming with the aid of two bladders, *duobus utribus,* see Sweet–Whitelock (1967), p. 233.

43/12–13. *þær . . . fledu wæs.* Or.'s addition, probably the result of the misapplication of a piece of information about the Ganges, such as Solinus 184, 16–17, 'minima Gangis latitudo per octo milia passuum, maxima per uiginti patet', see also Capella VI. 694, 'latitudo Gangis ubi diffusior uiginti milia passuum, ubi angustus octo milia.' Confusion between *viii* and *viiii* is not uncommon in Latin manuscripts. For confusion between *Gandes* (OH *Gyndes*, 'related' MSS *gandes*) and Ganges see Or. 9/25, OH I. ii. 13 and Glossary of Proper Names, also the Isidore map, where the Ganges is labelled *Gandes*.

43/21–3. *Ninus . . . rice.* OH II. vi. 7 'a Nino uel Samiramide reparatam'. See above, 36/26–7.

43/27–8. *hundseofontig . . . mile.* OH II. vi. 9 'quadringentis octoginta stadiis'. The stadium was one-eighth of a milliarium and thus 480 stadia should be the equivalent of 60 Roman miles. Even allowing for manuscript corruption and the possibility of the accidental incorporation of a hypothetical gloss 'septima (*for* octava) pars milliarii', it is hard to see how a figure of $70\frac{1}{7}$ Roman miles could be arrived at. However, an original figure of $77\frac{1}{7}$ would be much simpler to explain: see Grierson (1972), p. 29, where it is plausibly argued that 'a mile of 5000 feet, far shorter than the [legal mile of 8 furlongs], was what the translator of Orosius had in mind'.

43/29–30. *se mæsta . . . stream.* OH II. vi. 9 'fossa extrinsecus late patens uice amnis circumfluit.'

43/30–1. *wiðutan . . . weall.* This replaces OH II. vi. 10 'a fronte murorum centum portae aereae'. I have found no reference elsewhere to a second smaller wall outside the moat. However, Herodotus I. 178–81 describes a second one *within* the city, hardly less strong, though smaller, while Quintus Curtius, V. i. 28, claims that the Euphrates, which flows through Babylon, 'magnae . . . molis crepidinibus coercetur'. It is impossible to determine Or.'s source here, though the occurrence of the implausible figure of two cubits may point to a comment or gloss in which a larger numeral had been miscopied—maybe even the two hundred cubits of the great wall. For an instance of such miscopying see e.g. 21/13 and Commentary.

43/32. *stænenum wighusum.* OH II. vi. 10 *habitaculis defensorum.* The only references to stone in classical descriptions of Babylon are to a stone bridge: the city was otherwise constructed of baked brick and bitumen.

43/33–4. *Seo . . . westast.* Based on OH II. vi. 11, 'et tamen magna illa Babylon, illa prima post reparationem humani generis condita, nunc paene etiam minima mora uicta capta subuersa est', with *minima* construed with *Babylon*.

43/34–44/6. *Nu . . . mæge.* An effective expansion of OH II. vi. 13, 'quidquid enim est opere et manu factum, labi et consumi uetustate, Babylon capta confirmat; cuius ut primum imperium ac potentissimum exstitit ita ut primum cessit.' *Confirmat* is apparently taken to indicate speech on the part of the city. For Or.'s re-ordering of items here see Sweet–Whitelock (1967), p. 234.

44/8. *se Liþa cyning.* OH II. vi. 12 *rex Lydorum.* Potter (1952–3), p. 401, suggests that when the translator pronounced *Lyda* as *Liþa*, the copyist naturally took the word to be the weak form of the adjective *liðe*, 'gentle', and then added the definite article to bring it into line with current usage. However, the construction could be the translator's own: cf. *Cura Pastoralis* 39/13 'se Babylonia cyning' and Or. itself, 30/34 and 33/11 etc.

44/9–11. *Ac . . . rice.* According to OH II. vi. 12, Croesus, 'cum ad auxiliandum Babyloniis uenisset, uictus sollicite in regnum refugit'. The translator seems to have taken *uictus* to refer not to Croesus but to the Babylonians.

44/11. *he . . . ofslog.* OH II. vi. 12 'Croesum cepit captumque et uita et patrimonio donauit.' Or.'s version is based on the variant reading *damnauit* for *donauit* found in 'related' manuscripts; see Bately (1961), pp. 85, 92, and 100.

44/12–16. *Ond . . . niede.* OH II. vi. 14 'et nostri incircumspecta anxietate causantur, si potentissimae illae quondam Romanae reipublicae moles nunc magis inbecillitate propriae senectutis quam alienis concussae uiribus contremescunt.' The translator by taking *moles* to refer to the physical structure of Rome and by replacing an indirect question by a construction involving a causal clause strengthens the parallelism between Rome and Babylon. That Rome was preserved by its Christianity is an observation with numerous parallels in OH: see e.g. II. iii.

44/17–18. *an giong cyning . . . Damaris.* OH II. vii. 1 *Thamyris regina.* The young son is not mentioned in OH until II. vii. 2, where he is said to have been sent by Thamyris to pursue Cyrus. Nowhere is he given the rank of king.

44/19. *þæt londgemære . . . Araxis.* OH II. vii. 1 does not describe the Araxis river as the frontier of Scythia; however, the translator could have deduced its position from vii. 2 'Cyrus itaque Scythiam ingressus, procul a transmisso flumine castra metatus'.

44/20–3. *Ac . . . name.* According to OH II. vii. 2, Thamyris' intention was to hem in the enemy by using the river to block their retreat.

44/24–5. *þæm folce . . . dryncas.* Or.'s addition, possibly prompted by the belief, widely held in classical times, that the Scythians had milk as their staple diet. See above, 22/3–4.

44/26–9. *se gionga . . . metton.* Based on OH II. vii. 2 '[Cyrus] quasi territus refugisset'.

44/29–31. *Hie ðær . . . hæfdon.* OH II. vii. 3 'barbari ueluti ad epulas inuitati ebrietate uincuntur.'

44/32–3. *þæm twæm . . . folces.* See OH II. vii. 2, where the queen is said to have entrusted 'tertiam partem copiarum' to her son.

45/1–6. *hiere . . . mid him.* Cf. OH II. vii. 4 'paulatimque cedendo superbum hostem in insidias uocat. ibi quippe conpositis inter montes insidiis ducenta milia Persarum cum ipso rege deleuit.' Justinus' version, I. viii. 10–11, is that the queen led Cyrus *ad angustias*, where she had ambushes *conpositis in montibus*, while according to Frontinus, II. v.

5, the queen, feigning fear, lured Cyrus into a defile well known to her troops, then, suddenly facing about, turned to take the offensive. Or.'s description of the division of Thamyris' forces is probably inspired by OH's reference to an ambush. The inclusion of women in the army could be due either to OH's description of Thamyris herself as participating in the fighting, or to earlier references to the Amazons as warriors. See above, 29/19–35.

45/5–6. *twa þusend.* OH II. vii. 5 *ducenta milia.*

45/10–11. *twa hunde . . . iiiix.* OH II. viii. 1 has the reading *ccxlv.* An original *xlv* seems to have been misread or miscopied as *xiv.*

45/11. *Cambisis . . . rice.* According to OH II. viii. 1, it was Darius who came to the throne in the year given at the head of the chapter, Cambyses (529–522 B.C.) being mentioned only as his predecessor.

45/12–14. *gedyde . . . towearp.* OH II. viii. 2 'Cambyses . . . cunctam Aegypti religionem abominatus caerimonias eius et templa deposuit.'

45/15. *Caldei.* OH II. viii. 4 *Babylonam.*

45/17–18. *ægþer ge . . . forwiernde.* Cf. OH II. viii. 4–5 'Antyro, regi Scytharum, hac uel maxime causa bello intulit, quod filiae eius petitas sibi nuptias non obtinuisset.' That Darius was Cyrus' kinsman (*cognatus*) is a piece of information to be found in Bede, *De Temporum Ratione,* col. 536 and Freculph, *Chronicon,* col. 993. However, according to Justinus I. x. 14 he was his son-in-law, while Jerome, *Comm. in Danielem,* col. 518 refers to '*Darius* as Cyri regis Persarum avunculus'.

45/20–1. *Ac . . . slogan.* OH II. viii. 5 merely states that the Scythians tore his re* (rearguard)* *(extrema copiarum)* to pieces by their sudden attacks.

45/23. *þa brycge . . . wæs.* OH II. viii. 6 'ponte Histri fluminis'. In locating the bridge on the frontier, the translator may be making a contextual guess. See, however, Solinus 71, 7, 'finibus Thraciae a septemtrione Hister obtenditur.'

45/25–6. *þær forlet . . . sceoldon.* Probably a misunderstanding of OH II. viii. 6, 'amissis octoginta milibus bellatorum', prompted by OH's subsequent comment, 'hunc amissorum numerum inter damna non duxerit'. However, it is interesting to note that, according to Herodotus, Darius left Megabazus in Europe with 80,000 men.

45/27. *þa læssan Asiam.* OH II. viii. 7 *Asiam.* See 10/24 and Commentary.

45/28. *Ionas, Creca leode.* OH II. viii. 7 *Ionas.* See e.g. Isidore, *Etymologies* IX. ii. 28, 'Iones, qui et Graeci'.

45/30. *Mæcedoniam.* OH II. viii. 7 *Ionas.* In OH II. viii. 8 the Athenians are said to ask the help of the Lacedaemonians.

45/33. *ðære dune . . . Morotthome.* OH II. viii. 8 *campis Marathoniis.* For Or.'s use of *dun* here see Cornelius Nepos, I *Miltiades* 5. 3, 'sub montis radicibus acie regione instructa', also Lactantius Placidus, *in Stat. Theb.* V. 431 and XI. 644, 'Marathon mons'.

45/33–46/1. *Heora . . . Htesseus.* OH II. viii. 9 'Miltiades ei tunc bello praefuit.' According to Plutarch, *Theseus* xxxv, many of those who fought at Marathon against the Medes thought they saw the apparition of Theseus in arms rushing on in front of them against the barbarians. For possible Latin sources of Or.'s alteration, see Mela II. iii. 45, 'Marathon magnarum multarumque uirtutum testis iam inde a Theseo, Persica maxime clade pernotus', and Lactantius Placidus, *in Stat. Theb.* V. 431, 'Marathon . . . quam cum Persae invasissent, ab Atheniensibus Theseo duce caede magnorum virorum liberati sunt' (a passage which also contains a reference to Marathon as a mountain: see the preceding note). See further, Whitelock (1966), p. 91 and Bately (1971), p. 247.

46/1–2. *se . . . hæfde.* Cf. OH II. viii. 9, where Miltiades is described as 'celeritate magis quam uirtute fretus'.

46/2. *se geworhte . . . gefeohte.* Or.'s addition. According to Justinus II. ix. 14, 'in eo proelio tanta virtus singulorum fuit ut, cuius laus prima esset, difficile iudicium videretur'; see also Mela II. iii. 45.

46/8–9. *Læcedamania, Creca byrg.* OH II. ix. 1 *Lacedaemonius.* See 31/23, Commentary.

46/11. *viii c þusenda.* OH II. ix. 2 *septingenta.*

46/12. *iiii c m.* OH II. ix. 2 *milia . . . et trecenta.* For *trecenta* some of the 'related' manuscripts have the variant $\overline{cccc}$; see e.g. BNL 4877, Laud Lat. 4 and New College 151.

46/13. *þara miclena dulmuna.* OH II. ix. 2 *rostratas naues.* The Orosius Commentary, f. 9ᵛ explains *rostratas naves* as 'bellicas naves aere ferroque comptas pluras'. Or.'s ultimate source here seems to be Isidore, *Etymologies* XIX. i. 13–14, 'Rostratae naves vocatae ab eo quod in fronte rostra aerea habeant propter scopulos, ne feriantur et conlidantur. Longae naves sunt quas dromones vocamus, dictae eo quod longiores sint ceteris', with *longae naves* taken to refer back to *rostratae naves.* For the term *dulmuna* see 30/17, Commentary.

46/13–14. *þara scipa . . . bæran.* OH II. ix. 2 *onerarias,* i.e. transports or merchant vessels. See the Orosius Commentary, f. 9ᵛ, 'honerarias cum cibo et apparatu bellico'.

46/20. *Læcedemonia . . . byrg.* OH II. ix. 3 *rex Spartanorum.* See 31/23–5, and Commentary.

46/21. *on . . . londfæstenne.* OH II. ix. 3 'in angustiis Thermopylarum'. See Corpus T 91 *Thermofilas: faesten,* and Lindsay's note on this gloss.

46/22–8. *Xersis . . . men.* OH II. ix. 4 'Xerxes autem contemptu paucitatis obiectae iniri pugnam, conseri manum imperat. porro illi, quorum cognati et commanipulares in campis Marathoniis occubuerant, et certaminis simul et cladis exstitere principium.' That the survivors of Marathon should desire vengeance may be a contextual assumption on the part of the translator; see, however, Justinus II. xi. 3, 'Qui dum ulcisci suos quaerunt, principium cladis fuere.'

46/24. *þa ane . . . abolgen wæs.* Could this addition be based on a corrupt manuscript reading of *iniri*, resulting in confusion with *ira* 'anger'? For a similar lack of concord see e.g. 117/12.

46/29–32. *Xersis . . . geslægen.* OH II. ix. 5 'deinde succedens sibi turba maior ac segnior, cum iam neque ad procurrendum libera neque ad pugnandum expedita neque ad fugiendum prompta solis mortibus subrigeretur, triduo continuo non duorum pugna, sed caedes unius populi fuit.'

46/32–47/4. *He het . . . þeode.* OH II. ix. 6 'quarto autem die cum uideret Leonida undique hostem circumfundi hortatur auxiliares socios, ut subtrahentes se pugnae in cacumen montis euadant ac se ad meliora tempora reseruent; sibi uero cum Spartanis suis aliam sortem esse subeundam: plus se patriae debere quam uitae.' According to other classical sources, e.g. Frontinus II. ii. 13, the Spartans would not have been overcome had not the enemy been led around to the rear by a traitor.

46/35. *He . . . fæstre land.* Possibly based on the assumption that OH II. ix. 6, 'subtrahentes se pugnae in cacumen montis', referred to all Leonidas' army, not just the auxiliary allies. Some manuscripts of OH, including that used by Freculph, col. 999, have the variant reading 'hortatur auxiliares socios ut subtraherent se pugnae, in cacumen montis evadant', and it may be that the translator, using a manuscript with such a reading, misinterpreted *evadant* as indicative, referring to Leonidas and his army. However, Herodotus refers to the Spartans as withdrawing and taking up position on a little hill at the entrance to the pass before the final assault.

47/4–9. *Ac . . . gewyrcan.* According to OH II. ix. 7, Leonidas 'Spartanos admonet, de gloria plurimum, de uita nihil sperandum; neque exspectandum uel hostem uel diem, sed occasione noctis perrumpenda castra, conmiscenda arma, conturbanda agmina fore; nusquam uictores honestius quam in castris hostium esse perituros'.

47/8–9. *us . . . gewyrcan.* Potter (1952–3), p. 402, draws attention to the similarity between this sentiment and those of *Hávamál*

> ek veit einn at aldri deyr
> dómr of dauðan hvern

and *Alfred's Boethius* 28/11 'god word 7 god hlisa ælces monnes bið betra 7 deorra þonne ænig wela'. To these might be added quotations from OE poetry such as *Beowulf*, 1387–9 and *The Seafarer*, 72–3.

47/9–11. *Hu . . . gefliemde.* Based on OH II. ix. 8–10, but rather surprisingly omitting all details of the battle, including the description of the Spartans as 'uictores sine dubio, nisi mori elegissent' and the graphic account of their death: 'ad postremum uincendo fatigati, ubi quisque eorum deficientibus membris uisus est sibi mortis suae ultione satiatus, ibi inter impedimenta cadauerum campumque crasso et semigelato sanguine palpitantem lassus lapsus et mortuus est.'

47/15. *Ionas, Creca leode.* OH II. x. 1 *Ionas.* See 45/28.

47/15–16. *þeh . . . gecierdon.* Or.'s addition. See below, 47/20–8, Commentary.

47/16–18. *hie him . . . wæron.* Or. here combines material from OH II. x. 1 and 4.

47/19–20. *hie . . . cuman.* Or.'s addition, for which I have found no support in classical texts.

47/20–8. *Se Themestocles . . . gewyrcan.* According to OH II. x. 2, Themistocles rebuked and blamed his former allies and comrades in peril and persuaded them to respect the oaths of their old treaties. For the earlier alliance of Ionians, Athenians, and Lacedaemonians and the conquest of the Ionians by Darius see OH II. viii. 7 and x. 1.

47/30. *þe . . . getriewdon.* Or.'s addition.

47/33. *Xersis þegn . . . Marðonius.* According to Cornelius Nepos IV, *Pausanias*, 1. 2, Mardonius was *satrapes regius.* Cf. the Orosius Commentary, f. 9ᵛ, 'Mardonius id est dux Persicus'.

48/5. *sumum dæle his fultume.* Cf. 12/31 *sumne dæl Dene,* and Commentary.

48/6–13. *þa he . . . brohte.* OH II. x. 8 'rex Abydum, ubi pontem ueluti uictor maris conseruerat, cum paucis proficiscitur. sed cum pontem hibernis tempestatibus dissolutum offendisset, piscatoria scapha trepidus transiit.' Xerxes' bridge was made not of stone but of ships: see Isidore, *Etymologies* XIII. xvi. 3, 'ponte navibus facto' and Orosius Commentary, f. 9ᵛ, 'pontem de nauibus construxit'.

48/13–15. *Hu . . . geniðerade.* OH II. x. 9 refers not to God's hand in events but to *mutationes rerum.*

48/15–18. *se . . . generian.* OH II. x. 9 'exiguo contentum latere nauigio, sub quo ipsum pelagus ante latuisset et iugum captiuitatis suae iuncto ponte portasset'.

48/19. *forlet . . . wæron.* Or.'s addition. See above, 47/13–18.

48/20. *for . . . abræc.* A telescoping of two statements in OH: see II. xi. 1 'Olynthum . . . Graeciae oppidum expugnauit' and II. xi. 2 'incensa urbis parte in Boeotiam omnem belli apparatum deducit'. For the location of Boeotia in Greece see Isidore, *Etymologies* XIV. iv. 11. Olynthus was in Thrace.

48/22–4. *Atheniensum . . . gewurdon.* According to OH II. xi. 3, 'castra regiis opibus referta ceperunt, non paruo quidem antiquae industriae damno: nam post huius praedae diuisionem aurum Persicum prima Graeciae uirtutis corruptio fuit.'

48/27–8. *swa swa . . . sint.* Or.'s explanatory addition.

48/30. *nigon . . . anwealde.* OH II. xi. 8 'de uisceribus unius regni decies nouies centena milia uirorum'. See the Orosius Commentary, f. 9ᵛ, 'unius regni .i. persarum'.

48/31. *wiþerwinnum . . . Crecum.* OH II. xi. 8 refers to 'tribus proximis regibus tria bella', but identifies only Graecia, while the Orosius Com-

mentary, f. 9ᵛ names the three kings as Cyrus, Darius, and Xerxes. For
war with the Scythians see above, 45/16–26.

48/32–3. *þæt . . . deaðum.* Or.'s addition.

48/35–49/3. *Uton . . . sint.* OH II. xi. 9 reports Leonidas' words as
'Prandete, tamquam apud inferos cenaturi' and adds, 'auxiliaribus tamen,
quos excedere bello iubebat, misericorditer suasit, ut se ad meliora
tempora reseruarent.' Not only has the translator misunderstood his
source, but he or some intermediary seems to have interpreted the
inferos of Leonidas' speech in Christian rather than in classical Latin
terms.

49/3–9. *Leoniþa . . . ne nu.* OH II. xi. 10 'ecce cum ille promisit futura
meliora, isti adserunt meliora praeterita, quid aliud colligi datur utroque
in suis detestante praesentia, nisi aut semper bona esse sed ingrata aut
numquam omnino meliora?'

49/10–14. *Nu . . . Romane.* Orosius' actual reasons for returning to the
subject of Rome are very different: see II. xii. 1 'neque enim interuallo
miserarium ad alios transire conpellor, sed, sicuti se quondam efferue-
scentia ubique mala ipsis actibus conligarunt, ita etiam permixta referuntur: nobis quippe conferre inter se tempora Orbis, non cuiusquam
partis eius laboribus insultare propositum est.'

49/15–16. *ii . . . hundeahtatigum.* OH II. xii. 2 *cclxl.*

49/17. *þa hiora . . . eodon.* Or.'s addition, replacing a reference in OH
II. xii. 2 to a short interval of peace. Livy puts the defeat of the Fabii in
477 B.C., i.e. 14 years earlier. However, OH's account of Roman history,
II. v, had ended with the story of the defeat of the Fabii and had, like
II. xii, included reference to severe pestilence (see Or. 41/18–42/34). The
translator may thus be excused for assuming that the new section on the
Romans began just where the previous one had left off.

49/21–4. *hie . . . bringan.* OH II. xii. 3 gives a far less graphic description
of the effects of the plague: 'eo anno Aebutium et Seruilium ambo consules
pestilentia consumpsit, militares copias plurima ex parte confecit, multos
nobiles praecipueque plebem foeda tabe deleuit; quamuis iam etiam
superiore quarto anno oborta lues eundem populum depopulata sit.'
The detail that the survivors were too weak to bury the dead could be the
translator's own. However, see Livy III. vii. 3 with its reference to the
rotting carcasses of men and cattle in a stricken desert and to Rome with
her strength gone. See also, in connection with the war against the
Gauls, Livy V. xlviii. 3.

49/25–6. *ealle . . . winnende wæron.* OH II. xii. 5 'ciues exules seruique
fugitiui duce Herbonio, uiro Sabino, inuaserunt incenderuntque Capitolium.'

49/26–7. *heora heafodstedes . . . heton.* OH II. xii. 5 *Capitolium.* The
translator could have known of the function of the Capitol from a variety
of sources. See e.g. Isidore, *Etymologies* XV. ii. 31, 'Capitolium . . .

fuerit Romanae urbis et religionis caput summum', also Remigius, *in Capellam* V. 235. 15 and Servius, *Aen.* VIII. 652.

49/27–8. *þone ænne . . . hæfdon.* Apparently a contextual guess: in OH II. xii. 6 an allusion to *consul Valerius* follows an account of the death of the consuls Aebutius and Servilius.

49/29. *heanlicne sige.* OH II. xii. 6 explains that the victory was ignominious because gained against slaves.

49/30. *Fulcisci.* OH II. xii. 7 *Aequi Vulscique.* For manuscript variants see Glossary of Proper Names, and Introduction, p. lvii.

49/31. *on an fæsten.* OH II. xii. 7 *in Algido.* Algidus was the name both of a town and of a mountain range; see Orosius Commentary, f. 10, 'in algido .i. mons uel ciuium' and Jerome–Eusebius, col. 443, 'in Algido monte'.

50/2–3. *eal . . . læfed wæs.* Or.'s addition. According to Livy III. xxvii. 3, Cincinnatus called up all men of military age.

50/3. *anne earmne mon.* OH II. xii. 7 *Quintius Cincinnatus.* Cincinnatus' poverty is a familiar theme in Latin texts; see e.g. Valerius Maximus IV. iv *De Paupertate* and Augustine, *Civ. Dei* V. xviii. However, since Or. does not refer to Cincinnatus by name, it may be that he was previously unknown to the translator and that the latter either deduced his poverty from the reference to him ploughing or learned of it from a gloss or comment.

50/3. *consule.* OH II. xii. 7 *dictator.*

50/5. *Fulcisci.* According to OH II. xii. 8, it is the Aequi that are conquered. See above, 49/30, Commentary.

50/6–13. *Æfter þæm . . . hunger.* In OH this follows the section referring to the decemviri, Or. 50/14–22.

50/9. *besuncenum.* Sweet retains the manuscript reading *besuncen.* However, this does not seem to me a clear case of a parallel being uninflected when 'the case is clearly indicated in the expressions which it parallels': see A. Campbell, 'The Old English Epic Style', in *English and Medieval Studies presented to J. R. R. Tolkien* ed. N. Davis and C. L. Wrenn (1962), p. 22.

50/9–10. *hie selfe . . . wurden.* Or.'s addition.

50/11. *swa micel hæte.* Cf. OH II. xiii. 9 'ita iugis et torrida siccitas'.

50/10–13. *Æfter ðæm . . . hunger.* OH II. xiii. 9 merely states that, because of the drought (*torrida siccitas*), hope was then and there abandoned of raising crops on the land during that or the succeeding year. However, OH II. xiii. 1 refers to famine.

50/14–15. *Romane . . . hæfdon.* OH II. xiii. 2 'potestas consulum decemuiris tradita'. Cf. Eutropius I. xviii. 1, 'pro duobus consulibus decem facti sunt, qui summam potestatem haberent, decemviri nominati.'

50/15–22. *Hiera an . . . wergende wæron.* The translator has completely

failed to understand OH II. xiii. 3–5, 'nam primus ex decemuiris cedenti-
bus ceteris solus Appius Claudius sibi continuauit imperium, statimque
aliorum coniuratio subsecuta est, ut more contempto, quo insigne imperii
penes unum potestas autem communis erat, omnes omnia propriis
libidinibus agitarent. itaque inter cetera, quae insolentissime cuncti
praesumebant, repente singuli cum duodenis fascibus ceterisque im-
peratoriis insignibus processerunt: et nouo improbae ordinationis
incepto, ablegata religione consulum emicuit agmen tyrannorum, duabus
tabulis legum ad decem priores additis, agentes insolentissimo fastu
plurima, die, quo deponere magistratus mos erat, cum isdem insignibus
processerunt.' The story of Appius and Verginia that follows in OH is
omitted altogether.

50/20–1. *ealle . . . ofbeotan.* This appears to be the result of the misreading or miscopying of OH II. xiii. 4 *processerunt* as *percusserunt*,
possibly via a contraction such as the ꝓ of MSS Vienna 366 and Ricc.
627.

50/21. *saglum.* OH II. xiii. 4 *fascibus.*

50/21–2. *siþþan . . . wergende wæron.* Cf. OH II. xiii. 2 'magnam perniciem
reipublicae inuexit'.

50/23–4. *Iepelice . . . pleolecestan.* Orosius in fact says no such thing.
Sweet's edition takes Or.'s source here to be the reference in OH II.
xiv. 2, 'Sicilia . . . ut quam breuissime absoluam, requiem malorum nisi
nunc nescit.' However, the translator may have been influenced by OH
II. xviii. 4, 'Ecce paruissima pagina uerbisque paucissimis quantos de tot
prouinciis populis atque urbibus non magis explicui actus operum.' Like
the reference in OH II. xiv. 2 this is immediately followed by an account
of an eruption of Etna. This second account is omitted by Or.

50/25–30. *þæt . . . 7 bradre.* OH II. xiv. 3 'Aethna ipsa, quae tunc cum
excidio urbium atque agrorum crebris eruptionibus aestuabat, nunc
tantum innoxia specie ad praeteritorum fidem fumat.' That Etna was the
gate of hell and emitted sulphurous fumes was a commonplace in medieval texts; see e.g. Isidore, *Etymologies* XIV. viii. 14 'Mons Aethna ex
igne et sulphure dictus; unde et Gehenna', also Bede, *De Natura Rerum*,
col. 276. Isidore is quoted by the Orosius Commentary, f. 10. For the
continual spreading of the fires of Etna see *Gregorii Magni Dialogi Libri
IV*, ed. U. Moricca (Rome, 1924) IV. xxxvi and GD 315/4.

50/31. *iii . . . an.* OH II. xiv. 4 *cccxxxv.*

50/32–51/8. *Sicilie . . . geniedan.* A drastic abbreviation of OH II. xiv.
4–xviii. 1. See Introduction, pp. xciii f.

50/32–51/1. *healfe . . . healfe.* According to OH II. xiv. 7, these are the
inhabitants of Catina and Syracuse.

51/2. *þe ær . . . wæron.* Or.'s addition. See above, II. v.

51/5. *for . . . ieldrena.* Cf. OH II. xv. 4 'paterni auitique . . . odii'.

51/6–8. *Wæs . . . geniedan.* OH II. xv. 5 'mirum dictu, Atheniensium
tantas ea tempestate opes fuisse, ut, cum aduersus eos, hoc est aduersus

unam urbem, Graeciae Asiae totiusque Orientis uiribus incursum sit, pugnando saepe nec umquam cedendo consumpti magis uideantur fuisse quam uicti.'

51/9. *þy ilcan geare.* Cf. OH II. xvii. 4 'insignis hic annus et expugnatione Athenarum et morte Darii Persarum regis'. OH, however, is referring to the year 405 B.C., A.U.C. 348.

51/12–13. *se þær gingra wæs.* Presumably deduced from OH II. xviii. 2, where it is said that Cyrus was overwhelmed *a cohorte regia* and that as a result Artaxerxes 'potestatem regni parricidio firmauit'. Cf., however, Justinus V. xi. 2 'Regnum Artaxerxi, Cyro civitates, quarum praefectus erat, testamento legavit.'

51/13–14. *an burg . . . adrencte.* Cf. OH II. xviii. 7 'Tunc etiam Atalante ciuitas, Locris adhaerens terrae contigua, repentino maris impetu abscissa atque in insulam desolata est.' Atalante was a Greek town on the shore of *mare Euboicum.* Or.'s incorrect location of it in Africa may be the result of scribal error in an underlying Latin manuscript, since for *Atalante* a number of 'related' manuscripts read *Athlante,* while a common variant of the name *Atlas* (the African mountain) is *Athlans*: see 9/16 and Glossary of Proper Names. For an African people named the Atlantes see e.g. Mela I. iv and I. viii.

51/18–19. *mon . . . ham.* OH's reference, II. xix. 1, is merely to 'Romani repentinis saepe hostium eruptionibus comminuti'. However, Livy's account of these ten years refers to many wars instigated by or against the Romans.

51/20–4. *þæm cræfte . . . awestan.* Cf. OH II. xix. 2 'urbem nouissime sine ullo, digno Romanae uirtutis testimonio cuniculis et clandestina obreptione ceperunt.' The translator could have discovered the nature of *cuniculi* from a variety of sources; see e.g. Livy V. xix, Florus I. vi. 9, and Remigius, *in Capellam* V. 235. 12, 'Cuniculi sunt fossae subterraneae.' I have found no support for the translator's claim that the operation took place at night: see also below, 91/16–17.

51/27. *Senno þære byrig.* OH II. xix. 5 *Galli Senones.* These Gauls belonged to the tribe who gave their name to the town of *Senones,* mod. *Sens,* in Gallia Lugdunensis. See further, Glossary of Proper Names.

51/29. *on ðæm ilcan dæge.* Or.'s addition. According to Livy V. xxxvi, the battle broke out in the middle of the negotiations.

52/3. *gelice . . . mawe.* Cf. OH II. xix. 6 'quasi aridam segetem succidit'.

52/6–8. *Ne wene . . . gedydon.* Cf. OH II. xix. 6 'non enim facile aliquis similem ruinam Romanae militiae recenseret, etiam si Roma insuper incensa non esset.'

52/8–14. *þa feawan . . . gesealdon.* According to OH II. xix. 8–9, the survivors are those who had previously taken refuge on the Capitoline Hill: 'ibique infelices reliquias fame peste desperatione formidine terunt subigunt uendunt: nam mille libris auri discessionis pretium paciscuntur, non quo apud Gallos Roma parui nominis fuerit, sed quo illam sic iam ante detriuerint, ut amplius tunc ualere non posset.' Not only has the translator failed to realize that *uendunt* is to be interpreted in the context of the payment of a thousand pounds in gold, but he is apparently ignorant of the true outcome of the siege, with the arrival of Camillus before payment could be made and the subsequent defeat of the Gauls: see Livy V. xlix and Florus I. vii. 17. For a version of the story which describes the gold as paid and then recovered, see Eutropius I. xx.

52/15–16. *Hu þyncð . . . leahtriað.* This anticipates OH II. xix. 12, 'En tempora, quorum conparatione praesentia ponderantur', and Or. 52/23–4. For the construction see above 31/19–21, Commentary.

52/17–22. *þa þa . . . freond.* An effective rewriting of OH II. xix. 10, 'exeuntibus Gallis remanserat in illo quondam Vrbis ambitu informium ruinarum obscena congeries, et undique per impedita errantium et inter sua ignotorum offensae uocis imago respondens trepidos suspendebat auditus. horror quatiebat animos, silentia ipsa terrebant: siquidem materia pauoris est raritas in spatiosis.'

52/27–8. *hie eac . . . næren.* Cf. OH II. xix. 13 'Galli exstincto populo Vrbe deleta ipsum quoque Romae nomen in extremis cineribus persequentes'.

52/29. *for . . . ege.* Or.'s addition; see OH VII. xxxvii. 9 and Augustine, *Civ. Dei* I. i and vii.

52/32–3. *Ac . . . mosten.* Or.'s addition; see OH VII. xxxviii. 2.

52/34. *ænig.* OH II. xix. 13 'quemquam . . . senatorem'.

53/7–8. *iii . . . lvii.* OH III. i. 1 ccclxiv.

53/9. *bismerleceste.* As OH III. i. 3 explains, 'quid tam indignum liberis et fortibus uiris, quam longe remoti, saepe uicti, adhuc hostis et deinde minitantis imperio arma deponere pacique seruire?'

53/11. *iii winter.* Or.'s addition, for which I have found no support in classical texts. See, however, Cornelius Nepos XVII *Agesilaus*, II. iii, where a truce of three *months* is made between the Lacedaemonians and Tissaphernes, the *praefectus* of Artaxerxes. The peace referred to by OH is the so-called King's Peace of 387 B.C.

53/14. *for . . . gebead.* Cf. OH III. i. 3, quoted in 53/9, Commentary.

53/16–17. *swa . . . leaspellengum.* Or.'s addition. According to OH III. i. 3, the Greeks could not have acted as they did, 'si non in ipso tantum adnuntiatae pacis sono per corda cunctorum aegra belli tabuisset intentio et post diuturnas laborum uigilias oscitantes ac stupefactos quies inopina laxasset, priusquam ipsam quietem uoluntas pacta conponeret'. Could the translator have misinterpreted *sono* and *corda* as musical terms?

53/17–19. *Ne geþyncð . . . gestieran.* In spite of the specific attribution to Orosius, there is nothing to correspond to this at any point in OH III. i. For Or.'s theme see Introduction, pp. xciii f.

53/21–3. *hi . . . Asiam.* An expansion of OH III. i. 6, 'toto Orienti bellum mouentes'. For war with the Persians, see OH III. i. 6; for war with Asia Minor, see OH III. i. 11.

53/23–4. *Ahtene . . . gebune.* For the capture of Athens by the Spartans see OH II. xvii. 4; for the flight of the Athenians and their subsequent return see OH II. xvii. 8 and 13, sections not included in the translation of Book II.

53/25. *hæfdon . . . asponon.* Here, as in 53/28–9, Or. is anticipating OH III. i. 16, where, however, it is the Thebans who are said to attack, aided by the Athenians.

53/25–7. *Læcedemonie . . . habban.* Cf. OH III. i. 5 'Lacedaemonii, utpote homines et Graeci homines, quo plura habebant, eo ampliora cupientes, postquam Atheniensium potiti sunt, uniuersam Asiam spe dominationis hauserunt.'

53/28–9. *Ac . . . cnysedan.* See OH III. i. 16 and 53/25, Commentary.

54/1–8. *Sona . . . ealdormon.* An expansion of OH III. i. 6, 'qui cum sibi aduersus duos potentissimos Artaxerxis Persarum regis praefectos Farnabazum et Tissafernen pugnandum uideret, prouiso ad tempus consilio, ut pondus geminae congressionis eluderet, unum denuntiato bello adpetit, alterum pacta pace suspendit.'

54/9. *scire.* According to OH III. i. 7, Tissafernes was replaced as 'ducem nauali bello'.

54/15. *ænne wisne mon.* Or.'s addition. For Agesilaus' qualities of mind, see Cornelius Nepos XVII *Agesilaus, passim,* especially VIII. 1, Justinus VI. ii. 8 and Freculph, *Chronicon,* col. 1008, 'Agesila pede claudo, ingenio acerrimo'.

54/17–21. *Hie . . . gefuhten.* OH III. i. 9 'raro umquam ita pares omni industria duces in unum coiere bellum, qui acerbissimis inuicem proeliis fatigati et multo sanguine obliti uelut inuicti ab alterutro recesserunt.' OH does not refer to the decline of the Lacedaemonians till III. i. 15 (see Or. 54/28–9).

54/22–3. *Conon . . . aweste.* OH III. i. 10 'Conon . . . inuadit hostiles agros, turres castella ceteraque praesidia expugnat.'

54/30–1. *þæt hie . . . gemæne wæs.* Or.'s addition.

54/31–2. *hie 7 Thebane.* OH III. i. 16 gives the initiative to the Thebans, 'auxilio Atheniensium'.

54/33. *7 siððan besætan.* Or.'s addition, apparently a contextual guess.

55/2. *Ahtene.* OH III. i. 20 *Thebanos.* See 53/28 and 54/31–2, Commentary.

55/4–5. *þæm lytlan sige . . . hæfdon.* According to OH III. i. 21, the victory —which was over the Thebans—was *insperata,* 'unexpected'.

55/5–6. *Hie . . . getygþade.* OH III. i. 22 merely states that Conon, on hearing of the return of Agesilaus, turned back to lay waste the territory of the Lacedaemonians.

55/7. *mid micle sciphere.* Or.'s addition, possibly deduced from earlier allusions to Conon as naval commander; see, however, Cornelius Nepos IX *Conon*, IV. v, 'cum parte navium'.

55/8–9. *hi . . . unwræste.* Cf. OH III. i. 22 'Spartani . . . ultima propemodum desperatione tabuerunt.'

55/12–13. *he geniedde . . . tobræcon.* According to OH III. i. 24, Conon 'urbem . . . a Lacedaemoniis exinanitam Lacedaemoniorum praedis repleuit, Persis incendentibus concrematam Persis aedificantibus reformauit.'

55/13–14. *Læcedemonie . . . gehiersume wæron.* Or.'s addition. According to Cornelius Nepos XVII *Agesilaus*, vii. 1, after the battle of Leuctra, the Lacedemonians never regained their former hegemony.

55/16–18. *næs na . . . fullgongan.* OH III. i. 25 'non quia misericorditer fessis consuleret, sed ne se in Aegypto bellis occupato aliqua in regnum suum temptaretur inruptio'.

55/18–20. *Ac . . . fultumes hæfde.* Cf. OH III. ii. 1 'Lacedaemonii, inquieti magis quam strenui et furore potius quam uirtute intolerabiles'. The Thebans are not mentioned by OH at this point, though they are the chief enemy in following sections.

55/21. *hloðum . . . staledon.* Cf. OH III. ii. 1 'temptant furta bellorum'. According to the Laws of Ine, a *hloð* consisted of between 7 and 35 men: see Laws I, p. 94.

55/21. *Arcadum heora burg.* Cf. OH III. ii. 2 'speculati absentiam Arcadum castellum eorum repentina inruptione perfringunt'. The translator appears to have misconstrued OH III. i. 2 *Arcadum*, gpl. of *Arcades*, 'the Arcadians', as as. in apposition to *castellum eorum*.

55/24. *to Arcadium.* According to OH III. ii. 4, it is the Thebans, allies of the Arcadians, who gave the signal to cease fighting.

55/31. *Macedaniæ.* OH III. ii. 11 *Graecia.* See 61/7, and Commentary.

55/32–56/1. *on þa læssan . . . maran.* OH III. ii. 11 *Asia.*

56/1–2. *ic scæl . . . hæfde.* Or.'s addition.

56/11. *eaðmodegra . . . fiell.* OH III. iii. 3 'conseruatorem humilium et punitorem malorum'. Potter (1952–3), p. 404, sees in the Old English version an echo of *Luke* 1 : 51–2.

56/11–13. *Mare . . . þæt.* Cf. OH III. iii. 3 'haec ut commemorata sint magis quam explicita uerecundiae concesserim ut et qui scit recolat et qui nescit inquirat.'

56/14–16. *On . . . oferhergedon.* Cf. OH III. iii. 4 'Interea Romani, qui per septuaginta annos ab urbe Vulscorum, praeterea Faliscorum Aequorum et Sutrinorum subacti et adtriti adsiduis bellis conficiebantur, tandem in supra scriptis diebus Camillo duce easdem cepere ciuitates et rediuiuo finem dedere certamini.'

56/16. *Suttrian.* OH III. iii. 5 *Praenestinos.* For the Sutrini, see OH III. iii. 4, quoted in 56/14–16, Commentary.

56/17–19. *Hit . . . gefliemdon.* OH III. iii. 5 merely states that the Romans conquered (*uicerunt*) the Praenestini. That the latter were put to flight is reported by Livy VI. xxix. 3.

56/20–1. *iii . . . lxxxiii.* OH III. iv. 1 has the figure *ccclxxxiiii.*

56/21. *opre noman.* See Bately (1970), p. 436, and, for an explanation of this Roman practice, Servius, *Aen.* X. 655 ('licet possit fieri ut duo nomina unius sint, ut Numa Pompilius') and Festus, p. 136 *Binominis.*

56/23. *se micla moncwealm.* OH III. iv. 1 *ingens . . . pestilentia.* For a similar use of the demonstrative, see Augustine, *Civ. Dei* III. xvii, 'illa insignis pestilentia', referring to the same epidemic.

56/25. *reðre. Hrædre* would be closer to the *repentinus* of OH III. iv. 2.

56/26. *ungemætre . . . æfterhæpan.* OH III. iv. 2 refers to 'autumni diuitis indigesta inlecebra'.

57/1–3. *heora biscepas . . . don.* Cf. OH III. iv. 5 'auctores suasere pontifices, ut ludi scaenici diis expetentibus ederentur.' The translator may have derived his notion that the *ludi scaenici* were at first held in an amphitheatre (an anachronism, for which see Potter (1952–3), p. 405) from an entry in Isidore, *Etymologies* XVIII. xlii. 1 *De Theatro*: '[Eius] forma primum rotunda erat, sicut et amphitheatri; postea ex medio amphitheatro theatrum factum est. Theatrum autem ab spectaculo nominatum . . . quod in eo populus stans desuper atque spectans ludos (XV. ii. 34 ludos scenicos) contemplaretur.'

57/4. *hiora diofolgield . . . unclænnessa.* The obscenity of Roman stage plays is a recurrent theme in the writings of the early Fathers; see, e.g., Augustine, *Civ. Dei* II. xxvi and Tertullian, *De Spectaculis, PL* i, cols. 642–3 (where they are also said to be idolatries).

57/5. *cwæð Orosius.* What Orosius actually says, III. iv. 4, is that those who disparage the Christian era would complain at this point if he did not make reference to the ceremonies.

57/7–13. *buton . . . anfiteatra.* Or.'s addition; cf. OH IV. vi. 4, where *daemones* are described as 'operarios atque adiutores pestilentiae'. According to Isidore *Etymologies* IV. vi. 17 *Pestilentia*: 'Hoc etsi plerumque per aerias potestates fiat, tamen sine arbitrio omnipotentis Dei omnino non fit.' Or.'s assumption that the heathen gods were devils contrasts with that of Alfred in his translation of Boethius, where these gods are explained away as men.

57/13–16. *þa . . . witanne.* Cf. OH III. iv. 6 'uber nunc quidem mihi iste doloris atque increpationis locus est, sed, in quo iam reuerentia tua studium sapientiae et ueritatis exercuit, mihi super eo audere fas non est. commonuisse me satis sit et ex qualibet intentione lectorem ad illius lectionis plenitudinem remisisse.' Potter (1952–3), p. 406, takes *þa* to refer to *anfiteatra*; however, it need not have a specific antecedent, but may refer instead to the events, subjects or troubles ('these things') mentioned in the preceding section.

57/14. *fæder Agustinus.* OH III. iv. 6 *reuerentia tua,* glossed *Augustine* by 'related' MSS of Groups Biii, Cii, iii, and vii. Orosius addresses Augustine as 'beatissime pater Augustine' in his dedication: see OH I, prol. 1.

57/17. *on . . . geare*. OH III. v. 1 'proximo anno'.

57/18–20. *þa sædon . . . hæfden*. According to OH III. v. 3, it is the cruel earth which is not content to receive 'ex tanta pestilentia mortuos per sepulchra . . ., nisi etiam uiuos scissa sorberet'.

57/25. *gif . . . gewacadon*. Cf. OH III. vi. 1 'nisi otio et lentitudine tor-puisset'. I have adopted here the reading of MS C, although the *gewicadon* of MSS L and B (followed by Calendre l. 153) could be justified as prompted by OH 'Gallorum inundatio . . . ad quartum ab Vrbe lapidem consedit.'

57/26–7. *for þon . . . mehton*. OH III. vi. 1 merely states that Rome was thrown into perturbation and panic.

57/27. *þæs on morgenne*. Or.'s addition, possibly inspired by OH III. vi. 1 *consedit* (see 57/25, Commentary).

57/28. *ladteow*. OH III. vi. 2 *dictator*. See 41/13–14, and Bately (1970), p. 441.

58/1. *hiene ofslog*. Or.'s addition. The knowledge that Manlius Torquatus slew his Gallic adversary could have been derived from a number of sources; see, e.g., Livy VI. xlii. 5, Eutropius II. v, and *Gl. Ansileubi* TO 172.

58/2–4. *Be þæm . . . gefongen wæs*. Or.'s source, OH III. vi. 3, is referring to a completely different battle, against the Tuscans: 'conici datur quantum hominum caesum sit, quando octo milia sunt capta Tuscorum.'

58/7–8. *for þon . . . on Benefente*. Or.'s addition. No Carthaginians were in fact fighting in Italy at this time; however, Bede, *De Temporum Ratione*, col. 540, puts 'Carthaginensium bellum famosum' in the same year as Rome's conflict with the Galli Senones (see above, 51/26–7 and for Galli of unspecified origin, 57/24) while in Freculph, *Chronicon*, col. 1007, the comment 'Tunc etiam fuit Carthaginensium bellum illud famosissimum' immediately precedes the account (taken from OH III. vii. 6) of Artaxerxes' displacement of the Jews. For possible reasons for the location of the war in Beneventum see 102/12–13, Commentary.

58/11–12. *swa . . . cyþende wæron*. Or.'s addition, reflecting a common assumption in both classical and medieval times.

58/12. *oð midne dæg*. OH III. vii. 4 'ad plurimam diei partem'.

58/13. *ofer ealle Romane*. Or.'s addition.

58/14. *on Crecum*. Or.'s addition; see 61/7.

58/15. *ofer ealne middangeard*. OH III. vii. 5 'totius Orientis'.

58/15. *Persa cyning*. Or.'s addition; see OH III. vii. 8 'Persarum subiecit imperio'.

58/17. *he gefor . . . forhergeade*. Or.'s addition.

58/20. *mid bradum folcum*. Cf. OH III. vii. 7 'amplissimis generis sui incrementis'.

58/20–1. *on ðæm tohopan . . . lande*. A modification of OH III. vii. 7, 'exim quandoque erupturos opinio est', presumably influenced by knowledge of the prophecies that the Jews (whether of the Captivity or of the Dispersal) would eventually return home once more. See, e.g., Jeremiah 31 : 16 and 17, and the apocryphal 2 Esdras 13 : 40–7.

58/23–4. *ymbe Campena land*. OH III. viii. 1 'pro Campanis et Sedicinis'.

58/24–5. *longe . . . sigum*. According to OH III. viii, Pyrrhus took over 'Samniticum bellum ancipiti statu gestum'. For accounts of the Samnite wars, see below, 66/10–17 and 75/23–76/22. Eutropius II. ix gives the duration of the conflict as 49 years.

58/26–8. *þæt gewinn . . . angunnan*. OH III. viii. 1 merely comments that 'Pyrrhi bellum mox Punicum consecutum est.'

58/29–59/3. *Siþþan . . . caseres*. The translator leaves the sentence unfinished. Cf. OH III. viii. 3, where, in the course of a syntactically involved paragraph, Orosius challenges anyone who thinks Christian times should be decried to inquire into these matters.

59/2–3. *Octauianus . . . caseres*. OH III. viii. 3 *Caesare Augusto*. The reason for Or.'s alteration seems to be the fact that *Augustus*, like *Caesar*, had come to be used as a title: see, e.g., Isidore, *Etymologies* VII. vi. 43, 'apud nos Augusti appellantur reges, cum propriis nominibus [censentur]', and Einhard, *Life of Charlemagne*, ch. xxviii, 2, 'Imperatoris et Augusti nomen accepit'. Christian of Stavelot, col. 1280, similarly explains 'Caesare Augusto, videlicet Octaviano'.

59/3–11. *þæt hus . . . fotum*. Or.'s addition. The structure whose doors were opened in times of war and closed in times of peace seems to have been no more than a double barbican gate. However, there is ample precedent in Latin texts for Or.'s four-doored building: see, e.g., Augustine, *Civ. Dei* VII. 8 (following a reference to a four-faced Janus), 'Non habent omnino unde quattuor ianuas quae intrantibus et exeuntibus pateant interpretentur ad mundi similitudinem', Macrobius, *Saturnalia*, I. ix, 'Janus . . . ideo et apud nos in quattuor partes spectat' and Servius, *Aen*. VII. 607, 'inventum est simulacrum Iani cum frontibus quattuor . . . et quattuor portarum unum templum est institutum.' Servius goes on to discuss the term *Gabinus cinctus*, giving an explanation which seems to have prompted the second part of Or.'s comment on the significance of the gates of Janus: '*Gabinus cinctus* est toga sic in tergum reiecta, ut una (ima?) eius lacinia a tergo revocata hominem cingat. hoc autem vestimenti genere veteres Latini, cum necdum arma haberent praecinctis togis bellebant; unde etiam milites in procinctu esse dicuntur' (*Aen*. VII. 612). See also Festus, p. 191, 'apud antiquos togis incincti pugnitasse dicuntur.'

59/11–12. *Ac . . . betyneda*. See below, 130/26–7 and 131/23–4 etc.

59/14. *Perse.* Cf. OH III. viii. 5 *Parthicam,* and see below 150/22, Commentary.

59/17. *Romanisce cyningas.* OH III. viii. 5 refers to *iudices Romanos.*

59/21. *þe sibb . . . eorðwara.* Or.'s addition.

59/21–7. *þæt . . . gemægþa.* In his rendering of OH III. viii. 6–8, the translator appears to have been influenced by the story of Augustus' refusal of the title 'lord' on the grounds that he was only a man. This story is told in OH VI. xxii, but not repeated by Or. See further below, 133/29–134/2, Commentary. For Or.'s emphasis of the contrast between the lot of mankind before and after the birth of Christ, see Introduction, pp. xciv f.

59/28–9. *iiii hunde . . . viii.* OH III. ix. 1 *ccccviiii,* 'related' MSS, including Ricc. 627, *ccccviii.*

59/29–60/1. *On . . . ofslog.* Cf. OH III. ix. 1 'in quo bello unus consul interfectus est, alter exstitit parricida'. OH goes on to name Manlius Torquatus as the consul who slew his son; however, the translator appears to have overlooked or rejected this information, basing his identification on the earlier 'Manlio Torquato et Decio Mure consulibus' of OH, and taking *unus consul* to be the first named, and *alter* to be the second.

60/1–5. *for þon . . . ofslog.* Cf. OH III. ix. 2 'Manlius enim Torquatus filium suum, iuuenem, uictorem, interfectoremque Metii Tusculani, nobilis equitis et tum praecipue prouocantis atque insultantis hostis, occidit.' According to Livy VIII. vi–vii, the consuls proclaimed that no man should quit his place to attack the enemy; however, Torquatus' son, riding out to reconnoitre, was taunted by Geminus and accepted his challenge. That the son fought against his father's command is a piece of information found in a number of Latin texts other than Livy: see, e.g., Aurelius Victor 28, 4, Augustine, *Civ. Dei* I. xxiii and V. xviii, Frontinus IV. i. 40, Jerome–Eusebius, col. 473 and Freculph, col. 1010. That the youth was challenged to single combat is also a commonplace; however, this detail the translator could have deduced from OH. See further, Introduction, pp. lxi f.

60/5–7. *For . . . hæfde.* OH III. ix. 4 'Manlius quamuis uictor occursum tamen nobilium iuuenum Romanorum, qui legitime exhiberi solet, triumphans parricida non meruit.' Livy VIII. xii explains that only the seniors went to meet him.

60/8–10. *Minutia . . . alibban.* OH III. ix. 5 'Minucia uirgo Vestalis'. The goddess Vesta is identified with Diana in a number of Latin texts: see, e.g., *Mythographus I,* 112, and also, by way of two equations, by Isidore: see *Etymologies* VIII. xi. 57, where Diana is identified with Proserpina, and VIII. xi. 60, where Proserpina is identified with Vesta. However, the most likely source of Or.'s information is Jerome, *PL* xxiii, col. 270, where Minucia is said to be one of the innumerable 'sacerdotes Dianae Tauricae et Vestae'. For a second reference in OH to a *virgo Vestalis,* this time rendered 'heora goda nunne', see 88/5. An earlier reference, OH II. viii. 13, is omitted by Or., perhaps because OH merely describes the woman as *uirgo*.

60/12. *nugiet to dæge*. OH III. ix. 5 *nunc*.

60/18–20. *hie woldon . . . gesellan*. Or.'s addition.

60/21. *of ðære lyfte*. OH III. x. 2 explains: 'erat utique foedus ille ac pestilens annus inflictaeque iam undique cateruatim strages egerebantur et adhuc tamen penes omnes de corrupto aere simplex credulitas erat.'

60/22. *ænne þeowne mon*. The expected translation of OH III. x. 2, 'quadam ancilla', is either *ane þeow, ane þeowan*, or *ane þeowene*.

60/23. *beforan . . . gelaðede*. Or.'s addition. According to Livy VIII. xviii. 5 and 8, information about the crime having been given to the Senate, some twenty matrons were summoned to the Forum.

60/23–4. *iii hund 7 hundeahtatig*. OH III. x. 3 'trecentae septuaginta', 'related' MSS of Group C *ccclxxx*.

60/29–30. *æt . . . gesæt*. Or.'s addition, possibly a contextual deduction, based on the reference in OH III. xi. 1 to *finitimas Romae urbes*.

61/1–2. *Nu . . . beon*. According to OH III. xi. 2, it is consideration of events taking place during the reign of Alexander the Great's father, Philip, that is prompted by reference to Alexander, king of Epirus.

61/7. *on Crecum*. Or.'s addition. See 18/8–13, Commentary.

61/7–11. *binnan . . . hæfde*. OH III. xii. 1 merely comments that 'hos omnes acerbitatum aceruos cunctasque malorum moles struxit', though in III. xii. 10 it is claimed that Philip conquered *Graeciam prope totam* (Or. 62/9 *eall Creca folc*). All the peoples named by Or. are subsequently mentioned in OH as subdued by Philip with the exception of Moesia, for whose inclusion in *Creca land* see 18/9.

61/12. *cyninge*. OH III. xii. 2 describes Epaminondas as *imperatorem*.

61/13. *Læcedemonia*. OH does not name Alexander's kingdom, though from the context it is obviously Macedon; see also Justinus VII. iv. 8. For a similar error, see Freculph, *Chronicon*, col. 1011, where 'Philippo Lacedaemoniorum rege' appears for OH III. xi. 2 'Philippo Macedonum rege'. See also 78/15–16, Commentary.

61/16–17. *þeh . . . geligernesse*. Apparently a somewhat misleading selection of details from OH III. xii. 3, 'quamuis ea iam commisso adulterio et altero primum filio interfecto filiaque uiduata generi nuptias mariti morte pepigisset'. See, however, Justinus VII. v. 7, 'Indignum prorsus libidinis causa liberos a matre vita privatos'.

61/17. *Philippuses steopmodor*. Or.'s addition, perhaps prompted by OH's subsequent reference to a stepmother and half-brothers (see 63/5–6 and OH III. xii. 19). According to Justinus VII. iv. 5, Philip was Alexander's full brother, Eurydice being mother of both of them.

61/21–2. *him . . . wære*. Or.'s addition. According to Quintus Curtius IX. vi. 25, 'Philippus in acie tutior quam in theatro fuit; hostium manus saepe evitavit, suorum effugere non valuit.'

61/23. *Hiliricos, þe we Pulgare hatað.* The writer may well have in mind the great province of Illyricum, formed in the time of Constantine. This was divided into Illyricum Occidentale (which included Illyricum proper, Pannonia, and Noricum) and Illyricum Orientale (which included Dacia, Moesia, Macedonia, and Thrace). Later Croats invaded the west and Serbs the east. For the territory controlled by the Bulgars in the ninth century see 13/7–8, Commentary.

61/26–7. *for . . . ærest.* Cf. OH III. xii. 6 'ambitione habendorum equitum Thessalorum, quorum robur et exercitui suo admisceret'. Or. is here echoing the tradition that fighting on horseback was invented by the Thessali; see Pliny V. lvi. 202 and above, 28/20–1, Commentary.

61/27–8. *Hie . . . gecierdon.* Cf. OH III. xii. 7 'Thessalis ex inprouiso praeoccupatis atque in potestatem redactis'.

62/1. *Aruhes dohtor.* According to OH III. xii. 8, Olympias was Aruba's sister. For the form *Aruhes* see the Glossary of Proper Names, and Introduction, p. cix, n. 1.

62/3–5. *Ac . . . forlet.* Cf. OH III. xii. 8 'per hoc deceptus amisit priuatusque in exilio consenuit'. BT Suppl. suggests that *gebindan* here may denote 'ensnaring(?)' and translates the first part of the sentence 'got him in his toils thanks to this expectation'; however, it is possible that the Latin MS used by the translator contained a corruption of *deceptus*, such as *captus*.

62/6. *Othona . . . rice.* OH III. xii. 9 *Mothonam urbem,* 'related' MSS *Othonam* (see Bately (1961), pp. 81 and 89). There were several towns called Mothona in the classical world. The one referred to by OH lay on the Peloponnesian Gulf, north of Pydna, in Macedonia; however, Solinus 62, 12 confuses it with a second Mothona in Thessalian Magnesia: 'In regione Magnesia Mothona oppidum est, quod cum obsideret Philippus . . . damnatus est oculo iactu sagittae.' Could Or.'s location of the town in Theban territory have been inspired by OH III. xii. 14, where the Thebans are said to invite Philip to be their leader, 'quem hostem prius repellere laborabant'?

62/7–8. *eall . . . mette.* Or.'s addition. Justinus VII. vi. 16 claims the opposite: that far from being angrier with these people 'nec moderatus tantum, verum etiam mitis adversus victos fuerit'.

62/8–9. *æfter . . . folc.* OH III. xii. 10 'Exim Graeciam prope totam consiliis praeuentam uiribus domuit.'

62/16–21. *þa Crece . . . ahofan.* OH's account is very different: see III. xii. 10–11, 'quippe Graeciae ciuitates dum imperare singulae cupiunt, imperium omnes perdiderunt et dum in mutuum exitium sine modo ruunt, omnibus perire quod singulae amitterent oppressae demum seruientesque senserunt. quarum dum insanas conuersationes Philippus ueluti e specula obseruat auxiliumque semper inferioribus suggerendo contentiones, bellorum fomites, callidus doli artifex fouet, uictos sibi pariter uictoresque subiecit.'

62/21. *hie . . . ahofan.* Or.'s addition, presumably based on subsequent references in OH to fighting between Philip and various Greek states; see, e.g., OH III. xii. 14 and 15.

62/21–4. *he hiene . . . wunnon.* OH's version is again very different. According to III. xii. 14, Philip's help was sought by the Thebans and the Thessalians against the Phocians: 'Porro autem Thebani et Thessali omisso dilectu ciuium Philippum Macedoniae regem, quem hostem prius repellere laborabant, ultro sibi ducem expetiuerunt.' The Athenians were involved only as allies of the Phocians.

62/24–5. *hæfdon . . . belocene.* Cf. OH III. xii. 15 'angustias Thermopylarum . . . occupauere'. For an earlier equation *Thermopylae*: *londfæsten* see 46/21, Commentary For late Latin *clusa*, used of a narrow passage in mountainous country, which can be defended and closed, see P. Duparc, 'Les Cluses et la Frontière des Alpes', *Bibliothèque de l'École des Chartes*, cix (1951), 5–31. Calendre, LER 4647 interprets *cluse* as *chastel.*

62/27–9. *heora hergas . . . agene.* Cf. OH III. xii. 17 'templa quoque uniuersa subuertit spoliauitque', referring only to the temples of the states that Philip conquered.

62/29–31. *oþ . . . wearð.* Cf. OH III. xii. 17 'nec tamen umquam per xxv annos quasi iratis dis uictus est.'

62/32. *ealle þa cyningas.* Cf. OH III. xii. 18 *finitimos reges.*

63/3–4. *fæstast . . . rices.* According to OH III. xii. 20, Olynthus is 'urbem antiquissimam et florentissimam', while in II. xi. 1 it is described as 'Graeciae oppidum'. For its location in Macedonia, see Mela II. ii. 30.

63/11. *mid micelre firde.* OH III. xii. 22 'cum instructo exercitu'.

63/12. *ealle þa witan.* Or.'s addition. OH III. xii. 22 states merely that Philip 'inscios iuuenes uita regnoque priuauit'. However, some MSS read *insocios* for *inscios* and it may be that this or a similar reading is responsible for Or.'s expansion.

63/12–22. *Æfter þæm . . . awesten.* A rewriting and telescoping of OH III. xii. 23–8. According to OH, it is the Athenians and Phocians who are allies, hoping to prevent Philip from accepting the request of their enemies the Thessalians and Boeotians to be their leader in war against them. The principals are the Phocians and the Thessalians. The translator appears to have misconstrued OH III. xii. 25, 'cum Thessali Boeotiique poscerent Philippum, ut professum se aduersum Phocenses ducem exhiberet susceptumque bellum gereret, contra Phocenses adhibitis secum Atheniensibus et Lacedaemoniis uel differri bellum uel auferri et pretio et precibus laborarent', taking *Philippum* as the antecedent of *secum.*

63/14. *hie . . . beluce.* OH III. xii. 23 'qui prius Philippi ingressum Thermopylarum munitione reppulerant'. See above, 62/24–5.

63/19. *buta þa clusan.* OH III. xii. 27 'angustias Thermopylarum'. See above, 62/24–5, Commentary.

63/22–4. *þæm folce . . . dorstan.* Cf. OH III. xii. 31 'premit miseros inter iniuriarum stimulos superfusus pauor ipsaque dissimulatione dolor crescit hoc altius demissus quo minus profiteri licet timentium, ne ipsae quoque lacrimae pro contumacia accipiantur.'

63/24. *ealle þa ricestan.* OH III. xii. 28 *primos Phocenses.*

63/24-5. *sume . . . gesette.* According to OH III. xii. 32, 'alios populos . . . finibus hostium opponit; alios in extremis regni terminis statuit'.

63/29-30. *Philippuse . . . winnende.* Apparently the result of misunderstanding of OH III. xiii. 1, 'Sed haec cum per aliquantas Graeciae ciuitates exercuisset et tamen omnes metu premeret, coniciens ex praeda paucorum opes omnium, ad perficiendam aequalem in uniuersis uastationem utili emolumento necessariam maritimam urbem ratus'. The reason that OH gives for Philip turning pirate, III. xiii. 3, is 'ut pecuniam quam obsidendo exhauserat praedando repararet'.

63/31-2. *sona . . . gefengon.* OH III. xiii. 3 'captas itaque clxx naues mercibus confertas'. A number of 'related' MSS, including Ricc. 627, agree with Or. in reading *clxxx* or *centum octuaginta* for *clxx.*

63/33-64/2. *to ðon . . . winnanne.* According to OH III. xiii. 1, Philip thought Byzantium 'aptissimam . . . ut receptaculum sibi terra marique fieret'. His siege of that city is said by OH to precede his capture of the merchant ships, not, as in Or., to follow it.

64/5. *Læcedemonia ladteowe.* OH III. xiii. 2 'rege Spartanorum'. Cf. OH III. i. 17, where (another) Pausanias is described as 'dux alter Lacedaemoniorum'.

64/8-10. *þa ofþuhte . . . wæron.* See 63/29-30 and Commentary. According to OH III. xiii. 4, Philip divided his army 'propter agendam praedam et curandam obsidionem'.

64/11. *mid sumum hloþum.* OH III. xiii. 4 *cum fortissimis.*

64/11-12. *on Cheranisse, Creca folce.* OH III. xiii. 4 *Cherronesi.* For the location of the Chersonesus in Greece, see, e.g., Solinus 71, 4. Cherson was later to become one of the themes of the Byzantine empire.

64/13-14. *þe . . . gewinne.* According to OH III. xiii. 5, Philip attacked Atheas after the latter broke the treaty of alliance made between them when the Scythians were hard pressed in their war against the Istriani.

64/19-22. *mid þæm þæt . . . tofarene wæron.* This explanation of OH III. xiii. 6 *fraude* seems to be based on a misunderstanding of Frontinus II. viii. 14; 'Philippus veritus, ne impetum Scytharum sui non sustinerent, fidelissimos equitum a tergo posuit praecepitque, ne quem commilitonum ex acie fugere paterentur, perseverantius abeuntes trucidarent.' That Philip should place himself with the most loyal of his troops would seem natural to an Anglo-Saxon: see, e.g., *The Battle of Maldon,* 23-4. For the division of armies into three parts, see also above, 33/15-19.

64/23-4. *þær . . . wæpnedmonna.* OH III. xiii. 7 'in ea pugna xx milia puerorum ac feminarum Scythicae gentis capta'. No reference is made to the number of the dead.

64/24. *horsa.* According to OH III. xiii. 7 these were mares, *equarum*; the 'related' MS Ricc. 627, however, has the reading *equorum*.

64/24-6. *hie ðær . .. ahton.* OH III. xiii. 7 'auri atque argenti nihil repertum'.

64/28. *oðere Scippie.* Or.'s addition. The Triballi were in fact Thracians.

64/28-9. *Philippus . . . unweorð.* Or.'s addition.

64/29-30. *hiene . . . þeoh.* OH III. xiii. 8 'Philippus in femore uulneratus est.' Latin has two oblique stems for the noun *femur*: *femor-* and *femin-*. Did the translator have before him a gloss or comment *femore*: *femine* and did he subsequently interpret *femine* as part of the noun *femina?* Cf. glosses such as *Abavus* FE 4 *femur*: *femen* and *Arma* F 176 *femina*: *femora.*

64/30-1. *þa . . . afeoll.* OH III. xiii. 8 explains that Philip's men thought he had been killed.

64/32-4. *Wæs . . . ofsloge.* Or.'s addition.

65/8-11. *Philippuse . . . totwæmde wæron.* Has the translator misinterpreted OH III. xiii. 10, 'proelio commisso cum Athenienses longe maiore numero militum praestarent, adsiduis tamen bellis indurata Macedonum uirtute uincuntur'?

65/11. *on ungearwe.* Or.'s addition, without basis in OH.

65/19. *his agnum mæge.* OH III. xiv. 4 explains that this Alexander was brother of Philip's wife.

65/19-24. *þa . . . ofstang.* OH's account is very different: see OH III. xiv. 7 'die nuptiarum cum ad ludos magnifice apparatos inter duos Alexandros filium generumque contenderet, a Pausania nobili Macedonum adulescente in angustiis sine custodibus circumuentus occisus est.' The translator appears to have identified the games with the *ludi equestres* (see, e.g., Isidore, *Etymologies* XVIII. xxvii) and taken the verb *contendo* not in OH's sense of 'hasten on a journey', but in its alternative sense of 'strive', 'exert oneself'.

65/24 *ealdgefana sum.* OH III. xiv. 7 'Pausania nobili Macedonum adulescente'. This Pausanias was one of Philip's favourites and a member of his bodyguard. Or.'s assumption that he was an 'old enemy' was probably prompted by two earlier references to men called Pausanias (see OH III. i. 17, a passage without equivalent in Or., and III. xiii. 2, Or. 64/4-5, Commentary), of whom the second was founder of Byzantium, the city besieged by Philip.

65/25-66/3. *Ic . . . wære.* OH's comment is somewhat different: see III. xiv. 8-9: 'Adserant nunc multisque haec uocibus efferant quasi uirorum fortium laudes et facta felicia, quibus amarissimae aliorum calamitates in dulces fabulas cedunt, si tamen numquam ipsi iniurias, quibus aliquando uexantur, relatu tristiore deplorant. si uero de propriis querimoniis tantum alios audientes adfici uolunt, quantum ipsi perpetiendo senserunt, prius ipsi non praesentibus praeterita sed gestis gesta conparent et utraque ex auditu uelut alienorum arbitri iudicent.' For Or.'s theme see Introduction, pp. xciv f.

66/5–6. *eower . . . dagas.* See below, 156/16–18, OH VII. xxxix. 15.

66/6–8. *Philippuses . . . sunu.* See OH III. xv. 1 'sufficerent ista ad exemplum miseriarum insinuata memoriae nostrae gesta per Philippum, etiamsi Alexander ei non successisset in regnum', and III. vii. 5 'Alexander Magnus, uere ille gurges miseriarum atque atrocissimus turbo totius Orientis'.

66/11–12. *giet todæge is.* Or.'s addition.

66/13. *swa . . . sædon.* Or.'s addition, presumably inspired by the general reference to *Samniticum bellum,* OH III. viii. 1, Or. 58/23–8.

66/14. *þæm consule.* OH III. xv. 2 'magistro equitum'.

66/17–20. *þær . . . beforan.* Cf. OH III. xv. 2 'circumspectiore cura Samnites ac magis instructo apparatu apud Caudinas furculas consederunt; ubi . . . Veturium et Postumium consules omnesque copias Romanorum angustiis locorum armisque [clauserunt]'.

66/20–1. *hie siþþan . . . gan.* Or.'s addition.

66/23–4. *þone cyning . . . wæs.* OH III. xv. 3 'Herennium patrem'. According to Livy IX. iii. 4, Pontius first dispatched letters to his father, then sent for him.

66/25–9. *Hie . . . wæren.* Cf. OH III. xv. 5–6 'itaque Samnites uictoria potiti uniuersum exercitum Romanum turpiter captum armis etiam uestimentisque nudatum, tantum singulis uilioribus operimentis ob uerecunda corporum tegenda concessis, sub iugum missum seruitioque subiectum, longum agere pompae ordinem praeceperunt. sescentis autem equitibus Romanis in obsidatum receptis oneratos ignominia, ceteris rebus uacuos consules remiserunt.' The translator appears to have interpreted *sub iugum missum* in its non-literal sense of 'subjugated', possibly misapplying a comment or gloss stating that to be sent under the yoke was at that time the greatest of disgraces. See Introduction, p. lxii.

67/3–10. *Geornor . . . hæfdon.* A slightly expanded version of OH III. xv. 7, with OH's rhetorical question, 'Quid de exaggeranda huius foedissimi foederis macula uerbis laborem, qui tacere maluissem?', provided with an answer.

67/13. *deadlicne sige.* According to OH III. xv. 9, 'Romani pertinaciter moriendo uicerunt, nec caedi pariter uel caedere destiterunt.'

67/16–17. *Somnita cyning.* OH III. xv. 9 'duci eorum'.

67/17. *hie . . . gedydon.* According to OH III. xv. 9, 'iugum reposuerunt'.

67/24. *his ærestan ðegnscipe.* OH III. xvi comments that Alexander 'primam experientiam animi et uirtutis suae conpressis celeriter Graecorum motibus dedit'.

67/28–30. *Athene . . . hæfdon.* A misunderstanding of OH III. xvi. 2, 'Atheniensibus bellum deprecantibus remisit, quos insuper etiam multae metu soluit'.

68/1. *þætte . . . heafodstol.* Or.'s addition. Cf. Cornelius Nepos XV.

Epaminondas x. 4, where Thebes is said to have been 'caput . . . totius Graeciae' as long as Epaminondas was at the head of the state.

68/2–4. *ealle . . . gecirdon.* OH III. xvi. 2 'ceteras urbes Achaiae et Thessaliae uectigales fecit'. For the location of Achaia and Thessalia in Greece, see 18/12 and 24/33, Commentary.

68/7. *ealle . . . mehte.* OH III. xvi. 3 'omnes cognatos ac (*var.* ad) proximos suos'. The translator has interpreted *proximos* in terms of place not of relationship. The victims were, according to Justinus XI. v. 1, those relations of Alexander and of his stepmother that he thought might aspire to the throne during his absence.

68/9–12. *Nat . . . dorste.* OH III. xvi. 3 'hac tum parua manu uniuersum terrarum orbem utrum admirabilius sit quia uicerit an quia adgredi ausus fuerit incertum est.'

68/18. *Frigam, Asiam lond.* OH III. xvi. 5 *Phrygiae ciuitatem.* For the location of Phrygia in Asia minor see, e.g., Isidore. *Etymologies* XIV. iii. 38.

68/19–20. *þa . . . Persum.* Cf. OH III. xvi. 5 'nuntiato sibi Darii cum magnis copiis aduentu'.

68/21. *þære nearwan . . . wæs.* OH III. xvi. 5 'angustias quibus inerat locorum'.

68/22–3. *ungeliefedlicne . . . weg.* OH III. xvi. 5 'quingentis stadiis'.

68/23–4. *on Cilicium þæm londe.* Or.'s addition. That Tarsus was in Cilicia is a piece of information that could have reached the translator from a wide variety of sources, including the New Testament.

68/26–7. *him gescruncan . . . ædra.* OH III. xvi. 5 'contractuque neruorum'.

68/31–2. *þeh . . . ofercome.* OH III. xvi. 6 'quamuis iam pridem dc milibus hostium eadem paucitate superatis'.

69/3. *eahtatig m gefangenra.* OH III. xvi. 9 'capta autem xl milia'.

69/10. *Parmenionem his ladteow.* OH III. xvi. 11 *Parmenionem.* Cf. OH III. xiv. 4 where Parmenio is given the title *dux.*

69/11. *gefliemde.* According to OH III. xvi. 11, Parmenio was sent to attack the Persian fleet.

69/12. *mid eaþmodnessun.* Or.'s addition. OH III. xvi. 11 describes the kings as coming of their own accord, *cum infulis,* i.e. 'with fillets'. The wearers of fillets in Roman times included priests, sacrificial victims, and suppliants for protection.

69/13–14. *heora land . . . gesealde.* According to OH III. xvi. 11, 'ex multis sibi regibus . . . occurrentibus alios allegit, alios mutauit, alios perdidit.'

69/21. *Amones . . . sunu.* OH III. xvi. 12 *Iouis Hammonis.*

69/22–4. *to þon . . . wære.* OH III. xvi. 12 'ut mendacio ad tempus conposito ignominiam sibi patris incerti et infamiam adulterae matris aboleret'. Nectanebus is named as father of Alexander in several Latin

COMMENTARY 259

texts: see Julius Valerius I. viii (where 'Nectanabus' is described as *magus*), Fulgentius, *De Aetatibus Mundi et Hominis, Opera*, ed. R. Helm (Leipzig, 1898), p. 164 (extant MSS *Dictanabo*) and Lucan scholia, ed. Weber, X. 20, while a MS of OH, St. Gallen 621, has the gloss 'cum nectanabo: medico mago exule . . .'.

69/25. *þæt he . . . anlicnesse*. Or.'s addition, which Potter (1952–3), p. 410, sees as imaginative dramatization by the translator. However, according to Julius Valerius, I. iii and vii, Nectanabus assumed the form of Ammon to seduce Olympias, and it is possible that a gloss or comment 'he took the god's shape' was misapplied by the translator to the priest.

69/28–31. *Genoh . . . mihte*. Cf. OH III. xvi. 13 'ita certus Alexander fuit nobisque prodidit, dis ipsis mutis et surdis uel in potestate esse antistitis quid uelit fingere uel in uoluntate consulentis quid malit audire.'

69/32. *for . . . Darius*. OH III. xvii. 1 gives Darius the initiative. Although this is indeed the third battle mentioned by OH, the words *þriddan siþe* are Or.'s addition.

70/5–6. *Alexander . . . mehte*. Cf. OH III. xvii. 5 'xxxiiii continuis diebus castrorum praedam percensuit', beside Justinus XI. xiv. 8, 'Donatis refectisque militibus xxxiv diebus'. A number of 'related' MSS, including Ricc. 627, agree with Or. in giving the numeral *xxxiii*.

70/7. *giet*. Or.'s addition. The city of Persepolis was burnt by Alexander in B.C. 331 and never regained its former splendour; see Quintus Curtius V. vii. 9, 'Ac ne tam longa quidem aetate, quae excidium eius secuta est, resurrexit.'

70/8. *Darius . . . mægas*. According to OH III. xvii. 6, Alexander hastened to the king's side, 'Darium . . . cum a propinquis suis uinctum conpedibus aureis teneri conperisset'. For *hæfde* as a variant of *hæfden* see Introduction, p. lii.

70/9. *siex hund monna*. OH III. xvii. 6 'sex milibus equitum'.

70/10. *mid sperum tosticad*. OH III. xvii. 6 'multis confossum uulneribus'. According to Quintus Curtius V. xiii. 16, the wounds were caused by *tela*, i.e. darts, javelins, or spears.

70/11–15. *He . . . cild*. Cf. OH III. xvii. 7 'hunc mortuum inani misericordia referri in sepulchra maiorum sepelirique praecepit; cuius non dicam matrem uel uxorem sed etiam paruulas filias crudeli captiuitate retinebat.'

70/18. *fieftiene . . . monna*. OH III. xvii. 8 'quinquiens deciens centena milia peditum equitumque'.

70/20. *swa . . . sægð*. OH III. xvii. 8 *referuntur*. See 48/28–30.

70/22. *Asirie*. OH III. xvii. 9 *Syria*. This identification is not uncommon in Latin texts; see, e.g., Acron, *Comm. in Q. Horatium Flaccum*, ed. Hauthal, *Carm.* II. xi. 16.

70/25–6. *mid ealle awest*. According to OH III. xvii. 9, Rhodes submitted voluntarily, 'ultro ad seruitutem tremefacta successerit'.

70/29. *Antipater ... cyning.* OH III. xviii. 2 *Antipatri.* Antipater did not become king until after Alexander's death: see 81/10–11.

70/30. *þæs ... eam.* Or.'s addition; see 60/28.

70/32. *hrædlice.* Cf. OH III. xviii. 3 'post numerosa et grauia bella'.

71/1. *Ponto cyning.* OH III. xviii. 4 'praefectus Ponti'.

71/5. *Minotheo ... cwen.* OH III. xviii. 5 describes Halestris, or Minothea, as an Amazon. For the Scythian origin of the Amazons see 29/14–35.

71/6–7. *wið his ... cempan.* Or.'s addition.

71/10. *Paramomenas.* OH III. xviii. 7 *Parimas Parapamenos,* 'related' MSS *Parapamenos.* See Bately (1961), pp. 81, 89, and 100.

71/13. *scinlac.* OH III. xviii. 8 *rabies.* For a similar rendering of *rabies* by *scinlac* see 60/17.

71/14. *þa þe ... winnende.* An expansion of OH III. xviii. 8 *suos.*

71/15. *modrian sunu.* OH III. xviii. 8 *consobrinus.* Since Amyntas was son of Perdiccas, Philip's elder brother, he should have been described as Alexander's 'fæderan sunu'. However, although Isidore, *Etymologies* IX. vi, defines *consobrini* as 'qui aut ex sorore et fratre, aut ex duabus sororibus sunt nati', the original meaning of *consobrinus* and that given to it by a number of glossaries is 'maternal cousin'. See, e.g., *Abstrusa* CO 204 and *Abavus* CO 229, and the gloss in 'related' MSS of Group C 'consobrinus: sororis matris filius'.

71/15. *his broðor.* OH III. xviii. 8 'nouerca fratresque eius'.

71/16. *Parmenion his þegn.* OH III. xviii. 8 *Parmenio.* Earlier Parmenio is described as Alexander's *ladteow*: see 69/10 and Commentary.

71/18. *Clitus ... fæder.* OH III. xviii. 8 describes Clitus as 'annis grauis, amicitia uetus'. According to Quintus Curtius, VIII. i. 20–1, he was an old soldier of Philip's who had been given a province by Alexander.

71/19. *druncne.* Or.'s addition, possibly inspired by OH III. xviii. 9 *in conuiuio.* However, a number of classical texts describe Alexander as acting in a drunken rage: see, e.g., Quintus Curtius VIII. i. 43–4, Justinus XII. vi, Solinus 66, 17, and Pliny XIV. v. 58.

71/21. *for ealdre hyldo.* Potter (1952–3), p. 411, sees this as 'a characteristically heroic utterance raised above the level of Orosius's *cum ... memoriam patris tueretur*'. However, the translator may here be echoing OH III. xviii. 8 *amicitia uetus.*

71/22. *ahleop.* Or.'s addition. Cf. Quintus Curtius VIII. i. 43, 'ex lecto repente prosiluit'.

71/27. *him ... geniedde.* OH III. xviii. 11 'in deditionem accepit'.

72/2–3. *Nisan, India heafodburg.* OH III. xix. 1 *Nysam urbem.* That Nysa was the capital is probably a contextual guess; see, however, Mela III. vii. 66 'Urbium ... Nysa est clarissima et maxima.'

72/6–7. *anre byrg ... ymbweaxen.* OH III. xix. 2 'saxum mirae asperitatis et altitudinis, in quod multi populi confugerant'. It is tempting to see here confusion between *burg*, 'town', and *beorg*, 'hill', 'mound', in spite of the problems raised by the difference of gender between the two words, and there are precedents for this: see above 20/9 and Commentary. However, the translator may simply have misunderstood the Latin of OH. For a *town* that Hercules was unable to capture, see *Epitoma* ed. Thomas I. xlvi, 'Hinc profectus bagasdaram oppidum devenit, quod dicebatur Hercules expugnare non potuisse.'

72/11–12. *he . . . begeate.* OH III. xix. 2 merely claims that Alexander captured the rock 'cum summo labore ac periculo'. For references to heavy losses see Quintus Curtius VIII. xi. 12, 14, and 17.

72/16–20. *þa . . . comon.* OH III. xix. 3–4 'Alexander cum ipso Poro singulariter congressus occisoque deiectus equo concursu satellitum praesentiam mortis euasit; Porus multis uulneribus confossus et captus est.'

72/20–1. *for his þegnscipe . . . hiene.* OH III. xix. 4 'ob testimonium uirtutis'.

72/21–2. *he . . . atimbran.* According to OH III. xix. 4, it was Alexander who founded these cities: 'quo ob testimonium uirtutis in regnum restituto duas ibi condidit ciuitates Niciam et Bucefalen, quam de nomine equi sui ita uocari praecepit.' The translator may have been confused by OH's syntax, the main clause immediately preceding having as its subject not Alexander but Porus.

72/24. *on Ræstas.* OH III. xix. 4 *Adrestas*, apparently read as *ad Restas*, a division found in 'related' MSS including Ricc. 627.

72/25–6. *on India eastgemæra.* OH III. xix. 5 *ad Cofides*, Ricc. 627 *ad confines*. That Alexander had nearly reached the ocean is suggested by OH III. xix. 6; however, this ocean was not east but south of India.

72/28. *for þæm oftrædlican gefeohtum.* This may be an instance of the translator making specific what he imagines to be implied by OH: see III. xix. 5 *uiribus lassi.* Cf., however, Justinus XII. viii. 10, 'exercitus omnis non minus victoriarum numero quam laboribus fessus'.

72/29–31. *Siþþan . . . dyde.* OH III. xix. 5 'castra ob memoriam plus solito magnifica condiderunt'. Did the Latin MS used by the translator read *ob moram* in place of *ob memoriam*?

72/32–73/1. *Æfter þæm . . . eardedon.* OH III. xix. 6 'exim Alexander ad amnem Agesinem pergit; per hunc in Oceanum deuehitur: ibi Gesonas Sibosque . . . oppressit.' Alexander had not in fact yet reached the Ocean.

73/2–3. *þæm iglande . . . Subagros.* OH III. xix. 6 'Adros et Subagras (*var.* Mandros et Subagros)'. That these lived on an island seems to have been (incorrectly) adduced from the use by OH of the verb *nauigat.*

73/3–4. *eahta c m feþena.* OH III. xix. 6 *lxxx milibus peditum.* For the suggestion that the numeral *octoginta* may have been misread or misheard as *octingenti* see Potter (1952–3), p. 412.

73/6. *unweorðlicne sige.* See OH III. xix. 7 'tristem paene uictoriam', which is followed by the explanation that Alexander nearly lost his life in leading the assault on a city (an event described in 73/7–27).

73/7. *Æfter þæm.* OH III. xix. 7 *nam.*

73/8–10. *þa . . . abroden.* According to OH III. xix. 7, Alexander leapt down of his own accord: 'cum murum primus escendisset, uacuam ciuitatem ratus solus introrsum desiluit.' He was then surrounded by the enemy. That his action was a hasty one is implied by Quintus Curtius IX. iv. 30–32, though Curtius' account leaves Alexander stranded for some time on top of the wall.

73/11–13. *hie . . . wigcræftum.* OH III. xix. 8 refers merely to *multitudo hostium* and to *uis magna telorum.* What is incredible (*incredibile dictu*) is not the strength of the attack but Alexander's lack of fear. For the use of stones as well as weapons by the enemy, see Quintus Curtius IX. v. 7.

73/17. *hie . . . dydon.* Or.'s addition, possibly the translator's own deduction. See, however, Quintus Curtius IX. v. 16, where it is said that the Indi, having learned that Alexander was within the walls, ran to the spot.

73/20–7. *Nyte . . . metten.* Mainly Or.'s addition, the only details shared with OH III. xix. 8–10 being those involving Alexander's self-defence, his slaying of the man who wounded him and his resting wounded on his knees (OH *fixo genu*). That it should be a matter for wonder that Alexander's thegns should be determined to avenge their lord, alive or dead, seems a strange statement for an Anglo-Saxon to make. Could it have been inspired by Quintus Curtius IX. v. 19–20, where the Macedonians, on hearing rumours that the king had been killed, broke through the wall and slaughtered everyone they encountered till they had appeased their just anger, 'Terruisset alios quod illos incitauit'?

73/31. *on . . . niht.* Or.'s addition, as also the *on mergen* of the next sentence.

74/10. *he sæde . . . wolde.* Or.'s addition; see OH III. xv. 10, where the Romans are said to have heard that Alexander was arranging an expedition to occupy Africa and then to cross to Italy, also IV. vi. 21, where the Carthaginians are said to fear such an invasion.

74/11. *byrelas.* OH III. xx. 4 *ministri*, gs. See Justinus XII. xiv. 6, where the poison is said to have been administered by three brothers, who were accustomed to wait on the king at table, also Quintus Curtius X. x. 14–17.

74/13–26. *Eala . . . leahtrien.* An almost complete rewriting of OH III. xx. 5–13, which attacks Orosius' contemporaries for their callous indifference to suffering and then goes on to compare the respective viewpoints of conquered and conqueror and to remind its audience that their own sufferings are less than those of people in the past. See Introduction, pp. xciii ff.

74/20–1. *ægðer . . . gereordum.* Cf. OH III. xx. 8 'terrarum metas lustrans et utrique infeliciter notus Oceano'. *Westen* is associated with *wildeor* and *wyrmcynn* also in *Soul and Body* II. ll. 77–9.

74/24. *cotum.* OH III. xx. 9 *angulum* 'country seat', 'retreat', 'hole'.

74/25–6. *Ac . . . leahtrien.* Or.'s addition.

74/28–30. *oðer . . . consulatu.* Based on OH III. xxi. 1, 'Fabio Maximo v̄ Decio Mure iiii', with *v*, 'related' MSS *quinto*, taken to be a proper name. For Or's handling of *duo* and *tria nomina* see Bately (1970), p. 436, also below 95/12–13, Commentary.

75/8. *mid . . . hæfdon.* Or.'s addition.

75/10. *Cuintus.* OH III. xxi. 4 *Decius.* For the supposition that Quintus was the praenomen of Decius Mus, see 74/28–30, Commentary.

75/13. *oðer . . . m.* OH III. xxi. 6 *cxl milia cccxxx*, 'related' MSS including Vienna 366 and Ricc. 627 *clm cccxxx* and *centum quinquaginta milia trecentos triginta*.

75/14. *seofon m.* OH III. xxi. 6 *xlvii milia*. See the 'related' MS, Selden B 16, *vii milia.*

75/21–2. *þa . . . beran.* According to OH III. xxi. 8, 'triumphales pompas obuiae mortuorum exsequiae polluerunt', while 'tota ciuitas aut aegris suspiraret aut mortuis'.

75/28–9. *On . . . Papirius.* An expansion of OH III. xxii. 3 *Papirius consul.*

75/29–30. *heora biscopas.* OH III. xxii. 3 'pullariis auguribus'.

75/32–3. *swa . . . oferhirde.* OH's comment, III. xxii. 3, is quite different: the consul ended the war as resolutely as he had undertaken it, *quam constanter arripuit.*

76/1. *iiii m.* OH III. xxii. 4 *iii milia*; 'related' MSS, including Vienna 366 *iiii m.*

76/3. *mid deofolcræftum.* According to OH III. xxii. 5, the Romans thought they should consult the Sibylline Books. It is somewhat strange to find the Sibylline Books identified with devilry: according to Augustine, *Civ. Dei* XVIII. xxiii, the Sibyl of Erythrae or of Cumae was to be counted among those who belong to the City of God. See also Isidore, *Etymologies* VIII. viii and the *Oxford Dictionary of the Christian Church*, ed. F. L. Cross (London, 1957), *Sibylline Oracles.*

76/4–5. *Escolafius þone scinlacan.* OH III. xxii. 5 'ipso Aesculapi lapide'. Potter (1952–3), p. 413, suggests that the translator did not understand *lapis* in the restricted sense of 'statue'; however, he may have been misled by a comment such as Augustine, *Civ. Dei* III. xii: 'Aesculapius autem ab Epidauro ambiuit ad Romam, ut peritissimus medicus in urbe nobilissima artem gloriosius exerceret'; see also Lactantius, *Divinarum Institutionum libri septem, PL* vi, col. 290.

76/5. *þære . . . het.* OH III. xxii. 5 'horrendumque illum Epidaurium colubrum'.

76/6–7. *onlicost . . . become.* OH III. xxii. 5 'quasi uero pestilentia aut ante sedata non sit aut post orta non fuerit'. The translator appears to have misunderstood *sedata* 'settled', i.e. 'put an end to', perhaps confusing *sedo* with *sedeo*.

76/14–16. *þa . . . fultume*. Or.'s addition. According to OH III. xxii. 8, the father, seeing his son hard pressed, 'in medium se agmen . . . equo uectus ingessit'.

76/22. *lviiii wintra*. OH III. xxii. 10 'per quadraginta et nouem annos', 'related' MSS including Vienna 366 and Ricc. 627 *lviiii*.

76/25. *he 7 þa consulas*. OH III. xxii. 11 *ipse consul*.

76/28. *Gallie of Senno*. OH III. xxii. 12 'Etruscis et Senonibus Gallis'. For *Senno* see 51/27, Commentary.

77/1. *Gallie 7 Bryti*. OH III. xxii. 13 *Etruscis Gallisque*. The second omission of a reference to the Etruscans in this section; see 76/28, Commentary. For the *Bryti*, see 106/4 *Bruti*, OH *Bruttii*. If the *y*-spelling represents the alternative Latin form *Brittii*, then this may indicate that Or.'s insertion here comes from a source other than OH.

77/4–7. *ge Romane . . . þurhtugon*. This replaces an impersonal statement in OH III. xxii. 15, 'ut sub praesenti nunc concursatione Gotthorum magis debeat meminisse Gallorum'.

77/10–12. *Hit . . . byrnan*. In OH III. xxiii. 2 the simile is a military one: 'quorum ego tumultuosissimum tempus ita mihi spectare uideor, quasi aliqua inmensa castra per noctem de specula montis aspectans nihil in magno campi spatio praeter innumeros focos cernam'.

77/14. *ealle Libium*. OH III. xxiii. 3 'Libyaeque . . . maximam'.

77/14–15. *hit . . . gewinnum*. OH III. xxiii. 3 'horrendi subito bellorum globu conluxerunt'.

77/15–18. *þa . . . tofare*. The translator here keeps OH's simile but not its metaphor: see OH III. xxiii. 4, 'qui cum ea praecipue loca, in quibus exarsere, populati sunt, reliqua omnia terrore rumoris quasi fumi caligine turbauerunt'.

77/20–3. *his æfterfolgeras . . . gehrifnian*. OH III. xxiii. 6 'principes uero eius quattuordecim annis dilaniauerunt et ueluti opimam praedam a magno leone prostratam auidi discerpsere catuli, seque ipsos inuicem in rixam inritatos praedae aemulatione fregerunt'. I have retained the reading *seo leo* of MS L, although the appearance in OH of masc. *magno leone* and the use of possessive *his* suggest that the original translation may have been *se leo*: cf. GD 295/1 *seo leo . . . heo*, MS O *he*.

77/23–4. *Ptholomeus . . . Arabia*. OH III. xxiii. 7 'prima Ptolemaeo Aegyptus et Africae Arabiaeque pars sorte prouenit.'

77/25–6. *Laumenda . . . Hiliricam*. OH III. xxiii. 7 'confinem huic prouinciae Syriam Laomedon Mitylinaeus, Ciliciam Philotas, Philo Illyrios accipiunt.' See, however, Ricc. 627 'confinem huic provincie Syriam Laumedo. Thelenus Cyliciam. Phylotas Sylo. Illirios accipiunt', and Berne 576 'Laumedon Syria obtinuit Mithileneus Ciliciam'. For *Laomedon*

Vienna 366 reads *Lamedon*, and for *Philo* it reads *cum filio*, while certain other 'related' MSS are even closer to Or. with *Laumendo* for *Laomedon*, and with *Philo* omitted altogether. See further, Bately (1961), pp. 81, 82, 90, 92, and 100. For confusion between Syria and Assyria, see 70/22, Commentary.

77/26–7. *Iecrapatas . . . Asiam.* OH III. xxiii. 8 'Mediae maiori Atropatus, minori socer Perdiccae praeponitur.' See Ricc. 627 'Mediæ maiori Acropatus Stromen minori socer Perdicae praeponitur.' For the distribution in 'related' MSS of the form *Stromen* and its variant *Sinomen* and a possible explanation for it, see Bately (1961), pp. 81 and 90. The father-in-law of Perdiccas was in fact Atropatus. Perdiccas himself was assigned no province, since he had the supreme power, with Arrhidaeus being only nominal head of the Macedonian empire.

77/27–9. *Susana . . . Cariam.* OH III. xxiii. 8–9 'Susiana gens Scyno, Phrygia maior Antigono Philippi filio adsignatur. Lyciam et Pamphyliam Nearchus, Cariam Cassander, Lydiam Menander sortiuntur.' *Susiana*, Zangemeister's emendation of the *Susaniana* of the MSS, is the name of the province assigned to Scynus.

77/30–2. *Seleucus . . . eastlond.* OH III. xxiii. 10 'summa castrorum Seleuco Antiochi filio cessit.' See Justinus XIII. iv. 17, 'Summus castrorum tribunatus Seleuco . . . cessit.' That Seleucus became king of all the east is information provided by Justinus XV. iv. 7, Bede, *De Temporum Ratione* col. 541 and Jerome, *Comm. in Daniel*, col. 536.

77/32. *Cassander . . . Chaldeum.* OH III. xxiii. 10 'stipatoribus regis satellitibusque Cassander filius Antipatri praeficitur.' See also III. xxiii. 9 'Cariam Cassander'. I have found no explanation for the introduction of Chaldeans here, though they are referred to by Quintus Curtius X. x. 13 as taking charge of Alexander's corpse, while it could be argued that since Alexander died in Babylon, that was where his bodyguard and attendants were at that time. Other sources assign Babylon to Seleucus; see, e.g., *Epitoma*, ed. Thomas, I, 117.

78/2. *ðæt lond.* OH III. xxiii. 11 gives the name *Seres* here.

78/3. *Ithona . . . Indeum.* OH III. xxiii. 12 'in colonias *in* Indis conditas Python (*var.* Ithona) Agenoris filius mittitur.' Did the Latin MS used by the translator have a corrupt form of *colonias*—possibly *culonias* or *calonias*?

78/3–4. *Parapamenas . . . Caucasus.* OH III. xxiii. 12 'Parapamenos fine Caucasi montis Oxyarches accepit.' For *Parapamenos* a number of MSS have the reading *Parapemenos*; however, those apparently closest to Or. agree with OH. It is not clear whether the translator interpreted this name as subject or object, though -*as* for OH -*os* suggests that he took it as plural and therefore accusative. For the order OVS see 78/2 'ðæt lond . . . hæfde Itaxiles.'

78/4–5. *Arachasihedros hæfde Siburtus.* OH III. xxiii. 13 'Arachossi Chedrosique Sibyrti decernuntur.'

78/6. *Omintos hæfde Atrianus.* See OH III. xxiii. 13 'Bactrianos (MSS Atrianos) Amyntas sortitur.'

78/8. *Meþas.* OH III. xxiii. 13 *Persas.* See 10/3–4.

78/9. *Polausus hæfde Archos.* OH III. xxiii. 13 'Archon (MSS Archos) Pelassos'. For *Pelassos* 'related' MSS including Ricc. 627 have the variant *Palausus,* which the translator may well have interpreted as nominative singular. See 78/3–4, Commentary.

78/12. *þe he . . . hæfde.* Or.'s addition. OH III. xxiii. 14 refers merely to *omnes exules.*

78/15–16. *wiðsocon . . . wæs.* OH III. xxiii. 14 'a regno Macedonum defecerunt'. For a similar confusion of Lacedaemonia and Macedonia see 61/13, Commentary. Here, earlier references to Lacedaemonian supremacy may have had a part to play.

78/17–18. *angean Antigone . . . sceolde.* OH III. xxiii. 15 'cum Antipatro, cui Graecia sorte uenerat'. See further 78/21–3 and 79/6, Commentary, and, for the title 'King' applied to Alexander's successors, 81/10–11, Commentary.

78/18–19. *for þon . . . Alexandre.* Or.'s addition, presumably inspired by the statement of OH, III. xxiii. 14, that the origin of the wars was *epistula Alexandri.*

78/19–20. *gesetton . . . Demostenon.* OH III. xxiii. 15 merely says that the Athenians worked *per Demosthenen.* According to Justinus XIII. v, he acted as their ambassador.

78/21–3. *besæton . . . fultume.* OH III. xxiii. 15 'Antipatrum obsidione cingunt'. Or.'s additional comment seems to have been made necessary by the alteration in 78/17 above. In a later conflict Antipater does come to the help of Antigonus: see Justinus XIII. vi. 9.

78/23. *oðer heora ladteowa.* OH III. xxiii. 16 *dux eorum.* Or.'s alteration is necessitated by the assumption, 78/20, that Demosthenes was also a leader of the Athenians.

78/24. *flan.* OH III. xxiii. 16 'telo e muris iacto'. Leosthenes was in fact killed by a blow from a stone.

78/27. *Æfter þæm.* Or.'s addition. See the corresponding passage in Justinus, XIII. vi. 1, where the word *interea* is used.

78/27. *Perðica . . . hæfde.* OH III. xxiii. 17 *Perdicca.* See 77/26–7, Commentary.

78/28–9. *hiene . . . fæstenne.* Or.'s addition. See Justinus XIII. vi. 2, 'hostes ab acie in urbem recepti'.

78/31. *gebeotedan.* Or.'s addition.

78/31–2. *longe . . . wolden.* OH III. xxiii. 19 'diu deliberatum, utrum in Macedoniam bellum transferretur an in Asia gereretur'.

78/32–79/1. *monig . . . geteon.* A misunderstanding of OH III. xxiii. 18, 'grauissime multis prouinciis et insulis ob auxilia uel negata uel praestita dilaceratis'.

79/2–3. *for þon . . . cyninge.* Or.'s addition, apparently without any basis in fact. According to Justinus XIII. vi. 13, the attack was made 'ne in Macedoniam profectis Asia a Ptolomeo occuparetur'.

79/5. *twegen cyningas.* Or.'s addition. Neither Eumenes nor Neoptolemus had the title of king: see Cornelius Nepos, XVIII *Eumenes*, xiii. 2–3 'In quo quanta omnium fuerit opinio eorum qui post Alexandrum Magnum reges sunt appellati ex hoc facillime potest iudicari, quod, nemo Eumene vivo rex appellatus est, sed praefectus.'

79/6. *Antigone þæm cyninge.* OH III. xxiii. 21 *Antipatrum.* See also 78/17–18, Commentary. For *Antipatrum* a group of 'unrelated' MSS (Vat. 1976, Paris, Ars. 984, BNL 4878 etc.) have the reading *Antigonum.*

79/7–8. *þa . . . Polipercon.* Or.'s addition. OH III. xxiii. 22 names Polypercon as among the slain but does not say what side he was on. However, Justinus XIII. viii. 5 associates him with Antipater.

79/10–11. *forsætade . . . besætedon.* OH III. xxiii. 21 merely says that 'insidiantes insidiis capit'. According to Justinus XIII. viii. 6, 'qui securum adgressuros se putabant, securis in itinere et pervigilio noctis fatigatis occursum est.'

79/11–14. *Æfter ðæm . . . hie.* According to the corresponding passage of OH, III. xxiii. 23, these men were pronounced enemies by the Macedonians.

79/17. *Antipatre þæm cyninge.* OH III. xxiii. 24 *Antipatri.* For the title king see 70/29 and 81/10–11, Commentary.

79/22–3. *on ðæm tweon . . . fulleodon.* Cf. OH III. xxiii. 26 'qui fastidiose ducem in disponendo bello audientes'.

79/26. *hie selfe . . . Umene.* Or.'s addition.

79/27. *ymb . . . bismer.* OH III. xxiii. 27 *turpiter.*

79/31–80/2. *Ac . . . bena wæron.* OH III. xxiii. 28 'mox cum foedissima ignominia in exercitu Antigoni dispersi sunt.' Justinus XIV. iii. 9, referring to the period before the appeal to Antigonus, describes the Argyraspides as dispatched 'ab ipso limine patriae'.

80/3. *Æfter þæm.* OH III. xxiii. 29 *interea.*

80/4–7. *Cassander . . . cyninge.* OH III. xxiii. 29 'Cassandrum quem [Eurydice] flagitiose cognitum ad summum fastigium per omnes honorum gradus prouexerat'. According to Justinus XIV. v. 1, Eurydice wrote in the King's name to Polyperchon, asking him to deliver up the army to Cassander, 'in quem regni administrationem rex transtulerit'.

80/7–9. *heo . . . wiðerwearde.* According to the corresponding section of OH, III. xxiii. 29, Cassander 'ex libidine mulieris multas Graeciae ciuitates adflixit'.

80/9. *hie . . . Olimpeadum.* Cf. OH III. xxiii. 30 'adnitentibus Macedonibus'.

80/12. *Epira . . . hiere agnes rices.* OH III. xxiii. 30 *ab Epiro.* Or.'s addition here may merely be based on the knowledge that Olympias' brother was king of Epirus: see OH III. xi. 2. However, according to Greek sources, Olympias raised a faction against Antipater even before Alexander's death, and took Epirus (see, e.g., Plutarch, *Alexander*, LXVIII. 3), and this detail may well have been given in the missing section of Quintus Curtius, X. iv. 3.

80/14. *Cassander oðfleah.* Or.'s addition.

80/14–15. *Olimpiade . . . rice.* A safe deduction from the context; see, however, Justinus XIV. vi. 1, 'sed nec Olympias diu regnavit.'

80/16–17. *þa . . . laðade.* Henry Sweet in his edition assumes this addition to be based on OH III. xxiii. 31, 'Audito *adventu* Cassandri' (Sweet's italics).

80/17–19. *þa hio . . . gelastfull beon.* OH III. xxiii. 31 'diffisa Macedonibus'.

80/22–5. *þa burgleode . . . besittan.* Apparently inspired by OH III. xxiii. 32, 'filius Alexandri Magni cum matre in arcem Amphipolitanam custodiendus est missus.' It was in fact Cassander who sent him there: see Justinus XIV. vi. 13.

80/25–6. *him . . . rices.* Or.'s addition, probably deduced from the context. See, however, Justinus XV. i. 5, 'Cassandro parebat Macedonia cum Graecia', and Freculph, *Chronicon*, col. 1023, 'Cassandrum, qui Macedoniam obtinuerat'.

80/29–30. *Perþica . . . oðre.* OH III. xxiii. 33 'Perdicca Alceta et Polyperconte ceterisque ducibus, quos commemorare longum est'. Eumenes is included in the corresponding list in Justinus XV. i. 1. Antipater was still alive at this point: see below, 82/1–5 and OH III. xxiii. 56.

80/30–81/1. *Ac . . . gewealde.* All that OH III. xxiii. 34 says is that 'Antigonus ardens cupiditate dominandi liberandum bello Herculem regis filium ab obsidione simulat.' The reason given by Justinus XV. i. 3 is 'ut honestum adversus socios bellum suscipere videretur'.

81/2. *Seleucus þone eastcyning.* OH III. xxiii. 35 *Seleuco.* See 77/30–2, Commentary.

81/4–6. *On . . . Cassandre.* Or.'s addition.

81/6–7. *þær . . . sunu.* OH III. xxiii. 35 'Antigonus in eo bello cum filio Demetrio uincitur.' The context reveals that they lived to fight another day.

81/10–11. *for þon . . . ladteowas.* OH III. xxiii. 40 'quod exemplum omnes secuti regium sibi nomen dignitatemque sumpserunt.' See 79/5, Commentary.

81/12. *Antigones.* OH III. xxiii. 38 is referring to Cassander at this point. However, in Or., OH's section 38 is put after 40 and the unexpressed subject thus gets a new antecedent.

81/18. *his geþoftan.* OH III. xxiii. 42 'clarissimum inter omnes ducem'.

81/19–20. *for þon . . . eastlondum.* OH III. xxiii. 43 'hic siquidem Seleucus plurima per Orientem inter socios regni Macedonici bella gessit.'

81/21–2. *Indie . . . Alexandre.* OH III. xxiii. 45 *Indiam.* See 22/13–14 and Commentary, OH I. iv. 5.

81/23. *he . . . hiersumnesse.* Or.'s addition. According to OH III. xxiii. 46, Seleucus made a pact with the rebel Androcottus, allowing him to hold the kingdom.

81/24. *Antigones . . . sunu.* OH III. xxiii. 41 *Antigonum.*

81/25–6. *his sunu . . . adræfed.* Or.'s addition. See Justinus XV. iv. 22, 'Demetrius, filius eius, in fugam vertitur.'

81/26–7. *Ne . . . gefeoll.* What Orosius actually said, III. xxiii. 47, was that in that fight 'tunc totius paene Macedonici regni uires conciderunt.'

81/29–30. *þa . . . wære.* Or.'s addition. See 80/27–8.

81/32. *Philippuse Cassandres suna.* Of Philippus OH III. xxiii. 49 merely says that he succeeded his father. According to Justinus XVI. i. 1, he died very shortly afterwards.

81/33–82/1. *hie . . . angunnen.* Cf. OH III. xxiii. 49 'sic quasi ex integro noua Macedoniae bella nascuntur.'

82/6–8. *Æfter . . . wann.* OH III. xxiii. 52 'Lysimachus cum Dori regis Thracum infestissimo bello urgueretur, aduersus Demetrium pugnare non potuit.' There was no battle: Lysimachus made peace with Demetrius in order to avoid a war on two fronts. See Justinus XVI. i. 19.

82/9. *fird . . . Ptholomeuse.* According to OH III. xxiii. 53–4, it was Ptolemaeus who led an army against Demetrius: 'Demetrius . . . in Asiam transire disponit. Ptolemaeus autem et Seleucus et Lysimachus . . . bellum in Europam transferunt aduersus Demetrium.'

82/10. *Seleucus.* OH III. xxiii. 54 also names Lysimachus here.

82/12–13. *Pirrus to feng.* OH III. xxiii. 55 'regnum Macedoniae Pyrrhus inuasit.' See Justinus XVI. ii. 3 'regnum Macedoniae occupauit'.

82/14–15. *On . . . ealle.* OH III. xxiii. 57 refers less dramatically to an earthquake, though going on to say that the city became 'crudele sepulchrum'. Or.'s description of Lysimachia as *Lisimachus sio burg* seems to be the result of interpretation of an underlying *Lisimachi civitas* (as in the 'related' MS Ricc. 627) as a construction with epexegetic genitive of the type *Urbs Romae.* See further Bately (1961), pp. 85–6.

82/17. *his agene leode.* OH III. xxiii. 58 'omnes socii'.

82/22. *þreo . . . wintra.* OH III. xxiii. 59 *lxxiiii,* some 'related' MSS of Group C *lxxiii.*

82/22–3. *þæs ymb þreo niht.* Or.'s addition. According to Justinus XVII. ii. 4, Ptolomeus attacked 'post menses admodum septem'.

82/24–5. *diegellice . . . ofslog.* OH III. xxiii. 64 'insistente Ptolemaeo insidiis circumuentus occisus est.'

82/25–6. *Ða . . . geleornedon.* Or.'s addition.

82/27–8. *hæfdon . . . ealdgeferena.* OH III. xxiii. 61 'extinctis iam xxxiiii

Alexandri ducibus'. For the assumption of the title of king by Alexander's successors see 81/10–11, Commentary.

82/29–31. *Gemong . . . afslog.* OH III. xxiii. 62 'uel amissis uel interfectis prius ante hanc pugnam quindecim liberis'. Justinus XVII. ii. 1 says that the sons were lost 'variis casibus'.

82/32–83/6. *Ðyllicne . . . meder.* A rewriting of OH III. xxiii. 65–7, 'Haec sunt inter parentes filios fratres ac socios consanguinitatis societatisque commercia. tanti apud illos diuina atque humana religio pendebatur. erubescant sane de recordatione praeteritorum, qui nunc interuentu solius fidei Christianae ac medio tantum iurationis sacramento uiuere se cum hostibus nec pati hostilia sciunt; . . . nunc inter barbaros ac Romanos . . . tantam fidem adhibita in sacramentum seruant euangelia, quantam tunc nec inter parentes ac filios potuit seruare natura.' For Or.'s theme see Introduction, pp. xciv f.

83/2–3. *þonne . . . forlætað.* There is nothing to correspond to this in OH: indeed the situation in Rome in Orosius' day was very different. It therefore seems reasonable to suppose that the translator is referring here to conditions in his own time, and to raids by the Vikings. See further Introduction, p. xcii.

83/4–5. *nan . . . gebycggan.* Potter (1952–3), p. 414, sees here an allusion to wergild, which 'has, of course, no counterpart in Orosius'. However, a Latin source cannot be ruled out. See Justinus XVI. iv, where Clearchus of Heraclea is said to have demanded and received large sums of money as ransom from his prisoners, and then to have put them to death.

83/9–11. *Tarentine . . . irnan.* OH IV. i. 1 'Tarentini Romanam classem forte praetereuntem, spectaculo theatri prospectam hostiliter inuaserunt.'

83/14–15. *sume . . . gesealdon.* According to OH IV. i. 1, 'praefecti nauium trucidati, omnes bello utiles caesi, reliqui pretio uenditi sunt.' The translator, perhaps puzzled by the use of *caesi*, 'killed', alongside *trucidati*, has given the former its alternative sense of 'struck', and at the same time has interpreted a reference to selling into slavery as an allusion to ransoming. The word *pretio* is omitted by the 'related' MSS Vienna 366 and Ricc. 627.

83/18. *Ða . . . bismere.* OH IV. i. 2 says that they were *pulsati*, 'beaten'.

83/18–19. *swa . . . dydon.* Or.'s addition. See 83/14–15, Commentary.

83/24–5. *cwædon . . . mehte.* Cf. OH IV. i. 3 'quippe cum frustra de prole cura est, nisi rebus praesentibus consulatur'.

83/27–8. *þa . . . wendon.* OH IV. i. 5 merely states that the Tarentines were supported by large contingents of their neighbours.

83/28. *Pirrus, Epira cyning.* OH IV. i. 5 Pyrrhus. See 58/25–6 and 82/10.

83/29. *ægþer . . . sciphere.* Cf. OH IV. i. 6, where Pyrrhus is said to inspire terror 'terra mari, uiris equis, armis beluis'.

83/30–84/1. *He . . . wigcræfte.* Cf. OH IV. i. 5 'Pyrrhus . . . etiam in se ob magnitudinem uirium consiliorumque summam belli nomenque trans-duxit.' Florus Ì. xiii. 1 describes Pyrrhus as 'clarissimum Graeciae regem', while according to Justinus XXV. v. 3, 'satis constans inter omnes auctores fama est, nullum nec eius nec superioris aetatis regem conparandum Pyrrho fuisse.'

84/2. *Læcedemonium . . . wæs.* OH IV. i. 6 *Lacedaemoniis.* Lacedaemon was at no time ruled over by Pyrrhus, though for a short time he had control over Macedonia (see OH III. xxiii. 55 and 82/12–13, Commentary). Indeed, according to OH IV. ii. 7, he was killed 'Spartani regni auiditate seductus'.

84/7. *his godas . . . deofolgeld.* OH IV. i. 7 claims that it was the Delphic oracle that deceived him: 'Delphici illius uanissimi spiritus et mendacissimi nebulonis, quem magnum ipsi uatem ferunt'. The 'related' MS Vienna 366, however, replaces this passage with an account of Pyrrhus consulting Apollo. For the identification of idols with demons see, e.g., Tertullian, *De Spectaculis, PL* i, col. 720.

84/8. *begongende.* The reading of MS C; MS L *begonde* could be an error either for this or for *begande*: see GD 269/8.

84/8–11. *þa . . . næfst.* Although OH IV. i. 7 refers merely to the oracle's 'responso ambiguo', the translator probably found the words of the oracle inserted in his Latin exemplar. A number of 'related' MSS, including Vienna 366, have in either margin or text the words 'Aio te, [A]eacida, Romanos uincere posse', a response which seems to have been derived ultimately from Ennius, possibly via the lost thirteenth book of Livy, and is quoted by a number of Latin sources, including Cicero, *De Divinatione* II, 116 and *De Viris Illustribus,* 35. 2. For a slightly different wording see Augustine, *Civ. Dei* III. xvii. See further, Bately (1961), p. 97.

84/14. *þær . . . geslagen wæs.* Cf. OH IV. i. 8 'consumpta est grauissimo certamine dies, utrimque omnibus mori intentis, fugere nesciis.'

84/18–19. *He . . . ofstang.* OH IV. i. 10 'protentam in se manum beluae gladio desecuit'. Cf. OH IV. i. 21, where the Romans are said to attack with firebrands the elephants' *posteriora ac mollia*—the only soft part, according to authorities such as Pliny VIII. x and Solinus 112, 17, being the belly. J. E. Cross, 'The Elephant to Alfred, Ælfric, Aldhelm and Others', *SN*, xxxvii (1965), 367–73, suggests that the translator may here be recalling 1 Maccabees 6: 46, where Eleazar is said to have put himself underneath an elephant and slain it, and points out the most interesting verbal correspondence between Or.'s statement and Ælfric's translation of Maccabees (*Lives of Saints* II, p. 104, ll. 585–7), 'he to þam ylpe com 7 eode him under, stang ða hine æt ðam nauelan þæt hi lagon ðær begen heora egðer oðres slagen'. Ælfric also comments that 'ylpe is . . . eall mid banum befangen binnan þam felle butan æt ðam nauelan' (*ibid.,* l. 568), in connection with which Cross quotes Ambrose, *Hexameron, CSEL* XXXII, pars i (Prague etc. 1897), VI. v. 32 'ventre ceterisque iuxta mollioribus ad vulnus patet'.

84/20–2. *þa forwurdon . . . wæron.* OH IV. i. 10 merely says that the elephant in its rage turned against its own side, *in suos.* Nowhere are

Pyrrhus' elephants said to carry men, though OH IV. i. 21 refers to *machinas* on their backs. However, OH IV. xv. 3 describes Hannibal as mounted on an elephant and there are many other references in Latin texts to elephants with riders, including the moving account in Quintus Curtius VIII. xiv of the elephant that tried to protect its master, Porus.

84/23–4. *hie wæron . . . sceoldon.* Or.'s addition, possibly inspired by OH IV. i. 21, 'elephanti prima pugna uulnerari atque in fugam cogi posse deprehensi'.

84/24–7. *On . . . genumen.* Cf. OH IV. i. 11 'quorum tunc cecidisse referuntur peditum xiiii dccclxxx, capti icccx, equites autem caesi ccxlvi, capti dcccii, signa amissa xxii'.

84/28. *þeaw.* OH IV. i. 12 'scriptorum ueterum mos'.

84/29–30. *buton . . . ofslagen wære.* OH IV. i. 13 'nisi forte cum adeo pauci cadunt, ut admirationem terroremque uirtutis augeat paucitas perditorum'.

84/30–1. *on . . . feaht.* OH IV. i. 13 'prima Persici belli congressione'. See above, 68/13–17.

84/32–85/2. *Ac . . . eam.* According to OH IV. i. 14, 'Pyrrhus atrocitatem cladis, quam hoc bello exceperat, dis suis hominibusque testatus est, adfigens titulum in templo Tarentini Iouis, in quo haec scripsit:

> Qui antehac inuicti fuere uiri, pater optime Olympi,
> Hos ego in pugna uici uictusque sum ab isdem.'

85/2–3. *þa . . . þegnas.* According to OH IV. i. 15, Pyrrhus was in fact rebuked by his allies, 'a sociis increpitaretur'. For a similar interpretation of *socii* see 82/17, where *his agene leode* renders OH III. xxiii. 58 *omnes socii*.

85/5. *æt Romanum.* Or.'s addition.

85/5–6. *buton ælcon þegne.* OH IV. i. 15 'sine ullo milite'.

85/6. *Creca lond.* OH IV. i. 15 *Epirum.* For the location of Epirus in Greece, see 30/34, Commentary. According to Florus I. xiii. 25, Pyrrhus fled to *Graeciam suam.*

85/8. *xxiiii.* OH IV. i. 18 *xxx et iiii,* 'related' MSS, including Vienna 366 and Ricc. 627, *xx et iiii.*

85/13–15. *hie namon . . . hindan.* OH IV. i. 21 'subiectis inter posteriora ac mollia ignibus exagitati'. For the additional details given by Or. see OH IV. ii. 5 'Romani, adsueti iam pugnare cum beluis, cum malleolos stuppa inuolutos ac pice oblitos uncis insuper aculeis tenaces praeparauissent eosque flammatos in terga beluarum turresque uibrarent'.

85/17–19. *æt ælcon . . . sceoldon.* OH IV. i. 21 'ardentes insuper machinas furore trepido circumferentes exitio suis fuere'. See 84/20–2, Commentary.

85/19. *eahta þusend.* OH IV. i. 22 *v milia.*

85/21. *his guðfona.* In view of the reading of OH IV. i. 22 *signa . . . liii,* plural *guðfonan* might have been expected here. For loss of final *-n* see Introduction, p. xlviii.

85/23. *þæt rice . . . geniedde.* According to OH IV. i. 23, Pyrrhus was summoned to the rule of Sicily, 'ad Siciliae arcessitus imperium'. However, as Justinus XXIII. iii points out, although Pyrrhus was invited by the Sicilians, he had to fight the Carthaginians to win dominion over the island.

85/31. *Arosinis þære dune.* OH IV. ii. 3 *Arusinis campis.* Or.'s use of the term *dun* here may be the result of misunderstanding of the account of this battle given in Frontinus IV. i. 14, 'Pyrrhus primus totum exercitum *sub eodem uallo* continere instituit.' See also 121/22–3 and Bately (1972), p. 55, n. 5.

85/31–2. *Romane . . . gefeoht.* This reversal of the sense of OH IV. ii. 4 'Pyrrhi milites Romanorum inpressione trepidarent' is the result of the misconstruing of *Romanorum* with *milites.*

85/33–86/1. *hie hie . . . sceoldon.* OH IV. i. 21 'exitio suis fuere'. The translator (?) here omits OH's description of the preparation of the fire darts, which he has already used in 85/13–16.

86/1. *Pirruses . . . fleame.* Or.'s addition.

86/2. *v m.* OH IV. ii. 6 *vi milia;* 'related' MSS, including Ricc. 627, *v m.*

86/3. *xxxvi m.* OH IV. ii. 6 *xxxiii milia;* 'related' MSS, including Ricc. 627 and Vienna 366, *xxxvi m.*

86/3. *iiii hund.* OH IV. ii. 6 *mille trecenti;* 'related' MS Vienna 366 *ccc,* Ricc. 627 *c̄c̄c̄.*

86/4–5. *raþe . . . com.* Or.'s addition. According to OH IV. ii. 7, the incident at Argos took place 'post multa grauissimaque bella'. That Pyrrhus was attacking the city is confirmed by Justinus XXV. v. 1.

86/8. *on Affrice.* Or.'s addition.

86/10–11. *þær . . ne mehte.* Cf. OH IV. iii. 2 'ubi iam tunc Carthaginienses, quamuis nondum hostes adiudicati, uinci tamen a Romanis se posse senserunt'.

86/12–16. *hi . . . sceoldon.* OH IV. iii. 4 'octaua legio diffidens Romanae spei, nouum scelus ausa Reginenses omnes, quibus subsidio praeerat, interfecit, praedam sibi omnem atque ipsum oppidum uindicauit.'

86/19. *Sume he ofslog.* A safe deduction from OH IV. iii. 5 'exercuit digna supplicia'.

86/19. *geband.* Or.'s addition.

86/22–3. *feower . . . lxxvii.* OH IV. iv. 1 *cccclxxviii,* many MSS, 'related' and 'unrelated', *cccclxxvii.*

86/24. *heora . . . Iofeses.* OH IV. iv. 1 *aedes Salutis.* Salus was a female deity.

86/25. *on anre niht.* OH IV. iv. 2 *ante lucem.*

86/27. *oþ* . . *urnon*. OH IV. iv. 2 refers merely to *strepitu hominum*.

86/28–9. *on anre dune* . . . *Romebyrig*. OH IV. iv. 4 'apud agrum Calenum'. The Calenian Field was in southern Campania; see, e.g., Pliny II. ciii. Does a confusion between *ager* and *agger* underlie Or.'s use of *dun* here? See *Gl. Ansileubi* AG 37 'agger: monticulus uel aceruus' and Bately (1972), p. 55. For the confusion in spelling of *ager* and *agger*, see Servius, *Aen.* V. 273.

86/30–1. *fif æcra bræde*. OH IV. iv. 4 *quinque agri iugera*. The acre and the Roman jugerum were of a very different shape and size; however, they are equated in at least one Anglo-Saxon glossary: see Wright–Wülcker, 423, 9.

86/32. *Pencentes, Italia folc*. OH IV. iv. 5 *Picentes*. For the location of the Picentes in Italy, see, e.g., Pliny III. v. 38.

87/1–2. *ægðer* . . . *besincan*. Or.'s addition.

87/14–16. *þa* . . . *soðe*. OH IV. v. 2 'turpissimam rupti foederis labem praesumpto accumulauere peiurio'.

87/16. *Ulcinienses* . . . *folc*. OH IV. v. 3 'Vulsinienses, Etruscorum florentissimi'. The *and* of Or. may have originated in the first two letters of *Etruscorum*.

87/17–19. *hie* . . . *forgiefene*. According to OH IV. v. 3, the slaves were freed indiscriminately (*passim*), invited to banquets and honoured with marriage.

87/19–20. *þa* . . . *nolde*. OH IV. v. 4 'libertini in partem potestatis recepti plenitudinem per scelus usurpare meditati sunt et liberati seruitutis iugo, ambitu dominationis arserunt et quos dominos subditi aequanimiter dilexerunt, eos iam liberi, quod dominos fuisse meminerant, exsecrati sunt.' 'Libertini' OH here uses in its usual classical sense of 'freedman'; however, the translator has interpreted it according to the definition given by Isidore, *Etymologies* IX. iv. 47, 'Libertorum autem filii apud antiquos libertini appellabantur, quasi de libertis nati', a definition adopted in glossaries such as Corpus, L 205, 'Libertini: filii servorum lib-(eratorum)' and Wright–Wülcker 111, 23, 'libertinus: freolætan sunu'. In Anglo-Saxon society, the ceorl was the freeman, as opposed to the slave, or bondman.

87/28–88/4. *Ond* . . . *dyden*. OH IV. v. 7–8 'sed quantum superfuisset, inquireret: si uiolentia qua adfecerit, Sibyllini libri testes sunt, qui eam caelesti ira inpositam responderunt. sed, ne quemquam quasi temptatio cauillationis offendat, quod, cum Sibylla iratos deos dixerit, nos iram caelestem dixisse uideamur, audiat et intellegat, quia haec, etsi plerumque per aerias potestates fiunt, tamen sine arbitrio omnipotentis Dei omnino non fiunt.' For an earlier allusion by Orosius to the Sibylline Books and Or.'s handling of it, see 76/3 and Commentary.

88/5. *heora goda nunne*. OH IV. v. 9 *uirgo Vestalis*. See 60/8–10 and Commentary.

88/8. *ealle . . . hælan.* OH IV. v. 9 'consciique serui'.

88/11. *hu wene we.* See above, 31/19–21, Commentary.

88/12–13. *ægþer . . . ege.* Cf. OH IV. v. 11 'ne eosdem quibus haec et de quibus scribebantur offenderent auditoresque suos exemplis praeteritorum terrere potius quam instituere uiderentur'.

88/16. *Elisan þæm wifmen.* OH IV. vi. 1 *Helissa.* See 133/9, Commentary.

88/16. *lxxiitigum.* This form suggests an underlying *twa 7 seofontigum.*

88/16–17. *Swa some . . . awriten.* Based on a misunderstanding of OH IV. vi. 1, 'res ipsa exigit, ut de Carthagine . . . eiusque cladibus ac domesticis malis . . . uel pauca referantur.'

88/18. *Trogus . . . stærwriteras.* OH IV. vi. 1 'Pompeius Trogus et Iustinus'. The knowledge that these two men were historians could have been derived from the allusion in OH I. viii. 1, 'Pompeius historicus eiusque breuiator Iustinus'. However, that passage is rendered by Or. 23/23 as 'Sompeius se hæþena scop 7 his cniht Iustinus', a 'translation' which suggests that we must look for a different source here. See further Introduction, pp. lx ff.

88/22. *ða diofla þe.* I have here inserted from MS C the relative omitted by L: see Mustanoja (1960), p. 205, 'Non-expression of the object-pronoun in a relative clause has not been attested in OE. In ME it appears towards the end of the 14th century.'

88/28–9. *þæt . . . wunnon.* OH IV. vi. 7 refers to war of long duration only in connection with Sicily.

88/31. *heora latteowum . . . cempum.* OH IV. vi. 7 'ducem suum Mazeum et paucos qui superfuerant milites'.

88/33–89/1. *þæt hie . . . mehte.* OH IV. vi. 7 'ueniam petentes'.

89/3. *se ieldesta ladteow.* OH IV. vi. 8 *dux exulum.*

89/4. *on biscephade.* OH IV. vi. 8 describes Carthalo as *sacerdotem Herculis.* Cf. Justinus XVIII. vii. 9 'ornatus . . . purpura et infulis sacerdotii'.

89/6–7. *for þon . . . cyningum.* Or.'s addition. There are many allusions in classical texts to the royal purple; see, e.g., Servius, *Georgics* II. 495; see also *Cura Pastoralis* 85/9–10 'purpura, ðæt is cynelic hrægl'.

89/8. *ealle þa æltæwestan.* OH IV. vi. 9 'plurimis senatorum'. Justinus XVIII. vii. 17 gives the number as ten.

89/10. *besiered 7 ofslagen.* OH IV. vi. 9 merely says that Mazeus was slain; according to Justinus XVIII. vii. 18, however, 'ipse adfectati regni accusatus duplicis, et in filio et in patria, parricidii poenas dedit.'

89/15. *he . . . wende.* Or.'s addition, presumably a contextual guess.

89/19–21. *hie . . . sceolde.* Or.'s addition.

89/22–3. *mid* (2) *. . . gegierelan.* According to OH IV. vi. 14, he was 'sordida seruilique tunica discinctus'.

89/28. *þæt þær wyrrest wæs*. Or.'s addition, reflecting the Christian attitude to suicide.

90/4. *to gereordum*. According to OH IV. vi. 16, he planned to poison the senators' cups at a sham marriage of his only daughter.

90/7–8. *ealle . . . mehte*. An elaboration of OH IV. vi. 17 *seruitia*.

90/10. *xxiiii m*. OH IV. vi. 18 *uiginti milibus*, 'related' MSS, including Ricc. 627 and Vienna 366, *xxiiii m*.

90/10. *anre oþerre byrig*. OH IV. vi. 18 *castellum quoddam*. *Castellum* is equated with *oppidum* in a number of glossaries: see, e.g., Corpus O 202 and *Abavus* Op. 20.

90/11–13. *þa . . . gefliemdon*. A misunderstanding of OH IV. vi. 18–19, where it is said not only that Hanno occupied the fortress but also that it was he who 'Afros regemque Maurorum concitat'. There is nothing in OH or its source, Justinus, to suggest that the capture of Hanno took place outside or that his associates were put to flight.

90/13–15. *ærest . . . heafod*. Hanno's end was in fact much more unpleasant: see OH IV. vi. 19 'primo uirgis caesus, deinde effossis oculis et manibus cruribusque fractis, uelut a singulis membris poena exigeretur, in conspectu populi necatus est.'

90/25. *heora swicdomes*. Since the verb *fremman* normally governs the accusative, *swicdomes* is best interpreted as apl. See Introduction, p. xlvi.

90/28. *hiora heafedburg*. OH IV. vi. 23 'urbem Siciliae tunc florentissimam'. For Syracuse as the capital of Sicily, see, e.g., Solinus 49, 9 and Florus I. xxii. 33.

91/2–4. *Ac . . . hwile*. Or.'s addition. Cf. OH IV. vi. 24 'bene prouiso ac melius dissimulato consilio in Africam cum exercitu transiit'. That some troops remained behind is evident from the allusion in OH IV. vi. 28 to the defeat of a Carthaginian army in Sicily by Agathocles' brother; however, it is possible that Or.'s addition reflects knowledge of Justinus' comment, XXII. iv. 3–4, that Agathocles, having allowed all those who wished to depart to do so, furnished the rest with provisions and money for the necessities of a blockade.

91/5. *on Cartainense*. OH IV. vi. 24 *in Africam*.

91/6–7. *for þon . . . hæfde*. The reason given by OH IV. vi. 25 is that there should be no possible hope of retreat, 'ne qua spes refugiendi foret'.

91/7. *him . . . geworhte*. Like 91/9, *æt þæm fæstenne*, this addition is without basis in OH.

91/8–9. *Hanna . . . cyning*. OH IV. vi. 25 *Hannonem quendam*. The translator may have been influenced by a subsequent allusion in OH to (another) Hanno as *imperator*: see OH IV. vii. 5, Or. 92/12. However, the Carthaginian leaders are frequently described as kings: see 91/27, Commentary.

91/9. *xx m*. OH IV. vi. 25 *triginta milibus*, 'related' MSS, including Ricc. 627 and Vienna 366, *xx m*.

91/10–11. *his folces . . . æfterfylgende wæs.* A misunderstanding of OH IV. vi. 25–7, 'quem cum duobus milibus suorum interfecit; ipse autem duos tantum in eo bello perdidit . . . castra deinde ad quintum lapidem a Carthagine statuit.' Such a misunderstanding would be aided by a reading *ii m* for *duobus milibus* in the MS used by the translator. Cf. the 'related' MS Ricc. 627 *ii̅*.

91/13–14. *þonne . . . wæron.* Or.'s addition.

91/16. *þone . . . let.* Or.'s addition. OH IV. vi. 28 merely locates the action in Sicily. See 91/2–4 and Commentary.

91/16–17. *he besierede . . . ungearwe.* OH IV. vi. 28 simply says that Andro crushed 'Afrorum exercitu[m] . . . reuera incautum ac paene otiosum'. For other instances of the assumption that unexpected attacks happened at night, see 30/18 and 51/20–4.

91/17–19. *hit mæst . . . coman.* OH IV. vi. 28 describes the army as *deletus* and makes no mention of survivors.

91/20–2. *Agothocle . . . eodon.* What OH IV. vi. 29 in fact says is that 'non tributariae tantum urbes ab his, uerum etiam socii reges deficiebant.' No suggestion is made that any of them other than Afellas went over to Agathocles.

91/25–6. *Gif . . . begietan.* Or.'s addition.

91/27. *Amicor, Pena cyning.* OH IV. vi. 32 'Hamilcar dux Poenorum'. Or. habitually renders both *dux* and *imperator* by *cyning* when these terms are used of the Carthaginians, possibly influenced by a statement such as that of Cornelius Nepos, XXIII *Hannibal* vii. 4, 'ut enim Romae consules, sic Karthagine quotannis annui bini reges creabantur.'

91/28. *mid sibbe.* The basis for this surprising statement is OH's comment, IV. vi. 32, that the battle between Agathocles and the Carthaginians was so severe that had there not been a mutiny in Agathocles' army, Hamilcar and his forces would have deserted to the side of the enemy.

91/29. *he self ofslagen wearð.* Presumably deduced from OH's reference to a mutiny and a subsequent allusion, IV. vi. 33, to events 'post mortem Agathoclis'. Agathocles' death, however, occurred at a much later date, in Sicily; see Justinus, XXII. vii–XXIII. ii.

92/3. *wið Pena folce.* OH IV. vii. 1 'contra Hieronem Syracusanum regem et Poenorum copias Hieroni iunctas'.

92/5–6. *þa . . . genealæcten.* Based on a misunderstanding of OH IV. vii. 2 'tam celeriter Syracusanos Poenosque superauit, ut ipse quoque rex rerum magnitudine perterritus ante se uictum quam congressum fuisse prodiderit.' The king referred to is Hiero, the Syracusan.

92/7. *Hanna, Pena cyning.* OH IV. vii. 2 *rex*, referring to Hiero. Hanno is not mentioned until OH IV. vii. 5.

92/8–9. *7 him . . . siolfres.* According to OH IV. vii. 3, this fine was imposed on Hiero and the Syracusans (see preceding note). There is nothing to suggest that it was to be paid annually.

92/9. *On . . . punda.* Or.'s addition. See Leiden XXXIII. 1 'Talentum, habet pondera LXII quod faciunt LXXX libre attice', also Eucherius, *Instructionum Libri Duo*, ed. C. Wotke. *CSEL* XXXI, 158. For a talent of 70 pounds, see Bately (1971), p. 238, n. 3.

92/10. *Pena cyning.* OH IV. vii. 5 *imperator Poenorum.*

92/11. *he . . . swealt.* OH IV. vii. 5 is less specific, merely stating that he was reduced 'ad summam egestatem'.

92/12. *Pena oper cyning.* OH IV. vii. 5 'imperator nouus Carthaginiensium'.

92/12. *mid sciphere.* OH IV. vii. 5 refers to infantry, cavalry and elephants but not to ships. If Hanno came from Carthage, he must have come by ship; however, see above, 91/8, where the translator erroneously involves Hanno in the Syracusan war and thus presumably assumes that he was already in Sicily.

92/14. *on niht.* Or.'s addition.

92/15. *hundeahtatig.* OH IV. vii. 7 *septuaginta.*

92/16. *ærest.* Or.'s addition. Although the Romans' first fleet had in fact been built many years before, a number of Latin texts give Duilius the credit for being the first to win a naval triumph and Or.'s claim may well be a garbled version of this: see, e.g., Valerius Maximus III. vi. 4, and Jerome, *Adversus Jovinianum*, *PL* xxiii, col. 275. However, according to Eutropius II. xx, 'Primum Romani C. Duilio et Cn. Cornelio Asina coss. in mari dimicauerunt paratis navibus rostratis', while a Greek source (Polybius, *Histories*, ed. T. Büttner-Wobst (Leipzig, 1904), I. xxii. 1) comments that up to that time the Romans had no fleet of their own, first building one to fight the Carthaginians.

92/19–20. *ge mid mæste . . . segle.* OH IV. vii. 8 *in anchoris.*

92/22. *þa . . . hiene.* According to OH IV. vii. 9, Cornelius Asina 'ab Hannibale quasi ad conloquium pacis euocatus Punica fraude captus atque in uinculis necatus est'.

92/24. *iii hund.* OH IV. vii. 10 *tria milia.*

92/24. *xxx.* OH IV. vii. 10 *triginta et una.*

92/26. *Punici . . . Cartainense.* OH IV. vii. 11 *Carthaginienses.* In OH, the stem *Punic-* is used adjectivally only. See, however, Festus, p. 346, 'Punici dicuntur, non Poeni.'

92/29. *mid sciphere.* Or.'s addition, presumably deduced from OH's comment that Hanno was in charge of naval operations.

93/1. *Calatinus.* OH IV. viii. 2–3 names Calpurnius Flamma as the hero of this episode, Calatinus being merely the leader of the expedition: see 92/30, OH IV. viii. 1.

93/2–4. *on . . . þurhfor.* According to OH IV. viii. 2, Calpurnius Flamma 'insessum ab hostibus tumulum occupauit et in se Poenos omnes pugnando conuertit, donec Romanus exercitus obsessas angustias hoste non urguente transiret'. Did the Latin manuscript used by the translator have the variant *insensum*, found in Zangemeister's MS D, and was this interpreted by him as past participle of *sentio* with negative prefix *in*?

93/5. *ðæm consule*. OH IV. viii. 3 *Calpurnius*. See 93/1, Commentary.

93/9. *on ðæm fleame*. Or.'s addition.

93/12–13. *mid feower . . . þritigum*. OH IV. viii. 6 'trecentis triginta nauibus'. Or.'s reading is shared by a number of 'related' MSS: however, the figure 330 is found in the corresponding entry in the list of chapter headings 4/11. See Introduction, p. xxxviii.

93/13. *cyningas*. OH IV. viii. 6 describes Hamilcar as *imperator*.

93/15. *lxxxiiii*. OH IV. viii. 6 'sexaginta et quattuor naues', some 'related' MSS, including Ricc. 627 and Vienna 366, *lxxiiii*.

93/18. *Regulus se consul*. OH IV. viii 10 *Regulus*. Regulus was consul in 267 B.C. and again in this year, 256. He is described as consul by *De Viris Illustribus* 40. 1, Livy X. xxxii. 1, and Periocha XVII.

93/22–3. *þa . . . wæron*. OH IV. viii. 10 merely says that Regulus went *cum exercitu*.

93/24–5. *swelce . . . isen*. OH IV. viii. 11 'quasi per obliquam scutorum testudinem'. Or.'s alteration here is somewhat surprising. The translator could have known the meaning of *testudo* from a gloss such as *Gl. Ansileubi* TE 614 'coniunctio scutorum' or from Isidore, *Etymologies* XVIII. xii. 6. See also Corpus T 81 *testudo*: *bordðeaca* and Cotton Cleopatra A III *testudine*: *scyldreðan* (Wright–Wülcker 532, 8).

93/25–6. *palistas . . . fuhton*. OH IV. viii. 11 *ballistas*. In the Corpus Glossary B 8, *ballista* is glossed *staefliðre*; see also Cotton Cleopatra A III (Wright–Wülcker 357, 21) and *The Old English Riddles of the Exeter Book*, ed. C. Williamson (Chapel Hill, 1977), pp. 179–80.

93/27. *þwyres*. Or.'s addition. OH's only reference to angle here, IV. viii. 11 *obliquam*, is made in connection with the *testudo*: see 93/24–5, Commentary.

93/27. *an ribb*. According to OH IV. viii. 11, it is the creature's spine that was struck.

93/29–30. *heora mægen . . . ribbum*. According to OH IV. viii. 12, the creature rested on its ribs as if on legs.

93/30–1. *swa . . . fotum*. Cf. OH IV. viii. 13 'non enim ut uermis, cui spinae rigor non est, et in directum corpusculi sui partes gradatim porrigendo contractas, contrahendo porrectas motum explicat.' This passage is quoted by Isidore, *Etymologies* XII. v. 19; elsewhere in the section *De Vermibus* Isidore refers to creatures with legs such as the frog, scorpion, and millipede. See further 25/19, Commentary.

93/34. *cyningas*. OH IV. viii. 16 *imperatores*.

94/2–3. *wæs* (2) *. . genumen*. OH IV. viii. 16 'caesa sunt Carthaginiensium decem et septem milia, capta autem quinque milia, decem et octo elephanti abducti.'

94/6. *ungemetlic gafol.* OH IV. ix. 1 refers merely to 'intolerabiles et duras condiciones pacis'.

94/12–17. *he . . . fore.* An expansion of OH IV. ix. 2, 'Xanthippus, inspectis Poenorum copiis atque in campum deductis, longe in melius mutato apparatu pugnam cum Romanis conseruit', using material presumably derived ultimately from a lost book of Livy, probably via Frontinus. See Frontinus II. iii. 10 'Xanthippus . . . levem armaturam in prima acie conlocavit, in subsidio autem robur exercitus praecepitque auxiliaribus, ut emissis telis cederent hosti et, cum se intra suorum ordines recepissent, confestim in latera discurrerent et a cornibus rursus erumperent; exceptumque iam hostem a robustioribus et ipsi circumierent.' For a slightly different version of the stratagem see Silius Italicus, *Punica* VI. 326–8.

94/22. *Enilius . . . consul.* OH IV. ix. 5 'Aemilius Paulus et Fuluius Nobilior consules', the 'related' MS Vienna 366 'Emelius Paulus Fuluius Nobilior consul'. *et* is also omitted by other 'related' MSS.

94/23. *Clepeam þæm iglonde.* OH IV. ix. 5 *Clipeam.* Clypea, or Aspis, was in fact a city on the mainland of Africa.

94/24. *þær gefliemde wæron.* Or.'s addition.

94/25. *v m.* OH IV. ix. 6 'triginta et quinque milia'.

94/27. *on þæm iglande.* OH IV. ix. 7 *apud Clipeam.* See 94/23, Commentary.

94/28. *cyningum.* OH IV. ix. 7 *imperatores.*

94/29. *þa oþre gefliemed.* Or.'s addition.

94/29–30. *Mid . . . scipa.* Here, as below, 95/7, the translator (?) assumes that it is the amount of booty on board that is responsible for the sinkings, not, as in OH, the violence of a storm or the existence of dangerous rocks.

94/31. *ii cc 7 xxx.* For *cc 7 xxx* or *twa hunde 7 xxx*, OH IV. ix. 8 *ducentae uiginti*, 'related' MSS including Ricc. 627 and Vienna 366 *ccxxx*.

94/31. *lxx.* OH IV. ix. 8 *octoginta.* As Professor Potter observes (1952–3, p. 419), this alteration was necessary in order to put the arithmetic of the passage right. However, in view of the reading *lxx* of 'related' MSS such as Vienna 366, it seems to have been made by a copyist of the Latin not of the Old English version.

95/1. *cyning.* OH IV. ix. 9 *dux.*

95/2. *to gafolgieldum gesette.* OH IV. ix. 9 is more specific: 'mille argenti talentis et uiginti milibus boum reliquos condemnauit.'

95/3. *hie Regule . . . eodon.* OH's reason, IV. ix. 9, is that the people received Regulus *libenter.*

95/5. *iii hund scipa 7 lxgum.* OH IV. ix. 10 'ducentis sexaginta nauibus'.

95/7. *hiora scipa oferhlæston.* Or.'s addition. See 94/29–30, Commentary.

95/10–11. *þær . . . mehte.* OH's version, IV. ix. 13, merely states that

Cotta 'per totam Siciliam partim hostium, partim etiam sociorum in-humatas strages reliquit'.

95/12–13. On . . . Blaciduses. OH IV. ix. 14 'L. Caecilio Metello C. Furio Placido consulibus', 'related' MSS 'Lucio Cecilio (var. Elio) Metello Gaio Forio Placido consulibus'. This is the first passage used by the translator in which the Latin gives cognomen as well as nomen and prae-nomen. Much has been made of the way in which the translator, not understanding the Latin system of nomenclature, sometimes turns two men into three, as here. However, the reason for this is surely ignorance not of the number of names one man could have but of the number of men who could be consul at one time (see 50/14–15, 101/11, 117/26–7, 122/27), coupled with the fact that the formulae of this type are normally found without punctuation in Latin MSS and are preceded and followed by references to people with only two names apiece. Where the pairs of tria nomina have a separating et in OH no such error is made (see e.g., 119/23). See further below, 97/1, Commentary, and, for an instance of three names for two in the 'related' MSS of OH, 99/19, Commentary.

95/13. cyning. OH IV. ix. 14 imperator.

95/14. of Cartainum. OH IV. ix. 14 ex Africa.

95/14. Libeum þæt igland. OH IV. ix. 14 Lilybaeum, 'related' MSS Libeum. Lilybaeum was in fact located in Sicily. See the description of Sicily, 21/5–6, 'þone westsceatan man hæt Libeum, þær is seo burh neah þe man hæt Libeum'.

95/14. xxx m gehorsedra. OH IV. ix. 14 'equitum peditumque amplius triginta milibus'.

95/14–15. mid xxx elpenda 7 cgum. The strange form cgum suggests an underlying reading 'mid xxxgum elpenda 7 c' or 'mid c elpenda 7 xxxgum', and could result from a scribe giving phonetic realisation to the numeral as he copied.

95/15. Metellus þone cyning. OH IV. ix. 14 Metello consule.

95/23–96/3. he him . . . abead. Or.'s addition. The story of Regulus was a popular one and used as an exemplum by both classical and patristic writers. See further Bately (1971), p. 243.

95/23–5. he . . . gecyþan. That Regulus was bound by an oath to return to Carthage is a feature of a number of accounts, including Livy, Periocha XVIII, De Viris Illustribus 40. 4, and Silius Italicus VI. 346–550. Augustine, Civ. Dei I. xv further refers to the gods he swore by.

95/25–7. he . . . heolden. The request for peace is to be found in OH IV. x. For the suggestion of an exchange of prisoners see, e.g., Eutropius II. xxv (followed by Paulus Diaconus), Livy, Periocha XVII, and Florus I. 18.

95/28–31. he hie healsade . . . wurden. There are several versions of Regulus' reasons for urging rejection of the peace plan. For the argument that it would be unfair to exchange one for many, an old man for young men, see, e.g., Valerius Maximus I. i. 14, Cicero, De Officiis III. 26,

Tertullian, *Liber ad Martyres, PL* i, col. 625, Eutropius II. xxv, and Silius Italicus VI. 346–550. For the argument that the returned soldiers would not be the same afterwards see Horace, *Carm.* III. v, and Porphyrio's comment on this passage. Silius Italicus and Horace in addition stress the baseness and shame of such a transaction, while Augustine, *Civ. Dei* I. xv, records the argument that such an exchange would not be to the advantage of the Romans. For the possible implications of Or.'s combination of these themes see Introduction, p. lxiii.

95/31–96/2. *þa . . . þeow*. The suggestion that Regulus was offered the throne has of course no foundation in fact whatsoever; however, both Augustine and Eutropius (followed by Paulus Diaconus) give the reply that he could not live in the dignity of an *honest citizen* in Rome, since he had been a slave in Africa. See *Civ. Dei* V. xviii and Eutropius II. xxv, 'negauit se in ea urbe mansurum, in qua, postquam Afris seruierat, dignitatem honesti ciuis habere non posset.'

96/3. *asædon . . . abead*. Or.'s addition.

96/3–5. *þa . . . forlet*. OH IV. x. 1 'resectis palpebris inligatum in machina uigilando necauerunt'.

96/7. *Libeum þæt igland*. OH IV. x. 2 *Lilybaeum*, 'related' MSS *libeum*: see 95/14, Commentary.

96/8. *an fæsten*. OH IV. x. 2 'oppidum in promuntorio situm'.

96/8–9. *se geonga cyning*. Or.'s addition.

96/9. *ungearwe*. Or.'s addition.

96/11. *Hannibal*. OH IV. x. 3 does not name the commander of the Punic Fleet.

96/12–13. *Libeum þæm iglande*. OH IV. x. 3 *Lilybaeum*. See 95/14, Commentary.

96/13. *ix m*. OH IV. x. 3 *octo milia*, 'related' MSS, including Ricc. 627 and Vienna 366, *ix m*.

96/14. *on Affrice*. OH IV. x. 3 does not name Gaius Junius' destination.

96/16. *Hannibal*. OH IV. x. 4 refers merely to *classis Punica*.

96/18. *on Africe*. The most charitable interpretation of this is 'against the Africans', i.e. the Carthaginians.

96/19. *oþer cneow*. According to OH IV. x. 5, Lutatius was wounded in the thigh, 'transfixo femore'.

96/19–20. *þæs . . . firde*. Or. has here run together two quite separate events. OH IV. x. 6 'orta luce prior' refers not to the day after the battle of Drepana but to the day after the Roman and Carthaginian fleets arrived at the Aegates Islands. Enough time had elapsed between the two occasions for Hanno to travel 'cum quadringentis nauibus magnisque copiis ad Siciliam'.

96/21. *þeh . . . wære*. Or.'s addition, based on the erroneous supposition that this encounter took place on the day after Lutatius was wounded.

96/21–2. *him . . . byrg.* OH IV. x. 8 'Lutatius deinde ad Erycinam ciuitatem, quam Poeni tenebant, uenit.' Hanno had already fled to Africa: see OH IV. x. 7. For *ad Erycinam* the 'related' MSS closest to Or. have the reading *ad decinam*; in one MS, the word *ad* is written above the letters *de*, giving the impression that it is intended as a correction for them.

96/25. *þæt hie . . . Sardiniam.* Cf. OH IV. xi. 2 'ut Sicilia Sardiniaque decederent'.

96/26. *ælce geare.* According to OH IV. xi. 2, the money was to be paid 'aequis pensionibus per annos uiginti'.

96/29–30. *þa . . . siþþan.* OH IV. xi. 6 puts the flood before the fire, though first referring to 'diuersae ignium aquarumque clades'.

96/31. *þæra monna ondliefene.* Or.'s addition. Cf. OH IV. xi. 8 where it is the *fire* that is said to have destroyed 'tantum opum . . . quantum plurimae . . . uictoriae conferre non possent'.

97/1. *Titus . . . Gaius.* OH IV. xi. 10 'T. Sempronio Graccho C. Valerio Falcone', with *T.* and *C.* expanded to *Tito* and *Gaio* in many MSS. From this point pairs of *tria nomina* not clearly separated in OH or the translator's exemplar appear not only as sets of three *duo nomina* (see 95/12–13, Commentary) but also as pairs of *duo nomina*, as here, with the last two names lopped off and the remainder wrongly divided. It is possible that this is the result of 'correction' by a reviser, who deleted the name of the 'third' consul on grounds of historical inaccuracy, but overlooked a number of instances.

97/3. *xii m.* OH IV. xi. 10 *quindecim milia,* 'related' MSS including Ricc. 627 *xii m.*

97/4–5. *Gallie . . . Longbeardas.* OH IV. xii. 1 *Galli Cisalpini.* The Langobards, who were a Germanic people, did not invade Italy until A.D. 568. However, the Lombard kingdom in the ninth century coincided in part with *Gallia Cisalpina.*

97/6–7. *on . . . geare.* OH IV. xii. 1 *secundo,* i.e. *conflictu.*

97/7. *iiii m.* OH IV. xii. 1 *quattuordecim,* 'related' MSS, including Ricc. 627 and Vienna 366, *iiii m.*

97/10–11. *hie . . . wæron.* Or.'s addition, possibly inspired by OH IV. xii. 1 'aduersum [Gallos] uaria sorte bellatum est.'

97/12. *Titus . . . Bubulcus.* OH IV. xii. 2 'T. Manlio Torquato C. Atilio Bubulco', with *T.* and *C.* expanded to *Tito* and *Gaio* in the MSS. See 95/12–13, Commentary.

97/17. *æt . . . cirre.* See also 97/19 'æt þæm feorðan cirre'. OH IV. xii. 3 says that the ten leading men twice failed in their mission but that they finally obtained peace through the eloquence of Hanno.

97/19–20. *heora . . . þegn.* OH IV. xii. 3 'minimi hominis inter legatos'. There is no suggestion that Hanno went alone.

97/25–6. *l . . . hundum.* OH IV. xii. 7 *ccccxl,* 'related' MSS, including Ricc. 627 and Vienna 366 *cccccl.*

97/29. *eow Romanum.* Or.'s addition. For the construction *hu þyncð eow hu* see above, 31/19–21, Commentary.

97/29–98/1. *hwæþer . . . ontydre.* A rewriting of OH IV. xii. 8, 'stilicidium istud olei in medium magnae flammae cadens extinxit fomitem tanti ignis an aluit?'

98/3. *Cartaina cynig.* OH IV. xiii. 1 *dux Carthaginiensium.* See 91/27, Commentary. OH here begins a new section, with the formula 'Anno ab Vrbe condita'. Or. omits the formula and thus has no new chapter.

98/6. *On ðæm geare.* OH IV. xiii. 2 'Sequenti anno'.

98/7. *Fuluius . . . consul.* For once two consuls have been made into one: cf. OH IV. xiii. 2 'Fuluio Postumioque consulibus'. Or.'s error may have resulted from a misread, misinterpreted or miscopied abbreviation of *consulibus,* an obvious candidate being *consul.*

98/7–8. *fela . . . healfe.* Cf. OH IV. xiii. 2 'multis oppidis populisque deletis', referring to the Illyrians only.

98/10. *swelce niwe . . . gedydan.* Cf. OH IV. xiii. 3 'consuetudinem priscae superstitionis egressi'.

98/10–12. *þa . . . Pene.* Or.'s addition. See 97/26–8 and, for references to attacks by men from both Cisalpine and Further Gaul, OH IV. xiii. 5.

98/21–2. *þæt . . . hæfdon.* Cf. OH IV. xiii. 8–9 'octingenta milia Romanorum, nec saltem tanta quanta eos terrere debuit, caesa sui parte fugerunt . . . quod ideo ignominiosius turpiusque est, tam paucis amissis tanta agmina diffugisse, quia se in aliis uictoriis non uiribus animorum praeualuisse sed bellorum prouentibus prodiderunt.'

98/23. *ix m.* OH IV. xiii. 10 *quadraginta milia.*

98/24. *þæs . . . geare.* OH IV. xiii. 11 'Sequenti anno'. Or.'s reckoning depends on the error in 98/6, for which see Commentary.

98/26. *iii m.* OH IV. xiii. 11 'uiginti tria milia'.

98/26. *vi m.* OH IV. xiii. 11 *quinque milia*; 'related' MSS, including Vienna 366, *vi milia.*

98/28. *Piceno þæm wuda.* OH IV. xiii. 12 *in Piceno.* Does Or.'s description of Picenum as *wudu* reflect knowledge that in classical times this province was famed for its apples and olives? See, e.g., Horace, *Sermonum* II. 3. 272 and 4. 70, Juvenal, *Satires* I. xi. 74 and Pliny XV. iii. 16.

98/28. *an wielle weol blode.* OH IV. xiii. 12 merely says that 'flumen sanguine effluxit'. For a portent similar to that described by Or. see Livy XXII. i. 10.

98/28–9. *on Tracio þæm londe.* OH IV. xiii. 12 *apud Tuscos*; cf. the 'related' MS Vienna 366 *apud Taccos.* Could the intrusive *r* be derived from the alternative form *Etruscos?* Cf. 87/16, where OH IV. v. 3 *Etruscorum* is rendered *Thrusci,* also 75/2 *Ðrysci.*

98/29–30. *on Ariminio . . . dæg.* OH IV. xiii. 12 'Arimini nocte multa lucem claram obfulsisse ac tres lunas distantibus caeli regionibus exortas apparuisse'. See Julius Honorius, p. 35, *Ariminum oppidum.* Has the translator confused *offulgeo*, 'shine', with *offulcio*, 'stop up', or was the manuscript he used corrupt at this point? See, e.g., the reading of the 'related' MS Vienna 366, 'Arimini nocte *ultra* lucem claram obfulsisse', which could conceivably have been taken to refer to night lasting beyond normal sunrise.

99/2. *vii m.* OH IV. xiii. 14 *nouem milia*.

99/3. *Gælle.* OH IV. xiii. 15 *Gaesatorum*. Cf. OH IV. xiii. 5 'Gaesatorum, quod nomen non gentis sed mercennariorum Gallorum est'.

99/9–10. *v . . . xxxiii.* OH IV. xiv. 1 *dxxxiiii*, 'related' MSS, including Vienna 366, *dxxxiii*.

99/10. *Pena cyning.* OH IV. xiv. 1 *Poenorum imperator*.

99/12. *he . . . acwealde.* OH IV. xiv. 1 merely states that the townsfolk endured the tortures of hunger.

99/13–14. *hie firmetton . . . forleten.* Or.'s addition. That the Roman ambassadors were sent to request the end of hostilities against Saguntum is stated by Livy XXI. x, Eutropius III. vii, and Florus I. xxii. 5.

99/15 *he . . . nolde.* I tentatively interpret this as 'he himself was not prepared to see them', with *onseon* governing the genitive. However, there are other possibilities which cannot be ruled out: (i) we have here a rare instance of preposition *on* governing the genitive; (ii) *self* is (again exceptionally) a noun in the idiomatic singular with dependent genitive *heora*, acting as object of *onseon*. I am indebted to Dr. Bruce Mitchell for his most helpful comments on this construction, though for reasons of space I have been able to do no more than summarize his conclusions.

99/18. *þæt . . . freond.* Possibly no more than an expansion of OH IV. xiv. 3 'odio Romani nominis . . . iurauerat'. See, however, Hannibal's words as reported by Cornelius Nepos, XXIII *Hannibal* ii. 4: 'Pater meus . . . iurare iussit numquam me in amicitia cum Romanis fore.'

99/19. *Publius Cornelius . . . Longus.* OH IV. xiv. 3 'P. Cornelio Scipione et P. Sempronio Longo', with *P* expanded to *Publio* in many MSS. The 'related' MS Vienna 366 inserts *et* before *Sempronio Longo*.

99/20–1. *þa beorgas . . . Spaneum.* OH IV. xiv. 3 *Pyrenaeos montes*. The translator could have known of the location of the Pyrenees from OH I. ii. 73, where they are said to be east of Hispania citerior. However, the wording calls to mind comments such as Servius, *Georgics*, II. 374 'inter Gallias et Hispanias posito', and Lucan scholia, ed. Usener I. 689 'Pirineus mons qui Galliam ab Hispaniis dividit'. See also Isidore, *Etymologies* XIV. viii. 15 and the gloss to this passage in MS Stuttgart HB 410 'pyreneos terminos hispanie et gallie'.

99/24. *ofer munt Iof.* Or.'s addition. For other instances of this name in Old English see, e.g., *Alfred's Boethius*, Metre i. 8 and 14 *muntgiop* and Wright–Wülcker 355, 3, *munt iofes clifu*, glossing *Alpes*. The Latin equivalent, *mons Iovis*, again applied to part of the Alps, occurs in a number of texts, both classical and medieval. According to Livy, Hannibal's route over the Alps was a matter of controversy; however, Mela records a tradition linking it with *mons Iovis*: see Mela II. vi. 89, 'tum mons Iovis, cuius partem occidenti adversam, eminentia cautium quae inter exigua spatia ut gradus subinde consurgunt, Scalas Hannibalis adpellant'. See also the MS of OH, Stuttgart HB 410, where the *invias rupes* of this passage, OH IV. xiv. 4, is glossed *montis iovis*.

99/24–6. *Swa . . . heawan.* OH IV. xiv. 4 'inuias rupes igni ferroque rescindit.'

99/27. *an m.* OH IV. xiv. 5 *centum milibus.*

99/29–30. *Ticenan þære ie.* OH IV. xiv. 6 *Ticinum.* That the river, not the town of that name, was the site of the battle is information to be found in Valerius Maximus V. iv. 2 and Livy XXI. xxxix. 10.

100/1. *mid . . . fealh.* Or.'s addition. According to Livy XXI. xlvi. 7, the consul was rescued *intercursu . . . filii*, while Valerius Maximus V. iv. 2 says that the boy saved him *intercessu suo.*

100/4. *gefliemed.* OH IV. xiv. 7 merely says that they were *superati.*

100/6. *begen þa consulas.* OH IV. xiv. 7 refers only to Sempronius as involved here.

100/7. *gefliemed.* Or.'s addition. OH IV. xiv. 7 says that Sempronius 'paene solus evasit'.

100/9. *ofer Bardan þone beorg.* OH IV. xiv. 8 'in summo Appennino'. For *Mons Bardonis* see Steinmeyer and Sievers IV. 352 'Appenninicolę: bardtenberc'. In the thirteenth century Matthew Paris includes *Munt Bardun* in his itinerary to Apulia (see Miller, *Mappaemundi* III, 88), while Otto of Freising, *Gesta Friderici*, ed. G. Waitz (Hanover, 1884), II. xiii refers to 'Apenninum, qui modo mutato nomine mons Bardonis uulgo dicitur'. See also Servius, *Aen.* I. i, MS V² 'Rubiconem id est montem bardonem', cited in editio Harvardiana II (1946).

100/11. *horsa.* OH IV. xiv. 8 *iumenta.*

100/11. *þa elpendas . . . anum.* OH IV. xiv. 8 'elephanti paene omnes'. Cf. OH IV. xv. 3, where Hannibal is subsequently described as 'uni elephanto, qui solus superfuerat, supersedens'.

100/12. *uneaðe.* OH IV. xiv. 8 in fact claims that a large number of men died.

100/13–17. *he wiste . . . cile.* OH IV. xv. 2 merely says that Hannibal knew that Flaminius was alone in his camp, and 'quo celerius imparatum obrueret primo uere progressus arripuit propiorem sed palustrem uiam'. For a reference to an earlier attempt by Hannibal to cross the Apennines, which failed because of the cold, see Livy XXII. i. 1.

100/17–24. *Mid . . . hæfde.* An amplification of OH IV. xv. 4–5, 'uero proximus castris Flaminii consulis fuit, uastatione circumiacentium locorum Flaminium in bellum excitauit. haec pugna ad Trasumennum lacum facta est. ubi exercitus Romanus infelicissime arte circumuentus Hannibalis funditus trucidatus est.' The additional details given by Or. appear to be derived from Frontinus II. v. 24, 'Idem ad Trasumennum . . . simulata fuga per angustias ad (*mistakenly read* a?) patentia evasit

ibique castra posuit ac nocte dispositis militibus et per collem, qui
imminebat, et in lateribus angustiarum prima luce . . . aciem direxit.
Flaminius velut fugientem insequens (cf. 100/22–3 *buton truman*) cum
angustias esset ingressus, non ante providit insidias, quam simul a fronte,
lateribus, tergo circumfusus ad internecionem cum exercitu caederetur.'
See also Livy XXII. iv.

100/25. *vi.* OH IV. xv. 5 *sex milia*.

100/27. *Æfter þæm*. Or.'s addition. The corresponding passage in OH
IV. xiv. 9 precedes the account of the battle of Trasimene, the events
described in it actually occurring two years before the battle.

100/35–6. *ealle . . . blodege*. OH IV. xv. 1 does not specify the number of
ears when it reports 'apud Antium metentibus cruentas spicas in corbem
decidisse'.

101/2–3. *Lucius . . . Uarra*. OH. IV. xvi. 1 'L. Aemilius Paulus et
P. Terentius Varro', with *L* and *P* expanded to *Lucius* and *Publius* in
many MSS.

101/4–13. *Ac . . . gefeohte*. An expansion of OH IV. xvi. 1 'inpatientia
Varronis consulis infelicissime apud Cannas Apuliae uicum omnes paene
Romanae spei uires perdiderunt.' The source of the additional details in
Or. seems to be Valerius Maximus VII. 4, ext. 2, where Hannibal is said
to have ordered part of his forces to simulate flight in the middle of the
battle, 'quam cum a reliquo exercitu abrupta legio Romana sequeretur,
trucidandam eam ab his, quos in insidiis collocaverat, curavit'. For other
stratagems employed in the battle, see Livy XXII. xlviii and Frontinus
II. v. 27.

101/11. *ealle þa consulas*. Or.'s addition. See 101/13–14, Commentary.

101/11–13. *on Romanum . . . gefeohte*. Cf. OH IV. xvi. 2 'nullo tamen
Punico bello Romani adeo ad extrema internecionis adducti sunt.'

101/13–14. *þara consula . . . gefeng*. OH IV. xvi. 3 'periit enim in eo
consul Aemilius Paulus . . . Varro consul . . . Venusium fugit.' For the
splitting of the two consuls of the year into three, with the names Aemilius
and Paulus attached to two different men, see 101/2–3, Commentary. OH
also refers to the death of 'consulares aut praetorii uiri uiginti', a statement
which may have contributed to the translator's belief that a number of
consuls were involved.

101/17–20. *Be . . . wære*. Or.'s addition. Under the Republic, the gold ring
was the badge of the *equites*. See Livy XXIII. xii. 2 'neminem nisi
equitem, atque eorum ipsorum primores, id gerere insigne', also Florus
I. 22 and Augustine, *Civ. Dei* III. xix.

101/22. *þe . . . wæs*. Or.'s addition. According to Livy XXII. liii. 5,
Celius was merely one of the 'nobiles iuvenes'.

101/25. *þara cempena ieldest*. OH IV. xvi. 6 'tribunus tunc militum, idem
qui post Africanus'.

101/26–31. *swor . . . libban*. OH IV. xvi. 6 merely says that he forced the young man to swear that he would maintain the defence of his country, 'potius pro patriae defensione in sua uerba iurare'. That Scipio threatened with death any one who did not take the oath is a feature of the accounts of Valerius Maximus V. vi. 7, Frontinus IV. vii. 39 and Livy XXII. liii. That he himself took the oath is reported by Frontinus, Livy, and Silius Italicus X. 432 f.

101/32–102/1. *tictator . . . consulas.* OH IV. xvi. 7 *dictatorum.* See 41/13–14.

102/1–2. *He . . . seofontienewintre.* This statement is the result of the misconstruing of OH IV. xvi. 7, 'Decium Iunium . . . qui dilectu habito ab annis decem et septem immaturae inordinataeque militiae quattuor legiones undecumque contraxit'. It would not seem quite so strange to the Anglo-Saxons as it does to us: as Professor Potter points out (1952–3), p. 422), King Alfred became *secundarius* to his brother at the age of 17.

102/2. *Scipian . . . consule.* Or.'s addition, without basis in fact.

102/2. *ealle þa men.* OH IV. xvi. 8 limits it to those 'spectati roboris ac uoluntatis'.

102/3–4. *on þæt gerad . . . gelæsten.* They had to take the military oath, OH IV. xvi. 8 *sacramento militiae.*

102/7–8. *ealle . . . hæfdon.* OH IV. xvi. 9 'homines quicumque sceleribus ac debitis obnoxii'.

102/12–13. *þa gefor . . . gecirdon.* Or.'s addition. This could be based on two statements in OH: see IV. xvi. 10, 'Campania uero uel potius omnis Italia ad Hannibalem . . . defecit', and IV. xvii. 2, 'Hannibal de Campania mouit', with Campania identified with the ninth-century duchy of Beneventum as in the Ravenna Geographer, 248, 11–13, 'ab antiquis dicitur Campania, quae nunc Beneventanorum dicitur patria'. Alternatively, it could show knowledge of Livy XXIII. i. 1, where it is said that after the battle of Cannae Hannibal moved into Samnium. Beneventum was in Samnium: see Eutropius II. xvi, Regino of Prüm, s.a. 871, and the (inaccurate) comment by Dunchad, 78, 15, *Samius: Beneventanus.* For an earlier reference to Beneventum, see Or. 58/8, Commentary.

102/14. *feower legian.* Or.'s addition.

102/15. *þone consul.* OH IV. xvi. 11 *praetor.* Livy XXIII. xxiv describes Lucius Postumius as consul-elect; when he was defeated he had with him two Roman legions and a number of allied troops.

102/15–16. *þa Gallie . . . hæt.* OH IV. xvi. 11 *Gallos.* See 97/4–5, Commentary.

102/17. *gesetton . . . consule.* According to OH IV. xvi. 12, he was made *proconsule*, a word habitually rendered by *consul* in Or. See Isidore, *Etymologies* IX. iii. 8.

102/18. *se . . . gefera.* Or.'s addition. Did the translator or a hypothetical commentator have access to the information, given by Livy XXII. lvii, that after the defeat at Cannae Claudius Marcellus hastened to join the survivors at Canusium, the place where (again according to Livy) Scipio had made his stand against the proposals of Caecilius Metellus? Or did the translator misunderstand a comment drawing attention to similarities between Scipio and Marcellus as expressed by OH IV. xvi. 7, 'Romani ad spem uitae quasi ab inferis respirare ausi' (a statement immediately following the account of Scipio's intervention), and IV. xvi. 12, 'Claudius Marcellus . . . primus . . . post tantas reipublicae ruinas spem fecit Hannibalem posse superari'?

102/18–20. *He . . . gefliemde.* OH IV. xvi. 12 merely states that Claudius Marcellus 'Hannibalis exercitum proelio fudit'. This happened near Nola in 216 B.C. According to Frontinus II. iv. 8 and Livy XXIII. xvi. 8, Marcellus used campfollowers to give the appearance of a large force, a stratagem which Frontinus II. iv. 6 attributes also to another Marcellus, an officer of Marius engaged against the Teutons in 102 B.C. This second Marcellus was sent 'cum parva manu equitum peditumque nocte post terga hostium' and it may well be that these details are the source of Or.'s account of the tactics employed by the first Marcellus. See further Introduction, p. lxii.

102/24–5. *þa twegen . . . gebroðor.* OH IV. xvi. 13 *Scipiones,* i.e. P. Cornelius Scipio and Cn. Cornelius Scipio Calvus. See below, 104/18–22.

102/26. *Hasterbale . . . fædran.* OH IV. xvi. 13 'Hasdrubalem Poenorum imperatorem'. Hasdrubal Barca was Hannibal's younger brother and, although Or. claims that the Romans crushed him in this battle (OH *oppresserunt*), he in fact survived until 207 B.C. See below, 105/28–34. Could Or.'s incorrect identification—prompted by its erroneous interpretation of *oppresserunt*—be due to the fact that of the various Carthaginians named Hasdrubal one was brother of Hannibal and son of a man called Hamilcar (see, e.g., OH IV. xiv. 3 and IV. xvi. 20), while another was brother of a man called Hamilcar (see Justinus XIX. i. 1)? For *oppresserunt* 'killed' see below, 143/6 and Commentary.

102/27. *xxx m.* OH IV. xvi. 13 *xxxv milia.*

102/29. *se consul.* OH IV. xvi. 16 *centurio.*

102/31–3. *Æfter . . . geslagen.* This corresponds to OH IV. xvi. 17, where, however, the general is named as *Cn. Fuluius praetor.* The name Sempronius Gracchus comes from OH IV. xvi. 15, where it occurs in a reference to another incident, omitted by Or.

102/34–103/7. *Hu . . . hæfdon.* A rewriting of OH IV. xvi. 18–21, omitting Orosius' allusions to the Romans' wretchedness and depravity. For the themes of better times and better thegns see OH IV. xvi. 21, 'et tamen fortis in alterutrum desperatio in meliora profecit, nam in his omnibus desperando pugnarunt, pugnando uicerunt. ex quo euidenter ostenditur non tempora tunc fuisse tranquilliora otiis, sed homines miseriis fortiores', and Introduction, p. xcix.

103/2. *on Capadotia.* OH IV. xvi. 20 'in Sardinia contra Sardos', 'related' MS Vienna 366, 'in Sardia contra Sardinos'.

103/9. *Marcellus Claudius.* OH IV. xvii. 1 *Claudius Marcellus.*

103/9. *for . . . sciphere.* Or.'s addition, presumably based on the knowledge that Sicily was an island.

103/18–19. *cwædon . . . dorsten.* Or.'s addition, apparently prompted by OH IV. xvii. 3, 'cum senatu populoque diuersis curis trepido matronae quoque amentes pauore per propugnacula currerent et conuehere in muros saxa *primaeque pro muris pugnare gestirent*'.

103/19. *þæs on mergen.* Or.'s addition and possibly a contextual guess; see, however, Livy XXVI. xi. 1, *postero die*, also Silius Italicus, *Punica* XII 558.

103/21–3. *Ac . . . dorsten.* OH IV. xvii. 4 merely says that 'consules . . . non detrectauere pugnam'. See 103/18–19 and Commentary.

103/23. *butan þæm geate.* According to OH IV. xvii. 5, the battle-lines were drawn up in sight of Rome. See also Livy XXVI. x.

103/24–5. *þæt . . . gewealdan.* Cf. OH IV. xvii. 5 'uix armis retentis'.

103/27–9. *ðeh . . . geþafode.* A rewriting of OH IV. xvii. 7, 'tunc conuersus in religionem Hannibal dixisse fertur, potiundae sibi Romae modo uoluntatem non dari, modo potestatem.'

103/30. *Gesecgað me nu, Romane.* OH IV. xvii. 8 'Respondeant nunc mihi obtrectatores ueri Dei.'

103/30–104/3. *hwonne . . . bið.* Orosius' question is very different: was it Roman bravery or Divine compassion that prevented Hannibal from taking Rome? However, see IV. xvii. 10, with its story of a drought, when Gentiles and Christians alternately prayed for rain and only the latter's prayers were answered. For the theme of marked improvement after Christ's birth see Introduction, p. xciv.

104/9. *þa wæron gebroðor.* Or.'s addition. See below, 104/18–22.

104/10. *Hasterbale, Pena cyninge.* OH IV. xvii. 12 'a fratre Hasdrubalis'. Cf. Eutropius III. xiv. 2 'a fratre Hasdrubale'. Did the translator overlook the genitive inflection of OH *Hasdrubalis*, or did he have knowledge of the (correct) variant given by Eutropius?

104/11. *se consul.* OH IV. xvii. 12 *proconsule.* See 102/17, Commentary.

104/11–12. *ealle . . . men.* OH IV. xvii. 12 *senatum omnem.*

104/13–14. *for þon . . . beon.* Or.'s addition, possibly prompted by OH IV. xvi. 10 'Campania . . . ad Hannibalem . . . defecit'. See also Livy XXIII. vii.

104/17–18. *þa . . . gefaran.* OH IV. xvii. 13 'omnibus incusso pauore cunctantibus'. See also Livy XXVI. xviii, where it is said that a murmur arose that no one dared accept the Spanish command.

104/19. *se wæs cniht.* According to OH IV. xviii. 1, Scipio (already mentioned in OH IV. xvi. 6, Or. 101/24) was 24 years old at the time.

104/21–3. *he þæt færelt . . . hæle.* For Scipio's motives see OH IV. xviii. 1. OH does not suggest that he concealed them from the senate.

104/23. *Romane . . . geornfulle.* OH IV. xvii. 13–14 does not link the raising of money (through gifts on the part of the senators, not of all the Romans) with Scipio's Spanish campaign. Livy XXVI. xxxv indeed describes it as for the defence of Sicily and Italy.

104/28. *hoppan*. OH IV. xvii. 14 *bullas*, Vienna 366 *bollas*, with *u* written above *o*. The only other instance of the word *hoppe* recorded by BT occurs in the Laws of Edgar, where it refers to an object attached to a dog: *hundes hoppe*. A twelfth-century Latin version renders this *collarium canis*. Latin *bulla*, on the other hand, had as its general meaning something round, but was used especially of an amulet worn upon the neck by noble youths or hung upon the forehead of favourite animals. According to Isidore, *Etymologies* XIX. xxxi. 11, 'bullae a viris geruntur' and are so called 'quod similes sint rotunditate bullis quae in aqua vento inflantur'. However, if the translator chanced to refer to some of the other commentaries current in the early Middle Ages, he would have had a choice of interpretations. Thus, Paulus Diaconus, quoting Festus, described the *bulla aurea* as 'insigne . . . puerorum praetextatorum quae dependebat eis a pectore' (see Festus, p. 136). The Corpus Glossary, on the other hand, has three entries for the word *bulla*: B 169 'Bollas : ornamenta cinguli' (identified by Lindsay as originating from a gloss on this passage of Orosius), B 197 'Bulla: sigl' (an Old English word which is subsequently used, with *hringe*, to gloss *fibula*; see FI 170), and B 205 'Bullae: ornamenta regalium camellorum' (which Lindsay derives from the Abolita gloss 'Bullae: ornamenta regalium puerorum vel equorum vel camelorum' and which seems to have as its ultimate source the Vulgate, Judges 8:21 'bullas quibus colla regalium camelorum decorari solent'). On the evidence of these and related entries, it seems possible that the translator thought of the *bulla* not as an amulet but as some sort of collar.

104/29–30. *ðære niwan . . . hætt*. OH IV. xviii. 1 *Carthaginem Nouam*, i.e. Carthagena. Or.'s substitution of Corduba may have been inspired by the fact that while Carthagena was one of the most important cities in Spain in antiquity, Córdoba was the capital of the Spanish Caliphate in the ninth century, and thus the most important city in that part of Spain once held by the Carthaginians.

104/30–105/5. *he besætt . . . dælan*. OH IV. xviii. 1 'primo impetu Carthaginem Nouam cepit, ubi stipendia maxima, praesidia ualida, copiae auri argentique magnae Poenorum habebantur; ibi etiam Magonem fratrem Hannibalis captum cum ceteris Romam misit.' According to Livy XXVI. xlii f., Scipio made preparations for a siege, but succeeded in storming the town at the first attempt, while Florus I. xxii. 39 claims that it was captured on the very day the siege began. For the element of surprise, see Frontinus III. ix. 1, 'ad muros urbis accessit et cedente stagno, qua non exspectatur, inrupit', also Livy XXVI. xlvi. Neither of these texts describes what happened to the booty. However, Livy XXX. xliv, with reference to the end of the war, says that Scipio sent 133,000 pounds weight of silver to the treasury and distributed 400 asses apiece to his soldiers.

105/2–3. *monege . . . witena.* OH IV. xviii. 1 *ceteris.* According to Livy
XXVI. li, fifteen senators were sent to Rome with Mago.

105/10. *pone consul.* OH IV. xviii. 3 describes Cn. Fulvius as proconsul.

105/10. *eahta m.* OH IV. xviii. 3 *xvii milia.*

105/14. *for mid sciphere.* Or.'s addition. Livy XXVII. xv says that Fabius
Maximus *marched* to Tarentum, though he did make use of ships when
he got there.

105/15–16. *swa* (1) . . . *wæron.* Or.'s addition. According to Livy XXVII.
xii, Fabius Maximus urged his colleagues Marcellus and Fulvius to keep
Hannibal occupied elsewhere and then, having hidden himself on the
east side of Tarentum, attacked the city at first watch (*vigilia prima*) and
took it by surprise (*ibid.* xv–xvi).

105/17. *xxx m mid him.* Cf. OH IV. xviii. 5 'xxx milia hominum
captiuorum uendidit'.

105/18–20. *Hannibal . . . mid him.* OH IV. xviii. 6 merely says that
Claudius Marcellus 'ab Hannibale cum exercitu occisus est'. However,
according to Livy XXVII. xxvii, Hannibal sent some squadrons of
Numidian cavalry to conceal themselves deep in the woods near
Marcellus' camp, and when the consul left the camp to reconnoitre he
fell into Hannibal's trap.

105/20–1. *Hasterbal . . . broðor.* OH IV. xviii. 7 'Poenorum ducem Hasdrubalem'. See below, 105/28, OH IV. xviii. 9 'Hasdrubal Hannibalis
frater', and, for a reference to another brother, 104/30.

105/22–5. *Swa . . . sealde.* Apparently based on a misunderstanding of OH
IV. xviii. 7, 'Afris sub corona uenditis, sine pretio dimisit Hispanos'.
Potter (1952–3), p. 423, takes the misunderstanding to be of the phrase
sub corona vendere; however, see 68/2, OH III. xvi. 2, where it is obviously
understood. A more likely explanation is that the translator was puzzled
by the phrase *sine pretio*, and assumed that this meant that Scipio did not
keep the money.

105/29–30. *þa . . . Hannibal.* Cf. OH IV. xviii. 9 'ab exercitu Romano
ignorante Hannibale praeuentus'.

105/31. *ær . . . fluge.* Or.'s addition.

105/34. *liii m.* OH IV. xviii. 14 *l et viii milia;* 'related' MS Selden B 16
liii m.

105/34. *v m.* OH IV. xviii. 14 *v̄ cccc,* 'related' MSS of Group C *v m.*

106/3–4. *þa . . . Romanum.* Or.'s addition. Does this reflect the confession
attributed to Hannibal by Livy XXVII. li. 12 that he recognized
fortunam Carthaginis? or, in the words of Florus I. xxii. 53, ' "agnosco",
inquit, "infelicitatem Carthaginis." Haec fuit illius uiri non sine praesagio
quodam fati imminentis prima confessio'?

106/7–8. *Romanum . . . land.* Or.'s addition. Livy XXVIII. xl–xlv states
that Scipio urged the senate to allow him to go himself.

106/9–11. *raðe . . . wearð*. OH IV. xviii. 17 merely states that 'Hannonem Hamilcaris filium, ducem Poenorum, interfecit'. According to Livy XXIX. xxxiv, Hanno was lured out of the town of Salaeca by Masinissa and his troops, and then attacked by the Roman cavalry that had been concealed in the hills.

106/13–17. *Æfter . . . habban*. OH IV. xviii. 18 suggests that it was Scipio who was the aggressor, attacking 'hiberna Poenorum atque alia Numidarum quae utraque haud procul ab Vtica erant'.

106/17–27. *Ac . . . fleonde*. All that OH IV. xviii. 18–19 says of the battle of Utica is that Scipio 'hiberna . . . nocte concubia fecit incendi. Poeni trepidi cum casu accidisse ignem putarent, inermes ad extinguendum concurrerunt: quare facile ab armatis oppressi sunt.' Or.'s additional details here seem to be derived ultimately from Livy or Frontinus. According to Livy XXX. iv–vi, Scipio used spies to learn about the disposition of outposts and sentries. He then sent some of his men to set Syphax' camp on fire. The fire spread swiftly, and the troops who rushed out to extinguish it unarmed encountered an armed enemy. The Carthaginians from the other camp rushed over to help and ran straight into the Roman column. Frontinus too tells of spies sent to Syphax' camp (I. ii. 1) and of the setting fire to that camp which drew the unsuspecting Carthaginians from the other camp to their aid (II. v. 29).

106/25–7. *hie Scipia . . . fleonde*. Or.'s addition.

106/27–8. *hiera . . . byrg*. Though both *duces* escaped, only Hasdrubal imperator is said by OH IV. xviii. 20 to have made for Carthage. Livy XXX. vii confirms that they separated.

106/29–32. *ongean . . . gefeng*. A distortion of OH IV. xviii. 20–1, 'iterum cum Scipione congressi sunt, uictique fugerunt. Syphacem fugientem Laelius et Masinissa ceperunt, cetera multitudo Cirtam confugit, quam Masinissa oppugnatam in deditionem recepit.' Cirta was a city of Numidia about 48 miles from the sea; the 'related' MS Vienna 366, however, has the reading *Certam*, and such a reading seems to underlie Or.'s identification of the place with Crete.

106/32. *hiera ofer cyning*. According to Livy and other Latin sources, Syphax was indeed a king, but of the Numidians not the Carthaginians.

106/33. *to Rome . . . sended*. OH IV. xviii. 21 *perducendum*, 'related' MSS *perducendum Romam*.

106/34–5. *On . . . bemætan*. Cf. OH IV. xix. 1 'fessis Carthaginiensibus'.

107/3. *on þæm . . . com*. Or.'s addition, perhaps based on OH IV. xviii. 15 'anno tertio decimo quam in Italiam uenerat refugit in Bruttios'. In fact Hannibal had been away for 16 years: see Livy XXX. xxviii. 1.

107/7–9. *ane . . . worhte*. OH IV. xix. 1 'sepulchrum dirutum'. Could the translator have known of a description of the pyramids such as Porphyrio *Carm*. III. 30. 2, '*Pyramides* regum Aegyptiorum sepulcra sunt adeo ingenti mole saxorum in mediis harenis Aegypti structa'?

107/9–10. *þa . . . ondwyrdes*. OH IV. xix. 1 'abominatus dictum'. *Abominor* has two meanings: 'to deprecate something as an ill omen' and 'to hate'. Or.'s translation seems to hint at both of these meanings.

107/15–16. *hiera . . . gespræcan.* OH IV. xix. 2 refers merely to a *conloquium*. However, according to Livy XXX. xxx. 1, the two men met exactly half-way between the opposing ranks of armed men, each attended by an interpreter.

107/17. *raþe þæs.* OH IV. xix. 3 *diu.* See 29/18, Commentary.

107/18–19. *feowera sum.* OH IV. xix. 3 'quattuor equitibus'. Potter, (1952–3), p. 424, suggests that an original *iv* in an underlying Latin MS was misread or miscopied as *iii.* However, see 15/5, Commentary.

107/19. *Aþrametum þæm fæstenne.* OH IV. xix. 3 *Hadrumetum.*

107/19–21. *þa . . . wilnaden.* OH IV. xix. 4 makes Hannibal the instigator of the peace moves: 'Carthaginem . . . uenit consultantique senatui nullam esse residuam spem nisi in petenda pace persuasit.' However, Cornelius Nepos, XXIII. *Hannibal* vii. 1, says that the Carthaginians made peace while Hannibal was at Hadrumetum mustering a new army.

107/21–2. *Gaius . . . Publius.* OH IV. xix. 5 'C. Cornelio Lentulo P. Aelio Paeto', with *C* and *P* expanded to *Gaio* and *Publio* in many MSS. For the lopping off of the last two names, see 97/1, Commentary.

107/23–5. *on þæt gerad . . . aliefden.* Or.'s addition here sounds suspiciously like the terms of the treaty made at the end of the First Punic War; see 96/24–6. However, according to Livy XXX. xxxvii. 2, part of the peace terms was that the Carthaginians were to hold the territories which they had held before the war (see the earlier suggestion, XXX. xvi. 10, that 'insulis omnibus quae inter Italiam atque Africam sint decedant'), and were to pay out 10,000 silver talents in equal payments over 50 years. Sicily and Sardinia were in fact never conquered by the Carthaginians in this war.

107/26. *up ateon.* OH IV. xix. 5 'in altum productae'.

107/28. *se mæra . . . scop.* OH IV. xix. 6 'comicus, ex nobilibus Carthaginiensium captiuis'. Orosius has confused the playwright with a senator named by Livy as Quintus Terentius Culleo. *Comicus* is rendered by *scop* also in Old English glossaries; see, e.g., Wright–Wülcker 206, 17 and 283, 14.

107/28–31. *bær . . . freodom.* OH IV. ix. 6 describes Terentius as *pilleatus*, 'quod insigne indultae sibi libertatis fuit'.

107/32. *d wintrum* 7 *l.* OH IV. xx. 1 *dxlvi.*

108/1. *xiiii winter.* OH IV. xx. 1 'annis decem et septem'. Presumably an underlying MS, either Latin or Old English, had *uii* for *septem* and this was misread as *iiii.*

108/7–8. *Philippus, Mæcedonia cyning.* OH IV. xx. 1 *Philippo.* Cf. IV. xx. 5, where he is described as *regem.*

108/8–9. *Nauiða . . . cyning.* OH IV. xx. 2 describes Nabis, tyrant of Lacedaemon, merely as *dux.*

108/13. *Amilcores . . . broðor*. OH IV. xx. 4 'Hamilcare Poeno duce'. Hannibal had no brother of this name.

108/14–15. *Placentiæ . . . land*. OH IV. xx. 4 'Cremonam Placentiamque', referring to two towns.

108/16. *Claudius Fuluius . . . consul*. OH IV. xx. 4 refers to 'L. Fuluio praetore', with *L* expanded to *Lucio* or *Lutio* in many MSS.

108/17. *Flamineus se consul*. OH IV. xx. 5 'Flamininus proconsule'.

108/20. *vi m*. OH IV. xx. 6 *v milia*, 'related' MSS, including Vienna 366, *vi m*.

108/20–1. *Sempronius se consul*. OH IV. xx. 10 'Sempronius Tuditanus'. This Tuditanus never became consul; however, according to Livy XXXIII. xxv. 9, he was proconsul at the time of his death.

108/22. *on Etruria þæm lande*. OH IV. xx. 11 *in Etruria*.

108/25. *Lucius . . . Marcus*. OH IV. xx. 12 'L. Valerio Flacco M. Porcio Catone', with *L* and *M* expanded to *Lucio* and *Marco* in many MSS. See 97/1, Commentary.

108/28. *Hannibal . . . cyning*. OH IV. xx. 13 *Hannibal*. Although Or. uses the term *cyning* freely of other Carthaginian leaders (usually translating Latin *dux* and *imperator*; see 91/27, Commentary), this is the first time the translator has applied it to Hannibal. According to Cornelius Nepos, XXIII *Hannibal* vii. 4, the Carthaginians made Hannibal king when they recalled him to Carthage in 200 B.C., after the battle of Zama.

108/30–1. *þær . . . hæfde*. OH IV. xx. 13 merely describes Antiochus as 'apud Ephesum . . . cunctantem'. According to Florus I. xxiiii. 6, the king thought it enough just to set the war in motion.

108/31–109/1. *Ac . . . ongan*. In view of OH IV. xx. 13 'mox in bellum inpulit', it is tempting to adopt the reading of the Cotton MS here and omit the negative. See BT under the entries *lange* and *onginnan*. However, it is possible that the translator or his source confused *in bellum* with *imbellem*, 'without war', 'peaceful': see Corpus I 460 *inbellem*: *orwige*.

109/2–3. *þa . . . geandwyrde*. OH IV. xx. 18 merely says that Scipio 'etiam cum Hannibale conloquium familiare habuit'.

109/4–5. *Scipia . . . consule*. Cf. OH IV. xx. 20 'P. Cornelio Scipione M. Acilio Glabrione consulibus'. OH goes on to say that Glabrio defeated Antiochus; Scipio defeated the Boii. This Scipio is not Scipio Africanus but Scipio Nasica.

109/6. *Scipia*. OH IV. xx. 22 'Scipio Africanus'.

109/8–10. *swa . . . wearde*. Cf. OH IV. xx. 22 'quem utrum explorantem an in proelio cepisset incertum est'.

109/11. *Emilius se consul*. OH IV. xx. 23 'L. Aemilius proconsule'.

109/13. *Lucius . . . consul*. OH IV. xx. 24 L. Baebius. According to Livy XXXVII. lvii. 1, he was praetor.

109/13. *Etusci*. OH IV. xx. 24 *Liguribus*. See below, 109/26 'Ligor þæt land', and above, 21/19, where 'Tuscania þæt land' replaces OH I. ii. 103 'Ligusticum sinum' as north of Corsica.

109/15. *on Crece.* OH IV. xx. 25 'de Graecia in Gallograeciam, quae nunc est Galatia'. Could Or.'s alteration be due to a false identification of the Olympus mentioned here with the mountain of that name in Greece?

109/16–17. *on an fæsten.* Or.'s addition. See the reference to *castra* in the passage from Frontinus quoted in 109/19–25, Commentary.

109/19–25. *þa . . . eodon.* Cf. OH IV. xx. 25 'usque ad congressum hostium perruperunt: quadraginta milia Gallograecorum eo proelio interfecta referuntur.' Is Or.'s source here an account of the stratagem used by Q. Fulvius Flaccus against the Cimbri? see Frontinus II. v. 8 'Fuluius imperator Cimbrico bello conlatis cum hoste castris equites suos iussit succedere ad munitiones eorum lacessitisque barbaris simulata fuga regredi. Hoc cum per aliquot dies fecisset, avide insequentibus Cimbris, animadvertit castra eorum solita nudari. Itaque per partem exercitus custodita consuetudine ipse cum expeditis post castra hostium consedit occultus effusisque eis ex more repente adortus et desertum proruit vallum et castra cepit.' Livy XL. xxx–xxxii says that Q. Fulvius Flaccus used this stratagem against the Celtiberians in 181 B.C. In none of these accounts is there any reference to survivors.

109/28. *Marcus . . . Quintus.* OH IV. xx. 27 'M. Claudio Marcello Q. Fabio Labeone', with *M* and *Q* expanded to *Marco* and *Quinto* in many MSS.

110/1. *he his . . . senatos.* OH IV. xx. 28 'uelut Romanis amicum suique proditorem'.

110/4. *Quintius . . . consul.* OH IV. xx. 31 'Q. Fuluius Flaccus praetor'. See Glossary of Proper Names.

110/5. *þa firran Ispanie.* OH IV. xx. 31 'in citeriore Hispania', with *citeriore* written *ceteriore* in a number of MSS including Vienna 366. OH continues with a reference, omitted by Or., to 'Ti. Sempronius Gracchus in Hispania *ulteriore*'.

110/6. *þa . . . consul.* OH IV. xx. 34 'Lepido et Mucio consulibus'. See 98/7, Commentary.

110/6–8. *seo strengeste . . . Hungerre.* OH IV. xx. 34 'Basternarum gens ferocissima'. The Basternae were a Germanic people who appeared on the lower Danube *c.* 200 B.C. and subsequently occupied the country between the eastern Carpathians and the Danube. The Hungarians, or Magyars, were a Finno-Ugrian people, who appeared between the Carpathians and lower Danube at the very end of the ninth century. Both peoples are described as 'gens ferocissima': the Basternae here by Orosius, the Hungarians in the Chronicle of Regino of Prüm, s.a. 889. See further, Introduction, pp. lxxxix–xc.

110/8. *Hie woldon . . . cyninge.* OH IV. xx. 34 'auctore Perseo Philippi filio'. For the description of Perseus as king see OH IV. xx. 39.

110/12. *Plicinius . . . Casius.* OH IV. xx. 36 'P. Licinio Crasso C. Cassio Longino', with *C* expanded to *Gaio* in many MSS, but with *P* retained in a number of the MSS closest to Or. and merged with *Licinio* in the 'name' *Plicinio*.

110/19–20. *raðe . . . gefliemde.* According to OH IV. xx. 37, 'sequenti pugna paene pari clade partis utriusque in hiberna discessum est.'

110/21. *ealne þone gear.* Or.'s addition.

110/24. *Lucius Emilius.* OH IV. xx. 39 *L. Aemilius Paulus,* with *L.* expanded to *Lucius* in many MSS.

110/30. *Lucius . . . Aula.* OH IV. xxi. 1 'L. Licinio Lucullo A. Postumio Albino', with *L.* and *A.* expanded to *Lucio* and *Aulo* in many MSS. For *Licinio* the MSS closest to Or. read *Lucinio.*

111/1. *from Sceltiuerin.* Cf. OH IV. xxi. 1 'ingens Celtiberorum'. For another instance of metanalysis see 150/27 *Actesifonte.*

111/2. *Scipian þæm consule.* OH IV. xxi. 1 *P. Scipio.*

111/3–4. *for þon . . . dorste.* Or.'s addition. The translator seems to have confused this Scipio Africanus with his grandfather by adoption, who certainly undertook an expedition to Spain when everyone else held back (see 104/17–20) but who did not get the title Africanus merely as a result of that campaign: see, e.g., Livy XXI. xlvi and XXX. xlv, and Eutropius IV. iv. OH's reference to the death of this first Scipio Africanus, IV. xx. 29, is omitted by Or.

111/5. *on Asiam.* OH IV. xxi. 1 *in Macedoniam.*

111/7. *Scipian gefera.* OH IV. xxi. 3 refers to Sergius Galba as praetor, a word elsewhere translated by Or. as *consul.* He, like Scipio, was in Spain.

111/7–8. *Lusitaniam, Ispania folce.* OH IV. xxi. 3 *Lusitanis.* See OH IV. xxi. 10, where the Lusitanians are located *in Hispania.*

111/9–10. *bebudon . . . plegan.* According to OH IV. xxi. 4, it was the censors who ordered the building of a theatre. See, however, IV. xxi. 6 where it is said to be the gods and daemons 'qui ista petierunt'.

111/11–12. *þa . . . com.* See also 111/10 *ham.* Or.'s addition. The Scipio in question is not Scipio Africanus but P. Cornelius Nasica Corculum, who was at that time in Rome, and OH IV. xxi. 4 indeed names him as *Scipio Nasica.*

111/12. *se mæsta gedwola.* OH IV. xxi. 4 describes the measure as 'inimicissimum hoc fore bellatori populo ad nutriendam desidiam lasciuiamque commentum'.

111/14–16. *eall . . . sealdon.* OH IV. xxi. 4 'adeoque mouit senatum, ut non solum uendi omnia theatro conparata iusserit, sed etiam subsellia ludis poni prohibuerit.'

111/16–19. *Nu . . . gewunan.* This replaces a lengthy argument by Orosius, ending with the comment, IV. xxi. 9, 'quin potius Nasicae erubescant, qui Christianis exprobrandum putant et non nobis de hostibus, quos semper habuerunt, sed illi de theatro, quod haberi prohibuerat, conquerantur.' The reproach levelled against the Christians is that they have attempted to stop theatrical performances.

111/21. *beswac*. OH IV. xxi. 10 says that Galba treacherously put them to death, surrounding them with troops and destroying them while they were unarmed and off their guard.

111/21–3. *Seo dæd . . . wæs*. Cf. OH IV. xxi. 10 'quae res postea uniuersae Hispaniae propter Romanorum perfidiam causa maximi tumultus fuit.'

111/25. *Censorinus . . . Lucius*. OH IV. xxii. 1 'L. Censorino et M. Manilio', with *L* and *M* expanded to *Lucio* and *Marco* in many MSS. Was the name *Lucio* overlooked at some stage of the transmission of the text and then inserted in the margin or above the line?

111/27. *gif . . . oferwunne*. Or.'s addition. According to OH IV. xxii. 1, the intention was merely to order the abandonment of Carthage. However, other authorities use the terminology of war; see, e.g., Eutropius IV. x.

111/29. *he hie . . . Cartaina*. Or. here alters the true order of events. According to OH IV. xxii, what actually happened was that the two consuls and Scipio ordered the evacuation of Carthage. This provoked the resistance by the Carthaginians mentioned in 112/2–6 below. Then the consuls attacked and were driven back. Scipio, however, drove the enemy behind their walls.

112/1. *hiere*. OH IV. xxii. 3 '*a mari* decem milibus passuum'. See OH IV. xxii. 5, where Carthage is said to have been almost completely surrounded by the sea.

112/2–4. *him leofre . . . towurpe*. Cf. OH IV. xxii. 3 'aut defensuri ciuitatem aut cum ipsa per ipsam sepeliendi'.

112/5–6. *sume of seolfre . . . treowum*. OH IV. xxii. 4 'auri argentique metallis'. Potter (1952–3), p. 426, suggests that *metallis* may have been misheard or misread as *materiis*.

112/6. *cyningum*. OH IV. xxii. 3 *duces*. See 91/27, Commentary.

112/8. *ymbegong . . . xxx mila*. OH IV. xxii. 5 'uiginti duo milia passuum muro amplexa', 'related' MSS including Vienna 366 'uiginti milia'.

112/9. *xx fota ðicce*. OH IV. xxii. 5 'triginta pedes latum'.

112/10. *ofer læsse fæsten*. OH IV. xxii. 6 *arx*.

112/10. *on . . . clife*. Or.'s addition. OH IV. xxii. 6 refers to a wall that towered above the Stagnum Sea, 'imminens mari'.

112/10–11. *þæt . . . heah*. A misunderstanding of OH IV. xxii. 6, where the citadel of Byrsa is described as 'paulo amplius quam duo milia passuum', with reference, of course, not to its height but to its extent.

112/12–13. *Scipia . . . for*. Cf. OH IV. xxii. 7 'Censorinus in Vrbem rediit.' Scipio did indeed subsequently return home.

112/14. *Gneo . . . Lucinius*. OH IV. xxiii. 1 'Cn. Cornelio Lentulo L.

'Mummio', with *Cn.* and *L.* expanded to *Gneo* and *Lucio* in many MSS. Or. here omits OH's 'Anno ab Vrbe condita' formula and thus does not begin a new section.

112/14–15. *ða for* . . . *Affrice*. Or.'s addition. In fact it was his second expedition; for the first see 111/28. Before that he had campaigned in Spain: see 110/30–111/5. Could the translator (or some secondary source used by him) have included in his calculations the campaign in Africa by the first Scipio Africanus? See above, 106/7–107/27 and 111/3–4, Commentary.

112/16. *on þa burg*. OH IV. xxiii. 1 *Gothonem*, the war harbour of Carthage.

112/19. *xxvi m*. OH IV. xxiii. 3 *xxv milia*, the 'related' MS Selden B 16 *xxvi m*.

112/20. *Hasterbal* . . . *acwealde*. Apparently a misunderstanding of OH IV. xxiii. 4, 'se ultro dedit', i.e. voluntarily surrendered. Potter (1952–3), p. 426, suggests that the Latin *ultro* has been construed as dsn. of adj. *ultrum*, as if 'to the beyond, to the farther side', and so 'to death'.

112/21–2. *for* . . . *deaðe*. Or.'s addition. See 112/20, Commentary.

112/22–3. *Scipia* . . . *mehton*. OH IV. xxiii. 6 'diruta est autem Carthago omni murali lapide in puluerem conminuto.'

112/24. *xvi dagas*. OH IV. xxiii. 5 *decem et septem*, the 'related' MS Selden B 16 *sedecim*.

112/27–32. *þeh* . . . *aeargoden*. Or. omits Orosius' main point here, which is that the attack was completely unprovoked.

113/1–10. *Swa* . . . *heard*. Or. as usual rewrites Orosius' comments. Having discussed the reasons for the Third Punic War, OH IV. xxiii. 9–11 sums up:

causam non ex iniuria lacessentum Carthaginiensium sed ex inconstantia torpescentium Romanorum ortam inuenio. quod cum ita sit, cur Christianis temporibus imputant hebetationem ac robiginem suam, qua foris crassi, intus exesi sunt? qui porro ante sescentos fere annos, sicut sui prudentes timentesque praedixerant, cotem illam magnam splendoris et acuminis sui Carthaginem perdiderunt.
    Itaque finem uolumini faciam, ne forsitan conlidendo uehementius discussa ad tempus robigine ubi necessarium acumen elicere non possum, superuacuam asperitatem inueniam. quamquam obuiantem asperitatem nequaquam expauescerem, si interioris spem acuminis inuenirem.

Or.'s contrast between the fat and the lean appears to be based on OH's contrast *crassi, exesi*, with *exesi*, 'hollow, eaten away' interpreted in terms of hunger and not, as in OH, of corroding rust.

113/7–9. *Hit* . . . *geræceanne*. This comment is inspired by OH IV. xxiii. 9–11 (quoted above), but independent of it. Since the word *malm*, at least in more recent times, is used of a soft friable rock, consisting of chalky material, while whetstones are normally made of hard fine-grained rock, Or.'s point is that Orosius is faced with an impossible task.

113/14–17. *gelicost . . . gemæne.* Cf. OH V. i. 3 'quibus breuiter respondebitur et ipsos de temporibus solere causari et nos pro isdem temporibus instituisse sermonem, quae tempora non uni tantum urbi adtributa sed Orbi uniuerso constat esse communia.'

113/20–3. *Gif . . . c.* Cf. OH V. i. 7–8 'ipsa postremo dicat Italia: cur per annos quadringentos Romanis utique suis contradixit obstitit repugnauit, si eorum felicitas sua infelicitas non erat Romanosque fieri rerum dominos bonis communibus non obstabat? non requiro de innumeris diuersarum gentium populis diu ante liberis, tunc bello uictis, patria abductis, pretio uenditis, seruitute dispersis, quid tunc sibi maluerint, quid de Romanis opinati sint, quid de temporibus iudicarint.'

113/25. *hu him licade.* According to OH V. i. 9, to ask the kings their opinion would be foolish.

113/26. *on geocum.* OH V. i. 9 'sub iugum missis'. For an earlier instance of the translator's handling of this Latin idiom see 66/25–9.

113/28–9. *hie monege . . . life.* Or.'s addition, presumably inspired by OH V. i. 10 'maiores nostri bella gesserunt, bellis fatigati pacem petentes tributa obtulerunt: tributum pretium pacis est.'

113/30–114/3. *Ac . . . willaþ.* Cf. OH V. i. 12 'inquietudo enim bellorum, qua illi attriti sunt, nobis ignota est. in otio autem, quod illi post imperium Caesaris natiuitatemque Christi tenuiter gustauerunt, nos nascimur et senescimus.' For the theme of release from fear see OH V. ii. 4; for release from slavery see, e.g., Galatians 5:1. For Or.'s contrast between pre-Christian and Christian times see Introduction, pp. xciv f.

114/6. *Gneo . . . Lucio.* OH V. iii. 1 'Cn. Cornelio Lentulo L. Mummio consulibus', with *Cn.* and *L.* expanded to *Gneo* and *Lucio* in many MSS. See 97/1, Commentary. According to OH V. iii. 5, only Mummius attacked Corinth.

114/6–7. *ealra Creca heafedburg.* OH V. iii. 5 merely describes Corinth as 'urbem toto tunc Orbe longe omnium opulentissimam'; however, see, e.g., Isidore, *Etymologies* XIV. iv. 14, where in an entry on Achaia it is said that 'Huius caput est urbs Corinthus Graeciae decus', and Florus I. xxxii. 1, where Corinthus is said to be 'Achaiae caput, Graeciae decus', both comments being open to misconstruction.

114/9. *on pyttas besuncan.* OH V. iii. 7 refers to the metals as 'permixta in unum'. Isidore, *Etymologies* XVI. xx. 4, however, is more specific: 'omnes statuas aeneas et aureas et argenteas in unum rogum congessit et eas incendit.' *Rogus* has two meanings, 'funeral pyre' and 'grave', and it could be the second of these that is responsible for Or.'s reference to 'pits'.

114/9–11. *Giet . . . oþru.* Cf. OH V. iii. 7 'unde usque in hodiernum diem siue ex ipso siue ex imitatione eius aes Corinthium, sicut memoriae traditum est, et Corinthia uasa dicuntur.' For the high repute of Corinthian bronzework ('toto orbe laudatur'), see Florus I. xxxii. 6.

114/13. *wæs micel . . . reafere.* OH V. iv. 1 *latro.* The translator apparently does not consider the term *þeofmon* by itself adequate to describe a highwayman who ended up by devastating provinces and defeating the Roman army, although *latro* is translated by *þeof* (as well as *reafere*) elsewhere in Old English. According to the Laws of Ine, in Laws I, p. 94, 'Ðeofas we hataþ oð vii men.'

114/14–15. *monege tunas oferhergeade.* The corresponding passage in OH, V. iv. 1, reads 'infestando uias'; *tunas,* however, would suggest an underlying *uillas* or *uicos,* in place of *uias.*

114/17. *Uecilius þone consul.* OH V. ix. 2 'C. Vecilius praetor'.

114/19. *Gaius Folucius se consul.* OH V. iv. 3 *C. Plautium praetorem,* 'related' MSS, including Vienna 366, *Gaium Falucium praetorem.*

114/20. *Claudius se consul.* OH V. iv. 3 *Claudius Vnimammus.*

114/22. *uneaþe self com aweg.* Or.'s addition. It is Vecilius who is said by OH V. iv. 2 to have barely managed to slip away.

114/23. *Ueriatus.* OH V. iv. 5 *Lusitani.* Cf. OH V. iv. 1, where Viriatus is described as *genere Lusitanus.*

114/25. *ccc.* OH V. iv. 6 *cccxx.*

114/25. *On þæm fleame.* Cf. OH V. iv. 6 'cum uictores Lusitani sparsi ac securi abirent'.

114/26–7. *mon . . . ofsceat.* OH V. iv. 6 describes the man as a footsoldier, *pedes.* The translator (or an intermediary) seems to have supposed that the man was on foot because his horse had been killed. See further 115/1–2, Commentary.

114/27–115/1. *þa . . . gebindan.* Cf. OH V. iv. 6 'circumfusis equitibus'.

115/1–2. *þa slog . . . of.* In OH V. iv. 6 it is the horseman who is decapitated: 'unius eorum equo lancea perfosso ipsius equitis ad unum gladii ictum caput desecuisset'. Has *ipsius equitis* been construed with *lancea* and taken to refer to the Lusitanian? For the incorrect assumption that the latter was a cavalryman, see 114/26–7 and Commentary.

115/3. *þæt . . . dorstan.* OH V. iv. 6 'ut prospectantibus cunctis ipse contemptim atque otiosus abscederet'.

115/6. *vi m.* OH V. iv. 7 *quinque milia.*

115/7. *untreowlice.* According to OH V. vii. 1, Claudius' request was made *iuxta legem.* Or. omits the sequel to this refusal: that Claudius proceeded to celebrate a triumph at his own expense.

115/8–9. *for þon . . . næfde.* Cf. OH V. iv. 7 'propter superiora . . . damna'.

115/10–11. *þær . . . dorste.* According to OH V. iv. 9, the plague became so bad that it was impossible to live in Rome or even to approach it.

115/16. *hit wæs Godes gifu.* Or.'s addition. OH V. iv. 10 refers to *arcani iudicii.*

115/16–17. *ealle . . . sceoldon.* The reason given by OH V. iv. 10–11 is that

the plague abated before the usual expiatory sacrifices were made. The
translator seems to have identified the haruspices with the *ministri* of
OH V. iv. 8, 'ministri quoque faciendorum funerum primum non sufficerent deinde non essent'. Or. omits all reference to the expiatory sacrifice of a hermaphrodite which immediately preceded the plague and which
Orosius says was subsequently seen to be a vile and futile act.

115/19. *gefliemed wearð.* According to OH V. iv. 12, Fabius was the victor:
'Igitur Fabius consul contra Lusitanos et Viriatum dimicans Bucciam
oppidum, quod Viriatus obsidebat, depulsis hostibus liberauit.' Could
depulsis have been misread or miscopied as *depulsus*?

115/20–2. *he aspon . . . aceorfan.* Based on OH V. iv. 12, 'fecit facinus
etiam ultimis barbaris Scythiae . . . exsecrabile. quingentis enim principi-
bus eorum, quos societate inuitatos deditionis iure susceperat, manus
praecidit.' The translator has taken *eorum* to refer not to the Lusitanians
but to the Scythians.

115/22–3. *Numentinas, Ispania þeode.* OH V. iv. 13 *Numantinorum.* For
the location of Numantia in Spain, see 116/31–117/1 and OH V. vii. 2.

115/26–8. *þær . . . wenden.* OH V. iv. 14 'in hoc solo Romanis circa eum
fortiter agentibus, quod percussores eius indignos praemio iudicarunt'.

115/29–31. *Ic . . . gewinnum.* OH V. iv. 15 does not promise silence,
except by implication, merely stating that the crimes of the Romans were
such 'ut iure fastidiantur aliena'.

116/1. *þa wæron . . . anwalde.* Or.'s addition.

116/2. *Demetrias, Asia cyning.* Although OH V. iv. 17 assigns a kingdom
to Demetrius, it does not identify it. In fact Demetrius Nicator was king
of Syria.

116/3. *he wearð gefliemed.* Cf. OH V. iv. 16 'uicto Demetrii praefecto'.

116/4–5. *He . . . gesetton.* Or.'s addition. It was Demetrius Soter, his
father, who obtained recognition as king from the Romans.

116/6. *Numentine, Ispania folc.* OH V. iv. 20 *Numantiam.* See below,
116/31–117/1, OH V. vii. 2.

116/7–8. *hiene siþþan aweg bestæl.* OH V. iv. 20 states only that Mancinus
made a shameful peace.

116/8. *þa he ham com.* Or.'s addition.

116/9–13. *þa nawþer . . . forlet.* OH V. iv. 21 merely says that Mancinus
'ibi . . . usque in noctem manens, a suis desertus, ab hostibus autem non
susceptus lacrimabile utrisque spectaculum praebuit'. In fact Mancinus
survived the ordeal and was finally brought back to the Roman camp;
see, e.g., *De Viris Illustribus* 59 and Velleius Paterculus II. i. 4 f.

116/14. *Brutus se consul.* OH V. v. 12 *Brutus.* The translator may here be
identifying Decimus Junius Brutus Callaecus (consul 138 B.C.) with the
'D. Brutus uir consularis' of V. xii. 7.

116/14–16. *Brutus . . . gefeng.* OH V. v. 12 'Brutus in ulteriore Hispania

lx milia Gallaecorum, qui Lusitanis auxilio uenerant, asperrimo bello . . .
oppressit: quorum in eo proelio l milia occisa, sex milia capta referuntur.'
The translator has turned one battle into two and assigned the numbers
of dead and captured not to the Gallaeci but to their allies the Lusitani.

116/17. *se consul.* OH V. v. 13 *proconsule.*

116/18–19. *mid þæm mæstan bismre.* OH V. v. 13 relates that the survivors
stripped their camp and threw away their arms as a result of this shameful
disaster.

116/19–22. *Hwæþer . . . ungesælgestan.* A condensing and rewriting of OH
V. v. 14–16, with a question replacing Orosius' statement that he does
not intend to reveal the numbers of dead.

116/23. *Seruius Fuluius 7 Flaccus Quintus.* OH V. vi. 1 'Seruio Fuluio
Flacco Q. Calpurnio Pisone', with *Q* expanded to *Quinto* in many MSS.
See 97/1, Commentary.

116/26. *mare . . . dyde.* Or.'s addition. For a similar comment by the
translator see 50/30.

116/28–9. *swa . . . sædon.* Or.'s addition.

116/29–30. *nan . . . Furculus.* According to OH V. vii. 1, it was 'maior
paene infamia' than at Caudine Forks.

117/1. *on þæm norðwestende Ispania.* OH V. vii. 2 'Numantia autem
citerioris Hispaniae, haud procul a Vaccaeis et Cantabris in capite
Gallacciae sita, ultima Celtiberorum fuit.' See also OH I. ii. 71, where
the second 'angle' of Spain (which has in it *Brigantia, Gallaeciae ciuitas*)
is said to extend *circium*, i.e. 'north-west'.

117/3. *healf gear.* OH V. vii. 12 *diu.* See OH V. vii. 5, where Scipio is
said to pass part of the summer and the whole winter without attempting
battle.

117/4–5. *him . . . prowoden.* According to OH V. vii. 12, the Numantines
were 'saepe etiam orantes iustae pugnae facultatem, ut tamquam uiris
mori liceret'.

117/6–7. *þa het . . . aloccoden.* Or.'s addition. Frontinus III. x describes
several stratagems of this type, but not in connection with the siege of
Numantia.

117/7–10. *þa . . . geatum.* OH V. vii. 13 merely says that before they
burst through the two gates the Numantines drank their fill of *caelia*, a
drink which Orosius describes as made from moistened wheat, which is
at first heated, then dried, ground to powder, mixed with a mild juice and
allowed to ferment.

117/11. *On þæm swicdome.* Or.'s addition; see 117/6–7, Commentary.

117/13–14. *for ðon . . . fengon.* Or.'s addition. Cf. OH V. vii. 18, where it
is said that 'aurum uel argentum, quod igni superesse potuisset, apud
pauperes non fuit; arma et uestem ignis absumpsit.'

117/17. *an . . . Numentisc.* OH V. viii. 1 'Thyresum quendam, Celticum principem'. There is nothing in OH to suggest the age of the man. Has Thyresus, whose name is often spelt Tiresus, been confused with Tiresias, the blind seer who was renowned not only for his wisdom but also for his longevity? See e.g. Hyginus, LXXV, and Ovid, *Met*. III. 320 f.

117/17–19. *an hwy . . . wæron*. OH V. viii. 1 'qua ope res Numantina aut prius inuicta durasset aut post fuisset euersa'. The verb *duro* has not only the meaning 'last, endure', apparently intended here by Orosius, but also the meaning 'be hardened'.

117/19–22. *Đa . . . ealle*. Cf. OH V. viii. 1 'Thyresus respondit: concordia inuicta, discordia exitio fuit.'

117/26. *an þara consula*. OH V. ix. 1 'tribunus plebi'.

117/27. *winnan . . . ofslogon*. According to OH V. ix. 1–2, Gracchus stirred up riots among the people and was killed by the incensed nobles.

117/29–30. *vi . . . mehte*. OH V. ix. 4 refers to *quattuor milia* killed at Sinuessa, V. ix. 7 refers to more than *xx milia* killed by Rutilius, while V. ix. 6 gives the number killed by Piso at Mamertium as *octo milia*, and continues, 'quos autem capere potuit, patibulo suffixit.'

118/1. *dc wintrum 7 xxi*. OH V. x. 1 *dcxxii*, 'related' MSS including Selden B 16 *ccxxi*.

118/2. *Lucinius Crassus*. OH V. x. 1 *P. Licinius Crassus*, 'related' MSS, including Vienna 366, 'Publius (*var*. Puplius) Lucinius Crassus'.

118/3. *Aristonocuse þæm cyninge*. OH V. x. 1 *Aristonicum*. A safe contextual guess.

118/4. *þa læssan Asiam*. OH V. x. 1 *Asiam*, referring to the Roman province of that name. See 10/24, Commentary.

118/5. *to boclande*. OH V. x. 1 *per testamentum*. For the OE technical term *bocland* see E. John, *Land Tenure in Early England* (Leicester Univ. Press, 1964).

118/6–9. *An . . . Paflogoniam*. Or. here makes eight kings out of OH's four by interpreting their personal names as the names of countries. Cf. OH V. x. 2 'Nicomede Bithyniae, Mithridate Ponti et Armeniae, Ariarathe Cappadociae, Pylaemene Paphlagoniae', with *Nicomede* replaced by *Nicomedie* in a number of 'related' MSS (see Bately (1961), p. 76, note 29a). In some MSS the names *Ariarathe* and *Philemene* also have *æ* for final *e*; however, even without the *æ* spelling they could easily be mistaken for genitives in texts where Classical Latin *æ* had come to be written *e*. See further, Glossary of Proper Names.

118/11. *se oþer consul*. OH V. x. 4 'consul, qui Crasso successerat'.

118/12–13. *þa his fird eall tofaren wæs*. OH V. x. 4 'nudatumque omnibus copiis'.

118/13. *fæstenne*. OH V. x. 5 *Stratonicen urbem*.

118/14. *hiene . . . consule*. OH V. x. 5 merely says that he was forced to surrender.

118/15–16. *oþ he his lif forlet.* According to OH V. x. 5, Aristonicus was strangled.

118/17–18. *Antiochuse . . . næfde.* Cf. OH V. x. 8 'Antiochus, non contentus Babylona atque Ecbatana totoque Mediae imperio'. An earlier Antiochus is described as *Syra cyning* (108/26, OH IV. xx. 12 *rex Syriae*) and this may account for C's reading *Asiria*, a variant which is unsupported by any of the three lists of chapter headings. For the equation *Syria*: *Assyria* see 70/22, Commentary.

118/22–3. *for þon . . . æltæwra.* OH V. x. 8 says that his easy defeat was due to the fact that, although he had only 100,000 soldiers in his army, he carried along with him 200,000 servants and camp followers, among whom were prostitutes and actors.

118/24–5. *Scipia . . . þegna.* OH V. x. 9 'P. Scipionem Africanum'. The source of Or.'s description of Scipio Africanus seems to be the title given to Publius Scipio Nasica, who was 'a senatu vir optimus judicatus': see, e.g., *De Viris Illustribus* 44. 1, Solinus 28, 16, and Augustine, *Civ. Dei* II. v.

118/25–119/3. *mænde . . . Africe.* An expansion of OH V. x. 9, 'P. Scipionem Africanum pridie pro contione de periculo salutis suae contestatum, quod sibi pro patria laboranti ab improbis et ingratis denuntiari cognouisset, alio mane exanimem in cubiculo suo repertum'. See the following notes.

118/26. *on his ylde.* Scipio was in his fifties when he died.

119/1. *hu . . . þeowdome.* It was an earlier Scipio, Africanus Major, who defeated Hannibal, not the one mentioned here: see above, 107/12–27 and 109/6–7, OH IV. xix and xx. For Scipio's stand when Rome itself seemed in danger of falling see 101/21–31, OH IV. xvi. 6.

119/2–3. *hu . . . Africe.* For Scipio Africanus Minor's victories in Spain and Africa see 111/28–112/25 and 116/31–117/15, OH IV. xxii and V. vii. However, the first Africanus was also renowned for his conquests of these countries (see 104/29–105/22 and 106/7–107/27, OH IV. xviii) and the translator or an intermediary may again have been confusing the two men. This might explain the reference to Scipio's age, 118/26. See also Augustine's eulogy of Africanus Major, *Civ. Dei* III. xxi.

119/3–6. *On . . . alet.* According to OH V. x. 10, the rumour was that his wife had murdered him. That he was strangled as the result of a plot is suggested by Velleius Paterculus II. iv. 5; see also, *De Viris Illustribus* 58. 10, *Pro Milone*, Scholia Bobiensia 16, ed. P. Hildebrandt (Leipzig, 1907), 72, and Sidonius, *Opera* ed. P. Mohr (Leipzig, 1895), *Epistulae* VIII. xi, possibly following the now lost Livy lix.

119/4–5. *Romane . . . hæfde.* This typically wry Anglo-Saxon comment is turned by Calendre into a *proverbe au vilain*; see Introduction, p. xxxvi.

119/9. *Ða þa Emilius Orestes wæs consul.* Cf. OH V. x. 11 'M. Aemilio L. Oreste consulibus', with *L* expanded to *Lucio* in many MSS, and *M.* omitted by some 'related' MSS, including Vienna 366. For *consulibus* some MSS read *consul* (var. *cōsul*) and it is possible that such a reading occurred in Or.'s exemplar, causing the translator to suppose that only one consul was being referred to.

119/9–15. *Eþna . . . hǣte.* Or. here runs together descriptions of two separate volcanic eruptions, assuming incorrectly that the disaster on the island of Lipara was caused by the eruption of Etna. Cf. OH V. x. 11 'Aetna uasto tremore concussa exundauit igneis globis, rursusque alio die Lipara insula et uicinum circa eam mare in tantum efferbuit, ut adustas quoque rupes dissoluerit, tabulata nauium liquefactis ceris extorruerit, exanimatos pisces supernatantesque excoxerit, homines quoque, nisi qui longius potuere diffugere, reciprocato anhelitu calidi aeris adustis introrsum uitalibus suffocarit.' In this, the translator may have been influenced by Augustine, *Civ. Dei* III. xxxi, where the fires of Etna are said to have run down from the top of the mountain to the nearest shore and the sea reached such a boiling heat that the rocks were burnt and the pitch was melted in the ships.

119/12. *neah þǣm sǣ.* Cf. OH V. x. 11 'uicinum circa eam mare', the source also of 119/13 *neah þǣm sǣ.*

119/16. *Ða þa Marcus Flaccus wǣs consul.* OH V. xi. 1 'M. Plautio Hypsaeo M. Fuluio Flacco consulibus', with the first *M.* often expanded to *Marcio,* 'related' MSS *Marco,* and the second to *Marco.* A number of manuscripts again have *consul* or *cōsul* for *consulibus.*

119/16. *gǣrstapan.* OH V. xi. 2 *lucustarum.*

119/17–18. *ǣlc . . . growendes.* OH V. xi. 2 'non modo . . . cunctam spem frugum abrasissent herbasque omnes cum parte radicum, folia arborum cum teneritudine ramorum consumpsissent uerum etiam amaras cortices atque arida ligna praeroderent'. Cf. 25/32 'eall þæt on þæm lande wæs weaxendes 7 growendes'.

119/23. *Lucius Mella 7 Quintus Flamineus.* OH V. xii. 1 'L. Caecilio Metello et Q. Titio Flaminino', with *L.* and *Q.* expanded to *Lucio* and *Quinto* in a number of MSS.

119/23–4. *þa gewearð . . . Cartainam.* OH V. xii. 1 'Carthago in Africa restitui iussa'.

119/27–120/2. *þa men . . . getimbredon.* According to OH V. xii. 2, 'aliquamdiu haesitatum est, utrum Romanae paci expediret Carthaginem reformari.'

120/3. *Belearis þæt land.* OH V. xiii. 1 *Baleares insulas.*

120/4–5. *oferwan . . . forwurde.* OH V. xiii. 1 'piraticam infestationem, quae ab isdem tunc exoriebatur, plurima incolarum caede conpressit.'

120/6. *dc wintrum 7 xxvii.* OH V. xiv. 1 *dcxxviii.*

120/10. *Scipia Nasica 7 Lucius Calfurnius.* OH V. xv. 1 'P. Scipione Nasica et L. Calpurnio Bestia', with *L.* expanded in many MSS to *Lucio,* and *P.* omitted by some 'related' MSS, including Vienna 366.

120/12. *Mecipsuses mæg.* There is no reference to blood relationship in OH; see, however, Eutropius IV. xxvi and Sallust 5. 7.

120/13. *on his geogoðe.* Or.'s addition, possibly derived from Sallust 6. 1.

120/17-18. *he . . . fripe.* OH V. xv. 4 puts the request for peace after the sending of Calpurnius. However, according to Sallust 28. 1, Jugurtha's first approaches to the Romans were made long before this. See also Florus I. xxxvi. 4.

120/19-20. *he . . . purhteah.* Or.'s addition, apparently derived from Sallust 28. 7 and 29. 1, where Calpurnius is said to have fought at first, but to have quickly succumbed to bribery.

120/21-2. *diegellice . . . twywyrdige.* OH V. xv. 5 'omnibus pecunia aut corruptis aut adtemptatis seditiones dissensionesque permiscuit.'

120/24-5. *mon . . . ceapode.* Cf. OH V. xv. 5 'o urbem uenalem et mature perituram, si emptorem inuenerit!'

120/26-7. *Anilius Mostumius pone consul.* OH V. xv. 6 'A. Postumium, Postumii consulis fratrem', with *A.* expanded to *Aulum* in many MSS.

120/27. *lx m.* OH V. xv. 6 'quadraginta milium'. In Or.'s version an underlying *xl* appears to have had its constituent parts reversed.

121/2. *sippan lytle hwile.* Or.'s addition.

121/5-6. *he bedraf . . . lond.* Cf. OH V. xv. 7 'uidit praesente se et uastari Numidiam suam.' Metellus' campaigns in fact all took place in Numidia.

121/9-15. *for . . . pærbinnan wæs.* An expansion of OH V. xv. 8, 'Marius urbem Capsam . . . regiis tunc thesauris confertissimam dolo circumuenit et cepit.' The source of Or.'s additional material seems to be Sallust 91. According to Sallust, Marius, in order to conceal his real objective, made out that he was going to Lares. Then, marching by night until he was close to Capsa, he kept his army hidden until the Numidians, unsuspecting, came out of the town in force. Marius then ordered all his cavalry and the swiftest of his infantry to run and occupy the gates.

121/15. *his agnum folce.* OH V. xv. 9 'propriis rebus et uiribus'.

121/19-20. *lx m gehorsedra butan fepan.* Cf. OH V. xv. 9, where Bocchus is said to have provided cavalry, and V. xv. 10 where the joint forces of Jugurtha and Bocchus are said to include 60,000 cavalry.

121/21. *on . . . befangen.* Cf. OH V. xv. 11 'circumcursantium . . . equitum', and (referring to the third day of the battle) V. xv. 13, 'undique enim uelocior ad persequendum eques incluserat'.

121/22-3. *on sondihtre dune.* Cf. OH V. xv. 11, 'puluis caelum subtexuerit' and the reference in V. xv. 14 to the Roman army breaking out 'e uallo campoque'.

121/24-5. *Toeacan . . . hæte.* According to OH V. xv. 15, they were afflicted by heat and thirst on the third day.

121/28-9. *hie sume . . . mehten.* Cf. OH V. xv. 14 'uniuerso simul agmine prorupit e uallo campoque sese simul et proelio dedit', and the subsequent allusion, V. xv. 15 to 'agminis extrema' and 'media'. 'Vniuerso agmine' refers not to the enemy army but to the Romans.

121/29–30. *þa . . . hæfdon.* According to OH V. xv. 14, they were still surrounded by the enemy.

122/3. *lx m 7 an hund.* OH V. xv. 18 gives the figures as 'nonaginta milia', slaughtered almost to the last man.

122/5. *acwælon.* According to OH V. xv. 19, Jugurtha was strangled. Nothing is said of the fate of his sons.

122/7. *Mallius 7 Cuintinus wæron consulas.* OH V. xvi. 1 'C. Manlius consul et Q. Caepio proconsule', with *Q.* expanded to *Quintus* in many MSS and *C.* omitted by some 'related' MSS including Vienna 366.

122/8–9. *wið* (1) *. . . Gallium.* OH V. xvi. 1 'aduersus Cimbros et Teutonas et Tigurinos et Ambronas, Gallorum Germanorum gentes'.

122/9–10. *þær . . . þusenda.* OH V. xvi. 3 'lxxx milia Romanorum sociorumque . . . trucidata, xl milia calonum atque lixarum interfecta . . . ita ex omni penitus exercitu decem tantummodo homines . . . superfuisse referuntur.' The translator seems to have supposed that the *calones* and *lixae* were attached to the Romans.

122/10–11. *heora consul.* OH V. xvi. 2 'M. Aemilius consularis'.

122/13–14. *him . . . lond.* According to OH V. xvi. 9–10, the enemy 'Italiam petere destinarunt' and abandoning their attack on Marius departed.

122/17–19. *Eaþe . . . cuman.* Cf. OH V. xvi. 10 'aquam quidem in conspectu esse respondit, sed eam ferro uindicandam.' According to OH, the enemy held both plain and river.

122/22–3. *Æfter . . . consul.* Or. is here following OH V. xvii. 1. However, the events next described are those referred to by OH V. xvii. 1 as 'sexto consulatu eiusdem C. Marii', a statement apparently overlooked by the translator, if it occurred in his exemplar.

122/23–4. *mid . . . folcum.* Or.'s addition.

122/26–7. *ærest . . . Saturninus.* OH V. xvii. 3 'primus L. Apuleius Saturninus', with *L.* expanded to *Lucius* in many MSS. For Calendre's reading *Apuleius* see Introduction, p. xxxvii.

122/27. *hie.* OH V. xvii. 4 names the conspirators as Marius, *Glaucia*, and Saturninus.

123/1–2. *consul ær Marius.* Or.'s addition, possibly inspired by OH V. xv. 7–8, where first the consul Metellus, then the consul Marius are said to defeat the Numidians.

123/2–4. *Hit . . . mehton.* Cf. OH V. xvii. 6 'fremente pro tantis reipublicae malis senatu populoque Romano'. OH makes Pompey and Cato responsible only for proposing a decree that Metellus should be asked to return

(V. xvii. 11). Nothing is said of their status. However, see OH V. xviii. 18, where (another) Pompey and Cato are referred to as consuls.

123/4–5. *hie ofslogon Lucius 7 Saturninus.* According to OH V. xvii. 9, Saturninus was killed 'per equites Romanos'.

123/6–8. *him þa . . . ege.* Or.'s addition.

123/9. *vi c wintra 7 lxi.* OH V. xviii. 1 *dclviiii.* Presumably a reading *dclix*, miscopied *dclxi*, underlies Or.'s version.

123/9–11. *on . . . Martius.* A misinterpretation of OH V. xviii. 1, 'Sex. Iulio Caesare et L. Marcio Philippo consulibus', *Sex.* and *L.* being expanded to *Sexto* and *Lucio* in many MSS and *Philippo* being omitted. The translator's supposition that *Sexto* is a numeral, referring to the number of times Caesar had been consul, may have been prompted by a reading such as the *vi^{to}* of MSS Berne 160 and Vat. 1975; for the opposite error, see 74/28–30, Commentary. Sextus Julius Caesar was uncle of the Dictator.

123/11–13. *wearþ . . . diernden.* OH V. xviii. 1 'intestinis causis sociale bellum tota commouit Italia.' Neither Pompey nor Sextus Julius Caesar was in fact involved. It was the son of the one and the nephew of the other who were subsequently engaged in civil war. See below, 126/11–128/2. OH itself ascribes the troubles to Livius Drusus.

123/15. *on Tarentan.* OH V. xviii. 4 'apud Arretinos', 'related' MSS including Vienna 366, *Tarentinos.*

123/17. *hagolade.* According to OH V. xviii. 5, 'grando lapidum'.

123/18. *on Somnia þæm londe.* OH V. xviii. 5 'in Samnitibus'.

123/26. *Romana ealdormon.* OH V. xviii. 8 *praetorem. Praetor* is normally rendered *consul* in Or.

123/27. *aweddon . . . Somnitum.* OH refers neither to madness nor to Samnium: see V. xviii. 9 'omnium generum animalia, quae manus hominum blande perpeti atque inter homines uiuere solita erant, relictis stabulis pascuisque cum balatu hinnitu mugituque miserabili ad siluas montesque fugerunt. canes quoque . . . lacrimosis ululatibus uagi luporum ritu oberrarunt.'

123/28–9. *gefeaht . . . wearþ.* OH V. xviii. 10 'Cn. Pompeius praetor cum Picentibus . . . bellum gessit et uictus est.'

123/29–124/1. *Iulius . . . wearð.* Cf. OH V. xviii. 11 'Iulius Caesar Samnitium pugna uictus caeso fugit exercitu.' The Roman generals defeated by the Marsi were Rutilius and Caepio: see OH V. xviii. 11 and 14. Sabines and Marsi are linked by Pseud. Acr., *Carm.* III. 6. 38 'Aut Sabinis aut Marsis'. See *Pseudacronis scholia in Horatium vetustiora*, ed. Otto Keller (Leipzig, 1902, repr. 1967).

124/2. *hiene mon het casere.* OH V. xviii. 15 'ab exercitu imperator appellatus esset'. The name *Caesar* did not become a title until the time of Hadrian.

124/2-3. *þa bæd . . . brohte.* Or.'s addition. Cf. OH V. xviii. 15 'Romam . . . nuntios de uictoria misisset'.

124/3-6. *þa sende . . . com.* A misunderstanding of OH V. xviii. 15, 'senatus saga, hoc est uestem maeroris, quam exorto sociali bello sumpserat, hac spe adridente deposuit atque antiquum togae decorem recuperauit.' The colour black was probably suggested by the description of the sagum as 'uestem maeroris'. For the refusal of a triumph to the Dictator, Julius Caesar, see below, 126/11-12, Commentary.

124/7. *Silla . . . gefera.* OH V. xviii. 16 *Sulla*, cf. V. xviii. 23 *Sulla consul*. Sulla is linked with Pompey again in 125/6-7, though without support from OH. See Augustine, *Civ. Dei* III. xxx, where Pompey is described as a partisan of Sulla, whose power he equalled and even surpassed.

124/8. *Esernium þæm folce.* OH V. xviii. 16 *Aeserniam*, the name of the town where the Roman garrison was besieged.

124/9-13. *þa . . . geiecton.* OH V. xviii. 17 'qua uictoria senatus laticlauia et cetera dignitatis insignia recepit, cum togas tantummodo uictoria Caesaris primum respirante sumpsisset.' Or.'s misinterpretation follows logically upon its earlier erroneous assumptions, according to which dissension between Pompey and Caesar had already arisen and insult was intended to Caesar by the senate (see 123/11-12 and 124/3-6, and Commentary). It is again assumed that the situation was one requiring a triumph. Nowhere in OH is it suggested that Pompey's victory was the lesser one.

124/13-14. *Iulius 7 Pompeius.* OH V. xviii. 18 refers only to Pompey.

124/14. *Asculum þa burg on Mærsum.* OH V. xviii. 18 *Asculum ciuitatem.* Although the enemy are said by OH to be the Marsi, Asculum was in fact in Picenum.

124/19-20. *Mariuse þæm consule, Iuliuses eame.* OH V. xix. 3 *Marius.* Marius married Julia, the sister of the Dictator Julius Caesar's father: see Plutarch, *Marius* VI. 2. I have not found any reference to this relationship in Latin texts, and it may be that Or.'s ultimate source here is the now missing opening of Suetonius' *Life of Caesar.*

124/21-3. *for þon . . . ær wæs.* Or.'s addition.

124/23-4. *þa . . . Rome.* Or.'s addition.

124/24-5. *ealre his firde.* OH V. xix. 4 'quattuor legionibus'.

124/25-7. *Marius . . . agifan.* According to OH V. xix. 5 and 7, Marius, having first fled to the Capitol, then took refuge in the swamps of Minturnae, was captured there and taken to a prison, where it was intended that he should be put to death.

125/1. *þære ilcan niht.* Or.'s addition.

125/2. *suþ . . . mæst wæs.* OH V. xix. 8 *in Africam.*

125/3-5. *Him . . . ordfruman.* OH V. xix. 8 describes the consul Cinna as forming a criminal alliance with Marius. Sertorius, not a consul but according to OH 'ciuilis belli incentor et particeps', is said to be placed in command of part of Marius' forces.

125/7. *Pompeiuse.* OH V. xx. 1 refers only to Sulla as in Greece, Pompey having been killed by lightning (see OH V. xix. 18). However, see OH V. xx. 5 where a Cn. Pompeius (not the Pompey previously mentioned) is named as one of Sulla's generals.

125/8. *mid micelre geornfulnisse.* According to OH V. xx. 1, Sulla was *forced* by the senate's entreaties to bring help.

125/9. *hiene gefliemde.* OH V. xx makes no reference to Marius as actually fighting alongside his troops.

125/11. *Raðe . . . twæm.* Or.'s addition. See OH V. xxii. 4 'uiros consulares uiginti et quattuor . . . deleti sunt' and the reference in OH V. xxi. 3 to *quattuor consulares* on Sulla's proscription list.

125/11–12. *Marius . . . self.* The Marius of the preceding sections died of pleurisy: see OH V. xix. 23 'Marius . . . morte praereptus est.' As for Sulla, OH V. xxii. 16 does no more than report his death; according to other sources, e.g. Valerius Maximus IX. iii. 8, he burst a blood vessel.

125/12–13. *Cinna . . . byrg.* OH V. xix. 24 'Cinna . . . ab exercitu suo interfectus est.' According to other sources, e.g. *De Viris Illustribus* 69. 4, Cinna was killed near Ancona. The names Cinna and Smyrna are indeed linked in Latin texts, but the Cinna referred to is the poet and Smyrna the title of the poem for which he is famous. See, e.g., Servius, *Bucolics* IX. 35 and *Georgics* I. 288, Catullus, *Carmina*, ed. M. Schuster (Leipzig, 1949) XCV. 1, and Acron, *Art. Poet.* 388. See further Introduction, p. lxii. For the location of Smyrna in Asia, see, e.g., Isidore, *Etymologies* XIII. xxi. 22.

125/14. *þa . . . gewin.* A somewhat surprising introduction to an account of the Mithridatic Wars. Although Pompey is said by OH VI. iv. 9 to invade Parthia, this is not a fact given any prominence at all by Orosius.

125/14–15. *Metrepatis . . . lond.* According to OH VI. ii. 1, Mithridates is 'rex Ponti atque Armeniae'. For his conquest of Asia Minor see especially OH VI. ii. 1–2; for his conquest of 'cunctam . . . Graeciam' see VI. ii. 4.

125/17. *oþ . . . ofslogan.* OH VI. v tells of a revolt by Castor, prefect of Mithridates, the king's attempted suicide, and finally his offering of his throat to a passing Gallic soldier. There is nothing in the text of OH to suggest that Pompey was actively pursuing him at the time.

125/18. *geniedde . . . underþeow.* Archelaus is not mentioned by OH after his defeat by Sulla in the first Mithridatic War, OH VI. ii. 12, and his subsequent defection to Sulla.

125/19–22. *Hit . . . hungre.* Cf. OH VI. v. 11 'uerumtamen breuiter consulo: qualia tunc toto Orienti tempora uidebantur, cum per quadraginta annos miserae nationes alternis tantorum ducum uastationibus terebantur', etc. For the theme of starvation see OH VI. ii. 19.

125/23. *þa Pompeius hamweard wæs.* According to OH VI. vi. 1, Pompey, on hearing of the death of Mithridates, invaded Syria Coele and Phoenicia.

125/23–4. *þa noldan . . . Hierusalem.* OH VI. vi. 2 'a patribus urbe susceptus sed a plebe muro templi repulsus'. OH goes on to describe the Temple as 'non solum natura loci, uerum etiam ingenti muro fossaque maxima munitum'.

125/24. *Him . . . cyninga.* Cf. OH VI. vi. 4 'hoc bellum Orientis cum uiginti et duobus regibus sese gessisse', referring to the whole *bellum Orientis,* not just the campaign against Jerusalem.

125/26. *unwerig.* OH VI. vi. 3 'sine requie'.

125/30. *gebundenne.* OH VI. vi. 4 *captiuum.*

126/1–2. *vi . . . lxvii.* OH VI. vii. 1 *dcxciii,* var. *dclxliii.* Was an original *li* misread or miscopied as *u?*

126/2. *Gaiuse Iuliuse.* OH VI. vii. 1 *C. Caesare,* with *C* expanded to *Gaio* in many MSS. See below, 126/11, Commentary.

126/4. *for on Bretanie þæt iglond.* This replaces an account in OH of two separate invasion attempts: see OH VI. ix. 2 and VI. ix. 4.

126/5. *on . . . Centlond.* Or.'s addition. According to OH's account of the first invasion, VI. ix. 2, Caesar embarked from the territory of the Morini—an area from which OH I. ii. 76 suggests crossings were normally made to *Rutupi portus,* or Richborough in Kent.

126/6. *on Centlonde.* Or.'s addition.

126/8. *neh . . . Welengaford.* Cf. OH VI. ix. 6 'flumen Tamesim . . . quem uno tantum loco uadis transmeabilem ferunt'. It is interesting to note that Bede, *HE* I. ii, in quoting from OH, omits the reference to only one crossing point; see R. W. Chambers, *History,* N.S. iv (1920), p. 36.

126/9–10. *se cyning . . . Cirenceastre.* OH VI. ix. 8 'Trinobantum firmissima ciuitas cum *M*andu*b*ragio duce'. The Trinobantes lived in present-day Essex. For an attempt to explain Or.'s wrong identification here, see H. Nearing, 'The Legend of Julius Caesar's British Conquest', *PMLA,* lxiv (1949), 896: 'the words *Cirenceastre* and *Trinobantum* might look alike in a bad hand. Perhaps the author of this passage was influenced by a notion that Caesar had driven the Celts into the west, where they dwelt in his own day.' Nearing is presumably suggesting confusion between the initial syllables of these words, with *c* misread or miswritten *t.*

126/10. *ealle . . . wæron.* Cf. OH VI. ix. 9 'urbes aliae conplures'.

126/11. *Æfter . . . Rome.* Cf. OH VI. xv. 1 'rediens Caesar uictor ex Gallia', referring to a very much later occasion. Or. here as invariably elsewhere replaces OH *Caesar* by *Iulius,* presumably because for the translator *Caesar,* or *casere,* was a title, and no longer a proper name.

126/11–12. *bæd . . . ongean.* OH VI. xv. 1 'alterum consulatum poposcit.' That Caesar requested—or was refused—a triumph is a detail found in

a number of Latin texts: see, e.g., *De Viris Illustribus* 78. 5, Servius, *Aen.*
I. 286 and Acron, *Carm.* II. i. 2.

126/12–13. *þæt he . . . lete.* Cf. OH VI. xv. 1 'in Vrbem Caesar non nisi
dimisso exercitu ueniret'.

126/13–18. *Ac . . . hiene.* Based on OH VI. xv. 1–2, 'ad legiones, quae
apud Luceriam erant, Pompeius cum imperio missus est. Caesar Rauennam sese contulit. M. Antonius et P. Cassius tribuni plebis pro Caesare
intercedentes, interdicente Lentulo consule curia foroque prohibiti, ad
Caesarem profecti sunt Curione simul Caelioque comitantibus.' There
are several possible explanations for MS L *iii.* It may be a scribal error
for *ii*, (cf. LER 1523 *dui*). Alternatively it could be based on a MS reading
such as the 'marcus et antonius et publius cassius' of 'related' Group C
(see Bately (1961), p. 97), or even on the false assumption that Curio
and Caelius were one and the same person.

126/18. *to his agnum folce.* OH VI. xv. 3 says that he joined his five
cohorts at Ariminum.

126/20. *swiþost . . . forwurdon.* Cf. OH VI. xv. 3 'causam belli ciuilis, pro
restituendis in patriam tribunis, esse testatus est'; *þara monna* is gen. of
respect.

126/21. *legian.* OH VI. xv. 4 *cohortes.* OH refers also to three legions.

126/21. *on Silomone þæm londe.* OH VI. xv. 4 'apud Sulmonem'.

126/22. *Pompeius 7 Cato.* OH VI. xv. 4 *Pompeius.* Cato is not mentioned
by OII until VI. xv. 7, where he is said to have been driven from Sicily
by Curio.

126/23. *Thraci þære dune.* OH VI. xv. 4 *Dyrrachium*, mod. Durazzo. See
Lucan scholia VI. 14, 'Dyrrachium est mons, ubi est castrum munitis-
simum', and Vibius Sequester, in *Geographi Latini*, p. 156, under the
heading *Montes*: 'Petrae Dyrrachii castra Pompei Magni'.

126/24. *maðmhus.* OH VI. xv. 5 *aerario.*

126/24–6. *eall . . . ealles wæs.* OH VI. xv. 5 in fact states the amount of
gold and silver seized, but does not say what Caesar did with it.

126/26–7. *Marisiam þæt lond.* Cotton MS *Samariam.* OH's reference,
VI. xv. 6, is to *Massiliam*, mod. Marseilles.

127/3–4. *on Creca . . . onbad.* OH VI. xv. 18 'apud Dyrrachium'. See
above, 126/23 and Commentary.

127/4. *mid xxxgum cyningum.* OH VI. xv. 18 'multi Orientis reges'.

127/6. *Iuliuses ladteow.* Or.'s addition, a safe contextual guess.

127/7. *Tarquatus, Pompeius ladteow.* OH VI. xv. 19 *Torquatum.* See also
VI. xv. 20 'hoc periculo sociorum Pompeius cognito omnes eo copias
contraxit.'

127/11. *þær . . . gegaderade.* Or.'s addition, possibly a contextual guess.
See, however, Eutropius VI. xx 'in Thessalia . . . productis utrimque
ingentibus copiis'.

127/13–14. *coortana . . . m.* OH VI. xv. 23 *cohortes.* The strength of a cohort is given in a number of Latin texts: see, e.g., Isidore IX. iii. 51 'Cohors quingentos milites habet.'

127/14–16. *þis . . . senatuses*. Cf. OH VI. xv. 23 'praeterea reges multi, senatores equitesque Romani plurimi, absque leuium armaturarum magna copia'. Cato was in fact not present at the battle of Pharsalus, having been left in charge of Pompey's camp. For the linking of Pompey and Cato see also 123/2–4 and 126/22 and Commentary.

127/17–18. *hie selfe . . . hiera*. Or.'s addition. According to classical sources, Pompey was in the left wing at Pharsalus and was confronted there by Caesar: see Caesar, *De Bello Civili*, ed. F. Kraner and F. Hofmann, 13th ed. revised H. Meusel (Berlin, 1963), III. 88.

127/18–19. *ænne þara dæla gefliemed*. According to OH VI. xv. 26, 'equitatus Pompei pulsus sinistra latera nudauit.'

127/19–26. *þa . . . gemette*. The translator has completely misunderstood OH VI. xv. 26, 'deinde cum diu utrimque dubia sorte caederentur atque ex alia parte Pompeius inter hortandum diceret parce ciuibus nec tamen faceret, ex alia uero Caesar hoc faceret, quod urgeret dicens miles, faciem feri'.

127/29. *him . . . cyninge*. Or.'s addition, for which possible sources include Eutropius VI. xxi, Bede, *De Temporum Ratione*, col. 544, and Caesar, *Civil Wars* III. 103.

128/1–2. *hit siþþan . . . mid*. A contextual deduction.

128/3–4. *for þon . . . dagum*. Or.'s addition. Caesar's clemency was proverbial. See, e.g., Augustine, *Civ. Dei* IX. 5, Valerius Maximus V. i. 10, Solinus 27, 13–14.

128/5–6. *Photolomeus . . . gefangen*. OH VI. xv. 31 and 33 refer to two battles, in which the Egyptian forces were led by Achillas. That Ptolemy was taken prisoner is not stated, though it is implicit in OH VI. xvi. 1.

128/6–7. *ealle . . . ofslog*. OH VI. xv. 33 'omnes . . . interfectores Pompei interfecti sunt.'

128/8–9. *Æfter . . . þriwa*. OH refers to three battles, but two of these are said to occur before the restoration of Ptolemy.

128/11. *eft sette senatus*. Or.'s addition.

128/12. *he . . . tictator*. OH VI. xvi. 3 *dictator*. The translator had earlier explained the term as 'hiran ladteow þonne hiera consul wære, þone ðe hie tictatores heton'; see 41/13–15, Commentary.

128/13. *æfter Cato þæm consule*. Or.'s addition. According to OH VI. xvi. 3, Caesar, having crossed to Africa, fought and defeated Juba and Scipio. All that is said of Cato is that he committed suicide at Utica. See next note.

128/13–21. *þa . . . swealt*. An expansion of OH VI. xvi. 4, 'Cato sese apud Vticam occidit.' The details of Cato's speech before suicide are most probably to be derived from Augustine, *Civ. Dei*, I. xxiii, where it is said

that Cato commanded his son to hope for Caesar's clemency but refused
it for himself, possibly because he envied Caesar the glory he would win
by sparing him. However, *De Viris Illustribus* 80. 4 also tells how Cato
urged his son 'ut clementiam Caesaris experiretur', while Valerius
Maximus V. i. 10 reports Caesar as saying of the dead Cato, 'et se illius
gloriae invidere et illum suae invidisse'—using the same verb as
Augustine, *invidere*, the possible meanings of whose root include not only
'envy' but also (as in Or.) 'hate'. See also Capella V. 448, 'ut si deliberet
Cato, an se debeat, ne victorem aspiciat Caesarem, trucidare'. As for the
details of the suicide itself, these appear to be derived, as the result of
misunderstanding or careless reading, from a text in which the suicide of
Cato is linked with the suicide by leaping from a wall of a certain Cleombrotus. Such a text is Firmianus Lactantius' *Divine Institutions*, *PL* vi,
col. 408: 'Cato . . . antequam se occideret, perlegisse Platonis librum
dicitur, qui est scriptus de aeternitate animarum, et ad summum nefas
philosophi auctoritate compulsus est; et hic tamen aliquam moriendi
causam videtur habuisse, odium servitutis. Quid Ambraciotes ille, qui
cum eumdum librum perlegisset praecipitem se dedit, nullam aliam ob
causam, nisi quod Platoni credidit?' The suicide of Cleombrotus the
Ambraciot is linked with that of Cato also in a (spurious?) epistle of
Jerome, *PL* xxx, col. 263, but here Cato is correctly described as stabbing
himself to death with a sword. In Augustine, *Civ. Dei*, the two suicides
are referred to in adjacent chapters, I. xxii and I. xxiii, the manner of only
'Theombrotus's' death 'de muro' being described.

128/21–2. *Iulius . . . ofslog*. OH VI. xvi. 5 'Caesar Pompei Magni nepotes
filiamque Pompeiam simulque cum his Faustum Sullam et Afranium et
Petreium filium iussit occidi.'

128/23. *swa onddrysne*. Or.'s addition.

128/25–9. *þær . . . gebunde*. Caesar was in fact contemplating suicide: see
OH VI. xvi. 7 'Ultimum bellum apud Mundam flumen gestum est, ubi
tantis uiribus dimicatum tantaque caedes acta, ut Caesar quoque, ueteranis
etiam suis cedere non erubescentibus, cum caedi cogique aciem suam
cerneret, praeuenire morte futurum uicti dedecus cogitarit, cum subito
uersus in fugam Pompeiorum cessit exercitus.' Or.'s description of
Caesar's behaviour could be based either on Frontinus II. viii. 13, 'in
primam aciem pedes prosiluit', or on similar statements in Florus II. xiii.
82 and Velleius Paterculus II. lv. 3, though in the latter Munda is not
mentioned by name.

128/30–129/4. *ealle . . . xxvii*. OH VI. xvii. 1–2 'dum reipublicae statum
contra exempla maiorum clementer instaurat, auctoribus Bruto et Cassio,
conscio etiam plurimo senatu, in curia uiginti et tribus uulneribus
confossus interiit. in qua coniuratione fuisse amplius sexaginta conscios
ferunt.' For a different reason for Caesar's murder see, e.g., Augustine,
Civ. Dei III. 30, and Eutropius VI. xxv.

129/4. *xxvii*. OH VI. xvii. 1 'uiginti et tribus'. Although MS L now has
the 'correct' figure, as the result of alteration, I have restored the original

reading, which it shares with MS C. A number of 'related' MSS, including those closest to Or., have the reading *xxiiii* and this could well have been misread or miscopied as *xxuii*.

129/6-9. *feng . . . getyde*. As a result of omissions, it is made to appear as though Octavian came to power immediately. Cf. OH VI. xviii. 1 'Anno ab Vrbe condita dccx interfecto Iulio Caesare Octauianus, qui testamento Iuli Caesaris auunculi et hereditatem et nomen adsumpserat idemque, qui postea rerum potitus Augustus est dictus, simul ut Romam adulescens admodum uenit, indolem suam bellis ciuilibus uouit.'

129/6. *hiora unþonces*. Or.'s addition.

129/9. *he . . . getyde*. Or.'s addition. Octavian was in fact brought up by his grandmother, mother, and stepfather; however, Caesar apparently watched over his education with interest. See, e.g., Velleius Paterculus, II. lix.

129/10-12. *he siþþan . . . Lepidus*. OH VI. xviii. 2 'bella ciuilia quinque gessit: Mutinense Philippense Perusinum Siculum Actiacum. e quibus duo, hoc est primum ac nouissimum, aduersus M. Antonium, secundum aduersus Brutum et Cassium, tertium aduersus L. Antonium, quartum aduersus Sex. Pompeium, Cn. Pompei filium, confecit', with *M*. and *L*. expanded to *Marcum* and *Lucium* in many MSS. I have retained the reading of MS L here since the number of fights reported—five—is correct, although only four are named, and assumed that the version in MS C is the result of an attempt to impose some kind of order on the list. The reference to Lepidus seems to be in place of the reference to *L. Antonius*. For Lepidus' rebellion see OH VI. xviii.

129/10. *swa Iulius dyde ær*. Or.'s addition. See above, 123/11-12.

129/12-13. *þeh . . . wurde*. Possibly an assumption on the part of the translator, inspired by subsequent allusions in OH VI. xviii to Lepidus as a colleague of Octavian's. See, however, OH VI. xviii. 32, where Lepidus, having fallen out with Octavian, is said to have petitioned him and been granted his life and property.

129/14-15. *Octauianus . . . Antoniuse*. Or.'s addition. See OH VI. xix. 4.

129/16. *ealle Asiam*. Or.'s addition. See, e.g., Bede, *De Temporum Ratione*, col. 545, Eutropius VII. iii and VII. vi, and Acron, *Carm*. I. 37.

129/18-19. *he him . . . cwene*. Cf. OH VI. xix. 4 'Cleopatram sibi ex Alexandria occurrere imperauit.' Antony never married Cleopatra; however, she is described as *uxor* in a number of Latin texts: see, e.g., Bede, *De Temporum Ratione*, col. 545, Eutropius VII. vi and Servius, *Aen*. VII. 684.

129/19-20. *þa hæfde . . . Egypti*. Or.'s addition. For Caesar's involvement with Cleopatra, see, e.g., Bede, *De Temporum Ratione*, col. 544, Eutropius VI. xxii and Jerome–Eusebius, col. 538. For his restoration of Egypt to her, see OH VI. xvi. 2 (a passage not used in the corresponding section of Or.).

129/20–1. *hiene raðe gefliemde.* OH VI. xix. 7 'Antonius . . . uictus est.'

129/21. *þæs ymb iii niht.* OH VI. xix. 8 'tertio post pugnam die'.

129/22–3. *Octauianus . . . legian.* Cf. OH VI. xix. 8 'ducentae triginta rostratae fuere Caesaris naues et triginta sine rostris, triremes uelocitate Liburnicis pares et octo legiones classi superpositae, absque cohortibus quinque praetoriis.'

129/23–7. *Antonius . . . wætere.* Again a slight distortion of the facts. Cf. OH VI. xix. 9 'classis Antonii centum septuaginta nauium fuit, quantum numero cedens tantum magnitudine praecellens, nam decem pedum altitudine a mari aberant.' For *centum septuaginta* the 'related' MS Selden B 16 reads *lxx,* while other variants include *clxxx.*

129/29. *Antoniuses folces.* According to OH VI. xix. 12, the twelve thousand slain are *ex uictis.* The reference immediately following to Cleopatra as *his cwen* confirms that the reading *Octauianuses* of the two MSS of Or., LER 2034 *il,* i.e. *Octovianus,* is a slip for *Antoniuses.*

130/1–3. *Æfter . . . gefliemde.* Cf. OH VI. xix. 11 'inlucescente iam die uictoriam Caesar consummauit.'

130/3–4. *þæt . . . hlafmæsse.* Cf. OH VI. xix. 16 'kalendis Sextilibus', the date given not for the battle of Actium but for a somewhat later occasion, when Antony's fleet suddenly went over to Octavian, and Antony and Cleopatra killed themselves.

130/4–5. *Siþþan . . . hæfde.* Or.'s addition, apparently based on a misunderstanding of Bede, *De Temporum Ratione,* col. 351, 'Augustus mensis Sextilis antea vocabatur, donec honor Augusto daretur ex senatusconsulto, eo quod ipse die primo hujus mensis Antonium et Cleopatram superavit.' For a somewhat different rendering of this comment, see *An Old English Martyrology,* 132/16–19. OH itself assigns the title-giving to 6 January: see OH VI. xx. 2.

130/7. *on þæm Readan Sæ.* Or.'s addition. According to OH VI. xix. 13, Antony and Cleopatra sent their children to the Red Sea.

130/9. *to anum tune.* OH VI. xix. 16 'in regiam'.

130/9–10. *het . . . byrgenne.* Or.'s addition. OH VI. xix. 17 merely says that Cleopatra had concealed herself in *monumentum.*

130/11–14. *þa het . . . geendian.* Cf. OH VI. xix. 18 'serpentis, ut putatur, morsu in sinistro tacta bracchio exanimis inuenta est.' Or.'s additional material is based ultimately on Isidore, *Etymologies* XII. iv. 14, 'Hypnalis, genus aspidis, dicta quod somno necat. Hanc sibi Cleopatra adposuit, et ita morte quasi somno soluta est', possibly influenced also by XII. iv. 32, 'Dipsas serpens tantae exiguitatis fertur ut cum calcatur, non uideatur. Cuius venenum ante extinguit quam sentiatur, ut facies praeventa morte nec tristitiam induat morituri. De quo poeta . . . vix dolor aut sensus dentis fuit.' The first of these definitions is quoted by 'related' MSS of Group C. For identification of Cleopatra's asp with *dipsas* see the gloss 'dipsadem genus aspidis dictam' found in the 'unrelated' MSS Vat. ASP23E and BL Addit. 26623. Less close to Or.'s account is the 'hypnale, quod somno necat' of Solinus 122, 17 (quoted by Wyatt (1919), p. 212), a gloss based on which is to be found in the 'related' MS Balliol 125.

130/15–16. *hio nolde . . . weard.* OH VI. xix. 18 'se ad triumphum seruari intellexit.' For Or.'s conception of the triumph see 42/1–13, and Commentary.

130/16–18. *þa Antonius . . . alegde.* Or. has reversed OH VI. xix. 17 and 18.

130/18–20. *þa Octauianus . . . bringð.* Cf. OH VI. xix. 18 'frustra Caesare etiam Psyllos admouente, qui uenena serpentum e uulneribus hominum haustu reuocare atque exsugere solent'. The Psylli were in fact a tribe of African snake-charmers: see e.g. Dunchad 153, 14. Potter (1952–3), p. 432, suggests that Or.'s comment may have arisen from a careless reading of Solinus 124, 17–19, 'Super Garamantes Psylli fuerunt, contra noxium virus muniti incredibili corporis firmitate. soli morsibus anguium non interibant et quamvis dente letali appetiti incorrupta durabant sanitate.' However, MS St. Gall 621 glosses 'psillis admotis: serpentibus a victoribus ut vivesceret', while the Corpus Glossary has the entry, P 383, *P[hi]sillos: leceas,* the OE word *læce* having the two meanings 'doctor', 'leech' (species of worm) and a gloss could equally well have been Or.'s source here. For an asp which sucks the blood and at the same time removes any poison in it, see Isidore, *Etymologies* XII. iv. 15 (an entry which follows immediately on Isidore's comment on *hypnalis*).

130/21–2. *Alexandriam, Egypta heafedburg.* OH VI. xix. 19 'Alexandria, urbe omnium longe opulentissima et maxima'. Cf. Isidore, *Etymologies* XV. i. 34 'Alexandria . . . caput . . . regionis Aegypti'.

130/23–4. *mon . . . mehte.* OH VI. xix. 19 'Roma in tantum opibus eius aucta est, ut propter abundantiam pecuniarum duplicia quam usque ad id fuerant possessionum aliarumque rerum uenalium pretia statuerentur.'

130/25–6. *vii . . . xxxv.* OH VI. xx. 1 *dccxxv,* 'related' MSS including Selden B 16 and MSS of Group C *dccxxxv.*

130/26. *Octauianus Cesar.* OH VI. xx. 1 'imperatore Caesare Augusto'. The names *Caesar* and *Augustus* had both come to be used as titles: see 126/11 and 59/2–3, Commentary.

130/26. *on his fiftan consulato.* OH VI. xx. 1 *quinquies.* For other instances of the Latin loan word *consulatum* see 74/30 and 124/21.

130/28. *þa he cniht wæs.* Or.'s addition. Cf. OH VI. xviii. 1 *adulescens.*

130/29. *Iuliuses.* OH VI. xx. 5 *C. Caesare.* See 126/11, Commentary.

130/29–30. *þy . . . dyde.* Or.'s addition. The first portent in fact occurred when Octavian came to Rome on the death of Caesar, the second at the time when, according to OH VI. xx. 7, 'Caesari perpetua tribunicia potestas decreta est.'

131/1. *an gylden hring.* Cf. OH VI. xx. 5 'circulus ad speciem caelestis arcus'. Or.'s source here seems to be pseudo-Jerome on Luke, *PL* xxx, col. 569, *circulus aereus*, misread *circulus aureus*, possibly via an intermediary version with the reading *circulus aurei coloris*: see *Catéchèses Celtiques*, ed. A. Wilmart, *Studi e Testi*, lix (1933), 29–112, quoted by J. E. Cross, 'Portents and events at Christ's birth', *ASE*, ii (1973), 209–220, and Whitelock (1966), p. 91. For a similar account of this portent in the fifth Vercelli Homily, see *Die Vercelli-Homilien*, p. 115, 'þa wæs mannum on heofonum gesine gyldnes hringes onlicnes ymbutan þa sunnan.'

131/3–4. *se se . . . wære*. The corresponding passage of OH VI. xx. 5 reads 'qui ipsum solem solus mundumque totum et fecisset et regeret'. See *Die Vercelli-Homilien*, p. 115 'he mid his fægernesse gewlitgode þa sunnan, þe up nu dæghwamlice lyhteð'. For the source of this part of Vercelli V, see Cross, *ASE*, ii, 210. The Redeemer is referred to as shining more brightly than the sun in a homily for the First Sunday in Advent by Theophylactus: see M. F. Toal, *The Sunday Sermons of the Great Fathers* (Cork, 1954) I, 8.

131/4. *se ele . . . moncynne*. Cf. OH VI. xx. 6 'Christus enim lingua gentis eius, in qua et ex qua natus est, unctus interpretatur.' According to Jerome–Eusebius, col. 542, 'oleum terra erupit . . . significans Christi gratiam ex gentibus.' See also *PL* xxx, cols. 568 ff.

131/4–6. *Swa . . . bisene*. Or.'s addition.

131/7–11. *Sum . . . life*. Cf. OH VI. xxii. 6–7 'censum agi singularum ubique prouinciarum et censeri omnes homines iussit . . . in qua se et ipse, qui cunctos homines fecit, inueniri hominem adscribique inter homines uoluit.' A possible influence on Or. here is Bede, commentary on Luke, *PL* xcii, cols. 328–9.

131/12–14. *Oþer . . . weorca*. For the theme of peace see OH VI. xx. 1 and 8, and xxii. 5. For the theme of tribute see Bede on Luke, *PL* xcii, col. 328, 'censoribus suae profectionis, non ablatione pecuniae subjectos, sed fidei oblatione signare praecepit'. See further OH VII. ii. 16.

131/15–21. *þridde . . . ofslagen*. Cf. OH VI. xx. 7 'restituendosque per Caesarem omnes seruos, qui tamen cognoscerent dominum suum, ceterosque, qui sine domino inuenirentur, morti supplicioque dedendos' and VI. xviii. 33 'triginta milia seruorum dominis restituit, sex milia, quorum domini non exstabant, in crucem egit.' For the theme of the heavenly kingdom as man's true homeland, a common-place in medieval Christian writings see, e.g., Bede, *PL* xcii, col. 329. A different comment is provided by Vercelli V: see Cross, *ASE*, ii, 211.

131/22–3. *vii . . . xxxvi*. OH VI. xxi. 1 dccxxvi, 'related' MSS, including Selden B 16, dccxxxvi.

131/23. *sume . . . wiþerwearde*. According to OH VI. xxi. 1, *Caesar* decided to mount a campaign against the Spaniards.

131/25. *on anum fæstenne*. OH VI. xxi. 5 'in Vinnium montem natura tutissimum'.

131/25–6. *hie siþþan . . . acwælan.* OH VI. xxi. 5 refers only to famine; however, see OH VI. xxi. 8, 'igne ferro ac ueneno necauerunt', referring to a different siege, also on a mountain.

131/27–8. *monege . . . þeoda.* OH VI. xxi. 14 names also *Norici, Dalmatae, Moesi,* and *Thraces.*

132/1. *Quintillus . . . consul.* OH VI. xxi. 26 *Quintilius Varus.* Varus was consul in 13 B.C.

132/2–3. *buton . . . anum.* According to OH VI. xxi. 26, Varus 'deletus est'. Or.'s assumption that Varus survived seems to be based on Augustus' words, addressed to the (dead) governor, 'Quintili Vare, redde legiones': see OH VI xxi. 27.

132/4. *þonne . . . sæt.* Or.'s addition.

132/5. *þone . . . ofslean.* See 132/2–3, Commentary.

132/5–7. *Germanie . . . wiste.* According to OH VI. xxi. 29, it was the Parthians who made their peace with Augustus.

132/9–12. *eallum . . . bebead.* Or.'s addition. See OH III. viii. 5.

132/13. *swa . . . næron.* Or.'s addition.

132/14–15. *þæt wæs . . . rices.* See OH VII. ii.

132/17–19. *Nu . . . witum.* Cf. OH VI. xxii. 11 'ab initio et peccare homines et puniri propter peccata non tacui.'

132/19–22. *Nu ic . . . wæron.* Orosius, VI. xxii. 11, says he is about to refer to persecutions: 'nunc quoque, quae persecutiones Christianorum actae sint et quae ultiones secutae sint, absque eo quod omnes ad peccandum generaliter proni sunt atque ideo singillatim corripiuntur, expediam.'

132/22–3. *Her . . . siofoðe.* The translator appears to have forgotten that he has replaced OH's Books V and VI by a single Book V. Cotton, however, gives the correct numbering.

132/24–7. *Nu . . . gestodon.* The words are not in fact those of Orosius, who at this point recalls his comments at the beginning of the second book on the many points of similarity between the empires and then, VII. ii. 8, offers as proof, 'quo magis clareat unum esse arbitrum saeculorum regnorum locorumque omnium Deum', the recurrence of the number seven in the history of these empires. However, the statement that it was God's command is probably based on OH VII. i. 7, where it is said that it was in the power of God to make the Roman empire so large and exalted, but that his patience prevented it from reaching that state earlier.

132/24. *seofeþan.* Cotton MS *vi.* See 132/22–3, Commentary.

132/28–133/3. *Sio . . . m.* OH VII. ii. 12 'eundem duplicatum numerum mansisse Babyloniae, quae post mille quadringentos et quod excurrit annos ultime a Cyro rege capta est'. For Ninus and Sardanopolis see OH II. ii. 1 and 2, Or. II. i.

COMMENTARY

133/5. *lytle leng.* OH VII. ii. 9 *paulo minus.* It is the Carthaginian empire that is said to last 'paulo amplius'.

133/9–10. *þæs . . . consul.* Or.'s addition. For the foundation of Carthage by Dido, see, e.g., Isidore, *Etymologies* V. xxxix. 13, and Jerome–Eusebius, cols. 299 and 303. OH itself gives Dido her other name of Elissa, and this is the form found in the corresponding part of Or.: see OH IV. vi. 1 'ab Helissa', Or. 88/16 'from Elisan þæm wifmen'. For the overthrow of Carthage by Scipio, see 112/14–25, OH IV. xxii and xxiii.

133/11. *mæst.* Or.'s addition.

133/11–12. *Ymb . . . eacon.* Cf. OH VII. ii. 11 'septingentesimo conditionis suae anno', 'related' MS Vienna 366 'septicensimo condicionis suae in xiiii anno'.

133/13. *xv tunas.* OH VII. ii. 11 'quattuordecim uicos'.

133/14–15. *þær forwearð . . . aðstod.* Or.'s addition. Cf. OH VII. ii. 11 'nec umquam, ut ait Liuius, maiore incendio uastata est'.

133/15–20. *Mid . . . talentana.* Cf. OH VII. ii. 11 'post aliquot annos Caesar Augustus ad reparationem eorum, quae tunc exusta erant, magnam uim pecuniae ex aerario publico largitus est', and OH VII. vii. 7 'Vrbis, quam se Augustus ex latericia marmoream reddidisse iactauerat'. The use of the Latin term *talentana* may point to a commentary or gloss source in which that term occurred.

133/21–2. *Hit . . . anwaldas.* Or.'s addition.

133/22–4. *þa þa . . . Babylonia.* Or. has lost OH's parallelism while gaining a new one: cf. VII. ii. 13 'illius ergo Nini anno, postquam regnare coeperat, quadragensimo tertio natus est sanctus ille Abraham, cui dictae sunt repromissiones.' The number 42 is found in MSS of the 'related' group C; the reading of Vienna 366 here is *xlv*.

133/29–134/2. *þa hwile . . . ofrede.* Or.'s addition. Is the translator echoing OH VI. xxii. 4 'domini appellationem ut homo declinauit. nam cum eodem spectante ludos pronuntiatum esset in mimo O dominum aequum et bonum uniuersique, quasi de ipso dictum esset, exultantes adprobauissent, et statim quidem manu uultuque indecoras adulationes repressit et insequenti die grauissimo corripuit edicto dominumque se posthac appellari ne a liberis quidem aut nepotibus suis uel serio uel ioco passus est'? See also 59/21–4, Commentary and Tertullian, *Apology*, *PL* i, col. 450, 'Augustus imperii formator, ne dominum quidem dici se volebat; et hoc enim dei est cognomen.'

134/2. *þæs on . . . geare.* OH VII. iii. 4 'dum per duodecim . . . annos'. Orosius puts this expedition before the famine which, he says, took place in the 48th year of Augustus' reign, i.e. in the sixth year after the birth of Christ.

134/3. *on Siriæ.* According to OH VII. iii. 5, Gaius was passing by 'fines Palaestinae'. For Palestine as part of Syria see 10/20 and OH I. ii. 24.

134/7–8. *þæt . . . wæron.* Cf. OH VII. iii. 6 'ut Caesar lanistarum familias omnesque peregrinos, seruorum quoque maximas copias, exceptis medicis et praeceptoribus, trudi Vrbe praeceperit'.

134/8–10. *þa wearð . . . wurde.* According to OH VII. iii. 9, 'etsi sub extremis Caesaris temporibus apertus est Ianus, tamen per multa ex eo tempora, quamuis in procinctu esset exercitus, nulla bella sonuerunt.' Orosius also quotes the words of Tacitus, that Janus was opened in the old age of Augustus and remained so until the rule of Vespasian, 'dum apud extremos terrarum terminos nouae gentes saepe ex usu et aliquando cum damno quaeruntur': see OH VII. iii. 7.

134/13–14. *swa forgiefen . . . ær þæm.* OH VII. iv. 4 and 7 stress 'Tiberius' moderation, but no comparison is made with earlier regimes.

134/14. *Hierusalem.* Or.'s addition. Pilate's presence in Jerusalem would of course have been known from many sources including the Vulgate.

134/16–20. *Ac . . . noldon.* According to OH VII. iv. 6 'Tiberius cum suffragio magni fauoris rettulit ad senatum, ut Christus deus haberetur. senatus indignatione motus, cur non sibi prius secundum morem delatum esset, ut de suscipiendo cultu prius ipse decerneret, consecrationem Christi recusauit edictoque constituit, exterminandos esse Vrbe Christianos.'

134/22–3. *þara twa . . . patricius.* Cf. OH VII. iv. 8 'uiginti sibi patricios uiros consilii causa legerat'. Did an underlying MS have the abbreviation *xxti*, which was then misread or miscopied as *xxii*? And has the author, like Leiden XXXV. 272 (*Patricius: senator consiliarius*) taken *patricius* to have the meaning 'counsellor'?

134/24–6. *Hu . . . casere.* Cf. OH VII. iv. 10 'tanta libidinis et crudelitatis rabie efferbuit, ut, qui spreuerant Christo rege saluari, rege Caesare punirentur.'

134/26–8. *þeh . . . wæs.* Or.'s addition.

134/29–135/3. *On . . . cristendome.* The corresponding passage of OH, VII. iv. 11–12, describes the collapse of the seats of an amphitheatre at Fidenae, while the people were watching a gladiatorial performance, with the comment, 'dignum sane posteris tantae correptionis exemplum, tunc ad spectandas hominum mortes auidos homines conuenisse, quando pro salute hominum prouidenda Deus homo esse uoluisset'.

135/4. *eahtateoþan.* OH VII. iv. 13 'septimo decimo', 'related' MSS including Vienna 366 and Selden B 16 *xviii.*

135/5–8. *wearð . . . apeostrade.* OH VII. iv. 13–15 refers first to the earthquake and then to the darkness. Or.'s version may well be the result of a desire to follow the Biblical chronology, according to which the darkness preceded the earthquake.

135/6. *cludas feollon of muntum.* According to OH VII. iv. 13, the rocks were rent: 'saxa in montibus scissa'.

135/7. *þa se mona ful wæs.* Cf. OH VII. iv. 15 'quartam decimam ea die lunam'.

135/13–14. *hie . . . forsawon.* Based on OH's allusion, VII. v. 1, to 'Romanis blasphemantibus'.

135/15–16. *þæt he hiene . . . mehte.* Or.'s addition.

135/17. *swelc sacu.* OH VII. v. 2 refers less specifically to 'calamitatibus publicis'.

135/19–21. *Ungelice . . . forbugan.* A rewriting in general terms of OH VII. v. 3–4, which compares the period of unrest when mutinous slaves and runaway gladiators terrorized Italy with the period under consideration, when even Caligula could not break the peace. See Introduction, p. xcvii.

135/23. *betweonum him selfum.* Or.'s addition, perhaps inspired by OH's reference to *seditio.*

135/25. *hie . . . adrifan.* OH VII. v. 6 does not say who was responsible for driving the Jews out of Alexandria. According to Jerome–Eusebius, col. 575, it was Flaccus.

135/25–6. *hiora þone gelæredestan mon.* OH VII. v. 6 describes Philo as 'uirum sane in primis eruditum'.

135/26–7. *to þon . . . geærendian.* OH VII. v. 6 gives the reason as 'expromendarum querellarum causa'.

135/28. *bebead . . . mehte.* Or.'s addition.

135/29–136/1. *þæt mon . . . onlicnes.* Cf. OH VII. v. 7 'seque ibi ut deum coli praecepit'. That this involved the placing of a statue of Caligula in the Temple could have been known from a number of sources. See, e.g., Tacitus, *Histories* V. ix, Isidore, *Chronicon,* col. 1039 and Freculph, *Chronicon,* col. 1127.

136/3. *Raþe . . . slæpendne.* OH VII. v. 9 'ipse autem a suis protectoribus occisus est.' According to Suetonius, Caligula was attacked in a passageway. Could Or.'s version be the result of a confusion between *suis* and an abbreviation of *somnis?*

136/6. *þæt he . . . forgeate.* Calendre's source seems to have had these words, missing from L: see LER 2643.

136/8–10. *Ægþær . . . hæfde.* Cf. OH VII. v. 11 'Magnum reuera indicium miserentis Dei propter suffragium gratiae in populum continuo ex parte crediturum et propter irae temperamentum in populum tunc infideliter obstinatum, ut quanta multitudo hominum praeparatam mortem euaserit, ex multitudine interfectorum piscium disceretur omnibusque notesceret.'

136/12–13. *On . . . rices.* OH VII. vi. 2 merely refers to 'exordio regni eius'; however, according to Jerome, *De Viris Illustribus,* col. 607, Peter came to Rome in the second year of Claudius' reign, a date which appears to have been adopted by the *Anglo-Saxon Chronicle*: see Bately, *ASE,* viii, p. 183.

136/14–16. *þa . . . wæron.* According to OH VII. vi. 3, the Senate passed resolutions with a view to wiping out 'Caesarum uniuersa familia'.

136/16–20. *Ac . . . þohte.* According to OH VII. vi. 4, the forgiveness is all on Claudius' side: 'biduum illud, quo de reipublicae statu infeliciter consultatum actumque fuerat, memoriae exemit omniumque factorum dictorumue in eo ueniam et obliuionem in perpetuum sanxit.'

136/22–4. *Dalmatie . . . winnan.* Based on a misunderstanding of OH VII. vi. 6, 'Furius Camillus Scribonianus, Dalmatiae legatus, bellum ciuile molitus legiones multas fortissimasque ad sacramenti mutationem pellexerat.'

136/25–6. *swa . . . setton.* Or.'s addition, without foundation in fact.

137/3. *on Siria 7 on Palestina.* OH VII. vi. 12 'per Syriam'. The addition of Palestine seems to be based on knowledge that Jerusalem (referred to immediately afterwards) was in Palestine, coupled with ignorance that Palestine formed part of Syria. See, however, 10/20 and 134/3, Commentary, beside 140/18.

137/4. *þæm munucum.* OH VII. vi. 12 *Christianorum.*

137/7. *v mila brad . . . long.* OH VII. vi. 13 'triginta stadiorum'. Or.'s figures are most easily explained if we assume that the Latin MS used by the translator gave the figure as *xxxx stadiorum.* For the stadium as 1/8th of a mile, see 43/27–8, Commentary.

137/9. *þæm þe þær cristene næron.* OH VII. vi. 14 *Iudaeorum.* For the presence of Christians in Jerusalem see OH VII. vi. 12.

137/10–11. *swa . . . com.* Or.'s addition.

137/11–13. *On . . . wæron.* OH VII. vi. 15 puts the expulsion of the Jews in the year before the famine.

137/14–15. *he wearð . . . wæron.* There is no suggestion in OH VII. vi. 17 and 18 of any connection between the taunts hurled at Claudius during the famine and the executions subsequently ordered by the emperor.

137/15. *þe þær ieldeste wæron.* OH VII. vi. 18 *equites.*

137/16. *Romane . . . atre.* Cf. OH VII. vi. 18 'ipse . . . manifestis ueneni signis est mortuus.'

137/17–18. *viii hunde wintra 7 ix.* OH VII. vii. 1 *dcccviii.* Some MSS, though not those closest to Or., have the variant *dcccviiii.*

137/21–3. *bebead . . . opbrude.* According to OH VII. vii. 7, Nero's avarice was such that 'neminem ad reliquias rerum suarum adire permiserit; cuncta, quae flammae quoquo modo superfuerant, ipse abstulit'.

137/24–5. *ongon . . . bryne.* Based on OH VII. vii. 6 'tragico habitu Iliadam decantabat'.

137/25–7. *Ac . . . gemartredon.* OH VII. vii. 10 merely refers to the execution of Peter and Paul; the translator may have been influenced by OH VII. viii. 2 'Luit Roma caedibus principum excitatisque ciuilibus bellis recentes Christianae religionis iniurias', which is followed by a second allusion to the death of Peter.

138/2. *Galua se casere.* OH VII. viii. 1 *Galba.*

138/6–7. *swa wurdon . . . wæron.* Cf. OH VII. vii. 12 'in Oriente magnis Armeniae prouinciis amissis Romanae legiones sub iugum Parthicum missae, aegreque Syria retenta est.'

138/8. *Uitellus, Germania cyning.* This description of Vitellius is based on a misunderstanding of OH's allusions to him as made *imperator* in Germany, by *Germanicas legiones.* See OH VII. viii. 3 and 6, and, for the translation of *imperator* by *cyning* see 91/27, Commentary, also 61/12, etc.

138/8–9. *Uitellus . . . ongunnon.* According to OH VII. viii. 6, Otho was victorious in three battles againxt Vitellius' generals but was worsted in a fourth battle three months after he had begun to reign and killed himself: 'quarto . . . proelio cum animaduertisset suos uinci, mense tertio quam imperare coeperat sese interfecit.'

138/12–14. *he bebead . . . leng.* According to OH VII. ix. 5, Titus, who had been left in charge of the siege of Jerusalem by Vespasian, was at first undecided whether to destroy the Temple or preserve it as a memorial of his victory. However, 'Ecclesia Dei iam per totum Orbem uberrime germinante, hoc tamquam effetum ac uacuum nullique usui bono commodum arbitrio Dei auferendum fuit.'

138/14–15. *forbead . . . timbrede.* Or.'s addition.

138/21. *on anum tune buton Rome.* OH VII. ix. 12 'in uilla propria circa Sabinos'.

138/22–3. *viii hunde wintra 7 xxix.* OH VII. ix. 13 *dcccxxviii.*

138/23–139/2. *He . . . gedyde.* Or.'s addition. Titus' famous remark is recorded in a number of Latin texts, the versions closest to that of Or. being found in Jerome and Isidore. See Jerome–Eusebius, cols. 597–8, 'Titus . . . fuit . . . tantae bonitatis ut cum quadam die recordatus fuisset in coena nihil se illo die cuiquam praestitisse, dixit, Amici, hodie diem perdidi', Jerome, *Comm. in Epistolam ad Galatos*, PL xxvi, col. 433, 'Titus . . . tantae dicitur fuisse bonitatis, ut cum quadam nocte sero recordaretur, in cena, quod nihil boni die illa fecisset, dixerit amicis, Hodie diem perdidi' and Isidore, *Chronicon*, col. 1042, 'Porro in imperio tantæ bonitatis fuit, ut nullum omnino puniret, sed convictos adversus se conjurationis dimitteret, atque in eadam familiaritate qua antea habuerat retineret. Hujus etiam inter omnia fuit illud celebre dictum: perdidisse diem quo nihil boni fecerat.' See also Freculph, *Chronicon*, col. 1146. See further Whitelock (1966), p. 74, and Introduction, pp. xc. f.

139/3. *on þære ilcan adle.* OH VII. ix. 15 merely refers to 'morbo'.

139/7–8. *he bead . . . Gode.* Cf. OH VII. x. 2 'dominum sese ac deum uocari scribi colique iusserit'.

139/8–10. *he bebead . . . monnum.* OH VII. x. 5 merely states that 'beatissimus Iohannes apostolus in Patmum insulam relegatus fuit'. See, however, Jerome, *De Viris Illustribus*, col. 625 'movente Domitiano'.

139/13–14. *he . . . ofslagen.* According to OH VII. x. 7, Domitian was killed 'a suis . . . atque ignominiosissime sepultu[s] est'.

139/17. *Traianus þone mon*. OH VII. xi. 1 *Traianum*. Is the addition of *þone mon* here intended to distinguish *Traianus* from *Troianus*? See below, 142/10, Commentary.

139/17-20. *þa . . . laꝺ*. Or.'s addition, apparently derived from Jerome: see Jerome–Eusebius, cols. 603–4 *Nerva*: 'Senatus decrevit, ut omnia quae Domitianus statuerat, in irritum deducerentur', and Jerome, *De Viris Illustribus*, col. 625, of Domitian: 'actis ejus ob nimiam crudelitatem a senatu rescissis sub Nerva'.

139/20-2. *heton . . . wæs*. Cf. OH VII. xi. 2 'Iohannes apostolus hac generali indulgentia liberatus Ephesum rediit.'

139/24-5. *he . . . hæfdon*. According to OH VII. xii. 2, Trajan restored Germany beyond the Rhine and subdued many tribes beyond the Danube.

139/25. *his aldormonnum*. OH VII. xii. 3 'iudices'.

140/2. *he . . . syngade*. What Plinius Secundus is in fact reported as saying, OH VII. xii. 3, is that the Christians were harmless and doing nothing contrary to the Roman laws. Trajan accordingly modified his edict by rescripts couched in milder terms.

140/9. *Traianuses nefa*. OH VII. xiii. 1 'consobrinae Traiani filius'.

140/10-11. *þurh . . . haten*. In addition to Quadratus, OH VII. xiii. 2 names also Aristides and Serenus Granius.

140/11-14. *he forbead . . . þuhte*. Based on OH VII. xiii. 2, 'praecepit per epistulam ad Minucium Fundanum proconsule Asiae datam ut nemini liceret Christianos sine obiectu criminis aut probatione damnare.' Has the translator misunderstood *obiectu*, taking it in its sense of 'a placing before' and assuming that it referred to appearance before Hadrian himself?

140/14-16. *He . . . casern*. OH VII. xiii. 3 gives no reasons for the granting of the title: see, however, VII. xiv. 1, where it is said of Antoninus Pius 'gubernauit adeo tranquille et sancte, ut merito Pius et pater patriae nominatus sit.' The term *casern* for Latin *Augusta* (LER 3230 *cesara*) is, as far as I know, not found elsewhere in Anglo-Saxon texts: indeed, *Augusta* is rendered *caseres wif* and *caseres cwen* in glosses: see Wright–Wülcker, 155, 16 and 309, 24. However, a similarly constituted form is to be found among the Old High German glosses: see Steinmeyer and Sievers III. 134 and 182 *Augusta: keiserin*. LER 3230 here has the unique form *Cesara*.

140/18. *Palestina . . . lond*. Although this is the fifth occurrence of the name *Palestina* in Or., it is the first (and only) time a comment has been made on it. See, e.g., Christian of Stavelot, col. 1412 'illa omnis Palaestina provincia generaliter Judaea diceretur'.

140/19. *on operre stowe*. Or.'s addition, possible sources of which include Gregory the Great, *Hom. XL in Evangelia*, PL lxxvi, col. 1294, *Liber Nominum*, PL xxiii, col. 1301, and Christian of Stavelot, col. 1454.

140/22-3. *Ponpeius . . . Pius*. OH VII. xiv. 1 'Antoninus cognomento

Pius'. I know of no satisfactory explanation for the substitution of *Pompeius* for *Antoninus*. However, it is perhaps worth noting that the entry contains a reference to a writer called Justinus, and that (another) writer called Justinus is elsewhere associated with a man called Pompeius; see OH I. viii. 1 and IV. vi. 6, Or. 23/23 and 88/18.

140/23–5. *him . . . ende.* An expansion of OH VII. xiv. 2, 'Iustinus philosophus librum pro Christiana religione compositum Antonino tradidit benignumque eum erga Christianos homines fecit.' Calendre's source may have had the words *swa leof*, missing from L: see LER 3264f.

141/1. *dcccc wintra 7 iii.* OH VII. xv. 1 *dccccxi.*

141/2. *Marcus Antonius.* OH VII. xv. 1 'Marcus Antoninus Verus'.

141/2. *Aureliuse.* OH VII. xv. 1 'Aurelio Commodo'.

141/4. *xiiii winter.* OH VII. xv. 1 *decem et nouem,* 'related' MSS including Vienna 366, *xviiii.*

141/4–5. *mon . . . ofsloge.* OH VII. xv. 4 refers merely to persecutions carried on with great severity.

141/5. *Æfter þæm.* OH VII. xv. 4 puts the persecution during the Parthian War.

141/7. *frið.* OH VII. xv. 3 refers to the Romans as having victory over the Parthians.

141/8. *micel hungor.* Or.'s addition.

141/10. *þæt Deniscæ gewinn.* OH VII. xv. 6 'Marcomannicum bellum'. The Marcomanni inhabited Bohemia and part of Bavaria. However, by the eighth century the name had come to be used of the Vikings: see *De Inventione Linguarum* (attributed to Hrabanus), *PL* cxii, col. 1582, 'Marcomanni quos nos Nordmannos vocamus' and *MGHS rer. Merov.* VII. 18, n. 3.

141/11–12. *him com . . . þurst.* OH VII. xv. 8 refers only to thirst.

141/13. *þa . . . men.* OH VII. xv. 9 makes no mention of any request to the Christians, merely recording their action.

141/14. *ongeaton . . . wracu.* Or.'s addition. See Introduction, p. xcv.

141/16. *onufan þære dune.* Or.'s addition.

141/17. *fela þusend monna.* OH VII. xv. 9 'plurimi eorum'.

141/18–21. *þa . . . wolde.* According to the corresponding passage of OH, VII. xv. 11, 'exstare etiam nunc apud plerosque dicuntur litterae imperatoris Antonini, ubi inuocatione nominis Christi per milites Christianos et sitim illam depulsam et conlatam fatetur fuisse uictoriam.' Does Or.'s reference to temples (and its use of the Latin loan word) derive from a comment or gloss telling how Marcus Aurelius gave thanks in Rome's temples after this event? Cf. Claudian, *Sixth Consulship of Honorius,* II. 339–41.

141/21–2. *forgef . . . sceolde.* In OH VII. xv. 12 it is the arrears only that are remitted: 'praeteriti etiam temporis per omnes prouincias tributa donauit omniaque simul fiscalium negotiorum calumniosa monumenta congesta in foro iussit incendi.'

141/23. *on þæm æfterran geare.* OH VII. xv. 12 'postremo'.

141/26. *Lucius Antonius.* OH VII. xvi. 1 'Lucius Antoninus Commodus'.

141/27–8. *he wæs cene . . . anwig.* This corresponds to OH VII. xvi. 2, a passage in which Orosius relates with disapproval that 'gladiatoriis quoque armis saepissime in ludo depugnauit et in amphitheatro feris sese frequenter obiecit'.

141/28. *þe þær betste wæron.* OH VII. xvi. 2 'maxime quos animaduertit nobilitate industriaque excellere'.

142/1–2. *Capitoliam . . . diofolgield.* OH VII. xvi. 3 *Capitolium.* The knowledge that the statues of the gods were placed in the Capitol could have been derived from a variety of sources; see, e.g., Orosius Commentary f. 10, 'capetolium arx monita in roma in qua forma iovis habetur qui capud deorum omnium est', and Servius, *Aen.* II. 319, 'in Capitolio . . . omnium deorum simulacra colebantur.' For a different comment on the name Capitol see 49/26–7, Commentary.

142/3–5. *þær . . . boca.* Or.'s addition, probably derived directly or indirectly from OH VI. xv. 31, a passage omitted by the translator from the corresponding section of Or.

142/6. *dcccc wintra 7 xliii.* OH VII. xvii. 1 *dccccxliiii,* 'related' MSS including Vienna 366 and Selden B 16, *dccccxliii.*

142/7. *xvii.* OH VII. xvii. 1 *xviii,* 'related' MSS including Vienna 366, *xvii,* or *x et vii.*

142/7–10. *He besæt . . . Egypte.* An expansion of OH VII. xvii. 2, 'Pescennium Nigrum, qui in Aegypto et Syria ad tyrannidem adspirauerat, apud Cyzicum uicit et interfecit.'

142/10. *Albinus þone mon.* OH VII. xvii. 6 *Clodius Albinus* and *Albinus.* Could the somewhat unusual use of *þone mon* here have been inspired by a gloss intended to show that Albinus was the name of a man, not the common noun meaning 'plasterer'? See also 139/17 and 145/25–146/1, Commentary.

142/10. *on Gallium.* OH VII. xvii. 6 *apud Lugdunum,* immediately following a reference to Albinus as having made himself Caesar in Gaul.

142/12. *oft . . . Scottas.* Or.'s addition: cf. OH VII. xvii. 7 'magnis grauibusque proeliis saepe gestis'. The 'related' MS St. Omer 717 here glosses 'a ceteris indomitis gentibus: a pictis et scothis qui uastabant brittanniam multa temporis'.

142/13. *þwyres.* Or.'s addition. Cf. the *OE Bede,* 44/7–8 'þam dice . . . þæt Seuerus se casere het þwyrs ofer þæt ealond gedician', with *þwyrs* corresponding to *HE* I. xii *recto tramite.*

142/16. *Antonius.* OH VII. xviii. 1 'Aurelius Antoninus Bassianus idemque Caracalla'.

142/16. *vii ger.* OH VII. xviii. 1 'annis non plenis septem', the 'related' MS Vienna 366 'non plenis annis vii'.

142/16–17. *He hæfde . . . wifum.* OH VII. xviii. 2 'nouercam suam Iuliam uxorem duxerit'. Or.'s mistake is a very strange one. Knowledge of the correct meaning of the term *noverca* is shown in 63/5–6 and it is not one that should have caused any difficulty. According to the Tables of Kindred a man might not marry either his stepmother or his wife's sister—though King Æþelbald, Alfred's eldest brother, married his father's widow, Judith.

142/18–19. *from his agnum monnum.* According to OH VII. xviii. 2, he was killed 'ab hostibus'. The translator appears accidentally to have skipped to OH VII. xviii. 3 where it is said that 'Ophilus Macrinus . . . militari tumultu occisus est'; see Potter (1952–3), 435–6.

142/21. *Marcus Aurelius.* OH VII. xviii. 4 'Marcus Aurelius Antoninus'.

143/2. *Aurelianus Alexander.* OH VII. xviii. 6 'Aurelius Alexander'. I have kept the reading of MS L here since it has the support of 'related' MSS (see Glossary of Proper Names). However, MS C *Aureliu'nu'* (*Aureliusnus*) and chapter headings *Aurelius* suggest the possibility of the existence of an alternative reading in an underlying manuscript.

143/3. *xvi.* OH VII. xviii. 6 *tredecim.* For other instances of confusion of *ii* and *u* see 20/29 and 40/18.

143/3. *Mammea his sio gode modor.* OH VII. xviii. 7 'mater Mamea Christiana'.

143/3–4. *Origenise þæm gelæredestan mæssepreoste.* OH VII. xviii. 7 'Origenem presbyterum'. Origen is praised for his learning by Jerome, *De Viris Illustribus*, cols. 663–7.

143/5–6. *gedyde . . . hold.* Or.'s addition. See Bede, *De Temporum Ratione*, col. 551, 'Hic in Mammeam matrem suam unice pius fuit et ob id omnibus amabilis.'

143/6. *ofslog.* OH VII. xviii. 7 *oppressit.* For a similar assumption see 102/26 and 146/10, Commentary.

143/10–13. *bebead . . . Aegypte.* Cf. OH VII. xix. 2 'Maximinus . . . maxime propter Christianam Alexandri, cui successerat, et Mameae matris eius familiam persecutionem in sacerdotes et clericos, id est doctores, uel praecipue propter Origenem presbyterum miserat.' Maximinus indeed murdered Mammaea: see Ammianus Marcellinus XXVI. vi. Origen, however, fled not to Egypt but to Cappadocia, the reference to Egypt apparently being the result of knowledge that he was an Alexandrian: see, e.g., Jerome, *De Viris*, col. 663, Bede, *De Temporum Ratione*, col. 551, *Origenes Alexandriae*, and Freculph, *Chronicon*, col. 1176, where he is said to have gone from Rome to Alexandria (though no reason for this is given).

143/13. *Maximus ofslog his agen ealdormon. Ealdormon* is the subject of the sentence: see OH VII. xix. 2 'Maximinus . . . a Pupieno Aquileiae interfectus' and Or. 70/8 and 78/3–4, Commentary. Pupienus is subsequently said to usurp the imperium (VII. xix. 3), a statement which suggests that he was Maximinus' subordinate.

143/15. *dcccc wintra 7 xc.* OH VII. xix. 3 *dcccclxli.* In the 'related' MS Vienna 366, the final *li* has become attached to the name *Gordianus* that follows.

143/16–17. *he ofslog . . . ofslogan.* According to OH VII. xix. 3, the brothers 'in Palatio . . . interfecti sunt'. Gordianus had no hand in the murders.

143/17. *he self raþe þæs gefor.* According to OH VII. xix. 5, he was killed by his own men.

143/19–20. *He . . . dorste.* OH VII. xx. 2 'hic primus imperatorum omnium Christianus fuit.' The reference in Or. to concealment may be due to an attempt to reconcile OH's statement with the claim made by a number of writers that it was Constantine who was the first Christian emperor. See, however, Eutropius IX. iii, where Philip is said to have been ranked among the gods, i.e. deified, and therefore by implication to have been at least outwardly pagan.

143/20–144/4. *On . . . brucan.* A rewriting of OH VII. xx. 2–3, 'post tertium imperii eius annum millesimus a conditione Romae annus impletus est. ita magnificis ludis augustissimus omnium praeteritorum hic natalis annus a Christiano imperatore celebratus est. nec dubium est, quin Philippus huius tantae deuotionis gratiam et honorem ad Christum et Ecclesiam reportarit, quando uel ascensum fuisse in Capitolium immolatasque ex more hostias nullus auctor ostendit.' See also VII. xxviii. i, where Philip is said to have been Christian 'ut millesimus Romae annus Christo potius quam idolis dicaretur'. According to Jerome–Eusebius, cols. 645–6, the celebrations lasted for three days and three nights.

143/24. *palendsan.* Cf. *An OE Martyrology* 64/26 'on hire palatium, þæt is on hire healle'.

144/4. *Decius an rice mon.* OH VII. xx. 4 *Decii.* According to OH, Philip and the son who shared his throne 'diuersis locis tumultu militari et Decii fraude interfecti sunt'.

144/12. *m wintra 7 viii.* OH VII. xxi. 4 'millesimo septimo'.

144/21. *mid Emilitum þæm folce.* OH VII. xxii. 1 'in Raetia ab exercitu'. The form *Emilitum* is best explained as derived from a gloss or comment 'a militibus'.

144/22–3. *þa . . . wæs.* Or.'s addition.

145/1. *begen.* OH VII. xxii. 3 blames the persecution on Valerianus.

145/6–7. *he . . . gehæfde.* Cf. OH VII. xxii. 1 'mansit . . . Gallienus in regno infeliciter annis xv, respirante paulisper ab illa supra solitum iugi at graui pestilentia genere humano.'

145/7-8. *Germanie þe be Donua wæron.* Cf. OH VII. xxii. 7 'Germani Alpibus Raetia totaque Italia penetrata'.

145/9-10. *Gotan . . . Asiam.* OH VII. xxii. 7 'Graecia Macedonia Pontus Asia Gothorum inundatione deletur.' For *seo læsse Asia* see 10/24, Commentary.

145/10-11. *Sermende . . . Pannoniam.* According to OH VII. xxii. 7, 'Dacia trans Danuuium in perpetuum aufertur; Quadi et Sarmatae Pannonias depopulantur.' Dacia was in fact overrun by the Goths. The Huns did not appear in Europe until more than a hundred years after the reign of Gallienus, and it was not until the middle of the fifth century that they invaded Pannonia. See 13/9-10, Commentary.

145/14. *Medialane þære byrig.* OH VII. xxii. 13 *Mediolani.* See also 99/4, and Isidore, *Etymologies* XV. i. 57.

145/14. *from his agnum monnum.* Or.'s addition. See *Scriptores Historiae Augustae, Gallieni Duo* xiv.

145/17. *hie . . . Crecum.* Cf. OH VII. xxiii. 1 'Gothos . . . Illyricum Macedoniamque uastantes . . . deleuit.' For the inclusion of Macedonia in 'Greece' see 18/13, Commentary.

145/17-19. *him Romane . . . Capitoliam.* Based on OH VII. xxiii. 1, 'cui a senatu clipeus aureus in curia et in Capitolio statua aeque aurea decreta est'. The translator appears to have failed to recognize OH's use of chiasmus here, while his choice of verb, *ahengon*, seems more appropriate to the shield than to the statue!

145/24. *be norþan Donua.* OH VII. xxiii. 4 here refers to a campaign on the Danube and the subsequent restoration of Roman rule within its former boundaries.

145/25-146/1. *Tetricum þone mon.* OH VII. xxiii. 5 *Tetricum.* The addition of *þone mon* seems to be inspired by a gloss or comment, intended to show that *Tetricus* was a proper name, not the adjective meaning 'harsh, severe'. See Abstrusa TE 49 also 142/10, Commentary.

146/1. *for þy . . . anwalde.* A misunderstanding of OH VII. xxiii. 5 'Tetricum, in Gallia minime sufficientem sustinere seditiones militum suorum . . . ac per hoc proditorem exercitus sui'.

146/5. *Ponto þæm londe.* OH VII. xxiv. 1 *Ponto.* See also 71/1.

146/6-7. *on Tharsa þæm londe.* OH VII. xxiv. 1 'apud Tarsum'. There seems little excuse for Or.'s error here. Tarsus is correctly identified as a town in 149/4 and should in any case have been well known as the city of the Apostle Paul.

146/10. *Hunas.* OH VII. xxiv. 2 'a barbaris'. The Huns had not yet appeared in Europe: see 145/10-11, Commentary. However, in the mid fifth century they did indeed invade Gaul, where they were defeated by Aetius.

146/10. *he ofslog Saturninus.* Cf. OH VII. xxiv. 3 'Saturninum . . . oppressit et cepit' and see above, 143/6, Commentary. According to

Jerome–Eusebius, col. 655, 'Saturninus . . . postea imperium molitus invadere Apamiae occiditur.' He was in fact killed by the soldiers of Probus, though the emperor himself would have spared his life: see, e.g., *Scriptores Historiae Augustae, Firmus* xi. 1–3.

146/13. *on Sirmie þære dune.* OH VII. xxiv. 3 'apud Sirmium in turre ferrata militari tumultu'. Or.'s version seems to be the result of corruption in the underlying Latin MS. Possibilities include **torre* for *turre*, taken as the OE word *torr* 'rock, crag', and **tumulu* for *tumultu*, identified with Latin *tumulus*.

146/16. *tuwwa.* Or.'s addition, perhaps inspired by the reference to the taking of two towns.

146/16–17. *þa . . . ie.* Or. has misunderstood OH VII. xxiv. 4, 'urbes Cochem et Ctesiphontem cepit, super Tigridem in castris . . . interiit', taking 'super Tigridem' to refer not to the camp but to the towns.

146/17–18. *Numerianus . . . onwalde.* Or.'s addition; see OH VII. xxiv. 4, where Numerianus is referred to as co-ruler with his father.

146/21. *gingran casere.* OH VII. xxv. 2 *Caesarem.* Since the translator has already used *casere* to translate OH *imperator*, he now has to find some way of distinguishing between the two ranks.

147/3. *iii cyningas.* Only Narseus is described as *rex* by OH; however, Carausius is said to have assumed the purple: see OH VII. xxv. 3 and 4.

147/4. *iii caseras.* According to OH VIII. xxv. 5, Maximianus was promoted from Caesar to Augustus, while Constantius and Maximianus Galerius were made Caesars.

147/8. *he geeode. . .igland.* OH VII. xxv. 6 gives the credit for the recovery of Britain to 'Asclepiodotus praefectus praetorio'. However the province then came under Constantius' authority.

147/10–11. *hiene . . . ageafon.* OH VII. xxv. 8 merely says that after besieging him in Alexandria Diocletian 'Achilleum . . . cepit et interfecit'. For a similar, apparently unfounded, assumption, see 124/26–7 and Commentary.

147/12–13. *hiera naþer næfde sige.* Or.'s addition, apparently inspired by OH's observation, VII. xxv. 9, that in the third fight the Romans were defeated.

147/14. *mid micelre fyrhtnesse.* Or.'s addition.

147/18. *his wif . . . bearn.* Both *wif* and *bearn* are presumably intended as neuter plurals: see OH VII. xxv. 11 'uxores sorores liberosque'. The Old French version by Calendre, however, interprets *wif* as singular: see LER 4069 and Introduction, p. xxviii.

147/23–4. *woldon . . . weredon.* OH VII. xxv. 14 'purpuram imperiumque deponerent'.

147/25. *on seftnesse.* OH VII. xxv. 14 'in priuato otio'.

147/25–6. *Dioclitianus . . . byrig.* OH VII. xxv. 14 'Diocletianus apud Nicomediam, Maximianus apud Mediolanium potestatem imperii simul cultumque deposuerunt.' For the identification of Nicomedia and Mediolanium as towns see 145/14, Commentary and Isidore, *Etymologies*, XV. i. 57.

147/28–9. *Ilirice . . . middangeardes*. Based on OH VII. xxv. 15, 'Illyricum Asiam et Orientem'. For the belief that the continent of Asia was as large as Africa and Europe combined, see, e.g., Isidore, *Etymologies* XIV. ii. 2–3.

148/1–2. *Italie . . . Brettannie*. OH VII xxv. 15 refers merely to 'Italiam Africam et Gallias'. However, in a number of MSS the name *Hispaniam* is inserted before *et Gallias*. In the reign of Diocletian Britain was governed by a *vicarius*, subject to the *Praefectus Praetorio* of Gaul.

148/4. *cyningas*. OH VII. xxv. 16 *Caesares*. See 146/21, Commentary.

148/5. *Italiam 7 Africam*. According to OH VII. xxv. 16, Severus was only given Italy. However, since Maximianus got the Orient and Galerius himself remained in Illyricum, it might have seemed logical to the translator or commentator that Severus should also be assigned Africa. See *Anonymi Valesiani pars prior* (printed in *Ammianus Marcellinus*, ed. J. C. Rolfe, III), 3, 5 'Severus suscepit Italiam et quicquid Herculius obtinebat.'

148/10–11. *þa . . . Italiam*. OH VII. xxviii. 5 'praetoriani milites Romae Maxentium filium Herculii, qui priuatus in Lucania morabatur, Augustum nuncupauerunt.' Herculeus is immediately afterwards referred to as Maximianus Herculeus by OH.

148/11–12. *þe . . . wæs*. Or.'s addition. See above, 148/4–5.

148/13. *neah Rafenna þære byrig*. According to OH VII. xxviii. 8, 'ex eo fugiens Rauennae interfectus est'. Has the translator construed *Rauennae* with *fugiens*? For the identification of Ravenna as a town, see 145/8, and Julius Honorius, p. 35.

148/14–15. *he . . . wæs*. Or.'s addition. Cf. OH VII. xxviii. 5 'Herculii, qui priuatus in Lucania morabatur'.

148/16–17. *Ac . . . fæder*. Or.'s addition. According to OH VII. xxviii. 9, Maximianus was terrified by the open insults and rioting of the soldiers.

148/17. *fleah*. Cf. OH VII. xxviii. 9 'profectus est'.

148/21. *þa . . . Affricam*. OH VII. xxviii. 10 merely says that 'Galerius occiso Seuero Licinium imperatorem creauit.' For the extent of Severus' domains see 148/1–2 and Commentary.

148/21–2. *he . . . elþeode*. OH VII. xxviii. 12 merely says that Galerius intensified the persecutions of his predecessors and 'omni genere hominum exhausit prouincias'.

148/24. *monigne læce*. OH VII. xxviii. 12 *medici*.

148/27. *he gefor*. According to OH VII. xxviii. 13, he committed suicide: 'ipse autem cruciatus non sustinens uim uitae suae adtulit.'

148/27. *Lucinius feng to þæm onwalde*. Or.'s addition. See above, 148/21 and Commentary, also OH VII. xxviii. 14.

149/2–3. *binnan . . . het.* OH VII. xxviii. 16 'ad pontem Muluium'. The Mulvian Bridge was two miles north of Rome, carrying the via Flaminia over the Tiber. Or.'s additional information could have been derived from a gloss such as Leiden XXXV. 242, 'Ponte moluio; propter pontis iuxta roma'.

149/4. *Tharsa þære byrig.* OH VII. xxviii. 17 *Tharsum.* See 68/23, Commentary.

149/6. *on his hierede . . . færelte.* Cf. OH VII. xxviii. 18 'e palatio suo'.

149/8. *beheafdian.* OH VII. xxviii. 20 uses the neutral word *occidi.*

149/8–9. *siþþan* (2) *. . . onwalde.* Or.'s addition, a safe contextual deduction.

149/12. *hiene . . . amansumianne.* OH VII. xxviii. 25 merely refers to the convening of a council of bishops, 'per quos Arrianum dogma exitiabile et miserum esse euidentissime deprehensum, palam proditum ac reprobatum est'. For Arius' excommunication by the bishop of Alexandria, see OH VII. xxviii. 24.

149/14–15. *nan . . . anum.* Or.'s addition. Crispus and Licinius were in fact accused of high treason.

149/16–17. *het . . . Constantinopolim.* An expansion of OH VII. xxviii. 27 'urbem nominis sui . . . instituit'.

149/17–18. *He . . . timbrede.* Or.'s addition. Bede, *De Temporum Ratione* col. 556, gives the names of basilicas built by Constantine in Rome.

149/20. *on . . . byrig.* OH VII. xxviii. 31 'in uilla publica iuxta Nicomediam'. For Nicomedia identified as a town, see 147/25–6, Commentary.

149/21. *m wintra 7 xci.* OH VII. xxix. 1 *mxcii.*

149/24. *ealle þa gebroþor.* OH VII. xxix. 3 describes only Constantius as a heretic.

149/26. *ofslagen.* Cf. OH VII. xxix. 5 'a ducibus eius occisus'.

149/27. *Galliam 7 Italiam.* OH VII. xxix. 8 refers also to Africa.

149/27. *Ilirice.* See OH VII. xxix. 9 'in Illyrico . . . milites' and 153/28, Commentary.

150/1. *Ueteromonem þone mon.* OH VII. xxix. 9 'Vetranionem . . . uirum natura simplicem'.

150/1–2. *to þon . . . Magnentiuse.* Or.'s addition.

150/2–3. *hi . . . leornunga.* According to OH VII. xxix. 10, he studied the alphabet and syllables *inuitus.*

150/3. *Constantius.* Here and below, 150/7, and 12, the reading *Constantinus* is an error for *Constantius*: cf. OH VII. xxix. 10, 14, and 17. In 150/12, MS C has the correct reading.

150/6. *Luchina þære byrig.* OH VII. xxix. 13 *Lugdunum.*

150/6–7. *he . . . ofsticode.* OH VII. xxix. 13 'propria se manu interfecit'.

150/8. *se . . . gehalgod.* Or.'s addition. Julian the Apostate was so called because he renounced the Christian religion in which he had been brought up; he never entered religious orders. However, certain medieval sources describe him as monk (see Freculph, *Chronicon*, col. 1210) or *clericus* (see Isidore, *Chronicon*, col. 1049), a description taken up by Ælfric, both in his Catholic Homilies and elsewhere (see Benjamin Thorpe, *Homilies of Ælfric* (London, 1844), I. 448/23 sq. and Pope, *Ælfric*, viii, 132–3). For Or.'s use of the term *diacone* I have found no source, unless it is based on misunderstanding or careless reading of a text such as Bede, *De Temporum Ratione*, col. 557, where a reference to the emperor Julianus is followed by a reference to (another) Julianus as *Julianum diaconum*.

150/11–12. *mid . . . Parhte.* OH VII. xxix. 16 says that Julianus made his way through Italy and Illyricum while Constantine was away fighting in Parthia.

150/14–21. *þa . . . habbanne.* OH VII. xxx. 2–3 'Christianam religionem arte potius quam potestate insectatus, ut negaretur fides Christi et idolorum cultus susciperetur, honoribus magis prouocare quam tormentis cogere studuit. aperto tamen praecepit edicto, ne quis Christianus docendorum liberalium studiorum professor esset. sed tamen, sicut a maioribus nostris compertum habemus, omnes ubique propemodum praecepti condiciones amplexati officium quam fidem deserere maluerunt.' For *liberalium* MS Vienna 366 has the reading *liberarium*.

No satisfactory explanation has yet been put forward for 150/16 *fæste boc.* Thorpe and Bosworth both interpret it as fast-book or Penitential, but as Potter (1952–3), p. 436, points out, *fæst* for *fæsten* is unparalleled. His suggestion is that *fæste* may have the meaning 'serious'. However, the text that we have may be corrupt and *fæste* could be an error for *æfæste* (an emendation suggested to me by Professor Whitelock) or *arfæste*, either of which could have been inspired by a misconstruing of a statement such as Freculph, *Chronicon*, col. 1211, 'etiam contra Christianos conscripsit libros'.

150/22. *Perse.* OH VII. xxx. 4 *Parthos.* See for the association of Persia and Parthia see 10/8–9.

150/23. *eastane.* Or.'s addition.

150/27–151/2. *hiene . . . hæte.* According to the corresponding passage in OH, VII. xxx. 6, 'dolo cuiusdam transfugae in deserta perductus, cum ui sitis et ardore solis atque insuper labore harenarum confectus periret exercitus, imperator tanto rerum periculo anxius . . . per uasta deserti incautius euagatur.'

150/27–8. *for from Actesifonte þære byrig.* OH VII. xxx. 6 'a Ctesiphonte castra mouit.' The Latin preposition *a* appears to have been incorporated in the proper name: cf. the reading of the 'related' MS Vienna 366 *accessifonte*.

151/2. *an uncuð mon.* OH VII. xxx. 6 is slightly more specific, referring to 'quodam hostium equite'.

151/4–5. *Hiene . . . ofstong.* Cf. OH VII. xxxi. 1 'ab exercitu creatus cum et locorum iniquitate captus et hostibus circumsaeptus nullam euadendi facultatem nanciscetur'. According to Jerome–Eusebius, cols. 693–4, this happened *sequenti die*; see also Ammianus Marcellinus XXV. v. 1–4.

151/6. *healfe . . . lond.* OH VII. xxxi. 2 'partem superioris Mesopotamiae'.

151/10. *hit wæs ceald weder.* Or.'s addition, presumably deduced from the allusion in OH VII. xxxi. 3 to burning coals.

151/13. *m wintra 7 xcviii.* Based on OH VII. xxxii. 1, *mcxviii*, with *x* and *c* transposed.

151/15. *cempena ealdormon.* OH VII. xxxii. 2 'tribunus scutariorum'. Cf. 101/25 'cempena ieldest', OH 'tribunus militum'.

151/16. *þone his cristendom.* Cf. 35/14 *se heora cyning* and *St. Chad,* § 62.

151/16. *folgað.* OH VII. xxxii. 2 *militia.*

151/21. *þe þa ricsian wolde.* OH VII. xxxii. 4 *tyrannum.*

151/27. *Godenric Gotena cyning.* OH VII. xxxii. 9 'Athanaricus rex Gothorum'.

152/1–2. *Ualentinianus . . . lande.* According to OH VII. xxxii. 10, Valentinianus defeated the Saxons in the land of the Franks.

152/4–5. *Burgendum . . . fulwiht.* The corresponding passage of OH, VII. xxxii. 11–13, reports the settling of the Burgundians on the banks of the Rhine and briefly discusses their name and their history up to the time when Orosius was writing. The passage ends: 'eorum . . . esse praeualidam et perniciosam manum, Galliae hodieque testes sunt, in quibus praesumpta possessione consistunt; quamuis prouidentia Dei Christiani omnes modo facti catholica fide nostrisque clericis, quibus oboedirent, receptis blande mansuete innocenterque uiuant, non quasi cum subiectis Gallis sed uere cum fratribus Christianis.'

152/8–9. *m wintra 7 an hund 7 xxviiii.* OH VII. xxxiii. 1 *mcxxviii*, 'related' MSS including Vienna 366, *mcxxviiii.*

152/9–11. *feng . . . Ualense.* Based on OH VII. xxxii. 15, 'Gratianus filius Occidentis imperium tenuit, Valente patruo in Orientis partibus constituto.'

152/11–12. *He . . . hæfde.* Or.'s addition. See above, 151/23.

152/13–15. *bebead . . . monnum.* Cf. OH VII. xxxiii. 1 'legem dedit, ut monachi, hoc est Christiani qui ad unum fidei opus dimissa saecularium rerum multimoda actione se redigunt, ad militiam cogerentur.' Or.'s use of the word *yfel* is somewhat surprising here: see Introduction, p. c, n. 2.

152/15–16. *eal . . . gestaþelade.* OH VII. xxxiii. 2 merely says that at that time great numbers of monks lived in the Egyptian desert.

152/19. *Ualens.* OH VII. xxxiii. 6 *Valentiniano.* The substitution of names seems to have been deliberately made, on the assumption that Theodosius' campaign took place after Valentinianus' death; however, since it is possible that the Latin form was split by the intervention of the end of a line (cf., e.g., Vienna 366 *ualentia/no*) scribal error cannot be ruled out.

152/20. *þæs godan Theodosiuses*. OH VII. xxxiii. 6 *Theodosii*. See below, 153/25–6 and OH VII. xxxiv. 7.

152/21–6. *On . . . martyre*. Or. has here attached to Firmus OH's account of the death of Theodosius: see OH VII. xxxiii. 6–7 'ipsum Firmum afflictum et oppressum coegit ad mortem. post cum experientissima prouidentia totam cum Mauretania Africam meliorem pristinis reddidisset, instimulante et obrepente inuidia iussus interfici, apud Carthaginem baptizari in remissionem peccatorum praeoptauit ac postquam sacramentum Christi quod quaesierat adsecutus est, post gloriosam saeculi uitam etiam de uitae aeternitate securus percussori iugulum ultro praebuit.' Firmus in fact hanged himself: see Ammianus Marcellinus XXIX. v.

152/28. *fela m.* OH VII. xxxiii. 8 gives the number as 'plus quam triginta milia'.

152/28. *ðriddan geare his rices.* OH VII. xxxiii. 9 'Tertio decimo . . . anno imperii Valentis'.

153/1. *he . . . þeowas*. Like the date just given, this should refer to Valens not to Gratianus, whom OH VII. xxxiii. 8 indeed describes as 'fretus Christi potentia'.

153/1–2. *þa adrifon . . . earde*. According to OH VII. xxxiii. 10, it is the *gens Hunorum* that drives the Goths 'ab antiquis sedibus'.

153/3–5. *wilnedon . . . woldon*. OH VII. xxxiii. 10 'Gothi . . . a Valente sine ulla foederis pactione suscepti ne arma quidem, quo tutius barbaris crederetur, tradidere Romanis.' That the Goths asked for permission to settle could be a contextual guess. However, see Ammianus Marcellinus XXXI. iv. 1 and Jordanes, col. 1269.

153/5–6. *his gerefan . . . ealdormen*. OH VII. xxxiii. 11 refers to only one 'Maximi ducis'. However, according to Ammianus Marcellinus XXXI. iv. 9, the *comes* Lupicinus and *dux* Maximus, and others with their permission, were involved; see also Jordanes, col. 1270.

153/6. *nieddon hi æfter gafole*. OH VII. xxxiii. 11 says that Maximus was inspired by avarice.

153/8. *Antiochia þære byrig*. OH VII. xxxiii. 12 *Antiochia*. Antioch is described as a city by a number of Latin texts; see, e.g., Isidore, *Etymologies* XV. i. 14 'urbem . . . Antiochiam'.

153/9–13. *hu . . . gearian*. Cf. OH VII. xxxiii. 12 'sera peccati maximi paenitentia stimulatus episcopos ceterosque sanctos reuocari de exiliis imperauit', and VII. xxxiii. 19 'Gothi antea per legatos supplices poposcerunt, ut illis episcopi, a quibus regulam Christianae fidei discerent mitterentur. Valens imperator exitiabili prauitate doctores Arrian dogmatis misit.'

153/14. *feorþan*. OH VII. xxxiii. 13 'quinto decimo'. Cf. 152/28, where the numeral thirteen is replaced by three.

153/15. *anne tun.* OH VII. xxxiii. 15 *cuiusdam uillulae.*

153/16–17. *þær . . . ecnesse.* Inspired by OH VII. xxxiii. 19, 'iusto iudicio Dei ipsi eum uiuum incenderunt, qui propter eum etiam mortui uitio erroris arsuri sunt.'

153/18. *m . . . xxxiii.* OH VII. xxxiv. 1 *mcxxxii.*

153/20–2. *him geþuhte . . . oferswiþan.* Cf. OH VII. xxxiv. 2 'cum adflictum ac paene conlapsum reipublicae statum uideret'.

153/22–5. *Ac . . . geendade.* According to OH VII. xxxiv. 5–7, Theodosius first defeated the Alans, Goths, and Huns in a series of great battles, then made a treaty with Athanaric.

153/26–7. *ægþer . . . frið.* OH VII. xxxiv. 7 'uniuersae Gothorum gentes'. See also VII. xxxiv. 5 'illas Scythicas gentes'.

153/28. *Brettanie.* According to OH VII. xxxiv. 9, Maximus was proclaimed emperor 'in Britannia . . . ab exercitu'. See 138/8 and 149/27 and Commentary.

153/29–154/1. *Se . . . lare.* OH VII. xxxiv. 9 'uir . . . Augusto dignus nisi contra sacramenti fidem per tyrannidem emersisset'. Or.'s interpretation is presumably inspired in part by the description of Maximinus as being made emperor against his will.

154/1. *raðe þæs.* Or.'s addition.

154/8. *fird gelædde on Italie.* Cf. OH VII. xxxv. 4, where Theodosius is said to cross the Alps and go to Aquileia.

154/9. *Aquilegia þære byrig.* OH VII. xxxv. 3 *Aquileiae.* See Julius Honorius, p. 35 'Aquileia oppidum'.

154/9–13. *his . . . hindan.* Based on OH VII. xxxv. 3, 'Andragathius comes eius summam belli administrabat: qui cum largissimis militum copiis ipsamque magnarum copiarum fortitudinem praecellente consilio omnes incredibiliter Alpium ac fluminum aditus communisset, ineffabili iudicio Dei, dum nauali expeditione incautum hostem praeuenire et obruere parat, sponte eadem quae obstruxerat claustra deseruit.' Theodosius had earlier been described as in the east: see OH VII. xxxiv. 10. For the term *cluse* see 62/24–5, Commentary.

154/14–16. *funde . . . tobræc.* Cf. OH VII. xxxv. 4 'ita Theodosius nemine sentiente, ut non dicam repugnante, uacuas transmisit Alpes.' Did the translator assume that some soldiers must have been left to guard the passes and that as Theodosius crossed unopposed, they must have been 'yfele 7 earge'?

154/21. *þæs ymb ii ger.* Or.'s addition. In fact the murder took place four years after Valentinianus' restoration.

154/23–4. *gelicost . . . awierged.* Cf. OH VII. xxxv. 10 'ut uoluntariam sibi consciuisse mortem putaretur'. Was the manuscript used by the translator corrupt at this point, and *consciuisse* somehow confused with *inscius?* Or is *unwitende* itself an error for *witende?*

154/26-7. *for þon . . . Romanisc.* Or.'s addition.

154/27-8. *ac . . . beeode.* OH VII. xxxv. 12 refers only to Arbogastes as 'nixus . . . praecipuo culto idolorum'.

154/29. *þære . . . Maximus.* OH VII. xxxv. 13 'Alpium latera atque ineuitabiles transitus praemissis callide insidiis occuparant.' The translator, or a hypothetical commentator, seems to have assumed that the 'ineuitabiles transitus' must by definition be those previously used by Theodosius.

154/30-1. *þæt . . . tobræcon.* Or.'s addition.

155/1-2. *þa . . . beþridian.* OH VII. xxxv. 14 says the opposite: 'Theodosius in summis Alpis constitutus . . . sciens quod destitutus suis, nesciens quod clausus alienis'. Did Or.'s exemplar have *sciens* a second time, in place of *nesciens*, or did the translator read the passage carelessly?

155/2-4. *þa . . . gescotum.* Or.'s addition.

155/6-7. *ælc . . . eorþan.* OH VII. xxxv. 18 less plausibly refers to the weapons as all transfixing the unfortunate throwers.

155/10. *Æfter . . . Italie.* Or.'s addition, presumably based on OH's allusion to Theodosius as crossing the Alps.

155/11. *geendade he his lif.* OH VII. xxxv. 23 'diem obiit'.

155/18-20. *Ac . . . mehten.* OH's language is far less emotive: see VII. xxxvii. 1 'quid uterque egerit, quidue agere conatus sit, exitus utriusque docuit.'

155/23. *Rædgotan.* OH VII. xxxvii. 4 *Radagaisus.* See Introduction, pp. xcif.

155/25-6. *for . . . geboren wæs.* According to OH VII. xxxvii. 1, 'barbaras gentes ille inmisit, hic fouit.' See also OH VII. xxxviii. 1–3, where Stilico is said to be of Vandal stock and to have entered into alliances with Alaric and the Goths and also with Alani, Suebi, and Vandals, thinking that it would be as easy to repress the barbarian nations as it was to arouse them. Nowhere are Alaric and Radagaisus said to have been 'allowed' into Italy.

155/26. *Raðe . . . cristen.* OH VII. xxxvii. 9 states only that Alaric was a Christian, not that he became one.

155/28-9. *simle . . . Romanisce.* Or.'s addition.

156/14. *se mildesta.* According to OH VII. xxxvii. 9, Alaric was 'timore Dei mitis in caede'.

156/18. *ne wearð . . . forbærned.* Cf. OH VII. xxxix. 15 'facto quidem aliquantarum aedium incendio sed ne tanto quidem quantum septingentesimo conditionis eius anno casus effecerat'.

156/20-3. *Siþþan . . . Affrice.* Although OH, VII. xlii and xliii, alludes to the presence of Goths in Spain and Africa, the translator need not have derived his information from this source: see, e.g., Bede, *De Temporum Ratione,* col. 560.

GLOSSARY[1]

Entries are alphabetically arranged, except that all words beginning with the prefix *ge-* are listed according to their unprefixed forms. The ligature *æ* is treated like *ae*, following *ad*; *ð* is replaced by *þ*, which is treated as a separate letter between *t* and *u*. An asterisk indicates a form restored by emendation, where none of the manuscripts has the reading adopted in the text. Square brackets indicate the use as head-word of an infinitive form not recorded in the text; rounded brackets indicate that the gender suggested for a noun is not confirmed by morphological or syntactical features in the text. Abbreviations are conventional. The class of strong verbs is indicated by arabic numerals, that of weak verbs by roman numerals, while although I have used *pa. t.* to describe the past tense, I have retained the traditional description *pret. pres.* for verbs such as *wat*, *sceal*, and *mæg*.

In the arrangement of items and the number of references given I have followed the advice of EETS *Notes for Editors* (Oxford, 1972): thus, for instance, infinitives are normally cited as head-words only when they occur in the text, as are the nominative singulars of nouns with a choice of suffix (e.g. *-nes, -ness, -nesse, -nis*, etc.); inflexional forms other than those of strong verbs are not normally cited and not more than a single instance of each is usually given; elsewhere the number of references is normally limited to three or four, with *etc.* indicating the point at which selective citing begins. In the choice of references consistency has had to take second place to the need for maximum coverage. Where variant spellings occur, that used as the head-word is the most frequent one, even where this means listing related words, such as *ondwyrdan* and *geandwyrdan* at a distance from one another. Prepositions are treated summarily; postpositional adverbs and prepositions used elliptically are not normally given special treatment.[2] Lastly,

---

[1] The glossary is derived from a concordance which in its turn is based on a computer word-list and partial concordance, for the programme for which see A. J. T. Colin, 'The Automatic Construction of a Glossary', *Information and Control*, iii (1960), 211–230.

[2] The editorial decision as to whether to interpret a form as an adverb or a separable prefix is often an arbitrary one. For the magnitude of the problem see B. Mitchell, 'Prepositions, Adverbs, Prepositional Adverbs, Postpositions, Separable Prefixes, or Inseparable Prefixes, in Old English?' *NM* lxxix (1978), 240–57.

since Or. uses significant numbers of indisputably indicative forms where OE syntax conventionally requires the subjunctive, no attempt is normally made to identify subjunctive forms in the pa. t., except where they are distinctive.

GLOSSARY OF PROPER NAMES

As in the main glossary the number of references given is limited, with *etc.* marking the point at which selective citing begins. Case and number are determined mainly on syntactical grounds. Forms from OH or the 'related' MSS are normally cited only where they shed light on Or.'s forms.[1] When they apply to an entire entry they are placed with their English or Latin equivalent immediately after the head-word and normally in the nominative case. When they apply only to part of an entry, they are cited after the appropriate page and line reference. *V* is generalized in initial position in these Latin forms and *u* internally. Where a single form in OH has become two separate names in Or. these names are treated independently in the glossary with selective cross-references.

A

a *adv.* ever, always 14/23, 112/29. ~ *swa* quite as, just as 121/9, 142/4.

abæd, abædon see **abiddan**.

abead see **abeodan**.

abeden see **abiddan**.

abeodan 2 announce 95/24, 95/25, 95/27, 96/3. **abead** *pa. t. 3 sg.* 95/25. **aboden** *pp.* 95/27.

abiddan 5 obtain by prayer or asking 47/2, 97/17, 97/18, 97/20, etc. **abæd** *pa. t. 3 sg.* 80/13. **abædon** *pl.* 141/14. **abeden** *pp.* 46/12.

abitt 1 *pr. 3 sg.* bites 130/14. **abite** *pa. t. subj. sg.* should bite 130/12. *pl.* should devour 150/25.

ablon 3 *pa. t. 3 sg.* ceased 103/26.

aboden see **abeodan**.

abolgen see **abulge**.

abrecan 4 take by storm, destroy 43/20, 72/8, 86/5, 109/19, etc.; violate (peace) 97/16. ~ *ofer* force one's way over 4/29, 99/20, 99/23. **abræc** *pa. t. 3 sg.* 44/7. **abræcon**

pl. 31/5; **abræcan** 2/26. **abræce** *subj. sg.* 90/11. **abræcen** *pl.* 51/20.

abrocen *pp.* 4/6.

abroden 3 *pp.* dragged 73/10.

abugan 2 *w. dat.* bow 26/7.

abulge 3 *pa. t. subj. sg. w. dat.* should offend 140/12. **abolgen** *pp. in impersonal construction w. dat.* angered 46/24.

abylgþe *ds(f.)* injury 83/17 (v.l. æbylgþe).

ac, ah *conj.* but 9/19, 12/11, 12/23, 14/2, 69/6, etc.

acennes (*f.*) nativity 35/25.

aceorfan 3 cut down (timber) 92/19. ~ *of* cut off (head, hand) 40/22, 45/7, 106/1, 115/22. **acorfen** *pp.* 92/19. **acorfena** *npl. n.* 86/21.

acoren see **acuron**.

acræftan I devise, think out 30/14, 47/7.

geacsade, geacsian, etc. see **geascian**.

acsedon, acsiende see **ascian**.

acuron 2 *pa. t. pl.* chose, selected 45/31. **acoren** *pp.* chosen 134/23.

---

[1] For a detailed study of the distribution of the potentially most significant variants see Bately (1961).

acwælan, acwælon 4 *pa. t. pl.* died, perished 52/13, 119/14, 122/5, 131/26.
acwellan I kill, destroy 40/9, 60/19, 90/5, 136/6, etc. acwealde *pa. t. 3 sg.* 27/31. acwealdon *pl.* 104/12. acweald *pp.* 3/16. acwealde *npl.* 26/7.
acwencean I quench, extinguish 106/22.
acxe, asce, axe *wk.* (*f.*) (burnt) ash 23/11, 86/31, 119/13.
ad (*m. or n.*) funeral pyre 17/13.
adelfan 3 dig 130/9.
adl *f.* disease 139/3.
adon *anom. v.* remove, take away, banish 58/21, 65/6, 119/1, 146/10. adyde *pa. t. 3 sg.* 119/1.
adræfde I *pa. t. 3 sg.* drove out, banished 27/8, 69/14, 120/17, 148/17. adræfdon *pl.* 40/11 etc. adræfed *pp.* driven out 27/5. adræfde *npl.* 126/15. adræfdan *ppl. adj. dsm.* exiled 123/3.
adraf see adrifan.
adrencte I *pa. t. 3 sg.* drowned 51/14, 154/18.
adrifan I drive away, expel 87/22, 135/25, 137/12, 145/17, etc. adraf *pa. t. 3 sg.* 134/7. adrifon *pl.* 82/12. adrifen *subj. pl.* 24/8.
adrigde I *pa. t. 3 sg.* dried up 26/19.
adrincan 3 quench (thirst) 46/17; drown 26/23, 47/31, 119/19; sink 94/26, 94/27. adruncon *pa. t. pl.* 26/23. adruncen *pp.* 47/31. a-druncne *npl.* 119/19.
adwæscan I quench (fire) 97/31, 97/32.
adyde see adon.
æ *f.* law 50/15, 59/16, 132/11.
aeargoden II *pa. t. subj. pl.* should become slothful, remiss 112/32.
æcer (*m.*) field, cultivated land, acre 50/4, 86/30. æcra *gpl.* 86/30.
ædra *npl. f.* nerve, sinew 68/27.
ædre *wk.* (*f.*) nerve, sinew 96/4.
æfengifl (*n.*) supper 48/36.
æfre *adv.* ever 102/11, 128/17, 136/27. ~ ær ever before 116/26, 133/17.
æftemest, æftemæst *sup. adj.* last, hindmost 94/15, 133/7.

æfter *prep. w. dat.* after 16/26, 17/14, 23/20, 25/11, etc.; after, for 48/28, 54/34, 64/16, 74/22; in succession to 1/4, 24/31; in accordance with 1/12, 107/9, 111/18; *w. acc.* after 29/18. æfter þæm þe *conj.* after 33/23, 35/24, 37/12. æfter þæm þæt according as 113/8. æfter siextegum daga þæs þe etc. sixty days after etc. 92/18, 97/24.
æfter *adv.* after, afterwards 38/2, 39/2, 62/32, 81/21, etc.
æftera see æfterra.
æfterfolgere *m.* successor 77/20, 81/10.
æfterfolgiende II *pr. p. w. dat.* pursuing 29/6.
æfterfylgeaþ I *pr. pl. w. acc.* follow 24/14. æfterfylgende *pr. p. w. dat.* following, pursuing 26/12, 32/9, 44/11, 45/5, etc.
æfterfylgend *m.* successor 77/9.
æfterhæþan *wk. ds(m.)* subsequent parching by heat 56/26.
æfterra, æftera *wk. adj.* second, next 5/9, 24/4, 25/17, 35/27, etc.
*ægenu see agen.
æghwilc *pron.* each 15/17.
ægþer, ægþær *pron. adj.* each (of two), both. *as adj.* 31/31, 34/24, 39/12, 49/17, etc.; *as pron.* 15/19 33/7, 38/2, 40/28. ægþres ge . . . ge' (of) both . . . and 38/22, 38/24, 63/22; *as conj.* ægþer ge . . . ge . . . (ge) both . . . and . . . (and) 14/27, 19/2, 19/29, 21/11, 25/10, etc.
ægwern *adv.* everywhere 83/27.
æht (*f.*) possessions, property 15/7.
ælc *pron. adj.* each, every. *as adj.* 1/11, 10/26, 16/5, 17/2, etc.; *as pron.* 17/23, 17/25, 22/22, 89/18, etc. *pl.* all 38/15. buton ~ without any 38/20, 52/4, 85/6. ælcer(r)e *dsf.* 17/2, 62/10. ælcon *dsm. and n.* 62/18, 85/17; *pl.* 54/23.
ælmihtig *adj.* almighty 134/4. ælmihtegum *dpl.* 141/15.
æltæwe *adj.* excellent, honest 118/23.
æltæwest *sup.* most excellent 89/8.
æmenne *adj.* deserted 44/29, 73/9.
æmettig *adj.* empty 31/9.
æmod *adj.* disheartened 57/26.

ænig *pron. adj.* any. *as adj.* 14/6, 16/10, 27/16, 31/15, etc.; *as pron.* 33/16, 52/34, 81/26. ænegu *nsf.*, *npl. n.* 31/13, 114/11. ænegum *dsm.*, *dpl.* 104/1, 116/19. ænigan *dsm.* 27/15.

ænlicost *sup. adj.* most excellent, incomparable 42/24.

ænne see an.

ær *prep. w. dat.* before 31/12, 38/13, 103/31, 135/3, etc. *ær þon* (*þan*, *þæm*) *conj.* before 30/14, 38/20, 38/29, 85/32; *ær þæm* (*þam*) *þe* 21/23, 22/29, 23/12, 23/19, etc.

ær *adv.* before (in time), beforehand, previously 8/23, 9/19, 14/21, 31/11, etc. æror *comp.* earlier 90/9. ærest *sup.* first (in space and time) 1/3, 11/8, 11/28, 16/6, etc.; æst 62/12, 68/4, etc. ~ *beforan* earlier, previously 11/27, 24/1, 27/14, etc.

ær *conj.* before, sooner than 16/17, 16/19, 25/20, 30/17, etc.; *w. vb. to be inferred* 88/16, 105/30, 123/1.

ærdæg (*m.*) *on ærdagum* in former days 33/7, 54/31, 72/8, 90/19.

æren *adj.* made of bronze 52/36, 114/8.

ærende *n.* message, errand 78/19, 95/24. *in pl.* news, tidings 95/28, 96/3, 123/26; *gpl.* 54/7. ærenda *apl.* 96/3.

geærendian II obtain by negotiation 135/27.

ærend(d)raca *wk. m.* messenger 5/11, 28/26, 29/10, 51/28, etc. ærendwracan *npl.* 3/6. ærendracan *dpl.* 87/14.

ærest *adj.* see ærra.

ærest *adv.* see ær.

ærnaþ I *pr. pl.* gallop 17/21, 17/31. geærneþ I *pr. 3 sg.* gets by galloping 17/25.

æror see ær.

ærra *comp. adj.* previous, earlier 46/24, 47/20, 49/7, 65/25, etc. ærest *sup.* first 2/11, 17/22, 22/5, 35/29, etc. ærran *dpl.* 24/3.

æst see ær *adv.*

æt (*m.*) food 77/22.

æt *prep. w. dat.* at 9/8, 9/14, 45/23, 45/32, etc.; against 46/23; by 18/12; from 1/9, 22/2, 24/23; in, on 14/5, 34/4, 35/6; to 66/30, 98/34; with

37/5. ~ *ham*, ~ *nehstan* see ham, nearra; ~ *Hæþum* see Commentary, 16/13. et 9/7.

ætgædere *adv.* together 51/2, 71/28, 77/1, 100/24, etc.

geætred *ppl. adj.* poisoned 73/30.

ætsæmne, ætsemne *adv.* together 138/19, 144/11.

æþele *adj.* noble 101/20; excellent 14/32. æþelestan *sup. apl. wk.* most eminent 77/31; most noble 28/15.

æþeling *m.* prince, person of royal blood (OH tyrannus, regius iuvenis, etc.) 1/25, 2/6, 29/14, 29/20, etc.

æwielme (*m.*) source, head of river 11/4, 11/5, 11/14, 12/20, 12/24.

æwisce (*n.*) disgrace 95/29.

æxsum *dpl.* (*f*). axes 40/22.

afærde I *pa. t. 3 sg.* terrified 93/3.

afæstnian II fasten, infix 155/9.

afaran 6 depart 46/35, 47/1, 48/6, 68/17, etc. afor *pa. t. 3 sg.* 44/25. aforan *pl.* 52/16. aforen *subj. pl.* 109/21. afaren *pp.* 154/13.

afedde I *pa. t. 3 sg.* nurtured, brought up 25/4. *pp. npl.* 82/33.

afeoll 7 *pa. t. 3 sg.* fell down 64/31.

afielde see afyllan.

afleow 7 *pa. t. 3 sg.* flowed 6/3, 119/9.

afliemde I *pa. t. 3 sg.* put to flight, caused to flee 125/16, 148/20. afliemed *pp.* 1/25. afliemde *npl.* 29/14.

aflugon 2 *pa. t. pl.* fled 125/6.

afor, aforan, aforen see afaran.

afslog see ofslean.

afuhten 3 *pa. t. subj. pl.* should fight their way 121/29.

afyllan I fill 48/17, 100/35; *w. gen.* fill with 45/7. afielde *pa. 't. 3 sg.* 135/29.

afyrhtede I *pp. npl.* frightened, terrified 103/17.

agæled I *pp.* preoccupied 73/16.

agælwede I *pp. npl.* dismayed 103/17.

agan *pret. pres. vb.* possess, have 105/24. ahte *pa. t. 3. sg.* 151/19 (2 ×). ahton *pl.* 64/26.

ageaf, ageafan, etc. see agiefan.

agen *adj.* (*always decl. strong*) own 30/30, 38/5, 82/13, 82/27, etc.; *as substantive* one's own property

87/24. **agene** *asm.* 22/25. **ægenu*
nsf. 132/11. **agne** *apl. m.*, **agnes**
gsn. etc. 80/12, 113/21, etc.
agi(e)fan 5 give, give up, give back,
restore 39/10, 80/1, 124/27, 141/23,
etc. **ageaf** *pa. t. 3 sg.* 33/26.
ageafan *pl.* 118/14; **ageafon** 121/
14. **ageafe** *subj. sg.* 79/28. **ageafen**
pl. 112/1.
geagnian II secure possession of,
acquire 118/4, 118/20, 150/11.
agoldene 3 *pp. npl.* paid for 132/22.
agoten 2 *pp.* shed 22/3.
agylte I *pa. t. subj. sg.* should do
wrong 140/13.
ah see **ac**.
ahangan see **ahon**.
ahebban 6 lift up, raise (war), exalt
6/9, 53/21, 80/6, 121/32 etc. **ahof**
pa. t. 3 sg. 45/29. **ahofan** *pl.*
62/21; **ahofon** 53/21. **ahæfen** *pp.*
147/2; **ahafen** 47/35.
aheng, ahengon see **ahon**.
ahleop 7 *pa. t. 3 sg.* leapt up 71/22.
ahleopon *pl.* 129/2.
ahnescaden II *pa. t. subj. pl.* became
soft 117/18.
ahof, ahofan etc. see **ahebban**.
ahon 7 hang, crucify 89/5, 135/4,
145/19,154/23,etc. **aheng** *pa. t. 3 sg.*
117/30. **ahengon** *pl.* 88/7. **ahangen**
pp. 4/2.
ahredde I *pa. t. 3 sg.* saved 1/9, 24/23.
geahsade, geahsian see **geascian**.
ahsige see **ascian**.
ahte, ahton see **agan**.
ahwettanne I *dat. inf.* whet 113/10.
ahwet *pp.* excited 147/17.
alætan 7 lose (life) 66/21, 119/6;
leave 96/29. **alet** *pa. t. 3 sg.* 96/29.
aldormonnum see **ealdormonn**.
aleag 2 *pa. t. 3 sg.* was false to 60/12.
alugen *subj. pl.* had failed to
perform 67/6.
alecgan I put down, lay down 17/15,
17/30, 130/18, 147/24, etc. **aled**
pp. 17/17.
alegen 5 *pp.* brought low 54/20.
alesan see **aliesan**.
alet see **alætan**.
alibban III live 22/1, 22/18, 60/10.
alyfdon *pa. t. pl.* 22/18. **alyfden**
subj. pl. 22/1.

aliefan, I allow, grant 5/8, 65/1,
107/22, 107/25, etc.
al(i)esan I liberate, redeem (by
payment) 28/28, 31/18, 37/18, 114/3.
alle see **eall**.
alneg see **ealneg**.
aloccoden II *pa. t. subj. pl.* should
entice 109/22, 117/7.
alugen see **aleag**.
alyfden, alyfdon see **alibban**.
amansumianne II *dat. inf.* excom-
municate 149/12.
amber (*m., f.*, or *n.*) measure 15/18
(see Commentary).
ambyr *adj.* favourable 16/5 (see
Commentary).
ameldad II *pp.* betrayed 90/6.
ami(e)rran I destroy 75/6; waste
113/7; lead astray 87/28. **amirdon**
pa. t. pl. 87/28.
an *pron. adj.* one *as adj.* one, a certain,
single 1/17, 2/6, 3/7, 4/13, etc.; the
same 14/30; *placed after noun or
pron.* alone, only 29/7, 39/27, etc.;
as pron. one, a man 50/15, 60/3,
62/4, etc. **anra gehwelc** every one
63/26. *nales þæt an þæt see* **nales**.
ænne *asm.* 46/26.
an *prep.* see **on**.
anbid, onbid (*n.*) waiting, expectation 74/1, 108/30; interval 79/1.
anbugen see **onbugan**.
and see **ond**.
andefn(*f.*) amount 17/15.
andlang see **ondlong**.
andon *anom. vb. pp.* undone 134/8.
ondyde *pa. t. 3 sg.* undid 131/24.
andydan *pl.* 59/5.
andred, andredan see **ondrædan**.
andrysne, onddrysne *adj.* terrible
117/23; venerated 128/23.
geandwyrdan I answer 27/11, 57/5,
109/3. **geondwyrdon** *inf.* 57/5.
andydan see **andon**.
anfealdnesse *asf.* unity 117/21.
anfeng, anfengon see **onfon**.
anfiteatra *indecl.* (*sg.* or *pl.*) amphitheatre 57/3, 57/13.
anfiteatrum amphitheatre 150/23
(OH amphitheatrum).
anfon see **onfon**.
anfunde 3 *pa. t. 3 sg.* discovered
32/21, 33/13, 90/7, 148/17, etc.;

anfunde (*cont.*):
onfunde 32/18. anfundan *pl.* 86/
10; onfundon 23/17. anfunden
pp. 64/26.
angan(n) see onginnan.
ange *adv.* anxiously. *in impers.*
construction w. dat. (he) was anxious
48/10.
angeald 3 *pa. t. 3 sg. w. gen.* atoned
for, paid for 132/18. anguldon,
onguldon *pl.* 98/17, 134/6, 134/26.
angolden *pp.* 144/16.
angean see ongean.
angeat, angeatan, angeaton see
ongietan.
angin(n), onginn *n.* enterprise,
action 39/2, 92/17, 136/29; per-
severance 48/14, 73/23; beginning
38/16, 56/5; behaviour, proceedings
89/21.
anginnan see onginnan.
angitan, angite see ongietan.
angulden, angoldon see angeald.
angunnan, angunnen, angunnon
see onginnan.
anhagade II *pa. t. 3 sg. impers.*
suited, pleased *w. acc.* 102/5; *w.*
dat. anhagode 90/29.
anhende *adj.* requiring attention, on
hand 50/20.
anlicnessa, anlicnesse see onlicnes.
geanmette I *pa. t. 3 sg.* encouraged
76/18. geanmet *pp.* 82/9.
anrædnesse *asf.* unanimity 117/20.
anscunedon II *pa. t. pl.* detested
82/16.
anstyred I *pp.* agitated 89/18. onstyrede *npl.* 32/26.
anwald, anweald see onweald.
anwann see onwinnende.
anwendan see onwendan.
anwig (*n.*) single combat, duel
40/26, 42/29, 57/29, 60/4, etc.
anwigge *ds.* 49/17.
anwold see onweald.
anwyrde see ondwyrde.
apostol *m.* apostle 136/13, 139/9,
140/11.
ar¹ *f.* property, possessions 15/14,
33/26; honour, reverence 52/29,
151/18; mercy 34/18.
ar² (*n.*) bronze 34/6.

arad 1 *pa. t. 3 sg.* rode 65/24.
aræfnan I endure 65/32.
aræran I raise up 122/25.
arærnesse *ds(f.)* exalting 54/30.
aras 1 *pa. t. 3 sg.* arose 37/21.
areccean I relate 12/15, 27/27, 49/12.
argeotere *m.* bronze-founder 2/5,
34/2.
gearian II *w. dat.* honour 153/13.
ariman I enumerate 31/30.
arleas *adj.* impious 150/26 (2×).
arlease *apl. n.* 150/26.
arlic *adj.* honourable 51/25.
arung (*f.*) honour 124/6.
asæd, asæde, asædon see asecg-
(e)an.
ascade see ascian.
geascade, geascedon see geascian.
ascan see acxe.
asceat see asceotan.
ascedan see ascian.
asceotan 2 shoot 62/7, 155/6; rush
60/3. asceat *pa. t. 3 sg.* 60/3.
ascoten *pp.* 62/7.
ascian, acsian II ask 33/21, 41/6,
46/23, 66/23, etc. ahsige *pr. subj.*
sg. 97/26.
geascian, geacsian, geahsian II
find out, discover, learn 22/22,
40/9, 44/23, 64/16, etc.
ascop 6 *pa. t. 3 sg.* gave (name)
27/20, 42/27.
ascoten see asceotan.
asecg(e)an III tell, relate 27/27,
56/2, 96/3, 148/19, etc. asecgenne
dat. inf. 27/33. asæde *pa. t. 1, 3*
sg. 56/12. asædon *pl.* 88/11. asæd
pp. 88/17.
asende I *pa. t. 3 sg.* sent 28/26.
asettan I place, set 17/36, 135/30,
142/14.
aslawoden II *pa. t. subj. pl.* should
become sluggish 112/32.
aslog 6 *pa. t. 3 sg.* struck 152/26.
asmorodon II *pa. t. pl.* smothered
119/6.
aspanan 6 entice, persuade 39/23,
40/23, 69/9, 79/20, etc. aspon *pa. t.*
3 sg. 32/20. asponan *pl.* 50/32;
asponon 78/20. aspanen *pp.*
98/20; asponon 53/25.
aspended I *pp.* spent 17/27.
aspon, asponan, etc. see aspanan.

aspryngþ 3 *pr. 3 sg.* bursts forth 11/13. **asprong** *pa. t. 3 sg.* (*w. up*) erupted 50/26, 116/25.

astealde I *pa. t. 3 sg.* began 46/7. asteald *pp.* set 44/2.

astige 1 *pr. subj. sg.* should rise 77/18. astigen *pp.* raised up, puffed up 139/7.

atellan I enumerate, count 52/6, 76/25, 81/26.

ateon 2 draw, pluck 70/4, 107/26, 119/26, 130/19; deal with 156/9. atugan *pa. t. pl.* 119/26; atugon 70/4.

atimbran I build 69/19, 71/12, 72/22, 149/16.

at(t)or *n.* poison 60/19, 74/12, 130/20, 136/7 etc. attres *gs.* 136/4. atre *ds.* 3/16; attre 90/5.

atugan, atugon see ateon.

aþ *m.* oath 35/3, 41/26, 67/7, 67/10, etc.; oath taking 35/9.

aþencean I devise 30/13.

aþenian I stretch out 93/32.

aþeostrade II *pa. t. 3 sg.* became eclipsed 135/8.

aþer *pron. adj.* either. *as pron.* 73/5, 105/31; *as adj.* 35/18. aþer . . . oþþe . . . oþþe either . . . or . . . 153/4; *as conj.* 15/22. aþre *asf.* 35/18.

aþewde I *pa. t. 3 sg.* drove away 154/16.

aþreotan II *impers. w. dat.* of person make weary, displease 27/32; *w. gen.* of object of displeasure 115/30.

aþrysemodan II *pa. t. pl.* suffocated 119/6.

aþrytton I *pa. t. pl.* tired out, exhausted 125/27.

aþstod 6 *pa. t. 3 sg.* remained 133/15 (v.l. oþstod)

aþum (*m.*) son-in-law 82/14, 82/16, 148/18.

awæcnedon II *pa. t. pl.* arose 78/10.

aweddon I *pa. t. pl.* became mad 123/27.

aweg *adv.* away 44/4, 57/1, 85/9, 86/28, etc.

awende I *pa. t. 3 sg.* turned 45/15. awendan *pl.* changed 75/25. awende *subj. pl.* should turn 47/27. awende *pp. npl.* changed 132/21.

aweorpan 3 throw, cast down or out 76/10, 94/32, 106/1, 131/20. awurpon *pa. t. pl.* 94/32. aworpen *pp.* 131/20.

aweox 7 *pa. t. 3 sg.* grew 23/4.

awer *adv.* anywhere 62/28.

awerede I *pa. t. 3 sg.* defended 73/16, 73/21. aweredon *pl.* 112/12, 117/2.

awestan I lay waste 29/7, 30/27, 34/26, 51/7, etc. awested *pp.* 39/1; awest 53/8.

awierged I *pp.* strangled 154/24.

aworpen see aweorpan.

awrat 1 *pa. t. 3 sg.* wrote, recorded 46/10, 84/33. awriten *pl.* 141/19. awriten *pp.* written, recorded 11/25, 88/17, 90/23, etc. awritene *npl.* 136/5.

awurpon see aweorpan.

axan see acxe.

B

bad see bidan.

gebad see gebidan.

bæcbord *n.* port(side) 14/8, 14/24, 16/9, 16/16, etc.

bæd, bædan, etc. see biddende.

gebæde see gebiddan.

bæm see begen.

bær, bæran see beran.

bærnan I burn 52/26, 52/30, 66/4, 91/12, etc.

gebæro (*asf. or apl. n.*) behaviour, conduct 32/17. gebærum *dpl.* 103/16.

bæþ (*n.*) bath 153/10.

ban *n.* bone, a bone 14/32, 15/16, 17/32.

geband see gebindan.

barn see byrnan.

baþian II wash, bathe 68/26.

be, bi *prep. w. dat.* by 22/4, 35/9, 42/26, 83/23, etc.; near 14/4, 70/10; along 14/7, 14/13, 16/6, 17/30; past 14/19; according to 15/17, 34/19; in accordance with 98/14, 156/21; in comparison with 50/26; about, concerning 21/21, 25/4, 85/3; after 27/20, 72/22; from, by 59/6, 59/9; to 66/7. be norþan, be suþan, etc. see norþan, suþan. be twiefealdan twofold 130/23. be hiere cneowe up to her knees 43/11. be þæm to what extent 76/24. be þæm dæle þæt to the extent that 91/2.

bead 2 *pa. t. 3 sg.* offered, gave 69/5.
budon *pl.* 67/28, 95/31. bude
subj. sg. 140/2.
gebead 2 *pa. t. 3 sg.* offered, proposed 34/3, 53/14. gebudan *pl.* 55/
16; gebudon 3/6, 53/11, 58/7.
beæftan *prep. w. dat.* behind 33/16,
45/25, 83/22, 91/16, etc.
beæftan *adv.* behind 30/8, 33/18,
44/26, 76/15, etc.
beag see bugende.
beald *adj.* confident, bold 66/22.
gebealg 3 *pa. t. 3 sg. refl.* became
angry 89/5. gebulgon *pl.* 51/32.
gebolgen *pp.* angered 43/11.
beam *m.* beam, post. beames *npl.*
53/1.
bearn *n.* child 28/15, 29/31, 35/10,
36/2, etc.
bearnteam (*m.*) progeny 35/6.
bebead 2 *pa. t. 3 sg. w. dat.* of
person ordered 63/21, 64/20, 66/
29, 69/24, etc.; announced 90/22;
offered 27/11. bebudan *pl.* ordered
88/32, 108/27; bebudon 111/9,
141/4, etc. beboden *pp.* entrusted
154/10; commanded 131/19.
bebod (*n.*) command, decree 78/13,
132/25, 135/13, 139/13.
bebyrg(e)an I bury 3/8, 55/25,
70/12, 89/14, etc.
bec see boc.
becom, become, etc. see becuman.
becrupe 2 *pa. t. subj. sg.* should
creep 69/25.
becuman 4 come 24/7, 27/6, 79/7,
79/23, etc.; attain 57/11, 102/12,
etc. *w. dat.* befall 89/13. becumaþ
pr. pl. 83/2. becume *subj. sg.*
65/28. becom *pa. t. 3 sg.* 4/1.
becoman *pl.* 55/2. become *subj. sg.*
76/6. becomen *pl.* 102/12; become
98/2.
bedde *ds*(*n.*) bed 119/6.
bedraf 1 *pa. t. 3 sg.* drove (in flight)
78/28, 79/16, 81/8, 106/12, etc.
bedrifon *pl.* 54/33. bedrifen *pp.*
driven 49/31.
bedulfan 3 *pa. t. pl.* buried 60/12.
beeode, beeodon see began.
befeng 7 *pa. t. 3 sg.* seized 77/25.
befangen *pp.* surrounded 8/16,
10/27, 76/17, 112/8, etc.

befor 6 *pa. t. 3 sg. refl.* went 96/8.
beforan *pl.* 66/19; *utan beforan*
surrounded 66/20.
beforan *prep. w. dat.* before, in
front of 26/18, 40/21, 42/7, 45/3,
etc. *w. acc.* (*or dat.?*) into the
presence of 60/23, 99/17.
beforan *adv.* ahead 28/26. *ær* ~
previously 11/14, 11/27, 24/1, 27/14,
etc. *her* ~ above 70/20.
began *anom. vb.* practise, observe
135/2, 150/20, 154/28, 156/6. beeode *pa. t. 3 sg.* 154/28. beeodon
pl. 156/6.
begeat, begeatan, etc. see be-
gi(e)tan.
begen *adj. pron.* both. begen *napl.*
m. 63/11, 69/1, 79/11, 93/15, etc.
bæm *dpl.* 63/12, 69/1, 139/20, etc.
begeondan *prep. w. dat.* beyond
13/7, 147/28.
begi(e)tan 5 obtain, gain possession
of 31/15, 42/19, 57/25, 77/31, etc.
begeat *pa. t. 3 sg.* 62/1. begeatan
pl. 79/25; begeaton 39/7. begeate
subj. sg. 72/12. begeaton *pl.* would
have gained possession of 41/1;
begeate 94/9. begietena *pp. apl. f.*
39/35.
begongende see bigongaþ.
begunne 3 *pa. t. subj. sg.* began 37/5,
37/6.
behæfþ III *pr. 3 sg.* surrounds 8/18.
beheafdian II behead 149/8.
behealdan 7 protect 121/24. behealdanne *dat. inf.* observe 59/16.
behet 7 *pa. t. 3 sg. w. dat. of person*
promised 34/11. beheton *pl.* 67/9.
behlad 1 *pa. t. 3 sg.* closed 57/22.
behyldan I skin 93/31.
beladian II *w. gen.* clear in respect of
69/22.
beleac 2 *pa. t. 3 sg.* locked 89/29.
beluce *subj. sg.* should shut fast,
lock 149/18. beluce *pl.* 63/14.
belocen *pp.* shut fast 59/1. belocene *npl.* 62/25.
beled I *pp. w. gen.* invested with
67/19.
belifene 1 *pp. npl.* dead 49/21.
belimpeþ 3 *pr. 3 sg.* belongs 16/31.
beliþ 5 *pr. 3 sg.* surrounds 18/19.
belicgaþ *pl.* surround 18/21.

belocen, belocene see beleac.
beluce see beleac.
belytegade II *pa. t. 3 sg.* enticed 62/16.
bemætan 5 *pa. t. pl.* accounted, considered 63/28, 65/13, 70/1, 106/35; bemæton 95/20.
bemurciaþ II *pr. pl.* complain 31/2 (v.l. bemurcniaþ).
ben *f.* request, petition 39/6, 47/29, 107/2.
bena *wk. m.* petitioner. *bena wæron w. gen.* requested 80/1.
benæman I *w. gen. of thing* deprive 30/20, 79/24, 150/3.
benam, bename, benamon see beniman.
bend (*m., f., or n.*) bond 95/23, 125/1. gebende I *pa. t. 3 sg.* bound 125/1. gebend *pp.* 116/11.
beniman 4 take away, deprive *w. acc. of person and gen. of thing taken* 37/30, 38/1, 38/5, 38/22, etc., *w. dat. of thing* 133/3 (*v.l. w. gen*). benimþ *pr. 3 sg.* 16/35. benom *pa. t. 3 sg.* 54/9; benam 38/22. benoman *pl.* 49/26; benamon 52/31. bename *subj. pl.* 52/27. benumen *pp.* 37/30.
beon, bion *anom. vb.* be 15/26, 15/28, 28/19, 30/1, etc.; extend 14/1; happen, come to pass 25/9, 28/17, etc; *as auxil. w. pr. p.* keep on, continue 21/26, 29/27, etc; *to be rendered by corresponding simple tense* 11/6, 11/10, etc. ∼ *on* consist of 15/14. beonne *dat. inf.* 35/7. eam *pr. 1 sg.* 44/3. eart *2 sg.* 127/23. biþ *3 sg.* 11/19; is 8/16; ys 23/8. sindon *pl.* 8/24; sint 1/24; syndon 18/13; synd 16/7; synt 19/9; beoþ 15/4. sie *subj. sg.* 11/5; sy 15/19; beo 113/6. sien *pl.* 34/16; syn 21/30. wæs *pa. t. 1, 3 sg.* 2/3. wære *2 sg.* 45/8. wæran *pl.* 35/10; wæron 2/24. wære *subj. sg.* 21/23. wæren *pl.* 29/24; wæron 67/6; wære 36/23.
beorg, beorh *m.* hill, mountain, mountain range 4/29, 8/24, 9/16, 9/26, etc. beorgan *dpl.* 13/6.
beorhtte *adj. npl. of* beorgiht (?) mountainous 10/5.

beot (*n.*) promise, vow 60/11 (v.l. gehat).
gebeotode II *pa. t. 3 sg.* vowed, boasted 43/7, 43/9. gebeotedan *pl.* vowed 78/31.
bera *wk.* (*m.*) bear 15/18.
beran 4 bear (a burden), carry, wear (a hat) 15/36, 17/13, 75/22, 107/30, etc. byrþ *pr. 3 sg.* 17/27. beraþ *pl.* 15/36. berendes *ppl. adj. gsn.* pregnant 85/26. bær *pa. t. 3 sg.* 107/28. bæran *pl.* 46/14.
geberan 4 bear (a child) 31/16, 58/14, 59/21, 85/26, etc. geboren *pp.* 5/24. *of hiora lande geboren* native of their country 155/26. geborene *pp. npl.* 114/1.
bereafian II seize, despoil 64/11, 70/6, 83/3; *w. gen. of thing* rob, deprive of 66/27.
beren *adj.* belonging to a bear, bearskin 15/19.
berstende 3 *pr. p.* bursting, splitting open 25/29, 50/7.
besætan, besæton, besæt(t) see besittan.
besætedon II *pa. t. pl.* should lie in ambush for 79/10.
besanc see besincan.
besawon 5 *pa. t. pl.* gazed 52/19.
bescearen 4 *pa. t. subj. pl.* should shave 108/11.
besceat 2 *pa. t. 3 sg.* shot, plunged 3/3, 57/22.
besceawade II *pa. t. 3 sg.* should observe 90/22.
bescufan 2 cast 34/14, 118/15.
besencte I *pa. t. 3 sg.* sank 92/24.
besengdan I *ppl. adj. asf. wk.* burned 52/19.
beseten see besittan.
besi(e)rede, besyrede I *pa. t. 3 sg.* deceived, ensnared 44/31, 48/26, 64/19, 91/16, etc. besi(e)red *pp.* 76/17, 89/10. besierede *npl.* 66/18.
besincan 3 sink 11/7, 11/12, 50/10, 87/2, etc. besinca *inf.* 56/8. besincþ *pr. 3 sg.* 11/12. besince *subj. sg.* 11/7. besanc *pa. t. 3 sg.* 82/14. besuncan *pl.* 114/9; besuncon 56/5. besuncene *pp. npl.* 50/10.* besuncenum *dpl.* 50/9.

besittan 5 surround, besiege 4/8, 51/16, 54/33, 80/25, etc. **besæt** *pa. t. 3 sg.* 6/15; **besætt** 69/15. **besætan** *pl.* 35/3; **besæton** 2/25. **beseten** *pp.* 51/28.
besma (*wk. m.*) broom, rod. **besman** *dpl.* 40/22.
bespon 6 *pa. t. 3 sg.* incited 22/10.
bespricþ 5 *pr. 3 sg.* complains 44/12.
besprecaþ *pl.* speak about, complain of 34/15, 83/1; complain 31/3.
bestelan 4 steal (upon) 5/6, 30/19, 105/18, 154/12, etc.; *refl.* steal (away) 116/8. **bestæl** *pa. t. 3 sg.* 5/6. **bestælan** *pl.* 51/24.
besuncan, besuncen, etc. see **besincan.**
beswic, biswic (*n.*) treachery 63/1. *to beswice wearþ* played false 33/28.
beswican 1 deceive, betray, overcome by stratagem, circumvent 30/16, 32/20, 44/22, 47/8, etc. **beswicanne** *dat. inf.* 148/16. **beswac** *pa. t. 3 sg.* 2/4. **beswican** *pl.* 115/27; **beswicon** 49/16. **beswice** *subj. sg.* 82/18. **beswicen** *pp.* 37/30. **beswicene** *pp. npl.* 94/21.
beswiceden I *pa. t. subj. pl.* should overcome by stratagem 79/9.
besyrede see **besi(e)rede.**
bet *comp. adv.* better 19/28, 32/7, 34/12, 35/8, etc. **betst** *sup. adv.* best, most 47/30, 61/27, 64/1.
betæcan I *w. dat. of person* entrust, commit 124/20, 154/11, 155/16, 155/18, etc. **betæhte** *pa. t.* 48/1; **betahte** 155/11. **betaht** *pp.* 155/17.
betan I make, kindle (fire) 151/10.
ġebetan I make amends for, atone for 17/33, 38/20, 83/17; repair 55/13. **ġebette** *pa. t. 3 sg.* 83/17. **ġebetton** *pl.* 55/13.
betera *comp. adj.* better 40/19, 49/3, 49/5, 102/35, etc. **beteran** *dpl.* 49/3. **betst** *sup. adj.* best 6/2, 15/3, 47/8, 148/22, etc.
betoġen 2 *pp.* covered 121/31.
betst *adj.* see **betera.**
betst *adv.* see **bet.**
betuh, betux, betwux *prep. w. dat.* between, among 10/1, 10/2, 20/20, 115/32, etc. *w. acc.* 25/25,

29/16(?). **betwíh** 53/9. **betwuh** 22/27.
betweonum *prep. w. dat.* 2/27, 17/5, 51/3; *directly following pers. pron. in dpl.* 1/21, 2/7, 2/9, 2/18, etc. **betweonan** 17/5.
betynde I *pa. t. 3 sg.* closed, shut 6/18, 89/29, 130/27. **betyndan** *pl.* 138/19. **betyned** *pp.* 132/12. **betyneda** *npl. f.* 59/10, 59/12.
beþohte I *pa. t. 3 sg.* trusted 33/4. **beþohtan** *pl.* entrusted 94/11. **beþoht** *pp.* 81/19.
beþridian II force 62/18; circumvent 46/34; overpower 98/5, 155/2. **beþyddan** I *pa. t. pl.* thrust 85/15.
beweorpan 3 cast 45/7.
bewerian I defend, protect 54/25, 57/27, 75/7, 92/27, etc.
bewitan *pret. pres. vb.* administer, watch over 40/10, 42/18, 50/15, 155/17. **bewisten** *pa. t. subj. pl.* 42/18.
bewopene 7 *pp. npl.* in tears 52/18.
beworhte I *pa. t. 3 sg.* covered over 46/10. **beworht** *pp.* 43/32.
bewuna *indecl. adj.* wont, accustomed 64/9, 64/25.
bewundon 3 *pa. t. pl.* wound round 85/14.
bi see **be.**
bibliotheoco *n. and ds.* library 142/2, 142/5 (OH *as.* bibliothecam).
ġebicnede I *pa. t. 3 sg.* indicated 84/32.
bidan 1 remain 47/34, 57/20, 154/9; *w. gen.* wait for 14/13, 14/15. **bad** *pa. t. 3 sg.* 14/13. **bide** *subj. sg.* 47/34.
ġebidan I remain, wait 76/12, 76/15, 91/2, 103/5, etc. **ġebad** *pa. t. 3 sg.* 76/15. **ġebidon** *pl.* 87/3. **ġebiden** *subj. pl.* 76/12.
ġebiddan 5 pray 71/30, 134/2; *w. refl. dat.* 134/4. **ġebæde** *pa. t. subj. sg.* 134/2.
biddende 5 *pr. p. w. gen. of thing asked* asking, asking for 31/8, 39/15, 47/26, 48/17, etc. **bæd** *pa. t. 3 sg.* asked 47/23, etc. **bædan** *pl.* 57/18; **bæden** 107/1; **bæden** 55/24. **bæde** *subj. sg.* 31/13.
ġebidon see **ġebidan.**

gebielde I *pp. npl.* emboldened 84/23.
biernende see byrnan.
gebigan, gebiggiean I dislodge 155/4; subdue 117/29; subject 68/5.
gebigde *pa. t. 3 sg.* 68/5.
bigongaþ 7 *pr. pl.* worship 111/17.
begongende *pr. p.* worshipping 84/8.
bilwitnesse *ds(f.)* innocence 22/18.
gebindan 3 bind, tie up 40/21, 86/19, 115/1, 116/8, etc. geband *pa. t. 3 sg.* 62/4. gebundon *pl.* 124/27. gebunde *subj. sg.* 128/29. gebunden *pp.* 70/8. gebundenne *asm.* 79/30. gebundene *apl.* 42/8.
binnan *prep.* within *w. dat.* 10/12, 12/22, 42/16, 44/22, etc. *w. acc.* 52/11, 86/26. ~ þæm during that period 70/19.
binnan *adv.* within 12/10, 19/2, 64/1, 112/10. See also þærbinnan.
bion see beon.
birnende see byrnan.
biscep, bisceop, biscop *m.* bishop 149/12, 151/22, 153/10; priest (of non-Christian religions) 3/15, 5/29, 57/2, 57/18. biscepun *dpl.* 75/33.
biscephad (*m.*) priestly state. *on biscephade* in the guise of a priest 89/4.
bisen, bysen *f.* example, pattern, model 22/17, 24/21, 39/4, 44/2, 131/6.
bismer *n.* disgrace, infamy, shame 3/13, 38/21, 66/12, 66/25, etc.; *in pl.* disgraceful things 87/29, 88/10. bismre *ds.*, etc. bismra *apl.*, 66/26, 88/10, etc.
bismerlic, bysmerlic *adj.* disgraceful, ignominious 2/27, 27/29. bismerlecre *comp. nsf.* more shameful 116/29. bismerlecest-, bismerlicest- *sup.* most shameful 25/27, 53/9, 79/32, 87/14, 115/20.
bismerlice *adv.* shamefully 77/7.
bismrade II *pa. t. 3 sg.* mocked, put to shame 65/16, 75/31, 120/23, 135/27. bysmredan *pl.* 2/4.
gebismrade II *pa. t. 3 sg.* put to shame 47/10. gebismrad *pp.* 44/13. gebismrade *npl.* 103/3.
bismrung, bysmrung *f.* scorn 22/26; infamy 57/12.

bispel (*n.*) fable 25/5.
biswice see beswic.
bite (*m.*) bite 25/22.
bitresta *sup. adj. nsm.* most acrid 77/17.
biþ see beon.
blace *adj. asf.* black 124/4.
blæd (*f.*) fruit 23/9.
blædre (*wk. f.*) blister. blædran *dpl.* 25/29.
bleaþran *comp. adj. npl.* more inactive 48/24.
bleotan see blotan.
gebletsade II *pa. t. 3 sg.* consecrated 39/19.
blindlice *adv.* blindly 31/10.
bliþe *adj.* happy 52/16, 117/8.
bliþelice *adv.* merrily 65/30.
bliþnesse *dsf.* joyfulness 44/29.
blod (*n.*) blood 3/27, 22/3, 22/21, 25/17, etc.
bloddrync *m.* draught of blood 87/6.
blodege *adj. npl. n.* bloody 100/36.
blodgyte *m.* bloodshed 72/14, 87/4.
blodryne (*m.*) haemorrhage 152/7.
blot (*n.*) sacrifice 27/10, 27/31.
geblot *n.* sacrifice 1/18, 27/13, 115/13, 156/3, 156/7.
blotan 7 sacrifice 39/9, 88/22, 98/13, 115/15, etc. blote *pr. subj. sg.* 27/16. blotende *pr. p.* 155/27. bleotan *pa. t. pl.* 4/3. bloten *subj. pl.* 88/3 (v.l. blotten, cf. BTS *blotan*).
blotung *f.* sacrificing 57/6.
boc *f.* book 1/1, 32/3, 32/11, 35/26, etc. bec *ds.* 53/5; *npl.* 140/10.
bocland (*n.*) land held by charter 118/5.
gebod *n.* order, command 139/19, 147/22.
gebodade II *pa. t. 3 sg.* announced 42/32, 46/10, 89/17. gebodode should announce 109/14.
gebogene see gebugan.
gebohte see gebycggan.
gebolgen see gebealg.
geboren, geborene see geberan.
bot *f.* remedy 38/30.
brad *adj.* broad 15/27, 15/30, 15/31, 20/29, etc. bradre *comp. nsf. and nsn.* broader 15/27, 16/10, 50/30, etc. brædre *nsn.* 15/27. bradost

brad (*cont.*):
  sup. nsn. broadest 15/25. *mid bradum folcum* with widespread population 58/20.
bradiende II *pr. p.* extending 123/21.
bræce, bræcon see brecan.
bræd *f.* breadth. *fif æcra bræde* for a breadth of five acres 86/31.
gebræd 3 *pa. t. 3 sg. w. dat.* drew 101/25.
gebrædde I *pa. t. 3 sg.* extended 72/1, 116/1.
brædende I *pr. p.* stretching 89/25.
brædre see brad.
brægden *adj.* crafty 121/9.
bræþ (*m.*) vapour 151/12.
brecan 4 take by storm 109/17, 125/25; force one's way, break through 19/25, 93/26. brycþ *pr. 3 sg.* 19/25. bræcon *pa. t. pl.* 93/26. bræce *subj. sg.* 125/25.
bred (*n.*) tablet 46/10, 90/22.
bremust *sup. adj.* most renowned 40/7.
brengan see bringan.
gebrengan see gebringan.
breost *n.* breast 29/33, 73/19.
breþer see broþor.
bringan, brengan 3 I bring 42/5, 42/11, 49/24, 59/26, etc. ~ *on* bring to 84/5; ~ *ongean* bring to meet 73/3 etc.; ~ *to unsibbe* end in disagreement 107/16. bringþ *pr. 3 sg.* 77/21. brohte *pa. t. 3 sg.* 41/29. brohton *pl.* 15/1. brohte *subj. sg.* 108/29. brohten *pl.* 79/30. broht *pp.* 110/27.
gebring(e)an, gebrengan 3 I bring, lead 116/9, 139/21, 148/22, 154/8, etc. gebrohte *pa. t. 3 sg.* 73/1. gebrohten *subj. pl.* 66/30. gebroht *pp.* 70/25. *on fleame* ~ cause to flee 76/11.
broc *n.* affliction 30/31, 36/3, 65/27, 65/32, etc.
gebroc (*n.*) affliction 65/28; laborious effort 91/26.
brociende II *pr. p.* afflicting 41/22.
brocode *pa. t. subj. sg.* should oppress 143/11.
gebrocode II *pa. t. 3 sg.* afflicted, distressed 117/4. gebrocode *pp. npl.* 104/24; gebrocade 85/9.

gebroht, gebrohte(n) see gebring-(e)an.
broht(e), brohton etc. see bringan.
brosnien II *pr. subj. pl.* decay 44/13.
broþor *m.* brother 5/7, 7/4, 7/28, 39/17, etc.; *gs.* 39/3; *apl.* 40/19. breþer *ds.* 7/9.
gebroþor *coll. pl. m.* brothers 2/14, 23/25, 27/4, 39/1, etc. gebroþra *npl.* 27/4. gebroþran *dpl.* 27/3.
gebroþorscipe *m.* brotherhood 82/32.
gebrowen 2 *pp.* brewed 17/5.
brucan 2 *w. gen.* enjoy, partake of 23/4, 48/35, 144/4. brucende *pr. p.* 23/4.
brycg *f.* bridge 45/23, 48/7, 48/9, *149/3.
brycþ see brecan.
bryne (*m.*) burning, conflagration 50/27, 85/16, 114/7, 133/12, 137/25. ~ hæfdon received burns 26/30.
gebudan, gebudon[1] see gebead.
bude[1], budon see bead.
bude[2] I *pa. t. 3 sg.* lived 13/30 (2 ×), 14/7, 16/1, etc.
gebudon[2] I *pa. t. pl.* settled 29/16.
gebud *pp.* cultivated (v.l. gebun) 14/24.
bufan *prep.* above *w. dat.* 26/2, 43/31, 80/7, 129/27, etc. *w. acc.* 59/8. *w. acc. or dat.* 17/10, 107/8.
bugende 2 *pr. p.* turning 11/17. beag *pa. t. 3 sg.* turned 14/11, 14/15. bugan *pl.* 47/29. buge *subj. pl.* should turn 80/33.
gebugan 2 *pa. t. pl.* turned 33/20. gebogene *pp. npl.* defected 45/16.
gebulgon see gebealg.
gebun 7 *pp.* settled, cultivated 14/20, 14/21; occupied 37/13. gebune *npl.* 53/24.
gebunde, gebunden, etc. see gebindan.
burg, burh *f.* walled town, fortress, city 3/11, 4/6, 4/28, 17/1, etc. byrg *gs.* 46/20; burge 24/32. byrg *ds.* 3/5; byrig 2/2; burge 9/12. byrig *napl.* 1/7; byrg 5/20. burga *gpl.* 105/8.
burgen 3 *pa. t. subj. pl. w. dat.* should preserve 47/3.

burgleode *pl. m.* townsfolk, citizens 4/2, 55/10, 64/3, 80/22, etc.

burgware *pl. m.* townsfolk, citizens 39/5, 47/1, 51/32, 73/13, etc. **burgwarana** *gpl.* 39/26; **burgwarena** 88/17.

burne see **byrnan**.

geburnen 3 *pp.* burnt 86/31; caused by burning 142/4.

butan, buton *prep. w. dat.* without 22/26, 27/25, 31/19, etc.; outside 54/23, 90/12; besides 9/31, 9/32, 52/21; except, except for, but 14/22, 23/14, 24/21; free from 42/20. *w. acc.* without 50/29 (*v. l. w. dat.*). *conj.* unless 31/14, 31/16, 33/22; but, except 14/2, 14/12, 111/31. *ellipt.* but, except, only 52/25, 102/1, 124/12; than 46/24. *butan þæm þe* not to mention that 21/28, 51/18. *butan þæt* if . . . not, except that 57/7, 60/21, 89/20, 113/6.

butu, buta *adj. pron. common gender* both 10/2, 45/28, 63/19, 80/13, 106/6.

gebycgan I buy 83/5. gebohte *pa. t. 3 sg.* paid for 133/20.

byge (*m.?*) angle (of wall) 73/15.

bylwetlice *adv.* with simplicity 21/32.

byne *adj.* cultivated, inhabited 15/24, 15/25.

gebyrd(*f. or n.*) birth. *in pl.* parentage 15/17.

byrdest *sup. adj.* most well-born 15/17.

gebyrede I *pa. t. 3 sg. impers. w. dat.* befell 33/19, 65/23, 88/6.

byrele *m.* cup-bearer 74/11.

byrg, byrig see **burg**.

byrgde I *pa. t. 3 sg.* buried 60/13.

byrgenne *asf.* tomb, grave 107/7, 130/10, 130/17.

byrnan 3 burn 77/12, 98/29, 137/25, etc. **birnende** *pr. p.* 49/19; biernende 123/19; byrnende 86/29. barn *pa. t. 3 sg.* 112/24. burne *subj. sg.* 2/23.

byrþ see **beran**.

bysen see **bisen**.

bysmerlice see **bismerlice**.

bysmredan see **bismrade**.

bysmrung see **bismrung**.

C

calendas (*dpl. m.?*) Kalends. ∼ *Agustus* Kalends of August (OH Kalendis Sextilibus) 130/3.

carcern (*n.*) prison 113/27, 118/15, 122/5.

caru(*f.*) grief 42/34.

casere *m.* Caesar, emperor 1/27, 6/11, 6/18, 6/22, etc. **caseras** *gs.* 38/7.

casern(*f.*) empress 140/16.

cawel *m.* basket 100/35.

cealc *m.* plaster 151/11.

ceald *adj.* cold 68/25, 151/10.

ceap *m.* commodity 130/23.

geceapian II buy 114/1, 120/19, 120/21, 120/25, 130/24.

ceapode II *pa. t. sg. w. gen.* were to buy 120/25.

ceapscip (*n.*) merchant ship 63/32.

geceas see **geceosan**.

ceastra *apl. f.* cities 30/28, 30/29.

cempa *wk.* (*m.*) warrior 42/28, 71/7, 77/32, 79/21, 88/31, etc.

cendon I *pa. t. pl.* bore (child) 29/31.

cene *adj.* warlike 141/27.

ceorfæxsum *dpl.* (*f.*) executioner's axes 86/21.

ceoriaþ II *pr. pl.* murmur 77/5.

ceorl (*m.*) freeman 87/19.

ceosan 2 choose 29/12 (*w. part. gen.*), 42/28. curon *pa. t. pl.* 42/28.

geceosan 2 choose, elect 35/12, 36/1, 63/32, 81/13, etc. geceas *pa. t. 3 sg.* 3/11. gecuron *pl.* 30/14. gecoren *pp.* 67/19.

cesar *m.* caesar, emperor 123/29, 134/12, 136/15.

ciding(*f.*) rebuke 111/13.

ciefese *ds*(*f.*) concubine 148/9.

ci(e)le *m.* cold 51/17, 68/26, 100/12, 100/17.

gecierde, gecierdon see **gecirran**.

cierre see **cirr**.

gecierred see **gecirran**.

cild *n.* child 5/24, 39/14, 39/15, 70/15, 116/24.

cile see **ciele**.

ciningum see **cyning**.

cipemonn (*m.*) merchant 23/26.

cirdon see **cirrende**.

gecirdon see **gecirran**.

cirice *wk.* (*f.*) (Christian) church 149/18, 156/16; heathen temple 39/21; Jewish holy place, sacrarium 135/29. cirican *apl.* 149/18; ciricean 39/21. ciricum *dpl.* 156/16.

cirr, cierr, cyrr (*m.*) occasion 14/5, 47/12, 52/7, 53/2, etc. cierrun *dpl.* 121/5.

ġecirran, ġecyrran I turn 26/13, 50/18, 61/28, 80/18, etc.; *toġædere* ~ band together 29/26, 50/21. ġecierde *pa. t. 3 sg.* 130/8. ġecierdon *pl.* 47/16. ġecierred *pp.* 75/21. cirrende I *pr. p.* returning 64/27, 125/3. cirdon *pa. t. pl.* turned 14/18, 82/17.

cist *f.* chest 136/4.

clæne *adv.* completely 83/20.

claþa *gpl.* (*m.*) clothes 66/27.

cleopade, cleopode I *pa. t. 3 sg.* called out 55/23, 127/19.

clif *n.* cliff 112/10, 119/12; coast 11/4 (see Commentary), 11/13.

clud *m.* rock 72/7, 135/6.

cludiġ *adj.* rocky 15/23.

cluse *wk. f.* fortified pass, defile, cluse 62/25 (see Commentary), 63/14, 63/19, 154/29, 154/30, etc.

cneow *n.* knee 43/12, 59/8, 73/27, 96/19.

ġecneowe 7 *pa. t. subj. sg.* recognized 107/6.

cniht *m.* boy 26/5, 27/30, 61/11, 99/18, etc.; servant 23/23 (see Commentary).

cnihthad (*m.*) boyhood, youth 39/28.

cnysedan I *pa. t. pl.* overcame 53/29. ġecnysede I *pp. npl.* overcame 77/4.

com, come, etc. see cuman.

consul *m.* consul, man of consular rank 3/2, 3/17, 3/21, 4/8, etc.

consulatum *asm.* term as consul 124/21 (OH consulatum). consulato *ds.* 130/26; consulatu 74/30.

coortana, coortena *wk. gpl.* cohorts 127/13, 127/16 (OH cohortes).

ġecoren see ġeceosan.

corn *n.* grain, corn 100/35, 137/4.

costiġan II tempt 136/8.

cot (*n.*) cottage 74/24.

cræft *m.* power, might 33/5, 33/12; art, skill 23/30, 51/21, 51/24, 85/12, etc. *in pl.* forces 30/15, 34/23, 42/30, etc.

cræfteġa *adj. wk. nsm.* mighty 31/1. cræfteġast *sup. ns.* most powerful 42/24; cræftġestan *wk. as.* 30/26. ġecræftġade II *pp. npl.* made powerful 37/3.

crætwæn *m.* chariot 42/4, 42/7, 42/11.

creopendra 2 *pr. p. gpl.* crawling 93/30. crupon *pa. t. pl.* crawled 25/25, 52/18.

cristen *adj.* Christian 34/15, 38/23, 50/28, 56/9, etc. cristne, cristnum, etc. 44/12, 141/13, 141/18, etc.

cristendom *m.* Christianity, Christian faith 38/8, 44/14, 52/29, 104/4, etc.; Christian era 27/12, 31/3, 31/11, 103/31, etc.; Christian country 27/15.

crupon see creopendra.

cuca *adj.* alive, living 3/8, 57/19, 60/12, 73/24, etc. cwice *npl. f.* 36/4. cucan *dsm.* 128/20.

cuene see cwen.

cuma *wk.* (*m.*) stranger 1/19, 27/10.

cuman 4 come 14/25, 25/18, 25/21, 31/28, etc.; go 81/17, 83/11; attain 90/3, 101/15; get (to) 48/9; turn out, become 41/17; happen (to) 49/21. *aweg* ~ get away 57/1. ~ *up* land 107/12. cymeþ *pr. 3 sg.* 17/22; cymþ 16/8. cumaþ *pl.* 16/34. com *pa. t. 3 sg.* 4/16. coman *pl.* 16/19; comon 3/6. come *subj. sg.* 16/17. comen *pl.* 29/11; come 52/19. cumen *pp.* 4/24. cumene *npl.* 118/6.

cunnoden II *pa. t. subj. pl.* should try 65/6.

cunnon *pret. pres. vb. pr. pl.* know (are able?) 31/12. cuþe *pa. t. 3 sg.* knew 22/5. cuþan *pl.* knew 22/17; were able 88/1; cuþon 61/27. cuþen *subj. pl.* were able 113/16.

curon see ceosan.

ġecuron see ġeceosan.

cuþ *adj.* known, evident 19/19, 32/2, 79/13, 85/21, etc.; celebrated, famous 28/1, 52/4.

cuþan, cuþe, cuþon, etc. see cunnon.

cwaciende II *pr. p.* quaking 50/7.

cwacung *f.* quaking 56/7.

cwædon, cwæþ, etc. see cweþan.

ġecwæþ *pa. t. 3 sg.* proposed 40/25.
ġecwædan *pl.* agreed 39/30; ġe-
cwædon announced, proposed 35/8,
121/18, 121/28. ġecwæde *subj. sg.*
said 85/3. ġecweden *pp.* said 25/5;
agreed 60/2; proposed 67/21. ġe-
cwedene *npl.* called 21/29. *togædere* ∼ agreed to meet 94/13.
cwealdon I *pa. t. pl.* killed 88/24,
98/17.
cwealm *m.* pestilence, plague 3/18,
25/28.
ġecweden see ġecwæþ.
ġecwedræden *f.* agreement 60/2,
127/20, 127/21, 127/24. ġecwed-
rædenne *as.* 60/2.
cweman I *w. dat.* please 34/4.
ġecweman I *w. dat.* propitiate 63/30.
cwen *f.* queen 1/4, 22/8, 22/19,
30/1, etc. cuene *as.* 80/11.
cwene (*wk. f.*) woman 64/29.
cweþan 5 say 13/30, 19/31, 46/15,
49/1, etc. cweþaþ *pr. pl.* 52/23.
cweþe *subj. sg.* 44/3. cweþen
pl. 113/14. cwæþ *pa. t. 1, 3 sg.*
8/23. cwædon *pl.* 19/23. cwæde
subj. sg. 49/1.
cwice see cuca.
cwielmende I *pr. p.* torturing 34/1.
cyle *m.* cold 19/27, 19/28; freezing
17/34, 17/36.
cylle *m.* leather bag, skin 45/7.
cyme (*m.*) coming 133/22.
cymeþ, cymþ see cuman.
cyn see cynn.
ġecynd (*f.*) nature 93/29, 130/13.
ġecynde *adj.* belonging by in-
heritance 24/6.
cynecynnes *gs*(*n*). of royal race, of
royal family 40/12; kynekynnes
22/23. cynecynne *ds.* 40/20.
cynedom (*m.*) royal authority 90/2.
cynerice *n.* kingdom, sovereignty
61/8, 136/23.
cynesetl *n.* royal seat 64/7.
cynestol (*m.*) capital 70/7.
cyning *m.* king 1/3, 1/11, 1/14, 1/18,
etc. cyng 5/11. cyniġ 98/3. cyn-
inġc 15/8. kyning 21/24. kyninġc
26/13. ciningum *dpl.* 155/23.
cyn(n) *n.* race, family 24/23, 42/23,
59/18, 70/13, etc.; kind, species
23/9, 42/12, 130/19, 130/20.

cypren *adj.* of copper 114/9.
ġecyrran see ġecirran.
cyrre see cirr.
cyþan I make known, announce
58/11, 123/8, 134/19; practise 44/28.
ġecyþan I make known, reveal,
declare 37/2, 55/27, 67/24, 77/22,
etc.
cyþþe *a. and ds*(*f.*) native country
31/28, 78/11, 95/32; fellow country-
men 46/9.

D

dæd *f.* deed 43/13, 44/36, 46/1, 59/24,
etc. dædæ *ds.* 150/10; dæda 145/18.
dædbot *f.* penance, amends 135/2.
dæġ *m.* day 1/13, 5/5, 14/9, 14/11, etc.
lifetime, time 3/3, 4/16, 25/12, etc.
dagan *dpl.* 16/13. dæġ *endingless
loc.* in the phrases *on dæġ* in the
daytime, at that time 101/14, 119/25,
125/1; *ælce dæg* every day 50/7,
50/9; *þy ylcan dæg* on the same
day 17/12. dæġes *adv.* by day
26/4, 123/18, 125/25. to dæġe see
todæg.
dæġhwamlice *adv.* daily 155/27.
dæl¹ *m.* part, portion, region 1/11,
8/15, 12/26, 12/31, etc. *be sumum
dæle* to some extent 66/7, 77/8. *be
þæm dæle þæt* to the extent that
91/3. *sumne* ∼ *adv.* to some extent,
partly 12/31, 31/7.
dæl² (*n.*) valley 23/7.
dælan I share 39/23; distribute
105/5.
ġedælde I *pa. t. 3 sg.* distributed 126/
24. ġedæled *pp.* divided 63/10.
ġedæmde I *pa. t. 3 sg.* condemned
136/2.
ġedafenlice *adv.* fittingly, justly 150/
26.
ġedafenode II *pa. t. 3 sg. impers.* was
fitting 25/26.
daga, dagan, etc. see dæg.
dead *adj.* dead 17/7, 17/18, 17/29,
17/35, etc. *wk. as subst.* dead
(person) 55/25, 57/20.
deadlic *adj.* deadly 67/13.
deadwylle *adj.* barren 20/17.
ġedearf 3 *pa. t. 3 sg.* perished, sank
94/31. ġedurfon *pl.* 26/23, 95/7.
dearnenga *adv.* secretly 102/18.

deaþ (*m.*) death 3/23, 22/8, 22/24, 39/22, etc.
gedelf (*n.*) digging, excavation 43/16.
demde I *pa. t. 3 sg. w. dat.* judged 140/14.
dem(m) *m.* loss 142/4; harm 42/25, 52/7.
deofla, diofla *npl.* (*n.*) devils 57/9, 87/28, 88/22, 88/25; *gpl.* 144/1.
deofolcræft (*m.*) black magic 76/3.
deofolgi(e)ld, deofolgeld, diofolgi(e)ld *n.* idol 24/12, 84/7, 135/30, 142/2, etc.; idolatrous practice 2/20, 57/4, 57/7, 111/17, etc.
deor, dior *n.* animal 15/9 (2 ×), 15/15, 150/25.
derede I *pa. t. 3 sg.* harmed *w. dat.* 51/17. *w. acc.* 121/24.
deþ see don.
gedeþ see gedon.
diacon (*m.*) deacon 150/8.
dic *m.* ditch, moat 43/29, 43/30.
di(e)gel *adj.* secret 44/25, 93/2, 100/18. digle *asf.* 44/25.
diegellice *adv.* secretly 46/7, 82/24, 94/13, 106/19, etc.
diegelnessa *apl. f.* mysteries 38/3.
diernden I *pa. t. subj. pl.* concealed 123/13.
dierne *adj.* hidden, deceitful 80/5.
dierran see dyre.
digle see diegel.
diofla see deofla.
diofolgi(e)ld see deofolgi(e)ld.
diofolgieldhus *n.* heathen temple 149/19.
dior see deor.
do see don.
dogor (*m. or n.*) day 90/16.
dohtor (*f.*) daughter 30/9, 62/1, 62/3, 65/21, etc.; *npl.* 69/5. dohtra *gpl.* 39/5.
dom *m.* authority 54/20; glory, reputation 46/2, 67/19; sentence 153/16.
don *anom. vb. tr.* do, perform 27/14, 27/27, 34/20, 57/3, etc.; make 34/3, 61/25, 136/25; put 34/7, 84/14; give, offer 124/12; cause 30/28. *intr.* do, act 35/8, 76/6; *as substitute for preceding vb.* 34/5. ~ *to cyninge, consule,* etc. make king, consul, etc. 1/18, 87/22, 136/25; ~ *of*

free from 108/11; ~ *to gewealdon* bring into subjection 62/15, 63/20; unweorþ(ne) ~ have contempt for 64/29, 118/26; gieman ~ take care 73/17. deþ *pr. 3 sg.* 26/25. doþ *pl.* 34/20. do *subj. sg.* 19/26. doþ *imp. pl.* 152/25. donde *pr. p.* 27/27. dyde *pa. t. 3 sg.* 34/5. dydan *pl.* 115/13; dydon 29/24; dyde 35/8. dyden *subj. pl.* 29/11.
gedon *anom. vb. tr.* do, perform 24/11, 25/16, 34/10, 45/12, etc.; confer, give 145/17; show 70/11, 156/12; bring about, cause 39/16, 52/7; make 68/3, 72/19, 113/18. *intr.* act, do 82/16, 91/23; *as substitute for preceding vb.* do 52/8, 55/2. ~ *to* make into 68/3, 113/20; *to þon* ~ bring to such a state 55/8; *to nytte* ~ put to use 42/20; *to gewildum* ~ bring into subjection 72/6, 73/2; *on onwald* ~ bring into control 33/12, 37/16. gedeþ *pr. 3 sg.* 11/19. gedoþ *pl.* 18/1. gedyde *pa. t. 3 sg.* 8/10. gedydan *pl.* 83/13; gedydon 24/24. gedyden *subj. pl.* 39/16. gedon *pp.* 24/11. gedone *npl.* 113/20.
dorstan, dorste etc. see durran.
dream (*m.*) frenzy, ecstasy 60/18.
gedrefed I *pp.* troubled 29/20. gedrefde *npl.* 95/19.
gedrefedlic *adj.* troublesome, oppressive 26/4.
gedrefednesse *ds(f.)* distress 75/21.
dreogende 2 *pr. p.* carrying on (fight) 22/11, 32/12, 35/18, 41/11, etc.; suffering, enduring 32/4, 118/28.
drugon *pa. t. pl.* carried on 23/14.
drifan 1 drive, force to march or walk 42/8, 113/13, 113/26 etc.; speak often of 66/6. drifaþ *pr. pl.* 66/6. drifon *pa. t. pl.* 5/19. drife *subj. sg.* 130/15. drifen *pl.* 67/1.
drigan see dryge.
drinca *wk. m.* drink 122/18.
drincan 3 drink 17/4, 73/32, 74/12, etc.; absorb 122/2. drincaþ *pr. pl.* 17/3. drync *imp. sg.* 45/9. drincende *pr. p.* 44/30. druncne *pp. npl.* 71/17.
dropa *wk. m.* drop 97/30.
drugon see dreogende.

druncennysse (*dsf.*) drunkenness 25/10.

druncne see **drincan**.

dry *m.* magician 26/20. **drys** *gs.* 69/23.

ġedrycnede 1 *pp. npl.* dried up, emaciated 57/1 (v.l. gedrehte).

drycræft *m.* magical art 22/5, 23/27, 23/28, 23/31, etc.

dryġe *adj.* dry 56/25. **driġan** *dpl.* 26/19.

dryhten *m.* lord (here only the Lord) 2/11, 35/25, 36/5, 132/16, 136/2. **drihtnes** *gs.* 35/25.

drync *m.* drink 44/25, 60/19.

drync *imp.* see **drincan**.

ġedrync (*n.*) drinking 17/11, 17/14.

drype I *pr. subj. sg.* should drop 97/30.

drys see **dry**.

duguþ *f.* the flower, cream (of a people), nobility 33/12, 81/5, 101/18, 117/12. *pl.* virtues 30/10, 153/30.

dulfon 3 *pa. t. pl.* dug 51/22.

dulmunus (*m.?*) dromon, (Greek) warship 30/17. **dulmuna** *gpl.* 31/27, 46/13.

dun *f.* hill, mountain 45/33, 77/12, 85/31, 86/29, etc.

ġedurfon see **ġedearf**.

durran *pret. pres. vb. pr. pl.* dare 74/23. **dyrre** *subj. sg.* 136/28. **dorste** *pa. t. 3 sg.* dared 30/16 etc. **dorstan** *pl.* 63/24; **dorston** 14/19. **dorsten** *subj. pl.* 33/21.

duru (*f.*) door 6/18, 58/30, 59/5, 59/7, etc. **dure** *ds.* 84/33.

dust (*n.*) dust 121/23.

ġedwola *wk. m.* error 111/12, 149/10; heresy 149/24.

ġedwolmen *apl.* (*m*). heretics 153/11.

dydan, dyde etc. see **don**.

ġedydan, ġedyde, etc. see **ġedon**.

ġedynġed *pp.* manured 23/3.

dyre *adj.* dear of price, precious 15/10, 17/26. **dierran** *comp. npl.* more precious 114/11.

dyrre see **durran**.

dysiġ (*n.*) folly 87/17.

dysiġ *adj.* foolish 88/24, 88/27.

dysiġnesse *dsf.* folly 74/13.

E

ea *f.* river 8/25, 9/13, 9/30, 10/10, etc.; stream 43/14, 43/17. **ea** *gs.* 18/7; eas 14/20; **ie** 12/20. **ea** *ds.* 14/19; **ie** 8/19. **ea** *napl.* 10/8, 43/17. **ea** *gpl.* 43/14. **eaum** *dpl.* 115/32; ean 10/2.

eac *prep. w. dat.* in addition to 42/25.

eac *adv.* also, likewise 5/28, 9/9, 19/1, 22/13, etc. **eac swelce, swa eac** see swelce, swa.

eaca *wk. m.* addition. **eacon** *as.* more 133/12.

eaġe *wk. n.* eye 62/7, 90/14, 96/4, 116/25.

eahta *num.* eight 15/4, 19/11, 23/19, 24/29, etc.

eahtateoþa *wk. adj.* eighteenth 135/4.

eahtatiene, -tyne *num.* eighteen 77/3, 124/15, 124/16, 149/12.

eahtatiġ *num.* eighty 68/8, 69/2, 69/3, 84/25, etc.

eahteþa eahtoþa *wk. adj.* eighth 26/1, 86/13, 86/14, 151/7.

eal see **eall**.

eala *interj.* O, lo! 48/26, 74/13, 119/6.

ealaþ see **ealo**.

eald *adj.* old 12/5, 47/21, 82/20, 98/10, etc.; elder, senior 4/10, 93/7; ancient 30/27, 30/28, 47/24, 69/15. (For comp. and sup. see **ield-**.)

ealdcyþþe *ds(f.)* native country 55/10.

ealddæġ (*m.*) *ær on ealddagum* in days of old 47/25, 65/2.

ealddom (*m.*) old age 44/16.

ealdgefa *wk.* (*m.*) old foe 65/24.

ealdgefera *wk.* (*m.*) old comrade 82/28.

ealdgestreon (*n.*) ancient treasure 117/14.

ealdhlaford (*m.*) liege lord, hereditary lord 80/33, 155/19.

ealdordom (*m.*) authority 50/16.

ealdormon(n) *m.* great lord, OH praefectus, etc. 2/4, 32/18, 33/9, 37/30, etc. **ealdormen(n)** *ds.* 33/5, 154/9; *npl.* 78/1. **aldormonnum** *dpl.* 139/25.

ealdung (*f.*) old age 44/12.

eal(l), all *adj.* all, the whole of 1/2, 1/10, 1/19, 6/10, etc. *as subst.* everything, the whole 15/22, 18/20, 25/32, etc. **ealles** (*gs.*) *adv.* entirely 124/6. **ealle** (*instr.*) *adv.* altogether, entirely 135/12; *mid ealle* completely 23/14. **alle** *npl.* 81/24. **ealla** *apl.* 47/1.

eal(l) *adv.* all, entirely, completely
14/2, 14/20, 33/27, 34/10, etc.

(e)alneg *adv.* continually, always
66/5, 77/5, 97/23, 98/16, 113/14.

ealo (*n.*) ale 17/5. ealaþ *gs.* 17/36.
ealoþ *ds.* 117/9.

ealogeweorc (*n.*) brewing of ale
117/10.

ealoþ see ealo.

eam (*m.*) uncle 3/10, 33/3, 33/26,
36/33, etc.

eam see beon.

ean see ea.

ear *n.* ear of corn 100/35.

eard *m.* (native) land, dwelling place
29/17, 41/26, 79/24, 88/33, etc.;
region 79/32.

eardfæst *adj.* settled, remaining at
home 119/10, 152/3.

eardiaþ II *pr. pl.* dwell 15/25.

eardodon, eardedon *pa. t. pl.*
dwelt 16/18, 73/1.

eare *wk.* (*n.*) ear 116/25.

earfeþa, earfoþa *apl.* (*n.*) hardship,
difficulty, tribulation 6/2, 88/31,
118/25. earfeþan *dpl.* 61/19.

earfeþe *adj.* difficult 113/9.

earfeþlice *adv.* painfully 74/15.

earg *adj.* cowardly 103/21, 154/15.
eargran *comp. npl.* more vile 40/2.
eargast *sup.* most vile 40/4.

earm *m.* arm 85/11, 130/11; arm of
sea, bay, gulf 12/18, 13/14, 13/15,
13/19, etc.

earm *adj.* poor 29/3, 41/16, 48/18,
50/3; miserable, wretched 30/25,
30/32, 34/7, 113/29. earmran *comp.*
npl. poorer 41/16.

earmlice *adv.* piteously 82/2.

eart see beon.

east *adv.* east, eastward 11/6, 11/10,
11/21, 12/21, etc.; in the east 18/22,
155/21.

eastan *adv.* from the east, easterly
16/33, 16/34, 19/31, etc. *be* ~ *w.*
dat. to the east of 9/5, 9/31, 10/23,
11/2, etc. *wiþ* ~ to the east 9/4; *w.*
dat. to the east of 18/4.

eastane *adv.* from the east 11/28,
67/20, 147/21, 150/23.

eastcyning *m.* king of the east
81/2.

eastdæl *m.* eastern part, region, the

East 8/17, 11/10, 11/11, 43/4, 70/31,
etc.

eastemest *sup. adj.* easternmost
19/32, 132/28.

eastende *m.* eastern part, the East
9/21, 70/27, 147/29.

easteweard *adj.* the eastern part of
74/3, 74/22. *as subst.* eastern part
36/17.

eastewe(a)rd, eastweard *adv.* eastward 20/21; in the south 15/25,
15/26 (see Commentary)

eastgarsecg *m.* eastern ocean 72/2.

easthealf (*f.*) east side 10/27, 11/22,
12/11.

eastlond *n.* eastern land 77/32, 81/20,
115/30, 148/6.

eastgemære (*n.*) eastern boundary
72/26. eastgemæra *apl.* 72/26.

eastnorþ *adv.* north-east 12/28, 13/1.

eastrice *n.* empire in the east 37/20,
37/26, 64/7.

eastryhte *adv.* due east, eastwards
14/11.

eastsuþ *adv.* south-east 13/2.

eastsuþlang *adj. or adv.* extending
south-east 18/19.

eastweard *adv.* see easteweard.

eaþe *adv.* easily 46/15, 53/19, 57/25,
110/13, 122/17.

geeaþmedde I *pa. t. 3 sg.* humbled
38/21, 62/22.

eaþmetto *f.* humility 133/30.

eaþmodegra *adj. gpl.* humble 56/11.

eaþmodnessun *dpl.* (*f.*) acts of
humility 69/12.

eaum see ea.

eawenga *adv.* publicly 143/20.

ece *adj.* perpetual 66/29.

ecnesse *ds(f.):* *on ecnesse* for ever
153/17.

edwit (*n.*) disgrace 48/3.

eft *adv.* afterwards 4/24, 8/7, 25/11,
152/21, etc.; again 4/9, 4/18, 11/7,
81/15, etc.

ege *m.* fear, awe, dread, terror 5/14,
30/12, 42/34, 52/20, etc.

egefull *adj.* awe-inspiring 74/2.

egeslic *adj.* terrifying 89/17.

egsade II *pa. t. 3 sg.* terrified 77/
20.

geegsade II *pa. t. 3 sg.* terrified
41/2, 104/11; *pp. npl.* 45/22, 117/24.

ehtan I *w. gen.* persecute 138/5, 144/9; attack, harass 73/11.

ehtend (*m.*) persecutor 47/7, 137/28, 139/6, 140/1; pursuer (in vengeance) 101/27. ehtend *npl.* 140/1; ehtende 47/7.

ehtnes *f.* persecution 144/14, 144/23, 146/2, 147/20, 149/4. ehtnesse *as.* 144/23.

ele *m.* oil 97/30, 131/1, 131/4.

ellþeodge see elþeodig.

ellþiede see elþeod.

eln (*f.*) ell 15/3, 15/4, 15/5, 15/20; cubit 43/26, 43/27, 43/30, 112/9.

elpend, elpent *m.* elephant 84/15, 84/18, 84/21, 85/12, etc. elpendon *dpl.* 84/24.

elþeod, elþiod (*f.*) exile. *on elþeode* into exile 69/14, 123/1, 148/22. *on el(l)þiede* 88/32, 152/17.

elþeodig *adj.* foreign. el(l)þeodge *npl.* 30/25, 83/2. *as subst. on elþiodige, on ellþeodge* into exile 66/5, 68/2.

elþeodignesse *ds(f.)*: *on elþeodignesse* abroad 131/15.

elþiede, elþiod- see elþeod, elþeodig.

emdenes, emdemes *adv.* simultaneously 75/4, 103/1. *eal ~ all* without exception 49/12.

emfela as many (*w. gen.*) as (*w. dat.*) 25/20.

emleof *adj. w. dat.* equally dear 22/2.

emlice see emnlice.

emn *adj.* level 43/24.

emne *adv.* equally, evenly 63/10. emnar *comp.* more equally 54/21.

emnete *ds(n.)* plain 99/29.

emnlange *prep. w. dat.* stretching all along 15/24.

em(n)lice *adv.* equally, identically 37/24, 132/26; on equal terms 95/29; simultaneously 60/3.

emnreþe *adj.* equally cruel 40/17.

emnscolere (*m.*) fellow scholar 71/28.

emsarig *adj. w. dat.* equally sorry, just as sorry (as) 29/25.

ende *m.* end 20/20, 21/3, 38/18, 39/16, etc.; foot (of mountain), limit 78/4; part, district 36/15, 102/19, 106/21. *nanum ende* not at all 70/13.

endian II *intrans.* end 9/26, 18/22, 35/26, 83/6, 132/22.

geendian II *tr.* end, conclude 3/23, 5/9, 5/16, 30/10, etc.; carry out 153/16; complete 43/22.

endlefan *num.* eleven 45/32, 151/14. enlefan 85/20.

enlefta *wk. adj.* eleventh 152/6.

ent *m.* giant 30/15, 43/21, 72/7.

eodan, eode, eodon see gan.

geeode, geeodon see gegan.

eorþbeofung *f.* earthquake 3/1, 56/4, 72/9, 87/6, etc.

eorþe *wk. f.* ground 3/3, 3/27, 17/10, 26/2, etc.; earth 36/4. *to eorþan bringan* bury 49/23. *to eorþan beran* carry to place of burial 75/22.

eorþlic *adj.* earthly 59/18, 59/25.

eorþtyrewan *ds. wk.* (*m. or f.*) bitumen 43/28.

eorþwæstm *m.* fruit of the earth 11/20, 50/11.

eorþware *pl.* (*m.*) inhabitants of the earth. eorþwara *gpl.* 59/21.

eorþwela *wk. m.* fertility 23/20.

eow, eower, etc. see þu.

epistole *ds.* letter 78/10.

erian I plough 15/22. erede *pa. t. 3 sg.* 15/13, 15/14.

et see æt.

etanne 5 *dat. inf.* eat 28/16, 77/22.

ettan I graze 15/22.

F

facade II *pa. t. 3 sg.* desired to obtain 82/11.

fac(e)n *n.* crime, treachery 22/24, 30/32, 33/13, 46/9, etc.

facenlic *adj.* deceitful 2/27.

fæder *m.* father 3/10, 3/15, 28/8, 36/20, etc.; *gs.* 71/18; *ds.* 33/8. fæderas *apl.* 28/6. fæderum *dpl.* 39/10.

fæd(e)ra (*m.*) (paternal) uncle 102/26, 104/22.

gefæderen *adj.* born of the same father 63/6.

fægen *adj.* glad, joyful 117/8.

fæger *adj.* beautiful 23/9, 43/24. fægran *comp. npl.* 114/10.

fæhþ *f.* hostility, vendetta 47/21, 136/18.

fæmnhad (*m.*) virginity 60/10.

færelt *n.* (military) expedition 75/32, 81/17, 100/16, 103/11, etc.; expeditionary force 93/22, 96/14; retinue 149/6.

færende see **faran**.

færlic *adj.* unexpected, sudden 89/13.

fæst *adj.* secure 44/5, 46/32, 101/6; steadfast 113/5. **fæst boc** 150/16 (see Commentary). **fæstre** *comp. asn.* more secure 46/35, 80/24. **fæstast** *sup.* most secure 44/1, 63/3.

fæste *adv.* securely 72/7, 104/22, 132/12, 151/23; strictly 104/15.

fæsten, festen *n.* fortress, fortified town or camp 49/31, 52/11, 67/17, 78/22, etc. **fæstennes** *gs.*, **fæstenne** *ds.*, etc. 109/21, 109/24, etc.

fæstlecre *comp. adj. asn.* more vigorous 126/17.

fæstmod *adj.* steadfast, constant 151/26.

gefæstnad II *pp.* secured, concluded 97/29; **gefæstnod** 35/7, 129/8.

fæstness (*f.*) durability 43/25.

fætels *n.?* vessel 17/36 (see Introduction, p. lxxii n. 4).

fætt *adj.* fat 113/4, 113/5.

fandian II examine, explore 14/5; test, try 34/12.

gefandian II examine, test 89/1.

gefangen see **gefon**.

faran 6 go, travel, march 4/11, 4/14, 4/17, 30/3, etc. *togædere* ~ join forces 54/18, 103/26. **farenne** *dat. inf.* 154/12. **faraþ** *pr. pl.* 14/10. **farende** *pr. p.* 28/25; **færende** 43/18. **for** *pa. t. 3 sg.* 4/4. **foran** *pl.* 4/15; **foron** 83/23. **fore** *subj. sg.* 47/34. **foren** *pl.* 106/8; **fore** 83/25.

gefaran 6 *intr.* go, march 2/2, 58/17, 68/23, 81/22, etc.; die 46/5, 51/9, 81/28, 85/22, etc. *wel* ~ go well 88/19; ~ *him self* die a natural death 125/12. *tr.* obtain, receive 67/13, 67/16, 85/5; capture, overrun, attack 23/16, 29/15, 30/17, 62/27; *færelt* ~ carry out an expedition 75/32; *þa gefarenan* *ppl. adj. pl.* the dead 49/23, 87/27. **gefare** *pr. 1 sg.* 85/5. **gefor** *pa. t. 3 sg.* 22/14. **geforan** *pl.* 23/16. **gefore** *subj. sg.* 16/21. **gefaren** *pp.* 44/8.

fatu *apl. n.* (of **fæt**) vessel 114/10.

gefea *wk. m.* gladness, joy 55/10, 75/20, 117/9.

feaht see **feohtan**.

gefeaht see **gefeoht**.

gefeaht see **gefeohtan**.

fealh 3 *pa. t. 3 sg.* made his way, got away 100/1, 124/27. **fulgen** *subj. pl.* should leave 26/10.

gefeallen see **gefeol(l)**.

feallende see **fylþ**.

fearr (*m.*) bull 2/6, 34/6.

feawa, feawe *pron. adj. pl.* few, a few 25/8, 34/24, 35/17, 52/35, etc. **feawan** *wk. pl.* 52/8, 53/24. **feawum** *dpl.* 14/2.

gefecc(e)an I fetch, bring 3/19, 76/4, 94/2, 129/18; obtain 48/36. **gefetton** *pa. t. pl.* 76/4. **gefett** *pp.* 94/2.

fedan I rear 120/13. **feddon** *pa. t. pl.* 29/32.

feferadl (*f.*) feverish illness 106/6.

fel see **fell**.

fela *indecl. pron. and adj.* much, many. as *adj.* many 25/18, 141/17; as *pron.* a large number 98/7; *w. part. gen. sg.* much 19/24, 26/14, 27/22, 80/15, etc.; *w. part. gen. pl.* many 14/27, 16/18, 26/15, 35/18.

gefelan I feel 26/4.

feld *m.* plain. **felda** *ds.* 77/12.

fel(l) *n.* skin 15/15, 15/18 (2×).

fen see **fenn**.

feng, fenge, etc. see **fon**.

gefeng, gefenge, etc. see **gefon**.

fenlond (*n.*) marsh-land 29/7.

fen(n) *n.* fen, marsh 9/2, 12/8.

feoh *n.* cattle 42/12; goods or money 17/13, 17/24, etc.; money 31/16, 31/18, 48/23, 120/24, etc. *licgende feoh* treasure, gold and silver, property other than livestock 42/18, 64/25, 67/27, 69/3, etc.; *gemænan* ~ public money 102/7. **feos** *gs.* 17/15. **feo** *ds.* 17/21.

gefeoht *n.* fight, battle, war 4/13, 5/1, 21/29, 22/14, etc. **gefeaht** 125/9.

feohtan 3 fight 28/20, 31/30, 33/21, 46/33, etc. **feohtanne** *dat. inf.* 29/4. **feohtaþ** *pr. pl.* 45/2. **feohtende** *pr. p.* 21/26. **feaht** *pa. t. 3 sg.*

84/31. **fuhton** *pl.* 4/25. **fuhte** *subj.*
sg. 125/25. *pl.* 100/31.
gefeohtan 3 *intr.* fight 4/30, 5/5, 60/
31, 78/31, etc. *tr.* win 42/30, 47/30.
~ *anwig* fight single combat 72/16
etc. **gefeohtanne** *dat. inf.* 53/32.
gefeaht *pa. t. 3 sg.* 4/13. **gefuhton**
pl. 54/18. **gefuhten** *subj. pl.* 54/21.
gefeol(l) 7 *pa. t. 3 sg. intr.* fell (in
battle) 33/12, 81/4, 81/27, etc.; fell
(of kingdom, city, etc.) 37/11,
37/20, 133/8. *tr.* **gefeollan** *pa. t. pl.*
caused by falling 42/25. **gefeolle**
subj. sg. 133/1. **gefeallen** *pp.* 80/28.
feollon see **fylþ**.
feond *m.* enemy, foe 35/8, 51/19,
53/18, 58/26, etc. **fiend** *napl.* 33/18;
find 91/6.
feondscipe *m.* enmity, hostility 40/26,
47/6, 123/7, 129/18, 155/22.
feor *adv.* far 14/9, 14/10; far away
74/24; *w. dat.* far from 106/18.
firr *comp.* further 45/29; **fyr** 33/16.
firrest *sup.* furthest 14/9; *w. dat.*
furthest from 135/7.
feorh (*m. or n.*) life 48/18, 61/20,
83/5, 107/31, etc. **feores** *gs.* 82/2.
feore *ds.* 52/9.
feorm *f.* feast 123/16, 143/24.
feorþa *wk. adj.* fourth 25/23, 36/14,
36/19, 74/30, etc.
feos see **feoh**.
feower *num.* four 2/12, 6/21, 14/14,
31/22, etc. *feowera sum* with four
companions 107/18 (see Commentary).
feowerfete *adj.* four-footed, quadruped 42/5, 42/12.
feowerscyte *adj.* quadrangular 43/25.
feowerteo(g)þa *wk. adj.* fortieth
132/14, 133/23, 133/26.
feowertiene *num.* fourteen 77/20.
feowertig, -teg- *num.* forty 15/4,
22/10, 38/31, 101/2, etc.
gefera *wk. m.* colleague 102/18, 111/7,
124/7, etc.; follower, associate, com-
panion 39/4, 48/34, 74/9, 93/10.
feran I go 26/22, 29/30, 42/27,
50/5, etc. *w. refl. dat.* 29/13.
geferrædenne *asf.* fellowship 127/21.
fersc *adj.* fresh (of water, not salt)
15/36, 43/7, 43/15.
geferscipe (*m.*) company 74/6.

ferþan see **furþon**.
festen see **fæsten**.
fet see **fot**.
gefett, **gefetton** see **gefecc(e)an**.
feþa *wk.* (*m.*) infantry 68/17, 121/20;
infantryman, foot-soldier 68/29, 69/
2, 73/4, 75/14, etc.
feþe (*n.*) power of movement 93/30.
feþehere (*m.*) infantry 68/7.
feþer (*f.*) feather 15/15, 15/19. **feþra**
gpl. 15/19.
fieftiene see **fiftene**.
fiell (*m.*) fall, death 64/33, 75/11,
137/28, 154/19; downfall 56/11.
fiend see **feond**.
gefiend *npl.* (*m.*) enemies 65/5.
fi(e)rd, **fyrd** *f.* army 4/4, 4/9, 27/19,
33/15, etc. *on firde* campaigning,
in camp 85/7, 105/19.
fif *num.* five 14/17, 15/18, 16/13, 17/14,
etc.
fifta *wk. adj.* fifth 1/11, 6/9, 24/14,
25/28, etc.
fiftene, **fieftiene**, **fiftyne** *num.* 15/18,
16/32, 29/9, 70/18.
fiftig *num.* fifty 15/5, 20/32, 20/33,
21/7, etc.
fiftyne see **fiftene**.
filde *adj.* flat, level 43/23.
gefilde *n.* plain 10/25.
filosofum see **philosophus**.
find see **feond**.
findan 3 find 58/30, 104/17, 135/18,
136/3, etc.; decide 79/14, 80/9,
92/16; devise 51/25; obtain 34/18.
~ *æt me seolfum* bring myself (to
do something) 128/17. **findeþ** *pr.
3 sg.* 17/32. **funde** *pa. t. 3 sg.* 51/25.
fundon *pl.* 79/14. **funden** *pp.* 69/4.
finger *m.* finger 41/4.
fird see **fierd**.
firenlust *m.* sinful pleasure, lust
22/10, 22/26, 23/4, 23/5, etc.
firmetton I *pa. t. pl.* requested,
begged 99/14.
firr see **feor**.
firra, **fyrra** *wk. adj.* further 11/20,
19/7, 20/1, 109/11, 110/5. *w. dat.*
19/7.
firrest see **feor**.
first, **fyrst** *m.* space of time 42/15,
48/29, 104/32, 147/22, etc.; time
50/18.

fisc *m.* fish 119/14, 136/7.
fiscaþ (*m.*) fishing 14/4, 17/2.
fiscere *m.* fisherman 14/22, 14/26, 48/13.
fla *wk. f.* arrow, dart 62/7, 73/19, 78/24. flana *gpl.* see flan.
flan *m.* and *f.* arrow, dart 22/7 (*f.*), 155/6, 155/8 (*m.*), 93/23, 109/18, 155/4 (*m.* or *f.*).
fleah see fleon.
fleam (*m.*) flight 85/32, 86/1, 92/7, 95/17, etc. on *fleame gebringan* cause to flee 76/10.
flede *adj.* flooded, in flood 43/13, 48/9, 96/30. fledu *nsf.* 43/13; flede 48/9.
geflemde, geflemed see geflieman.
fleoge *wk.* (*f.*) winged insect, fly 25/24.
fleon 2 flee 2/5, 33/10, 33/22, 80/20, etc.; *trans.* flee from 28/11; decline 59/24, 133/31. fleonne *dat. inf.* 33/20. fleonde *pr. p.* 27/6. fleah *pa. t. 3 sg.* 64/33. flugon *pl.* 64/31. fluge *subj. sg.* 33/17. flugen *pl.* 64/21.
fleot (*m.*) estuary, water 19/1.
gefleow 7 *pa. t. 3 sg.* flowed over 23/7.
flex (*n.*) flax 85/14, 85/16.
fliema *wk. m.* fugitive 150/28.
geflieman I put to flight 5/22, 29/6, 33/25, 46/3, etc. geflemde *pa. t. 3 sg.* 105/20. geflemed *pp.* 93/15.
geflit *n.* strife 140/4, 153/6; dispute 78/33.
floc(c)mælum *adv.* in droves 45/21, 106/25.
flod *n.* flood 1/13, 9/3, 11/20, 23/2, etc.
floweþ *pr. 3 sg.* flows 9/4. flowaþ *pl.* flow 10/2. flowende *pr. p.* flowing 11/7, 11/19.
fluge, flugen, etc. see fleon.
fodrere (*m.*) forager 85/9.
fol see full.
folc *n.* folk, people, nation 1/15, 1/19, 2/7, 4/7, etc.; army, troop of soldiers 26/12, 33/17, 45/24, 46/22, etc.
folcgefeoht (*n.*) pitched battle 45/20, 65/9, 70/17, 121/18; war 48/29.
folgade II *pa. t. 3 sg. w. dat.* followed 89/25. folgodan *pl.* 143/12.
folgaþ (*m.*) service 151/16, 151/17.
folgere *m.* follower, successor 80/28, 81/30, 82/20.

folnæh, folneah *adv.* almost 30/30, 30/31, 37/29, 37/33.
fon 7 catch 15/11; ~ *to* succeed to (kingdom etc.) 3/11, 3/14, 6/17, 6/24, etc. (*w. refl. dat.*) 63/12, 144/5; inherit 129/9; turn to 11/25; adopt 156/6; take possession of 117/14. ~ *ymb* turn to 88/14. foþ *pr. pl.* 15/11. feng *pa. t. 3 sg.* 1/4; fengc 22/8. fengon *pl.* 117/14. fenge *subj. sg.* 95/32. *pl.* 156/6.
gefon 7 capture, seize 41/2, 64/23, 100/29, 128/26, etc. gefeng *pa. t. 3 sg.* 44/11. gefengon *pl.* 33/25. gefenge *subj. sg.* 108/28. gefangen *pp.* 30/22; gefongen 58/3. gefongene, gefongne *npl.* 42/8, 83/13. gefangenra *gpl.* 69/3.
for (*f.*) march 91/14.
for *pa. t. 3 sg.* see faran.
gefor see gefaran.
for *prep.* for *w. dat.* because of, for the sake of, on account of 14/31, 19/29, 22/23, 24/7, etc.; in place of 124/4. *w. acc.* on behalf of, on account of 88/24, 98/13; as, for 25/12, 55/8, 98/22, etc. *w. instr.* because of, for 147/22; *for hwi, for hwy* why 34/15, 65/25, 65/27 etc. *for þam, for þæm, for þon adv.* for, for this reason, therefore 24/9, 32/1, 40/8, 40/21, etc.; *for þy* 16/36, 17/26. *for þæm, for þon conj.* because, since, for 14/15, 14/19, 32/1, etc. *for þy* 75/23, 154/27; *for þæm* (*þam, þan, þon*) *þe* 19/24, 19/25, 19/28, 24/6, etc.; *for þy þe* 146/1; *for þæm . . . þy* 44/21.
foran see faran.
geforan see gefaran.
foran *adv.* in front 11/18, 29/33, 100/1.
forbærnan, forbærnnan I burn, consume by fire, cremate 1/6, 17/12, 17/32, 91/5, etc. forbærneþ *pr. 3 sg.* 17/28.
forbead 2 *pa. t. 3 sg.* forbade 133/31, 138/14, 140/3, 140/11, 150/16. forbuden *subj. pl.* 75/30. forboden *pp., w. dat. of person forbidden* 104/15.
forberan 4 endure 63/23.
forbleow 7 *pa. t. sg.* blew 119/18.
forboden see forbead.
forbræcon 4 *pa. t. pl.* violated 67/11.

forbuden see forbead.

forbugan 2 avoid 135/21.

forburnan, forburnon 3 *pa. t. pl.* burned, were consumed by fire 119/13, 133/13, 142/3, 142/5.

forbyrd (*f.*) abstention 22/27.

forceorfan 3 cut through 135/16.

forcurfon *pa. t. pl.* 96/3.

forcuþ *adj.* wicked 118/22. forcuþran *comp. npl.* more wicked 40/1.

forcwædon 5 *pa. t. pl.* called (in reproach), reviled 103/22.

ford *m.* ford. forda *ds.* 126/8.

fordemede I *pp. npl.* condemned 102/7.

fordon *anom. vb.* bring to ruin, destroy 23/18, 28/28, 30/19, 62/27, etc. fordyde *pa. t. 3 sg.* 25/10. fordydon *pl.* 23/18. fordyden *subj. pl.* 112/29. fordon *pp.* 65/17.

fordrifan 1 banish 152/17. fordraf *pa. t. 3 sg.* drove off course 43/9. fordrifen *pp.* driven out of its usual course 11/18.

fordyde, fordyden, etc. see fordon.

fore, foren see faran.

fore *prep. w. dat.* (*always in post-position*) on account of 1/26, 4/24, 97/23, 113/14.

gefore see gefaran.

foreweard *m.* sentry, outpost 106/17.

foreweard *adj.* forepart of 132/24.

forgan *anom. vb.* forgo 152/13.

forgeaf 1 *pa. t. 3 sg. w. dat.* of person forgave, remitted 132/6, 136/19; forgef 141/21. forgeafon *pl.* 102/8, 136/18. forgeafen *subj. pl.* 76/12.

forgeald 3 *pa. t. 3 sg. w. dat.* of person paid back for 48/21. forguldon *pl.* 22/1, 56/18. forgulde *subj. sg.* 27/7.

forgeatan, forgeate see forgyt.

forgef see forgeaf.

forgiefen *adj.* indulgent 87/19, 134/13.

forgifnesse *asf.* forgiveness 34/20.

forgulde, forguldon see forgeald.

forgyt 5 *pr. 3 sg.* forgets 24/27. forgeatan *pa. t. pl. w. gen.* forgot 50/19. forgeate *subj. sg.* should forget 136/6.

forher(g)iung(*f.*) devastation, ravaging 44/13, 47/22, 125/21.

forherigan I ravage, lay waste 29/1, 58/17, 114/16, 145/9, etc. forhergede *pa. t. 3 sg.* 58/17; forhergeade 45/27. forhergedan *pl.* 34/26; forhergedon 145/12.

forhiened I *pp.* humbled, brought low 65/13, 65/17, 133/16. forhiende *npl.* 106/34.

forht *adj.* fearful 57/26.

forhwæga *adv.* somewhere, somewhere about 17/16, 17/20.

forlædde I *pa. t. 3 sg.* led to destruction 33/11.

forlæg 5 *pa. t. 3 sg. refl.* had illicit intercourse 60/10, 88/6. forlæge *subj. sg.* 69/23.

forlætan 7 leave 40/10, 44/26, 101/23, etc.; let go 83/19, 88/33; relinquish 147/24; abandon 41/10; lose 82/29; release 87/7; restore 72/20; omit from narration 28/2; grant 24/26. *lif* ~ lose one's life 47/6. *up* ~ divide up 43/13. forlæte *pr. 1 sg.* 28/7. forlætaþ *pl.* 83/3. forlet *pa. t. 3 sg.* 35/30. forleton *pl.* 29/12. forlete *subj. sg.* 78/12. forleten *pl.* 39/32.

forleosan 2 destroy 41/8; lose 83/24, 113/2, 139/1. forluran *pa. t. pl.* 113/2. forlure *subj. sg.* 139/1. forluren *pl.* 83/24.

forlet, forleten, etc. see forlætan.

forlignessa *apl. f.* adulteries 28/7.

forlor (*n.*) loss 72/11.

forluran, forlure, etc. see forleosan.

forma *wk. adj.* first 25/17, 35/26, 36/17, 40/16, etc. (For sup. see fyrmest.)

formulton 3 *pa. t. pl.* melted away, burned up 119/13.

fornæh, forneah *adv.* very nearly, almost 10/16, 25/2, 50/24, 62/18, etc. ~ *mid ealle* almost completely 25/10, 30/27, 39/11.

forneþdon I *pa. t. pl. refl.* risked their lives 117/4.

fornome 4 *pa. t. subj. sg.* should carry off 94/8.

forod *adj.* broken 93/27.

foron see faran.

forsacende 6 *pr. p.* renouncing 33/27. forsoc *pa. t. 3 sg.* renounced 41/28.

forsætade I *pa. t. 3 sg.* caught in an ambush 79/10.

forsawon see **forseah**.

forscapung *f.* mishap, mischance 26/34, 32/5.

forscurfon 3 *pa. t. pl.* gnawed off 119/17.

forseah 5 *pa. t. 3 sg.* held in contempt, rejected with scorn 2/20, 46/23, 98/33, 99/15, 111/18. **forsawon** *pl.* 135/14.

forsende I *pa. t. 3 sg.* banished 62/5, 63/25, 66/5.

forseten 5 *pp.* obstructed 92/31.

forsewennesse *ds(f.)* contempt. *for his forsewennesse* out of contempt for him 89/6.

forslean 6 slaughter, inflict heavy casualties on 41/27, 48/22, 49/30, 63/24, etc. **forslog** *pa. t. 3 sg.* 30/19. **forslagen** *pp.* 46/29; **forslægen** 45/25. **forslægene** *npl.* 39/11; **forslagene** 34/24.

forsoc see **forsacende**.

forspendaþ I *pr. pl.* use up 17/29.

forspillan I destroy 70/3, 117/15. **forspildon** *pa. t. pl.* 117/15.

forstod 6 *pa. t. 3 sg.* stood in front and protected 100/1.

forsugiende II *pr. p. w. gen.* keeping silent about 67/4. **forsugedon** *pa. t. pl. w. gen.* passed over in silence 88/12.

fortendun I *pa. t. pl.* burned off, burned away 29/33. **fortende** *pp. npl.* burnt 29/35.

forþ *adv.* forth, onwards, forward 9/3, 9/6, 11/15, 101/15, etc. *secgan ~ go on to say* 132/19. *~ ofer þæt well beyond that* 61/3.

forþohte I *pp. npl.* filled with depair 91/20, 101/21.

forweorþan 3 perish, die 25/2, 31/30, 48/29, 51/20, etc. **forwearþ** *pa. t. 3 sg.* 4/19. **forwurdon** *pl.* 26/30. **forwurde** *subj. sg.* 47/4. **forworden** *pp.* 151/1; **forwordene** *npl.* 39/12.

forwiernan I *w. gen. of thing and dat. of person* refuse, deny 44/20, 45/18, 89/2, 115/8, etc.

forworden(e), **forwurde**, etc. see **forweorþan**.

forwyrcan I destroy 45/23. **forworht** *pp. refl.* committed a crime 102/8.

fot *m.* foot 23/2, 39/15, 59/11, 93/31, etc. **fet** *apl.* 116/24. **fotan** *dpl.* 26/19.

foþ see **fon**.

fracoþast *sup. adj.* most abominable 40/3.

frægn see **frine**.

fræton 5 *pa. t. pl.* devoured 26/1.

gefrætwed II *pp.* adorned 133/19. **gefrætwedum** *ds.* 42/5.

fram see **from**.

frecenlice *adv.* dangerously 99/30.

frefelice *adv.* cunningly, shamelessly 71/4.

fremde *adj., as subst. (wk. and strong)* stranger, foreigner 17/30, 71/13, 83/2.

gefremman I accomplish, effect 47/14, 71/20, 92/17, etc. *gewin ~ engage in battle* 27/29. **gefremede** *pa. t. 3 sg.* 27/29. **gefremedon** *pl.* 79/30. **gefremed** *pp.* 71/20.

fremmende I *pr. p.* committing 22/22, 90/25.

freode, -on see **freogean**.

freodom *(m.)* liberty, freedom 37/13, 37/31, 65/14, 107/31.

gefreodon II *pa. t. pl.* set free 87/18, 102/3.

freogean II set free 102/5. **freode** *pa. t. 3 sg.* 87/20. **freodon** *pl.* 102/7.

freond *(m.)* friend 17/7, 52/22, 99/18, 129/13 (2×). **friend** *ds.* 89/19.

freondscipe *(m.)* friendship 47/24, 140/24.

gefriend *npl. (m.)* friends 65/4, 83/5.

frig *adj.* free 131/17.

frine 3 *pr. subj. sg.* let one ask 97/23. **frinende** *pr. p.* inquiring 89/19. **frægn** *pa. t. 3 sg.* asked 117/17.

friþ *m.* peace, protection 3/6, 5/8, 31/13, 31/15, etc. *~ geniman* make peace 5/23, 29/29, 39/32, etc.

friþian II defend 86/16, 86/18.

from, fram *prep. w. dat.* from 14/21, 16/15, 17/16, 17/21, etc. as a message from, on behalf of 75/30; by 27/2, 37/30, 39/1, 53/1, etc.; of 30/12, 67/30, etc.; at the hands of 109/13; at the instigation of 67/26; through 143/5; about, concerning 23/22, 50/8. *ellipt. or adv.* 70/4.

frox *m.* frog 25/18.

fruma *wk.* (*m.*) on *fruman* at the beginning 39/17, 39/20.

frumcenned *ppl. adj.* firstborn 26/6.

frumslæp (*m.*) first sleep 51/23.

frymþ (*f.*) beginning 35/23, 132/17.

fugel (*m.*) bird 15/15.

fugelere *m.* fowler 14/23, 14/26.

fuhte, fuhton see feohtan.

gefuhten, gefuhton see gefeohtan.

ful see full.

fulgan *anom. vb. w. dat.* carry out, accomplish 22/26, 79/23; help 102/9. fulleodon *pa. t. pl.* 79/23. fuleoden *subj. pl.* 102/9. See also ful(l)gongan.

fulgen see fealh.

fulgongan see fullgongan.

fuliaþ II *pr. pl.* decompose 17/35.

ful(l) *adj.* full 135/7; complete 152/24. *w. gen.* full of 17/36, 136/4.

ful(l), fol *adv.* fully 32/6, 50/6 (v.l. fullice), 56/28; very 11/6, 98/10.

ful(l)gongan 7 *w. dat.* carry out 55/18; follow 114/3.

fultum *m.* help, assistance 23/22, 29/25, 44/8, 84/3, etc.; army, reinforcements 33/14, 46/8, 46/24, 80/12, etc. fultome *ds.* 90/12.

gefultuman II *w. dat.* help 63/15, 63/16.

fultumleas *adj.* without help 35/6.

fulwade II *pa. t. 3 sg.* baptized 152/24.

gefulwade II *pa. t. 3 sg.* baptized 152/22. gefulwad *pp.* 152/23.

fulwiht (*n.*) baptism 152/5, 153/10.

funde, funden, etc. see findan.

fundedon II *pa. t. pl.* hastened 79/4.

furþon, furþum, ferþan, *adv.* even 26/2, 74/24, 83/5, 101/23.

furþumlic *adj.* remarkable?, corrupt? 32/16 (see Commentary).

fyll *f.* fill 45/9.

gefylled I *pp.* filled 135/11; destroyed 93/31.

fylst (*m.*) assistance. on *fylste beon* assist 32/21.

fylstan I *w. dat.* help, aid 34/5, 39/8, 79/3, 82/11, etc.

gefylste I *pa. t. 3 sg. w. dat.* helped, assisted 91/32, 151/18. gefylstan *pl.* 87/24. gefylste (*subj.*) *sg.* should help 80/10, 82/4.

fylþ 7 *pr. 3 sg.* penetrates 16/9.

feallende *pr. p.* falling 39/15.

feollon *pa. t. pl.* fell 105/12.

fyr *n.* fire 1/6, 6/3, 22/31, 23/6, etc.

fyr *adv.* see feor.

fyrbryne *m.* fire 4/21, 96/28.

fyrcyn (*n.*) kind of conflagration 133/12 (v.l. fyrbryne)

fyrde see fierd.

fyren *adj.* fiery 123/14.

fyrhtnesse *dsf.* fear 147/14.

fyrhto (*f.*) terror 74/20.

fyrmest *sup. adj.* foremost 94/15.

fyrmest *sup. adv.* best, of the greatest importance 77/15. swa *micel swa we hit fyrmest witon* to the best of our knowledge (or ability) 12/15–16.

fyrra see firra.

fyrsmeortende *ppl. adj.* smarting like a burn 25/22.

fyrst *m.* see first.

fyrst *sup. adj.* foremost 15/11.

fyrþran I further, promote 111/18.

G

gaderade II *pa. t. 3 sg.* assembled 68/6.

gegaderade, -ode II *pa. t. 3 sg.* gathered, assembled 24/3, 33/14, 46/8, 61/28, etc. gegaderedon, gegaderodon *pl.* 50/2, 65/7, etc.; *refl.* assembled 54/32; gegaderede 69/26. gegaderod *pp.* 46/4; gegaderad 100/15.

gærsciþ *m.* blade of grass 26/1.

gærstapa *wk.* (*m.*) locust 119/16.

gæþ see gan.

gafol *n.* tax, tribute 1/11, 15/14, 15/15, 24/15, etc.

gafolgielda (*wk. m.*) payer of tribute 67/17, 68/3, 71/27, 91/21, etc.

gan *anom. vb.* go 51/23, 107/28, 128/18, 130/10, etc. on *hand* ~ surrender, submit 66/21, 73/14, 91/22, etc. gæþ *pr. 3 sg.* 19/17. eode *pa. t. 3 sg.* 50/4. eodon *pl.* 49/17; eodan 52/13.

gegan *anom. vb.* conquer, overrun 61/24, 62/9, 68/10, 99/4, etc. geeode *pa. t. 3 sg.* 61/8. geeodon *pl.* 30/3. gegan *pp.* 30/25.

ᵹanᵹan 7 go 42/29. ᵹonᵹende *pp.*
npl. 26/24. ᵹonᵹendre *gpl.* in-
fantry(men) 61/30.
ᵹanᵹehere (*m.*) infantry 83/29.
ᵹara *wk.* (*m.*) gore, angular point of
land 19/3.
ᵹarsecᵹ, ᵹarseᵹc, ᵹarsæcᵹ, ᵹar-
seᵹᵹ *m.* ocean 8/12, 8/16, 18/27,
18/30, etc.
ᵹe *pron.* see þu.
ᵹe *conj.* and 17/8, 19/1, 36/3, etc. *as
correl.* ᵹe ... ᵹe ... (ᵹe) both ...
and ... (and) 1/23–4, 1/26–7, 80/14,
etc. *ægþer* ᵹe see æᵹþer.
ᵹeafon 5 *pa. t. pl. w. dat. of person*
granted 96/25.
ᵹear, ᵹer *m. and n.* year 1/10, 1/11,
5/20, 50/6, etc. *apl.* 86/4. ᵹeare *gpl.*
97/11. ᵹearan *dpl.* 24/3.
ᵹeare *adv.* well 27/22, 35/29. ᵹearor
comp. more certainly 131/8.
ᵹearo *adj.* ready. ᵹearora *gpl.* 92/19.
ᵹearrim (*n.*) reckoning by years,
chronological order 61/3 (v.l. geargerime).
ᵹegearwod, ᵹegearod II *pp.* prepared 25/20, 144/3.
ᵹeat *n.* gate 50/25, 103/20, 103/23,
116/9, etc. ᵹeata *napl.* 42/26, 56/17.
ᵹeat *pa. t. 3 sg.* poured 136/6.
ᵹelp see ᵹielp.
ᵹeoc (*n.*) yoke 113/26.
ᵹeoᵹoþ (*f.*) youth 120/13.
ᵹeomorlic *adj.* miserable 89/21.
ᵹeomriende II *pp.* lamenting 47/5.
ᵹeond, ᵹiend, ᵹind *prep. w. acc.*
throughout, over 15/36, 24/33, 25/
18, 36/2, 50/11, etc.
ᵹeong, ᵹiong *adj.* young 44/17,
44/20, 44/23, 96/8. ᵹingra *comp.*
younger 51/13, 70/14; junior 146/21.
ᵹingst *sup.* youngest 23/24.
ᵹeongra *wk.* (*m.*) disciple 140/11.
ᵹeorn *adj. w. gen.* eager, anxious for
67/14. ᵹeornran *comp. npl.* more
eager 26/10.
ᵹeorne *adv.* eagerly, earnestly 47/33,
75/4, 104/19; well 74/23; diligently
154/28. ᵹeornor *comp.* more willingly 54/5, 67/3; better 36/24.
ᵹeornfull *adj.* desirous 150/15; *w.
gen.* eager for 104/23. ᵹeornfulran
comp. npl. m. more eager for 46/27.

ᵹeornfullnesse, -nisse *dsf.* eager-
ness 68/32, 125/8.
ᵹeornlic *adj.* desirable 113/7.
ᵹeotere *m.* bronze-founder 34/3,
34/11.
ᵹer see ᵹear.
ᵹerede I *pa. t. 3 sg.* prepared 130/16.
ᵹeredon *pl.* 107/16; ᵹiredon 59/8.
ᵹiddian II sing, recite 35/15, 53/16.
ᵹieldanne see ᵹyldan.
ᵹ(i)elp *m.* boast 113/11; glory, fame
5/17, 88/10, 113/27.
ᵹi(e)lpaþ 3 *pr. pl.* boast 97/23,
113/14, 116/21. ᵹulpon *pa. t. pl.*
4/24.
ᵹielpword (*n.*) boast 54/16.
ᵹiemde I *pa. t. 3 sg.* was concerned
about 118/21.
ᵹieme *wk. f.* care 73/17.
ᵹiend see ᵹeond.
ᵹeᵹiered see ᵹeᵹierwan.
ᵹeᵹierela *wk.* (*m.*) clothing 89/23.
ᵹierndon, ᵹiernende see ᵹyrnen.
ᵹeᵹierwan, ᵹeᵹyrwan I prepare
25/19, 33/8, etc. ᵹeᵹyrede *pa. t. 3
sg.* 27/32. ᵹeᵹiered *pp.* adorned
42/12. ᵹeᵹieredne *as.* clothed
89/4.
ᵹiet, ᵹyt *adv.* yet, still, even 14/10,
23/8, 24/25, 36/14, etc. See also
nugiet, þagiet.
ᵹif, ᵹyf *conj.* if 16/4, 17/32, 33/16,
33/21, etc.
ᵹifu (*f.*) grace 115/16. ᵹifan *dpl.*
gifts 63/30.
ᵹilpaþ see ᵹielpak.
ᵹimstan (*m.*) gem, precious stone
42/5, 133/19.
ᵹind see ᵹeond.
ᵹingra, ᵹingst see ᵹeong.
ᵹiniende II *pr. p.* gaping 57/20.
ᵹiniᵹendan *wk. asf.* 3/3.
ᵹiong see ᵹeong.
ᵹiredon see ᵹerede.
ᵹirela *wk.* (*m.*) clothing 89/5.
ᵹirnde, ᵹirndon, ᵹirnende see
ᵹyrnen.
ᵹisl (*m.*) hostage 61/11, 66/28, 108/7,
121/7.
ᵹitsunᵹ *f.* avarice 22/16.
ᵹlad I *pa. t. 3 sg.* glided, slid 93/24.
ᵹleawra *comp. adj.* wiser 23/24.
ᵹleawast *sup.* most skilled 84/6.

gleawestan *asm.* wisest 90/21.
gleawra *ofer hie ealle* wiser than them all 23/24.
gnætt *m.* gnat 25/21.
gnide 1 *pr. subj. sg.* should rub 113/7.
gnornung *f.* grief 44/35; discontent 67/4.
god¹ *m. and n.* God, (heathen) god 4/3, 24/11, 24/25, 25/26, etc. godas *npl.* 57/2; godu 24/12.
god² *n.* good 24/27, 35/30, 38/17, etc.; benefit 55/17. *is.* in *nane gode* of any help 148/24.
god *adj.* good 2/12, 15/1, 35/29, 49/7, etc. gode *apl. as. subst.* good things 104/2. godan *dpl.* 97/21.
godcund *adj.* divine 23/22, 23/31.
godgield (*n.*) heathen rite, heathen idol 45/13.
gold (*n.*) gold 31/15, 42/4, 52/9, 104/27.
goldhord (*m. or n.*) treasure 121/13.
gong (*m.*) path, course 43/17.
gongende, gongendre see gangan.
gegremedan II *pa. t. pl.* provoked, enraged 85/34.
gremede II *pa. t. 3 sg.* provoked, enraged 84/21.
gretan I attack 115/3. grette *pa. t. 3 sg.* touched 23/8.
grimlic *adj.* bloody. grimlecan *wk. asm.* 28/14. grimlicran *comp. npl.* more grievous, more cruel 22/16.
grimme *adv.* dearly, cruelly 22/1.
gegripen 1 *pa. t. subj. pl.* should seize 137/22.
grom *adj. w. dat.* angry 43/10, 137/14.
grot (*n.*) particle 133/15.
growendes *pr. p. gs.* growing 25/32, 119/18.
grund *m.* ground 125/29.
guldon see gyldan.
gulpon see gielpaþ.
guþfona *wk. m.* military standard 84/27, 85/20, 85/21, 136/25.
gydenne *ds* (*f.*) goddess 60/9.
gyf see gif.
gyldan 3 pay 15/18, 33/32, 131/13, etc.; pay for 102/6. gieldanne *dat. inf.* 29/5. gylt *pr. 3 sg.* 15/17. gyldaþ *pr. pl.* 15/15. guldon *pa. t. pl.* 29/9.

gylden *adj.* golden 70/9, 101/17, 101/19, 114/8, etc.
gylt *m.* crime, offence 34/20, 60/5, 60/11, 60/12, etc.
gylt see gyldan.
gegylte I *pr. subj. sg.* should sin 34/19.
gegyrede see gegierwan.
gyrnen I *pr. subj. pl. w. gen.* desire 27/17. gi(e)rnende *pr. p.* desiring 4/5, 90/2, 148/2. girnde *pa. t. 3 sg.* desired 80/30. gi(e)rndon *pl.* 54/24; ~ *æfter* desired, longed for 146/12.
gegyrwan see gegierwan.
gyt see giet.

H

habban III have *as independent vb.* possess, enjoy, experience, have 13/3, 14/32, 15/8, 17/20, 18/33, etc.; hold, consider (as) 38/28, 98/22, 134/19; obtain 53/27, 62/10, 63/27; allow to be 70/15; have in marriage 82/23. *w. part. gen.* have 31/7, 46/2, 46/15, 55/19. *as auxiliary vb.* have 12/14, 19/25, 19/27, 21/21. habbanne *dat. inf.* 33/30. hæbbe *pr. 1 sg.* 9/18. hæfst *2 sg.* 57/14. habbaþ *pl.* 13/3; hæbbe *1 pl.* 11/25. *pr. subj. sg.* 19/28. hæbben *pl.* 52/24. hæfde *pa. t. 1, 3 sg.* 4/6, 56/2. hæfdon *pl.* 25/12; hæfden 35/2. *subj. sg.* let him have 83/25. hæfden *pl.* 31/20; hæfde 55/20. hafa *imp. sg.* 85/1.
hacele *wk. f.* mantle 124/4.
gehæfde III *pa. t. 3 sg.* held 145/7.
hæftnied (*f. or n.*) captivity 70/15.
hæl 4 *pa. t. 3 sg.* concealed 151/23. hælan *pl.* 88/8. hæle *subj. sg.* 104/23.
gehæled I *pp.* healed 73/33.
hælende *ppl. adj.* healing, Saviour 132/16.
hærfestwæte *wk. f.* autumnal wetness 56/26.
hæt (*m.*) hat 107/28, 107/30.
hæt see hatan.
hæte *wk. f.* heat 19/26, 26/33, 50/11, 121/25, etc. hæton *as. or pl.* 26/32.
hæto *f.* heat 19/28, 26/28, 26/31, 119/15, etc.

hætt see hatan.

hæþen *adj.* heathen 23/23, 45/12,
52/32, 69/24. hæþnan *ds. wk.*
69/24; *npl.* 69/29.

hæþenisc *adj.* pagan, heathen 57/3,
107/9, 156/5. hæþeniscan *dpl.*
156/5.

hæþenscype (*m.*) heathen times
27/13.

hafa, hafaþ see habban.

hagol *m.* hail 25/30, 26/3.

hagolade II *pa. t. 3 sg.* hailed 123/17;
hagalade 58/13.

hal *adj.* well, healthy 88/24.

gehalgedon II *pa. t. pl.* consecrated
2/16. gehalgod *pp.* 39/17, 150/8.

halig *adj.* holy 144/9. halgum *dpl.*
144/9.

ham (*m.*) home *loc.* 14/21. æt ~ at
home 30/2, 50/2, 51/19, 61/22,
etc.; home 35/4. *as adv.* homeward,
home 29/11, 30/6, 35/9, 74/7, etc.

hamfærelt (*n.*) home-going 79/19.

hamweard *adv.* homeward, on the
way home 29/7, 29/13, 41/29, 42/6,
etc.

hand, hond *f.* hand 23/10, 41/3,
89/25, 90/15, etc. *on* (*an*) ~ *gan*
submit, surrender 73/14, 91/22,
94/4, 95/3, etc. *on ægþere* (*aþre*) ~
on both sides, on either side 31/31,
34/24, 35/18, 140/6.

hat *adj.* hot 34/6.

[hatan] 7 bid, order, command 3/14,
6/4, 29/3, 40/21, 41/4, etc.; call
name (*w. name in either nom. or acc.*)
1/26, 8/25, 9/2, 9/22, etc. hæt *pr. 3
sg.* 9/17; hætt 9/4; hateþ 8/13.
hataþ *pl.* 11/8. het *pa. t 3 sg.* 1/18;
hett 59/31. heton *pl.* 3/19; hetan
24/18. hete *subj. sg.* 81/9. haten
pp. 19/33; hatan 54/15. hatene
npl. 16/27. hatenu *nsf.* 62/2. hatte
pass. is called, was called 9/8,
19/4. hatton *pl.* were called 41/20.
gehaten etc. see gehet.

he *m.*, heo *f.* hit *n. pron. 3rd person*
he, she, it. he *nsm.* 3/11. hiene *asm.*
1/19; hine 5/26. his *gsm. and n.
and poss. adj.* 1/4, 15/22; hys 26/9.
him *dsm. and n.* 1/5; hym 16/19.
heo *nsf.* 10/22; hio 8/23. hie *asf.*
31/25; hi 38/5. hiere *gdsf. and poss.*

adj. 10/1; hyre 18/34; hire 9/10.
hit *nasn.* 11/14, 12/10; hyt 17/17.
hie *napl.* 1/10; hi 3/18; heo 52/18;
hig 23/10; hy 15/35; he 107/15.
heora *gpl. and poss. adj. and pron.*
1/11, 47/8, 66/1; hiora 1/10;
hiera 8/19; hyra 15/14. him *dpl.*
1/8; heom 25/12.

hea see heah.

heaf (*m.*) lamentation 41/30, 89/18.

heafod *n.* head 45/6, 90/15, 106/1,
108/11, etc.; capital 36/27, 64/7.
heafda *napl.* 40/22, 86/20.

heafodburg, heafedburg(*f.*) capital,
chief city 72/2, 90/28, 93/17, 114/7,
130/22.

heafodrice *n.* empire 36/15. heofodricu *apl.* 37/24. heafedrica *gpl.*
6/21, 132/26.

heafodstede (*m. or n.?*) chief place
49/26.

heafodstol (*m.*) capital 68/1, 78/16.

heah *adj.* high 43/27, 43/31, 112/9,
112/11. heare *dsf.* 77/12. hea
npl. n. 129/27. hierra *comp. nsm.*
of higher rank 128/12. hiran *asm.*
41/13. hierre *nsn.* 124/23. hehsta
sup. nsm. highest 10/30. hiehstan
g. and ds. highest, most important
86/24, 137/24. hehste *nsn.* 64/7.

heahþungen *adj.* of high rank,
illustrious 17/8.

gehealdan 7 guard, defend 91/3;
maintain 117/20, 133/30. geheold
pa. t. 3 sg. 133/30. geheoldon
pl. 117/20.

healdanne 7 *dat. inf.* hold, defend
30/3, 154/10; healdonne 30/7,
154/11; healdenne keep, observe
132/11. heoldon *pa. t. pl.* observed,
maintained 82/32,99/11.heolde*subj.
sg.* should govern 40/14. heolden
pl. should maintain 95/27.

healf *f.* side, part 4/25, 8/19, 10/26,
14/20, etc. healfe *napl.* 98/11,
127/9.

healf *adj.* half 8/17, 17/10, 50/32,
134/8. *fifte* ~ four and a half 68/8,
117/30–1. *oþer* ~ one and a half
75/13.

healf *adv.* 28/16 (2×), 28/20 (2×).

healfcucne *adj. asm.* half alive 70/10.

gehealp 3 *pa. t. 3 sg. w. dat.* helped

23/22. ȝehulpan *pl.* 115/16. *w.*
ȝen. ȝehulpon *pa. t. pl.* 57/7.
ȝehulpe *subj. sg.* 99/31; *pl.* 50/1,
55/1. ȝehulpen *pl.* 141/14.
healsade II *pa. t. 3 sg.* implored
95/28.
healt *adj.* lame 54/15, 54/17 (2×).
hean *adj.* mean, of little worth 55/9,
95/30; *w. gen.* brought low through
156/7.
heanlic *adj.* shameful, ignominious
48/14, 49/29, 85/3, 156/2.
heanlice *adv.* ignominiously 76/9.
heap (*m. or f.*) troop, band 127/17.
heapmælum *adv.* in droves 91/21.
heard *adj.* hardy, hard 113/10,
117/18, 117/19; harsh, severe, hard
121/20, 128/31, 134/20. heardestan
sup. wk. npl. hardiest 21/30.
heardlic *adj.* grievous 125/9.
heardlice *adv.* hard 113/7.
heardost *sup. adv.* most greatly
62/22.
heardsælnesse *f.* misfortune 58/10.
heardsælþa *asf.* hard fate 89/27.
heare see heah.
hearȝ, herȝ *m.* altar, temple 9/1,
62/28, 69/20, 69/26.
hearm (*m.*) harm 111/22.
heawan 7 hew 99/26.
hefenisc see heofenisc.
hefon see heofen.
hehsta, hehste see heah.
hell *f.* hell 48/36, 49/2, 50/25, 50/28.
help (*m. or f.*) help 56/11.
ȝehendast *sup. adj.* most conveni-
ently placed, nearest 64/2.
heo see he.
heofen, heofon, hefon *m.* heaven
2/22, 3/28, 28/10, etc. *in pl.* the
heavens 49/18, 87/11.
heofenisc, hefenisc *adj.* heavenly
1/6, 53/2.
heofodricu see heafodrice.
heofonlic *adj.* heavenly 22/31.
heofonrice (*n.*) kingdom of heaven
131/20, 152/24.
heofonware (*m.*) *pl.* inhabitants of
heaven 59/21.
ȝeheold, ȝeheoldon see ȝehealdan.
heolde, -en, -on see healdanne.
heom see he.
heora see he.

heorte *wk.* (*f.*) heart 132/21.
her *adv.* here, at this point, in this
place 1/1, 27/14, 57/4, 61/1, etc.
here *m.* army, particular kind of
armed force (e.g. cavalry, infantry)
26/14, 30/2, 30/5, 30/8, etc.
herede see herȝeaþ.
herefeoh *n.* booty 64/31.
herehyþ *f.* plunder 30/6, 94/30.
heretoga *wk.* (*m.*) general 3/22.
herga, hergas see hearȝ.
ȝehergeadon II *pa. t. pl.* ravaged
96/17. ȝehergad *pp.* 78/12; ȝeher-
ȝead made prisoner 95/26.
hergean, hergi-, heriȝ- II *intrans.*
make raids 15/34, 15/37, 51/18,
65/10, etc. *trans.* make raids on
29/10, 52/4, 63/21, 86/15, etc.
herȝenne *dat. inf.* 100/20.
heriende *pr. p.* 21/26.
herȝeaþ I *pr. pl.* praise 65/27.
herede *pa. t. 3 sg.* praised 134/5.
herg(i)ung, heriung *f.* plundering,
raid 42/19, 56/18, 70/21, 71/13, etc.,
hergiunga *ds.* 42/19.
hering *f.* praise 88/10 (2×).
het see hatan.
ȝehet 7 *pa. t. 1, 3 sg.* promised 9/19,
39/23, 63/16, 63/18, etc.; summoned, called 148/23. ȝeheton *pl.*
promised 47/16. ȝehete *subj. sg.*
should invite 90/4. ȝehaten *pp.*
promised 60/9 etc. ȝehatene *npl.*
called 81/11. ȝehatenu *nsf.* 64/6.
hetan, hete, etc. see hatan.
hete *m.* hatred, enmity 77/15, 99/17.
hetelic *adj.* evil 28/7.
heton, het(t) see hatan.
hi see he.
hider *adv.* hither 16/19.
hie see he.
hiehstan see heah.
hienan I destroy, ill-use, oppress
66/3, 71/14, 71/24, 86/15, etc.
hiene see he.
hiera see he.
hieran, hir-, hyr- I hear 4/6,
75/15, 84/17, 90/18, 100/4, etc. *w.*
in (on), to belong (to), be subject
(to) 16/14, 16/20, 16/25, 16/28; *w.*
dat. obey 78/13, 78/16.
ȝehieranne I *dat. inf.* hear 65/26,
66/1. ȝehierde *pa. t. 3 sg.* heard

ġehieranne (*cont.*):
41/10, 92/22, etc.; *w. dat.* listened
to 48/5. ġehierdon *pl.* heard 125/5.
hi(e)rde *m.* herdsman 5/21, 114/12.
hiere see he.
hiered (*m.*) household, court 82/33,
149/6.
hierra *wk. m.* lord 101/32 (*or comp.
of* heah).
hierra *comp. adj.* see heah.
ġehiersum, ġehyrsum *adj. w. dat.*
obedient 26/8, 27/19, 35/12, 55/14.
hiersumedon II *pa. t. pl. w. dat.*
obeyed 36/22; hirsumedan submitted to 53/14. hirsumeden *subj.
pl.* 42/17.
ġehiersumedon II *pa. t. pl. w. dat.*
obeyed 63/1.
hiersumnesse *ds*(*f.*) subjection
81/23.
hiewestan *m.* hewn stone 112/22.
hiġ see he.
him see he.
hindan *adv.* from the rear 83/12,
154/13; in the rear 85/15.
hine see he.
hio see he.
hiora see he.
hiran see heah.
hirde see hierde.
hirdon see hieran.
hire see he.
hirsumedan, hirsumeden see
hiersumedon.
his see he.
hit see he.
hiwunġ (*f.*) marriage 39/3.
hlæfdian *wk.* (*f.*) *pl.* ladies, mistresses
87/23.
hlæne *adj.* lean 113/4 (2 ×).
hlaf *m.* loaf 123/16.
hlafmæsse (*wk. f.*) Lammas, the
first of August 130/4.
hlaford *m.* lord, master 5/27, 13/29,
49/25, 49/28, etc.
hlafordhyldo *f.* loyalty 155/18.
ġehleat 2 *pa. t. 3 sg.* obtained by lot
108/3.
hliepe *wk.* (*f.*) horse-block 145/5.
hlihhan 6 *w. gen.* laugh at 65/30.
ġehlot (*n.*) determination, lot 69/30.
hloþ (*f.*) band 55/21, 64/11, 65/10.
hluton 2 *pa. t. pl.* cast lots 108/2.

hlynn *m.* noise 34/7.
hlytta *wk.* (*m.*) one who divines by
casting lots 98/33.
hnescestan *sup. adj. asm. wk.* softest
113/8.
hnesclic *adj.* effeminate 32/16.
hofon 6 *pa. t. pl.* raised 23/14.
hol (*n.*) hole. holan *dpl.* 52/18.
hold *adj. w. dat.* well disposed 140/25,
141/19, 143/6.
hond see hand.
hoppe *wk. f.* ornament 104/28 (see
Commentary).
hors *n.* horse 17/20, 17/22, 17/26,
28/20, etc. horsan *dpl.* 15/14.
ġehorsad-, ġehorsed- *ppl. adj.*
mounted (of cavalry) 68/8, 69/2,
72/27, 73/4, etc.
horshwælum *dpl.* (*m.*) walruses
14/31.
hrædlic *adj.* short 29/18.
hrædlice *adv.* soon, quickly, shortly
26/12, 33/23, 48/21, 51/19, etc.
hrægl (*n.*) garment, clothing 17/28,
59/8, 59/11.
hran *m.* reindeer 15/9, 15/11, 15/18.
ġehreas 2 *pa. t. 3 sg.* fell 86/25,
98/32. ġehroren *pp.* fallen 44/3.
hreoh *adj.* rough 21/11.
hreosende 2 *pr. p.* falling into ruin
44/15.
hreow *f.* regret 38/20.
hreowlice *adv.* painfully 25/29;
miserably 65/29; wretchedly, in a
way to excite pity 28/5, 116/11.
hreowsian II repent 135/1.
hreowsung *f.* penitence 26/10.
*hricġ (*m.*) back 145/5.
hrif *n.* belly 33/23.
ġehrifnian II be gorged? (*or* become
ferocious? cf. BTS *hrifnian*) 77/23.
hring *m.* ring 101/17 (2 ×), 101/20,
104/28, etc.; globe, circle 123/15,
123/20, 131/1.
hrof (*m.*) roof 42/18.
ġehroren see ġehreas.
hryre *m.* fall, downfall 54/30, 114/5;
destruction 85/8; collapse (of building) 98/31.
hryþer (*n.*) horned cattle 15/12.
hu *adv.* how 1/2, 1/3, 1/4, 1/6, etc.;
what 38/12, 48/26, 74/13. *to þon . . .
hu* in such a way that 34/7. *hu . . . hu*

(*hwelce*) 31/19, 74/17, etc. see Commentary on 31/19.
hulic *pron.* of what sort 118/22; hulucu 112/7.
gehulpan, gehulpe, etc. see gehealp.
hund¹ *m.* dog 25/24, 123/27.
hund² *num.* hundred 22/30, 35/24, 86/3, etc. *w. part. gen.* 15/9, 26/16, etc. *as adj.* 27/1, 40/15, 61/5, etc. hunde *a. and dpl.* 4/14, 4/15, 4/19, etc. hunda 4/11. hundum *dpl.* 97/26.
hundeahtatig *num.* eighty 28/23, 35/24, 49/16. *w. part. gen.* 45/25, 60/23, 92/15.
hundseofontig, -syfantig *num.* seventy 20/28, 20/32, 21/8, 23/13. *w. part. gen.* 43/27.
hund twelftig *num.* one hundred and twenty 68/17; *w. part. gen.* 93/33.
hunger, hungor *m.* famine, hunger 23/21, 24/5, 24/16, 32/4, etc. hungres *gs.* 41/21. hungre *ds.* 1/10. hungrig *adj.* hungry. hungregum *dpl.* 77/21.
hunig (*n.*) honey 17/2.
hunta *wk.* (*m.*) hunter 14/23, 14/26.
huntoþ (*m.*) hunting 14/3.
huru *adv.* about, at least 16/32.
hus *n.* house, temple 17/11, 52/32, 59/3, 86/24 etc.
hwa¹ *m.* hwæt *n. interr. pron.* who, what 3/15, 27/26, 31/30, 58/3, etc. *w. gen.* what proportion of, what 14/28, 31/30, 84/27, 87/27. hwy *instr.* 117/17. *for hwi, for hwy* why 34/15, 65/25, 65/27, 87/13.
hwa² *m.* hwæt *n. indef. pron.* someone, something 24/26, 34/16, 34/19, 77/22; anyone 56/12. *lytles hwæt* some small amount, some small thing 65/28, 74/14, 83/3.
gehwa *indef. pron.* any one 57/15.
hwæl *m.* whale 15/2, 15/16, 15/20. hwales *gs.* 15/16. hwalas *npl.* 15/2.
hwælhunta *wk.* (*m.*) whaler 14/9.
hwælhuntaþ *m.* whaling 15/4.
hwær *adv.* where 27/14, 27/16, 31/12, 31/14, etc.
hwærfigiende II *pr. p.* wandering 150/32.

hwæt *pron.* see hwa.
hwæt *adv.* why 46/23; why, lo! 44/4, 67/5.
hwæthwara *adv.* a little 33/19.
hwætra *comp. adj.* braver 64/18. hwatest *sup.* bravest 30/26, 30/33. hwætscipe (*m.*) bravery, valour 30/10, 31/6, 113/3.
hwæþer *pron. adj.* which (of two) *as adj.* 55/27. *as pron.* 14/12, 14/16, 78/33, etc. hwæþre *npl.* 32/7. *w. the alternatives introduced by* þe 66/24, 68/9, 71/20, 84/8, etc.; *w. three alternatives* 73/20.
hwæþer, hweþer *conj.* whether (or not), if 35/14, 85/27, 89/1, 97/29, etc. *w. the alternatives introduced by* þe whether . . . or 112/28. *w. main clause unexpressed* say whether, ask yourself whether 116/19.
hwæþ(e)re *adv.* however, nevertheless 26/7, 26/16, 38/1, 45/19, etc.
hwalas, hwales see hwæl.
hwam see hwa.
hwara *adv.* where 103/31.
hwatestan see hwætra.
hwearf 3 *pa. t. 3 sg.* returned 73/34; *w. refl. dat.* 128/11. hweorfendum *pr. p. dpl.* changing *on hweorfendum sigum* with varying degrees of success 58/25.
gehwearf 3 *pa. t. 3 sg.* passed 27/26, 36/30. gehwurfe *subj. sg.* was averted 136/30.
hwelc *pron. adj. as interr. adj.* what sort of, how much 2/16, 31/19, 32/3, 38/11, etc.; of what sort, what kind (of people, place, time) 69/29, 83/4; *as interr. pron.* which (of many) 77/22, 108/2. *as indef. adj.* any, some 42/1, 42/9, 107/30; *pron.* 59/7. *swa ~ swa rel. adj.* whatever 32/2. hwelcun *dpl.* 74/16.
gehwelc, gehwilc *indef. pron. adj.* each, every *as pron.* 24/14, 63/26; *as adj.* 64/2.
hwelchugu *adj.* some 61/4.
hwelp (*m.*) whelp 77/21.
hwene *adv. w. comp.* a little 15/27, 111/5.
hweol *n.* wheel 26/24.
hweorfendum see hwearf.
hwetstan *m.* whetstone 113/2, 113/9.

hweþer see hwæþer *conj.*
hwi see hwa.
hwider *adv.* whither 33/22, 59/6.
hwierfan I turn 49/10.
hwil *f.* time, while 16/5, 17/11, 35/12, 37/31, etc. *sume hwile* for a certain time, for a while 47/27, 58/27, 66/8, 85/31. *þa hwile* meanwhile 41/20, 43/2, 55/19. *læssan hwile* for a shorter time 52/28. *þa hwile þe conj.* while 43/1, 65/1, 68/6, etc. See also hwilum below.
gehwilc see gehwelc.
hwilum, hwylum *adv.* sometimes 15/34, 15/35, 17/8, 17/15, etc.
hwit *adj.* white 42/6. *feowerfetes twa* ~ two white species of quadruped 42/6.
hwon *adv.* somewhat, a little 14/13, 31/4; little 148/2.
hwonan, hwonon *adv. and conj.* whence 60/20, 96/29, 133/13, 137/10.
hwonne *adv. and conj.* when 50/10, 103/30.
gehwurfe see gehwearf.
hwy *adv. and conj.* why 73/9, 77/6, 85/3, 118/26, etc. *an* ~, *for* ~ see hwa.
hwylum see hwilum.
gehwyrfed I *pp.* changed 26/11.
hy see he.
hyd *f.* hide, skin 15/1, 15/16, 15/20, 93/32, etc.
gehydde I *pa. t. 3 sg.* concealed 64/20. gehyd *pp.* 152/12.
hyldo *f.* friendship 71/21; favour 132/9.
hym see he.
hyra see he.
hyraþ, hyrþ see hieran.
hyre see he.
gehyrsume see gehiersum.
hys see he.
hysecild *n.* male child 29/32.
hyspton I *pa. t. pl.* scorned 135/13.
hyt see he.

I

ic *pron. 1st pers.* I etc. 8/23. me *ds.* 27/11. min *gs.* (as possessive) 113/6. we *npl.* we etc. 11/25. us *adpl.* 36/5, 122/19. ure *gpl.* (as possessive, decl. strong) 1/2, 122/17.

ie see ea.
geiecte I *pa. t. 3 sg.* increased 114/22. geiecton *pl.* 124/13. geieced *pp.* enlarged 64/6.
ieldra, yldra *comp. adj.* senior 92/10; elder 27/4. ieldest *sup.* senior, most important 5/28, 89/3, 101/25, 104/11, etc. ieldstena *gpl.* 97/18.
ieldran, yldran *wk. (m)pl.* ancestors 1/2, 8/11, 38/26, 51/5, etc.
ierfweard (*m.*) heir 115/12.
iergþe *ds(f.)* cowardice 74/23.
ierming *m.* poor wretch 52/17.
iermþo *pl. f.* calamities, miseries 39/31, 41/22, 58/10; *as. or pl.* 117/5. iermþa *npl.* (*or s.?*) 58/10.
i(e)rnan 3 run 33/20, 39/14, etc.; flow 11/6, 12/21, 43/15, etc.; sail, run (of ship) 3/24, 83/11, etc. irnþ *pr. 3 sg.* 8/25. i(e)rnende *pr. þ.* 8/24, 33/20; yrnende 16/22. orn *pa. t. 3 sg.* 123/17. urnon *pl.* 86/27.
i(e)þ *comp. adv.* more easily 51/7, 120/24. þe ~ the more easily 39/9, 40/24, 54/4, 87/12, etc.
ieþe *adj.* pleasant 134/21. ieþre *comp. nsf.* easier 46/18.
ieþelice *adv.* easily 50/23, 62/18, 118/19, 147/2, 154/18.
igland, ygland, -lond *n.* island 9/8, 9/16, 9/25, 9/31, 20/26, etc.
ilca, ylca *pron. adj. always decl. wk.* same. *as adj.* 8/20, 9/10, 10/29, 17/12, etc. *as pron.* 38/14, 73/22, etc. ilcan *dpl.* 13/6.
in *prep.* in. *w. acc.* to, into 23/27, 71/1, etc.; *w. dat.* in 8/19, 9/1, etc.
in *adv.* ~ *on* on to, into 11/12, 14/12, 14/16, 14/18, etc.; to 16/14. *þær in* inside 73/10, 73/18.
ingewinn *n.* internal conflict, civil war 50/24.
inn (*n.*) dwelling 89/28.
innan *adv.* within, inside 88/19, 113/4 (2×).
inne *adv.* inside 17/7, 17/11, 17/30, 25/21, etc. ~ *on* within, inside 69/25, 129/3.
inneweard *adj.* inside part of 112/24.
into *prep. w. dat.* into 52/2, 79/16, 106/12, 106/30, etc. *w. acc.* 124/25.
iower, iowra, iowre see þu.

ipnalis a kind of adder, *Lat.* hypnale
130/11.
irnan, irnende, etc. see iernan.
irre *n.* anger 52/36, 109/30.
irre *adj. w. dat.* angry 62/29, 62/30,
84/19, 88/3.
is (*n.*) ice 110/10.
is see beon.
isen (*n.*) iron 93/25, 112/4.
isen *adj.* iron 85/14.
istoria history, *Lat.* historia 56/2.
iþ see ieþ.
iu *adv.* formerly 13/9.

K

kynekynnes see cynecynnes.
kyning(c) see cyning.
kyrtel *m.* garment, coat 15/19.

L

ġelacnad II *pp.* healed 65/3.
ladedon II *pa. t. pl.* excused 115/8.
ladteow, latteow *m.* leader, general,
Lat. dux etc. 6/15, 40/13, 41/13,
54/21, etc.
læce *m.* doctor 148/24.
lædan I lead, conduct 1/15, 25/15,
100/23, 110/24, etc.
ġelædan I lead 33/15, 43/4, 45/4,
46/35, etc.; bring 46/31, 140/13.
læfed I *pp.* left 50/3.
læg, lægan, etc. see licgan.
ġelærde I *pa. t. 3 sg.* urged, advised
67/27, 106/8; taught 129/9; persuaded 80/6. ġelærdan *pl.* gave
(counsel) 98/9; ġelærdon urged,
instructed 4/23, 88/23, 97/14.
ġelæred *pp.* taught 61/14, 151/22.
ġelærede *npl.* 71/28.
ġelæredest *ppl. adj. sup.* most learned
61/12, 135/26, 143/4.
lærende I *pr. p.* urging 47/33; *w. dat.*
teaching 87/29. lærde *pa. t. 3 sg.*
urged, instructed 128/14, 154/27.
læs *adv.* less *as sb.* fewer, smaller
number 84/29, 129/25. na þy ~
none the less 121/7. þy læs *conj.*
lest 90/15. See also þylæs.
læssa *comp. adj.* less, lesser 48/3,
52/28, 59/27, 65/32, etc.; smaller
15/2. *seo* læsse *Asia* Asia Minor, the
Roman province of Asia 10/24 etc.

læst *sup.* smallest, least 17/18,
17/24, 43/34, 70/14.
læstan I observe 127/20.
ġelæstan I perform, fulfil, carry out
29/5, 44/36, 67/8, 67/10, etc.; *w.
dat.* accompany 102/4.
laf *f.* widow 80/20, 80/31, 82/2. *to
lafe beon* (*weorþan*), survive, remain
17/14, 23/15, 25/8, 34/24, etc.
lamp 3 *w. dat.* befell 91/25.
land, lond *n.* land 3/4, 10/4, 10/5,
10/6, etc. *be lande* along the coast
14/17.
landleode, lond- *mpl.* inhabitants
of a country 11/29, 29/18, 39/33,
60/30, etc.
landġemære, lond- *n.* boundary,
confine 9/12, 12/14, 12/15, 44/19,
etc. landġemæro *napl.* 19/21,
19/22.
landmen *npl.* (*m.*) local population
11/9.
landġemirce *n.* boundary 8/19, 9/7,
9/11; *gpl.?* 9/7.
landrice *n.* territory 39/26; region
9/20.
lang, lange see long, longe.
ġelang, ġelong *adj.* attainable 122/
18; ~ *on* owing, attributable to
105/32, 117/18.
lar *f.* advice, prompting 80/8, 94/20,
108/13, 111/13; instruction 98/15,
136/14, 152/23. *æt þære lare wæron*
advised, counselled 128/7.
lareow *m.* teacher 24/13, 153/10.
ġelastfull *adj.* helpful 80/19.
late *adv.* late, late in the day 73/5,
105/32, 153/13. lator *comp.* later
56/2.
latteow see ladteow.
laþ (*n.*) harm, injury 30/32, 80/15,
151/7, 153/12.
laþ *adj. w. dat.* hateful, displeasing
67/9, 105/22, 107/10, 139/20, etc.
laþran *comp. npl.* more hateful
40/2. laþost *sup. nsn.* most hateful
127/24. laþesta *nsm. wk.* 128/16.
laþade II *pa. t. 3 sg. w. dat.* was
hateful 80/17.
ġelaþaþ II *pr. 3 sg.* invites 131/10.
ġelaþede *pp. npl.* summoned 60/
23.
laþspel *n.* sad tidings 42/32.

geleafa *wk. m.* belief, faith 104/7, 131/
13, 149/11, 151/25, etc.

geleafsum *adj.* to geleafsuman so as
to produce belief 70/16.

leahtriaþ II *pr. pl.* blame 38/11, 52/16.
leahtrien *subj. pl.* 74/26. leahtrade
þa. t. 3 sg. reproved 134/6.

lean *n.* recompense 115/28, 119/7.

leaspellengum *dpl.(f.)* fables, empty
or false talk 53/17.

leasungspell (*n.*) fable 26/33.

leat 2 *þa. t. 3 sg.* bent forward 152/25.

gelec 7 *þa. t. 3 sg.* played a trick,
deluded 62/23.

legan see legie.

gelegen see gelicgean.

leger (*n.*) lying 17/29.

legie *wk. f.* legion 6/14, 86/13, 102/14,
125/26. legean *npl.* 126/16. legan
apl. 126/2. legian *gpl.* (?) 86/14;
dpl. 132/2.

lenctenhæte *dsf.* springtime heat 56/
25.

gelende I *þa. t. 3 sg.* went, arrived
55/9, 90/10. gelendon *pl.* 35/9.

leng, lencg *comp. adv.* longer 17/9,
45/26, 47/34, 48/2, etc. lengest
sup. longest 82/27.

lengra see long.

lengþ (*f.*) length. on lengþe at length
77/31.

leo *mf.* lion, lioness 28/16, 77/21.

leod (*f.*) country, race 25/8.

leode *mpl.* people of a country,
country 1/8, 1/21, 2/24, 13/20, etc.

leof *adj. w. dat.* dear 23/30, 140/15.
leofre *comp. nsn.* preferable *him
leofre wæs* etc. he (they) preferred
29/4, 39/30, 54/16, 59/17, etc.
leofast *sup.* dearest 127/23; most
preferable 155/28.

leofaþ see libban.

leoht *adj.* light 15/38. leohtra *comp.
nsm.* brighter 131/3; *apl.* less
oppressive 128/31.

leornode II *þa. t. 3 sg.* learned 150/5,
150/16.

geleornode II *þa. t. 3 sg.* learned,
acquired 23/28, 23/31. geleornodon *pl.* 22/2; geleornedon 82/26;
thought about, worked out 74/10.
geleornad *pp.* learned, acquired
85/12; geleornod 140/24.

leornung *f.* learning. leornunga *ds.*
150/3.

leoþ (*n.*) song 28/1, 42/24, 53/16.

leoþcwide (*m.*) poem 65/26.

let 7 *þa. t. 3 sg.* left 91/16, 101/6,
126/27, etc.; kept 14/7; allowed
136/9. leton *pl.* left 30/7, 147/27;
regarded 55/8; let 59/10, 91/2;
letan left 93/4. lete *subj. sg.* should
leave 126/13.

gelette I *w. gen.* hindered from 43/6.

libban III live 36/4, 66/25, 75/27,
101/31, etc. leofaþ *pr. 3 sg.* 128/16.
libbaþ *pl.* 22/4. libbende *pr. p.*
38/20. libbendne *asm.* 153/13.
libbendes *gs.* 85/26. lifde *pa. t. 3
sg.* 82/19. lifdon *pl.* 74/16; lyfedan
27/4.

lic *n.* corpse 17/11.

gelic (*n.*) similitude 139/7.

gelic *adj. w. dat.* similar 38/16, 56/5,
76/6, 83/1, etc.

gelica *wk.* (*m.*) equal 95/31, 97/23.

licade see licien.

gelicade II *þa. t. 3 sg. w. dat.* pleased
59/15, 63/33, 84/32, 132/11. gelicoden *subj. pl.* 113/22. gelicad *pp.*
liked, pleasing 65/26.

gelice *adv.* equally, alike 56/28, 71/13,
105/12. gelicost *sup. þæm gelicost
(þe)* just as (if), in the very same
way (as) 77/11, 77/21, 97/30, etc.
gelice 7 as though 44/1, 52/3,
62/19; just as 122/2.

licgan, licgean, licggean 5 lie,
stretch, flow 9/12, 9/21, 9/33, 70/10,
etc. lie dead 59/2, 75/28, etc. liþ
pr. 3 sg. 11/21; ligeþ 9/6. licgaþ
pl. 8/20; licgeaþ 8/22. læg *pa. t. 3
sg.* 14/18. lægan *pl.* 59/2; lægon
113/27. læge *subj. sg.* 14/6. licgende *ppl. adj.* 42/18 etc. (see
feoh); licggende 105/3.

gelicgean 5 cease 82/19. gelegen *pp.*
laid 130/10.

lichoma *wk.* (*m.*) corpse 86/26.

licien II *pr. subj. pl. w. dat.* please
32/8. licade *pa. t. 3 sg.* pleased
113/25.

gelicoden see gelicade.

licost *sup. adv. þæs licost þe* as though
81/33.

gelicost see gelice.

ġeliefanne I *dat. inf.* believe 46/19.
ġeliefen *pr. subj. pl. w. gen.* admit
113/21; *w. dat.* believe 113/23.
ġelifde *pa. t. 3 sg.* believed 156/8.
ġeliefdon *pl.* 88/23; *w. dat.* 57/10.
ġeliefedlice *adv.* trustfully 48/5, 54/6.
lif *n.* life 21/32, 22/18, 30/10, 39/31,
etc.
lifde, lifdon see libban.
ġelifde see ġeliefanne.
ġelig(e)re *n.* illicit intercourse 22/22,
22/25, 22/27, 40/5, etc.
ġeliġernesse *ds(f.)* illicit intercourse
22/23, 61/17.
liġette *ds.* (*m. f. or n.*) lightning 142/3.
liġeþ see licgan.
lim *n.* limb 25/25, 130/12.
ġelimplice *adv.* fittingly 38/13.
liþ see licgan.
liþe *adj.* mild, pleasant 44/26. liþran
comp. apl. milder 128/31; lyþran
npl. 19/17.
loca *npl.* (*n.*) locks 132/13.
locian II look, observe 43/24, 107/6.
logan 6 *pa. t. pl. w. dat.* of *person*
dissuaded, spoke with disapproval
98/34.
ġelomlicost *sup. adv.* most frequently 88/29.
ġelomp 3 *pa. t. 3 sg.* happened 37/17,
37/24. ġelumpan *pl.* 87/10.
lond see land.
londfæstenne *ds(n.)* landfastness,
natural fortress 46/21.
londleode see landleode.
londgemære, londgemæro see
landgemære.
long, lang *adj. w. gen.* long 9/5, 14/2,
15/3, 15/4, etc. lengra *comp. nsm.*
longer 15/3.
ġelong see ġelang.
longe, lange *adv.* long, far 14/5,
17/35, 35/6, 55/14, etc.
longian II *impers. w. acc.* cause
longing 48/28.
longsum *adj.* long drawn out, pro-
tracted, tedious 32/2, 70/1, 76/3,
105/31, 110/28, etc. longsumere
dsf. 41/17. longsumast *sup.* most
long lasting 47/9.
longsumlice *adv.* for a long time 36/1.
lotwrenc (*m.*) cunning, stratagem
57/8, 64/19, 64/34.

lufaþ II *pr. 3 sg.* loves 36/6. lufiaþ
pl. love 111/17. lufade *pa. t. 3 sg.*
loved 32/17. lufedon *pl.* 59/16.
lufu *f.* love. lufe *as.* 59/19. lufan *wk.*
ds. 34/19, 36/6, 39/15, etc.
ġelumpan see ġelomp.
lustbære *adj.* agreeable 53/17.
lustbærlic *adj.* pleasant 48/26.
lustfull *adj.* desirous 56/12.
lustlice *adv.* willingly, gladly 31/7,
53/13, 65/32, 69/16.
lustsumlic *adj.* pleasant 23/9, 65/26.
lutedan II *pa. t. pl.* lay hidden 52/18.
lyfedan see libban.
lyft *f.* air, sky 60/21.
lyst I *pr. 3 sg. impers. w. acc.* of
person causes desire 57/15. lyste
subj. sg. 32/2.
lyt *n. w. part. gen.* few 57/20.
lytel *adj.* little, small 15/38, 21/12,
22/11, 24/22, etc.; short 24/26,
35/11, etc. lytle *instr. used adverbially* a little, somewhat 70/20,
133/5. lytles hwæt some small
thing, some small amount 65/28,
etc. lytlan *dsm.* 48/29.
lytiġ *adj.* cunning 88/26, 121/9.
ġelytlade II *pa. t. 3 sg.* diminished,
decreased 36/5; ġelytlode 26/17.
ġelytladu *pp. nsf.* 100/30.
lyþerlic *adj.* mean 89/23.
lyþran see liþe.
lyþre *adj.* vile, wicked 154/11.

M

ma *adv.* more, rather, to a greater
extent 29/25, 44/15, 47/34, 74/23;
ne . . . þon ~ any more than, nor . . .
either 53/18. *as sb.* more 15/12,
17/15; *w. gen.* 24/20, 46/33, 47/3,
57/16, etc.
mæd *as(f.)* meadow 52/3.
mædena see mæġden.
mædencild *n.* girl 29/32 (2×).
mæġ *m.* kinsman 45/17, 65/19, 68/7,
120/12, etc. mæġas *napl.* 46/26.
mæġa *gpl.* 47/22. magum *dpl.*
17/7.
mæġ *pret. pres. vb. 1, 3 sg.* can, is
able, may 15/22, 15/26, 49/11,
110/13, etc. magon *pl.* 17/34;
magan 38/25. mæġe *subj. sg.*
16/11. mæġen *pl.* 47/8. mehte

mæg (cont.):
pa. t. 3 sg. could, might, was able
14/17; mæhte 33/14; meahte
14/10; mihte 15/28; myhte 22/23.
mehton pl. 30/13; mehten 31/18;
mehtan 38/29; meahtan 26/22;
mæhte 44/9. mehten subj. pl.
29/26; mæhten 30/14; mehte
53/27; elliptically, with inf. to be
inferred 19/28, 62/25, 72/17. ~ to
can serve as 112/23. ~ wiþ can
prevail against 35/14, 65/9, 87/12,
etc. mehten hi if they might 65/6.
mægden (n.) maiden 2/10. mædena
npl. 26/5.
mægdenmenn npl. m. maidens 35/1.
mægen (n.) power, might, (military)
force 37/23, 46/2, 46/30, 55/19, etc.
mæggemot (n.) assembly of kinsmen
131/10.
mægrædenne ds(f.) kinship 129/9.
mægþ f. family, race 17/34, 131/8,
136/16, 137/29.
ġemæġþ f. family 59/27.
mæġþhad (m.) chastity, virginity
30/11.
mæhte, mæhten see mæġ.
ġemænaþ I pr. pl. lament, complain
about 65/29, 74/15.
ġemæne adj. w. dat. common (to),
shared (by) 54/31, 65/6, 102/6,
104/24, 113/17.
ġemænelice adv. in common 42/20,
65/5.
mænende I pr. p. lamenting 128/3.
mænde pa. t. 3 sg. lamented,
complained about 6/2, 118/25, 122/
15, 126/19, 135/16.
mæniġ see moniġ.
mære adj. famous, glorious 30/23,
31/26, 66/11, 70/23, etc. se mæra
Alexander wk. nsm. Alexander the
Great 1/27, 3/14, 4/6, 90/18 (see also
mara). mærast, mærest- sup.
most famous 44/1, 71/7.
ġemære n. boundary, frontier 44/22,
45/23, 60/30, 62/24; as. or apl.
9/20. ġemæro napl. 9/29, 116/2.
mærlic adj. glorious 76/1. mærlecra
gpl. splendid 71/20.
ġemærsad II pp. glorified 83/30.
mærþ f. glory 42/13; glorious or
wonderful thing 93/32. mærþa pl.

mighty or glorious deeds 42/8,
72/11.
mæssepreost (m.) mass-priest 143/4,
152/23.
mæssepresbyter m. mass-priest 149/
10 (v.l. mæssepreost).
mæst m. mast 92/19, 107/6.
mæst sup. adj. (of size or degree,
incl. fig.) greatest, very great,
largest 15/5, 17/16, 17/23, 23/21,
etc. elliptically as sb., us. w. gen.
the greatest, the greatest number
43/7, 43/15, 47/8, etc. mæstra ælcne
heora flana almost all their arrows
155/8. mæste nsm. 5/14. mæsta
nsf. 52/21. mæst sup. adv. chiefly,
especially, most 9/8, 15/14, 22/4,
24/33, etc. ~ eall almost all 43/3,
46/28, etc. swa hie ~ mehten as
much as they could 137/22. is ~ on
consists mostly of 15/14.
mæþ (f.) degree 34/20.
maġan see mæġ.
maġister (m.) master, teacher. magi-
stre ds. 71/29.
maġon see mæġ.
maġum see mæġ.
ġemalic adj. wanton, shameless 29/2.
man¹ see mon(n).
man² (n.) wickedness 2/16, 27/17.
man adj. false 87/16.
mancwealm see monncwealm.
mancyn see moncyn.
mandæd (f.) wicked deed 28/4.
maneġa see moniġ.
maniġ see moniġ.
maniġfeald see moniġfeald.
mann see monn.
manslyht see monsliht.
mara comp. adj. greater 13/17, 17/9,
36/10, 46/23, 48/23, etc. þæs maran
Alexandres, þæm maran Alexandre
(for nom. sg. see mære) Alexander
the Great 3/9, 3/10, 60/28, 61/2,
67/20; as sb. mare n. a greater quantity, more 19/27, 47/14, 56/11, 56/12,
etc. maran dpl. 13/17.
ġemartrade II pa. t. 3 sg. martyred
143/11. ġemartredon pl. 137/27.
martyre (m.) martyr 144/9, 147/22,
152/1, 152/26.
martyrunġ f. martyrdom, passion.
martyrunga as. 134/15.

mattuc (*m.*) mattock. **mattucun** *dpl.* 99/26.

maþmhus (*n.*) treasury 126/24, 136/4.

mawe 7 *pr. subj. sg.* should mow 52/3.

me see **ic**.

meahtan, meahte see **mæg**.

mealmstan *m.* malmstone 113/8 (see Commentary).

mearc *f.* territory 63/25.

ǥemearcian II note, record 55/30. **ǥemearcod** *pp.* marked out 119/26.

mearþ (*m.*) marten 15/18.

meder see **modor**.

medo (*m. or n.*) mead 17/4, 17/6.

ǥemedren *adj.* born of the same mother 63/6 (v.l. gemedred).

medselþ *f.* bad fortune 89/1.

mehtan, mehte, etc. see **mæg**.

men see **monn**.

ǥemenǥed I *pp.* mingled 25/31.

menǥeo *f.* multitude 46/17. **men(i)ǥe** *a. and ds.* 26/17, 47/13, 68/30.

menn see **monn**.

meolc (*f.*) milk 3/27, 17/3, 22/4, 87/11.

mere *m.* lake 15/37, 16/33, 16/36, 20/7, etc.

merǥen (*m.*) morning. *on* ~ 73/32, 96/20, 103/19, 121/25. See also **morǥen**.

ǥemetan I meet, find, encounter 78/32, 89/3, 114/23, etc. **ǥemette** *pa. t. 3 sg.* 68/24. **ǥemetton** *pl.* 69/33.

mete *m.* food 25/19, 25/20, 27/32, 33/8, etc.

meteliest (*f.*) lack of food 66/21, 91/1.

ǥemetǥian II moderate, control 38/25.

ǥemetǥung (*f.*) moderation 44/30.

ǥemeting see **ǥemetting**.

ǥemetlic *adj.* sufficient 66/7.

metseacsum *dpl.* (*n.*) meat-knives 129/3.

mette I *pa. t. 3 sg.* met, found, encountered 14/20, 62/8, 62/28, 65/24. **metton** *pl.* 44/29 etc. **metten** *subj. pl.* 64/25.

ǥemette, -on see **ǥemetan**.

ǥemet(t)ing (*f.*) (hostile) meeting, encounter 66/16, 94/21, 100/7 (v. l. gemitting), 120/27 (v. l. gemittincg). **ǥemetingǥe** *ds.* 101/5.

mettrymnesse *dsf.* illness 148/27.

meþiǥ *adj.* weary, exhausted 73/26. **meþie** *npl. m.* 49/23.

micel, mycel, micl-, mycl- *adj.* much, great, large 1/10, 1/13, 3/2, 3/18, 17/2, etc. *as subst. w. gen.* much 29/28, 47/9, 110/23, etc. **micellre** *dsf.* 145/6. **miclana** *gpl.* 31/27; **miclena** 46/13. **miclan** *dsn.* 61/18; *dpl.* 61/19. **micclan** *gs. wk.* 23/3.

micelness (*f.*) magnitude, great size 43/25.

micle *adv.* much 15/2, 17/9, 26/9, 44/27.

miclian II increase, become greater 37/10, 133/5.

ǥemiclian II increase 32/29, 62/3, 88/26.

miclum *adv.* greatly, much 17/33, 26/29, 65/16, 140/2.

mid *prep.* with *w. dat.* together with, along with, accompanied by 1/5, 2/2, 3/19, 4/4, etc.; by, by means of, through 1/10, 2/16, 8/16, 11/19, etc.; among 15/11, 17/33, 23/19; because of 24/3, 45/22, 56/25; in regard to 46/1, 84/30; against 120/18. *w. instr.* together with, along with 17/25, 64/31, 68/11, 72/11; by 86/6; through, by means of, because of 23/22, 57/9. *w. acc.* with 114/1. *mid ealle adv.* altogether, completely 23/18, 25/10, 33/11, 44/31. *mid þæm þæt, mid þæm* (*þam*) *þe conj.* when 39/4, 48/33, 58/8; because 84/23, 94/32, 150/26. *mid þon*(*þan*) *þe* when 33/2, 45/11; because 55/11. ~ *ellipt.* with (it, them, etc.) 15/11, 64/20, 128/2.

middanǥeard *m.* the earth, the world 1/2, 1/4, 2/13, 6/21, etc.

middeldæl (*m.*) middle part 9/21 (v. l. middele).

middeweard *adj.* the middle of, middle 23/2, 37/27, 43/16, 43/23; in the middle 15/27.

midmest *sup. adj.* central 127/18.

midne *adj. asm.* middle *oþ* ~ *dæg* until midday 58/12, 98/30.

mierde I *pa. t. subj. pl.* should obstruct 138/14.

miht (*f.*) might, power 37/3, 59/23, 69/31.

mihte see **mæg.**

mil *f.* mile 3/4, 15/27, 15/29, 16/12, etc.

milde *adj.* mild, merciful, kind 87/18, 134/13, 134/21. **mildesta** *sup. nsm.* *wk.* most merciful 148/7, 156/14. **mildelice** *adv.* mildly, in a kindly manner 27/7, 39/16.

mildheortast *sup. adj.* most merciful 128/4.

mildheortnes(s) *f.* mercy, compassion, clemency 38/29, 70/11, 82/25. **mildse** *asf.* clemency 135/26.

mildsung, miltsung *f.* mercy, compassion 8/10, 38/11, 131/4, 136/9, etc.

min see **ic.**

misdæd *f.* misdeed 137/26, 153/9, 156/13.

mislamp 3 *pa. t. 3 sg. impers. w. dat.* turned out badly, went wrong 88/30.

mislic *adj.* varying, various kinds of 32/5, 111/6. *on mislecum sigum* with varying degrees of success 111/6.

missenlic *adj.* various, different kinds of 32/26, 34/3, 74/21, 77/10, 97/11. **missellican** *dpl.* 77/10.

misspeowe 7 *pa. t. subj. sg. impers. w. dat.* should go ill with 48/4.

gemitting (*f.*) (hostile) meeting 121/22.

miþ *prep. w. dat.* (v. l. mid, q. v.) with, along with 76/20, 91/4; by, through 109/22; *as conj. miþ þæm þe* when 59/7, 86/32.

mod (*n.*) mind, heart, spirit 22/2, 29/19, 43/11, 48/10, etc.; spirits, courage 35/16, 147/17.

modor *f.* mother 37/1, 44/18, 44/32, 69/4; *gs.* 82/4. **meder** *ds.* 61/16.

modrie *wk.* (*f.*) mother's sister, maternal aunt 71/15.

mon see **monn.**

mona *wk. m.* moon 100/31, 135/7.

monaþ (*m.*) month 16/4, 17/8, 138/3, 138/9, etc. *apl.* 29/30, 52/25, 99/12.

moncwealm see **monncwealm.**

moncyn(n), mancyn *n.* mankind 25/6, 35/30, 44/3, etc.; men, number of people, population 25/24, 50/2, 62/8, 110/23. **monkynne** *ds.* 26/25.

moneaca *wk. m.* increase of population 85/27.

monega, monegena etc. see **monig.**

monfultum *m.* reinforcements, army 65/7, 102/22, 114/14, 121/17.

gemong *prep. w. dat.* among, in the course of, in the midst of 39/14, 52/33, 81/11, 82/29. ~ *þæm* in the meanwhile 106/23. *as conj.* ~ *þæm þe* while 86/12.

monig, manig, moneg- maneg- *adj.* many, much, many a 1/19, 3/26, 4/26, 17/1, etc. many of 128/22. **mænig** 16/12. **monog** 70/26. **monegena** *gpl. wk.* 115/29.

monigfeald, manig- *adj.* manifold, numerous, complicated 22/21, 22/32, 30/10, 36/3, etc. **manigfealdon** *dpl.* 22/10. **monigfealdeste** *sup. nsf.* most extensive 85/25.

monigfealdlecor *comp. adv.* more extensively 37/22.

monkynne see **moncynn.**

monmenie *asf.* multitude of people 64/18.

mon(n), man(n) *m.* man, person, *in pl.* people 1/3, 1/17, 2/11, 4/5, etc. *as indef. pron.* one (*nom. sg. only, introducing the equiv. of a passive construction*) 1/1, 8/12, 9/16, 9/22, etc. **men(n)** *ds.* 43/19, 48/18; *napl.* 4/3, 8/14.

mon(n)cwealm, mancwealm *m.* pestilence, slaughter, death of men 3/2, 4/1, 25/7, 32/26, etc.

monncynn see **moncynn.**

monog see **monig.**

monsliht, manslyht *m.* manslaughter, murder 25/11, 32/4, 95/10, 155/28.

monþe see **monaþ.**

monweorod (*n.*) army, band 65/23.

mor *m.* high waste ground, mountain 15/24, 15/25, 15/29, 15/32, etc.

morgen (*m.*) morning. **morgenne** *ds.* 57/27. See also **mergen.**

morþ *n.* murder, destruction 27/14.

moste, mosten, moston see **motan.**

gemot *n.* meeting, council 63/11, 112/28, 118/26, 119/27.

gemotærn (*n.*) council hall 129/3.

motan, moton *pret. pres. vb. pr. pl.* are permitted, may, must 17/25, 36/21. **moten** *subj. pl.* may 31/9, moste *pa. t. 1, 3 sg.* might 22/26, 85/1, etc. moston *pl.* 49/22 etc. mosten *subj. pl.* 39/8 etc.; moste 67/5. *elliptically w. inf. of vb. of motion to be supplied* 76/12.

gemulton 3 *pa. t. pl.* melted 114/7.

gemun *adj. w. gen.* mindful of 30/31.

gemunan *pret. pres. vb. w. gen.* remember 38/26. gemyne *imp. sg.* 127/21. gemunende *pr. p.* 61/2. gemunde *pa. t. 3 sg.* 33/6. gemunden *subj. pl.* 47/23.

munt *m.* mountain 70/26, 71/11, 93/2, 98/12, etc.

munuc *m.* monk 137/4. munecas *napl.* 152/13, 152/16.

munuclif *n.* monastic foundation 152/16.

murciaþ II *pr. pl.* complain 67/7 (v. l. murcniaþ).

muþa *wk. m.* (river) mouth 9/22, 9/23, 9/25, 9/27.

mycel see micel.

mydd *n.* measure, *Lat.* modius 101/16.

myhte see mæg.

gemyndgian II call to mind 56/11; *w. gen.* 61/1, 77/8; remind someone (*acc.*) of something (*gen.*) 47/21.

gemyndgung *f.* monument, memorial 55/11.

gemyne see gemunan.

mynster (*n.*) monastery 139/20.

myre *wk. (f.)* mare 17/3.

N

na *adv.* no, not, by no means, not at all 27/25, 38/20, 49/2, 96/1, etc. ~ ma no more 82/19, 84/31.

nabbaþ see næfst.

nædre *wk. f.* snake, serpent 3/20, 4/12, 76/5, 93/20, etc.

næfde, næfden etc. see næfst.

næfre *adv.* never 31/28, 35/4, 76/6, 87/15, etc.

næfst III *pr. 2 sg.* have not 84/11. nabbaþ *pl.* 44/5. næfde *pa. t. 3 sg.* had not 15/12, 32/30, etc. næfdon *pl.* 111/1. næfden subj. pl. 33/22.

nægl *m.* nail 85/14, 85/16.

nænig *adj.* not any 17/5.

nænne see nan.

næran, nære, etc. see nis.

næs *adv.* not ~ *na* not at all 19/24, 42/32, 55/16, 57/9.

næs see nis.

genæson 5 *pa. t. pl.* survived 100/12.

nafela *wk. m.* navel 84/19.

nahton *pret. pres. vb. pa. t. pl.* did not have 52/21.

nales *adv.* not at all, by no means 24/12, 37/23, 56/23, etc. ~ *þæt an þæt(te)* . . . *ac (eac)* not only . . . but (also) 22/20, 26/28, 31/17, 91/20, etc. ~ *na* certainly not 44/13.

nam, naman, etc. see niman.

genam, gename, etc. see geniman.

nama see noma.

nan *pron. adj. as adj.* no 14/21, 16/2, 22/13, 22/17, etc. *as pron.* none 41/26, 52/31, 62/10, 84/4, etc.; no one 100/16, 109/14. nænne *asm.* 88/19, 111/1.

nanuht (*n.*) nothing 44/5, 80/1, 85/26, 95/28, etc. *as adv.* not at all 134/6.

nat *pret. pres. vb. pr. 1 sg.* do not know 65/25, 68/9, 113/5. nyte *1 pl.* 73/20. nyton *3 pl.* 74/15. nyste *pa. t. 3 sg.* did not know 14/28 etc.; nysse 14/12. nyston *pl.* 105/16. nysten *subj. pl.* 45/24.

naþelæs *adv.* none the less 69/13.

naþer, naþær, nawþer *pron.* neither 49/8, 49/9, 54/19, 147/13. naþer ne . . . ne neither . . . nor 38/6, 48/10, 52/21, 113/10, etc.

ne *particle* not 14/20, 14/25, 14/29, 15/2; *as conj.* nor 30/14, 37/3, 53/18, 156/16, etc. *as correl.* ne . . . ne . . . (ne) neither . . . nor . . . (nor), nor . . . nor 30/13, 70/13, etc.

neadinga *adv.* forcibly 27/30.

neah, neh *adv. and prep. w. dat.* near 8/24, 9/3, 9/26, 11/4, 84/13, etc.; almost, nearly 14/30, 50/12, 54/18, 71/8, etc. near *comp.* nearer, more nearly 11/1, 19/17, 49/10, 87/15, etc. nihst, nyhst *sup.* nearest 12/11, 17/18, 17/24, 37/14.

neahþeod *f.* neighbouring people 30/13, 53/27.

nealæcte I *pa. t. 3 sg. w. dat.* approached 125/6. nealæhtan *pl.* 35/14.

genealæcten I *pa. t. subj. pl.* drew 92/6.

near see neah.

nearo *adj.* narrow 21/11. nearwan *ds. wk.* 46/21, 68/21.

nearonesse *dsf.* narrowness, strait 9/5.

nearra *comp. adj.* nearer 11/23, 18/32, 19/8, 19/33, etc. nihst *sup.* nearest 60/30, 81/17; last 48/32, 133/2. æt *nihstan, nehstan, nyhstan* finally, at last 22/6, 22/24–5, 35/2, 49/22, etc.

nearwan see nearo.

neawest (*m. or f.*) neighbourhood 29/23.

ġenedde see ġeneþan.

nefa *wk. m.* nephew 33/1, 33/5, 33/15, 33/29, etc.; descendant 128/22.

neh, nehstan see neah, nearra.

nele *anom. vb. pr. 3 sg.* is unwilling, is not prepared to 131/20; nyle 113/10. nellaþ *pr. pl.* are unwilling 31/12, 67/9; nyllaþ 74/16, 77/6. nolde *pa. t. 3 sg.* would not, did not wish 26/7 etc. noldan *pl.* 38/20; noldon 31/28, etc. nolde *subj. pl.* 78/16.

ġenemde *pp. npl.* named 12/12.

nemneþ I *pr. 3 sg.* calls 1/1, 9/16, 9/27. nemnen *subj. pl.* call 10/4. nemnede *pp. npl.* named 42/26.

ġener *n.* refuge 33/22.

ġenerian I save 48/18, 94/32.

ġeneþan I venture 30/16. ġenedde *pa. t. 3 sg.* 84/18; ġeneþde 100/12. neþing *f.* daring, risk 74/19.

nicealt *adj.* newly plastered 151/9 (v. l. niwcilctan).

nied (*n.*) compulsion, time of distress or need 44/16, 94/8, 94/9.

ġeniedan I force, compel 29/8, 40/5, 42/10, 47/23, etc. ġenyd *pp.* 21/27.

nieddon I *pa. t. pl.* forced 150/2, 153/6.

niede *adv.* of necessity 115/29.

niedling, nydling *m.* slave 24/24, 39/29, 67/1.

niedþearf(*f.*) necessity 118/28.

nieten, nyten *n.* cattle, beast 22/3, 25/22, 25/28, 85/26, etc.

nigan, nigon, nygan *num.* nine 21/19, 43/12, 48/30, 68/17, etc.

nigantiene *num.* nineteen 70/20.

nigeþa, nygoþa *wk. adj.* ninth 26/3, 137/11, 138/21.

nigon see nigan.

nigonwintre *adj.* nine years old 99/17.

nihst see neah, nearra.

niht *f.* night 16/22, 47/1, 58/12, 86/25, etc.; *ds.* 1/17; *apl.* 82/23.

nihtes *adv.* by night 26/4, 30/18, 51/23, etc.

ġenihtsumnisse *dsf.* condition of plenty 97/22.

niman 4 take 34/13, 73/31, 85/13, 130/11; *wicstowa* ~ set up camp 44/23. ~ *to suna* adopt 32/30. ~ *to wife* marry 156/20. nimþ *pr. 3 sg.* 17/24; nymþ 23/10. nimaþ *pl.* 17/31. nime *subj. sg.* 97/30. nam *pa. t. 3 sg.* 32/30; nom 118/21. namon *pl.* 8/4; naman 29/21. name *subj. sg.* 44/23. namen *pl.* 152/14.

ġeniman 4 take, take possession of 17/24, 22/25, 29/17, 31/24, etc.; seize, capture 23/26, 27/30, 84/27; ~ *ġeþoht* get an idea 156/2; ~ *friþ* make peace 5/23. ġenam *pa. t. 3 sg.* 5/23; ġenom 80/19. ġenamon *pl.* 23/26; ġenaman 59/14; ġenoman 28/15. ġename *pa. t. subj. 3 sg.* 54/3. ġenamen *pl.* 39/32. ġenumen *pp.* 2/1.

nirewett *n.* narrow place 66/19.

nis *anom. vb. neg. pr. 3 sg.* is not 32/1. næs *pa. t. 3 sg.* was not 24/20, 27/25, etc. næran *pl.* were not 106/18; næron 43/6. nære *subj. sg.* should not be, were not 22/27. næren *pl.* 35/9; nære 87/15. þær *Mutius nære* had it not been for Mucius 41/1.

niþ *m.* hostility, ill will, rancour 22/12, 82/18, 99/16, 132/6, 156/14.

niþer *adv.* down 123/21, 125/29.

ġeniþerade II *pa. t. 3 sg.* brought low 48/15, 63/26; ġeniþrode 25/27; ġenyþerode 26/18.

niwan *adv.* newly 49/28.

niwe *adj.* new 4/17, 95/13, 98/10, 101/5, etc. niwu *apl. f.* 30/29.

niwlice *adv.* newly, recently 107/29, 137/5, 139/24, 147/1.

ġenog, ġenoh *adj.* enough 17/6, 118/18, 137/4, 141/16.

ġenog, ġenoh *adv.* sufficiently, very 31/9 (2×), 35/28, 69/28.

noht (*n*.) nothing 63/28, 70/1, 98/22, 106/35, etc.; as *adv*. not at all 53/17.
noldan, nolde, etc. see nele.
nom see niman.
genom, genoman see geniman.
noma, nama *wk. m.* name 16/36, 20/3, 20/18, 20/31, etc. namon *as.* 54/29. nomon *ds.* 140/22.
norþ *adv.* north 10/15, 10/16, 11/13, 11/16, etc. norþor *comp.* the further north 15/26. norþmest *sup.* northmost 13/30.
norþan *adv.* from the north 8/16, 14/13, 123/15. be ~ to the north 9/29; *w. dat.* north of 9/25, 9/27, 10/21, 10/22 etc. wiþ ~ north of. *w. acc.* 12/21; *w. dat.* 12/24.
norþaneastan *adv. be* ~ to the northeast 19/9; *w. dat.* north-east of 13/10.
norþanwestan *adv. be* ~ *w. dat.* to the north-west of 12/29.
norþdæl *m.* northern part 1/24, 8/18, 8/24, 19/27, etc.
norþeastende *m.* north-east end 12/2.
norþeastlang *adj.* extending to the north-east 19/11.
norþerne *adj.* northern 11/18.
norþ(e)weard *adj.* to the north of, the northern part of 14/1, 15/33 (2×). on norþeweardum in the northern part 36/18.
norþeweard *adv.* northwards, in the north 15/28.
norþhealf(*f.*) north side 10/28, 18/14, 19/14.
norþland *n.* northern land 21/29.
norþgemæro *npl. n.* northern boundaries, northern limits 10/6, 10/12.
norþmest *sup. adj.* furthest north 26/31, 133/5.
norþmest *sup. adv.* see norþ.
norþor see norþ.
norþryhte *adv.* in a northerly direction, directly northwards 12/18, 14/6, 14/7, 14/10.
norþsceata *wk. m.* northern promontory 21/3.
norþweard see norþeweard.
norþwest *adv.* north-west 19/5.
norþwestende (*m.*) north-west end 117/1.

norþwestgemære (*n*.) north-west boundary 9/14.
notu *f.* use 31/10.
nu *adv.* now 9/18, 9/19, 10/8, 12/12, etc. as *conj.* (*often in correl. w. adv.*) now that, since 11/25, 44/3, 49/6, 61/1, etc.
nugiet, nugyt *adv.* still 24/13, 26/23, 38/7, 44/14, etc.
genumen see geniman.
nunne *wk. f.* nun (used of Vestal Virgin) 3/7, 4/2, 60/9, 88/5.
genyd see geniedan.
nydling see niedling.
nygan see nigan.
nygoþe see nigeþa.
nyhst see neah, nearra.
nyle, nyllaþ see nele.
nymþ see niman.
nysse, nyste, etc. see nat.
nyte, nyton see nat.
nyten see nieten.
nytt (*f.*) use 42/20.
nyt(t) *adj.* useful, helpful 51/24, 113/5.
genyþerode see geniþerade.

O

oeþel (*m. or n.*) country, home 101/27, 131/16, 131/20. repr. by rune ᛟ 90/20.
of *prep. w. dat.* out of, from, from among, of 3/21, 3/27, 25/15, 35/13, 46/12, etc.; by 19/2, 56/8, 68/32; on 28/18, 65/20; about, concerning 14/27, 14/28, 28/2; because of, through 23/5, 23/28, 23/30, 56/24; off (from) 45/7, 106/1, 115/22. *w. instr.* out of 40/12. *ellipt. and quasi-adv.* off 40/22, 86/21.
ofbeotan 7 *pa. t. pl.* beat to death 50/21.
ofdune *adv.* down 59/11.
ofer *prep. w. acc.* over, across 1/15, 4/29, 9/12, 9/13, etc.; contrary to, against 8/5, 47/15, 70/3; after 121/16; throughout 6/10, 59/12, 106/27; after comp. in excess of, more than 23/25 (*for* 101/32 *see* hierra); *w. dat.* over 23/7, 110/10. *as adv.* over, across 16/10, 48/13.
oferbrec 4 *imp. sg.* violate 127/22.
oferbræc *pa. t. 3 sg.* violated 60/1.

oferclom 3 *pa. t. 3 sg.* climbed upon, over 73/10.

ofercuman 4 overcome, subdue 54/4, 93/23, 95/16, 131/30, etc. ofercom *pa. t. 3 sg.* 6/6. ofercome *subj. sg.* 68/32. ofercumen *pp.* 42/2. ofercumene *npl.* 95/19.

oferdrencton I *pa. t. pl.* intoxicated 117/9.

oferdrifen 1 *pa. t. subj. pl.* cover by driving 26/26.

ofereode *anom. vb. pa. t. 3 sg.* passed away 115/13, 115/17.

oferfæreld (*m. or n.*) passage 43/6, 44/20.

oferfaran 6 cross 43/8, 43/14, 99/27, 105/30. oferfor *pa. t. 3 sg.* 43/14. oferfaren *pp.* 105/30.

oferferan I cross over 15/30, 15/31, 26/19.

oferfleow 7 *pa. t. 3 sg.* overflowed 23/2.

oferflitanne 1 *dat. inf.* confute 149/12.

oferfon 7 seize 89/5.

oferfor see oferfaran.

oferfroren 2 *pp.* frozen over 18/1, 110/9.

oferfunden 3 *pp.* put to the test 155/23.

oferfyrre *dsf.* excessive distance 19/20.

ofergongen 7 *pp.* passed 87/3. See also ofereode.

oferhebban 6 omit 27/22.

oferheortnesse *ds(f.)* excessive feeling 89/26.

oferherge(a)de II *pa. t. 3 sg.* ravaged, laid waste, overran 4/15, 45/28, 69/13, 95/2, etc. oferhergedon *pl.* 31/4; oferhergedan 57/24; oferhergodon 3/4.

oferhi(e)rde I *pa. t. 3 sg.* overheard 34/10; *w. dat.* disobeyed 75/33. oferhierdon *pl.* 111/13.

oferhlæstan I overload 94/30, 95/7, 129/27.

oferhogode III *pa. t. 3 sg.* disdained 153/4.

ofermæte *adj.* immense 26/17, 48/7, 58/9.

ofermætlic *adj.* immense 32/25.

ofermetto *f.* pride, arrogance 25/26, 26/17, 48/14, 48/15, etc.

ofermodig *adj.* proud 56/11. ofermodgan *gs. wk.* 40/27. ofermodgast, -gest *sup.* proudest 37/19, 40/4.

ofermycel *adj.* excessive. ofermycelo *nsf.* 26/28.

oferstag 1 *pa. t. 3 sg.* scaled 93/2.

oferswiþan I overcome, conquer 22/15, 62/14, 86/10, 89/1, etc.

ofersylefredan I *pa. t. pl.* covered with silver 75/26. ofersylefreda *pp. npl. n.* 79/22.

oferwadan 6 wade across 43/12.

oferwinnan 3 overcome, subdue 3/18, 5/12, 6/5, 63/16, etc. oferwinnanne *dat. inf.* 46/18. oferwan(n) *pa. t. 3 sg.* 22/5; oferwon(n) 3/16. oferwunnan *pl.* 113/12; oferwunnon 5/18. oferwunne *pa. t. subj. sg.* 111/27. oferwunnen *pl.* 63/17; *pp.* 53/11. oferwunnene *npl.* 117/29.

oferwlenced *adj.* excessively opulent 29/2.

oferwon(n) see oferwinnan.

oferworhte I *pa. t. 3 sg.* covered over, overlaid 90/23.

oferwunnan, oferwunne, etc. see oferwinnan.

offeallen 7 *pp.* destroyed 137/29.

offor 6 *pa. t. 3 sg.* overtook, intercepted 64/27 (*w. pl. subject*). offoran *pl.* 83/12.

of(f)rung *f.* sacrifice, sacrificial offering 2/10, 57/10.

ofgeafan 5 *pa. t. pl.* gave up 23/16.

ofre *ds(m.)* bank 12/20.

ofrian II make offerings 35/1, 59/22, 88/3, 98/16, etc. ofrede *pa. t. 3 sg.* 134/2. ofredan *pl.* 98/16. ofreden *subj. pl.* 35/1.

ofsceat 2 *pa. t. 3 sg.* shot down 114/27. ofscoten *pp.* 22/7, 78/24.

ofscotod II *pp.* shot 109/18.

ofslean 6 kill, slay 5/11, 5/23, 33/8, 81/14, etc. ofslog *pa. t. 3 sg.* 4/12; ofsloh 22/5; afslog 82/31. ofslogan *pl.* 28/7; ofslogon 5/26. ofsloge *subj. sg.* 15/5. ofslagen *pp.* 5/10; ofslægen 46/3; ofslegen 27/25. ofslægene *npl.* 29/18; ofslagene 96/10; ofslegene 23/14. ofslagenre *gpl.* 52/36. *ofslagen wære* would have been killed 99/31.

ofsmorode II *pa. t. 3 sg.* strangled 154/22. ofsmorod *pp.* suffocated 151/12.

ofstang see ofstong.

ofsticade II *pa. t. 3 sg.* stabbed 130/16. ofsticedon *pl.* 129/3.

ofstong, ofstang 3 *pa. t. 3 sg.* stabbed 65/24, 84/19, 136/2, 137/27, etc.

ofswungon 3 *pa. t. pl.* flogged to death 83/15.

oft *adv.* often, frequently 10/4, 53/10, 98/10, 103/5, etc. oftost *sup.* very often, most often 88/28, 103/3, 108/4, 117/2. *swa oft swa conj.* whenever 98/16, 115/25, 145/4.

oftorfod II *pp.* stoned to death 109/19.

oftrædlica *adj. npl. n.* frequent 149/7. oftrædlican *dpl.* 72/28.

oftrædlice *adv.* frequently 21/28, 62/20, 65/9, 88/30, etc.

oftredd I *pp.* trampled on 137/10.

oftsiþ *m. on oftsiþas* frequently 153/12.

oftyrfdon I *pa. t. pl.* stoned to death 93/9.

ofþyncendum I *pr. p. ds. impers. w. dat.* causing displeasure to 33/2, 46/29, etc. oþþyncende *ns.* 123/2. ofþuhte *pa. t. 3 sg.* caused regret to 64/8; caused displeasure to 87/19, 124/19.

ofworpen 3 *pp.* stoned to death 86/6.

olecung (*f.*) flattery 61/28.

on, an *prep.* on, in *w. acc.* to, onto, into 1/2, 2/2, 3/3, 8/13, etc.; on, in 8/18, 10/26, 14/8, 46/26; upon 5/6; according to 3/15, 30/30, 34/17; against 4/25, 27/19, 29/3, 45/17. *w. dat.* in 1/3, 1/13, 1/17, 8/18; on 3/24, 46/10, 76/6; into, to 139/9, 154/8; at a distance of 3/4 (*or acc.?*), 17/20; against 127/9; from 44/4, 48/36, 53/14, 79/28; by, at 72/9, 82/8; in respect of 51/17, 51/18; among 42/32. *w. instr.* on, in 67/24, 117/17. *on dæg* during the day 119/25. *on niht* by night 16/4. *on siml* see simbel. *as adv.* (*w. ellipsis*) on 23/9, 84/33; from 113/9.

on *conj.* see ond.

onbad 1 *pa. t. 3 sg. w. gen.* awaited 127/4.

onbærnan I burn, ignite 78/29, 85/14, 106/21, 137/21, 142/2.

onbead 2 *pa. t. 3 sg.* announce, send word 79/28, 111/11, 134/14; declare 129/17. onbudon *pl.* ordered 126/12.

onbide see anbid.

onbudon see onbead.

onbugan 2 bow 139/8; submit 34/2. anbugen *pa. t. subj. pl.* 34/2.

onbutan *adv.* about 65/10.

oncnawan 7 know, understand, perceive 26/15, 38/13, 44/4, 53/15. oncnewen *pa. t. subj. pl.* 38/13.

ond, and *conj.* and (*almost always 7 in the MSS*) 8/20, 11/9, 15/4, 91/4, etc. on 9/1. *gelice 7* just as. See gelice.

onddrysne see andrysne.

ondliefen *f.* sustenance 96/31.

ondlong, andlang, ondlang *prep. w. gen.* along 8/20, 10/14, 12/2, 18/14, etc.

ondrædan 7 dread 45/22, 90/20, etc.; *w. refl. dat. pron.* 27/16, 48/12, 62/22, 74/18 etc. ondrædende *pr. p.* 41/13. ondrædendum *dpl.* 23/25. ondred, andred *pa. t. 3 sg.* 32/21. ondredan, andredan *pl.* 74/4; ondredon 26/15; ondrædan 75/3.

ondrædenlic *adj.* fearful 87/2.

ondræding *f.* terror, dread 50/10, 128/27.

ondwlita *wk. m.* face 127/25.

ondwyrdan I *w. dat. of person and gen. of thing* answer 29/1, 69/27, 84/10, 85/4, etc.

ondwyrde *n.* answer 29/4, 107/10 (2×), 117/22, 117/23. anwyrde 95/25.

geondwyrdon see geandwyrdan.

ondyde see andon.

onemn *prep. w. dat.* during. ~ *þæm* at the same time 70/28.

onfon, anfon 7 receive, accept *w. acc.* 25/4; *w. dat.* 69/16, 141/20, 147/18, etc.; *w. gen.* 27/7, 79/31. onfeng, anfeng *pa. t. 3 sg.* 37/18, 54/7; onfengc 25/4. onfengon, anfengon *pl.* 136/17, 69/12. onfengen *subj. pl.* 40/20. onfangen *pp.* 55/11.

onfunde, onfundon see anfunde.
ongan(n) see onginnan.
onge(a)n, angean *prep. w. acc.*
towards, opposite 19/3, 19/4, 19/5,
19/6, etc.; against 6/12, 33/24,
51/11; to meet 42/3, 46/21. *w. dat.*
towards, to meet 9/21, 21/16, 41/29,
41/31; against 5/29, 33/10, 40/27,
41/25. *w. ellipsis* 76/15, 99/6.
ongean *adv.* opposite 16/11.
ongeanweard *adj. w. dat.* going
towards 150/13.
ongeat, ongeatan etc. see ongietan.
ongen see ongean.
ongi(e)tan, angitan 5 realize, understand 36/24, 44/4, 58/3, 88/1, etc.
w. gen. know of 49/13. angite *pr. 1
sg.* 49/13. ongeat *pa. t. 3 sg.* 109/19;
angeat 79/18; onget 117/5.
ongeatan *pl.* 74/9; angeatan 57/8;
ongeaton 141/14; angeaton 153/
25. ongeaten *subj. pl.* 38/10.
onginn *n.* see anginn.
on-, anginnan 3 begin, proceed to
11/28, 35/15, 53/5, etc.; undertake,
attempt 72/9, 72/10, 82/1, 109/1;
attack 30/17, 68/11. onginþ *pr. 3
sg.* 8/23; onginneþ 1/1. onginnaþ
pl. 9/11. ongan(n) *pa. t. 3 sg.* 21/24;
angan(n) 32/19, 60/29; ongon(n)
1/3. ongunnon *pl.* 6/8; angunnan
53/21; angunnon 71/19. angunnen *subj. pl.* 64/21. *pp.* 56/2;
ongunnen 108/31.
ongitan see ongietan.
ongon(n) see onginnan.
onguldon see angeald.
ongunnen, ongunnon see onginnan.
onhætan I heat 34/10, 99/26.
oninnan *prep. w. dat.* in the middle
of 26/22. See also þæroninnan.
oninnan *adv.* inside 23/4, 34/7.
onlicnes *f.* image, statue 53/1, 69/25,
114/7, 136/1. onlicnesse *as.* 2/6;
anlicnesse 34/6. onlicnessa,
anlicnessa *napl.* 34/3, 114/7.
onlicost *sup. adv.* most like. ~ *swelce*
just as though 76/6.
onsægden III *pa. t. subj. pl.* should
offer sacrifice 35/1.
onsendan I send out, send forth
54/5, 104/5, 106/20, 109/8, etc.

onseon 5 look on 99/15.
onsien *f.* sight 138/18.
onstealde I *pa. t. 3 sg.* instituted
138/6. onsteled *pp.* originated
55/29.
onstyrede see anstyred.
ontydre I *pr. subj. 3 sg.* should
nourish 98/1.
onufan *prep. w. dat.* upon 64/30,
84/20, 85/17, 141/16.
onwalda *wk. m.* ruler 134/13.
onw(e)ald, anw(e)ald, anwold *m.*
jurisdiction, rule, power, dominion,
empire 2/12, 4/5, 6/1, 21/25, 37/32,
51/6, etc. anwaldas *gs.* 69/34.
onwealdun *dpl.* 36/11.
onwealg *adj.* whole, safe and sound
38/1.
onwendan, anwendan I change
139/18; convert 104/4; overthrow
30/30, 150/16.
onwinnende 3 *pr. p. w. dat.* attacking, fighting against 98/11, 145/6.
anwann *pa. t. sg.* attacked 61/20,
64/4.
onwocan 6 *pa. t. pl.* awoke 86/27.
onwoce *subj. sg.* arose 112/31.
open *adj.* open, public 59/6, 59/7,
129/18.
openlice *adv.* openly, publicly 57/4,
123/8, 123/11, 150/16, 152/12.
ordfruma *wk. m.* author 27/5, 122/26,
125/5.
orgyte *adj.* manifest 26/23.
ormæte *adj.* enormous 47/13.
orn see iernan.
ortriewe *adj.* despairing 85/27.
geortriewe I *pr. subj. sg. w. dat.*
doubt, fail to trust 49/2.
orwene *adj.* despairing 102/11.
oþ *prep. w. acc.* until 17/12, 47/1,
50/17, etc.; up to, as far as 9/13,
10/10, 11/11, 56/17, etc.
oþ *conj.* until 5/26, 16/8, 17/23, 21/26,
etc.; oþ þe 17/17; oþ þæt, oþþæt
37/7, 37/15; oþ þætte 40/2.
oþbrudon 3 *pa. t. pl.* rescued 80/22.
oþbrude *subj. sg.* 137/23.
oþer *pron. adj. strong* other, another,
second, one (of two). *as adj.* 1/19,
5/26, 14/11, 73/19. *as pron.* 18/1,
32/9, 54/3, 54/5, etc. *correl. oþer . . .
oþer* one . . . another, the other

15/20, 30/2–3, 54/1, 72/22. oþer . . .
oþþe . . . oþþe either . . . or 28/27–8,
29/11, 41/8, 66/20; oþer þara . . .
oþþe . . . oþþe 63/15, 74/15, 155/6–7.
~ healf hund one hundred and
fifty 75/13. oþþre npl. m. 125/17.
oþran dsm. and n. 66/15, 85/11.
oþewde I pa. t. 3 sg. appeared 110/3;
revealed, showed 152/12. oþ(i)e-
wed pp. revealed 2/22, 73/31, 85/7,
137/6.
oþfleon 2 flee away, escape 52/11,
52/32, 53/24, 63/3, etc.; w. dat. flee
from, escape from 23/17, 52/34.
oþfleah pa. t. 3 sg. 76/9. oþflugon
pl. 25/3. oþflogen pp. 109/17.
oþhydan I hide from 52/34.
oþiewed see oþewde.
oþra, oþran, etc. see oþer.
oþsace 6 pr. subj. sg. deny 136/28.
oþsworan 6 pa. t. pl. denied on oath
87/14.
oþþæt see oþ.
oþþe conj. or 14/12, 14/16, 14/26,
15/19, etc. correl. oþþe . . . oþþe . . .
(oþþe) either . . . or . . . (or) 31/15,
42/19, 73/24, etc. See also oþ þe.
oþþre see oþer.
oþþringan 3 w. dat. of person and acc.
of thing deprive of 74/11.
oþþyncende see ofþyncendum.
oþwitaþ 1 pr. pl. taunt with 97/22.

P

palendsan wk. ds. palace 143/24.
palistas ballistae dpl. 93/25 (OH apl.
ballistas).
patricius n. or apl. (or sg. ?) patricians
134/23 (OH apl. patricios).
philosophus m. philosopher, orator
140/23. philosofum as. 71/27;
filosofum 78/20. philosophe ds.
61/13, 67/27.
piniende II pr. p. tormenting 25/23.
pinedon, pa. t. pl. tortured 41/3,
140/18.
pinung f. torture 34/1, 34/4.
plega wk. m. sport, game, play 17/12,
17/14, 34/9, 135/2, etc.
plegedon II pa. t. pl. played, diverted
themselves 3/25, 65/20, 83/9.
pleo ds(n.) peril 61/18.

pleolecestan sup. adj. npl. wk. most
dangerous 50/24.
port m. port 16/2, 16/13; promontory? 9/24 (2×, see Commentary),
9/26, 9/27.
preost m. priest 143/12.
pretorium as(m. ?) praetor 77/1 (OH
praetor).
proletarii npl. (m. ?) the proletarii
83/21.
pund n. pound 52/9, 92/9, 104/28.
purpure wk. f. purple garment 89/4,
89/7, 147/16, 147/24, 150/4.
pyle pillow (m. ?) 124/23.
pytt m. pit 114/9.

R

racente wk. f. chain 70/9, 113/26.
racentan dpl. 106/33.
gerad n. intention, condition. on þæt
~ þæt with the intention that 33/16,
66/28; on condition that 96/24,
102/3, 107/23; on hwelc ~ with what
intention 124/24.
gerad adj. w. gen. expert in 21/32.
geræcan I obtain 54/19, 73/5, 113/
9; seize 68/7; capture 43/18. geræceanne dat. inf. 113/9. geræhte
pa. t. 3 sg. 73/6; gerahte 43/18. See
also gereccan.
ræd m. counsel 90/4, 98/10, 106/8.
ræde 7 pr. subj. sg. let him read 32/3.
redon pa. t. pl. took counsel 35/5.
rædehere (m.) mounted force, cavalry
68/17, 83/29.
rædlecre comp. adj. nsn. more ad-
visable 54/3, 112/28.
rædþeahtere m. counsellor 42/16,
134/23.
rædþeahtung (f.) counsel 83/31.
rædwæn (m.) chariot 147/16.
geræht, gerahte see geræcan,
gerecc(e)an.
rap (m.) rope 154/23.
raþe adv. quickly, soon 24/24, 26/11,
35/5, 39/2, 52/1, etc. raþor comp.
sooner 41/17. raþost sup. most
quickly 135/16. ~ þæs immediately,
shortly after 11/6, 49/20, 75/29,
78/16, etc. swa ~ swa as soon as, as
readily as 33/18, 89/13–14. ~ þæs þe
conj. as soon as 86/4, 86/9, 91/5,
91/18, etc.

read *adj.* red (always ref. to *mare rubrum*) 1/16, 10/7, 10/14, 11/14, etc.

ġereafade II *pa. t. 3 sg.* stole 79/28.

reafere (*m.*) bandit 114/13.

reaflac (*m. or n.*) robbery 114/14.

reafunġ *f*, plundering 48/22.

reccan I interpret 23/29.

ġerecc(e)an I set forth, show 9/20, 132/25. **ġeræht** *pp.* reproved (so BTS, with comment that it 'might be taken under geræcan') 33/24.

reccend (*m.*) ruler, guide 36/6, 36/9.

redon see **ræde**.

ġerefa *wk.* (*m.*) public or royal official 153/6.

ren *m.* rain, rainstorm 103/24, 103/26, 103/27, 104/1, etc.

ġerenian II put. *to bismre* ~ humiliate 66/25.

ġereord (*n. or f.*) language 74/21; meal 90/4.

ġerestan I *pa. t. pl. refl. w. gen.* desisted from 41/21.

repe *adj.* fierce, cruel 1/27, 30/34, 56/25.

repnesse *dsf.* cruelty 1/5.

ribb (*n.*) rib 93/27, 93/30.

rice *n.* kingdom, dominion, empire 1/4, 3/14, 7/11, 7/12, 36/9, etc.; rule, reign 27/25, 37/27, etc.

rice *adj.* powerful, mighty, important 41/16, 107/8, 144/4. **ricost-, ricest-** *sup.* most important, most powerful 17/3, 63/24, 71/17, 136/5.

ricsian II reign, rule, hold sway 1/3, 5/21, 21/24, 33/34, etc. **ricsade** *pa. t. 3 sg.* 24/18; **ricsode** 24/30. **ricsedon** *pl.* 36/11.

ridan I ride 17/25, 42/7, 61/29. **ridep** *pr. 3 sg.* 17/25. **ridendra** *pr. p. gpl.* 61/29.

rihtwis see **ryhtwis**.

ġerimanne I *dat. inf.* reckon 46/18.

rimde I *pa. t. 3 sg.* counted, should count 84/29.

ġerimes *gs*(*n.*) in number 118/21.

rinan I rain 3/27, 87/10, 141/15.

ripon I *pa. t. pl.* reaped 100/35.

ġerise I *pa. t. subj. sg., impers. w. dat.* became, befitted 34/12.

ġerisenlicre *comp. adj. nsn.* more fitting 48/1.

ġerisna *npl.* (*n.*) what is fitting.

hiora ~ *nære* it was not fitting for them 95/30.

rustega *adj. npl.* (*n.*) rusty 132/13.

ġeryht (*n.*) straight line. *on geryhte* directly 19/6.

ryht *adj.* right, just, upright, true 2/12, 35/29, 140/14, 149/11, etc. **ryhtcynecynn** (*n.*) legitimate royal family 81/13. **ryhte** *adv.* directly 12/27; exactly 43/25. **ryhtor** *comp.* more accurately 113/18. **ryhtlicran** *comp. adj. dsf.* more fitting, more proper 36/6. **ryhtnorþanwind** (*m.*) due north wind 14/15. **ryhtwestende** (*m.*) extreme western limit 9/15. **ryhtwis, rihtwis** *adj.* righteous, just 1/9, 23/22.

ryne (*m.*) course 131/8.

S

sacu *f.* strife 98/2, 122/25, 135/17.

sæ *m. and occas. f.* sea 1/16, 3/24, 4/18, 9/4, etc.; inland sea, lake 11/8, 11/9, 11/12. **se** 96/14.

ġesæd, ġesæde see **ġesecgan**.

sæde, sæden, -on see **secgan**.

sæearm *m.* arm of the sea 18/6.

sæfæreld (*m. or n.*) sea-passage 26/22.

sæflod (*m. or n.*) sea flood 51/14.

ġesægd see **ġesecgan**.

sægde, sægden, -on see **secgan**.

sægen *f.* statement 59/24, 71/23, 75/31, 98/33.

sægþ see **secgan**.

sæl *m.* occasion 88/19.

ġesælig *adj.* happy, fortunate. **ġesælgum** *dpl.* 116/21.

ġesæt, -on see **ġesittan**.

sæt(t), sæte etc. see **sittan**.

saġlum *dpl.* (*m.*) cudgels 50/21.

sam *conj. correl.* ~ ... ~ whether ... or 18/1.

same see **some**.

ġesamnode see **ġesomnedon**.

samod *adv.* together 16/34.

sand, sond *n.* sand 11/6, 11/7, 11/8, 11/10, etc.

sariġ *adj.* sorrowful 29/19, 132/3, 153/9.

gesawan, gesawe etc. see geseon.
sawlum dpl.(f.) souls 57/11.
scæl see sculan.
scamlicost sup. adj. most shameful 25/24.
gesceadwislice adv. wisely, discreetly 29/1. gescadwislecor comp. more clearly 36/23.
sceal(l) see sculan.
sceap (n.) sheep 15/13.
scearp adj. sharp, rough 10/5, 85/14, 113/10.
sceat see scyt.
sceata wk. m. corner, angle 21/3, 21/7.
sceawigean II see 32/11. sceawode pa. t. 3 sg. looked carefully at, scrutinized 34/11.
sceawung (f.) surveying, inspection 14/31.
sceld, scield m. shield 100/33, 121/31, 145/18.
gescend I pp. put to shame 47/12.
sceolan, sceolde etc. see sculan.
gesceop 6 pa. t. 3 sg. created 35/29, 36/5. gesceope subj. sg. 2/12.
sceorfende 3 pr. p. gnawing 26/2.
sceorp n. apparel 75/26, 89/6.
scield see sceld.
sciet see scyt.
scildan I w. dat. protect 85/18.
gescildan I protect 44/15, 49/3, 56/9, 93/28. gescylde pa. t. 3 sg. 24/4.
gescildnisse ds(f.) protection 104/5.
scinendra ppl. adj. comp. ns. more brightly shining 131/3.
scinlac (n.) rage, frenzy 60/17, 71/13.
scinlac adj. magical, phantasmal 3/19 (v. l. scinlæc-)
scinlaca wk. m. magician, sorcerer 3/19, 76/4.
scinncræft (m.) magic 57/8.
scip, scyp n. ship 4/10, 4/11, 4/20, 25/3, etc. scipa napl. 15/38. scipe gpl. 4/14. scipun dpl. 30/17.
scipgebroc (n.) shipwreck 32/5.
scipfierd (f.) naval force 47/14.
sciphere (m.) naval force, war fleet 5/4, 55/7, 69/11, 92/29, etc. scipehere 54/12.
sciphlæst (m.) body of (fighting) men on a ship 96/12.

sciprap m. ship-rope, cable 15/1, 15/16, 15/19.
scir f. district 16/1; office 54/9, 150/20.
sciran I w. gen. get rid of 63/23.
scole dsf. school 150/5.
gescomian II impers. w. acc. put to shame 111/16, 156/1.
scond (f.) disgrace 48/23.
scondlic adj. shameful 30/24, 60/16.
scondlicost sup. most shameful 51/21; scondlicestena gpl. 27/28.
scondlice adv. humiliatingly 33/24.
scop m. poet 23/23, 24/8, 31/31, 35/12, etc.
scopleoþ (n.) poem 35/15, 42/33, 137/24.
scortlice adv. briefly 9/18, 12/14, 21/21, 35/22, etc.
scot (n.) shot 73/12.
gescot (n.) shooting 155/4; missile 73/30.
gescruncan 3 pa. t. pl. contracted 68/26.
[sculan] pret. pres. vb. shall, must, ought, have to, be obliged to, supposed to, destined to 17/11, 17/31, 27/23, 28/2, etc. w. to, wiþ, ut or hwider and ellipsis of inf. of vb. of motion must go etc. 49/2, 54/3, 151/1. in pa. t. w. inf. denoting assertion that is matter of report and may be untrue was supposed to, was said to 60/9, 109/10. sceal(l) pr. 1, 3 sg. 15/17, 16/6, 27/22; scæl 37/22. sculon pr. pl. 152/13; sceolan 47/6; sceolon 17/19. scyle subj. sg. 66/8. sceolde pa. t. 3 sg. 14/14. sceoldonpl. 83/22; sceoldan 40/10. sceolden subj. pl. 28/27.
gescylde see gescildan.
scyle see sculan.
scyll (f.) scale (of a serpent) 93/24.
scyp see scip.
gescyrtan I curtail 27/23.
scyt 2 pr. 3 sg shoots, moves rapidly, thrusts 9/15, 10/15, 11/10, 12/3, etc.; sciet 9/8. sceat pa. t. 3 sg. shot 64/29, 93/24.
scyte (m.) shooting 29/34.
scytta wk. (m.) archer 93/22.
se see sæ.
se m., seo f., þæt n. pron. adj. def.

se (*cont.*):
art. the one, that, the, this *as adj.*
and *art.* 1/8, 1/15, 1/19, 11/9, 15/2,
etc.; *as pron.* 10/1, 18/24, 20/33,
23/9, etc.; he, that man 17/24, 80/30.
as rel. pron. who, which, what 1/6,
8/12, 8/23, 8/24, etc.; se se 131/3,
131/10. þæt sint these are 9/29.
þæt wæron these were 14/23; who
were 30/21. þæs from that time,
after this 76/8, 105/18, 120/26. þæs
on morgenne on the following morning 57/27. þæs þe conj. after, after
which 138/9. raþe þæs, sona þæs see
raþe, sona. þæs þe swiþor all
the more 128/27. þy for this reason
17/34. þy, þon, þe w. comp. the
29/34, 40/24, 53/18, 137/19. þy
conj. because 72/20. For compound
conjunctions see æfter, for, mid,
to, etc. Forms: se nsm. 1/9; þe
133/9. þone asm. 1/11; þæne 17/17.
þæt n. and asn. 1/6. þæs gsm. and
n. 1/13, 23/7. þæm dsm. and n. 1/4,
2/6; þam 8/8. þy instr. m. and
n. 16/36, 17/12; þe 128/27; þon
28/20; þan 17/25. seo nsf. 1/1;
sio 2/27. þa asf. 3/3. þære g. and
dsf. 3/4, 9/13. þa napl. 1/6. þara
gpl. 6/20; þæra 41/4. þæm dpl.
4/24; þam 51/17.
ᵹeseah see ᵹeseon.
ᵹeseald, ᵹesealde, etc. see ᵹesellan.
sealde, sealden, -on see sellan.
sealt adj. salt 10/27, 20/6, 20/11.
seara see searu.
searawrenc (m.) crafty trick 47/26.
seariᵹende II pr. p. pining away
96/5.
searu (f. or n.) treachery, stratagem.
sear(e)we ds. 33/11, 68/15. seara
apl. 29/18. searwum dpl. 42/31;
searewan 62/9.
sec(e)an I seek, go to, visit 44/23,
45/31, 56/13, 74/25 etc. sohte þa. t.
3 sg. 15/9. sohton pl. 74/22. sohte
subj. pl. 31/2.
ᵹesecan I seek out, visit, attack
41/26, 53/13, 71/5, 74/24, etc.; eard
~ return home 41/26. ᵹesohte þa.
t. 3 sg. 54/26. ᵹesohton pl. 27/10;
ᵹesohtan 1/19.

secᵹ(e)an III say, speak, relate,
inform 3/15, 11/5, 13/29, 14/1, etc.;
speak of, announce 11/27, 24/2, etc.;
impersonal be said, related 11/14,
27/14. sæᵹþ pr. 3 sg. 32/6. sæ(ᵹ)de
þa. t. 1, 3 sg. 13/29, 31/31; sede
70/7. sæ(ᵹ)don pl. 11/27, 37/25;
sæᵹden 36/25; sedon 88/18.
sæ(ᵹ)den subj. pl. 8/14, 75/30.
ᵹesecᵹ(e)an III say, speak of 32/24,
36/23, 43/19, 50/23, etc. ᵹesæ(ᵹ)d
pp. 9/18, 35/22. ~ be speak about
21/21.
secþ see sec(e)an.
sede, sedon see secᵹ(e)an.
seftnesse ds(f.) leisure 147/25.
seᵹl (m. or n.) sail 16/23, 92/20.
seᵹlde I þa. t. 3 sg. sailed 107/5.
seᵹlian II sail 16/6, 16/13, 16/15.
ᵹeseᵹlian II sail 16/4.
seldon adv. seldom, rarely 90/27.
seldsiene adj. unfamiliar 44/24.
selest see soelest.
self, seolf, sylf pron. adj. self decl.
strong in agreement w. noun or pers.
pron. myself, yourself, himself, etc.
3/16, 14/29, 27/15, etc. in ns.
agreeing w. subj. sometimes preceded
by refl. dat. pron. him self himself
27/31, 39/19, 56/13, etc. uninfl.,
referring to pl. noun or pron. hie self
themselves etc. 28/10, 53/26, 88/9.
syluum dsm. 27/20.
sellan I give 28/16, 60/25, 67/7,
67/26, etc.; hand over, deliver up
62/20, 113/23; give in marriage 62/3,
65/18, 65/21. sealde þa. t. 3 sg.
57/19. sealdon pl. 6/14. sealden
subj. pl. 120/15.
ᵹesellan I give, grant 1/11, 52/9,
52/14, 54/14, etc.; sell 23/26, (wiþ feo)
68/2, 69/14, 83/15. ᵹesyllaþ pr. pl.
24/15. ᵹesealde þa. t. 3 sg. 33/29.
ᵹesealdon pl. 23/26; ᵹesealdan
23/26. ᵹesealden subj. pl. 96/26.
ᵹeseald pp. 36/1.
ᵹeseman I settle 33/9; reconcile
39/13, 41/17, 63/15, 63/19, etc.
senatorum gpl. senators (OH senatores) 137/15, 141/28.
senatus npl.(m.) members of the
senate 42/3, 42/6, 101/22, 104/17,
etc.; apl. 104/22. senatum npl.

76/11; apl. (or s.) 42/14. senatos
apl. 111/27. senata gpl. 107/23;
senatusa 134/21; senatuses 127/
16; senatum 88/13; dpl. 109/30.
sendan I send 5/3, 5/25, 6/12,
29/10, etc.
seo see se.
geseo see geseon.
seofan, seofon, syfan num. seven
1/9, 15/3, 16/22, 35/26, etc.
seofeþa, seofoþa, siofoþa, syfeþa
adj. seventh 25/30, 43/27, 124/21,
132/23 etc.
seofonteoþa adj. seventeenth 145/21.
seofontienewintre adj. seventeen
years old 102/1–2.
seofontig num. seventy 82/21, 82/22.
seoles, sioles gs(m.) seal's 15/17,
15/20.
seolfe, -ne, -um see self.
seolfre, siolfre ds(n.) silver 31/15,
42/12. seolfres, siolfres gs. 92/9,
104/28.
seon 5 see 16/11. seonne dat. inf.
look 23/10.
geseon 5 see, behold, observe 14/29,
26/20, 28/18, 73/8, etc. ~ swelce see
what looked like, as it were 123/14,
131/1. geseo pr. 1 sg. 77/12. geseah
pa. t. 3 sg. 3/27. gesawan pl. 3/24;
gesawon 22/3; gesawen 28/21.
gesawe subj. sg. 107/7. gesewen
pp. 49/18. gesewene npl. 4/26.
geset see gesettan.
geseten, -e, -um see gesittan.
setl n. seat 124/23, 132/4; siege 41/10,
51/16, 79/18. gan on ~ set 19/17.
gesetnesse g. and dsf. decree, law
1/12, 24/13. gesetnessa apl. 128/30,
129/2, 139/18.
settan I establish, set up 30/29,
38/14, 38/15, 136/26; set down 88/9;
appoint 42/17, 128/11.
gesettan I set, establish, appoint
32/18, 42/14, 46/25, 73/1, etc.; decree
22/27, 88/21, 107/29; make 95/2;
place 106/18; settle 109/30. gesettan pa. t. pl. 50/14. geset(t) pp.
107/29, 145/3, etc.
86/14 etc.
seþþan see siþþan.
gesewen(e) see geseon.
sibb f. peace 2/27, 31/17, 52/33, 59/19,

etc.; friendship 54/7; relationship,
kindred 22/28.
gesibbe adj. apl. as subst. relatives,
kin 131/9.
sibbsum adj. friendly 31/7.
gesib(b)sum adj. friendly, peaceable
31/19, 136/17.
sicaþ 1 pr. pl. sigh 52/23.
sie, sien see beon.
gesiene, gesyne adj. visible, evident
26/26, 52/36, 87/6, 98/18, etc.
sierwan I plot 32/19, 61/20, 65/10,
78/32, etc. sierede pa. t. 3 sg. 61/20.
siredon pl. 75/4.
siex, syx num. six 15/9, 15/10, 15/31,
17/14, 28/12, etc. syxa sum 15/5
(see Commentary).
si(e)xta, syxta wk. adj. sixth 6/10,
25/28, 123/10, 132/22, 146/4.
siextegum see syxtig.
sige m. victory 28/15, 41/15, 41/27,
49/29, etc.; success 58/25, 97/11,
111/6.
siglan I sail 14/13, 14/16, 14/19.
gesiglan I sail 14/11, 14/14, 14/17.
simbel, siml, symbel adj. on (an)
~ always, continuously 22/20, 63/30,
71/14, 99/11, 144/22, etc.
simbel, simle, symle adv. always,
ever 15/26, 42/15, 115/26, 125/26,
etc.; constantly 137/22.
simbelfarende ppl. adj. ever-
journeying, nomadic 20/14.
sindon see beon.
singan 3 sing 23/24, 35/15, 42/24,
42/33. singende pr. p. 23/24.
sungen pp. 42/24.
sint see beon.
sinþyrstende I pr. p. w. gen. continually thirsting for 71/25.
sio see se.
siofoþe see seofeþa.
sioles see seoles.
siolfre(s) see seolfre.
siredon see sierwan.
sittan 5 sit 64/30, 73/27, 132/4, etc.;
remain, stay 69/13; camp 35/10,
72/31, 99/12, 105/19, etc.; settle
52/33, 156/20. sitte pr. subj. 1 sg.
77/11. sittende pr. p. 31/29. sæt(t)
pa. t. 3 sg. 64/10, 94/21. sæton
pl. 96/9; sætan 71/19. sæte subj. sg.
112/1,

gesittan 5 camp 60/30; inhabit, settle 21/22, 58/19, 71/11, 153/4, etc. gesæt *pa. t. 3 sg.* 147/26. gesæton *pl.* 156/22. geseten *pp.* 148/15. gesetene *npl.* 58/19. gesetenum *dpl.* 9/32.

siþ (*m.*) time, occasion 34/25, 81/29, 96/24, 111/4, etc.; expedition 48/8, 72/2. siþan *dpl.* 128/23. siþ(e)mesta *sup. adj. wk.* last 2/3, 32/15, 36/20, 49/14, 133/24. siþþan, seþþan, syþþan *adv.* afterwards 1/10, 12/20, 22/14, 23/6, etc. *as conj.* after 14/21, 22/19, 27/29, 31/16, etc. siþþan . . . siþþan after (when) . . . then 50/28 etc. sixtan, -e see siexta. slæd *n.* valley 45/4. geslægen see geslog. slæp (*m.*) sleep 130/14. geslagen see geslog. slapan 7 sleep 96/5, 136/3. slæpendne *pr. p. asm.* 136/3. [slean] 6 slay, kill 29/27, 29/32, 85/18, etc.; strike 93/23, 132/4; fix by striking 85/13. sleanne *dat. inf.* 152/22. sleande *pr. p.* 29/27. slog *pa. t. 3 sg.* 40/18; sloh 25/31. slogan *pl.* 45/21; slogon 29/32. sloge *subj. sg.* 33/18. slege (*m.*) killing, murder 39/3, 44/35, 45/17, 60/6, etc. sliht (*m.*) slaughter 47/22, 125/22. slog, slogan etc. see slean. geslog 6 *pa. t. 3 sg.* slew, inflicted (slaughter) 101/12. geslogan *pl.* 54/28. geslagen *pp.* slain 68/16, 84/14, 99/7, etc.; geslægen 46/32. sloh see slean. smæl *adj.* narrow 15/21. smælre *comp. nsn.* narrower 15/26. smalost *sup.* most narrow 15/28. smeþe *adj.* smooth, level 77/12, 93/25. smic *m.* vapour 77/18. snawgebland *n.* snowstorm 100/10. snelra *comp. adj.* braver, bolder 46/1. snoru *f.* daughter-in-law 80/19, 80/23. snyttro (*f.*) wisdom 67/25. soelest, selest *sup. adj.* best 107/20, 113/8, 118/24, 144/3. gesohtan, gesohte etc. see gesecan. sohte, sohton see sec(e)an. somcucre *adj. dsf.* half-dead 130/18.

some, same *adv. swa* ~ similarly 88/16. *swa* ~ *swa* the same as 45/2. gesomnedon II *pa. t. pl.* gathered, assembled 108/13. gesomnad *pp.* 94/11, 111/14; gesomnod 136/24. gesamnode *npl.* 17/19. sona *adv.* immediately, within a short time 24/27, 29/5, 32/9, 33/10, etc. ~ *þæs* shortly afterwards 67/11, 86/31, 98/9, etc. *sona swa conj.* as soon as 54/1, 65/3, 85/24, etc. sond see sand. sondiht *adj.* sandy 121/23. sorg (*f.*) anxiety, trouble 100/14. soþ (*n.*) truth 14/29, 49/9, 87/16, 102/34. soþ *adj.* true 24/12, 57/9, 75/15 (*or subst.*), 104/7. soþfæst *adj.* truthful, pious 56/8. sped *f.* wealth 15/7, 17/9, 17/29. spedig *adj.* wealthy 15/7. spell *n.* story 14/27, 27/23, 27/28, 28/1, etc.; news 89/17, 91/19. spellcwide (*m.*) historical narrative 55/30. gespeow 7 *pa. t. 3 sg. impers. w. dat.* profit, avail 90/10, 90/28. spere (*n.*) spear 70/10. spon 7 *pa. t. 3 sg.* persuaded 79/7. sponan *pl.* 82/18. gespon 7 *pa. t. 3 sg.* enticed, persuaded 22/23, 47/15. spræc *f.* speech 38/25. spræc, spræcon, etc. see sprecan. gespræcon 5 *pa. t. pl.* agreed 75/1, 139/17; gespræcan spoke 107/16. gesprecen *pp.* agreed 51/30. sprecan 5 speak, say 37/22, 47/5, 48/34, 113/6, etc. sprecanne *dat. inf.* 30/24. sprece *pr. 1 sg.* 38/10. sprecaþ *pl.* 31/10. sprecende *pr. p.* 6/20. spræc *pa. t. 3 sg.* 5/17. spræcon *pl.* 14/30. spræce *subj. sg.* 109/3. spynge (*wk. f.*) sponge 122/2. staca *wk.* (*m.*) stake 119/25, 119/27. stælhran *m.* decoy deer 15/10 (see Commentary). stænc see stenc. stænen *adj.* made of stone 43/32. stærwritere *m.* historian 37/5, 88/18. stalade II *pa. t. 3 sg.* went stealthily 121/17. staledon *pl.* 55/21.

stale *ds(n.) on ~ beon (w. dat.)* be of help to 123/4.

stalung *f.* stealing, robbery 114/13.

stan *(m.)* stone 48/7, 58/13, 73/12, 86/6, etc.

standan, stondan 6 stand, remain 9/15, 36/28, 65/2, 112/30, etc. stent *pr. 3 sg.* 16/14; standeþ 16/33. stondaþ *pl.* 9/9; standaþ 20/21. standende *pr. þ.* still, stagnant 23/6. stod *pa. t. 3 sg.* 36/28.

staniht *adj.* stony 10/6.

staþe *ds (m. or n.)* shore 16/34, 26/24; bank 146/17.

gestaþelade II *pa. t. 3 sg.* established 152/16.

staþol *(m.)* foundation, 133/15; position 103/6.

stellende I *pr. þ.* setting 39/4.

stenc, stænc *(m.)* stench 50/27, 119/12, 119/21.

stent see standan.

steopfæder *(m.)* stepfather 28/9.

steopmodor *(f.)* stepmother 61/17.

steopsunu *(m.)* stepson 28/9.

steorbord *n.* starboard 14/8, 14/22, 16/6, 16/16, 16/17, etc.

sticade, -ode II *pa. t. 3 sg.* stabbed, gouged out 84/21, 90/14.

sticung *(f.)* pricking, goading 85/16.

gesti(e)ran I *w. dat. of person and gen. of thing* restrain from 53/19, 101/24, 152/4, 152/5, 155/25; get under control 115/14. *him wæs gestiered* they were restrained 152/5.

stigan 1 mount, climb 107/5.

gestihtade II *pa. t. 3 sg.* ordained 143/21.

stihtung *(f.)* dispensation 133/21.

gestihtung *(f.)* dispensation, disposing, providence 37/4, 37/24.

gestillan I still, abate, halt 58/27, 76/4, 88/25, 136/29.

stilnesse *a. and dsf.* stillness, tranquillity 106/5, 106/6.

stincan 3 stink, give off fumes 151/11.

gestirde see gestieran.

stod see standan.

gestod 6 *pa. t. 3 sg.* remained, lasted 132/28, 133/5, 133/29; *w. refl. dat.* stationed himself 137/23. gestodon *pl.* were 132/27. gestode *subj. sg.* lasted 97/27.

stondan, stondaþ see standan.

gestop 6 *pa. t. 3 sg.* went 73/15.

stow *f.* place 3/12, 14/3, 15/23, 15/29, etc.

stream *m.* stream 43/30; current 43/9.

streng(e)st, strengran see strong.

gestreon *n.* wealth, treasure 17/27, 129/8, 130/22.

strienan I *w. gen.* beget 29/31, 35/10, 71/7, 83/23.

strong *adj.* strong 44/5; powerful 61/12; resolute 113/5; severe, hard 128/31, 132/25. strengran *comp. asm.* more powerful 29/34. streng-(e)st *sup.* most powerful 3/17, 72/13, 75/1, 110/6.

gestrongade II *pp.* strengthened 153/21.

stupian II stoop 145/4.

styccemælum *adv.* here and there 14/3; to bits 86/27.

gesugian see geswigian.

sulh *(mf. or n.)* plough 50/4.

sum *pron. adj.* some, a certain, one; *in pl.* some, certain (ones). *as adj.* 3/15, 6/19, 8/14, 12/31, etc. *as pron.* 52/11, 52/13, 65/24, 131/7, etc. *w. noun or pron. preceding or following in same case* some of 15/1, 50/18, 52/12, 100/19, etc. *syxa sum* 15/5 see Commentary. *sume . . . sume* some . . . others 52/12–13 etc.

sumdæl somewhat, some portion 13/2, 13/19, 18/29. See also dæl.

sumor *(m.)* summer 14/4, 18/1, 56/25. sumera *ds.* 14/4. sumerum *dpl.* 56/25.

sumorhæte *dsf.* summer-heat 72/28.

suna see sunu.

sund *(n.)* swimming 43/8.

gesund *adj.* safe and sound 47/2–3.

sunderfolgeþa *gpl. m.* of special offices 150/18.

sundorspræc *f.* private conversation, private conference 92/21, 107/15.

sungen see singan.

sunne *wk. f.* the sun 19/16, 100/31, 131/3, 135/7, etc.

sunu *m.* son 1/18, 22/25, 24/5, 27/3, etc.

susl *n.* torture 34/8.

suþ *adv.* south 8/20, 9/5, 9/12, 10/2, etc.

suþan *adv.* to the south, from the south 8/16, 16/35. be ~ to the south 9/30, 10/29, etc.; *w. dat.* to the south of 11/3, 12/25, 12/26, etc. *wiþ ~ w. acc.* south of 16/9.

suþaneastan *adv. be ~ w. dat.* to the south-east of 9/24.

suþdæl *m.* southern part 1/24, 11/25, 19/26, 19/27, 28/24.

suþeast *adv.* south-east 18/7.

suþ(e)weard *adj.* southern part of, southern 15/32, 16/3. *on suþweardum* in the southern part 36/18.

suþgarsecg *m.* southern ocean 9/13.

suþhealf (*f.*) south side 10/7, 11/21, 11/22, 18/8, 18/10.

suþgemæro *npl.* (*n.*) southern boundaries 10/13.

suþmest *sup. adj.* southernmost 26/30, 133/8.

suþryhte *adv.* due south, directly south 9/1, 14/15, 14/17.

suþsceata *wk. m.* southern corner 21/4.

suþweard *adj.* see suþ(e)weard.

suþweard *adv.* southwards 11/30.

suþwest *adv.* south-west 19/3.

swa *adv. and conj.* so, as. *as adv.* in this way, so, thus, consequently, accordingly 8/17, 17/23, 17/35, 19/25, 29/5, etc.; just as 94/24; exceedingly, very 23/29, 23/30, 24/24, 24/33, etc. *as conj.* as, just as 4/23, 8/23, 9/19, 19/31, etc.; as if 71/30; so that, in such a way that 27/20, 90/22, 133/13, 137/10; since 49/12; as soon as, when 64/20, 99/24, 105/30; though, yet 156/10; where 23/7, 25/26. *swa swa* just as, as 17/15, 25/6, 37/25; like 67/1; as if 36/22; as far as 14/14, 14/17. *correl. swa . . . swa* as . . . as 12/15, 14/9, 14/10, 15/30, 15/31; so . . . as 73/11; whether . . . or 59/5. *swa þæt* so that 22/22, 25/8. *swa +comp. . . . swa +comp.* the . . . the 15/26. *sona swa . . . (swa)* as soon as . . . (so) 54/1-2, 65/3, 85/24. *swa cuce* alive as she was 60/12; *swa swatigne* sweaty as he was 68/26, *swa hie mæst mehten* as much as they could

137/22. *swa hwelc swa*, etc. see hwelc. *swa some* see some. *swa þe(a)h* see swaþeah. *a swa* see a.

geswac see geswican.

swætan I sweat 100/33.

swatig *adj.* sweaty 68/26.

swaþe(a)h, swaþeah *adv.* however, nevertheless 23/15, 39/7, 73/13, 73/25, etc. *as conj.* swa þeh þe even if 74/14.

swealt 3 *þa. t. 3 sg.* died 92/11, 128/21. swulton *pl.* 106/6, 113/28.

sweflen *adj.* sulphurous 23/6, 50/25.

swefn (*n.*) dream 23/29, 73/31.

sweg (*m.*) noise 123/15.

swelc, swilc, swylc *pron. adj.* such, the same, the like. *as adj.* 46/14, 53/17, 65/27, 89/6, etc. *as pron.* 65/22, 90/16; such as 107/8, 135/12. *correl. swelc . . . swelc* such . . . as 27/14, 65/31, 84/16, 135/17. *æt swelcum* on such occasions 65/22.

swelce, swilce *adv. eac ~* likewise 37/9, 37/33, 44/2; also 22/21. *as conj.* as though, as if 2/22, 45/3, 49/18, 76/6, etc.; as it were 123/14, 131/1.

swelgend *m.* glutton, whirlpool 66/7. See Commentary.

swencende I *pr. p.* afflicting 110/21.

swenctan *pa. t. pl.* afflicted 57/10.

geswencton I *pa. t. pl.* harassed 113/28. geswencte *pp. npl.* afflicted 26/29.

gesweop 7 *pa. t. 3 sg.* took possession of, swept up 77/24.

sweor *m.* father-in-law 39/18, 39/21, 39/22, 40/18, 146/18.

sweora *wk. m.* neck 135/15, 154/23.

sweord (*n.*) sword 101/25, 115/1.

sw(e)ostor, swiostor (*f.*) sister 40/7, 69/5, 82/23, 129/17, etc. *gs.* 149/14.

gesw(e)ostor (*f*)*pl.* sisters 30/21, 142/17.

sweotol *adj.* obvious, clear 103/4, 104/4, 144/8.

gesweotolad II *pp.* made clear, explained 49/19.

sweotole *adv.* clearly 53/15, 57/15, 59/18, 59/22, etc.

sweotollice *adv.* clearly 69/28. sweotelicost *sup.* most clearly 31/31.

swete *adj.* sweet 44/26.

geswican I *w. dat.* deceive, turn
traitor, desert 32/22, 123/25, 139/25,
150/31; *w. gen.* cease from 73/25,
74/9, 103/5, etc. geswac *pa. t. 3
sg.* 150/31. geswicon *pl.* 102/10.
geswicen *subj. pl.* 55/25; *pp.* 32/22.
swicdom *m.* treachery 39/7, 44/28,
90/25, 117/11. swicdomes *apl.*
90/25. *heora swicdomes* treasonable
practices against them 90/25.
swift *adj.* swift 17/26. swiftost,
swyftost *sup.* swiftest 17/19, 17/22.
geswigian, gesugian II *w. gen.* be
silent about 27/28, 28/4, 66/8,
115/29.
swilc, swilce see swelc, swelce.
geswinc *n.* labour, toil 99/27, 113/6,
118/27, 119/4.
swingan 3 flog 40/22, 90/14. swong
pa. t. 3 sg. 90/14.
swiostor see sweostor.
swiþe, swyþe *adv.* very, greatly
2/11, 2/12, 3/12, 10/5, etc. swiþor
comp. more 19/26, 32/17, 51/17,
etc.; rather 68/14, 69/30, 135/2,
etc. swiþost *sup.* chiefly, most,
especially 14/30, 17/28, 23/1, 61/25,
etc. swiþor micle much more, far
more 44/27, 52/32.
swiþlic *adj.* very great 89/18.
swiþlice *adv.* very greatly 29/20.
swiþra *comp. adj.* right 8/18, 29/33.
geswiþrad II *pp.* abated 50/28.
swong see swingan.
swor 6 *pa. t. 3 sg.* swore 101/26.
sworan *pl.* 101/30, 102/4.
geswor 6 *pa. t. 3 sg.* swore 95/23,
99/17. gesworan *pl.* 31/28, 35/3,
41/26. gesworen *pp.* sworn 41/8.
swostor see sweostor.
geswostor see gesweostor.
swulton see swealt.
swyftoste see swift.
swylc see swelc.
swyn (*n.*) pig 15/13.
swyþe see swiþe.
sy see beon.
syfan see seofan.
syfeþe see seofeþa.
syl *f.* pillar 9/9, 9/15, 20/21, 111/15.
sylf see self.
sylfren *adj.* silver 114/8.
gesyllaþ see gesellan,

syluum see self.
symbel see simbel *adj. and adv.*
symble *ds(n.)* feast 71/19.
symle see simbel *adv.*
syn, synd, syndon see beon.
syndrig *adj.* exceptional 52/20; exceptional?, standing apart? 99/25.
gesyne see gesiene.
syngade II *pa. t. 3 sg.* sinned 140/2.
synn *f.* sin 26/33, 132/18, 135/1.
synt see beon.
syþþan see siþþan.
syx see siex.
syxta see siexta.
syxtene *num.* sixteen 21/19.
syxtig *num.* sixty 15/6, 15/20, 15/26,
22/30, etc. siextegum *dpl.* 92/18.

T

tacen, tacn *n.* sign, indication,
miracle, prodigy 26/25, 48/8, 49/19,
85/7, etc.; proof, evidence 52/4;
distinctive feature 24/13.
tacnade II *pa. t. 3 sg.* signified,
indicated 48/32; portended 87/6,
120/1; showed symbolically 50/25,
131/9, 131/13, 131/18.
getacnade II *pa. t. 3 sg.* signified,
indicated 59/22, 131/4. getacnad,
getacnod *pp.* marked out 38/3;
shown, shown symbolically, indicated 56/10, 59/18, 131/2; portended
130/28.
tacnung *f.* sign 50/29; miracle 134/15;
dispensation 36/16. *as.* 50/29.
tæcan I *w. dat.* refer, direct 57/15.
tælaþ I *pr. pl.* revile 38/30. tælde *pa.
t. 3 sg.* treated with contempt
120/23.
talentan *dsf. wk.* talent 92/9. talentena *gpl.* 107/25; talentana 92/9,
96/26, 133/20.
tam *adj.* tame 15/9.
getawade II *pa. t. 3 sg.* put, treated
66/26.
tawian II treat 57/12, 83/14, 83/18.
teah see teonde.
geteah see geteon.
getellan consider, recount, ascribe
24/11, 61/4, 110/14. geteled *pp.*
61/4. getealde *npl.* 24/11.
templ *n.* temple 138/13, 141/19.

tengden I *pa. t. subj. pl.* would proceed to the attack 60/3.

getenge *adj. w. dat.* oppressing 122/16, 137/14, 144/15.

teola *adv.* well 90/28.

geteon 2 draw, bring 1/23, 35/21, 61/26, 79/1, etc. geteah *pa. t. 3 sg.* 60/31. getugon *pl.* 35/21. getogen *pp.* 35/2.

teona *wk. m.* injury, wrong, harm, damage 31/29 33/6, 54/31, 91/13, etc.

teonde 2 *pr. p.* taking 50/16. teah *pa. t. 3 sg.* attracted, took, annexed 125/15, 146/1; accused 109/32. tugon *pl.* raised 59/8; accused 90/24. tugen *subj. pl.* should annex 96/25.

teoþa *wk. adj.* tenth 26/5, 94/18, 103/13.

teþ see toþ.

theatrum *a. and ds.* theatre 3/25, 111/10, 134/30. þeatra *ds.* 83/10.

tibernessa *apl. f.* destruction, sacrifice of life 32/3.

tictator (*m.*) dictator 5/2, 51/25, 101/32, 128/12. tictatores *n. or as.* 41/14 (OH dictatorem). tictatore *ds.* 41/15.

tid *f.* time, period 4/31, 24/32, 29/14, 29/18, etc.; season 11/17. tidan *dpl.* 4/24; tidun 49/3.

tidlice *adv.* quickly, in good time 55/1, 92/17, 130/20.

tiema see tima.

tiene *num. suffix* vtiene fifteen 35/26.

tigelan *ds. or pl. wk.* (*f.*) brick 43/28.

tigþade II *pa. t. 3 sg.* granted 153/5.

tihtle *wk. f.* accusation 90/26.

tima *wk. m.* time 91/15, 100/16, 149/11. tieman *as.* 100/10.

timber *n.* material, timber 92/18.

timbran I build 30/29, 43/21, 138/15, 140/19, 149/18.

getimbran I build 1/7, 2/14, 6/4, 21/23, etc.

getimbrum *dpl.* (*n. or f.*) buildings 96/32.

tintrade II *pa. t. 3 sg.* tormented 65/16. tintredon *pl.* 30/33. tintregad *pp.* tortured 90/13.

tintrego *apl. n.* tortures 34/10.

to *adv.* too 22/11, 95/29.

to *prep. w. dat.* to 1/4, 1/23, 3/6, 3/11, etc.; at 39/15, 57/11; alongside, by 10/14, 13/5, 130/17, 144/10; as, for 1/11, 1/18, 5/2, 8/5; as regards, in respect to 84/6, 135/23; from, of 57/24, 74/7, 91/11, 119/5; according to 38/15; next to, after 40/8, 80/7; among 110/13; in addition to 64/16; in 33/4, 45/20, 90/6. *to þæm* so 49/23. *w. instr.* to 144/5, 145/3. *to þon* so 34/23, 48/8, 88/24; for this reason 55/8. *as conj.* to *þon þæt* because 63/33, 69/22, 71/6; in order that, so that 31/8, 67/19, 72/1. *ellipt.* to it 82/12. *to dæge* see todæg.

tobærst 3 *pa. t. 3 sg.* burst open, burst apart 123/19, 128/19.

tobeatan 7 smash 112/23.

tobræd I *pp.* scattered 100/21.

tobrecan 4 take by assault 69/15, 154/16, 154/30; overthrow 129/2; destroy 112/12; damage, break 55/13, 107/7. tobræc *pa. t. 3 sg.* 69/15. tobræcon *pl.* 55/13. tobrocen *pp.* 112/12. tobrocene *asf.* 107/7.

tobrudon 3 *pa. t. pl.* tore to pieces, rent 86/27.

todæg, todæge *adv.* today 23/8, 42/24, 60/12, 66/12, etc.

todæleþ I *pr. 3 sg.* separates 21/12. todælaþ *pl.* divide 17/13; separate 20/16. todælde *pa. t. 3 sg.* divided 45/1, 64/10; dispersed 63/21. todældon *pl.* divided 1/2, 8/13, 30/2, etc. todæled *pp.* 19/25. todælde *npl.* 50/19.

toe(a)can *prep. w. dat.* in addition to 14/31, 30/9, 48/11, 88/20, etc. ~ *þæm þe* in addition to the fact that 71/23.

toemnes *prep. w. dat.* alongside 15/32, 15/33, 73/18.

[tofaran] 6 disperse 64/22, 77/18, 103/27, 118/13, etc. tofare *pr. subj. sg.* 77/18. toforan *pa. t. pl.* 103/25. tofaren *pp.* 82/25. tofarene *npl.* 45/21.

tofeoll *pa. t. 3 sg.* fell in ruins, collapsed 134/31.

toforan see tofaran.

togæd(e)re *adv.* together 8/20, 8/22, 29/26, 50/20, etc.

togædereweard *adv.* towards each other 79/4, 92/4, 155/2–3; going towards each other 107/15–16.

toge *n. or as.* toga (OH *gs.* togae) 124/5.

getogen see geteon.

tohlad 1 cracked open 57/17, 86/29.

tohliden *pp.* split open 100/34.

tohopa *wk.* (*m.*) hope 58/20.

toliþ 5 *pr. 3 sg.* runs in different directions 11/16; divides 16/30. tolicg(e)aþ *pl.* lie (extend) in different directions 9/20, 19/22, 19/23.

tomiddes *prep. w. gen.* in the middle of 150/30.

tonemne I *pr. subj. sg.* name separately 12/10. tonemdon *pa. t. pl.* distinguished by name 8/13.

torfung (*f.*) pelting, stoning 73/12.

tornwyrdon I *pa. t. pl.* addressed abusively 33/21.

torr (*m.*) tower 137/24.

tosetene 5 *pp. npl.* widely dispersed 12/6.

toslog 6 *pa. t. 3 sg.* struck to pieces 86/24, 142/1.

tosomne *adv.* together 29/30, 101/7, 110/19. ~ cuman engage in battle 101/7.

tosticad II *pp.* pierced through 70/10.

totæron 4 *pa. t. pl.* tore to pieces 77/21.

totugon 2 *pa. t. pl.* pulled apart 77/20.

totwæman I separate, divide 65/11, 75/4.

toþ (*m.*) tusk 14/32. teþ *apl.* 14/32.

toweard *adj.* to come 131/11; approaching 49/4 (see BT p. 1010), 107/6? (see BT p. 1009).

toweard *prep. w. dat.* towards 17/21. See also toweard *adj.*

toweorpan 3 cast down, overthrow, destroy 62/28, 112/16, 112/22, 152/15, etc. towearp *pa. t. 3 sg.* 45/14. towurpon *pl.* 30/28. towurpe *subj. sg.* 111/28. toworpen *pp.* 114/5. toworpenu *nsf.* 70/24. toworpena *npl. f.* 5/20.

treahtigean II discuss 71/20.

treow¹ (*f.*) covenant 47/24.

treow² *n.* piece of wood 85/13, 112/6.

treowþa, triewþa *fpl.* terms, pact 89/20; honour 115/26. *dydon lytla*

~ showed a certain amount of honourable behaviour 115/26.

getriewde I *pa. t. 3 sg.* was confident 80/18. getriewdon *pl.* trusted 47/30.

getriewe *adj. w. dat.* faithful to 62/26. getrywestan *sup. ds. wk.* most faithful 119/8.

triumphan *a. and dsm.* triumph (OH triumphus, triumphum) 5/18, 41/29, 41/31, 42/1, etc. triumpheum *ns.* 42/13.

trog (*m.*) boat, tub 48/17.

truma *wk. m.* band, troop, cohort 46/26, 100/23, 121/29, 127/13. *buton truman* in random order 100/23.

getruwade II *pa. t. 3 sg. w. dat.* believed, trusted 44/21, 86/14, 111/22, 121/15. getruwedon *pl.* 26/21, 42/29, 110/9.

truwian II trust 119/7.

getrymede I *pa. t. 3 sg.* fortified 35/16; drew up 103/20. getrymedon *pl.* encouraged 26/20. getrymed *pp.* drawn up for battle 86/33.

trymedon I *pa. t. pl.* drew up for battle 103/23.

tu see twegen.

tua see tuwwa.

tugen, -on see teonde.

getugon see geteon.

tun *m.* estate, villa (OH villa etc.) 130/9, 138/21, 139/2, 149/20, etc.; town (OH oppidum) 94/4, 107/12; homestead, settlement, town? 17/16, 17/18, 17/24, 114/15; group of houses, district 133/13.

tunecan *asf. wk.* tunic 124/5 124/12.

tungul *npl. n.* stars 28/10, 58/11.

tuw(w)a, tua *adv.* twice 97/16, 116/3, 132/28, 146/16.

twegen *m.*, twa *f.n.*, tu *n.* two 5/20, 8/15, 21/16, 21/20, etc. twegea *g.* 43/30; twegra 3/2. twæm *d.* 10/2; twam 39/1. *twegen fætels* 17/36 (see Commentary). *twa 7 twentigra gpl.* of twenty-two 134/22.

twelf *num.* twelve 26/19, 29/30, 76/1.

twelfta *wk. adj.* twelfth 134/2, 134/29.

twelftig *num. hund* ~ hundred and twenty 68/17, 93/33.

twentig *num.* twenty 15/12, 15/13, 20/29, 134/22, etc.
tweo *wk.* (*m.*) uncertainty, state of indecision 79/22; doubt 115/15.
tweode I *pa. t. 3 sg. impers. w. acc.* seemed doubtful 102/22, 121/27.
getweode I *pa. t. 3 sg. impers. w. acc.* seemed doubtful 35/14.
tweogendlic *adj.* uncertain. tweogendlican *dsn.* 108/30.
tweolice *adv.* ambiguously 84/10.
twiefeald *adj.* twice as much. twiefealdan *dsn. as subst.* 130/23.
twywyrdig *adj.* making contradictory statements, at variance 49/6, 120/22.
getyde I *pa. t. 3 sg.* educated 129/9; *pp. npl.* 82/33.
tydriend (*m.*) propagator 25/6.
getygþian II *w. dat. of person and gen. of thing* grant 47/29, 65/7, 69/7, 79/29, etc. getygþade *pa. t. 3 sg.* 55/6. getygþedon *pl.* 39/9.
tyhtan I educate 120/13.
tyn *num.* ten 15/18, 24/30.
tyncen (*n.?*) small cask?, bladder? 43/9 (see Commentary).

þ

þa *pron. adj.* see se.
þa *adv.* then 16/17, 16/19, 21/31, 22/2, etc. *conj.* when, since, as, although 3/25, 22/15, 27/7, 57/19, etc. *þa þa* (then) when 30/33. *correl. þa . . . þa* when . . . then 16/15, 26/22–3, 35/1–3, etc. *þa giet, þa gyt* see þagiet.
þæh see þeah.
þæm see se.
þæne see se.
þænne see þonne.
þær, þar *adv.* there 8/14, 8/19, 9/8, 9/21; 17/32, etc. *conj.* where 9/15, 11/8, 11/10, 12/3, etc.; if 41/1, 41/17, 50/1, 51/20, etc. *þær þær* (there) where 9/26, 9/29, 18/30.
þæra see se.
þæræfter *adv.* after that 24/2.
þæræt *adv.* therein 154/14.
þærbinnan *adv.* therein 62/25, 78/30, 83/10, 91/2, etc.
þære see se,

þærinne *adv.* therein, inside 51/17, 52/22, 57/3, 62/8, etc.
þærof *adv.* thereof 114/10.
þæron *adv.* therein 14/25, 34/8, 34/13, 68/26, etc.
þæroninnan *adv.* therein 57/22, 130/10.
þæronufan *adv.* thereon 84/22; in addition 96/26.
þærryhte *adv.* immediately 60/25.
þærto *adv.* thereto, there, for that end 46/30, 57/15, 111/14, 112/16, etc.
þærtomiddes *adv.* in the midst 135/30.
þærute *adv.* outside 52/22, 89/29.
þærymbutan *adv.* round about 39/34; þær ymbutan 91/12.
þæs see se.
þæt *pron. adj.* see se.
þæt *conj.* that 2/11, 4/6, 4/23, 16/21, etc.; so that 4/10, 25/2, 26/19; because, since 17/35, 31/12; in that, when 103/4; it happened that 87/10; in order that 45/26, 154/30; that they 32/21 (*or indecl. rel.*); *as element in various compound conjunctions* e.g. mid þæm þæt, to þon þæt, see mid, to, etc.
þætte, þæt þe *pron.* that, which 9/8; what 49/13, 135/6.
þætte *conj.* that 28/17, 29/21, 29/24, 30/13, etc.; it happened that 40/16, 45/11, etc.
þafiende II *pr. p.* enduring 121/25.
geþafiende II *pr. p. w. dat. of person* being in agreement with 50/17.
geþafode *pa. t. 3 sg. w. dat. of person and acc. of thing* allowed 38/6, 40/6, 103/29.
þagi(e)t, þa giet, þagyt, þa gyt *adv.* still, yet 15/8, 22/11, 27/4, 39/26, etc.
þam, þan see se.
þanc see þonc.
geþanc *m.* thought, intention 26/11.
geþancodon II *pa. t. pl. w. dat. of person and gen. of thing* thanked for 119/4.
þanon see þonan.
þar see þær.
þara see se.
þas see þes,

þe *pers. pron.* see þu.

þe *demonstr.* see se.

þe *instr. neuter pron. with comparatives* see se.

þe *indecl. particle* that *as rel.* that, who, which, etc. (sometimes implying a prep.) 1/1, 1/19, 1/25, 1/26, etc. þe . . . *hi* etc. which etc. 11/29. *as conj.* as, because 2/5. þe . . . þe whether . . . or 120/1. For þæs þe, þy þe, þeah þe, etc. see se, þeah, etc.

þeah, þeh, þæh *conj.* though, even though 11/4, 12/10, 24/25, 26/7, etc. þeah þe, þeh þe even if, although 8/14, 10/4, 17/36, 24/17, etc. *as adv.* however, nevertheless 10/20, 14/1, 15/12, 15/23, etc. *correl.* þeah . . . þeah although . . . nevertheless 49/1–2 etc.

þeahhwæþre see þehhwæþ(e)re.

þearf (*f.*) need, necessity 31/14, 32/1, 104/3, 144/23.

þeatra see theatrum.

þeaw (*m.*) custom, practice 17/6, 17/31, 24/17, 29/29, etc.; mode of conduct, habit 141/27.

þegn *m.* noble, minister, one engaged in a king or queen's service 6/2, 40/27, 71/16, 118/25, etc.; soldier 43/8, 43/10, 85/6, 114/26, etc.; brave man 65/31, 103/4.

þegnscipe (*m.*) bravery 67/24, 72/20.

þeh see þeah.

þehhwæþ(e)re, þeah- *adv.* nevertheless 33/19, 47/7, 118/9.

geþenc(e)an I consider, bear in mind, think about 24/27, 31/12, 67/9, 77/6, etc.; intend 85/32, 107/12, 136/10, etc. *w. gen.* consider 32/7, 77/11. geþohte *pa. t. sg.* 153/9. geþohten *subj. pl.* 95/30. geþoht *pp.* 79/10.

þencþ I *pr. 3 sg.* thinks 97/32. þence *subj. sg.* should intend, intends 97/31, 113/8. þencende *pr. p.* thinking 44/35, 100/22, 154/7. þohte *pa. t. 3 sg.* thought, intended 34/4, etc. þohtan *pl.* 52/10; þohton 29/22; þohte 136/20.

þeod, þiod *f.* nation, people, district 12/11, 20/3, 20/5, 20/9, etc.

geþeode *n.* language 14/30; nation, nationality 17/32.

þeofmon (*m.*) thief, brigand 114/13.

þeoh *n.* thigh 25/25, 64/30.

þeos, þeosan see þes.

þeosternes, þysþernes (*f.*) darkness 26/4, 135/5.

þeow *m.* slave, servant 5/27, 49/25, 66/29, 87/19, etc.

þeow *adj. w. dat.* in bondage to 67/6, 96/2; bond 60/22, 131/16.

þeowa *wk.* (*m.*) slave 17/4.

þeowdom, þiow- (*m.*) servitude, slavery 31/18, 31/19, 37/17, 42/21, etc.

þeowiende II *pr. p. w. dat.* serving 38/23, 62/19.

þeowot (*m. or n.*) servitude 62/20, 70/25.

þes *m.*, þeos *f.*, þis *n. dem. pron. and adj.* this. þes *nsm.* 56/27. þisne *asm.* 1/2; þysne 51/24. þis *n. and asn.* 16/8, 38/10; þiss 36/31; *w. pl. vb.* 55/31. þises *gsm. and n.* 2/13; þyses 19/23; þisses 6/21. þissum *dsm. and n.* 16/7, 74/3; þysum 21/25; þeosan 55/15; þiosan 1/3; þysan 27/12. þeos *nsf.* 27/12. þas *asf.* 36/4. þisse *dsf.* 47/8; þysse 24/25. þas *napl.* 10/11, 113/6. þissa *gpl.* 32/7. þysan *dpl.* 24/21; þyson 21/30.

þicce *adj. w. gen. of measurement* thick, abundant 11/20, 23/2, 112/9.

þicgeanne I *dat. inf.* eat 123/16.

þigedan *pa. t. pl.* partook of, ate 60/24; þigedon 143/24, 144/1.

geþicgeanne I *dat. inf.* eat 60/19.

þiclice *adv.* thickly 75/22.

þider, þyder *adv.* thither 14/31, 16/3, 85/23, 86/17, etc.; whither 125/7.

þiderweard *adv.* on the way, in that direction 16/15, 100/21, 106/25, 130/7, etc.

þigedan, þigedon see þicgeanne.

þine, þinum see þu.

þing *n.* thing, matter, respect 111/16, 132/22, 152/13, etc.; thing of value 95/6; condition 111/31. *for . . . þingum* on . . . account 126/20, 136/15. *mid nanum þinge* (þingum) not at all, in no way, by no means 39/12, 135/21. þingun *dpl.* 54/23; þingan 135/21; þingon 19/29.

geþingade II *pa. t. 3 sg.* made an agreement 156/20.

þiod see þeod.
þiosan see þes.
þiowdome see þeowdom.
þis(s), þisses, etc. see þes.
geþofta *wk. m.* comrade 64/13, 115/21.
geþoftade II *pa. t. 3 sg.* entered into
  an agreement, joined 81/1; *w. refl.
  dat.* 121/16. geþoftedan *pl.* 81/31.
geþoht *n.* thought 156/2; intention
  150/26.
geþoht, geþohte etc. see ge-
  þenc(e)an.
þohtan, þohte see þencþ.
geþoledon II *pa. t. pl.* suffered 78/15.
þolige II *pr. subj. sg. w. gen.* should
  fail to get 24/27. þoliende *pr. p. w.
  acc.* enduring 39/30.
þon see se.
þonan, þonon, þanon *adv.* thence
  9/1, 9/5, 15/37, 44/27, etc.
þonc, þanc (*m.*) thanks 85/1. *an þance*
  pleasing 49/8. þonces *gs. used as
  adv.* in (someone's) favour, for
  (someone's) sake 143/24, 144/1.
þoncung *f.* thanks 24/22.
þone see se.
þonne, þænne *adv.* then 8/18, 8/20, 8/
  21, 9/3, 135/28, etc. *as conj.* when 32/
  25. *correl.* þonne... þonne when...
  then 17/27, 23/10, 28/18–19, 29/31.
  after comp. than 19/18, 19/26, 19/27,
  19/28; *w. part. gen.* 46/1, 55/20, etc.
þonon see þonan.
þrang, þrong 3 *pa. t. 3 sg.* pressed
  73/15, 128/27.
geþrang 3 *pa. t. 3 sg.* pressed 73/22.
þreatung (*f.*) ill-treatment, ill-usage
  136/1.
þreo, þreora see þrie.
þreoteoþon *wk. adj. ds.* thirteenth
  107/3.
þridda *wk. adj.* third 17/17, 19/4,
  19/23, 24/31, etc.
þrie *m.*, þreo, þrio, þry *f. and n.*
  three 1/2, 8/13, 16/16, 25/20, 82/23,
  101/16, etc. þreo *m.?* 125/27 see
  Sievers–Brunner, § 324. þreora
  gpl. 9/19; þriora 4/16. þrim *dpl.*
  4/11.
þriereþre *adj. used as noun* trireme.
þriereþrena *gpl.* *54/14, 129/23.
þritig *num.* thirty 12/11, 15/27, 21/13,
  93/13. þritti 21/13.

þriwa *adv.* three times 128/9, 138/8.
þrong see þrang.
þrowiende II *pr. p.* suffering 34/8.
þrowoden *pa. t. subj. pl.* should
  suffer 117/5.
þry see þrie.
þrymlicran *comp. adj. npl.* more
  splendid 42/9.
þryscyte *adj.* triangular 19/1, 21/2.
þrysmde I *pa. t. 3 sg.* oppressed
  77/19.
þu *pron. 2nd pers.* thou, you, etc. þu
  ns. 45/8. þe *ds.* 53/17. ge *npl.* 31/2.
  eow *a. and dpl.* 31/3, 31/4. eower
  gpl. 66/5; iower 31/5. *gs. and gpl. as
  possessive adj. decl. strong* thy, your
  þine *asf.* 45/9. þinum *dpl.* 57/14.
  eower- 31/6, 113/2, 156/5, etc.;
  eowr- 65/32, 113/3; iowr- 31/5,
  31/6, 67/6. iowra *apl.* (*n.*) 67/6.
þuhte see þyncan.
geþuhte see geþyncþ.
þunor *m.* thunderbolt, thunder 85/8,
  86/24, 141/17, 142/1, 146/17.
þurfe *pret. pr. vb. pr. subj. sg.* needs
  27/15.
þurh *prep. w. acc.* through, because
  of, by 11/10, 29/18, 38/2, 43/15,
  52/29, etc.
þurhfor 6 *pa. t. 3 sg.* passed through
  93/4.
þurhsceat 2 *pa. t. 3 sg.* pierced
  through 73/23. þurhscoten *pp.*
  73/19.
þurhteon 2 carry through, carry out,
  perform (*w. dat. of person* against)
  22/16, 38/29, 104/21, 108/4, 111/6,
  etc.; achieve 48/8. þurhteah *pa. t.
  3 sg.* 91/27. þurhtugon *pl.* 123/4.
  þurhtogen *pp.* 92/18.
þurhwunigean II persist, continue
  38/2, 44/5, 155/27.
þurst *m.* thirst 46/17, 74/8, 121/24,
  122/16, etc.
þus, þuss *adv.* thus 17/27, 23/23,
  38/3, 39/19, etc.
þusend *n.* thousand *as pure num.
  undeclined us. w. part. gen.* 21/24,
  22/29 23/12, 27/24, etc. *decl. as pl.
  noun* 26/16, 58/3, 64/34, 118/19.
geþwære *adj.* gentle, agreeable 136/
  17.
geþwærnes (*f.*) concord 132/20.

þwyres *adv.* at an angle 142/13; on the flank, obliquely 93/27, 94/16, 100/24.

þy see se.

þyder see þider.

þylæs *conj.* lest 47/34. See also læs.

þyllic *pron. adj.* such. *as pron.* 88/9. *as adj.* 82/32, 88/10.

þyncan I *w. dat.* seem (to) 52/15, 52/27, 66/1, 66/7, etc. þuhte *pa. t. 3 sg.* 14/30; *subj. pl.* 66/1.

geþyncþ I *pr. 3 sg. w. dat.* seems to 53/17. geþuhte *pa. t. 3 sg.* seemed to 48/15, 54/3, 63/29, 65/8, etc.

þyrstende I *pr. p. w. gen.* thirsting for 22/20, 45/8.

þysan, þysse etc. see þes.

þysþernes see þeosternes.

U

ufane *adv.* from above 60/21.

ufera *comp. adj.* later 90/16.

uht see wiht.

uissillus 130/19 for OH *apl.* Psyllos (Vienna 366 phisillus). See Commentary.

unablinnendlice *adv.* without cease 39/34. unaablinnendlice 25/23.

unar *f.* dishonour 126/19.

geunaredon II *pa. t. pl.* dishonoured 24/24.

unarimed *adj.* countless 57/13.

unarimedlic *adj.* boundless, immeasurable 47/24.

unarimedlice *adv.* innumerably 50/7, 119/1.

unasecgendlic *adj.* ineffable 36/16.

unbeboht *adj.* unsold 15/9.

unclænnessa *napl. f.* uncleanness, obscenity 38/26, 57/4.

geunclænsade II *pa. t. 3 sg.* defiled 39/3.

uncuþ *adj.* unknown, unfamiliar 44/24, 113/30, 151/2. uncuþre *comp. nsn.* more unfamiliar 66/18.

under *prep. w. dat.* under, beneath 42/18, 51/22, 114/27, 152/11, etc.; in the course of, during 29/28, 98/2, 111/21; in the time of, under the rule of 3/17, 3/21, 41/19; among 104/17. ~ þæm meanwhile 39/24. *as conj.* ~ þæm þe while 21/31. *w. acc.*

under 84/18. ~ þæt on these grounds 115/8.

underfeng 7 *pa. t. 3 sg.* undertook 39/25, 93/18, etc.; received, took in 66/28, 120/13. underfengon *pl.* undertook 42/22. underfenge *subj. sg.* should undertake 108/3; should accept 95/28. underfongen *pp.* undertaken 103/1.

undergeaton 5 *pa. t. pl.* realized 62/17.

underi(g)ende *adj.* harmless 22/13, 25/9.

underneoþan *prep. w. acc.* underneath 73/19.

undernmete (*m.*) breakfast 48/35.

underngereord (*m. or n.*) breakfast 48/34.

underþeow *m.* subject 52/11, 112/17, 125/18, 128/10, 132/10.

underþeow *adj. w. dat.* (*or subst.*) subject 110/23, 111/23.

underþiedde I *pa. t. 3 sg. w. dat.* of *person* subjected (to) 139/24, 149/15. underþieded *pp.* 28/24, 36/22, 59/15, 62/1; underþiedd 31/16; underþied 62/11. underþiedde *npl.* 99/8.

uneaþe *adv.* with difficulty, barely 48/13, 52/34, 70/16, 72/27, etc.; scarcely 133/15.

ungeferlic *adj.* divisive, internecine 6/10, 123/11.

ungeferlice *adv.* divisively, in civil war 129/10.

ungefoge *adv.* excessively 17/26.

ungefoglecest *sup. adj.* most immense 43/29.

unforbærned *adj.* unburnt, uncremated 17/7, 17/10, 17/33.

unfriþ (*m. or n.*) hostilities 14/19.

ungearwe *adj. napl.* unprepared 55/2, 91/17 (*pl. for sg. or for on ungearwe?*), 96/9. on ~ unprepared 30/19, 65/11, 90/9 etc. ungearone *asm.* 118/12.

ungeorne *adv.* reluctantly 79/22.

ungyltig *adj.* innocent 98/17.

unhæle *ds(f.)* ill health 88/23.

unieþe *adj.* difficult 32/23; unpleasant 74/14.

unieþnesse *dsf.* harshness 83/14; trouble, difficulty 145/7.

ungelic *adj.* unalike, dissimilar 38/18, 135/19.

ungeliefedlic *adj.* incredible 43/19, 43/26, 68/22, 73/11, etc. ungeliefedlicne *asm.* *possibly in error for* ungeliefedlice *adv.* 68/22.

ungemæte *adj.* immoderate 56/26.

ungemætlic *adj.* immeasurable, excessive 21/25.

ungemet (*n.*) immense number 46/14, 76/24. *mid* ungemete excessively 80/30, 90/2, 151/11, etc.; in excessive numbers 106/6. ungemettan *dpl.* *used adverbially* immensely 72/6.

unmetlic *adj.* excessive. unmetlican *dpl.* 36/10.

ungemetlic *adj.* immense, very great 4/12, 4/21, 28/13 (*or adv.*), 46/17, 69/3 (*or adv.*, v.l. ungemetlice), etc.; excessive 22/21, 34/1, 76/2, etc. ungemetlican *dsm.* 127/12.

ungemet(t)lice *adv.* excessively 31/2, 54/18, 68/25, 96/17, etc.

unmiltsung *f.* impiety, pitilessness 38/27.

unmyndlenga *adv.* unexpectedly 79/7.

ungeniedde *adj.* without compulsion 132/6.

unoferwunnen *adj.* unconquered 85/2.

unoferwunnendlic *adj.* invincible 61/30.

ungerad *adj.* at variance 50/32; *w. dat.* at variance with 134/10.

unræd *m.* ill-advised course 91/27, 111/12.

ungerædnes *f.* discord, disagreement 91/29, 117/21, 117/25, 138/7. ungerædnesse *as.* 117/21.

geunret I *pp.* troubled 76/2.

ungerisno(*f. or n.*) what is unseemly, improper things 110/1.

unryht *n.* wrong, evil 38/19, 136/19.

unryhtlic *adj.* wrong, unjust 29/2.

unryhtwisest *sup. adj.* most unjust 37/19. unryhtwisestana *gpl.* 37/19.

ungesælgest *sup. adj.* most unhappy 113/19, 116/22.

unsarast *sup. adj.* most without pain 130/12.

unsibb *f.* enmity, strife, variance 6/8, 6/10, 38/27, 51/11, etc.

unspedig *adj.* poor 17/3. unspedgestan *sup. npl. wk.* most indigent 21/31.

unstillnessa *apl. f.* disturbances, breaches of the peace 55/19.

ungetæsran *comp. adj. npl.* more obnoxious 40/2.

untidlican *adj. dpl.* unseasonable 56/24.

ungetina *napl.* (*n.?*) foul injuries 32/3, 41/18, 50/29 (v. l. ungetima; see Dahl (1938), pp. 112–13).

untreowlice *adv.* perfidiously 91/23, 115/7.

untreowþ *f.* perfidy 79/19, 91/25. untreowþa *as.* 91/25.

untrumnesse *dsf.* sickness 148/23.

untweogendlice *adv.* without doubt, for a certainty 47/5, 73/23, 87/1, 89/19, 100/15; unequivocally 28/27.

unþanc, unþonc (*m.*) displeasure 107/10. heora (*eoweres*) *unþances* against their (your) will 26/8, 31/6, 39/7, 129/6.

unþeaw (*m.*) vice 135/12, 137/19.

ungeþwærnes *f.* discord, division 47/35, 135/23, 137/8. ungeþwærnesse *as.* 135/23.

unwærlice *adv.* unwarily 106/10.

unwæstmbærnesse *ds(f.)* barrenness 12/7.

ungewealdes *adv. his* ~ involuntarily 137/26.

unwenlic *adj.* unpromising, giving little hope of success 103/6.

unweorþ *adj. w. dat.* little esteemed by 39/28, 48/25, 115/27. *dyde* ~ made light of 64/29; held in little esteem 118/26. unweorþestan *sup. asm.* least important 97/19.

unweorþlic *adj.* of little importance 73/6. unweorþlicost *sup.* most disgraceful 25/27.

unweorþlice *adv.* with contempt 75/33, 99/14; ignominiously 139/14.

unweorþnesse *dsf.* indignity 145/7; contempt 147/15.

unwerig *adj.* unwearying 125/26.

ungewilde *adj. w. dat.* independent of 149/16.

unwilla *wk.* (*m.*) *his unwillan* against his will 156/22. *his* (*hiora*) *unwillum* against his (their) will 6/17, 89/15.

unwis *adj.* ignorant 26/32.

ungewis(s) *n.* ignorance 66/19; uncertainty 74/20.

unwitende *ppl. adj.* unwitting 131/5; out of his senses 132/3, 154/24.

unwræst *adj.* weakly, ignoble 55/9.

ungewunelic *adj.* unusual, unaccustomed 26/31.

up, upp *adv.* up 6/3, 6/8, 9/9, 11/7, 11/8, etc.

upahebban 6 raise up 41/16, 41/24, 117/22, 136/25; become puffed up, be arrogant 53/26. upahofon *pa. t. pl.* 41/16. uppahæfene *pp. npl.* 53/26.

uphofan 6 *pa. t. pl.* raised up 33/4.

uppon upon. *wiþ* ~ *adv.* above 15/24.

uppweardes *adv.* upwards 89/25.

ure, urra, etc. see ic.

urnon see iernan.

us see ic.

ut *adv.* out 9/4, 9/6, 9/22, 12/3, etc.

utan, uton *adv.* from without, outside 8/12, 12/19, 14/28, 19/1, etc. *ymb* . . . *utan* see ymbutan.

utancymen *adj.* foreign 115/11.

utane *adv.* from without 61/19; abroad 88/20.

ute *adv.* out 109/6; abroad 61/21; outside 25/21.

utera *comp. adj. gpl.* foreign 50/19.

utfæreld (*n.*) exodus, departure 26/9.

utgan *anom. vb.* leave 112/19.

uton *adv.* see utan.

uton *hortatory auxiliary (subj. 1 pl. of witan* to go) let us 47/7, 48/35.

utscyt 2 *pr. 3 sg.* flows out 18/31.

utsiht (*f.*) dysentery 138/20, 140/7.

utsionde 1 *pr. p.* oozing out 25/30.

uþe *pret. pres. vb. pa. t. 3 sg.* wished 47/3. uþon *pl.* 117/13. uþen *subj. pl. w. dat. of person and gen. of thing* 55/17.

ġeuþe *pret. pres. vb. pa. t. 3 sg. w. dat. of person and gen. of thing* granted 38/24. ġeuþen *subj. pl.* should grant 39/5.

W

waa *adv. w. dat. of person, gen. of source* woe 63/22.

ġewacadon II *pa. t. pl.* had become sluggish 57/25.

wædl *f.* barrenness 24/2.

wædla *wk.* (*m.*) beggar 113/20. wædlan *dpl.* 113/20.

wæl *n.* slaughter, the slain, number of corpses 46/32, 54/28, 68/16, 98/22, 136/7, etc.

wælgrimlice *adv.* with the utmost bitterness 87/3.

wælhreowlice *adv.* cruelly 65/12.

wælstow *f.* battlefield 64/25.

wæpn *n.* weapon 17/28, 57/21, 79/21, 103/25, etc.; *napl.* 75/26. wæpna *apl.* 29/21; wæpena 152/14; wæpeno 111/31.

wæpned *adj.* male 60/18.

wæpnedmon (*m.*) male, man 98/14, 103/16, 104/28, etc. *napl.* wæpnedmen 29/23, 103/19. wæpnedmonna *gpl.* 32/17.

wær (*f.*) compact 91/24.

wæran, wære, etc. see beon.

wærscipe (*m.*) circumspection 66/16.

wæs see beon.

wæstdæle see westdæl.

wæstm *m.* fruit of the earth, produce 1/11, 22/32.

wæs(t)mbære *adj.* fertile 20/16, 22/30.

wæstmbærnesse *asf.* fertility 24/1.

wæstmbæro *asf.* fertility 36/4.

wæstmberende *ppl. adj.* fruitful 23/8.

wæt *adj.* wet 56/24.

wæta *wk.* (*m.*) moisture 121/32, 122/2.

wæter *n.* water, body of water 11/15, 23/6, 25/17, 46/16, etc. wætre *ds.* 10/27. wætrum *dpl.* 9/20.

wæterflod *n.* flood 24/33.

wag *m.* wall 132/4.

waldend (*m.*) lord 25/13.

wanade II *pa. t. 3 sg.* injured 156/16.

wand 3 *pa. t. 3 sg.* flew 115/2.

wanian II *w. refl. dat.* lament 89/26, 128/20.

wann see winnan.

ġewann see ġewinnan.

wansped *f.* poverty. wanspeda *npl. w. sg. verb* 64/27.

ġewarhte see ġewyrcan.

ware *a. and dsf.* heed, care 118/22; defence 52/4, 93/4.

ġewarnedon II *pa. t. pl. refl.* were on their guard 64/15.

wat see **witan**[1].
ġewat 1 *pa. t. 3 sg.* went 45/27.
ġewiton *pl.* 33/23. **ġewiten** *pp.*
passed 44/4.
we see **ic.**
weal see **weall.**
weald *m.* high land covered with
wood, *Lat.* saltus 19/9, 56/27.
ġeweald *n.* power, control 21/27, 22/
19, 42/10, 44/31, etc. **ġewealdon**
dpl. him to ~ under his control
62/15, 63/20, 129/16.
wealdan 7 *w. gen.* exercise, control
36/21, 80/25. **weold** *pa. t. 3 sg.* 80/25.
ġewealdan 7 *w. gen.* wield 103/25.
ġewealden *ppl. adj.* inconsiderable
75/5, 102/18.
weal(l) *m.* wall 39/21, 43/25, 43/29,
125/29, etc. **wealles** *npl.* 44/12.
weallan 7 rise, flow, (*w. dat.*) flow
with, well with 3/27, 12/17, 87/10,
etc. **wilþ** *pr. 3 sg.* 11/30; **wielþ**
11/8. **weol(l)** *pa. t. 3 sg.* 98/28, 131/1.
weallġebrec (*n.*) breaking down of
a wall 73/25.
weard[1] (*m.*) guard, sentry 106/19.
weard[2] (*f.*) watch, guard 109/10.
weard *in comb. wiþ . . . weard prep.*
w. gen. towards 5/19, 106/22, 113/
27, 125/3, etc.
wearp 3 *pa. t. 3 sg.* cast 119/19.
wurpe *subj. sg.* should strike 93/27.
wearþ see **weorþan.**
ġewearþ see **ġeweorþan.**
weax (*n.*) wax 46/10, 90/23.
weaxan 7 grow, increase, develop
29/33, 37/10, 123/7, 133/4, etc.
weaxende *pr. p.* 58/11. **weaxendes**
gs. 25/32. **weox** *pa. t. 3 sg.* 114/15.
wedd *n.* pledge 35/7, 67/7.
wedende I *pr. p.* raging. *foran* ~ ran
amok 85/16.
weder (*n.*) weather 19/17, 151/10.
wedera *npl.* 19/17.
weg *m.* way, distance 14/8, 14/22,
16/8, 68/23; etc.; route, road 17/30,
92/31, 99/24, etc.; path 26/19,
26/22. *hys* ~ on his way 17/25.
wel, well *adv.* well 14/24, 23/29,
25/26, 65/26, etc.; properly 36/21.
wela *wk.* (*m.*) prosperity 23/3, 133/29.
ġewelgade II *pa. t. 3 sg.* enriched
130/22.

weliġ *adj.* wealthy 69/15, 90/1, 113/18.
welġe *asf.* 113/18. **weleġan** *asf.*
wk. 69/15. **weleġre** *comp. nsf.* 43/5.
weleġran *npl.* 48/23. **weleġast**
sup. 58/22, 63/3, 70/7. **weleġestan**
as. 103/10.
welġelæred *ppl. adj.* well instructed
143/5.
well see **wel.**
wen (*f. or m.*) likelihood 97/31.
wenan I believe, imagine, suppose,
expect 31/19, 35/28, 36/10, 44/27,
etc.; *w. gen.* expect, hope for 68/27,
79/19, 83/28, etc.
wendan I go, turn 29/8, 62/26, 63/2,
107/11, etc.; change 38/15; *w. refl.*
dat. go 75/6; *w. refl. acc.* 117/16.
ġewendan I turn 33/24, 61/4.
wenung *f.* expectation 62/4.
weol(l) see **weallan.**
weold see **wealdan.**
weorc *n.* work, task 25/19, 34/12,
111/15, 119/27, etc.; deed 131/14;
fortress 44/1.
weorod, werod *n.* band, army 46/23,
60/4, 68/11, 130/9, etc.
weorþ *n.* price 105/24.
weorþ *adj. w. dat.* held in esteem (by)
140/15. **weorþesta** *sup., wk. nsm.*
most esteemed 51/21.
weorþan 3 become, happen, come
about, be 1/25, 3/26, 5/14, 30/8,
39/13, etc. ~ *to* turn into 11/12,
23/10. **wyrþ** *pr. 3 sg.* 11/12.
weorþaþ *pl.* 23/10. **wearþ** *pa. t. 3*
sg. 2/1. **wurdon** *pl.* 1/17. **wurde**
subj. sg. 23/30. **wurden** *pl.* 65/4.
wurdon would have been 50/1.
ġeweorþan 3 happen, come about
5/12, 25/15, 56/14, 56/23, etc.;
become 30/23, 48/24; *impers. w. acc.*
agree 109/4, 111/26, 119/24, 123/24.
ġewearþ *pa. t. 3 sg.* 3/18. **ġewurdon**
pl. 4/30. **ġewurde** *subj. sg.* 31/12.
ġeworden *pp.* 24/10. **ġewordene**
npl. 37/23.
weorþfulnesse *dsf.* honour 124/10.
weorþianne II *dat. inf.* worship
69/29. **weorþedon** *pa. t. pl.* worshipped 87/28.
weorþlic *adj.* worthy 75/32.
weorþlice *adv.* honourably 39/16,
147/19.

weorþmynt (*m. or f.*) honour 145/18.
weorþscipe *m.* honour 99/1, 124/11, 140/16.
weotan, weotum see wita.
weox see weaxan.
ǥeweox 7 *pa. t. 3 sg.* grew up 33/2.
wepan 7 weep at, weep 65/30, 89/23, 89/24, 107/2, 126/18. wepende 89/23.
wer *m.* husband 2/5, 29/22, 29/26, 31/20, etc.
werede etc. see werian¹,².
ǥewerǥade II *pp. npl.* wearied 121/31.
werǥende see werian¹.
werian¹ I defend, protect 74/25, 103/ 18, 103/22, 121/28. werǥende *pr. p.* defending 50/22.
werian² I wear 89/6, 89/7, 101/20, 147/24, 150/4.
weriǥ *adj.* weary 41/22.
werod see weorod.
west *adv.* west, westward 10/10, 10/16, 11/15, 12/3, etc.
westan *adv.* west 20/30. *wiþ* ~, *be* ~ *w. dat.* to the west of 9/30, 9/33, 10/1, 13/27, etc.
westane *adv.* in the west 18/21, 147/21.
westannorþan *adv.* to the north-west 18/20. *be* ~ *w. dat.* to the north-west of 13/27, 18/6, 19/18.
westansuþan *adv. be* ~ to the south-west 18/26, 18/29, 20/22. *w. dat.* to the south-west of 18/12.
westanwind (*m.*) wind from the west 14/13.
westast see weste.
westdæl (*m.*) west part 43/2, 70/31. wæstdæle *ds.* 155/15.
weste *adj.* waste, uncultivated, unpopulated 14/2, 14/8, 14/22, 14/25, etc.; deserted, desolate 52/20. westast *sup.* most desolate 43/34.
west(e)mest *sup. adj.* most westerly 133/11, 133/25.
westen *f. and n.* wilderness, desert 11/11, 18/17, 18/32, 151/5, etc. westenne *asf.* 9/13; *dsn.* 13/7. westennes *gsn.* 150/30. westennum *dpl.* 74/20.
westende (*m.*) western extremity 9/10, 11/5.
westende I *pr. p.* laying waste 29/10.

westenne etc. see westen.
westeweard *adj.* western 9/7. *on westeweardum* in the western part 36/19, 74/4, 74/18.
westhealf(*f.*) western side 9/1, 10/28, 11/22, 18/8, etc.
westlang *adv.* in a westerly direction 21/8.
westmest see westemest.
westnorþ *adv.* north-west 12/30.
westnorþlang *adv.* extending north-west 18/19.
westrice *n.* western empire 8/9, 37/21.
westryhte, westrihte *adv.* due west 11/28, 11/31, 18/6.
westsceata *wk. m.* western promontory 21/5.
westsuþende *m.* south-west extremity 9/7.
westwe(a)rd *adv.* westwards 19/31; travelling westwards 48/6.
ǥewician II camp 14/26, 46/16, 93/19, 100/18, etc.
wiciaþ II *pr. pl.* camp 14/3. wicode *pa. t. 3 sg.* camped 16/5.
wicing *m.* pirate 6/5, 63/31, 120/4.
wicstow *f.* camp, encampment 44/22, 44/25, 51/22, 70/5 etc.
wide *adv.* widely 12/6; far and wide 77/18.
ǥewidere (*n.*) weather. *dpl.* ǥewideran 56/24.
widmære *adj.* celebrated 3/12.
widsæ *f.* open sea 14/8, 14/23, 16/16.
wieldre *comp. adj. nsf.* more powerful 84/29. wyldran *npl.* 87/21.
wi(e)lle (*f.*) spring 98/28, 131/1.
wiernde I *pa. t. 3 sg. w. gen. of thing and dat. of person* refused 153/5. wyrndon *pl.* prevented 26/9.
wierp (*m.*) blow 93/27.
wierþe see wyrþe.
wietena see wita.
wif *n.* wife 2/1, 29/19, 29/20, 31/24, etc.; woman, female 1/25, 32/17, 60/18, etc.
wiflic *adj.* feminine 22/12.
wifmon *m.* woman 43/11, 60/8, 98/14,104/27,etc. wifmen *ds.* 88/16; *napl.* 2/4, 112/19. wifmenn *npl.* 45/2. wifmonna *gpl.* 64/23. wifmonnum *dpl.* 30/12.

wig *n.* war 59/8, 84/6; fighting force 64/29.

wigcræft *m.* military skill 21/32, 22/1, 61/26, 84/1; military force 73/13, 94/12.

wighus (*n.*) tower, military fortification 43/32.

wigwægn (*m.*) war-chariot 26/14, 26/24.

wiht *n.* creature, thing 19/28. *w. gen.* wuht 119/17; uht 130/13. wyhta *npl.* 36/4.

wilde *adj.* wild 15/11, 15/23.

gewilde *adj.* captive 72/19.

wildeor (*n.*) wild animal 74/20, 119/21.

wildrum *dpl.* (*n.*) wild animals 15/8.

gewildum, gewildon *dpl.* (*n.?*) him to ~ gedon subjugate 72/6, 73/2, 73/28, 80/11, 83/13.

wile see willan.

gewill *n.* pleasure, will 34/9. *on his (hiora) gewill* according to his (their) wish 3/15, 30/30, 34/17, 69/27.

willa *wk. m.* will 8/5, 34/19, 47/15, etc.; desire 52/30, 53/15, 156/21; consent 90/3, 107/23. *his (hiora) agnum willan (willum)* of his (their) own accord 110/2, 148/3, 156/18. *hiere willum* voluntarily 31/13.

[willan] *anom. vb.* wish, intend, desire, will, *pa. t.* would, would like 3/17, 12/14, 14/5, 18/3, 27/11, etc.; to be used 122/2. wil(l)e *pr. 1, 3 sg.* 9/19, 122/2; *1 pl.* 11/25. willaþ *1, 3 pl.* 38/26, 114/3; wyllaþ 17/13. willen *subj. pl.* 152/25. wolde *pa. t. 1, 3 sg.* 1/23, 38/10. woldon *pl.* 2/5; woldan 59/4. wolden *subj. pl.* 35/5; wolde 155/24.

wilnian II *w. gen.* desire 6/1, 33/34, 47/13, 49/4, etc.

gewilnung *f.* desire 21/25, 61/25, 135/27. gewilnunga *ds.* 135/27.

wilþ see weallan.

win *n.* wine 44/24, 44/30, 117/11.

wind *m.* wind 11/18, 16/5, 26/25, 56/26, etc.

gewin(n) *n.* conflict, war 1/20, 2/21, 5/9, 5/12, etc.

winnan 3 fight 1/22, 2/8, 2/9, 21/31, etc. winnanne *dat. inf.* 30/3.

winnende *pr. p.* 2/24. won(n) *pa. t. 3 sg.* 3/9, 103/13; wann 82/8. wunnon *pl.* 1/8; wunnan 5/27. wunne *subj. sg.* 4/10. wunnen *pl.* 112/31.

gewinnan 3 conquer, capture 62/21, 71/9, 73/33, etc.; fight 80/28, 82/6. gewann *pa. t. 3 sg.* 62/7; gewonn 71/3. gewunnan *pl.* 80/28; gewunnon 82/6. gewunnen *pp.* 22/12. gewunnene *asf.* 35/11.

winter (*m. and*) *n.* year 2/25, 21/23, 21/24, 21/26, etc.; winter 14/3, 18/2. wintra *ds.* 14/3. wintran *dpl.* 27/1.

wintersetl (*n.*) winter quarters 100/14, 106/16.

gewintred *ppl. adj.* old in years, aged 150/3.

wintregum *adj. dpl.* wintry 11/17.

wiotodlice *adv.* truly 97/21.

wis *adj.* wise 35/28, 54/15.

wisdom *m.* wisdom 1/10, 23/31, 24/3.

wise *wk. f.* fashion, way 60/9, 75/26, 132/12, 141/14; condition 88/19. *in pl.* affairs 81/19, 90/22.

wislecre *comp. adj. nsn.* wiser 83/24.

wisse, wiste, etc. see witan¹.

wita *wk.* (*m.*) counsellor, senator 90/25, 118/24, 118/25, 119/8, etc. weotan *npl.* 117/23. wietena *gpl.* 90/3. weotum *dpl.* 6/2.

witan¹ *pret. pres. vb.* know, realize 22/18, 32/3, 32/25, 36/6, etc.; show, feel 24/23, 132/7. witanne *dat. inf.* 56/13. wat *pr. 1 sg.* 27/22. witan *pl.* 36/5; witon 12/16. wite *subj. sg.* 35/29. witende *pr. p.* deliberately, knowing 76/3. wiste *pa. t. 3 sg.* 44/9; wisse 14/12. wiston *pl.* 59/6. wisten *subj. pl.* 113/16.

witan² 1 *w. dat. of person* blame for 88/31. witan *pa. t. pl.* 137/13. witen *subj. pl.* would blame 116/19.

wite (*n.*) punishment 132/19.

gewiten see gewat.

witena see wita.

gewitgad II *pp.* prophesied 56/7.

witgan *npl.* (*m.*) prophets 139/12.

witnade II *pp.* tortured 86/20.

gewitnesse *dsf. on þære ~ wære* should be a witness 63/10.

witon see witan.

ǥewiton see ǥewat.

witum see wita.

wiþ, wyþ *prep. w. acc.* against, with 3/9, 5/23, 5/26, 19/28, 81/2, etc.; towards 133/30; from 104/22, 151/ 23; by, beside 9/23, 11/13, 14/1. *w. dat.* against, with 59/14, 92/28, 111/7, 123/29; by, beside 21/11; in exchange for 52/9, 83/15, 94/7, 111/ 31. *w. gen.* towards 64/21, 89/26, 103/18. *as conj. wiþ þæm þe* on condition that, in return for the concession that 67/27, 102/8, 151/7. *wiþ eastan* etc. see **eastan** etc. *wiþ . . . weard* see **weard**.

wiþæftan *prep. w. dat.* behind 42/7.

wiþcwædon 5 *pa. t. pl. w. dat.* of person and gen. of thing refused 64/3.

wiþerflita *wk.* (*m.*) opponent 38/26, 48/27, 57/6.

wiþerweard *adj.* hostile 134/17; *w. dat.* hostile to, opposed 4/22, 80/9, 97/4, 131/23, 136/27.

wiþerwinna *wk. m.* opponent 55/15, 138/6, 147/6, etc.; *w. dat.* 3/22, 6/19.

wiþhabban III *w. dat.* restrain, withstand 48/16.

wiþsacen see **wiþsoc.**

wiþsawon 5 *pa. t. pl. w. dat.* rebelled against 87/20.

wiþsoc 6 *pa. t. 3 sg. w. dat.* renounced 45/13. wiþsocon *pl.* (*w. neg. clause*) rejected 78/15. wiþsocen *subj. pl.* 67/28. wiþsacen *pp.* declared hostility? 41/5.

wiþstondan 6 *w. dat.* resist, withstand 30/14, 35/17, 67/20, 82/7, etc. wiþstod *pa. t. 3 sg.* 46/22. wiþstodon *pl.* 53/28. wiþstode *subj. sg.* 33/5.

wiþutan *prep. w. dat.* outside 43/30.

wiþwinnende 3 *pr. p. w. dat.* resisting, fighting against 62/30.

wlenco (*f.*) wealth 113/20.

wod *adj.* mad 60/17.

woh *n.* injustice, wrong 140/2, 153/1.

wol *m. and f.* plague 24/7, 41/23, 56/27, 75/17, 85/2ɓ.

wolbærnes (*f.*) pestilence 38/12.

wolbryne (*m.*) plague-fire, pestilence 49/20.

woldan, wolde, etc. see **willan.**

wolǥewinn (*n.*) pestilential conflict 38/27.

won, wonn see **winnan.**

ǥewonn see ǥewinnan.

wop (*m.*) lamentation 89/18, 128/3.

word *n.* word 41/2, 53/19, 95/31, 113/6, etc.; statement, saying 49/1, 55/26; story 26/32; opinion 101/28, 150/19; fame, (good) report 47/8.

ǥeworden(e) see ǥeweorþan.

ǥeworht, ǥeworhte see ǥewyrcan.

worhte, worhton see wyrcan.

worms *n.* pus 25/30.

worold, world, woruld *f.* world 24/22, 24/25, 24/33, 30/29, etc.

woroldlic *adj.* worldly 152/13.

woroldlice *adv.* after the manner of this world, temporally 153/16.

woroldgesælþon *dpl.* (*f.*) worldly goods, earthly blessings 21/30.

woroldþing (*n.*) worldly thing 148/2.

*woruldiermþum *dpl.* (*f.*) miseries of this life 139/21.

wraciende II *pr. p.* carrying on 32/6.

wraco, wracu *f.* vengeance, persecution, retribution, misery 23/5, 25/27, 41/17, 88/1, etc.

wræc, wræce see **wrecan.**

ǥewræc, ǥewræce, etc. see ǥewrecan.

ᵂræcc(e)a *wk. m.* exile 46/8, 54/11, 78/11.

wræcsiþ *m.* exile 63/25, 88/32, 139/9.

wræne *adj.* licentious 32/16. wrænast *sup.* most licentious 40/4.

wrænnesse *dsf.* licentiousness 1/5, 22/21.

wrat I *pa. t. 3 sg.* cut 123/16. writon *pl.* wrote 88/9.

wraþ *adj. w. dat.* hostile to, cruel to 134/20.

wrecan 5 avenge, take vengeance for 29/22, 29/26, 46/4, 151/24, etc. wrecende *pr. p.* 36/1. wræc *pa. t. 3 sg.* 98/15. wræce *subj. sg.* 90/16.

ǥewrecan 5 avenge, take vengeance for 43/10, 44/36, 54/31, 73/26, etc. ǥewræc *pa. t. 3 sg.* 134/25. ǥewræce *subj. sg.* 62/26. ǥewræcen *pl.* 31/29. ǥewrecen *pp.* 35/4.

wrenc *m.* stratagem 84/16, 101/4, 155/2.

ǥewrit *n.* document, deed, book 58/30, 129/8, 136/5, 141/22, etc. ǥewrito *npl.* the scriptures 10/4. ǥewritun *dpl.* 58/30.

writon see wrat.

wrixleden I *pa. t. subj. pl.* should exchange 95/29.

wroht *f.* strife 137/11.

wucu (*f.*) week 15/30. wucena *gpl.* 144/4.

wudu (*m.*) wood, forest 98/28, 114/24.

wuht see wiht.

wulf *m.* wolf 86/25, 119/26.

ǥewuna *wk. m.* custom 59/23, 60/7, 62/9, 72/30, etc. *swa hit ∼ is* as is customary 56/24.

wunade see wuniende.

wund (*f.*) wound 72/18, 129/4.

wund *adj.* wounded 65/1, 85/11, 93/6, 96/19, 96/21.

wunder see wundor.

wunderlecast *sup. adj.* most wonderful 44/1.

ǥewundod II *pp.* wounded 69/1, 84/19, 99/31, etc. ǥewundodne *asm.* 72/18. ǥewundedum *dpl.* 73/32.

wundor, wunder *n.* wonder, portent 2/22, 3/26, 4/26, 51/6, etc. wundra *gpl.* 135/6. wundrum *dpl.* 25/16.

wundrianne II *dat. inf.* wonder at 24/22, 73/20. wundrade *pa. t. 3 sg.* wondered 73/8. wundredan *pl. w. gen.* wondered at 92/6.

ǥewunian II remain 47/1, 100/14; be accustomed 23/28.

wuniende II *pr. p.* living, waiting 42/16, 44/33. wunode *pa. t. 3 sg.* lived 73/29; wunade should remain 95/32.

wunnan, wunnon, etc. see winnan.

ǥewunnan, ǥewunnen, etc. see ǥewinnan.

wurde, wurden, etc. see weorþan.

ǥewurde, -on, see ǥeweorþan.

wurpe see wearp.

wyhta see wiht.

ǥewylde I *pa. t. 3 sg.* subjected 119/2.

wyldran see wieldre.

wyllaþ see willan.

wyn (*f.*) pleasure 52/21.

wyrc(e)an I make, build, form 9/2, 11/8, 34/13, 46/7, 119/26, etc.; compose 137/24; perform 23/29, 24/7, 25/19. wyrcenne *dat. inf.* 23/29. worhte *pa. t. 3 sg.* 24/7. worhton *pl.* 92/16.

ǥewyrcan I make, build, construct 15/20, 34/6, 43/20, 43/28; obtain, achieve 46/2, 47/9, 47/28; carry out, perform 47/21, 88/7. ǥeworhte *pa. t. 3 sg.* 2/5. ǥeworht *pp.* 15/16. ǥewarhte *npl.* 114/10.

wyrd *f.* chance, accident 37/3, 37/23.

ǥewyrd *f.* determination 69/30.

ǥewyrht (*n.*) desert. ǥewyrhton *dpl.* 126/19. *∼ habban* deserve 41/30.

wyrhta *wk.* (*m.*) craftsman 34/13.

wyrm (*m.*) crawling animal 25/19 (see Commentary), 93/30.

wyrmcynna *gpl.* (*n.*) species of reptile 74/21.

wyrndon see wiernde.

wyrs *comp. adv.* worse 31/3, 35/8.

wyrse *comp. adj. n. and asn.* worse 31/11, 36/1; *nsf.* 27/12. wyrsan *napl.* 26/11, 34/16, 52/24. wyrrest *sup.* worst 65/29, 89/28.

wyrt (*f.*) herb 73/31.

wyrttruman *apl.* (*m. or f.*) roots 26/2.

wyrþ see weorþan.

wyrþe, wierþe *adj.* deserving 135/13; *w. gen.* deserving of 104/5, 153/29.

wyrþig *adj.* fitting 134/31.

wyscte I *pa. t. 3 sg.* wished 135/15.

wyþ see wiþ.

Y

yfel *n.* evil, wickedness, misery, affliction 31/21, 34/17, 49/11, 63/23, etc. yfles *gs.* 125/5. yflum *dpl.* 88/20.

yfel *adj.* evil 90/8, 141/27, 154/15; bad, ominous 49/4, 85/7 etc.; infamous 116/28. yflan *npl. wk.* 3/26.

yflian II harm 52/31, 156/16. yfelade *pa. t. 3 sg.* 156/16.

yǥland see iǥland.

ylcan, ylce see ilca.

ylde *ds*(*f.*) old age 118/26.

yldra, yldran see ieldra.

ymb, ymbe *prep. w. acc.* around 11/16, 25/1, 35/11, 37/31, etc.; after 35/25, 37/33, 131/8, etc.; about,

concerning 9/18, 12/14, 18/3, 37/24;
at, about (a stated time) 91/15,
100/9, 100/16. *þæs ymb an gear* etc.
one year later 75/23. *ymb fíf gear
þæs þe* etc. five years after 86/4. *in
postposition w. dat.* 81/17. *ymb . . .
utan* see **ymbutan.**
ymb(e)ġong *m.* circumference 43/27,
43/31, 112/8.
ymbfanġen 7 *pp.* surrounded 19/16.
ymbfaran 6 surround 46/33, 154/31.
ymbfaren *pp.* 154/31.
ymbhæfd III *pp.* surrounded 19/1,
19/2.
ymbhwyrft *m.* circle 8/11.
ymbliġeþ 5 *pr. 3 sg.* surrounds 8/12;
ymbliþ 12/19.

ymbsæton 5 *pa. t. pl.* besieged 40/29.
ymbseten *pp.* 39/29, 64/17, 91/17.
ymbutan *prep. w. acc.* around 13/14,
43/29. *as adv. east* ~ round in an
easterly direction 154/12. *ymb hie
utan* etc. round about them 14/28,
18/20.
ymbweaxen 7 *pp.* surrounded 72/7.
yndse *f.* ounce 104/27.
ġeypped I *pp.* disclosed 60/22.
yrnende see **i(e)rnan.**
ys see **beon.**
yst (*f.*) whirlwind 58/15.
ytemest *sup. adj.* furthest, extreme
19/19, 79/32.
yterenne *adj. asm.* of otter's skin
15/19.

GLOSSARY OF PROPER NAMES

A

Abbenas *npl. Lat.* Auenae (promunturium) 20/19 (Ricc. 627 and other
rel. MSS habennae, habenae).
Abrahame *ds.* Abraham 133/22,
133/25.
Abulia *ds.* Apulia 85/10.
Achie *ns.* Achaia (common var.
achia) 18/12; *ds.* 18/13, 56/4.
Achaie *ds.* 1/13, 3/1.
Achileus *nas.* Achilleus (common var.
achileus) 147/3, 147/9.
Actesifonte *ds.* Ctesiphon 150/27
(OH *abl. s.* a Ctesiphonte, Vienna
366 and other rel. MSS accesifonte,
actesifonte).
Ad(d)riaticum *ns.* Adriatic, *Lat.
neut. adj.* Hadriaticum (mare) 21/2;
n. or as. 20/5, 20/31, **21/9.* **Atriaticum** 18/16 (Vienna 366 and other
rel. MSS atriaticum).
Adipsus *ns.* Oedipus 28/8 (Vienna
366 and other rel. MSS *as.* odip-
pum).
Adrianus *ns.* Hadrian, *Lat.* Hadria-
nus 7/6, 140/9.

Adriaticum see **Addriaticum.**
Adrumetis *ns.* Hadrumetus 20/9. See
also **Aþrametum.**
Ægypta see **Egypti.**
Ægyptus, Aegyptus *nsf.* Egypt,
Lat. Aegyptus (*f.*) 11/1, 11/21,
11/23, 19/33, etc. **Ægyptum** *as.*
127/28; **Egyptum** 58/16. **Ægypte**
as. or pl. 29/7; **Egypte** 10/18.
Egyptum *ds.* 19/32 (OH *as.*
Aegyptum); *ds. (or dpl. of* Egypti)
24/7. **Ægyptum** *dpl.* Egypts 11/23.
See also **Egypti.**
Ælfe *gs.* of the Elbe 12/30, 13/18. Cf.
ODu. Elve, *OHG* Elbe.
Ælfrede *ds.* Alfred 13/29.
Æpira see **Epira.**
Æquitania, Aequitania, Equitania
ns. Aquitania (Vienna 366 and
other rel. MSS aequitania etc.)
18/28, 18/32; *ds.* 18/28; *npl.* the
people of Aquitania? 19/9.
Æsperos *n. or apl.* Hesperian 20/23
(OH *adj., asm.* Hesperium).
Æthiopes *npl.* the Ethiopians, *Lat.*
Aethiopes 20/14. See also **Æthio-
piam.**

Æthiopiam *as.* (*or pl.?*) Ethiopia 22/13 (OH *as.* Aethiopiam). Æthiopian *ds.* (*or pl.?*) 25/7. See also Æthiopian.

Æthiopian *npl.* the Ethiopians 26/30. See also Æthiopiam.

Æthiopica, Ethiopica *adj., as.?* Ethiopian, *Lat. adj.* Aethiopica (deserta) 9/13, 11/11. Æthiopicum *n. or as.* 19/34 (see Commentary); *ds.* 19/35 (OH gentes Libyoaethiopum). Æthiopicus *n. or as.* 20/1 (OH *nsm.* Aethiopicus).

Ætiubena *gpl.* of the Adiabeni 137/4 (OH *gpl.* Adiabenorum).

Æþna see Eþna.

Afdrede, Afrede *npl.* the Abodriti 13/1, 13/18, 13/20.

Affrica *nsf.* Africa (OH Africa, common var. Affrica) 8/22, 19/29, 19/31, 21/20, etc.; *as.* 19/22; *gs.* 9/14; *ds.* 51/13. Affricam *as.* 4/14, 8/14 (OH *as.* Africam); Africam 125/2 (OH *as.* Africam). African *as. or pl.* 74/10. See also Affrice.

Affricanisce *adj., nsn.* African 36/22.

Affricanum *adj., nsn.* African 36/13, 36/18 (OH *adj., nsn.* Africanum, rel. MSS affricanum).

Affricanus *nas.* Africanus (common var. affricanus) 109/2, 111/3.

Affrice, Africe *napl.* the Africans, Africa (*Lat. adj.* Africus, no exact equivalent in OH). *npl.* 121/3; *apl.* (*or as.* of Affrica) 4/15, 86/8, 93/12, 95/5, etc. Affrica *gpl.* (*or gs.* of Affrica) 25/8. Affricum, Africum *dpl.* (*or ds.* of Affrica?) 133/7, 152/18. See also Affrica.

Affricum *adj., n. or as.* African 21/10 (OH *abl. s.* Africo).

Agathocles, Agothocles *ns.* Agathocles (Vienna 366 and other rel. MSS often agothocles) 85/21, 91/10, 91/23; *gs.* 91/15. Agothoclen *as.* 82/13 (OH *as.* Agathoclem). Agathocle, Agothocle *ds.* 90/29, 91/20.

Ageselaus *ns.* Agesilaus (Ricc. 627 and other rel. MSS ageselaus etc.) 54/16. See also Iesulause.

Agidis *ns.* Hagis 70/28 (OH *gs.* Hagidis, common var. agidis).

Agothocles see Agathocles.

Agrigentum *as.* Agrigentum 105/7. See also Argentine.

Agustinus *ns.* Augustine, *Lat.* Augustinus 57/14.

Agustus[1] *nas.* Augustus 130/4, 131/27, 132/1, 132/3, etc. Agustuses *gs.* 131/28. Agustuse *ds.* 6/19.

Agustus[2] August, *Lat. adj.* Augustus 130/3. See calendas.

Ahtena, Ahtene, etc. see Athena, Athene, etc.

Alamanni *apl.* the Alamanni 147/7. Alomonne *dpl.* 152/27 (v.l. alamanne).

Albani *npl.* the Albani 12/12 (OH *ns.* Albania).

Albinus *as.* Albinus 142/10.

Alceta *ns.* Alceta 79/13. See also Alciþen.

Alciþen *ns.* Alceta (Vienna 366 and other rel. MSS alcita) 80/29. See also Alceta.

Alexander *nas.* Alexander 3/9, 22/14, 30/34, 31/23, 70/1, etc. Alexandres *gs.* 3/10; Alexanderes 70/30. Alexandre *ds.* 61/13.

Alexandria *n. or as.* Alexandria 69/20, 71/12; *ds.* 8/21, 9/11, 135/24, etc. Alexandriam *as.* 130/21.

Alomonne see Alamanni.

Alpeam *as.* Clypea 93/16 (OH *as.* Clipeam, Ricc. 627 alpeam). See also Clepeam.

Alpis *n. or as. or pl.* the Alps, *Lat. pl.* Alpes 12/18, 13/5, 18/17, 18/21, 18/25, etc.; *dpl.* 99/22.

Alrica *ns.* Alaric 37/34, 155/26, 156/13. Alrican *gs.* 156/19; *ds.* 155/23.

Amazanas, Amozenas *n. or apl.* the Amazons, *Lat.* Amazones 1/26, 29/35.

Ambictio *ns.* Amphictyon (Vienna 366 ampiction, Ricc. 627 and Selden B 16 ampictio) 24/30. Ambictiones *gs.* 1/13, 24/32.

Ambira *ns.* Ambira 73/29.

Ambogestes *ns.* Arbogastes 154/22. See also Arbogastes.

Ambronos *apl.* the Ambrones 122/8 (OH *apl.* Ambronas).

Amilcor, Amicor, Amilchor *nas.* Hamilcar (common var. hamilchar)

90/21, 91/27, 93/14, 94/1, etc.

Amilcores gs. 96/9, 108/13.

Amilius ns. Aemilius 101/2. See also **Emilius**.

Amintas as. Amyntas 71/15. See also **Omintos**.

Amon ns. Ammon 10/19.

Amones gs. Amun's 69/21, 69/25 (OH gs. Hammonis, Vienna 366 and other rel. MSS amonis).

Amoses n. or as. Amasis 24/17 (OH Amosis, Vienna 366 and other rel. MSS amoses).

Amozenas see **Amazanas**.

Andra ns. Antander (OH Andro, MSS of rel. group A andra) 91/15.

Andregatia ds. Andragathius (Vienna 366 andragatius) 154/10.

Angle see **Ongle**.

Anilius as. Aulus 120/26. See also **Aula**.

Annianes n. or as. the Anio 103/15 (OH as. Anienem, var. ann-).

Anthiopa ns. Antiope (Ricc. 627 and Vienna 366 anthiope) 30/21.

Antigones, Antigonus nas. Antigonus 77/28, 78/30, 79/8, 79/14, etc. **Antigones** gs. 79/19. **Antigone** ds. 78/17.

Antiochia ds. Antioch, Lat. Antiochia 153/8.

Antiochus ns. Antiochus 6/1, 108/26, 109/7, 118/20. **Antiochuses** gs. 109/5. **Antiochuse** ds. 108/29, 109/2, etc.

Antipater nas. Antipater 70/29, 80/29, 82/1, 82/14. **Antipatrum** as. 78/22 (OH as. Antipatrum). **Antipatre** ds. 79/17; **Antipatrume** 78/25.

Antonius[1] nas. Antonius 129/16, 129/11, 129/13, etc. *Antoniuses gs. 129/29. **Antoniuse** ds. 129/15.

Antonius[2] ns. Antoninus (Vienna 366 and other rel. MSS antonius) 7/8, 7/12, 141/2, 141/21, etc.

Apis ns. Apis 24/20.

Apius ns. Appius 115/4 (Vienna 366 and other rel. MSS apius). **Appius** as. 92/3.

Apulcius ns. Apuleius 122/27.

Aquilegia ds. Aquileia (MSS of rel. groups A, B, and C gs. aquilegie) 143/14, 154/9, 154/17.

Arabia nas. Arabia 10/15, 77/24; ds. (or as.) 22/32.

Arachasihedros apl.? the Arachossi and Chedrosi (OH npl. Arachossi Chedrosique) 78/4.

Araxis ns. the Araxes 44/19 (OH gs. Araxis).

Arbatus ns. Arbatus 2/4, 32/18, 36/28. **Arbate** ds. 37/30.

Arbis ns. Arbis 10/8.

Arbogastes, Arbogestes ns. Arbogastes 155/3, 155/9. See also **Ambogestes**.

Arcadium dpl. the Arcadians, Lat. Arcades 55/24.

Arcadiusan see **Archadius**.

Arcadum as. OH Arcadum, gpl. of Lat. Arcades, the Arcadians, apparently taken as the name of a town 55/21.

Archadius ns. Arcadius 8/8, 155/14, 155/17 (Selden B 16 and MSS of rel. groups B, C, and D archadius).

Arcadiusan as. 56/9 (OH gs. Arcadii).

Archalaus as. Archelaus (MSS of rel. groups B and D archalaus) 125/18.

Archolaus ns. 78/9 (prob. under influence of preceding name Archos).

Archimepes gs. Archimedes' 103/12.

Archolaus see **Archalaus**.

Archos apl.? (or ns.) Archon, personal name, possibly taken as name of people (Vienna 366 and other rel. MSS archos) 78/9.

Areas apl. the Arei 78/5 (OH apl. Areos).

Arfatium n. or as. Carpathian 20/30 (OH abl. s. Carpathio, frequent var. carphatio).

Arge see **Argus**.

Argeatas ns. Ariarathes (Vienna 366 and other rel. MSS ariarates) 110/16. See also **Ariarata, Argeate**.

Argeate ds. the name of the king, Ariarathes, taken as a place name 118/8 (OH abl. s. Ariarathe, MSS of rel. group D ariathe). See also **Argeatas, Ariarata**.

Argentine ds. Agrigentum 33/34 (OH apl. Agrigentinos, MS Vienna 480 argentinos), 92/11. See also **Agrigentum**.

Argi *n. or apl.* the Argives, people of Argos 24/19 (OH *apl.* Argiuos, Ricc. 627 argios).

Argiraspides *npl.* the Argyraspides, 'armed with a silver spear' 79/21 (OH *apl.* Argyraspidas).

Argus *as.?* the town of Argos 86/5 (OH *apl.?* Argos). **Arge** *as. or pl.* 27/6 (OH *apl.?* Argos)

Arianiscan see **Arrianiscan.**

Ariarata *ds.* Ariarathes 78/28 (OH *ds.* Ariarato). See also **Argeatas, Argeate.**

Ariminio *ds.* Ariminum 98/29 (OH *ds.* Arimini, common var. arimino).

Aristobolus *as.* Aristobulus 125/29 (Vienna 366 and other rel. MSS *as.* aristobolum).

Aristonocuse *ds.* Aristonicus 5/29, 118/3.

Aristotolese *ds.* Aristotle 71/28 (OH *as.* Aristotelen).

Aripeusses *gs.* Arridaeus' 80/3 (v.l. Aripeuses, OH *gs.* Arridaei, common var. aridei).

Armenan *as.* Armenes 108/9 (OH *as.* Armenen).

Armenia *ns.* Armenia 10/23; *gs.* 11/29; *ds.* 118/8. **Armenie** *nas. or pl.* 10/17, 10/22, 125/17. **Armeniam** *as.* 141/7 (OH Armeniam). See also **Armenie.**

Armenie *apl.* the Armenians, *Lat.* Armenii, 78/8. See also **Armenia.**

Arocasia *ns.* Arachosia (Ricc. 627 and other rel. MSS arocasia) 10/3.

Arosinis *ds. or pl.* Arusini (campi) 85/31 (OH *dpl.* Arusinis, Ricc. 627 and other rel. MSS arosinis).

Arpellas *ns.* Harpalus (Ricc. 627 and other rel. MSS (h)arpall-) 33/28. **Arpelles** *ds.* 33/4.

Arpis *ds. or pl.* the city of Arpi 100/32 (OH *apl.* Arpos).

Ar(r)ianiscan *adj., ds. wk.* Arian 149/24, 151/22. **Arrianisce** *apl. m. strong* 153/10.

Arrius *ns.* Arius (common var. arrius) 149/10.

Arrunses *gs.* Arruns' 40/27 (OH *abl. s.* Arrunte). See Commentary.

Artabatus *ns.* Artabanus 48/25.

Artecserses *ns.* Artaxerxes 51/10.

Artecsersis *ns.* 58/21; *n. or as.* 58/16.

Aruhes *ns.* Aruba (Ricc. 627 and other rel. MSS arucha) 62/2; *gs.* 62/1.

Arzuges *n. or apl.* the Arzuges 20/3.

Asculum *as.* Asculum 124/14.

Asia *ns.* Asia 1/24, 8/15, 8/16, 10/26, etc.; *gs.* 6/1. **Assia** *ds.* 108/26. **Asiam** *ns.* (v.l. asia) 30/13; *as.* 8/14 (often for OH Asiam); *gs.* 28/24; *ds.* 10/26 (OH Asiam), 30/5. **Asian** *gs.* 11/25; *ds.* 29/16. *seo læsse* ~ OH Asia minor 10/24, 118/4, etc.

Asilia *ns.* Assyria (Ricc. 627 and other rel. MSS asiria) 10/3. See also **Asiria.**

Asina *ns.* Asina 92/20.

Asiria *n. or as.* Assyria (Ricc. 627 and other rel. MSS asiria) 10/4; *ds.* 2/3, 32/14, 37/20; *gs.* (or gpl. of Asirie) 1/3. See also **Asilia, Asirie.**

Asirie, Asyrie *napl.* the Assyrians, *Lat.* Assyrii (common var. asyrii, asirii) 27/23, 32/23, 49/14, 70/22, etc. **Asiria, Asyria** *gpl.* 36/28; *gpl.* (or gs. of **Asiria**) 1/3, 21/24. **Asiriæ** *apl.* 45/15. **Asirium** *dpl.* 132/27; **Assirin** 24/19. See also **Asiria.**

Assapias *apl.* the Adaspii 71/10 (Ricc. 627 and other rel. MSS *apl.* assapios).

Assia see **Asia.**

Assirin see **Asirie.**

Asterbal see **Hasterbal.**

Astiai *ns.* Astyages 32/30 (OH *ds.* Astyagi, common var. astiagi), 33/4.

***Astrixim** *ns.* (or pl.) Astrixis 20/16 (OH *as.* Astrixim).

Asyrie see **Asirie.**

Athanaricus *as.* Athanaricus 153/23. See also **Godenric.**

Athaniense see **Atheniense.**

Atheas *ns.* Atheas 64/13.

Athena *nas.* Athens, *Lat. pl.* Athenae 18/11, 55/30; *ds.* 24/30. **Ahtene** *as.* 51/7, 53/20, 53/23, etc. **Ahtena** *ds.* 54/11. See also **Athene.**

Athene, Ahtene *napl.* the Athenians, *Lat.* Athenienses 55/2, 62/23, 63/18, 67/28, etc. **Ahtenum** *dpl.* 54/30. See also **Athena, Atheniense.**

Atheniense, Athenienses, Ahteniense *napl.* the Athenians, *Lat.* Athenienses 45/29, 45/30, 51/1, 53/28, etc.; *dpl.* 28/14. **Athaniense** *npl.* 1/21. **Atheniensium** *npl.* 2/7, 34/22 (OH *gpl.* Atheniensium); *dpl.* 35/20. **Atheniensa** *gpl.* 28/15. **Atheniensum** *dpl.* 47/25. **Atheniensem** *dpl.* (*or ds.*) 35/13 (OH *adj.*, *as.* Atheniensem). See also **Athena, Othinentium.**

Athium *ns. or pl.* Antium (common var. anthium) 100/34.

Athlans *nas.* Atlas (OH Athlans) 9/16, 20/22; *ds.* 11/6.

Atilius *ns.* Atilius 93/11, 96/6. See also **Atirius.**

Atirius *ns.* Atilius 97/12. See also **Atilius.**

Atregsas *n. or gs.* Atreus 28/6 (OH *gs.* Atrei; Laon 137 atregi).

Atrianus *ns. or apl.* Bactriani 78/6 (Ricc. 627 *apl.* atrianos). See also **Bactriana, Pactriane.**

Atriaticum see **Addriaticum.**

Attalis *ns.* Attalus 118/4 (OH *gs.* Attali). See also **Catulusan.**

Aprametum *ds.* Hadrumetum 107/19 (Vienna 366 *as.* atrimetum). See also **Adrumetis.**

Aula *ns.* Aulus 110/30 (OH A., MSS *abl. s.* aulo). See also **Anilius.**

Aulolum *ns.* the Autololes 20/23 (OH *gpl.* Autololum, Ricc. 627 and Vienna 366 aulolum).

Aurelianus *ns.* Aurelius 143/2 (MSS of rel. group C aurelianus). See Commentary.

Aurelius¹ *ns.* Aurelius 7/14, 142/21. **Aureliuse** *ds.* 7/8, 141/2.

Aurelius² *ns.* Aurelianus 7/22, 145/23 (BN 17567 aurelius).

B

Babylonia *nas.* Babylon, Babylonia, *Lat.* Babylon, Babylonia 10/11, 37/11, 37/15, 37/17, etc.; *ds.* 43/4. **Babyloniam** *as.* 115/31 (OH *as.* Babyloniam). **Babylonie** *as.* 36/27. See also **Babylonie.**

Babylonicum *adj.*, *nsn.* Babylonian, *Lat.* Babylonicum 36/12, 36/16 (OH *adj.*, *nsn.* Babylonium). See also **Babylonisce.**

Babylonie *npl.* the Babylonians, *Lat.* Babylonii 38/18, 81/21 (*or apl.*). **Babylonias** *apl.* 78/9 (OH *apl.* Babylonios). **Babylonia** *gpl.* (*or gs. of* Babylonia) 36/29, 36/30. **Babylonium** *dpl.* 44/8. See also **Babylonia.**

Babylonisce *adj.*, *nsn.* Babylonian 36/19 (OH *adj.*, *asn.* Babylonium). See also **Babylonicum.**

Bachinum *ns.* Pachynum 21/5 (Stuttgart 19 bachinum).

Bactriana *gpl.* of the Bactriani 22/4. See also **Atrianus, Pactriane.**

Bægware, Begware *napl.* the Bavarians 12/26, 13/4. **Begwara** *gpl.* 13/6. Cf. *Anglo-Saxon Chronicle* s.a. 891 Bægerum, Begerum, OHG Baiari, Beiere, Peigirae, etc., *Lat.* Baiovarii.

Bæme *npl.* the Bohemi 12/27. See also **Behemas.**

Bagrada *ns.* Bagrada 93/20.

Balearis *npl.* the Balearic Islands, *Lat.* Baleares (insulae) 21/17 (*or apl.*) 21/18, 21/20. See also **Belearis.**

Baleus *ns.* Baleus 24/18.

Bardan *as.* Bardo 100/9. See Commentary.

Basterne *n. or apl.* the Basternae 110/7.

Begware see **Bægware.**

Behemas *apl.* the Bohemians 13/3. See also **Bæme** and cf. *OHG* Beheima, Beheime, 9th- c. *Lat.* Boemi, Behemi and Steinmeyer and Sievers III. 206 Boemi: beheima. See further Introduction, p. lxx.

Belearis *as. or pl.* the Balearic Islands 120/3 (OH *apl.* Baleares insulas). See also **Balearis.**

Bellica *ns.* Belgic, *Lat.* Belgica (Vienna 366 and other rel. MSS bellica) 18/24 (*or as.*), 19/13. Cf. *OE Bede* 26/2 Gallia Bellica.

Benefente *as. or pl.* Beneventum 58/8, 102/12.

Beormas *npl.* the Biarmians, *ON* Bjarmar 14/24, 14/27, 14/30. See Commentary.

Betuitusan *as.* Bituitus 6/6, 120/7.

Beuius *ns.* Baebius 109/13.

Biþþinia *ds.* Bithynia 118/7.

Bizantium[1] *nas.* Byzacium 20/6, 20/9 (Selden B 16 and other rel. MSS bizantium).

Bizantium[2] *nas.* Byzantium 3/11, 63/33, 64/4.

Blaciduses *gs.* Placidus' 95/13.

Blecingaeg *ns.* Blekinge 16/27.

Blesus *ns.* Blaesus (common var. blesus) 95/4.

Boeti *apl.* the Boetians, *Lat.* Boeotii (common var. Boetii) 55/31. Boetium *dpl.* 35/19, 48/20.

Boho *ns.* Bocchus 121/19, 122/3. Bohan *as.* 121/16 (OH *abl. s.* Boccho).

Bonorum *as.* Bonosus 146/11 (OH *as.* Bonosum: cf. Vat. Lat. 3339 bonorum).

Bore *ns.* Boreum 12/3.

Bosiridis *ns.* Busiris 1/18. Bosiriþis *gs.* 27/9 (OH *gs.* Busiridis, Vienna 366 and other rel. MSS bos(s)iridis).

Bothmose *ds.* Patmos 139/9 (OH *as.* Patmum, MSS of rel. groups A and C pathmos).

Bretlande *ds.* Britain 147/3.

Brettanie *npl.* the Britons 8/4, 153/28. For possible *apl.* forms see Brettannia.

Brettannia, Brittannia, Bryttania *nas.* Britain, *Lat.* Britannia (common var. brittan(n)ia) 12/19, 13/15, 18/27, 19/11, etc. Brettannia *ds.* 19/18. Brettaniam *as.* 147/8; Brettannie 148/7; Bretanie 126/4. Brettanie *apl.* the British Isles 142/11 (OH *apl.* Britannias), 148/1 (*or apl. of* Brettanie).

Brettas *apl.* the Britons, *Lat.* Britanni 126/4, 126/6, 142/12.

Brigantia *as.* Brigantia 19/5.

Brittanisca *adj.*, *nsm. wk.* British, *Lat.* Britannicum (common var. brittanicum) 18/26.

Brobus *ns.* Probus 146/9. See Probus.

Bruti *napl.* the Bruttii (Vienna 366 and other rel. MSS *npl.* bruti) 76/28, 106/4. See also Bryti.

Brutus *nas.* Brutus 2/16, 40/9, 40/16, 40/17, etc. Brutuses *gs.* 40/6. Brutuse *ds.* 40/25.

Bryti *npl.* the Bruttii? 77/1. See Commentary.

Bryttania see Brettannia.

Bubulcus *ns.* Bubulcus 97/12.

Bucefal *ns.* Bucephala 72/17, 72/22 (OH *as.* Bucefalen).

Burgendan *napl.* the inhabitants of Bornholm 13/22 (2×). Burgenda *gpl.* 16/25, 16/26. Cf. ON Borgundarholmr, Bornholm.

Burgende *napl.* the Burgundians 18/35. Burgendum *dpl.* 152/4 (OH *gpl.* Burgundionum). Cf. OE Martyrology 178/22 Burgenda, OE Bede 142/20 Burgundena.

C

Calabria *ds.*, *gs. or gpl.?* Calabria, Calabrian 56/26 (OH *abl. pl.* Calabris [saltibus]).

Calatinus *ns.* Calatinus 4/8, 92/30, 93/1.

Caldea *ns.* Chaldaea 10/11 (Vienna 366 and other rel. MSS caldea).

Caldei *napl.* the Chaldaeans, *Lat.* Chaldaei (common var. caldei) 37/13, 45/15; *dpl.* 37/32. Caldeum *dpl.* 32/25; Chaldeum 77/32.

*Calfurnius *ns.* Calpurnius (MSS of rel. groups B and C calfurnius, calphurnius) 120/10. Calfurnan *as.* 120/18.

Caligardamana *n. or as.* Caligardamana 9/24.

Calonie *apl.* OH colonias, interpreted as proper name 78/3. See Commentary.

Calpis *ns.* Calpe, the Rock of Gibraltar 20/19 (OH Calpes, Ricc. 627 and other rel. MSS calpis).

Cambisis *ns.* Cambyses 2/20, *45/11.

Camerinam *ds.* Camerina 92/31 (OH *as.* Camerinam); Camerinan 4/9.

Camillis *ns.* Camillus 51/25 (OH *gs.* Camilli).

Campaina *ds.* Campania 103/14, 104/12; Compania 84/13.

Campena *gpl.?* of the inhabitants of Campania 58/24 (OH *dpl.* Campanis).

Canone *ds.* Caranus 133/6 (OH *abl. s.* Carano, MSS of rel. groups A, B, and C carono).

Capadoca *gpl.* the Cappadocians', *Lat. pl.* Cappadoces (common var. capadoces) 78/28. See also **Capadotia.**

Capadotia, Capodocia *ns.* Cappadocia (common var. capadocia, capodocia) 10/22, 70/24; *ds.* 10/23, 10/24, 10/25, etc. **Capadocia** *gs.* (or *gpl.*) 110/16. **Capodotia** *ds.* 10/23; **Cappadocia** 118/8. **Capadotiam** *as.* 62/32; *a. or ds.* 29/16; *npl.* 63/1 (OH *as.* Cappadociam). **Capodotiam** *as.* 141/6.

Caperronie *ns.* Caparronia 88/5; **Caperrone** 4/1.

Capitoliam *n. or as.* the Capitol, *Lat.* Capitolium, arx Capitolina 49/26, 52/12; *as.* 142/1 (v.l. capitolium); *ds.* 145/19 (v.l. capitolium).

Capu *ds.* Capua 104/13.

Carendre *ns.* Carentania 13/5. **Carendran** *g. or ds.* 13/7. **Carendan** *ds.* 18/18. Cf. Steinmeyer and Sievers III. 207 Carentani: kerendra.

Cariam *as.* Caria 77/29 (OH *as.* Cariam). **Caria** *ds.* 98/31.

Cartaginenses *npl.* the Carthaginians, *Lat.* Carthaginienses 86/10, 87/11, 89/18; *dpl.* 86/8. See also **Cartaine, Cartainiense.**

Cartaina *nas.* Carthage, *Lat.* Carthago, Carthaginis 5/20, 6/4, 20/10, 89/8, etc.; *gs.* (or *gpl.* of **Cartaine**) 3/6; *ds.* 4/2. **Cartainam** *as.* 119/24; **Cartainan** 112/15. Cf. *Alfred's Soliloquies* 48/13 Cartaina. See also **Cartaine.**

Cartaine *napl.* the Carthaginians, *Lat.* Carthaginienses 4/5, 96/7, 96/24, 97/15, etc. **Cartaina** *gpl.* 3/6. **Cartainum** *dpl.* 5/7. See also **Cartaina, Cartain(i)ense.**

Cartain(i)ense *napl.* the Carthaginians, *Lat.* Carthaginienses (common var. t for th) 91/5, 91/12, 94/5, 95/19, etc. **Cartain(i)enses** *npl.* 90/18, 90/27, 91/30, etc. **Cartainiensa** *gpl.* 94/3. **Cartainiensium** *dpl.* 91/19. See also **Cartaginenses, Cartaine.**

Cartalon *as.* Carthalo 105/16 (OH *abl. s.* Carthalone, common var. cartalone).

Cartanense *ds.?* Carthage 91/11. See also **Cartaina.**

Carus *ns.* Carus 7/25, 146/15.

Casius *ns.* Cassius 110/12. See also **Cassus.**

Caspia *n. or as.* Caspian, *Lat.* Caspium 12/4, 58/19; *ds.* 12/7.

Cassander *nas.* Cassander 77/32, 80/4, 80/14, 80/16. **Cassandres** *gs.* 81/32. **Cassandre** *ds.* 81/6.

Cassus *as.* Cassius 129/12. See also **Casius.**

Cathenas *apl.* the Cattheni 72/24 (OH *apl.* Catthenos, Ricc. 627 and other rel. MSS cathenas).

Cathma *ds.* Cadmus 28/2 (OH *abl. s.* Cadmo, Vienna 366 and other rel. MSS cathmo).

Cato *ns.* Cato 126/22. **Caton** *gs.* 127/15; *ds.* 123/3, 128/13.

Catulusan *as.* Attalus 71/16 (Ricc. 627 and Vienna 366 catulus). See also **Attalis.**

Caucarius *ns.* Carausius 147/3 (MSS of rel. groups A, B, and C caurasius).

Caucasus *ns.* Caucasus 9/29; *gs.* 78/4; *n. or apl.* 11/26; *apl.* 71/11; *dpl.* 10/6, 12/5. **Caucasis** *ns.* 9/26. **Caucaso** *ds.* 10/13.

Caudenes *nas.* ∼ **Furculus** the Caudine Forks, *Lat.* Caudinae Furculae 3/12, 66/11, 66/17 (Vienna 366 and other rel. MSS *apl.* caudenas furculas); *ds.* 116/30.

Cecilium *as.* Caecilius 77/1. See also **Celius, Eliuses.**

Celius *ns.* Caecilius 101/22 (Vienna 366 and other rel. MSS *abl. sg.* celio). See also **Cecilium.**

Cenomanni *npl.* the Cenomanni 108/12.

Censorinus *ns.* Censorinus 111/25.

Centauri *n. or apl.* Centaurs 28/19.

Centenus *ns.* Centenius 102/29 (Selden B 16 and other rel. MSS centenus).

Centlond *n. or as.* Kent 126/5. **Centlonde** *ds.* 126/6.

Cepio *ns.* Caepio (common var. cepio) 95/4.

Cerene *dpl.* the Cyrenae 91/22.

Cesar *ns.* Caesar 130/26.

Chaldeum see **Caldei**.

Chalisten *as.* Callisthenes 71/27 (OH *as.* Callisthenen, MSS of rel. group C challisten).

Cheranisse *dpl.* Chersonese 64/11 (OH *gs.* Cherronesi, Vienna 366 cerronisi).

Chorasmas *apl.* the Chorasmi 71/26 (OH *apl.* Chorasmos).

Ciarsathi, Ciarsæthi *npl.* the Caryatii 1/8, 23/13 (Ricc. 627 and other rel. MSS ciarsathii, ciarsati).

Ciclades *n. or apl.* the Cyclades 20/33.

Cicrope *ds.* Cecrops 24/31 (OH *abl. s.* Cecrope, Selden B 16 and other rel. MSS cicrope).

Cilia *ns.* Cilicia 10/26. **Cilium** *as.* 12/1. See also **Cilicia**.

Cilicia *nas.* Cilicia 20/27 (*or ds.*), 70/24. **Cilicium** *as.* 69/17 (OH *as.* Ciliciam), 77/25 (OH *as.* Ciliciam); *ds.* 68/24.

Cimbros *apl.* the Cimbri 122/8 (OH *apl.* Cimbros).

Cinam *ds.* Erycina 96/22 (Ricc. 627 and other rel. MSS *as.* decinam). See Commentary.

Cinna *ns.* Cinna 125/4, 125/12.

Cipros *ns.* Cyprus, *Lat.* Cypros (common var. cipros) 20/26.

Cirenceastre *ds.* Cirencester 126/10.

Cirimacia *ns.* Cyrenaica 19/33 (Ricc. 627 cirinacia, Vat. Lat. 1975 cirimaca).

Cirinen *as.* Caenina, OH Caeninensium oppidum 39/29 (Ricc. 627 and other rel. MSS *gpl.* cyrinensium). See also **Cirinensa**.

Cirinensa *gpl.* of the inhabitants of Caenina, Caeninenses 39/25 (OH *gpl.* Caeninensium, Ricc. 627 and other rel. MSS cyrinensium). See also **Cirinen**.

Cirspinus *as.* Crispinus 105/26.

Cirus *ns.* Cyrus (common var. cirus) 2/18, 33/1, 33/15, 33/26 etc. **Ciruses** *gs.* 45/17. **Ciruse** *ds.* 33/32.

Cipnus *ns.* Cydnus (common var. cidnus) 68/25.

Clafrione *ds.* Glabrio 109/4 (OH *abl. s.* Glabrione, Laon 137 clabrione).

Claudius *nas.* Claudius 4/17, 4/26, 5/22, 7/21, etc.; *gs.* 60/14. **Claudium** *as.* 50/21. **Claudiuses** *gs.* 137/1. **Claudiuse** *ds.* 137/13.

Cleoffiles *gs.* Cleophylis' 72/4.

Cleopatra, Cleopatro *ns.* Cleopatra 129/29, 130/6, 130/9. **Cleopatron** *as.* 129/18, 130/2.

Clepeam *ds.* Clypea 94/23 (OH *as.* Clipeam, Ricc. 627 and other rel. MSS clepeam). See also **Alpeam**.

Climax *n. or as.* Climax 11/3.

Clitus *ns.* Clitus 71/18, 71/21.

Coelle *ns.* Coele 10/19.

Colima *ds.* Calama 121/1.

Collina *n. or as.* Colline, *Lat.* Collina 103/21.

Colosus *ns.* Colossus (common var. colosus) 98/32.

Comagena *ns.* Commagena 10/18.

Compania see **Campania**.

Conon *nas.* Conon 54/11, 54/22, 54/26, 55/9, etc. **Conone** *ds.* 55/5.

Constans *nas.* Constans 149/25, 149/26. **Constante** *ds.* 149/23.

Constantinopolim *ns.* Constantinople 56/6 (OH *as.* Constantinopolim), 64/6, 149/17 (*or as.*); *ds.* (OH *as.* Constantinopolim) 9/5, 18/4, 18/5, 153/24.

Constantinus *nas.* Constantinus 148/18, 149/2, 149/7, 149/13, etc. **Constantinuse** *ds.* 148/8; **Constantino** 64/5; **Constantine** 149/22.

Constantius *nas.* Constantius 147/5, 148/1, 148/7, etc. **Constantiuse** *ds.* 147/27.

Cordofa *n. or as.* Córdoba, *Lat.* Corduba 104/30. See Commentary.

Corintus *ns.* Corinth, *Lat.* Corinthus 18/11. **Corinthum** *ns.* 5/21 (based on 114/6 *as.*); *as.* 78/21 (OH *as.* Corinthum), 114/6. Corinton *ds.* 18/12.

Cornelius *nas.* Cornelius 92/20, 99/6, 99/19, 107/21, etc.

Corrinthisce *adj., n. or apl. n.* Corinthian 114/9 (v.l. corinthisce, OH *adj., npl. n.* Corinthia).

Corsica *nas.* Corsica 21/12, 21/17 (2 ×). **Corsicam** *as.* 92/28.

Cotta *ns.* Cotta 4/15, 95/9.

Craccus *ns.* Gracchus 5/26, 102/32, 117/26. See also **Gratias.**

Crassus *ns.* Crassus 110/12, 118/2. **Crassuse** *ds.* 118/5.

Crecas *napl.* the Greeks, *Lat.* Graeci 31/27, 45/29, 46/11, 126/23, etc. **Creacas** *n. or apl.* 23/17. **Creca** *gpl.* 1/21. **Crecum** *dpl.* 48/31. See also **Crece.**

Crece *napl.* the Greeks, *Lat.* Graeci 62/16 (2×), 108/10, 109/15. See also **Crecas.**

Crecisc *adj., asn.* Greek 29/35. **Crecisce** *nsn. wk.* 36/17, 36/21.

Cremone *as.* Cremona 108/15.

Cretan see **Creto.**

Cretense *npl.* the Cretans, *Lat.* Cretenses 1/21, 28/14; *dpl.* 28/13. **Creticum** *adj., ns.* Cretan, *Lat. neut.* Creticum 20/30.

Cretisca *adj., nsm. wk.* Cretan 21/1.

Creto *ns.* Crete, *Lat.* Creta 20/29. **Cretan** *ds.* 106/30 (OH *as.* Cirtam, Vienna 366 certam; see Commentary).

Crispum *as.* Crispus 149/13 (OH *as.* Crispum).

Crist *ns.* Christ, *Lat.* Christus 31/16, 56/10, 59/20, 104/4, etc. **Cristes** *gs.* 133/22. **Criste** *ds.* 104/3.

Croesus *ns.* Croesus 44/8.

Cuintinus *ns.* Quintus 122/7 (OH Q., MSS Quintus).

Cuintius see **Quintius.**

Cuintus see **Quintus.**

Curius *ns.* Curius 76/23, 85/30.

Curtius *ns.* Curtius 3/3, 57/21.

Cwenas *npl. m.* the Lapps 15/34, 15/36. **Cwena** *gpl.* 15/34. Cf. *ON* Kvænir.

Cwenland *nsn.* land of the Lapps 13/26. Cf. *ON* Kvænland.

Cwensæ *n. or as.* Lappish Sea 12/22. See Commentary.

Cwintus see **Quintus.**

D

Dacos *apl.* the Dahae 71/26 (OH *apl.* Dahas, Ricc. 627 and Vienna 366 dachas, other rel. MSS dachos).

Dædolas *n. or apl.* Daedalian 72/3 (OH *adj., apl. m.* Daedalos).

Dalamentsan *npl.* the Daleminzi 13/10; *dpl.* 13/11 (2×). Cf. *OHG* Dalemintzi, Talaminzi.

Dalmatia *ns.* Dalmatia 18/14; *ds.* 18/15, 18/23.

Dalmatie *npl.* the Dalmatians 136/22 (OH *gs.* Dalmatiae).

Damaris *ns.* Thamyris 44/18 (MSS of rel. group C thamaris); **Dameris** 44/34 (Vienna 366 tameris, MSS of rel. groups A, B, and C thameris).

Damascena *ns.* the region about Damascus, *Lat.* Damascena 10/19.

Dameraþ *ns.* Demaratus 46/9 (Vienna 366 and other rel. MSS demarathus).

Danai *ns.* the river Don, *Lat.* Tanais 8/25; *ds.* 8/19, 8/20, 8/23. **Danais** *as.* 12/8; *gs.* 12/11; *ds.* 12/17. Cf. Freculph, col. 1019 Danaim, Remigius *in Capellam* VI 304. 6 Danaum.

Danaus *ns.* Danaus 27/5.

Dara *n. or as.* Dara 11/9.

Darius *nas.* Darius 3/16, 45/15, 45/31, 51/4, etc.; *gs.* 68/31. **Dariuses** *gs.* 2/21.

Datia *npl.* the Dacians 13/9 (OH *ns.* Dacia). **Datie** *apl.* (*or s.?*) 145/11.

Dauides *gs.* David's 139/11.

Decius[1] *ns.* Decius 7/18, 74/30, 75/12, 144/4, etc. **Detius** *n. or as.* 59/31.

Decius[2] *ns.* Decimus 102/1 (Vienna 366 and other rel. MSS *as.* decium).

Demetrias *nas.* Demetrius 81/3, 81/7, 81/24, 81/31, etc. **Demetriase** *ds.* 82/7.

Demostenon *as.* Demosthenes 78/20 (OH *as.* Demosthenen). **Demostanase** *ds.* 67/26.

Denamearc *ns.* Denmark 16/16. **Denemearce** *ds.* 16/20; *gs.* Denemearcan 16/25.

Dene *napl.* the Danes 12/31, 16/15.

Deniscæ *adj., nsn.* Danish 141/10. See Commentary.

Deprobane *ns.* Taprobane 9/25. See also **Taprabane.**

Detius see **Decius.**

Dianan *ds.* Diana 60/10.

Diocles *ns.* Diocles 32/29. **Diocle** *ds.* 32/30.

Dioclitianus *ns.* Diocletianus (common var. dioclitianus) 7/26, 146/20, 147/9, 147/19, etc. **Dioclitiane** *ds.* 147/14; **Dioclitie** 147/2.

Dissifarnon *ns.* Tissafernes 54/1 (OH *as.* Tissafernen).

Diþa *ns.* Dido 133/9.

Diulius *ns.* Duilius (common var. diulius) 92/17, 92/22.

Dolabella *ns.* Dolabella 76/27.

Domitianus *ns.* Domitianus 7/4, 139/5, 139/19.

Domitius *ns.* Domitius 76/27.

Donua *nas.* the Danube, *Lat.* Danuvius 12/20, 110/9, 153/2; *gs.* 12/24 etc.; *ds.* 18/3. Cf. *OHG* duonowa, tuonouwe, etc., *ON* Dúná.

Dorus *ns.* Dorus 82/7.

Drancas *apl.* the Drangae 71/9 (Ricc. 627 and other rel. MSS *apl.* drancas).

Dranceas *apl.* the Dranchei 78/5 (OH *apl.* Drancheos, Vienna 366 dranceos).

Dryhten the Lord. See main glossary.

E

Eacedam *as.* Aeacida 80/13.

Ealdseaxan *npl.* the continental Saxons, the Old Saxons 12/28. **Ealdseaxna** *gpl.* 13/18. **Ealdseaxum** *dpl.* 12/29. Cf. *Anglo-Saxon Chronicle* s.a. 779E Eald-Seaxe.

Eastfrancan *npl.* the East Franks, Franci orientales 12/25. Cf. *Anglo-Saxon Chronicle* s.a. 891 East-Francum.

Ebora *ns.* Ebora 56/4.

Effesum *as.* Ephesus 30/4, 139/21 (OH *as.* Ephesum for both instances).

Eforwicceastre *ds.* York, *Lat.* Eboracum 142/14.

Egeum *n. or as.* Aegaean 18/11 (OH *adj.*, *asn.* Aegaeum).

Eginense *ns.* the river Acesines 72/33 (OH *as.* Agesinem, Vienna 366 egessinem).

Egisca *adj.*, *nsm. wk.* Aegaean 21/2.

Egypti, Egipti, Egypte, Ægypte *napl.* the Egyptians, *Lat.* Aegyptii 24/8, 24/22, 26/20, 45/12, etc. **Egypta, Ægypta** *gpl.* 1/9, 11/19.

Egyptum *dpl.* (*or ds.* of Ægyptus) 23/20; **Egyptan** (*or ds.* of Ægyptus) 27/9. See also Ægyptus.

Egyptiscan *adj.*, *napl. wk.* Egyptian 2/20, 24/9.

Egyptum see Ægyptus, Egypti.

Elena *nas.* Helena 2/1, 31/25, 137/3. **Elenan** *ds.* 148/9.

Elice *ns.* Helice 56/4.

Elisan *ds.* Helissa (common var. elisa) 88/16.

*****Eliuses** *gs.* Caecilius' 95/12 (OH *abl.* Caecilio, MSS of rel. group C elio). See also Cecilium, Celius.

Ellaspontus *ns.* Hellespont 10/29.

Emilianus *ns.* Aemilianus (common var. emilianus) 144/17.

Emilitum *dpl.* 144/21. See Commentary.

Emilius *ns.* Aemilius (common var. emilius) 109/11, 110/24, 119/9. See also Amilius, Enilius.

Eneas *ns.* Aeneas 2/2, 32/9.

Engle *npl.* the Angles 16/19. See Commentary.

Englisc *adj.*, *asn.* English 29/35.

Enilius *ns.* Aemilius (common var. emilius) 4/13, 5/12, 94/22. See also Emilius.

Eowland *ns.* Öland 16/28.

Epira *gs. or pl.* of Epirus 58/26, 70/30, 80/12, 82/10, etc.; **Æpira** 65/19 (v.l. epira).

Epirotarum *gpl.* the Epirotes' 60/28 (OH *gpl.* Epirotarum).

Epithaurus *n. or as.* Epidaurian 76/5 (OH *adj.*, *asm.* Epidaurium, Ricc. 627 and other rel. MSS Epidaurum).

Equitania see Æquitania.

Ercol *nas.* Hercules 30/15, 72/7, 73/1. **Ercoles** *as.* 80/20, 81/12; *gs.* 9/9, 9/15, 20/21, 72/11, etc.

Escolafius *as.* Aesculapius 76/4 (MSS of rel. groups A, B, and C *gs.* escolapii); Escolapius 3/19.

Esernium *dpl.?* the Aesernians? 124/8 (OH *as.* Aeserniam, common var. eserniam).

*****Estland** *ns.* the land of the Ests 17/1. *****Estlande** *ds.* 16/34.

Estmere *nas.* Świeży Zalew or Frisches Haff 16/32 (2×), 16/33, 16/34.

Estum *dpl.* the Ests 16/31, 17/5, 17/6, 17/31, *17/34. Cf. *Lat.* Aestii.

Ethiopica see Æthiopica.

Etruria *ds.* Etruria 108/22.

Etrusci *npl.* the Etruscans, *Lat.* Etrusci 41/23. See also Etusci, Thrusci, Tuscea, þrysci.

Etusci *dpl.* the Etruscans 109/13 (OH *abl. pl.* Liguribus). See Commentary, and see also Etrusci.

Eþna *ns.?* Aetna (common var. aethna, ethna) 50/25; *gs.* 6/3, 119/9. Æþna *gs.* 116/25.

Eudomane *ns.* Eudaemon 10/15 (Ricc. 627 and other rel. MSS eudomen).

Eudoxius *ns.* Eudoxius 151/22.

Euergetas *apl.* the Euergetae 71/10 (OH *apl.* Euergetas).

Eufrates *nas.* the Euphrates (common var. eufrates) 10/10, 11/30. Eufrate *as.* 43/15; *ds.* 10/16, 29/8, 43/7.

Eugenius *nas.* Eugenius 154/24, 155/3, 155/9.

Eumen, Eumenis *ns.* Eumenes (common var. in related MSS eumenis) 77/30, 79/13, 80/29, 110/16. Umenis *nas.* 79/5 (2×), 79/7, etc. Umenes *as.* 79/29. Umene *ds.* 79/26.

Euoi *npl.* the Boii 108/12.

Euredica *ns.* Eurydice 80/3.

Eurilohus *as.* Eurylochus 71/16 (Vienna 366 eurilohus).

Europe *nas.* Europe, *Lat.* Europa 8/15, 8/23, 30/13, 108/27, etc.; *gs.* 9/7. Europem *as.* 8/14 (v.l. europam, OH *as.* Europam).

Euxinus *nas.* the Euxine 9/4, 10/28, 18/6, 18/8, 21/28.

Exantipus *ns.* Xanthippus (common var. xantipus) 94/19. Exantipuse *ds.* 94/10, 94/12.

F

Fabiane *n. or apl.* the Fabii 42/23 (OH *gpl.* Fabiorum).

Falisci *npl.* the Falisci 56/14, 100/33. Faliscis *dpl.* 97/2 (OH *abl. pl.* Faliscis).

Falores *ns.* Phalaris (common var. falaris) 33/35.

Falster *ns.* Falster 16/24.

Farnabuses *ns.* Pharnabazus (common var. farnabuzus, farnabusus) 54/1.

Fauius *ns.* Fabius (common var. fauius) 6/6, 74/28, 75/10, 76/11, etc. Fauiuses *gs.* 52/5. Fauia *ds.* 66/14. See also Uauius.

Fefles *ns.* Afellas (common var. affellas) 91/22.

Fenitia *ns.* Phoenicia (common var. fenitia) 10/19; *gs. or pl.* 58/22.

Fetontis *gs.* Phaeton's 26/34 (OH *gs.* Phaetontis).

Feucestas *ns.* Peucestes 78/8.

Fiaminius *ns.* Flaminius 98/33. See also Flamineus[1].

Filimine *ds.* Pylemene (name of king taken as place name) 118/8 (Munich 22025 and MSS of rel. groups A and B Phylemene, Philimene, etc.). See Commentary.

Filiotes *as.* Philotas 71/16 (Ricc. 627 and other rel. MSS philiotas, filiotas). See also Filotos.

Filonem *as.* Philo 135/25 (OH *as.* Philonem, var. filonem).

Filotos *ns.* Philotas (common var. filotas) 77/26. See also Filiotes.

Finnas *npl.* the Lapps 14/3, 14/23, 14/29, 15/14, etc. Finnum *dpl.* 15/10. Cf. *ON* Finnar, 'Lapps', and *Widsith* 76.

Firmus *ns.* Firmus 152/18, 152/21.

Fiþnam *n. or as.* Pydna 80/21 (OH *as.* Pydnam, Ricc. 627 and other rel. MSS fydnam, fidnam).

Flaccus *ns.* Flaccus 60/15, 98/25, 108/25, 116/23, etc.

Flamineus[1] *ns.* Flaminius (Vienna 366 flamineus) 100/13. See also Fiaminius.

Flamineus[2] *ns.* Flamininus 108/17 (Vienna 366 and other rel. MSS flaminius), 119/23 (Selden B 16 and other rel. MSS *abl. s.* flaminio). See also Flaminius.

Flaminius *ns.* Flamininus (common var. flaminius) 108/3, 108/6. See also Flamineus[2].

Floriam *ns.* Florianus 146/5.

Focenses, Focense *npl.* the Phocenses (common var. focenses) 61/10, 63/18. Focenses *dpl.* 63/1?.

Folucius *ns.* Plautius 114/19 (OH *as.* Plautium, Vienna 366 and other rel. MSS falucium).

Foriuses *gs.* Furius' 95/13 (OH *abl. s.* Furio, Ricc. 627 and other rel. MSS forio). See also **Furius.**

Fortunatus *n. or as.* Fortunate 9/17 (OH *apl.* Fortunatas).

Fraortes *ns.* Phraortes (common var. fraortes) 32/28. **Fraorte** *ds.* 32/29.

Fratauernis *ns.* Phrataphernes (common var. fratafernes) 78/7.

Frigam *as.* Phrygia (common var. frigia) 68/18; **Frigan** 77/28, 77/29. *þa læssan* ~ Phrygia minor 77/29. *þa maran* ~ Phrygia major 77/28.

Frisan *npl.* the Frisians 12/29. Cf. *Anglo-Saxon Chronicle*, s.a. 885 Frisan.

Frisland *nsn.* Frisia 12/30.

Fulcania *ns.* Vulcania 110/3 (OH Vulcani [insula], MSS of rel. groups A, B, and C uulcania).

Fulcisci *apl.* the Volsci (OH Vulsci, Ricc. 627 uulcisci) 49/30; *dpl.* (*or s.*) 50/5. See also **Wulchi.**

Fuluius *nas.* Fulvius 98/7, 98/24, 104/11, 105/10, etc.

Furculus see **Caudenes.**

Furius *ns.* Furius 108/23, 123/6. See also **Foriuses.**

G

Gades, Gaþes *ns.* Gades, *Lat. pl.* Gades (insulae) 9/8, 19/4, 21/20.

Gælle *apl.* the Gauls, *Lat.* Galli 99/3 (v.l. gallie), 115/4. See also **Galli, Gallie.**

Gaius *nas.* Gaius 4/18, 96/14, 97/1, 107/21, etc. **Gaiuses** *gs.* 95/13. **Gaiuse** *ds.* 6/14.

Galerius *nas.* Galerius 147/5, 147/11, 147/13, 147/28, etc. **Galeriuse** *ds.* 147/19.

Galli *npl.* the Galli, Gauls 75/2, 77/3. See also **Gallie.**

Gallia[1] *ns.* Gaul, *Lat.* Gallia, 18/24 (*or as.*), 19/13; **Galliam** *ns. or d.* (OH *as.* Galliam) 149/27; *as.* 145/9. *in pl.* **Gallie,** the Gallic provinces, *Lat.* Galliae, *apl.* 147/1, 148/1 etc. **Gallium** *dpl.* 146/10. See also **Gallie.**

Gallia[2] *gs. or pl.* Galaecia 19/5) OH *gs.* Gallaeciae, Ricc. 627 and other rel. MSS *gs.* gallie).

Gallica *ns.* Caligula (common var. gallicula) 135/11.

Gallie *napl.* the Gauls, Gaul, *Lat.* Galli 4/21, 4/24, 51/30, 52/25, etc. **Gallia** *npl.* 51/27; **Galliæ** 2/26. **Gallia** *gpl.* 4/27. **Gallium** *dpl.* 4/26; **Galleum** 99/21. See also **Galli, Gallia.**

Gallienus *ns.* Gallienus 144/20, 145/13. **Gallienuse** *ds.* 145/5.

Gallisc *adj., nsm.* Gallic, *Lat.* Gallus 98/13, 98/14. **Galliscne** *asm.* 58/1. **Galliscum** *dsn.* 53/1.

Gallus *nas.* Gallus 7/19, 144/13, 144/17.

Galua *ns.* Galba 7/1, 111/7, 111/20, 138/2.

Gandes *ns.* the Gyndes 43/5 (Ricc. 627 and Vienna 366 gandes).

Gandis *n. or as.* the Ganges 9/22 (OH *gs.* Gangis, Ricc. 627 and Vienna 366 gandes). **Gandes** *gs.* 9/25.

Ganemeþis *as.* Ganymede 27/30 (OH *as.* Ganymedem).

Gangeridas *apl.* the Gangaridae 72/25 (OH *apl.* Gangaridas).

Garamantes *apl.* the Garamantae 20/7 (OH *apl.* Garamantas, Ricc. 627 and other rel. MSS garamantes).

Gaþes see **Gades.**

Geames *ns.* Jamnes 26/20. Cf. Isidore, *Etymologies* VII. vi. 44 Iannes, OE fragment, Cockayne, *Narrat.* p. 50 Iamnes.

Genutius *nas.* Genucius (common var. Genutius) 56/21, 86/17.

Geothulas *apl.* the Getuli 20/7 (Ricc. 627 and other rel. MSS *apl.* gethulos).

Geoweorþa *ns.* Jugurtha 120/12, 120/19, 120/20, etc. **Geoweorþan** *a., g. and ds.* 6/7, 120/15, 120/27, 121/13.

Germania *n. or as.* Germania 12/23.

Germanie *napl.* the Germans, Germany, *Lat.* Germani 132/1, 132/5, 145/7. **Germania** *gpl.* (*or gs.*) 30/34, 138/8. **Germanium** *dpl.* 141/11.

Gneo *ns.* Gnaeus 112/14, 114/6 (OH

abl. s. Cn., rel. MSS gnaeo, gneo).
Gneus *as.* 105/9 (OH *as.* Cn., rel.
MSS gnaeum, gneum). See also
Grease.
God *nas.* God 8/10, 24/25, 25/26,
26/16, etc. **Godes** *gs.* 23/5. **Gode**
ds. 24/12. See also main glossary.
Godenric *ns.* Athanaricus 151/27. See
also **Athanaricus.**
Gomorre *ns.* Gomorra 1/7, 22/30.
Gordianus *ns.* Gordianus 7/16, 143/
16.
Gotan *napl.* the Goths, *Lat.* Gothi
1/26, 13/10, 30/33, 31/4, etc.; *dpl.*
155/25. **Gotena** *gpl.* 151/27;
Gotene 154/30; Gotona 37/34. Cf.
Alfred's Boethius Gotan 7/1, etc.
Gotland[1] *ns.* Gotland 16/28. Cf. *ON*
Gotar, the inhabitants of Gotland.
Gotland[2] *ns.* Jutland 16/11 (see Com-
mentary), 16/18.
Gratianus *nas.* Gratianus 8/4, 152/27,
153/19, 154/7, etc.
Gratias *ns.* Gracchus 97/1 (OH *abl. s.*
Graccho, Ricc. 627 gracio). See
also **Craccus.**
Grease *ds.* Gnaeus 41/25 (OH *abl. s.*
Gn., rel. MSS gneo). See also **Gneo.**
Gurius *ns.* Gurges 76/9.

H

Hæfeldan *npl.* the Havolans 13/22;
n. or apl. 13/1. Cf. Bavarian Geog.
2 Hehfeldi, Adam of Bremen, col.
513 Heveldi, *Ann. Quedlinburgenses,*
s.a. 996 Heveldun etc.
Hæþum *ds. or pl.* Hedeby 16/17,
16/21. *æt* ~ 16/14 (see Commentary).
Cf. *ON* Heðeby, *Chronicle of
Æthelweard,* p. 9, Haithaby.
Halgoland *ns.* Hålogaland 16/1. Cf.
ON Hálogaland.
Hanna *ns.* Hanno 4/5, 90/2, 91/8,
92/7, etc.; **Hanno** 106/10. **Hannan** *as.* 90/12; **Hannonan** 92/26;
Hannonam 105/7 (OH Hannonem). **Hannan** *npl.* 94/28.
Hannibal *nas.* Hannibal 4/28, 92/14,
96/8, 96/11, etc. **Hannibalan** *as.*
4/8. **Hannibales** *gs.* 5/7. **Hanni-
bale** *ds.* 92/21.
Hasterbal *nas.* Hasdrubal (common

var. hastrubal) 4/16, 95/13, 95/17,
105/20, etc.; **Asterbal** 5/6. **Haster-
bale** *ds.* 102/26, 104/10, 106/1.
Hasterbalas *apl.* 94/1.
*Heliam *n. or as.* Aelia 140/20.
Hettulf *ns.* Athaulfus 156/19.
Hierusalem *as.* Jerusalem, *Lat.*
Hierusalem 140/19; *ds.* 125/24,
134/5, 134/14, etc.
Hiliricam *as.* Illyria, *Lat.* Illyricum
77/26 (OH *apl.* Illyrios, MSS of
rel. groups A, B, and C illiricos,
iliricos).
Hiliricos *apl.* the Illyrians 61/23 (OH
apl. Illyrios, MSS of rel. groups A,
B, and C illiricos, iliricos). See also
Ilirice.
Himelco, Himeolco *ns.* Himilco
(common var. himelco) 4/4, 89/12.
Hisdriana *gpl.* of the Histriani 64/13
(OH *gpl.* Histrianorum).
Honorius *ns.* Honorius 8/8. **Onorius**
ns. 155/15, 155/17; *gs.* 156/19.
Horigti *npl.* the Chorwati 13/11
(v.l. horithi). **Horoti** *dpl.* 13/12
(v.l. horiti). Cf. *Serbo-Croat* Hrvati.
Htesseus *ns.* Theseus 46/1.
Hunas *napl.* the Huns 145/11, 146/10.
Cf. *Elene* 21 Hunas etc.
Hungerre *n. or apl.* the Hungarians
110/8. See Commentary.

I

Ianes *gs.* of Janus 6/18, 130/27, 131/
24, 132/12. **Ianas** *npl. or gs.?* 58/30,
59/12.
Ibærnia, Ibernia, Igbernia *ns.*
Ireland, *Lat.* Hibernia 19/14, 19/15;
ds. 19/18.
*Icarisca *adj., nsm. wk.* Icarian 21/1.
See Commentary.
Idumei *npl.* the Idumaei 10/19.
Iecrapatas *ns.* Atropatus (common
var. acropatus) 77/26.
Iersomas *npl.* the Gesonae 72/33
(Ricc. 627 and other rel. MSS *apl.*
gessonas).
Iesulause *ds.* Agesilaus 54/34. See
also **Ageselaus.**
Igbernia see **Ibærnia.**
Ilfing *ns.* the Elbing 16/33, 16/34,
16/35. See Commentary.

Ilirgus *ns.* Illyrius 79/13.

Ilirice *napl.* the Illyrians *Lat.* Illyrii (common var. illirii, illirici) 98/6, 108/18, 110/18, 110/22, etc. See also **Hiliricos, Nilirice.**

Indeas *apl.* the Indians, *Lat.* Indi 22/13. **Indea** *gpl.* 9/31, 25/9, 72/14. **Indeum** *dpl.* 74/3, 78/1, 78/3. **India** *ds.* India 11/27.

Indie *as. or pl.* the Indians, India, *Lat.* Indi 43/3, 72/1, 72/5, 81/21. **India** *gs. or pl.* 9/29, 72/2, etc. See also **Indeas, India.**

Indisc *adj., n. or as.* Indian, *Lat.* Indicus 9/23.

Indus *ns.* the Indus 9/30; *ds.* 9/33, 10/1. **Induse** *ds.* 78/2, 115/32.

Iobeses *gs.* Jove's 69/21 (OH *gs.* Iouis). See also **Iof, Iofes.**

Iof *as.* Jove. *munt* ~ Mount Jove, *Lat.* mons Iovis 99/24. See Commentary.

Iofes *ns.* Jove, *Lat.* Iuppiter, Iouis 85/1. **Iofeses** *gs.* 86/24. See also **Iobeses, Iof.**

Iohannes *as.* John, *Lat.* Iohannes 139/8, 139/20.

Ion *n. or as.* the Gihon 11/11.

Ionas *apl.* the Ionians 45/28, 47/15 (OH *apl.* Ionas), 47/21 (OH *apl.* Iones, MSS of rel. Group C ionas).

Iordanis *ns.* the Jordan, *Lat.* Iordanis 23/1.

Ioseph *nas.* Joseph 1/9, 23/22, 23/24, 23/26. **Iosepes** *gs.* 24/5, 24/13. **Iosepe** *ds.* 23/23, 24/23.

Iraland *ns.* Ireland 16/6. **Iralande** *ds.* 16/7. See Commentary.

Ircaniam *as.* Hyrcania (common var. hircania) 12/6, 33/29, 71/4; *ds.* 58/18.

Ircanus *apl. (or as.?)* the Hyrcanii 78/7 (OH *apl.* Hyrcanios, Ricc. 627 and other rel. MSS hyrcanos).

Ircclidis *ns.* Hircylides 53/30.

Ispania *nsf.* Spain, *Lat.* Hispania 18/32, 19/7, 19/8, 21/21, etc.; *ds.* 5/10. **Ispanie** *ds.* 109/11. *seo us fyrre* ~ Hispania ulterior 19/7. *seo us nearre* ~ Hispania citerior 19/8.

Ispanie *napl.* the Spaniards, *Lat.* Hispani 6/19, 94/10, 104/18, 104/20, etc. **Ispania** *gpl.* 5/23; *gpl., (or gs. of* **Ispania***)* 4/28. **Ispanium** *dpl.* 4/30. See also **Spaneum, Spenum.**

Israhela *gpl.* of Israel, *Lat.* Israel 1/15, 25/15. Cf. *OE Bede* 92/6 Israhela.

Issaurio *ns.* Isauria 10/26 (Vienna 366 *ns.* issauria); *d. or as.* 20/27.

Istria *ns.* Istria, *Lat.* (H)istria 18/15; *ds.* 18/16.

Isþrie *npl.* the Istrians, *Lat.* Istri, Histri, 99/5, 99/7 (v.l. istrie).

Itacanor *ns.* Itacanor 78/7.

Italiam *ns. (or d.)* Italy, *Lat.* Italia 149/27 (OH *as.* Italiam); *as.* 32/10 (OH *as.* Italiam), 67/21 (OH *as.* Italiam), 101/24, etc.; *ds.* 2/15. **Italia** *as. (or apl. of* Italie*)* 123/11; *ds.* 21/11. See also **Italie.**

Italie *napl.* the Italians, *Lat.* Itali 5/7, 6/10, 103/13, 113/21, etc. **Italiam** *npl.* 102/10. **Italia** *gpl. (or gs.)* 18/19. **Italium** *dpl.* 74/30. See also **Italiam.**

Itaxiles *ns.* Taxiles 78/2.

Ithona *ns.* Pithon 78/3 (Ricc. 627 ythonam, MSS of rel. groups B and C hythona, ithona). See also **Pison.**

Iþasfe *ds.* the Hydaspes 116/1 (OH *as.* Hydaspem); **Iþasfene** 78/2 (OH *as.* Hydaspem). See also **Iþaspes.**

Iþaspes *ns.* the Hydaspes 10/8 (OH *as.* Hydaspem). See also **Iþasfe.**

Iudan *napl.* the Jews, *Lat.* Judaei 137/12, 140/4; **Iuþan** 135/22. **Iudena** *gpl.* 138/15, 140/18; **Iudana** 58/17; **Iudea** 125/28.

Iudea *ns.* Judaea 10/20. See also **Iudan.**

Iudiscan *adj., apl. m. wk.* Jewish 140/17.

Iulianus *nas.* Julianus 150/7, 150/13, 151/2, 151/5. **Iulianuses** *gs.* 151/15.

Iulius *ns.* Julius 1/27, 6/11, 6/15, 31/1, 123/10, etc. **Iuliuses** *gs.* 124/19. **Iuliuse** *ds.* 123/12.

Iunius *ns.* Junius 96/14, 102/1.

Iustinianus *ns.* Justinus 88/18.

Iustinus *ns.* Justinus 23/23, 140/23.

Iuþan see **Iudan.**

Iuuinianus *ns.* Jovianus 8/1, 151/4, *151/11 (Selden B 16 and other rel. MSS iouinianus).

L

Læcedemonia *gs.* of Lacedaemon 46/20; *ds.* Lacedaemon 31/25, 35/19, 55/29; **Læcedamania** 46/8 (v.l. læcedamonia); **Læcedomonia** 2/1. **Læcedemoniam** *ds.* (*or dpl.* of **Læcedemonie**) 47/25. See also **Læcedemonie**.

Læcedemonie, Læcedemoniæ *napl.* the Lacedaemonians, *Lat.* Lacedaemonii 2/9, 34/28, 47/27, 51/1, 53/10, etc. **Læcedemonia** *npl.* 35/3; *gpl.* 34/30. **Læcedemonium** *dpl.* 2/28. See also **Læcedemonia**.

Læland *ns.* Laaland 16/24. Cf. Adam of Bremen, col. 631 Laland.

Lampida *ns.* Lampeto (Ricc. 627 and other rel. MSS lampito) 30/1.

Langaland *ns.* Langeland 16/24. Cf. *ON* Langaland.

Lapidus *ns.* Lepidus 110/6, 116/16. See also **Lepidus**.

Lapithe *npl.* the Lapiths, *Lat.* Lapithae 28/17, 28/18.

Larisan *as.* Larissa 61/24 (OH *as.* Larissam, Ricc. 627 and other rel. MSS larisam).

Latina *a. or ds.* Latin 12/12.

Latine *napl.* the Latins, *Lat.* Latini 3/7, 59/29, 60/3. **Latina** *gpl.* 60/3.

Latinus *ns.* Collatinus 40/9; *gs.* 40/6.

Laucius *ns.* Lucius 56/21 (OH L., Vienna 366 and Ricc. 627 *abl. s.* laucio). See also **Lucius**.

Laumenda *ns.* Laomedon (Selden B 16 laumendo) 77/25.

Lemniaþum *gpl.* of the Lemnian women 28/4 (OH *gpl.* Lemniadum).

Lentulus *ns.* Lentulus 107/21, 112/14, 114/6.

Leonantius *as.* Leonnatus 78/25 (Ricc. 627 *abl. s.* leonantio). See also **Leonontus**.

Leoniþa *ns.* Leonidas 46/20 (OH *ns.* Leonida), 46/34, 47/10, etc. **Leoni-þan** *gs.* 2/21; *ds.* 47/19.

Leonontus *ns.* Leonnatus (Ricc. 627 leonanthus, Vienna 366 leonnanthus) 77/29 (v.l. leomontus). See also **Leonantius**.

Leostenas *ns.* Leosthenes (common var. leostenes) 78/23.

Lepidus *as.* Lepidus 129/12. See Commentary and see also **Lapidus**.

Leptan *ds.* Leptis 107/12 (OH *as.* Leptim).

Leuinus *ns.* Laevinus (common var. leuinus) 105/6.

Liber *ns.* ~ *Pater* father Liber, Liber Pater 25/9.

Libeum *n. or as.* Lilybaeum (Ricc. 627 and other rel. MSS libeum) 21/6 (2×); *as.* 95/14, 96/7; *ds.* 4/17, 96/12.

Libia *ns.* Libya (common var. libia) 11/2, 19/33; *n. or as.* 19/34; *ds.* 19/35. **Libium** *as.* 77/14.

Libius *ns.* Livy, *Lat.* Liuius (Ricc. 627 and other rel. MSS libius) 75/13.

Liciam *as.* Lycia 77/28 (OH *as.* Lyciam).

Ligor *as.* Liguria 109/26 (OH *apl.* Ligures, the Ligurians, Vienna 366 and other rel. MSS ligores).

Ligore *ds.* the Loire, *Lat.* Liger 18/28 (OH *gs.* Ligeris, Vienna 366 and other rel. MSS ligeri).

Liparum *as.* Lipara, *Lat.* Lipara 93/11 (OH *as.* Liparam, Jes. 34 liparum). **Liparis** *as.* 92/21 (MSS of rel. groups B and C liparim).

Lipare *ds.* 119/11

Lisimachus¹, Lisimahhus *nas.* Lysimachus (common var. lisimachus) 77/29, 81/2, 82/6, 82/13, 82/23, etc. **Lisimachuse** *ds.* 81/33; **Lisimache** 81/18.

Lisimachus² *ns.* Lysimachia 82/14 (OH Lysimachia ciuitas, Ricc. 627 lisimachi ciuitas). See Commentary.

Lisum *n. or as.* the Liris 84/13 (OH *as.* Lirim, BN 4879 lirum).

Liþa *gpl.* the Lydians' 44/8 (OH *gpl.* Lydorum, common var. lidorum).

Liubene *n. or apl.* 12/13. See Commentary.

Longbeardan *n. or apl.* the Langobards 102/16. **Longbeardas** 97/5. Cf. *Anglo-Saxon Chronicle*, s.a. 887 Longbeardna londe etc.

Longus *ns.* Longus 99/19.

Lucani *npl.* the Lucani 76/28, 123/24 (*or apl.*). **Lucanum** *dpl.* 124/2.

Lucaniam *ds.* Lucania 85/30 (OH *as.* Lucaniam).

Luchina *ds.* Lyons, *Lat.* Lugdunum 150/6 (v.l. lucthina). Cf. Steinmeyer and Sievers III. 610 Luctuna: Liutona.

Lucinius *nas.* Licinius (Vienna 366 and other rel. MSS lucinius) 5/28, 110/30, 112/14, 118/2, 148/27, etc. See also **Lucinuse.**

Lucinuse *ds.* Licinius 148/21 (Vienna 366 and other rel. MSS lucinio). See also **Lucinius.**

Lucio *ns.* Lucius 114/6 (OH *abl.* Lucio). See also **Lucius.**

Lucius *nas.* Lucius 5/3, 7/10, 101/2, 102/15, etc. **Luciuses** *gs.* 95/12. See also **Laucius, Lucio.**

Lucretie *ns.* Lucretia 40/8; **Lucrettie** 40/6 (v.l. lucretie, OH *gs.* Lucretiae).

Lucullus *ns.* Lucullus 110/30.

Lusitanie *apl.* the Lusitani 111/20, 116/15. **Lusitaniam** *dpl.* (*or s.*) 109/12, 111/7, 116/15.

Lutatia *ns.* Lutatius 4/19, 96/17, 96/19, 96/21.

M

Macedaniæ, Macedonie see **Mæcedonie.**

Macheus *ns.* Mazeus (Vat. Lat. 1975 maceus) 89/3.

Mæcedonia *ds.* Macedonia 103/2, 105/6. **Mæcedoniam** *as.* 45/27 (OH *as.* Macedoniam); *ds. or pl.* 45/30. See also **Mæcedonie.**

Mæcedonie, Macedonie, Macedaniæ *napl.* the Macedonians, Macedonia (*Lat.* Macedones) 18/10, 55/31, 61/10, 80/8, etc. **Macedonia** *gpl.* (*or sg.*?) 3/11; **Mæcedoniæ** 108/19 (v.l. mæcedonia). **Mæcedonium** *dpl.* 68/4, 133/5 (*or ds.*); **Mæcedoniam** 71/17 (v.l. mæcedoniam). See also **Mæcedonia.**

Mæcedonisce *adj., nsn.* Macedonian (OH Macedonicum) 5/11, 110/13.

Mægelan see **Megelan.**

Mægþa *gpl.* (*or gs.*)? ~ *land* Land of Women? 13/12, 13/13. See Commentary.

Mærsum *dpl.* the Marsi 124/14. See also **Marse.**

Mæse *as.* Messena (MSS of rel.

group C mesena) 35/3. See also **Messene.**

Mæsi, Mesii *npl.* the Moesians (*Lat.* Moesi) 18/9 (OH Moesia, MSS of rel. groups B and C mæsia), 61/10.

Mæþe *napl.* the Medes (OH Medi) 27/26, 32/23, 37/14, 37/16, etc.; *gpl.* 32/29 (v.l. mæþa), 33/30. **Mæþum** *dpl.* 32/24. See also **Meþas.**

Magentsan *ds.* Mainz (OH Mogontiacum, Selden B 16 and other rel. MSS magontiacum) 143/7. Cf. Steinmeyer and Sievers III. 611 Maguncia. i. Maginza; *ibid*, p. 125 Mogontia: Magenze.

Magnentius *ns.* Magnentius 149/26. **Magnentiuse** *ds.* 150/2, 150/5.

Magonem, *as.* Mago 100/28, 104/30 (OH *as.* Magonem).

Maiores see **Syrtes.**

Mallius¹ *ns.* Manlius (Ricc. 627 and other rel. MSS mallius) 57/29, 59/30, 96/6, 97/12, 98/24, 122/7.

Mallius² *ns.* Manilius 111/25 (OH *abl. s.* Manilio, Selden B 16 Manlio, MSS of rel. groups B and C mallio).

Malosorum *gpl.* of the Molossi 62/1 (OH *gpl.* Molossorum, Vienna 366 and other rel. MSS malos(s)orum). See also **Molosorum.**

Malua *ns.* Malva 20/15, 20/19.

Mambres *ns.* Mambres 26/21. Cf. Isidore, *Etymologies* VII. vi. 45.

Mammea *ns.* Mamea (Vienna 366 and other rel. MSS mammea) 143/3. **Mammeam** *as.* 143/11 (OH *gs.* Mameae).

Mandos *apl.* the Mandi 71/3 (OH *apl.* Mandos).

Mandras *n. or apl.* the Madri or Mandri (OH *apl.* in Adros, Ricc. 627, Vienna 366 etc. mandros, BNL 17567 mandras) 73/3.

Manfeld *n. or as.* Field of Wickedness, *Lat.* Campus Sceleratus 60/13.

Mantius *ns.* Mancinus (Vienna 480 mancius, other rel. MSS mantinus) 5/22, 116/6, 116/28.

Marcellus¹ *nas.* Marcellus 5/4, 60/15, 102/17, 102/20, etc.

Marcellus² *ns.* Marcellinus (MSS of rel. group C marcellus) 127/5.

Marcolia *ns.* Marcus Livius 105/27 (OH *abl. s.* M. Livio, var. Marco Livio, Vienna 366 marcolio).

Marcus[1] *ns.* Marcus 3/3, 7/8, 7/13, 57/20, 108/25, etc. **Marcuse** *ds.* 41/25.

Marcus[2] *ns.* Marcius (Vienna 366 and other rel. MSS marcus) 109/25.

Margas *apl.* Argos 78/21 (OH Sicyonam Argos, MS D siciona margus).

Marisiam *as.* Marseilles 126/26 (OH *as.* Massiliam, Vienna 480 Marsiliam). See also **Masiliam.**

Marius *nas.* Marius 6/9, 121/8, 121/11, 121/12, etc.; *n., a., or ds.* 123/2; *a. or ds.* 125/9. **Mariuse** *ds.* 124/19.

Maroara *npl.* the Moravians 13/3 (2×); *gpl.* 13/8; *dpl.* 13/10. Cf. *OHG* Marhara, *Slav.* Morawa.

Marrucine *n. or apl.* the Marrucini 123/24.

Marse *n. or apl.* the Marsi 123/23; *dpl.* 123/29. See also **Mærsum.**

Marsepia *ns.* Marpesia (Ricc. 627 and other rel. MSS marsepia) 30/1, 30/7.

Marseus *nas.* Narseus 147/4, 147/12, 147/18.

Martius *ns.* Marcius 123/11.

Marþonius *ns.* Mardonius 47/33. See also **Morþonius.**

Masiliam *as.* Marseilles (OH Massilia, MSS of rel. group C masilia) 148/20. See also **Marisiam.**

Masinissa *ns.* Masinissa 110/17.

Mauritania *ns.* Mauretania (Ricc. 627 and other rel. MSS mauritania) 20/12; *ns. or ds.* 20/14, 20/18.

Mauritaniam *as.* 95/2 (OH *as.* mauretaniam).

Mauritanie *apl.* the inhabitants of Mauretania, *Lat.* Mauri 90/11. **Mauritaniæ** *npl.* 121/30 (v.l. mauritanie). **Mauritania** *gpl.* 121/16 (*or gs.*), 122/2.

Maxentius *nas.* Maxentius 148/10, 149/2. **Maxentiuse** *ds.* 149/1.

Maximianus[1] *nas.* Maximianus 147/5, 147/6, 147/20, 147/26, etc. **Maximianuses** *gs.* 148/10.

Maximianus[2] *as.* Maximus 153/28. **Maximianum** *as.* 8/5 (v.l. maximum).

Maximinus *nas.* Maximinus 148/6, 149/3.

Maximus[1] *nas.* Maximus 74/29, 105/14, 154/9, 154/17, etc.; *a. or ds.* 154/29.

Maximus[2] *ns.* Maximianus 146/21 (Vienna 366 maximum).

Maximus[3] *nas.* Maximinus (Vienna 366 and other rel. MSS maximus) 7/15, 143/10, 143/13.

Mecipsuses *gs.* Micipsa's 120/12 (OH *gs.* Micipsae).

Mediolane *ds.* Milan, *Lat.* Mediolanum 147/26 (OH *ds.* Mediolani); **Medialane** (v.l. mediolane) 145/14 (Trier 1095 *ds.* medialani). See also **Megelan.**

Megelan *as.* Milan, Lat. Mediolanum 99/4. **Mægelan** *ds.* 155/11 (v.l. mægelange). Cf. Steinmeyer and Sievers III. 611 Mediolanum: Meilan, and Introduction, p. cxiv. See also **Mediolane.**

Melitam *as.* Melita 93/11 (OH *as.* Melitam).

Mella *ns.* Metellus 119/23 (OH *abl. s.* Metello, MSS of rel. group C mello). See also **Metellus.**

Membraþ *ns.* Nimrod (OH Nebrot, Selden B16 and other rel. MSS nembroth) 43/21.

Meore *ns.* Möre 16/27.

Meotedisc *adj., n. or asn.* Maeotis (palus) 9/2, 12/8 (OH *apl.* Maeotidas, common var. meotidas).

Meroen *n. or as.* Meroe 11/16 (OH *as.* Meroen).

Merothonia *ds.* the plain of Marathon, *Lat.* Marathonii campi, 46/25.

Morotthome *n. or as.* 45/33 (MSS of rel. groups B, C, and D morothoniis).

Mesana *ns.* Messana (Ricc. 627 and other rel. MSS mesana) 21/4.

Mesiane *npl.* the Messenii 2/9, 34/29, 34/30; *ds. or pl.* 35/19. **Mesiana** *gpl.* (*or s.*) 35/16. See also **Messene.**

Mesicos *n. or as.* Issicus (sinus) 20/28 (OH *as.* Issicum Ricc. 627 misicum, MSS of rel. group A mesicum).

Mesii see **Mæsi.**

Mesopotamia *ns.* Mesopotamia 10/
11. **Mesopotamiam** *as.* 78/9 (OH
as. Mesopotamiam), 145/12 (OH
as. Mesopotamiam), 151/6.
Messene *apl.* Messenii 35/13. See
also **Mæse, Mesiane.**
Metellus *nas.* Metellus 6/5, 95/15,
95/16, 101/22, 120/3, 123/1, 123/5.
Metelluses *gs.* 95/12. See also
Mella.
**Metredatis, Metreþatis, Mitri-
datis** *nas.* Mithridates (common
var. mitridates, metridates) 6/12,
115/31, 124/18, 125/14.
Meþas *apl.* the Medes, *Lat.* Medi
32/19, 36/30, 78/8 (v.l. mæþas).
Meþa *gpl.* 33/3, 33/12, 36/29,
37/31. **Meþen** *dpl.* (*or s.*) 32/28. See
also **Mæþe.**
Meþia *nas.* Media 10/3, 10/4 (v.l.
media). **Meþian** *as.* 77/26, 77/27.
Minores see **Syrtes.**
Minotauro *ds.* the Minotaur 28/16
(OH *abl. s.* Minotauro).
Minotheo *ns.* Minothea 71/5.
Minturnan *ds. or pl.* Minturnae
117/30 (OH *loc. pl.* Minturnis).
Minutia *ns.* Minucia 60/8.
Minutius *nas.* Minucius 84/17, 99/6.
Mitridatis see **Metredatis.**
Moab *ns.* Moab 10/19.
Molosorum *gpl.* of the Molossi
80/13 (OH *gpl.* Molossorum, Ricc.
627 and other rel. MSS molo-
sorum). See also **Malosorum.**
Moluia *n. or as.* Mulvian, *Lat.* pons
Mulvius 149/3 (Selden B16 and
other rel. MSS *as.* moluium).
Momertine *npl.* Mamertini 92/2.
Monelaus *gs.* Menelaus' 31/24.
Morotthome see **Merothonia.**
Morþonius *ns.* Mardonius 48/19
(Vienna 366 mortanius, mordanio).
See also **Marþonius.**
Mostumius *as.* Postumius 120/26
(OH *as.* Aulum Postumium). See
also **Postumius.**
Moyses *nas.* Moses 1/15, 24/5, 24/8,
25/15. **Moyse** *ds.* 26/9, 26/16, 26/18.
Mulieses *gs.* Amulius' 36/33 (OH
gs. Amulii).
Mure *n. or as.* Mus 60/1 (OH *abl. s.*
Mure).

Mutius *ns.* Mucius (Vienna 366 and
other rel. MSS mutius) 41/1,
110/6.

N

Narbonense *nas.* Narbonensis 19/4,
19/10; *gs.* 18/29; *ds.* *18/22, 18/30.
Nasica *ns.* Nasica 120/10.
Natabres *apl.* the Nathabres (com-
mon var. natabres) 20/7.
Nauiþa *ns.* Navis 108/8 (OH *gs.*
Nauidis).
Nearchus *ns.* Nearchus 77/28.
Nectanebuses *gs.* Nectanebus' 69/23
(St. Gall 621 *abl. s.* nectanabo).
See Commentary.
Neoptolomus *nas.* Neoptolemus
79/5, 79/6.
Nerfa *ns.* Nerva 7/5, 139/16, 139/23.
Nero *ns.* Nero 6/25, 137/18, 138/5.
See also **Nerone.**
Nerone *ns.* Nero 105/27 (OH *abl. s.*
Nerone). See also **Nero.**
Nicea *ns.* Nicaea 72/23 (OH *as.*
Niciam).
Nicomedia *ds.* Nicomedia 118/7
(OH *abl. s.* Nicomede, name of a
king; MSS of rel. groups A, B, C,
and D nicomedie, interpreted as
place name). See Commentary.
Nicomedio *ds.* Nicomedia 149/20
(v.l. nicomedia); **Nicomidio** 147/26
(v.l. nicomedia). See also **Nico-
media.**
Nilirice *apl.* the Illyrians: *an Nilirice*,
for *an Ilirice* 68/5. See also **Ilirice.**
Nilus *nas.* the Nile, *Lat.* Nilus
9/12, 11/3, 11/15, 19/32.
Ninus *ns.* Ninus 1/3, 21/24, 22/4,
24/19, etc. **Ninuses** *gs.* 37/7.
Ninuse *ds.* 37/5, 133/1.
Nisan *as.* Nysa 72/2 (OH *as.* Nysam).
Nissibi *as.* Nisibis 151/6 (OH *as.*
Nisibi).
Noe *ns.* Noah, *Lat.* Noe 25/6.
Norþdene *npl.* the North Danes
13/16, 13/19.
Norþmen(n) *napl. m.* the Nor-
wegians 13/27, 15/34, 15/35, 15/37.
Norþmanna *gpl.* 15/21; **Norþ-
monna** 13/29.
Norþweg *ns.* Norway 16/9. Cf. *ON*
Norvegr.

Nuchul *n. or as.* Nuhul (common var. nuchul) 11/9.

Numantie *apl.* the Numantines, *Lat.* Numantini 116/31. **Numantia** *gpl.* 117/11. **Numaantium** *dpl.* (*or ds. of* Numantia) 116/28 (v.l. numantium, OH *as.* Numantiam). See also **Numentiæ, Numentinas.**

Numedia, Numeþia *ns.* Numidia (common var. numedia) 20/10, 20/15; *gs.* (*or gpl. of* Numeþe) 6/7, 110/17, 120/11, etc.; *ds. or gpl.* 21/16. **Numedian** *as.* 95/1; **Numeþiam** 121/6 (OH Numediam). See also **Numeþe.**

Numentiæ *npl.* the Numantines, *Lat.* Numantini 117/18. **Numentia** *gpl.* 116/9. See also **Numantie, Numentinas.**

Numentinas, Numentine *apl.* the Numantines, *Lat.* Numantini 115/22, 116/6. See also **Numantie, Numentiæ.**

Numentisc *adj., nsm.* Numantine 117/17. See also **Numentiæ.**

Numerianus *ns.* Numerianus 146/17.

Numetores *gs.* Numitor's 36/31, 36/33, 39/18 (OH *gs.* Numitoris, Vienna 366 numetoris).

Numeþe *npl.* the Numidians, *Lat.* Numidae 106/15. See also **Numedia.**

O

Oceanus *ns.* the Ocean, *Lat.* Oceanus 8/12. **Oceano** *ds.* 8/16 (OH *abl. s.* Oceano).

Octauianus *ns.* Octavian, *Lat.* Octavianus 6/17, 6/18, 59/11, 59/21, 129/6, etc.; *gs.* 59/2. **Octauianuses** *gs.* 129/17. **Octauianuse** *ds.* 130/8; **Octauiane** 129/14.

Ocus *ns.* Ochus (common var. ocus) 58/15.

Ohthere *ns.* Ohthere 13/29, 16/1.

Olimpiade *ns.* Olympias (common var. olimpias) 80/12, 80/14; **Olimpiadas** 80/29; **Olimphiade** 62/2. **Olimpiadum** *as.* 80/22. **Olimpeadum** *ds.* 80/9.

Olimpus *ns.* Olympus 10/30. **Olimphus** *n. or as. or pl.* 109/16 (occas. *Lat.* var. olimphus).

Olinthum *as.* Olynthus 63/3 (OH *as.* Olynthum, common var. olinthum).

Omarus *ns.* Homer, *Lat.* Homerus 31/31 (v.l. omerus).

Omintos *ns.* Amyntas (common var. amintas) 78/6. See also **Amintas.**

Ongle *n. or as.* Angeln 12/31 (v.l. angle). **Angle** *ds.* 16/14 Cf. *ODan.* Angul.

Onorius see **Honorius.**

Orcadus *ns. for Lat. pl.* Orcades 19/15 (OH *apl.* Orcadas).

*Orestes *ns.* Orestes 119/9.

Origenis *n. or as.* Origen, *Lat.* Origenes 143/12 (OH *as.* Origenem). **Origenise** *ds.* 143/3.

Orithia *ns.* Orithyia (common var. orithia) 30/21, 30/22.

Orosius *ns.* Orosius 1/1 (*or as.*), 2/11, 8/12, 27/11, 27/22, etc.

Osti *npl.* the Osti 13/20, 13/21. For 13/25 see Commentary.

Ostilianus *ns.* Hostilianus 144/13.

Ostsæ *n. or as.* the East Sea 13/16, 13/20. See Commentary.

Othinentium *dpl.* the Athenians 28/5 (OH *gpl.* Atheniensium, Ricc. 627 athinentium). See also **Atheniense.**

Othon *nas.* Otho 138/3 (OH *abl.* Othone), 138/8 (*or ds.*)

*Othona *as.* Mothona 62/6 (Ricc. 627 and other rel. MSS *as.* othonam).

Ottorogorre *n. or as.* the Ottorogorra 9/28 (OH *gs.* Ottorogorrae).

P

Pactriane *n. or apl.* the Bactriani 81/21. See also **Atrianus, Bactriana.**

Pactrium *dpl.* the Bactriani, Bactria 78/1 (OH *abl. s.* Bactriana).

Paflagoniam *as.* Paphlagonia (common var. paflagonia) 77/30. **Paflogoniam** *ds.* 118/9.

Palestina *ns.* Palestine, *Lat.* Palaestina (common var. palestina) 10/20; *ds.* 22/32, 137/3, 140/18. **Palastine** *ns.* 11/1 (v.l. palestine).

Paminunde *ds.* Epaminondas 61/12 (Ricc. 627 and other rel. MSS *as.* epaminundam).

Pamphiliam *as.* Pamphylia (common var. pamphilia) 77/28 (OH *as.* Pamphyliam).

Pannoniam *as.* Pannonia 145/11 (OH *apl.* Pannonias), 152/6 (OH *apl.* Pannonias).

Pannonii *npl.* the Pannonians, *Lat.* Pannonii 131/28.

Papirius *nas.* Papirius 67/18, 75/29, 75/31. **Papiria** *ds.* 67/12 (OH *abl. s.* Papirio).

Paramomenas *apl.* the Parapameni 71/10 (OH *apl.* Parapamenos). See also **Parapamenas.**

Parapamenas *apl.* (*or ns.*) the Parapameni, name of people, possibly interpreted as personal name, 78/3 (OH *apl.* Parapamenos). See also **Paramomenas.**

Parcoadras *n. or apl.* the Parchoatrae 11/29, 11/31 (OH *apl.* Parcohatras).

Parhte see **Parthe.**

Parmenionem *as.* Parmenio 69/10 (OH *as.* Parmenionem); **Parmenion** 71/16 (OH *ns.* Parmenio).

Parnasus *n. or as. or pl.?* Parnassus 25/1 (OH *abl. s.* Parnasso, common var. parnaso).

Parthe *napl.* the Parthians, *Lat.* Parthi 118/18, 118/19, 142/18, etc.; **Parhte** 150/12. **Parthos** *apl.* 78/7 (OH *apl.* Parthos). **Partha** *gpl.* 6/1. **Parthim** *dpl.* 71/8.

Parthia *ns.* Parthia 10/3; *n. or as.* 10/9.

Pater see **Liber.**

Paulus *nas.* Paulus 94/22, 101/2; St Paul 137/27.

Pausanias *as.* Pausanias 71/17. **Pausania** *ds.* 64/4 (OH *abl. s.* Pausania).

Peligni *n. or apl.* the Peligni 123/23.

Pelopensium *npl.* the Peloponnesians 34/22 (OH *gpl.* Peloponnensium, MSS of rel. groups A, B, and C pelopensium).

Pencentes *apl.* the Picentes 86/32 (Ricc. 627 pencentes). See also **Pincente.**

Pene *napl.* the Carthaginians, *Lat.* Poeni 4/23, 92/5, 92/31, 94/28, etc. **Pena** *gpl.* 4/7.

Pentesilia *ns.* Penthesilea (MSS of rel. group C pentesilia) 30/22.

Penula *ns.* Penula 102/29.

Percopiosus *as.* Procopius 151/21.

Perdica, Perþica *ns.* Perdiccas (common var. perdica) 78/27, 78/30, 79/1, 79/12, etc. **Perdice** 77/27 (OH *gs.* Perdiccae). **Perdican** *gs.* 79/14.

Perenei *n. or apl.* the Pyrenees, *Lat.* Pyrenaei 99/21; *apl.* 4/29. See also **Pireni.**

Perpena *ns.* Perpenna (Vienna 366 perpena) 118/11.

Perse *napl.* the Persians, *Lat.* Persae 45/22, 47/29, 53/11, etc. **Persi** 27/21 (MSS of rel. groups A and B persi). **Persa** *gpl.* 37/16; **Persea** 33/15; **Perseo** 33/11. **Persum** *dpl.* 2/28; **Perseum** 33/2; **Persan** 33/1.

Perseus *nas.* Perseus 5/12, 27/18, 110/21, 110/25, etc. **Perseuse** *ds.* 110/8; **Perseo** 28/2 (OH *abl. s.* Perseo).

Persi see **Perse.**

Persipulis *as.* Persepolis 70/6 (Vienna 366 and other rel. MSS *as.* persipolim).

Persiscan *adj., gsn. wk.* Persian, OH Persicus 48/22.

Persiþa *ns.* Persida 10/3.

Perþica see **Perdica.**

Petrus *nas.* St. Peter, *Lat.* Petrus 136/13, 137/27.

Pharaon *n. or as.* Pharaoh, *Lat.* Pharao, *gs.* Pharaonis 24/18. **Pharon** *ns.* 26/13. **Pharones** *gs.* 26/17. **Pharaone** *ds.* 23/30.

Philippus *nas.* Philip, *Lat.* Philippus 3/10, 5/10, 7/17, 61/5, 61/11, etc. **Philippuses** *gs.* 61/17. **Philippuse** *ds.* 62/3.

Philopes *gs.* of Pelops 27/28 (OH *gs.* Pelopis); *as. or gs.* 27/32.

Pholomeus, Phtolomeus, etc. see **Ptholomeus.**

Piceno *ds.* Picenum 98/28 (OH *abl. s.* Piceno).

Pilatus *nas.* Pilate, *Lat.* Pilatus 134/14, 136/1.

Pincente *n. or apl.* the Picentes

123/23. **Pincentes** *dpl.* 124/9. See also **Pencentes.**

Pireni *ns. or pl.* the Pyrenees 19/9 (OH *npl.* Pyrenaei). See also **Perenei.**

Pirrus *nas.* Pyrrhus (common var. pirrus) 1/26, 30/34, 82/10, 82/11, etc. **Pirrusan** *as.* 58/25. **Pirruses** *gs.* 84/27. **Pir(r)use** *ds.* 85/21, 91/31.

Piscenius *as.* Pescennius 142/8 (v.l. pisceninus; Vienna 366 and other rel. MSS piscennium).

Pison *ns.* Pithon (Ricc. 627 pyson) 79/13. See also **Ithona.**

Pissandor *ns.* Pisander (MSS of rel. group B pissander) 54/25.

Pius *n. or as.* Pius 140/23.

Placentiæ *as.* Placentia 108/14.

Plenius[1] *ns.* Plynos (Ricc. 627 and other rel. MSS plenius) 29/15.

Plenius[2] *ns.* Pliny 140/1 (OH *gs.* Plinii, Vienna 366 and other rel. MSS pleni, plenii).

Plicinius *ns.* Publius Licinius 110/12 (OH *abl.* P. Licinio, Selden B 16 and other rel. MSS plicinio). See also **Lucinius.**

Polausus *ns. or apl.* the Pelassi, name of people possibly taken as a personal name, *ns.* 78/9 (OH *apl.* Pelassos, Ricc. 627 and Selden B 16 palausus).

Polipercon *nas.* Polypercon 79/8, 80/29.

Polores *n. or as.* Pelorum, *Lat. also* Peloris 21/4 (OH *ns.* Pelorum).

Pompeius[1], **Pompeus** *nas.* Pompeius 23/27, 24/9, 115/22, 123/28, 127/10, etc.; *gs.* 127/7. **Pompeiuses** *gs.* 6/15. **Pompeiuse** *ds.* 123/3. See also **Sompeius.**

Pompeius[2] *ns. for* OH Antoninus 7/7. **Ponpeius** 140/22.

Ponthionis *gs.* of Pandion 28/4 (OH *gs.* Pandionis).

Pontius *nas.* Pontius 66/23, 76/16, 76/18.

Ponto *gs.* of Pontus 71/1 (OH *gs.* Ponti); *ds.* Pontus 118/7 (OH *gs.* Ponti, Vienna 366 ponto), 146/5 (OH *abl. s.* Ponto). **Pontum** *a. or ds.* 29/16 (OH *gs.* Ponti).

Poros *nas.* Porus 72/15 (OH *abl. s.*

Poro), 72/16, 72/18 (OH *ns.* Porus). **Porose** *ds.* 72/13 (OH *abl. s.* Poro).

Porsenna *ns.* Porsenna 40/24, 40/29, 41/10. **Porsennes** *gs.* 41/9.

Postumius *nas.* Postumius 98/7, 102/15. See also **Mostumius.**

Presidas *apl.* the Praesidae 72/24 (OH *apl.* Praesidas).

Priamises *gs.* Priam's, *Lat.* Priamus, *gs.* Priami 31/23.

Probus *ns.* Probus 7/24. See also **Brobus.**

Procos *ns.* Procas 36/31, 36/33, 37/8; *gs.* 37/10. **Procose** *ds.* 37/6.

Proculus *as.* Proculus 146/11.

Profentse, Profentsæ *ns.* Provence, *Lat.* Provincia 18/31, 18/33.

Proponditis *ns.* the Propontis 18/5 (OH *gs.* Propontidis, BNL 4875 proponditis); *n. or as.* 10/29 (OH *abl. s.* Propontide).

Pt(h)olomeus, Ph(o)tolomeus, Pholomeus, Tholomeus *nas.* Ptolemy, *Lat.* Ptolemaeus (common var. Ptholomeus) 6/16, 77/23, 79/2, 79/3, 79/12, etc. **P(t)holomeuse** *ds.* 81/33, 127/29. **Ptolome** *npl.* the Ptolemies 36/13.

Publia *ns.* Publius 41/20 (OH P., rel. MSS *abl. s.* publio).

Publius *ns.* Publius 99/19 (2×), 101/2, 107/22.

Pulgare *npl.* the Bulgarians 18/15; *apl.* 61/23. **Pulgara** *gpl.* 13/7. ***Pulgarum** *dpl.* 18/18. Cf. *OHG* Pulgar, *Lat.* Bulgari, *Gregory's Dialogues* 300/21 Bulgarisc.

Punice *napl.* the Carthaginians, *Lat.* Punicus (*only as ᵃadj.*) 4/9, 4/18, 93/7, 94/24, etc. **Punici** *npl.* 58/27. **Punica** *gpl.* 88/14. **Punicum** *dpl.* 94/18.

Q

Quadratus *ns.* Quadratus 140/11.

Quintillus[1] *ns.* Quintillus 145/20.

Quintillus[2] *as.* Quintilius 132/1.

Quintius[1] *ns.* Quintius 57/28, 108/3, 108/6. **Cuintius** 58/2.

Quintius[2] *ns.* Quintus 110/4 (v.l. quintus. OH Q., usual expansion Quintus, MSS of rel. groups B and C quintius).

Quintus *ns.* Quintus 56/22, 109/28, 116/23, 119/23. **Cwintus** 74/29. **Cuintus** 75/10, 104/11. See also **Cuintinus, Quintius**[2].

R

Rædgota *ns.* Radagaisus 155/27. **Rædgotan** *ds.* 155/23. Cf. *Alfred's Boethius* 7/2 Rædgota and Introduction, pp. xci f.

Ræstas *apl.* the Adrestae 72/24 (OH *apl.* Adrestas, Ricc. 627 and other rel. MSS ad restas, Trier 1095 adræstas).

Rafennan *as.* Ravenna 145/8 (OH *as.* Rauennam). **Rafenna** *ds.* 148/13.

Se Reada sæ *m.*, seo **Reade sæ** *f.*, the Red Sea, *Lat.* mare rubrum 1/16, 9/30, 10/2, 10/7, 10/14, etc.

Regiense *dpl.*? the Reginenses 86/13.

Regnesburg *n.* or *as.* Regensburg or Ratisbon 12/27. Cf. *OSaxon* Reginesburg.

Regulus *nas.* Regulus 4/12, 93/18, 93/22, 93/34, etc. **Reguluses** *gs.* 94/16. **Regule** *ds.* 94/6, 95/3.

Remus *ns.* Remus 2/14. *Remuses* *gs.* 37/1. **Remuse** *ds.* 39/2.

Riffen *as.* or *pl.* Rhipaean, OH Riphaei 13/13 (v.l. riffin). **Riffeng** *ds.* or *pl.* 8/24 (v.l. riffing).

Rin *n.* or *as.* the Rhine, *Lat.* Rhenus 18/25; *as.* 12/17. **Rines** *gs.* 12/20. **Rine** *ds.* 12/24. Cf. *Anglo-Saxon Chronicle* s.a. 887 Rin, *OHG, ON* Rin.

Rochouasco *ds.* or *pl.*, or *gpl.* the Rhobasci 9/1 (OH *gpl.* Rhobascorum, Ricc. 627 and other rel. MSS rochobascorum).

Rodan *ns.* the Rhône, *Lat.* Rhodanus (common var. rodanus) 18/30.

Rogathitus *ns. for Lat. pl.* the Trogodytae (MSS of rel. group C rogodite) 20/2. **Rogathite** *as.* or *pl.* 20/4.

Roma *nas.* Rome, *Lat.* Roma 2/17, 37/18, 38/4, 44/12, etc.; *ds.* 37/21. **Rome** *as.* 96/16; *ds.* 3/2. See also **Romeburg.**

Romane *napl.* the Romans, *Lat.* Romani 2/18, 2/25, 3/9, 3/17, 36/20

(OH *adj.* Romanum), etc. **Romana** *gpl.* 3/4; **Romano** 3/24; **Romane** 122/10. **Romanum** *dpl.* 2/22. See also **Romware.**

Romanisc *adj., nsm.* Roman 154/27. **Romanisce** *napl. m.* 59/17, 155/29. **Romaniscan** *npl. m. wk.* 108/9.

Romeburg, Romeburh *nas.* the city of Rome 2/14, 21/17, 21/23, 27/1, etc. **Romebyrg, Romebyrig** *ds.* 42/16, 42/27. See also **Roma.**

Romulus *ns.* Romulus 2/14, 2/16, 39/2, 39/20, etc. **Romuluses** *gs.* 39/18; **Romules** 37/1. **Romuluse** *ds.* 39/2, 40/1.

Romware *npl.* the Romans 31/2, 39/27. See also **Romane.**

Roþum *nas.* Rhodes, *Lat.* Rhodus (common var. rodus) 23/16 (OH *as.* Rhodum), 69/17 (OH *as.* Rhodum), 70/25 (OH *ns.* Rhodus); *ds.* 98/31 (OH *ns.* Rhodus).

Roxan *as.* Roxa 80/19.

Rufinus *ns.* Rufinus 155/20. **Rufinuse** *ds.* 155/17.

S

Sabei *ns.* or *pl.* Sabaea (or its inhabitants, the Sabaei) 10/15.

Sabini *napl.* the Sabines, *Lat.* Sabini 39/5, 42/31, 43/2, 49/16. **Sabine** *npl.* 2/18. **Sabinan** *a.* or *dpl.* 76/24. **Sabina** *gpl.* 42/29.

Sabinisce *adj., nasn.* Sabine 41/12, 42/22.

Saguntum *as.* Saguntum 4/28, 99/10.

Salinatore *ns.* Salinator 105/27 (OH *abl. s.* Salinatore).

Samera *ns.* Samara 9/27.

Sameramis *ns.* Semiramis, OH Samiramis (common var. sameramis) 1/4, 22/8, 22/19, 36/26, etc.

Sapan *as.* Sapores 145/2 (OH *abl. s.* Sapore, Trier 1095 sapone); *ds.* 145/3.

Sardanopolus *ns.* Sardanapallus (common var. sardanapalus) 2/3, 32/14, 32/15; **Sarþanopolim** 27/25 (OH *as.* Sardanapallum). **Sardanopolum** *as.* 36/29 (OH *as.* Sardanapallum), 37/12; **Sardanopolim** 133/2.

Sardina *nas.* Sardinia 21/12, 21/13.
Sardine *ns.* 21/18; Sarþinia 107/
24. **Sardiniam** *as.* 92/28, 96/25.
Sardinium *ds.* (*or dpl.*?) 88/28. See
also **Sardinie.**
Sardinie *npl.* the Sardinians, *Lat.*
Sardi 4/22, 97/13. **Sardinium** *dpl.*
(*or ds.*?), 100/32. See also **Sardina.**
Sardis *n. or as.* Sardis 68/19.
Sarmondisc *adj.*, *nsm.* Sarmatian
8/25 (OH *abl. s.* Sarmatico).
Sarracene *npl. as s.?* the Saracens,
Lat. Saraceni 10/20, 11/2.
Sarþanopolim see **Sardanopolus.**
Sarþinia see **Sardinia.**
Saturninus *nas.* Saturninus 122/27,
123/5, 146/10.
Sceltiuerin, Sceltiferin *dpl.* the
Celtiberians, *Lat.* Celtiberi 5/14,
111/1 (OH *gpl.* Celtiberorum). See
Commentary.
Scene *n. or as.* the Shannon, *Lat.*
Scena 19/7 (OH *gs.* Scenae).
Scipia, Scipio *ns.* Scipio 4/29, 6/1,
99/30, 100/27, etc.; **Scipa** 99/19.
Scipian *as.* 5/2; *gs.* 100/27; *ds.* 5/8;
npl. 102/24.
Sciringesheal *n. or as.* Skiringssalr
16/3; *as.* 16/9. Scirin(c)gesheale *ds.*
16/8, 16/12, 16/15. See Commentary.
Sciþþie *napl.* the Scythians, Scythia,
Lat. Scythae 1/24, 21/29, 22/6,
26/31, etc. **Sciþþia** *gpl.* 12/10.
Sciþþium *dpl.* 1/25; **Sciþþian**
29/14 (*or ds.*?). Cf. *Alfred's Boethius*
43/10 Sciþþeas. See also **Sciþ-**
þian *as.?*
Sciþþian *as.?* Scythia 12/6. See also
Sciþþie.
Sciþþisce *adj.*, *nsf.* Scythian 71/5.
Scolopetius *ns.* Scolopetius 29/15.
Sconeg *ns.* Skåne 16/24. Cf. *ON*
Skáney.
Scotland *nas.* Ireland 9/10, 19/5,
19/15. See Commentary.
Scribanianus *as.* Scribonianus 136/
27. **Scribanianuse** *ds.* 136/23.
Scridefinne *npl.* the Lapps 13/27
(v.l. scridefinnas) Cf. Adam of
Bremen, *col.* 641 Scritefinorum,
and *ON* skríþa, slide in snow-
shoes.

Seaxan *apl.* the Saxons, *Lat.* Saxo-
nes 152/2. **Seaxum** *dpl.* 16/14.
Seleucus *nas.* Seleucus 77/30, 81/2,
81/23, 81/31, etc. **Seleucuse** *ds.*
81/19.
Seleutia *ds.* Seleucia 140/7.
Sempronius *nas.* Sempronius 5/10,
86/32, 95/4, 97/1, etc.
Senno *ds.* Sens, *Lat. pl.* (Galli)
Senones, the people of Sens 2/26,
3/21, 51/27, 76/28. Cf. *Ann. Senon-*
ensis MGHS V/I s.a. 895 Sennis.
Serfilius *ns.* Servilius 56/22, 95/4.
Sericus *n. or as.* Sericus 9/28.
Serius *ns.* Sergius (occas. var. serius)
111/7, 111/20.
Sermende *napl.* the Sarmatae 13/13,
13/24, 13/26, 131/28, 145/10, 152/6
(v.l. sermenne).
Sertorius *ns.* Sertorius 125/4, 125/13.
Seruius *nas.* Servius 116/23, 123/25.
Seuerus *nas.* Severus 7/11, 142/7,
148/5, 148/11.
Seuges *ns.* Zeugis (common var.
zeuges) 20/9.
Siburtus *ns.* Sibyrtus (possibly taken
as *apl.*) 78/5.
Sicheus *ns.* Scythaeus (Ricc. 627
and other rel. MSS sicheus) 78/6.
Sicilia *ns.* Sicily, *Lat.* Sicilia 21/2,
107/23; *ds.* 33/35, 50/26, 85/22.
Siciliam *as.* 96/25. **Sicilium** *ds.*
(*or dpl.* of **Sicilie**) 88/28. See also
Sicilie.
Sicilie, Siciliæ *napl.* the Sicilians,
Lat. Siculi 4/16, 50/32, 89/12,
90/27, etc. **Siciliae** 4/4. **Sicilia**
gpl. 2/24. **Sicilium** *dpl.* 51/3; *dpl.*
or *a.* or *ds.* of **Sicilia** 100/5. See
also **Sicilia.**
Sicilium *ns.* Sicilian 20/31.
Sidonem *as.* Sidon 58/22 (OH *as.*
Sidonam, Vienna 366 sidonem).
Sifax *ns.* Syphax (common var.
sifax) 106/28, 106/32.
Sihonas *apl. Lat. sg.* Sicyona 78/21
(Ricc. 627 and other rel. MSS *as.*
sichonam, sychonam).
Silla *ns.* Sulla (common var. silla)
124/7, 124/15, 124/23, etc. **Sillan**
as. 6/12; *ds.* 124/27.
Sillende *ns.* Sinlendi 12/31, 16/11,
16/18. See Commentary.

Silomone *ds.* Sulmo 126/21 (OH *as.* Sulmonem, Vienna 366 salomonem, other rel. MSS sulomonem etc.).

Siluie *ns.* Sylvia 37/1 (OH *gs.* Sylviae, common var. silviae, silvie); **Siluian** *gs.* 36/33.

Sinope *ns.* Sinope 30/9 (2 ×).

Siraccusa *gpl.* of the Syracusans 85/22 (OH *adj., abl. s.* Syracusano). See also **Siracussana.**

Siracuses *nas.* Syracuse, Lat. Syracusae 90/28, 103/10 (OH *apl.* Syracusas, common var. siracusas).

Siracussana *ns.* Syracusan (taken as name of town?) 21/5 (OH *adj., nsf.* Syracusana, common var. siracusana). See also **Siraccusa, Siracuses.**

Siria, Siriam, Sirie see **Syria.**

Sirie, Siriæ *apl.* the Syrians, Syria, Lat. Syri 134/3 (*or as.* of **Syria**), 145/12, 145/24. **Sira** *gpl.* 108/26, 108/29. **Sirium** *dpl. or as.* of **Syria** 69/11 (OH in Syriam).

Sirmie *ds.* Sirmium 146/13.

Sirtes see **Syrtes.**

Siuos *npl.* the Sibi 72/33 (OH *apl.* Sibos).

Smyrna *ds.* Smyrna 125/12.

Sodome *ns.* Sodom, Lat. Sodoma 1/7, 22/30.

Somnia *ds.* Samnium 123/18 (OH *abl. pl.* Samnitibus).

Somnite *napl.* the Samnites, Lat. Samnites 3/21, 58/25, 60/31, 75/9, etc. **Somnita** *gpl.* 66/14; **Somnite** 60/29. **Somnitum** *dpl.* 66/19.

Somniticum *adj., asn.* Samnite 58/23 (OH Samniticum).

Sompeius *ns.* Pompeius 23/23. See also **Pompeius.**

Soroastrem *as.* Zoroaster 22/4 (OH *as.* Zoroastrem).

*Sostianos *apl.* the Sogdiani 78/6 (OH *apl.* Sogdianos, Ricc. 627 and other rel. MSS sosdianos; also sostianos).

Spaneum *dpl.* the Spaniards, Lat. Hispani (MSS of 8th and 9th centuries frequ. spani) 74/1, 99/21. See also **Ispanie, Spenum.**

Spartani *dpl.* the Spartans, Lat. Spartani 28/3. **Spartana** *gpl.* 70/28.

Spenum *dpl.* the Spaniards 98/4. See also **Ispanie, Spaneum.**

Stileca *ns.* Stilico 155/21. **Stilecan** *ds.* 155/18 (OH *ds.* Stiliconi).

Stontos *ns.* Statanor (Ricc. 627 and other rel. MSS stantanor, Trier 1095 stantanos) 78/5.

Stromen *ns.* Stromen 77/26. See Commentary.

Subagros *n. or apl.* the Subagrae 73/3 (OH *apl.* Subagras, occas. var. subagros).

Subres *npl.* the Insubres (MSS of rel. groups B and C subres) 108/12.

Sulcanum *as.* Uscana, OH Sulcamum (common var. sulcanum) 110/22.

Surfe, Surpe *npl.* the Sorbs 13/12, 13/24. Cf. *OHG* Surbi.

Susana *ns.* OH Susiana, *adj.*, 'of Susa', taken as personal name 77/27.

Suttrian *npl.* the Sutrini 56/16.

Suþdenum *dpl.* the South Danes 13/14.

Swæfas *npl.* the Alamanni or Suebi 12/25, 145/9 (OH *npl.* Suebi, common var. suaeui). **Swæfa** *gpl.* 13/6. Cf. *Widsith* 44 Swæfe, *OHG* Swaba.

Sweoland *ns.* Sweden 15/33. See also **Sweon.**

Sweon *napl.* the Swedes 13/23, 13/24; *dpl.* 16/28. Cf. *Ein. Ann.* s.a. 813 Sueones, *ON* Svíar.

Syria *n. or as.* Syria 10/20; *ds.* 10/21. **Siriam** *as.* 141/7. **Siria** *ds.* 137/3, 138/7; **Sirie** 142/9. See also **Sirie.**

Syrtes *nas.* Syrtes. ~ *Maiores* the Greater Syrtes 19/35, 20/4. ~ *Minores* the Lesser Syrtes 20/6, 20/11.

Sysyle *npl.* the Siusli 13/12; *n. or apl.* 13/2. Cf. *OHG* Siusili, Suisli, Siusli.

T

Tacitus *ns.* Tacitus 7/23, 146/4.

Taprabane *ds.* Taprobane 9/31. See also **Deprobane.**

Tarcuatus, Tarcwatus, Tarquatus *nas.* Torquatus (occas. var. tarquatus) 6/15, 58/1, 59/31, 98/24, etc. See also **Torcuatus.**

Tarcuinius *ns.* Tarquin, *Lat.* Tarquinius 40/3, 40/23, 40/26, 40/29.
Tarcuinie *ds.* 41/5; *n. or apl.* the
Tarquins 37/20.
Tardanus *a. or gs.* Dardanus 27/33.
Tarente *ns.* Tarentum 84/1. **Tarentan** *ds.* 83/10, 105/14, 123/15 (OH
apl. Arretinos, Vienna 366 and
other rel. MSS tarentinos).
Tarentine *napl.* the Tarentini 3/24,
83/9, 83/12, 83/20, etc. **Taren-
tinum** *dpl.* 84/1.
Tarquatus see **Tarcuatus.**
Tauros *n. or as. or pl.* Taurus 10/17;
n. or apl. 10/21, 12/1; *as.* (*or pl.*)
12/9; *apl.* 70/26. **Taurasan** *as.*
68/22. **Tauro** *ds.* 10/13.
Temes *n. or as.* the Thames, *Lat.*
Tamesis 126/8.
Temeseras *n. or as. or pl.* Themis-
cyrian 10/25 (OH *apl.* Themiscyrios
[campos], common var. t(h)eme-
scerios).
Tenelaus *ns.* Sthenelus 27/6 (OH *as.*
Sthenelan, Ricc. 627 and other rel.
MSS tenelaum).
Terfinna *gpl.* the Ter-Lapps' 14/25.
Terrentius *ns.* Terentius (Vienna
366 and other rel. MSS terrentius)
101/2, 107/28.
Tetricum *as.* Tetricus 145/25 (OH
as. Tetricum).
Teutonas *apl.* the Teutonae 122/8
(OH *apl.* Teutonas).
Tharsum *ds.* Tarsus (common var.
tharsus) 68/23 (OH *as.* Tharsum);
Tharse 69/33; **Tharsa** 146/7, 149/4.
Thasalia *ds.* Thessaly, *Lat.* Thes-
salia (common var. thesalia) 24/33.
See also **Thesaliam.**
Thebane *napl.* the Thebans, *Lat.*
Thebani, 53/25, 54/32, 55/20, 55/22,
etc. **Thebana** *gpl.* 53/28. **Theba-
num** *dpl.* 61/11; **Thebani** 28/3.
Thelenus *ns.* OH *adj.* Mytilenaeus,
the Mytilenaean, taken as a personal
name (Ricc. 627 and other rel. MSS
thelenus) 77/25.
Theleomommos *ns.* Tlepolemus
(Ricc. 627 and other rel. MSS
thleponmos, thelponmos, thelopon-
mos) 78/8.
Thelescises *npl.* the Telchines, OH

Telchises (Ricc. 627 and other rel.
MSS thelscises) 23/13; **Thelesci**
1/8. **Thelescisa** *gpl.* 23/15.
Themestocles *ns.* Themistocles 47/
18, 47/20.
Theodosia *n. or as.* Theodosia 9/4.
Theodosius *nas.* Theodosius 8/6,
152/19, 153/20, 153/22, etc. **Theo-
dosiuses** *gs.* 152/20. **Theodosiuse**
ds. 154/3.
Theram *a. or ds.* Thera 137/7 (OH
as. Theram).
Therasiam *a. or ds.* Therasia 137/7
(OH *as.* Therasiam).
Thesali *napl.* the Thessalians, *Lat.*
Thessali (common var. thesali)
28/17, 28/18, 61/9, 61/25, etc.;
Thesalii 62/23.
Thesaliam *as.* Thessaly, *Lat.* Thes-
salia (common var. thesali) 127/11
(OH *as.* Thessaliam); **Thesalium**
as. or pl. 84/3. See also **Thasalia.**
Theuhaleon *ns.* Deucalion 25/2,
*25/3; *ds.* 25/5.
Thigesþres *n. or gs.* Thyestes 28/6.
Thila *n. or as.* Thule, *Lat.* Thyle
19/19.
Tholomeus see **Ptholomeus.**
Thraci[1] *ds.* Dyrrachium, mod.
Durazzo 126/23.
Thraci[2], **Traci** *napl.* the Thracians,
Lat. Thraces 18/9, 68/5, 108/18,
110/18. **Thracea** *gpl.* 82/7.
Thraciam *as.* Thrace, *Lat.* Thracia
77/29. **Tracia** *ds.* 63/7 (v.l. thracia).
Thrusci *npl.* the Etruscans 87/16
(OH *gpl.* Etruscorum, occas. var 7
truscorum). See also **Etrusci.**
Tiber *ns.* the Tiber, *Lat.* Tiberis
21/15, 96/29.
Tiberius *nas.* Tiberius 6/22, 134/12,
134/20, 135/8, etc. **Tiberiuses** *gs.*
134/29.
Ticenan *ds.* the Ticinus 99/29 (OH
as. Ticinum, Vienna 366 and other
rel. MSS ticenum).
Tigris *ns.* the Tigris 10/1; *gs.* 146/16.
Tigres *ds.* 10/10.
Tingetana *n. or as.* Tingitana 20/18.
Tirrenum *n. or as.* Tyrrhenian 21/15
(OH *adj.* Tyrrhenicum, var. tir-
renicum); **Tirenum** 21/10 (OH
Tyrrhenum).

Tirus *nas.* Tyre, *Lat.* Tyrus (common var. tirus) 69/14, 70/23. **Tirum** *as.* 4/6, 90/19 (OH *as.* Tyrum).
Titus *ns.* Titus 7/3, 57/28, 58/1, 97/1, etc.; **Tita** 41/20 (OH T., MSS *abl. s.* tito). **Tituses** *gs.* 7/4, 139/5. **Tituse** *ds.* 138/12, 138/18.
Tontolus *ns.* Tantalus 27/29. **Tontolis** *gs.* 27/28 (OH *gs.* Tantali).
Torcuatus *ns.* Torquatus 97/12. See also **Tarcuatus.**
Traci see **Thraci.**
Tracia see **Thraciam.**
Tracio *ds.* Thrace? 98/28 (OH *apl.* Tuscos).
Traianus *nas.* Trajan, *Lat.* Traianus 139/17, 139/23, 140/6. **Traianuses** *gs.* 140/9.
Trefia *ds.* the Trevia 100/3, 100/7.
Tribaballe *npl.* the Triballi 64/28 (OH *npl.* Triballi).
Tribulitania *ns.* Tripolis 20/3 (OH Tripolitana provincia).
Trogus *ns.* Trogus 88/18.
Troia *ns.* Troy, *Lat.* Troia 38/31.
Troiana *gpl.* of the Trojans 27/33, 31/26; *gpl. or ds.* 31/24.
Troianiscan *adj., dsn. wk.* Trojan 30/23, 32/10.
Truso *ns.* Druzno? 16/33; *ds.* 16/21. See Commentary.
Tuscania *ns.* Tuscany, *Lat.* Tuscania 21/19.
Tuscea *gpl.* the Etruscans' 40/23 (OH *gpl.* Etruscorum, var. tuscorum). See also **Etrusci.**
Tusci *as.* Tuscia 51/28.

þ

þrysci *napl.* the Etruscans 75/2, 75/5. See also **Etrusci, Thrusci,**
þyringas *napl.* the Thuringians 12/28, 13/3. Cf. *Lat.* Thuringi, *OHG* Duringa.

U

Ualens *ns.* Valens 8/3, 151/22, 152/9, 152/11, etc. **Ualenses** *gs.* 153/3. **Ualense** *ds.* 152/11; **Ualente** 151/20 (OH *as.* Valentem).

Ualentinianus *nas.* Valentinianus 8/2, 8/6, 151/14, 152/1, etc. **Ualentinianuses** *gs.* *152/9, 152/10.
Ualerianus *ns.* Valerianus 144/21, 145/1.
Ualerius *ns.* Valerius 108/25; *gs.* 60/15.
Uarra *ns.* Varro 101/3.
Uauius *ns.* Fabius (common var. fauius) 51/33. See also **Fauius.**
Uecilius *as.* Vecilius 114/17.
Ueigentes *npl.* the Veientes (MSS of rel. groups B and C veigentes) 41/23.
Ueiorum *as.* (*or gpl.*) *for* OH *gpl.* Veiorum, of the Veii 2/25, 51/16.
Ueriatus *nas.* Viriatus (Vienna 366 and other rel. MSS veriatus) 5/21, 114/12, 114/23, 115/18, etc. **Ueriatuses** *gs.* 114/25.
Uesoges *ns.* Vesozes (Ricc. 627 and other rel. MSS vesoges) 1/23, 28/23, 28/25.
Uespasianus *ns.* Vespasian, *Lat.* Vespasianus 7/2, 138/11. **Uespasiane** *ds.* 138/17. See also **Wespasianus.**
Uestine *n. or apl.* the Vestini 123/23.
Ueteromonem *as.* Vetranio 150/1 (OH *as.* Vetranionem, MSS of rel. groups A, B, C, and D veteranionem).
Uitellus *ns.* Vitellius (Vienna 366 and other rel. MSS vitellus) 138/8.
Ulcinienses *npl.* the Volsinians 87/16 (OH *npl.* Vulsinienses, MSS of rel. group C vulcinienses).
Ulsca *ns.* Vulsco (Vienna 366 and other rel. MSS ulsco) 96/6.
Umbri *npl.* the Umbrians, *Lat.* Umbri 75/2. **Umbre** *apl.* 75/5.
Umene(s), Umenis see **Eumen.**
Utica *n. or as.* Utica 106/14.
Uxiarches *ns. or apl.* Oxiarches 78/4 (Ricc. 627 axiarches).
Uzera *npl.* Uzerae Montes 20/13.

W

Wascan *npl.* the Basques 18/33, 18/35. Cf. *Lat.* Wascones, Steinmeyer and Sievers III. 610 Equitania: uuasconolant.

Welengaford *n. or as.* Wallingford 126/8.

Wendelsæ *nasm.* the Mediterranean Sea 9/6, 9/9, 10/16, etc.; *ds.* 9/10. **Wendelsæs** *gs.* 8/21. Cf. *Anglo-Saxon Chronicle* s.a. 885 Wendelsæ.

Weonoþland, Weonodland *nas.* territory of the Wends 16/23, 16/29, 16/30. **Weonodlande** *ds.* 16/31; **Winodlande** 16/35. Cf. Steinmeyer and Sievers III. 132 Sclavi: winida and see **Winedas.**

***Wespasianus** *ns.* Vespasian, *Lat.* Vespasianus 138/20 (v.l. uespassianus). See also **Uespasianus.**

Westsæ *asf.* the sea west of Norway 14/1.

Wilte *npl.* the Veletians or Vilci 13/1. Cf. *Lat.* Wilti, *OHG* Wilzi.

Winedas *apl.* the Wends 13/22. **Wineda** *gpl.* 13/2. **Winedum** *dpl.* 16/14. See **Weonoþland.**

Wisle *nsf.* Vistula, *Slav.* Visla 16/30, 16/31, 16/35; *as.*(?) 16/35; *gs.* 13/9. **Wislemuþa** *nsm.* the mouth of the Vistula 16/37. **Wislemuþan** *as.* 16/29.

Witland *nas.* 'Witland' 16/30, 16/31. See Commentary.

Wulchi *npl.* the Vulsci 56/14 (v.l. fulchi). See also **Fulcisci.**

Wulfstan *ns.* Wulfstan 16/21.

X

Xersis *nas.* Xerxes (common var. xerses) 46/6, 46/11, 46/21, 46/22, etc.; *gs.* 2/21. **Xersan** *as.* 143/6 (OH *as.* Xerxem). **Xerse** *ds.* 47/26.

Z

Zoffirion *ns.* Zopyrion 70/32 (Vat. 1975 Zoffirion).

EARLY ENGLISH TEXT SOCIETY

LIST OF PUBLICATIONS
1864–1980

DECEMBER 1980

Orders from non-members of the Society should be placed with a bookseller. Orders from booksellers for volumes in part 1 of this list should be sent to Oxford University Press, Press Road, Neasden, London NW10 0DD. Orders from booksellers for volumes in part 2 of this list should be sent to the following addresses: orders for E.E.T.S. reprints to Oxford University Press, Press Road, Neasden, London NW10 0DD; orders for Kraus reprints from North America to Kraus Reprint Co., Route 100, Millwood, N.Y. 10546, U.S.A., from other countries to Kraus Reprint Co., FL 9491 Nendeln, Liechtenstein.

EARLY ENGLISH TEXT SOCIETY

The Early English Text Society was founded in 1864 by Frederick James Furnivall, with the help of Richard Morris, Walter Skeat and others, to bring the mass of unprinted Early English literature within the reach of students and to provide sound texts from which the New English Dictionary could quote. In 1867 an Extra Series was started of texts already printed but not in satisfactory or readily obtainable editions. In 1921 the Extra Series was discontinued and all publications were subsequently listed and numbered as part of the Original Series. In 1970 the first of a new Supplementary Series was published; unlike the Extra Series, volumes in this series will be issued only occasionally, as funds allow and as suitable texts become available.

In the first part of this list are shown the books published by the Society since 1938, Original Series 210 onwards and the Supplementary Series. A large number of the earlier books were reprinted by the Society in the period 1950 to 1970. In order to make the rest available, the Society has come to an agreement with the Kraus Reprint Co. who reprint as necessary the volumes in the Original Series 1–209 and in the Extra Series. In this way all the volumes published by the Society are once again in print.

Membership of the Society is open to libraries and to individuals interested in the study of medieval English literature. The subscription to the Society for 1981 is £7·50 (or for U.S. members $20.00, Canadian members Can. $23.00), due in advance on 1 January, and should be paid by cheque, postal order or money order made out to 'The Early English Text Society', and sent to Mrs. Rachel Hands, Assistant Executive Secretary, Early English Text Society, 35 Beechcroft Road, Oxford. Payment of this subscription entitles the member to receive the new book(s) in the Original Series for the year. The books in the Supplementary Series do not form part of the issue sent to members in return for the payment of their annual subscription, though they are available to members at a reduced price; a notice about each volume is sent to members in advance of publication.

Private members of the Society (but not libraries) may select in place of the annual issue past volumes from the Society's list chosen from the Original Series 210 to date or from the Supplementary Series. The value of such texts allowed against one annual subscription is £12·00, and all these transactions must be made through the Executive Secretary. Members of the Society may purchase copies of books O.S. 210 to date for their own use at a discount of 25% of the listed prices; private members (but not libraries) may purchase earlier publications at a similar discount. All such orders must be sent to the Assistant Executive Secretary.

Details of books, the cost of membership and its privileges, are revised from time to time. The prices of books are subject to alteration without notice. This list is brought up to date annually, and the current edition should be consulted.

December 1980

LIST 1

ORIGINAL SERIES 1938–1980

O.S. 210   **Sir Gawain and the Green Knight,** re-ed. I. Gollancz, with introductory essays by Mabel Day and M. S. Serjeantson. 1940 (*for* 1938), *reprinted* 1966.   £3·25

211   **The Dicts and Sayings of the Philosophers:** translations made by Stephen Scrope, William Worcester and anonymous translator, ed. C. F. Bühler. 1941 (*for* 1939), *reprinted* 1961.   £8·75

212   **The Book of Margery Kempe,** Vol. I, Text (*all published*), ed. S. B. Meech, with notes and appendices by S. B. Meech and H. E. Allen. 1940 (*for* 1939), *reprinted* 1961.   £8·25

213   **Ælfric's De Temporibus Anni,** ed. H. Henel. 1942 (*for* 1940), *reprinted* 1970.   £4·75

214   **Forty-Six Lives translated from Boccaccio's De Claris Mulieribus** by Henry Parker, Lord Morley, ed. H. G. Wright. 1943 (*for* 1940), *reprinted* 1970.   £6·00

215, 220   **Charles of Orleans: The English Poems,** Vol. I, ed. R. Steele (1941), Vol. II, ed. R. Steele and Mabel Day (1946 *for* 1944); *reprinted as one volume with bibliographical supplement* 1970.   £7·25

216   **The Latin Text of the Ancrene Riwle,** from Merton College MS. 44 and British Museum MS. Cotton Vitellius E. vii, ed. C. D'Evelyn. 1944 (*for* 1941), *reprinted* 1957.   £5·00

217   **The Book of Vices and Virtues:** A Fourteenth-Century English Translation of the *Somme le Roi* of Lorens d'Orléans, ed. W. Nelson Francis. 1942, *reprinted* 1968.   £8·75

218   **The Cloud of Unknowing and The Book of Privy Counselling;** ed. Phyllis Hodgson. 1944 (*for* 1943), *corrected reprint* 1973.   £5·75

219   **The French Text of the Ancrene Riwle,** British Museum MS. Cotton Vitellius F. vii, ed. J. A. Herbert. 1944 (*for* 1943), *reprinted* 1967.   £6·00

220   **Charles of Orleans: The English Poems,** Vol. II; *see above* O.S. 215.

221   **The Romance of Sir Degrevant,** ed. L. F. Casson. 1949 (*for* 1944), *reprinted* 1970.   £5·75

222   **The Lyfe of Syr Thomas More, by Ro. Ba.,** ed. E. V. Hitchcock and P. E. Hallett, with notes and appendices by A. W. Reed. 1950 (*for* 1945), *reprinted* 1974.   £7·25

223   **The Tretyse of Loue,** ed. J. H. Fisher. 1951 (*for* 1945), *reprinted* 1970.   £4·75

224   **Athelston: a Middle English Romance,** ed. A. McI. Trounce. 1951 (*for* 1946), *reprinted* 1957.   £4·75

225   **The English Text of the Ancrene Riwle,** British Museum MS. Cotton Nero A. xiv, ed. Mabel Day. 1952 (*for* 1946), *reprinted* 1957.   £5·75

226   **Respublica:** an interlude for Christmas 1553 attributed to Nicholas Udall, re-ed. W. W. Greg. 1952 (*for* 1946), *reprinted* 1969.   £3·50

227   **Kyng Alisaunder,** Vol. I, Text, ed. G. V. Smithers. 1952 (*for* 1947), *reprinted* 1961.   £8·75

ORIGINAL SERIES 1864–1938

O.S. 131   The Brut, or the Chronicles of England . . . from Bodleian MS. Rawl. £6·00
B. 171, ed. F. W. D. Brie. Vol. I 1906, *reprinted* 1960. (See O.S. 136 for Vol. II.)

132   The Works of John Metham, ed. H. Craig. 1916 (*for* 1906), *reprinted* $15.00 Kraus 1973.

133, 144   The English Register of Oseney Abbey . . . *c.* 1460, ed. A. Clark. $20.00 Vol. I 1907, Vol. II 1913 (*for* 1912); *reprinted as one volume* Kraus 1971.

134, 135   The Coventry Leet Book, ed. M. D. Harris. Vol. I 1907, Vol. II $38.75 1908; *reprinted as one volume* Kraus 1971. (See O.S. 138, 146 for other parts.)

136   The Brut, or the Chronicles of England, ed. F. W. D. Brie. Vol. II $21.25 1908, *reprinted* Kraus 1971. (See O.S. 131 for Vol. I.)

137   Twelfth Century Homilies in MS. Bodley 343, ed. A. O. Belfour. £3·25 Vol. I Text and translation (*all published*) 1909, *reprinted* 1962. *Paper*.

138, 146   The Coventry Leet Book, ed. M. D. Harris. Vol. III 1909, Vol. $27.50 IV 1913; *reprinted as one volume* Kraus 1971. (See O.S. 134, 135 for other parts.)

139   John Arderne Treatises of Fistula in Ano etc., ed. D'Arcy Power. £5·00 1910, *reprinted* 1968.

140   John Capgrave's Lives of St. Augustine and St. Gilbert of Sempring- $12.50 ham and a sermon, ed. J. J. Munro. 1910, *reprinted* Kraus 1971.

141   The Middle English Poem Erthe upon Erthe, printed from 24 manu- £3·50 scripts, ed. H. M. R. Murray. 1911, *reprinted* 1964.

142   The English Register of Godstow Nunnery, Vol. III. See above, O.S. 130.

143   The Prose Life of Alexander from the Thornton MS., ed. J. S. West- $7.50 lake. 1913 (*for* 1911), *reprinted* Kraus 1971.

144   The English Register of Oseney Abbey, Vol. II. See above, O.S. 133.

145   The Northern Passion, ed. F. A. Foster. Vol. I 1913 (*for* 1912), $17.50 *reprinted* Kraus 1971. (See O.S. 147, 183 for other parts.)

146   The Coventry Leet Book, Vol. IV. See above, O.S. 138.

147   The Northern Passion, ed. F. A. Foster. Vol. II 1916 (*for* 1913), $15.00 *reprinted* Kraus 1971. (See O.S. 145, 183 for other parts.)

148   A Fifteenth-Century Courtesy Book, ed. R. W. Chambers, and Two £3·50 Fifteenth-Century Franciscan Rules, ed. W. W. Seton. 1914, *reprinted* 1963.

149   Lincoln Diocese Documents, 1450–1544, ed. A. Clark. 1914, *re-* $25.00 *printed* Kraus 1971.

150   The Old English Versions of the enlarged Rule of Chrodegang, the $8.75 Capitula of Theodulf and the Epitome of Benedict of Aniane, ed. A. S. Napier. 1916 (*for* 1914), *reprinted* Kraus 1971.

151   The Lanterne of Liȝt, ed. L. M. Swinburn. 1917 (*for* 1915), *reprinted* $22.50 Kraus 1971.

152   Early English Homilies from the Twelfth-Century MS. Vespasian D. $16.00 xiv, ed. R. D.-N. Warner. 1917 (*for* 1915), *reprinted* Kraus 1971.

153   Mandeville's Travels . . . from MS. Cotton Titus C. xvi, ed. P. $16.25 Hamelius. Vol. I Text 1919 (*for* 1916), *reprinted* Kraus 1973. *Paper*.

154   Mandeville's Travels . . . from MS. Cotton Titus C. xvi, ed. P. £4·50 Hamelius. Vol. II Introduction and notes. 1923 (*for* 1916), *reprinted* 1961. *Paper*.

155   The Wheatley Manuscript : Middle English verse and prose in British $10.00 Museum MS. Additional 39574, ed. M. Day. 1921 (*for* 1917), *reprinted* Kraus 1971.

156   The Donet by Reginald Pecock, ed. E. V. Hitchcock. 1921 (*for* 1918), $20.00 *reprinted* Kraus 1971.

O.S. 157 **The Pepysian Gospel Harmony,** ed. M. Goates. 1922 (*for* 1919), $12.50
reprinted Kraus 1971.

158 **Meditations on the Life and Passion of Christ,** from British Museum $8.75
MS. Additional 11307, ed. C. D'Evelyn. 1921 (*for* 1919), *reprinted*
Kraus 1971.

159 **Vices and Virtues** [from British Museum MS. Stowe 240], ed. F. £3·00
Holthausen. Vol. II Notes and Glossary, 1921 (*for* 1920), *reprinted*
1967. (See O.S. 89 for Vol. I.) *Paper.*

160 **The Old English Version of the Heptateuch** etc., ed. S. J. Crawford. £8·50
1922 (*for* 1921), reprinted with additional material, ed. N. R. Ker
1969.

161 **Three Old English Prose Texts** in MS. Cotton Vitellius A. xv, ed. S. $11.25
Rypins. 1924 (*for* 1921), *reprinted* Kraus 1971.

162 **Pearl, Cleanness, Patience and Sir Gawain,** facsimile of British £22·50
Museum MS. Cotton Nero A. x, with introduction by I. Gollancz.
1923 (*for* 1922), *reprinted* 1971.

163 **The Book of the Foundation of St. Bartholomew's Church in London,** $6.25
ed. N. Moore. 1923, *reprinted* Kraus 1971. *Paper.*

164 **The Folewer to the Donet by Reginald Pecock,** ed. E. V. Hitchcock. $25.00
1924 (*for* 1923), *reprinted* Kraus 1971.

165 **The Famous Historie of Chinon of England by Christopher Middleton,** $12.50
with Leland's Assertio Inclytissimi Arturii and Robinson's translation, ed. W. E. Mead. 1925 (*for* 1923), *reprinted* Kraus 1971.

166 **A Stanzaic Life of Christ,** from Harley MS. 3909, ed. F. A. Foster. $27.50
1926 (*for* 1924), *reprinted* Kraus 1971.

167 **John Trevisa Dialogus** inter Militem et Clericum, Richard Fitzralph's $17.50
'Defensio Curatorum', Methodius' 'þe Bygynnyng of þe World and
þe Ende of Worldes', ed. A. J. Perry. 1925 (*for* 1924), *reprinted* Kraus
1971.

168 **The Book of the Ordre of Chyualry** translated by William Caxton, ed. $11.25
A. T. P. Byles. 1926 (*for* 1925), *reprinted* Kraus 1971.

169 **The Southern Passion,** Pepysian MS. 2334, ed. B. D. Brown. 1927 $15.00
(*for* 1925), *reprinted* Kraus 1971.

170 **Boethius De Consolatione Philosophiae,** translated by John Walton, $40.00
ed. M. Science. 1927 (*for* 1925), *reprinted* Kraus 1971.

171 **The Reule of Crysten Religioun by Reginald Pecock,** ed. W. C. Greet. $31.25
1927 (*for* 1926), *reprinted* Kraus 1971.

172 **The Seege or Batayle of Troye,** ed. M. E. Barnicle. 1927 (*for* 1926), $15.00
reprinted Kraus 1971.

173 **Stephen Hawes The Pastime of Pleasure,** ed. W. E. Mead. 1928 (*for* $30.00
1927), *reprinted* Kraus 1971.

174 **The Middle English Stanzaic Versions of the Life of St. Anne,** ed. R. E. $11.25
Parker. 1928 (*for* 1927), *reprinted* Kraus 1971.

175 **Alexander Barclay The Eclogues,** ed. B. White. 1928 (*for* 1927), £6·00
reprinted 1961.

176 **William Caxton The Prologues and Epilogues,** ed. W. J. B. Crotch. $20.00
1928 (*for* 1927), *reprinted* Kraus 1973.

177 **Byrhtferth's Manual,** ed. S. J. Crawford. Vol. I Text, translation, £7·25
sources, and appendices (*all published*) 1929 (*for* 1928), *reprinted* 1966.

178 **The Revelations of St. Birgitta,** from Garrett MS. Princeton Uni- $7.50
versity, ed. W. P. Cumming. 1929 (*for* 1928), *reprinted* Kraus 1971.

179 **William Nevill The Castell of Pleasure,** ed. R. D. Cornelius. 1930 $8.75
(*for* 1928), *reprinted* Kraus 1971.

180 **The Apologye of Syr Thomas More, knyght,** ed. A. I. Taft. 1930 $25.00
(*for* 1929), *reprinted* Kraus 1971.

181 **The Dance of Death,** ed. F. Warren. 1931 (*for* 1929), *reprinted* **Kraus** $8.75
1971.

O.S. 182 **Speculum Christiani**, ed. G. Holmstedt. 1933 (*for* 1929), *reprinted* $31.25
Kraus 1971.

183 **The Northern Passion** (Supplement), ed. W. Heuser and F. A. Foster. $10.00
1930, *reprinted* Kraus 1971. (See O.S. 145, 147 for other parts.)

184 **John Audelay The Poems**, ed. E. K. Whiting. 1931 (*for* 1930), *re-* $20.00
printed Kraus 1971.

185 **Henry Lovelich's Merlin**, ed. E. A. Kock. Vol. III. 1932 (*for* 1930), $20.00
reprinted Kraus 1971. (See E.S. 93 and 112 for other parts.)

186 **Nicholas Harpsfield The Life and Death of Sr. Thomas More**, ed. £11·75
E. V. Hitchcock and R. W. Chambers. 1932 (*for* 1931), *reprinted*
1963.

187 **John Stanbridge The Vulgaria and Robert Whittinton The Vulgaria**, $12.50
ed. B. White. 1932 (*for* 1931), *reprinted* Kraus 1971.

188 **The Siege of Jerusalem**, from Bodleian MS. Laud Misc. 656, ed. E. $10.00
Kölbing and M. Day. 1932 (*for* 1931), *reprinted* Kraus 1971.

189 **Christine de Pisan The Book of Fayttes of Armes and of Chyualrye,** $20.00
translated by William Caxton, ed. A. T. P. Byles. 1932, *reprinted*
Kraus 1971.

190 **English Mediaeval Lapidaries**, ed. J. Evans and M. S. Serjeantson. £5·75
1933 (*for* 1932), *reprinted* 1960.

191 **The Seven Sages of Rome** (Southern Version), ed. K. Brunner. 1933 $16.25
(*for* 1932), *reprinted* Kraus 1971.

191A R. W. Chambers: **On the Continuity of English Prose** from Alfred to £3·00
More and his School (an extract from the introduction to O.S. 186).
1932, *reprinted* 1966.

192 **John Lydgate The Minor Poems**, ed. H. N. MacCracken. Vol. II £8·50
Secular Poems. 1934 (*for* 1933), *reprinted* 1961. (See E.S. 107 for
Vol. I.)

193 **Seinte Marherete**, from MS. Bodley 34 and British Museum MS. £5·75
Royal 17 A. xxvii, re-ed. F. M. Mack. 1934 (*for* 1933), *reprinted* 1958.

194 **The Exeter Book**, ed. W. S. Mackie. Vol. II Poems IX–XXXII. 1934 $17.50
(*for* 1933), *reprinted* Kraus 1973. (See O.S. 104 for Vol. I.)

195 **The Quatrefoil of Love**, ed. I. Gollancz and M. M. Weale. 1935 (*for* $6.25
1934), *reprinted* Kraus 1971. *Paper.*

196 **An Anonymous Short English Metrical Chronicle**, ed. E. Zettl. 1935 $17.50
(*for* 1934), *reprinted* Kraus 1971.

197 **William Roper The Lyfe of Sir Thomas Moore, knighte**, ed. E. V. $23.75
Hitchcock. 1935 (*for* 1934), *reprinted* Kraus, 1976.

198 **Firumbras and Otuel and Roland**, ed. M. I. O'Sullivan. 1935 (*for* $17.50
1934), *reprinted* Kraus 1971.

199 **Mum and the Sothsegger**, ed. M. Day and R. Steele. 1936 (*for* 1934), $11.25
reprinted Kraus 1971.

200 **Speculum Sacerdotale**, ed. E. H. Weatherly. 1936 (*for* 1935), *re-* $18.75
printed Kraus 1971.

201 **Knyghthode and Bataile**, ed. R. Dyboski and Z. M. Arend. 1936 (*for* $17.50
1935), *reprinted* Kraus 1971.

202 **John Palsgrave The Comedy of Acolastus**, ed. P. L. Carver. 1937 (*for* $17.50
1935), *reprinted* Kraus 1971.

203 **Amis and Amiloun**, ed. MacEdward Leach. 1937 (*for* 1935), *reprinted* £5·75
1960.

204 **Valentine and Orson**, translated from the French by Henry Watson, $25.00
ed. A. Dickson. 1937 (*for* 1936), *reprinted* Kraus 1971.

205 **Early English Versions** of the Tales of Guiscardo and Ghismonda and $20.00
Titus and Gisippus from the Decameron, ed. H. G. Wright. 1937
(*for* 1936), *reprinted* Kraus 1971.

206 **Osbern Bokenham Legendys of Hooly Wummen**, ed. M. S. Serjeantson. $20.00
1938 (*for* 1936), *reprinted* Kraus 1971.

O.S. 207 The Liber de Diversis Medicinis in the Thornton Manuscript, ed. £4·75
M. S. Ogden. 1938 (*for* 1936), *revised reprint* 1969.

208 The Parker Chronicle and Laws (Corpus Christi College, Cambridge £16·50
MS. 173); a facsimile, ed. R. Flower and H. Smith. 1941 (*for* 1937),
reprinted 1973.

209 Middle English Sermons, from British Museum MS. Royal 18 B. £8·75
xxiii, ed. W. O. Ross. 1940 (*for* 1938), *reprinted* 1960.

EXTRA SERIES 1867-1920

E.S. 1 The Romance of William of Palerne, ed. W. W. Skeat. 1867, *reprinted* $35.00
Kraus 1973.

2 On Early English Pronunciation, by A. J. Ellis. Part I. 1867, *reprinted* $15.00
Kraus 1973. (See E.S. 7, 14, 23, and 56 for other parts.)

3 Caxton's Book of Curtesye, with two manuscript copies of the treatise, $8.00
ed. F. J. Furnivall. 1868, *reprinted* Kraus 1973. *Paper.*

4 The Lay of Havelok the Dane, ed. W. W. Skeat. 1868, *reprinted* Kraus $20.00
1973.

5 Chaucer's Translation of Boethius's ' De Consolatione Philosophiæ', ed. £4·50
R. Morris. 1868, *reprinted* 1969.

6 The Romance of the Cheuelere Assigne, re-ed. H. H. Gibbs. 1868, $5.00
reprinted Kraus 1973. *Paper.*

7 On Early English Pronunciation, by A. J. Ellis. Part II. 1869, *reprinted* $15.00
Kraus 1973. (See E.S. 2, 14, 23, and 56 for other parts.)

8 Queene Elizabethes Achademy etc., ed. F. J. Furnivall, with essays on $20.00
early Italian and German Books of Courtesy by W. M. Rossetti and
E. Oswald. 1869, *reprinted* Kraus 1973.

9 The Fraternitye of Vacabondes by John Awdeley, Harman's Caveat, $8.75
Haben's Sermon etc., ed. E. Viles and F. J. Furnivall. 1869, *reprinted*
Kraus 1973.

10 Andrew Borde's Introduction of Knowledge and Dyetary of Helth, with $35.00
Barnes's Defence of the Berde, ed. F. J. Furnivall. 1870, *reprinted*
Kraus 1973.

11, 55 The Bruce by John Barbour, ed. W. W. Skeat. Vol. I 1870, Vol. IV £7·25
1889; *reprinted as one volume* 1968. (See E.S. 21, 29, for other parts.)

12, 32 England in the Reign of King Henry VIII, Vol. I Dialogue between $40.00
Cardinal Pole and Thomas Lupset, ed. J. M. Cowper (1871), Vol. II
Starkey's Life and Letters, ed. S. J. Herrtage (1878); *reprinted as one
volume* Kraus 1973.

13 Simon Fish A Supplicacyon for the Beggers, re-ed. F. J. Furnivall, $12.00
A Supplycacion to . . . Henry VIII, A Supplication of the Poore
Commons and The Decaye of England by the great multitude of shepe,
ed. J. M. Cowper. 1871, *reprinted* Kraus 1973.

14 On Early English Pronunciation, by A. J. Ellis. Part III. 1871, *re-* $25.00
printed Kraus 1973. (See E.S. 2, 7, 23, and 56 for other parts.)

15 The Select Works of Robert Crowley, ed. J. M. Cowper. 1872, *re-* $15.00
printed Kraus 1973.

16 Geoffrey Chaucer A Treatise on the Astrolabe, ed. W. W. Skeat. 1872, £4·50
reprinted 1968.

17, 18 The Complaynt of Scotlande, re-ed. J. A. H. Murray. Vol. I 1872, $35.00
Vol. II 1873; *reprinted as one volume* Kraus 1973.

19 The Myroure of oure Ladye, ed. J. H. Blunt. 1873, *reprinted* Kraus $40.00
1973.

20, 24 The History of the Holy Grail by Henry Lovelich, ed. F. J. Furnivall. $45.00
Vol. I 1874, Vol. II 1875; *reprinted as one volume* Kraus 1973. (See
E.S. 28, 30, and 95 for other parts.)

E.S. 21, 29 The Bruce by John Barbour, ed. W. W. Skeat. Vol. II 1874, Vol. £10·00
III 1877; *reprinted as one volume* 1968. (See E.S. 11, 55 for other part.)

22 Henry Brinklow's Complaynt of Roderyck Mors, The Lamentacyon of a $10.00
Christen agaynst the Cytye of London by Roderigo Mors, ed. J. M.
Cowper. 1874, *reprinted* Kraus 1973.

23 On Early English Pronunciation, by A. J. Ellis. Part IV. 1874, *re-* $30.00
printed Kraus 1973. (See E.S. 2, 7, 14, and 56 for other parts.)

24 The History of the Holy Grail by Henry Lovelich, Vol. II. See above,
E.S. 20.

25, 26 The Romance of Guy of Warwick, the second or 15th-century £8·50
version, ed. J. Zupitza. Vol. I 1875, Vol. II 1876; reprinted as one
volume 1966.

27 John Fisher The English Works, ed. J. E. B. Mayor. Vol. I (*all pub-* $30.00
lished) 1876, *reprinted* Kraus 1973.

28, 30, 95 The History of the Holy Grail by Henry Lovelich, ed. F. J. $26.25
Furnivall. Vol. III 1877; Vol. IV 1878; Vol. V The Legend of the Holy
Grail, its Sources, Character and Development by D. Kempe 1905;
reprinted as one volume Kraus 1973. (See E.S. 20, 24 for other parts.)

29 The Bruce by John Barbour, Vol. III. See above, E.S. 21.

30 The History of the Holy Grail by Henry Lovelich, Vol. IV. See above,
E.S. 28.

31 The Alliterative Romance of Alexander and Dindimus, re-ed. W. W. $8.75
Skeat. 1878, *reprinted* Kraus 1973.

32 England in the Reign of King Henry VIII, Vol. II. See above, E.S. 12.

33 The Early English Versions of the Gesta Romanorum, ed. S. J. H. £11·25
Herrtage. 1879, *reprinted* 1962.

34 The English Charlemagne Romances I: Sir Ferumbras, ed. S. J. H. £6·00
Herrtage. 1879, *reprinted* 1966.

35 The English Charlemagne Romances II: The Sege of Melayne, The $20.00
Romance of Duke Rowland and Sir Otuell of Spayne, ed. S. J. H.
Herrtage. 1880, *reprinted* Kraus 1973.

36, 37 The English Charlemagne Romances III and IV: The Lyf of £6·00
Charles the Grete, translated by William Caxton, ed. S. J. H. Herrtage.
Vol. I 1880, Vol. II 1881; *reprinted as one volume* 1967.

38 The English Charlemagne Romances V: The Romance of the Sowdone £5·75
of Babylone, re-ed. E. Hausknecht. 1881, *reprinted* 1969.

39 The English Charlemagne Romances VI: The Taill of Rauf Coilyear, £4·75
with the fragments of Roland and Vernagu and Otuel, re-ed. S. J. H.
Herrtage. 1882, *reprinted* 1969.

40, 41 The English Charlemagne Romances VII and VIII: The Boke of $60.00
Duke Huon of Burdeux translated by Lord Berners, ed. S. L. Lee. Vol. I
1882, Vol. II 1883; *reprinted as one volume* Kraus 1973. (See E.S. 43,
50 for other parts.)

42, 49, 59 The Romance of Guy of Warwick, from the Auchinleck MS. £11·50
and the Caius MS., ed. J. Zupitza. Vol. I 1883, Vol. II 1887, Vol. III
1891; *reprinted as one volume* 1966.

43, 50 The English Charlemagne Romances IX and XII: The Boke of $25.00
Duke Huon of Burdeux translated by Lord Berners, ed. S. L. Lee.
Vol. III 1884, Vol. IV 1887; *reprinted as one volume* Kraus 1973.

44 The English Charlemagne Romances X: The Foure Sonnes of Aymon, $21.25
translated by William Caxton, ed. O. Richardson. Vol. I 1884, *re-*
printed Kraus 1973.

45 The English Charlemagne Romances XI: The Foure Sonnes of Aymon, $35.00
translated by William Caxton, ed. O. Richardson. Vol. II 1885, *re-*
printed Kraus 1973.

46, 48, 65 The Romance of Sir Beues of Hamtoun, ed. E. Kölbing. Vol. I $31.25
1885, Vol. II 1886, Vol. III 1894; *reprinted as one volume* Kraus 1973.

E.S. 47   **The Wars of Alexander,** an Alliterative Romance, re-ed. W. W. Skeat. $45.00
1886, *reprinted* Kraus 1973.

48   **The Romance of Sir Beues of Hamtoun,** Vol. II. See above, E.S. 46.

49   **The Romance of Guy of Warwick,** Vol. II. See above, E.S. 42.

50   The English Charlemagne Romances XII: **The Boke of Duke Huon of Burdeux,** Vol. IV. See above, E.S. 43.

51   **Torrent of Portyngale,** re-ed. E. Adam. 1887, *reprinted* Kraus 1973. $15.00

52   **A Dialogue against the Feuer Pestilence by William Bullein,** ed. M. W. $10.00
and A. H. Bullen. 1888, *reprinted* Kraus 1973.

53   **The Anatomie of the Bodie of Man by Thomas Vicary,** ed. F. J. and $22.50
P. Furnivall. 1888, *reprinted* Kraus 1973.

54   **The Curial made by maystere Alain Charretier,** translated by Caxton, £1·40
ed. P. Meyer and F. J. Furnivall. 1888, *reprinted* 1965.

55   **The Bruce by John Barbour,** Vol. IV. See above, E.S. 11.

56   **On Early English Pronunciation,** by A. J. Ellis. Part V. 1889, *reprinted* $60.00
Kraus 1973. (See E.S. 2, 7, 14, and 23 for other parts.)

57   **Caxton's Eneydos,** ed. W. T. Culley and F. J. Furnivall. 1890, *reprinted* £5·75
1962.

58   **Caxton's Blanchardyn and Eglantine,** ed. L. Kellner. 1890, *reprinted* £7·25
1962.

59   **The Romance of Guy of Warwick,** Vol. III. See above E.S. 42.

60   **Lydgate's Temple of Glas,** ed. J. Schick. 1891, *reprinted* Kraus 1973. $20.00

61, 73   **Hoccleve's Works: The Minor Poems,** Vol. I ed. F. J. Furnivall £7·25
(1892), Vol. II ed. I. Gollancz (1925 *for* 1897); reprinted as one volume
and revised by Jerome Mitchell and A. I. Doyle 1970.

62   **The Chester Plays,** ed. H. Deimling. Vol. I 1892, *reprinted* 1967. (See £3·75
E.S. 115 for Part II.)

63   **The Earliest English Translations of the De Imitatione Christi,** ed. J. K. $21.25
Ingram. 1893, *reprinted* Kraus 1973.

64   **Godeffroy of Boloyne,** or the Siege and Conqueste of Jerusalem by $26.25
William, archbishop of Tyre, translated by William Caxton, ed. M. N.
Colvin. 1893, *reprinted* Kraus 1973.

65   **The Romance of Sir Beues of Hamtoun,** Vol. III. See above, E.S. 46.

66   **Lydgate and Burgh's Secrees of old Philisoffres:** a version of the $15.00
Secreta Secretaorum, ed. R. Steele. 1894, *reprinted* Kraus 1973.

67   **The Three Kings' Sons,** ed. F. J. Furnivall. Vol. I Text (*all published*) $15.00
1895, *reprinted* Kraus 1973.

68   **Melusine,** ed. A. K. Donald. Vol. I (*all published*) 1895, *reprinted* $40.00
Kraus 1973.

69   **John Lydgate The Assembly of Gods,** ed. O. L. Triggs. 1896, *reprinted* $20.00
Kraus 1976.

70   **The Digby Plays,** ed. F. J. Furnivall. 1896, *reprinted* 1967. £3·00

71   **The Towneley Plays,** re-ed. G. England and A. W. Pollard. 1897, $25.00
reprinted Kraus 1973.

72   **Hoccleve's Works: The Regement of Princes and fourteen minor poems,** $18.75
ed. F. J. Furnivall. 1897, *reprinted* Kraus 1973.

73   **Hoccleve's Works: The Minor Poems,** Vol. II. See above, E.S. 61.

74   **Three Prose Versions of the Secreta Secretorum,** ed. R. Steele and $20.00
T. Henderson. Vol. I (*all published*) 1898, *reprinted* Kraus 1973.

75   **Speculum Gy de Warewyke,** ed. G. L. Morrill. 1898, *reprinted* Kraus $20.00
1973.

76   **George Ashby's Poems,** ed. M. Bateson. 1899, *reprinted* 1965. £3·50

E.S. 77, 83, 92   **The Pilgrimage of the Life of Man**, translated by John Lydgate $53.75
from the French by Guillaume de Deguileville, Vol. I ed. F. J.
Furnivall (1899), Vol. II ed. F. J. Furnivall (1901), Vol. III introduction, notes, glossary, etc. by K. B. Locock (1904); *reprinted as one
volume* Kraus 1973.

78   **Thomas Robinson The Life and Death of Mary Magdalene**, ed. H. O.   £3·50
Sommer. 1899. *Paper.*

79   **Dialogues in French and English by William Caxton**, ed. H. Bradley. $6.25
1900, *reprinted* Kraus 1973. *Paper.*

80   **Lydgate's Two Nightingale Poems**, ed. O. Glauning. 1900, *reprinted* $8.75
Kraus 1973.

80A Selections from Barbour's Bruce (Books I–X), ed. W. W. Skeat, $35.00
1900, *reprinted* Kraus 1973.

81   **The English Works of John Gower**, ed. G. C. Macaulay. Vol. I   £7·00
Confessio Amantis Prologue–Bk. V. 1970. 1900, *reprinted* 1978.

82   **The English Works of John Gower**, ed. G. C. Macaulay. Vol. II   £7·00
Confessio Amantis V. 1971–VIII, *In Praise of Peace.* 1901, *reprinted*
1978.

83   The Pilgrimage of the Life of Man, Vol. II. See above, E.S. 77.

84   **Lydgate's Reson and Sensuallyte**, ed. E. Sieper. Vol. I Manuscripts,   £5·75
Text, and Glossary. 1901, *reprinted* 1965. (See E.S. 89 for Part II.)

85   **The Poems of Alexander Scott**, ed. A. K. Donald. 1902, *reprinted* $10.00
Kraus 1973.

86   **The Poems of William of Shoreham**, ed. M. Konrath. Vol. I (*all* $26.00
published) 1902, *reprinted* Kraus 1973.

87   **Two Coventry Corpus Christi Plays**, re-ed. H. Craig. 1902; *second*   £3·50
edition 1957, *reprinted* 1967.

88   **Le Morte Arthur**, a romance in stanzas, re-ed. J. D. Bruce. 1903, $11.25
reprinted Kraus 1973.

89   **Lydgate's Reson and Sensuallyte**, ed. E. Sieper. Vol. II Studies and   £4·00
Notes. 1903, *reprinted* 1965. (See E.S. 84 for Part I.)

90   **English Fragments from Latin Medieval Service-Books**, ed. H. Little- $5.00
hales. 1903, *reprinted* Kraus 1973. *Paper.*

91   **The Macro Plays**, ed. F. J. Furnivall and A. W. Pollard. 1904. Superseded by O.S. 262.

92   The Pilgrimage of the Life of Man, Vol. III. See above, E.S. 77.

93   **Henry Lovelich's Merlin**, ed. E. A. Kock. Vol. I 1904, *reprinted* Kraus $27.50
1973. (See E.S. 112 and O.S. 185 for other parts.)

94   Respublica, ed. L. A. Magnus. 1905. Superseded by O.S. 226.

95   The History of the Holy Grail by Henry Lovelich, Vol. V. See above,
E.S. 28.

96   **Mirk's Festial**, ed. T. Erbe. Vol I (*all published*) 1905, *reprinted* Kraus $26.00
1973.

97   **Lydgate's Troy Book**, ed. H. Bergen. Vol. I Prologue, Books I and II, $27.50
1906, *reprinted* Kraus 1973. (See E.S. 103, 106, and 126 for other
parts.)

98   **John Skelton Magnyfycence**, ed. R. L. Ramsay. 1908 (*for 1906*), $30.00
reprinted Kraus 1976.

99   **The Romance of Emaré**, ed. E. Rickert. 1908 (*for 1906*), *reprinted*   £3·50
1958.

100   **The Middle English Harrowing of Hell and Gospel of Nicodemus**, $17.50
ed. W. H. Hulme. 1908 (*for 1907*), *reprinted* Kraus 1976.

101   **Songs, Carols and other Miscellaneous Poems from Balliol MS. 354**, $25.00
Richard Hill's Commonplace-book, ed. R. Dyboski. 1908 (*for 1907*),
reprinted Kraus 1973.

E.S. 102 **The Promptorium Parvulorum**: the First English–Latin Dictionary, $36.25
ed. A. L. Mayhew. 1908, *reprinted* Kraus 1973.

103, 106 **Lydgate's Troy Book**, ed. H. Bergen. Vol. II, Book III, 1908; $45.00
Vol. III, Books IV and V, 1910; *reprinted as one volume* Kraus 1973.
(See E.S. 97, 126 for other parts.)

104 **The Non-Cycle Mystery Plays**, ed. O. Waterhouse. 1909. Superseded by S.S. 1.

105 **The Tale of Beryn,** with a Prologue of the Merry Adventure of the $25.00
Pardoner with a Tapster at Canterbury, ed. F. J. Furnivall and W. G.
Stone. 1909, *reprinted* Kraus 1973.

106 **Lydgate's Troy Book,** Vol. III. See above, E.S. 103.

107 **John Lydgate The Minor Poems,** ed. H. N. MacCracken. Vol. I £8·25
Religious Poems. 1911 (*for* 1910), *reprinted* 1961. (See O.S. 192 for
Vol. II.)

108 **Lydgate's Siege of Thebes,** ed. A. Erdmann. Vol. I Text. 1911. £5·25
reprinted 1960. (See E.S. 125 for Vol. II.)

109 **The Middle English Versions of Partonope of Blois,** ed. A. T. Bödtker. $45.00
1912 (*for* 1911), *reprinted* Kraus 1973.

110 **Caxton's Mirrour of the World,** ed. O. H. Prior. 1913 (*for* 1912), $22.50
reprinted Kraus 1978.

111 **Raoul Le Fevre The History of Jason,** translated by William Caxton, $15.00
ed. J. Munro. 1913 (*for* 1912), *reprinted* Kraus 1973.

112 **Henry Lovelich's Merlin,** ed. E. A. Kock. Vol. II 1913, *reprinted* £5·00
1961. (See E.S. 93 and O.S. 185 for other parts.) *Paper.*

113 **Poems by Sir John Salusbury and Robert Chester,** ed. Carleton Brown. $11.25
1914 (*for* 1913), *reprinted* Kraus 1973.

114 **The Gild of St. Mary, Lichfield:** Ordinances and other documents, $9.00
ed. F. J. Furnivall. 1920 (*for* 1914), *reprinted* Kraus 1973. *Paper.*

115 **The Chester Plays,** ed. Dr. Matthews. Vol. II 1916 (*for* 1914), *re-* £3·75
printed 1967.

116 **The Pauline Epistles** in MS. Parker 32, Corpus Christi College, $35.00
Cambridge, ed. M. J. Powell. 1916 (*for* 1915), *reprinted* Kraus 1973.

117 **The Life of Fisher,** ed. R. Bayne. 1921 (*for* 1915), *reprinted* Kraus $10.00
1973.

118 **The Earliest Arithmetics in English,** ed. R. Steele. 1922 (*for* 1916), $7.50
reprinted Kraus 1973.

119 **The Owl and the Nightingale,** ed. J. H. G. Grattan and G. F. H. $12.00
Sykes. 1935 (*for* 1915), *reprinted* Kraus 1973.

120 **Ludus Coventriæ,** or The Plaie called Corpus Christi, Cotton MS. £7·00
Vespasian D. viii, ed. K. S. Block. 1922 (*for* 1917), *reprinted* 1961.

121 **Lydgate's Fall of Princes,** ed. H. Bergen. Vol. I 1924 (*for* 1918), £7·25
reprinted 1967.

122 **Lydgate's Fall of Princes,** ed. H. Bergen. Vol. II 1924 (*for* 1918), £7·25
reprinted 1967.

123 **Lydgate's Fall of Princes,** ed. H. Bergen. Vol. III 1924 (*for* 1919), £7·25
reprinted 1967.

124 **Lydgate's Fall of Princes,** ed. H. Bergen. Vol. IV 1927 (*for* 1919), £10·00
reprinted 1967.

125 **Lydgate's Siege of Thebes,** ed. A. Erdmann and E. Ekwall. Vol. II $22.00
Introduction, Notes, Glossary etc. 1930 (*for* 1920), *reprinted* Kraus
1973.

126 **Lydgate's Troy Book,** ed. H. Bergen. Vol. IV 1935 (*for* 1920), *re-* $50.00
printed Kraus 1973. (See E.S. 97, 103, and 106 for other parts.)